W.H.K. Pollock

W.H.K. Pollock

A Chess Biography with 523 Games

Olimpiu G. Urcan *and*
John S. Hilbert

McFarland & Company, Inc., Publishers
Jefferson, North Carolina

ALSO OF INTEREST AND FROM MCFARLAND

OLIMPIU G. URCAN

Adolf Albin in America: A European Chess Master's Sojourn, 1893–1895 (2008; paper 2014)

Julius Finn: A Chess Master's Life in America, 1871–1931 (2010)

(and Peter Michael Braunwarth) *Arthur Kaufmann: A Chess Biography, 1872–1938* (2012)

JOHN S. HILBERT

Walter Penn Shipley: Philadelphia's Friend of Chess (2003; paper 2012)

The Tragic Life and Short Chess Career of James A. Leonard, 1841–1862 (2006; paper 2014)

(and Peter P. Lahde) *Albert Beauregard Hodges: The Man Chess Made* (2008; paper 2013)

Emil Kemeny: A Life in Chess (2013)

Frontispiece: W.H.K. Pollock in Montreal, 1893 (John G. White Chess and Checkers Collections, Cleveland Public Library).

FIRST EDITION, *first printing*

LIBRARY OF CONGRESS CATALOGUING-IN-PUBLICATION DATA

Names: Urcan, Olimpiu G., 1977– author. | Hilbert, John S., 1953– author.
Title: W.H.K. Pollock : a chess biography with 523 games /
Olimpiu G. Urcan and John S. Hilbert.
Other titles: William Henry Krause Pollock
Description: Jefferson, North Carolina : McFarland & Company, Inc.,
Publishers, 2017 | Includes bibliographical references and index.
Identifiers: LCCN 2016042233 | ISBN 9780786458684
(library binding : alk. paper) ∞
Subjects: LCSH: Pollock, W. H. K., 1859–1896. | Chess players—
England—Biography. | Chess—History.
Classification: LCC GV1439.P64 U73 2016 | DDC 794.1092 [B]—dc23
LC record available at https://lccn.loc.gov/2016042233

BRITISH LIBRARY CATALOGUING DATA ARE AVAILABLE

ISBN 978-0-7864-5868-4 (print)

Printed in the United States of America

Edited by Robert Franklin
Designed by Robert Franklin and Susan Ham
Typeset by Susan Ham

*McFarland & Company, Inc., Publishers
Box 611, Jefferson, North Carolina 28640
www.mcfarlandpub.com*

To selfless librarians

Table of Contents

Preface and Acknowledgments

"A brilliant man was poor Pollock, an enemy to no one but himself, and decidedly a chess genius, in whose company none could be for a moment dull. He has left many marks of his brilliant chess genius, and it may possibly be the work of some enthusiast to gather his gems together, and present them to the chess world as a most appropriate monument to his memory." —*Leeds Mercury (Weekly Supplement),* October 10, 1896

The words above, taken from one of William Henry Krause Pollock's many obituaries, speak to his geniality and genius, his brilliancy and Bohemianism, and why the reader is reading these words. The authors were by no means the first to gather Pollock's gems together, and in this respect owe much to their predecessor, Frideswide F. Rowland, of Kingstown, Ireland, and her host of contributors who responded to her requests for information, anecdotes and games regarding her fallen friend. Rowland's efforts resulted in the memorial volume *Pollock Memories* (Dublin, 1899), still considered by many as one of the kindest and warmest tributes to a chess talent of the Old School—before, as some might say, the "pawn grubbing tactics" of Steinitz had completely and forever changed the game at the highest level.

The present work is, however, more ambitious. Rowland's work included 145 full games, and 19 additional positions. The book in your hands includes 510 Pollock games and 13 game fragments. Computer databases we have seen show no more than 100 to 150 games attributed to Pollock. And as might be expected of someone whose keenest delight lay in opening the lines and pursuing attacks, the number of decisive games among Pollock's published oeuvre is overwhelming: 90 percent. Even his draws, few as they are, were hard fought, with rarely a trace of the grandmaster variety in sight.

As he was described in the *British Chess Magazine* at the time of his death (November 1896, pages 441–446), Pollock was an idealist, in life as well as chess, and with all the shadings of purity and impracticality that word conveys. Trained for the medical profession, the son and grandson of Anglican ministers, Pollock could have taken up his role as a prosperous, middleclass professional, with a life dedicated to more conventional duties, a growing family, and thoughtful pastimes. Instead, he made his hobby his life, his first and only love. He never practiced medicine. He never married. Chess became his precarious living, and one that barely afforded him the chance even to return to the home of his youth to die.

In chess Pollock loved sacrifice, tactical complications, and a rollicking game full of wit and adrenaline, a fireworks display of personality and daring. He lived in an age that considered chess a mere pastime and among full-time chess players who mostly valued whatever let them win, however mundane or prosaic. Pollock agreed neither with his age nor with his peers. It is doubtful he would have wanted it otherwise.

This book is offered to the reader interested in curious personalities, on and off the board, to those who wish to understand a player's life and thought. It traces Pollock's family life, for often to understand a man, to understand where he was heading, it is necessary first to understand something of where he came from. It covers his chess playing career, both professional across the board with the finest players of the day, and as a chess entertainer performing simultaneous exhibitions. And it provides his games: the serious, the playful, the thoughtful and carefree, complete with brilliancy and blunder, just as his imagination, and his opponents' nerves, called them forth.

Pollock's appetite for sacrificial chess grew alongside his remarkable skill for writing and reporting. Through his contributions to the *British Chess Magazine* and columns in the *Baltimore Sunday News* and *Albany Evening Journal*, he provided his readers with exceptionally rich reports. While today he is chiefly remembered for some of his remarkable combinations over the board, Pollock's mark on chess journalism in the late 1890s cannot be overstated. His writing was a pioneering effort, executed with remarkable energy, style and impeccable expertise seldom seen today. Samples of his witty annotations and more ample writing are present throughout this work.

The authors wish to thank a wonderful group of people who made this work possible. We are indebted to Joost van Winsen and Alan Smith for assisting with the recovery of a significant number of difficult-to-reach newspaper columns and game scores. Tim Dyas has been particularly generous in sharing with us his decade-long research on the genealogy of William Henry Krause. We are grateful to Martin Frère Hillyer for sharing with us a rare Pollock photograph from Walter Frère's collection. We are immensely grateful to Kelly Ross Brown (John G. White and Special Collections Librarian, Cleveland Public Library) for processing our countless requests for photographs over the years.

Other specialized librarians from Europe and the United States proved equally helpful: Henk Chervet (Royal Library in the Hague), Damon Talbot (special collections archivist, Maryland Historical Society), Eben Dennis (Maryland Department, Enoch Pratt Free Library), Inez J. Fletcher (librarian, National Library of Ireland), Keith Murphy (National Library of Ireland), Berni Metcalfe (National Library of Ireland), and Williams Rosie (University Centre Hastings) were all exceedingly prompt, courteous and productive in dealing with our email enquiries.

Kati Halden, Lucy Nash and C.S. Knighton, researchers associated with the Old Cliftonian Society, Clifton College, aided us greatly in extracting a number of basic details of Pollock's studying years. They were joined in this task by Robert W. Mills (librarian, Royal College of Physicians, Ireland). Help and kindness also came our way from Sarah Taylor (Bristol Record Office), Drew Westerman (Bath Record Office), and Siân Mogridge (Hackney Archives, Dalston CLR James Library).

Several chess players and researchers responded enthusiastically to our calls for assistance and they fully deserve mention here: Jonathan O'Connor, Alan Papier, Graham Mill-Wilson, Myron Samsin, Harrie Grondijs, Hans Renette, and Peter Michael Braunwarth.

We are particularly grateful to Edward Winter for giving space to our enquiries related to this project in his *Chess Notes* column, for offering us a number of quality illustrations, and for his unparalleled expertise in the field.

Errors are, of course, the fault of the authors alone.

Olimpiu G. Urcan • John S. Hilbert
Singapore; Buffalo, New York 2017

Abbreviations and Annotation Symbols

Annotation Symbols

!	strong move
!!	brilliant move
!?	interesting move
?!	dubious move
?	weak move
??	blunder
+	check
1–0	White wins
0–1	Black wins
½–½	draw
+	victory
–	loss

Abbreviations

BCM	*British Chess Magazine*
BCA	British Chess Association
CCA	Counties' Chess Association
ICM	*International Chess Magazine*
PM	F.F. Rowland's *Pollock Memories*
Rev.	Reverend (ecclesiastical title)
$	Dollar (American currency)
£	Pound (British currency)
C.N.	*Chess Notes* (Edward Winter)
USCA	United States Chess Association
NYSCA	New York State Chess Association

PART ONE

Life and Chess Career (1859–1896)

1. The Irish Connection, 1859–1881

The story of William Henry Krause Pollock begins with his maternal grandfather, William Henry Krause, to whom Pollock owed the first three-quarters of his name. William Henry Krause was born on July 6, 1796, on the island of St. Croix, West Indies. Brought to England at an early age, he was educated at schools in Fulham and Richmond. At 18 he decided to become a professional soldier and obtained a commission in the 51st infantry, then in the south of France. In June 1815 he fought with the Allied armies against Napoleon at Waterloo. After the war, placed on half pay, he returned to St. Croix where his father still lived. In January 1822, at the age of 26, William Henry Krause visited Annefield, County Kildare, Ireland, to attend the marriage of his friend, Captain Joseph Dyas, to Elizabeth Ridgeway. Converted to Evangelism by Joseph's eldest sister, Krause remained in Ireland.

His decision to stay in Ireland was likely prompted by more than religious conviction. A year after his conversion, Krause married Elizabeth's sister, Angelina Ridgeway. Eliza Angelina, the only child of William Henry Krause and Angelina Ridgeway Krause, and the chess player's future mother, was born on November 23, 1823, at Annefield. But the family's happiness was short-lived. On September 17, 1824, only ten months after giving birth to her daughter, Angelina Krause died of consumption. Whatever his private feelings were of this loss, Krause shortly thereafter left for Herefordshire to seek, without success, his ordination. He left baby Angelina with her uncle and aunt to be raised with her cousin, Joseph Henry, and her cousin's younger sister, Eliza Anne Dyas (born in 1826).

Eventually, Krause found work with Lord Farnham at Cavan, being appointed as his "moral agent" over his Irish estates, and Angelina was able to rejoin her father. Full of anti–Catholic zeal, Krause, while working for Lord Farnham, enrolled at Trinity College, Dublin, on April 5, 1826. He graduated with a bachelor of arts degree in 1830. Eight years later, on February 27, 1838, he received a master's degree. He was ordained for the curacy of Cavan by the Bishop of Kilmore, and it was at Cavan that Krause ministered for two years. In 1840, he was appointed incumbent of the Bethesda Chapel, Dublin, and emerged as one of the city's leading evangelical clergymen.[1] He became an active member of the Orange Order, a Protestant fraternal organization founded in 1796, together with his brother-in-law Captain Joseph Dyas. Krause, at 55 years of age, died on February 27, 1852, in Dublin.

---

1. For general assistance and leads on the Irish side of W.H.K. Pollock's family, thanks are owed to Tim Dyas, a descendant of the Dyas family living in Mallorca, Spain [emails to Urcan, October 2011]. Some of the information on William Henry Krause is also available in his entry in the *Oxford Dictionary of National Biography* [online edition]. The entry is largely based on Charles Stuart Stanford's *Memoir & Correspondence of the Late Reverend William Henry Krause, with Selections from his Correspondence* (Dublin, 1854).

Eliza Angelina Krause, now approaching 30, apparently met her husband-to-be about this time. Although details are difficult to secure, some notable dates survive marking the church career of her future husband, William James Pollock (1830–1919). Born in London about 1830, according to database records of the Scottish Episcopal Clergy, Pollock received a bachelor of arts degree from Trinity College, Dublin, in 1853. In mid–June 1854, he was licensed as a deacon in Bootle, a small town on the English west coast in Lancashire.[2] A year later, in June 1855, he was ordained as a priest by the bishop of Chester at Chester Cathedral.[3] In February 1856, he was licensed by the Lord Bishop of Manchester to the stipendiary curacy of St. Mathias's Church, Salford.[4] The next year, he was sent to work as a senior curator to the Parish Church of Cheltenham, a large spa town in Gloucestershire.[5] Here the couple's first son was born on Monday, February 21, 1859. In memory of Angelina's father, who had died almost exactly seven years earlier, he was named William Henry Krause Pollock.

The Reverend William Henry Krause (1796–1852), a family ancestor to whom W.H.K. Pollock owed so much of his name (*Memoir and Correspondence of the late Rev. W.H. Krause, A.M.*, edited by Charles Stuart Stanford, Dublin, 1854).

Census records indicate the Pollocks, soon blessed with two very young children, continued to move from one city to another, no doubt following the ecclesiastical missions with which the Episcopal Church entrusted the father. The early 1860s were spent in Montrose, 430 miles up north on the eastern coast of Scotland, where the Rev. William James Pollock was appointed to the St. Peter's Episcopal Church in October 1860.[6] "Mr. Pollock, " the *Cheltenham Chronicle* of October 19 reported, "will leave the scene of his labours here, attended by the good wishes of all who have known him." Four days later, the same newspaper reported that on the Sunday afternoon of his departure, "there was a large and attentive congregation assembled on the occasion" of Pollock's farewell.

In Montrose, the Pollocks lived at Panmure Terrace, a residential area congenial to the pockets and pretensions of the clergy and medical professions. It was there on August 21, 1861, Angelina gave birth to another boy, John, and, on February 17, 1863, to Margaret, their second daughter.[7] That they enjoyed at least some of their time on the Scottish coast is suggested by a brief testimonial letter written by Angelina to a daily

---

2. *Blackburn Standard*, June 21, 1854. • 3. *Carlisle Patriot*, June 16, 1855. • 4. *Lancaster Gazette*, February 2, 1856. • 5. As noted by the *Jackson's Oxford Journal* of July 2, 1859. • 6. *Sherborne Mercury*, October 30, 1860. • 7. John's birth was announced in the *Dundee Advertiser* of August 26, 1861, and even in the *Cheltenham Chronicle* of August 27, 1861; Margaret's birth was announced in the *Dundee Courier* of February 19 and the *Dunfermline Saturday Press* of February 21, 1863.

Clifton College, with the Guthrie Memorial Chapel on the right (*Illustrated London News*, October 26, 1867, page 465).

newspaper praising the accommodations provided on one occasion.[8] But despite such pleasant interludes, Angelina's health suffered, possibly because of the strain of giving birth to four children in quick succession. Although her precise cause of death remains obscure, we know Angelina Pollock died on July 3, 1863, in Rathmines at the house of her father-in-law.[9] It appears that immediately after this tragic event, William Pollock was dispatched as a curate to the Parish Church in Crosthwaite, Cumbria.

On June 9, 1864, William James Pollock received his bachelor and master of arts degrees from Wadham College, Oxford.[10] He also remarried, this time to Eliza Ann, Angelina's first cousin and the only daughter of his father's late friend, Captain Joseph Dyas, on November 15, 1864, at All Souls' Church, Langham-place, London.[11] In 1865, while in Crosthwaite, they had a son, Joseph Dyas, named in memory of Eliza Ann's brother and father.

In July 1872, the Bishop of Bath appointed the Reverend Pollock rector of St. Saviour's in the ancient city of Bath, Somerset.[12] The city became the family's new home and, while the Reverend Pollock attempted to establish a firm reputation in the city, a more stable family house was erected at 10 Grosvenor Road.[13]

By this time William Henry Krause Pollock was 13, and his early education took place at

8. From the *Dundee Advertiser* of August 2, 1862: "A Furnished Flat to Let at the Railway Station, Brechin, belonging to James Smith. The above was occupied for a short time by the Rev. Mr. Pollock, Montrose. Mrs. Pollock writes as follows: 'Dear Mrs. Smith—I write a line to say how very comfortable we were during the time we had your apartments. We very much enjoyed being at your House, and were delighted with the pretty view from the windows. The situation seems particularly healthful.—Believe me, yours truly. [Signed] A. Pollock, July 25, 1862.'" • **9.** According to the *Dublin Evening Mail*, July 4, 1863, the *Freeman's Journal* of July 7, 1863, and the *Dundee Advertiser*, July 11, 1863; her in-laws address was given as 8 Kenilworth Square, Rathmines. • **10.** As announced by the *Morning Post* (June 10, 1864), *London Standard* and the *Oxford Journal* (June 11, 1864). • **11.** A marriage announcement appeared in the *Manchester Courier and Lancashire General Advertiser* of November 23, 1964. • **12.** Announced by the *Derby Mercury* (July 17, 1872), the *Worcester Journal* (July 17, 1872), and the *Western Gazette*, August 16, 1872. • **13.** The Rev. Pollock was of the opinion that the clergy should not interfere with politics at all. In this respect he wrote a telling letter to the *Bath Chronicle* in mid–1873. It drew a vast response from individuals of different political stripes and interests and, in some of these replies, Pollock was called a "newcomer" to the city. See, for instance, the *Bath Chronicle* of July 7, 1873.

Clifton College, Bristol.[14] He joined the Junior School at Clifton College in September 1871 and, as a member of one of the highest forms, he lived in Town House, Harris House, and then Oakeley's House. He left the school at the end of Michaelmas Term in July 1876.[15] Various accounts note that Pollock also studied at Somersetshire College, Bath, although the details remain vague.[16]

In 1880 the Pollock household in Bath was flourishing with Angeline, Margaret, John, William Henry Krause and Joseph Dyas all living in the parental home. The household was looked after by Margaret Shanks, a 39-year-old Scottish parlor maid, Henrietta Philips, a 59-year-old cook, and Isabella Grant, a Bath-based 15-year-old housemaid.[17] It was in that very year that all of them, family and servants, wished safe journey to the 21-year-old W.H.K. Pollock when he was sent to study medicine at the prestigious Dr. Steevens' Hospital in Dublin, one of the top medical establishments in Ireland.[18] Perhaps the Irish blood inherited from his mother made Pollock feel at home in the Irish capital; certainly, later in life he returned there with joy on several notable occasions. In 1882 he graduated as a licentiate of the Royal College of Surgeons in Dublin but did not embrace the career of a practicing surgeon right away; nor did he attempt to further advance his studies. The sibling who did seize the moment to advance his career was not William Henry Krause, but rather his step-brother, Joseph Dyas, who in July 1883 gained admission to the Royal Military College in Sandhurst. In the late 1880s and early 1890s Joseph Dyas served with the Connaught Rangers, "the Devil's Own," an Irish regiment with the British Army with a long history of notable interventions in various overseas colonies.[19]

There can be little doubt that the Reverend Pollock, now in his early 50s, prayed for all his sons and that his prayers may well have included his hopes that at least one would follow his lead and serve the Church. That his eldest chose medicine instead would not have stopped him praying for William's success in that profession. While the 19-year-old John would eventually serve the Church, both he and William fell in love with the game of chess during their student years. The

---

14. Clifton College was founded in September 1862 under the leadership of Dr. Percival, the bishop of Hereford. At the time it opened, it had 69 boys (28 boarders and 41 town-boys). By April 1863, there were two schools: Preparatory School and the Junior School. The first took boys up to 11 years, at which age they passed into the Junior School where they remained until 14. By Pollock's time at Clifton's Junior School, the latter had six classes (16 to 20 boys each) and the following subjects were mandatory: Latin, English subjects, scripture, science and drawing. Depending on the class level, French, Greek, and mathematics were also taught. Among the sports encouraged at the Junior School were cricket, soccer and rugby. ● **15.** The basic information about Pollock's time at Clifton College was contributed by Kati Halden of the Old Cliftonian Society, Clifton College [email to Urcan, January 21, 2010] and by Lucy Nash of The Old Cliftonian Society [email to Urcan, November 23, 2010]; the information is confirmed also by E.M. Oakeley in *Clifton College Register, a list of Cliftonians from September 1862, to July, 1880* (London: Rivingstons, Waterloo Place, 1887), pages 88 and 141. ● **16.** According to Howard Staunton's *The Great Schools of England* (London: Strahan and Co. Publishers, 1869 edition), Somersetshire College was founded in 1858 and was intended to offer the same level of education as the best public schools in England. Besides classics and mathematics, special attention was given to history, geography and French. In addition, a natural science class was formed by the late 1860s and every effort was made "to instruct the Pupils in the Holy Scriptures, and to render that instruction practical" (page 557). Noted here is the rare occurrence of a chess biography quoting information from a general reference work composed by an exceedingly talented chess player. ● **17.** The details of the Pollock household in 1880 are extracted from the *Census Returns of England and Wales, 1881*; Kew, Surrey, England: The National Archives of the UK (TNA): Public Record Office (PRO), 1881. Class: *RG11*; Piece: *2439*; Folio: *132*; Page: *20*; Line; GSU roll: *1341587;* Also provided by Ancestry.com and the Church of Jesus Christ of Latter-Day Saints. *1881 England Census* [database on-line]. Provo, UT, USA: The Generations Network, Inc., 2004. ● **18.** Dr. Steevens' Hospital was founded under the terms of the will of Dr. Richard Steevens (1653–1710), a well-known physician in Dublin. Designed by Thomas Burgh, the hospital became one of the top medical establishments in Ireland, especially after the Dublin School of Medicine was transferred to it in 1857. At that time it was renamed Steevens' Hospital Medical College. Many notable Irishmen sought treatment on its premises. See T. Percy C. Kirkpatrick, *The History of Dr. Steevens' Hospital, Dublin 1720–1920*, (Dublin: University of Dublin College Press, 2008 edition); see also *www.rcsi.ie*. ● **19.** *The Bath Chronicle*, July 26, 1883.

game in all likelihood had been taught to the boys by their father, who, like many other ecclesiastical figures of the period, was educated at least in the game's basics. Indeed, there is some reason to believe the elder Pollock was yet more talented at chess.[20]

In the early 1870s, during the brothers' childhood years, Paul Morphy's fame was still a recent memory. His games were considered models of play by more than one generation of enthusiasts. Undoubtedly the elder Pollock played often with his sons, and in doing so influenced his oldest boy perhaps much more than he intended. Unlike his younger brother John, who eventually chose the study of scripture over the more geometrically straightforward movements of wooden bishops, William became utterly fascinated with chess. Given William's training as a physician, with its great promise, and given the difficult and suspect life of a Victorian chess professional, it seems almost equally certain that the more William became fascinated with the game, the more devoutly his father prayed that his son's passion for it would subside. In this respect, at least, prayers failed the Reverend Pollock, as the rest of this book devoutly attests.

---

20. William James Pollock's ability to play chess was at least suggested, if not demonstrated, in the chess column of the *Baltimore Sunday News* of July 26, 1891: "Pollock's brother and father were excellent chess players."

2. Early Chess Play, 1882–1885

Dublin, Bath and Bristol

Chess fully captured the heart and mind of only the eldest of the Reverend Pollock's sons. Following the brothers' friendly encounters over the board during their student days in Dublin, John returned to his books, while William remained fascinated with the chessboard. For John Pollock, the game remained throughout life a simple distraction, a pleasant way of momentarily escaping the hardships of study and work. For William, regardless of parental hopes, chess became the object of deeper and deeper study. In time, the game became his foremost passion. Ultimately, it became his life.

Studious efforts directed at chess intensified during the winter of 1880-81. According to the *Bath Chronicle and Weekly Gazette* of January 6, 1881, on Saturday, January 1, both Pollock brothers, as members of the Bath Chess Club, took part in simultaneous exhibitions played at the Athenaeum by the well-known player the Rev. William Wayte. In a first series of ten games, William lost but John drew against the more experienced player. In a second series of three games conceding the first move, it was John again who succeeded in drawing Wayte while William lost once again.[1] John may or may not have been a stronger player than his brother William at that date; it is impossible to say. John certainly played a greater role than his brother in the Bath club's hierarchy. According to the *Bath Chronicle* of March 18, 1882, John was elected at that time to be the Bath Chess Club's honorary secretary.

While studying in Dublin, William frequently visited the Dublin Chess Club, the most active club in the Irish capital.[2] One influential figure in Pollock's development as a player and, perhaps, in the formation of his combinative, Morphy-like style, was Robert Fitzmaurice Hunt (1824–1907). The following was written in the *British Chess Magazine* (September 1907, page 417) at Hunt's death in 1907. Note how the passage both praises Hunt for his beneficial influence on Pollock's game, and simultaneously absolves him of responsibility for Pollock's choosing chess as a profession:

---

1. From the *Brighton Guardian* of May 4, 1881: "The second annual handicap tournament, in connection with the Bath Chess Club, has resulted in Mr W.H. Pollock (Class A) winning the first prize with a score of 11½ won games, out of a possible 16; Mr W. Hill (class B) the second, scored 10 won games. There were nine competitors. Class A gave the odds of a Kt to Class B." • **2.** Several sources state that Pollock's first published chess problem and game allegedly appeared in *The Practical Farmer* ["the only newspaper in Dublin which then contained Chess news"] in 1882. This was mentioned in Pollock's obituary in the *British Chess Magazine* (November 1896, page 411) and by F.F. Rowland in *Pollock Memories* (Dublin, 1899) at page 2. Efforts to track down this publication at the National Library of Ireland were unavailing. Thanks are owed to Inez J. Fletcher for the attempt [email to Urcan, November 1, 2010].

[...] On the occasion of Paul Morphy's visit to London, Mr. Hunt made his acquaintance, and became his personal friend; and it was Mr. Hunt who introduced the famous American to the St. George's Chess Club, of which he was then a member. He always spoke with great admiration of Morphy both as a chess player and as a man. He admired brilliancy in chess, though his own play was rather solid than brilliant, and he was, we believe, stronger in defence than in attack. He always picked out and encouraged young players of promise at the club, and when Mr. W.H.K. Pollock was a member of it, Mr. Hunt probably contested more games with him than with any other member. And when Mr. Pollock decided on devoting his talents to chess (a choice which Mr. Hunt regretted) there can be no doubt that he had learned lessons from Mr. Hunt's strong and steady defence, which proved useful to him in his subsequent career and prevented him from indulging in many unsound sacrifices. Mr. Hunt was a general favourite at the club. He knew how to win and how to lose, and always held a high rank among its best players; and to have been the personal friend of Morphy, and it might be said the preceptor of Pollock, is a distinction that has fallen to the lot of few chess players. [...]

The Reverend William Wayte, circa 1893–1894 (Dalston CLR James Library, Hackney Archives).

Pollock's apprenticeship unfolded not only in Dublin, but also in Bath and Bristol. Both cities have on record an active and lengthy chess history. John's allegiance to Bath was evident when in May of 1882 he joined a chess team representing the city in its traditional match against the unified teams of Bristol and Clifton Chess Associations.[3] The match took place at the Imperial Hotel in Clifton on Wednesday afternoon, May 3. Although John won both his games on board eight against F. Burford, the Bath team lost the match 11–12. In the return match, played on June 3 at the Grand Pump Room Hotel in Bristol, according to the *Bath Chronicle and Weekly Gazette* of June 8, 1882, the Bath team again lost by a narrow margin 12–13, with both Pollocks losing their games.

Like his brother John, William also played against the Bristol players when he was at home, as well as match games in Dublin at the city's strongest chess club. In early January 1883, according to the *Bath Chronicle and Weekly Gazette* of January 4, 1883, Wayte gave another simultaneous exhibition, this one involving nine boards. One of his two losses was to William.[4]

On Wednesday afternoon, March 14, 1883, the Pollock brothers played together for Bath once again. William took third board against the Rev. N. Tibbits, representing the Bristol and

3. Pollock's earliest involvement with the Bath Chess Club's team against those from Bristol and Clifton Chess Association in early May 1882 was signaled by the May 4, 1882, issue of the *Bristol Mercury and Daily Post*. • **4.** According to the newspaper account, Wayte finished with 4 wins, 2 losses and 1 draw; the remaining two games were abandoned due to the late hour.

Clifton Chess Associations. He won his game with a Vienna Opening, while his younger brother, playing on board seven, scored 1½ out of two games, one in a Ruy Lopez and the other in a King's Gambit. Incidentally, William's presence on the Bath team meant, for the first time, a severe defeat for Bristol. Noting the overall score of 13–8, the newspaper chess columnist for the *Bristol Mercury and Daily Post* of March 15 wrote that "this result was unexpected, the Bath eleven not being considered by their opponents a very strong one; hence, probably the latter somewhat undervalued their skill in the Royal game, and paid the penalty." The president of the Bristol and Clifton Chess Associations "congratulated the Bath gentlemen upon their well-earned victory, and promised that next time the Bristol side would exert their very utmost to retrieve their position." The growing strength of the Pollock brothers made the Bath team a new county powerhouse. At the end of that month, during the annual meeting of the Bath Chess Club, William was elected a member of the club's committee, according to the *Bath Chronicle* of March 29, 1883.

A rematch between Bath and Bristol took place Thursday, June 7, 1883, at Bath's Grand Pump-room Hotel. The Bristol team could not do much better than in the spring. William, this time playing on board four against the Rev. J.E. Vernon, scored 1½ out of two games, the draw adjudicated because of the late hour. John, on board seven, drew both games against A.T. Perry. The *Bristol Mercury and Daily Post*'s chess columnist could not quite let go of his favoritism, even in the face of his team's second defeat at the hands of Bath, this time by an overall score of 6–9, when he stated in his June 15 column that "this result must be very gratifying to the visitors, as the high reputation of their antagonists is well known." Another report, this one from Bristol's *Western Daily Press* of June 8, 1883, recorded Bath's achievement in slightly more positive terms:

> This is the second occasion on which the Bath representatives have conquered their opponents since the formation of the Bristol and Clifton Chess Association, and it is highly creditable to the former that, undeterred by successive defeats, and undismayed by the high reputation—gained in many arduous encounters—of their antagonists, they came forward time after time with unsubdued spirit and energy, and manifested such an Antaeus-like faculty of deriving strength from being overthrown that at last they have succeeded, not once, but on both occasions this year, in plucking the laurels of victory from the brows of their experienced adversaries.

Somewhat revealing about the chess work put together by the Pollock brothers and as an early example of William's journalistic efforts, the *Bath Chronicle and Weekly Gazette* of June 14, 1883, offered the top-board game score between N. Fedden and E. Thorold with sketchy annotations by "W.H.K. and J. Pollock."[5]

Thus, William's early fame as a competent chess player, although generally formed in Dublin, also grew through play in smaller cities in England, like Bath, Clifton and Bristol. While inter-city team matches provided some playing opportunities for amateurs in England, another step was to

---

5. **N. Fedden–E. Thorold [C56], Bath vs. Bristol Match, Bath, Grand Pump-room Hotel, Board 1, 7 June 1883: 1. e4 e5 2. Nf3 Nc6 3. Bc4 Bc5 4. 0–0 d6 5. c3 Nf6 6. d4 e×d4 7. c×d4 Bb6 8. Nc3 Bg4 9. Bb5 B×f3 10. g×f3** W.H.K. and J. Pollock: "Best! If 10. Q×f3 0–0, for if 10. ... B×d4 11. e5 d×e5! 12. B×c6+ b×c6 13. Q×c6+ Nd7 14. Nd5 Rc8! 15. Bg5 [*sic*] f6 16. Qe6+ Kf8 17. Bc1 and Black will have an awkward game." **10. ... 0–0 11. Be3 Ne7 12. Qd2** W.H.K. and J. Pollock: "12. Kh1, with Rg1, seems to be a preferable line of play." **12. ... c6 13. Bd3 Qd7 14. Ne2 Ng6 15. Kh1 Qh3 16. Ng1 Qh5 17. Be2 Nh4 18. Bg5 h6 19. B×h4** W.H.K. and J. Pollock: "19. f4 would have been much better, as 19. ... N×e4 will cost Black a piece, and if 19. ... Ng4 20. h3 h×g5 21. B×g4 Qg6 22. f5." **19. ... Q×h4 20. a4 Rae8 21. Ra3 Bc7 22. Bd1 Nh5 23. Ne2 f5 24. Ng3 f×e4 25. N×h5 Q×h5 26. f×e4 Qh4 27. f3** W.H.K. and J. Pollock: "This costs White a pawn." **27. ... R×e4 28. f×e4 R×f1+ 29. Kg2 Rf6 30. Bf3 Rg6+ 31. Kh1 Ba5** W.H.K. and J. Pollock: "Possibly overlooking White's skillful rejoinder." **32. b4** W.H.K. and J. Pollock: "If he had taken the bishop, Black would of course have mated him by ...Qf2, etc." **32. ... Bd8 33. Bg2 Bg5 34. Qe2 Bf4 35. Rh3 Qf6 36. Rd3 Rg5 37. Qf3 a5 38. b×a5 R×a5 39. Qd1 Qh4 40. Bh3 Qf2 41. Bg2 Rh5 42. h3 Rg5 43. Qf1 R×g2** W.H.K. and J. Pollock: "Black has conducted his attack with admirable pertinacity and skill from the tenth move to the end." **0–1**

engage in the annual tournaments of the Counties' Chess Association. Possibly much inspired by the great tournament held in London between May and June 1883, an event that featured 14 of the world's best masters, that summer William tried his luck in his first larger tournament.

Birmingham 1883: Counties' Chess Association

Whereas John remained an average player occasionally appearing in annual match events between Bath and neighboring cities, William had greater chess ambitions. For any young provincial player the tournaments organized by the Counties' Chess Association, established in 1870, offered an opportunity to meet stronger opponents. Unlike the chess events organized in London's famous resorts or the master tournaments run by the British Chess Association, the meetings organized by the Counties' Chess Association targeted mainly provincial amateurs. Indeed, entry in the first class tournaments was restricted to amateur players. Because the prize money in these "amateur" events was in fact relatively appealing, the restriction against professionals created indignation in the circles of London-based, master-class players. The controversy around not allowing professional players to compete for the organization's prizes, a stance loudly supported by the Rev. Arthur Bolland Skipworth (1830–1898), filled the pages of the leading chess journals, such as the *Chess Player's Chronicle* and *Chess-Monthly*, as well as appearing in a dozen or more provincial columns. While Skipworth's decision to keep out professional players brought him little sympathy in London, the success of the Counties' Chess Association tournaments remains a telling one: except in 1888 and 1889, between 1870 and 1893 the tournament was held annually. Furthermore, in 1885 at Hereford and in 1886 at Nottingham, the Counties' Chess Association ran a masters tournament alongside the traditional class events reserved for the strongest provincial amateurs. However the established masters felt about being denied this potential revenue, the Association's tournaments proved a good training ground for up-and-coming players such as William Pollock.

In the summer of 1883, Pollock played in the Second Division (Class II) of the Counties' Chess Association's annual tournament, that year held in Birmingham between July 30 and August 5. The city had hosted the event earlier, in 1874 and 1877. The *British Chess Magazine* prefaced the event with the expectation that "the liberality and spirit of the Birmingham Club will doubtless ensure a large gathering of the leading amateurs in the kingdom." Pollock was one of the many players gathered in the rooms of the Midland Institute on July 30, when G.E. Walton, the president of the Birmingham Chess Club, opened the proceedings. While Walton's words filled the overcrowded room and were occasionally interrupted by courteous applause, Pollock may well have admired the floral decorations of the walls and the collection of water drawings by Samuel Standidge Boden (1826–1882), one of the strongest English players of the 1850s.[6]

---

6. The quote from the *British Chess Magazine* regarding the Counties' Chess Association at Birmingham in 1883 is taken from the August & September 1883 issue, page 269. The detailed proceedings are based on accounts which appeared published in the *Birmingham Daily Post* of July 31, 1883, and the *British Chess Magazine* of August–September 1883, pages 299–300. Detailed descriptions of Pollock's play in this event are based on chess columns from the *Birmingham Daily Post* of early August 1883. The final report published by the *British Chess Magazine* mentioned Pollock as the winner of the Class II section with the note that he represented the Croydon Club. In the January 21, 1882, *Illustrated Sporting and Dramatic News*, G.A. MacDonnell wrote that many of Boden's paintings "would compare not unfavourably with the smaller productions of Birket Foster."

The competitors at Birmingham were ranked in three classes according to strength, with prizes varying for each class: for the first class, prizes of £15, £7 10s., and £5 were offered; for the second class, the prizes were £6, £4, and £2; and for the third class, £5, £3 and £2. Besides the main tournaments for each class, the organizers also planned a handicap event and other varieties. After a welcoming address by the Reverend Skipworth, honorary secretary of the Association, and some debate regarding the best way to arrange the games between the combatants in the first class event, Pollock eventually was asked to make his first move in this tournament, and press the American-made Yale Gem chess clock exactly at 8:00 p.m.[7]

While taking a turn about the playing hall between moves, Pollock may well have studied carefully the faces and gestures of the well-known English players in the first class section. He would have seen there, among others, the Rev. C. Ranken, Amos Burn, the Rev. J. Owen, and the Rev. Skipworth. He also would have seen a certain Fischer, hailing from Cheltenham, Pollock's native town. As stated in the *Birmingham Post*, July 31, 1883: "As these gentlemen constitute the pick of our amateur performers, and most of their names were rendered familiar in chess circles by success in other contests," a contemporary noted, "they will no doubt produce some exceedingly interesting games. They went to work last night with much spirit, advancing their forces into the open field with a boldness which is often wanting in champion practice."

In Pollock's own section, 14 players entered the contest. Among the strongest were the familiar names of C.D. Locock, president of the Oxford University Chess Club, A. Rumboll, Miss Thorold and Herbert Jacobs. Pollock had little trouble defeating most of his opponents. The local chess columnist wrote that "in Class II, Mr. Pollock, of Bath, is carrying everything before him. He is said to be a player of such proficiency that his proper place would be in Class I, but having been admitted in the lower division, he has already won nine games out of the fourteen set down, without meeting a single reverse. Since nearly all his opponents have so many defeats as victories against their names, the first prize seems within his grasp." By Thursday evening, August 2, Pollock had 11 points out of 14 games and lost his first game to the Reverend Huntsman of Nottinghamshire. But with only two games left to play, it was virtually impossible for anyone to catch him. On Saturday evening, August 4, Pollock concluded his games and won the first prize, with 11 points, followed by Locock (10), and Huntsman and Wildman (tied at 9).

Team Matches, Simultaneous Exhibitions and Handicap Events

Pollock's success did much to encourage the 23-year-old to visit the famed chess resorts while in London. It was here, through countless offhand encounters with the leading metropolitan masters, that the game could be quickly learned. He visited Simpson's Divan and Purssell's Restaurant, two of the most famous. Often he produced games abounding in brilliancies. In late 1883 and early 1884, Pollock was still active in Bath and Bristol. William and John were two of the

---

7. The presence of the clocks was noted by the local press: "In order to check the time occupied with the moves, at each table was provided a pair of toy clocks, ingeniously united together on a framework, in such a manner that when one set [was] going the other stopped. This operation was performed by a mere touch of the hand, each player, when he had made his move, putting the timepiece of his adversary in motion. The clocks are American production of the 'Yale Gem' pattern" (*Birmingham Daily Post*, July 31, 1883).

four Bath players who turned up at the Stork Hotel in Birmingham to play a match against the local club at the end of November 1883. The Pollocks took the top boards and, according to the *Bath Chronicle and Weekly Gazette* of October 4, William scored 1 win, 1 loss on board one while John lost both his games. The double-round match ended in a draw.

But Pollock was still not strong enough to compete on equal terms with recognized masters. For instance, on Saturday, November 5, 1883, according to the *Bath Chronicle* of November 8, both brothers were part of a ten-board simultaneous exhibition given by Edmund Thorold at the Athenaeum (+6 −4). William lost but John won. Then, on November 14, the Pollock brothers took part in another 10-board simultaneous exhibition given by the Rev. G.A. MacDonnell when he visited the Bath Chess Club. MacDonnell scored +9 −1, and this time both Pollock brothers had to acknowledge defeat. The *Bath Chronicle* of December 27, 1883, noted too that the Pollock brothers took part in a seven-board simultaneous exhibition given in Bath by D.Y. Mills on December 21 (+3 −2 =2). William won his game and his brother John was one of two players to draw.

Finally, on the Wednesday after Christmas 1883, as the *British Chess Magazine* reported, the two brothers were part of another simultaneous exhibition, this one a display at the Athenaeum given by the seemingly ever-ready Wayte. The latter played on eight boards as White, winning all his games. Afterward, he played four more simultaneously, all with the Black pieces, and managed to score +2 =2. While William Pollock lost both his games, one of the draws was scored by his brother John.[8]

In late February 1884, this time without his younger brother, Pollock again played for the Bath team in its traditional match against Bristol. Late Wednesday evening, February 20, he was present at Clifton's Imperial Hotel, located on Queen's Road. The playing room was filled with spectators, most of them desirous of seeing revenge for Bristol's recent match losses to Bath. This time the Bristol organizers did everything possible to gather the strongest players in the city.

Although Pollock won a fine Vienna game by announcing a long forced mate, the Bath team lost the match 7½–11½. As was also customary, the Bath team challenged the Bristol players to a return match in the coming months.[9] If there was any good news for Pollock and his teammates, it was the announcement made, following the conclusion of play, that the next year's edition of the Counties' Chess Association meeting would be held in Bath.

About a week later, according to the *Bristol Mercury and Daily Post* of March 8, 1884, the fifth edition of a traditional handicap tournament at the Bath Chess Club was won by William, with John finishing a close second.[10] The Pollock brothers were by now clearly among the strongest players in Bath. According to the *Bath Chronicle and Weekly Gazette* of March 13, 1884, during the general meeting of the club held on Saturday, March 8, at the Athenaeum, Orange Grove, William and John were elected members of the club's committee. Besides noting the club's "prosperous finances," the final report stated that the past year had been the most active in the club's

---

8. The Pollock brothers' appearance in the 10-board simultaneous exhibition given by the Rev. G.A. MacDonnell at the Bath Chess Club on November 14, 1883, is memorialized by a note in the *British Chess Magazine* of December 1883, page 415. The Pollocks' appearance in the Reverend Wayte's exhibition séance at the Bath Chess Club on December 26, 1883, is mentioned in the same source for February 1884, page 61, as well as in the *Bath Chronicle and Weekly Gazette* of January 3, 1884. • **9.** The match was reported in the *Chess-Monthly* of March 1884, page 195, the *Bristol Mercury and Daily Post*, February 21, 1884, and the *Western Daily Gazette*, February 21, 1884. • **10.** This was reported almost simultaneously in the chess columns of the *Nottinghamshire Guardian* (March 7, 1884), the *Bristol Mercury and Daily Post* (March 8, 1884), and the *Sheffield Independent* (March 8, 1884).

history. Further progress in cultivating the game in Bath was expected during the upcoming year, as the club was hosting the Counties' Chess Association meeting.

April 1884 saw William involved with an unusual innovation in Bath. The city organized a traditional May fair at the Assembly Rooms under the title "Olde Englishe Maye Fayre" in order to raise money for the local hospital. An exciting novelty planned for the fair was a chess game with living pieces. The following detailed description appeared in the *Bath Chronicle* of May 1, 1884, which also listed the names of each piece—including that of the White King, William Pollock:

> [...] Upon a raised platform in the tea-room is marked out a large chess board, and on their respective squares stand at the specified times, a body of 32 ladies and gentlemen who form the "pieces" with which the game is played. The dresses of all are handsome, while each has some distinctive article of attire which denotes the character assumed. On Tuesday evening a rehearsal took place. Some games were played and various movements and evolutions gone through by the pieces, the effect of whose picturesque appearance was heightened by the flood of lime light directed upon them by Mr. J.A.R. Rudge. The game played is, of course, one pre-arranged, and thus the patience of the audience is not tried by the tedious "waits" which would inevitably take place were two skillful players placed in opposition. The movements, indeed, are rapid, while the manner in which the game is played makes the exhibition very interesting. Mr. Wilkinson, of Birmingham, and Mr. C.W. Dymond, a member of the committee, direct the games, and immediately a move is called the character referred to marches to the square indicated and takes up his position thereon if it be vacant, if not—except in certain cases—he engages in a terrific combat with its possessor, and of course becomes the victor. The fighting is not confined to the Knights, but is engaged in by the Castles, and the humble but useful Pawn, while even the King himself does not sometimes disdain crossing weapons with an adventurous foot soldier of the opposite side. Indeed the fights are sometimes rather severe, and often, unequal, and those spectators who know nothing of chess may perhaps wonder how it is that a little Pawn with his spear is occasionally powerful enough to vanquish the Knight with its battleaxe, the Rook with his sword, and even to make the Royal head himself, armed as it he is with a kingly sword, fly away in terror at his approach. The weapons of the Bishops are not carnal, and any Knight, Rook, or Pawn who sees a Rev. Father approach immediately kneels and peacefully delivers up his arms; courtesy also demands that the Queen should not be opposed, while both Queen and Bishop, if they recognize that the odds are against them, gracefully retire, and yield up possession of the coveted ground. A clanging discordant sound from the band announces that the King is in check, while a series of the same noises are emitted when his Majesty, vainly endeavouring to find a place of safety, darts hither and thither distractedly, and checkmate is signalled by the kneeling of the defeated forces, and the strains of the "The Conquering Hero" played by the band. The sword of the defeated King is then taken by the Marshal (who also leads the disabled combatants from the "field"), and handed to the Royal victor, who subsequently returns it when another game is begun. It will be seen that when the pieces are well coached this is a most interesting performance, and doubtless large numbers will witness it during the progress of the bazaar [...].

That Pollock had a significant hand in organizing the exhibition is proven not only by his leading role as the White King. When a city official enquired on whose authority a large hoarding (a billboard) was erected on the north wall of a shop on Old Bond Street, where the living chess exhibition was going to take place, according to the *Bath Chronicle* of May 15, 1884, Pollock stepped forward and acknowledged his responsibility in the matter. As the representative of the Living Chess Tournament committee, he sought and obtained permission of the shop owner, who was an ex-mayor of the city. Upon further protests, Pollock noted that "The hoarding may have prejudiced the minds of the people, as it is a frightful thing, but it would be posed artistically and would be almost an ornament to the street for a week or so." The city officials had none of it and considered such an unapproved construction a "piece of impertinence." They ordered it to be taken down. Evidently, Pollock's sense of artistry went unappreciated. It was neither the first nor the last time his willful enthusiasm would lead him into conflict with others, whether family, friends or authorities.

Before attending the Counties' Chess Association's meeting, the Pollock brothers played for Bath in the rematch against Bristol. Gathered in the banquet room of the Guildhall in Bath, a venue allowed by express permission of the city's mayor, the teams commenced play at 4:30 Thursday afternoon, June 26. A "considerable number of spectators" witnessed the exciting play. William scored only 1–1 at third board in his two games against a player named Franklin, losing a Scotch Gambit with Black and winning a Sicilian as White. John, however, scored 1½–½ against a Mr. Hunt on board five, and helped the Bath team tie the match 11½–11½.[11]

Bath 1884: Counties' Chess Association

A month after this return match, Bath hosted the annual meeting of the Counties' Chess Association. The meeting began Monday, July 28, and lasted until August 9.[12] Skipworth, the heart and soul of the organization, mailed the meeting's preliminary program to the *British Chess Magazine*. Along with Skipworth, six other players entered in the Class I (Division I) section: H.E. Bird, C.E. Ranken, G. MacDonnell, E. Thorold, W. Wayte, and J.L. Minchin. In the second division of the same class, Pollock was in the company of the Rev. M. Pierpoint, J. Burt, C.J. Lambert, J. Coker, J.H. Blake, C.D. Locock, T.H.D. May, the Rev. W.L. Newham, and W.E. Hill. His brother John played in the Class II section with ten other amateurs.[13]

As signaled by the *Bath Chronicle and Weekly Gazette* of July 31, both Pollocks played in the Association's handicap tournament. In the first round, William Pollock defeated Thorold while John lost to Pierpoint. In the main tournament, by the Wednesday evening of July 30, after four rounds, Pollock had scored against Fedden and Loman but had lost to Burt and Lampert. The next day he scored his third point, against May. For the rest of the tournament, Pollock lost only one more game, to the strong Blake, and scored against Coker, Huntsman, Locock and Pierpoint, finishing 7–3. Since Fedden and Loman matched Pollock's score, tiebreak games were necessary.

Ordinarily such a close finish would produce further excitement for spectators and players, but it seems at Bath the expected pleasure was marred. Pollock won his tiebreak game against Loman, but an incident took place in his other tiebreak game against Fedden, of the Bristol and Clifton Chess Association. Several columnists did not shy away from voicing criticism at the way the referees conducted themselves. Apparently they left the city on Saturday morning, way ahead of the final round of all competitions, leaving some of the players on their own in critical situations. One such case was Pollock's decisive last round game against Fedden in the Class I, Division II tournament. Pollock claimed that Fedden exceeded the time limit but there was no referee to

11. Reports of the match appeared in the *Western Daily Gazette* (June 27, 1884), *Bristol Mercury and Daily Post* (June 27, 1884) and *Bath Chronicle and Weekly Gazette* (July 3, 1884). • **12.** The preliminary program of the Counties' Chess Association tournament held in Bath in July–August 1884 appeared in the *British Chess Magazine* of July 1884, page 285, the *Sheffield Independent* of July 26, 1884, and the *Bath Chronicle and Weekly Gazette* of July 31, 1884.The latter two noted that John Pollock was one of the members of the organizing committee. Several newspaper reports mentioning William Pollock's play were found in the chess columns of the *Bristol Mercury and Daily Post* of July 29 and July 31 and the columns of the *Western Daily Gazette* of early August 1884. • **13.** A sample of John Pollock's play was found in Bristol's *Western Daily News*, July 30, 1884: **J. Pollock–E.L. Raymond, Counties' Chess Association (Class II), Bath, 28 July 1884: 1. e4 e5 2. Nf3 Nc6 3. Nc3 Nf6 4. Bb5 Bb4 5. 0–0 0–0 6. Nd5 N×d5 7. e×d5 Nd4 8. N×d4 e×d4 9. c3 Bc5 10. d3 Qf6 11. b4 Bb6 12. c4 c6 13. d×c6 d×c6 14. Ba4 Bf5 15. c5 Bc7 16. Bb3 Qg6 17. Bc4 Rae8 18. f4 Bg4 19. Qd2 Re2 20. f5 Qh5 0–1.**

decide upon the matter.[14] While the Class I (Division 1) section of the event was clearly won by Wayte, followed by Skipworth and Bird, deciding who actually won Pollock's division was no easy matter, with several accounts indicating a tie while others specified there were additional playoff games between the two. As for John, Pollock's brother, he played well in the Class III tournament, finishing second with 8½ points, just half a point behind the winner.[15]

In the main handicap tournament, 20 players competed. John was knocked out in the first round by Pierpoint, while William, after eliminating Thorold in the first round, knocked out MacDonnell and Hill in the second and third rounds and finished in a respectable third place.

Just a few days prior to the start of the Counties' Chess Association in Bath, on July 24, Leopold Hoffer (1842–1913), the chess organizer and influential columnist for *The Field*, was busy at Simpson's Divan in London forming the British Chess Association. About 70 chess clubs in the country sent representatives, and the meeting's final report showed good signs for increased chess activity at the master level in England. The constitution and the program of the newly founded association were finally drafted at the end of January 1885 and published in the country's leading chess journals.[16] Pollock himself would be a keen participant in the events organized by the British Chess Association the very next summer.

Pollock returned to Bath for the winter of 1884–1885. On Wednesday, February 25, a few days after he turned 24, he took a trip to Bristol, this time without his brother John, to lead the Bath team once again in the traditional interclub match held at the Imperial Hotel. Playing second board, Pollock won only one game against W.H. Harsant. Nevertheless his play was considered impressive. "A few years ago Mr. W.H.K. Pollock, Mr. T.H.D. May, and Messrs. F.A., and W.E. Hill, especially, were, comparatively speaking, novices in the game," the columnist of the *Bristol Mercury and Daily Post* wrote on February 26. "Now they are qualified to take rank amongst the amateurs of the kingdom, and the first-named, indeed, at the meeting of the Counties' Chess Association, in August last tied for the first prize with Mr. N. Fedden, of this city, and Mr. Loman, of London and formerly of Belgium [*sic*]. The three prizes, first, second and third, were divided between the gentlemen mentioned, after a second undecided trial."

The rematch against Bristol and Clifton was played on Wednesday evening, May 20, in the Council Chamber of the Guildhall in Bath. The plan was for 13 boards, rather than the previous 10, and for each pair of players to conduct two games. If need be, at nine o'clock p.m. adjudication would begin. While two ladies graced the proceedings, Miss Thorold for Bath and Miss Mary Rudge for Bristol and Clifton, officers from both clubs were also among the spectators. At 6:15

---

14. The incident between Pollock and Fedden was described in the *Bristol Mercury and Daily Post* of August 4, 1884, and the *Bath Chronicle and Weekly Gazette* of August 7, 1884. The *Bristol Mercury* column gave Pollock and Fedden as tied for the first and second place. The *Leeds Mercury* chess column for August 16 stated the following: "Messrs. Fedden, Loman and Pollock, made equal scores, seven each. We do not know the result of the play in deciding their respective positions." The column of the *Nottinghamshire Guardian* of August 15 gave Pollock and Fedden as tied for the top two positions. The column of the *Sheffield and Rotherham Independent* of August 18 noted that Pollock finished first, followed by Fedden, but the September 6 issue revised its announcement, acknowledging that Pollock, Fedden and Loman tied for the top three positions. The London *Times* of August 9 announced that all three players earned the right to participate in the Class I tournament of next year's meeting in Hereford. *The Chess-Monthly* (September 1884, page 5) noted that "the result was a tie and division of the prizes between Messrs. Fedden, Loman, and W.H.K. Pollock, in equal shares of £5 6s. 8d. each." A more detailed report published by the *British Chess Magazine* (August–September 1884, pages 324–327) made no mention of the Pollock-Fedden incident, stating instead that no tiebreak games were played at all. • **15.** According to the *Bath Chronicle and Weekly Gazette* of August 7, 1884, and *The Chess Player's Chronicle* of August 3, 1884 (page 73). • **16.** Detailed reports about the inaugural meetings of the British Chess Association appeared in the *Chess Player's Chronicle*, January 21, 1885, pages 319–320 and the *British Chess Magazine* of March 1885, pages 101–104.

play was interrupted by a short break for tea, coffee and other refreshments, at which time eight games had been decided, the majority (5½) in favor of Bath. At nine o'clock, three or four games that were adjudicated made the score even more in Bath's favor, the final tally being 16 to 8. William scored 1½–½ at second board against L.J. Williams, thereby contributing to the Bath Chess Club's victory.[17]

Between February and April 1885, Pollock played chess in Bath and Bristol but also in London and Dublin, mostly informal encounters with some of each city's best players. In mid–June 1885 he went to London to play in the first congress of the newly formed British Chess Association, staged at Simpson's Divan between June 15 and July 3. The tournament would be Pollock's most severe test thus far during a time labeled as the "beginning of a new era in the history of English chess."

London 1885: British Chess Association Tournament

Hoffer's yearlong efforts to provide the metropolitan chess scene with an all-encompassing event were rewarded, although the full slate of hoped for events did not come off. The major attraction was the British Chess Association tournament, which attracted entries from 16 strong players: Bird, Isidor Gunsberg, G.A. MacDonnell, J. de Soyres, Loman, W. Donisthorpe, G.E. Wainwright, A. Guest, Thomas Hewitt, James Mortimer, H.A. Reeves, A. Rumboll, W. Wyllis Mackeson, D.Y. Mills, R. Rabson and the young Pollock. Five money prizes were offered, of 25, 15, 10, 5 and 4 guineas, respectively. In addition, the Association planned to hold an Association Cup event, open to all clubs and associations federated with the British Chess Association. As it turned out, however, there were not enough entries for this particular section. Another feature of the meeting that unfortunately had to be cancelled was a blindfold match involving Blackburne and Zukertort. Neither master was in London at the time.[18]

More successful were other features of the congress that ran in parallel: a problem solution tournament "for the quickest and most correct solution to problems," and a small consultation tournament between a "chess master and amateur v. chess master and amateur." Pollock signed up for both the problem solution tournament as well as for the consultation tournament. In the latter he played the role of the "amateur" accompanying the more established MacDonnell. Another attractive feature was a small tournament for the Lord Tennyson's Prize which consisted of the works "of the poet laureate and president of the B.C.A., with his autograph inscription." This event was, curiously enough, reserved for those belonging to the bar, the field of medicine, or the church. Pollock entered to play next to Donisthorpe, Heppell, MacDonnell, S.F. Smith, the Rev. de Soyres, Reeves and Trenchard. John Ruskin offered a similar prize for those belonging to the realms of art, science and literature, with the top prize being won eventually by James Mortimer.

When, on the afternoon of Monday, June 15, Pollock entered the commodious rooms of

---

17. Reports appeared in the *British Chess Magazine* of June 1885 (pages 213–214), the *Bristol Mercury* (May 21, 1885), the *Morning Post* (May 25, 1885), and the *Sheffield and Rotherham Independent* (May 30, 1885). ● **18.** It is a pity that Blackburne was not present for the inaugural British Chess Association meeting in June 1885. The *Leeds Mercury* of June 27 revealed the reason for his absence: he was on his way from the Antipodes through the Suez Canal but was greatly delayed by its stoppage due to the sinking of a barge. He expressed a great interest to compete in the Association's tournaments once back in England.

Simpson's Divan, the boards and men, stop-clocks and score sheets were already arranged. Games were to be played from 2:00 p.m. to 5:00 p.m. and from 7:00 p.m. to 11:00 p.m. daily, at a rate of twenty moves per hour. On that Monday Pollock lost his first game to Bird in a Dragon Sicilian, but bounced back in the evening with a quick win against Rumboll. On the next day, Tuesday, June 16, he lost quickly to Gunsberg in the morning and succumbed in the evening to Donisthorpe's powerful kingside attack. On Wednesday, June 17, Pollock lost his fifth round game to MacDonnell. His start, at 1–4, had to be disappointing, but Pollock was not discouraged. On Thursday, June 18, he recorded two wins, against Mackeson in the sixth round and against Mills in the seventh. On Friday, Pollock demolished Mortimer and on Saturday morning, June 20, he scored against Hewitt. That afternoon Pollock defeated Loman in the tenth round to score his fifth consecutive win, reaching an overall score of 6–4. After a break on Sunday, June 21, the next day Pollock drew against Guest, and the day after defeated de Soyres in the twelfth round. On Saturday, June 27, Pollock won another game, this time from Rabson.

No games in the chief tournament were scheduled for the weekend of June 27–28. Instead, on Saturday the problem solution tournament took place. Hoffer's initial plan was to have a number of fresh compositions crafted especially for the occasion by some foreign composers. Apparently, he received none that he could use. Instead, he selected two puzzles from a contest run in the problem section of *The Chess-Monthly.* "A four-mover and a three-mover, from the set '*Set Sapienti*' were printed on clear diagrams" read the extensive report of the same magazine, "and supplied to the competitors. The competitors were Messrs. Bird, Horwitz, Pollock, Mortimer, Raymond, Gunsberg, Jacobs, Lowe and others." The two compositions, widely reproduced through Britain's chess columns of mid–1885, are given below (solutions appear at the end of the chapter).

British Chess Association Solution Tourney, June 27, 1885

FIRST PROBLEM

White to move and mate in four moves

SECOND PROBLEM

White to move and mate in three moves

(Both problems are from *Chess Player's Chronicle*, July 1, 1885)

Gunsberg, who entered for only one problem, was the first to deliver the correct solution for the four-mover (first problem above) and thus secured the first prize in that section, followed by Bird. Herbert Jacobs won the top prize for the three-mover after he used only ten minutes to crack the puzzle. If Pollock did solve either of these two problems, he did not do so quickly enough to win a prize.

After the weekend, on Tuesday, June 30, Pollock scored against Wainwright, reaching the overall score of 9½ before his final game against Reeves. On Wednesday, July 1, Pollock won his final game, too, thus scoring 10½–4½ despite his miserable start. When the tournament came to its conclusion on Friday, July 3, Pollock finished a respectable fourth, behind Gunsberg (14–1), Bird and Guest (tied for second/third with 12–3). "Mr. Pollock," a correspondent wrote in the *British Chess Magazine*, "by his play in this Tourney has proved himself to be a formidable opponent, as his score shows." His finish was all the more remarkable, given his 1–4 start.[19]

On July 4, the small consultation tournament involving four teams was played. The teams were James Mason and Donisthorpe, Bird and Hewitt, Gunsberg and Hunter, and MacDonnell and Pollock. The crowds of spectators watched the play eagerly for hours, until some of the games had to be adjourned. Twenty moves an hour, the move rate afforded the players, proved to be too slow for convenient finishes. At any rate, the first prize of £5 5s was won by Mason and Donisthorpe, the only team not losing a single game, scoring 2½–½. Pollock's partnership with MacDonnell proved unproductive, and they lost all three of their games. Pollock fared much better in the Lord Tennyson's tournament, which he qualified to enter based on his training in medicine. Facing Donisthorpe, Heppell, MacDonnell, Smith, de Soyres, Reeves and Trenchard, he scored 6½–½, winning first prize: the autographed copy of Alfred Lord Tennyson's works. Three of Pollock's entertaining victories from this event have been found.

This first Congress of the British Chess Association received somewhat mixed reviews in the chess press. Regardless of how the congress was perceived, Pollock's play was clearly his best to date. And yet even the praise for his play included something of the similarly qualified reception the British Chess Association as a whole received. The *Leeds Mercury* of July 11, for instance, wrote that "Mr. Pollock, too, comes in with great credit. His play has always been original—sometimes, indeed, even to oddness—but then, without losing in originality, he has shown a steadiness and soundness that mark him out as a player worthy of the position he occupies." A brief announcement of Pollock's success in London also appeared back home in Bath in the *Bath Chronicle and Weekly Gazette* of July 9.

Hamburg 1885

A few days after the conclusion of the British Chess Association tournament, the young Pollock, encouraged by this success, traveled nearly 450 miles east to Hamburg to play in the

---

19. The description of the first congress of the British Chess Association in June and July 1885 as "the beginning of a new era in the history of English chess" comes from the *Northern Echo* of June 22, 1885. The brief reports cited in the text in relation to the British Chess Association Solution Tourney for 1885 come from *The Chess-Monthly* (June 1885) and *The Chess Player's Chronicle* of July 1, 1885, page 37. The quote about Pollock as a "formidable opponent" originates from the *British Chess Magazine* for July 1885, at page 271. The description of the small consultation tournament played on July 4, 1885, comes from *The Chess-Monthly* of July 1885, page 324. Further reports on the first congress of the British Chess Association that mentioned Pollock appeared in the following chess columns: *London Standard* (June 15; June 18–20; June 22–24; June 26–27; June 29–30; July 1–4), *Morning Post* (June 15–17; June 19; June 22–23; June 25–26; June 29–30; July 1; July 3–4; July 6), *Sheffield and Rotherham Independent* (June 16–17; June 20; June 29; July 4), London *Daily News* (June 17; June 27), *Northern Echo* (June 22), *Nottinghamshire Guardian* (July 3; July 10).

Hauptturnier, scheduled for July 12–26, 1885. He undoubtedly witnessed the masters section at Hamburg, which included the names of 18 strong players, among them Tarrasch, Gunsberg, Bird, Blackburne, Mason, Mackenzie, Schallopp, and Schottländer. Gunsberg won the top prize (1000 marks), followed by Blackburne, Englisch, Mason, Tarrasch and Weiss (all tied for second through sixth prizes).

Pollock entered the secondary tournament in order to try and forge the start of a Continental reputation. The secondary tournament was reserved for the young, aspiring talents battling for recognition as master players. Indeed, by tradition the winner of the annual Hauptturnier event earned the title of master among chess players. The players who signed up for the Hauptturnier at Hamburg were arranged in four different groups of eight players each. Pollock landed in the First Group, along with F.H. Brillow (Amsterdam), Benjamin (Hamburg), C. Doppler (Leipzig), A. Ehrenberg (Hamburg), Mandelssohn (Breslau), S.R. Rocamora (Hamburg) and P. Seufert (Berlin). Other remarkable players from the other groups were Max Harmonist (Berlin) and Jacques Mieses (Leipzig), both disputing matters in the third group. Only the two top players out of each group qualified for further play.

Unfortunately, little has been found regarding Pollock's performance in Hamburg. It is known, however, that he met his opponents in the following order and with the following results: a win over Benjamin, a loss to Mandelssohn, Ehrenberg (win), Brillow (draw), Seufert (win), Doppler (win), and finally Rocamora (loss). Before his loss to Rocamora in the last round, Pollock had 4½ points. A final round win would have given him the same score that allowed Mandelssohn and Seufert to qualify for further play. As it was, Pollock finished third and thus missed a chance to qualify for the competition's next stage. In the end, Max Harmonist finished first in the secondary tournament's finals. He cashed the 300 marks awarded to the victor and was followed by Wilhelm Bauer and Hermann Neustadtl. Only one game of Pollock's has survived from this event: his win over Doppler in the sixth round.[20] In addition, some years later, Pollock recollected the following fragment from an offhand game played against Schottländer on July 18, 1885, at Hamburg:

Pollock–Schottländer
Offhand, Hamburg, July 18, 1885

Black to move

"Herr Schottländer," noted Pollock, "who has just made one of his characteristic blunders and lost a piece, here shows his remarkable position-judgment by winning the game in eight

20. The Hamburg 1885 tournament book, J. Minckwitz's *Der Vierte Kongress des Deutschen Schachbundes, Hamburg 1885* (Leipzig, Verlag von Weit & Comp., 1886), has little information on the Hauptturnier section and presents no games played by Pollock. Pages 23–28 reveal Pollock's opponents round-by-round. Regrettably, at the time of research and writing the present authors had no access to the chess columns from the Hamburg dailies of 1885.

moves, as follows": **15. … Ba5 16. Qd4 d5 17. e×d5? e×d5+ 18. Be2 Qe7 19. 0–0–0 Qa3+ 20. Kd2 B×c3+ 21. Q×c3 R×e2** and Black won.[21]

Hereford, August 1885: Counties' Chess Association

Despite playing in London and Hamburg in quick succession, Pollock returned to England ready for more chess. His brother John joined him for play in the annual meeting of the Counties' Chess Association (August 3–13). The event started on Monday, August 3, in Hereford, at the Green Dragon Assembly Rooms, where "A.B. Skipworth of Tetford Rectory, Horncastle, [had], as usual, obtained the patronage and cooperation of a great number of noblemen, ladies, and gentlemen residing in all parts of the kingdom." An element of novelty, "for the first time in the history of the association," was a masters' tournament open to all in the world. But to offer such an event is one thing; to see it to successful fruition another. And that could only happen if some significant money prizes were placed on the table. The fact that the Association was celebrating 20 years of existence provided a fortunate context for this to take place. The first prize in the masters' tournament was £60, the second £25, the third £15, and the fourth of £5.

The *British Chess Magazine*, August–September 1885, page 330, announced:

> But in addition to these special prizes the zeal and the liberality of the Hereford Committee, headed by the President for this year, Mr. C. Anthony, enabled them to increase also the ordinary prizes of the Association very considerably. Naturally, the prospect of reward for success thus held out attracted a large number of entries, more indeed at first in one or two of the classes than the Committee well knew what to do with, and though some of them did not turn up, there were still enough to make it necessary to divide the ordinary first and second classes into two sections.

When the Congress was opened by the president at 6:00 on that Monday evening, August 3, Pollock was one of the many players in attendance listening to the eloquent address about the history of the Counties' Chess Association. An hour later the games in both first and second class sections commenced, while the masters were scheduled to have their first clash the next morning.

While his brother John played in the Class I tournament, Pollock, for the first time, was in the Masters Tournament in the company of some of the strongest players of his time: Bird, Blackburne, and Gunsberg were there, as was the American champion, George Mackenzie. Mason played, as did the Rev. J. Owen, the Rev. Ranken, Schallopp, the Rev. Skipworth, and Thorold. "This," the London *Times* noted, "is stated to be undoubtedly the strongest competition of play yet held under the auspices of the Counties' Chess Association." Notably, even Tarrasch manifested an interest in playing, but eventually did not make an appearance.[22]

Unlike modern tournaments, well organized with conditions known long in advance, the players in the masters' section had yet to agree on whether to play a single or a double-round tournament, as well as what time control to use. Nine of the players voted for a single-round tournament at 15 moves an hour, while Pollock and Bird voted for a double-round tournament at 20 moves an hour. Eventually, the majority prevailed and a single round resulted.

---

21. This fragment appeared, years after the game was played, in the *Baltimore Sunday News* of May 13, 1893. •
22. The cited reports regarding the Counties' Chess Association meeting at Hereford in 1885 come from the *Daily News* of August 3, 1885, and *British Chess Magazine* of August–September 1885, pages 330 and 333–334. The quote from London *Times* comes from the August 7, 1885, edition.

The Counties' Chess Association Meeting at Hereford, the Masters Tournament, 1885. Sitting (left to right): J. Mason, J.H. Blackburne, Charles Anthony (the president), G. Mackenzie, the Rev. C.E. Ranken; standing (left to right): I. Gunsberg, E. Thorold, H.E. Bird, W.H.K. Pollock, T. Smith, E. Schallopp, the Rev. J. Owen, the Rev. A.B. Skipworth (*Illustrated London News*, August 29, 1885, page 209).

The tournament was not a success for Pollock, who scored a disappointing 3 out of 10 (winning only from Ranken, Mason and Thorold) and tied with Ranken and Thorold at the crosstable's bottom. In the Class I section, his brother John did not place his name among the prize winners either. Both brothers also played in the handicap tournament which attracted 24 entries.

William was a first class player in that tournament and had to give pawn and move to second class players, and pawn and two moves to third class players. He did not reach the third round before his particular section came to an abrupt end due to some absences.

The annual meeting ended with a special tribute to Skipworth and his efforts on behalf of the Association. Then, all the participants were invited to Charles Anthony's private residence for an exuberant dinner in a tent erected on the lawn. Several toasts were made, the main ones being to the Queen, to the Counties' Chess Association by the mayor, to the chess masters, and to the president of the Association. Besides friendly chess games, there was plenty of whist and billiards and fine music enlivened the enjoyable evening.

Ireland: Irish Chess Association 1885

After brief stays in London where he played offhand games or matches at odds against various leading English players such as Francis J. Lee, Pollock planned a fall trip to Dublin, the city of his student years. In the earliest months of 1885 the city's chess life was revitalized. As

A drawing representing the chess activities at the Simpson's-in-the-Strand (*Punch*, April 4, 1885, page 167).

T.B. Rowland reported in the *British Chess Magazine* April 1885, page 143, "the distinct revival" of the Dublin Chess Club started in February:

> The first social gathering of Chess-players known to have taken place in Dublin since the International Tournament of 1865—when Herr Steinitz gained first prize, the Rev. G.A. MacDonnell second, and Mr. Bolt third—took place at Byrne's Restaurant, Nassau Street, on the 28th February last. By Mr. Porterfield Rynd's invitation upwards of one hundred Chess-players met and enjoyed a most delightful evening. About fifty boards were in use at one time, and an unceasing supply of refreshments was served during the entertainment. Much credit is due to Mr. Rynd for the very spirited manner in which he has marked a distinct revival of Dublin Chess.

On April 7, 1885, another meeting took place at Byrne's Restaurant, this one headed by Thomas Long and held with the express aim of organizing an event around Easter. About 35 preeminent members attended. Rowland was appointed honorary secretary and treasurer. He revealed the dual goals of their meeting (*British Chess Magazine* article, page 144):

> The meeting to be held is intended to assume the two-fold character of a conversazione, open, without any charge for admission, to all Chess-players in Dublin at the time; and a conference, which, it is hoped, will lead to the formation, on a permanent and healthy basis, of an association of Irish Chessists. Some of the objects of the conversazione are, as suggested by Mr. Porterfield Rynd, (1) the holding of it periodically for the promotion of intercourse between the Chess-players of Dublin; (2) the formation of another and more widely popular Chess club

in Dublin; and perhaps (3), the establishment in Dublin of a good café like Gatti's in London, for the public practice of Chess.

The club was to be called "St. Patrick's Chess Club," and the project was heavily aided by the owners of the restaurant on Nassau. They "decided upon giving facilities for public practice at their rooms. They will provide boards and men as in the London chess resorts, and give every necessary accommodation—including bedrooms, of which there are eight—to Chess-players visiting Dublin." Things seem to have been going in the desired direction. Six parts of a *St. Patrick's Chess Club Pamphlet*, "a weekly representative of Irish chess" as it was called, were made available containing games, problems and chess intelligence for Irish fans. By June 1885 the major chess publications published the constitution and the program of the Irish Chess Association. Thomas Long was announced as its president, followed by four vice-presidents and a 20-man council. The preliminary program of the association envisioned a main tournament, along with several other contests for clubs, as well as contests for problem and endgame solvers.[23]

The new Irish Association meeting was expected to be but a small affair compared with the size of the recently concluded British tournaments, but Pollock had sufficient reasons to make the trip to the Irish capital. Wrote the *British Chess Magazine* (November 1885, page 401):

> Great magnitude for the first Irish meeting was hardly to be expected, bearing in mind the present state of affairs political in that country, and therefore it was with pleasurable surprise we learned of its considerable size and scope. Had the city and County of Dublin Chess Club, as a Club, joined in the undertaking, it is reasonable to suppose the dimensions would have been larger still. As it was, however, and having only the assistance of some individual members of the club just named—Mr. W.H.S. Monck the most notable—in conjunction with the strong support of the newly formed St. Patrick's Chess Club, the Dublin University Club, the Richmond Club (Dublin), and the newly formed Limerick Club, the association may well be congratulated on the success of its first meeting.

According to Dublin's *Freeman's Journal and Daily Commercial Advertiser* of early October, Pollock, a "valiant Knight of the board" as he was called by the *British Chess Magazine*, was confirmed as one of the participants in the annual championship. Play took place under the patronage of Lord General Viscount Wolseley. Besides Pollock only five other players were to compete in the main, round-robin tournament, to be played at the Richmond Club: W. Nicholls, Rynd, A.S. Peake, Mackeson and J. Murphy. By Wednesday, October 7, Pollock had defeated Mackeson and Murphy, thus early establishing himself as tournament leader. Eight days later he pocketed the first prize of £8, scoring an impressive 9 points out of 10 games. His one loss was to Rynd, who finished second with 8½–1½.

The new Irish Association also ran a handicap tournament, and Pollock enlisted as well. Included were all the players in the championship tournament except Peake, and with the addition of T.B. Rowland, D. Cudmore, J.C. Newsome, T. Kenny, and Parker Dunscombe. This event saw a reversal of the finish in the championship: Rynd took first with 8 points, while Pollock finished second with 6½. His score was good enough to pocket a £2 prize. But Pollock was not finished. On Friday evening, October 16, he gave what may well have been his first simultaneous exhibition. While the final result against the 20 players he faced remains unknown, the moment was significant for Pollock: he now began to perform the role of an acknowledged master.

Pollock also won a two-move solution tourney "for the quickest and most correct set of solutions to the problems submitted to be solved at the meeting." Pollock only entered the three move

---

23. It was published in the *British Chess Magazine* of August–September 1885, pages 282–283.

problem category, although both the two and three move problems are reproduced here (solutions are at the end of the chapter; for samples of Pollock's original problems, see Appendix F).

Irish Chess Association Solution Tourney, October 16, 1885

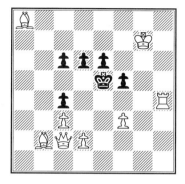

[FIRST] TWO MOVE PROBLEM

White to move and mate in two moves

[SECOND] THREE MOVE PROBLEM

White to move and mate in three moves

Solved quickest by W.H.K. Pollock

(Both problems are from *Leeds Mercury*, October 17, 1885)

On Saturday evening, October 17, at 8:00, a final business meeting was arranged at Byrne's Restaurant on Nassau Street. Various chess entertainments were enjoyed and, more importantly, Mrs. Rowland distributed the prizes. There is little doubt that both she and her husband were delighted to see Pollock as "Irish champion." It was during this time that Pollock's long-lasting friendship with the Rowlands was further strengthened.[24]

---

24. Mrs. Rowland, Frideswide Fanny Beechey, was born in Galway in the early 1840s. Her year of birth is unclear. In an article on pages 48–63 in the 6/2005 issue of the *History Studies*, a journal of the University of Limerick History Society (available online at *http://www.ul.ie/historystudies/node/9*), Tim Harding argued she was born on April 18, 1845, while Jeremy Gaige's *Chess Personalia* gives April 18, 1843. ¶ By the 1870s she had discovered a strong interest in chess problems and in the early 1880s was a constant solver of problems given in newspaper columns. In late 1882 she began a chess column herself in the *Matlock Register*. The next year she published a collection of chess problems entitled *Chess Blossoms* (1883). That same year, 1883, she met Thomas Rowland. The couple married and moved to Dublin, where they began working on book projects and edited chess columns for various newspapers, including the *Irish Sportsman*. ¶ Thomas Rowland was born in Dublin on June 1, 1850. In 1885 he was the chess editor of the Dublin *Evening Mail*. "As an organizer and one skilled in stirring up and infusing spirit," F.R. Gittins wrote, "he was instrumental in founding in Dublin, near where he resides, the Irish Chess Association in 1885, the Kingstown Chess Club in 1886, the City Chess Club in 1889, the Clontarf Chess Club in 1888, the Rathmines Chess Club in 1889, the Club of Living Chess in 1891, the Hibernian Chess Association, the Irish Chess Club in 1892, and the Glengeary Chess Club in 1893. In 1885, he promoted the first Irish Chess Congress held after a lapse of twenty years. He also promoted successful chess congresses and tournaments in Dublin in 1892 and 1893." ¶ The Rowlands continued to write chess columns both in England and in Ireland in the late 1880s and to publish books dealing with

At the start of the winter of 1885, the eyes of the chess world were focused on Zukertort, who was scheduled to leave for America on Saturday, December 5, to settle the matter of the world championship with Steinitz. On November 31, 1885, a farewell dinner was given for the traveling master by the City Chess Club. A large number of well-known chessists participated: Pilkington (in the chair), the Revs. G.A. MacDonnell and J. Scargill, Dr. Mackenzie, and Messrs. Adamson (honorary secretary), Black, Cunningham, Down, Laws, Lord, Manning, Pollock, Stevens, Wainwright, and others attended. After supper Pilkington proposed a toast to Zukertort's health, and bid him Godspeed on his journey.

An emotional Zukertort replied with gratitude and then referred to the stakes of the forthcoming match,

> which were got together without either himself or Mr. Steinitz making any public appeal, and he therefore considered the outside public had no occasion to grumble whether they were heavy or light. Neither was it a case of England against America, for he was able to state that, whilst the bulk of his own stakes were raised in England, the greater part of Mr. Steinitz's was raised in this country and India.

Frideswide F. Rowland in the late 1880s (John G. White Chess and Checkers Collections, Cleveland Public Library).

Zukertort's statement prompted loud cheers, followed by songs and recitations, those also interrupted by more toasts. One of them was made by Pollock. When to the slight disappointment of those in attendance Zukertort left the gathering rather early, Pollock, like the rest of the men present in the room, gave the master a standing ovation.[25]

The clash between Zukertort and Steinitz was followed in all corners of Britain. Pollock

---

(footnote 24 continued) chess problems. They were also very interested in correspondence chess and entertained an active exchange of chess columns from different parts of the world. After their marriage on June 5, 1884, the Rowlands ran a club in Victoria Terrace, Clontarf, which was open to all religions and both sexes. In 1893 the Rowlands moved to Kingstown where they lived until 1903. Here they launched a newspaper, the *Kingstown Monthly*. ¶ According to Harding's research, the Rowlands may have split around 1904–5, but Mrs. Rowland continued to head strong initiatives on behalf of Irish chess. By 1914–1916 her activity as a columnist diminished considerably because of the War and health problems. She died on February 25, 1919 (an obituary appeared in the *Irish Times* of March 22, 1919). It mentioned she was a "graphologist of no mean order and an ardent student of fine arts." (Graphology involved the analysis of handwriting, often associated with a psychological analysis; as a pseudoscience, today it has been almost entirely debunked.) ¶ Thomas Rowland died on August 13, 1929. Brief profiles of both (with illustrations) appeared in *The Chess Bouquet* (London, 1897, pages 77–80). Following Pollock's death, F.F. Rowland authored and published *Pollock Memories: A Collection of Chess Games, Problems, &c, &c.* (Dublin, 1899), a 160-page tribute to the former Irish champion. • **25.** The details of the farewell supper in the honor of Zukertort at the City Chess Club come from a report published in the chess column of *Leeds Mercury* of December 5, 1885.

spent the winter of 1885-86 in Bath, and there, besides engaging in correspondence chess,[26] he likely studied the game scores between the two titans. He may very well have fantasized about the scene of their battle far across the water. We do not know if he envisioned that early a future transatlantic voyage, following in the steps of Zukertort. It is, however, known that his next three years were spent on British soil. Occasionally, he traveled to London, where the major chess resorts beckoned. And once again, in the first month of 1886, Pollock would engage in competitive master play.

Problem Solutions:

Page 22:
First problem: **1. Qc2**
Second problem: **1. Qg6**
Page 29:
First problem: **1. Qb3**
Second problem: **1. Nf7**, **1. Ne3** or
    1. Nc6

Johannes Zukertort vs. William Steinitz during the 1886 world title match (John G. White Chess and Checkers Collections, Cleveland Public Library).

---

26. From the *Sheffield and Rotherham Independent* of 21 November 1885: "A match by correspondence has been arranged between the Sussex Chess Association and the Irish Chess Association. It will be of considerable interest, as the players selected on each side are strong. Amongst those on the Irish side are: Messrs. T. Long, W.H.S. Monck, P. Rynd, W.H.K. Pollock, G.F. Barry, G.D. Soffe, J. Murphy, M.S. Woollett, A.S. Peake, P. Dunscombe, Charles Drury, and Mrs. T.B. Rowland." A complete list of players and pairings was given in the *Dublin Daily Express* of December 24, 1885. According to the February 3, 1886, issue of the same newspaper, Pollock lost to L. Leuliette in 34 moves.

3. In England and Ireland, 1886–1888

London 1886: Master Contests

After spending the winter of 1885-86 in Dublin, Pollock returned to London for another opportunity to face leading experts. By at least one account, he was in "excellent form" and "won some pretty games."[1] The occasion was offered by a masters tournament at the British Chess Club between February 17 and March 13. George Newnes suggested the tournament, and contributed 20 guineas out of the total £42 prize fund (first prize was £18, second prize £12 and third prize £8). Pollock and seven others, namely Blackburne, Bird, Mason, Gunsberg, MacDonnell, Reeves and Guest, entered the masters tournament. In the first round, played on February 17, Pollock won from Reeves in a Giuoco Piano. In the next, not played until Saturday afternoon, February 20, he lost to Gunsberg after he misplayed the opening on the Black side of a Ruy Lopez. On Tuesday, February 23, Pollock's third round opponent, Guest, failed to appear in time for the game, and Pollock successfully claimed the forfeit. With his score 2–1, Pollock met MacDonnell

---

1. Reports of the time chronicle some of the festivities in which Pollock participated. In the winter of 1885-1886, Pollock maintained close relations with Dublin's chess circles: "CHESS IN IRELAND—The Dublin University Chess Club commenced its winter session with a meeting presided over by the Rev. Dr. Salmon, Dr. W.H.K. Pollock, Mr. J.B. Pim, Mr. Porterfield Rynd, Mir Aulad Ali, Major Shaw (late Hon. Sec. Dublin Club), Dr. W.A. Murray (Hon. Sec. St. Patrick's Club), Mr. T.B. Rowland (Hon. Sec. I.C.A.), Mr. Parker Dunscombe, Mr. Cudmore and others were amongst the visitors present. A Club tourney with 32 entries is now in progress. The St. Patrick's Chess Club having made an advantageous change of quarters from 29, Nassau Street, to 9, Merrion Row (corner of Stephen's Green), a large muster assembled for the house-warming. The capacious Club-hall was filled with visitors and members, who enjoyed a varied entertainment. At one end Mr. Porterfield Rynd contented *sans voir* against Mr. John Pollock, Mr. Soffe, Mr. Peake, Mr. Hanrahan, and Mr. Gerrard, but started the games so late that a conclusion could not be reached. Mr. Pollock succumbed when a piece behind, more on account of the lateness of the hour than by reason of any hopelessness of defence. Mr. Rowland in another part of the room with a large party, kept up 4-handed Chess as recently introduced by Major Verney. A winter Handicap of considerable dimensions and novel features is on foot with an attractive 1st prize—a beautiful set of Ivory men presented by Mr. Cudmore—a 2nd prize value of £ 2s presented by another member, and other inducements" (*British Chess Magazine*, January 1886, page 24). ¶ In January and February 1886, Pollock was also busy in London: "A little tournament is in progress at Purssell's rooms which is attracting some attention. Amongst the players are Messrs. Bird, Fenton, Guest, Gunsberg, Hooke and Pollock. All these are strong players and some good games are likely to ensue" [*British Chess Magazine,* February 1886, pages 65–66]. ¶ The following was recorded in the *Morning Post* of January 18, 1886: "Some interesting play has taken place in Purssell's chess tournament during the past week. In Section A Mr. Gunsberg, after declining a draw, was defeated by Mr. Anger, to whom he gave pawn and move, the latter having previously lost to Mr. Guest, who gave him two moves. Messrs. Hooke and Lee are playing well. In Section B Mr. Fenton, receiving pawn and two moves, defeated Mr. Bird, who, however, had more than one opportunity to draw. Mr. Pollock, who is in excellent form, has won some pretty games, notably against Mr. H. Jacobs. The contest will probably conclude this month."

in the fourth round on Saturday, February 27. The latter declined Pollock's Evans Gambit and a balanced strategic game ensued. Both players displayed good skill at purposeful maneuvering, but when a tactical melee broke out just before move 30, Pollock was more precise and won. Thus, before the fifth round Pollock had an excellent score of 3–1.

Difficult contests, however, were rapidly approaching. He faced his strongest opponents in the next few games. His good start faltered on Tuesday, March 2, against Mason. Pollock's most difficult game was against Bird, in the sixth round on Saturday, March 6. The game opened poorly for Pollock, and Bird secured very active play. The older player elegantly countered Pollock's attempts to confuse matters, so much so that even Pollock was reportedly impressed as the older player took the game toward checkmate. Two days later, on Monday, March 8, Pollock played his seventh round game against Blackburne. It was Pollock's third consecutive loss. When the tournament came to an end the next day, Pollock had tied for fourth-fifth with Mason (both with 3 out of 7) behind Blackburne (6½), Bird (5) and Gunsberg (5).

Henry Edward Bird (1829–1908), one of Pollock's most difficult opponents in the 1880s (courtesy Edward Winter).

In his final report for the *Illustrated Sporting and Dramatic News* (March 27, 1886, column), MacDonnell wrote ambivalently regarding the event:

> The Masters' Tournament recently concluded at the British Chess Club was in many respects a remarkable event. It comprised eight combatants, all of them more or less distinguished, and the majority of them of world-wide reputation. It produced several brilliant parties, and was conducted from first to last without a hitch of any importance. The prizes being small and differing but little in value, the contest may be regarded as simply one amongst amateurs, but the rules that were laid down for it, and moreover, strictly enforced, raised it, considering the strength of the players, to the display of a—I hate the word—"Masters" tournament.

He was less ambivalent regarding Pollock. In his April 3 column, MacDonnell severely criticized Pollock's play in this event, although some of his wrath appears to have been fuelled by his own loss to the younger man:

> Mr. Pollock came out next to Mason with a score of 3 games. His play disappointed me very much. It was only episodically good. He frequently drifted into a bad position without knowing it. Having formed a plan, and, finding himself foiled in his endeavour to carry it out, he seemed to lose heart and "go in" for random shots. To my mind's eye the chess board presents no grander sight than a battle fought out by a wounded player who with utmost force and spirit perseveres against desperate odds. A little more earnestness and enthusiasm, Mr. Pollock, in your play, if you would do justice to your great ability, and win what you naturally aspire to—a foremost place amongst our greatest players. Mr. Pollock's score was better than his play. He had one or two strokes of luck. Thus he won a game of Mr. MacDonnell, in which the chances were largely against his getting even a draw. He

also scored a game against Mr. Guest, owing to the latter failing to present himself at the time appointed for the combat.

Computer-assisted analysis of MacDonnell's loss to Pollock reveals that at no point during the game did MacDonnell have even the smallest advantage. MacDonnell's measure of "luck" was certainly inconsistent, especially when he viewed his own poor score of 2 out of 7 as a "small mess ... owing more to ill-luck than bad play." MacDonnell was hardly the first, or the last, commentator to evaluate the play of others through the lens of his own ego.

On Saturday evening, April 10, both Pollock brothers were again called on to support the Bath team against their Bristol counterparts. Play commenced at the Clifton Chess Club on Queen's Road in Clifton, with 12 man teams. "There was a good attendance of ladies and gentlemen who journeyed from the sister city," a copy of the *Bristol Mercury and Daily Post* of Monday, April 13, read, "and the play at the various boards was watched and—of course, privately—criticized with keen interest." Play commenced shortly after 4:00 o'clock in the hotel's large assembly room. Bristol quickly scored three victories in the first two hours, but "this was their last success during the match. In quick succession defeat followed defeat, and the Bath representatives once more showed themselves fully entitled to a high rank among the leading clubs of the kingdom." John defended a Scotch Gambit on the eleventh board against H.M. Prideaux, and by 6:20 p.m. had a two pawn advantage when his opponent resigned. Fifteen minutes later, just as a break for refreshments was taken, Bath scored two more points at boards six and ten. After the break, the Bath player at the fifth board won his game and made the score 4–3 for the visiting team. The Bath players scored win after win and at 7:40 in the evening they were leading 8–3. After the second round of games were played the Bath team triumphed 15–5 in one of the most convincing wins in match history between the two cities. Pollock's game on board three against L.J. Williams, an Evans Gambit Declined, had to be adjudicated as a draw, as were a good number of games, by 8 o'clock in the evening "when the Bath players had to leave to catch the train for their return home."[2]

Early in May Pollock took a top board for Ireland in a series of correspondence matches against Sussex. By May 27, it was known that Pollock had lost his game against L. Leuliette. The Irish team, however, led by F.F. Rowland, was leading the match 4½–3½ with six games still to be played. The *British Chess Magazine* offered the following résumé of Pollock's unfortunate postal debacle:

> In the correspondence match between Associations of Ireland and Sussex, two games have been already decided— one in favour of Sussex and the other in favour of Ireland. Mr. W.H.K. Pollock (Irish C.C.) succumbed to Mr. Leuliette (Sussex C.C.) in a Scotch gambit wherein he adopted a very queer defence. After the opening moves **1. e4 e5 2. Nf3 Nc6 3. d4 e×d4 4. Bc4** Mr. Pollock played **4. ... Qe7** and **5. ... Qc5**. The main feature in the game, as might be supposed, was the tackling of the Black Queen by White's minor pieces on the Queen's side until she was caught securely; and after the accomplishment of that task, which was creditably performed by Mr. Leuliette, the forcing of a win was not difficult, although Mr. Pollock bravely held out while there was any hope.[3]

Sometime shortly before the start of these correspondence series, the Irish Chess Association was invited to hold its annual meeting at Belfast in the second half of September. Although some argued for an earlier date, the annual tournament of the British Chess Association was scheduled

---

2. Detailed reports on this match appeared in the *Bristol Mercury* of April 12, 1886, and the *Bath Chronicle and Weekly Gazette* of April 15, 1886. • **3.** Pollock's encounter with Leuliette is remarked upon in the *Belfast News-Letter* of May 27, 1886; the cited report from the *British Chess Magazine* comes from page 96 of the March 1886 issue. A report was also published in *The Chess Player's Chronicle* of May 12, 1886, pages 497–498.

for July and the usually wide participation in this event forced the Irish organizers to settle for a later date in order to avoid conflicts.

On Thursday afternoon, May 27, the return match between the teams of Bristol and Clifton and those from Bath and Neighborhood Clubs was played at the Castle Hotel in Bath. The Bath team won 11½–9½, with William playing on the second board against Fedden. The two men split their games. John scored a point against Williams on the fifth board in a Four Knights' Game. During the usual concluding toasts, according to the *Bristol Mercury* of May 28, the president of the Bath Chess Club "expressed his pleasure at seeing them in Bath, and said he was all the more pleased that they had pulled up a little. They would have been very sorry to beat the visitors very badly (laughter)."[4]

In June, quite possibly to improve his form for the forthcoming British congress, Pollock played frequently in London. He participated in a spring handicap tournament at the London Chess Club. Preparations were needed for the Congress of the British Chess Association, whose executive council met on May 13 and decided the program. The tournament was to be held in mid–July in the Criterion's Victoria Hall, Piccadilly; the first prize would be £80, second £50, third £40, fourth £25, fifth £15, while the whole of the entrance fees (£2 each) would be divided among the non–prize winners in order of merit. Among the secondary events were the smaller tournaments prized with autographed copies of Tennyson's and Ruskin's works, consultation matches, a blindfold play exhibition, a problem competition and four-handed chess.[5]

Many strong players entered the British Chess Association's Master Tournament, which began play on Monday, July 12. Bird, Blackburne, Burn, Gunsberg, Hanham, Lipschütz, Mason, Mortimer, Schallopp, Taubenhaus and Zukertort were all on hand. Skipworth arrived late and could not join the event, while Louis Paulsen, Samuel Rosenthal, Riemann and Fritz also intended to join, but did not arrive in time. Even so, Pollock had never been in stronger company. The *British Chess Magazine* of August–September 1886 (page 340) wrote that

> Mr. Pollock is a rising amateur who is fast making his mark as a player. He took part in the last year's B.C.A. Tourney, coming out fourth prize-winner. Since then he has made considerable progress and is now nearly—if not quite—P[awn] and move stronger than in 1885. He possesses great originality of style with good position-judgment, and is in every way a valuable addition to the English section.

In the first round Pollock won from Blackburne in an excellently played game. He then drew with Gunsberg, but lost in the third round to Zukertort. In the fourth, Pollock won in brilliant style from Lipschütz. After a bye, he lost to the outsider Mortimer in the sixth round and to Taubenhaus after that. In the eighth, Pollock rebounded with a quick victory over the American Hanham, while in the ninth he bowed his king once again, this time against Bird. The tenth round brought Pollock more bad news, as he fell before Amos Burn. Schallopp was his opponent in the eleventh, and after a grueling eight hours Pollock once more resigned. In the last two rounds, as if to round out his inconsistent play, he lost against Mason but won from Mackenzie.

When the tournament finished on July 29, Pollock found himself in tenth place with what might have been considered a rather disappointing score of 4½–7½. But as a learning experience, the tournament must have been invaluable. Pollock had shown flashes of excellence, and had won against not only Blackburne, who was thereby forced to win a playoff against Burn in order

---

4. Another brief report appeared in the *Bath Chronicle and Weekly Gazette* of June 3, 1886. • **5.** Reported in the London *Daily News* of July 10, 1886.

A 1886 group engraving featuring the "sixteen leading players in the world." Sitting (from left): J.H. Blackburne, W. Steinitz, J.H. Zukertort, B. Englisch. Standing: G. Mackenzie, I. Kolisch, H.E. Bird, J. Arnous de Rivière, S. Rosenthal, J. Mason, W. Norwood Potter, E. Schallopp, L. Paulsen, G.A. MacDonnell, I.A. Gunsberg (*The Graphic*, July 17, 1886, pages 56–57).

to claim first place, but also in a fine game against Mackenzie. Blackburne and Mackenzie were then two of the world's strongest masters. This is how Cunningham summarized the young man's play, and his potential, in the *British Chess Magazine* (August–September, pages 356–357):

> POLLOCK's career in the Tournament has been more disappointing perhaps than any other of the unsuccessful players. In game after game he acquired advantages only to throw them away again, and commencing his score by a fine win against Blackburne he finished it by having only 4½ to his credit. His play against Blackburne was all that could be wished, but his victory over Lipschütz was the result of a stupid blunder on the part of the latter, whilst Hanham lost to him by a slip owing to pressure of time-limit. His game with Mackenzie was a very fine one, and its result had important effects upon the score, for had Mackenzie won he would have tied with Mason for fifth prize.

The *Morning Post* of July 28 concluded that "Pollock, although he did not win a prize, has played some extremely good games."

Nottingham 1886: Counties' Chess Association

Immediately after the British Chess Association Congress, Pollock traveled to Nottingham to play in the Counties' Chess Association's Masters tournament, starting August 3 at the Mechanics' Lecture Hall. Skipworth decided at the last minute to add an international masters section to his usual Counties' Chess Association meeting. He approached many of the masters playing in the British Chess Association Congress, and most of them accepted the rather sudden invitation. But when the exact schedule became known, disagreements surfaced. The requirement that two games a day be played unfortunately led to the withdrawal of Blackburne, Mackenzie and Mason.

The prizes Skipworth offered were £40 for first, £20 for second, £10 for third and £5 for fourth. The entry fee of £2 was, as in the just concluded British Chess Association tournament, used as a consolation prize fund for the non–prize winners. The ten competitors who eventually started play were Pollock, Bird, Gunsberg, Burn, Zukertort, Schallopp, Taubenhaus, Hanham, Thorold and Rynd. Despite the nonparticipation of Blackburne, Mason and Mackenzie, the tournament was still very strong. Pollock finished seventh with 3 wins and 6 losses, his only remarkable game being registered against Schallopp, who finished second with 7 points. Burn won the event with a score of 8–1, his two draws coming against Zukertort and Bird. Pollock's win over Schallopp significantly aided Burn's quest for first prize. Pollock also participated in a handicap tournament organized for the Counties' Chess Association.[6]

Triumph in Dublin

Pollock had to wait only a few weeks until another competition attracted his interest: the second congress of the Irish Chess Association (September 20–30). Local chess columns suggest that by the end of August, Pollock was already taking short trips to Ireland, giving simultaneous exhibitions there between his appearances in London's chess resorts. As reports mailed in by the Rowlands to the *British Chess Magazine* (July 1886, page 290) suggested, chess life in the Irish capital was revitalized in mid 1886:

> Not since the days of Tuatha de Dannianx, who introduced Chess into the Emerald Isle, has there been more interest taken in the game than what there is at present. The Chess clubs of Dublin, Belfast, Lurgan, Dundalk, and Limerick, are, notwithstanding the summer season, in full life and activity, and Tournaments are the order of the day with each, a case which is without precedent in the annals of Irish Chess.

The 1886 Irish Chess Association annual tournament took place in Belfast, starting September 20, at the Examination Hall of Queen's College. Unfortunately, the Association's meeting coincided with an extended period of rioting and unrest between Catholics and Protestants that had been tormenting the population since the end of July. The *Illustrated London News* of October 2, 1886, opined with heavy sarcasm that the tournament's venue affected its success: "the local riots must have greatly interfered with the success of the meeting; few persons are likely to have been attracted to Belfast in the face of the probability of martyrdom in the cause of chess." Some concern was also expressed in the *British Chess Magazine* (August–September 1886, page 365). Although writing before the Congress, the correspondent had greater hopes than his *Illustrated London News* counterpart for a more successful event:

> Great political excitement dwarfs the affairs of Chess; and the general election of July must no doubt answer for some abatement of the symptoms of Chessic affection now prevalent in Ireland. But the abatement has been small and temporary; for Ireland, in view of her important coming congress at Belfast—and 2nd of the I.C.A.— would not submit to more than was absolutely unavoidable.

A.S. Peake, the Association's new honorary secretary, planned multiple events, beginning with a main tournament open to all Association members, with an entry fee of £1, to decide the

---

6. Detailed reports on the 1886 Counties' Chess Association's meeting appeared in the *Nottingham Evening Post* (August 3–5, 7, and 9–10, 1886), and the *Nottinghamshire Guardian* (August 6, 13, and 20, 1886).

Participants in the Irish Chess Association, Belfast, 1886. Sitting: Amos Burn (left) and J.H. Blackburne; standing (left to right): William Steen, J.L. Downey, J.D. Chambers, S.J. Magowan, W.H.K. Pollock, J.S. McTear, R.W. Barnett, R. Barnett, W. Nicholls, N. Oakman, W.C. Palmer, A.S. Peake, R. Boyd, James Neill (*Illustrated London News*, October 23, 1886, page 424).

championship of Ireland. In addition, Peake planned a handicap tournament, blindfold matches between top experts, and an interclub tournament. The masters tournament was the main attraction, with Burn, Blackburne, Pollock, Barnett, Chambers, Harvey, Palmer, Nicholls and Peake as competitors. A 15-player handicap tournament, which Pollock also entered, ran parallel with the main event. This is how the *Belfast News-Letter* of September 20, 1886, introduced the strongest players:

> First and foremost among those competing in the even tourney comes Mr. J.H. Blackburne, the English champion by many considered the finest player of the day. This year, we believe, he has taken first place in every tourney in which he has competed. The entries also include Mr. Amos Burn, of Liverpool, who has recently scored such brilliant successes. In the late British Chess Association tourney he tied with Mr. Blackburne, but the champion defeated him on the tie being played off, and he only secured second place. Since then, however, at the meeting of the Counties' Chess Association, at Nottingham, he came out first with a phenomenal score of 8 of a possible 9, not losing a single game, a truly marvellous performance when we remember that he was opposed to such renowned masters as Zukertort, Schallopp, Taubenhaus, Pollock, Gunsberg, and Bird. Messrs. Blackburne and Burn have not met since the late B.C.A. Congress, and the result of their contest is looked forward to with much interest. Another great name among the competitors is that of Mr. W.H.K. Pollock, the well-known English master, renowned for the soundness and brilliancy of his play, never far below the winner in the tourneys in which he competes. Last year he won the Irish Chess Association even tourney in Dublin. Among the other entries are Mr. J.D. Chambers, of Glasgow, one of the strongest of the Scotch players; Mr. R.W. Barnett, president of the Oxford University Chess Club; Mr. W. Nicholls, of Strabane; Messrs. W.C. Palmer and A.S. Peake, of Dublin; and Mr. Ernest Harvey, of Belfast.[7]

---

7. The *Belfast News-Letter* published reports on the Irish Chess Association's tournament on September 20, 24, 27–30 and October 1–2 and October 8, 1886.

Given Pollock's erratic play in both his last tournaments, to emphasize his "soundness" and his results' being "never far below the winner," took some significant license with the facts. But perhaps facts were less important than spirit, in this case, and Pollock as well as the local players certainly brought a great deal of dash to a chess event surrounded by political chaos. An extensive report subsequently published in the *British Chess Magazine* (November 1886, pages 412–416) noted the inspiring effect the Irish Chess Association had on local chess, and noted, too, in passing, that the threat of riot had in the end perhaps not materially hindered the meeting:

The Irish Chess Association

Until recently Chess was comparatively little practised in Ireland. Clubs languished, individual players were few and lukewarm. The foundation of the Irish Chess Association marks the commencement of a new era. In Dublin first, afterwards in Belfast, Limerick, Lurgan, Derry and elsewhere, its invigorating influence has come to be felt. Among existing clubs the more prosperous have attained an additional prosperity, the less prosperous have been rescued from extinction. New clubs have sprung into existence, at least one which had died of inanition has been revived. By its constitution the Association is to hold annual meetings alternately in Dublin and some Irish provincial town. Of these meetings the first was held in Dublin last year; the second, of which we are about to speak, has just concluded in the capital of Ulster. Some of the English papers wondered some time ago whether any reckless persons would venture into the home of the Belfast riots in pursuit of Chess. A goodly number have gone and returned in safety; indeed we strongly suspect that some of those who did go are profoundly convinced that the much talked of riots are a myth: we know that certain friends of ours while attending the meeting went in quest of a riot in vain.

When play ended in Examination Hall of Queen's College, Pollock had scored the most brilliant victory of his tournament career to date. He won the first prize of £12 with a perfect 8–0, a remarkable performance when one considers the presence of Blackburne (6 points) and Burn (7) in the event. While he had shown flashes of brilliance before, never had he played so consistently. Nor was his good form limited to the masters tournament. In the handicap event, Pollock finished second with 11½ points behind Burn, who won with 13. Pollock lost only two games out of his 15, against Barnett and Burn. The *British Chess Magazine*:

Irish air, his native air we believe, seems to agree with Mr. Pollock. Last year, in Dublin, he was first in the even tourney. Again, at the meeting just concluded, he has out-distanced all competitors, taking first with an unbeaten score, a feat of which he has good reason to be proud when we remember that he was opposed by such formidable antagonists as, for instance, Messrs. Blackburne and Burn.

The *Nottinghamshire Guardian* of October 8 printed the following remarks about Pollock's play:

The even tourney was remarkable for the brilliant performance of Mr. Pollock, who defeated all the other competitors, including of course Messrs. Blackburne and Burn, the most successful players of the present year. This places Mr. Pollock beyond doubt among the very finest players of the day.

Although Pollock came in first, the particulars of his residence did not allow him to be crowned as Irish champion. The same *British Chess Magazine* article remarked:

We congratulate the winner on his brilliant success. He is we believe by blood an Irishman, but not being "resident" in that country is, by the terms of the programme, ineligible for the "Irish Championship" which falls to his latest antagonist the accomplished young Belfast player Mr. R.W. Barnett. Mr. Barnett, as our readers probably know, is President of the Oxford University Chess Club.

The *Belfast News-Letter*'s columnist reached the same conclusion on October 1: "Mr. Pollock, is, we believe, by birth an Irishman, but not being an Irish resident is ineligible for the Irish championship, which falls on our talented townsman, Mr. R.W. Barnett[...]." On that very Friday when such comments made their way into print, a dinner was given for the tournament visitors at Royal Avenue Hotel. W.A. Robinson, president of the Belfast Chess Club, presided alongside the president of Queen's College, and Burn, Pollock and Chambers were among the honored guests. According to the *Belfast News-Letter* of October 2, drinks and Irish songs prevailed:

> After dinner, which was served in Mr. Haussler's best style, the chairman gave "The Queen," which was loyally honoured. "The Lord Lieutenant and Prosperity to Ireland" having been drunk, the next toast was "Our Visitors," which was proposed by the chairman in happy terms. Messrs. Burn, Pollock, Chambers, and Nicholls individually responded, and drunk in the heartiest manner. Mr. James Henderson and Mr. Thomas MacKnight responded.... The next toast was the "Irish Champion," which was drunk with enthusiasm. Mr. R.W. Barnett responded in a most telling speech. The health of the President of the Queen's College was proposed by Dr. Barnett, and responded in suitable terms. "The Chairman," "The Vice-Chairman," and several other toasts followed. During the evening the pleasure of the proceedings was much enhanced by vocal solos rendered by several gentlemen of the company. Several of the speakers to the toasts referred to the very successful tournament just concluded, and expressed a strong hope that it would give a great impetus to the game of chess in the North of Ireland.

Growing Reputation

A week later, the *Belfast News-Letter* announced that "a match between Mr. Burn and Mr. Pollock to be played here, was proposed, and failed of accomplishment only through the unwillingness of one of the players to engage in it at present. We hope it has only been deferred." In fact, after Pollock gave a couple of simultaneous exhibitions in various Irish clubs that October, the two men instead played a long series of offhand games during 1887, although their overall score is unknown. Before then, Pollock found an opponent in Skipworth, with whom he disputed a match in December 1886. At this time Pollock was once more active at Simpson's Divan. The practice the young Pollock received with Burn, however, was undoubtedly priceless regarding the cultivation of his growing chess powers.

In early 1887 Pollock's reputation as one of England's promising young masters was growing and he found strong allies to vouch for it.[8] In May, Pollock fought a match with F.J. Lee at Simpson's Divan. As it turned out, Lee was much too strong to be given pawn and move odds.[9] Such individual and team matches, along with continuous playing sessions from May through July, helped prepare Pollock for play in the annual meeting of the Counties' Chess Association, this year held in Stamford in mid–August. In June–July he played in the first section of the City

---

8. When an articled called "The Chess Masters of the Day" written by Leopold Hoffer in the pages of *The Fortnightly Review* (December 1886) failed to mention a number of leading amateur players (among them Pollock), the *British Chess Magazine* (April 1887, page 152) pointed out the lapse. In regard to Pollock, in particular, the *British Chess Magazine* was astonished at Hoffer's omission: "The advent of a new Chess master after a lapse of twenty years is in itself an event of considerable interest in the Chess world. W.H.K. Pollock was early last year admittedly a master, in the opinion of many considered competent to judge. In August [*sic*] of last year he won the first prize in the 'Irish Chess Association one game Master Tournament,' winning from Blackburne, Burn, and six leading Irish players. He is most modest and very chivalrous, always ready to play on convenient occasions for pure love of the game and credit of victory alone. This is truly a strange omission." ¶ H.E. Bird sent a letter to *The Fortnightly Review* (January–June 1887, pages 471–472) in which he wrote his displeasure of "the omission of two out of the four genuine British-born masters, viz. the Rev. G.A. MacDonnell and W.H.K. Pollock. The latter was winner of the last masters' tournament, and is the first new master in this country for twenty years. The great interest in the chess circle at Mr. Pollock's success, and the encouragement afforded to the rising generation of chess-players by the advent of a new master, are considered to render the suppression of his name both significant and unfortunate." • **9.** "The little match between Mr. F.J. Lee and Mr. W.H.K. Pollock, in which the latter gave the odds of P[awn] and move, has been decided in the favour of the odds-receiver, the final score being Lee 6, Pollock 1. When Mr. Pollock's score at the same odds in the City Tournament is considered, this performance of Mr. Lee's points him out to be a strong and rising player" (*British Chess Magazine,* July 1887, page 301).

of London Chess Club's handicap event, where he had to give the odds of pawn and move to all his opponents. He finished third with 7–2, "a very excellent performance indeed considering the odds given," the *British Chess Magazine* duly remarked (July 1887, page 300).[10] Finally, another telling sign of Pollock's growing prowess was his presence at the top board in the City of London's team vs. St. George's Club encounter that took place on May 19. Although his team lost 8–7, Pollock drew his encounter against the Rev. W. Wayte, the same master who a few years earlier routinely defeated him in simultaneous exhibitions back home in Bath.[11]

CCA Meeting (Stamford, August 1887)

At the Counties' Chess Association's meeting that summer, held in Stamford at the Stamford Hotel between August 1 and 6, Pollock played in the company of Bird, MacDonnell, Blake, Thorold, D.Y. Mills, and Locock. Bird and Pollock were the favorites, but the tournament was won by the young Blake, who defeated them both and finished undefeated at 5–1, followed by Mills a full point behind. Pollock tied for third through fifth at 3–3 with Bird and Thorold, his only wins being against MacDonnell and Locock. Given his recent showing, Pollock likely considered his performance disappointing. As so often the case during these years, Pollock also participated in the association's handicap tournament. According to a detailed report in the *Lincoln, Rutland and Stamford Mercury* of August 12, the 16-player handicap event did not finish and the prizes were withheld.[12]

In the fall of 1887, Pollock oscillated between London and Bath, engaging in chess play while waiting for another congress of the British Chess Association. Occasionally, he gave simultaneous exhibitions in the neighboring towns. He did so at the Grantham Chess Club on November 21. According to the *Lincolnshire Chronicle* of November 25 and the *Grantham Journal* of the following day, he gave two 16-board simultaneous exhibitions (+15 –1 and +14 –2).[13] Then, on November 24, as reported by the *Morning Post* of November 28, he gave a ten-board simultaneous exhibition at the Grimsby and District Chess Club (+7 –2 =1).[14]

Between November 29 and December 8 Pollock played in the Third Congress of the British Chess Association, held at Convent Garden. The other participants were Lee, Bird, Zukertort, Guest, Mortimer, Mason, Blackburne and Gunsberg. The tournament winner would be crowned British Chess Association Champion and hold the Challenge Cup for 1887-1888. As at the previous Congress, there was another edition of the Tennyson and Ruskin tournaments. "On the opening day," the *Leeds Mercury* of December 3 noted, "play did not commence till about three

---

10. The *Morning Post* of May 30, 1887, wrote of this as an "excellent performance" by Pollock. ● **11.** The match was reported by the *Nottinghamshire Guardian*'s chess column of May 20, 1887. ● **12.** On the other hand, the column of the *Nottinghamshire Guardian* of August 20 noted that "Nearly all the visitors entered for the Handicap Tourney, which resulted in Bird taking the first prize and Pollock the second." The contradiction has not been resolved. ● **13.** In addition to calling Pollock "one of the leading chess-masters of the day," the *Grantham Journal* of November 26, 1887, recorded the following: "At the conclusion, a few minutes before twelve, Mr. Cockman (captain), in proposing a vote of thanks to Mr. Pollock for his kindness in coming amongst them, remarked that it would strike all present as wonderful that one so young should have attained so high a position in the chess world. It proved conclusively that youth was no bar to success, and should act as a great encouragement to the younger members of the Club. He hoped Mr. Pollock's name would become a household word, and rank with those of Steinitz, Zukertort, Blackburne, Skipworth, and other giants. Mr. Pollock thanked Mr. Cockman for his kind words, but he thought he had complimented him too highly." ● **14.** According to the *Lincolnshire Chronicle* of December 2, 1887, Pollock was accompanied by Skipworth during his visit at the Grimsby and District Chess Club. It remains unclear to what degree the two individuals were associated in the late 1880s.

o'clock, instead of twelve. All the masters were present, and many of the amateurs, as well as a considerable body of interested spectators. The master-tourney naturally attracted most attention, and the bulk of spectators gathered to that end of the room where masters sat within a roped space."

The tournament would not be one of Pollock's most memorable. In the first round, he once more faced the redoubtable Blackburne and attempted to surprise him with an early gambit. The experiment failed, and Pollock was routed in 22 moves. In the next round Pollock offered another Evans Gambit, this time to Guest, who accepted it and eventually won the game. Confronted with such a poor start, Pollock came back in the third round with a quick win against Lee, only to immediately drop another point, this time to Gunsberg. In the fifth round, played on Saturday, December 3, Pollock met Zukertort. "Pollock adopted an old opening—the Ponziani," the *Birmingham Daily Post* wrote on December 5, "and certainly accomplished a creditable performance in drawing with such a skillful master as Zukertort."

Interest in the tournament remained strong. According to the *Daily News* of December 6 and 9, while Pollock faced Bird,

> the crowded state of the large room in which the contest is being carried on testified to the unabated interest taken in the proceedings as the final issue draws nearer. From two o'clock until six, when no less than three of the five games were adjourned for the usual two hours' interval, the throng of spectators stood in close ranks around the space set apart for the ten combatants, and watched with eager attention the fluctuations of the different battles going on under their eyes.

Pollock's game against Bird was the longest of the day, finishing at 10:30 that evening in a draw after six and a half hours play. On Tuesday, December 5, Pollock defeated Mortimer in the seventh round in a Three Knights' Game. The next day Pollock met Mason. "Nothing daunted by his previous failures in the Giuoco, [Pollock] played it against Mason, but did not follow it up quite in the normal line, and the position became exceedingly interesting. Pollock played brilliantly and won."

The tournament's final round commenced in a "room crowded with spectators," as the *Daily News* reported. Pollock sat across from his opponent of so many games, Burn, the latter leading the tourney together with Gunsberg. Burn's victory assured him the first prize with 8 points, ahead of Gunsberg who, although he scored the same number of points as Burn, had lost their individual encounter. Pollock finished fifth with a score of 4–5. His up and down play was summarized by the *British Chess Magazine* (January 1888, page 42):

> The fifth place was taken by POLLOCK, who has certainly not added to his reputation during the present encounter. His playing the Greco counter—a recognised risky defence—so many times did not show good generalship, and doubtless had a good deal to do with his comparatively poor score. His play against Lee, however, was of a high order. The latter, defended by a French, and taking his Q out of the game, on the vain supposition that he could thereby win a Pawn, he allowed Pollock to get up an attack from which he never recovered. We have already mentioned his draw against Zukertort, and we can only add that he fairly earned the half-point, for his play was exceedingly good. His game also with Bird, was well and correctly played. The latter opened with a Giuoco Piano, and, as usual with him, early advanced P to Kt4, but he never got more than equal terms with Pollock, who at last forced a draw by perpetual check in an ending, when each had a Q and equal Pawns. His play against Mortimer was dashing and brilliant. The opening was a three Kt's, and Pollock got a strong attack before the first dozen moves had been played. "Horse, foot, and artillery" rushed to the charge, and at last Pollock, by a sacrifice of his Queen, had a mate in two in sight, and Mortimer resigned. Invigorated, doubtless, by his now rising score, Pollock sat down in good spirits to play Mason, and this may have had something to do with his adopting once more the Greco Counter—2. ... f5—despite his defeats by Blackburne and Gunsberg in the same opening. Be that as it may, however, he had better fortune with it this time, for Mason did not get by any means a good game, and

Pollock playing very elegantly, won. This, however, was his first [*sic*: last] victory, for in the final round Burn defeated him as we have already said, and he therefore came in fifth, with 4 out of a possible 9.

After a brief visit to London for more simultaneous exhibitions,[15] in mid–December Pollock gave a few simultaneous exhibitions in Ireland. As some accounts of games played in the Bristol area would suggest, Pollock spent much of the winter of 1887-1888 in Bath or Bristol. This may have been, in part, for family reasons. His brother John, who by now was a clergyman, did not give up chess playing altogether. Accounts find him as part of the Swansea chess team in a six-player match against Aberdare. John was the only player on his team to win both his games, and saved his team from an otherwise even more humiliating defeat, 3½–7½.[16]

From Bath or Bristol, Pollock traveled regularly to London. In the same month he was no doubt delighted to be added as collaborator to the editorial team of the *British Chess Magazine*. He also entered in a very strong handicap tournament at Simpson's Divan with Bird, Gunsberg, Lee, Mortimer, Müller, and Zukertort. Gunsberg won with a near perfect 16½ out of 17 games, followed by Mason with 15, and Bird. A small consolation for Pollock, who finished further back, was his one guinea award for the best game of the tournament. This singular success may have been enough to encourage him to enter another handicap tournament at the British Chess Club later that summer, if any encouragement was needed for a young master who relished his art.

The handicap tournament at the British Chess Club started in late May, and besides Pollock included Zukertort, Blackburne and Gunsberg, as well as Wainwright and several other amateurs. Pollock started badly with only one victory in four games, although his one win was over Gunsberg, winner of the handicap event earlier at Simpson's. By late June, Zukertort was leading 7–1, but on Tuesday, June 28, 1888, the master who had for so many years battled Steinitz on and off the board, suddenly died. The tournament was suspended. When it resumed a few days later, Gunsberg was in the lead and Pollock had only an even score. In the end, Pollock finished sixth with 8½, behind Blackburne and Gunsberg (who tied for first with 11 points), and Bird, Wainewright and Zukertort. The last named had played so well that, ironically enough, he won a prize despite dying before finishing his schedule.

In early August Pollock took a train to Bradford where the British Chess Association arranged its fourth annual congress, held August 6 through 18. In addition to the entries of the well-known British masters, a few international players appeared as well: Taubenhaus (Paris), Curt von Bardeleben (Berlin), Captain George H. Mackenzie (United States), and Max Weiss (Vienna). At the end of a long series of hard fought games, Pollock tied with Bird for the ninth and tenth positions with 7 points, behind Gunsberg, the winner with 13½, Mackenzie (12), von Bardeleben (11), Mason (11), Burn (10½), Blackburne (10), Weiss (10), and Taubenhaus (10). Five of Pollock's points were scored against strong masters: von Bardeleben, Taubenhaus, Bird, Mortimer and Lee.

---

15. From the *British Chess Magazine*: "Mr. Pollock set himself a difficult task on the 18th Dec. He visited the new London Banks Club, and played simultaneously against 21 of the members. As this club has something like 150 names on its books, one may imagine that our youngest master did not find matters very easy. He won eleven games, lost seven, and drew three" [*British Chess Magazine*, January 1888, page 4]. The same information is confirmed by the *Morning Post* of December 26, 1887. ● **16.** The Rev. John Pollock's play for the Swansea chess team is documented by a note in the Cardiff's *Western Mail* of March 5, 1888. Since November 1887 he played top board for the Bath team in regional encounters (see the *Bristol Mercury and Daily Post* of November 9 and 12, 1887, and the *Bath Chronicle and Weekly Gazette* of November 19, 1887). The *Bristol Mercury* of November 28, 1887, called John Pollock "the champion of Wales" and stated he was engaged in simultaneous exhibitions in Bristol.

Following his short stay in Bradford Pollock returned to London, where in November and early December he appeared regularly at Simpson's Divan, competing in two handicap tournaments, giving simultaneous exhibitions and drafting original annotations for a tournament book of the Bradford 1888 tournament.[17] In the middle of these events, and quite possibly aided by the Rowlands, with whom he had close ties, he embarked on a weeklong tour in some of the important Irish cities.

An Irish Tour

The initiative for this short tour appears to have been an invitation issued by the Belfast Chess Club. The *Belfast News-Letter* of December 6 stated, "A proposal has been made by some interested in the royal game to invite Mr. Pollock to Belfast to play for two nights all comers simultaneously. Nothing definite has yet been arranged in the matter. It is hoped, however, that some well-known master will visit our city during the winter and give an additional impetus to the study of the game." Two days later the same column noted that "W.H.K Pollock will make a tour through Ireland, and amongst the clubs he will visit are the Belfast, Dublin, Clontarf, Kingstown, and Rathmines."

In mid–December 1888 Pollock crossed the Irish Sea to start his Irish tour, but his first stop was not Belfast. It was Dublin. On Wednesday, December 12, the *Irish Times'* chess column announced the master's presence in the city. It did so recognizing Pollock, the two time Irish Chess Association Congress winner, as a particular draw for his fellow Irishmen:

THE DUBLIN CHESS CLUB

We have just heard with much satisfaction that the Dublin Chess Club have made arrangements with W.H.K. Pollock, the well-known player, who is passing through Dublin this week, to hold a reunion at their rooms on next Friday, 14th inst., for that afternoon and evening when we may anticipate some novel performance. It is not so many years since Mr. Pollock, when a student, was a member of the club, and often then ranked with their leading players. His games were always full of deep research, subtle in the extreme, and his combinations carried out with the accuracy of a master. We have no doubt his old opponents will largely turn up for the occasion to greet him, and to have again the pleasure of measuring their strength with the accomplished master. We learn also that the committee has allowed members the privilege of bringing a friend with them for the event.

Pollock arrived in Ireland on the day the *Irish Times* announced his imminent presence, and was ready for work the following day, Thursday, December 13. Fortunately for Pollock, then in his mid-to-late twenties, his energy and enthusiasm carried him through what many would have considered a daunting gauntlet of events. His first stop was at Clontarf, the ancient coastal town best known historically for the Battle of Clontarf, which took place on Good Friday, in 1014, against the Vikings. He paid a visit at the Clontarf Chess Club for a simultaneous exhibition. Pollock played 21 opponents and won 19 games. From the chess column of the *Irish Times* of December 13, 1888:

---

17. According to the *Morning Post* of October 22, 1888, on October 15 he gave a 17-board simultaneous exhibition at the Somerset House Chess Club (+14 −2 =1). The November 12 edition of the same newspaper printed the following: "A pamphlet containing a selection of the games played in the Bradford tournament, together with an account of the various competitions, has just been issued from the office of the *British Chess Magazine* at Leeds. The games chosen are 52 in number, and are for the most part copiously annotated by Mr. W.H.K. Pollock, who in a few cases has had the assistance of the Rev. C.E. Ranken, Mr. J.H. Blake, and Mr. J.S. West. A careful selection has been made of the most interesting games played in the Masters Tournament, and the book forms an interesting memorial of the Bradford meeting."

Mr. W.H. Pollock's Visit—The distinguished chess master, Mr. W.H.K. Pollock, who won first prizes in the Dublin Chess Congress, 1885, and the Belfast Chess Congress, 1886, defeating Mr. A. Burn and the English champion, Mr. J.H. Blackburne, in the latter, arrived in this city yesterday. On this (Thursday) evening he will visit the Clontarf Chess Club, Victoria terrace, and by simultaneously contesting the members and their friends, will perform one of those feats of skill for which he is noted. There being many strong players in the club, the entertainment promises to be of unusual interest. As already announced, Mr. Pollock will on tomorrow (Friday) afternoon and evening visit the old-established Dublin Chess Club, 35 Molesworth street, when we anticipate some novel performances between him and such players as Messrs. W.H. Baker, C. Drury, E.F. Geraghty, R.F. Hunt, W. Hillos, Rev. D.D. Jeremy, Dr. T. Mason, Rev. J. Maxwell, Captain M.S. Woollett, Messrs. W.H.S. Monck, J.B. Pim, Dr. T. Stack, Mr. M. Wilson, and other members and friends. On Saturday evening Mr. Pollock will visit the newly formed Rathmines Chess Club, which meet at the residence of the president, Cambridge House; and amongst those whom he is likely to contest simultaneously are Mir Aulad Ali, Sir Charles Cameron, W.J. Chotwodo Crawley, B.A., L.L.D., J. Dobson, J. P, J.J. Doherty, L.L.D., G.V. Patton, L.L.D., T. Mason, M.D., A. Quill, B.L., Captain M.S. Woollett, T. Eyre Powell, William Beckett, D. Cudmore, C. Conaty, J. Deheny, E.P. Du Cros, T.M. Kenny, F. Trager, B.A., J.J. Jones, B.A., J. Sandes, J. Wheatley, solicitor; A.G. Bagot, T.B. Rowland and other members. The visit will prove to be a great treat to chess-players here, and as it is so seldom such an event occurs, the committee of each club will allow members to bring friends.

On Friday afternoon, December 14, according to the *Irish Times* of December 17, Pollock was a guest of the Dublin Chess Club, the most important Irish organization of its kind. With a large gathering of members and friends who came to greet Pollock in the famous Leinster Hall (where Zukertort was entertained during his visit to Dublin), play commenced at 3:30 p.m. Pollock started the exhibition with six consultation games against the club's strongest players (first round: Peake & Miley, Fitzpatrick & Drury, Jones & Newcomb; second round: Fitzpatrick & Wellington Colomb, Baker & Woollett, Peake & Hobson). He won all three games in the first round. In the second, which lasted until 7:00 p.m., he gave up only one draw, against Peake & Hobson. In the evening, Pollock gave an 11-board simultaneous exhibition, scoring 8–3. Pollock had now given three long exhibitions in two different locations in little more than 24 hours.

The next night, Saturday evening, December 15, Pollock gave a "wonderful display of his power of simultaneous play" at the Rathmines Chess Club, according to the December 15 issue of the *Freeman's Journal and Daily Commercial Advertiser* and *Irish Times*. It was a somewhat unusual display, staged at the private residence of J. Dobson, an influential justice of the peace in the city. Pollock scored 9–3, with 3 draws, on the 15 boards. The use of chessmen of different patterns and sizes increased Pollock's effort considerably and two of the games he lost were blamed on slips made due to the difficulty of using such unusual and visually confusing sets. That he had given four exhibitions in half as many days apparently went overlooked, at least as an excuse for his slips.

On Tuesday, December 18, Pollock agreed to another simultaneous exhibition at the City Chess Club, in the Concert Hall of the Coffee Palace on Townsend Street. When Pollock entered the hall, accompanied by an elderly Dr. J.T. Pollock (a Dublin-based uncle of his), he saw 21 players ready to cross swords with him. He was briefly introduced by Dr. M. Dowell Cosgrave, the president of the club, and received a warm greeting from players and visitors alike. Among the notable visitors there was Mir Aulad Ali, an Indian Muslim who married an English-woman and became a professor of Persian, Arabic and Sanskrit at Trinity College, Dublin. As for the 21 opponents pitted against him, Pollock scored 17–4. Following the conclusion of play, Pollock received special thanks from Porterfield Rynd while Mir Aulad Ali was exceedingly impressed with Pollock's "grand display of simultaneous chess," according to the *Irish Times* of December 19.

Pollock gave no displays on the Wednesday that followed, but on Thursday, December 19, he visited the Kingstown Chess Club at 3 Haigh Terrace as documented by the *Irish Times* of December 20. The club was certainly "one of the strongest" in Ireland according to several accounts. After a warm welcome given to Pollock by all those present, play commenced at 7:30 p.m. Pollock had to battle 18 opponents across as many tables. After two hours of play Pollock scored his first victory. Then, from 9:00 p.m. to 11:15 p.m., Pollock continued to win point after point. Eventually, he scored 13 wins, 3 losses and 2 draws. Writing in his December 21 column of the *Stamford Mercury*, Skipworth made note of Pollock's "very successful tour of Ireland."

While contemplating an engagement in Liverpool, Pollock spent two more days in Dublin. On either the Friday or Saturday that followed, Pollock gave another 20-board simultaneous exhibition at the Phoenix Chess Club, at Morphy's Chess Divan on Grafton Street (scoring 16–4). As chronicled by the *Irish Times* of December 24, the attendance was so large that the resources of the club were severely taxed to accommodate the players and spectators.

For the Christmas holidays, Pollock interrupted his Irish tour and went to Bristol on Monday, December 24. He remained there with some family friends for Christmas and then left for London to complete some of his games at the Simpson's Divan Tournament. He planned to return to Ireland on January 8 so as to fulfill his engagements with the Belfast Chess Club.[18]

Pollock kept his promise and returned to Ireland in early January 1889, reaching Belfast on Tuesday, January 8. According to the *Belfast News-Letter* of January 10, he gave a simultaneous display the next day at the Belfast Chess Club. "Mr. Pollock, the eminent chess master, visited Belfast Chess Club on Wednesday evening," the *Belfast News-Letter* read, "and contested nineteen simultaneous games with the members. On Mr. Pollock entering the room he received a hearty welcome from those present. The place was crowded during the time of play with interested spectators." Pollock scored 9 wins, 4 losses and 6 draws. On the next day he planned to visit Portadown, on Friday to make a stop at the Victoria Chess Club, and on Saturday, January 12, to return to Belfast for another exhibition. He agreed to a number of simultaneous contests at Derry Club for Monday, January 14. During his visit at Londonderry Pollock received a "hearty welcome." In a 14-board simultaneous exhibition, in which he took White in every game, he scored 13–0, with 1 draw. A 15-board display followed and Pollock, this time handling Black at all boards, scored 11–4.

While in Belfast, Pollock experienced the deep gratitude and good wishes Irish chess players felt for him. The *Belfast News-Letter* of January 24, favored its readers with a recounting of how, as the visiting master's tour came to an end, the Belfast players united to show their appreciation. The account also gave something of Pollock's plans:

> We understand that a few of Mr. Pollock's friends and supporters among the chessplayers of Belfast have determined to unite in subscribing to a small testimonial to be presented to him before leaving the district, not only as a token of their appreciation of his disinterested efforts in the cause of the game in the North of Ireland, but also in some measure to contribute to his project of crossing over to America in order to compete in the great international tournament which is to commence in the first week of April. In thanking Mr. Neill, who, in behalf of himself and the other players made known the movement at a chess party given last Friday by an influential member of the Belfast Chess Club, Mr. Pollock expressed the pleasure it would afford him to be allowed to connect the object of the presentation with the expedition to New York, as he felt that ties of personal friendship rendered it especially opportune for him to accept such substantial support from his chess brothers in Ireland.

---

18. According to the dates given by the *Belfast News-Letter* on December 20 and 28, Pollock was scheduled for two simultaneous exhibitions at the local club on Wednesday, January 9 and Saturday, January 12. Additionally, on Friday, January 11, he was also contracted for a similar display in the rooms of the Victoria Chess Club. The members of the local chess club were exceedingly anxious to observe and compete against the young master. The club had, after all, been the first to issue an invitation to Pollock at the start of the previous December.

The Irish support mentioned here led many to view Pollock as representing Ireland at the Sixth American Chess Congress. The *Irish Times* of January 29 encouraged subscribers to contribute to Pollock's expenses on his trip to America for this very reason:

> The Irish Champion—Mr. W.H.K. Pollock, will attend and compete at the forthcoming American Chess Congress as Irish representative. The Belfast players, deciding that the burden of travelling expenses will not be borne on him solely, have united in subscribing towards such, and, in order that other Irish players may have an opportunity of joining, a subscription list has been opened by the hon. Secretary of the Clontarf Chess Club, viz.— Mr. T.B. Rowland, 9 Victoria terrace, Clontarf, Dublin.

While Pollock may not have met the residency requirements to officially obtain the Irish Chess Association title the previous two years, his Irish blood, his winning of those events, combined with his pleasant manners and willingness to take on all comers while on tour, made him "Irish Champion" in the hearts of those who came to know and appreciate him.

Pollock's prolonged stay in Ireland was connected to his participation in the Third Congress of the Irish Chess Association, played at Dublin, March 5–9, 1889. Besides Pollock, only two other recognized masters entered the competition, Amos Burn and James Mason. The field was completed by the following Irish amateurs: Captain F.O.C. Beaman, Peake, Morphy, J. White, S. Fitzpatrick, and M.S. Woollett. Play took place at the Dublin Chess Club in the morning and at Morphy's Chess Divan in the evening. In the first round Pollock had a bye, while in the second round, on March 5, he was paired with Mason, the result being a draw. The struggle for the first prize was an obvious fight between Burn and Pollock, the latter losing the decisive encounter and thus missing the opportunity to claim a third Irish Chess Association victory. Pollock had to be satisfied with the prize of £10 for second place, scoring 6½, a full point behind Burn.

From the start of 1886 through early 1889, Pollock's play began to show substantial improvement. Although his results would remain erratic, his overall play strengthened greatly during this time. The Irish and English chess public, in particular, had seen his status grow from that of a relative unknown to that of a player whose abilities, at their best, rivaled those of the recently departed Zukertort's. They had witnessed, as had his family, Pollock's transformation from an amateur to a professional.

Less than 24 hours after the Irish Chess Association prize ceremony came to an end, both Burn and Pollock began the lengthy journey to America to take part in the Sixth American Chess Congress, about to be staged in New York City. While Burn would eventually return home and remain one of the pillars of British chess throughout the decades to come, Pollock's life was irreversibly changed by this trip. In fact, as many of his closest confidants would one day argue, it may well have also severely shortened his life.

4. Two Months in New York,
March 25–May 25, 1889

Arriving in the New World

Pollock's romantic, "brilliant" style of aggressive king hunts and spectacular displays of ingenuity at the board may have been better suited for an earlier time in the history of chess, when defenses were less well developed and before Steinitz appeared to ordain the steady accumulation of small, strategic advantages as the orthodox means of proper play. Yet in individual encounters, as we have seen, Pollock could be an extraordinarily dangerous opponent. He would also be one of only seven men (the others being Chigorin, Blackburne, Burn, Mason, Bird and Gunsberg) to participate in the two greatest tournaments of his time: New York 1889 and Hastings 1895. His participation in both was well founded. Erratic as his results often were, he rarely failed to excite spectators—and later, readers—with exciting play, especially when he faced the grandest masters of his age. This chapter is about Pollock's adventures in his first, great, international tournament, and of his first two months in the country that would be his home for much of the remainder of his short life.

Accompanied by the 40-year-old Amos Burn, Pollock left Dublin on Monday, March 11, heading to Queenstown, a seaport on the Irish south coast (now Cobh, Ireland). From there the pair embarked for America aboard the steamer *Wisconsin*. Although Burn traveled in the exclusive Liverpool Saloon onboard the ship, while Pollock traveled in second class, a revealing detail concerning the two men's relative financial situations, there can be little doubt the two spent most of the trip either engaged in offhand games or discussing chess matters.[1] They reached New York on March 22, three days before the start of the Sixth American Chess Congress.

The great tournament had been advertised in all the major chess journals and newspaper columns. The following announcement appeared in the *New York Sun* of March 3, a newspaper that paid particular attention to the event:

FAMOUS PLAYERS TO MEET IN THE TOURNAMENT OF THE SIXTH AMERICAN CHESS CONGRESS

Players and lovers of the game of chess, both in this country and in Europe, are looking forward with the greatest interest to the Sixth American Chess Congress, which begins in this city on March 25. The international

---

1. Information extracted from the *Ancestry.com*. New York Passenger Lists, 1820–1957 [database online]. Provo, UT, USA: The Generations Network, Inc., 2006. Original data: Passenger Lists of Vessels Arriving at New York, New York, 1820–1897; (National Archives Microfilm Publication M237, 675 rolls); Records of the U.S. Customs Service, Record Group 36; National Archives, Washington, D.C.

The *Wisconsin*, a Guion Line steamship launched in 1870 and scrapped in 1892, took W.H.K. Pollock and Amos Burn to New York in March 1889 (authors' collection).

Section of the *Wisconsin* passenger list showing W.H.K. Pollock and Amos Burn (*Passenger and Crew Lists of Vessels Arriving at New York, New York, 1897–1957*; Records of the Immigration and Naturalization Service; National Archives, Washington, D.C., Microfilm M237_530).

tournament which this congress has arranged promises to be the greatest event of its kind in the history of chess playing. The masters of the game in America, England, Germany, France, Russia, and Austria will contend for the championship of the world and a prize of $1,000. There will be more than twenty players entered, and each will play two games with each of the others. Seven prizes are offered, ranging from $1,000 to $200. Messrs. Fred Wehle and Frank Rudd, who are on the Congress Committee, have offered a special prize of $50 for the best played game. Any chess player may enter the tournament upon paying an entrance fee of $25. A deposit of $25 is also required, which will be returned after the first or second round of the tournament. This is meant to prevent any player from withdrawing before he has played all his games. The congress will very likely last over six weeks.

The rules which the congress have adopted are the American code as laid down in the books of the Fifth American Chess Congress. These are some of the special rules of the tournament: In the first round drawn games shall count half for each player; In the second round the first draw shall not count, but a second game shall be played (in which the first move shall be drawn by lot), and if it results in a draw it shall count half for both players; If two players tie for the first prize they shall play a match; Any player withdrawing from the tournament before the completion of either round, save with the sanction of the committee, will forfeit his deposit of $25 and any prize he may be entitled to; The time limit is fixed at fifteen moves an hour, and will be regulated by stop clocks. The player who exceeds the time limit forfeits the game, which will be scored as won by his opponent.

The most important rule of the Congress, however, is that the winner of the tournament shall be bound to play a championship match if duly challenged. He shall not be obliged to play for stakes, but may insist upon the maximum sum of $500 a side. To insure compliance with this rule, one-fourth of the amount of the first prize will be retained as a forfeit until the championship match is completed or the time for challenge has expired. If less than four European players enter, the match will not involve the championship of the world, but only that of the Sixth American Chess Congress.

The judges of the games, who will also award the prizes, are Messrs. Thomas Frère, Philip Richardson, and William M. de Visser. A jury of twelve good players has been appointed to decide any question that does not come within the jurisdiction of the Congress Committee.

Among the players who are expected to enter are Capt. Mackenzie, Lipschütz, Judd, Hanham, Delmar, Loyd, and Halpern of the United States; Vázquez of Havana, C. Golmayo of Mexico, Gunsberg, Blackburne, Mason, Burn, and Bird of England. Von Bardeleben of Germany, Weiss and Bauer of Austria, Taubenhaus and Rosenthal of Paris, and Chigorin of Russia.

Mr. William Steinitz will not enter. He is busy preparing a book on chess openings, and this, with his duties as editor of a chess magazine, he says, makes it impossible for him to devote six days a week to a tournament. It is thought, however, that he will challenge the winner. The best score ever made against Steinitz, by any one player was made by Chigorin in the recent match in Havana. Steinitz out, the favorites will probably be Chigorin and Gunsberg.

Originally the brainchild of the energetic and influential Max Judd, the congress proved popular and the preparations for it ran relatively smoothly as it attracted subscriptions from around the world. Heralded by the *New York Tribune* of March 17 as "the most important occurrence in chess circles since the time [of] Paul Morphy," the event gathered the following 20 strong players: nine United States–based players (the Baird brothers, C.F. Burille, E. Delmar, J.M. Hanham, Max Judd,[2] S. Lipschütz, D.M. Martinez, and J.W. Showalter), seven players from England

---

2. Max Judd's contribution to the congress was underlined in the *New York Sun* of March 10, 1889: "The idea of this tournament was first suggested to American players by Mr. Max Judd of St. Louis in a speech at the annual dinner of the New York Chess Club three years ago, in reply to a toast in his honor, when he eloquently appealed to the chess players assembled, among whom where Messrs. Steinitz, Zukertort, Mackenzie, Loyd, Cook, Perrin, Delmar, and others, to start a scheme for a sixth American Chess Congress that would be greater than any hitherto held, and that would interest all lovers of the noble pastime on this continent and elsewhere. This speech had the effect of interesting many present in the subject. A committee was formed, and the New York Chess Club elected three delegates to represent the club—Dr. O.F. Jentz and Messrs. W.W. Ellsworth and C. Schubert. The committee worked with zeal and fidelity, overcoming all obstacles, and they are proud of the triumphant success of their efforts. More than $5,200 has already been subscribed to the Congress fund, nearly $1,000 of which came from sources outside of the United States. Europe, China, Japan, East India, Canada, and Australia are represented on the subscription list. Thirty States and one Territory also sent in subscriptions. The State of New York heads the list with over $2,000." ¶ An article titled "How the Sixth American Congress Has Been Organized" was published (with some fine line-drawings of the key players) in the March 24, 1889, edition of the *St. Louis Republic*, under the signature of a "special

(H.E. Bird, J.H. Blackburne, Amos Burn, G.H.D. Gossip, I. Gunsberg, J. Mason, and Pollock), one Canadian (N. MacLeod), one Frenchman (J. Taubenhaus), one Russian master (M. Chigorin) and one Austrian (Max Weiss). Among the notable absentees there were von Bardeleben, Tarrasch, Mackenzie and, indeed, Steinitz.[3]

The commodious hall over the Union Square Bank at No. 8 Union Square, two buildings away from the Union Square hotel, was to be the stage for one of the greatest tournaments in chess history,[4] a double–round robin with 20 players. As second round draws had to be replayed once, the overall number of games per participant varied between 39 and 47. At a very rapid pace of six games a week, the tournament was to last over two months, until the end of May, an unimaginable amount of time for an over-the-board tournament in more recent times.

The 30-year-old Pollock, who was almost invariably referred to by American columnists as "the Irish champion," and often—and mistakenly—as "of Irish birth," participated with 19 other master class players in an event which, even a dozen decades later, would still be

The English master Amos Burn traveled to America together with Pollock in March 1889 (courtesy Edward Winter).

correspondent." There should be little doubt that this "special correspondent" must have been either Max Judd or someone who had his complete cooperation. Although he must have appreciated Steinitz's efforts on behalf of the congress, a little bit of sarcasm was inevitable: "'Who killed Cock Robin?,' 'I,' said the sparrow, etc. 'Who got up the Sixth American chess congress?,' 'I,' said Herr Wilhelm Steinitz, and so fourth so fifth [*sic*]. This may sound a little egoistical—cock robinish—but all the same, it is true that Steinitz did get up this congress, and in spite of big obstacles and opposition." • **3.** Steinitz' decision not to participate was massively decried. From the official report of the tournament committee: "[...] the non-participation of Mr. Steinitz was a great disappointment to the majority of Chess amateurs. The Committee beg to say on this subject that they would have been highly gratified if Mr. Steinitz had been one of the contestants, and they are of opinion that whatever the result of his competition might have been, it would have in no way affected his impartiality as a critic in the Book of the Congress, which had been confided to his editorship. They also wish to state that they would have taken the fullest responsibility for any decision in matters of dispute in which eventually the interest of Mr. Steinitz might have been directly or indirectly involved, and being conscious that all their members only wished fair play to prevail, they would not have been embarrassed or influenced in the least by the fact that Mr. Steinitz had been one of the principal promoters of the Congress. However, Mr. Steinitz seems to have entertained different opinions in the matter, and having previously announced in the *International Chess Magazine*, in consequence of some adverse criticism in the press, that he did not intend to join the contest, he adhered to that resolution. The Committee, though they respect the motives of Mr. Steinitz, beg to say that his participation would have greatly added to the interest in the tournament." ¶ The tournament book Steinitz authored, in which the above-mentioned committee report appeared as well, was reprinted in 1982: *The Book of the Sixth American Chess Congress: Containing the Games of the International Chess Tournament held at New York in 1889*, by Wilhelm Steinitz (Zurich: Edition Olms, 1982). • **4.** In his excellent *Amos Burn: A Chess Biography* (Jefferson, N.C.: McFarland, 2004, page 346), Richard Forster argues that New York 1889 was the strongest chess tournament of all time, followed closely by London 1883 and Vienna 1898.

considered among the strongest chess tournaments the world has ever seen. Various day-by-day accounts place Pollock at one of the ten tables in the tournament hall.[5] This is how the chronicler of the *Sun* of March 26 saw the proceedings in the first round, played on Monday, March 25[6]:

> When President J. Spencer Turner of the Sixth American Chess Congress opened the tournament yesterday in the hall over the Union Square Bank he was surrounded by the brightest galaxy of chess players ever seen in this town[...]. The main part of the hall was railed off and ten tables set inside the railing, five in a row, as it was expected that twenty players would begin play in the first round of games, but Mr. Showalter of Kentucky, who was drawn to play against Max Judd of St. Louis, did not appear. This gave Mr. Judd a game at the start, so only nine tables were used. When play began at 1:30 lines of spectators three deep peered over each other's shoulders at the players. At table No. 1 they saw the modest lad McLeod of Quebec pitted against the black-haired veteran Taubenhaus, champion of France. At table No. 2 the venerable London champion, H.E. Bird, with high forehead and bald head, faced young J.W. Baird of New York, who looked over the miniature battle field from under a bulging forehead. At table No. 3 the handsome and keen-eyed Russian champion, Chigorin, faced Eugene Delmar's broad and dome-like brow. At table No. 4 compact Isidor Gunsberg of London, with full high forehead and ministerial aspect, faced with fellow countryman Amos Burn of Liverpool, who shaded his penetrating eyes under his hat. At table No.5 sat England's great player, J.H. Blackburne, wearing his hat and smoking his pipe, the smoke curling over the silk hat of Major Hanham, the Englishman's able opponent. Over table No. 6, loomed the finely proportioned head, covered with black hair, of Max Weiss of Vienna, who was pitted against young and pale-faced Burille of Boston. At table No. 7, the patriarchal head of Champion Gossip of Australia towered above the derby-covered head of Mr. Mason from London. At table No. 8 Mr. Martinez, a tall veteran with a high forehead and bald head, from Philadelphia, played against young and fair-faced Mr. D.G. Baird of New York; at table No. 9 Mr. Lipschütz, New York State's pale and fair-faced young champion, opposed Ireland's auburn-haired and intellectual expert, Mr. Pollock.

A Lackluster Start

"Closely watched by a group of experts," Pollock's game against Lipschütz was considered to be of interest "as showing the comparative strength of the New York champion and the champion of Irish birth." The score of the game, reproduced in the *Sun* of March 26, reveals that Pollock, handling the Black side of a Vienna Game, equalized rather easily in the opening and middlegame. After multiple exchanges in the first twenty moves, Pollock was still in a fine position:

Lipschütz–Pollock
Sixth American Chess Congress
March 25, 1889, Round 1

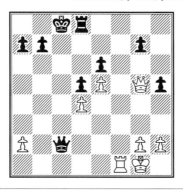

After 22. Rf7–f1

5. Among his first visits in New York, it appears Pollock paid a visit at the Eden Musée to play against Ajeeb, the famed automaton possibly at that time operated by Albert Beauregard Hodges. From the *Baltimore Sun* of April 5, 1889: "It is said that Pollock, the Irish champion, visited a museum where there is a chess automaton this week, and was beaten in two games he tried with the inanimate player." • **6.** The daily reports in the *New York Sun's* chess column provided the tournament's best coverage. Several are made extensive use of in this chapter.

Steinitz praised Lipschütz's last move in the tournament book: "This is a *coup of repos* of the kind that, in our opinion, denotes greater mastery than the conception of brilliant terminations. Such a winning retreat with its consequences in actual play alone could not be easily conceived nor anticipated by the opponent. Black's game is now absolutely lost." While the last sentence might be something of an exaggeration, the position requires care. White's move threatens the straightforward Rc1, and there is little active tack that Black can pursue. Pollock played the rather passive **22. ... Qh7?!** which allowed Lipschütz to take over the game with **23. Qe7! Qh6?** Black tries to control e6 and c1 simultaneously, but it doesn't work. After **24. h3 h4 25. Kh2 Qe3 26. Q×e6+** Lipschütz won in a few more moves. Instead of his choice for his 22nd move, in the diagrammed Pollock should have prevented the immediate Qg5–Qe7 with **22. ... Kd7!** which would have maintained the balance: 23. Q×g7+ Kc8 24. Qe7 Qc6!

The second round, played on Tuesday, March 26, brought another enthusiastic crowd to the playing hall. One object of attraction in the hall was a chessboard used by Paul Morphy, on which the Englishman Blackburne won his first game against Major Hanham. From the *New York Times* of March 27:

> A more studious assembly of men could not be found yesterday than the celebrated chess players who are competing for prizes in the Sixth American Chess Congress at 8 Union Square. Cups of coffee were placed next to the chess boards, and, occasionally, a pony of brandy was deemed necessary for proper exhilaration of the mind. The cigars the players smoke are strong, and two or three of them affect well-burned pipes[...].
>
> The games between Pollock and Blackburne, Burn and Chigorin, and Hanham and Gunsberg attracted the most attention from spectators. Chess players sat back of them and carefully noted down the various moves. They winked at one another at what they considered good plays, and acted as though they wanted to ask questions in many instances. There were many visitors during the afternoon.

In the second round, Pollock was paired against Blackburne, the most watched player, whom he had met on several occasions during his time in England. Until his 38th move, Pollock's play on the White side of a Giuoco Piano was nearly flawless. He placed consistent pressure against Blackburne's queenside, where the Englishman had castled his king. Deft strokes against Black's queenside pawns led to a clear advantage for Pollock. Blackburne's king was forced into exile and at move 38 Pollock was faced with this position:

Pollock–Blackburne
Sixth American Chess Congress
March 26, 1889, Round 2

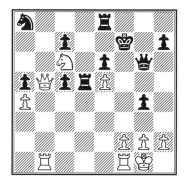

After 37. ... Rd8–e8

Here Pollock had to choose between hunting Black's king and securing some significant material advantage by capturing the a5-pawn. An instinctively combinative player, Pollock chose the first option: **38. Qb7?! Kg8 39. Rb3!?** with the intention to continue the king hunt by transferring the rook to the other side of the board. After **39. ... Qc2** Pollock engaged in some tactical fireworks with **40. Ne7+ R×e7 41. Qc8+ Kg7 42. Rg3?**, with the final move being a misconception which brought Pollock down quickly: **42. ... h5 43. Q×a8 Rd1! 44. Qf3 Red7** and Blackburne won a few moves later. Instead of this mishandled king hunt, Pollock could have obtained a nearly won position with 38. Q×a5, followed by the simple plan of pushing the passed a-pawn. But pragmatic play, so cherished by Steinitz, had little attraction for the Romantic-style players of the late–nineteenth century, and Pollock was certainly one of the most Romantic.

At the start of the third day of play, Wednesday, March 27, Morphy's influence over the gathering was manifest in an unusual way. The following two descriptions come from the *New York Times* and *New York Sun*, respectively, of March 28:

While a group of veteran players were looking at the excellent portrait of Paul Morphy, belonging to the Manhattan Chess Club, and which hangs on the wall opposite the entrance to the room in which the champions are now striving for superiority, the question arose as to whether the masters of the game today could stand against Morphy's sweeping play. The opinion was unanimous that while there were more great players at present than there were thirty years ago, there is no second Morphy [*Sun*].

Silence held its usual sway yesterday at the chess tournament that is going on at 8 Union Square. Among the spectators was Paul von Frankenberg U. Proschlitz, President of the Breslau (Germany) Chess Club, who came over as the representative of his club to witness the tournament. Years ago he lived in this city, and was one of the organizers and President of the New York Chess Club. Whether the strain of the two days' play has affected some of the players or not, at least two of the contestants were not looking well yesterday. Bird looked feeble, and his ailing health may have been the cause of his losing a game to Burn in a short time, for he resigned on the twenty-second move. Gossip, the Australian player, was also out of sorts. [...]

Many of the spectators and the managers were disappointed in Mason. He was pitted against D.G. Baird, but when he came into the hall he was laboring under excitement, and it was said that he had been imprudent enough to visit a barroom with some friends. Nevertheless he insisted on playing, but after making eight moves he had to retire, giving up his game to his opponent [*Times*].

Joseph Henry Blackburne, early 1892 (*Records of the Copyright Office of the Stationers' Company, January–March 1892***; photograph by David James Scott).**

To say it plainly, the start of the round was disturbed by an inebriated Mason.[7] But play at the rest of the boards began smoothly enough. Pollock had to cross swords with Gunsberg,

---

7. Mason's drunken state was also alluded to by the *New York Sun* of March 28, 1889, which phrased it a little more diplomatically: "Mason had made a draw with the Australian champion, Gossip, on Monday, and won a game from Mr. Showalter on Tuesday, and stood a good chance to add another game to his score. But Mr. Mason was not himself. He had stimulated his brain to an extent that dazed him and rendered his language incoherent. In brief, he was unfit for chess company, so he was persuaded to leave the room. This gave the game to Mr. Baird. Mason has wonderful insight in planning attacks, and is as cool and patient as a poker player when he sits down to win; but his unsteadiness has prevented him from winning the highest honors in the ranks of chess."

another well-known master on the British circuit. Various chess columns noted that Pollock, on the Black side of a Ruy Lopez, was expected to win based on his strong play in this game, but an error allowed Gunsberg to escape with perpetual check. Indeed, with his typical competence in such matters, Pollock concocted a powerful kingside attack, abundant in mating threats:

Gunsberg–Pollock
Sixth American Chess Congress
March 27, 1889, Round 3

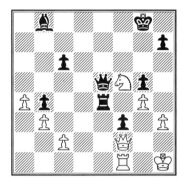

After 41. ... Rd4–e4!

Here, as Pollock threatened the forceful Re2, Gunsberg made a last effort to escape: **42. Qd2**, threatening the capture of the g5-pawn and infiltrating with the queen on the back rank. Steinitz commented: "Both parties have exercised their ingenuity in attempts to win, but each player was carefully on the watch, and a forced draw is now the result." But Steinitz's assessment was not entirely accurate. Pollock's move choice was certainly unfortunate: **42. ... Re2??** and Gunsberg got away with a perpetual after **43. Q×g5+ Kf8 44. Qh6+ Kg8 45. Qg5+ Kf8 46. Qh6+ Kg8** etc. Instead, contrary to Steinitz's verdict, Pollock could have won with 42. ... Bc7! quietly covering the crucial d8 square, and after 43. Q×g5+ Kh8 Gunsberg would have had nothing at hand to avoid either mate or heavy material loss.

Pollock was playing with great verve and imagination, but the excellent positions he had reached in rounds two and three, which might with luck and sounder play have netted him two points, had been frittered away into a mere half point. After such a disappointing start, Pollock had to meet no less a player than Chigorin in round four. The Russian had lost in the first round to New York's Delmar, but had won his next two games, against Burn and Hanham. Not surprisingly, Pollock's luck remained the same. The *New York Sun* of March 29 wrote that Chigorin won "by splendid play," while the *New York Times* of the same day recorded that the "fight continued hotly for nearly three hours, when Pollock gave up because he had suffered heavily and was surrounded by foes." The loss was in fact the result of uncharacteristically timid play from Pollock, whose game collapsed due to a serious oversight at move 20. In a Four Knights' Game, Pollock overlooked "a beautifully-conceived and finely worked-out combination," according to Steinitz.

In the fifth round, played on Friday, March 29, Pollock met Bird, another English player with whom he was well acquainted. Some accounts indicate Bird was feeling ill during this round, the *New York Times* suggesting the English master was bearing "his sufferings with great patience and fortitude." Pollock attempted to surprise his veteran opponent with a Scandinavian Defense and matters proved quite lively for a good portion of the game. At his 40th move, at a time in play that was becoming almost predictable, Pollock blundered and lost the exchange in a position slightly in his favor. In fewer than 20 more moves, and despite his determined efforts, he had to concede the point.

Breaking the Ice

The next day, Saturday, March 30, Pollock finally achieved his first tournament victory, earned at the expense of 18-year-old Nicholas MacLeod, the young Canadian player watched with great intensity by the majority of spectators, and whose only point so far had been scored against Delmar. According to the *New York Sun* of March 31, "the last day of the first week's play in the chess tournament attracted more visitors than on any previous day" and

> Among them was Mr. Thomas Workman, a millionaire of Montreal, who is an admirer and liberal patron of the royal game; Mr. H. Keyes, champion of the New Jersey State Chess Association; Charles V. Edwards of New Orleans, the veterans Thomas Frère and William M. de Visser, and Mr. William Steinitz, the foremost player in America. Mr. Steinitz walked slowly about the enclosed space set apart for the players, stopping to make a brief inspection of each game. As the great master noted the positions of the mimic armies he would shake his big, round head and lower his massive forehead as though he would like to have the next move and rearrange the plan of battle. He tarried longer than usual at the table occupied by Max Judd, champion of the West, and M. Chigorin, Russia's strongest player.

Before Steinitz's eyes, Pollock won a "very interesting Ruy Lopez" from MacLeod. The opening play was in fact more interesting for MacLeod than for Pollock, as the latter, having White, had soon to struggle to deny Black a decisive advantage.

Pollock–MacLeod
Sixth American Chess Congress
March 30, 1889, Round 6

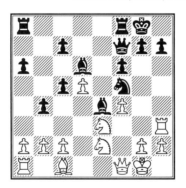

After 21. ... Nh6–f5

Here Pollock, who agonized throughout the opening, cleverly sacrificed his d5 pawn, with **22. Ng3!? N×e3 23. B×e3** and MacLeod grabbed the pawn with **23. ... Q×d5?** only to be rebuffed by **24. Rd1 Qe6 25. f5!** which gave White a decisive advantage: **25. ... Qe8 26. Qc4+ Kh8 27. N×e4** and Pollock won. It is evident that MacLeod would have done much better with 23. ... B×d5!?.

In the seventh round, played on April 1, Pollock scored another victory, this time over the American J.W. Baird at the end of a short, intriguing battle in a rare Evans Gambit line. Pollock selected a non–text book continuation at his seventh move, and Steinitz commended him for it, writing in the tournament book that "There is always refreshing originality in Mr. Pollock's play. The innovation will hardly strengthen the attack theoretically, but in practice it was well worth adopting exceptionally." Pollock's move (**7. N×d4** instead of the more common **7. 0–0**), had at least the merit of throwing Baird out of well-trodden paths. But the American did well to survive the assault Pollock mounted upon his king in the first 20 moves:

Pollock–J.W. Baird
Sixth American Chess Congress
April 1, 1889, Round 7

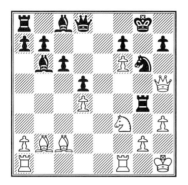

After 22. h3

In this position Baird played **22. ... R×g2 23. Ng5 R×c2?** and Pollock mated in two moves. Steinitz noted the following after Baird's 23rd move: "A blunder, but his game was anyhow gone." Pollock's attack was not entirely precise, however. A closer look reveals that **23. Ng5** was not the best move. Instead 23. B×g6! would have been the most precise follow-up: 23. ... R×g6 (23. ... h×g6 fails to the simple 24. Qh4!) 24. Ng5 h6 25. N×f7! K×f7 26. Rae1 with an immediate and beautiful win. After Pollock's 23rd move, Baird could have defended better with 23. ... R×g5! and while White's position is certainly better, Black's game was not entirely "gone," as Steinitz opined.

A Mixed Bag

The proceedings of the eighth round, played on Wednesday, April 2, were threatened by Chigorin's potential withdrawal from the tournament. As the chronicler of the *Sun* revealed on April 3, the controversy during his game against Max Judd came to an end with Chigorin mutely accepting the committee's decision:

The twenty players in the international chess tournament took their places at the little tables yesterday to engage in the eighth series of battles of brains with an air of quiet dignity, equal to that of members of the Supreme Court when in session. The Russian champion, Mikhail Chigorin, who had assumed a very war-like front on the announcement of the first decision in his postponed game with Max Judd, and had threatened to retire from the field on Monday evening after forfeiting his game to Mason on the time limit, reappeared serene and handsome as usual, to play against Boston's young champion, Constant F. Burille. The other players were MacLeod against Judd, Bird against Mason, Gunsberg against Weiss, Blackburne against Gossip, Lipschütz against Showalter, D.G. Baird against Taubenhaus, Martinez against J.W. Baird, Pollock against Delmar, and Hanham against Burn. The games were long and characterized by pertinacity and endurance. When the gavel of the umpire sounded for recess at 5 pm, no less than eight games had not progressed much beyond what is known as the middle game, and all were hopeful to ward off defeat by good play during the evening session. The sound of the gavel immediately liberates the players whose turn it is not the move. The others are at liberty to take sufficient time to consider the next move, which must be placed in an envelope, sealed, and delivered to the umpire, to be opened in presence of both players at the opening of the evening session. The umpire has to see that the record of time and other things is correct.

The full story of why Chigorin appeared "serene and handsome" after this incident was because he had, in fact, triumphed. As explained in detail nearly a month later, in the *New York Sun* of May 1:

> One case in point [regarding conflicts] is that which arose between Messrs. Chigorin and Judd, when Mr. Judd claimed the fifty-move rule on Mr. Chigorin. The umpire decided that it was a fifty-move position, which meant a mate in fifty moves, irrespective of exchanges or advancement of pawns. This decision was sustained by the jurors though there were several pawns on the board. The Russian was so annoyed and angered by this action that he allowed a pending game to go by default, resigned from the tournament, and made preparations to return to Russia. Judges Richardson, de Visser, and Frère, then examined the position where the fifty-move rule to mate was applied by the umpire, and reversed the decision. Thereupon, Mr. Chigorin returned to the tournament.

Nor would this be the last spat between Committee and players.[8]

Once things settled and the round proceeded as normal, Pollock was defeated by Delmar. The American was the author of some very energetic opening play, but Delmar failed to get any significant advantage in that phase of the game. Pollock defended carefully as the endgame was reached. The critical juncture came after Pollock's 38th move:

Mikhail Chigorin in 1895 (*Records of the Copyright Office of the Stationers' Company, July–September 1895***; photograph by William James Donald).**

---

8. The "fifty-move" rule as appeared in the Charles A. Gilberg's *Fifth American Chess Congress* (New York, 1881): "Counting Fifty Moves—If, at any period during a game, either player persist in repeating a particular check, or series of checks, or persist in repeating any particular line of play which does not advance the game; or if 'a game-ending' be of doubtful character as to its being a win or a draw, or if a win be possible, but the skill to force the game questionable, then either player may demand judgment of the Umpire as to its being a proper game to be determined as drawn at the end of fifty additional moves, on each side; or the question: 'Is, or is not the game a draw?' may be, by mutual consent of the players, submitted to the Umpire at any time. The decision of the Umpire, in either case, to be final. And whenever fifty moves are demanded and accorded, the party demanding it may, when the fifty moves have been made, claim the right to go on with the game, and thereupon the other party may claim the fifty move rule, at the end of which, unless mate be effected, the game shall be decided a draw" (pages 167–168). ¶ The same rule was discussed as follows in the "Revised International Chess Code" as appeared in J.I. Minchin's *Games Played in the London International Chess Tournament, 1883* (London, 1883): "A player may at any time call upon his adversary to mate him within fifty moves (move and reply being counted as one). If by the expiration of such fifty moves no piece or Pawn has been captured, nor Pawn moved, nor mate given, a draw can then be obtained" (page iv).

Delmar–Pollock
Sixth American Chess Congress
April 2, 1889, Round 8

After 38. ... Be4–b7

In this position, Delmar went for **39. Rd6+! K×d6 40. B×b4+ Kc6 41. B×a3**, and Black was lost. Pollock could have maintained equality easily with 38. ... R×b3, instead of 38. ... Bb7.

With a frustrating score of 2½–5½, Pollock found himself among the tournament's bottom dwellers together with Burille, Hanham, MacLeod (2) and Martinez (½), while Chigorin and Weiss led with 6 points, followed by Blackburne, Gunsberg, and Lipschütz with 5½ each. D.G. Baird, Delmar and Taubenhaus (5), Bird and Burn (4½), Judd and Mason (4), J.W. Baird, Gossip and Showalter (3½) rounded out the field. Once again, Pollock's lack of consistency, coupled with serious lapses late in the middle game and in the endgame, haunted him.

In the ninth round, played on April 3, Pollock and Burn met for the first of their two games. The *New York Times* of April 4 mentioned something of a change from the ordinary for the tournament that round:

Yesterday was ladies' day at the American Chess Congress, and preparations had been made to make the visitors as comfortable as possible. Notices were put up asking visitors to abstain from smoking, but the injunction was not extended to the players, and several of them took a few puffs at their cigars. Very few ladies appeared during the day, but there was a fair representation present in the evening, and they generally watched the progress of the games as intently as did their escorts. Among those who were present were Mrs. W.F. Eno of Brooklyn, the Misses Cobb of Brooklyn, Mrs. Schreyer, Mrs. Max Judd, Mrs. H. Worrall, Mrs. Maltzan, Miss Ruthven, Mrs. Schubert, Mrs. Ettlinger, and Miss Teed.

Exhibiting again some original opening play, Pollock, on the White side of a Giuoco Piano, fell victim to some serious oversights in the middle-game. Heavy material losses forced him to resign to Burn before move 40.

The next day Pollock faced Hanham. The result was a much needed win, and one based on some forceful play:

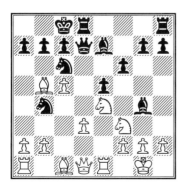

Hanham–Pollock
Sixth American Chess Congress
April 4, 1889, Round 10

After 12. ... 0–0–0

Hanham continued here with **13. a3** imagining perhaps some material gains after **13. ... N×d3 14. B×d3 Q×d3 15. Nd6+** but Pollock found an excellent way to get ahead: **15. ... R×d6! 16. c×d6 Q×d1 17. R×d1 B×d6** with superior piece activity for Pollock, who capitalized on it rather easily.

In the eleventh round, played on April 5, Pollock drew the Frenchman Taubenhaus after a long game that lasted well into the evening. Although he may well have expected to win their game, he failed to do so. From the *New York Sun* of April 6:

> Messrs. Pollock and Taubenhaus played the Morphy variation in the Two Knights Defense to a draw after a six hours' struggle. Mr. Pollock obtained the advantage of a pawn in the opening and was looked upon to win, but Mr. Taubenhaus secured a draw in the end game by the ingenious sacrifice of a bishop.

On Saturday, April 6, Pollock lost his 12th round game to Martinez, and after a rest day found himself paired with Judd. Taking advantage of the free day, the *Sun's* chronicler, interviewing an insider, published on April 7 a detailed report filled with many interesting remarks regarding the tournament's setting. The description appears to be penned by someone unfamiliar with chess, but its originality and detailed portraitures call for an extended passage, offered here:

> How many New Yorkers realize that the chess contest now reported every day in the newspapers is the greatest tournament of its kind ever held in the world? For other chess tournaments few players have been induced to go from one hemisphere to another; for this tournament ten have come—one each from as far away as Australia and Russia. At other tournaments the prizes have been small sums; here four thousand dollars is raised for division into six prizes, ranging from $1,000 for the best player to $300 for the sixth best.
> The tourney is being held at 10 [*sic*] Union Square or Fourth Avenue opposite Union square. The best way to give an idea of what the tourney hall looks like outside is to say that the place suggests a political campaign head-quarters. It is the second story of an ordinary house, over a store. It has a plate-glass front and a big chromatic transparency such as a political club would put up. But once the visitor enters the hall door down stairs this impression vanishes. The floor is neatly and newly clothed and the walls are as neat as fresh paint can make them. As the doorway to the playroom a man stands with tickets, which he exchanges for fifty cents. Only the players, who have deposited an entrance fee of $50 each, and the reporters actually recording the play are admitted without tickets.
> "We need to sell tickets in order to meet the expenses," says the very gentlemanly young man at the door. It is notable that all the people one sees, from him at the door to the last man in the rear of the hall, display gentlemanly attributes. Nearly all are neatly dressed, all are intellectual looking, all move quietly, and converse in whispers. Gentleness and decorum distinguish the gathering.
> "It costs forty dollars a day to maintain this tournament," says the doorkeeper "and the play will last seven weeks. There are twenty contestants, and each must play twice with each other one; twice, so that each player will have the advantage of the first move against each other player. The first round of games will take three weeks, beginning with Monday a week ago, March 23 [*sic*: 25]. The second round will last four weeks, in all probability because there is to be what we call a by-day [*sic*: bye day] for the playing out of all drawn and contested games. These may take several days, of course. Mr. Steinitz, who got up the tournament, will publish a book containing an account of each of the three hundred and eighty games that will be played. He announced this in advance and got subscriptions at $10 a volume from all over the world. The Baron Rothschild subscribed and other sub-scriptions came from as far away as Calcutta and Australia. On this money we opened the contest. If what the book brings in, less a small amount for Mr. Steinitz, and what we get in gate money and entrance fees do not meet the cost of the tournament there are many wealthy men who will make up for the shortage. Some have already put their hands in their pockets for this end."
> The hall of the tournament is very little altered from what it was when it was leased—a rectangular room the length of the ordinary house. The floor is softened with strips of thin carpet, and the whitewashed walls bear a few photographs of groups of chess players, an oil painting of Paul Morphy, and a few stenciled announcements on cardboard. The lower half of the hall is where the contestants sit, and they are roped in by means of what pugilists call a ring, made of pine posts, from one to another of which runs a line of red picture cord. Five feet apart in two rows stand the tables—plain white pine kitchen tables, each with a huge chess board on it heaped with chessmen. On the two sides of each table are varnished high-backed chairs. There is a space around this

roped-in enclosure, between it and the walls, and here the spectators congregate—one or two near the greater number of players, and a dozen or a score huddled together close to the more skillful players, or the players whose games happen at the moment to be acutely interesting to those who are masters of the subtle game. There is a big card swung overhead the enclosure. It reads: "Conversation Strictly Prohibited." [...]

All is silence. Often there is only one man at a table. His opponent has gotten up to stretch his legs. Perhaps he has gone out for a walk. Think of a game so slow as that! Compare it in the mind with a horse race or a game of baseball. Without looking at an encyclopedia to verify the thought, it seems to an onlooker that chess must have originated in China or India. Where there are two players seated over their board the only way a spectator has of knowing which man is playing is by looking at the tumble clocks on the table. The one that is ticking is, of course, next to the man who is playing. But both men are leaning back in their chairs, and both are apt to be pulling their moustaches or biting their lips. Here and there one sees both players staring at the board between them, but more often the only display of interest in the board is seen in an occasional glance at it by the man whose clock is ticking. When the *Sun* reporter was present there was what might be called wild excitement over a game between Taubenhaus of Paris and Baird of New York. By wild excitement is meant a pressure of a score of persons against the enclosure close to the table of these players. It was also expressed in the tendency of strangers to come up to the reporter and whisper: "Big game, eh?" or "He'll lose a rook, see if he don't," "He's got a tough job there." Who had the tough job or who would lose a rook the reporter will never tell, for all he could see was a natty young New Yorker, with a big bulging forehead and a large scarf pin, seated opposite a sallow, black-haired Hebrew from Paris ... [who] moved a bishop and threw over the see-saw board under the clocks so as to stop his own and set his opponent's clock going. This movement was followed by a buzz among the spectators, but the Hebrew took this opportunity to get up and walk around the hall.

Chess is a great equalizer. The greatest player in the world, Mr. Mackenzie, strolled in during the afternoon, and proved to be a man of only ordinary appearance, and, if one was to judge by appearances, not a wealthy man. He, like many another great player, lives by following the royal game. He wanted to enter the contest, but took ill in Havana and he was not able to play. All who were in the hall sympathized with him, for all admire him, and feel that no one in the contest is a match for him. Chess brings the poor and the rich together in a poetic hodge-podge of pure democracy. Any one can see this at places like the Café Cosmopolitan in Second Avenue, where broadcloth sits by homespun, and mechanics play against the richest men of the east side. Any one can see it in this tournament, where yesterday a man in shabby clothes, with a greasy red worsted muffler around his neck, played at one table against a stout man in broadcloth, well-barbered and portly, and as sleek as Col. Shepard.

Pollock's game against Judd was played on Monday, April 8, and the *Sun* the next day summarized it as follows: "Mr. Judd lost a Ruy Lopez opening to Mr. Pollock. Mr. Pollock gained a piece early in the game. Yet Mr. Judd defended so well that all thought he would win; but the Irish champion proved himself a great chess player and won his game very dexterously." The game, with Pollock handling the Black pieces, was a hypnotizing affair right from the opening:

Judd–Pollock
Sixth American Chess Congress
April 8, 1889, Round 13

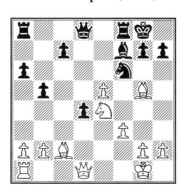

After 19. Nc3–e4

Here Pollock continued with **19. ... d3** and Judd, faced with quite a number of selections to pick from, followed up with a less than fortunate retort: **20. N×f6+? g×f6 21. B×f6 d×c2 22. Q×c2 Qd4+** and Black was winning. Judd could have maintained a competitive game with 20. e×f6! d×c2 21. Q×c2 Qd4+ 22. Kh1 Bd5 23. Nc3. Judd posed an obstinate resistance, but, after some hesitations despite being a rook up, Pollock drove home his advantage.

Falling Again

The tournament was close to finishing the first cycle, with interesting play continuing unabated as the *Sun* of April 10 noted:

> The fourteenth day of the international chess tournament bristled with interesting incidents. Now that the first round of the twenty players is drawing to a close, every game is watched with absorbing interest, and each player's head appears to be as full of thought as that of wise old Ben Franklin's when he first brought the game into public notice in America by playing it in Philadelphia more than a century ago. The masters who faced each other at the ten tables within the intellectual arena yesterday were Blackburne against Chigorin, Taubenhaus against Gunsberg, Lipschütz against Bird, Delmar against Gossip, Burn against Weiss, Pollock against Mason, Martinez against Judd, Hanham against Burille, J.W. Baird against Showalter, and D.G. Baird against MacLeod[...].
>
> Messrs. Pollock and Mason played a safe and steady Giuoco Piano opening. Pollock developed a very strong attack. Mason met the attack ingeniously, and succeeded in coming out a pawn ahead, but the position was still so critical for the defence that Mason promptly accepted an offer to declare a draw, after a well-played game of thirty-three moves.

Indeed, Pollock obtained a sizeable opening advantage, but a few inexactitudes allowed Mason to equalize. In the next round Pollock, with 5½ points, was pitted against Burille who had so far had a similar performance. Unfortunately for Pollock, he badly misplayed a Vienna Game and ended up completely outplayed. Round 16 took place on Friday, April 12, and saw Pollock playing one of the strongest players: the Austrian Weiss, who was only half a point behind Blackburne, then the leader with 12 points. In an unusual Queen's Pawn opening, Pollock played uninspired chess, and after losing his queenside, found his transparent attempt at mounting a kingside attack well anticipated.

In the next round Pollock tried to punish Gossip for daring to play the Steinitz Gambit against him. He began a sharp king hunt, yet despite sacrificing many pawns for it, the attack failed to build a mating web and Gossip eventually triumphed. From the *New York Sun* of April 13:

> The attendance at the chess tournament fell off somewhat yesterday, and several of the players appeared as though they could enjoy a brief rest from their brain work. They will have a short respite next week, when renewed interest will be aroused in the second and final round of battles. Drawn games will not count half a game in the second round, as in the first, but will have to be played off. Thursdays will be bye days, on which drawn and adjourned endgames will be played[...].
>
> Messrs. Gossip and Pollock played a Vienna game which resolved itself into a Steinitz gambit. Mr. Pollock made some errors in the defence which enabled Mr. Gossip to obtain a winning position, when Mr. Pollock resigned.

In the 18th round, played on April 13, Pollock, on the White side of a Ruy Lopez, again essayed risky opening play and got into serious trouble against Showalter. The American obtained a decisive advantage right from the start, but after several errors failed to convert his advantage. Pollock survived by drawing a simple rook endgame. He played a much better game in round 19, the last before the break, when pitted against D.G. Baird. Handling the Black pieces in a Vienna Game, Pollock found a good opportunity to get a clear advantage based on some eye-pleasing tactics:

D.G. Baird–Pollock
Sixth American Chess Congress
April 15, 1889, Round 19

After 19. Bf4×e5

Here Pollock continued correctly with the powerful **19. ... R×f3!** and after the more or less forced **20. R×f3 B×d4 21. Re1 Q×e5 22. Q×e5 R×e5 23. R×e5 B×f3 24. Re8+ Kf7 25. Rd8 Bf6 26. Rd7+ Ke6 27. R×c7 Be4**, Pollock should have had enough advantage for a win. Yet Baird defended well, and in what must have been another frustrating experience for Pollock, drew the game at move 75.

Stronger Play

At the halfway mark, the tournament paused for two days, on April 16 and 17. What would have been more than sufficient play for a large tournament in itself represented only the first round of play at New York, and with the replaying of draws required for the second portion of the tournament, the players could look to an even longer second half combat. Pollock managed only 6½ points out of 19 games. He won from MacLeod, J.W. Baird, Hanham, and Judd, drew against Gunsberg, Taubenhaus, Showalter, D.G. Baird, and Mason, and lost to Lipschütz, Blackburne, Chigorin, Bird, Delmar, Burn, Martinez, Burille, Weiss, and Gossip. While the fight for the first prize was heavily contested between Weiss (15½), Blackburne (15), Gunsberg (14) and Chigorin (14), Pollock, after three weeks of continuous play, found himself tied for 15th–17th place with Gossip and Hanham. Would he improve his place significantly in the tournament's second half? Or would he remain perilously near the bottom of the crosstable, his trip across the Atlantic a chessic disaster?

Play resumed Thursday, April 18. It appears the break served Pollock well, as he immediately scored an important victory against Lipschütz, as recounted by the *Sun* of April 19:

> Earnest play began in the international chess tournament at 1 p.m. yesterday, when the champions faced each other in the second and final round of games. Before the first skirmishing round was half finished it was expected that at least half a dozen of the American team would withdraw at the finish of the round, as the rules would permit them to do and furthermore they could have drawn $25 each, or half of the entrance money.[9] But the

---

9. Such a curious rule was indeed present in the tournament rules: "Rule V: At the close of the first round any player may withdraw from the Tournament, and his deposit of $25. 00 will then be returned to him. He shall be entitled to any prizes falling to him according to his score."

home team remained in to a man, although the ten foreigners had scored 108 games in the initial round against 79 for the Americans. [...]

At 2:25 all the games were in full blast in the following order, the first-named player in each pair handling the whites: Taubenhaus against MacLeod, J.W. Baird against Bird, Delmar against Chigorin, Burn against Gunsberg, Pollock against Lipschütz, Martinez against D.G. Baird, Showalter against Judd, Burille against Weiss, Hanham against Blackburne. [...]

Mr. Pollock played a Ruy Lopez game on Mr. Lipschütz, which was the longest and hardest of the day, and was adjourned at 11:30 pm. Mr. Pollock with king and rook, Mr. Lipschütz with king and three pawns—Mr. Lipschütz struggling for a draw, with the chances in favor of Mr. Pollock winning. Mr. Pollock played the endgame in a style that commanded the admiration of all the experts present.

It was indeed a masterful performance by Pollock throughout the opening and the middlegame. In the endgame matters became slightly more complicated:

Pollock–Lipschütz
Sixth American Chess Congress
April 18, 1889, Round 20

After 63. ... Rg3–g8

Here Pollock played the erroneous **64. Kc7**, which was met by Lipschütz with **64. ... R×d8?!**
65. K×d8 Nc6+ 66. Kc7 N×a5 67. Kb6 and Lipschütz gave up the knight for the pawn with **67. ... N×b3 68. R×b3**, with good prospects to save the game. After a series of correct moves by both sides, the following critical position was reached at move 75:

White to move

Pollock continued with **76. Rh2+**, a forced move, and Lipschütz erred decisively with **76. ... Kf1??** after which the e2-pawn was lost: **77. Rh1+ Kf2 78. Kd2.** Steinitz commented on Lipschütz's error: "Black, most injudiciously, is not satisfied with a draw which he could easily secure by Ke3, and he has to bear the usual penalty for attempting to win a game drawn by its nature, for after the opponent's reply his own game can no more be saved."

On Friday, April 19, Pollock lost a Vienna game with Black against Blackburne, again after unsuccessfully giving up pawns for attacking chances which simply did not materialize. Another, even more premature attack, brought him another defeat at the hands of Gunsberg on the next day. "Messrs. Pollock and Gunsberg played a very interesting and intricate game," wrote the *Sun*'s chronicler on April 21. "Mr. Gunsberg had the defence and selected the seldom played Fianchetto di Donna defence. Mr. Gunsberg obtained a pawn with a good game, but left a strong counter game for the attack. Mr. Pollock was pressed for time and overlooked his best moves, and, unfortunately, lost what could have been a drawn game had he played correctly." Indeed, as Steinitz remarked in the tournament book, Pollock could have saved the game at move 23.

On Monday, April 22, after the break provided by a Sunday rest day, Pollock's unfortunate lapses in winning positions continued. He drew with Chigorin who before the round started stood third with 17 points. "Mr. Chigorin played his celebrated Evans Gambit," read the *Sun*, in giving the full score of the game, against "the young British [*sic*] champion, Mr. Pollock, by whom he was outplayed in the early part of the game. At the twenty-eighth move Mr. Pollock had a clearly won game. He then neglected his chances, and, after a hard struggle, agreed to a draw in a position where he had a slight advantage."

Chigorin–Pollock
Sixth American Chess Congress
April 22, 1889, Round 23

After 33. ... Re5–e2

Here Chigorin, in serious trouble, played **34. Rf2**, and Pollock replied **34. ... R×f2?** Instead Pollock could have scored the point with 34. ... R×d2! 35. R×d2 Qe4! 36. Rf2 (36. f×g6 is met by the simple 36. ... Qe1+ 37. Kh2 Q×d2+ 38. Kg1 Qe1+ 39. Kg2 h×g6) 36. ... Nf4! when the best White has is returning the exchange, in light of the threat ...Qe1+. Steinitz did not mention this continuation in his tournament book. Instead, Pollock's move allowed one of the world's strongest players to escape with a draw. To add to Pollock's misery, as draws in the second cycle had to be replayed, the game was replayed on Thursday, April 25. Chigorin employed the same opening but with better success. Pollock resigned after 37 moves.

Pollock battled Bird in round 24, played on Tuesday, April 23. After insipid opening play, he took advantage of a serious error by his opponent at move 29 and scored easily. With the same apparent effortlessness, in the next round Pollock played cat and mouse with the young MacLeod after winning a piece in the opening and—according to the *Sun* of April 25—announced mate in ten.

MacLeod–Pollock
Sixth American Chess Congress
April 25, 1889, Round 25

After 34. f3
Black to move and force a mate

Pollock's announced mate was close to being accurate: he wrapped up the game with **34. ... R×g2+ 35. Kh1 R×h2+ 36. K×h2 Qh5+ 37. Kg3 Qg5+ 38. Kf2 Qg2+ 39. Ke3 Qe2+ 40. K×f4 Bd6+ 41. Kg4 Qg2+** and MacLeod resigned. With **35. ... Rg1+!**, Pollock could have mated one move earlier than in the game.

Now with 9½ points, Pollock met J.W. Baird on April 26. With a witty though not decisive queen sacrifice, Pollock pushed back against the American's attack and, benefiting from a pressing material superiority, he closed matters in 36 moves. Surely, with three points in the last three games, Pollock must have felt his form improving.

Blackburne vs. the Committee

The next day the preparation for the celebrations of the 1889 Washington Inaugural Centennial in New York literally altered the playing hall, while perhaps simultaneously reflecting its mood. A description appeared in the April 28 edition of the *Sun*:

> The depressing atmosphere, together with a high partition that has been built across the Union Square end of the long room in which the chess tournament is held, made the quarters of the champions somewhat dull and gloomy yesterday, and the players sat down to the games which marked the close of the fifth week of the tourney in a rather weary way that spoke of needed rest that will come today. The partition was erected so that the players and others can obtain uninterrupted views of the centennial processions from the large windows that face the square and line of march.

Pollock defeated Delmar that day for his fourth win in a row, but only after the latter ruined a perfectly won position and ended up in a hopeless bishop vs. knight endgame. The increasing appearance of such errors in a tournament requiring extraordinary endurance is not all that surprising. Following the free Sunday, Burn ended Pollock's winning streak. He defeated his traveling companion after Pollock's inexact play in a Ruy Lopez. The next two days were both public holidays, which allowed the masters a breather from their marathon.

Not all was running as smoothly as the holidays in honor of the nation's first president might have suggested. Dissatisfaction with some of the umpires again emerged, as it had before with Chigorin and the fifty move rule. This time, Blackburne occupied center stage, though the matter also tangentially involved Pollock.

First, Blackburne claimed that a number of unrelated exchanges with various tournament committee men had led to bad feelings toward him. The *New York Times* of May 3 would list these allegations in its columns. One can only assume that Blackburne himself was the source for the paper's inside knowledge:

> Yesterday was by-day [*sic*: bye day] at the American Chess Congress, and the players looked refreshed by their two days' rest. Blackburne, however, seems to be considerably annoyed over some difficulties that he has had with the Managing Committee. One arose out of a disagreement between him and one of its members as to the manner of resuming play after the afternoon recess. Another committeeman wanted Blackburne to play some blindfold games in Brooklyn, but he would not accept the price offered. Still another official, it was said, wanted to engage Blackburne to travel over the country and give chess exhibitions, but Blackburne remarked that he could manage himself. On a remark being made several days ago to Blackburne with regard to something that the committee has said about him, Blackburne replied: "If the committee say so they say what is not true." He soon received a note from the Room Committee stating that, inasmuch as he had been pleased to call the committee liars, the latter considered themselves released from all considerations of courtesy which otherwise they should have been willing and glad to show him. This letter he received in the place of a ticket to a seat in the hall to see the parade.

Retaliation against Blackburne, the press reported the English master as alleging, took not only the form of petty refusal to give him tickets to watch the inaugural centennial celebrations like the other competitors, but also a more sinister shape in regard to important tournament matters. From the *New York Sun* of May 1:

TROUBLE IN THE CHESS CAMP
WHY THE LONDON GIANT WAS NOT INVITED TO SEE THE PARADE

> Instead of playing in the tournament yesterday the chess champions looked at the grand movements of this great nation in commemoration of the inauguration of the first President 100 years ago. They will continue to admire these patriotic demonstrations today, but intend to resume play tomorrow, which will be a bye day for playing off adjourned and tie games.
>
> During their brief rest, chat among the players leads to the belief that all is not rosy and fraternal in the camp, and that there is danger of trouble breaking out. It is said that the Congress Committee, or umpire, has made several decisions that have already threatened to break up the tourney in part. [After a discussion of the earlier controversy between Chigorin and the Committee regarding the fifty move rule in his game with Judd.] Now, it is said, Mr. Blackburne has suffered by rulings to which he objects. One case occurred on the last bye day, when Mr. Blackburne was scheduled to play two games, one an adjourned game with Mr. Mason, which occupied only ten minutes, and the other game was with Mr. Hanham. The last game, it is said, was untimely adjourned, and that advantage was taken of the adjournment to analyze the game and defeat Mr. Blackburne after the recess. Mr. Blackburne has the reputation of being well versed on tournament rules, and is considered a sensible, fair man by our players. Of course, he made critical remarks about the case at which the umpire took umbrage. The effect of this, it is said, was that when the committee sent notes to other players, inviting them to use the windows of the tournament room during the parades, they informed Mr. Blackburne that the courtesy would not be extended to him, because he had called the committee a set of liars. The English giant was so annoyed by this action that he was unable to play up to his full strength in his game with Mr. Showalter on Monday, and lost the game on account of the perturbed state of his mind. Mr. Blackburne has written to the committee denying the charge.[10]

And as for Pollock? The *Sun* article immediately added that "A leading member of one of the city chess clubs said last evening that members of the committee had also threatened to curtail

---

10. Rule XII of the tournament referred to adjournment thusly: "At the hour fixed for adjournments the player whose turn it is to move must deliver his next move in writing, in a closed envelope, to the member of the Committee present. Such envelopes will be opened after the adjournment by the member of the Committee then present, in the presence of both the competitors, and such member will make on the board the move as written down. Consultation and analyzing moves on a Chess board during the adjournments are strictly prohibited, and any competitor proved guilty of the same shall be expelled from the Tournament by a three-fourths vote of the Jury" (page xviii of the tournament book). What specific charge Blackburne made against the Tournament Committee for allowing improper adjournment in his game against Hanham, and what his evidence was to suggest Hanham improperly analyzed their game during the recess, are unknown.

courtesies to Mr. Pollock, the popular player from Dublin, because he has exercised his right of private judgment."

Pollock could not let this latter comment stand unaddressed. His letter to the editor was promptly published in the *New York Sun* of May 3. His solidarity with his fellow Englishman was manifest, yet so was his diplomatic skill with the pen. Pollock's writing ability, as revealed here, would prove a great help to his further stay in the United States.

To The Editor of the Sun:

Sir:—A statement appeared in The Sun of Wednesday to the effect, briefly, that Mr. Blackburne had been excluded from the hall of the chess tournament during Tuesday and Wednesday this week (non-play days), and that I had been threatened with similar treatment. I have been assured on the behalf of the committee, at whose hands I may say I have met personally with nothing but courtesy and consideration throughout, that in my case there were no grounds for the report; but that owing to Mr. Blackburne's disagreements with that body of gentlemen having assumed too personal a development, they declined to permit him to join what was a private gathering in the hall for the exchanges of hospitalities and witness the centennial celebrations.

The power of punishing a British champion by excluding him from joining, upon the area of his marvellous exploits, in so great and noble a celebration of the nation we Britons are still proud to call our cousins, and the exercise of restrictions, on the two procession days, upon the privileges of the press in the congress hall, are being questioned and censured now, however acquired, as serious and dangerous precedents in the management of international chess tournaments.

W.H.K. Pollock
Chess Congress, 8 Union Square, May 2, 1889

The congress committee had a meeting on the evening of May 4. Thomas Frère presided and among the committee members present were the following: Vice-president Westerfield, Dr. D'Oench, Frank Rudd, Fred Wehle, R.W. Ferguson, C.C.H. Bruel, A.W. Shepard, R. Colwell, A. Moehle, H. Davidson, C. Schubert, Steinitz, Dr. Cohn, F. Rose and Dr. Mintz:

The Treasurer, Mr. Rose, told the story of window privileges during the centennial parade, and alluded to his action in reference to the Blackburne episode and press comments thereon. The letter of Mr. W.H.K. Pollock to The Sun was read, and the sentiments were warmly applauded. The committee approved of the final ruling of the umpire in the Judd–Chigorin controversy awarding the game to the Russian champion. A motion of approval of the Room's committee's action was amended so as to avoid approving of their action in the Blackburne affair, yet otherwise thanking them for general efficiency. There being no formal complaint before the committee from Mr. Blackburne, no official action was taken. It will rankle for the remainder of the tournament. The rule proposed in the international code of 1883, having received the consent of all players, was adopted, thus killing the rule of the fifth American Chess Congress after the mischief it had wrough[t].[11]

---

11. This was not the end of it in the American press. Upon his return in England, Blackburne made statements about the way he was treated, that other players didn't get their money prizes and that he intended to sue the committee. Some of these remarks appeared printed in the *New York Herald* of July 3, 1889. According to Blackburne, "what really affected him, and others as well, was the treatment he received at the hands of certain people in New York." ¶ The July 6 issue of the same newspaper printed a lengthier piece on the matter, this time with strong words from some American officials: "The dispatches printed in the *Herald* recently, to the effect that J.H. Blackburne, the chess player, had complained most bitterly of his treatment at the hands of the committee having charge of the recent chess congress in this city, have caused much talk in chess circles here. Mr. Blackburne's friends claim that his complaint is well founded, while officials of the congress say that any ill-treatment that Mr. Blackburne received is due to his own actions. Among Mr. Blackburne's friends is Mr. J.H. Todd, secretary of the Columbia Chess Club. Mr. Todd was one of the subscribers to the chess congress and claims to represent the sentiment of a large number of other subscribers. Mr. Todd declares that Blackburne would undoubtedly have won the first prize in the tournament had not the offensive actions of the committee unnerved him and impaired his wonted skill. In support of his theory Mr. Todd instances the fact that in the second series of games which followed the alleged insults to the committee Mr. Blackburne lost six games to players from whom he had won in the first series. The crowning slight to Champion Blackburne, however, was the following letter, which he received from the committee. It says: 'Sir—Being reliably informed that you reviled the entire committee by remarking that the committeemen "are all liars," we hereby inform

A Forceful Finish

Play off the board having subsided for the moment, the games on the board resumed Thursday, May 2. Replay games were the point of interest. Pollock was back at the board only on the next day, when he was pitted against Hanham. At his 26th move the latter, handling the Black pieces, committed a serious mistake which gave Pollock the point instantly. With 12½ points, Pollock was way behind the closely bunched leaders, Weiss, Burn, Blackburne, Chigorin and Gunsberg, but ahead of Burille (12), Showalter (11), Martinez (9), Hanham (8½), Gossip (7), J.W. Baird (5) and MacLeod (4½). The scoring was somewhat clouded by adjourned games as well as games that required replay due to draws.

In the next round, the tournament's 30th, Pollock won with Black from Taubenhaus after the latter, too eager to finish his development, overlooked some easy tactics in a Ruy Lopez. The following day, Pollock played a tough game against Philadelphia's Martinez. Although neither player gained a palpable advantage, the endgame proved exciting (with Pollock's three Black pawns against Martinez's bishop). The players finally chose safety and shared honors. The game would be replayed on Thursday, May 9, when Pollock lost in fewer than 30 moves after carelessly walking into his opponent's mating web, admirably executed by Martinez. Then, on Tuesday, May 7, Pollock suffered another loss, this time at the hands of Judd in an endgame of pawns with bishops of opposite colors.

Pollock bounced back with a victory over Mason the next day by speculating on the latter's hesitant opening play:

---

you that we consider ourselves released from all considerations of courtesy which we would otherwise have been willing and glad to show you. (Signed) Frederick Rose, Joachim Maltzan, Room Committee.' When the news of the letter got out, Mr. Todd says that an effort was made by a few subscribers to get Mr. J. Spencer Turner, president of the Congress, to make reparation to Mr. Blackburne, but this, it is said, Mr. Turner refused to do unless Mr. Blackburne himself made a formal complaint. Mr. Todd was particularly bitter in his denunciation of the way Dr. F. Mintz, a member of the Tournament Committee, acted toward Blackburne. Mr. Blackburne, he says, repeatedly expressed the wish that Dr. Mintz 'would keep outside the ropes' which surrounded the chess tables. Dr. Mintz, who is a director and member of the Manhattan Chess Club, emphatically denies these charges. He says the difficulty with Mr. Blackburne was wholly due to the ungentlemanly conduct of the latter and the offensive way in which he let everyone know that he was 'down on Americans.' The occurrence which led to the sending of the obnoxious letter to Mr. Blackburne was, Dr. Mintz says, a dispute about the committee permitting one of the players to begin play one day at three o'clock instead of one. Prior to the beginning of play Mr. Blackburne wanted to insist upon certain things which were not even suggested when he gave his consent to the change of time. Afterward he said that if the committee asserted that they did not hear him mention these conditions they were all liars. When the committee heard of this language they gave him a week to apologize. He refused to make any further apology than to say that he had not intended to use the word liar. On the strength of this response the committee sent him the letter excluding him from the rooms during the centennial. Mr. J. Spencer Turner, president of the Sixth American Chess Congress, says: 'I was made president of the congress because I have always taken the deepest interest in the game of chess, and also because Mr. Max Judd, of New Orleans, and myself guaranteed the expenses of the tournament, to the tune of $5,000. I never saw such a fellow as this Blackburne, and it's about time the American side of the story had an airing. Blackburne behaved like a systematic blackguard throughout the tournament. He was always kicking against the rules. He refused frequently to seal his moves at the sound of the gong, although the rules distinctly provided this should be done. On one occasion he kept a committeeman waiting half an hour after the gong sounded before he would consent to seal his move as the other players were obliged to do. On another occasion Blackburne came to me and said he and a fellow player had arranged to draw a game, so that the third and fourth prize could be divided between them. I told him I wouldn't permit such a thing; that he was to play to win and not to draw games.' Mr. Turner laughed at the idea of Mr. Blackburne suing the committee. 'He has no cause of action against us,' said he. 'He went home with $600 in cash in his pocket, and I cannot see what he has to go to law about. As to the charge that prizes were withheld from the less successful players there is absolutely no truth in it.'" ¶ See also the detailed coverage Steinitz gave Dr. Frederick Mintz's version of the Blackburne controversy, *International Chess Magazine*, June 1889, pages 173–177.

Mason–Pollock
Sixth American Chess Congress
May 8, 1889, Round 33

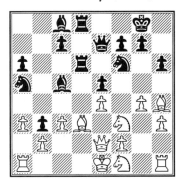

After 18. ... Rb6–d6

In this position, Mason should have played 19. 0-0-0, which was the only way to solve the critical problems he was facing. Instead, he played **19. Rd1**, only to be rebuffed by Pollock's energetic **19. ... Nc4!!**, a move called "ingenious and powerful" by Steinitz, and one clearly Mason missed. The game continued **20. Nd4 e×d4 21. B×c4 d×c3 22. R×d6 Q×d6 23. b×c3 b2! 24. Ba2 N×e4!** and Pollock mated Mason a few moves later. The *Sun* called the game "one of the most brilliant Ruy Lopez of the tournament."

Another good game by Pollock was against Burille in the next round. The latter attempted to surprise Pollock with an attack, but failed to impress. On move 14 Burille made an error that gave Pollock chances for an elegant finish:

Pollock–Burille
Sixth American Chess Congress
May 10, 1889, Round 34

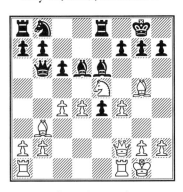

After 14. c2–c4!

James Mason, a close friend of Pollock's and a future coauthor (John G. White Chess and Checkers Collections, Cleveland Public Library).

Here Burille erred with **14. ... Bc7??** (14. ... c5! was much stronger) which allowed

Pollock a sparkling finish: **15. f5! B×e5 16. c5 Qc7 17. f×e6 B×h2+ 18. Kh1 f6 19. B×f6! Qf4 20. Be5!** and the American resigned. Games like this one, and the one the round before against Mason, were the reason players, commentators, and spectators alike found Pollock's play fascinating to watch.

Pollock's Immortal

On Saturday, May 11, Pollock had to play against Weiss. The latter, often referred to in the American press as "the little man with a grey coat," was leading with 25½ points after 34 rounds, followed closely by Burn (25), Chigorin (25), Blackburne (23) and Gunsberg (22½). With just a few rounds left in this seemingly-endless event, any loss or draw could have been decisive for these players.

Pollock's ingenuity surfaced in this particular game, which had a profound impact on the tournament's outcome. Perhaps Pollock's improving form over the past few days should have alerted Weiss to his danger. In any event, Pollock defeated Weiss in a Ruy Lopez that the *Sun* called a "treat to the beholders." The combination that brought Pollock the point is featured today in many game collections, and has long been heralded as a brilliancy. The next day's *New York Times* announced that Pollock's effort had likely earned him the tournament's brilliancy prize:

> POLLOCK'S DASHING GAME
> HE DEFEATS CHAMPION WEISS IN THE CHESS TOURNAMENT
> It was generally conceded at the chess tournament yesterday that Pollock of Dublin played one of the most dashing and brilliant games, and the committee are inclined to award to him the fifty-dollar prize for brilliancy of play. He was pitted against Weiss, who handled the White pieces and had the advantage of the attack. However, Pollock in his sixth move brought out his bishop, adopting the tactics of the old school against the modern and coming out into the open to the attack. A little later Pollock sailed down with his queen into the enemy's stronghold, and compelled Weiss to accept a sacrifice and to step upon very dangerous ground. Weiss's king was driven to the wall, surrounded by enemies on all the other sides, and he was finally compelled to resign.

Weiss–Pollock
Sixth American Chess Congress
May 11, 1889, Round 35

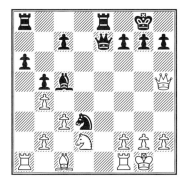

After 17. b4

Pollock played the excellent **17. ... B×f2+!**, a move that Weiss must have at least in part anticipated. But what the Austrian did not foresee was the following series of entertaining sacrifices. One can only imagine what the spectators thought of Black's next few moves: **18. Kh1 Qe1!!**—in Steinitz's own words, "the prelude to a most ingenious and splendidly conceived line of attack."—**19. h3 N×c1 20. R×e1 R×e1+ 21. Kh2 Bg1+ 22. Kg3 Re3+**—"Here," Pollock would write later in the *Baltimore Sunday News*, "we finally determined to go for a checkmate, and the most problematic one we could conceive of." **23. Kg4 Ne2 24. Nf1 g6 25. Qd5 h5+ 26. Kg5 Kg7 27. N×e3 f6+** with mate in two to follow.

This brilliancy and his 16½ points placing him at the middle of the crosstable, coming as it did after such an unfortunate start in March and his erratic play in April, must have given Pollock some satisfaction. Sunday likely was his most enjoyable rest day since sailing to the United States.

On Monday, Pollock returned to play and to his fluctuating results. He lost a game to Gossip based on faulty middle-game play. On Tuesday, he suffered another loss, this time to Showalter, as the result of uncharacteristically timid play. In round 38, played on Wednesday, May 15, Pollock drew against D.G. Baird and had to replay the game on Friday. Having the White pieces, Pollock won the game. In three replayed games in the tournament, he managed only one point.

On Tuesday, May 21, after all outstanding draws were replayed, the final standings were known: Chigorin and Weiss tied for first place with the remarkable score of 29 points each, followed by Gunsberg (28½), Blackburne (27), Burn (26), Lipschütz (25½), Mason (22), Judd (20), Delmar (18), Showalter (18), Pollock (17½), Bird (17), Taubenhaus (17), D.G. Baird (16), Burille (15), Hanham (14), Gossip (13½), Martinez (13½), J.W. Baird (7) and MacLeod (6½). Between May 22 and 27, following four playoff games between Chigorin and Weiss, all four ending in draws, the two decided to split the money prize. The grandest chess tournament to take place on

American soil had ended. It would be another fifteen years, and well after Pollock's death, before a comparable American event would take place, at Cambridge Springs. Only Chigorin and Delmar, of the 20 participants at New York 1889, would return to play there, as by then another generation of chess players had gained international fame and standing.

Pollock's 11th place finish was an enormous achievement considering the strength of his opponents. During the tournament, Pollock managed to score victories against Weiss, Lipschütz, Mason, Judd, Delmar, Bird, Taubenhaus, the Baird brothers, Burille, Hanham, and MacLeod. Only five of his games finished as draws (not including the three initial, second round draws). For his brilliancy over Weiss, Pollock was honored with the $50 prize donated by Professor Isaac L. Rice for the "most brilliant game of the tournament." Pollock also received a $50 prize for the best second-round scores against the top prizewinners (3 points).

Max Weiss, the leading master Pollock defeated in style during the Sixth American Chess Congress (*Chess-Monthly*, June 1888, page 289).

By May 21, the congregation of masters

gathered in the city for two months was finally disbanding. Some were choosing to spend time giving exhibitions throughout America while others were rushing back to Europe for more tournaments. Gunsberg, Weiss, and Chigorin were ready for simultaneous and blindfold exhibitions at the Manhattan Chess Club. Blackburne was invited to play at the Columbia Chess Club and made plans to visit the Franklin Chess Club of Philadelphia, as well as elsewhere.

Amos Burn, who had sailed to America with Pollock, sailed back home on the *Wyoming* on Tuesday, May 21, at 10:00 a.m. Pollock did not sail with him. Instead, he remained in America looking for engagements. That Pollock was determined to remain in America long before the tournament finished was succinctly, and unequivocally, stated in the *Cincinnati Commercial Tribune's* April 20, 1889, chess column: "W.H.K. Pollock intends to make this country his home." (How many lives had radically changed their course through the utterance of similarly concise words?)

While Blackburne was invited for an exhibition at the Baltimore Chess Club, Pollock was invited to give an exhibition of simultaneous chess at the Brooklyn Chess Club on Tuesday, May 28. The *New York Times* of June 16 published the following pen-portrait of Pollock, offering a curious combination of positive and negative attributes:

> Pollock is a young man of about 30 years, blond, and sports a good-sized, reddish-golden mustache. While playing he crosses his legs and with one hand holds a cigar to his lips and supports the other with the other hand [*sic*]. Although of a good-natured disposition he is very earnest in whatever he undertakes and, unlike most Irishmen, for he was born in Dublin [*sic*], where his family belongs, he is not very quick to perceive the point of a dry joke. He has studied the games of almost all the great players of past and modern times, and is always willing to explain the intricacies of any game, although he is inclined to enter too much into details. He played one of the most brilliant games with Weiss, to whom he sacrificed two important pieces and then forced him toward a mate.

Although his friends back in England and Ireland knew very well that Pollock, despite some Irish blood in his veins, was not born in Dublin, they would have undoubtedly nodded in agreement regarding his personality.

Then, with an abruptness that appears almost a product of whim rather than planning, however rushed, word leaked out that Pollock was going to remain in the United States. Hazeltine in his July 27, 1889, *New York Clipper* column remarked that "The best news in American chess this week is the positive announcement that the brilliant Irish champion, Dr. W.H.K. Pollock, is definitely settled to be 'one of us.' He has an engagement with the Baltimore Chess Association," and was to take over as chess editor of the *Baltimore Sunday News*.

While a few of Pollock's intimates, such as the Rowlands and his brother John, may have received letters, or known in advance, of Pollock's intentions to remain in the United States, perhaps they were as surprised as were most of his acquaintances. Why Pollock would have chosen to remain in the comparative wastelands of chess play in America rather than return to advance his chess career in Europe remains a mystery. After all, he could have given a few exhibitions to refill his coffers, and then returned to a much more active chess environment. Yet his staying on, like some of his earlier decisions in life, would not have come as a total surprise to anyone who knew him at all well. Unlike most professional players, Pollock sought few riches through his chess exploits. As his years in Bath and Dublin attest, despite the comforts provided by a well-to-do parental home, Pollock turned his back on a potentially lucrative career in medicine, one for which he had trained, but for which he would never live.

We will likely never know why he chose the path he did, either for his life's work or for his home. Perhaps America fascinated him as a country in which to seek a new chess identity, or perhaps he simply found a change of locale too tempting to pass up. Perhaps it was easier to love his family from a distance, given his decision to follow chess rather than the socially approved and trained-for vocation of a physician. All we know for sure is that he did stay. He had decided, whatever his motives, to pursue his own version of the American dream: a life lived for chess brilliancy in its most artistic and romantic sense, in the land, both literally and metaphorically, of Paul Morphy.

5. A Baltimore Man, June 1889–May 1890

Stopovers in Brooklyn and Philadelphia

By the end of the Sixth American Chess Congress, Pollock had accepted the invitation to visit and offer several exhibitions at the Brooklyn Chess Club. His first exhibition took place on the next Friday, May 31, and the Brooklyn Chess Club took special measures to make it a success. "Mr. Pollock, the Irish chess champion, will be the guest of the Brooklyn Chess Club on Friday evening next with members of the club, beginning at 7:30 pm," announced the *Brooklyn Daily Eagle* of Wednesday, June 1. Pollock scored only 7 wins, with 4 losses and 1 draw, as the same *Eagle* column explained, no doubt much to the pleasure of the club members mentioned:

> The Brooklyn Chess Club last night were given the privilege of the use of the large lodge room adjoining their club parlor over the Post Office, on the occasion of the chess reception given the Irish chess champion, Mr. Pollock, by the club and the result was that the series of simultaneous chess games played by Mr. Pollock were watched by a larger crowd of invited guests than was possible at the previous club gatherings of the kind, there being ample room for the spectators as well as players. Mr. Pollock had twelve of the club members as his opponents, and he won from the strongest of the club's players in the night's tourney, he defeating Messrs. Eno, Murray, Simis, Olly, Sprowers and Pruden [Barrett was also defeated but unmentioned], while he lost to Messrs. Broughton, Park, Rolfe and Shepard. Mr. Rolfe played "the game of his life" on the occasion, and the genial old gentleman was heartily congratulated. Mr. Seely will have to look to his laurels. There was but one game drawn and that was by Mr. Edwards.

As often happened on such occasions, the visiting master had to play some consultation games in the company of the club's most influential players. Although ill and forced into the reduced boundaries of his house for several months, Charles A. Gilberg, Brooklyn's top chess promoter and the club's president, was able to lead the festivities on the occasion of Pollock's exhibition. Pollock, in consultation with Gilberg, played against Philip Richardson and G.F. Murray on May 31. Pollock and Gilberg, on the Black side of a Hampe-Allegaier-Thorold Gambit, won after some "very fine play" and a "very neat ending."

On his way to Baltimore, Pollock also stopped in Philadelphia for a few days, as a brief report in the *Philadelphia Times* of June 23 reveals:

> Mr. W.H.K. Pollock, the well-known London exponent of the sixty-four squares and participant of the late congress, tarried in Philadelphia a few days, en route to Baltimore, where he may, if opportunity offers, locate permanently. He played quite a number of parties with local experts, the most notable being two with Priester (in which Pollock won one and drew one), two with Voigt (which Pollock lost) and one with Wilson (a draw). In a simultaneous séance of six games he lost to W.C. Wilson, E. Stark and Charles Eccles. Mr. Pollock has been awarded the $50 brilliancy prize of the late congress for his game with Weiss.

A New Home in Baltimore

Immediately after his appearance at the Brooklyn Chess Club, Pollock departed for Baltimore, the city on the Patapsco River. His trip was the product of successful negotiations with some of the city's chess leaders, especially fruitful being the discussions with Edward L. Torsch, president of the local chess club.[1] On June 29, an executive committee of the Baltimore Chess Association elected Pollock as a member. Very shortly thereafter, he was also offered the editorship of the chess column of the *Baltimore Sunday News*. Indeed, it is quite possible that this opportunity to become a chess editor for a city newspaper acted as part of the inducement for his move to the city. The weekly newspaper began publication in 1874 and, according to several newspaper directories, appeared on Sunday morning containing all the news before 5:00 a.m. but also a consistent section on literature and other entertaining information. It would continue publication only through 1894.

On June 30, 1889, Pollock opened his first *Baltimore Sunday News* column as follows:

> Having decided to take up my residence in this city, I have great pleasure in announcing that I have been engaged by the publishers of THE BALTIMORE SUNDAY NEWS to undertake the editorship of this column. While my endeavors will be first and foremost to present the ideas and wishes of the chess players of Baltimore and to give prominence to every feature of interest in local news, it is at the same time my aim to promote the highest interest of the game as a first-class science; in fact, with the kind assistance of our readers, to make interesting and popular reading matter, but to take also the utmost care that this column shall hold its own against the world as regards the quality of work.
>
> Chess players are, therefore, invited to cooperate with this enterprise and to come up as one man with games, problems, solutions, notes, news and queries and rely on every effort being made to do justice to each department.
>
> The former esteemed chess editor, my friend, Mr. L.H. Wieman, who is so well known to have the interests of the game at heart, has most generously undertaken to set me on the right track by the aid of his valuable experience and has promised me his advice and cooperation, so that I start with every confidence that this column will be a success[...].
>
> W.H.K. Pollock

In taking over Wieman's column (which had been suspended in mid–May), Pollock understood well the importance of balancing local and international coverage. Chess players, then and now, wanted to be kept abreast of developments everywhere, but also wanted their own chess world highlighted. In his July 7 column Pollock wrote: "While endeavoring to prove that the mantle of our able and successful predecessor has fallen upon us, we are not going to forget our promises to give the fullest attention to the claims of chess at home and to strive to promote the

---

1. According to the *American Chess Bulletin* of May-June 1921 (pages 114–115), it was indeed Edward L. Torsch who persuaded Pollock to settle in Baltimore. Torsch was featured, with a portrait, in the *Bulletin* on the occasion of the young Samuel Reshevsky's exhibitions in the city that summer: "Edward L. Torsch is one of the few remaining original members of the Baltimore Chess Association, a native of Baltimore and graduate of the Baltimore City College in the class of 1868. His first knowledge of chess was gained from his grammar school principal, who taught the willing ones chess during recess and after school hours. Though Mr. Torsch never sought an office, he has nevertheless held some position for over forty years. For ten years he was president, from 1885 to 1895. He has had the pleasure of knowing nearly all the great chess masters who visited this country and his city during that time, from Steinitz to Capablanca. He was an intimate friend of the late Alex G. Sellman, chess master and native of Baltimore, and of the late William H.K. Pollock, who played in New York in the Sixth American Chess Congress. He induced Mr. Pollock to take up his abode in Baltimore, and thereby greatly advanced the interests of the game in that city. Mr. Torsch never attempted to gain great proficiency in the game, but devoted most of his efforts to work in and for the association, to increase its membership and widen its popularity. In the business world, Mr. Torsch is president and treasurer of the Torsch & Franz Badge Co. of Baltimore, which house has been known all over the country for the past forty years, and he is also secretary and treasurer of the Torsch Packing Company of Baltimore, another large corporation in its line." Torsch was also elected treasurer of the United States Chess Association, a short-lived organization associated with the Eighth American Chess Congress held in July 1921 [see *New York Times*, July 11, 1921, and also the *American Chess Bulletin*, May-June 1921 (pages 111–112)].

highest interests of the game and its devotees and to do justice to both in every branch." In the same column, at the insistence of some of his Baltimore friends, Pollock published the score of his brilliant win over Weiss from the Sixth American Chess Congress, along with his own annotations.

In addition to such tasks demanding his penmanship, Pollock also began in earnest to aid the life of the local club: he gave two simultaneous exhibitions, one of 13 boards (9 wins, 1 loss, 3 draws), and one of nine boards (5–2, with 2 draws), giving knight-odds in one of the games. Pollock also played many games in consultation, "at which his record is still unbroken." As he would state with his dry humor, he remained, "however, open to defeat any night at the chess rooms." As with any at least semi-professional player, Pollock found it both to his personal as well as civic advantage to promote the game in his new hometown however possible.

Pollock's column met with immediate approval, not only from readers but contributors. And those came from both sides of the Atlantic. In less than a week he received original problems from Charles A. Gilberg, Samuel Gold and James Mason, as well as from German and Swedish composers.[2]

Pollock's influence in the Baltimore Chess Association, or at least his connections with the

Edward L. Torsch was instrumental in convincing Pollock to settle in Baltimore in mid–1889 (*American Chess Bulletin*, May-June 1921, page 114).

European masters, may well have been instrumental in getting Henry E. Bird to visit the city and offer some exhibitions in July 1889. Bird arrived Saturday evening July 8, on the final part of his tour through Canada and parts of America. "Mr. Bird has made himself a general favorite in Baltimore," Pollock wrote in his July 14 column, "and the fact that his visit having been a private and sociable one (no formalities) seems rather to have enhanced the enthusiasm of his reception, though we think the phenomenal quickness and freshness of his play over the board did a great deal towards enticing players to brave the sweltering hot evenings and emulate the energy and courage of the brave old Islander." Such words would have been pleasing to the ears of both Bird and his opponents, and it was this ever-present tact, among other things, that dramatically distinguished Pollock from his new homeland's greatest practitioner, Steinitz. After Bird played two simultaneous exhibitions (9 wins, no losses, 1 draw, and 6 wins, 2 losses), a "soul-stirring Evans Gambit" in consultation was played between Pollock and J. Hinrichs teamed against Bird and Uhthoff. The game ended a draw

---

2. A brief note published in the *Columbia Chess Chronicle* of August 30, 1889 (page 39) is suggestive: "A correspondent from the Baltimore Chess Association writes of the impetus to Chess arising from the Sixth American Chess Congress and the visits of Mess. Blackburne and Bird, and especially from the permanent settlement of the genial gentleman and scholar, Mr. W H.K. Pollock. Membership has increased greatly, and members of the B.C.A. have such opportunities of studying Chess that they have only to find an 'unattached' Chess-player to show him a move or two that is too much for his limited experience."

in 46 moves. On Wednesday, July 10, Pollock accompanied Bird to a dinner at the Hotel Rennert, arranged for Bird by Torsch. Many enthusiasts, even Baltimore's mayor, attended. Baltimore was the final stop of Bird's United States tour, and no doubt a highly satisfactory conclusion to what had to be an otherwise grueling experience for the often ill, veteran player.

Whereas Bird returned to New York via Philadelphia, sailing back to England on board the *Celtic*, Pollock continued his work in Baltimore. He opened correspondence with various American chess clubs in order to set up team correspondence play, and did his best to create a livelier local chess life, including making himself available for consultation games as well as games at odds. In addition, besides publishing the numerous problems contributed by a host of international problemists (and sometimes with the problems dedicated to the new chess editor), Pollock published some of his own creations. The one below first appeared in the September 1, 1889, issue of the *Baltimore Sunday News*. Steinitz enjoyed it, writing Pollock that he thought it "very fine," commending the younger man for his efforts. (Solutions to problems appear at the end of this chapter.)

By W.H.K. Pollock
White to mate in two

When players such as Professor Simon Newcomb, the famous astronomer and mathematician, then of Washington, or Hermann Voigt, the very strong player out of Philadelphia, passed through the city, Pollock met them at the chessboard. On Thursday, September 26, Pollock also gave a 14 board simultaneous exhibition at the club, winning every game. He admitted in his September 29, 1889, column that he had never accomplished such a sweep, even while he complimented three of his opponents for their excellent fighting spirit. All in all, things went smoothly for Pollock as he settled into his new life in Baltimore. That he was aware of his good fortune, and grateful for it, can be seen from the October 20 *News*, when he prefaced his column with the following observation:

> We pause here, on presenting our sixteenth column, and at the end of our first half-year's labor in the field of American Chess, to offer our warmest thanks both to our readers, friends, and to the chess press of the New World, for the touchingly noble and generous reception and support given us from a continuance of your indulgence, favor and good-will, which we shall still try to merit, striving here as we strove elsewhere to aid in the spread of so powerful a bond of civilization as our noble game has for ages been recognized to be. "Honesty is our policy," not because (like the Scotchman in the proverb) "we've tried baith," but because we like it and the style of friends we make by it![3]

---

3. Something of Pollock's honesty, high journalistic standards and idealism, as well as his capacity to place blame to some degree on both parties, was manifest in the context of the acrimonious exchanges between Hoffer's *Chess-Monthly* and Steinitz's *International Chess Magazine* during this period. This, for instance, is what he wrote in his November 10, 1889, column: "The October *Chess-Monthly* has disgraced English journalism by replying to the bitter 'Personal and General' attacks of the *International* with a quantity of obscene poetry, the style of which jars also against International Chess harmony, a public offense that cannot pass uncensored, for the better the feeling between nations the more they will struggle for chess supremacy—over the board." This condemnation of public bickering suggests something of Pollock's character, as well.

In November 1889, Pollock was instrumental in arranging and advertising a team match between Washington and Baltimore, with the capital players taking the trip to Maryland. The match was set to take place in the Eutaw Association Rooms, and admission was free. Pollock acted as referee in this, the first such match between the two cities, played on Saturday, November 9 (the match finished 5–5). In addition, Pollock penned detailed reports in his column and annotated the cleverest games.

For the rematch, scheduled for November 28, Pollock and others were recommended to be placed on the Baltimore team "so to increase their fighting chance." Eventually this idea was dropped, to the detriment of the Baltimore team. No doubt Pollock was so far beyond the strength of the club players involved that his playing would have seemed somehow unfair, and certainly not in keeping with his desire to promote the game in every aspect. In the end, Pollock acted as referee and chronicler—the latter, not without his witty humor as appeared in the *Baltimore Sunday News* of December 1:

> It was a strong and enthusiastic team of Knights of the chequered field that journeyed "on to Wash" or watch on Thanksgiving afternoon, to "see how things would go" for the Monumental City players were not finally separated from the spectators until just before the match commenced when it was decided to play 11 a side.
>
> The contest which ensued proved one of the most brilliant of the kind on record in the Western World, regarded from every point of view except as to the final result, which was—12½ to 5½ in the favor of the Capital—an altogether unexpected denouement.
>
> The arena of battle was thronged at 6:45 pm when play commenced, nearly 50 persons being present. It was computed that at least 100 people visited the rather limited space where the novel and interesting encounter took place during the evening, 47 being entertained at 9 o'clock lunch [*sic*] recess, at which period it was *finally* decided that the World's Fair would be held in Washington[...].
>
> The Washington men played a splendid game throughout, and we only regret that we have not the honor of being numbered among the vanquished heroes—our estimate of the cause of the defeat of Baltimore this time being their lack of backbone in not *insisting* on their strongest men (e.g., Dalla, Han [*sic*], Pollock, &c.) supporting them in practical warfare—the want of practice shown by several of the Maryland veterans—a somewhat inferior light, boards and men to those in use at the B.C.A. [Baltimore Chess Association]—the powerful moral support afforded Washington through their brilliant gathering of spectators (even "the force" was represented at lunch at a late hour)—the consistently intellectual Chess form exhibited by the players of the Delphi of the New World—and—the Thanksgiving Turkey.

Pollock, during "a very pleasant reunion [with] several ladies present and a good number of consultation games as well as 'skittles' indulged in," gave a simultaneous exhibition in Washington on December 14 (15 wins, 5 losses, 2 draws). In his Christmas column of December 22, Pollock offered his readers another one of his original problems. This time he published a three mover, accompanied by the following challenge: "We promise, as prize, a nightmare to any Chess Poet who solves this just before supper on Xmas Day; also *Games of the Vienna Tournament* by A.G. Sellman (for local solvers)":

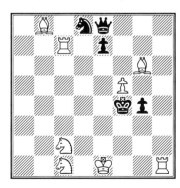

By W.H.K. Pollock
White to mate in three

In the same column, Pollock gave space to a Christmas essay focused on the young underdogs of chess populating his workplace: the newsboys who sold the newspaper. Although the exact author remained unknown even to Pollock, it is a remarkable piece and Pollock's decision to include it just three days before Christmas certainly reveals something of his character, and perhaps how that character was formed in the house of his father, the Reverend Pollock:

A BEAUTIFUL CHRISTMAS MOVE
"YE DID IT UNTO ME"

What's novel in chess? Let us drop the platitudes about it being older than Pyramids and discover where it is youngest. Where last has the infection broken out? Perhaps you would least guess. Down on Baltimore, St. No. 218, right opposite THE SUNDAY NEWS office is the Newsboys' Residing Room, the evening resort of those bread-winners who are as essential a part of the newspaper business as the printing press itself. Evening after evening, especially at this time of the year, the rooms are crowded with them. And kind, noble-hearted ladies, moved by the example of Him who said "Suffer little children to come unto Me," sacrifice their drawing-rooms to come down here and teach these little fellows, often friendless and homeless, to sing Christmas hymns and pass pleasant hours. In a recent conversation, one of the ladies referred to the subject of amusements furnished the boys. The ever-present question arose in the mind. "How can this be turned to the advantage of Chess?" An offer to spend an occasional evening there, met with hearty appreciation and acceptance. This will explain the presence of Chess in the Newsboys' Reading Room of our city. They learn more quickly than grown people. Explaining the names and moves of the pieces once, is ample. They crowd around each other. They climb up on the big table to peep over at the players. That they are bright and sharp goes without saying. They are improving rapidly in the rudiments. After which, they will hold a little Tournament, and it's going to be a success, too. After the tournament they may challenge the Baltimore Chess Association, or, bred with a spirit of *revanche*, visit—Washington. Who knows? Remember that one of the brightest geniuses in the world, James Mason, of London, was once a little newsboy in New York, and who will deny that chess has a high moral influence and value if it can draw them from the streets to spend their evenings in the fascination of the noblest of games?[4]

Given Mason's alcoholism and its occasional public displays as evidenced during the New York 1889 tournament, when for at least one round he had to be removed from the playing room—the writer of the newsboy essay might better have refrained from associating "high moral influence" and Mason in the same sentence. Still, the uplifting intention was clear, as was the goodwill extended toward the troubled genius.

Pollock spent much of January 1890 following the great contest between Chigorin and Gunsberg taking place in Havana, annotating the games for his audience both in Baltimore and, as the influence of his column spread through exchanges, throughout the nation.[5] He gradually established himself as one of the better game annotators in the country, although not of the depth of Steinitz—but then who was? That it was about time he played chess seriously, in a tournament or match, must have crossed his mind, given all the time he was spending giving his readers updates on various tournaments, both American and European. One notable event proved to be the third championship of the short-lived United States Chess Association (USCA), a tour-

---

4. As appears evident from his subsequent January 5, 1890, column, Pollock was not the original architect of this gesture towards the Newsroom's homeless boys, but he clearly felt for them. • **5.** Pollock also published news from home, with a valuable personal touch. Here is an example from the *Baltimore Sunday News*, January 5, 1890: "Mr. Blackburne played 28 games simultaneously at Swansea, a week before Xmas, winning 22 and drawing one—a remarkable feat against strong selected opponents. The Rev. J. Pollock, who alone escaped defeat, and who is one of the strongest English amateurs, makes the following interesting observations: 'I ought, as Blackburne acknowledged, to have won, but you know the difficulty of playing well when everyone is crowding round telling you the best moves, which are always the worst. Blackburne thinks double. He thinks over the board and he thinks blindfold. He comes to your board and says: "Let me see, I can win Queen for two Rooks, then play Kt–Kt5, B there, and win another pawn" (sotto voce) and then he immediately plays something quite different. He must have thought of the combination he spoke of and he must have thought of the combination he did not speak of. Ergo, he thought blindfold and he thought over the board.'"

nament about to begin in early February 1890, in St. Louis. During a general meeting of the Baltimore Chess Association on January 18, headed by Torsch, Pollock was entrusted with representing the State of Maryland at the event.

In St. Louis: Third USCA Championship

The next day, January 19, Pollock published in his column a full announcement of the USCA's plans, including details of the program: the St. Louis tournament would commence Tuesday, February 4.[6] The first prize was $250, second $150, third $75, fourth $50, and fifth, $25. The championship tournament was open only to one representative from each state. For a state to qualify as a member of the USCA, at least 20 residents had to join the organization. The representative of each state had to be nominated by the state association where one existed, or, if there was none, by the individual state members. The entry fee was $20. The organizers also planned a free-for-all tournament, as they termed it, open to all members of the association without any entry fees or conditions.

Charles F. Nordhoff of Cincinnati, the USCA's secretary and treasurer, sent a private note to the Baltimore Chess Association, which Pollock provided his readers. Because of the convoluted ways in which various players were put forth for possible participation by a smorgasbord of "organizations" at the state, city, club and even individual level, Pollock's comments made rather broad fun of the resulting confusion:

> "We sincerely hope that the Baltimore Chess Association may be represented at the meeting and in the Championship tournament, as this will undoubtedly be the largest meeting yet held by the Association" [wrote Nordhoff], and reminds us [so Pollock continued] that Baltimore is represented by only six members, fourteen short of the required number. New York lacks six of filling the quota and Massachusetts thirteen, but they will undoubtedly fill the same and send a champion. Those likely to enter are Max Judd and W. Haller (Missouri), S. Ruphrat and Maurice Judd, or C. Miller (Ohio), J.W. Showalter (Kentucky), H.C. Brown and R.N. Whiteford (Indiana), and the New York and Massachusetts delegates. "We are not certain about Gunsberg, Chigorin and Mackenzie. It all depends on concluding their match in time. The New Orleans Club may enter a representative as may also Mr. Uedemann of Chicago, who is trying to organize an Illinois Chess Association," wrote Nordhoff. Other "possibilities" are Canada and Georgia, the latter encouraged by Mr. [Isaac] E. Orchard of Atlanta. Over $100 will be divided in prizes for the free-for-all tussle.
>
> The enterprise of St. Louis is admirable, and it behooves us all to further to our utmost so good a programme. The management, however, should state which State *Chigorin* will represent, or is there to be an International Tourney, in which case it will easier for some of us to enter.

Despite the confusing possibilities, matters quickly coalesced, and on January 26, Pollock reported that his correspondence with the USCA's organizers suggested that "St. Louis is jubilant over the outlook" of the congress being a success. He listed the following individuals as confirmed for play: Lipschütz (New York), Max Judd (Missouri), Pollock (Maryland), Maurice Judd (Ohio), H.C. Brown (Indiana), and Louis Uedemann (Illinois). Most of these players had alternates in case they could not attend. Others interested in entering were the following: Jackson W. Showalter (Kentucky), W.A. Haller (Missouri), Isaac E. Orchard (Atlanta, Georgia) and Charles A. Moehle (Chicago). During the January 18 meeting of the Baltimore Chess Association, a key speaker was L.H. Wieman, the former editor of the *Baltimore Sunday News* column and now a

---

6. The circular for the third USCA championship, signed January 4, 1890, with the tournament details appeared published in full in the *Columbia Chess Chronicle* of January 15, 1890 (pages 137–138).

vice-president of the USCA, who "argued the claims of that body with such efficacy, that ten of those present became members of it on the spot and paid up the $1 subscription. Sixteen of the required quota of 20 having now joined, it was decided that Mr. W.H.K. Pollock represent the Baltimore Chess Association in the forthcoming Championship Tournament at St. Louis."

Pollock's name was given as confirmed by the *St. Louis Republic* of January 26, 1890, whose editor three days later wrote about looking forward to a grand event:

GREAT CHESS TOURNAMENT

The United States Chess Association, composed of delegates from different State associations, will meet in St. Louis on Tuesday, February 4. At this meeting, which will be held in the Emilie building at Ninth and Olive streets, a tournament will be held for the United States' championship and other prizes. It will last about 10 days and about 10 States are expected to be represented by from 50 to 60 delegates.

The citizens of St. Louis have contributed $600, which will be distributed as prizes. As some of the best players in the country will be present, some excellent games may be witnessed. Chess players throughout the country are interested as well as those in St. Louis, and the coming tournament is exciting considerable interest in chess-playing circles.

For connoisseurs, however, the fact that some advertised names could not play in the tournament, as will be seen, must have been disappointing. In the end, seven players participated in the championship tournament: Pollock (Maryland), Showalter (Kentucky), Lipschütz (New York), H.C. Brown (Indiana), Louis Uedemann (Illinois), William Haller and A.H. Robbins (both of St. Louis). But the road to this final set proved more rocky than expected. Pollock left for St. Louis on Friday, January 31:

Mr. Pollock, our editor, left Friday, Jan. 31, to take part in the match as a representative of the State of Maryland in general and more particularly as a representative of the Baltimore Chess Association. Mr. Pollock said he felt in good form when leaving, and we predict for him a high score in the Championship Match. Though he has three of the strongest players in the United States against him, we will be very much surprised if Mr. Pollock does not hold at least second place in the Tournament. The Nottingham *Guardian* says: "Some of the most brilliant games we have met with have been when such masters as Blackburne and Pollock have been playing a number of games simultaneously, when genius has been substituted for analysis, and when the time limit, though not enforced, has been perhaps sixty or eighty moves an hour." We hope to have one of Mr. Pollock's brilliant games properly annotated in our next issue.[7]

When E.S. Rowse, the president of the St. Louis Chess, Checker and Whist club, sat at his office desk on February 1, he began receiving brief telegraphic notes from some of the country's best players announcing their participation. The first was a note from Lipschütz informing him that he had just left New York. That was good news since some strong players were unavailable, including the local master, Max Judd, who was in Europe on business. As for Maryland's entry, "Mr. Pollock is an Englishman," wrote the *St. Louis Republic* chronicler on the second day of February, "who came over last spring and entered the lists of the international chess congress of May in New York, and did himself credit. He adopted this country and is now the chess editor of the *Baltimore News*." The brief report, adorned with Max Judd's and Lipschütz's line-engravings, noted the coincidence that many of the participants were ex–St. Louisans: Uedemann used to live in the city before he went to Chicago; the same was said of Charles Moehle, who went to Chicago from St. Louis, and became "noted as an eccentric and blindfold player [...] and created so much interest with a machine which played a strong game automatically." Interestingly, Maurice Judd, Max Judd's oldest brother, was given as a player possibly representing Ohio. Otherwise,

---

7. Just who was writing the column, especially this report dated February 9, in Pollock's absence is unclear. L.H. Wieman, the *Sunday News'* previous chess editor, acting as substitute is one possibility.

Albert White would have taken up the task. Others were expected as late as the night before the tournament began.

The following was written in the *St. Louis Republic* of February 4 before such hopes proved overly optimistic, and contains more than a grain of self-congratulation as well as city puffery, including as it does describing the long-forgotten St. Louis resident and second USCA champion, William Haller, as having an "international" reputation. This sort of local boosting and resulting inaccuracy often appeared in articles written by reporters who themselves were not chess players, but who were expected to emphasize a local angle in their reports, while also advertising the national or international importance of such an event. The *Republic*'s piece did provide a good deal of color regarding the forthcoming St. Louis event:

> Twenty tables have been spread in the Emilie building, Ninth and Olive streets, for the bounteous chess feast that the lovers of that game from all parts of America will sit down to at 10 o'clock this morning, and from six to 10 hours a day for probably a week the devotees will sit in silence over these tables and ponder how to checkmate adversaries.
>
> It is anticipated that this will be by far the most brilliant collection of chess players ever seen in America. It is but the third time the United States associations have assembled through their representatives, and this will be in reality the first stubborn conflict, as in the other meetings, though the playing was good, the attendance was comparatively very small. Now the lists are full, and many have already arrived. And the men who will marshal their little armies of chess men in this fight are preeminently the best in the land, and all these who will take part in the championship tourney bear the title of champions in contests for State, United States, international or world supremacy.
>
> THE BIG FOUR
>
> There is a quartet particularly whose ability has carried their names around the world. They are: S. Lipschütz (New York), W.H.K. Pollock (Baltimore), J.W. Showalter (Kentucky), and William H. Haller (St. Louis). The relative strength of the members of the "big four," according to the estimates of the delegates who have arrived, corresponds, to the above arrangement[...].
>
> THE MASTER TOURNEY
>
> The master tourney, of course, is the one that evokes the chief interest. The players, in most cases, have more than individual reputations at stake, for they are selected to represent their respective sections. They all feel the honor reposed in them and are coming prepared to fight and finish for their constituents, and so well have the selections been made that no section will have a walk over. That it will go to St. Louis, New York, Baltimore or Kentucky is certain, unless a "dark horse" should set his wits most violently to work. Of these four places St. Louis stands a splendid chance, Lipschütz will fight for New York, Pollock for Baltimore and Showalter for Kentucky. The first two are representatives, while the latter goes on his own hook by virtue of having won the championships which give him entrée to any game. A.C. Robbins, the widely known problem composer, is the elected representative for St. Louis as alternate for Max Judd. Should Mr. Robbins, who is a strong player, lose, St. Louis has a second chance of keeping the championship at home through the efforts of Will Haller, who, like Showalter, goes in on his own account, by right of having won the championship of the second annual tournament last year at Indianapolis. [...] Mr. Pollock arrived yesterday morning and in the evening was joined by Messrs. Showalter and Lipschütz, who constitute a trio of chums from friendships formed in numberless tourneys. Col. Showalter is a typical Kentuckian and states that an unexpected contestant, Mr. Hodges, now champion of Tennessee, formerly of St. Louis, is en route. Mr. Pollock is a newspaper man, from Dublin, and will be recognized at once as an Englishman of culture. Mr. Lipschütz, besides being a player, is a noted chess author, and is the only one of the trio who is small of stature.
>
> Mr. H.C. Brown, the representative of Indiana's interests, also came in. Though he has won the State championship twice, this is his first venture outside of his State. He was accompanied by Dr. E.R. Lewis, one of the vice-presidents of the United States association, and by Mr. W.H. Ripley of the executive board, both of whom will assist the local officers in entertaining the players and arranging the games, besides taking a hand in the free-for-all if time permits.

Some of the players who had not yet arrived were nevertheless paired for the morning of February 4, but the masters' tournament eventually comprised only Pollock, Lipschütz, Showalter,

Robbins, Haller, Uedemann (who arrived early in the morning of the first round) and Brown. "It will be observed," noted the *St. Louis Republic* the next day, "that Maj. Hanham was entered by the committee, but that the gentleman at the time the players were paired off had not arrived in the city. The committee thought best to enter him, however, in the hope that he would arrive in time to play a portion of his games." Hanham in the end never appeared.

Although, as suggested by subsequent snippets of information in the *Sunday News* column, Pollock caught a cold on his journey, once he camped at Hotel Moser, he fared very well as the competition started.[8] The fact that he was paired in the first round against an absent Hanham gave Pollock some extra hours for recovery (he was awarded a win after an hour passed, although eventually Hanham was dropped from the scoring). The second round commenced in the evening, and Pollock was paired against Haller on the third board in what constituted his first actual game in the tournament. After he took Haller out of the books with a rarely explored opening line (**1. e4 e5 2. Nc3 Nf6 3. Bc4 N×e4!?**), Pollock finished the game with his typical tactical artistry:

Haller–Pollock
U.S. Chess Association Championship
St. Louis, February 4, 1890

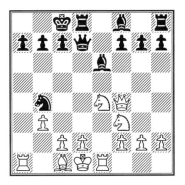

After 12. a2×b3

Pollock continued with **12. ... N×c2!** and after **13. R×a7** (13. K×c2 allows mate in two, with ...Qd3+ and ...Q×b3) **13. ... Kb8 14. Ne5 Qb5 15. Nc3** he delighted the spectators with **15. ... B×b3!** after which the game's conclusion in Black's favor was a simple formality.

The second day of play, Wednesday, February 5, Pollock played Uedemann in the morning, even though he had not originally been scheduled to play him then. Because of Hanham's continued absence, Uedemann, like Pollock the day before, found himself without an opponent. Accordingly, the two men were paired, with the next day's *St. Louis Republic* somewhat obscurely observing that doing so "completes the first round." Apparently the decision had already been made to omit Hanham from the tournament's crosstable, and thus Pollock's first round default win was eliminated from the scoring.

The solution the organizer's found of pairing Pollock with Uedemann led to something of a controversy, which occurred when the following position was reached:

---

8. The sources for recovering most of the games played by Pollock during this tournament are the *Baltimore Sunday News* and *St. Louis Republic* chess columns, but also the *Third Annual Report: United States Chess Association with Forty-Two Games Played at St. Louis and Seven Games Played at Indianapolis* (Indianapolis: Carlon & Hollenbeck, Printers and Binders, 1891). In an undated *Baltimore Sunday News* column in the possession of Olimpiu G. Urcan, Pollock later wrote that the report was a "handsome 64-page pamphlet containing 42 games played at St. Louis and 7 at Indianapolis," although he criticized the quality of the game annotations provided.

Pollock–Uedemann
U.S. Chess Association Championship
St. Louis, February 5, 1890

White to move

Here Uedemann claimed a draw based on the 50-move rule, as summarized in William Cook's *Synopsis of Chess Openings* (American edition). As the *Republic* of February 6 noted:

> The committee, after considerable deliberation, decided to disallow Mr. Uedemann's claim, upon the ground that the win was not doubtful, owing to the presence of White's pawn at a7. The game then proceeded as follows: **1. Nb6 Bb7 2. a8Q Ba8 3. N×a8.** At this point, Mr. Uedemann again claimed that the rule be applied, but his claim was not allowed, as the mate is a well-known one in 28 moves, hence the position could not come within the rule as doubtful. The decision of the committee upon the point adjudicated practically nullifies the 50-move rule, and will no doubt lead to some legislation upon the subject by the association before its adjournment. Mr. Pollock won the game, however, forcing Uedemann to resign upon the eighty-fifth move.[9]

---

9. The critical passage from William Cook's *Synopsis of Chess Openings* (Cincinnati: Robert Clarke & Co, 1884) is the following: "Counting Fifty Moves: If, at any period during a game, either player persist in repeating a particular check, or series of checks, or persist in repeating any particular line of play which does not advance the game; or if '*a game ending*' be of doubtful character as to its being a win or a draw; or if a win be possible, but the skill to force the game be questionable; then either player may demand judgment of the Umpire as to its being a proper game to be determined as drawn at the end of fifty additional moves, on each side; or, the question: 'Is, or is not the game a draw?' may be, by mutual consent of the players, submitted to the Umpire at any time. The decision of the Umpire, in either case, to be final. And whenever fifty moves are demanded and accorded, the party demanding it may, when the fifty moves have been made, claim the right to go on with the game, and thereupon the other party may claim the fifty move rule, and the end of which, unless mate is effected, the game shall be decided a draw" (page 253 of the section entitled "Chess Code of The Chess Association of the United States of America, Adopted in New York, January 28th, 1880, during the session of the Fifth American Chess Congress"). ¶ The *Baltimore Sunday News* of March 2, 1890, which reproduced the whole excerpt, added the following: "It is a pity that the fifty-move rule is either not abolished altogether or else some active steps should be taken by the United States Chess Association and the different State Associations to formulate some rule in its place to which there can be no doubt expressed as to its actual meaning. The same rule caused trouble at the Sixth American Congress." Whether these were actually Pollock's words, or whether they simply gave the sense of his position, for his own column, is unknown. Further to this point, the remark that the "mate is a well-known one in 28 moves" is not precise: from any starting position, the side with the bishop and knight manage to checkmate in at most 33 moves regardless of the opponent's best defense. ¶ Pages 22–23 of the pamphlet of the third USCA congress had the following on this incident: "His [Uedemann's] right to demand the fifty move count was disputed, and the question was submitted to Messrs. [W.C.] Cochran, [J.W.] Hulse and [W.H.] Ripley, the three members of the executive committee present. Under Rule XXII of the London Chess Club, published in Staunton's Handbook, p. 39, and Agnel's Book of Chess, p. 119, or under Rule XI of the British Chess Association as published in Gossip's Manual, p. 32, the right to demand the fifty move count would have been beyond dispute; but, unfortunately for Mr. Uedemann, it was expressly announced that play in this tournament would be governed by the Chess Code as found in Cook's Synopsis (Am. Ed.). The framers of this code, for some reason best known to themselves, discarded the British Chess Association Rule, which is at least easily understood and applied, and adopted instead one which is ambiguous in its terms and has led to much controversy whenever appealed to. The only part of which is applicable to the case in hand, is the following: 'If "a game ending" be of *doubtful* character as to *its being a win or a draw*; or if *a win be possible, but the skill to force the game be questionable*; then either player may demand judgment of the Umpire as to its being a proper game to be determined as drawn at the end of fifty additional moves, on

That evening after supper Pollock played Robbins. "Pollock and Robbins settled down to a Three Knights game," wrote the columnist of the *St. Louis Republic* the next day, "which was won by the former just before the close of play after a hard-fought contest." On Thursday, February 6, Pollock faced his sternest task: the undefeated Showalter. In effect, this was the culmination of the tournament, although taking place only in the fifth round, as recounted by the *St. Louis Republic* of February 7:

> As Pollock and Showalter were tied for first and second places at the opening of the tournament yesterday morning, an intense interest, amounting almost to anxiety, was manifested by the spectators as these two redoubtable champions of the chess arena assumed their respective positions at the board preparatory to playing. Pollock had the move and opened up with a Four Knights game. Showalter played with rapidity and in fine style. The game, so far, is the shortest and the most brilliant of the tourney.

Objectively, it was no brilliancy. Pollock blundered, overlooking a simple mate in two, and resigned at his fifteenth move. For Pollock, obviously, it was a debacle, but hardly an adequate test of strength against Showalter.

That afternoon, Pollock played his sixth round opponent, Lipschütz, and the game, a Vienna, was drawn in 46 moves. After playing his two strongest opponents on the same day, Pollock that evening, at 7:00, observed a problem solving contest. Samuel Loyd provided a special three mover for the occasion, the prize being an elegant scarf pin with chess motif. Fourteen participants took part, mainly those from the free-for-all section of the championship, as the masters were not allowed to enter this particular contest. The participants had one hour to solve Loyd's chessic conundrum, but no one succeeded in doing so. "The time given by those who returned what they supposed to be solutions," said the February 7 *St. Louis Republic*, "varied all the way from five minutes to an hour. When the time had expired and the contest closed, it was ascertained that not a single solution had been reported. The problem was solved, however, within a few minutes after the time limit by several who failed in the contest."

Chess Problem by S. Loyd
Specially composed for U.S. Chess Association Championship at St. Louis, February 6, 1890

White to mate in three[10]

(*footnote 9 continued*) each side.' Now, the ending was not '*of doubtful character*,' as White has a forced win; and as the win *was possible*, the committee had no right to act unless they regarded Mr. Pollock's '*skill to force the game questionable*.' Strictly construed the rule could only be applied, in cases like this, where it is manifest that a player does not know how to mate, and the game would be indefinitely prolonged to no good purpose. The committee could not so reflect on Mr. Pollock, and he justified their confidence by forcing mate in twenty-eight moves. If the ruling of the committee has been otherwise, the result would have been the same, but the incident should call attention to the imperative necessity of revising this wrangle-breeding and wholly unsatisfactory rule" (italics in original). • **10.** The frontispiece of the *Third Annual Report: United States Chess Association with Forty-Two Games Played at St. Louis*

In round seven, played the morning of February 7, Pollock defeated the little known and less remembered H.C. Brown from Indiana in a Two Knights Defense in about an hour and a half. Thus, at the end of the double round event's first cycle, Pollock stood second with 4½ points, behind Showalter (who scored a perfect, and perfectly impressive, 6 out of 6, in the process earning Pollock's utmost admiration—to the point he compared the Kentucky Lion with Blackburne), but tied with Lipschütz (4½), and ahead of Haller (2), Brown (1½), Uedemann (1½) and Robbins (1).

In round eight, played the next morning, Pollock had a bye (due to the absence of Hanham). That evening he faced his ninth round opponent, Uedemann, garnering the point in sparkling fashion, although the game didn't finish until 1:10 a.m.:

Uedemann–Pollock
U.S. Chess Association Championship
St. Louis, February 8, 1890

After 20. Ke1–f2

Pollock closed matters swiftly with **20. ... Qe2+ 21. Kg1 Nf3+! 22. g×f3 Q×e3+ 23. Qf2 Q×f4 24. N×e4 B×f3** and Uedemann's game was beyond redemption. "The game is one of the most interesting yet played and will repay the trouble of an examination," wrote the *St. Louis Republic's* reporter, while giving the score in full.

In the tenth and eleventh rounds, Pollock won from Haller and Robbins, improving his standing in the crosstable. In the next round, played the afternoon of February 10, Pollock again met Showalter. Quite understandably, the local press played up the drama between the two men, making the most of it for the readers:

The game between Showalter and Pollock in the thirteenth round was a Ruy Lopez and commenced immediately with the afternoon session. The score of these gentlemen was so close that the loss of a single game by Showalter greatly endangered his chances for first place and rendered it within the range of possibilities for Pollock to take first prize. As the game progressed Showalter entered into a combination of considerable depth and beauty, but of which his wily antagonist was fully aware. The conception, however, was faulty, and the result was that Showalter was compelled to abandon his scheme and put himself upon the defensive. At the middle stage of the game a quiet fell upon the room that was positively painful in its stillness. It was the first time in the whole series of his

and Seven Games Played at Indianapolis (Indianapolis: Carlon & Hollenbeck, Printers and Binders, 1891) has the following to say about Loyd's problem: "This problem was afterwards published in the leading chess columns and 'baffled' an unusually large number of solvers, who wondered why the United States Chess Association was so slow." This somewhat unclear statement may be interpreted to mean that prior to seeing Loyd's problem, readers around the nation thought the failure by those present at the USCA tournament to solve the problem within the allotted 60 minutes reflected poorly on the solvers' abilities. Once the problem was published nationally, however, it became apparent how difficult Loyd had set the task, and the failure of anyone in St. Louis to solve the problem within the time limit was more understandable.

games that the Kentucky champion's prospects were at an ebb. In all his preceding encounters his advantages had been so pronounced that success was certain. The game was finally drawn and secures to Showalter the first prize of $250 and the championship of the association. The second and third prize now lie between Lipschütz and Pollock with the latter to draw and tie or win both the games he has yet to play and come in second.

Showalter–Pollock
U.S. Chess Association Championship
St. Louis, February 10, 1890

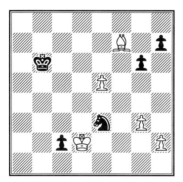

After 46. f4×e5

After a tense battle, the game was drawn as follows: **46. ... Kc5 47. Kc1 Nf1 48. K×c2 N×h2 49. Kd3 Nf1 50. Ke4 N×g3+ 51. Kf4 Nh5+** and after a few more moves the players shared the point.

As in the first cycle, Pollock immediately met Lipschütz after facing Showalter. The game was "an Evans gambit declined," reported the local chronicler, who added that "Pollock played the attack with great spirit and vigor, but Lipschütz's defense was both judicious and accurate. The game was finally won by Lipschütz." Due to an unexpected loss by Lipschütz to Robbins, the final standings were as follows: Showalter (11½) $250, Pollock (9) $150, Lipschütz (8½) $75, Haller (5) $50 and Robbins (4) $25. Pollock won both his games against Brown, Haller, Robbins, and Uedemann and lost ½–1½ in his encounters with both Showalter and Lipschütz.

Pollock's performance satisfied his fellow Baltimoreans, who, as evidenced in the *Baltimore Sunday News* of February 16, clearly added a little excuse for Pollock that he was not claiming for himself:

> We are glad to find that our expectations of last issue in regard to Mr. Pollock have been fulfilled. He contracted a very heavy cold shortly after his arrival, but managed to fulfill his duties as representative of Maryland and Baltimore Chess Association very creditably, both to himself and to those whom he represented.

"Gentlemen, chess *must* be boomed"

The *St. Louis Republic* of February 12 noted that Showalter, Lipschütz and Pollock left for Indianapolis that very morning, where they would make a stopover at the invitation of the local club. Afterwards Lipschütz and Showalter traveled to Louisville where the two planned to play a short match. According to the February 23 column of the *Baltimore Sunday News*, Pollock spent a few days in Cincinnati and gave some simultaneous exhibitions at the Mount Auburn Chess Club. Immediately after his stay in Cincinnati, Pollock returned to Baltimore. Then, on February 21, he gave a series of much praised simultaneous exhibitions in Washington: a 12-board simultaneous lasting nearly three hours, with a score of 10–2, and another simultaneous with the same number of boards, which began at 10:30 p.m. that same evening. In the latter Pollock, who must have been feeling something of the strain of playing for so many hours, won "about three-fourth of the games." The following fragment from this exhibition was given in the March 2 column:

Pollock–Unknown
12-board simultaneous exhibition
Washington, February 21, 1890

White to move

Pollock continued with **1. g6!**—threatening 2. Rh8+ and 3. g×f7—and Black collapsed swiftly after **1. ... N×f6+? 2. Kf5!** Clearly, Black could have defended better with 1. ... f×g6 2. R×g6+ Kf8 3. Kf5 Re2 4. Be5 c4!

Much inspired by the USCA proceedings in St. Louis, Pollock and Wieman called for a Baltimore Chess Association meeting in the first week of March 1890 for the purpose of founding the Maryland Chess Association. The body was established on Saturday, March 8, at the rooms of the city's Association. Among those present were many to be expected, but also some, such as Halpern, who might come as something of a surprise: A.L. Huggins, L.H. Wieman (chair), E.L. Torsch (president of the Baltimore Chess Association), Pollock, J. Halpern (New York), J.H. Park (Brooklyn), A Schofield, Hughes, F.W. Koch, Bennett, J. Hinrichs (vice-president of the Baltimore Chess Association), J. Uhthoff, Barrett, Fuechsl and Tanhauser.

Wieman, whose position in the USCA already established his interest in organizing chess, opened the meeting with the words: "Gentlemen, Chess *must* be boomed." The "booming" of an organization involved not only its leading members but also the rank and file in a concerted effort to publicize and promote the game. It was the spirit of the age throughout the nation, and those attracted to chess had the "booming" fever as well. The group obviously shared Wieman's enthusiasm, for "the motion to found the Maryland Chess Association was carried by storm," reported Pollock on March 16. Pollock, Uhthoff and Park were elected as the new Association's executives and the *Sunday News* was appointed its official organ. In a sense, between his work as an Association officer and his chess column, Pollock had become the voice of chess statewide. In addition, on April 14, a general meeting decided to search for better rooms and a deal was cut (for $300 rent annually) with the Haydn Musical Association, 306 W. Fayette Street, a few doors down from the Baltimore Chess Association's old rooms. In his *Baltimore Sunday News* column of April 20, 1890, Pollock wrote:

> While the resources of the Association are powerful enough to guarantee the maintenance of such a club-room for the coming year, its eventual permanent establishment in such quarters, as well as adequate furnishing of the Hall as a comfortable first-class Chess resort, will largely depend upon the way Baltimore patronizes the "game of science and culture" by increase of membership and private liberality.

With matters progressing well in Baltimore, and with the Maryland Chess Association founded and club rooms newly situated, one might have thought Pollock would settle down to enjoy the growth of the game in his newly adopted home. That, however, was not the case. Pollock remained an untiring traveler. Within weeks, he would be traveling "out West," at least as far as St. Louis, and within the course of the following 12 months he would find himself stopping in Springfield and Kansas City, and then in Chicago, Cincinnati, Pittsburg[11] and New York City. The last named could hardly be a surprise. In chess, in the United States, all roads in the nineteenth century led back to New York City.

Problem Solutions:

Pages 78 and 79:
Pollock's problems: **1. Nb5** and **1. Rc5**
Page 86:
Loyd's problem: **1. Ne3**

---

11. Between 1891 and 1911, Pittsburg (without an h) was the city's official spelling.

6. Going West,
May 1890–June 1891

On the Road

On Monday, May 10, 1890, Pollock boarded a train heading to St. Louis, Missouri, a city located more than 740 miles west of Baltimore. Ever since his arrival in the "Monumental City," Pollock's efforts in chess had been fruitful. His yearlong journalistic work on behalf of the *Sunday News* had produced a chess column that had quickly emerged as one of the best in America, and perhaps much farther abroad. As expected, given his appetite for travel since his days in England and Ireland, Pollock could hardly be shackled to reporting matters from a desk in some building in downtown Baltimore. Besides traveling for his own play in tournaments and matches, Pollock also traveled to report on events of national importance involving leading American players. Nor was his employer slow to make use of its chess newsman in such fashion, while indulging in some self-boosting as well:

> Mr. W.H.K. Pollock, the Chess Editor of The Baltimore Sunday News, left for St. Louis, Monday, 10th inst., to report the Showalter–Judd match for the The News. Mr. Pollock is a live editor and works for a live paper. After a careful comparison of the leading chess columns both in this country and in Europe, we feel that we are making no mistake when we say that dollar for dollar The News through the agency of Mr. Pollock gives its readers more genuine chess information and news than any other chess paper or magazine in the world.

In an age where information provided in chess columns was often simply recycled from other sources, themselves often secondary, such quality work required the hand of a chess professional like Pollock who did not hesitate to pack his bags, ride a train for hundreds of miles and report from the actual site of matches and tournaments. In the second part of May 1890 he "was on a professional visit to Chicago and St. Louis." The match between Max Judd and Jackson W. Showalter began on May 19, and Pollock telegraphed his copy analyzing the match for both the *Sunday News* and *St. Louis Republic*.[1] On days without match games, Pollock gave simultaneous exhibitions at the St. Louis Chess Club. For instance, on May 22 he played against 12 amateurs, scoring 8 wins, 2 losses and 2 draws, in less than three hours. He repeated such performances

---

1. After some lengthy negotiations throughout February–April 1890, the match between Judd and Showalter finally started on May 19, 1890, in the rooms of the local St. Louis chess club. The match was for $250 a side, the first to win seven games (draws not counting) to be declared the victor. The games began at 4:00 p.m., and five games a week were required. According to the *St. Louis Republic* of May 4, a full report of the match, including games, was to be published on a daily basis in the news column of that newspaper. The match ended on June 3, with Judd the winner, 7–3.

several times during the match. The following report, which highlights more of Pollock's work and travels, was printed in the June 8, 1890, issue of his *Sunday News* column:

CHESS IN THE WEST

Besides the Judd–Showalter match, chess in the West is not very lively. Still in spots it is occasionally heard from. Owing to the fact that the Associated Press failed to report the St. Louis match little information regarding it can be obtained and consequently it has failed to arouse much enthusiasm. I quote in this regard the words of a prominent Cincinnati business man and a strong chess player: "We have had but one dispatch since the match begun. Four or five columns daily of baseball—giving the results of games in every cross-roads town; two or three columns daily on horse-racing, giving the performances of every two or three-year-old *colt*, and not a line for the intellectual performance of two of the best chess players in the United States!" Quite right as far as it goes, but do not the chess players of the United States have themselves to blame for this state of affairs to a certain extent? Newspapers may be called the barometers of popular opinion. They print what the people want. If every man who played chess in the United States refused to buy a paper unless it contained dispatches of his favorite game, we think the papers would shortly be giving a column a day to chess. The fact that chess is daily becoming more powerful is shown by the increased number of papers which are printing weekly chess columns throughout the country. Tho' chess is dull, as we have stated, through the West, still a few disciples of the game are steadily preaching its merits to any who will listen. Foremost among these is our editor [Pollock], who at last accounts was moving in a straight line for the Indian Territory, bent on instructing Lo in the mysteries of the game. We have heard, however, that he received a heavy *check* at Springfield, Mo., which had the effect of turning his course in the direction of Kansas City, where he again received a check, and now with considerably abated momentum, is moving on St. Louis.

In Springfield, more than 200 miles southwest of St. Louis, Pollock gave three simultaneous exhibitions, in total playing 23 games and winning all but one of them. Besides playing some consultation games against Showalter and some local St. Louis experts, Pollock partnered with the Kentuckian in giving some simultaneous exhibitions in Kansas City, more than 190 miles north of Springfield, playing an eight-board simultaneous, for instance, giving the odds of a knight (5 wins, 2 losses, 1 draw). Pollock gave three exhibitions on three successive evenings at the Kansas City Chess Club. Out of 25 games he scored 20 wins, 4 losses and 1 draw. According to the *St. Louis Republic* of June 15, Pollock was also invited by the Topeka Chess Club for exhibitions, but due to another commitment he had to decline.

A Match against Moehle

In early June, Showalter and Pollock traveled about 260 miles to Chicago, to the northeast of St. Louis. On June 12 a small tournament began at the Chicago Chess Club with prizes amounting to $100. The tournament lasted only a week, and is one of the more underreported tournaments in the literature. Besides Pollock and Showalter, the other players involved were Blanchard, Daly, Herman, C.O. Jackson (who retired halfway through the tournament), Philips, and Uedemann.

As the Chicago press largely ignored the event, there was some confusion about the final standings. According to the *Cincinnati Commercial Tribune* of June 21, Showalter finished first with 11 points, followed by Pollock with 9½, and then Philips and Uedemann with 9 wins each. But according to a crosstable mailed by Pollock himself to the *Baltimore Sunday News* and which appeared in the June 29 edition of that newspaper, it was obvious this was a double-round event and that Pollock won both games against Blanchard, Daly, Herman, and Jackson, scored 1½ against Philips and Uedemann and lost both his games against Showalter. The crosstable indicates rather that Showalter won with 13 points, followed by Uedemann with 11½ and Pollock in third place with 11 points.[2]

In late June, on his way back from Chicago, Pollock traveled about 260 miles south and stopped in Cincinnati. Here he intended to play a match against the 30-year-old Charles A. Moehle, one of the visitors at the Chicago Chess Club during the recently concluded tournament and a man famed for being the less-than-secret operator inside one of the Ajeeb automatons.[3]

The match would be decided by the first to win seven games, or seven points with draws being taken into consideration as half points only after each player reached 4 points. The stakes were $100, the winner to receive two-thirds. One of the local chess columns also stipulated that at least two games had to be played daily, despite the hot weather and, a curious fact, the lack of chess clocks:

> This evening at 7 o'clock a great chess match will be commenced between these celebrated professionals. Charles Moehle is world renowned as a prize winner in the principal American tournaments since 1880 and more recently

---

2. Louis Uedemann wrote to the *Cincinnati Commercial Tribune* to correct the score and the following was published in its July 5 editions: "Mr. Uedemann sends us the following as the correct result of the recent tournament to Chicago. First: J.W. Showalter of Kentucky, won 13 games, lost 1; Second: L. Uedemann of Chicago, won 11½ games, lost 2½; Third: W.H.K. Pollock of Baltimore, won 11 games, lost 3; Fourth: Dr. D.L. Philips, with 8 wins; Fifth: O.M. Blanchard, with 6½ wins." The *Baltimore Sunday News* of July 13, 1890, took pleasure in announcing that it was one of the few sources that gave the correct results: "The *News* seems to have been the only paper which gave the Chicago score correctly. But this is solely the fault of the Windy Press of 'Garden' City. Showalter played by far the best, while Pollock was 'chicagoed' into third place." ● **3.** According to J. Gaige's *Chess Personalia*, Charles A. Moehle (occasionally spelled "Möhle") was born on November 26, 1859, in New York. In 1880 Moehle took part in the Fifth American Chess Congress and finished third (13 points), behind George H. Mackenzie (13½) and James Grundy (13½). In the early 1880s, Moehle was very much a traveler looking for profitable chess engagements. The *St. Louis Globe-Democrat* of March 11, 1883, noted that Moehle passed through St. Louis and crossed swords with Max Judd and gave, not very successfully, some exhibitions at odds at the St. Louis Chess, Checker and Whist Club. Supplementary information, provided by the *Globe-Democrat* of March 25, 1883, noted that Moehle had for the past year been living "on a farm about sixteen miles south of St. Louis." In August of 1884, Moehle met Zukertort over the board in St. Louis and lost a game to the famous master. While it is not clear when Moehle left St. Louis, by 1886 or 1887 he was in St. Paul, Minnesota. Various hints and asides in historical chess columns also place Moehle in Chicago during this period. It was during this period that various columnists disclosed the fact that Moehle was the man hidden inside Ajeeb, the automaton chess player. ¶ The *St. Louis Republic* of February 2, 1888, called Moehle "the brains of Ajeeb." As John Hilbert and Peter Lahde documented in *Albert Beauregard Hodges: A Man Chess Made* (Jefferson, N.C.: McFarland, 2008), this particular automaton was a second version of Ajeeb (the first remaining in New York City), the peripatetic one which started its journey in September 1887 at the Milwaukee Industrial Exposition. When Ajeeb played in Chicago, Moehle was pointed out as the man within the machine. In mid–1888, Moehle camped in Cincinnati: "We are glad to hear that Mr. Charles Moehle will remain in Cincinnati for some time, with headquarters at the Queen City Club, of which he has been elected an honorary member," stated the *Cincinnati Commercial Tribune* of August 25, 1888. The account continued: "There are few men living who have as much genius for chess as Mr. Moehle. The privilege of playing with him is prized accordingly." In that year, during the Centennial Exposition in Cincinnati, Ajeeb was one of the attractions. ¶ When signing up for the first United States Chess Association championship planned for September 1888, Moehle was given as representing Minnesota. He played next to Hanham, Burns, Judd, Tomlinson, and Showalter and finished tied for second and third with Hanham, behind Showalter. Although given as a potential participant in the Sixth American Chess Congress, Moehle did not play. The same thing happened in the third congress of the USCA in February 1890 in St. Louis, when he was announced as an alternate player. Moehle died on March 27, 1898, in Cincinnati, and his death was announced in many columns countrywide. According to Ohio's *The Repository* of April 1, 1898, "His death resulted of consumption in a hospital several days ago, and only the charity of a friend saved him from a pauper's grave." The *New York Tribune* of April 10, 1888, called him "one of the strongest Metropolitan players." ¶ Following his successful match against Moehle, Pollock maintained a courteous and positive impression of Moehle's capabilities as a player. He wrote in the *Baltimore Sunday News*, October 10, 1890: "Mr. Charles A. Moehle, alias 'Ajeeb,' is contemplating a Western tour. Probably no chessplayer in the new world is so thoroughly equipped for 'exhibition' work as Master Moehle, his remarkable faculty for blindfold play enabling him to combine amusement with instruction in a rare manner. He is moreover absolutely second to none in the branch of oddsgiving. His 'blindfold record' is ten games simultaneously. Western exchanges please note."

famous as the manipulator of the wonderful automaton "Ajeeb," while his opponent, W.H.K. Pollock, of London, who has conducted the celebrated chess column of the *Baltimore Sunday News* for the last year, has won numerous prizes in international tournaments in Europe. The first game will be played at the old Queen City Club-rooms, southwest corner of Twelfth and Vine Streets, and a big attendance of chess enthusiasts is expected.

Pollock, playing Black, lost the first game against Moehle, a 24-move Bishop's Opening, due to a seductive yet inaccurate sacrifice which eventually backfired. He won the second game, a Two Knights Defense, the next afternoon, while the third game was a "long steady Evans Gambit in which the American had the attack and outplayed Pollock in a fine ending." Pollock hit back in the afternoon with another win, a 24-move Sicilian. The score now stood 2–2, with play resuming on Thursday, June 26, at 2:00 p.m. Pollock won both games on that day, making the score 4–2 in his favor, but he drew the seventh game, played on June 27, a complicated Petroff of 61 moves with Moehle attacking wildly. With the score 4½–2½, the eighth game began at 8:00 p.m. on the same day and "was an interesting battle of three hours' duration." Pollock, as usual, obtained a favorable opening with the attack, which was repulsed, and the game looked drawish. In the ending, which Moehle played admirably, "the Saxon slipped and allowed Ajeeb to queen a pawn," as described by the *Cincinnati Commercial Tribune* of June 28.

Pollock appears to have lost the next two games, the ninth and tenth, and so trailed Moehle by a point. On June 29, he bounced back winning both games, and thus led 6½–5½ with one of the draws not counting. "The eleventh game," wrote the *Tribune*, "in which [Moehle] played the attack, was a 'Scotch,' and the twelfth was the only 'Vienna' which has occurred during the match." The latter game was marked by particularly brilliant play on Pollock's part. On Monday, June 30, Pollock lost an Evans Gambit, but on the next day, he won a quick game to make the final score 7–6 in his favor (draws, finally, not counted). The brilliancy prize, donated by two local enthusiasts, was equally divided between the two players. Below is the key moment of Pollock's highly praised game:

Pollock–Moehle
Twelfth Match Game
Cincinnati, June 29, 1890

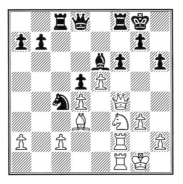

After 19. ... f6

In this balanced position, Pollock continued with **20. Nh4!**, intending to increase his control over the weakened light squares on the kingside, and Moehle replied with the apparently promising **20. ... Bh3**. Instead of retreating, Pollock pushed forward with a brilliant exchange sacrifice: **21. Nf5!! B×f1 22. Qg4**. Here Moehle panicked and instead of 19. ... Qc7, which would have maintained some fighting chances, he played **22. ... Kf7?** allowing Pollock to feature his imaginative attacking play: **23. Q×g7+ Ke6 24. R×f1 Rc7 25. Ne7!!** and shortly thereafter Moehle resigned.

A brief account of the match was provided by the July 13 edition of the *Baltimore Sunday News*:

> Nothing is proved by the match except that there is nothing to choose between the two players when at their best, and that both continually evinced combination powers and brilliancy of the highest order. Moehle is perhaps a little rusty on openings, but has, with few exceptions, evinced a most wonderful mastery in the endgames. The match was conducted in a spirit of fairness and chivalry throughout. The games, most of which we hope to publish, will be found vivacious enough. The fact that 14 being played in 8 days, during tropical heat, will account for some weakness of fitful play, while at the same time the absence of a time-limit indubitably gave power and finish to several combinations.

Unfortunately, for whatever reason, very few of the match games against Moehle were ever published, either in the *Sunday News* or elsewhere. Only five, all that could be located, are included in the present work.

A Match with McCutcheon

Following the conclusion of his match with Moehle, Pollock journeyed 420 miles home to Baltimore. Here, after nearly two months away from the city, he continued to work closely with the active members of the Maryland Chess Association, although he was not adverse to meeting other masters in proposed matches, such as Lipschütz.[4] With his Baltimore connections, Pollock enjoyed some lighter chess-related matters, too:

A MEMORABLE DAY

> Last Tuesday saw the annual steamboat [party] of the [Baltimore Chess Association] sailing down Chesapeake bay to Miles river in a drizzle. It mattered little to the selected band of chess enthusiasts who represented the old Association and inaugurated festivities to the new [Chess Association members] that the elements were adverse and that the good *S.S. Tolchester* steamed through 150 miles of "Prohibition Territory," for the gallant company were for Chess without exception, and brought good cheer with them in brains and baskets. An informal State free-for-all was held on board; out of a dozen combatants Mr. Hughes took first place, Mr. Schofield second and Mr. J. Hinrichs third. Mr. Pollock played and won two bright little blindfold games played simultaneously. Brother Wieman played 54 skittles at a fearful rate of speed. President Torsch made everybody happy; even brilliant Uhthoff, whose hard-fought battle occupied two hours, and the Hall-Pollock combination worked wonders in odds-giving. The ladies present evinced a lively interest in the five or six boards which kept racing all day, though only the undaunted Mrs. Morrow dared her skill in the chess arena.

On returning to the club rooms after the boat excursion, Pollock and company played the following handicap game:

W.H.K. Pollock & Robert Hall–A Syndicate of
three strong players of the Baltimore Chess Association
Odds Game / *Remove Nb1*

1. e4 e5 2. Nf3 Nc6 3. Bc4 Bc5 4. b4 B×b4 5. c3 Ba5 6. 0–0 Nf6 7. Ng5 0–0 8. f4 d6 9. d3 B×c3 10. Rb1 Bd4+ 11. Kh1 Rb8 12. f5 Ne7 13. Qf3 c6 14. Qh3 h6 *(see diagram)*

---

4. In mid–August 1890 Pollock challenged Lipschütz to a match, a challenge apparently left unanswered. From the *Pittsburg Dispatch* of August 17, 1890: "There is every prospect of an important chess match between Pollock of Baltimore, and Lipschütz, of New York. Pollock has published his défi."

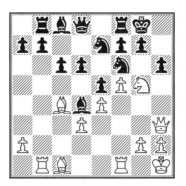

After 14. ... h7–h6

15. Qh4!! h×g5 16. B×g5 d5 17. Bb3 Qd6 18. Rf3 d×e4 19. Rh3 Ng6 20. f×g6 B×h3 and White mates in four (*Baltimore Sunday News*, August 3, 1890).

With no further chess excursions outside the city through the end of November, Pollock monitored with great interest the tournament in Manchester, England, as well as the heated exchanges between Steinitz, Gunsberg and Mason on the matters of a top level match. On Tuesday, December 2, 1890, he took a nearly 200 mile trip to Pittsburg, Pennsylvania, where he gave three simultaneous exhibitions at the Allegheny Chess Club (finishing overall with 22 wins, 3 losses, 3 draws) and a few consultation games. The *Pittsburg Dispatch* of December 6 wrote:

> Mr. Pollock arrived in the city on December 2, in the afternoon he played a number of off-hand games at the Pittsburg Library, winning them all. In the evening he played 11 simultaneous games at the Allegheny Chess Club, of which he won 7, lost 3 and drew 1. The local winners were Messrs. Lutton, Johns, Patterson and Cromble; the latter gentleman took Mr. Patterson's place, who was obliged to leave at an early hour. He left his game in good shape. Mr. Watts drew his second game and lost his first. On the evening of December 2 Mr. Pollock played ten simultaneous games, winning all except the one with Mr. Anderson, which was drawn. On the evening of December 3 he played seven simultaneous games, winning all except the one with Mr. Collins, President of the club, which was drawn. As soon as these games were finished he played a number of consultation games, winning all except the one with Messrs. Johns, Bippus and Watts, which was drawn. Mr. Pollock's visit has been greatly enjoyed by the local players, several of whom have requested the editor to make arrangements for another visit. We shall take great pleasure in doing so, and hope Mr. Pollock will carry away pleasant impressions of our city.

"Success" in a simultaneous exhibition—for the exhibitioner—could be a more subtle matter than simply an excellent record of wins versus losses. And the selection above illustrates this nicely. Not only did Pollock naturally win a majority of his games, but he managed, somehow, to draw the club president during one exhibition when he defeated everyone else. And he managed, again somehow, to find a number of men anxious to invite him back for another exhibition. In this fashion the give and take of performance and entertainment, coupled with some success on the part of the club members and a positive response from the local press, creates almost a paradigm for how a master might cultivate a circuit for future exhibitions. Of course, one might legitimately ask whether Pollock ever intentionally, for instance, drew a won game. Or dropped a draw. No one knows. All that can be said is that greater masters than he occasionally found ways to "help along" men of local club importance.[5]

One of Pollock's opponents at a simultaneous exhibition given at the Pittsburg Library Chess Club was the 33-year-old lawyer John L. McCutcheon, the inventor of a line of play in

---

5. See, for example, the following suggestive comment regarding several setbacks sustained by world champion Lasker against local unknowns during one of his United States tours: "A somewhat careful study of the achievements of travelling chess masters leads to the remark that they usually lose or draw a game with the local secretary." Source: *Checkmate*, February 1903, page 104 (referring to three games published in the January 1903 issue, pages 87–88).

the French Defense which proves reliable even today and that bears his name (**1. e4 e6 2. d4 d5 3. Nc3 Nf6 4. Bg5 Bb4!?**). Pollock won the game in an elegant manner.[6] The *Pittsburg Dispatch* of Saturday, December 13 printed the following:

> Our Late Guest—Mr. Pollock—left for Baltimore on Tuesday evening last. He enjoyed his visit here very much, and we assure him that he will receive a hearty welcome whenever it suits his convenience to make us another visit. He was in good form and the games were above the average. Mr. J.L. McCutcheon and he will begin at an early date three [*sic*] games by correspondence to test the validity of a rare line of play in the French defense, to which the former gentleman has devoted considerable attention.

In fact, as announced too by the December 21 *Baltimore Sunday News* column (and subsequent columns), Pollock began a thematic four-game postal match with McCutcheon for $20 a side to further test the variation. (In this December 21 column, Pollock referred to the match as being of three games. In later columns

John Lindsay McCutcheon (John G. White Chess and Checkers Collections, Cleveland Public Library).

---

6. John Lindsay McCutcheon was born on May 28, 1857, the son of Scottish immigrants who settled in the Pittsburgh area and early became deeply involved with the processing of iron. As an adolescent McCutcheon studied law at Columbia University, graduating in 1881. He passed his examinations in June that year and was admitted to the bar in Allegheny City, near Pittsburgh. He practiced in his father's firm. McCutcheon's first chess exploits (among them a victory over J. Zukertort in an 1884 simultaneous exhibition) brought him for a time to the Brooklyn Chess Club. While it remains unclear the exact date of his invention in the French Defense, it is known that the first extant game dates from a simultaneous exhibition game won by McCutcheon against Steinitz in November 1885. McCutcheon's job in the Smoky City prevented him from extensive travels for chess and also kept him away from the main centers of activity such as New York and Philadelphia. Thus he found in correspondence chess an ideal substitute for over-the-board play. ¶ In 1894 he entered the Continental Correspondence Chess Association Tournament, run by Walter Penn Shipley and others out of Philadelphia, and also contested postal (and often thematic) matches with several strong American players. In an effort to promote his variation, McCutcheon sponsored money prizes for the best games played with this particular line in the French at the Monte Carlo international tournaments in 1902 and 1903. In this sense, he might be considered a minor version of Isaac Rice, who extensively proselytized for the gambit that bears his name. The main difference, of course, is that the McCutcheon variation, unlike the Rice Gambit, is sound. McCutcheon persisted in his habit of motivating leading masters to test his variation. Harry N. Pillsbury played a two-game match (by correspondence) against McCutcheon on the Black side of the opening, winning 1½–½. So did Emanuel Lasker in 1904. Lasker scored only 1–1, losing a McCutcheon variation game with Black against its inventor and winning the other against it with White. ¶ According to an obituary in the *New York Times* of July 17, 1905, McCutcheon, who had been ill for some time, died on July 16, 1905 (Gaige gives July 17, 1905, in his *Chess Personalia*, which may be based on other, possibly more reliable sources, such as the *National Cyclopaedia of American Biography*). "Mr. McCutcheon was one of the best known chess players of America," the obituary said, "and had a world-wide reputation both as a player and patron of the game." A little known fact is that, one of McCutcheon's sisters was the third wife of Thomas De Witt Talmage (1832–1905), at the time one of the most pre-eminent religious figures of nineteenth century America. An excellent article on McCutcheon was published by Neil Brennen in *The Pennswoodpusher*, May 2006. The sharp McCutcheon Variation in the French Defense remains even today a popular variation.

H.E. Bird, I.A. Gunsberg and J.H. Blackburne in early 1894 (*Records of the Copyright Office of the Stationers' Company, January–March 1894*; photograph by William James Donald).

he confirmed the match as of four games.) The match ended in early August 1891, Pollock winning 3–1. For purposes of testing McCutcheon's variation, Pollock was given White in three of the four games. Pollock's own thoughts on the McCutcheon Variation appeared in the July 12 issue of the *Baltimore Sunday News*, prefacing the fourth game of the match: "We never thought much of the merits of Mr. McCutcheon's variation, but it is singularly productive of fresh and unheard of positions—the match in question swarms with them."

At the end of December 1890 and early January 1891, Pollock was involved in a handicap tournament organized by the Baltimore Chess Association. In fact, as indicated by the January 4 column, the most active chess players in the city celebrated the new year together, and in doing so memorialized something about their feelings for the master in their midst:

> Genial President Torsch kept open house on New Year's Day, every member of the association being invited through the medium of a fascinating design of "silver on silk," which an authority declared the prettiest invitation card he had ever seen. Considering the weather, a good number of strong members availed themselves of the mental and material enjoyment amply provided, and in the evening an adjournment was made to the rooms where those assembled received Mr. Pollock's New Year wishes, which we believe, were as heartily given as if he were not, upon the occasion, the unexpecting recipient of a very handsome New Year's gift from a number of the members, many of whom are not "notorious" chessists, nor under any obligations to Mr. Pollock as a "chess instructor," but Mr. D. Kemper explained it thus: "Mr. Pollock, you have a great many friends in Baltimore."

With Gunsberg in Baltimore

During the annual meeting of the Maryland Chess Association on January 10, it was decided Pollock should represent the state at the USCA's 1891 Congress, to be held that March in Lexington,

Kentucky. Two days later, Gunsberg was invited to Baltimore once his match with Steinitz was over, with a tentative arrival date set for February 2.[7] A committee formed by Torsch, Habersham, Hinrichs and Pollock was entrusted with the negotiations. They began collecting subscriptions for Gunsberg's planned exhibition in order to defray expenses. Gunsberg's first Baltimore exhibition took place on Monday, February 2:

> The first evening, Monday, 2nd inst., was devoted to a "peripatetic exhibition" which proved to be of sensational nature, as Mr. Gunsberg encountered no less than 31 players simultaneously, and in the marvelously short space of 3½ hours finished the whole series, mating the last man, Mr. D. Kemper, on the stroke of twelve, while he suffered but one defeat, at the hands of Mr. Harry Dallam, and this was due to a slip.

Pollock's detailed column notes gave a list with all the players and the exact time of their resignation. He had learned well the benefit a columnist derived from as often as possible naming in print his friends and fellow club members. In the end, Gunsberg scored 23 wins, 1 loss and 7 draws, while nearly 100 people witnessed the exhibition. On Tuesday, February 3, Gunsberg gave another exhibition, this time six simultaneous games (each with three Baltimore players playing in consultation) out of which he won 5 and drew 1 in two hours and a half.[8] Early on the next day, Wednesday, February 4, Gunsberg "gave some interesting examples of his skill at rendering the odds of the Knight, winning six out of eight games in about two hours." In the evening, Gunsberg gave a 30-board simultaneous exhibition against a stronger crowd, scoring 23 wins, 1 loss and 6 draws. Either that very night or early the next day, Pollock met Gunsberg in an exhibition game at H.S. Habersham's residence, "for a prize generously offered by that gentleman." The following position, with Pollock threatening Gunsberg's queen, was reached between the two masters:

Pollock–Gunsberg
Exhibition Game
Baltimore, February 4, 1891

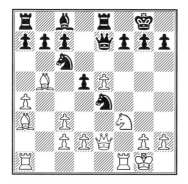

After 11. Bc1–a3

The opening was a Vienna Game in which Pollock obtained almost everything he wanted. In the position above, Gunsberg played the inferior **11. ... Qe6** and after Pollock's powerful

---

7. From the *New York Sun*'s chess column of January 17, 1891: "After his present match with Steinitz is over Gunsberg contemplates a tour through the United States and Canada before returning to London. He is in communication with many of the leading clubs in this country, and in all probability will play a series of games with Max Judd of St. Louis, and will also encounter Pollock in Baltimore. He intends, if possible, to include the cities of Philadelphia, Chicago, New Orleans, and Montreal in those which he will visit and it is understood that negotiations are in progress with that end in view." • **8.** It is possible Gunsberg's performance was a blindfold séance, although it is unclear; a note in the *Baltimore Sunday News* of February 22, 1891, citing the *Evening Post* to that effect, is the support for thinking so. That Pollock, however, in his own coverage of the event would fail to mention it as a blindfold exhibition makes the remark suspect.

12. c4!, Gunsberg continued with **12. ... Nd6**. Pollock played the normal **13. B×d6**, and Gunsberg blundered with **13. ... Q×d6**—an "hallucination," as Pollock wrote in his column—**14. e×d6 R×e2 15. c×d5** and he resigned. Interestingly, Pollock could have won in an elegant manner with **13. e×d6! Q×e2 14. c×d5**, and despite his queen, Gunsberg would have been unable to save the game against Pollock's domineering pieces.

In general, Gunsberg's exhibitions in Baltimore were well-received: "Socially speaking," wrote Pollock in the *Baltimore Sunday News* of February 8,

> Mr. Gunsberg created a most favorable impression upon everybody, players, press and audience, by his urbane and gentle demeanor and his modesty in regard to his achievements, and he may safely count himself as a "favorite" in Baltimore. He is now fulfilling an engagement with the Franklin and Germantown Clubs in Philadelphia, and sails for England on the 14th. Mr. Gunsberg and the officers of the club were entertained at a supper given by Mr. E.L. Torsch at Brevis's restaurant, S. Liberty-st., on Thursday evening and many speeches and much cordiality prevailed.

In addition to some games in consultation, with the two English masters on the same side, Gunsberg crossed swords with Pollock one more time after the dinner. This time he won.

In early April 1891 Pollock visited the Brooklyn Chess Club for some exhibitions, being the guest of J.H. Park, a player with excellent connections both in Brooklyn and Baltimore. The *Brooklyn Daily Eagle* of April 5 printed the following impressions:

> W.H.K. Pollock, the Irish champion and chess editor of the Baltimore *Sun[day News]*, created a sensation last night at the Brooklyn chess club at 315 Washington Street. He played against F. Rose, D.J. Finlay, E. Loessor, J.D. Elwell, G.F. Murray, C.W. Eccles, R. Bonu, A.J. Souweine, C.F. Thompson, J.J. Sprowers, E. Colinel and W.F. Eno. At 11 pm he knocked out Eccles, and the impression of Secretary Broughton was the Irish champion would knock out all the others.[9]

A more thorough summary of Pollock's play in Brooklyn was offered by the April 12 column of the *Sunday News*:

> Mr. W.H.K. Pollock was the guest of the enterprising and hospitable Brooklyn Chess Club on the 3rd and 4th insts., and encountered a picked team of 12 players simultaneously on the Saturday evening, ten of whom succumbed, while Messrs. Fred Rose and Souweine scored their games, the former winning in an ending after 90 moves. The team was a strong one and the attendance was large and appreciative. Mr. Pollock was entertained by the members of the club, and especially by the President, Mr. Charles A. Gilberg, with unlimited hospitality. The Brooklyn Chess Club is in a remarkably prosperous condition. There are about 100 members and a "perpetual tournament," in which 40 players are engaged, is in progress. Each competitor plays as many games as he pleases, and if defeated hands over a check which he has to purchase and which goes towards the prize fund.

During his trip, Pollock also visited the Manhattan Chess Club, where some consultation games were played on April 5. After he returned to Baltimore, he was finally crowned as the winner of a lengthy handicap tournament—amusingly called by Pollock the "Dragging Tournament, 1890-1-2(?)"—that started at the end of the previous year and from which quite a number of games proved extant. He continued to give simultaneous exhibitions at the local club, as he did on May 14 (13–3), as well as participating in at least one consultation correspondence game.[10]

---

9. It appears that Pollock was engaged for various exhibitions, and not only the standard simultaneous display: "Mr. Pollock, the chess expert of Baltimore, has been the guest of the Brooklyn Chess Club under an engagement for chess exhibitions during the last three days, which terminated yesterday with a simultaneous performance" [*New York Tribune*, April 5, 1891]. • **10.** Among Pollock's communications with other leading columnists or experts in America there was his correspondence with Boston's Preston Ware. The discussions were mainly focused on the merits of the so-called "Stone-Ware" Defense in the Evans Gambit (**1. e4 e5 2. Nf3 Nc6 3. Bc4 Bc5 4. b4 B×b4 5. c3 Bd6!?**) Not surprisingly, a correspondence match highlighting this line was played between Baltimore and Boston (represented by the Deschapelles Club). With Ware's death during this period, Boston's Deschapelles Club

Pollock's frequent play in some of the country's top chess clubs was at least in part meant to keep him in good form for an important forthcoming event: in July 1891 the New York State Chess Association's midsummer meeting planned to include an attractive match between him and the well-known Eugene Delmar. For this, Pollock had to make arrangements for yet more travel: this time to Skaneateles, on the Western border of Onondaga County, located in New York's Finger Lake Region.

ceased to exit and thus only one game—out of the planned five—was finished. It was given in the May 31, 1891, edition of the *Baltimore Sunday News*. It is probable Pollock played a part in formulating the Baltimore replies, although to what extent he did so remains unknown. The game: **Baltimore–Boston, Correspondence Game, 1890–1891,** 1. e4 e5 2. Nf3 Nc6 3. Bc4 Bc5 4. b4 B×b4 5. c3 Bd6 6. d4 h6 7. 0–0 Nf6 8. d×e5 B×e5 9. N×e5 N×e5 10. Bb3 d6 11. f4 Ng6 12. Ba3 0–0 13. e5 Ne8 14. Qd3 Kh7 15. Nd2 b6 16. Rae1 f5 17. Re3 a5 18. g4 Qh4 19. Rg3 f×g4 20. e6 Ba6 21. c4 c5 22. h3 Nf6 23. Rf2 Kg8 24. Nf1 Ne7 25. Bb2 d5 26. h×g4 d×c4 27. B×c4 Rad8 28. Qc2 B×c4 29. Rh2 Q×g3+ 30. N×g3 B×e6 31. Re2 B×g4 32. R×e7 Rf7 33. R×f7 K×f7 34. B×f6 K×f6 35. Qb2+ Kf7 36. Q×b6 Rd3 37. Ne4 Be6 38. a4 c4 39. Q×a5 Bd5 40. Nc3 Be6 41. Qe5 g6 42. a5 Rd7 43. a6 Black resigned.

7. Six Days in Skaneateles, July 20–25, 1891

A Long Walk

On Friday, July 17, 1891, Pollock left Baltimore for Syracuse, New York, taking a train north for the 240 mile journey. As announced in the chess press throughout the month of June, the New York State Chess Association's (NYSCA) midsummer gathering was initially planned for Chittenango, New York, between July 21 and 25. The plan fell through because the White Sulphur Springs Hotel's management unexpectedly announced the hotel was unavailable for the summer, and the NYSCA had to search for another venue. This was speedily found in the Packwood House, in Skaneateles. As with all the NYSCA midsummer gatherings to that date, a location in central New York was found in order to encourage both statewide competition and to entice New York City metropolitan players to take a cooling, lakeside vacation in an age long before air conditioning.

Three events dominated the NYSCA agenda during this end of July: the traditional contest for the *Staats-Zeitung* Trophy, a handicap tournament, and a match between Pollock and Eugene Delmar. Five strong players entered the Trophy competition, a double–round robin event: A.E. Blackmar (Brooklyn Chess Club), J.M. Hanham (Manhattan Chess Club), Emil Kemény (City Chess Club), Albert B. Hodges (Staten Island Club), and Howard J. Rogers (Albany Chess Club). The first class of the Handicap tournament had nine players, with Hanham and Hodges choosing to play in this event as well. No less significant a fact, certainly from the historical perspective, is that the *New York Tribune* commissioned Steinitz to draft daily reports of the competition and his presence at Skaneateles was certainly a welcome addition for the participants and organizers.[1]

Traveling advice was given by the *Albany Evening Journal* of July 11: "Skaneateles is situated at the head of Skaneateles Lake and is only 18 miles on the Auburn branch of the New York Central railroad. It is just as convenient to reach as Chittenango from all parts in the center of the state and more easy of access to New Yorkers and Albanians [i.e., those in Albany] as they can take the fast limited trains to Syracuse and then change to the Auburn branch."

Pollock had his own peculiar traveling itinerary. Howard J. Rogers, one of the chief organ-

---

1. The authors are particularly grateful for the attention Steinitz gave the Pollock and Delmar match through his *New York Tribune* and *International Chess Magazine* reports. His insightful comments and annotations form this chapter's backbone.

izers of the NYSCA and a man who played an important role in Pollock's life in the near future,[2] remembered the following a few years later:

> As an added attraction to the midsummer meeting of the Association at Skaneateles, N.Y., we hit upon a match between the New York State Champion, Eugene Delmar, and Mr. Pollock, the Champion of the South. I conducted the correspondence, which was very pleasant, and awaited with much interest my first meeting with Mr. Pollock. The match was to begin on Monday, and up to Sunday noon we were uncertain of the whereabouts of the Southern Champion. About five o'clock a few of us were sitting on the broad piazza overlooking the beautiful waters of Skaneateles Lake, when a dusty figure in brown suit, freckled face and wealth of reddish chestnut hair, approached the hotel: "Pollock," we shouted in a breath, "where on earth did you come from?" "Well, you see," said he, shaking hands all around with beaming cordiality, "I brought up in Syracuse early in the morning; I really couldn't spend the day loafing around there, so I thought I would take a bit of a tramp across the hills and tone myself up a little for the match." His "bit of a tramp" was a hard walk of over 20 miles in a hot August day.[3]

Pollock's unusual workout may have surprised many, but it did not surprise his fellow chess players back in Baltimore. The following description of Pollock appeared in the July 26 *Baltimore Sunday News*:

> In personal appearance, Mr. Pollock is of powerful frame for a young man, and of average height; an intellectual face, a piercing eye, charming freedom of manner, devoid of the faintest trace of personalism and modest to a fault. He is nowhere esteemed higher than among his friends in this city. He is almost as fond of athletic sports as of his chosen profession, and those of us who know his feats on the cricket field and pedestrianism were not amazed at this walk of twenty miles from Syracuse to Skaneateles, in way of exercise.

Delmar, no longer an athletic man, and about to turn fifty the next month, was still very much a competent match for Pollock over the board. Steinitz, for instance, introduced the combatants as follows in his July 21 column in the *New York Tribune*:

> The Chess-master Delmar, accompanied by his second son, Eugene, a boy twelve years old, and his rival, Pollock, were landed at Syracuse on Sunday morning. Not finding any railway connection with Skaneateles, Pollock, who strongly believes in severe physical exertion as preparation for the mental contest, seized the opportunity of tramping it all the way to Packwood House, a distance of twenty-three miles. He accomplished the feat in about eight hours, arriving before 6 pm. His opponent came about an hour later, and both appeared to be in excellent condition.

The games began on Monday, July 20, and Rogers, while writing the following in a report of the association, gives us a suggestive impression of the general atmosphere:

> The Packwood House was invaded and complete possession taken by Tuesday morning. Play was carried on in the reading room, parlors, verandas, and the boat-house pavilion. The owners of the house were untiring in their efforts to please the guests and a universal good time was the result. Mr. Bruel, ex-president of the Association, spared neither time nor expense in making the visit a pleasant and enjoyable one to the members, preparing for them boat rides, carriage drives and various other entertainments.[4]

---

2. Howard Jason Rogers (1861–1927) was born in New York in November 1861 and, graduating from Williams in 1884, was admitted to the bar in 1887. His main career developed in the field of education. He was the head of the New York educational exhibit during the Chicago World's Fair. Between 1895 and 1899, he was New York's superintendent of public instruction and in 1900 he went to Paris as the head of the American commission of the department of education and social economy. He headed the New York exhibits at the St. Louis Exhibition (1904) and at Seattle (1909). During World War I, Rogers worked with the Red Cross and military relief efforts. By the 1920s, he was an executive of the Red Cross. A great chess enthusiast, Rogers was active in various NYSCA events in the mid–1890s. His work as an organizer on behalf of the NYSCA as secretary and later, starting in 1893, as president, was respected by the members. He authored chess columns for the *Albany Evening Journal* and *Sunday Express* for several years in the 1890s. An obituary appeared in the *New York Times* of September 30, 1927. ● **3.** Howard J. Rogers' words about Pollock's walk to Skaneateles comes from a private letter to F.F. Rowland, January 7, 1898; reprinted on pages 10–11 of F.F. Rowland's *Pollock Memories* (Dublin, 1899). ● **4.** Rogers' description of the tournament atmosphere was published in *New York State Chess Association 1878–1891: History and Report*, edited by Howard J. Rogers (Albany, NY: Riggs Printing Co., 1891), page 35.

Further details appeared in the *Baltimore Sunday News* of July 26, no doubt with bits of intelligence telegraphed by Pollock himself: "The locality is a charming one. The hotel is situated directly at the lake, and separated from it by only twenty yards of lawn and grounds. The lake is eighteen miles long, with nearly half of it in sight. Boating is a favorite sport."

A Match against Delmar

While the Trophy and the handicap events saw an exciting battle between three key players (Hanham, Hodges and Kemény),[5] the main attraction of the midsummer meeting was the match between Delmar and Pollock. "As was perfectly natural," wrote Rogers in the yearly report of the NYSCA, "the chief interest of the meeting centered in the contest between Eugene Delmar, the New York Champion, and W.H.K. Pollock of Baltimore, the Maryland champion." The match consisted of the best of nine games. In case of a tie, the first to win a game in the play-off would be declared the victor. The time limit was 20 moves an hour and draws counted as half-points. Both players' expenses were paid by the NYSCA and the winner would receive $70, while the loser would receive $40. Charles A. Gilberg was selected to be Delmar's umpire while August Vorrath fulfilled the same duty for Pollock.

Rogers also explained the NYSCA's choice of Pollock as Delmar's opponent, and in doing so revealed the selection was based on much more than mere chess strength:

> In selecting a contestant to meet the Champion of the Association, the Board of Managers aimed to secure a player who could meet in kind the brilliant and dashing style of play to which Mr. Delmar is addicted, and thus make the match of greater interest to spectators than more conservative play would be. Mr. Pollock's record as champion of Ireland, winner of the brilliancy prize in the Sixth American Chess Congress, and subsequent fine play in the United States Chess Association meetings, convinced the mangers that he was the best person available. Their choice was not misplaced. The match was well contested, replete with interesting positions, and the conclusion of every game viewed by an eager and excited crowd.

Steinitz, who chronicled with exceptional detail the encounter between the two masters, agreed with the general idea that the match proposal was exciting.[6] He also evaluated the oppo-

---

5. The *Staats-Zeitung* Trophy was won by Hanham (6 points of 8 games), followed by Kemény (5½), Hodges (5), Blackmar (2½), and Rogers (1), the last named being forced to default his second round games due to his event-management duties. Hanham also managed to finish first in the Handicap event (6½ out of 8), followed by Hodges (6) and W.F. Eno (6). • **6.** A majority of New York–based chess columns reported daily on the event, with Steinitz's reports in the *New York Tribune* being the most detailed and eventually reprinted in the *International Chess Magazine* for June and July 1891. Hartwig Cassel was also present and he reported for the *New Yorker Staats-Zeitung*. A supplementary picture was painted by a correspondent for the *New York Herald* of July 26, 1891: "The number of visitors is legion. The most noticeable is the short figure of the world's undaunted chess champion, William Steinitz. He closely watches the games, and if a move is made which he does not approve of he hums almost inaudibly and turns to watch some other game. Among the players Hanham, with his silver beard, attracts general attention. Delmar is incessantly yawning, while his opponent, Pollock, is blessed with a marvellous appetite. E. Kemény, the representative of the city club, who astonished everybody by his precise and excellent play, is a six-footer who cruelly murders the Queen's English." ¶ This passage is from the *Oswego Daily Times* of late July (exact date unidentifiable): "Among the names familiar to the public, that of Wilhelm Steinitz, who for twenty years has held the world's championship stands preeminent. Steinitz was present in his capacity as chess editor of the *New York Tribune*, which paper published daily reports of a column or more per day. Steinitz is a man of diminutive stature, little more than five feet in height, but with an unusually large head. He has a round ruddy face, well covered with whiskers, and bright twinkling eyes. He was accompanied by his secretary, who reported full scores of all the games to his employer." ¶ The same report noted that "He [Pollock] is a prepossessing young man who speaks English with a melodious accent and frequent use of the expression 'don't you know'[...]. One of the interesting features of the Skaneateles meeting was the analysis of games in the Delmar–Pollock match by other players after the games were finished. Steinitz analysed the games

nents through his experienced eyes, and in the process provided many insightful details in his July 19 column in the *Tribune*:

The arrangement of the Delmar–Pollock match was a happy thought, and no two players could have been found in the States whose rivalry would have excited more general interest. Both belong to the dashing and brilliancy school, and a series of games may be expected which will form an enjoyable treat to the large and constantly growing number of amateurs who are now closely studying the progress of important chess events. The two players have had an almost entirely different training as a preparation for their coming contest, and in their previous record against each other, have come out pretty nearly even, with a slight advantage in favor of Delmar. Pollock is much the younger of the two, but has frequently coped with first-class masters in great European tournaments, like that at Hamburg, 1885; London, 1886; Bradford, 1888, and some of minor importance. In one of the later, at Dublin, 1889, he won the chief prize, but though this tourney was only a small one his performance was highly creditable, considering that two of his competitors were Burn and Mason. In the International Tournament of the Sixth American Chess Congress, held in New York in 1889, he gained the special brilliancy prize for a game which he won in most elegant style against Max Weiss, who ultimately tied with Chigorin for the two chief prizes. In the same tournament he met his present opponent for the first time, but in the general score, which is undoubtedly the superior test, as far as tournaments can prove anything, Delmar came out with half a point ahead. In match play, which is

Eugene Delmar, one of America's leading players in the 1880s and 1890s (John G. White Chess and Checkers Collections, Cleveland Public Library).

now universally held to be a closer proof of relative strength than that of tournaments, Pollock has had only one opportunity of showing his skill, namely against Charles Moehle, whom he defeated in Cincinnati last year by the odd game of seven up. Delmar, on the other hand, is well seasoned in match contests for over twenty years, when he first defeated Loyd. Within recent years his most notable hand-to-hand encounters were fought against his young rival, Lipschütz, who, however, came out the better in two matches out of three. His tournament training was not of such a severe character as that of his opponent, for he entered an International Chess Congress for the first and only time in New York in 1889. Yet his record in smaller tourneys is a very successful one, for he won twice the championship of the New York State Chess Association and several times that of the Manhattan Chess Club and of other clubs to which he belonged. He has also had the advantage of frequent skittle practice at the Manhattan Chess Club with such players as Lipschütz, Hanham, Hodges, Ryan, and other strong opponents, while Pollock, who lives in Baltimore, very rarely finds an opponent against whom he can sharpen his wits. The coming contest cannot be called a match in its proper sense, as the number of games to be played is limited to nine, and only in case of a tie one more decisive game will settle the victory. Unless, therefore, either player should win by a large majority, the question of superiority between the two players will still remain undecided. But the contest is sure to be productive of excellent and attractive games, and the managers of the New York Chess Association deserve great credit for having organized it.

---

from the score sheets and dictated his comments to his secretary. Those who attempted to point out mistakes in his analysis generally came to grief."

The difficult task of predicting the final result contributed to the excitement. Steinitz wrote in one of his reports in the *International Chess Magazine* of June 1891,

> Some connoisseurs expressed the opinion that the ultimate result of the contest between the two players could only be guessed at, but there was much curiosity as to the kind of game that would begin the fight. Caution is usually the order of the day in the first round of such a struggle, and generally a sort of "feeler" for strength is sent out by both parties. This tends to effect a drawn battle, and the whole affair serves only as a preliminary for getting into form. It was considered doubtful, however, whether in a limited contest this policy would be advisable for either player, and a hot open fight was therefore anticipated by some in the first game.

Play started Monday, July 20, at 2:00 o'clock in the afternoon. Pollock won the toss and so had the White pieces. In his description of this Vienna Game (**1. e4 e5 2. Nc3 Bc5 3. f4 d6 4. Nf3 Bg4 5. Bc4 Nc6**) in the July 21 edition of the *Tribune*, Steinitz labeled Pollock's sixth move (**Bc4–b5** just after he developed his bishop to c4 on the previous move) as a "serious waste of time" and, in his actual game annotations, recommended instead an ingenious line of play he himself had played before in Havana in 1889: 6. f×e5 d×e5 7. d3 and if 7. ... Nd4 then 8. B×f7+! The fact that Pollock spent 25 minutes over his tenth move indicated the degree of trouble he was in. Steinitz summarized play in general:

> He [Pollock] played **1. e4** and the rapid answer of his opponent, by making the same move, contrary to the practice which he often adopts of selecting the French Defence, verified at once the predictions of connoisseurs who expected a lively struggle from the start. The game soon developed into a Vienna Opening in which Pollock, however, lost time on the 6th move. This led to an exchange, reducing his attack. A counter attack on the kingside was then promptly taken in hand by the farsighted opponent, which evidently caused White great trouble. Pollock's clock marked thirty-seven minutes after his 10th move, he having taken twenty-five minutes over his last, while Delmar's clock showed altogether sixteen minutes. White's 13th move was not a good resource, but on the next turn Black missed an opportunity of strengthening his attack. On the 20th move Delmar offered to give up a pawn, which his opponent did not venture to take, though it seems to me that it would have been safe and Black could hardly get up sufficient attack to cover the loss of material.

Pollock–Delmar
Skaneateles, July 20, 1891
First Match Game

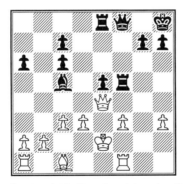

After 20. ... Kg8–h8

Here, Steinitz advocated 21. Q×c6, writing that "we see no clear reason why White on this or his next move does not capture the c6-pawn." While the world champion's suggested move was certainly justified and perfectly playable, Pollock preferred **21. Bd2**, developing his queenside, anticipating transferring his king to a safer square, and neutralizing Black's bishop, all at the price of his f3-pawn. Even Steinitz seemed impressed:

> However, it soon became evident that Pollock was pursuing another very ingenious plan whereby he intended to clear the centre at the expense of a Pawn and to confine the adverse Bishop to inactivity. The scheme required

more attention than Delmar apparently bestowed upon it when he indiscriminately tried to force on his b-pawn instead of endeavoring to attack the adverse queenside pawns in the rear. The result of the omission was that when the game adjourned at 5:00 pm Pollock was on the point of winning two pawns on the queenside, threatening also to win the confined Bishop soon, while he could stop easily with his king or bishop the adverse advanced b-pawn.

After Delmar's 35. ... Kh8–g7.
Pollock to seal his 36th move

Here the move Pollock sealed was **36. Kf3?**, trying to stop Black's kingside pawns. As Steinitz correctly pointed out, this move threw away the advantage obtained through Delmar's inferior **35. ... Kg7?** instead of the stronger 35. ... g2. Pollock could have won with 36. Re7+! Kg8 37. R×c7 g2 38. R×a7 Rh4+ 39. Kf3 Rh3+ 40. K×g2 R×e3 41. d5 and there is no hope for Black. Steinitz, who lost interest in annotating the rest of the game in detail, wrote the following:

> Things took a different aspect when the game was resumed at 7 o'clock. Pollock's sealed move, as it is not unfrequently the case, sealed his fate, at least so far as his winning chances were concerned. Instead of playing for the gain of the pawns on the queenside, White had aimed at a clearance, of the other wing from Pawns, which presented no danger. Delmar then gained time, and made good use of it by attacking and winning two pawns on the adverse queenside and ultimately obtaining a passed a-pawn. At various stages in the interim Pollock had good prospects for a draw, if he had systematically played for it, but he tried to win and wasted valuable time in his effort. Some feeble moves on his part allowed his opponent to queen his pawn, and though White fought hard afterward, he had to yield to superior force at about 9:00 p.m.

After 40. ... R×a4

Pollock's failure to check on e7, as he had also failed to do at adjournment, this time cost him the game. In the diagram above, Pollock continued with the dubious **41. Bd8?** Instead, with 41. Re7+ Kg6 (41. ... Kf8? would have lost immediately to 42. Ke5!) 42. Bd2!, White continues with chances for a win. Following this second omission of Re7+, as Steinitz noted, Pollock's game continued to worsen, until he was forced to resign on move 64, mate in two being unavoidable.

Time being precious at the NYSCA midsummer meeting, after a break of only an hour, Delmar and Pollock began their second game. Then, after only 25 moves, the game was adjourned at 11:30 p.m. until the next morning. While Steinitz praised Delmar's evening opening play, a close look at the game reveals that Pollock's opening play was no less remarkable. Besides maintaining the balance with Black, Pollock's play secured him means that eventually allowed a powerful kingside attack. Steinitz summarized it thusly in his July 22 column:

> The second Pollock–Delmar game began last night. Delmar being the first player, he started with the Ruy Lopez Opening, which took a normal and authorized turn up to the 8th move for Black, who posted his queen['s bishop] rather disadvantageously at b7. With little exception, the manner in which Delmar obtained the pull, owing to the slight weakness in the opponent's game was highly praiseworthy. Not minding a temporary attack on the adversary against his kingside, he alternately operated on both wings until on the 19th move he succeeded in blocking that ill-placed queen's bishop. The game was adjourned at 11:30 pm, yesterday on White's 25th move[...].

Delmar–Pollock
Skaneateles, July 20 and 21, 1891
Second Match Game

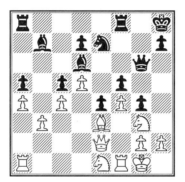

After 24. ... a6–a5.

Delmar to seal his 25th move

The American's sealed move was **25. Bc1**, clearly intending to pressure Pollock's kingside after reshuffling pieces. While such closed positions are seldom favored by tactical players such as Pollock, he did put forward some clever positional ideas combined with tactics when the game was resumed the next day: **25. ... Kg8 26. Bb2 Qh6 27. Qd2 Ng6 28. Ne2 Ra6!**—with the idea of engineering a transfer of this rook to the kingside—**29. g3** (Steinitz recommended 29. Qc3) **29. ... Ne5!?** and, with such imaginative efforts, Pollock took the initiative. Yet the game was complicated. Steinitz wrote that

> [...] the sealed envelope being opened at the resumption of play at 1:30 p.m. today, the move made revealed a transfer of the attack straight against the king, which had been cleverly prepared previously. Pollock tried to neutralize matters by a counter demonstration with his heavy forces on the same wing and was assisted in his design by weak play on the part of his opponent on the 29th move, at a point when the latter could have secured his advantage by a strong diagonal threat of his queen to c3, instead of adopting the feeble advance of g2–g3, which allowed Black a cleverly conceived entrance of the knight in the centre by means of which Pollock soon effected a powerful formation of pawns close to the adverse king's quarters. But soon after, on the 33rd move, Pollock impetuously rushed in for the attack, overlooking an ingenious sacrifice of the exchange, which allowed the adversary to escape with great advantage in position.

Indeed, from his 32nd move onward, for nearly a dozen moves, Delmar held a decisive advantage. Yet Pollock played on. The player from Baltimore succeeded in hanging on to the slimmest of hopes, and a critical moment arrived after Delmar's 52nd move, **52. Nd6**.

After 52. Nb5–d6

Pollock continued with **52. ... Re7** and Delmar faltered, throwing away his advantage with **53. Be5??** allowing Pollock the brilliant **53. ... Kg4!!** Steinitz, as well as the other experts present, noted Delmar could have easily won as late as his fifty-third move:

> Delmar had a clear draw in hand at his own option, but after some repetition moves he decided on a course which led to an exchange of queens, with a winning advantage for his side, for subsequent analysis proved that White could have won as late as the 53rd move by **Bf6**, a line of play suggested by Mr. Charles A. Gilberg, the President of the Association. Delmar's actual play, **53. Be5**, however, gave the ingenious Pollock an opportunity of developing, at the expense of a bishop, a profound ending plan which he initiated by supporting with his King his far advanced f3-pawn. He then opened an irresistible attack with his rook on the h-file, which he carried out with masterly exactitude. Within a few moves he cleared a road for queening his f-pawn, and soon afterward he forced the gain of the knight, the only piece which the opponent had left for defence.

While all the above remains both insightful and accurate, as far as it goes, it was not pointed out then or later that Pollock's rebound with **53. ... Kg4** was in truth sufficient only for a draw. It took another serious error on Delmar's part to lose the game. After **54. N×b7 Rh7 55. N×c5 Rh2+**, Delmar continued with the losing **56. Ke3?** Perhaps it would have taken a computer to find the line 56. Ke1! Re2+ 57. Kd1 Re3 58. Kd2 f2 59. K×e3 f1Q 60. N×d7, when White has enough resources to avoid loss.

A few hours after Delmar resigned, the third game began.[7] With the score 1–1 and the first two games indicating a very capable Delmar, Pollock attempted to stage a little surprise on his very first move. Steinitz described the matter well in the July 23 edition of the *Tribune*:

> Never before within my recollection was there such a surprise effected in the first two moves of an opening as in the third game of the Delmar–Pollock match played yesterday. In reply to the irregular **1. f4**, Delmar, as second player, offered to give up a pawn by **1. ... e5**, which constitutes a gambit named after its inventor, the Danish player, Herr From. Pollock did not allow himself to be outbidden in chivalry, and by his answer, **2. e4**, a regular King's Gambit position, which is of the rarest occurrence in match playing, was presented to the astonished onlookers, who were wondering which of the multitudinous varieties of this brilliant opening would be the sequence. Delmar cut speculation short by declining the gambit with **2. ... Bc5**. The usual course of this form of the opening was altered on Black's 4th move, ...Nc6, which after the developing process remained slightly in favor of White, until Delmar, on the 11th move, allowed his opponent to isolate and double the c6/c7 pawn[s] in a sort of position which has been called "Winawer's trade mark," after the celebrated Russian master, who had first shown, in the Paris Congress of 1867, how to operate against this weakness in kindred situations.

---

7. Steinitz' descriptions of the fourth, fifth and sixth games of the match Pollock vs. Delmar appeared in the *International Chess Magazine* of June 1891, pages 182–183, page 185 and page 187. The champion's take on the seventh game appeared published in the *International Chess Magazine*, June 1891, pages 187–188 and *New York Tribune* of July 26. Steinitz' analysis of the eighth game appeared in the *International Chess Magazine* of July 1891, pages 209–210 and *New York Tribune* of July 27.

Some lively skirmishing for attack and defense followed up to the 20th move. Then came some indifferent maneuvering on Pollock's part, while Delmar, after some attacking attempts on the kingside, properly directed his attention toward dissolving the double c-pawns, which was the sore point of his game and the only hindrance to his forming a strong centre and obtaining the advantage of the queen's wing. Pollock could easily have prevented the execution of such a plan at an early stage by maneuvering one of his knights to a4 or b3, and then seizing the open c-file with one of his Rooks, but he altogether neglected to guard that point on the Queenside. He clustered his pieces instead on the kingside, thus giving his opponent an opportunity to break in on the other wing. On the 24th move Pollock's defence became extremely difficult and his blocked up rook at g5 was made the mark of a finely conceived attack by the advance of the adverse d-pawn which ultimately lost Pollock the exchange.

Pollock–Delmar
Skaneateles, July 21, 1891
Third Match Game

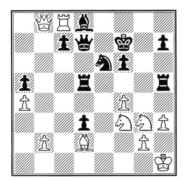

After 41. Ne4–g3

Here Delmar, faced with Pollock's new threat, **41. Ng3**, played the dubious **41. ... Rhf5** instead of the more powerful 41. ... Nd4! Pollock recovered some material with **42. N×f5 R×f5 43. Qa8 Rd5 44. Rb8 Be7** and began a clever maneuver to distract Delmar from the kingside with **45. b4.** Delmar failed to notice the danger on his back rank and the kingside when he played **45. ... B×b4?** (best was 45. ... a×b4, keeping the dark-squared bishop next to his king) and after **46. B×b4 a×b4 47. Rh8**, Delmar was completely lost. Steinitz wrote of the matter as follows:

> After having thus obtained a decisive superiority of material, Delmar's attention began, however, to relax, and there was little of his usual vigorous aim in his play. He neglected for a series of moves to seize the key of the adverse position, by the capture of the f4-pawn, which would soon have opened for him a powerful attack. Pollock fought the uphill battle with tenacity and ingenuity of resource. Having recovered the exchange, owing to the opponent's weak play, he made a stubborn defence for a long time, but ultimately he sacrificed a pawn on the queenside in order to tempt his opponent to exchange Bishops and then to institute an attack with his rook at h8, which was very difficult to parry. Delmar incautiously effected the exchange of Bishops, and then selected a defence with his rook at a4, which allowed his opponent to spring a mine on the 48th move by the advance of the f-pawn, the very pawn whose capture Black had previously neglected for a long time, although he had several favorable opportunities for getting rid of it. Black's game then broke up in a few moves and Delmar resigned after six hours' play.

Leading 2–1, Pollock had good reason to feel comfortable in the fourth game, played later that same day. His opening play was original and strong in a little-explored opening line (**1. e4 e5 2. Nf3 Nc6 3. c3 Nf6 4. d4 N×e4 5. d5 Bc5!**). In his game notes Steinitz called the line "too hazardous for a match game." In fact, Pollock obtained an excellent position up to his 16th move as Steinitz showed in the June edition of his *International Chess Magazine*:

In an English opening played by Delmar a bold line of counter attack was adopted by Pollock on the 5th move. The sacrifice of the piece for two pawns which he instituted at that point is a well-known variation invented by G.B. Frazer, of Dundee, which leads to lively complications, but can hardly be recommended for soundness. On the 9th move Black deviated from the usual course, but the alteration in the counter attack did not seem to improve Pollock's position greatly, and Delmar, who, after getting his king into safety, began a vigorous attack against the adverse kingside, gained ground step by step and pressed hard on the opponent with his superior forces. Pollock afterward expressed the opinion that he chose a bad square for the retreat of his queen on the 17th move, but it must be considered very doubtful at least whether any other move would have improved the position to such an extent as to balance Delmar's superiority of material, for Black had only two Pawns for the piece lost, of which one was doubled. On the 20th move, Pollock made a rash attempt at breaking through on the e-file, thereby exposing himself to a powerful adverse assault, which ended the game in three moves.

Delmar–Pollock
Skaneateles, July 21, 1891
Fourth Match Game

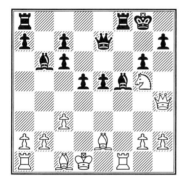

After 16. Rh1–f1

Here Pollock played **16. ... Rad8**, a normal-looking move, but which proved to give White a forceful kingside attack which forced Black to resign in a few moves: **17. Nf3! Qe6 18. Bh6 Rfe8 19. Ng5 Qd7 20,g4 d4 21. Bc4+** and it was all over. Instead, at the critical 16th move, Pollock could have maintained good prospects with 16. ... Be6!? 17. R×f8+ R×f8 18. Nf3 Q×h4 19. N×h4 e4. With this quick victory, Delmar equalized the score after four hotly contested games. The decision to invite Pollock to face Delmar in the match certainly had turned out a judicious one, measured by the onlookers' pleasure.

But after four wild contests, the players settled down, for a time, to more subdued play. Spectators witnessing the fifth match game waited almost 60 moves for something dramatic to unfold. Their most knowledgeable spectator though, Steinitz, described the game (and some of his own frustration with its play) in the following terms in his magazine:

The fifth [game] opened with a dull variation of the Four Knights' game. On the 10th move Delmar effected an unfavorable exchange of a Bishop for a Knight, and the following move was still worse, for he exposed himself to the loss of a pawn by 12. B×f6, followed by Qh5, which line of play, however, Pollock also overlooked. An exchange of Queens soon ensued, of which, as usual, a long ending was the issue. Pollock had a slight advantage with his two Bishops, which he could have further materialized on the 28th move by exchanging the knight and the centre pawn, followed by Rb4, since the adverse centre was practically cut off from the support of Black's king, and could also be easily broken by the advance of White's c-pawn. As matters proceeded Bishops of opposite colors were left on the board, and either party could easily produce a drawing position if aiming at it. But neither seemed to be content with such result, and Pollock especially endeavored to press by liberating an isolated a-pawn. The pursuance of this plan cost him, however, two pawns on the kingside, and Delmar was left with two combined passed pawns, whose advance could no doubt be hampered for some time, but which could be surely worked up in the end. On the 46th move Delmar neglected to play his rook in the rear of the advancing adverse pawn, which would have saved him a great deal of trouble. In a similar manner he omitted several times to play his bishop at a8, which would have stopped the Pawn and left him freedom for operations with his rook and pawns. He instead made some useless maneuvers against Pollock's king, and finally, on the 66th move, he allowed himself to be caught in a drastic manner, having needlessly run into a position which exposed him to a mate in a few moves, or, as the only other alternative, allowed Pollock the queening of his pawn. On perceiving his error too late after the check of the rook given by Pollock, at the 67th move in the diagrammed position below, Delmar resigned.

The position Steinitz found most damning:

Pollock–Delmar
Skaneateles, July 22, 1891
Fifth Match Game

After 66. Be5–b8

In this position, at 11:00 p.m., Delmar played his final blunder, **66. ... Bg2??**, which Pollock promptly answered with **67. Rf6+**, forcing the New Yorker's resignation. In his annotations Steinitz noted "The position is a very curious one. If 67. ... Kg5 68. Bf4+ and mates next move by Rh6. Black therefore has no other move than 67. ... Ke4, whereupon White queens with a check."

Leading again, this time 3–2, Pollock faced another Ruy Lopez in game six, played on July 23. While little came of the opening, as Steinitz remarked, Pollock made a few doubtful decisions in the middle-game, which led to severe material losses:

There was nothing remarkable in the opening of the sixth game, which was a Ruy Lopez, with Delmar as first player, up to Black's 13th move, **13. ... Nd4**. This seems an excellent innovation, giving the defence the superiority on the queenside, and though, as actually happened, White could tear up the adverse Pawns on the other wing, this was of no import, and Black's attack soon materialized into the advantage of a pawn plus. Delmar made a capital defence, and especially his 23rd move, **23. Kf1**, showed extraordinary depth of calculation as explained in our notes. Pollock did not seem to see the attack on the Queenside which it prepared and which he could have avoided by 23. ... Qc8. His actual play, **23. ... Qd7**, allowed Delmar to isolate Black's queen's bishop and thus to neutralize in a great measure Pollock's advantage. The latter still more weakened his position on his 26th and 28th moves, and then Delmar directed his attack against the queenside with sure aim, which ultimately not only recovered his pawn, but gained one extra. Pollock offered a stubborn resistance, and for a long time it seemed as if he would effect a draw in spite of the hostile majority of pawns. But on the 41st move he virtually destroyed his last chance by retaking the Bishop with the Pawn instead of with the queen. His object was apparently some sort of perspective kingside or centre attack, but the weakened King's Pawn soon became the mark of White's heavy forces and could not be sufficiently defended. After this Pawn had fallen, Black's rooks were blocked and pinned, and finally Delmar formed a position in which he was bound to force mate, whereupon Pollock resigned. The score therefore stood 3 all.

Delmar–Pollock
Skaneateles, July 23, 1891
Sixth Match Game

After 40. ... Nd7–e5

Delmar's decision to exchange bishop for knight with **41. B×e5** was met by Pollock with the inferior **41. ... f×e5**, instead of the better 41. ... Q×e5 with good drawing chances. "He could have made a better fight for a draw by retaking with the Queen," Steinitz commented, "and he could then stand exchanging pieces, as his King would afford protection for his Pawns in the ending. His weak e5-pawn now becomes the mark of attack and must soon fall, which practically ends the game."

The seventh game proved devastating for Pollock. Facing Delmar's French Defense, Pollock tried a little-explored line, which bought him nothing more than equality. Some complications ensued and he was faced with a powerful kingside assault. He should have sacrificed the exchange to avoid trouble and might have enjoyed good prospects, but uncharacteristically he chose passive defense. In what was a rare instance for the Baltimore master, passive play proved his undoing. Even then, the endgame provided several good chances to reestablish equality, but he missed them. Steinitz wrote that

The seventh game of the match played at Skaneateles, July 24th between Delmar and Pollock was in many respects remarkable. The adoption by Pollock of a new line of attack against the French Defence, which was first introduced by Dr. Tarrasch at Manchester last year, made the opening interesting to experts as well as to students. In the early development Pollock disdained gaining a small advantage by isolating the adverse d-pawn, and he played on the crowding system. The issue of this was a position in which Black, on the twelfth move, gave up a pawn for an attack which in turn crowded White's pieces very inconveniently to all appearance. Still, in my opinion, the pawn ahead had analytically the best of it, and even in practical play a master of Pollock's calibre should not have hesitated much to sacrifice the exchange for another pawn, with an excellent attack on a third, for which he had several opportunities. Instead of thus relieving himself he, in a feeble manner, created holes on the kingside and allowed the opponent to accumulate heavy forces against that wing, in pursuance of a deeply and finely conceived plan, which ripened on Delmar's twenty-fourth move into a powerful as well as beautiful sacrifice of a knight for two pawns. On the twenty-ninth move Delmar, as he himself pointed out, could have won on the spot by a check of queen at g4, instead of the more quiet **29. ... Qf3** [Delmar's and Steinitz's suggestion, confirmed by computer analysis, would have forced a mate in ten.] Later on he could have proceeded effectively with his attack, though a piece minus, without exchanging heavy forces. But he evidently wished to make sure of it by playing to recover his piece, though this line of play led to a rather lengthy ending. After the exchange of the queens, Black kept his pawn ahead and easily gained access for attacking other weak pawns. Pollock fought hard, and at one time threatened to draw a mating net with his rook and knight. But Delmar had no difficulty in liberating his king and ultimately leading his passed d-pawn to victory.

Pollock–Delmar
Skaneateles, July 24, 1891
Seventh Match Game

After 50. Kg3–f2

Pollock could have rebounded in the endgame, the part of the game left unanalyzed by Steinitz. After seriously diluting his advantage, Delmar played **50. ... Nd1+** and Pollock responded with **51. Ke2?**, permitting Delmar to regain the upper hand with **51. ... N×c3+ 52. Kd2 Rg3**, eventually winning. Instead, Pollock had a better alternative: 51. Ke1!, which still threatens the mate on h8 and the d5 pawn—for instance 51. ... Rg1+ 52. Kd2 K×h4 53. R×d5 with equal chances.

As it happened, Delmar took the lead 4–3 with only two games to go. And in a way it was worse than a simple defeat. Delmar had played the game with blazing speed, according to the *Baltimore Sunday News* for August 9, 1891. Pollock had used nearly two and a half hours for the game; Delmar a mere 35 minutes.

In order to win the match Pollock had to win the remaining two games. What energy he might have had left for such an ambitious comeback was undermined by weak opening play in the eighth game, played on the same day immediately after his seventh round debacle. The ex-world champion wrote that

> The eighth and [as it turned out] last game of the contest at Skaneateles can only be properly described as one of those collapses which sometimes occur at critical stages of a game or match. Pollock appeared overweighted by the odds against which he had to fight in the circumstance that his opponent was a game ahead and had only one more game to win or two to draw in order to come out the victor of the series. His play bore the mark of that depression which not infrequently overtakes chess experts as the result of anxiety and overwork. Pollock had adopted the Sicilian Defence, to which he had joined the queen's fianchetto, followed by ...a7–a6. In defiance of all modern principles he had thus moved, as second player, three wing pawns early in the game. Still more ill-favored was the aspect of his operations with his king's knight and queen, and on the 11th move he had wasted no less than four moves with the former and two moves with the latter; and those two pieces had to go home to their original squares. Delmar's development, on the other hand, was reasonable and intelligent, and there was always some point gained in concentration or aggressive movements. On the 12th move the superior position judgment which he displayed in the early part of the game produced an attack which came to a fine head four moves later by a beautiful combination, after an elegant sacrifice of a knight. The entanglement cost Black the exchange and a pawn in a bad position, from which Pollock tried to extricate himself by a counterattack on the queenside, on which wing White had castled. It was, of course, useless, and he had to sacrifice two more pawns in order to keep up some temporary irritation. Delmar could have won with still greater ease already on the 23rd move by Ne5[...].

Delmar–Pollock
Skaneateles, July 24, 1891
Eighth Match Game

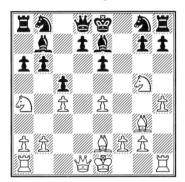

After 13. ... Bf8–e7

Here Delmar, already enjoying a considerable advantage, played **14. Bh5+** instead of the much stronger 14. Qb3! Pollock continued with **14. ... g6** and Delmar replied with the powerful **15. N×h7!** Pollock defended with the hopeless **15. ... B×e4** and after **16. Qg4! R×h7 17. Q×e4 R×h5 18. Q×g6+ Kf8 19. Q×h5** his position was beyond redemption. Yet he continued to fight until 8:00 p.m., when he finally resigned. After Delmar's Knight sacrifice, Pollock's best chance was 15. ... Kf7!? 16. Qf3+ Nf6 17. Ng5+ Kg7 18. B×g6!? K×g6 19. 0–0–0. Even though White's chances still look superior, there was room for some resistance. The match had, in fact, been lost during the seventh game, the eighth being but an afterthought ... at least psychologically. Such a break from his usual fighting optimism was rare in Pollock's play.

As a ninth game could not change the outcome, the players agreed to stop the match. Defeated 5–3, Pollock did not lose his sense of humor, although some of his frustration did show through in his comment afterward: "I have played worse in the games which I won in this match than in those that I lost in the Sixth American Chess Congress. But I must be glad of an opportunity even of losing a match for I am entirely out of the way of good practice all the year round." The party following the conclusion of the midsummer meeting at Skaneateles on Friday, July 24, may have offered him some consolation. Pollock's impressions were recorded in his *Sunday News* column of August 2:

> All the tournaments were brought to a close on Friday evening, July 24, largely owing to the indefatigable efforts of Secretary Rogers, to whom the success of the meeting from a business point of view is as largely due as it was to Mr. and Mrs. Bruel, of Skaneateles, from a social. That lady and gentleman placed a steamboat at the disposal of the Association on Saturday, July 25, and a large party enjoyed a most glorious excursion on the lake, feasting and conversation being varied with minstrel songs, chess, cards, a visit to Dr. Calthrop's mountain camp (where the hale old astronomer and sage took Mr. Steinitz a row, where he could best view the Swiss like scenery, and where Gen. Congdon and the Editor [Pollock] quickly discovering the log-kitchen, were seen discussing cups of fragrant tea), and a landing at fashionable Glen Avon. The trip was found to be an admirable antidote to the somewhat fierce festivities of the previous night, when everyone made a speech and even Steinitz sang a song, and Messrs. Rose and Gilberg "symposiarchized" as the music and the weird "laughing song" spread for miles over the moonlit lake.

In his final report in the *New York Tribune* of July 27, Steinitz cited Pollock's own words of appreciation:

> In reference to the general arrangements of the meeting and the private hospitalities extended to the visitors by prominent members of the committee, I need only quote the opinion of Mr. Pollock, who has attended a great number of European tournaments, and who said: "This beats anything of the kind that I have ever witnessed,

and is only equaled by the Hereford (England) meeting, held in 1886. But the latter was, after all, an international tournament, organized on a much larger scale, and it is hardly fair to compare the two." Other members of the association and visitors expressed themselves equally delighted with the entertainments of the meeting.[8]

Even though Pollock lost the match, he had gained in more than one fashion. First, he had relatively serious play with a strong adversary, something his situation in Baltimore, pleasant as it was in other respects, did not afford. Second, and perhaps even more importantly—and as this chapter makes clear—his play was deeply critiqued by no less a player than the world champion, whose annotations and commentary on the games must have formed a useful and valuable lesson for the young man. Seen from this perspective, the match with Delmar had been extremely useful for Pollock, even though the outcome of play had not been in his favor.

Pollock was hardly finished with chess for the year. Following his summer idle at Skaneateles, however possibly marred by the unfortunate outcome of his play, Pollock returned to Baltimore only for a few hours. Following his brief stay, he traveled more than 700 miles southwest to Lexington, Kentucky, where the Fourth Congress of the USCA would be played in the heat of a Southern August. The chess column of the *Baltimore Sunday News* of August 2, 1891, cited the following from the *Cincinnati Commercial Gazette*: "It is not true, as rumored, that Mr. W.H.K. Pollock intends to walk all the way from Skaneateles, N.Y. to Lexington, Ky., to put himself in good condition for play. This rumor probably grew out of the fact that he walked twenty-three miles to Skaneateles on the eve of his match with Delmar. He is now walking away from the latter."

---

8. Pollock's exact words about his performance at Skaneateles were reproduced in the NYSCA meeting report at page 37. In addition, the following comes from the *New York Clipper*, August 15, 1891: "The grand match, Delmar vs. Pollock, was won by the veteran master, Delmar 5 to 3. It is only justice to note that, several of the games are seriously marred by mistakes and miscalculations. Dr. Pollock is reported as averring that his victories in this match were worse specimens of chess than his defeats in Sixth Am. Congress, attributing this comparatively poor showing to his utter lack of competent practice. In fact, he is too easily first in his present surroundings."

8. In Bluegrass Country, August–December 1891

Sharpening Claws

In late July 1891, Pollock arrived in Lexington, Kentucky, the site of that year's battle for the USCA fourth annual congress. He and six other players signed up for the championship tournament: Showalter, Delmar, Major Hanham (the winner of the *Staats Zeitung* meeting at Skaneateles in July), Uedemann, Otto Fick (a physician hailing from St. Louis), Warwick H. Ripley (an Indianapolis lawyer), and S.F.J. Trabue (a local amateur from Louisville). Toledo's C. Locke Curtis, the champion of Ohio, failed to attend the meeting because of business commitments.[1] The global prize fund of $250 was collected through the effort of the citizens of Lexington who liberally contributed to the success of the event. The first prize for the main championship was $100, second $75 and third $25. Samuel Loyd and Charles A. Gilberg were supportive of the event. The former, sticking close to his traditions, offered all participants (including those 18 players attending the free-for-all secondary tournament) the chance to win one of his medals for solving the problem, below, extracted from one of his games (solutions to both the problem and Loyd's question regarding White's previous move, appear at the end of the chapter):

"Looking Backward"
By S. Loyd

Black resigns.

What move has White just made?

---

1. That he had intended to participate is confirmed by Ohio's *The Evening Repository* of June 25, 1891: "Mr. Curtis is now champion of the State, and will uphold the honor of Toledo and Ohio in the great chess contest at Lexington, Ky., in August, when he will be pitted against such national celebrities as Max Judd, Lipschütz, Pollock and other players of equal note."

As announced in the *Baltimore Sunday News* of August 16:

> This no-move problem was submitted to the members of the United States Chess Association, assembled at Lexington, Ky., by Mr. Samuel Loyd, of New York. To the first player announcing its solution he offered as a prize a beautiful chess pin set with diamonds. The successful one was Prof. R. de Roode, of Lexington, who handed in the solution in just forty-five minutes. Considering that no limit had been placed on the time, this was considered quite remarkable.

This small six-round event in Lexington was mainly a battle between Showalter, Pollock, Hanham and Delmar, the only master class players with realistic chances of winning the title. Showalter, in addition to having won the USCA title each of the previous two times he had played, was literally Lexington's hometown favorite.

Showalter had in fact hosted Pollock before the event, and the two men clearly enjoyed playing against one another. The November 15, 1891, column of the *Baltimore Sunday News* indicated Pollock had played a match with Showalter prior to the start of the championship:

> For a week previous to the recent meeting of the USCA at Lexington, Ky., Mr. W.H.K. Pollock was the guest of the Showalter family, at their lovely farm home near Georgetown. By way of sharpening their claws for the championship tourney, J.W. and W.H.K. agreed to play a match of twelve games, the winner of the majority, draws counting ½ a game, to be the victor. Showalter won the series by 6½ to 5½, the two games in the Lexington Congress being reckoned in. Considering that the Kentuckian champion scored the first three games of the match and had the first move in both the Tournament games, this was a fairly close call. The run of the games was peculiar, Showalter failing to win a game from the 4th to 9th. Three games were drawn. Neither stakes nor clocks were employed.

The seven extant games from this obscure match (played mostly at night, ten games in six days) prove the men enjoyed a close affair indeed. Faced in the first game with a King's Gambit and some wild tactical play that brought his king to the center of the board, Pollock admitted defeat just before move 50. In the second game, Pollock misplayed a tactical Ponziani and suffered a much quicker defeat. This scenario repeated itself in the third game. After a quick draw in the fourth game, Pollock was fortunate to draw the fifth after his attacking impetus produced a risky sacrifice that nearly backfired. Pollock's first win occurred in the sixth game when he took advantage of Showalter's weak opening play and trapped his queen at his 19th move. He won again the next game at the end of precise play against Showalter's King's Gambit:

Showalter–Pollock
July 1891, Georgetown, Seventh Match Game

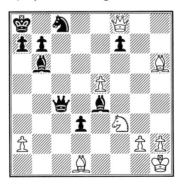

White to move

In this position, Showalter played **33. Bb3?** allowing Pollock a fine retort: **33. ... d2!** Instead, White should have played 33. Bd2! B×f3 34. B×f3 Ba5 35. Be3 2 36. Qc5 with good chances to maintain the balance. Pollock pressed home his advantage after **34. h4 B×f3 35. g×f3 Qf1+ 36. Kh2 Qf2+ 37. Kh3 Q×f3+ 38. Kh2 Kb8 39. B×d2 Qf2+ 40. Kh3 Q×d2** and won at move 57.

In the eighth game, eventually drawn, Pollock missed capitalizing on a big advantage and allowed Showalter an ingenious way out of a very difficult situation: in a rook vs. two knights endgame, the Kentuckian sacrificed his rook for Pollock's last pawn, trying to make it impossible for Pollock to win. It appears Pollock won the ninth game and Showalter the tenth, although the two games have not survived. At this point the score stood 5½–4½ in Showalter's favor. At this point, the two men decided to let their two games in the forthcoming USCA encounter decide the outcome of the match, which in the end gave the contest to the Kentuckian.

Another USCA Championship

Following this friendly warm-up, Pollock began participation in the USCA championship.[2] "The play on the first day was marked by some close, careful play, and some notable surprises," reported the small tournament book published later. "Mr. Showalter was defeated by Mr. Pollock in his first game, and Mr. Hanham, who came like a conquering hero fresh from the New York State tournament, was glad to draw his games with Dr. Fick and Mr. Uedemann, and lost to W.H. Ripley. He evened up matters next day by defeating Mr. Pollock." Pollock's first round victory over Showalter was a seven-hour battle with both masters patiently maneuvering on both sides of the board.[3] The following position was reached at move 49:

Showalter–Pollock
August 4, 1891, Round 1
Fourth USCA Congress

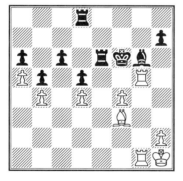

After 49. ... Kg7–f6

Showalter continued with the impatient **50. f5?**, giving away a pawn in the hope of infiltrating behind Black's queenside pawns with one of his rooks. It turned out, rather, that Pollock's more active king helped with liquidating White's queenside pawns, and decided the game in

---

2. Probably unaware yet of the friendly encounter between Showalter and Pollock from late July to early August 1891, Isaac E. Orchard, writing in the *Atlanta Sunny South* of August 15, suggested a match between the two. It's possible that Orchard meant a serious match (with stakes and clocks). Writing in the December 6, 1891, *New York Tribune*, Steinitz commented that the match as played was a "friendly" one. • **3.** The duration of the Pollock vs. Showalter (first round game) in the USCA's Fourth Annual Congress was mentioned by the *Chicago Herald* and *New York Sun* of August 5, 1891. The exact order of Pollock's rounds/games in this tournament has been determined thanks to daily brief reports from the *New York Herald*.

Black's favor after **51. ... B×f5 52. R×f5+ K×f5 53. Bg4+ Kf6 54. B×e6 K×e6 55. Rg7 Rd7 56. Rg8 Kf5! 57. Ra8 Ke4.**

Pollock's excellent start in defeating the hometown favorite in the first round was followed by a 22-move victory over Trabue, and then by a characteristic lapse in the third round, at a moment when a little self-restraint would have been wise. But Pollock wasn't thinking of restraint of any sort when on the morning of August 5 he faced the dangerous New Yorker, Hanham. Playing White, Pollock essayed a spectacularly unclear sacrifice. He had obtained the following comfortable position after 20 moves:

Pollock–Hanham
August 5, 1891, Round 3
Fourth USCA Congress

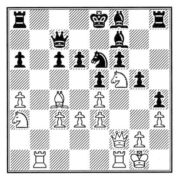

After 20. ... a6

Jackson Whipps Showalter (John G. White Chess and Checkers Collections, Cleveland Public Library).

Pollock continued with the sharp **21. N×d6+?! B×d6 22. Q×f6.** While it posed some serious problems for Black, this line was not decisive. Throughout this complicated 51-move game, Hanham held on remarkably well and, benefiting from a serious error at Pollock's 39th move, even managed to turn the tables on his opponent. Instead of the text move, in the diagram above Pollock could have chosen the far more efficient 21. Nd4!?—certainly equally spectacular, yet with a clear plus for White.

Next, Pollock outplayed Ripley in an Evans Gambit that lasted 25 moves. By Thursday morning, August 6, with three wins and one loss, Pollock was leading in the tournament. But the time had arrived to face a stronger opponent: Louis Uedemann, a man Pollock had faced before during the previous USCA championship in St. Louis. The game, "watched with fervor" by spectators, was another hard-fought encounter. Pollock, having Black, defended with the same original knight sacrifice that he used in the fourth game of his match with Delmar at Skaneateles less than a month earlier (**1. e4 e5 2. Nf3 Nc6 3. c3 Nf6 4. d4 N×e4 5. d5 Bc5!?**). After 27 moves, the following bewildering position was reached:

Uedemann–Pollock
August 6, 1891, Round 5
Fourth USCA Congress

After 27. ... Rf4–a4

Here Uedemann could have continued with the mind-boggling 28. Nh6!! which would have gotten him out of any serious trouble. Instead he chose the sharp line **28. Ne3 d2 29. B×d2 R×a3+ 30. b×a3 Q×a3+ 31. Kb1 Rb8+ 32. Kc2 Rb2+ 33. Kd1 Q×a1+ 34. Ke2 Qa6+ 35. Nc4 Rb8** and after some rich tactical play that gave both players chances, Pollock came out on top in 60 moves.

Pollock, with four wins out of five games, disposed of Fick, his sixth round opponent, rather easily with an energetic kingside offensive. He tied Showalter for the top prize, both players scoring five points. The tournament's executive committee decided to have an extra game between the two players as a tiebreaker. It started as a traditional Two Knights Defense, but with his fifth move (**5. Ng5** after 1. e4 e5 2. Nf3 Nc6 3. Bc4 Nf6 4. d4 e×d4) the Kentuckian seems to have surprised Pollock. The latter annotated the game, published in the August 16 edition of the *Sunday News*, and expressed surprise at the move. Despite sailing unexplored waters, Pollock obtained a good opening position once his king castled and reached safety. His sacrifice of the queenside pawns was meant to be followed by some great pressure upon Showalter's king, but things didn't turn out as planned. Allowed to mobilize quickly, the American champion succeeded in neutralizing Pollock's incipient attack and—according to Michigan's *Bay City Sunday Times* of August 30—after three hours and twenty minutes, pushed home the material advantage offered by his extra pawns.

Thus, Pollock finished second, taking home the $75 prize.[4] But he did not immediately leave Lexington.

---

4. This is how *The Evening Bulletin* of August 10, 1891 (Maysville, Kentucky) summarized the event: "CHAMPION CHESS PLAYER: The chess contest at Lexington last week for the championship of this country resulted in the victory of J.W. Showalter, an ex-citizen of Mason County. This is the third time in succession he has won the championship. Showalter's defeated opponent in this last tournament, W.H.K. Pollock, is a chess player of international reputation. He was born in Ireland [*sic*], and first came into conspicuous notice by winning the championship of that nation about five years ago. Afterwards he won the International Tournament at Belfast, making the remarkable record of winning every game and both rounds, defeating such players as Blackburne, of England; Gunsberg, of Hungary [*sic*]; and Burn, a Scotchman [*sic*]." From the *Philadelphia Inquirer* of August 9, 1891: "A very peculiar feature was commented on by President [W.C.] Cochran. The representatives of Kentucky, Maryland and New York now occupy the same relative positions as they did at the close of last year's tournament at St. Louis, namely: Showalter, of Kentucky, first; Pollock, of Maryland, second; and Hanham, of New York, third."

A Triangular Affair

Colonel Frank Williams, the president of the Lexington Chess Club, had the idea of organizing a triangular tournament involving Hanham, Showalter and Pollock in the last week of August 1891. According to the *Sunday News* of August 30, Williams' motivation was simple: during the USCA's fourth championship he was 1300 miles away and missed the action. "Determined to see some match play," Williams sponsored a purse of $100 to be played for by the three players. Each player had to contest four games against each other (with draws counting as half-points). The tournament commenced on August 23 at the Lexington Turf Club, with some prestigious members of the local clubs in attendance. Reporting for the *Sunday News*, Pollock offered some revealing details of the proceedings, starting with the following matter:

> The first incident of note was the desire of Maj. Hanham to set the clocks of *both* his antagonists, who arrived somewhat later than 10 a.m., the appointed hour of play, in motion. Mr. C.W. Charles, the well-known "Cincinnati Charles," formerly chess editor of the *Commercial Gazette*, was umpire on the occasion and arranged matters amicably, Showalter being drawn against Hanham, and being mulcted of 40 minutes of his time—a 40 minutes that the genial USCA champion would not, unless his nature strangely changed, willingly gain by forfeit in 40,000 games against as many opponents [Showalter won the game nevertheless in 31 moves].
>
> The rules empowered him [Hanham] to do this, as Pollock and Showalter on two occasions failed to turn up at the absurdly early hour of play (arranged especially to suit Major Hanham) i.e., 9:30 a.m. Mr. Showalter resided with friends, at a considerable distance from the Turf Club. The score up to Monday afternoon stood: Showalter 1½, Hanham 1, Pollock ½.

Pollock started a game against Hanham and after only 20 moves it was adjourned in the following position:

Hanham–Pollock
Triangular Tournament
August 1891

After 20. ... Qg6–g5

On resumption of play the next morning, Pollock was late 59 minutes and the following incident took place:

> Pollock made a blunder while endeavoring to make 20 moves in ¾ of a minute. When moves are made instantaneously the unwritten code of chess players as opposed to sharps is not to turn the clock of the player who is pressed in such a way. Major Hanham, however, worked by counting the ticks of the clock, and in several cases actually turned the clock *after* his opponent had moved; A good deal of "feeling" occurred, and some of the boys threatened to have the gallant Major tied up with a string and his clock set in motion. Perhaps the Major would consider *this* "sharp practice."

Such little absurdities aside, Pollock played some good chess. The sequence below was considered a "Pollock gem," the tactical play revealing an "extraordinarily deep plot":

Pollock–Showalter
Triangular Tournament
Lexington, August 1891

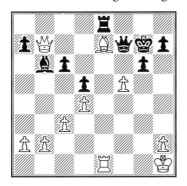

White to move

Here, according to the August 30 *Sunday News* column, Pollock played **1. Kg2** (intending 2. f×g6 and 3. Rf1). After Showalter played **1. ... g×f5**, the game continued with **2. Kh1 Bd8 3. Rg1+ Kh8 4. B×d8! Q×b7 5. Bf6+** and White won.[5]

While Showalter and Pollock spent some agreeable time together in Georgetown (Showalter's home for many years),[6] according to the September 6 column in the *Sunday News*, the triangular tournament was unfortunately brought "to a sudden and insatisfactory termination, on account of some disagreement between the players and the prize contributor." As Pollock made it clear in his September 13 column, it was Hanham's inflexibility regarding play in the morning hours that ruined the tournament.

On his way back home, Pollock made a stop in Pittsburg where he spent seven days at McCutcheon's house. "No public exhibitions of play were given," wrote the *Pittsburg Dispatch* on September 12, one day after Pollock's departure. Before the end of the month, Pollock was back in Baltimore. The *Sunday News* of September 20 announced that Pollock offered a simultaneous exhibition to all comers at the club (18–2, with 3 draws). He also took part in a continuous handicap tournament in the city. That fall he remained in Baltimore taking good charge of

---

5. Pollock appears not to have noticed that 1. Bf6+! wins in more straightforward fashion: 1. ... K×f6 (1. ... Kg8 2. R×e8+ Q×e8 3. Qg7 mate) 2. Q×c6+ Kg7 3. Q×e8. ● **6.** More than one incident illustrates the joking fun Showalter and Pollock had together. From the August 30 issue of the *Baltimore Sunday News* (citing Lexington's *Morning Transcript*): "The two chess champions, Pollock and Showalter, were borrowing the latest novel from Mr. McGuire, the genial co-manager of the Georgetown Lancaster Hotel. Mr. McG[uire] was trying to explain that he wished he was a bird, like the Irishman, so as to be in 'two places at wanst,' otherwise he could not attend the bar and office simultaneously. One of the chess champions (the Irish one we believe) at once replied, 'Mr. McGuire, you're too ambiquitous.'" And, again, from the September 20 edition: "A really curious coincidence. Mr. Pollock, while a guest of Mr. J.W. Showalter at Georgetown last month, set up the chess men as for commencing a game, observing: 'In the first round of the New York Congress of 1889, I played **1. d4** in my game with Max Weiss, who replied **1. ... d5**. I will, on the supposition that you have not seen the game, give you sixteen guesses as to what my second move was.' Showalter failed to discover the move. On trying the same experiment with Arthur Peter, who won the free-for-all at Lexington, the gentleman found the move on his first guess! On repeating the experiment with Dr. E.W. Keeney, the brilliant chess and checker editor of the *Kentucky Commonwealth*, at Newport, Ky., the Doctor also guessed the move first shot! Neither of the three gentlemen had seen the game in question. The move was **2. Qd3**. The game was a good one but escaped publication at the time. It was almost a stroke of genius on the part of Cols. Keeney and Peter, but the point of the joke is not lost on dear old Jack, who still holds the championship all the same." Pollock's 2. Qd3 didn't impress Steinitz, who wrote in the tournament book "Eccentric and not commendable." By move 17, despite his odd second move, Pollock had managed to regain the initiative, losing later only because of an unsound sacrifice [**see Game 259**].

his column. Before Christmas 1891 he offered the following amusement to his readers (playfully alluding to Loyd's "Looking Backward" problem; solution appears at the end of the chapter):

"Lacking Book"
(With apologies to Mr. S. Loyd)
By W.H.K. Pollock

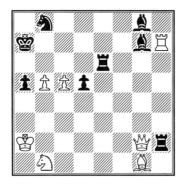

Black has just made an atrociously bad move;

What is the *worst* move that White can make in reply?

Pollock spent a good deal of time that fall and early winter entertaining his Baltimore friends at the local club, where he participated in various light pastimes, including, for instance, team alternation chess, where one player after another on the team, without consultation, would make a move. With the start of 1892, however, Pollock found more competitive chess further north, as his attention turned to Brooklyn.

KEY TO LOYD'S PROBLEM:

Page 117: White played **K×g3+** (after Black played f×g3+, an *en passant* capture). The position was taken from a game S. Loyd vs. E. Bellamy; the problem appeared in the *Baltimore Sunday News* of August 16, 1891, and *Pittsburg Dispatch* of August 15, 1891. Sam Loyd had as early as 1859 anticipated in one form or another "retrograde analysis" and problems.[7]

KEY TO "LACKING BOOK":

Page 124: Black played **1. ... d5**; White's worst move is **2. c×d6+** allowing mate in one.

---

7. See "To Know the Past One Must First Know the Future: Raymond Smullyan and the Mysteries of Retrograde Analysis," by Bernd Graefrath, in *Philosophy Looks at Chess*, edited by Benjamin Hale (Chicago and La Salle, Ill.: Open Court, 2008), page 3.

9. With the Holy Trinity: Chigorin, Steinitz and Lasker, January–December 1892

In Brooklyn

In late January 1892, while offering extensive coverage in his column of the world championship match between Steinitz and Chigorin, Pollock gave simultaneous exhibitions in Baltimore. By the end of February, Steinitz had triumphed in Havana (+10 –8 =5) and retained the title. When this high profile match was over, Pollock headed to New York. He stopped at the Manhattan Chess Club in early March where he played games against Lipschütz and Ryan. But, as the March 13 column in the *Sunday News* had it, the Brooklyn Chess Club "was the centre of attention at present." The club was going to hold its annual championship. The tournament was initially set to begin on February 1, but some discussion about the prizes delayed the proceedings. The *Brooklyn Daily Eagle* of February 2 explained:

THE BROOKLYN CHESS CLUB TOURNAMENT POSTPONED

The gift of an elegant set of metallic chessmen plated with gold and silver as a prize for the annual club tourney has aroused a special interest in the contest for the honor of being the champion player of the Brooklyn chess club for 1892, and the prospects that the entry list will include the strongest players who have entered for a similar event in the history of chess in Brooklyn. The executive committee of the club expected to open the tourney on the 1st of the new month, but there is a division of opinion on the subject of arranging the tourney, and the opening has been deferred. The majority of the leading players of the club favor a tournament for a money prize, leaving the president's gift of the elegant chessmen as the chief prize for an additional tourney. The first class of the club list of players for 1892 includes such noted experts as Messrs. Teed, Gilberg, Eno, Densmore, Elwell and others of the last tourney, with the addition of Messrs. Hodges, Delmar, de Visser, Richardson, Pollock, Blackmar, Kemény, Russell and others of the new class of the present year. It will be seen, therefore, that the coming tourney will be one of the most interesting the club has as yet had.[1]

The club's annual tournament would, as suggested, involve some of the strongest players not only of Brooklyn, but of the nation. And, in all likelihood, to attract at least some of them,

---

1. The following appeared in the *Brooklyn Standard-Union* of February 6: "It is expected that the strongest players of Brooklyn and New York will compete and one of the finest contests that has yet been played in Brooklyn will be the result. W.H.K. Pollock, of Baltimore, who is a member of this club, will be invited to enter, and with his antagonist of last year, Eugene Delmar, in, some good playing may be looked for. The list will be about ten, though everyone can enter who desires. The other entries will probably be A.B. Hodges, E. Kemény, Philip Richardson, A.E. Blackmar, George Russell, Edward Olly, W.M. de Visser, and F.M. Teed."

prize money, more than chess sets, was of value. The event finally started a month later, on March 5, with Pollock, Hodges, Delmar, Kemény and Hanham among the favorites, and the field fleshed out with George Russell, Olly, Finlay, Souweine and Blackmar. First prize was $40, second $25, and Charles Gilberg's gold and silver plated chess set demoted to third. Two additional money prizes of $5 each were on the table, for the best score against prizewinners and for the best game by nonprizewinners. Each player had to play at least two games per week. Eno, Elwell and Olly formed the tournament committee.

After a rather slow start (3 out of 5), Pollock found his stride in the following rounds, in his case played much more quickly than at the leisurely pace of two games a week, to accommodate his out-of-town status. By March 28, Pollock had scored 12–3 with 2 draws (which according to the tournament rules had to be replayed). His consistent play got him a profile, accompanied by a fine engraving, in the March 26 issue of the *Brooklyn Standard-Union*:

> W.H.K. Pollock, who has during the past few years edited the chess department of the Baltimore "Sunday News," made his debut in chess circles in 1885 [*sic*] in England. A student of medicine, with no love for his profession, he left it to follow the pleasant but unprofitable pathway of Caissa. That he has made good use of his opportunities is shown by the successes which have followed him. Occasionally the inequalities of his temperament have interfered with the full accomplishment of his endeavors, but the general results have been so that that he is recognized as one of the leading players of this country.
>
> Were we to refer to any one particular of Mr. Pollock's playing it would be that of ingenuity, that element which is so necessary in those to whose style may be applied the term brilliant. Very fertile in conceptions and deep in combinations his playing develops some of the most interesting games that have graced the tournaments and chess congresses in which he has taken part[...].

Pollock's two replay games in the Brooklyn Chess Club championship had to be postponed due to an important occasion. Steinitz and Chigorin, two of the world's top masters, were paying a visit to Brooklyn. Steinitz arrived first in the last days of March. After several private visits to the homes of some of the more well-to-do Brooklyn club members, on March 26 Steinitz gave a small simultaneous blindfold exhibition at the club against a strong threesome: Abel E. Blackmar, William M. de Visser and Philip Richardson. Pollock, among the many spectators crowding the room, saw Steinitz, sitting with his back to his opponents, lose the first game to Blackmar, next defeat de Visser and, by 10:45 p.m., force Richardson to resign as well. Like all those present, Pollock joined the loud applause that greeted Steinitz's success. Curiously, Pollock was not listed as one of the 18 special guests who accompanied the champion to the Clarendon Hotel late that same evening, where Steinitz was entertained in high style. "Speeches and songs were the order, and merriment reigned," wrote the *Brooklyn Standard-Union*.[2]

Shortly thereafter, on Wednesday, March 30, Mikhail Chigorin also paid a visit to the Brooklyn Chess Club. According to the *Standard-Union* for February 6, Chigorin from Havana had corresponded in Russian with Edward N. Olly, and arranged for the Brooklyn visit. This time Pollock was not merely a spectator. With obvious reluctance, he took a board against the Russian master in the latter's 12-board simultaneous exhibition. According to the April 10 issue of the *Sunday News*, Pollock and Halpern "were unwilling to play, but the spectators loudly insisted on their occupying the vacant boards, and treated them to quite an ovation on their acquiescence."

---

2. The *Brooklyn Standard-Union* of April 2, 1892, gave the names of the 18 guests (including Steinitz): Charles A. Gilberg, A.E. Blackmar, S.B. Chittenden, Dr. F.W. Wunderlich, J. Josephson, A.B. Hodges, W.F. Eno, Dr. Broughton, J.D. Elwell, Henry Chadwick, Philip Richardson, W.M. de Visser, Juan Sabater, F. Rose, W. Duval, E. Olly, and E. Kemény. Were we to fully trust this report (and Pollock's name was not omitted by error), why a columnist of Pollock's reputation did not attend such a party would remain a mystery.

Pollock managed to defeat Chigorin, although clearly he did not think very much of his accomplishment. He certainly did not publish in his own column his win against the single performer. How could he? As a player of master status himself, participating in such a display had to feel uncomfortable for the Baltimore resident, even though doing so was relatively common during displays in his adopted homeland. He had much more reputation to lose in such a loss to Chigorin, than did Chigorin in such a loss to him. As a club member, yet essentially the guest of his Brooklyn friends, Pollock had no real alternative. He either took a board, and risked his reputation for no significant reward, or refused to play, and risked alienating his Brooklyn friends. The *Brooklyn Daily Eagle* of March 31 reported in greater detail:

> The rooms of the Brooklyn Chess Club were last night crowded to excess by club members and invited guests, on the occasion of the club's special reception to the Russian chess champion, Mr. Chigorin, on his return to the metropolis from his great contest with the world's champion, Mr. Steinitz. He was cordially greeted on his arrival at the club by President Gilberg, who introduced him to the officers and members of the club, and shortly afterward the special entertainment of the evening was commenced, it being a simultaneous games tourney, in which the champion played singly against twelve members of the club, the latter being seated at the tables in two rows of six players on each side, the single player walking from table No. 1 to No. 12 in regular order. His opponents included such noted experts as Messrs. Pollock, Eno, Kemény, Hanham, Haghorn and Olly, and it was the strongest team the club had ever before presented in any previous tourney of the kind. The games had not proceed far before it became manifest that the champion had every opening at his fingers' ends, the rapidity of his moves being exceptional. When the book moves, too, had been gone through with each and each game had been fully developed, his rapid calculations and quick moves were an exceptional feature, and his adversaries were put on their mettle to keep up with the pace he gave them. The contest began at 8:15 p.m. and in an hour afterward things began to approach a crisis at several of the tables. But it was 10 p.m. before the first player succumbed to the champion's rapid fire and strong attacks, and the first victim was Mr. Halpern, the champion of the City chess club of New York, who is now a member of the Brooklyn club. The next to retire was Mr. Breckenridge, the champion's attack being a brilliant one in this game. The third game to end was that of Mr. Pollock, the Baltimore chess editor, who successfully played the Two Knights' Defense opening and won a creditable victory. Then came Mr. Eno's victory, after [*sic*] the best played game of the evening, his skillful working of the King's Gambit resulting in a won game. The fourth game finished was that of Major Hanham, who played a Giuoco Piano opening very successfully. Mr. Kemény then drew his game and, after that, all the others fell down rapidly, the tourney ending before 11 o'clock. After the close of the reception at the club rooms Mr. Chigorin became the special guests of President Gilberg at the Clarendon Hotel, with a few invited guests, and thus ended the most enjoyable reception the club has ever had.[3]

On Saturday morning, April 2, Pollock, together with Charles Devide and von Taube, accompanied Chigorin as he boarded the steamer *La Touraine*, heading to Europe. Then, wasting no time in Brooklyn, Pollock returned to Baltimore. He had finished all his games in the Brooklyn Chess Club's championship, including the two draws that had to be replayed, completing his

---

3. The chess editor of the *Standard-Union* wrote the following on April 2: "His [Chigorin's] lack of knowledge of our language did not seem to be a bar to friendliness, for his intelligent appearance, and interest in all about him, carried with it the idea that he intentively [*sic*] understood all that was said. Mr. Chigorin is about five feet seven inches in height, with very dark hair and fair skin; high forehead, and with a general air of prosperity about him that is quite pleasing to chess players. He has a bright, kindly eye that looks directly to the questioners and his hand-shaking has that warm, brotherly pressure that draws one to him. His chess-playing in the simultaneous performance, with which he entertained the club, was very fine, rapid, and with seemingly a perfect knowledge of the openings; his moves were considered and decided upon almost at a glance. The Brooklyn C.C. feels very proud in winning three games and drawing one of the twelve, for in New Orleans a week ago he only lost three games, of forty-three played, at three different exhibitions. Messrs. Eno, Pollock and Hanham, won and E. Kemény drew." This quotation suggests another reason Pollock, though a master himself, could not turn down taking a board against the internationally known visitor: club pride. Clearly, the Brooklyn Club took pleasure in comparing itself in terms of results with the New Orleans Chess and Checkers Club, an organization built on a much larger scale than that of even Brooklyn's flourishing organization.

schedule with an impressive 15–3. Although the leisurely pace required of the local competitors meant the final determination of Pollock's placing was several months in the future, there was little doubt he would win the Brooklyn title, and he did so, with Emil Kemény taking second place.[4] As for his time in Brooklyn, "Mr. Pollock's visit was a very pleasant one," wrote the *Standard-Union* of April 9, "and the instruction and entertainment his playing gave to the club members will make the trip a pleasing memory. He made a remarkable score in the tournament, winning fifteen games and losing three; he did not lose a game in the second round."

Back home in Baltimore Pollock expected to meet Showalter and his wife, who were on their way for the Kentucky Lion to meet Lipschütz in a match in New York. The couple had planned a brief stay in Baltimore in early April. Due to health issues, Showalter delayed his trip to Baltimore for a week and only arrived in the city on Monday afternoon, April 11. From the April 17 issue of the *Baltimore Sunday News*:

> Mr. J.W. Showalter arrived in Baltimore on Monday afternoon, April 11th, for a few days visit en route to encountering Mr. Lipschütz in New York, the match having been postponed until tomorrow. On the same evening, the Kentuckian being somewhat fatigued with his long journey, did not indulge in any heavy chess, but, in company with Mr. Pollock played six simultaneous consultation games against strong members, the peripatetic pair winning four and losing two games. On Tuesday, chess was out of question until the evening on account of the ball match, Mr. Showalter being a very deep-dyed baseball crank and a player of great skill besides. In the evening a game was played between him and Mr. Pollock for a prize generously offered by Mr. Robt. C. Hall. The game was of a very interesting nature and resulted in a draw.

The Showalters left the city for New York on April 17. Showalter had played more than 50 games while in town, most of them simultaneous or consultation games, but also some training and exhibition games with Pollock. All his efforts at regaining form would be in vain, however, as Lipschütz would defeat him and claim Showalter's "title" as United States champion. (Even though by the rules of the USCA, Showalter's title belonged to the Association, and could only be gained through annual tournament competition.) In the last week of May, Pollock traveled to New York and, while meeting Showalter, had some words of comfort for the Kentuckian. By the end of May, Showalter lost the championship match against Lipschütz +1 –7 =7 and the purse of $1,500. In his June 5 *Baltimore Sunday News* column Pollock wrote:

> Mr. J.W. Showalter postponed his departure from the scene of the match until the 28th ult., when he left with Mrs. Showalter direct for home. We had the pleasure of an hour's conversation with him on the afternoon of 28th. To say that he is dissatisfied with the result of the match would be slightly inadequate. He is simply but absolutely dumbfounded and utterly unable to account for his succession of blunders and repeated failure to win his won games or draw his drawn ones. He confidently expects to defeat Lipschütz in the return match in the West, as he has never felt at home, chessically, in New York, and undoubtedly his play may have suffered from the subtle influence of being surrounded by his opponent's backers and partisans. Mr. Showalter referred in the warmest terms to Mr. Lipschütz's gentle and agreeable demeanor. The victor presented the loser with a handsome gold cigar cutter.

Back to facing the local enthusiasts in Baltimore, Pollock produced (and published) entertaining fragments like the one below that appeared in his *Baltimore Sunday News* column of May 28:

---

4. The *Baltimore Sunday News* of July 24, 1892, published the full crosstable of the event: Pollock won the top prize with +15 –3, followed by Kemény (+14 –4), and with a tie for the third position between Blackmar, Hanham and Hodges (+12 –6); all the draws in this event had to be replayed.

Pollock–Mr. C.
Baltimore Chess Association
May 1892

Black to move

Pollock noted that the game continued with **1. ... d2 2. R×c5+ b×c5 3. Rc1+ Kd3 4. Rc3+ Ke4 5. Re3+ Kd5**, when Black missed the winning move 5. ... Kf5! and allowed White to force a draw: **6. Re5+ Kc4 7. R×c5+ Kd3 8. Rc3+ Ke4 9. Re3+ Kd5 10. Re5+ Kd6 11. Re6+ Kd7 12. Re7+ Kd8** (12. ... Kc6! and heading with the king to f4 was also winning for Black.) **13. Re8+ Kc7 14. Rc8+ Kb6 15. Rc6+** and the game was drawn.

In July and August 1892, Pollock was busy studying the games played by the world's top masters at the Dresden international tournament. "We have a private opinion that this congress is, for pure chess, the strongest one held in the Fatherland," wrote Pollock in his August 14 column. "We want all our readers to join us in the study of the finest of the 135 games which we can select." He published analysis of the most entertaining games throughout the summer.

With Steinitz: Work and a Shooting Incident

At the end of August, Pollock was a guest of Steinitz at his house at Upper Montclair, New Jersey. According to Kurt Landsberger, Steinitz moved there either in 1889 or 1890 and lived there for a few years.[5] It appears that Steinitz liked not only Pollock's chess knowledge, but also his good relations with many figures on the American scene, and used him to conduct correspondence with various collectors and men of letters in American chess. It also appears Pollock helped Steinitz work on the second part of his *The Modern Chess Instructor* manuscript, and possibly with considering a never consummated resurrection of the champion's *International Chess Magazine*. Things seem to have gone smoothly for a while, and Pollock found himself in the middle of the country's greatest chess stories. On September 27, for instance, both Pollock and Steinitz, along with Hodges, Gilberg, Lipschütz, Janusch and others, took part in a dinner given by the New York City Chess Club when it moved its premises to Café Europa. Then on Thursday, October 6, Emanuel Lasker arrived in America for the first time, for his month long engagement at the Manhattan Chess Club. Three days later, Lasker visited Steinitz at his residence in Upper

---

5. Some basic information regarding Steinitz's stay at Upper Montclair and the incident described in the text can be found in *The Steinitz Papers: Letters and Documents of the First World Chess Champion*, ed. Kurt Landsberger (Jefferson, N.C.: McFarland, 2002, pages 159–160) and also Landsberger's *William Steinitz, Chess Champion: A Biography of the Bohemian Caesar* (Jefferson, N.C.: McFarland, 1993, pages 273–275).

Montclair, together with Adolph Brodsky, the famed violinist, and Hartwig Cassel. They then spent the evening at the New York City Club. There is little doubt that Pollock, too, spent a good deal of time at the Manhattan Chess Club throughout October and early November to witness Lasker's extraordinary play against New York's finest.

But trouble arrived in early November 1892. A shooting incident, of all things, occurred at Steinitz's house around the time Pollock was there. It remains rather mysterious. Steinitz dismissed his first secretary, Nathaniel W. Williams, and replaced him with Ernest Treitel. The rivalry between Williams and Treitel, both still living under the same roof, led to a physically charged dispute early that November. One morning Williams used a firearm to shoot Treitel in Steinitz's house. Treitel was taken to Mountainside Hospital, where eventually his left arm was amputated, and Williams was arrested by police and locked up at the police station. In his *William Steinitz, Chess Champion* (1993), Landsberger consulted a number of Montclair newspapers and recounted how various versions of the incident (varying from attempted murder to accidental shooting) were published as well as brief descriptions of the trial that followed. Pollock's involvement remains unclear. A letter dated November 4, 1896, from F.J. Lee to F.F. Rowland, who was collecting material for a biographical work on Pollock, stated that Pollock lived with Steinitz for several months and that both Pollock and Steinitz were called as witnesses at the trial. According to Lee, the shooting incident and its aftermath altered for the worse the relationship between the two chess players:

> Steinitz and Pollock were not friends since the unfortunate catastrophe in Steinitz house in 1892. W. Steinitz lived for several years in a very secluded house at Upper Montclair, New Jersey. I called on Steinitz at his house with Lasker in August 1893, so you can depend on my description. Upper Montclair is about thirty miles from New York City; and Steinitz's house was stationed in the middle of a good sized wood and over a mile from the nearest house and the Railway Station. This solitude suited Steinitz, who lived in the house with three Secretaries, one a German whose name I forgot, another an American named ... and the third was for several months W.H.K. Pollock.
>
> The American used very often to amuse himself shooting birds and rabbits in the wood, but one morning he returned to the house from an early ramble and went into the bedroom with his gun, which went off, and the German Secretary was killed [*sic*]. This incident caused a great sensation at Upper Montclair, and although the American firmly declared that it was an accident, he was arrested on a charge of "Manslaughter."
>
> The case was tried in New York and Pollock as well as Steinitz had to appear in the trial as witnesses. Over this trial Steinitz and Pollock had very serious differences, and they took different views as to the action of the American (who, by the way, was sentenced to five or six years), and directly after this Pollock left the house of Steinitz and the latter [Pollock], I know, never made it up with Steinitz.[6]

There are some obvious factual problems with Lee's account, starting with the rather basic fact that no one died: Ernest Treitel was not killed on the spot; he lost his left arm due to the shooting but he was still alive during the trial; the latter did not take place in New York but in Newark; and no newspaper account describing the trial made any mention of Pollock testifying as a witness.[7] Once the incident made it into the Montclair and Newark newspapers in early

---

6. F.J. Lee's letter to F.F. Rowland appeared published in full in *Four Leaved Shamrock*, spring 1911, No. 32–33. It also appears cited on page 276 of *William Steinitz, Chess Champion* and page 159 of *The Steinitz Papers*. Landsberger wrote: "None of the accounts indicated that he [Pollock] ever lived with Steinitz, but this is quite possible since they were friendly. He was the guest of Steinitz at the Manhattan Chess Club in November 1884 [*sic*: this is wildly inaccurate since Pollock came to America only in 1889], and he, too, received a copy of the Congress book as a gift from Steinitz." Evidence that Pollock indeed lived with Steinitz for some time is provided by the *Baltimore Sunday News* of August 28, 1892: "Mr. W.H.K. Pollock is a guest of Mr. W. Steinitz in the rural castle of the champion at Upper Montclair, N.J." • **7.** Worth noting too is that no court records have been located concerning the shooting or the trial, and what for now passes as fact is based only on various newspaper accounts published between early November 1892 and early March 1893.

November, a reporter of the *New York Sun* was dispatched to report on it as well. This (until now overlooked) report of the whole episode unfolding in Steinitz's house saw print in the *New York Sun* of November 20, 1892. Besides containing details unmentioned elsewhere, it contains a possible reference to Pollock (in mentioning the "professional chess player"), although the matter is somewhat clouded by references to Steinitz's second secretary, Treitel, as well. In any event, the *Sun's* reporter no doubt felt he was entertaining his readers by making fun of both the short Steinitz and the possibly even shorter Williams, despite the severe and permanent harm Treitel endured:

DONNERWETTER, GADZOOKS!
THE LIFE OF A FAMOUS CHESS PLAYER
AND HIS SECRETARY

Nathaniel Williams's Great Versatility and the Unpleasant Things Which Resulted from the Discovery that it was Limited

Nathaniel Williams, who for five years has been the private secretary of Steinitz, the chess player, was removed last week to the jail at Newark from Montclair, where he was arrested on Nov. 4 for shooting Ernest Treitel, a German, who had succeeded him in Steinitz's employ. Williams entered

William Steinitz, the reigning world champion, circa 1883 (John G. White Chess and Checkers Collections, Cleveland Public Library).

Treitel's room early that morning dressed for hunting and carrying a gun. Steinitz was sitting a short distance from the closed door of the room. He says that he heard the two men talking angrily together. A few moments later he heard the muffled sound of a shot followed by a second louder report. Immediately Williams left Treitel's room and passed out of the house.

Treitel cried out that he had been shot by Williams, and Steinitz found him in bed, badly wounded in the left arm. Williams, when arrested, insisted that the shooting was accidental, and accounted for his presence in Treitel's room by saying that it was necessary for him to pass through that room in order to get out of the house. On Monday or Tuesday of the next week he will be taken before Justice Milligan at Montclair for examination. If released he will be again arrested on complaint of Steinitz, who alleges that Williams has repeatedly threatened his life. This Williams denies. Treitel, who has lost his arm as a result of the shooting, will soon be discharged from the Mountain Side Hospital at Montclair.

It develops that condition of affairs existed for some time previous to the shooting in the Steinitz household. The great chess player is a widower and lives at Upper Montclair. Williams is an Englishman who has long been an intimate friend of Steinitz. During his five years' service as the great chess player's secretary he lived in Steinitz's home, directing the affairs of the household and managing Steinitz's business. He appears to have combined the duties of private secretary, butler, and business manager in a satisfactory manner. He occasionally did a little gardening for Steinitz, and has been known to cook dinner in an emergency, as well as wait on the table and kill the chickens. The compensation he received for such versatility was small, but until the end of last August both he and Steinitz were apparently satisfied with the arrangement.

At that time Steinitz engaged another man, a professional chess player [clearly a reference to Pollock], to assist him in the preparation of a work he is now writing. The help he required was of a more literary character than Steinitz believed Williams could render him. It appears that there was a limit to Williams's usefulness, although he himself would not acknowledge it. The Englishman chafed under the presence of the new secretary, and his conduct, Steinitz says, became as unusual as it was exasperating. He domineered over Steinitz, and made life so unpleasant that Steinitz dismissed him, giving him permission, however, to remain in his household until he found another situation.

Williams stayed with Steinitz on apparently the same footing as before, with no special unpleasantness until Oct. 12. Then a little scene occurred at the breakfast table which is variously described. Williams says that he intimated a desire to come to New York to see the Columbus parade. He felt justified in the wish, he says, because it was the first day off he had taken in five years. Steinitz did not agree with him, and said if Williams came to the city he'd better stay, for he would never get inside that house again. Then Williams said something, and Steinitz says he rose in his seat to answer the remarks.

It takes Steinitz some little time to rise in his seat, and it is an impressive act. He is suffering at present with a lame knee, and moves with difficulty on two canes. At all events Williams was so frightened when Steinitz was rising from his seat that he ran up to the second story and brought down a weapon which Steinitz describes as a "bludgeon." By the time Williams got back to the dining room Steinitz had resumed his seat, and the bludgeon was laid aside.

Breakfast and the discussion of Williams's plans for the day were continued together. In a short time the argument took such a direction that Steinitz was compelled for the second time to rise in his seat. This time one of his canes rose higher than he did and came down on Williams's head. Reports vary as to how the cane descended. Steinitz says it fell with a gentle tap. Williams says it came down with a thud. He says that it rose and fell again, this time dislocating the thumb on the hand he stretched out to protect himself from Steinitz's gentle tap.

Well. Williams came to New York and saw the parade..., and he took with him then news that almost made Steinitz rise in his seat again. He said, as Steinitz tells it, that he had brought suit for $1,000 damages and $20 a week while the injury to his thumb continued, and that he had levied an attachment on the royalties of Steinitz's books and on his bank account. He demanded the immediate payment of $120 back salary, and, by the way of emphasis, threatened Steinitz's life at various points in the narrative of his day's doings.

The next day Steinitz came to New York to investigate. Apparently the result was satisfactory, for Williams continued to live with Steinitz, who says he hadn't the heart to turn his old friend out. Williams says he wouldn't leave because Steinitz owed him money. For two weeks longer they lived together, although some frigidity marred the serenity of the household. One day Steinitz wouldn't eat at the same table with Williams. Then, when Steinitz was mollified, Williams would refuse to eat with him.

One night, after Treitel had arrived at the house, Steinitz and he started to play a little game of cards. Williams waited until they were well under way, and then walked into the room where the men were playing and swept chips and cards off the table, with some accompanying language that was not soothing. That was the night before the shooting.

In such little ways as these, Williams let it be seen that he was not pleased with the presence of Treitel. Then he became more vigorous in his objection and refused to hand over Steinitz's books and papers to the new secretary. Steinitz says that on the day of the shooting Williams threatened again his life. After he found Treitel wounded in his room, Steinitz cried "Murder" from his stoops, front and rear. At the front door Williams stood guard with the gun and threatened to shoot him unless he kept quiet. The gun was empty, and Steinitz knew it, but the threat was not the less terrifying.

Williams is about five feet in height, and his appearance is as mild as a June day. But according to Steinitz's excitable imagination his ex-secretary lives on hate. His breath is flame and slaughter, and he threatens murder with every respiration. The chess player is afraid for his life, even when Williams's bloodthirsty spirit is curbed by the stout steel of Newark jail, and he believes that if the Englishman is released he himself will be in instant and constant danger of portentous fate.

Williams claimed the shooting of Treitel was nothing but an accident. The trial continued on the last day of November and a report in the *Sun* of December 1 summarized the proceedings. Once again, the writer made his audience supremely aware of the absurd as well as the ironic twists embedded in the affair:

WILLIAMS AND TREITEL HELD

The One for Doing the Shooting and the Other as a Witness

Another move in the war of the chess players was made yesterday, when Nathaniel Williams, charged with atrocious assault on Ernest Treitel, was examined before Justice Milligan at Montclair. William Steinitz, the champion of the world, assisted at the maneuvers, and was a more interesting figure than either of the principals.

But as a witness his tactics were not those of a champion. His testimony differed in such important features from that given by the other witness for the State that Williams's counsel has little apprehension that the Grand Jury will find an indictment against the great chess player's former secretary.

When it was discovered several years ago that Montclair needed a Police Headquarters, somebody built a shed in the rear of the hose company's building in Main street and divided it into two small rooms by a flimsy wooden wall. In one of these Justice Mulligan [*sic*] holds court. In the other are two iron cages and a stove with a capacity for heating that no one would suspect from its modest appearance. In the Justice's room are a desk, three clocks, and a cot. There are also two chairs, one of which his Honor occupies during business hours, and another for the witness while he is testifying. At other times witnesses, lawyers, officers and spectators all sit on the cot.

Both iron cages were occupied yesterday at 3 o'clock, the hour appointed for Williams's examination. In one of them was Ernest Treitel, detained as a witness, and in the other sat Williams smoking a cigar. A few minutes after 2 Steinitz hobbled in on two canes, and a quarter of an hour later the Justice arrived. All hands crowded into his room. Treitel got the witness chair, and the others, including Williams, found places on the cot. Treitel, who left the Mountainside Hospital on Tuesday, appeared very faint and nervous as he began his testimony. Toward the end he recovered, and before he concluded a pleasant atmosphere of amiability pervaded the room, caused by defendant Williams, who produced a box of candy and passed it along the cot. Most of the onlookers crunched in unison during the rest of the examination. Before Treitel began to testify Williams's counsel requested that the other witnesses for the State be required to leave the room while Treitel was on the stand. This meant Steinitz, who was the only other witness. So the champion was compelled to go out and sit in one of the cages. Treitel testified that he was awakened at 7 o'clock on the morning of Nov. 4 by a blow to the head. He never gets up until 10, so the blow startled him. He opened his eyes and saw Williams at the head of his bed with a gun.

"I'm going to shoot you," said Williams.

"All right," answered Treitel: "I can't help it."

Treitel said that Williams then shot him and he felt a pain in his left hand. His sleeve and the bedclothes were burning. He got up to look for Steinitz, and Williams passed into the kitchen. Treitel said he found Steinitz in the front hall. He asked Steinitz to go for a physician, but the chess player said that nobody could leave the house as Williams was standing in front of the door with a gun threatening to destroy the first person who left the house.

When Treitel finished Steinitz was called in. He first enquired of the Court how long the proceedings would last.

"I have a cab at the door," he said, "and he charges by time."

He was assured that the examination would soon conclude, and took the witness chair. He told the story of the assault, beginning with a little game of pinochle between himself and Treitel. Williams twice interrupted the game, he said, by sweeping the cards to the floor and addressing the players by names which Steinitz characterized as "real bad." He said that after the shooting he found Treitel in bed. His story differed from Treitel's in other points. Steinitz admitted that he had once assaulted Williams and still owed him money.

Dr. Oliver Soper of Upper Montclair, who attended Treitel, testified as to the nature of his injuries and the statement that Williams made to him at the time. Williams said that a gun had exploded and he didn't know that it was loaded. E.B. Gould, a New York lawyer, residing in Montclair, appeared for Williams. Justice Milligan held Treitel as a witness and Williams to wait the action of the Grand Jury in default of $10,000 bail.

The most puzzled man in New Jersey yesterday was Treitel. He has lost an arm in the embroglio, and now finds himself locked up for ten days, until the Grand Jury meets again. He can't understand it.

Another report in the *New York Sun* summarized the court proceedings from January 5, 1893. According to this report, published on January 6, Williams's defense argued that Williams intended only to pass through Treitel's room on his way out to his hunting session. Treitel tried to chase him out and grabbed his gun. In the struggle that ensued the gun discharged and wounded Treitel. Anna Dietrich, a housekeeper in Steinitz's house, testified that Treitel himself confessed to her the shooting was accidental. The newspaper report also mentioned that Steinitz testified again, but did not specify as to what effect. However, according to a detailed account of this court session, appearing in the *Montclair Times* of January 7, 1893, Steinitz refused to be sworn in prior to his testimony.[8]

---

8. Landsberger wrote the following about Steinitz's refusal to be sworn in on pages 275–276 of his *William Steinitz, Chess Champion*: "Court records still exist, but since no detailed records were kept, no further information could be gained. It is interesting that Steinitz refused to be sworn in. Authorities with the New Jersey court system offered the opinion that this was probably due to the wording of the oath of that time."

In the weeks that followed, and despite the confusion regarding the publicized facts, Williams was found guilty of "assault and battery, with intent to kill." His counsel made argument for a new trial and the judge's decision on this request was to be announced in mid–March 1893. In early March of that year, according to several New York newspaper reports, Treitel died "from scarlet fever while under treatment at Bellevue Hospital." Although Treitel's death wasn't directly related to the shooting, certainly sympathy for his plight was on the mind of the men most directly responsible for Williams's fate. On March 13, and with Treitel's death now known, Williams was sentenced to five years' imprisonment.

None of the newspaper reports mention Pollock as a trial witness. If Lee was at least correct that Pollock's fallout with Steinitz in the autumn of 1892 was due to their differences regarding the Williams trial testimonies, then at least if nothing else can be said, Pollock's position must have in some fashion disagreed with, or failed to back up, Steinitz's version of the facts. We likely will never know precisely what the two chess players disagreed on, but at least Pollock seems to have avoided any public stain from this affair being attached to his name, regardless of how bad were relations between him and the chess champion of the world. This did not, however, free him from private vilification by Steinitz, who in writing another chess player in passing referred to the "black ingratitude and daily hostility of the drunken Pollock" as among his woes, while attempting to explain two years later the loss of his title to Lasker.[9] This is the only reference appearing in the record of any suggestion Pollock might have had trouble handling alcohol. Its worth can be weighed in light of its source, and the absence of any other public record of such a condition. Pollock, as far as is known, never referred to either the shooting or his falling out with the aging champion.

An Encounter with Lasker

Pollock's whereabouts in November 1892 are not entirely clear. It appears he returned to Baltimore only at the end of that month, when he met Emanuel Lasker over the board. In mid–November, the members of the Baltimore Chess Association held a meeting to discuss how to invite Lasker to visit Baltimore and play "a short match" with Pollock in the process. The November 16 issue of the *Sunday News* announced that Lasker's visit to Baltimore was to take place beginning November 28, and it was arranged the German master would give a series of exhibitions in the city. "No chess player in Baltimore should miss the opportunity of seeing, and if possible, playing against him," the column read. Lasker arrived in Baltimore as announced, while the local chess column the day before stated that "Mr. Pollock will pay us a flying visit during the week. For him to be absent would be similar to playing 'Hamlet' with the king left out." Whether

---

9. Steinitz's animosity toward Pollock seems to have been lasting. In a letter to Walter Penn Shipley over a year and a half later (and dated June 23, 1894), Steinitz wrote: "My private life has been an unhappy one and I have never been in good health since about 1875. The last two years have however been exceptionally unfortunate and especially the murder (virtually) committed in my house soon after my wife's death the narrow escape which I had with my own life the black ingratitude and daily hostility of drunken Pollock whom I had treated like a brother the loss of *The Tribune* and other troubles had so affected me that as my friends well know and as Lasker was well aware of I could not concentrate my attention fully on the game for any length of time." [Extract from the full letter published in *The Steinitz Papers*, pages 187–189.] Steinitz's libel of Pollock was but one link in a chain of explanations for his failure against Lasker in their then recent 1894 title match. Earlier in the same letter Steinitz had categorically asserted that "I consider it clearly *proven beyond a doubt* just from the match on record that my former best play would have been sufficient to beat Lasker by about *10 to 2 or 3* and some draws" (page 188; emphasis in the original).

Pollock was still living with Steinitz in New Jersey as late as the end of November or not, he apparently had been away from Baltimore for some time.

On the evening of November 28, Lasker gave a 24-board simultaneous exhibition at the Baltimore Chess Association. The next day, after asking to be excused from giving a planned blindfold performance, Lasker conducted an exhibition game against Pollock. Curiously enough, the star of the hour was willing to play the one game blindfolded, if his opponent was as well. The Maryland *Sun* of November 30 described the encounter as follows:

> Mr. W.H.K. Pollock played a "blindfold" game of chess with Emanuel Lasker at the rooms of the Baltimore Association last night, and after a contest of over two hours resigned the game to Mr. Lasker on the forty-second move. The eyes of the two players were not blindfolded. Mr. Lasker seated himself before a window in the rear of the building, while Mr. Pollock faced a bare wall. In the other end of the room the members of the association followed the play by means of board and chess men.

Emanuel Lasker in 1892 (*Records of the Copyright Office of the Stationers' Company, July–September 1892*; photograph by Frederick Thomas Downey).

Lasker–Pollock
Baltimore Chess Association
Double Blindfold Game,
November 29, 1892

Black to move

Here Pollock went astray with **28. ... Bd4?!**, a move that made Lasker's task infinitely easier after **29. B×d4 R×d4 30. Rh1 b5? 31. Rh7** and the German won. With 28. ... Kd8!? Pollock had a good chance to maintain the balance.

The *New York Sun* of December 1, 1892, reported:

> Tonight the members of the [Baltimore] club were treated to a novelty by Lasker encountering Maryland's champion, William H.K. Pollock, both playing without seeing board and men. A large crowd watched the progress of the game with interest, and when at the end of the party a veritable race ensued between the opposite pawns to be first at queening the crowd was wild with excitement. Lasker's final maneuver, especially the intended sacrifice of his queen, brought forth a volley of applause.[10]

---

10. According to the Montreal *Morning Herald* of November 30, 1892: "The game which lasted two hours (with a 10-minute recess) was exciting as well as interesting. Lasker became confused at one time as to the position of his bishop, and had to be set aright by the tellers. Pollock, however, went straight through without a mistake, as far as his positions were concerned. Prof. D. Melamet was teller for Lasker, and Mr. William E. Arnold for Pollock."

The next day, Lasker won 6 games against 14 players in consultation (with Pollock consulting on the first board) and played various games against a dozen club players.[11] He won them all. At least in this instance, unlike earlier in the year when forced to take a board alone against Chigorin in Brooklyn, Pollock limited his role, and his reputation's exposure, to participating with a group.

Once Lasker moved on to his next club engagement, Pollock remained in Baltimore much preoccupied with local chess matters. On December 23, he was invited to give a simultaneous and blindfold exhibitions in Hagerstown, Maryland, 60 miles northwest of Baltimore. Pollock's record for his exhibitions in the "Hub City" was remarkable: out of 30 games played, regardless of the kind of exhibition, he lost none. His presence among the chess fans in Hagerstown prompted the latter to form "the first regular chess club ever organized in the State outside of Baltimore." In late January a club was indeed founded with 13 initial members. It was fittingly called "The Pollock Chess Club of Hagerstown," with J.B. Taylor as its elected president and Justus Scheffer as vice-president. "The title," wrote the editor of the January 29, 1893, column in the *Baltimore Sunday News*, "though highly complimentary to Mr. W.H.K. Pollock, is not wholly flattering or nonsignificant, as the 'Maryland Chess champion,' who represents his State dutifully, had a hand in promoting this, the first chess club in Maryland outside of Baltimore, and is besides chess editor of the journal which is the official organ of the Maryland Chess Association."

This may have been a very fitting end for a very busy and possibly uncomfortable 1892 for Pollock. The following year would bring yet more personal changes in his life.

---

11. From the *New York Sun* of December 2, 1892: "The German surprised the chess community by performing another astounding feat, which has not been tried heretofore. Last night he encountered fourteen of the strongest Baltimore players who consulted against the visitor on six boards. The leading spirits at the single table were: Pollock, the champion of Maryland, Ireland, and Brooklyn; Hall, who distinguished himself in several tournaments of the United States Chess Association; Uhthoff, and the veteran Major Venable. Notwithstanding this array of talent, Lasker made a clean sweep, winning all six games after a great battle." Lasker's visit inspired some in the Baltimore chess fraternity to have similar arrangements with Pollock. From the December 18 edition of the *Baltimore Sunday News*: "We fail to see why the Baltimore Chess Association should not, with a good membership roll and annual dues of $10, eight times as high as that of the London clubs, try the experiment of instituting a series of match games between any member desirous of improving their game and Mr. Pollock. The contest might be conducted on the same lines as Mr. Lasker's at the Manhattan Chess Club. The games should be on even terms, the first move alternating. Played at fixed hours and with a fixed time-limit. The games could be analysed subsequently with great advantage. A prize might be offered for those making the best score at the end of say a month. That brilliant and instructive parties would result goes without saying—likewise that not a few of our local amateurs would find their strength on strength increased in a way that would surprise the oldest of them." The plan apparently did not come to fruition.

10. Moving Up North, January–August 1893

"Acquisition of New Ideas"

The heavily advertised plans for a Columbian Chess Congress, first suggested for 1892 and then shifted to 1893, first suggested for Chicago and then shifted to New York, in connection with the World's Fair commemorating the 400th anniversary of Columbus's arrival in the New World drew the attention of a number of European and American chess experts. The very last issue of Lasker's *London Chess Fortnightly*, dated July 30, 1893, indicated the congress would begin September 25, 1893, "or at the latest early in October."

That no location was mentioned should have been taken as a warning. Any number of international players were expected, at least on rumor, including the likes of Blackburne, Mason, Albin, Marco, Weiss, Chigorin, Tarrasch and Lasker, not to mention the usual American players, which in the *Fortnightly's* brief communication included Pollock. The vague notion that such a glittering array of chess personalities would assemble at an unspecified location at a not fully specified time might have been taken as another warning. A third warning might have been seen in the single paragraph devoted to the matter. While some only contemplated crossing the water for a hefty money-prize, guaranteed, others actually sailed for the New World before the congress plans were confirmed.

Accordingly, Lasker and Steinitz were joined in the greater New York metropolitan area by a number of other, lesser, European-based masters throughout the spring and summer of 1893. What happened to the Columbian Chess Congress will be discussed in detail in the next chapter. For now, though, it is sufficient to note that Pollock, while following the developments on this project, more realistically began play in a local handicap tournament of the Baltimore Chess Association in February 1893. Then he embarked on a brief tour to the North, including Canada. In the *Sunday News* of April 1, he called it somewhat mysteriously "a tour of acquisition of new ideas."

During the first week of March, Pollock traveled to Pittsburg, where he was the guest of the Allegheny Chess Club on the evening of March 9. On Thursday, March 10, he gave a 12-board simultaneous exhibition at the Pittsburg Library (9–2, with 1 draw), followed by a 14-board simultaneous on the following day (11–2, with 1 draw). On Saturday, March 12, Pollock gave a four-board blindfold simultaneous performance (3–1).[1]

---

1. Regarding this blindfold simultaneous exhibition, the *Sunday News* of March 18 wrote: "One of the games was little more than an old familiar catch. The moves ran thus: **1. e4 Nc6 2. d4 d6 3. Nf3 e5 4. Bc4 Bg4 5. Nc3 N×d4 6. N×e5 B×d1** and White gave mate in two moves. The other games were well contested, boards 2 and 3 holding out for rather over two hours."

Then, via the Lake Shore route, he was off to Buffalo, New York's Queen City, where he was engaged for a week by the Buffalo Chess Club. His play here lasted throughout the week of March 13–18. He played games against the top players at the club: George C. Farnsworth, T.N. Wilcox, James A. Congdon, George H. Thornton, S. Langleben, and Henry E. Perrine.

Against the last named, he created one of his typical entertaining samples:

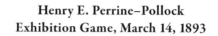

Henry E. Perrine–Pollock
Exhibition Game, March 14, 1893

White to play

According to the *Buffalo Morning News* of March 15, Perrine played **23. f4** and Pollock replied with **23. ... e×f3** but after **24. Q×g6**, Pollock shocked his opponent with an unusual retort: **24. ... f×e2!?** The game, called by the local columnist, "one of the most brilliant played in Buffalo," continued with **25. Qb1 Bc4?** (Far more precise was 25. ... e×f1N+! 26. R×f1 Rde8.) **26. Rg1?** (Perrine missed the spectacular 26. R×f6 R×f6 27. Re1 Rf2 28. Kg3 Rdf8 29. Qc2 Rf1 30. R×e2 with clear winning chances.) **26. ... e×d1Q 27. Q×d1 Ne4 28. Qc2 Bd5 29. Nf3 Rf6 30. Qb2 Rdf8 31. Qd4 a6 32. Rb1 h6 33. Rb2 Kh7 34. Qd1 g6 35. Qd4 h5 36. Qe5 d6 37. Qd4 g5** and eventually Pollock won.

Pollock also gave simultaneous exhibitions, a blindfold séance and games-at-odds against local players. The following description of his first simultaneous exhibition appeared in the *Buffalo Morning Express* of March 14:

BATTLING AT CHESS

Dr. W.H.K. Pollock Defeats 21 Out of 22 Players in Simultaneous Games

Dr. W.H.K. Pollock, one of the most noted and most scientific chess players in this country, opened a series of games at the Chess Club yesterday afternoon at 1:30 o'clock. Mr. G.C. Farnsworth of this city was his first opponent, and at 3:30 o'clock, after two hours of hard battle, the game was adjourned unfinished, honors easy. Mr. T.N. Wilcox, Dr. Pollock's next contestant, withdrew from the struggle after the 19th move, having been checkmated in less than an hour.

Last evening at 7:30 o'clock 22 games were started, and Dr. Pollock played them all simultaneously. His method of playing is very fascinating. He moves along the line of chess tables, smoking a cigar and pauses before one of the players. After surveying the board for a few moments, he suddenly makes his move, and after one last look at the table, as if to impress upon his memory the position of every piece, he moves on to the next table. [...]

Dr. Pollock won 21 out of the 22 games.

Pollock's blindfold simultaneous exhibition at five boards on March 16 was exuberantly, if not particularly accurately regarding the quality of the result, described thusly in the *Buffalo Morning Express* of March 17:

PLAYING CHESS BLINDFOLDED

DR. POLLOCK TRIED FIVE GAMES THUS ALL AT ONCE—HE WON TWO OF THEM

Dr. Pollock played five simultaneous games of chess blindfolded last night at the Chess Club and won two of them. This is one of the best records ever made in the city of Buffalo, and among the best, it is said, ever made anywhere. He sat in a corner of a darkened room facing the wall and the tables were in the two rooms beyond. He used no notes, and kept all the moves made and each table separate in his memory and still won two out of five games. When it is remembered that there are 64 squares and 32 men on each board and that there were five of these, it will be seen that this was no ordinary feat. His opponents were Urban Broughton and George Sickels, who lost, and G.B. Pierce, A.B. Kellogg and L.G. Sellstedt, who won. The contest lasted about two hours, and was witnessed by a large number of men and women.

The *Buffalo Courier* of March 19, 1893, gave further insights and a Pollock interview in regard to his presence in Buffalo in early March 1893. The journalist, after erring on Pollock's roots in a brief summary of his career ("Pollock is of Scotch descent") reported:

[...] Dr. Pollock in the course of his talk with the COURIER writer said that he was a very bad hand at most other games, but plays to some extent cricket, the piano-forte, checkers, billiards, and baseball. He has performed in the leading cities of America and in London, Hamburg, Amsterdam, Nottingham, Hereford, Belfast, and Dublin. Dr. Pollock said that he was no great scorer in large tournaments of the highest caliber, as a rule, though in the days of Zukertort, Gunsberg, Blackburne, Mason, and Bird from 1887 to 1889 he ranked as about the fourth best player in London. Dr. Pollock had a hand in the founding of the first chess club organized in Maryland, outside of Baltimore, at Hagerstown. It is called the "Pollock Chess Club."

As to his style as a player he is known as the "Brilliancy Master" in some circles. He plays all sort of openings, but only recollects adopting the Ruy Lopez attack once in his life, except in connection with the Four Knights Opening. He is partial to the Evans Gambit, Ponziani Opening, 1. f4, or Bird's, or the Dutch Opening, Vienna or Queen's Knight Opening, Giuoco Piano in its 12 forms, such as Max Lange's Attack, the Four Knights Opening and the Two Knights Defense.

He is somewhat of a problemist and a great friend and admirer of Loyd, Shinkman, Babson, Wainwright, Gilberg, Teed, and other great American composers.

"What do you think of the Buffalo Chess Club" the writer asked.

"It is about the best organized club," was the reply, "has the nicest rooms, and one of the largest memberships of any club outside of New York City. The six leading players of Buffalo, Messrs. Farnsworth, Congdon, Langleben, Thornton, Perrine, and Wilcox are brilliant amateur players, and I think that some who are not ranked with these six play equally well. If I had any criticisms to make I should say that one or two of the gentlemen are rather rash in their playing at times."

"What nationality do you rank as the leading one in the art of chess playing, Doctor?"

"I consider the Germans to be the best chess players in the world, and naturally so, for they spend much time in that occupation, and they have what they call the café system, which, to explain, means that they play the game over their coffee."

"Yes, I like Buffalo immensely; its climate suits me very well, and it is possible I may stay here permanently if I can make certain necessary business arrangements."

Yesterday afternoon and evening Dr. Pollock made his last appearance at the headquarters of the Chess Club. (...)

The members of the Club as a body express themselves as much gratified with the tournament, and as particularly pleased with Dr. Pollock. His style of playing is much admired, and his manner is unassuming and courteous. He is characterized as playing with great brilliancy and variety of style, the beauty of the combinations with which he terminates his games being a revelation to all his opponents. From this city he will go to Montreal where he has an engagement for a short time.

Pollock himself summarized his sojourn in the *Baltimore Sunday News*, March 25:

CHESS IN BUFFALO

The Buffalo programme which we printed last week was strictly carried out. The result proved the wisdom of a good business arrangement, and everything was pleasant to the visitor and the club. The ladies' night was a pleasing episode. Dr. Pollock contested 63 games winning 48 during the week, losing nine, with four unfinished.

The concluding event was the unanimous election of Dr. Pollock as an honorary member of the club. Many happy speeches were made and the doctor responded with modesty. He is the first gentleman who has received this compliment from the club. The arrangements were splendidly carried out by Mr. G.C. Farnsworth and Gen. Congdon.

A Brief Montreal Visit

Following his stay in Buffalo, Pollock traveled the 380 miles northeast to Montreal, Canada. He arrived in Montreal in the last week of March and was the guest of Joseph Ney Babson, the well-known Canadian problem composer, at the Windsor Hotel. The visit was billed as "of a social nature" without a formal engagement by the club.[2] Despite this, Pollock played some offhand games against some of the leading players and also gave some exhibitions at the Montreal Chess Club, including a blindfold performance at the French-Canadian Chess and Checker Club on March 29 "before a numerous and enthusiastic audience."[3]

Joseph Ney Babson, a notable problemist and columnist in Montreal, Canada (John G. White Chess and Checkers Collections, Cleveland Public Library).

During his play in Montreal, Pollock met Frank James Marshall, the future United States champion. Although Marshall and his family were United States citizens, Marshall himself having been born in New York City on August 10, 1877, by 1885 the family had moved to Montreal, where they lived for the next eleven or so years. The Montreal-raised American was only 15 when Pollock met him, but he had been visiting coffee houses for chess play and other events for the past four or more years. Pollock was not unaware of the young man's promise. According to Babson's April 22 column in the *Montreal Daily Herald*, Pollock said the following about Marshall: "That young lad makes some astonishingly fine moves."[4]

Two incidents marred Pollock's visit in Montreal, as he reported to his Baltimore readers

---

2. Joseph Ney Babson (1852–1929) was the chess editor of the *Montreal Daily Herald* in the early 1890s. He was also a notable problem composer and was instrumental in arranging the Montreal leg of the 1894 Steinitz–Lasker world championship match. See *American Chess Bulletin*, December 1909, page 275 and March 1930, page 59. • 3. According to the *Baltimore Sunday News* of April 8, 1893, among his opponents were J. Robertson, J.N. Babson, R. Fleming, R. Short and Cook, "each of whom taxed Mr. Pollock's skill severely before he could score a majority of games." Another relevant fragment about Pollock's time in Montreal (and especially with Babson) comes from the May 13, 1893, issue of the same newspaper: "The Pollock Chess Club (Hagerstown, Md.) held a special meeting on the 5th inst., Mr. J.B. Taylor and Prof. R. Wallis respectively resigned as president and vice-president, Prof. J. Scheffer and Mr. W.R. Hamilton took Prof. Scheffer's place as secretary. A letter from W.H.K. Pollock of Baltimore, says the *Hagerstown Daily Mail*, presenting a photograph of himself and J.N. Babson of Montreal, was read, and Professor Wallis kindly offered to have the picture framed for the club." • 4. *Montreal Daily Herald*, April 22, 1893. See also *Young Marshall: The Early Chess Career of Frank Marshall, with Collected Games 1893–1900*, by John S. Hilbert (Moravian Chess, 2002), page 7.

Members of the Canadian Chess Association, Montreal 1889. Sitting (left to right): J. Nolan, J. Henderson, J. Barry, H.A. Howe, J.G. Ascher (half-seated), Prof. Hicks, R.G. Hutchison. Standing: T. Taylor, R. Short, M. St. John, J.P. Cooke, J.W. Shaw, G.M. Liddell, J.R. Robertson, J.E. Narraway (McCord Museum Archives).

in the April 8 edition of his column. Both were violent in nature, with the second one taking place near Pollock's hotel, as he reported in his April 8 *Baltimore Sunday News* column:

> Two grave misfortunes marred the otherwise unalloyed pleasure of our visit to Montreal. One was the total demolition by fire of the Herald office—for the fourth time—which occurred on the evening of 27th ult. and which temporarily deprives us of Mr. Babson's entertaining chess column in that paper. The second was an accident of a sadder nature, which took place later in the week. Mr. St. John, one of the most genial gentlemen of a genial chess circle, who had only the day before joined us in a couple of consultation games, was returning home in company with his wife. A passing electric car obscured a runaway tram, close by the Windsor Hotel, and, while Mr. St. John miraculously escaped injury, Mrs. St. John was knocked down and instantly killed. Mr. St. John is widely known and respected in Canadian chess circles and the event cast quite a gloom over Montreal.

Part of Pollock's appeal as a chess journalist was his ability to incorporate such instances, important to the local chess community and of interest to a broader circle of readers as well. And readers were not long deprived of Babson's "entertaining chess column." On April 15, 1893, only a week after Pollock's remarks were printed in Baltimore, Babson wrote the following in his *Montreal Herald* column about Pollock's visit to the Canadian city:

> After a ten days' pleasant sojourn in Montreal, Dr. Pollock left on Tuesday last for Albany, where he was booked to give exhibitions on Thursday and Friday. During his visit here the Doctor enlivened our chess circles by numerous exhibitions of simultaneous play, both with and without sight of the board. On Wednesday evening of last week, he displayed his remarkable powers of memory in blindfold play by successfully carrying through six games simultaneously, though the adjoining room seemed to be a perfect pandemonium, and this too, notwithstanding that the moves were irregularly incorrectly called by the teller. The Doctor is a genial good hearted fellow, and

won the hearts of all who had the pleasure of meeting him and it is hoped that at no distant day our local players may have the pleasure of seeing him again in this city.

Down to Albany

After leaving Montreal, Pollock spent a few days at Saratoga Springs, New York, on his way to Albany, the capital of New York. He played no games at this resort, but he took advantage of the renowned baths and relaxed thoroughly. He arrived in Albany on April 6 where he spent three days at the Albany Chess Club playing 26 official games (finishing 19–4, with 3 draws). Pollock's total included six blindfolded games, five of them played simultaneously on April 8 against a team stronger than the one met in Buffalo, according to Pollock's own admission in his *Sunday News* column. This was followed by a 15-board simultaneous (11–1, with 3 draws), Howard J. Rogers being the only winner against the master. Pollock enjoyed his time in Albany and it appears he liked Rogers and the city. In fact, he liked what he found very, very much. He also found himself confronted by some fairly new technology, as will be seen. This is what Pollock wrote in his April 15, 1893, column in the *Baltimore Sunday News*:

W.H.K. Pollock with Joseph Ney Babson, with a dedication to James D. Séguin (John G. White Chess and Checkers Collections, Cleveland Public Library).

Professor Rogers, while being president of the New York State Chess Association and chess editor of the *Albany Journal*, the official organ of that body, is, with Prof. Deyo, the leading Albany player. He will not find it easy to obtain an efficient substitute in these capacities during his absence in Chicago, for which city he has already left. Professor Rogers holds the high office of manager of the education exhibit for the State of New York at the [Columbian] exposition. One of the most pleasant features of our Albany visit was a "phonographic concert" given by the Professor at his office in the Capitol. He is busy collecting some hundreds of choruses, glees and solos, vocal and instrumental, from the various educational centers for reproduction by phonograph at the World's Fair. Perhaps the most striking and distinct of those we heard was a vocal exercise by children of 5 years at Syracuse. The teacher at one stage asks the little chorus if they sang rather difficult passages well, and the infants all reply, "No, Sir!" Then they try it again. And all this reproduced by an instrument, from a wax cylinder, anywhere and at any time!

In return, his friends from Albany wrote the following in the *Albany Evening Journal* of April 15: "The Albany Chess Club had a delightful visit from Dr. W.H.K. Pollock last week. His games were lively and entertaining and his genial manner and freedom from affectation won him many friends."

While back in Baltimore, Pollock was eager for a match against Walbrodt. According to Steinitz in the *New York Tribune* of April 16, "A proposition from Mr. Pollock to play a short match with Herr Walbrodt has been accepted by the latter provided all details can be arranged satisfactorily. Walbrodt wishes to play the match at Baltimore during the week following his engagement." Unfortunately, the match never took place, as Walbrodt was busy in New York and never visited Baltimore before leaving America.

Pollock also seems to have been instrumental in suggesting the formation of a second chess club in Baltimore. A coterie of players, mainly those who desired to meet more than once a week, as provided for by

Howard J. Rogers (1861–1927), one of Pollock's closest associates and friends in Albany, New York (photogravure from a photograph as appeared in the *International Congress of Arts and Science*, edited by H.J. Rogers, St. Louis: University Alliance, 1904, Vol. 1).

the Baltimore Chess Association, met at Charles Schneider's German café on Eutaw Street on the evening of April 22. Pollock was elected secretary of the new establishment.

But an important change was about to sweep through Pollock's life. Despite leading the Baltimore team in May to victory against the Washington Chess, Checker and Whist Club, and despite his many activities on behalf of the city's chess players in general, Pollock was looking for a more vibrant chess scene. Baltimore, as pleasant as it was for the master, was limited in what it could offer a strong player still interested in improving his game. Pollock often felt the urge to make changes in his life, including his giving up a career in medicine and his decision to stay in America after New York 1889. Perhaps, too, the growing number of foreign masters making their presence felt in the New York area suggested to Pollock a change was in order. In addition, if one is to believe G.H.D. Gossip, there was another, much more mundane but no less pressing reason for Pollock's departure from Baltimore. At the time, according to an article by Gossip in *Frank's Leslie's Popular Monthly* (July–December 1894 volume, page 250), Pollock was employed in the central freight office of the Baltimore and Ohio Railroad Company as a statement clerk. Gossip concluded Pollock left Baltimore "on account of the lowness of his salary."

This one reference to Pollock's occupation as a railroad statement clerk tells us as much as we need to know about the plight of a quasi-professional chess player in America in the 1890s. The same easily applies to almost any decade in the United States. Chess players had to find other work to make a living. They may have lived for chess, but they paid the bills as bank employees (Delmar), nursing home administrators (Hodges), printers (Lipschütz), or railroad clerks (Pollock, and also Kemény). In only very rare instances were American-based masters free to follow their muse exclusively. Showalter could do so largely because of his family's ranching and farming interests, while Steinitz and later, Pillsbury, were still poorly paid exceptions to this very cruel rule. Whatever the precise details, Pollock's leaving Baltimore was certainly in part fueled by his desire to improve his situation.

That he improved his circumstances only marginally was made known almost in passing several years later in a letter penned by Pollock's key contact in Albany, Howard J. Rogers. The latter would recall his encounter with Pollock when the master visited Albany:

> [...] In the early spring of 1893, my duties as Superintendent of New York's Educational Exhibit at the Chicago Exposition took me to that city for eight months. I proposed to Pollock that he come to Albany, take charge of my chess column in the *Albany Evening Journal*, and try life in the North for a time. His letters to me had shown a desire to leave Baltimore, and during a professional tour the winter previous he made Albany a visit, liked the city, and made a great hit with our chess players. The year '93 I think was Pollock's most prosperous year in America. He edited both the *Baltimore News* and *Albany Journal* chess columns, and was also given a half-time assignment as reporter on the Journal staff. This combined, gave him a weekly income of about sixteen dollars. His life in Albany seemed very pleasant, and on my return from Chicago in November of that year, I found him established quite like an old resident[...].[5]

Sixteen dollars weekly, made up here and there from assorted part-time employment, was not a princely sum even in 1893. By one measure (and none take into account all the multiple variables involved), it amounts to roughly $450 a week in 2015 dollars.[6] Even for someone living alone today, such a sum would hardly produce a lavish lifestyle. For it to represent Pollock's "most prosperous year in America," as Rogers indicates, suggests something of how difficult Pollock must have found life in the New World.

Pollock left Baltimore for Albany in early June 1893. Indeed, he was still editing the chess column in the *Baltimore Sunday News* in parallel with his newer tasks in Albany. Following a blindfold simultaneous of four boards (3–1) and a 14-board simultaneous exhibition at the Baltimore Chess Association (11–2, with 1 draw), Pollock gave a 24-board simultaneous exhibition in Washington that lasted for five hours (21–2, with 1 draw).

Then, he was off to Albany. Although still not the heart of American chess culture, Albany represented a step toward that center and its two important wings (New York and Brooklyn, at the time still separate cities; flanked north and south by Boston and Philadelphia). It was Albany that Pollock represented in that year's edition of the New York State Chess Association's midsummer meeting held at Staten Island.

While there were plans for a potential match between Pollock and Pillsbury, the former was busy adapting in Albany and preparing for the midsummer meeting. Unfortunately, no match

---

5. Letter from H.J. Rogers to F.F. Rowland, January 17, 1898; cited in *Pollock Memories*, page 11. • **6.** Any estimate of money's relative worth has very limited value without extensive comparison to other factors, such as the relative cost of basic housing, food and clothing, or in terms of technology, how recently an improvement has been introduced, and whether it has become commonly available or not. (Consider, for instance, the scarcity and high cost and newly introduced presence of ballpoint pens in the mid–1940s compared to their cost today.) The estimate of Pollock's weekly salary's worth was calculated using data from www.measuringworth.com/ppowerus/.

with Pillsbury ever took place, as interesting as it likely would have been. Although Pillsbury was not yet the Pillsbury of Hastings 1895, he was a very strong player and it would have been interesting to see how Pollock's style matched up in individual play with the 20-year-old Bostonian.[7]

NYSCA Midsummer Meeting

The NYSCA midsummer meeting was held August 7–12. Unlike earlier midsummer meetings, this one was held downstate, at Staten Island's Hotel St. George. Albert Hodges, then acting in place of Rogers for the Association and himself a Staten Island resident, had taken upon himself initiating this change in venue when time had grown short for preparing the event. In addition to the usual handicap tournament, there was a tournament for the silver cup presented by the *New Yorker Staats-Zeitung* (won by Hanham in 1891 and by Kemény in 1892). Besides Pollock, representing the Albany Chess Club, the following players signed up for the contest: Hanham (Manhattan Chess Club), Jacob Halpern (City Chess Club), Edward N. Olly (Brooklyn Chess Club) and Albert B. Hodges (Staten Island Chess Club).

The *Brooklyn Standard-Union* of August 5 noted Pollock's debut in this event, underlining that "if he be in form Albany has a good chance to hold the trophy during the next year." Pollock described the meeting as follows in his August 12, 1893, column in the *Albany Evening Journal*:

> The meeting is a very pleasant one, even if the surroundings are not so picturesque as at Skaneateles last year. Among the spectators on the opening day were S. Lipschütz, who is about to make a fresh trip, probably to Los Angeles, for the benefit of his lungs; veteran H. Frere [*sic*], E. Hoffmann, H. Cassel, C. Devide, F.G. Janusch, F. Rose, G.A. Barth of the *Staten Islander*, H. Schweitzer, and G. Holt, treasurer of the Manhattan Chess Club. Most of the players are old friends, and came from great distances.... Play at night proceeded in the cool and well-lighted roof gardens of the hotel, and some of the New York visitors indulged in games of cards in quiet corners. The main room for play is delightfully situated, overlooking the bay. The massive silver trophy was on view during the sessions, and created the usual admiring interest.

The double–round robin that commenced on August 8 proved a walkover (in Pollock's own words) for Hodges, who won the top prize with the score 6–0, with 2 draws, followed at great distance by Hanham and Olly, each with 3½–3½, and finally Halpern and Pollock, each with the depressing score of 2½–5½. (Hanham and Olly played only seven games, their second round game being found unnecessary, as neither man could catch Hodges.) Pollock was in surprisingly poor form in this particular event. The *Brooklyn Standard-Union* of August 12 published the following critique:

> Regarding the form displayed by the players the greatest disappointment is in the Albany representative, Mr. Pollock. He remarked that the reason for his poor score was his lack of practice with strong players. His games are beautiful, as usual, in parts; but as a whole they lack steadiness. He will require considerable practice to put him in shape to give him a chance for a prize in the Columbian tournament. Mr. Pollock seems in good physical condition, and, were it not for a seeming reluctance to train properly, he might have improved his score.

---

7. From the *New York Herald* of June 11, 1893: "The Irish champion chess player, [W.]H.K. Pollock has challenged Pillsbury, the champion of Boston, to play a match. There is every likelihood of these cracks meeting within the next few weeks." And from the *Baltimore Sunday News* of July 1, 1893: "A match between H.N. Pillsbury and W.H.K. Pollock has been bruited. Both are willing to play, but it is very unlikely that any meeting will be arranged between these players before they meet at the International Chess Congress, where Mr. Pillsbury will represent Boston in all probability. Mr. Pollock has his hands full at Albany, which city he will represent at the Staten Island tournaments August 7–12."

The *Standard-Union*'s assessment that Pollock had "a seeming reluctance to train properly" presupposes, of course, the opportunity to do so. That Pollock blamed his poor showing on lack of practice against strong opposition may well have merit, but Pollock's history of erratic performance despite his often acknowledged and impressive imaginative ability leaves reasonable room for a more complicated explanation. The move from Baltimore to Albany had taken Pollock out of the railroad clerks' office and put him into regular reporting work, if only part time, but work consistent with his editing two chess columns. His livelihood now was earned entirely with his pen, and his attention to the literary side of his life would have left less room for the energetic and all-consuming dedication to chess development he would have needed to reach another level in his play.

Consider, too, that he was already 34 years old. Even for the times, when many chess masters developed much later than they do today, this would have been a period in his life when the full fruits of earlier dedication would have been expected. Yet it had already been four years since New York 1889, Pollock's last international appearance. Had he made the decision to return to Europe soon after the Sixth American Chess Congress, he might have played at Breslau 1889 (as had, for instance, Blackburne and Mason, both present with Pollock at New York 1889), followed by Manchester 1890, London 1892, and Dresden 1892, to name just the most likely major events, let alone the constant play residence in a great chess center like London or Berlin would have afforded. That he had not returned, that he had turned aside from trying to earn his living fully from playing the game, was of course a decision he could place on no one other than himself.

A good sample of Pollock's aggressive tactical play comes from his encounter with Edward Olly:

Olly–Pollock
NYSCA Midsummer Meeting, August 1893

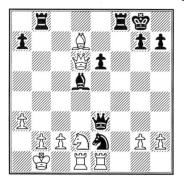

After 19. ... Bb7–d5

Olly proceeded **20. Nf1** to which Pollock no doubt calculated the possible 20. ... R×b2+ 21. K×b2 Qc3+ 22. Kb1 Ba2+ leading to a quick draw. Instead, he opted for **20. ... Qe4** and after **21. Qc5** (defending against Ne2–c3+) he essayed **21. ... Qe5!?**, threatening Bd5–a2+, encouraging White not to resist temptation to some obvious tactics: **22. B×e6+ Q×e6** and now Olly failed to exhibit accurate calculation: **23. Ne3?** (Instead, 23. R×d5! Nc3+ 24. Q×c3 Q×d5 25. Ne3 was White's lifeline.) **23. ... Rfc8!** and White collapsed quickly under Pollock's forceful offensive.

Pollock did play somewhat better in the handicap section, finishing second, behind a young Hermann Helms, but ahead of the 15-year-old Louis Karpinski and Major Hanham (Pollock defeated Hanham twice in the A class section). Among other illustrious spectators at Staten

Island were Lasker and Pollock's newly acquired detractor, Steinitz. The latter promised to give a simultaneous exhibition to those present but eventually denied them the pleasure claiming he was indisposed. He may well have been dwelling on the wrong done him regarding his *New York Tribune* column, the loss of which took place simultaneously with Staten Island 1893. At least this would have given the old master another target for his wrath than his onetime assistant. Pollock, whatever his personal difficulties with Steinitz, expressed nothing but regret for both Steinitz's and the chess world's loss of the *Tribune's* column.[8]

A few weeks after the Staten Island midsummer meeting ended in mid–August, word appeared that the fate of the planned Columbian Chess Congress was sealed: indefinite postponement meant cancellation and most of the chess players in America knew it by mid–September, although the news would apparently not reach Europe with any speed. The masters began looking for other engagements. Throughout August, before and after the NYSCA summer meeting, Pollock spent his time at Café Bondy, 49 Bowery Street in New York. Immediately after his play at Staten Island, Pollock entered a handicap tournament at the café, along with such relatively minor chess figures as Captain Pinkham, M. Lissner, W. Frère, Stephen G. Ruth and other players from the City and Brooklyn chess clubs.

The 25 players who eventually enlisted were divided into five classes, the fifth receiving rook odds from Pinkham, Lissner and Pollock, who represented the first class. "The second, third and fourth classes," wrote Pollock in his *Sunday News* column for August 26, 1893, "are particularly strong, probably as vigorous, keen and well-posted a gang as in the famous tournaments at Pursell's in London, and stronger than those receiving the odds in the divan handicaps." Such statements, accurate or not, could not but be well received by the men who played in the event.

At some point, Sobernheim was leading with 15 points out of 18 games, the best score, but he was forced to retire due to "persistent insomnia." That left the 23-year-old Hermann Helms in the lead with a score of 12–2 with 5 draws, followed by Pollock who, after a rough start, had won 20 of the 28 games he had played. By early September, Pollock had scored 27½ out of 36, and he received the $15 given to the second prize winner. Helms, who would in October 1893 start what became his famous chess column in the *Brooklyn Daily Eagle*, which with some interruption would continue until the *Eagle* closed more than 60 years later, in 1954, scored slightly better (32–8) and pocketed the $20 first prize.

Such café-based activities kept Pollock busy, but they certainly did not offer him any "proper training" for master-class encounters. Very soon thereafter, however, in mid–September 1893, the leading experts in the New World decided to take matters into their own hands and arrange for a tournament of their own. Pollock happily joined them.

---

8. Steinitz's column in the *New York Tribune* was discontinued on August 8, 1893, after his refusal to take a $5 deduction from his weekly salary. Although at the time of writing his column Pollock did not know the exact reasons for Steinitz's withdrawal from the *Tribune*, he was sympathetic to the world champion's decision. He wrote the following in the *Baltimore Sunday News* of August 12: "An editorial notice appeared in the *Tribune* of the 6th inst. to the effect that Mr. Steinitz would no longer be able to conduct the chess column in that paper. A well deserved tribute is paid to the champion's work and the opinion expressed that the discontinuance of his beautiful weekly chess studies will be widely regretted. No reason is given for this disaster to chess literature, but an impression prevails in New York that it is part of a plan to reduce expenses."

11. An Impromptu Misadventure, September–October 1893

"The collapse of the Columbian Chess Congress," the *Brooklyn Standard-Union* of September 20, 1893, wrote,

> owing to the inability of the committee to raise more than $2,800, has left several prominent European chess players in New York in an annoying position; they came to this country under heavy expense, and some of them will be in difficulty about returning. In order so that their trip shall have some result, a project was set under way last evening at the Manhattan Chess Club to arrange a tournament with prizes in proportion to the amount of money that can be raised.

Indeed, Adolf Albin, F.J. Lee, N. Jasnogrodsky, J. Taubenhaus, A. Schottländer and G.H.D. Gossip had been in New York since August or mid–September 1893, and they were terribly disappointed (and, some, shocked) by the cancellation of the Columbian Chess Congress. So were a number of other leading masters from Europe who contemplated crossing the Atlantic but eventually did not. Officials of the Brooklyn Chess Club joined ranks with those of the Manhattan Chess Club and gathered enough funds to at least offer a master-class tournament in New York to whet the appetite of these foreign masters as well as that of quite a number of local experts, ready to do battle at any time.

On September 19, a tournament committee was elected[1] and money was raised rather quickly: $300 was promised from newspapers, the Manhattan Chess Club subscribed $100, the Brooklyn Chess Club $50, and City Chess Club another $50. Individual subscriptions raised the total to $700, and there were men hopeful of raising it to $1,000. Among the players who expressed a clear interest in joining the event were Albin, Taubenhaus, Gossip, Lee, Showalter, Pollock, Hanham, J.W. Baird, D.G. Baird, Pillsbury, Delmar, Lipschütz, Amos Burn, J.S. Ryan and Kemény. Some of the foreign experts were busy either on the premises of the Manhattan or the Brooklyn chess clubs, engaged in short matches for stakes, or offering various

---

1. The tournament committee was the following: President, Charles A. Gilberg; Vice-president, A. Foster Higgins; Treasurer, George Holt; Secretary, F.G. Janusch; Associated with the committee were also J. Sabater, Wesley Bigelow, Dr. Broughton, M. Frankel, Dr. E.W. Dahl, H. Caswell, A. Vorrath, L. Goldmark, and J. Livingston. Charles Gilberg was instrumental in getting the loyalty and support of the foreign players between September 19 and September 30. And this he accomplished in part through entertaining them. For instance, in the week prior to the start of the event (when confirmation of players was still ongoing), Gilberg took some of his chess friends on an excursion down the bay and outside Sandy Hook, a few miles beyond the Scotland Lightship. Gilberg's boat passed by Staten Island on the way back to New York that same afternoon. Among the players (and some of their wives) on board were Emanuel Lasker, William de Visser, Hartwig Cassel, Major J. Moore Hanham, F.G. Janusch, and George Holl. Lasker played two games on board with de Visser (+1 =1) (*Brooklyn Daily Eagle*, September 20, 1893).

exhibitions.[2] Bringing them together in a tournament was not exactly a daunting task, especially with the prize fund creeping up to $800, with promises to increase it at least to $900, if not more.

The tournament was set to start on September 30 at the Manhattan Chess Club, and perhaps for understandable reasons, given its genesis, was dubbed the "impromptu tournament." The name stuck. The tournament was a single round, round-robin event, with the hours for play set for 2 to 6, and 7 to 9 p.m. The time limit was twenty moves an hour; the entrance fee, $10. Pollock, Pillsbury and Showalter telegraphed the playing committee that they would be on hand. They were joined by Lasker, Gossip, Olly, Jasnogrodsky, Louis Schmidt, Jr., Ryan, Taubenhaus, Hanham, Delmar, Lee and Albin. The playing hours were adjusted for Delmar and Ryan (to start at 4:00 instead of 2:00 p.m.) and Hodges made a similar request but for much later playing hours. Since it was impossible to accommodate him, Hodges didn't play. According to the October 7 column of the *Sunday News*, Pollock was disappointed that the tournament was not a double–round robin, as he considered himself such a slow starter that he was required "to lose four or five games before finding his gait." But he also expressed confidence that he would play some quality games and take a high place in the final crosstable.

The first round started on Saturday, September 30, but only six games were in progress.[3] The game between Pollock and Showalter, who had not arrived yet in New York, was rescheduled to be played on October 4. This is how the *Brooklyn Standard-Union* of October 2 summarized the tournament's opening:

> The games of the Impromptu International Tournament commenced at 2 p.m. on Saturday, in the presence of as large a gathering of local chess players as that of the Sixth American Chess Congress in 1889; the interest evinced by the spectators at the six boards was not less than that of the crowds which watched the games of that congress, and is an indication of the truth of the assertion that chess of a high class is as attractive to the amateur players of today as it ever was. The large mass of chess literature which has been published during the past five years has spread the game in this section more than ever before, the evidence of this being the large number of new faces seen at the chess gatherings. [...] Among the spectators were Charles A. Gilberg, W.M. de Visser, William Steinitz, S. Loyd, E. Hymes, winner of the Intercollegiate Chess Cup for Columbia College last winter, and Walter Frere.

The second round was played on Monday, October 2 and had Pollock pitted against Albin. "[Albin] is a player of the old school," Pollock described him for his readers of the October 7 *Sunday News*, "daring and chivalrous in attack. He is likely to win one of the five chief prizes,

---

2. One of the most active was Jasnogrodsky; he played several short matches against Albin and others in August 1893; in the week before the "Impromptu" tournament, he offered to play a 12-board simultaneous exhibition and a six-board blindfold exhibition at the same time at the Manhattan Chess Club. Pollock was right to be skeptical (*Baltimore Sunday News*, September 30, 1893: "Next Saturday N. Jasnogrodsky will give one of his haircurling performances. He will endeavour to play 14 men simultaneously, and six others sans voir at the same time. He might as well throw in a match with Steinitz too, for good luck"). The *Brooklyn Standard-Union* of September 25 reported Jasnogrodsky's troubles even if he downgraded his blindfold séance: "Mr. Jasnogrodsky, the Polish expert, gave an exhibition of simultaneous play over the board and blindfold playing at the Manhattan C.C. Saturday evening. He played twelve games over the boards and four blindfold. Of the sight games he won eight, lost two and drew two; the sans voire [*sic*] games were not a success; he made missplays and seemed not to be able to retain the positions clearly, even with the use of a board without pieces and notes in hieroglyphics. Mr. Jasnogrodsky won only one and lost three of the blindfold games." ● **3.** A brief description of the playing room comes from the *New York Recorder* of October 2, 1893: "The room in which the fight is going on is 'roped' for the occasion; that is, divided by a stretched rope into two parts, the public being allowed only on one side of the rope, the contestants being on the other. At a separate table the ever-hustling and untiring chess reporter, H. Cassel, reigns supreme, having Mr. S. Rocamora for assistant. They represent about a score of newspapers, in both English and German tongues. The *Recorder* and the Russian chess papers are represented by Mr. E.N. Olly."

being in excellent practice. He is an enthusiast and a great sitter, though somewhat fidgety. In his 79-move game with Taubenhaus, on Saturday, the latter was asked why he went on fighting a drawn position against the Austrian. 'Oh,' replied Taubenhaus, 'that amuses him.'" Against Albin, Pollock played excellent chess:

Albin–Pollock
October 2, 1893, New York
Impromptu Tournament, Round 2

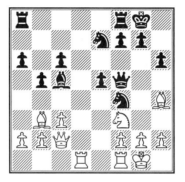

After 21. ... Qf6×f5

In the position above, Albin played **22. B×e7** only to be surprised by Pollock's typical ingenuity: instead of capturing the bishop with 22. ... B×e7, Pollock continued with **22. ... Qg4!?** Albin replied with **23. g3** perhaps hoping that Pollock would settle for a draw after **23. ... Nh3+ 24. Kg2 Nf4+ 25. Kg1 Nh3+ 26. Kg2 Nf4+ 27. Kg1**, but Pollock wanted more and went for **27. ... Q×f3! 28. g×f4 Qg4+ 29. Kh1 Qf3+ 30. Kg1 Qf3+ 31. Kh1 Qf3+ 32. Kg1 B×e7!** Profoundly unsettled by Pollock's resistance, Albin committed an error on the very next move, **33. Rd3?** (instead of the more powerful 33. f×e5), and Pollock went on to win in nearly a hundred moves. The game took six hours and eight minutes.

On Tuesday, October 3, Pollock was paired with Gossip for his third round. A player with a constellation of immigration stamps on his passport, Gossip was referred to by Pollock in the *Sunday News* as "Gossip of the Three Continents." Pollock also emphasized Gossip's literary output. The game was unconventional, as the *Brooklyn Standard-Union* observed on October 4:

Adolf Albin, circa 1896. The Romanian-born master shared with Pollock a similar appetite for dashing chess (John G. White Chess and Checkers Collections, Cleveland Public Library).

Nicolai Jasnogrodsky and Adolf Albin during the New York Impromptu tournament, 1893 (John G. White Chess and Checkers Collections, Cleveland Public Library).

Pollock and Gossip had a curious Evans Gambit declined, Pollock having the move; the game developed in an odd way, and was drawn by a continued attack on Gossip's Queen after twenty-three moves had been played. Mr. Pollock remarked later that he had a fear of Mr. Gossip; he couldn't play Mr. Gossip's style; Gossip defeated Pollock in both their games in the Sixth American Congress, though their positions in the final score were widely separated.[4]

Wednesday, October 4, was a rest day for the masters. Only Pollock and Showalter had to play out their postponed first round encounter. Having the move, Pollock's choice of opening was eccentric: **1. e4 e5 2. d3**. Perhaps he recognized his talented opponent was better versed in more conventional lines. He may have reached this conclusion following their earlier, informal match. In any case, the game was a hard fought draw in four hours and seven minutes. Thus, after three games played, Pollock had two points to his credit and was well placed for a good showing.

On Thursday, October 5, Pollock played his old antagonist, J. Moore Hanham. The two had known one another since the British Chess Association meeting in 1886, almost seven years earlier. "Major Hanham, another bearded veteran, will as usual give everybody a hard tussle,"

---

4. While offering this game score, the *New York Recorder* of October 7, 1893, noted: "Among the impromptu curiosities of the impromptu congress, the following game should be entitled to take the cake. Mr. P[ollock] says he was afraid of Mr. G[ossip]. What kind of feeling was predominant on the other side is unknown."

wrote Pollock in the *Sunday News*. "The Major seems to be the only non-smoker in the tournament, but he is also about the hardest man to tire out." In their encounter, Pollock made no attempt to tire out Hanham. He played an apathetic game and lost two pawns right after the opening, without any compensation. He acknowledged defeat at move 39.

On Friday, in the fifth round, Pollock played Ryan in what turned out to be a highly disappointing affair. After 26 moves in a Ponziani Opening, Pollock obtained the following, dominating position:

Pollock–Ryan
October 6, 1893, New York
Impromptu Tournament, Round 5

After 26. ... Bc4–e6

Pollock continued correctly for a time with **27. Ne7+ Kh8 28. d5!** (Stronger than 28. Ng6+ R×g6 29. Q×f8+ Kh7), but after **28. ... Re8**, he missed the brilliant 29. f×e6! R×e7 30. Q×e7! Q×e7 31. f×e7, with a simple win for White. Instead, Pollock played the inferior **29. d6**, allowed Ryan to sacrifice the exchange to release the pressure, and then blundered severely, allowing his queen to be trapped. The game lasted three hours and 48 minutes and was a complete collapse for the unfortunate Pollock, who thereby lost what easily could have been one of his cleanest wins in the tournament.

In round six, played on Saturday, October 7, Pollock met Delmar. Once again, Pollock's lack of staying power proved to be his major weakness. Following excellent opening play, he secured a decisive advantage only to collapse spectacularly in the following position:

Delmar–Pollock
October 7, 1893, New York
Impromptu Tournament, Round 6

After 30. Rg3–g4

W.H.K. Pollock (right) in New York, 1893; his opponent is unidentified (courtesy Martin Frère Hillyer).

Pollock continued with **30. ... R×c2** and still maintained a solid advantage before he reck-lessly allowed Delmar to win the g7-pawn with his heavy pieces. A closer study of the position above reveals how clean-cut Pollock's win would have been: 30. ... b3! 31. Rc4 Qa5 32. Qf3 Qa2 33. Qe3 b×c2 34. Qc1 Qb1 34. Rf×c2 Q×c1 35. R×c1 Rd7 and Black's two extra pawns are sufficient to earn the point. This was Pollock's third defeat in a row and his morale must have been quite low, especially given how erratic his play had been. Good positions were ruined by blunders, and it is hard to see how his confidence could not have been shaken.

The seventh round, played on Monday, October 9, did nothing to improve the situation. Pollock played Louis Schmidt, Jr., and by the 30th move had once more obtained a winning posi-tion, only to once again snatch defeat from the jaws of victory.

On Tuesday, October 10, during the eighth round, an incident apparently marred the pro-ceedings. A scheduling dispute with Pollock's opponent, Edward N. Olly, resulted in a forfeiture for Pollock. The official score of the tournament stood as a default win for Olly. Pollock would, however, have something more to say about the matter in one of his published columns following the conclusion of the event.

On Wednesday, October 11, Pollock met Lee in the ninth round. Following a badly played Scandinavian with White, Pollock had to acknowledge his fifth consecutive defeat. On Thursday, the play moved to the Brooklyn Chess Club where Pollock met Lasker. The latter had an incredible run (9 wins out of as many games). While Pollock was simply not in good enough shape to pose serious problems for the German master, he did try his best and Lasker had his most difficult game in the tournament. According to the *Brooklyn Standard-Union* of October 16, "in the Pollock game Lasker had much the worse position at one stage, and only by the most cautious play did he win; Mr. Pollock refused a draw, and eventually lost." As Lasker would go on to win the tournament with his famous 13–0 performance, Pollock's refusal of a draw offer takes on added significance, if only as a curiosity emerging from the event. But did Lasker really offer a draw? Another, lengthier, column from the October 21 *Standard-Union* had the following: "In his game with Pollock, he [Lasker] was in quite a hard scrape in the middle game, and would probably have accepted a draw, but with Mr. Pollock it was win or lose, and disdaining a draw, he fought on to defeat." This is a far cry from the certainty of an actual draw offer. The two statements were apparently written by the same reporter, in the same newspaper, only five days apart.

As for the game itself, after exceedingly accurate opening play, the following position was reached:

Emanuel Lasker (John G. White Chess and Checkers Collections, Cleveland Public Library).

Lasker–Pollock
October 12, 1893, New York
Impromptu Tournament, Round 10

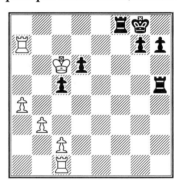

After 38. Kd5–c6

In this difficult but not necessarily hopeless endgame, Black faltered, and continued **38. ... Rhf5?! 39. a5 h5? 40. a6 h4?** Lasker eventually won easily by capturing Pollock's kingside pawns.

Following this round, Charles A. Gilberg introduced the participants to the solving contest challenge: a three-mover composed by the ever-ready Sam Loyd. The received solutions were to be adjudicated by Nellie Showalter. According to the *Baltimore Sunday News*, Loyd made the following remarks before the participants started to have a go at the problem: "Owing to the impromptu nature of the contest the problem would hardly be considered a difficult one and might be hit upon at a glance by an expert. The prizes, therefore, should be rather for correct solving, therefore when six solutions have been received the contest closes, and the prize will be awarded according to the correctness. Those giving the most complete solution being declared winners."

An Impromptu for the Occasion
By S. Loyd

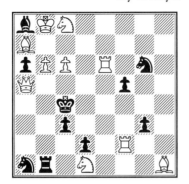

White to mate in three

Pollock finished solving the problem in 45 minutes, but he was too late for the top two prizes. According to the *New York Recorder* of October 16, Lasker and Pillsbury were faster:

> Mr. Lasker seems bound to be first in everything, for in this contest as well he won the first prize by handing the first correct solution to the honorary umpire, Mrs. J.W. Showalter. His time was thirty-five minutes. Within the next ten minutes Messrs. Pillsbury and Pollock presented their solutions, securing the second and third prizes.

Pollock's redemption in the tournament belatedly began in the eleventh round, on October 13, when play was resumed in the rooms of the Brooklyn Chess Club. In his game with Pillsbury, Pollock made a splendid rebound. The *Brooklyn Standard-Union* column noted that "the game between Pollock and Pillsbury was one of the most stubbornly contested of the tournament. Mr. Pollock won the exchange early, and thereafter Mr. Pillsbury worked for a draw. After six hours' play the game was adjourned in a position that seems drawn." Yet Pollock eventually won:

Pollock–Pillsbury
October 13–16, 1893, New York
Impromptu Tournament, Round 11

After 32. ... Qe6-e7

In the diagram above, Pollock demolished Pillsbury with the precise **33. B×d5! R×d5 34. Rf×g6!** and despite his long resistance (81 moves in six hours and 24 minutes) the Bostonian had to acknowledge defeat.

The last two rounds brought the players back to the Manhattan Chess Club. On October 16, Pollock defeated Taubenhaus and on the next day he began his last round game, against Jasnogrodsky. The latter game was finished only on October 18, a 114-move win for Pollock in

New York 1893 Impromptu Tournament, players and officials. Sitting (left to right): J.M. Hanham, J. Ryan, E. Delmar, N. Jasnogrodsky, J.W. Showalter, L. Schmidt, E. Lasker, J. Taubenhaus, E.N. Olly. Standing: W.H.K. Pollock, H. Cassel, G.H.D. Gossip, F.J. Lee, A. Albin, H.N. Pillsbury, M. Frankel, A.F. Higgins, W. Bigelow, E.W. Dahl, F.G. Janusch, S. Lipschütz and L. Goldmark (*Harper's Weekly*, October 28, 1893, page 1041).

which Jasnogrodsky claimed the 50-move rule (in a case of king vs. king, knight and bishop) but resigned after 23 moves in a nearly nine-hour marathon.

Emanuel Lasker's perfect 13–0 earned him the $300 first prize. He was followed at a great distance by Albin, who with an 8½–4½ score secured $185. Delmar won the $115 third prize with 8 points, followed by Lee ($90) and Showalter ($60). As it turned out, Pollock had been one of the two players to consume the most time during tournament play.[5] And his rebound came too late to help him do more than avoid an utterly catastrophic performance. As it was, he could do no better than a tie for 9th through 11th place with Ryan and Schmidt, with four victories, two draws and seven losses. As the *New York Recorder* of October 19 put it, "Pollock played good chess only at the very finish, in spite of the saying 'Better never than too late.'"

A final report regarding the tournament appeared in the *Brooklyn Standard-Union* of October 21. It revealed a discriminatory practice in regard to the chess press, and illustrates what must be a very rare instance of a privileged member of that vocation tattling on his own benefactors. The passage also provides some insight into how well regarded Lasker was at the time, and how only Showalter and Pollock gave him much difficulty:

> The Impromptu International Chess Tournament which has just been finished at the Manhattan C.C. was a great success. Credit is due to the projectors, and praise to the committee in charge. Few hitches, and only one dispute occurred, and everything went through on scheduled time. The whole matter was arranged in so short a time that if there were not some causes for complaint, it would be strange; yet, it is to be hoped in future tournaments in this country, the management will have more time in which to consider the advisability of excluding some representatives of the press; or, if admitting them, denying to them privileges which were accorded to others. The writer has nothing to complain of; being a member of the committee, all privileges were permitted; yet, it was distinctly understood to be upon sufferance; and the feeling was not entirely pleasurable. There seemed

---

5. From the *Baltimore Sunday News* of April 7, 1894: "In the Impromptu Tournament in which Lasker made a clean score of 13, the shortest amount of time was consumed in deliberation by Lasker and Ryan, whose total was about 11 hours. Pollock and Showalter, who consumed the most time, occupied over 23 hours each."

to be a belief that the newspapers of New York, which had contributed to the fund, though no mention of this was made in the meeting of the committee, except that the games were to be sent to them by the secretary in time for publication, and even the games were not stated to be exclusive property. After the tournament was started, the sub-committee in charge of the rules took upon themselves the privilege of admitting representatives of such papers as they pleased. The reporter of the "Evening Post," Charles Devide, was excluded, although he follows chess reporting as a business; the representative of the New York "Herald" and "Mail and Express" was politely informed that while he would be welcomed, he must not publish news of the tournament. Other papers which had not contributed were permitted to publish daily reports, and the whole matter was one of personalism. The writer has the greatest respect for the gentlemen composing the sub-committee, and believes that had they discussed the matter, they would have acted differently; nevertheless, their arbitrary action was without sanction of the whole committee; was unwarranted by the powers conferred upon them, and injurious to the best interests of the game of chess.

Regarding the results of the tournament and the form displayed by the participants, some surprises have occurred, but as a whole, the expected happened. The playing of Emanuel Lasker in the thirteen games was as usual of a high class; in a few instances his opponents secured better positions, but his wonderfully accurate play gave him the victory. In his game with Pollock, he was in quite a hard scrape in the middle game, and would probably have accepted a draw, but with Mr. Pollock it was win or lose, and disdaining a draw, he fought on to defeat. Showalter worked very hard, but the noise of the large crowd in the Brooklyn C.C. distracted him; had his surroundings been more conducive to study he would have taken advantage of a golden opportunity, and at least have drawn. Lasker is a grade better than anyone who competed in the tournament, and the score justified the belief that Mr. Lasker is gaining in chess strength. [...]

In his own *Albany Evening Journal* column of October 14, Pollock also voiced criticism:

THE NEW YORK TOURNAMENT

The Impromptu International Master Tournament at the Manhattan Chess Club has proved a signal success, especially in regard to the quality of the play, keenness of the competition and the good feeling between the players. Great credit is due to the managers and members of the club generally for the smoothness with which the machinery of the contest has worked. Failures there have been of course on the part of individual players, strings of "duck's eggs," insomnia, hallucinations and blunders the sad memory of which will be effaced only in the grave, but wounds are the property of other battlefields besides those of chess.

The tournament is of a semi-private character—admission is by courtesy—the invited contestants were selected at the discretion of the committee—the privileges of publishing the games, etc., had to be purchased. Thus, in a sense, reporters were barred, and some heart-burnings resulted as a matter of course. The New York evening paper expressed itself very strongly at the opening of the tournament. It said that the Manhattan Chess Club was getting its fun very cheap, as the press had contributed $400 and the players $140 (by entrance fees) out of the $800 odd found by the Manhattan and Brooklyn clubs. History will justify or condemn the criticism.

In the *Baltimore Sunday News* column of October 28, Pollock gave voice to an even stronger criticism, this time addressed to the playing committee for their decision in his game against Olly in the event's eighth round:

Considerable has been said and written about various actions of the committee—a body of honest and honorable gentlemen, but one hardly competent to manage an international chess tournament satisfactorily to itself, the players, press or visitors. We have not space to do more than epitomize the shortcomings of management.

The forfeiting of the game on time-limit question by Pollock to Olly was upheld by the committee without even a hearing from the former or examination of a letter written by the latter asking for privilege in time from his adversary, the tacit granting of which caused the loss of the game—an unheard-of departure, at least from the accepted traditions and uses of courtesy. Regarding the press, we have nothing personally to add to the subjoined [see the quotation immediately above] opinions of our talented and careful confrere of the *Standard-Union*.

The Impromptu tournament in New York was followed by another master tournament at Café Manhattan in December 1893, this time organized by the City Chess Club. The event featured five players from the Impromptu tournament (Pillsbury, Showalter, Albin, Hanham and Delmar) joined by five others: Hodges, J.W. and D.G. Baird, Halpern and Ettlinger. According to the *New York Evening Post* for December 9, 1893, the tournament had been suggested by Julius Livingstone, president of the City Chess Club, for the express purpose of seeing that two of its members, Hodges and Hanham, could participate. Hodges, it must be remembered, had not participated in the earlier, Impromptu Tournament because of a conflict regarding hours of play. The *Evening Post* claimed the management of the Café Manhattan tournament had originally been bungled, and among the unfortunate results, Pollock, stationed in Albany, hadn't even been invited to play.

As it happened, the failure to invite Pollock to play in the Café Manhattan event had an additional unfortunate consequence for him: on the very day the Café Manhattan tournament started in New York, December 9, 1893, Pollock fell on the ice in Albany. In a letter briefly quoted in the *New York Evening Post*, published four days later, on December 13, Pollock wrote: "I am at present enjoying a visit to the Albany Hospital, owing to the fracture of the tibia, sustained through slipping during the snow-storm on Saturday."

Several years later, on January 17, 1898, Howard J. Rogers wrote a letter to Frideswide F. Rowland, then in the process of writing *Pollock Memories*, about her subject's time in America. He misremembered Pollock's broken leg as occurring in January of 1894, rather than on December 9, 1893, but there is little doubt he remembered correctly that Pollock, while in Albany,

> had the misfortune to slip on an icy pavement, and break the small bone of his leg just above the ankle. This laid him up in the city hospital for nearly five weeks, where his chief amusement was annotating chess games and chatting with his daily callers, of whom he had many. Pollock roomed in the house of Dr. Southworth, who took a most kindly interest in him, on Eagle Street, and after he left the hospital spent most of his time in his room for a number of weeks. I had many long visits with him at that time, and he told me in confidence much of his past history. It was during this spring that his throat seemed to trouble him, but with the coming of warm weather it seemed to disappear.

While Pollock recovered from his fracture, he must have read with great interest the news of another big tournament scheduled to take place in the United States, although this time somewhere in Indiana, and promoted by a little-known organizer.

KEY TO LOYD'S PROBLEM:

Page 155: **1. Re1**

12. In Montreal,
May 1894–July 1895

An Indiana Swindle

Although he did not play in the masters' event held at the Café Manhattan in December 1893, Pollock was so eager to engage in tournament play that he nearly became ensnared in one of the more appalling absurdities that occurred on the national chess front.

One seemingly enticing option that quickly emerged, as if by magic, was for playing in the "Continental Chess Congress," a large tournament scheduled to be held in Terre Haute, Indiana—a location hitherto unknown to the national chess community. The event, said to be open to all world players, was the work of one Charles O. Jackson of Kokomo, Indiana, the alleged president of the State Association. The prize fund was announced as $1,800, together with $1,200 reserved for an entertainment fund and $700 for a special prize. The entertainment fund was meant to defray the expenses of board and lodging for the contestants. The entrance fees were to be divided among the prizewinners, with first prize set at $500. The tournament was restricted to 40 participants, each of them to pay the entrance fee of $25 to Jackson before January 27, and in exchange receive an acknowledgment receipt.

The tournament program, published in full by Pollock in his December 16, 1893, *Baltimore Sunday News* column, stated that the prizes would remain the same even if fewer than 40 players signed up. It also announced attractive prizes for the best-played games, starting with a $150 prize for the most brilliant game, as well as including a list of prizes for best score against the prize winners by a non–prize winner, announced mates, and shortest games ending in mate. A secondary tournament, limited to 20 players, was open to all for a fee of $10. The top prize for this secondary event was $250 (almost as much as Lasker's prize for winning the New York Impromptu tournament) and the total secondary tournament prize fund was $750.

Jackson's program also announced that the Indiana Chess Association championship was to be held between February 21 and 24 at Terre Haute with "elegant prizes" offered. Jackson announced that he had secured the services of famous masters like Pollock, Gossip and Showalter to entertain the members and visitors with simultaneous, consultation and blindfold chess. "It is quite probable many other eminent masters will be present during the meeting, and a cordial invitation is extended to 'all lover of chess' in Indiana to be present and participate," the program concluded. With such attractive prizes at a time when sponsored cash in hand for chess was a problematic venture in the United States, as soon as the program was released, many players were tempted to enter. Jackson duly raised the initial limit of 40 players to 70. Among the first players who signed up were Pollock, Congdon, Pillsbury, Burille, Albin, Uedemann, Haller, Lee, Frère, the Baird brothers, Gossip, Taubenhaus, Orchard and Ballard. Jackson certainly must have been pleased with his success. And chess players in general must have been delighted with the emergence of a hitherto unknown chess sponsor. It all seemed too good to be true.

And it was. By early January 1894, some New York players began to wonder how it was possible for an obscure figure like Jackson to raise such funds and offer such superlative conditions for a tournament in an area that had until now, to say the least, no ambitious association with the game. In short, Jackson's "Terre Haute Tournament" finally attracted some real scrutiny. The *New York Times* of January 1, 1894, broke the story:

> Within these last few weeks a certain person called Jackson, a former President of the Indiana Chess Association, has been sending out circulars asking chess players to enter for a tournament, for which Jackson alleges that some $3,000 has been subscribed, and that all players will get free board and lodging should they send their $25 entrance fee to Jackson. Major Hanham wrote to Jackson asking him to forward particulars as to how the prizes have been guaranteed, and he received an answer that particulars would be sent to him in a few days. Instead of the particulars he received an abusive letter. Lasker told the following story to a *Times* reporter about Jackson: "When I was asked to play Showalter at Kokomo Jackson wrote me, to New Orleans, that I would get my expenses. After the match I made out a bill, but I did not get a cent, and I had also to pay my hotel bill." Showalter told a *Times* reporter the following story: "I was present at the last meeting of the Indiana Chess Association, and I know it to be a fact that Jackson was not elected President. If in the printed circulars Jackson claims to be President, I must nail that as a lie. Jackson wrote me to come to Kokomo to play Lasker, and that he had my stakes ready. When I arrived at Kokomo I was told by Jackson that my backers had gone to San Francisco, and that he had not my stakes, I was obliged to write to my father, who put up the stakes."
>
> Whether chess players would do well to forward any money to Jackson after hearing the stories from Hanham, Lasker and Showalter is rather doubtful.

Still wanting to believe Jackson's tournament was legitimate, Pollock responded on behalf of the denigrated sponsor: "It is the last sentence [in the *New York Times* article] that seems to render it necessary for the promoters of the tournament to protect themselves from aspersions of their good faith, which must appear to the general chess public as unwarrantable and outrageous," wrote Pollock in his January 6 *Baltimore Sunday News* column.

But the *New York Times* of January 15 added further details to the story, exposing Jackson as a "swindler of great ingenuity." Following the January 1 *Times* report, some New York players wrote to C. Gerstmeyer, the actual president of the Indiana Chess Association whose name appeared on Jackson's advertising program. Gerstmeyer wrote back stating that he and his organization did promise help to Jackson, but only in terms of playing rooms and some little money for the printing of circulars. Jackson himself, reached for comment, claimed he had the total $4,500 fund secured. It appears he had contacted for sponsorship some of the influential chess club officials around the country, but without success. Gerstmeyer was compelled to explain Jackson's background to men like Pillsbury and L.D. Broughton in private letters. His portrayal of the promoter was less than flattering. Jackson hit back with press releases sent to the *New York Tribune* and other newspapers claiming he had the support of the Terre Haute Chess Club and he would certainly have the prize money in hand as soon as at least 26 players signed up. In case of failure to achieve this, those who already signed up were sure to receive a refund.

In his column of January 13 *Sunday News*, Pollock continued to give Jackson the benefit of doubt:

Mr. Jackson also writes to us in the greatest indignation at the reported statements of Hanham, Lasker and Showalter, republished in THE NEWS last week. We cannot go into the details of the Lasker–Showalter match, but regarding the statements concerning Jackson and the Terre Haute programme we implicitly believe his assertion that he never wrote an abusive letter to any chess player in his life and that he was elected president of the Indiana Association in November, 1893. Meantime, the date of January 27 (this day fortnight) still holds good as the latest day for entries.[1]

On January 27, a day before the above-mentioned deadline, the *New York Times* published the following follow-up on the story:

C.O. Jackson, whose operations among Western chess players led to his being characterized as a chess fraud, says he was induced by Western racing men to make up the "fake" tournament for Terre Haute. That he did not succeed in his endeavors to swindle the players and patrons of the game was largely due to the *New York Times*, which exposed Jackson from the very start. The Terre Haute Chess Club, after investigating the story told in *The Times*, at once severed its connection with Jackson, and the "fake" tournament was a thing of the past.[2]

Also on January 27, writing in his *Sunday News* column, Pollock finally found himself in a position to give a most expansive account of the whole Jackson matter:

THE TERRE HAUTE FIASCO

The sudden, complete and utterly causeless collapse of the Terre Haute Congress demands immediate explanation and falling that, a swift investigation. An international tournament had been announced on a magnificent scale, printed programmes have been distributed and press notices printed and quoted over Europe and America; players have been invited to send in their $25 entrance fees and participate, and—presto—on account of a questioning note in the corner of an article in a paper which has no regular chess column nor chess editor and an alleged cabal in the East the congress is "declared off" without another word! For a second time within six months [the first likely being the aborted Columbian Chess Congress] chess players have been fooled, the chess press hoaxed and the names of the redoubted hospitality of America, taken in vain through the fainheartenedness and instability of an incompetent management. Now the public are loudly calling for names of those who are responsible for this tampering with the character of the blameless institution of chess. And before proceeding further we wish distinctly to exonerate the Terre Haute Chess Club, through its president and treasurer, from responsibility either for the funds stated to be on hand or from the falling through of the programme. The former, Dr. C. Gerstmeyer, sent three communications to Dr. L.D. Broughton of the *Brooklyn Standard-Union*. In the first of these, dated January 6, he states that Mr. Jackson, as president of the Indiana State Chess Association, first got the Terre Haute players to raise a certain sum to engage one or two masters to attend the annual meeting of the association in that city. Subsequently he said that the USCA (which was long before defunct) would hold its meeting there and provide an entertainment fund of $1,200 and considerable prize money besides. Gradually the scheme of a masters' congress on a large scale was sprung upon the local club, which, however, refused any responsibility beyond the furnishing of a suite of rooms at the Terre Haute House. This refusal was emphasized

---

1. Pollock's reaction is curious since the *New York Sun* of January 16, 1894, had already published the following: "THE TERRE HAUTE CHESS MATCH IS OFF, Kokomo, Ind., Jan. 15—The Terre Haute Chess Club, as backers of the 'Masters' Continental Chess Congress,' have declared the tournament off and instructed the Treasurer to refund promptly all entrance fees so far received. The reason given for this action is the misunderstanding regarding the entrance fees and moneys which seems to have prevailed among the players to such an extent as to seriously cripple the arrangement of the necessary details." In all likelihood Pollock's column was written and published before he had access to this information from New York. • **2.** Regarding these "Western racing men," the *Daily Inter Ocean* of January 19, 1894, had the following to add: "Were to Sell Pools on Chess Games. Promoter Jackson's Admissions Scandalize the Disheartened Terre Haute Club, Terre Haute, Ind., Jan. 18—Special Telegram.—The Terre Haute Chess Club, which has abandoned the Masters' Continental Chess Congress, was scandalized today by the admission of Charles O. Jackson, of Kokomo, Ind., promoter of the congress, that he was backed by a syndicate of gamblers, whose names he refuses to divulge, who were to reimburse themselves by selling pools on the games in New York, Chicago, and other large cities." Of course, given Jackson admitted setting up the "tournament" for such purposes and people, his admission itself raises serious questions. It may well have been there was no group of "Western racing men," and Jackson concocted this bit of information to lay the blame at more feet than his own. One wonders if he had not been caught out in his endeavor, whether players arriving for the tournament would have ever met the conman in the first place.

by the holding of a meeting of the club upon the advertisement in the *Terre Haute Gazette* which they considered calculated to lead to the belief that the Congress proposed had the sanction and endorsement of the club. The latter only refrained from publicly disavowing this position from a desire not to interfere with the success of the meeting. Dr. Gerstmeyer concludes: "We have drifted into this muddle by slow process, but we will let daylight into it shortly." The president's second letter (January 8) says that the club had met Mr. Jackson and stated its refusal to assume any responsibility beyond the furnishing of a place for play and money for the circulars issued. It regretted the prejudices existing in certain quarters against him, but could not endorse him nor guarantee the money he had agreed to raise. It only agreed to assume responsibility for the entrance fees and other funds when turned over to Dr. Baker, treasurer of the club, and to receive further entrance fees after January 7. In his third letter, written one hour later, Dr. Gerstmeyer says that in consequence of information just received he exceedingly regrets having ever met Mr. Jackson.

Writing to the Chess Editor [Pollock], under the date Jan. 15, Dr. W.H. Baker, Treasurer Terre Haute C.C., reiterates, in different form, the statements of Dr. Gerstmeyer's first letter, strongly disclaiming on the part of the club any responsibility for the purse of the larger tournament.

Both gentlemen admit their desire to have the Indiana State meeting at Terre Haute and admit to raising of a fund for the expense of exhibitions, etc., from Messrs. Pollock and Showalter during the meeting, but consistently maintain that the International Congress as explained on the programmes issued was Mr. Jackson's affair solely.

Pollock, as well as others, had been the victims of their own desire to see chess flourish. In the end, it appears little if anything was lost, other than a bit more of the game's reputation in the eyes of the general public. Chess in America hardly needed charlatans to help further marginalize it. That Pollock appears somewhat gullible in this whole exchange cannot be denied, but then such a lapse is consistent with "his erratic and bohemian ways," as Professor Rogers described them to Frideswide Rowland after Pollock's death. As Rogers characterized him, Pollock "was of a nervous temperament, easily impressed, and would often dwell strangely on one idea." Perhaps the "easily impressed" aspect of his personality had taken sway when Jackson's offer appeared, and explain accounts of Pollock's seeming reluctance, until so late, to be swayed by the mounting evidence of disaster.

The NYSCA Midwinter Meeting

Pollock's desire for some genuine chess playing early in 1894 was finally met—not in Terre Haute, but in New York. On February 22, Washington's Birthday, Pollock arrived in Gotham to play in the 16th annual midwinter meeting of the New York State Chess Association held at Assembly Hall in the United Charities Building, 105 East 22nd Street. The winter meetings of the NYSCA had traditionally been the forum for a one day tournament to decide the Association's next champion. The attendance in the championship tourney was excellent: Pollock was joined by Hanham, Hodges, the Baird brothers, Gossip, Hymes, Halpern, Showalter, Delmar, Olly, G. Simonson, E.E. Burlingame, A.J. Souweine, A.C. Clapp, and W.E. Scripture. This was a strong field, but one that would have been eminently stronger had Emanuel Lasker and Pillsbury entered the tournament, as had apparently been possible at one point.[3] The tournament offered its actual participants five prizes ($50, $20, $15, $10 and $5) and the committee decided to introduce a time limit for the games: 30 moves an hour. S. Loyd and Pillsbury acted as umpires.

---

3. From the *Brooklyn Standard-Union* of February 24, 1894: "The strength of the players in the championship tournament was greater than in any previous event, and the pairing in the different rounds brought the stronger players together early. Mr. Lasker considered the advisability of entering, but at the last minute decided not to do so; had he entered Mr. Pillsbury would also have competed. There was a question as to the eligibility of both players, the rules providing for active membership in a chess club or residence in the State; but the committee would have admitted both gentlemen upon their statement that New York was to be their residence."

According to the *New York Sun* of February 23, Pollock lost in the first round to the ever-present Hanham. He won from Burlingame in the next in a French Defense, and from Delmar in the third, in a Vienna Game. In the fourth round, played at City Chess Club, according to the *New York Recorder*, Pollock lost to Halpern and, according to the rules, had to drop out. The tournament was won by Hodges, followed by J.W. Baird, with Halpern, Simonson and Showalter tying for third through fifth.

A problem-solving tournament was arranged too. In about an hour's time, Pollock won the first prize, followed by Hanham, Charles Nugent and E. Hoffmann. The problem composed by Loyd for this occasion appeared for the general public in the *Brooklyn Standard-Union* of February 24 and the *New York Herald* of February 25:

Problem Solving Contest
NYSCA Meeting, February 22–23, 1894
By S. Loyd

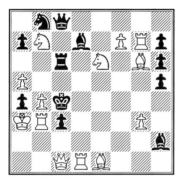

White to mate in three

According to the *Brooklyn Standard-Union* of March 3, 1894, Pollock and Hanham solved this problem in ten minutes.

Heading to Montreal

Immediately after the end of this small event, the eyes of the chess world focused on the fight about to break out between two elite masters: the world championship match between Steinitz and Lasker. Although begun in New York City, the match shifted locations, and in early May it moved from Philadelphia to Montreal. At that time the score stood Lasker 7, Steinitz 2, with 2 drawn games. Pollock, who painstakingly annotated the games in his newspaper columns, dined with Howard J. Rogers, his benefactor in Albany, and then boarded a train for Montreal. As Rogers wrote four years later, he would never see the young chess master again.

Pollock arrived at the Cosmopolitan Club in Montreal, along with Pillsbury, no doubt a visit facilitated by his friend Babson. A close associate of Lasker's during this time, with whom he dined at the Windsor Hotel, Pollock wrote the following for the *Sunday News* of May 12. It reveals something of Pollock's eye for curious detail, selected to engage his reader's interest:

A feature of the match was the reproduction of the game by wire, move for move, in the window of the Star office downtown. This idea emanated, as a matter of course, from the ever-fertile brain of J.N. Babson, who furnished the board, which was affixed on an easel. It almost became a question whether the Star people would not find it necessary to withdraw the board, as during parts of the play two policemen were required to keep the crowd moving, and on Saturday afternoon St. James', which is a wide street, became impassable for vehicles for a short time. A gentleman told the writer that the time-honored incident which occurred to Zukertort in Paris was repeated. An officer asked a spectator who was standing in the clearing of the footway to move. "It's your move," replied the enthusiast, without removing his eyes from the board.

The enthusiasm of such Montreal citizens, regardless of their knowledge, or lack of knowledge, about the game, was made further evident in the following statement attributed to Pillsbury, as it originally appeared in the *Boston Herald* and as reprinted in Pollock's May 19 *Sunday News* column:

> It is hard to be obliged to admit that the leading cities of the United States, including those of our own modern Athens, are so far behind the methods of popularizing what is universally admitted as the most scientific game of the age. Everybody here seems to know about this as a world's championship, and to follow the fortunes of the players, whether they know the game or not.
>
> No end of persons have learned the game and picked up a respectable knowledge of its science within the past week since Steinitz and Lasker have been playing. It is the common talk. Persons who have not the slightest knowledge of the game go to the Cosmopolitan Club to see the masters play, or else form parts of the vast crowd which has so blocked the way in St. James street at times that the carriages and cabs have been obliged to drive around another street.
>
> At the opera performance here on Saturday last a chess scene was introduced, one of the players being designated Steinitz and the other Lasker, and the crowd applauded wildly. In the hotels at dinner every one discusses the match with great zest, and yet I venture to say that not over 25 per cent of them know even the moves.

Understandably, Pollock felt at home with such an atmosphere. His detailed reporting of the match for the American newspapers showed his reporting skills at their best. Consider the following piece of fine chess journalism, both for its technical content but also for its colorful detail regarding the seventeenth game of the match, which appeared in his *Sunday News* column of May 26:

W.H.K. Pollock in Montreal, 1893 (John G. White Chess and Checkers Collections, Cleveland Public Library).

The World's Championship Match

The 16th game having been won by Lasker the score read: Lasker 9, Steinitz 4, drawn 3. Intense interest prevailed in Montreal on Saturday, May 19, when Steinitz, with the move against him and the sword of Damocles hanging over his head, and [*sic*: had] to sit down and face the youth who was apparently certain of ultimately wresting the world's championship from its holder for over a quarter of a century. The game proved to be all that the most enthusiastic admirers of a stubborn fight could wish. Lasker opened with a quiet form of the Giuoco Piano, but failed to obtain any pull at any time. After 51 moves an adjournment was taken until Monday, the following being the position:

Lasker–Steinitz

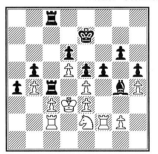

After 51. ... f6–f5

Lasker did not turn up for nearly half an hour after the hour for resumption of play, and the room presented

William Steinitz vs. Emanuel Lasker, World Championship Match, Cosmopolitan Club, Montreal (*Le Monde Illustré*, May 26, 1894, page 37).

a somewhat disconsolate appearance, the little time-piece ticking ominously, while Steinitz leaned out of the open window abstractedly, apparently figuring out what debut he should adopt in his 18th game. When at length Lasker arrived, it was only to hand in a resignation without even sitting down to the board. Steinitz then explained that his intended continuation was, if 52. Ng3 (best; if 52. e×f5 B×f5+ winning the exchange.) 52. ... f×e4+ 53. Kd2 (if 53. N×e4 Bf5 wins) 53. ... Bd7 afterward playing it to e8 and then to f7.

A neat illustration of the use of a chess editor occurred just before the adjournment at 11 p.m. on Saturday. The sporting editor of a well-known Montreal paper asked the chess editor at the office whether Lasker or Steinitz would win the game. The chess editor replied that he did not see what answer Lasker could make if his opponent played f5, though he could not undertake to explain all the variations. So the sporting editor hied himself down to the window of the Star office, wherein the moves are repeated from the Cosmopolitan Club by wire. There he found five policemen on guard keeping back the crowd, and everybody speculating on a different move for Black. So the sporting editor began to assert what Steinitz's next move would be with such emphasis that bets were offered in order to preserve quiet. Just as the odds against the move proposed reached 7 to 3 the operator made the chess editor's suggested advance of the f–pawn, and, of course, the sporting editor scoops the stakes and exits chuckling.

On Saturday, June 2, after Lasker had won the match, Pollock visited Montreal's Cosmopolitan Club. There Pillsbury gave a successful 12-board blindfold simultaneous exhibition which lasted throughout the night. At its conclusion, Steinitz was presented with "a substantial purse of gold" subscribed by his admirers in the city and amounting to $125. The gesture was followed by felicitous speeches and toasts.[4]

---

4. According to the *Montreal Daily Star* of June 4, 1894, Pillsbury's exhibition at the Cosmopolitan Club finished +8 –4. Those winning were Marshall, Lindsay, Cochenthaler and Falconer. Apparently, Pollock kibitzed for Cochenthaler as the *Montreal Daily Star* of June 12 recorded: "It has been ungraciously said that Mr. M. Cochenthaler got 'tips' on his game from Babson, Pollock and Steinitz. He was at all events urged to continue by those gentlemen, for about one o'clock he remarked:

In mid–June, Pollock was a key player in the formation of a new chess club in Montreal. On June 19, a coterie of players met at the Hope Coffee House and formed the Chess and Checker Club of Montreal. According to the *Montreal Daily Star*, Pollock was one of the experts elected for the Executive Council, and the 16-year-old Marshall acted as secretary. Clearly eyeing each other for a match, Pollock and Marshall planned to cross swords. Pollock challenged Marshall to a match of five games, offering his younger opponent increasing odds with each game.[5] Most local players believed the odds were risky to offer a player of Marshall's caliber. "Local players think the odds are too heavy," the *Montreal Daily Star* of June 8 recorded, "as Mr. Marshall can hardly be given the knight odds and is quite capable of snatching a game on even terms. The challenger, however, is confident of winning either the match or return match[…]." The match did not materialize.

Although he continued to edit his chess columns for the *Albany Evening Journal* and *Baltimore Sunday News*, Pollock chose not to return to Albany. He now made his headquarters in Montreal, although his move there was not yet certain. In early August, he received an invitation to play in the midsummer NYSCA meeting held in Buffalo. Although initially a larger number of players were announced, in the end only Showalter, Pillsbury, Albin and Farnsworth took part. Pollock offered extensive coverage of the event in his *Albany Evening Journal*, but for some reason decided not to play.

Finally, in late summer of 1894, Pollock officially moved to Montreal, leaving Albany behind. Rogers wrote the following on Pollock's time in Albany, which casts light on one interpretation of his character, while also suggesting a reason for the move[6]:

> Of his life in Albany, I must touch lightly, or I shall become prolix. He was a steady attendant at the Chess Club, and many were the struggles we had over the board. He was of a nervous temperament, easily impressed, and would often dwell strangely on one idea. He often called me a mind-reader, because I seemed to anticipate his line of play in Chess, and block it. Curiously enough, although he was easily my superior at the game, it was with difficulty that he made even games in our personal tilts. His erratic and Bohemian ways were the delight of his brethren on the reporting staff of the "Express," the morning edition of the "Journal." Pollock would usually appear at the reporting rooms about 10 or 11 p.m., and calmly settle himself for a deep Chess analysis or other work. He was ready to chat with anybody, from managing editor to galley-boy, at any time, and finally when the morning editions were going to press in the small hours of the night, he would betake himself to his rooms and go to bed. He never arose till about 10 a.m. When assigned to report a particular occurrence, he was as likely to report another totally different, which happened to take his fancy, or perhaps forget about it entirely. As might be imagined, this resulted in the end in his discharge from the reporting staff. As an instance of his delight in pursuing investigations of a scientific nature may be mentioned his interest in meteorology and in the practical working of the Weather Bureau. He struck up a warm acquaintance with Mr. Sims, Chief of the Department at Albany, and himself a chess player, and might be found many a night occupying the signal tower in the government building with his friend.

During the period September through November 1894, Pollock gave a number of simultaneous exhibitions throughout Montreal. On September 22, he gave a 19-board exhibition at the Central Chess Club. The *Montreal Daily Herald* of September 29 recorded the following:

> Few pleasanter evenings have been passed than that enjoyed by the Central Chess Club on Saturday last. As was announced in this column, Dr. Pollock undertook to lick all that portion of creation that playeth chess at the Hope Coffee House; and he did it too, but with that uniform geniality and courtesy which make him a universal

---

(*footnote 4 continued*) 'If I don't go home now I'll get killed.' When he lost a bishop he offered Pillsbury a draw. The latter replied: 'I'm a piece ahead.' Five minutes later Pillsbury asked if Mr. C. would draw. The reply came pretty quickly: 'You've left your Queen en-prise.'" ● **5.** The first game would have been even; in the following games, Pollock would offer in succession pawn and move, pawn and two moves, knight, and, in the last game, a rook. ● **6.** Letter from H.J. Rogers to F.F. Rowland, January 17, 1898; cited in *Pollock Memories*, pages 11–12.

favorite. The following nineteen gentlemen were the venturesome wights who played black against the doctor: Messrs. O.L. Fuller, president of the Central Club; O. Trempe, chess editor of *La Presse*; O.N. Mintz, P. Dale, F.J. Marshall, Victor Koefoed, J.M. Ferres, P. Farrell, J.T. Bolt, R.J. Logan, C. Germain, St. Pierre Chess Club, Gabriel Breeze, B. Hayes, Jas. West, W. Farquharson, Wayland Williams, F.H. Pitt, Montreal Chess Club; A.C. Wurtele and H. Hamilton. Two of these gentlemen were unable to finish their games, as they had to leave early, they were V. Koefoed, and Mr. A.C. Wurtele. The remainder all prosecuted their games to the bitter end, but all with the same dire result, a win for White. This, however, must not imply that the play was weak. There were some very good games, more especially those of Mr. C. Germain and F.J. Marshall, who both pressed Dr. Pollock very hard. [...] Among those present were Mr. J. Henderson, Chess Editor of the Gazette; the English player, Mr. Gossip, and the genial secretary of the Montreal C.C., Mr. Barry.

The same column reproduced the score of Pollock's win over Marshall. The latter eventually lost in 56 moves but in the opening he could have gotten the better of Pollock had he played a different move in the position below:

Frank J. Marshall (*Le Monde Illustré*, December 2, 1893, page 371).

Pollock–Marshall
Simultaneous Exhibition at 19 boards
Montreal, September 22, 1894

After 11. 0–0–0

After Pollock castled long, Marshall played **11. ... Qe8**. Instead, he could have gone for the powerful 11. ... b5! forcing Pollock to give up the bishop for a couple of pawns: 12. B×b5 Rb8 13. c4 a6 14. a4 a×b5 15. a×b5, and if White had any hopes of salvaging this position, those hopes would have been dashed by the clever 15. ... N×d5! 16. c×d5 R×b5, and Black has a decisive advantage.

In October, Pollock was still contributing to the chess life of the city even if he wasn't the only expert performing at the clubs. The *Montreal Gazette* of October 11 summarized it:

> The autumn season of chess in Montreal has already assumed a lively appearance. The French Canadian Chess Clubs are in a flourishing condition; the Central Chess Club inaugurated the season with a very successful entertainment of simultaneous chess by Dr. Pollock; the Montreal Chess Club had an exhibition by Mr. Gossip; and the "Heather Chess Club," a Cote-St. Antoine, after adding a reading room to the other entertainments is busy preparing for something else. We learn that the chess club in connection with the Y.M.C.A., is also busying itself preparing for a great performance in the near future. This is as it should be and argues well for the future of chess in Montreal.

On November 10, Pollock gave another exhibition at the Montreal Chess Club, this time against 22 opponents (19–3). The *St. John Globe* of December 7 described the event, as well as a slight twist in play rarely seen on this side of the Atlantic:

> The tables were arranged for Dr. Pollock and his opponents to take first move alternately, so that every player had the choice of Black or White, according to the position he selected in the arena. This is the continental fashion, most of the English players who have visited Montreal taking advantage of the first move.

The exhibition ran for nearly five hours, from 8:00 p.m. to 1:00 a.m., and Gossip took a special interest in the proceedings, analyzing some of the games for the local columns. Pollock lost a game to Marshall during this exhibition. The game is notable because it featured one of Marshall's "swindles," which would become famous in his later years.

Marshall–Pollock
Simultaneous Exhibition at 22 boards
Montreal Chess Club, November 10, 1894

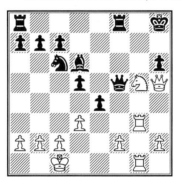

After 19. Qe2–h5

At his 16th move, Marshall sacrificed a bishop for some attacking chances on Pollock's king. After his 19th move, Marshall had to struggle considerably to stay in the game, since the sacrifice seemed futile. But Pollock, who had to dedicate effort and attention to the other 21 games as well, failed to find the correct defense. He continued with **19. ... B×g3?** and after **20. Q×h6+ Kg8 21. R×g3 Rf6 22. N×e4+** he was completely lost. Instead, Pollock should have played 19. ... Bf4+! 20. Kb1 Rf6! (not 20. ... B×g5 due to 21. R×g5 Qh7 22. Rg6 Rg8 and the game is equal) and White's attack would have been gone.

On November 29, Pollock gave yet another simultaneous exhibition, this one on 21 boards (+14 –5 =2), and again lost a game to Marshall. In addition to making a presence in the Montreal clubs for various simultaneous exhibitions,[7] Pollock spent evenings at the private residences of

---

7. From *New York Evening Post* of November 24, 1894: "A correspondent writes from Montreal as follows: 'Chess is flourishing here. Pollock and Gossip are daily at the Montreal Chess Club, the Rev. J. de Soyres of St. John, N.B., long prominently connected with practical and theoretical chess in England, and S.G. Ruth of Brooklyn are also

several notable Montreal players, including that of Joseph Babson. In early November, during such a sitting at the house of J.W. Shaw, Pollock defeated the 53-year-old Gossip in a 31-move game for a small prize offered by the host. Another game between the two was played on Thanksgiving Day, November 22, at a private residence. It appears these two encounters were part of a three-game match arranged by Shaw between Pollock and Gossip. This time Pollock won in 41 moves.[8] Such encounters served as the preliminary steps for a formal match between Pollock and Gossip in December 1894.[9]

In early December, he also played in a handicap tournament at the Montreal Chess Club. In one of the early rounds, Pollock, who had to give odds of pawn and two moves to all first class players, defeated Marshall in 43 moves. In the end, Pollock finished fourth, with +14 −6, behind T.R. Davies (17–3), Robert Short (16–4), C. Gerstner (15½–4½).

J.W. Shaw (*Le Monde Illustré*, April 28, 1894, page 622).

visitors at the above club. The YMCA has started a large handicap, and the Heather and Central Chess Clubs opened the season by a couple of team matches and some successful exhibition play." ● **8.** From the *British Chess Magazine* of January 1895 (page 9): "In a little match of three games up, for a prize offered by the well-known Montreal amateur, Mr. J.W. Shaw, all three parties were won by Dr. W.H.K. Pollock from Mr. G. Hatfeild D. Gossip, of chess 'manual' and 'theory' fame, who has been for some time sojourning in the Canadian capital." ● **9.** George H.D. Gossip (1841–1907) was born in New York as the son of English parents and between 1870 and 1895 was active in a series of tournaments, often competing against the best players of the time. His mother died soon after his birth and his father took him to England two years later. He lived in Barlborough Hall, Derbyshire and at Hatfield, in Yorkshire. He earned a scholarship to Oxford University, but he couldn't attend because his family was ruined by a lawsuit. He did some translation work and writing in France, Germany and England in the late 1870s and early 1880s. In 1868 he married and in 1871 he lived in Ipswich with his wife and four children. In 1882, after the death of his father, Gossip moved to Australia where he contributed articles to many newspapers. In 1888 he moved (apparently alone) to the United States and lived for a while in San Francisco. The next year he relocated to England where he lived until 1894. He moved to Montreal, Canada soon afterwards. Although Gossip, who took part in a great number of chess events starting with 1864, never scored impressive results, and writers often mocked his habit of finishing in the lower half of crosstables, his playing strength in fairness needs to be re-evaluated. Notable efforts in the direction of reevaluation include G.H. Diggle, "The Master Who Never Was," *British Chess Magazine*, January 1969, pages 1–4, and Edward Winter in his feature article titled "Gossip" at www.chesshistory.com. Gossip's best result, as Winter points out, seems to be his otherwise largely neglected performance in the Sixth American Congress, New York, 1889 where he scored + 11 −22 =5, winning from Lipschütz, Judd, Delmar, Showalter, Bird, the Baird brothers, Hanham and Pollock (in both games). But he did finish last in five tournaments: London 1889, Breslau 1889, Manchester 1890, London 1892 and New York 1893. In parallel with his career as a player, Gossip also published a large number of chess books. Among the most important are *The Chess Player's Manual—A Complete Guide to Chess* (1874) and *Theory of the Chess Openings* (1879). Gossip did not take criticism of his books lightly and often made enemies in both the chess playing and writing world. A controversial figure, sometimes accused (without consistent proof) of publishing fabricated game scores that put him in a good light, Gossip deserves far more diligent scrutiny.

G.H.D. Gossip (on the right) across from F.J. Lee (John G. White Chess and Checkers Collections, Cleveland Public Library).

An Unpleasant Match

The match between Pollock and Gossip appears to have been one of the slender opportunities in Montreal for the two to make money directly through chess. Gossip did not speak well of the largess of his Montreal hosts, and suggested Pollock's plight was hardly better. In a letter to a friend dated October 20, 1894, and included by G.H. Diggle in an article on Gossip (published in *Newsflash*, April 1, 1983, page 13), Gossip was quoted as saying:

> The French Canadian Chessplayers here are the poorest, meanest humbugs I ever met—all Jesuits. An old priest promised me 10 dollars for a simultaneous, but of course a Jesuit can only be relied on not to keep his word. Another club treated me similarly. The only real patron of Chess here is an American, Mr. J.N. Babson. I have only made 27 dollars in 6 weeks, 18 dollars thanks to him. A Manchester paper has published already four columns of articles by myself, for which of course I expect payment, if I am not dead before the money can reach me. A very nice man, Mr. Cox, Professor of Physics at the University here, who had promised to take a course of chess lessons off me, has OF COURSE been laid up with lumbago, so I have not made a cent with him. If I go to Cuba I shall have to swim there according to present prospects.... *Pollock is not much better off*.... [emphasis added]

Pollock's match against Gossip started in mid–December. It generated significant interest in the Canadian chess press, with newspaper columns reporting promptly on the developments of this long encounter. The match began on Saturday afternoon, December 15, at the premises of the Montreal Chess Club (No. 55 University Street) under the following conditions: the winner of the first seven games would receive two-thirds of a purse sponsored by J.W. Shaw, the other one third going to the loser; games were to be played starting at 4:00 p.m. on Tuesday, Thursday and Saturday of each week.

The first game, played on the afternoon of December 15, was won by Pollock in 25 moves. Having the Black pieces, Pollock took advantage of Gossip's unimpressive opening play in a King's Gambit Declined and pushed home a powerful kingside attack that eventually forced Gossip to give up his queen to avoid an immediate disaster. On December 18, Pollock won again although his opening play was much less inspired. In fact, Gossip got a solid, decisive advantage and only some serious errors allowed Pollock to escape defeat and then, finally, score the full point. The third game, played on December 20, was a very similar story: Gossip, having the White pieces, reached a relatively equal rook endgame with good chances for a draw, but instead of avoiding a rook exchange proposed by Pollock, he accepted it only to realize a few moves later he was completely lost. Thus, after the first three games, Pollock was leading 3–0.

The fourth encounter, played on Saturday, December 22, saw a vicious clash between the two men in an Evans Gambit Declined. Pollock, playing White, launched a formidable sacrificial attack against Gossip's king and after 25 moves, the following position was reached:

Pollock–Gossip
Montreal Chess Club, Fourth Match Game
December 22, 1894

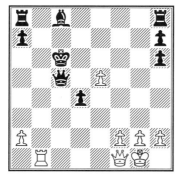

After 25. Qc4–f1

Pollock's attack had run its course, and Gossip could have simply played 25. ... Q×e5! in order to secure the whole point. Instead, he played the dubious **25. ... Bf5?!** allowing Pollock to recover some of his material with **26. Qa6+ Kc7 27. Qb7+ Kd8 28. Q×a8+ Bc8 29. Qe4** and suddenly Gossip had to work very hard for a win. After strenuous efforts in a fierce 60-move long battle, Pollock managed to escape with a draw.

In the fifth game, played on the same day, Gossip missed a clever win at his 19th move as a result of Pollock's risky play. Instead, Pollock obtained two rooks for Gossip's queen and, helped by his extra passed pawns, scored another point to make the score a nearly overwhelming 4½–½ in his favor.

Perhaps Pollock's lead was too large for him to maintain focus and concentration. After five games, play was briefly suspended and with its resumption, Pollock's erratic nature quickly made its appearance. Following the break for Christmas celebrations, on December 27 the match resumed with the sixth game. Pollock, commanding the White side of an Evans Gambit Declined, played a risky game and gave Gossip some serious counterplay. This time the latter grasped his chances and scored his first point in the match.

In the seventh game, Pollock defended with what modern authorities call today the Sicilian Dragon. Following some complex tactical play, Pollock could have twice obtained a decisive advantage, but now it was his turn to watch winning games unravel. The rook and pawns endgame that resulted was drawn. Pollock briefly recovered this by winning the eighth game, on December 27, thus making the overall score 5–1, with two draws. It was during this particular game, lost by Gossip in a surprising fashion, that, oddly enough, signs of trouble for Pollock became more visible. After **1. e4 e5 2. f4 e×f4 3. Nf3 g5 4. Bc4 Bg7 5. 0–0 d6 6. d4 Nc6**, a well-known line in the King's Gambit, Pollock employed the inferior **7. N×g5?** (instead of the commonly met 7. c3), which seems to have troubled Gossip. The latter followed up with **7. … B×d4+ 8. Kh1 Q×g5** but after **9. R×f4** he panicked and played the very weak **9. … Qg6** (instead, 9. … Nf6! would have allowed him a big advantage) allowing Pollock a decisive advantage with **10. B×f7+ Q×f7 11. R×f7 K×f7 12. Qh5+** and eventually, after some further exchanges, Pollock's queen migrated to the queenside and captured Black's pawns, creating a speedy, and decisive, passed pawn.

It was at this point, according to the *Montreal Gazette* of January 26, 1895, Gossip vehemently protested matters *off* the board, "on account of interruptions during play, caused by talking, etc., while he was studying his moves." In a move very rarely, if ever, seen in what passes for a serious chess match, "The managing committee, after enquiring into all the particulars of the case, upheld his demand and ordered the game to be cancelled."

Thus, with this game discarded, Pollock was still leading 4–1, with two draws, before the ninth game was to be played. While the exact exchanges between the two players have not survived, it is not difficult to imagine Pollock's discontent with the managing committee's decision to erase his victory in the eighth game. On January 16, when the eighth game's replay commenced, one can clearly see a different Pollock at play: an uncharacteristically timid opening with White got him in trouble early and after 24 moves the game was adjourned. When the game was about to resume by revelation of the sealed move, according to the *Montreal Gazette* of January 26, Pollock refused to continue. The arbiters revealed his sealed move, Gossip replied, and the game was scored for Gossip after an hour of waiting for Pollock's time to expire.

Pollock then failed to make an appearance for the ninth game, which was duly scored in Gossip's favor, making the score 4–3, with two draws. Although explicit reasons for Pollock's failure to resume play in the eighth game and his failure to appear for the ninth were never made public, the most reasonable conclusion was that he had serious disagreements either with Gossip or with the management committee—or perhaps both. It appears Pollock intended refusing to finish the match. The January 26 issue of the *Montreal Daily Herald* continued the story:

> Notwithstanding his previous decision not to continue the match with Mr. Gossip, Dr. Pollock, at the request of the Committee, and, as he states, "out of personal respect to the Vice-President, and in the absence of the President," consented to proceed, and the tenth game was commenced on the afternoon of Saturday last; meanwhile the Doctor had lost the ninth game by default. Now the question is, how does the score stand? At the close of the seventh game the position was: Pollock 4, Gossip 1, drawn 2. Then the eighth game was played which was also won by the Doctor; but Mr. Gossip appealed to the committee to have it cancelled on the ground that there had been too much talking while he was making his moves, which talking caused him to lose the game. After much letter writing on the part of Mr. Gossip and much talking on the part of everybody the committee at last agreed to cancel the game. Another game was then played which at the adjournment in the middle of the game was apparently a won game by Gossip, but as his opponent did not come to time it went to Mr. Gossip by default. It was agreed to call this the eighth game of the match. Score: Pollock 4, Gossip 2, drawn 2. The next game, as has already been said, the doctor lost by default. Score: Pollock 4, Gossip 3, drawn 2. The tenth game commenced

on Saturday last was not finished until Tuesday evening when it was won by Mr. Gossip. Score: Gossip 4, Pollock 4, drawn 2. Another game was promptly commenced, and when adjourned till Thursday afternoon looked to be in Dr. Pollock's favor. However, when play was resumed on Thursday, a very dull game ensued and the game at last ended in a draw. Score: Gossip 4, Pollock 4, drawn 3.[10]

Although he agreed to play the tenth game, Pollock's state of mind, and his play, were clearly affected. He blundered in a difficult endgame and lost the game in 59 moves. In an extraordinary turnaround, Gossip had tied the score 4–4, with two draws (and one cancelled game). Now both players did their utmost to bring home the match, as well as the lion's share of the $100 purse.

The 11th game was a tense battle ending up eventually in a draw, an equitable result considering the quality of play of both players. The 12th game was an even more tense affair. After 43 moves, the following even position was reached:

Pollock–Gossip
Montreal Chess Club, Twelfth Match Game
January 1895

After 43. ... Bf8–h6

Here, Pollock played **44. g5** and a sharp sequence followed: **44. ... Bg7 45. f5! g×f5 46. Q×f5 Qe5?!** (Instead, 46. ... Qe2+ was the safer path.) **47. g6!+ Ke7 48. Q×e5 d×e5 49. Kh3** and, suddenly, due to Black's chronic weakness on the light squares, Pollock was in a great position and scored convincingly.

But Pollock, ever erratic, lost the next game quickly and so Gossip tied the match 5–5. In the 14th game, Pollock won neatly in a Giuoco Piano as a result of excellent tactical play. After

---

10. The same source recorded the following: "In connection with this match and the reasons alleged by cancelling the eighth game, the wags of the Club are making much fun over the question as to whether a man should be allowed to talk or not while he is playing. One gentleman—who, by the way, is not a member of the Club, but ought to be—went so far as to say that the man who could say nothing during his game but 'Check! Check!! Check!!!' was an 'Unspeakable Turk.' Such a libel on the Turk has evoked the following lines from a correspondent, which we give for what they are worth: 'The grim unutterable Turk is but/A shadow to be human wreck/Who playing chess can utter naught/But, now and then, a 'check'/His visage sour's enframed between/Two bloodless hands; his scrawny neck/With wasted vocal chords is full/That only croak a 'check.'/His back is bent just like a little 'C,'/Of that he doth but little reck/He only lives to move a piece,/And then to howl a 'check'/What Turk so void of soul as this/On bloody field or pirate deck/No fiend can beat the silent fiend/Who speaks no but to a 'check.'" It appears that Gossip didn't like these verses at all and threatened to sue the *Herald*. According to the February 16 issue of the *Herald*, Gossip's decision to sue was met with amusement at the Montreal Chess Club. Its May 4 issue postulated: "This reminds us that a sigh of great relief has gone up from the management of the *Herald*. Mr. Gossip has written that he no longer intends to press his libel suit against this paper on account of certain verses which he claimed to be a scurrilous diatribe against himself. Since this announcement, there has been a tremendous boom in *Herald* stock." Reactions to Gossip's treatment of the disagreement even reached Baltimore, where Pollock had included the *Herald*'s ditty as well as the scornful laughter with which Montreal chess players greeted Gossip's hue and cry (see *Baltimore Sunday News* for February 9 and February 16, 1895).

another draw in game 15, Pollock continued his rollercoaster play when he blundered away a piece, allowing Gossip to once more tie the match, this time at 6–6, with four draws. In the end, according to the *Albany Evening Journal* of February 16, Gossip proposed that the match be declared a draw, a conclusion Pollock accepted. The two men then split the purse provided by Shaw. "The Pollock–Gossip match has been declared a draw," wrote the *Montreal Daily Herald* of the same day, "much to the regret of those who thought to have a lively time over the last game."

F.F. Rowland published in her *Four Leaved Shamrock*[11] bits of her correspondence with James Fish, an amateur chess player and businessman who knew Pollock well while in Canada. Fish's comments also suggest something of Pollock's very limited circumstances while in Montreal.

> Although I had the pleasure of playing many games with him, Dr. Pollock, I am sorry none of them, as far as I know, have been preserved. When Dr. Pollock first struck Montreal, I had removed to Toronto, but business brought me back for a few weeks, and as a matter of course, we met at the Chess Club, after which we each made our way towards our respective boarding house, which turned out to be in the same direction. Without asking each other, we found ourselves going to the same street, eventually we stopped, both of us, at the same house, and we were somewhat amused to find that we both roomed at the same flat, and after a while, for economical and other reasons, we made one room for the both of us, and a jolly time it was, for anyone who knew our friend knew that he was lively or nothing.

Then Rowland cited the following extract from a letter from Pollock to Fish, dated January 9, 1895. It gives us a rare glimpse of Pollock, the man, writing privately to a friend, as well as his opinion of Gossip given, it appears, literally in the middle of the final discussions to declare the match drawn:

> It is very wintry indeed, here, a vast lot of snow has been falling and the drifts are something immense, it has been as low as about 25 below zero some few days ago, it suits me very well, though at present I have a bad cold. A coincidence, nearly as curious as the one when you and I discovered we were living in opposite rooms occurred the other day to me.... On going down to get some hot water, a fellow lodger whom I just knew to speak to, asked me if I knew anything about Bath and Clifton. I said "I should think I did, having for one thing been educated at Clifton College." He said, "Then I daresay, you have heard of my brother, a master there." I had, in 1873, when for half a year I was in his form! I was rather a favourite of his, as he was nothing but a classical man, and I, as a boy, was a bit of a fool at most other subjects. I came out head of his form the term I left that school. I could see a distinct likeness in the present man. I and Gossip are 6 each, and may draw the match. He has proved a terrible crank and has had several games by forfeit, and one "cancelled." He has now a libel suit against the Chess column of the "Herald," Babson is in California, his business you might know, got into bad shape, and his health was much affected. Wheeldon, you hear from I suppose, we often speak of you. He is a man I like better every time I meet him. We have (Gossip and I), just agreed, per the committee, to call the match a draw. Whereby all parties are relieved.
>
> There have been a few considerable fires here, one at the Mercantile Library in James' Street. Glad you did so well with Narraway, taking it all together, most of us agreed that when you were here your play was not anything near as strong as it usually is. Your work is of a trying nature.
>
> Short is winning the handicap. I have about 10 out of 16 played, which is fair, as I give Pawn and two to First Class. I beat Marshall, Falconer, and Cameron at the odds, and I have not played any other of the class.

Immediately after the match, Gossip returned to the United States and stopped in Buffalo, New York, where he would reside for a number of years. Evidently, given his attitude throughout this match and his threat to sue the chess editor of the *Montreal Daily Herald*, his relationship with the Montreal chess media deteriorated badly. As for Pollock, who turned 36 soon after the match ended, it appears his opportunities in Montreal were indeed meager, offering him little chance of a comfortable and pleasant home. Writing to F.F. Rowland, Rogers later recollected[12]:

---

11. Copy in the authors' possession; undated, although clearly appearing after Pollock's death. • **12.** Cited in *Pollock Memories*, page 12.

His [Pollock's] letters to me from Montreal were frequent, and I edited the local news of his Chess column. The tone of his letters, however, indicated discouragement, and I could see that he was not getting on well in Canada. He seemed to dislike the idea of returning to the States, though he undoubtedly would have done so had a good opportunity presented itself. Of his life in Montreal, I know little, as his letters said scarcely anything concerning his personal affairs.

Discouraged or not, Pollock remained in Montreal for the first part of 1895. In the early months that year he continued to offer various exhibitions in the city, but in May he traveled to Saint John, New Brunswick, where he reunited with an old friend from England, the Reverend John de Soyres.[13] He continued to send missives to Baltimore and Albany so as to take care of his two chess columns.

Pollock also sent letters to the *British Chess Magazine* focused on miscellaneous news from Canadian chess clubs. In one such letter, published in the January 1895 issue (pages 17–18) but clearly written and mailed at the end of 1894, Pollock noted with characteristic humor his hunt for game scores from the October–November 1894 New York tournament:

> There is quite a demand for the New York *Sun*, which assiduously prints all the games in the New York Tournament, which will have reached its last round by the time this is mailed, and will doubtless be won by Steinitz. Having failed to obtain a copy of the paper at any of the usual bookstalls the other day, I tried the "Windsor," the principal hotel here. The *Tribune*, *Herald*, and *World* were in evidence, but no *Sun*. "Quite a number of people have been asking for the *Sun* to-day, since I sold my last copy," said the clerk, "is there anything special going on connected with that paper?"

Despite the financial hardships he likely experienced in Canada during this period, Pollock's journalistic standards in his approach to chess writing remained unaltered. Both his Baltimore and his Albany columns abound in original analysis of important or interesting games, brief book reviews, insightful comments and useful news and reports for the amateur. Every now and then, too, Pollock's hat as an instructor in his columns was replaced by that of an entertainer. The following appeared in the *Baltimore Sunday News* of April 6, 1895, under the headline "THE COMIC SIDE OF CHESS":

> We have the best authority for the following amusing instance of the difficulty many players experience in surmounting the P takes P en passant imbroglio. They fail to grasp the sense of the rule that gives a humble pawn a privilege denied to a Rook or Bishop, or even to their majesties. The game in question was played in a Canadian chess club:

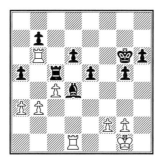

Mr. J vs. Dr. G

13. John de Soyres (1847–1905), the son of a clerk in Exeter, was born on April 26, 1847, and admitted to Cambridge in 1869. He also studied in Munich and Berlin. He was admitted at the Middle Temple on November 21, 1870, and was called to the Bar in 1874. In 1873, de Soyres played in the first Inter-University Chess Match (he also took a board in the 1874 edition). He was ordained as a deacon in London in 1877 and as a priest in 1878. Between 1881 and 1886, de Soyres taught modern history at Queen's College, London, and was a select preacher at Cambridge, 1885. Between 1885 and 1905, the Rev. de Soyres was posted to St. John's, New Brunswick, Canada. He died on February 3, 1905, at Halifax while undergoing an operation. [Source: *Alumni Cantabrigienses*, A Cambridge Alumni Database, www.venn.lib.cam.ac.uk/Documents/acad/intro.html] At the time of his death, de Soyres was remembered as one of Canada's greatest speaking clergymen, and his life illustrated a devotion to profession that Pollock, who as we know so quickly broke off from medicine, may have admired but never emulated.

White has just played P from QB2 to QB4 [c2–c4]. Black replied R to B6 [...Rc3], capturing the P "en-passant." Upon White remonstrating that the R could not hop over the pawn's head, Black claimed that the pawn could not have reached c4 without going to B6 [c3] and that he had captured it on the latter square. White admitted the claim and continued with QKtP to QB4 [b2–c4], capturing the Rook "en-passant," on the ground that the R could not have reached B6 without putting himself en prise to that White pawn. Seized with an idea, Black consented to this very logical, but somewhat Lynch-like lore and continued with B×R! [Bd4–d1] But he lost his Bishop and the game, by the answer R×Pch!! [Rb6–d6] All hands agreed that the laws governing the ancient game were all too crude and none too well framed for such odd emergencies.

On April 24, Pollock sent another letter to the *British Chess Magazine*. It revealed a certain movement, of which he was no doubt actively involved, to revitalize Canadian chess. A championship of the Canadian Chess Association was discussed as was a plan to establish a chess league for interclub matches inspired by the Metropolitan Chess League of New York. After some meetings held in April in Montreal, although some interclub matches were still arranged, it was decided to postpone the league project until the fall. Pollock's letter ended characteristically on a lighter note:

> We are in the midst of the April showers at last, but there are yet plenty of traces of snow to be seen, especially in the vicinity of the St. Lawrence river, which is about opening for traffic commencing with the brisk and active ferry boats. The grass, from a collective point of view, has been green for about a week, and I have seen watercress at 13 cents a bunch, about the first evidence of vegetable life since the arctic winter; but this is not about chess, so I must wind up with the ancient and fish-like hope that I may be able to write again shortly, and wish your readers a happy chess and cricket season.

By the time Pollock's letter appeared in the *British Chess Magazine* (June 1895, pages 262–265), the English chess amateurs needed no reminder that they were less than six weeks away from one of the greatest tournaments ever held. And, to the great satisfaction of English fans, the tournament was to be held in the historically rich Hastings, East Sussex, located about 55 miles southeast of London, along the English coast. Pollock, who could not have missed witnessing, and indeed acting in, such a grand struggle on British soil, mailed an application to the tournament officials in Hastings as a potential representative of Canada. When a letter of acceptance finally informed him he was one of the 22 selected players, Pollock began preparations for his 3,300-mile journey. Not only would Pollock once again face the finest players of his age. He would also be going home. Which element of his itinerary offered the most food for his imagination remains unknown.

KEY TO LOYD'S PROBLEM:

Page 163: **1. Q×h6**

13. At Hastings,
July 1895–February 1896

On the English Coast

On July 27, 1895, after being confirmed as one of the 22 masters invited to Hastings, Pollock, as Canada's representative, sailed to England from Montreal onboard the steamer *Labrador*. For a chess journalist of his caliber, the 36-year-old Pollock must have clearly realized the magnitude of the chess battle soon to commence through the efforts of the Hastings and St. Leonard's Chess Clubs. Heavyweights such as Lasker, Steinitz, Tarrasch, and Chigorin would clearly be favorites, while youthful geniuses such as Walbrodt, Schlechter, Pillsbury, Teichmann, and Janowski were hoping to score as well as possible, if not win a high prize. Experienced masters like Albin, Bird, Marco, Burn, Blackburne, Gunsberg, Mason, Schiffers, and von Bardeleben would help round out the field.[1] As always, no matter how brilliant the field, a few strong tournament players would be missing—in the case of Hastings, Englisch, Winawer and Weiss come to mind—but rarely would such a glittering cast be assembled. And never again would Pollock find himself so closely associated with the game's elite.

---

1. Also selected to participate were S. Tinsley, B. Vergani and J. Mieses. Along with Pollock himself, they completed the field of 22 players selected out of the 38 applicants. Pollock's selection was defended by the *British Chess Magazine* of August 1895 (pages 327–328): "In announcing the competitors' names, our contemporary *The Field* says: 'The sixteen not admitted are sure to be disappointed, but the committee have made the selection with good judgement, except, perhaps, in two instances, being probably guided by the desire of having all countries represented. If, however, Herr Emil Schallopp is amongst the rejected, we are of opinion that he should have taken Pollock's or Vergani's place.' We do not agree with this view of the matter. Mr. Pollock plays as the only representative of one of the most important of the British Colonies—Canada—and one moreover that has done no small service to chess, as witness, for example, the way the Montreal chess-players supported the late Lasker–Steinitz match, and we think the committee has done well in admitting the chosen representative of the Dominion to the Tournament. We have every respect for Herr Schallopp alike as a player, a chess journalist, and a gentleman, but seeing that Germany is already represented by four players, and indirectly—but very really—by Herr E. Lasker, who we believe is still a Prussian, we fail to see, on any grounds, why the Fatherland should be allowed another competitor at the expense of ignoring Canada. Herr Schallopp may be a stronger player than Mr. Pollock, and the same remark may apply to Sig. Vergani, but we think that in selecting competitors for an International Tournament, as wide an area of representation as possible should be secured. From this point of view we regret that Herr van Lennep, a Dutch player, is not one of the actual competitors instead of a reserve. A great International Tournament is not intended solely as a test of supremacy of any individual player, but as a test of the relative strength of the players of various countries. Indeed we are of opinion that an ideal International Chess Tournament would be one wherein every chess-playing country was represented by its chosen champion. Under any circumstances the suggestion that such an important section of the British Empire as the Dominion of Canada should be deprived of its sole representative in order to give our Teutonic friends an additional chance of the prize-money is a suggestion in bad taste, and one which will not commend itself to British chess-players, who will welcome Mr. Pollock's inclusion in the list of competitors."

Participants in the Hastings Tournament 1895. Standing (left to right): Albin, Schlechter, Janowski, Marco, Blackburne, Maróczy (winner of the minor tournament), Schiffers, Gunsberg, Burn and Tinsley. Sitting: Vergani, Steinitz, Chigorin, Lasker, Pillsbury, Tarrasch, Mieses and Teichmann. Five players are missing from this photograph: Pollock, Mason, Bird, Walbrodt and von Bardeleben (*Records of the Copyright Office of the Stationers' Company, October–December 1895*; **photograph by William James Donald**).

The single–round robin tournament was staged at Brassey Institute, very near the sea. The Institute, founded by Thomas Brassey in 1879, featured a Venetian Gothic style building which at the time hosted the Public Reference Library, the Town Museum, and the Schools of Science and Art. The game sessions were scheduled for 1:00 to 5:00 p.m., and 7:00 to 10:00 p.m. Play would proceed at a rate of 30 moves in two hours and, if subsequently needed, 15 moves per hour thereafter. A prize fund of £500 was complemented by consolation money for non–prize winners (£1 per win, 10s. per draw against a prize-winner, £1 for wins against any of the top three players) and several other prizes.[2]

---

2. 1st prize £150, 2nd 115, 3rd 85, 4th 60, 5th 40, 6th 30 and 7th 20. According to the September 1895 *British Chess Magazine* (pages 366–367), several other prizes were included: the winner of the most Evans Gambits (accepted) would receive a ring and Carlo Salvioli's *The Theory and Practice of Chess* (valued at £40); the first winner of seven games received an enlarged photograph (valued at £4, 45) given by G.W. Bradshaw, the tournament's official photographer; £5 would be the prize for the non–prize winner making the highest score against the seven prize winners. A letter to the editor from Herbert E. Dobell published in *The Hastings and St. Leonards Observer* of July 20, 1895, also recorded the following: "The charge for admission to the Brassey Institute will be 1s. per day, 4s. per week, 10s. 6d. for the whole Congress; family ticket to admit three, one guinea. The Committee appeal to the townspeople at large to show their sympathy with the movement by attending the Congress, and, as it lasts for a whole month, it is not too much to ask everyone to go at least once during the time. They will have an opportunity of seeing such a gathering of chess players as they are not likely to have again in their lives, and even if they know nothing of chess it is something to be able to say that they have seen the best players from America, Austria, Germany, France, Italy, Russia, Canada, and England." This particular newspaper carried several detailed reports on the tournament throughout August and September 1895.

The tournament began on Monday, August 5, in the tournament hall of the Brassey Institute with several speeches by tournament and city officials. An eyewitness described the playing area for the *British Chess Magazine* (October 1895, pages 410–417):

> [...] Arriving at the Institute half-an-hour before play time afforded me the opportunity to inspect the room, which was moderate in height, and about 70 feet by 45 feet; the walls, soft in colour, were adorned with about a score of large exquisite pictures (lent by Mr. Thomas Mann, of Hastings), and the floor was carpeted, which imparted a feeling of comfort of a social character, rather than the bareness of a public hall. At the West end was a platform, with table and a few chairs; about five feet distant was a range of four tables, each 4 feet by 3 feet, and separate from each other about 5 feet, this being the space for the players. On either side of the range of tables, and half a yard away, was a line of twenty chairs forming the seating accommodation for the four tables, and leaving ample walking space all round; about five yards away there was another set of four tables with seating, and then a similar three tables, giving space for a large number of onlookers between the lines of chairs. These eleven tables were handsome and substantial, and each was furnished with chess-boards and men, timing clocks, ash trays and match-box, and adjacent, on the floor, spittoons. Having observed these details, my attention was attracted to a gentleman decorated with a red white and blue rosette (the director of play for the day), placing the names of the players, clearly printed on handsome cards, at the left-hand corner of the tables at which they were to sit for that day[...].

Carl Schlechter (John G. White Chess and Checkers Collections, Cleveland Public Library).

While a cold rain fell on the sidewalks outside, as Pollock informed his *Sunday News* readers in his first report, a peculiar way of deciding the pairings took place before the first round commenced: although every round pairing, and assignment of color, would be known before the tournament began, the order of the individual rounds, and hence the day's opponent, would not be known until the actual day of play:

> The president [John Watney] then made the draw of the names to match with the numbers with which the pairings had been arranged, and as the names were called the players were cheered, Blackburne, of Hastings, naturally coming in for the chief ovation: this draw determined the first moves and the pairings of all the rounds, but not the order in which the rounds were to be played. The draw was then made for the round of the day, and the president explained that he, or in his absence the director in charge, would make this draw each day before play commenced. By 1:15 all were at work with eleven clocks ticking away, and not a single competitor absent or late. Mr. [Norman] van Lennep, the reserve man, was also present, but as there was no vacancy he was constrained to play the *rôle* of an onlooker.
>
> The pairing of the opening day gave promise of some fine games, and the spectators were not disappointed. Imagine a very large room covered with red baize and the walls hung with pictures of the best artists; eleven tables in two rows of four and one of three, whilst rows of chairs cause about 100 spectators to keep a sufficient distance from the players [*tournament book*, page 11].

With his "health far from being good" (according to Rowland), Pollock met Carl Schlechter in the first round, the 21-year-old Austrian who at the time was causing a sensation in Viennese chess circles and who in time would climb to the top of the chess world. Pollock avoided the main lines in the Ruy Lopez and forced Schlechter to find concrete ways to get the upper hand with the White pieces. The critical juncture of the game was reached at move 15:

Schlechter–Pollock
Hastings, Round 1
August 5, 1895

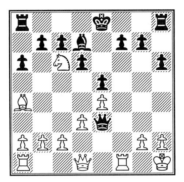

After 14. ... Be6–d7

Here Schlechter played **15. N×e5** and after **15. ... B×a4 16. N×f7 0–0!** Pollock was able to quickly equalize and eventually draw the game after 36 moves. In the tournament book, Emanuel Schiffers stated that 15. Nb4 would have not given Schlechter any superiority, but this is arguable. In fact, 15. Nb4 was a very good idea, one considered "tempting" by Pollock himself in his *Sunday News* column. For instance, 15. ... B×a4 16. Nd5 Qc5 17. b4! (Schiffers overlooked this sharp retort) 17. ... Qc6 18. Qg4! and Pollock's position would have been completely compromised.

On Tuesday, August 6, in his second game, Pollock again found himself with the Black pieces, this time against another Vienna-based master, the 32-year-old Georg Marco, one of the most knowledgeable theoreticians of his time. Pollock's opening play was hesitant and starting with his tenth move he made errors which allowed Marco a quick win. The next day he reversed the scenario against the 32-year-old Beniamino Vergani, an Italian expert, who managed at least four suspect moves in his first 11, and whom Pollock caused to resign at move 23. At least Pollock had scored the whole point, although Vergani was outclassed and at the conclusion of the event would bring up the tournament's rear.[3]

On August 8, as reported in Horace F. Cheshire's tournament book, a full day's excursion took place:

> Today the masters are taken to Battle in wagonettes, and by the kind permission of the Duchess of Cleveland and Lord Brassey visit Battle Abbey and Normanhurst Court. A party of fifty-five, including all the masters (except Lasker and Burn) and many press-men, start in splendid weather, which keeps up all day. They drive to the Abbey, where they are photographed, go over Normanhurst Court, which is much admired, and, driving back, arrive at six o'clock, having thoroughly enjoyed the day. In the evening the masters are taken to

---

3. For some details of Vergani's selection and reactions in Italy following his finish as last, see the *British Chess Magazine*, November 1895, page 467. The tournament book describes him as being "slight of figure and lame, but always with a smile." *The Hastings Chess Tournament 1895*, ed. by Horace F. Cheshire (G.P. Putnam's Sons, 1896; reprint Dover, 1962), page 362.

a special concert on the pier, and the enjoyment manifested proved the oft-made assertion that chess-players are generally musicians. The masters had the option also of seats at the theatre to see *Charley's Aunt*, but all chose the music [*tournament book*, page 59].[4]

When play resumed the next day, Pollock, handling Black for the third time in four rounds, faced the young American, Pillsbury. The latter was eager to avenge his loss to Pollock during the Impromptu tournament in New York two years earlier. A highly theoretical Ruy Lopez commenced with both players following well known book recommendations. Just before 30 moves were made, Pollock succeeded in capturing one of Pillsbury's pawns. The capture, however, came with a price: his piece development lagged and the American threatened to take over the game through a precise strategy executed on the board's dark squares. Initially, at his 32nd move, Pillsbury missed a simple win and permitted Pollock to escape from a difficult position and compli-

Steinitz in August 1895 (*Records of the Copyright Office of the Stationers' Company, July–September 1895;* **photograph by William James Donald).**

cate matters. Finally, just when the complications seemed to favor him, Pollock blundered dramatically and lost.

During the fifth round, on August 10, Pollock met Richard Teichmann, a 26-year-old German player who would later emerge as one of the world's top masters. The 32-move Ponziani they contested was balanced, and Pollock secured the draw with a neat combination at his 26th move. Thus, after the first week of play, Pollock stood with a score of 2–3, the same as that of Albin, Schlechter, Gunsberg, Blackburne and Janowski. Overall, Steinitz was leading (4½), followed by Chigorin and von Bardeleben (4), Pillsbury and Schiffers (3½), Lasker, Tinsley and Mieses (3). Interestingly enough, after five rounds no player remained with a clean score, and 20 of the 22 masters had lost at least one game. (The two exceptions were Steinitz and von Bardeleben.)

---

4. With this occasion a group photograph was taken in front of the entrance to Battle Abbey but not all participants were present. It was published on page 221 of *The Sketch*, August 21, 1895. In an article for the *Birmingham Gazette* and reproduced in the *Chess Player's Chronicle* of September 4, 1895 (pages 258–260), R.J. Buckley gave a thorough description of the excursion and noted the following: "James Mason and W.H.K. Pollock, who had declined the ride, reclining on the sands in derisive mockery, claiming the prestige of having been able to rest on the day of rest, and to devote their spare time to a little skittle chess, preparatory to the renewed contest of the morrow" (information provided in Edward Winter's *CNs* 5836, 5841, 7354 and 7879). For unknown reasons, Pollock also does not appear in the other well-known group photograph taken at Hastings.

On Monday, August 12, Pollock began the tournament's second week of play with Black against the tournament's leader, Steinitz. Given their past relations, and Steinitz's clear animosity toward the younger man, it is difficult to speculate whether the two exchanged any words prior to the game, or, for that matter, during the tournament. Since the shooting incident at Upper Montclair, the two had parted ways despite their earlier cooperation. They did exchange hard-hitting moves over the board that day at Hastings, however, in what turned out to be Pollock's only official tournament game against Steinitz. Pollock made use of a little explored idea in the Giuoco Piano (**4. ... Qe7**), which he had previously tested in a series of offhand games against Lasker at the Manhattan Chess Club prior to the latter's world championship match against Steinitz. Pillsbury later annotated the game for the tournament book.

Steinitz–Pollock
Hastings, Round 6
August 12, 1895

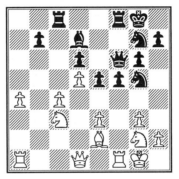

After 27. Nb5–c3?!

About Steinitz's last move, Pillsbury commented: "A violation of an old-time principle that the pieces should not be left loose and unguarded. Black takes advantage of this misplay with great precision, and obtains a winning advantage. White should have played 27. Qc2 Ne4 28. Nc3 Nc5 29. a5 with a fair prospect of attack on the weak b-pawn." After Steinitz's inexactitude, Pollock got a first chance to prove the superior mobility of his pieces with **27. ... f4!!**, a brilliant pawn push that seemed to have surprised Steinitz. His weak reply, **28. Qc2?**, allowed **28. ... f3!** after which Steinitz's position seems to be beyond redemption despite some defensive resources: **29. Nh4 Nf5!** and Pollock eventually won in 58 moves. According to multiple newspaper accounts, loud applause from the large throng of spectators watching this particular game rocked the hall. The game must have been quite satisfying for Pollock, and undoubtedly galling to his chief detractor and opponent.

The next day, Pollock had to battle another giant: Lasker, the reigning world champion. The latter, no doubt keenly aware of Pollock's appetite for an early offensive, wisely declined Pollock's Evans Gambit offer and proceeded to an exact and swift win as a consequence of Pollock's neglecting the development of his pieces, a mistake highlighted by Tarrasch in his annotations for the tournament book.

With 3 points out of seven games, Pollock had Black against Albin in the eighth round on August 14. He had defeated the Romanian-Austrian master during the second round of the Impromptu tournament in New York and they must have known each other well since Albin spent nearly three years in America before his arrival in England.

Albin–Pollock
Hastings, Round 8
August 14, 1895

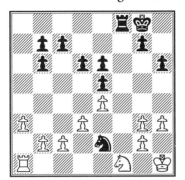

After 21. Nh2–f1

After 21 moves and massive simplifications, Pollock here went for **21. ... R×f1+ 22. R×f1 N×g3+ 23. Kg1 N×f1 24. K×f1**. Teichmann commented in the tournament book: "Black is eager to simplify the game and reduces it to what he most likely thought an easily won pawn ending. His two double pawns, however, ought to have given him some apprehensions about the possibility of winning. 21. ... Nd4 followed by 22. ... Rf2 would have given Black a won game in a few moves." Albin eventually mismanaged the endgame and lost, but Teichmann took considerable space to prove he could have drawn the pawn endgame despite being a pawn down.

After a day off, spent with more entertainment and various visits, Pollock sat again at the playing table on August 16, this time across from 34-year-old Curt von Bardeleben. The German must have remembered well his loss to Pollock during the international masters tournament at Bradford in 1888. Following a highly original treatment of the opening (**1. d4 c5**—which made Blackburne comment in the tournament book: "This bizarre defense is not to be commended."), Pollock obtained a good position, but soon thereafter he got in hot water and resigned before his 26th move.[5] In round ten, played the next day, Pollock drew the 27-year-old Janowski when in fact he should have won easily from the following position:

Pollock–Janowski
Hastings, Round 10
August 17, 1895

After 38. ... f5–f4?

---

5. In fact, Pollock's decision to play **1. d4 c5** was exceedingly "modern" for the 1890s and in contemporary chess would eventually become known as part of the "Benoni system" of openings.

Janowski could have done better with 38. ... Qe1! instead of the impulsive text move. Pollock was quick to appreciate his opponent's error, and made the most of it by playing **39. Re4!** and suddenly Janowski's king was in danger of being checkmated. Janowski replied with **39. ... Qb1**, a move which received an "!" from Curt von Bardeleben in his tournament book annotations, convinced this move saved Janowski's game. In fact, Janowski was completely lost after Pollock's 39th move, but after **40. Re6+ Kh5** Pollock played a relatively poor move **41. Bf2?**, and after **42. ... Ng3** followed it up with the error **42. Be1?**, which allowed Janowski to draw immediately by perpetual check. Instead, Pollock could have won beautifully with 41. Rc8! (threatening mate on the h-file) 41. ... Q×b2 42. Bd4!! Q×d4 43. R×e2 and Janowski could have resigned on the spot.

Pollock lost his next two games to two of his closest chess friends. In the 11th round, he met Amos Burn, who had just returned from the United States after a long business sojourn in that country. Pollock appealed again to the then-eccentric **1. d4 c5**, and a tense battle ensued. For about 30 moves, the play was exceedingly balanced, but then Pollock missed some fine tactics that could have given him the full point. Instead, his errors did not go unpunished and Burn eventually won in 38 moves. Then, with only a 4½–6½ score, Pollock met the 46-year-old James Mason. The latter's insistent kingside attack forced Pollock to make a careful defense. But he couldn't hold. Several errors left his position a shambles, and he resigned after White's 37th move.

Round 13 was played on August 21, and found Pollock with White against the 33-year- old Siegbert Tarrasch. As strong as Tarrasch was, Pollock could not have asked for a better opponent to face when in the mood to play his highly unorthodox chess. And Pollock started the fireworks

Dawid Janowski (John G. White Chess and Checkers Collections, Cleveland Public Library).

with his second move. After **1. e4 e6**, Pollock played **2. e5**, a move that he previously used against Blackburne in 1886. As Pollock confessed, the main idea was to take "both Tarrasch and *himself* out of the books" (emphasis in the original) and play an original game. Instead of the common-sense 2. ... d5, Tarrasch replied with **2. ... f6**, following a path similar to Blackburne's. In April 1896, Pollock was asked to annotate this game for the *St. John* (New Brunswick) *Globe* chess column. In addition to elaborate annotations, Pollock prefaced the game with remarks that let us consider how he explained the play to himself:

A Memorable Game

When two strong players meet in an important single contest over the board for the first time, there are several reasons why the unexpected should be expected to occur. The stronger, or the one bearing the greatest repute, is less likely to be prepared for the style of the weaker than vice versa, and is more likely to be caught off his guard. The weaker, particularly if (as in my case in the game about to be considered) he has undergone some galling reverses just previously and is looking for more trouble, will be furnished with a nervous stimulus or goad to a strenuous cerebral effort—a stimulus such as produces what are called "inspired games," and which cannot by any effort of will be "called up" by the player. I cannot explain this "inspiration," but its effects on a man's play are usually that his moves are made with nearly twice the ease and rapidity of ordinary occasions and he feels confident of producing something new—up to the point of mental exhaustion.

Ordinarily, however, an inspired game is brief—the brilliancy partie in a tournament rarely exceeds 30 moves at the resignation point. The very natural question arises: suppose the other player is *also* breathed upon by the celestial afflatus and equally sits down at the board with the *conviction* that he is able to win the game? It will hardly ever happen that two players endowed with powers of originality shall, from the start of a game, be possessed of equal "form," an equally well distributed lubrication of the cephalic machinery, and the player who is "there first" will obtain a superior position, especially if opposed by a tolerably firm resistance, which a few skilful and problem-like touches will suffice to turn brilliantly into a winning advantage.

It may be interesting to mention partly as illustrating the above remarks (although I am not going to give myself away as having been the weaker player on *each* occasion) that, upon my first meeting them in tournament play I have succeeded in defeating Steinitz, Pillsbury, Tarrasch, Mason, Lipschütz, and Bardeleben, and amongst stars of somewhat lesser magnitude but not lesser brilliancy, Lee, Mortimer, Hanham, Mills, Locock, Thorold, Loman, Hodges, and Albin, while drawing with Showalter and having really stubborn battles with Lasker, Zukertort, Weiss, Bird, and Mackenzie. Others I forget and I am glad of it, for I have already blown my own trumpet harder than is good for my bronchitis.

Most of your readers will know Dr. Tarrasch as a short and slightly-built man of keenly intellectual but very kindly mien, very courteous in demeanour and outwardly "cool and collected" over the chessboard. In some of these respects, as also in his vivacity, habit of wearing a beard and spectacles, he reminds me of the late Dr. Zukertort, but Dr. Tarrasch is by no means *diminutive* in stature, and I may say, with apology for comparisons, that in conversation with the latter the most timid "duffer" would be at home and there is never any need to try to "humour" the great "Nuremberg medicine man."[6]

After twenty moves Pollock and Tarrasch reached the following position:

Pollock–Tarrasch
Hastings, Round 13
August 21, 1895

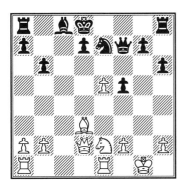

After 18. … b7–b6?

Siegbert Tarrasch (*Records of the Copyright Office of the Stationers' Company, July–September 1895*; photograph by William James Donald).

---

6. Pollock's notes (cited above) and original annotations to this game appeared in the *St. John Globe* of April 10, 1896, and subsequently in the *Baltimore Sunday News* of April 25, 1896.

Looking for ways to conclude development and secure his king, Tarrasch committed a fatal error. Instead, 18. ... Nc6 would have allowed him some chances to resist the forthcoming assault. Pollock swiftly scored with **19. Nf4 Bb7 20. Bb5 Nc6 21. e6!** and Tarrasch was forced to resign a few moves later.

On the evening of Thursday, August 22, Pollock participated in the banquet at the Queen's Hotel designed to entertain the masters and the press. He listened to heartfelt speeches from Lasker, Steinitz, Chigorin (through an interpreter), Tarrasch (in German), and Bird.

On August 23, Pollock won against Gunsberg, an old acquaintance. Pollock, "in a masterly manner," as Albin remarked, took advantage of Gunsberg's weak opening play. With similar ease, Pollock took down another one of his compatriots, Bird, in the 15th round. In just three rounds he had improved his score to 7½–7½.

But with six games remaining, Pollock's comeback ground to a halt. On August 26, when the 16th round was played, Pollock faced the 24-year-old Carl A. Walbrodt. A clever sacrifice of the exchange allowed Pollock serious counterplay and the game was called a draw after 36 moves, a fair result considering the final position. But over the next two rounds, Pollock lost to Mieses and Blackburne. Then in round 19, played on August 30, he met Chigorin, one of the leaders. An eyewitness reported for the *British Chess Magazine* (October 1895, pages 410–417), giving a detailed account:

> [...] Visitors and players have gradually arrived, and taken their places; punctually as the room clock strikes one, the director rings his bell, play-time has arrived, and now passing from table to table the director ascertains that all players are at their games, moving with more or less promptness or consideration; Mr. Pollock and Mr. Bird are, however, not yet present, but he sets their clocks in motion. [...]
>
> The room was now crowded with spectators, chess players in social or friendly converse, or eager onlookers; and although notices "requested visitors to be as quiet as possible, and not to make remarks in the hearing of players" were prominent, a low hum of conversation pervaded the room, not enough to distract the players, but friendly greetings of visitors from all parts of the Continent as well as the United Kingdom; indeed it was a social function, free but orderly. Here was Alapin the Russian master, there Rosenthal the French master, yonder, Minckwitz the German master, Maróczy the Hungarian, and many whose names are household words in the chess world, all, in the intervals of onlooking, exchanging greetings, introductions, and friendly talk. A marked feature too was the large attendance of the fair sex, who, with their gayer costumes, gave brilliancy and colour to the assembly, and although their mood evidently was not so much the rigour of the game as the opportunity for social and friendly intercourse, their presence added greatly to the pleasure of both the Masters and spectators. Occasionally some earnest and eager onlooker would draw his chair forward or stand up in the arena of play, when the steward, with blue and white rosette, who was responsible for the particular table would repress this over-eagerness with "Kindly keep your seat in line, or stand outside the chairs, we must study the comfort of the players first, and the convenience of onlookers next"; this was quite sufficient to immediately restore the original orderliness or arrangement. [...]
>
> Returning after an interval of nearly two hours, the confusion attendant on the adjournment has been restored to order, the stewards are distributing the scoring pads, adjusting clocks to the times marked on the sealed envelopes, and making ready for the resumption of the games. Punctually at the stroke of seven o'clock the director's bell rings, the forces are placed in correct position, the move recorded on suspending play is made, the clocks set in motion, and the games are in progress. During the interval, I have heard reports of several critical positions, and visit first board 2, where W.H.K. Pollock, a tallish good looking fellow, courteous and pleasant, with poetic fancies both in chess and words, and who sits far back with arms resting on his knees and face almost touching the board, so that it seemed hardly possible for him to view the whole, is faced by M. Chigorin, the Russian master, of moderate height, well-knit frame, dark olive complexion, high round forehead, jet black hair and most penetrating eyes, very quiet and affable in manner, with hands clasped and the fore part of the arms resting on the table, and whose slight trembling of the right leg resting on the toes indicates the excitement of mind.

Pollock offered Chigorin an Evans Gambit and the Russian accepted. A tactical slugfest ensued and just before move 20, the following position was reached:

Pollock–Chigorin
Hastings, Round 19
August 30, 1895

After 19. ... Bb6–a5

Pollock continued with the very ambitious **20. Rd7** but after **20. ... Nb6! 21. R×c7 Rhc8 22. R×b7 B×c3 22. Ba3+?** (22. Bh4+ was a slightly better choice) **22. ... Kf6**, the Russian master was in charge, and Pollock eventually lost in 40 moves. Instead, with 20. Re4!, Pollock would have gotten a much better result. With this win against yet another Evans Gambit, Chigorin secured the special prize of the "special emerald ring, set in diamonds" and a copy of Salvioli's book for his seventh win against this opening.

Pollock's wavering finish concluded with a blunder against Tinsley on August 31 and, on September 2, a final game and a final loss, this time to Schiffers. Pollock finished the tournament in 19th place, with 8 points out of 21 games (6–11, with 4 draws). In the last six rounds, after finally battling back to an even score, he had managed a paltry one draw. Curiously, despite his dismal finish, Pollock (along with Pillsbury) was the only player to defeat both Steinitz and Tarrasch, players who finished fourth and fifth, respectively. Certainly Hastings 1895 represented another characteristically erratic result for the master of erratic play. For his efforts he collected £6 10s. as consolation money.[7]

At the same time, Pollock had nothing but praise for the youthful, American conqueror of Hastings. Taking Pollock's words from the *Albany Evening Journal,* Hazeltine in his September 21, 1895, *New York Clipper* column published the following:

> In view of the importance and rank of the tournament, the winning of first prize by a genuine Plymouth Rock American, with no naturalization papers in his pocket, is a matter of honest pride to the American people. ...

---

7. Horace F. Cheshire, who authored the English version of the tournament book, had the following to say about Pollock: "POLLOCK, W.H.K.—36 at the time of the tournament, Pollock was born February 21, 1859, at Cheltenham. Educated at Somersetshire College, Bath, and Clifford College, he took his medical qualifications in Ireland in 1882. There he acquired much of his chess, being a favorite at the Dublin Chess Club, especially on account of his great ability in the direction of simultaneous play. Later, he and his brother (the Rev. J. Pollock) were well known at Bath, but we hear of him in a great variety of places in the British Isles and America. He has played in numerous tournaments with varying success. Crossing the Atlantic five years ago, on the occasion of the American Congress, he settled in Canada and became the chief representative of that country, but up until now he has not returned from England. He beat Moehle in 1891, and could probably take a better position by treating the game more seriously. Pleasant in manners, brilliant in style, and an agreeable companion or opponent, he still lacks staying power. Many of his games are of the highest order, and the one against Weiss at the 1889 Congress has become historic. He is a good writer, and is the chess editor of several columns, and has contributed to many others. Many brilliancy prizes at various times have fallen to his lot" [*tournament book*, page 360]. Aside from suggesting to readers that Pollock had immediately moved from Europe to Canada, and had lived there for five years, ignoring his years in Baltimore and Albany, Cheshire's write-up regarding Pollock is not only accurate factually but perceptive psychologically.

The victory does not carry with it, as stated in some papers, the championship of the world; that still remains between Lasker and Steinitz; but it does carry with it the honor of defeating in open competition the picked talent of the world, a task of greater powers of endurance, nerve, and knowledge of chess than the winning of a set match. His victory marks a new era also in American chess, inasmuch as it holds up to the world the high character of play prevalent on this side of the Atlantic. There has been a disposition in certain foreign quarters to sneer at American chess as "imported"; but the routing of all Europe by an American, who has just left the amateur ranks, will speak volumes on the progress of the game in this country.

Brief Visits at Home and Ireland

On September 5, three days after the tournament concluded, Pollock took part in a special dinner for the champion of Hastings, Pillsbury, at the Metropolitan Chess Club. Present also were Steinitz and Chigorin. In the evening, Pillsbury gave a 14-board simultaneous exhibition at the Ladies' Chess Club, conceding the odds of a knight to all but one of the women (11–2, with 1 draw). Following a few more séances in London, Pillsbury sailed to New York on September 21, where he would receive a hero's welcome. While Chigorin, Lasker, Steinitz and others left London rather quickly, Pollock, noted the October 1895 issue of the *British Chess Magazine*, "is staying with his friends in the West of England." It was time for him to pay a visit to Bristol, Clifton and Bath.

On Thursday, September 18, Pollock was in Bristol and residing "with his relatives" at 5 Berkeley Square, Clifton. He met with the members of the chess circle of the Literary and Philosophic Club and gave them a 15-board simultaneous exhibition, scoring 12–3.[8] But, even when he was finally at home, Pollock remained a peripatetic character. On October 2, Pollock visited his former club and gave a simultaneous exhibition.[9] In the latter part of September, according to the *Newcastle Weekly Courant* of September 29, Pollock addressed a letter to chess circles in Newcastle proposing some exhibitions in the city. The visit was announced in the October 12 edition of the same newspaper column, informing its readers that Pollock would give a simultaneous exhibition at the Newcastle Chess Club on Monday, October 14, followed by a visit at the Art Gallery the next day when he would play against all comers. According to the *British Chess Magazine* (November 1895, page 470), on the first day of his visit in Newcastle Pollock gave a 20-board simultaneous exhibition (18–1, with 1 draw) and on the next day at the Art Gallery, he again played simultaneously against 20 players, scoring an identical result.

His trek across the countryside was punctuated by one performance after another. From Newcastle, Pollock proceeded in the last week of October to Yorkshire. According to the *Liverpool Mercury* of November 2, citing a report from the *Bradford Observer*, on October 18 Pollock stopped at Harrogate where he gave a 14-board simultaneous exhibition against the members of the Harrogate Chess Club at the St. James's Hotel, winning all games. The next day he visited the Leeds Chess Club where he played three games in consultation against the strongest players of the club (1–0, with 2 draws). In the evening, in a room crowded with spectators, according to the *Liverpool Mercury*, he faced ten players simultaneously. The same newspaper column noted that Pollock was surprised by the strength of his opponents, who gave him one of his lowest

---

8. Three players played two games against the master; from Bristol's *Western Daily Press* of September 20, 1895: "No less remarkable than the accuracy, was the quickness with which his [Pollock's] varying designs were elaborated and carried out." • **9.** This was mentioned in a club report in the *Bath Chronicle* of March 26, 1896, but without a score.

exhibition results ever: 3 wins, 5 losses, 2 draws. He then gave simultaneous exhibitions at Farsley Chess Club (7–0, with 3 draws), Woodlesford Chess Club (22–0, with two games unfinished), and Bradford Chess Club (13–0, with 2 draws and four games unfinished).[10]

As announced by the *Weekly Irish Times* on October 19, Pollock was planning to visit Ireland as well. It appears that his visit to Dublin materialized only in the second half of December. Pollock spent most of November in Bristol attending the club's meetings and, as evidenced by the *Bath Chronicle* of November 21, serving as adjudicator in the traditional match between Bath and Bristol, a match that launched his chess career a decade earlier.

His trip to Ireland took place in late December. The December 26 edition of the *Weekly Irish Times* noted:

Harry N. Pillsbury in August 1895 (*Records of the Copyright Office of the Stationers' Company, July– September 1895***; photograph by William James Donald).**

> The chess-loving public of Dublin will be glad to hear that Mr. W.H.K. Pollock, Canada's representative at the recent international tournament at Hastings, is staying at Avoca House, Blackrock, and we hope may be able to give an exhibition of simultaneous play at some of the numerous chess clubs in the district this week.

Two days later, the same newspaper announced:

> The secretaries of the Dublin chess clubs have now a grand opportunity of giving their members a first-class Christmas entertainment, owing to the fact that Canada's representative at the recent international chess tournament, W.H.K. Pollock, is at present staying at Avoca House, Blackrock, and will be happy to give exhibitions of simultaneous play during his short sojourn amongst his old friends.

But there was no exhibition until after the New Year's Eve celebrations. The reason was disclosed by the *Bristol Mercury and Daily Post* of January 18: Pollock was ill. F.F. Rowland remembered the reaction upon seeing Pollock: "His friends were, however, much pained with his altered appearance, for signs were evident that the fell disease, consumption, was sapping his constitution."[11] Yet, against the recommendation of his medical advisor, on Thursday, January 2, 1896, Pollock was in Dublin at the Coffee Palace, 6 Townsend Street where he spent a "most enjoyable evening" in the company of a large meeting of players who came to greet the master. He would not disappoint his old friends. Pollock gave a 15-board simultaneous exhibition scoring 10–3, with 2 draws, in two hours and 45 minutes, according to the *Weekly Irish Times* of January 11. A

---

10. Various newspaper columns gave slightly different numbers for Pollock's exhibitions in October 1895; the chess column of the *Bristol Mercury and Daily Post* of November 2 gave a summary of Pollock's exhibitions and summarized his record: he played 127 games and scored +102 −9 =10, with 6 games left unfinished. • **11.** F.F. Rowland, *Pollock Memories*, pages 5–6.

great number of Irish chess players were present at the séance, including T.B. Rowland, one of his closest friends. Nine days later, on January 11, Pollock also gave a simultaneous exhibition at the Blackrock Chess Club at the Parochial House, Blackrock.

After nearly two weeks of recovery, on January 24 Pollock left Dublin for Bristol on board the steamship *Argo*. He must have spent some weeks at home with his father, now a chaplain for the Bristol Blind Asylum, and his brother John, who, the local chess column noted, was still a player in county matches. No record survives of his reception at home. Evidently, he kept in touch with his Dublin friends, too. In early March, together with his friend and future chronicler, F.F. Rowland, he acted as a referee for a Ladies' Chess Tourney in the city. The *Weekly Irish Times* of March 7, in announcing Pollock's role in the affair, also published the following poem by J. Paul Taylor titled "The Pilgrim of Chess":

> Why cherish for chess such intense predilection,
> And the openings and endings so painfully learn?
> Ah! I linger awhile o'er some tale of affection
> And the leaves of a novel luxuriously turn.
> Nay! Nay! Cries the student, mid toil and distress,
> No rest but the grave for the Pilgrim of Chess.
> Though deaf unto music, and blind to the beauty
> Of painting or sculpture, then surely can't feel
> The power of ambition or dictates of duty?
> Then spare for these trifles some share of thy zeal,
> He was too much engrossed to reply—as you'll guess,
> How blind and how deaf is the Pilgrim of Chess.
> I paused, for reception could scare have been colder;
> But then came a touch from some tresses of hair;
> For a sweet girlish face had peeped over my shoulder,
> While the voice of its owner rang out in the air—
> "Ah, dreamer, awake! Then will have to confess
> That the spirit of Love is more potent than chess."
> As the sound of that voice came a change o'er the player,
> And he smiled as he gazed at her radiant face;
> No partner in waltzes could then have been gayer,
> Of the lines on his forehead scarce lingered a trace.
> Through the rest of his life he had reason to bless
> The love that awakened the Pilgrim of Chess.

One cannot help wonder how differently Pollock's life might have turned out had he fallen in love with one of the chess-playing ladies orbiting around his friend Mrs. Rowland. But for Pollock, one of the game's most devoted pilgrims, chess proved more potent than anything else. Despite the insistent requests from his family and closest friends not to proceed with such a plan, by mid–March 1896 Pollock was back in Montreal, via Halifax. While his family in Clifton must have wondered how many years were to pass before they would see him again, he would return to the family much sooner than expected. But the unexpected return would be a most unfortunate one. And all too brief.

14. Towards an Early Endgame, March–October 1896

A Sudden Farewell

Pollock arrived in Montreal shortly before St. Patrick's Day, March 17, 1896. Writing to F.F. Rowland in Ireland that afternoon, he shared his love for "dear old Ireland":

I received the little tin box of real Irish Shamrocks about mid-day to-day, quite fresh too. You cannot think how proud I felt and so sweet a remembrance of dear old Ireland. It was very kind of you, I think they are meant to grow, but I could not help plucking off some little sprigs to wear, and to give to one or two of my Irish friends here. Why, I don't suppose there are six people in the city have had such a present, as they do not generally keep fresh. This is a great St. Patrick's Day. Processions all over the city. People come from the Eastern States, but to-day is better than usual.[1]

In April Pollock was giving more exhibitions in Montreal. On April 18, for instance, in addition to a chess lecture he gave a 10-board simultaneous exhibition for the players of the Heather Chess Club. On May 9, according to the *Montreal Gazette*, Pollock gave another simultaneous exhibition at the Cercle St. Dennis and delivered a short address on openings.

Pollock also spent many hours annotating the games played in St. Petersburg, where the four giants, Lasker, Pillsbury, Steinitz and Chigorin were competing, and some of his annotations appeared in the *British Chess Magazine*. Later his work became part of the tournament book he coauthored with his friend, James Mason. Howard J. Rogers recollected the following in his letter to F.F. Rowland:

I tried hard, not knowing the extremity of his health, to induce him to come to the midsummer tournament of the New York State Association, held at Ontario Beach, on Lake Ontario, in July 1896. His last letter to me, from which I quote, was written on July 24th, and throws much light on his physical condition and upon his unsatisfactory life in Montreal. "To me nothing would be more delightful than a trip to Rochester for the Ontario Beach meeting, though it would be questionable if I could play decently. But it is impossible; I cannot seem to get the better of my trouble. Barring incidents, I must sail on August 1st. Three or four days in the land of Cousin Jonathan, who, for the most part treated me exceedingly well, would indeed have been a pleasure to take the taste of these half-breeds out of my mouth before sailing. Please convey to the committee my extreme regret at being prevented from coming, through illness."[2]

Considering Pollock's language as recollected by Rogers, and the sense of bitterness in some

---

1. Cited by F.F. Rowland in *Four Leaved Shamrock* [undated clipping on file]. • **2.** F.F. Rowland, *Pollock Memories*, page 12; the fragment from Pollock's letter to Rogers also appeared in the *Albany Evening Journal* of October 24, 1896.

of his words, his last days on Canadian soil were far from idyllic. Given his stay in that city as a whole was disappointing, one might wonder why he returned from England to Montreal in the first place.

The reasons for his return to his homeland, however, were sadly transparent. The *Montreal Gazette* of July 25, published the day after Pollock penned his letter to Rogers, announced Pollock's actual departure:

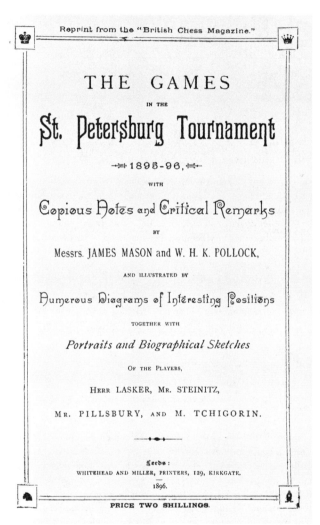

Reprint from the "British Chess Magazine."

THE GAMES

IN THE

St. Petersburg Tournament

1895–96,

WITH

Copious Notes and Critical Remarks

BY

Messrs. JAMES MASON and W. H. K. POLLOCK,

AND ILLUSTRATED BY

Numerous Diagrams of Interesting Positions

TOGETHER WITH

Portraits and Biographical Sketches

OF THE PLAYERS,

HERR LASKER, MR. STEINITZ,

MR. PILLSBURY, AND M. TCHIGORIN.

Leeds:
WHITEHEAD AND MILLER, PRINTERS, 129, KIRKGATE.

1896.

PRICE TWO SHILLINGS.

The title page of James Mason & W.H.K. Pollock's *The Games in the St. Petersburg Tournament 1895–96* (Leeds: Whitehead and Miller, 1896); Pollock provided in-depth annotations for 20 out of the 36 featured games (courtesy Edward Winter).

DR. POLLOCK RETURNS HOME

We are very sorry to hear that Dr. Pollock's health is so much impaired that he will be compelled to return to the old country at an early date. His prowess over the board and his personal popularity have made him many friends in Montreal, and he will leave us with many good wishes for restored health, and prosperity in chess and every other department of human activity.

On August 8, Pollock announced his departure from the pages of the *Baltimore Sunday News*, where he had for years entertained his readers and chess friends alike:

Baltimore, August 8, 1896

TO ALL READERS—IMPORTANT NOTICE

With very great regret I have to announce that I am obliged to abdicate the chair of chess editor of this column. Serious and prolonged trouble of (at least) a bronchial nature has compelled my severance from my many delightful chess associations in this country and I am due to sail to my paternal home in Bristol on this day, if perchance complete rest and home treatment may effect a restoration.

Any personal communications must be addressed to me at 5 Berkeley square, Bristol, Eng., only

FAREWELL![3]

Even as health necessitated his return home, Pollock annotated for his readers the first game he received from the Nuremberg tournament: the first round draw between Blackburne and Teichmann. Pollock found

---

3. Notice of Pollock's departure appeared in various other American newspaper columns, and in the September 1895 *British Chess Magazine*, page 352 prefaced as follows: "We greatly regret to find that owing to ill-health Mr. W.H.K. Pollock is obliged to resign the editorship of his able chess column in the *Baltimore News*, and to come to his paternal home at Bristol for complete rest."

the game extremely interesting for the problem-like draw Blackburne discovered. On the very Sunday his last *Sunday News* column appeared, Pollock stepped aboard the *Vancouver*, a 5000-ton transatlantic passenger liner.

An Unfortunate Collision

Pollock's troubles, however, were far from over. At about 11:30 p.m., off Father Point, Rimouski, Quebec, during a night made deadly by dense fog, the *Vancouver* suffered a head-on collision with the ship *Lake Ontario*, a 4500-ton Beaver liner.[4] The *Daily Mail and Empire* (Toronto) of August 11 reported the accident as follows:

THE VANCOUVER
IN COLLISION WITH THE STEAMER LAKE
ONTARIO—BOTH VESSELS DAMAGED—
PUTTING INTO PORT FOR REPAIRS

Father Point, Que., August 10—R.M.S. Vancouver, that sailed from Quebec on Sunday morning at 9:20, received the British mails and some passengers off here and proceeded for Liverpool at 10:30 p.m. Sunday. A dense fog prevailed, and the Father Point fog signal was fired steadily from 7 p.m. until 3 o'clock this morning. The Vancouver had to feel her way in here by the use of her lead, aided by the fog signal. About an hour and a half after passing here,

W.H.K. Pollock in mid–1895; a photograph by George Bradshaw that was also featured in the Hastings 1895 tournament book (*Sportfolio: Portraits and Biographies of Heroes and Heroines of Sport and Pastime*, London, 1896, page 138).

while she was proceeding slowly with her whistle sounding regularly, all at once she was run into bow on by an inward-bound steamer. Her bow on the starboard side was badly smashed in almost down to the water line. Both her anchors were carried away with the hawser pipe, and her windlass broken, but her collision bulkhead remained intact. [...]⁵

Passengers on the *Vancouver* provided details summarized in the Quebec *Daily Telegraph* of August 8:

In an interview with passengers of the *Vancouver* it was learned that owing to the thick fog the tender with the mails had considerable difficulty in finding the steamer on arriving off Rimouski, shortly after 10 o'clock, that the *Vancouver*'s whistle was kept almost continuously blowing, with Captain Williams on the bridge and other officers of the ship at their posts. The crash came after 11 o'clock, when all the passengers had retired or were

---

4. The *Vancouver* was an ill-fated liner. According to data provided by Merseyside Maritime Museum (National Museum of Liverpool), the ship was built by Charles Connell and Company in Glasgow in 1884. In that year, she left Liverpool for her maiden voyage to Montreal and became the second largest ship on Canadian service. By 1890, the ship was modernized to match the standards of *Labrador*, the other leading Canadian ship. In August 1890, during a journey marred by fog, she struck an iceberg near Belle Isle but escaped with little damage. In October of the same year, *Vancouver*'s commander and quartermaster were swept overboard and drowned during a storm. In 1894, she was stranded at the entrance to Lough Foyle, Northern Ireland, and had to be towed to Liverpool for repairs. After her August 1896 collision with *Lake Ontario*, in which Pollock suffered, *Vancouver* was out of service for three months. • **5.** The same report saw print in *The Evening Record* (Windsor, Ontario) of August 11, 1896.

A postcard featuring the steamer *Vancouver* in the 1890s (private collection).

about to retire, and was of such force as to cause the passengers to believe that the vessel had gone on some rocks, as the big ship shook from stem to stern. But a few minutes elapsed between the time *Lake Ontario*'s whistle was heard and the collision occurred, and the latter vessel was so close to the *Vancouver* for a moment or so afterwards that a person could have boarded her without difficulty, but the force of the shock, it is thought, veered her around and after the officers of the vessels had exchanged a few words she was again lost in the fog. In the meantime there was very little excitement on the *Vancouver* and although everybody was aware that the damage sustained must be considerable, there was not the slightest sign of panic, the ladies particularly remaining quite cool and following out the instructions given by the chief officer. Commander Williams also maintained perfect discipline among the crew and had the life boats ready to launch at once in case they were required which happily he found they were not after a hurried examination of the damage sustained and put back the vessel to Father Point, where a pilot was secured before proceeding to Quebec.

A passenger from *Lake Ontario* was also interviewed for the same newspaper:

A saloon passenger, who occupied the foremost stateroom at the starboard side, corroborates these particulars, and adds that he had just retired when he heard a crash, and looking out of the port hole saw a large steamer passing close by. On going on deck, he found that the *Lake Ontario* had been run into. About half the passengers had gone to their staterooms at the time, but the collision of course brought them out again to ascertain what had occurred. There was, however, very little confusion, and the passengers did not exhibit symptoms of great alarm. He heard an officer say that if the other ship's damage had been further aft she must have sunk in seventy feet of water. The escape of both ships was regarded as a very narrow one. [...]

The passenger already alluded to was in his berth at the time when suddenly and without any warning he saw a steamer looming down on the *Lake Ontario*. Both steamers met with their own momentum. He was knocked up against his cabin door and went on deck to see what had happened. He had first seen a green light and then a red one. The *Lake Ontario*'s bow was then badly damaged and pieces of plate from the *Vancouver* were on the former's deck. There was very little confusion at the time and engines were immediately reversed.

Both ships had to stop at Quebec for repairs. The *Vancouver*, Pollock's ship, was expected to reach port at 1:00 a.m., but because of its damage it took until at 7:00 a.m. Since the news of

The damaged *Vancouver* as it appeared in the *Strand Magazine*, July–December 1896.

the collision spread quickly, hundreds of citizens anxiously awaited the arrival of the steamer, flocking to her side. There they learned the following:

> The *Vancouver* suffered a great deal more damage than the *Lake Ontario*. The vessel was undoubtedly struck on the port side, carrying away the stem completely, and crushing into her desk. Portions of the plating on the starboard side is still hanging on. The anchors are also gone and the water is flowing into the vessel to the first bulkhead. The damage is quite extensive and it will be several days before she will be removed to the docks to undergo repairs. [...]
>
> The passengers, of which there are a large number including several men of the British army, with few exceptions, will remain on the steamer until the *Scotsman* arrives down from Montreal when they will be transferred and proceed on their journey. In the meantime they are being well cared for by the officers of the company.
>
> Two seamen were injured as a consequence of the collision, one having a foot badly cut with broken glass and the other several ribs broken, while a cabin boy had a more miraculous escape. He was hurled from the bunk in which he was sleeping on to a table in the room and the next minute his bunk was carried away.[6]

A brief report, accompanied by an image of the damaged liner, appeared in *The Strand Magazine* (July–December 1897, page 554). Pollock, for whom the shock and the delay must have

---

6. The same report was printed in several other Quebec newspapers.

been distressing, especially given his poor health, eventually reached England aboard another ship. According to one account appearing in the *Western Daily Press* (Bristol) of October 7, a day after his death, "the shock so affected Mr. Pollock, in his weak state of health, as to hasten his end."

Pollock's Final Days

Pollock arrived in Bristol on August 27. As written later on in the *British Chess Magazine*, a close associate remarked that Pollock "was taken straight to his father's house in Clifton, and tended with all care that love could bring to his aid." By this time, his farewell notice from his last column in the *Baltimore Sunday News* and his return to England were brought to the attention of various English columnists. On August 29, the column of the *Nottinghamshire Guardian* noted: "We regret to hear that Mr. Pollock, the brilliant chess master and chess editor, has been compelled by ill health to relinquish his editorial work. We hope that his return to England will result in his final recovery. His native land will welcome back her most dashing and daring chess player."[7] Pollock's farewell to his American readers was also reprinted in the September 5 issue of the *Bristol Mercury and Daily Post*. The editor added: "We sincerely hope that Mr. W.H.K. Pollock's indisposition is but temporary, and that America's loss may be England's gain." But on September 18, just two weeks later, and possibly with more precise knowledge than earlier, the same newspaper reported Pollock's condition was quite serious:

> All chessmen in Clifton and a very large number of friends outside the circle of those devoted to the royal game, will learn with deepest regret that since his return from America and his resignation of a prominent position he held there in literary and chess circles, Mr. W.H.K. Pollock has found his health still more impaired. Mr. Pollock, who is the son of the Rev. Wm. James Pollock, M.A., the well known chaplain of the Blind Asylum, is lying in a really serious condition of health at the residence of his father, Berkeley square. He is certainly one of the most brilliant chess players of his time, and it will be remembered that that winter when he came over from America on a visit, he gave an evening of simultaneous play at the Clifton Chess Club.

A sad irony was that while Pollock lay seriously ill in Clifton, an important tournament was being held a short distance away at the Imperial Hotel, the habitual headquarters of the Bristol and Clifton Chess Club. The event started September 7 under the auspices of the Southern Counties' Chess Union, headed by the Rev. J.F. Welsh. It brought together representatives from Surrey, Kent, Hants, Wilts, Somerset and Gloucestershire Associations. The Class I championship was won by Henry E. Atkins, followed by J.H. Blake, two players who would leave their own marks on British chess as the next century started.[8]

Pollock was too sick to attend any of the proceedings, even as a spectator, in the room of the Imperial Hotel where a decade earlier, as a young member of the Bath Chess Club, he had often come to do battle against the Bristol team. Although Pollock still hoped for a recovery, this too was to be denied him. After suffering slightly more than a month, he declined further,

---

7. Such brief announcements of Pollock's return to England appeared in multiple columns in the Kingdom. *The Falkirk Herald* of September 2, 1896, noted: "Dr. W.H.K. Pollock, the Montreal expert, is returning to the old country on account of a serious break down in his health. He has been very popular in Canada, and leaves many friends, who trust he will sooner recover at home. It will be remembered that he represented Canada worthily last year at the Hastings tourney." Pollock's return was also announced briefly in the *Morning Post* of September 7, 1896.
● 8. Reports on the championship appeared in the November 1896 issue of the *British Chess Magazine* (pages 388–390) and in the chess column of the *Bristol Mercury* of September 11, 1896.

and died on Monday, October 5, 1896.[9] The 37-year-old chess master and journalist was gone. His death was announced on October 7 by the *Western Daily Press*. An announcement also appeared in the *Bristol Mercury and Daily Post* of the same day:

> It is with deepest regret—a regret which all chess players, not only in this country, but in America will share—that we have to announce the death of Mr. W.H.K. Pollock, the brilliant chess player, who has delighted members of the Clifton Chess Club and others further afield, especially by his feats of simultaneous play. Mr. Pollock, who was the son of the Rev. William J. Pollock, M.A., chaplain of the Blind Asylum, died on Tuesday at his father's residence, No. 5, Berkeley square. Three or four weeks ago we mentioned his return from America, where ill-health compelled him to resign a prominent position he held in literary and chess circles. It was known when he reached his father's residence that his recovery was hopeless, so serious were his lungs affected, and despite every medical care and good nursing he succumbed yesterday. Mr. Pollock, who was 37 years of age, spent his early life in Bath, whence his father came to Bristol some few years ago. The funeral has been fixed for Friday.

According to F.F. Rowland's correspondence with an unnamed Canadian confrere, Pollock's health problems had worsened following one of his characteristically impulsive, altruistic acts:

> As to the announcement of the trouble, I am inclined to date it further back than others. Sometime in the late winter—I have not the exact date—in February or in March 1895, on returning from a long drive out to a Scotch entertainment in the suburbs, when the thermometer was down to 20 below zero, he found a fire in progress near his lodgings. A poor woman was being burnt out of house and home, and his quick sympathies being excited, he did much to help in saving both her, and her little sticks of furniture. He got home sodden with water, which was hanging icicles from his hair, hat, and coat. No wonder he caught a severe cold, which laid him up for some time, and from which I do not believe he ever really recovered. For he suffered all that summer, from what he euphemistically called "Hay fever." Anyway, I firmly believe that he came by his death in the service of others.

Whether or not any specific incident could be said to be the cause of his death, it was well known that Pollock had long suffered from compromised health, and that his primary weakness was his lungs.

Under the heading "Pollock Memories," an extensive obituary in the *Dublin Daily Express* of October 16 (re)published the following burial details along with a prescient reflection:

> [...] Why Dr. W.H.K. Pollock did not follow the medical profession we do not know. It may have been that it was distasteful to him, or it may have been that his great love for chess caused him to give up all other pursuits. As it was, the course he adopted did not serve him, and we do not know of a single instance of any man being successful as a chess professional.
>
> The remains were interred at Arno's Vale Cemetery on Friday morning. The funeral left Berkeley square at noon, and reached the cemetery shortly before one. The mourning coaches were occupied as follows: first coach, the Rev. W.J. Pollock, the Rev. J. Pollock and Miss Pollock; second coach, the Rev. Marcus Bickerstaff and Mrs. Bickerstaff; third carriage, the Revs. Leonard Bickerstaff and S. Day. The service was conducted by the Revs. Marcus and Leonard Bickerstaff. Amongst those at the graveside were the following gentlemen: Messrs. N. Berry and T. Furber, representing the Clifton and Literary and Philosophic Clubs; and Mr. H.H. Davies, representing the City Chess Club, and a number of local chess players.[10] Amongst the many floral offerings and wreaths was one "In loving memory" from T.B. and F.F. Rowland, Kingstown, Ireland.

---

9. Pollock's death is generally cited as "October 5, 1896" in a majority of sources (including Gaige's *Chess Personalia*). His extensive obituary that appeared published in the *British Chess Magazine* of October 1896 mentioned that he died on October 5. Other sources are less uniform. The two Bristol newspapers in the text above suggest he died on Tuesday, October 6. The *Yorkshire Evening Post* of October 7, 1896, announced his death as taking place on Monday, October 5. The same was reported by the October 7 *Lichfield Mercury*. The London *Morning Post* of October 12, however, claimed that Pollock died on Tuesday, October 6. • **10.** Similar information was offered in the *Western Daily Press* and *Bristol Mercury* of October 10, 1896.

CERTIFIED COPY OF AN ENTRY OF DEATH GIVEN AT THE **GENERAL REGISTER OFFICE**

Application Number   7282555-1

REGISTRATION DISTRICT		BRISTOL	
1896 DEATH in the Sub-district of St Augustine		in the City and County of Bristol	

Columns:— 1   2   3   4   5   6   7   8   9

No.	When and where died	Name and surname	Sex	Age	Occupation	Cause of death	Signature, description and residence of informant	When registered	Signature of registrar
361	Fifth October 1896 5 Berkeley Square u.D.	William Henry Krause Pollock	Male	37 57 Years	Surgeon L.R.C.S.I	Pulmonary Phthisis 2 years Pneumothorax 10 hours Certified by R.Shingleton Smith M.D.	W.I Pollock Father present at the death 5 Berkeley Square Bristol	Seventh October 1896	William Peirce Registrar	one H.Imof Sly No.2 cp

CERTIFIED to be a true copy of an entry in the certified copy of a Register of Deaths in the District above mentioned.

Given at the GENERAL REGISTER OFFICE, under the Seal of the said Office, the   6th   day of   April   2016

DYE 002282   See note overleaf

CAUTION: THERE ARE OFFENCES RELATING TO FALSIFYING OR ALTERING A CERTIFICATE AND USING OR POSSESSING A FALSE CERTIFICATE ©CROWN COPYRIGHT
WARNING: A CERTIFICATE IS NOT EVIDENCE OF IDENTITY.

RJW

A certified copy of W.H.K. Pollock's death certificate courtesy of UK's General Register Office, reproduced here with permission. Pollock's death was registered in the Bristol registration district (sub-district of St. Augustine) during the October–December quarter of 1896, volume 6a, page 35. His occupation was given as "surgeon" and it stated he died on October 5, 1896, at 5 Berkeley Square. Cause of death, certified by R. Shingleton Smith, M.D.: "pulmonary phthisis; pneumothorax." The certificate also stated that William James Pollock was present at the death of his son.

Pollock was buried on Friday, October 9, at Arno's Vale Cemetery, Clifton.[11] On the day of his funeral, the *Bristol Mercury* published the following:

> The funeral of Mr. W.H.K. Pollock, the eminent chess player, whose death we noticed on Tuesday, is fixed for one o'clock to-day at Arno's Vale, the mourning carriages leaving Berkeley square at twelve. We may add that Mr. Pollock, educated at Clifton College in the time of Dr. Percival, subsequently studied for the medical profession. He was a licentiate of the Royal College of Surgeons, Ireland, but did not practice. In 1878 he joined the Bath Chess Club, and soon rose in fame as a player of exceptional merit. He afterwards went to America, where he at once took a prominent part in chess circles. He played many games with well known performers, and frequently scored brilliant victories. He was also the editor of the chess columns in the "Baltimore News." He afterward resided in Albany and Montreal, but his health gave way, and he came to England to take part in the Hastings tournament. In February he returned to Canada, but his condition became worse, and about six weeks ago he decided to make the voyage to England. Unfortunately the steamer in which he sailed met with an accident in the St. Lawrence, and the shock apparently contributed not a little to hasten his end.

A day after Pollock's burial, the annual meeting of the Bristol and Clifton Chess Association took place. "Special votes of sympathy and respect were passed at all the annual meetings," it was

---

11. The location of Pollock's grave seems to have been lost. We are thankful to Graham Mill-Wilson (Bristol) who took a trip to the Arnos Vale Cemetery in May 2008 but due to many graves being overgrown with ivy and brambles, and some simply vandalized, the attempt to find and recondition Pollock's grave failed [email to Urcan, May 5, 2008]. We are also thankful to John Richards, David Collier and Alan Papier regarding this matter.

reported in the *British Chess Magazine* (November 1896, page 428), "and his loss will be greatly mourned in Bath and Bristol, where he was well known." Numerous obituaries appeared in the British press throughout October 1896.[12]

News of Pollock's death reached America as well, and a number of leading newspapers recollected the man in their late October editions. The Baltimore Chess Association held a special meeting on October 24.[13] A special official ("engrossed") copy of the following letter was delivered to the Reverend William James Pollock, the chess player's father:

BALTIMORE CHESS ASSOCIATION

Whereas the Association has learned of its loss through death of an esteemed and highly gifted member, Dr. William H.K. Pollock, which occurred in Bristol, England, October 5th, 1896, and, whereas we deem it proper to place upon the record this expression of our sorrow, therefore be it resolved—That we have lost in him a true friend, endowed with the deepest sense of honour, a generous nature, and a modest and unassuming disposition; resolved, that as an organisation devoted to the ennobling game of Chess, we record our indebtedness, as well as that of the whole Chess playing world, to him as one of the most brilliant and original Chess Masters of his time, whose labours as Chess editor of the "Baltimore News," and as a Chess instructor, have done much to elevate the standing of the Association, and improve the play of the members. Resolved, furthermore, that a page of our minutes be set apart for recording these resolutions, and that a copy be sent his bereaved family.

E.L. TORSCH, President
JOHN HINRICHS, Vice-President
HARRY E. GARNER, Secretary.[14]

In what spirit, and possibly with what regrets, the Reverend Pollock received this tribute to his son from exponents of the game that had taken his child from a career in medicine and had formed the subject of his "Bohemian" travels, remains unrecorded.

The most heartfelt tribute in the United States seems to have been that of Miron Hazeltine, the longtime editor of the *New York Clipper's* chess column. This is what he wrote in the November 7 edition:

DR. W.H.K. POLLOCK—"He was my friend, faithful and just to me."—We are not ashamed to record thus publicly that tears dimmed our eyes on receipt of the startling news of the decease of everyone's friend—dear, social, delightful Dr. Pollock. We over here hoped that the fears he evidently felt when he penned that pathetic "Farewell" to his American friends would not for many years be realized. Hence the pang of grief when the news came with the suddenness of surprise. [Hazeltine then cited Pollock's obituary from the *Leeds Mercury* found in Appendix B.] Our friend was educated at Clifton, though he took his surgeon's degree at Dublin, a profession he did not practice very long, Caissa's charms proving more powerful than those of Aesculapius. Thrice endeared to us now are the two beautiful portraits of our decades friend, one singly, and one grouped with Bro. Babson. *Vale, a longe vale, mi amice. In matrix* [*sic*: matris] *molle* [*sic*: molli] *fremio* [*sic*: gremio] *dormit; in immortalitate resurget*.[15]

The November 1896 issue of the *British Chess Magazine* (pages 441–446) published an extensive obituary of Pollock, including a fine portrait and his famous win over Weiss.[16] We reproduce its essential parts below:

We deeply regret to announce the death of our esteemed friend and co-worker, Mr. W.H.K. Pollock, who died at 5, Berkeley Square, Clifton, Bristol, the residence of his father, on October 5th, lamented most by those who

---

12. See Appendix B for further transcripts. • **13.** According to the *Baltimore Sun* of October 24, 1896; However, Rowland stated the Baltimore Chess Association letter was signed on October 21. • **14.** Reprinted in *Pollock Memories*, page 15. • **15.** Asclepius was the god of medicine in Greek religion. His serpent-entwined rod is a symbol used in modern times associated with medicine and health care. Hazeltine's Latin expression in translation: "Farewell, long farewell, dear friend/ He rests smoothly in the lap of the mother [i.e., Mother Earth]/ He will resurrect in immortality." The authors are grateful for the assistance of Dr. Peter Braunwarth and Dr. Alfred Dunshirm, of Vienna University, for the translation as well as the corrections. • **16.** According to F.F. Rowland's *Pollock Memories*, this obituary was authored by I.M. Brown, an individual closely associated with chess activities in Leeds.

knew him best—who knew his strength and his weakness, his best qualities and his worst. William Henry Krause Pollock was a son of the Rev. William J. Pollock, M.A., formerly Rector of St. Saviour's, Bath, but now Chaplain of the Blind Asylum, Bristol. He was born in Cheltenham, on February 21st, 1859, and was educated at Clifton College and Somersetshire College, Bath. He was intended for the medical profession, and made considerable progress with his studies from 1880–2, during which period he was a resident pupil at Dr. Steeven's Hospital, Dublin. He qualified in 1882 as a licentiate of the Royal College of Surgeons, Dublin.

Pollock learnt to play chess early in life; in 1878 he had a reputation as a good player in the local chess circles of Bristol and Dublin. His first published game and problem appeared during 1882 in *The Practical Farmer*, the only newspaper in Dublin which then contained chess news.

Why Mr. Pollock did not follow the medical profession we need not enquire, suffice for us to record the fact that the year 1885 found him competing in the Master Tournament of the British Chess Association's first congress, and this tournament was the first really important contest in which he took part. [A summary of Pollock's results up to 1889 followed here, his win over Weiss, and his results up through Hastings 1895.]

After the tournament, Mr. Pollock made a professional tour through the Midlands and the North of England, giving several exhibitions of simultaneous play. His friends were, however, much pained with his altered appearance, for signs were evident that the fell disease consumption was sapping his constitution. Despite the appeals of his relatives and many friends, ourselves included, Mr. Pollock returned to Canada early this year, and resumed his chess work, again taking up his abode in Montreal. Not for long, however, was he destined to remain abroad. His physical weakness grew apace, and about two months ago he bade farewell to his Canadian friends and took passage for England. Unfortunately the steamer on which he voyaged collided with another vessel in the St. Lawrence, and possibly the delay in going back to Quebec, and waiting there a week, hastened the course of his disease. Taking passage in another vessel he reached England in due course, but reached it only to die. He was taken straight to his father's house at Clifton, and tended with all the care that love could bring to his aid. But it was too late, for he sank slowly but surely, until death released him on the 5th of October, in the 38th year of his age. To the last he himself was hopeful of partial recovery, and in a letter to us, written only a few days before his death, he expressed his "intention to contribute some light chess to the *B.C.M.* very shortly." Man proposes but a Higher Power disposes, and "poor genial Pollock" will write no more. He has edited his last column, and played his last game, and British chess suffers an irreparable loss by his death.

A scholar and a gentleman, Mr. Pollock was an excellent writer on all subjects connected with chess. He had a "sweet turn" for literary effect, and a happy wit that made his writings enjoyable. As a chess expert he was brilliant rather than profound. He was a fanciful player, delighting in prettiness, and therefore apt to lose games to the dull players of the exact school. He had a habit of over-refining his play, which not unfrequently resulted in defeat. In a word he was an artist rather than a scientist, and the poetry of chess was more to him than its prose. In tournaments he was always "a dreaded antagonist," even for the strongest masters to meet, yet he threw away games to weaker players; but with all these faults of his environments, his best efforts reached the high water mark of genius. He won good games in many important tournaments from most of the masters he met, notable exceptions being Messrs. Lasker and Zukertort. He constructed a few problems, but they are only vagaries, at least he so termed them. During his chess editorship in the States he won two of Loyd's prizes in New York, against the best solvers.

In the early days of Mr. Pollock's chess career, many people thought that in him a future English champion would be forthcoming, and the glories of Staunton and Blackburne be revived if not eclipsed. But this expectation was not fulfilled, and Pollock's chess career must be regarded as a fragment rather than a whole. Yet it is a fragment no British lover of chess would willingly part with, for it is full of beautiful promise and adorned with many chess gems of rare brilliancy. With great gifts for the game he never attained the highest rank among the Masters, though it may be doubted whether one of them excelled him in actual and potential genius for the game. In chess, however, as in life, he was an idealist. He worshipped at the shrine of the beautiful. He was not content to do what he could do easily and well, but strove after the absolute—his own perception of the perfect. He was above all an artist at the chess-board. It was not merely "the mate" that he pursued, but the beauty of the mate; he did not merely want to win, he always wanted to win in the most artistic manner. And in this pursuit of the ideal, the practical often suffered. Had he been more self-seeking, the chess world would have heard more of him personally. Neither nature nor art had fitted him to be his own trumpeter; he loved chess for its own sake, and not for the gain it might bring him, or the reputation he might attain by its means.

We have spoken of the chess player, we must now speak of the man, and at the grave of all that is mortal of our lamented co-worker, we desire to pay the last tribute of affection and esteem to the memory of one whom we ever found upright, true, and gentle; generous, high-spirited, and unselfish. Not without faults—who is?—yet with and above all faults, an Englishman of a noble type.

The mortal remains of Mr. Pollock, who was unmarried, were interred at Arno's Vale Cemetery, Clifton, on Friday, October 9th. Amongst those at the graveside, in addition to the members of the family, were Messrs. N. Berry and T. Furber, representing the Clifton Literary and Philosophic Clubs; Mr. H.H. Davis, representing the City Chess Club; and a number of local chess players.

On page 447 of the same magazine, F.F. Rowland published the following, composed by her on October 20, two weeks after Pollock's death.[17] No doubt Pollock would have enjoyed seeing the playfulness of his long, full name spelled out letter by letter by his friend through such a tribute:

> **IN MEMORIUM** [*sic*]
> **W.H.K. POLLOCK. AN ACROSTIC**
>
> **W**hen round Caissa's board we meet,
> **I**n peaceful evening's hour;
> **L**oved friends once more to warmly greet,
> **L**inked by her magic power.
> **I**n vain we seek amidst the scene
> **A** genius rare, as thou hast been,
> **M**arvels to weave with insight, quick and keen.
> **H**allowed by fires divine thou wert—
> **E**'er bright thy smile—thy heart
> **N**e'er changed. Through all the waste of years—
> **R**emembered still thou art—
> **Y**et is that memory drenched with mourner's tears.
> **K**een critic! Oft thy sparkling wit
> **R**egilt the classic page,
> **A**nd in chess lore thy games are writ,
> **U**ndimmed by time or age,
> **S**oon passed thy life—an April day
> **E**arly its radiant sunshine died away.
> **P**erchance the brightness of that life,
> **O**'er shadowed oft by gloom,
> **L**ay far above this vain world's strife,
> **L**ightened beyond the tomb.
> **O**utlived in its effect, a skill
> **C**loudless; with us to linger still.
> **K**ind friend, farewell, we bow to God's own will.

Tributes did not stop even in January 1897. Joseph Ney Babson, one of Pollock's long lasting friends in Canada, published a long composition that mentioned Pollock in the January 9, 1897, edition of the *Clipper*:

[...] Poor POLLOCK! Alas, a true friend I did love,
Always gentle and kind as the angels above;
His loss the world mourns, but he's left here for aye,
A glorious record and fine samples of play. [...]

---

17. A slightly different version of Rowland's acrostic opened her *Pollock Memories*.

On January 27, the Dublin Chess Club passed the following vote on behalf of the managing committee with a copy dispatched to Pollock's father[18]:

> The following vote was passed by the Managing Committee (Dublin Chess Club) on behalf of the Club, Jan. 27, 1897:—Proposed—"That this club do place on record its deep sense of the loss the cause of Chess has recently sustained by the death of our brilliant young Master, Mr. W.H.K. Pollock, who represented Ireland in the game, and who, for several years, while studying medicine in Dublin, was a member of this Club, and even then showed great originality and grasp of the game, and by his genial and warm-hearted nature had won for himself the esteem of his fellow-members, to all of whom his after—though too short career—was a matter of lively interest."

Epilogue

In Bristol and Bath, the sites of his very first chess battles, Pollock was not forgotten. In September 1900, shortly before the fourth anniversary of his death, during the Southern Counties' meeting of amateurs that concluded in the first half of that month, the Reverend John Pollock sponsored a special prize of £5 as a memorial to his deceased brother in the third division of the competition.[19] In the early months of 1900, F.F. Rowland brought out *Pollock Memories*, a 159-page work featuring a collection of Pollock's best games.[20] It provided the journalistic chess circles with another opportunity to remember Pollock's genial creativity.

Although not included in the volume itself, F.F. Rowland did include in one of her letters to Miron Hazeltine, with whom she kept in close contact throughout the preparation of *Pollock Memories*, a description of Pollock's grave, as seen in a photograph she had received: "It is marked by a large white cross, cut in classic simplicity, and under the cross is a scroll, with his name, date of death, and the words, I believe, he wrote: 'In possession of Eternal Life.' On St. Patrick's Day, 1896, I sent him some Irish shamrocks out to Montreal, and he wore them in his coat. On St. Patrick's Day, '97, I sent his sister a basket full of shamrocks, which she placed on his grave, and there they still remain!

> Upon his grave, the shamrocks bloom,
> And in our hearts, for e'er
> His memory lives beyond the tomb,
> Fresh as those shamrocks fair.
> *New York Clipper*, May 8, 1897[21]

Whether Pollock's career was a fragment, as suggested by the *British Chess Magazine*, or whether it amounted to more, let each reader decide. Pollock's moments of genius on the board have been known to the chess world since they first saw print in the newspapers and magazines of his day. His life, though short, was no fragment. He turned his back on conventional success, a success for which his family and education had prepared him. He did so at high personal cost, in terms of the goods of the world. What he purchased instead with his life was freedom to follow his one true love, wherever it led him. And those of us who admire his games are glad he did.

---

18. According to page 39 of the November 12, 1919, London *Times*, William James Pollock died in Clifton at age 90. • **19.** This information is culled from the London *Times* of September 17, 1900. • **20.** See Appendix C: "*Pollock Memories*: Inception & Reception." • **21.** When *Pollock Memories* appeared, Hazeltine praised it highly, as he did the man: "This is a gem of a book that should be in the hands of every American player who admires and honors the best type and exhibition of chess genius, and most especially of those who knew this most genial of chess masters, whom to know was to love." (*New York Clipper*, September 15, 1900)

PART TWO

1882–1896: Games 1–518

A Note on Games

This section contains 518 games played by Pollock between 1882 and 1896, *all* the game scores found during our research we were able to date (the 11 not dated are in an appendix). Structured in 13 sections, they encompass a wide variety: games from simultaneous exhibitions, consultation games, offhand encounters, games at odds and handicap games, serious tournament games and games by correspondence. They are arranged in chronological order.

We attempted to provide an exact historical source for each of the games in this collection. Wherever this proved impossible, we have specified this accordingly **(see games 241 and 242)**. Similarly, wherever possible, exact details in regard to venue and date have been offered. Appendix K contains 11 additional game scores (games 519–530) in which a venue or an exact date (or both) have been difficult to ascertain with precision. Appendix L offers six endgame positions from Pollock games (531–536).

All games herein contain brief annotations by various historical authorities (Pollock and Steinitz included) and by us. The exact authorship of such notes has been credited accordingly within quotation marks. Annotations without a specified authorship (and, hence, without quotation marks) are ours. The purpose of our succinct, if not at times terse, annotations is simply to tempt readers to look deeper on their own.

Throughout the work on these games, we have made use of specialized chess software such as Fritz 15, Houdini 3 and Rybka 3. We hope to have done this without abusing either the silicon creatures or Pollock's all-too-human chessic imagination. Thus we have attempted a balance, where luring readers into reflecting further on certain positions may be a forgivable intrusion, but where completely taking the thrill out of Pollock's tactical melees is not. Readers are invited to investigate further on their own terms.

Part Two, Section I
(January 1882–October 1885)

GAMES IN DUBLIN, BATH AND BRISTOL

1. Roberts–Pollock [C45]
Dublin Chess Club, Dublin, 1882

1. e4 e5 2. Nf3 Nc6 3. d4 e×d4 4. N×d4 Bc5 5. Be3 Qf6 6. c3 Nge7 7. Bb5 a6 8. Bc4 Ne5 9. Bb3 d6 10. 0–0 Qg6 11. Kh1 Q×e4 12. Nd2 Qh4 Better was 12. ... Qg4!? 13. f3 Qh5 14. Ne4 0–0. **13. N4f3 N×f3 14. N×f3 Qh5 15. B×c5 Q×c5** A very good alternative was 15. ... d×c5 16. Re1 Bg4. **16. Re1 Q×f2?** An ill-conceived pawn grab, but it was late for Black: 16. ... Qf5 17. Re3 Qf6 18. Qe2 Kd8 19. Re1 Re8 20. Ng5! Q×g5 21. B×f7 Rf8 22. R×e7 with a clear plus for White. **17. Qd5 Be6** *(see diagram)*

After
17. ... Bc8–e6

17. ... Rf8 18. Rad1 Kd8 19. Qg5 Be6 20. Rd2 Qb6 21. Nd4 with a winning position for White. **18. R×e6!** The alternative was 18. Q×b7 0–0 19. Q×c7 Nd5 20. Q×d6. **18. ... f×e6 19. Q×e6 Kd8 20. Ne5 d×e5 21. Rd1+ Ke8 22. Qd7+ Kf8 23. Qd8+ R×d8 24. R×d8 mate 1–0** [*Illustrated London News*, February 25, 1882]

2. Pollock–A. Rumboll
Odds Game, Bath, 1882
Remove Nb1

1. f4 d5 2. Nf3 e6 3. e3 b6 4. Be2 Bb7 5. 0–0 Bd6 6. b3 Qf6 7. Rb1 Qh6 Pollock: "Although, curiously enough, Black has not yet moved a Knight, he has opened with spirit and maneuvered the queen and two bishops into menacing positions to the castled king." **8. Bb2 Nf6 9. Qe1 Ne4 10. h3 Nd7 11. c4 0–0 12. Kh2 g5** Pollock: "Vigorously played. This advance would, however, be safer with the king housed on the other side, as White has his forces ready for concentration on this." **13. Ne5 N×e5 14. f×e5 Bb4 15. Rd1 d×c4 16. a3** Pollock: "White appears to have exchanged his dangerous position on the kingside for worse troubles in the centre." **16. ... B×d2 17. R×d2 N×d2** Pollock: "17. ... c3 was much better. It is difficult indeed to see what White could have done in reply." **18. Q×d2 c×b3 19. Rf6 Qh4** Pollock: "A grave for the Queen! Black had here a beautiful stroke in 19. ... Rfd8 (in order in certain contingencies to liberate the Queen, via f8) and if then 20. Q×d8+ R×d8 21. R×h6 Rd2 22. Rh5 R×e2 23. R×g5+ Kf8 B[ishop] moves and b2 wins." **20. Bg4 Rad8 21. Qe2** *(see diagram)*

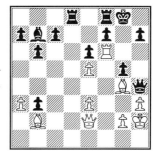

After
21. Qd2–e2

21. ... B×g2! Pollock: "Surely the bishop could be put to a better use, if not a nobler death, than this." Pollock underestimated this move. It's actually one of the best in this position. The alternative was 21. ... Ba6! 22. Q×a6 h5 23. Rh6 Qf2 24. R×h5 Q×e3 with a clear advantage for Black. **22. K×g2 Kg7?!** Pollock: "It is indeed no easy matter to see what Black is driving at." After 22. ... Rd5 23. Bc3 Rfd8 24. R×f7 K×f7 25. Qf3+ Ke8 26. B×e6 Rd2+ 27. B×d2 R×d2+ 28. Kf1 Qf2+ 29. Q×f2 R×f2+ 30. K×f2 b2 31. Bf5 h5 it would appear White has nothing more than a draw. **23. Bc3 Rd5 24. Qf1** Pollock: "A very skilful move. Not only does it prevent Black from doubling rooks on account of the attack on the f7–pawn, but were White incautiously to move Be1, to win the queen, the reply b3–b2 would turn the tables. See also White's next move." Objectively, best was 24. Be1 b2 25. B×h4 b1Q 26. B×g5 R×e5 27. h4 Qb5 28. Qf3 with some chances of survival for White. **24. ... b2 25. Qb1 Rb5?** 25. ... Rfd8! 26. Rf2 Rd3 was winning for Black. **26. B×b2 h5 27. Be2 Rb3 28. Rf3 Rd8 29. Qc2** (*see diagram*)

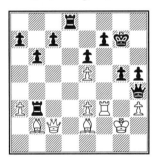

After
29. Qb1–c2

29. ... Qa4?? Pollock: "Black does not see all dangers of the position. There is a marked contrast between his opening and ending play." 29. ... R×b2! 30. Q×b2 Qe1 kept the game wide open. After the text blunder, Pollock mated in five. **1–0** [*Bristol Mercury and Daily Post*, March 30, 1888].

3. Pollock–A. Rumboll
Odds Game, Bath, 1882
Remove Nb1

1. e4 e5 2. Nf3 Nc6 3. d4 e×d4 4. Bc4 Bc5 5. Ng5 Nh6 6. Qh5 Ne5 A more precise defense was 6. ... Qf6 7. 0–0 Qg6! **7. Ne6!** Pollock: "This beautiful move, which wins a piece by force, is mentioned in [George H.] Selkirk's *The Book of Chess* but in very few, if any, more recent works in English." **7. ... Bb4+** Pollock: "Producing a verita-

ble vortex! It would have been better to play 7. ... d×e6, and the game would be about even." **8. c3** (*see diagram*)

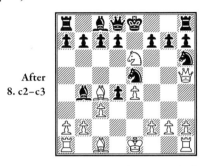

After
8. c2–c3

8. ... Nd3+? Giving away the advantage. Black could have maintained the edge with 8. ... d×e6! 9. Q×e5 Be7 10. Q×g7 Bf6 11. Q×h6 d×c3 12. Be3 c×b2 13. Rb1 Bc3+ 14. Ke2 Qd6. **9. B×d3 d×c3?** Best was 9. ... d×e6! 10. Qb5+ c6 11. Q×b4 e5 with chances for both sides. **10. N×g7+! Kf8** 10. ... Ke7 is met by 11. Qe5+ Kf8 12. B×h6 c×b2+ 13. Ke2. **11. B×h6 c×b2+ 12. Ke2 b×a1Q 13. R×a1 Qf6** 13. ... Kg8 is met by 14. Qg4 Kf8 15. Ne6+ Ke8 16. Qg7! **14. Ne6+ Kg8 15. e5 Q×e6** and White mates in three moves. Pollock: "Ein sehr lebhaftes Spiel" ("A very lively game.") **1–0** [*PM*, pages 79–80]

4. Pollock–A. Rumboll [C29]
Match Game, Bath, 1882

1. e4 e5 2. Nc3 Nf6 3. f4 Nc6 4. f×e5 N×e5 5. d4 Nc6 6. e5 Ng8 7. Nf3 d5 8. Bb5 a6 9. Ba4 f6? This was too provocative. A more diligent path was 9. ... Nge7 10. 0–0 Be6 11. Ng5 Qd7. **10. 0–0 Be6 11. Be3** 11. e×f6! was winning by force after 11. ... N×f6 12. Re1 Qd7 13. Qe2 Ke7 14. Ng5. **11. ... Bb4?** 11. ... Qd7! would have been sufficient to hold his game together. **12. Qe1 Bf8?** 12. ... Qd7 13. Qg3 0–0–0 was perhaps Black's only chance to attempt some resistance. **13. Qg3 Nge7 14. Nh4 g5** (*see diagram*)

After
14. ... g7–g5

15. Nf3 A forceful approach was 15. Qf3! f5 (15. ... g×h4? 16. Q×f6 Qd7 17. Q×h8 Nf5 18. Bh6 0–0–0 19. B×f8 Qf7 20. Qg7) 16. B×c6+ N×c6 17. N×f5 h5 18. Rad1! **15. ... Nf5 16. Qf2 g4 17. Nd2** Very inventive would have been 17. Nh4! g3 18. h×g3 N×h4 19. Q×f6! Q×f6 20. R×f6 Nf5 21. R×e6+ Kd7 22. R×c6 b×c6 23. N×d5 N×e3 24. N×e3 and White's pawns assure a clear edge in the endgame. **17. ... Rg8** 17. ... f×e5! could have launched some tactical fireworks: 18. N×d5!? Q×d5 19. Bb3 Bh6! 20. B×d5 B×e3 21. B×e6 Nc×d4 22. B×f5 N×f5 23. Rae1 B×f2+ 24. R×f2 0–0–0 and Black's fine. **18. N×d5! g3** *(see diagram)*

After
18. ... g4–g3

If 18. ... Q×d5, 19. Bb3 N×e3 20. B×d5 N×d5 21. e×f6 0–0–0 gives White the upper hand. **19. Q×f5 g×h2+** If 19. ... B×f5, then 20. N×f6+ Kf7 21. Bb3+ Be6 22. N×g8+ K×g8 23. B×e6+ Kh8 24. Nf3 g×h2+ 25. Kh1 Qe8 26. Ng5 is crushing. **20. Kh1 B×f5** 20. ... Q×d5 is met by 21. Qh5+! Bf7 22. Q×h2 Qd7 23. c4. **21. N×f6+ Ke7 22. d5 N×e5 23. N×g8+ 1–0** [*Baltimore Sunday News*, December 21, 1890]

5. W.L. Harvey–Pollock [C00]
Match Game, Dublin Chess Club, November 1882

1. e4 e6 2. e5 Pollock: "Introduced by Steinitz at Vienna Tournament, 1882. The *Chess-Monthly* considered the innovation, in common with the authorities, of questionable value." **2. ... d5 3. e×d6 B×d6 4. d4** Pollock: "This move, followed by the Queen's Fianchetto, is preferred to 4. ... Nc6." **4. ... Nf6 5. Bd3 0–0 6. Bg5 h6 7. Bh4 c5 8. d×c5 B×c5 9. Nf3 Nc6 10. a3 e5 11. Nc3 g5** *(see diagram)*

12. N×g5?! 12. Bg3 e4 13. B×e4 Q×d1+ 14. K×d1 (14. R×d1? Re8!) 14. ... N×e4 15. N×e4 Bb6 and Black's better. **12. ... h×g5 13. B×g5 Qd4 14. Qf3 Ng4** Even stronger was 14. ... e4! 15. B×e4

After
11. ... g7–g5

N×e4 16. Be3 Re8 17. B×d4 N×d4 with a strong attack for Black. **15. 0–0** Pollock: "15. 0–0–0 would give White a powerful, if not a winning attack." Not quite so, because of Black's excellent 15. ... f5! **15. ... f5** *(see diagram)*

After
15. ... f7–f5

16. Rad1?? Best was 16. Nb5! Qd7 (16. ... e4 17. N×d4 e×f3 18. N×f3 with equal play.) 17. Bc4+ Kh8 18. Rad1, with unclear play. **16. ... e4! 17. B×e4 f×e4 18. R×d4 e×f3 19. Rd5 f×g2 20. K×g2 N×f2 0–1** [*PM*, pages 84–85]

6. Pollock–N. Tibbits [C25]
Bath vs. Bristol Match, 14 March 1883

1. e4 e5 2. Nc3 Bc5 3. f4 e×f4 4. Nf3 g5 5. d4 Bb4 6. Bc4 d6 7. h4 B×c3+ 8. b×c3 Qe7? Better was 8. ... f6 9. h×g5 f×g5 10. e5 d5 11. Bd3 Qe7. **9. N×g5 Nh6 10. Qh5 Qf6 11. 0–0 Bg4 12. R×f4!** **Q×d4+ 13. c×d4 B×h5 14. g4?!** Most precise was 14. Rf6 Ng4 15. Rf5 Bg6 16. Rf4 h5 17. Rb1 Nc6 18. R×b7 0–0–0 19. Rb1 N×d4 20. c3 Nc6 21. N×f7. **14. ... B×g4** The alternative 14. ... N×g4 15. N×f7 Rf8 16. Ng5 R×f4 17. B×f4 Kd7 18. Rb1 would have left White with an indisputable plus still. **15. Rf6 Ng8 16. R×f7 Nd7 17. Rf4** 17. N×h7 0–0–0 18. Bg5 was more decisive. **17. ... Nh6 18. Be6 B×e6 19. N×e6 Rc8 20. Rf3 Rg8+! 21. Bg5 Nf7 22. Raf1 N×g5 23. h×g5 Ke7 24. d5 Ne5 25. Rh3 Rh8 26. Rf4 Ng6?!** 26. ... c6! was an excellent choice. **27. Rf6** *(see diagram)*

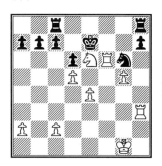

After
27. Rf4–f6

27. ... h6? Decisively wrong. One possible defense was 27. ... a6 28. Rb3 b5 29. Rh3 b4 30. Kf1 a5 31. Ke2 c6! **28. R×g6 Rhg8 29. Rg×h6 1–0** [*Clifton Chronicle*, April 25, 1883]

7. Pollock–J.N. Burt [C51]
Bristol, May 1883

1. e4 e5 2. Nf3 Nc6 3. Bc4 Bc5 4. b4 Bb6 5. b5 Na5 6. B×f7+ Pollock: "This is altogether unsound, not so much on account of the sacrifice of material as in that the attack is premature and short lived." **6. ... K×f7 7. N×e5+ Kf8 8. Ba3+ d6 9. d4 Be6 10. 0–0 Ne7 11. Qf3+ Ke8 12. Qh5+ g6 13. Qg5 d×e5 13.** ... B×d4 14. Nd2 B×e5 and Black is clearly winning. **14. Q×e5 B×d4 15. Q×e6 B×a1 16. Nd2 Bc3 17. Rd1 Rf8?** 17. ... Qd7! 18. Q×d7+ K×d7 19. Nb1+ Ke6 20. N×c3 Rhd8 and Black wins. **18. Nf1** Pollock: "White has contrived, deftly enough, to win the queen, but of course at an exorbitant price." **18. ... Rf7 19. R×d8+ R×d8 20. Ne3 Rd2 21. h3 R×f2?** 21. ... Bd4!? 22. B×e7 R×e7 23. Qg8+ Kd7, with equal play. **22. Nd5** 22. B×e7! Rf1+ 23. N×f1 R×e7 24. Qg8+ Kd7 25. Qd5+ Ke8 26. Ne3 and White would have won. **22. ... Bd4 23. N×c7+ Kf8 24. Qc8+?** Chasing ghosts. 24. Kh2 or 24. Kh1 were the best moves. The text move loses. **24. ... Kg7 25. Ne6+ Kh6 26. Qb8** Pollock: "Truly a strange plight! This is the only move to prevent the immediate loss of the game." **26. ... Rf1+ 27. Kh2 Bg1+** (*see diagram*)

After
27. ... Bd4–g1+

Black misses an aesthetic way to wrap things up: 27. ... Nac6!! 28. b×c6 N×c6 29. Bf8+ R×f8 30. Q×f8+ R×f8 31. N×f8 and Black wins. **28. Kg3 Bf2+ 29. Kg4 Nc4 30. Bc5 B×c5 31. N×c5 Ne3+ 32. Kg3 R7f2 33. Qe5 R×g2+ 34. Kh4 g5+ 35. Q×g5+ R×g5 0–1** [*Sheffield and Rotherham Independent*, June 3, 1887]

8. J.E. Vernon–Pollock [C45]
Bristol vs. Bath Match, Bath, 7 June 1883

1. e4 e5 2. Nf3 Nc6 3. d4 e×d4 4. N×d4 g6 5. Be3 Bg7 6. c3 Nf6 7. N×c6 b×c6 8. Bg5?! 8. Bd3 or 8. Nd2 were more logical options. **8. ... h6 9. B×f6 Q×f6 10. Bc4** (*see diagram*)

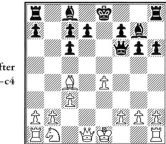

After
10. Bf1–c4

10. ... Qg5 10. ... Rb8! 11. Bb3 Ba6 was stronger. **11. 0–0 0–0 12. Nd2 d5 13. Nf3 Qf4! 14. g3 Q×e4 15. Bd3 Qg4 16. Re1 Be6 17. Be2 Qf5 18. Nd4 B×d4 19. Q×d4 Qc2! 20. Rab1 Bf5 21. g4 Rfe8 22. g×f5 R×e2 23. f×g6 Q×g6+ 24. Kh1 Rae8 25. Rbd1 Qe6 26. R×e2 Q×e2 27. Kf1 Re4 28. Qd3 Rg4+ 29. Kh1 Q×f2 30. Qh3 Qe2 31. Q×g4+ Q×g4 32. Rg1 Q×g1+ 33. K×g1 0–1** [*Clifton Chronicle*, June 13, 1883]

9. Pollock–J.E. Vernon [C55]
Bath vs. Bristol Match, Bath, 7 June 1883

1. e4 e5 2. Nf3 Nc6 3. Bc4 Nf6 4. Qe2 Be7 5. d4 d6 6. d5 Nb8 7. Nc3 Nbd7 8. Bd2 Nb6 9. Bb3 Bd7 10. Nd1 a5 11. a3 c6 12. c4 c5 13. 0–0 0–0 14. Ne1 Ne8 15. f4 Bf6 16. f5 Bg5 17. Ne3 B×e3+ 18. B×e3 g6 19. Bh6 Ng7 20. f6 Nh5 (*see diagram*)

21. B×f8?! White should have tried 21. Qf2! Kh8 22. Rc1 Rg8 23. Bd1. **21. ... K×f8 22. Qe3 N×f6 23. Nf3 Ng4 24. Qd2 Kg7 25. Ng5 Nh6 26. Rf2 Qe7 27. Raf1 Rf8 28. h4 a4 29. Ba2 and**

After
20. ... Ng7–h5

the game was adjudicated as a draw. ½–½ [*Clifton Chronicle*, June 20, 1883]

BIRMINGHAM (CCA, JULY 1883)

10. Pollock–F.P. Wildman [C49]
Counties' Chess Association (Division II), Birmingham, July 1883

1. e4 e5 2. Nf3 Nc6 3. Nc3 Nf6 4. Bb5 Bb4 5. 0–0 0–0 6. Nd5 Bc5 7. d4 Pollock: "A powerful attack, invented by Blackburne." **7. ... N×d4** Pollock: "7. ... N×d5 can be played here; 7. ... e×d4 is also better than the text move." **8. N×d4 e×d4 9. Bg5 Be7 10. N×e7+ Q×e7 11. Q×d4 d6 12. f4 c5** Pollock: "Black's game is badly constrained, nor does this help matters. If 12. ... Rd8 13. e5 d×e5 14. Q×e5 Qd6 15. Rad1 Qb6+ (15. ... Q×d1 16. B×f6. Pollock is wrong here—15. ... Q×d1 is a good move: 16. B×f6 g×f6!—*authors*) 16. Kh1 Bg4 with a much better prospect." **13. Qc3 Q×e4 14. B×f6 g×f6 15. Q×f6 Qg6** Pollock: "White threatened both Rg3 and Bd3." **16. Qh4** (*see diagram*)

After
16. Qf6–h4

16. ... Bf5? Pollock: "If 16. ... Q×c2 17. Rf3 Q×b2 18. Rd1 with a crushing attack. 16. ... Qg4, however, held out some slight chances." Pollock's conclusion may be too radical. Black would still have resources: 18. ... Bf5 19. Rg3+ Bg6 20. Bf1

Qc2 21. R×d6 Rae8 with equal chances. **17. Rf3 Kh8 18. Rg3 Qe6 19. Bd7** Pollock: "Neat and conclusive. 19. Bc4, on the other hand, would have enabled Black to prolong the game by 19. ... d5." **19. ... Qg6 20. R×g6 f×g6 21. B×f5 R×f5 22. Re1 1–0** [*PM*, page 20]

11. Pollock–C.D. Locock [C29]
Counties' Chess Association (Division II), Birmingham, July 1883

1. e4 e5 2. Nc3 Nf6 3. f4 d5 4. f×e5 N×e4 5. Nf3 Bg4 Pollock: "5. ... Be7 is perhaps the safest move here." **6. Qe2** Pollock: "In order to dislodge the knight from e4." **6. ... Nc6** Pollock: "If 6. ... N×c3 7. b×c3 greatly strengthening White's centre. Another move is 6. ... Ng5." **7. N×e4 Nd4? 8. Qd3 B×f3** (*see diagram*)

After
8. ... Bg4×f3

9. g×f3 Pollock: "Immediately after the game Mr. Locock pointed out that retreating the Kt to f2 (or g3) wins a clear piece. The position is very peculiar, and well illustrates Steinitz's rule, 'When you have found a very good move, don't make it, but look for a better one.' Not only did I make the very same oversight in an offhand game in London a year or two later, but the identical position occurred between Blackburne and Paulsen in the Breslau tournament seven years later, the self-same mistake being again perpetrated by Black and overlooked by White. Mr. Hoffer on that occasion pointed out White's proper reply, 9. Kf2. It is easy to discern the process of thought which led to the 'let-off.' White, whether failing to reckon on the opponent's extremely ingenious 10th move, or not, sees that the plan in his game is a good one, and that he will remain with a strong pawn centre and both bishops on the board." **9. ... d×e4 10. Q×e4 Qh4+! 11. Kd1 Q×e4 12. f×e4 Nf3** (*see diagram*)
13. e6 Pollock: "In order to isolate a pawn. Black ought of course to have taken it." **13. ... f6?** Better was 13. ... f×e6 14. Bg2 Ne5 15. Bh3 Bc5 16. B×e6

After
12. ... Nd4–f3

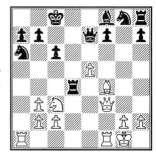

After
13. ... Rd8×d4

Ke7 17. Bf5 Rhf8. **14. d3 0-0-0 15. Bh3 Kb8** 15. ...
Be7 looks somewhat stronger. **16. Rf1 Ne5** Pollock: "If 16. ... N×h2 17. Rf2 Bd6 18. Bf4 B×f4
19. R×f4 g5 20. R×f6 g4 21. Bg2 or White might
play 21. Rf2." **17. Be3** Pollock: "White ought to
play Ke2 at once." **17. ... Nc4 18. Bc1 Bc5 19. Ke2
Ne5 20. Be3 B×e3 21. K×e3** Pollock: "The king
is now well-posted and victory merely a matter of
time." **21. ... Rd6 22. Rg1 Rc6** 22. ... Ng6 23. Bf5
Rc6 24. c3 Rb6 25. b3 Re8 26. h4 Rc6 27. B×g6
h×g6 28. R×g6 Rc×e6 29. Rag1 with clear advantage for White. **23. R×g7 R×c2 24. Rag1 Ng6
25. e7 R×h2 26. Bd7 N×e7 27. R×e7 R×b2
28. R×h7 Rf8 29. Rf7 Rd8 30. R×f6 R×a2 31. e5
c5 32. e6 Kc7 33. Rg7 Ra3 34. Ba4+ Kb8 35. Bb5
c4 36. B×c4 1-0** [*PM*, pages 19–20]

VARIOUS GAMES, LONDON (1883/1884)

12. G.A. MacDonnell–Pollock [C37]
London, Simpson's Divan, 1883

1. e4 e5 2. f4 e×f4 3. Nf3 g5 4. Bc4 d5 Pollock:
"This, in conjunction with the seventh move and
sequel, forms something of a novelty in the defence
to the Muzio Gambit." **5. B×d5 g4 6. 0-0 g×f3
7. Q×f3 Qe7 8. Nc3 c6 9. Bb3 Be6 10. d4 B×b3
11. a×b3 Na6 12. e5 0-0-0 13. B×f4** The exchange sacrifice with 13. R×a6 b×a6 14. Q×c6+
Kb8 15. Qe4 might have not been quite enough
after 15. ... Qb7! 16. Qd3 Bc5. **13. ... R×d4** (*see diagram*)
14. R×a6! Pollock: "Perhaps a little rushed, but
he must make some show of attack." **14. ... R×f4!**
14. ... b×a6 15. Q×c6+ Qc7 16. Q×a6+ Qb7 17. Qe2
Bh6 was the other alternative, but White has significant compensation. **15. R×c6+! Kb8** 15. ...
b×c6!? 16. Q×c6+ Qc7 17. Qa8+ Qb8 18. Q×b8+
K×b8 19. R×f4 leads to a fascinating and wildly
unclear position. **16. Q×f4 b×c6 17. e6+ Qd6
18. Q×f7 Ne7** 18. ... Nh6 19. Qd7 Q×d7 20. e×d7

Kc7 had to be preferred. **19. Kh1 Ng6 20. Qe8+
Kc7 21. Rd1** (*see diagram*)

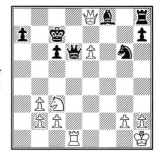

After
21. Rf1–d1

21. ... Be7! 22. Qf7 Rf8 It's rather surprising
that Pollock did not mention 22. ... Q×d1+!
23. N×d1 Rf8 24. Kg1 R×f7 25. e×f7 Bc5+ 26. Kf1
Ne5 where Black keeps decent winning chances.
23. R×d6 K×d6 Pollock: "Probably done for a
jest." **24. Ne4+ Ke5?** This is just too optimistic.
24. ... Kc7! 25. h3 R×f7 26. e×f7 Kd7 would have
allowed Black to continue to press. **25. Qg7+ K×e4
26. g3 Bc5 27. Q×h7 Rf6 28. h4 Ke3 29. h5 Ne5
30. e7 Rf1+ 31. Kg2 Rf2+ 32. Kh3 Rf1** 32. ...
B×e7 was losing too after 33. Q×e7 Rf5 34. g4 Rf3+
35. Kg2 Kd4 36. c3+ Ke4 37. Q×e5+. **33. Qd3+
1-0** [*Leeds Mercury*, June 23, 1883; *PM*, page 43
(in this source F.F. Rowland gave "July 1887" as the
date of the game)]

13. E.P. Griffith–Pollock
**Odds Game, London Chess Club,
London, 1883**
Remove f7 pawn

**1. e4 Nc6 2. d4 d5 3. e5 Bf5 4. Nf3 Qd7 5. Bd3
0-0-0 6. a3 h6 7. Bb5 e6 8. Be3 Nge7 9. Nbd2
g5 10. Nb3 Qe8 11. Qe2 Qg6 12. Nc5 Nb8 13. a4**
(*see diagram*)
13. ... Nec6!? 14. N×b7 Nb4! After 14. ... K×b7
15. B×c6+ N×c6 16. Qb5+ Kc8 17. Q×c6 Qe8
18. Qb5 White has the edge. **15. Nc5** 15. N×d8
promises only edgy play: 15. ... N×c2+ 16. Kf1

After
13. a2–a4

N×a1 17. Nc6 N×c6 18. Qd1 Nb4 19. Q×a1 a6 20. Be2 Bd3 21. B×d3 Q×d3+ 22. Kg1 Qe2. **15. ...** **B×c5 16. 0–0** 16. d×c5 could have been met by 16. ... d4 17. N×d4 R×d4 18. 0–0 (18. B×d4 N×c2+ 19. Kf1 N×a1 seems to favor Black.) 18. ... Rd5 19. Rad1 Rhd8 and Black has more pleasant play. **16. ... Be7 17. Bd2 g4 18. Ne1 N4c6** Very good was 18. ... c6! 19. B×b4 B×b4 20. Ba6+ Kc7. **19. Be3 h5 20. c4 h4 21. c×d5 e×d5 22. Rc1** *(see diagram)*

After
22. Ra1–c1

22. ... g3! 23. f×g3 h×g3 24. h×g3 24. h3 could have led to the following sharp exchange: 24. ... Nb4 25. Bf4 a6 26. e6! Rd6! 27. Qd2 a×b5 28. Q×b4 Q×e6 29. Q×b5 Rc6 30. Nf3 R×c1 31. R×c1 Bd6 and Black's clearly better, although not yet decisively so. **24. ... Be4 25. Nf3 Rdf8 26. B×c6 N×c6?** 26. ... R×f3!? 27. g×f3 Bd3 28. Qf2 N×c6 29. Rfd1 Kb7 with plenty of compensation. **27. Qa6+ Kd7 28. e6+ Q×e6 29. R×c6 Bd6 30. Ne5+** Even stronger was 30. Rfc1 R×f3 31. R×c7+ B×c7 32. R×c7+ K×c7 33. Q×e6 R×e3 34. Qe5+. **30. ... Ke7 31. R×c7+ Kd8 32. Rc6??** *Shoreditch Citizen:* "This is indeed a pity, Mr. Griffiths has carried on his attack with the skill of a master, but now, unware of his impending doom, he makes a waiting move, when 32. Bg5+ would have forced the game at once. Mr. Pollock's mate is very pretty, and we leave it for our junior readers to find out for themselves." **0–1** White could have easily won with 32. Bg5+ Rf6 33. B×f6+ K×c7 34. Q×a7+ Kc8 35. Rc1+. [*Shoreditch Citizen,* December 11, 1887]

14. Amateur–Pollock [C59]
Offhand Game, London(?), 1883

1. e4 e5 2. Nf3 Nc6 3. Bc4 Nf6 4. Ng5 d5 5. e×d5 Na5 6. Bb5+ c6 7. d×c6 b×c6 8. Be2 h6 9. Nf3 e4 10. Ne5 Qd4 11. f4 Bc5 12. Rf1 Bd6 13. c3 Qb6 14. b4 Nb7 15. Qa4 B×e5 16. f×e5 Nd5 17. Na3 0–0 18. Bb2 *(see diagram)*

After
18. Bc1–b2

18. ... Qc7 An appealing alternative was 18. ... Nc5!? 19. b×c5 Q×b2 20. Rd1 e3 21. Nc4 e×d2+ 22. R×d2 Qb1+ 23. Kf2 N×c3. **19. c4 Nb6 20. Qb3 Be6 21. Qg3 Rad8 22. Rf6!? Kh7 23. Rf4?!** 23. R×e6 f×e6 24. Qe3 Kh8 25. Q×e4 Qe7 26. Nc2 c5 might not have offered quite sufficient compensation, but was superior to the hesitation in the text. **23. ... Na4 24. Bc3 N×c3 25. d×c3 Q×e5 26. Nc2?** *(see diagram)*

After
26. Na3–c2

After 26. Rf2 Q×g3 27. h×g3 c5 Black is much better. **26. ... Rd3!! 27. B×d3 e×d3+ 28. Ne3** 28. Qe3 Q×c3+ 29. Qd2 Q×c2 30. Rc1 Q×d2+ 31. K×d2 g5 and Black should win without much difficulty. **28. ... Q×c3+ 29. Kf2 Qb2+ 30. Kf3 Qe2+ 31. Ke4 f5+ 32. Ke5 Qb2+ 33. K×e6 Qf6+ 34. Kd7 Qd6 mate 0–1** [*Shoreditch Citizen,* March 17, 1883]

15. S. Tinsley–Pollock [A01]
London, Purssell's, 18 October 1883

1. b3 e5 2. Bb2 Nc6 3. e3 d5 4. Bb5 Bd6 5. f4 f6 6. B×c6+ Pollock: "White may have purposed subsequently sacrificing his B for KP, but found it would not work." **6. ... b×c6 7. g3** Pollock: "This move makes it the more likely, as its only possible object could be to prevent Qh4+. It is of course very bad chess." **7. ... Ne7** Pollock: "Nh6 would answer present purposes equally well, and is very probably a better move." **8. Qe2 Ng6 9. Nc3 0-0 10. 0-0-0 a5 11. a4 Ba6 12. Qf3 Qe7 13. Kb1 Rab8 14. f5** Pollock: "Mr. Tinsley does not often play in this manner. The game is only given on account of the very interesting play arising from White's 16th move." **14. ... e4 15. Qf2 Ne5 16. Ka2** *(see diagram)*

After
16. Kb1–a2

16. ... R×b3! Pollock: "Sound or unsound, this sacrifice of a rook is particularly startling, as there appears to be nothing whatever in it, viewing the game at this stage." 16. ... Bd3 wins in an equally startling manner: 17. c×d3 N×d3 18. Qg2 R×b3 19. K×b3 Rb8+. **17. c×b3** Pollock: "If 17. K×b3 Bc4 mate." **17. ... Nd3** Pollock: "The only move to save the queen." **18. Qg2 Nb4+ 19. Ka1** Pollock: "19. Ka3 would of course mean submitting to Black the choice of a draw. Or he might proceed as follows: 19. ... Bd3 20. Nge2 Rb8 21. Nd4 Be5 22. Nb1 Nc2+ 23. Ka2 B×d4 24. B×d4 Qb4 and wins; If 19. Kb1 Bd3+ and the result is practically the same as in the actual game." **19. ... Nc2+ 20. Kb1 Bd3 21. Kc1 Ba3 22. Nb1** The only available move. **22. ... Qc5** Pollock: "He could also win by 22. ... B×b2+ 23. K×b2 Rb8." **23. B×a3 N×a3+ 24. Kb2 N×b1 25. R×b1 Qc2+ 26. Ka3 Q×b1 27. Ne2 Qc2 28. Nd4 Qc5+ 29. Ka2 Rb8 30. Qg1 Qb4 31. Qc1 Bc4** Pollock: "This apparently was a slip, for White could take off the Bishop and victory would again hang in the balance." 31. ... c5 was stronger. **32. Qc2 Q×a4+ 0-1** [*PM*, pages 17–18]

16. Pollock–Mr. W. [C37]
London, Simpson's Divan, 1884

Pollock: "It is curious to note, how a little novelty in a well-worn opening often succeeds in com-

pletely leading the opponent astray." **1. f4 e5** Pollock: "Starting for From's Gambit, which White, by refusing, converts into a King's Gambit; and presently the regular Muzio appears." **2. e4 e×f4 3. Nf3 g5 4. Bc4 g4 5. 0-0 g×f3 6. Q×f3 Qf6 7. e5 Q×e5 8. d3 Bh6 9. Bd2 Ne7** Pollock: "If 9. ... Q×b2 10. Qe4+ Ne7 11. Bc3 Qb6+ 12. Bd4 and wins a piece." Pollock's reasoning is not very clear, as after 12. ... Qa5 13. B×h8 d5 14. B×d5 Q×d5 15. Q×h7 Qg5 16. Bb2 Nbc6, Black is very much ahead. **10. Re1 Qf5** Pollock: "This seems unsuitable in the present instance. The idea of White's novelty, 10. Re1, is to abandon the assault up on the blocked KB file, and to seize instead a file which is more open and valuable." **11. Nc3 0-0** *(see diagram)*

After
11. ... 0-0

12. R×e7 Pollock: "Probably quite unexpected." **12. ... Qc5+ 13. Kh1 Q×e7 14. Nd5 Qd8** Pollock: "If 14. ... Qh4 then 15. Bc3 threatening 16. Bf6." **15. Bc3 d6 16. Bf6 Nc6 17. B×d8 N×d8 18. Ne7+ Kh8 19. N×c8 1-0** [*Baltimore Sunday News*, May 25, 1895]

BATH (EARLY 1884)

17. J.N. Burt–Pollock [C77]
Bath, January 1884

1. e4 e5 2. Nf3 Nc6 3. Nc3 Nf6 4. Bb5 a6 5. Ba4 Pollock: "5. B×c6 d×c6 6. N×e5 affords a strong attack." **5. ... Bb4 6. 0-0 0-0 7. d3 d6 8. h3** Pollock: "A weak move." **8. ... Ne7** Pollock: "Black should have taken the knight off first, although it makes a pretty good case of it as it is." **9. Ne2 Ng6 10. Ng3 d5 11. Qe2 Bd6 12. Bg5 h6 13. B×f6** Pollock: "The attack to which he is subjected shows the gain of the pawn to be a loss." **13. ... Q×f6 14. e×d5 Nf4 15. Qe4 g5 16. Nh2 h5 17. Qf3 g4 18. h×g4 h×g4 19. N×g4 Qh4 20. Ne3 f5 21. Nh1?** White should have tried 21. Rfe1 Rf6 22. Nef1 Rh6 23. c3 with prospects to resist Black's offensive. **21. … e4!** Pollock: "Leading to a comical and evidently unexpected crisis." **22. Qg3+** *(see diagram)*

After
22. Qf3–g3+

22. … Kf7! 23. Q×h4 23. Rae1 was to be met by 23. … Qh6! 24. Nc4 Rh8 25. N×d6+ c×d6 26. f3 Rg8. **23. … Ne2 mate 0–1** [*Illustrated Sporting and Dramatic News*, February 22, 1884; *PM*, page 21]

18. Pollock–Mary Rudge [C30]
Bath vs. Bristol Match, Clifton,
Imperial Hotel, 20 February 1884

1. e4 e5 2. Nc3 Bc5 3. f4 d6 4. Nf3 Nc6 5. Bb5 a6 6. Ba4 Nf6 7. d3 7. f×e5 d×e5 8. N×e5 Qd4 9. B×c6+ b×c6 10. Nd3 Ba7 11. Qf3 0–0 did not offer White much. **7. … Bd7 8. f5 h6 9. Qe2 Nd4 10. N×d4 B×d4 11. Bb3 B×c3+ 12. b×c3 Bc6 13. g4 Qe7 14. Bd2 0–0–0 15. c4! b6 16. a4 Bb7** 16. … a5 was almost mandatory. **17. a5 Rhf8** This is too passive. Instead, 17. … h5! 18. g5 Nd7 19. h4 Nc5 was playable. **18. a×b6 c×b6 19. Qe3?!** 19. Ba4! Qc7 20. 0–0 Nd7 21. B×d7+ gives White a clear edge. **19. … Qc7 20. 0–0 Nd7** 20. … N×g4 21. Qf3 h5 22. Rfb1 Rg8! was more ambitious, seeking counterplay. **21. Qf2 Nc5 22. Rfb1 f6 23. Be3 Kd7 24. Ba2 Qc6 25. Rb2** *(see diagram)*

After
25. Rb1–b2

25. … N×e4? 25. … Rb8 or 25. … Ba8 were sufficient to keep the balance. The text move is based on a miscalculation. **26. d×e4 Q×e4 27. Kf1!**

Qh1+ 28. Qg1 Qf3+ 29. Ke1 Qe4 30. R×b6 Kc8 31. Rab1 Rf7 32. c5 Rc7 33. Be6+ Rdd7 34. c6 R×c6 35. R×b7 Rc3 36. Rb8+ Kc7 37. R1b7+ Q×b7 38. R×b7+ Kc6 "Pollock announced a mate in nine [*sic*]." **1–0** [*New York Clipper*, October 9, 1897 (citing the *Irish Weekly Times*)]

BATH (CCA, JULY/AUGUST 1884)

19. Pollock–E. Thorold
Counties' Chess Association (Handicap Tournament), Bath, 29 July 1884
Remove f7 pawn

1. d4 Nf6 2. Nf3 e6 3. e3 d5 4. c4 Bb4+ 5. Nc3 0–0 6. Bd3 Nc6 7. 0–0 B×c3 8. b×c3 Qe7 9. a4 Ne8 10. Ba3 Nd6 11. e4 d×e4 12. B×e4 Rf4 13. Re1 Qf6 14. Bd3 Bd7 15. Bc1 Rf8 16. B×f4 Q×f4 17. c5 Ne8 18. Re4 Qf6 19. Qd2 h6 20. Rae1 Ne7 21. Ne5 B×a4 22. Qa2 Nd5 23. Ng4 Qf7 24. R×e6 N×c3 25. Qd2 25. Qc4 was good too. **25. … Nd5 26. Rg6 Qf4 27. Qe2 Kh8 28. g3 Q×d4** *(see diagram)*

After
28. … Qf4×d4

29. N×h6 An even more entertaining finish was 29. c6 b×c6 (29. … B×c6 30. R×c6 b×c6 31. Q×e8) 30. Q×e8 R×e8 31. R×e8+ Kh7 32. R×h6 mate. **29. … Nef6** 29. … g×h6 would be met by 30. R×h6+ Kg8 31. Rh4. **30. R×g7 Be8 31. Qd2! Ne4 32. Rh7+! K×h7 33. B×e4+ Q×e4 34. R×e4 1–0** [*Illustrated Sporting and Dramatic News*, August 30, 1884]

20. F.A. Hill–Pollock
Counties' Chess Association (Handicap Tournament), Bath, July/August 1884
Remove f7 pawn

"The following capital game (hitherto unpublished) will, we are sure, command much local as well as general interest, the winner being well and favourably known to many readers of this paper. The game was played at the Counties' meeting at Bath in 1884, in the handicap, Mr. Pollock carrying off the first prize." **1. e4 d6 2. d4 Nf6 3. Nc3 e5 4. d×e5 d×e5 5. Q×d8+ K×d8 6. Bg5 c6 7. 0-0-0+ Kc7 8. f4** 8. Nf3 was better. **8. ... h6 9. Bh4 e×f4 10. e5 g5 11. e×f6 g×h4 12. Nf3 Bg4 13. Be2 Nd7 14. Nd4 N×f6 15. B×g4 N×g4 16. Ne6+ Kb6 17. Na4+ Ka5 18. Rd4 h5 19. Re1 Ne3 20. N×f4 Re8 21. Kd2** (*see diagram*)

After
21. Kc1–d2

21. ... N×c2! 22. R×e8 N×d4 23. Re4 Bb4+ 24. Kd3 c5 25. b3 Rd8 26. Ke3 Nc2+ 27. Kf3 Ne1+ 27. ... b5 **28. Nb2 Rd2 29. Nbd3 Nd4+** 30. Ke3 R×a2 was also possible. **28. Kf2 b5 29. Nb2 Rd2+ 30. Re2 R×e2+ 31. K×e2 Ba3 32. Nbd3 N×d3 33. K×d3 c4+ 34. b×c4 b×c4+ 35. K×c4 Bd6 36. g3?** 36. N×h5 B×h2 37. Ng7 would have secured a draw. **36. ... h×g3 37. h×g3 h4 38. Ng2 h3 0–1** [*The Lincoln, Rutland and Stamford Mercury*, May 11, 1888]

21. N. Fedden–Pollock [C51]
Counties' Chess Association (Class I, Division II), Bath, 30 July 1884

1. e4 e5 2. Nf3 Nc6 3. Bc4 Bc5 4. 0-0 Nf6 5. b4 B×b4 6. c3 Be7 7. d4 0-0 8. d5 Nb8 9. Bd3 d6 10. h3 Nbd7 11. Be3 Re8 12. c4 Nf8 13. Nc3 Ng6 14. Ne2 Bd7 15. Ng3 Qc8 16. Nh2 Nf4 17. B×f4 e×f4 18. Nf5 N×e4 19. B×e4 19. N×e7+! R×e7 20. Re1 Bf5 21. Qc2 Qe8 22. Re2 Bg6 23. Rae1 f5 24. f3 Bh5 25. f×e4 B×e2 26. R×e2 was much better for White. **19. ... B×f5 20. B×f5 Q×f5 21. Rb1 b6 22. Nf3 Bf6 23. Qa4 h5 24. Rfe1 Be5 25. Qc6 Rac8 26. Rb3 g5 27. Nd4 Qf6 28. Nb5 f3?!** 28. ... a6! **29. Nd4 g4 30. h×g4 h×g4 31. Qd7 g3 32. Re4 Qg6 33. R×e5 d×e5 34. Ne2 Red8 and Black wins. 29. R×f3 Qg6 30. N×a7 Ra8 31. Q×c7 Bh2+ 32. K×h2 R×e1 33. Nc8 Qg7 34. Ne7+ Kh8 35. Nc6** 35. Q×d6! Re8 36. Nc6 h4 37. Rf5 allows White to fight on. **35. ... Qa1** (*see diagram*)

N. Fedden (London Borough of Hackney Archives).

After
35. ... Qg7–a1

36. Q×f7?? and Black forced a mate in four. **0–1** 36. Q×d6 Rh1+ 37. Kg3 R×h3+ 38. K×h3 Qh1+ 39. Qh2 g4+ 40. Kg3 h4+ 41. Q×h4 Q×h4+ 42. K×h4 g×f3 43. g4 R×a2 44. Kg3 Rc2 and White could have tried his luck in the endgame. [*Bristol Mercury and Daily Post*, August 1, 1884; *Chess Player's Chronicle*, August 13, 1884; *New York Clipper*, October 20, 1900]

22. Pollock–J.N. Burt [C49]
Counties' Chess Association (Class I, Division II), Bath, August 1884

1. e4 e5 2. Nc3 Nc6 3. Nf3 Nf6 4. Bb5 Bb4

5. 0–0 0–0 6. Nd5 Ba5 7. d4 N×d5 8. e×d5 N×d4 9. N×d4 e×d4 10. Q×d4 d6 11. Qa4 Bb6 12. Bd2 Bf5 13. Rae1 Qf6 14. Qb3 Qg6 15. Ba4 15. Bd3 was more natural. **15. ... Rab8 16. Bf4 Bc5** (see diagram)

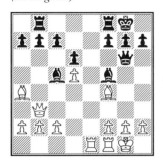

After
16. ... Bb6–c5

17. Re7? Preparing what turns out to be a losing tactical trap. White could have tried 17. Qc3 Be4 18. g3 Qf5 19. b4 Bb6 20. Bd7 Q×d5 21. Be3, but Black's position is still better. **17. ... b5 18. Rfe1 h6** Evidently, 18. ... b×a4? loses to 19. Q×b8 R×b8 20. Re8+. **19. B×b5 a6 20. c4 a×b5 21. c×b5 Bc2 22. Qf3 R×b5 23. b3 Bb6 24. Qe2 R×d5 25. h4 Qf5 26. Bg3 Qd3 27. Qg4 Rd4 28. Qh3 Qf5 29. Qh1 Rd2 30. Kh2 B×f2 31. B×f2 Q×f2 32. R7e3 Q×h4+ 0–1** [*Sheffield and Rotherham Independent*, November 1, 1884]

23. Pollock–R.J. Loman [C48]
Counties' Chess Association (Class I, Division II), Bath, August 1884

1. e4 e5 2. Nc3 Nc6 3. Nf3 Nf6 4. Bb5 Bc5 5. N×e5 N×e5 6. d4 Bd6 7. d×e5 7. f4 is another aggressive idea typical for that time. **7. ... B×e5 8. 0–0 B×c3 9. b×c3 0–0 10. e5 Ne4** Pollock: "Black has played the opening indifferently. His 4th, 6th and 8th moves are open to question, and here Ne8 is safer." **11. Qh5 Qe7** Pollock: "If 11. ... N×c3 12. Bd3 g6 13. Qh6 followed by Bg5 and wins." **12. Re1** (see diagram)

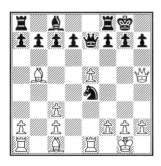

After
12. Rf1–e1

12. ... N×f2 Pollock: "The loss of the piece can hardly be prevented; thus, if 12. ... Qc5 13. R×e4 Q×b5 14. Rh4 h6 15. B×h6 and wins; if 12. ... N×c3 13. Bd3." Pollock likely overlooked 13. ... g6 14. Bg5 g×h5 15. B×e7 Re8 16. Bf6 Kf8 17. B×h7, where Black saves the piece, although he still faces serious difficulties. Pollock also suggested that 12. ... Nc5 can be met by 13. Bg5 Qe6 14. Re3 c6? (14. ... h6! 15. Bf6 Kh7 16. Rd1 Rg8 17. Rh3 d5 and Black can defend.) 15. Bf6!! and White wins. **13. Bf1!** Pollock: "It will be noticed that White made the only move. If 13. Ba4 Qc5 14. Be3 Qc4 15. Bb3 Qg4!" **13. ... f6** Pollock: "Black now makes desperate efforts to retrieve matters, and the greatest care becomes necessary to prevent it, for he obtains a third pawn for the piece minus." **14. K×f2 g6?** After 14. ... f×e5+ 15. Kg1 d6 16. Rb1 White's edge is very clear. **15. Qh6 f×e5+ 16. Kg1 d6 17. Bc4+ Be6 18. Bg5 Qd7 19. B×e6+ Q×e6 20. Rf1 d5 21. Rae1 e4 22. Be3 b6** Pollock: "In order to drive away the bishop when it reaches d4. But it does not improve his pawn position." **23. Bd4 Qe7 24. R×f8+ R×f8 25. Rf1 R×f1+ 26. K×f1 Qf8+** Pollock: "Labouring under the impression that he could draw the game." **27. Q×f8+ K×f8 28. Be5 c6 29. Ke2 Ke7 30. Ke3 Ke6 31. Bb8 a6 32. g4 g5 33. c4 Kd7 34. c×d5 c×d5 35. Kd4 Ke6 36. a4 b5 37. a5 1–0** [*PM*, pages 24–25]

24. J.H. Blake–Pollock [C45]
Counties' Chess Association (Class I, Section II), Bath, August 1884

1. e4 e5 2. Nf3 Nc6 3. d4 e×d4 4. N×d4 Bc5 5. Be3 Qf6 6. c3 Nge7 7. Qd2 B×d4 8. c×d4 d5 9. Nc3 d×e4 10. d5 Ne5 11. Nb5 (see diagram)

After
11. Nc3–b5

11. ... Bf5?? It appears Pollock mixed his move order here. His sacrifice—a good idea—could have worked with 11. ... 0–0! 12. N×c7 Bf5 13. N×a8 R×a8 14. Rc1 Rd8, leaving Black with pleasant

J.H. Blake (London Borough of Hackney Archives).

compensation. **12. N×c7+ Kd7 13. N×a8 R×a8 14. Bb5+ Kd8 15. d6 N7g6 16. Qa5+ b6 17. B×b6+ a×b6 18. Q×b6+ Kc8 19. Qc7 mate 1–0** [*Sheffield Independent*, September 20, 1884]

25. J. Coker–Pollock [C49]
Counties' Chess Association (Class I, Section II), Bath, August 1884

1. e4 e5 2. Nc3 Nf6 3. Nf3 Nc6 4. Bb5 Bb4 5. B×c6 d×c6 6. Qe2 Bg4 7. h3 B×f3 8. Q×f3 Qd7 9. 0–0 0–0–0 10. a3 Bd6 11. d3 Rdg8 12. Be3 h5 13. Rfb1 h4 14. b4 Nh5 (*see diagram*)

After
14. ... Nf6–h5

15. B×a7!? A risky idea. 15. b5 was a reasonable alternative. **15. ... b6 16. Na4** Better was 16. b5 Kb7 17. b×c6+ Q×c6 18. B×b6 c×b6 19. Q×f7+ Bc7 20. Nd5 with clear compensation. **16. ... Kb7 17. B×b6 c×b6 18. Qe3?** More incisive was

18. Nc5+! b×c5 19. b×c5+ Kc7 20. c×d6+ K×d6 21. Rb6 g5 22. d4 and, due to his exposed king, Black may be in some danger here despite the extra knight. **18. ... Bc7 19. c3 g5 20. f3 f5! 21. e×f5 Ra8 22. Nb2 Q×f5 23. Qe4 Qd7?!** 23. ... Q×e4! 24. d×e4 Ng3 25. Kf2 Rad8 26. Rd1 b5 was a more technical resolution. **24. a4 Ng3 25. Qe3 b5 26. a5 Qd6 27. Re1 Rae8 28. Nd1 Nh5 29. Nf2** (*see diagram*)

After
29. Nd1–f2

29. ... e4! 30. a6+ After 30. N×e4 Black wins by force: 30. ... Qh2+ 31. Kf1 Ng3+ 32. Kf2 N×e4+ 33. d×e4 Bg3+ 34. Kf1 Qh1+ 35. Qg1 Q×g1+ 36. K×g1 B×e1 37. R×e1. **30. ... Ka8 31. N×e4 Qh2+ 32. Kf2 Nf4 33. Rg1 N×h3+ 34. Ke2 N×g1+ 35. R×g1 h3 36. Qc5 Re6 37. Kf2 g4! 38. Qf5 Bb6+ 39. d4 Rhe8 40. Q×g4 R×e4!** 40. ... B×d4+ 41. c×d4 R×e4 42. f×e4 Rf8+ was possible too. **41. f×e4 Rf8+ 42. Ke2 Q×g1 43. Qd7 0–1** [*Illustrated Sporting and Dramatic News*, November 1, 1884]

26. C.D. Locock–Pollock [C84]
Counties' Chess Association (Class I, Division II), Bath, August 1884

1. e4 e5 2. Nf3 Nc6 3. Bb5 a6 4. Ba4 Nf6 5. d4 e×d4 6. 0–0 Be7 7. e5 Ne4 8. N×d4 0–0 9. Nf5 (*see diagram*)

After
9. Nd4–f5

9. ... d5 Pollock: "This game was played in Section 1B. It was of considerable importance, and the last game of the tournament. By winning it Mr. Pollock tied for first place with Messrs. Fedden and Loman. Had he lost it he would have tied for fourth place with Mr. Burt, half-a-point below Mr. Blake. Hence 'the heroic treatment' of the defence. Black deliberated 20 minutes over this move, the time limit being one hour for 20 moves." **10. e×d6 B×f5 11. B×c6 B×d6 12. B×b7 Qh4?!** Pollock: "The plan, of course, seems a bold one, if not at first blush a desperate one. But Black was in no humour to reck of a sacrifice of the exchange. It may just be noticed that 12. ... N×f2 would be foiled by 13. Qf3." 12. ... Rb8 13. B×e4 B×e4 14. Nc3 Bg6 15. Nd5 Re8 was better for Black. **13. g3 Qh3 14. Qf3?** Pollock: "It must be confessed that here reality coincides with appearances. White seems to gain nothing by disdaining to take the rook. It is, of course, 'another thing' in actual play, with the clocks ticking away their warning of the approach of the hour's expiration, when many things that are not are seen. After 14. B×a8 R×a8 (14. ... Bg4! 15. Qd3!) 15. Qf3 Re8 16. Qg2 Qh5 17. Re1 Black has no better move than 17. ... Re6. A comparison then of this position with that after Black's 17th move in the actual game will show at once which of the two is the more manageable game to play." **14. ... Rae8 15. Be3 Re6 16. Nd2 Nf6 17. c4 c6 18. B×c6 Bb4 19. Bd5 B×d2 20. B×e6 f×e6 21. Qg2 B×e3 22. f×e3 Qh6** Better was 22. ... Q×g2+! 23. K×g2 Bd3 24. Rf2 B×c4. **23. Rfe1** 23. Rf4! Qg5 24. Re1 e5 25. Rh4 Qg6 26. c5 with equal chances. **23. ... Be4** 23. ... Bd3! 24. Rad1 B×c4 25. b3 Bd5 26. Qe2 Qg6 27. Rd4 Ne4 28. Rf1 R×f1+ 29. K×f1 Qf6+ and Black wins. **24. Qd2 Bf3 25. Rf1 Ne4 26. Qd4** *(see diagram)*

After
26. Qd2–d4

26. ... N×g3! 27. Qe5 Ne2+ 28. Kf2 Qh4+ 29. Qg3 N×g3 0–1 [*PM*, pages 23–24]

27. Pollock–R.J. Loman [B30]
Counties' Chess Association (Class I, Division II, Playoffs), Bath, August 1884

Pollock: "A very curious and interesting game, of its kind." **1. e4 c5 2. Nc3 Nc6 3. Nf3 g6 4. Bb5** Pollock: "Strangely enough this excellent move seems to have passed out of memory, and does not seem to have been had recourse to at all in the days of the revival of the Sicilian Defence by Messrs. Bird, Lasker, and others, in the form of the King Fianchetto, in conjunction with d2–d3." **4. ... Bg7** Pollock: "4. ... Nd4 is preferred by some, but the move at least gives White considerable latitude." **5. B×c6 d×c6** Pollock: "The capture with the b–pawn would leave the doubled pawns more awkwardly fixed, unless the c–pawn could be advanced to c5 and supported with the d–pawn. In the Ruy Lopez the doubled c–pawn is considered no disadvantage to Black. But in the present case both pawns are advanced a square, and therefore the two front pawns of the phalanx of three cannot both be defended by pawns, unless the foremost is advanced to c4. It is on the forced position of these adverse pawns that White gives up his bishop, and we shall see how far he was justified in trying so fine a plan." **6. Ne2 Nf6 7. d3 0–0 8. Be3 Ng4 9. Bc1 f5** Pollock: "This gives Black considerable freedom for his pieces, but does not improve his pawn position." **10. e×f5 B×f5 11. 0–0 Qc7 12. Ng3 Ne5 13. N×e5** Pollock: "There was also 13. Ng5 to be considered, but White is determined upon following the plan indicated, remote as it seems." **13. ... B×e5 14. f4 Bg7 15. Qe2 Rae8 16. N×f5 R×f5 17. Qe6+ Kh8 18. g4 Rd5 19. Rb1 Rd6** Pollock: "Black makes great efforts to advance his king's pawn. Could it have been played on e5 on the 15th move?" **20. Qe1 Qd7 21. Qg3 e5 22. f5** Pollock: "This will leave White two pawns to one on the king's side for the ending." **22. ... g×f5 23. R×f5 Rg6** Pollock: "This move and the next (especially) is very well managed by Black, and the position of the first player becomes exceedingly precarious." **24. Be3 e4** *(see diagram)*

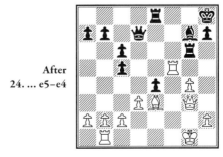

After
24. ... e5–e4

25. Bd2? Pollock: "It is remarkable that White

should succeed in repairing a mistake of such magnitude as that of his 24th move." **25. B×c5 e×d3** (According to Pollock, 25. ... Bd4+ 26. B×d4+ Q×d4+ 27. Kh1 e×d3 should win for Black. Black certainly enjoys an edge in the ensuing endgame, but it's far whether a winning one.) 26. c×d3 Bd4+ 27. B×d4+ Q×d4+ 28. Kh1 R×g4 29. Qf2 Q×f2 30. R×f2 with approximately equal play. **25. ... e×d3 26. c×d3 Qd4+** 26. ... c4! 27. Kh1 Q×d3 28. Q×d3 c×d3 29. Rf3 Rd8 30. h3 Rd7 and Black enjoys a clear advantage. **27. Kh1 R×g4 28. Qf3** Pollock: "Threatening to win a piece by Bc3." **28. ... Rg8 29. Bc3 Qa4 30. Rf8** (*see diagram*)

After
30. Rf4–f8

Pollock: "Both sides play most ingeniously, and the attack changes like a kaleidoscope." **30. ... B×c3 31. b×c3 Q×a2 32. R×g8+ Q×g8 33. c4** Pollock: "To prevent the exchange of queens." **33. ... Rg6 34. Qf5** Pollock: "Threatening to exchange the c5-pawn safely." **34. ... b5 35. Qe5+ Rg7 36. Rf1 Qd8??** Pollock: "This loses the game forthwith." 36. ... b4! 37. Q×c5 b3 38. Rf8 Rg1+ 39. Q×g1 Q×f8 40. Qd4+ Kg8 41. Qg4+ and anything can happen still. Pollock recommended 36. ... h6! and he was right: 37. Q×c5 Qe6 38. c×b5 c×b5 39. Q×b5 a5 and Black seems to have a draw in hand. **37. Rf7 Qg8 38. Re7 b4 39. Re8 Q×e8 40. Q×e8+ Rg8 41. Qe5+ Rg7 42. Q×c5 Rb7? 43. Qf8 mate 1–0** [*PM*, pages 21–23]

28. N. Fedden–Pollock [C45]
Counties' Chess Association
(Class I, Division II, Playoffs),
Bath, August 1884

1. e4 e5 2. Nf3 Nc6 3. d4 e×d4 4. N×d4 N×d4 5. Q×d4 Ne7 6. Bc4 Nc6 7. Qd5 Qf6 8. 0–0 d6 9. Bb5 Bd7 10. Nc3 Be7 11. Qd3 Bd8 12. Nd5 Qh4 13. f4 0–0 14. Bd2 f5 Somewhat safer was 14. ... a6 15. Bc4 Re8 16. a4 Qh5. **15. e×f5 B×f5 16. Qc3 Qh5 17. Rae1 Bd7 18. Bc4 Kh8 19. Rf3 Bg4 20. Rg3 Bh4** (*see diagram*)

After
20. ... Bd8–h4

21. h3! B×g3 22. Q×g3 Bd7 23. Bc3 White's compensation is evident. **23. ... Rf7 24. b4 Bf5?** 24. ... Qg6 or 24. ... Re8 were two viable alternatives. **25. b5 Qg6 26. Q×g6 B×g6 27. b×c6 b×c6 28. f5 R×f5 29. N×c7 Raf8** 29. ... Rc5 would have been a last attempt but White has an easy solution here too: 30. N×a8 R×c4 31. Re3 d5 32. Nc7 d4 33. Rf3 h6 34. Bb2 B×c2 35. Rf8+ Kh7 36. Ne6. **30. Re7 Bf7 31. Ne6 d5 32. N×f8 d×c4 33. R×a7 Kg8 34. Ra8 Bd5 35. Ne6+ Kf7 36. g4 c5 37. Ra7+ 1–0** The *Field* gave the game score as a victory for White, but several newspaper accounts suggest Pollock claimed a win on time, a fact disputed by Fedden. [*The Field*, December 6, 1884]

VARIOUS GAMES (LATE 1884/ EARLY 1885)

29. R.J. Loman & Pollock–Block [A42]
London, Simpson's Divan,
Consultation Game, October 1884

1. c4 g6 2. d4 Bg7 3. Nc3 e6 4. e4 d6 5. Be3 c6 6. Bd3 Ne7 7. Rc1 Qc7 8. Nf3 Nd7 9. 0–0 0–0 10. Qd2 e5 11. Ne2 f5 12. d×e5 d×e5 13. e×f5 g×f5 14. Bh6 e4 15. B×g7 K×g7 16. Ng5 Nf6 17. Nd4 Qd6 18. Be2 Rd8 19. Rfd1 Ng6? Better was 19. ... h6! 20. Nde6+ B×e6 21. Q×d6 R×d6 22. R×d6 B×c4 23. B×c4 h×g5 with reasonable compensation for Black. **20. c5** It's unclear why the players handling White missed this simple path to victory: 20. N×f5+! B×f5 21. Q×d6 R×d6 22. R×d6. **20. ... Q×d4** (*see diagram*)

21. Qf4?? With 21. Q×d4 R×d4 22. R×d4 h6 23. Nh3 Nd5 24. g3 White has a clear advantage. **21. ... Nd5** The columnist called this "Potent and admirable." However, simpler is 21. ... N×f4 22. R×d4 N×e2+ 23. Kf1 N×d4. **0–1** [*Illustrated Sporting and Dramatic News*, January 10, 1885]

After
20. ... Qd6×d4

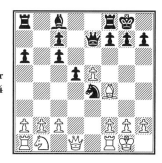

After
12. Bc1–f4

30. Pollock–W.H. Harsant [C47]
Bath vs. Bristol Match, Clifton,
25 February 1885

"A strange little story enough!" **1. e4 e5 2. Nc3 Nc6 3. Nf3 Nf6 4. d4 e×d4 5. N×d4 Bb4 6. Bg5 d6 7. Bb5 Bd7 8. 0–0 B×c3 9. b×c3 0–0 10. f4 N×d4 11. B×d7 Q×d7 12. B×f6 Nc6 13. Qh5 g×f6 14. Rf3** (*see diagram*)

After
14. Rf1–f3

14. ... f5?? Instead, Black could have defended with 14. ... Rfd8 15. Qh6 Ne7 16. f5 Qc6 17. Rg3+ Ng6 18. f×g6 Qc5+ 19. Kh1 f×g6 with equal play. **15. Qg5+ Kh8 16. Qf6+ Kg8 17. Rg3 mate 1–0** [*PM*, pages 25–26]

31. W.H. Harsant–Pollock [C84]
Bristol vs. Bath Match, March 1885

1. e4 e5 2. Nf3 Nc6 3. Bb5 a6 4. Ba4 Nf6 5. d4 e×d4 6. 0–0 Be7 7. e5 Ne4 8. N×d4 0–0 9. Nf5 d5 10. B×c6 b×c6 11. N×e7+ Q×e7 12. Bf4 (*see diagram*)

12. ... g5!? 13. Be3 Interesting would have been 13. f3 g×f4 14. f×e4 d×e4 15. Qh5 f5 16. e×f6 Q×f6 17. Nc3 Qd4+ 18. Kh1 e3 19. Ne2 Q×b2 20. Rae1. **13. ... Q×e5 14. Bd4 Qf4 15. f3 Nd6 16. Re1 Nf5** 16. ... Bd7!? was a viable option too. **17. Be5 Qb4 18. Nd2** 18. Bf6!? h6 19. Nc3 Be6 (19. ... Q×b2?! is just too risky: 20. N×d5 Qb5 21. Ne7+ N×e7 22. R×e7 Be6 23. h4) 20. a3 Qb6+

21. Kh1 c5. 18. ... Qc5+ 19. Kh1 Qb6 20. Nb3 (*see diagram*)

After
20. Nd2–b3

Again, attempting some active play on the king-side was a better idea: 20. Bf6 h6 21. f4!? **20. ... Ne3?** Losing almost on the spot. Better was 20. ... f6! 21. Bc3 Rb8 with chances for both sides. **21. Qd2 f6 22. R×e3 f×e5 23. R×e5 h6 24. Re7** 24. Qd3! was even more decisive. **24. ... Bf5 25. Qc3 Rf7 26. Rae1 Raf8 27. Nd4 Bg6 28. R1e6 R×e7 29. R×e7 c5 30. Ne6 d4 1–0** After 31. Qe1, Black's position is hopeless. [*Bristol Times and Mirror*, March 7, 1885]

32. Pollock–J.N. Burt [C57]
Bristol, April 1885

1. e4 e5 2. Bc4 Nf6 3. Nf3 Nc6 4. Ng5 d5 5. e×d5 N×d5 6. N×f7 K×f7 7. Qf3+ Ke6 8. Nc3 Nce7 9. d4 c6 10. Bg5 Qa5? Pollock: "A somewhat unusual move." 10. ... h6 was necessary. **11. d×e5 Ng6 12. 0–0** 12. 0–0–0 was even stronger. **12. ... Bb4 13. Rfe1?!** Pollock: "White preserves his e–pawn for the persecution of the adverse king as soon as it set free." 13. Nb5! Rf8 14. B×d5+ c×d5 15. Nd4+ K×e5 16. Qe3+ Kd6 17. a3 with a powerful attack for White. **13. ... B×c3 14. Qg4+ Kf7 15. e6+ Ke8 16. b×c3 Q×c3 17. Rad1 Rf8 18. B×d5 c×d5 19. Qa4+ Qc6 20. R×d5! Ne7 21. Rd7!** Pollock: "The game is not without its pretty points. White again threatens mate, in three moves." **21. ... Rf6 22. B×f6?!** 22. R×e7+! K×e7

23. B×f6+ g×f6 24. Qb4+ Qd6 25. Qe4 Qd2
26. Kf1 Qh6 27. h3 Qg6 28. Qb4+ Ke8 29. Qb5+
and White must win. **22. ... g×f6** Pollock: "If
22. ... Q×a4, [then] 23. R×e7+ Kf8 24. Rf7+ Ke8
25. R×g7 B×e6 26. R×e6+ Kf8 27. Ree7; White
cannot lose and ought to win." A correct assessment by Pollock. For instance, 27. ... Q×c2
28. Ref7+ Ke8 29. h4 Qc1+ 30. Kh2 Qf4+ 31. Kh3
Q×f2 32. R×b7 Qf5+ 33. Kh2 Qf4+ 34. Rg3 and
White's pressure is consistent. **23. Qg4** 23. Red1
was needed. **23. ... B×d7 24. e×d7+** *(see diagram)*

After
24. e6×d7+

24. ... Q×d7?? Pollock: "An oversight." 24. ...
Kf8! 25. Qh4 Qd6 26. Qh6+ Kg8 27. Qe3 with
equal play. Pollock recommended 24. ... Kd8
25. Qg7 Q×d7 26. Q×f6 and concluded White
"would not find it easy to win." But 26. Qh8+!
Qe8 27. Q×f6 b6 28. Qd4+ Qd7 29. Qh8+ Qe8
30. Rd1+ Kc7 31. Qe5+ Kb7 32. Re1 Rd8
33. Q×e7+ Q×e7 34. R×e7+ Kc6 would have assured White of a winning endgame. **25. Qg8 mate
1–0** [*PM*, page 26]

33. Pollock–L.J. Williams [A03]
**Bath vs. Bristol Match, Bath,
20 May 1885**

1. f4 d5 2. e3 c5 3. Nf3 Nc6 4. b3 Nh6 5. Bb2
f6 6. Be2 e6 7. 0–0 Bd6 8. Nc3 a6 9. Qe1 Qe7
10. Qh4 Bd7 11. a4 Nb4 12. Ne1 0–0–0 13. Nd3
Nf5 14. Qf2 d4 15. Ne4 d×e3 Possible too was
15. ... N×c2 16. N×d6+ Q×d6 (16. ... N×d6?
17. Rac1 d×e3 18. d×e3 Ne4 19. Qf3 Nd2 20. Qg3
Ne4 21. Qh3 e5 22. f5 and White should prevail.)
17. Rac1 d×e3 18. d×e3 Nc×e3 19. N×c5 Bc6
20. Rfe1 Qd2. **16. N×d6+ Q×d6 17. d×e3** *(see diagram)*
17. ... Nc6 There was nothing wrong with 17. ...
N×c2 18. Rac1 Nc×e3 19. N×c5 Kb8 20. Ba3
Qd4, although the tactical complications can grow
daunting: 21. N×b7!? N×f1 (21. ... K×b7? allows
22. Bc5! Qe4 23. Bf3) 22. Bd6+ K×b7 23. Bf3+
Bc6 24. B×c6+ Kc8 25. Bb5+ Kb7 26. Rc7+ Kb6

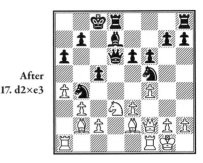

After
17. d2×e3

27. Bc5+ K×c7 28. B×d4 R×d4 29. B×f1 Rhd8
and Black has a real fighting chance. **18. Ba3 b6?**
18. ... Nb4 was necessary. **19. a5! Nb4 20. Rfd1
Qc7 21. N×b4 c×b4 22. B×a6+ Kb8 23. B×b4
Bc6 24. Bd3 g5 25. a×b6 Qb7 26. Bc5 1–0**
[*Hereford Times*, May/June 1885]

1st British Chess Association
(June/July 1885)

34. Pollock–H.E. Bird [B72]
**1st BCA Tournament, London,
Simpson's Divan, Round 1,
15 June 1885**

1. e4 c5 2. Nc3 Nc6 3. Nf3 g6 4. d4 Pollock:
"An excellent move here is 4. Bb5." **4. ... c×d4
5. N×d4 Bg7 6. Be3 d6 7. Bc4 Nf6 8. 0–0** 8. f3
is the more common path today. **8. ... 0–0
9. Qd2?! Ng4! 10. N×c6 b×c6 11. Rad1 Be6
12. B×e6 f×e6** *(see diagram)*

After
12. ... f×e6

Pollock: "The opening appears to result a little
in Black's favour." **13. Bg5 Rf7 14. h3 Nf6 15. Qe2**
Pollock: "Intending to proceed with e4–e5 or
Qe2–c4." 15. e5!? Nd5 16. e×d6 Q×d6 17. Ne2
would have dented Black's pawns. **15. ... Qa5
16. Bd2 Qb4 17. Rb1** Pollock: "It does not appear
that White missed anything here ... by Nd5. The
text move is therefore a good one, and the least

disturbing to his pawn position." 17. e5 was again a good choice. **17. ... Raf8** Pollock: "This prevents Nd5 and Nc7, etc." **18. Nd1 Qa4** 18. ... Q×e4 was safe. Why Bird didn't take the e4–pawn is unknown. **19. b3 Q×a2** *(see diagram)*

After
19. ... Qa4×a2

20. Rc1 Pollock: "White seems to have fallen into the temptation of playing for a trap hoping to have time to play Bc3 and win the queen by Ra1. He also perhaps preferred to sacrifice the pawn for a kingside attack, for he could have recovered it by 20. Nc3 Qa5 21. Ra1 Qc7 22. Qc4 Qd2 23. Ra6, bringing the pressure from the queenside. The play now becomes animated enough." 20. Nc3 Qa5 21. Nd5 Qc5 22. Bc3 Qb5 23. c4 Qb7 24. N×f6+ B×f6 was better than the path followed in the game. **20. ... Qa3 21. f4?** 21. f3 was somewhat better. **21. ... Nd7** 21. ... Nh5! 22. Qg4 Qc5+ 23. Kh2 Qd4 was very strong for Black. **22. Qg4 Nc5 23. Nf2 Bd4 24. f5 e×f5 25. e×f5 B×f2+** 25. ... Qb2! and Black has a decisive advantage. **26. R×f2 R×f5 27. R×f5 R×f5 28. Qd4?** 28. Re1!? Qa2 29. R×e7 Q×c2 30. Qd4 and White seems to survive. **28. ... Ne6 29. Qh4 Qc5+ 30. Kh1 Rf6** Pollock: "Black holds his pawns together very skilfully." **31. Qe4 d5 32. Qa4 Qf2 33. Qb4 c5 34. Qb8+ Rf8 35. Qe5 Qf5 36. Qe2 Rf7** Pollock: "White gives a great deal of trouble, but the end of it is fairly visible." **37. Qa6 Ng5 38. Q×a7 d4 39. Qc7 Kg7 40. Ra1** 40. B×g5 Q×g5 41. Re1 e6 42. Qb8 was perhaps a last attempt to fight for a draw. **40. ... e6** Bird missed a tactical finish: 40. ... N×h3! 41. Qg3 (41. g×h3 Q×h3+ 42. Kg1 Qg4+ 43. Kh1 Qe4+ 44. Kg1 Rf3) 41. ... Nf2+ 42. Kg1 Ne4 43. Qe1 Qf2+ 44. Q×f2 R×f2 45. Ba5 R×c2 and Black wins. **41. Qb8 Ne4 42. Ba5 e5?!** More incisive was 42. ... Nf2+! 43. Kg1 Q×c2 44. Qe5+ Kh6 45. Q×e6 Rf5. **43. Bc7 Nf2+! 44. Kg1 e4** 44. ... N×h3+! again was a finish Pollock likely wouldn't have missed. **45. Be5+ Kh6 46. Kh2 e3 47. b4 N×h3! 48. g×h3 Q×c2+ 49. Kh1 Qe4+ 50. Kg1 Rf2 51. Bg7+ K×g7 52. Ra7+ Kh6 53. R×h7+ K×h7 0–1** [*PM*, pages 26–28]

35. Pollock–A. Rumboll [C51]
1st BCA Tournament, London,
Simpson's Divan, Round 2,
15 June 1885

1. e4 e5 2. Nf3 Nc6 3. Bc4 Bc5 4. b4 B×b4 5. c3 Bc5 6. d4 e×d4 7. 0–0 d6 8. c×d4 Bb6 9. Nc3 Bg4 10. Bb5 a6 11. Ba4 Bd7 12. e5 Ba5 13. Bg5 f6 14. e×f6 g×f6?! The alternative was 14. ... N×f6 15. Re1+ Kf8 16. Rc1 h6 17. Bd2 Bb6. **15. Re1+ Kf8 16. Bd2! h5?** *(see diagram)*

After
16. ... h7–h5

16. ... B×c3? would not help either: 17. B×c3 Kg7 18. d5!; After 16. ... Kg7 17. d5 Ne5 18. B×d7 Q×d7 19. Nd4 Re8 20. Qh5 and White maintains a comfortable edge. **17. Nh4 Kg7 18. Qf3 Nce7 19. Qg3+ Kf8 20. Bb3 Nf5** 20. ... Be8 would run into 21. Qf3! Rh7 22. R×e7 R×e7 (22. ... N×e7? loses quickly to 23. Q×f6+ Bf7 24. B×f7 R×f7 25. Qh8+ Ng8 26. Ng6+ Ke8 27. Q×g8+ Kd7 28. Q×f7+ Kc8 29. Re1) 23. Qd5 Bf7 24. Q×a5. **21. Qg6 Ngh6 22. N×f5** and a mate in four is impossible to defend. **1–0** [*Chess Player's Chronicle*, June 24, 1885]

36. I.A. Gunsberg–Pollock [C22]
1st BCA Tournament, London,
Simpson's Divan, Round 3,
16 June 1885

1. e4 e5 2. d4 e×d4 3. Q×d4 Nc6 4. Qe3 Nf6 5. Bd2 d6 6. Nc3 Be6 7. 0–0–0 d5!? 8. e×d5 N×d5 9. Qg3! Bd6?! A rather risky venture. An even sharper option was 9. ... N×c3 10. B×c3 Bd6 11. Q×g7 Bf4+ 12. Bd2 Be5. **10. Q×g7 Be5 11. Qh6 Qd6?** 11. ... Rg8 12. Q×h7 Nf6 13. Qh4 Rg4 could be met by the powerful 14. Bg5! **12. Ne4 Qe7 13. Nf3 0–0–0 14. N×e5 N×e5 15. Bg5! Nb4** An inventive if insufficient resource. The tactics seem to work only in White's favor: 15. ... Qb4 16. B×d8 Q×e4 17. f3 Qa4 18. Bf6 Bf5 19. Rd2 Re8 20. Qg5 Nd7 21. Bb5! **16. R×d8+ R×d8** *(see diagram)*

After
16. ... Rh8×d8

17. Bc4!! Qd7 18. B×e6 f×e6 19. B×d8 Qc6 20. Nc3 Nd5 21. Bf6 Nd7 22. N×d5 e×d5 23. Bg5 Qc4 24. Qe6 1–0 [*London Evening Standard*, June 19, 1885; *Chess Player's Chronicle*, July 1, 1885; *Chess-Monthly*, February 1886, pages 176–177]

37. W. Donisthorpe–Pollock [A01]
1st BCA Tournament, London,
Simpson's Divan, London, Round 4,
16 June 1885

1. b3 f5 2. Bb2 e6 3. e3 Nf6 4. Be2 Be7 5. Bh5+ N×h5 6. Q×h5+ Kf8 6. ... g6 7. Qh6 Bf6 8. B×f6 Q×f6 9. Nc3 b5 would have been an alternative perhaps more to Pollock's liking. 7. Nh3 Bf6 8. d4 Nc6 9. Nf4 g5 10. Nd3 d6 11. Qe2 Bd7 12. Nd2 Be8 13. g4 Bg6 14. g×f5 e×f5 (*see diagram*)

After
14. ... e6×f5

15. h4! g×h4 A better alternative was 15. ... h6 16. 0-0-0 a5 17. Rdg1 a4. **16. Nf4 Qd7?** Better was 16. ... Bf7 17. 0-0-0 Rg8 18. Qb5 Qc8. **17. 0-0-0 Qf7? 18. Kb1 Kg7 19. Nf3 Rhe8 20. N×h4 B×h4 21. R×h4 d5 22. Rdh1 Rh8 23. Qf3 Ne7 24. Qg3 Ng8 25. Ba3 Nf6 26. Qg5 Rhg8 27. Rh6 a5** 27. ... Rh8 is best met by 28. f3! Nd7 29. Rg1 c5 30. N×g6. **28. R×g6+! Q×g6 29. N×g6 h×g6 30. Be7 Ne4 31. Qf4 1–0** [*The Field*, June 20, 1885]

W. Donisthorpe (London Borough of Hackney Archives).

38. Pollock–G.A. MacDonnell [C49]
1st BCA Tournament, London,
Simpson's Divan, Round 5,
17 June 1885

London Evening Standard (June 18, 1885): "Pollock vs. MacDonnell was a Four Knights' opening, which lasted five hours and was adjourned at seven [*sic*] o'clock. (The *Morning Post* of that day remarked the game was adjourned at 5 o'clock and resumed at 7.) MacDonnell was a pawn ahead, but it required the very best play to win. On resuming the game MacDonnell won, the game lasting altogether six and a half hours." **1. e4 e5 2. Nc3 Nc6 3. Nf3 Nf6 4. Bb5 Bb4 5. 0-0 B×c3 6. d×c3 Qe7 7. Qe2 a6 8. Bd3 d6 9. h3 h6 10. Be3 Be6 11. a4 Qd7 12. Nd2 g5 13. f3 Nh5 14. Qf2 Ne7 15. g4?!** Too committal. 15. Rfd1 Nf4 16. Bf1 was safer. **15. ... Nf4! 16. B×f4 e×f4 17. Qd4** 17. e5 d×e5 18. Ne4 0-0-0 19. Qa7 would have been a subtle way to snatch the initiative. **17. ... Ng6 18. Rfe1 Ne5 19. Kg2?** White's position is precarious, especially as he lacks counterplay. **19. ... Ke7** Very forceful would have been 19. ... h5! 20. Be2 c5 21. Qf2 0-0-0 22. b4 B×g4! **20. Nc4**

Nc6 21. Qf2 f6 22. b3 h5! 23. Rh1 A more careful approach was 23. Be2 B×c4 24. b×c4 Rh6 25. c5 Ne5 26. c×d6+ c×d6 27. Qb6 h×g4 28. h×g4 Rah8 29. Rh1. 23. ... h×g4 24. h×g4 (*see diagram*)

After
24. h3×g4

24. ... B×g4! 25. Qe2 Bh3+ 26. Kf2 Ne5 27. N×e5 f×e5 28. Rag1 Rag8 29. Bc4 Rg7 30. Qd1 Qc6 31. Qd2 Qc5+ 32. Ke1 Kf6 32. ... g4! was an excellent breakthrough. 33. Bd5 c6?! Again, 33. ... g4 was winning. 34. b4 Qb6 35. Bc4 Qc7 36. Bf1 Rgh7 37. B×h3 R×h3 38. Qg2 R×h1 39. R×h1 R×h1+ 40. Q×h1 Kg6 41. Qh8 Qf7 42. Qb8 Qe7 43. Qg8+ Kf6 44. Kf2 Qe6 45. Qh7 Qe7 46. Qg8 b5 47. a5 Qe6 48. Qa8 d5 49. Q×a6 d×e4 50. f×e4 Qd7 (*see diagram*)

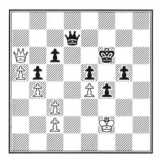

After
50. ... Qe6–d7

51. Qb6?? The losing move. 51. Ke1!! was not an easy move to find to maintain equality: 51. ... f3 (51. ... g4 52. Qa8 Kg5 53. a6 f3 54. Qb7 Qd8 55. Qh7!, with equality; 55. a7? Kf4! 56. a8Q f2+ and Black mates first.) 52. Qb6 g4 53. Qb8 f2+ 54. K×f2 Qd2+ 55. Kg3 Qf4+ 56. Kh4 Qh2+ 57. K×g4 Qg2+ 58. Kh4 Qh2+ 59. Kg4 with a very likely draw. 51. ... Qd2+ 52. Kf1 Qd1+ 53. Kg2 Q×c2+ 54. Kf1 Qb1+ 55. Kf2 Qc2+ 56. Kf1 Qd3+ 57. Kf2 Qd2+ 58. Kf1 Qd3+ 59. Kf2 g4! 60. Q×c6+ Kg5 61. Qd5 g3+ 62. Ke1 Q×c3+ 63. Kd1 Kg4 64. a6 g2 65. Qd7+ Kg3 66. Qg7+ Kf2 67. a7 Qa1+ 0–1 [*Chess-Monthly*, November 1885, pages 74–76]

D.Y. Mills (London Borough of Hackney Archives).

39. D.Y. Mills–Pollock [C22]
1st BCA Tournament, London, Simpson's Divan, Round 7, 18 June 1885

London Evening Standard (June 19, 1885): "The last game was finished at 10:55 [PM], when Mills surrendered to Pollock." 1. e4 e5 2. d4 e×d4 3. Q×d4 Nc6 4. Qe3 Nf6 5. e5 Nd5 6. Qe4 Nb6 7. Nf3 g6 8. Bg5 Be7 9. Bf4 0–0 10. Nc3 d5! 11. e×d6 B×d6 12. B×d6 Q×d6 13. Rd1 (*see diagram*)

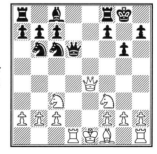

After
13. Ra1–d1

13. ... Bf5! 14. Qh4 14. R×d6 B×e4 15. Rd2 B×f3 16. g×f3 Rad8 favors Black. 14. ... Rfe8+

15. Be2 Qb4! 16. 0–0 Q×b2 17. Ng5 h5 18. Qg3?
Better was 18. Nge4 B×e4 19. N×e4 Kg7 20. Bf3
Qe5 21. Nd2. **18. ... f6! 19. Rb1 Q×c2 20. Rbc1
Qb2 21. Bd3 B×d3 22. Q×d3 Ne5 23. Qb5
Q×b5 24. N×b5 c6 25. Ne4 c×b5 26. N×f6+
Kf7 27. N×e8 R×e8 28. Rfe1 Nbc4 29. a4 Nd3
30. R×e8 K×e8 31. Rc3 Nf4 32. Rc2 Na3
33. Rc7** (*see diagram*)

After
33. Rc2–c7

**33. ... b4! 34. R×b7 a5 35. Kf1 Nd5 36. Ke2
Nc3+ 37. Kd2 N×a4 38. f3 Kd8 39. h4 Kc8
40. Rg7 b3 41. Rg8+ Kd7 42. Rg7+ Ke8 43. R×g6
Kf7 44. Ra6 b2 45. Ra7+ Ke6 46. Rb7 b1Q
47. R×b1 N×b1+ 48. Kc2 Nac3 49. g4 h×g4
50. f×g4 a4 51. Kb2 a3+ 52. Ka1 a2** 52. ... Nd2!
would have mated more quickly. **53. h5 Kf6 0–1**
[*Chess-Monthly*, November 1885, pages 82–83]

40. Pollock–J. Mortimer [C46]
1st BCA Tournament, London,
Simpson's Divan, Round 8,
19 June 1885

1. e4 e5 2. Nc3 Nc6 3. Nf3 Bc5 4. N×e5 Pollock: "Nearly always the *coup juste* in kindred positions, as leading to rapid development of the pawn centre especially. Black should have played the other knight. This game is a good example of the rule: Black's king's bishop quickly becomes embarrassed and presently he is fain to exchange it off for an inferior piece." **4. ... N×e5 5. d4 Bd6
6. d×e5 B×e5 7. Bd3** Pollock: "The bishop is snugly placed here should Black, as in the present case, take off the queen's knight, which, however, is by no means commendable." **7. ... B×c3+?!** A possible path to equal play was 7. ... Nf6 8. 0–0
0–0 9. Nd5 d6 10. c3 c6 11. Ne3 d5 12. f4 Bc7. **8. b×c3 d6 9. 0–0 h6 10. e5! d5** 10. ... d×e5 11. f4
e×f4 12. Qf3 with a strong initiative for White.
Pollock: "10. ... d×e5 is perhaps as good. The pawn, however, could in no way be held." **11. Ba3 Ne7
12. f4 g6 13. Qf3 c6 14. Rae1 Be6 15. g4?!** Pol-

lock: "White's opening is perfectly played, and the attack which he pursues, without respite from this to the mate, is absolutely sound." **15. ... h5! 16. h3
h×g4 17. h×g4 Ng8** 17. ... Rh4! 18. Rb1 (18. f5?
N×f5!) 18. ... b5 19. Kf2 B×g4 with advantage for Black. **18. f5! g×f5 19. g×f5 Qh4 20. Rf2 Bc8
21. e6 f6** (*see diagram*)

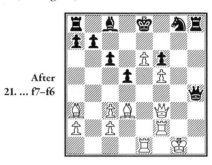

After
21. ... f7–f6

**22. Ree2! Ne7 23. Rh2 Rg8+ 24. Reg2 Qe1+
25. Bf1 B×e6** 25. ... R×g2+ loses too after
26. Q×g2 B×e6 27. f×e6 0–0–0 28. B×e7 Re8
29. B×f6 Q×e6 30. Qg3. **26. R×g8+ B×g8
27. Re2** Pollock: "The moves all explain themselves. The late Herr B. Horwitz expressed himself several times as greatly pleased with White's management of this game." **27. ... Qh4 28. R×e7+
Kd8 29. Qe2 Qg5+ 30. Bg2 Q×f5 31. Bd6 Qg6**
and White mates in three with 32. Rd7+. **1–0**
[*Chess-Monthly*, November 1885, page 80; *PM*,
page 28]

41. Pollock–J. Hewitt [C25]
1st BCA Tournament, London,
Simpson's Divan, Round 9,
20 June 1885

**1. e4 e5 2. Nc3 Bc5 3. f4 e×f4 4. Nf3 Bb6 5. d4
g5 6. Bc4 d6 7. 0–0 Be6 8. Nd5 Nd7 9. N×b6
N×b6** (*see diagram*)

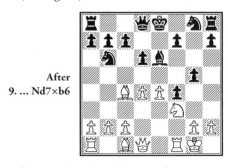

After
9. ... Nd7×b6

10. d5! N×c4 11. d×e6 f6? A careless attempt to save some pawns. Instead, Black would have gotten really promising play after a forced sequence of the following kind: 11. ... f×e6 12. Qd4 Ne5 13. N×e5 d×e5 14. Q×e5 Qf6 15. Q×c7 (15. Qb5+!? Kf7 16. Bd2 e5 17. Bc3 Qb6+ 18. Q×b6 a×b6 19. B×e5 Nf6 20. g3 Rhg8 21. g×f4 g×f4+ 22. Kh1 Ke6 23. B×f6 K×f6 24. R×f4+ Ke6! with equal play.) 15. ... Qd4+ 16. Kh1 Nf6 17. Qg7 Rg8 18. Q×b7 Q×e4 19. Q×e4 N×e4 20. Re1 0-0-0. **12. N×g5! Ne5** 12. ... Qe7 is answered by 13. Qh5+ Kf8 14. Nf7 Q×e6 15. N×h8 Kg7 16. R×f4 K×h8 17. Rh4 Qe7 18. Qd5 Nb6 19. Q×b7 Re8 20. Bd2. **13. Qh5+ Ke7** 13. ... Kf8 fails too after 14. B×f4 Qe8 15. Qh3 h6 16. B×e5 d×e5 17. Rad1! **14. B×f4 Qe8 15. Q×e8+** 15. Qh4 or 15. Qh3 were stronger alternatives. **15. ... R×e8 16. B×e5 d×e5 17. Rad1?** Probably caught up in the excitement, White errs almost decisively. Pollock had to play the following endgame at this point: 17. Nf7 K×e6 18. N×h8 Ne7 19. Rf3 R×h8 20. Rd1. **17. ... f×g5 18. Rf7+ K×e6 19. R×c7 Re7** Even more precise was 19. ... Nf6 20. R×b7 Re7. **20. Rc8 Kf7 21. Rdd8 Kg7 22. c4 h5 23. b4 Re6 24. c5 Re7 25. b5 Re6?** Black was forced here to a very exact defense, but it was possible to hold it. Not by 25. ... Kf7?! because of 26. Ra8! (26. c6!? b×c6 27. b×c6 Re6 28. Rc7+ Kf6 29. Rcc8 Kf7 30. Rd7+ Re7 31. Rd6 Rh6 32. R×h6 N×h6 33. c7 Ke6 34. Rh8 R×c7 35. R×h6+ Ke7 36. R×h5) 26. ... Rc7 27. R×a7 R×c5 28. R×b7+ Kg6 29. b6; But by 25. ... h4! 26. c6 Kf6 27. c7 Ke6 28. a4 Rd7 29. a5 b6 30. a×b6 a×b6 31. R×g8 R×g8 32. R×g8 R×c7 33. R×g5 Rc4. **26. c6** Even more decisive was 26. Ra8! Re7 27. R×a7 Rh7 28. c6! Kh8 29. b6! b×c6 30. Raa8 Rhg7 31. a4 Rb7 32. a5. **26. ... b×c6 27. b×c6** *(see diagram)*

After
27. b5×c6

27. ... Ne7? The final error. 27. ... Kh6! 28. Re8 Rd6 29. c7 Rc6 30. R×e5 g4 31. Kf2 Rh7 32. R×g8 Rh×c7 would have given Black some chances for a draw. **28. R×h8 N×c8 29. R×c8 Kf6 30. c7 Rc6 31. Rf8+ 1-0** [*Knowledge*, June 26, 1885]

42. R.J. Loman–Pollock [C80]
1st BCA Tournament, London, Simpson's Divan, Round 10, 20 June 1885

1. e4 e5 2. Nf3 Nc6 3. Bb5 a6 4. Ba4 Nf6 5. 0-0 N×e4 6. d4 b5 7. N×e5 N×e5 8. d×e5 Bb7 9. Bb3 Nc5 10. Nc3 N×b3 11. a×b3 Bc5 12. Qg4 *(see diagram)*

After
12. Qd1–g4

12. ... Qe7! 13. Q×g7 0-0-0 14. Qf6 Rdg8 15. g3 Qe8 15. ... Q×f6!? was playable too: 16. e×f6 h5 17. Re1 h4 18. Be3 Bd6 19. Bd4 Re8 20. Kf1 c5 21. R×e8+ R×e8 22. Be3 h×g3 23. h×g3 B×g3 24. B×c5 Be5 with equal chances. **16. Be3 Be7?!** More convincing was 16. ... B×e3! 17. f×e3 h5 18. Rf4 h4 19. R×h4 R×h4 20. Q×h4 Q×e5. **17. Qf4 h5! 18. h3 h4 19. g4 Qd8?** Pollock missed a fine resource: 19. ... Rh5! 20. Rad1 Bg5 21. Qf5 f6 22. f4 Bh6 23. Qd3 f×e5 24. f5 B×e3+ 25. Q×e3 d6. **20. Ne4! Rg6 21. Rfd1** 21. c4! would have given White the initiative. **21. ... Rhg8 22. Rd2 Re6 23. Nc5 B×c5 24. B×c5 Qe8 25. Be3 R×e5 26. Rad1 Re4! 27. Qf5?** After 27. Qh2 Black takes over with 27. ... d6! 28. Rd4 f5! **27. ... R×e3! 28. f×e3 Q×e3+ 29. Rf2 Q×h3 30. Re2 R×g4+ 31. Kf2 Qg3+** and mates next move. **0-1** [*The Field*, June 27, 1885]

43. J. de Soyres–Pollock [C51]
1st BCA Tournament, London, Simpson's Divan, Round 12, 23 June 1885

1. e4 e5 2. Nf3 Nc6 3. Bc4 Bc5 4. b4 B×b4 5. c3 Bc5 6. 0-0 d6 7. d4 e×d4 8. c×d4 Bb6 9. d5 Na5 10. Bb2 N×c4 Pollock believed in this particular variation. Other options are 10. ... Nf6 and 10. ... Ne7. **11. B×g7 f6 12. Qa4+ Qd7 13. Q×d7+ B×d7** *(see diagram)*
14. Nbd2? 14. Rc1 Kf7 15. B×h8 Na5 16. Nc3 Ne7 17. B×f6 K×f6 still favors Black. **14. ... N×d2**

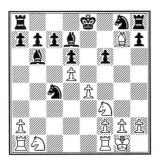

After
13. ... Bc8×d7

After
17. Bc1×f4

15. N×d2 Kf7 16. B×h8 Ne7 17. B×f6 K×f6 18. Nc4 Bc5 19. Rab1 b5 20. Nd2 a5 21. e5+!? A well thought out practical chance. **21. ... K×e5?** 21. ... Kf5! 22. e×d6 B×d6 23. Rfd1 N×d5 wins. **22. Rfe1+ Kf6 23. Ne4+ Kf7 24. Rb3?** White's only chance was 24. Ng5+! Ke8 25. Rb2 Bg4 26. h3 Bh5 27. Ne6 Kd7 28. N×c5+ d×c5 29. R×b5, with good chances for an open fight. **24. ... N×d5 25. Rf3+ Kg7 26. Rg3+ Kh8 27. Rg5 Re8** 27. ... Bb4 28. Rc1 c6 was more precise. **28. R×d5 Bc6 29. R×c5 d×c5 30. f3 c4 31. Kf2 b4 32. Ke3 Rd8 33. Nf6 Kg7 34. Ne4** (see diagram)

After
34. Nf6–e4

34. ... B×e4 35. f×e4 c3 36. Re2 c5 37. Rf2 c4 38. Rc2 Rd3+ 39. Ke2 a4 40. h4 a3 0–1 [*The Field*, June 27, 1885]

44. Pollock–R. Rabson [C66]
1st BCA Tournament, London, Simpson's Divan, Round 13, 27 June 1885

1. e4 e5 2. Nc3 Nc6 3. Nf3 Nf6 4. Bb5 d6 5. 0–0 Bd7 6. d3 Be7 7. Ne1 Nd4 8. Bc4 c6 9. h3 b5 10. Bb3 a5 11. a4 b4 12. Ne2 N×b3 13. c×b3 c5 14. Ng3 Qc8 15. f4 Qb7 16. Nf3 e×f4 17. B×f4 (see diagram)

17. ... 0–0–0?! A risky plan that paradoxically solves all White's opening problems. 17. ... Be6 18. Nd2 0–0 was much safer. **18. Rc1 Bc6?** Another error. More precise was 18. ... h6 19. Nd2

Rhe8 20. Qe2 Qa6 21. Nc4 Be6 with a defendable position. **19. Qe2** Very forceful would have been 19. Nf5 Bf8 20. N3d4! Be8 21. Qf3 g6 22. Bg5 with a big plus for White. **19. ... Kb8?** A third consecutive error. A good defense was 19. ... Rhe8 20. Nd2 Qa6 21. Nf5 Bf8. **20. R×c5 Qb6 21. d4 Ka8 22. Rc2 d5 23. Nf5 d×e4 24. Ne5 Bb7 25. N×e7 Q×d4+ 26. Kh1 Rhe8 27. Qb5! Qa7 28. Rc7 Qa6 29. N5c6 Nd5 30. Q×a6+ B×a6 31. Ra7 mate 1–0** [*Morning Post*, June 29, 1885]

45. W. Donisthorpe–Pollock [C20]
Lord Tennyson's Competition, London, Simpson's Divan, 25 June 1885

1. b3 e5 2. e4 Nf6 3. Nc3 Bb4 Pollock: "A Ruy Lopez 'au second.' 3. ... b6 has, by the way, been suggested as a defence to the Ruy Lopez. So that White is 'second player with a move ahead.' I doubt if it is a move of much use to him." **4. Bd3 0–0 5. Nge2 d5 6. Bb2 d×e4 7. B×e4 N×e4 8. N×e4 f5 9. N4g3 Nc6** Pollock: "Besides having both bishops, Black has the freer game so far." **10. c3 Ba5** Pollock: "Preventing d2–d4." **11. Qc2 e4 12. 0–0–0** Pollock: "There seems no available means of preventing the damaging entry of the knight to d3." **12. ... Ne5 13. Nf4 Nd3+ 14. N×d3 e×d3 15. Qb1 f4 16. Ne4 Bf5 17. f3 b5 18. b4?** Pollock: "Rather desperate, as it obviously plays Black's game." White had to try 18. Rhe1 Bb6 19. g4 f×g3 20. h×g3 Be6 but even so, Black's control is impeccable. **18. ... Bb6 19. a4** (see diagram)

19. ... a5!! Pollock: "This practically settles matters, as White's stronghold on the queenside is destroyed, and he can never escape across the invested centre of the board." **20. Qa2+ Kh8 21. b×a5?** 21. a×b5 a×b4 22. Qb3 b×c3 23. Q×c3 Qe7 24. Rhe1 was much better than the text move. **21. ... R×a5 22. h4 R×a4 23. Qb3 Qa8 24. Ng5 c5 25. Q×b5** 25. Nf7+ fails to the obvious 25. ... R×f7 26. Q×f7 Ra1+ 27. B×a1 Q×a1 mate. **25. ...**

After
19. a2–a4

Rb8 **26. Nf7+ Kg8 27. Nd6 Bc7 28. Ba3** Pollock: "A dying thrust! If Black took the bishop instead of the queen, White would deliver mate in seven moves—the well-known smothered mate." **28. ... R×b5 0–1** [*PM*, page 30]

46. G.A. MacDonnell–Pollock [A02]
Lord Tennyson's Competition, London, Simpson's Divan, 26 June 1885

1. f4 f5 2. b3 e6 3. Bb2 Nf6 4. e3 Be7 5. Nf3 0–0 6. c4 Ne4 7. Qc2 Bh4+ Pollock: "The object of this is to open the entire diagonal for the action of the queen's bishop." **8. g3 Bf6 9. d4** Pollock: "In this kind of opening it is essential to remember that the pawns constitute the framework of the game, and should be self-supporting. White has therefore already a slight disadvantage in position." **9. ... b6 10. Bg2 Bb7 11. Nc3 c5 12. 0–0–0 Qe7 13. Rhg1 a6** Pollock: "It is true that Black is violating the rule just laid down. But the rule naturally applies to fixed pawns, and Black is here advancing with a view of exchanging pawns for attack against the castled king." **14. Qe2 N×c3 15. B×c3 b5 16. Nd2 Nc6 17. Nb1 c×d4 18. e×d4 b×c4 19. d5 Nd8** Pollock: "Any other move with the knight loses a piece." **20. d6 Qf7 21. b×c4 B×g2 22. R×g2 Nc6 23. Qd3 Rfb8 24. Rdd2 Nb4 25. B×b4 R×b4 26. Rc2 Rab8 27. Nc3 Qh5** Pollock: "Threatening B×c3 and Rb1+." **28. Rgd2 e5** Pollock: "Here is a gross violation of the principle! The proper method of pursuing the attack is 28. ... Qh3, followed by the advance of the h–pawn. The text move was made without due preparation and should have cost the game." Pollock's comment is too harsh. Black's position is still winning. **29. Rb2** Pollock: "Well devised. (29. f×e5 Bg5, winning the exchange)." **29. ... e4?!** This, on the other hand, is a clear error. 29. ... R×b2! 30. R×b2 R×b2 31. K×b2 Q×h2+ 32. Kb3 e×f4 33. g×f4 Q×f4 and Black wins. **30. Qd5+ Kf8 31. R×b4 R×b4 32. N×e4**

Qe8 **33. N×f6 g×f6 34. Kc2 Qe1 35. Kc3** (see diagram)

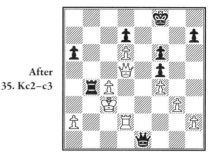

After
35. Kc2–c3

35. ... Ra4?? 35. ... Rb8! 36. Q×f5 Qa1+ 37. Kd3 Qb1+ 38. Rc2 Qf1+, with equality. **36. Qg2??** Pollock: "This extraordinary double blunder is accountable to both of the parties being much pressed by the time limit. Black's move is a blunder, and White could have won the rook by simply attacking it with his king." Indeed, 36. Kb3! traps the Black rook. **36. ... Qe3+ 37. Kc2 R×a2+ 38. Kd1 Qb3+ 0–1** [*PM*, pages 29–30]

47. A. Hvistendahl–Pollock [C51]
Lord Tennyson's Competition, London, Simpson's Divan, June 1885

1. e4 e5 2. Nf3 Nc6 3. Bc4 Bc5 4. b4 N×b4 5. c3 Nc6 6. d4 e×d4 7. 0–0 d6 8. c×d4 Bb6 9. d5 Pollock: "The d–pawn should never be advanced beyond the 4th square without great caution; especially early in the game. This is all but a case in point, and the text move has for many years been discarded in favour of Morphy's attack, 9. Nc3." **9. ... Na5 10. Bb2 N×c4 11. Qa4+** Pollock: "[Black's previous move] looks almost like a blunder, but it is not. The usual move is 10. ... Ne7. The idea of 9. ... N×c4 is shown in the following variation: 11. B×g7 f6 12. Qa4+? Qd7 13. Q×d7+ B×d7 14. B×h8 Kf7. I have adopted it several times with success." **11. ... Bd7 12. Q×c4 f6 13. a4** Pollock: "An ingenious but harmless continuation." **13. ... Ne7 14. a5 Bc5** (see diagram)

After
14. ... Bb6–c5

15. e5?! A slower (and safer) path was 15. Nbd2 0–0 16. Nb3 b6 17. a×b6 a×b6 18. Nfd4. **15. ... f×e5 16. N×e5 0–0 17. Nd3 b6 18. N×c5?!** A dubious exchange. Better was 18. Nc3 Ng6 19. Ne4 Qh4 20. Rae1 Rae8 21. g3. **18. ... b×c5 19. Nc3 Rb8! 20. Rab1?** Pollock: "Hardly a good move, as Black could also gain an advantage by Bf5." **20. ... Rb4 21. Qe2 Ng6! 22. Ba1** Pollock: "It is curious to note that 22. Bc1 instead, with a view of preventing ...Nf4, would have given Black another opportunity of winning the exchange by 22. ... Bb5." **22. ... Rg4! 23. g3 Nf4 24. Qd2 Qh4 25. Ne2** Pollock: "Another defence lay in playing the king, but Black's attack would remain very strong." **25. ... Nh3+ 26. Kh1** Pollock: "If 26. Kg2 Black may continue 26. ... Ng5, threatening Q×h2." **26. ... Bf5! 27. f3** *(see diagram)*

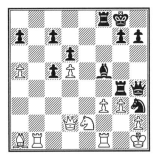

After
27. f2–f3

Pollock: "If 27. g×h4 Be4+ 28. f3 R×f3, and mates directly." 27. Rb3 loses too after 27. ... Be4+ 28. f3 Ng5 29. Ng1 R×g3 30. Qe2 B×d5. **27. ... B×b1** Pollock: "It is rare indeed that we meet with a case where one party, in a winning combination, sacrifices queen, rook, and knight in three consecutive moves." **28. g×h4** Pollock: "White will otherwise lose the game, more prosaically, through loss of material." **28. ... R×f3! 29. R×f3** Pollock: "29. Ng3 would not redeem the game." **29. ... Nf2+! 30. R×f2 Be4+ 31. Rg2 R×g2 32. Nc3** Pollock: "32. Qf4 prolongs but does not save. Thus: 32. ... Rg4+ 33. Q×e4 R×e4 34. Ng1 Ra4 35. Bc3 Ra3 36. Be1 Rd3 37. Kg2 R×d5 38. Ne2 Kf7 39. Kf3 Rd1 would probably be the 'modus op.'" **32. ... R×d2+ 0–1** [*Morning Post*, October 5, 1885; *PM*, pages 31–32; the game also appeared in the *Hereford Times* of March 4, 1899, with the following note: "We are indebted to Mr. H.E. Bird for the following remarkable game played by the late Mr. W.H.K. Pollock at Simpson's on October [*sic*] 1st, 1885. Mr. Bird is of the opinion that the game has not hitherto been published."]

48. Gunsberg & Hunter–MacDonnell & Pollock [C22] BCA Meeting, London, Simpson's Divan, Consultation Game, 26 June 1885

1. e4 e5 2. d4 e×d4 3. Q×d4 Nc6 4. Qe3 Bb4+ 5. c3 Ba5 6. Qg3 Qf6 7. Bf4 d6 8. Nd2 h6 9. Bb5 Bb6 10. Nc4 g5 11. Be3 Qg6 12. 0–0–0 e5!? could have been met by 12. ... d5 13. N×b6 a×b6 14. Ne2 Qc2. **12. ... Q×e4! 13. B×b6 a×b6** *(see diagram)*

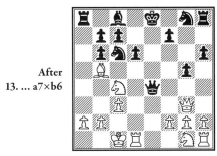

After
13. ... a7×b6

14. Q×d6!? Bf5! 15. Qe5+ Q×e5 16. N×e5 R×a2 17. N×c6 b×c6 18. B×c6+ Kf8 19. Nf3 Ne7 20. Nd4 Bg6 21. Rhe1 N×c6 22. N×c6 Kg7 23. Re7 Rha8 24. R×c7 Ra1+ 25. Kd2 R1a2! 26. Ke3 R×b2 27. Rd2 R×d2 28. K×d2 Ra1! 29. Ne5 Rh1 30. g3 R×h2 31. Ke3 h5 32. Nf3 Rh1 33. N×g5 Rd1 Possible too was 33. ... h4!? 34. g×h4 R×h4 35. Ne6+ Kf6 36. Nd4 Re4+ 37. Kd2 Kg5. **34. Ne6+ Kf6 35. Nf4 Rd6 36. c4 Kg5 37. f3 h4 38. Nh3+ Kh5 39. Rc8 Bh7 40. Rh8 Kg6 41. g×h4 Kg7 42. Rb8 Bd3 43. Ng5 B×c4 44. Ne4 Rd3+ 45. Kf4 b5 46. Rb6 Rd5 47. Nf6 Rd1 48. Ne8+ Kh7 49. Nd6 Rd4+ 50. Kg5 Be6 51. f4 Kg7?** A likely draw would have emerged after 51. ... Rd5+ 52. f5 Kg7! 53. R×b5 (53. Rb7 R×d6 54. f×e6 R×e6 55. R×b5 Rg6+ 56. Kf5 Ra6, with equal chances.) 53. ... f6+ 54. Kg4 Rd4+ 55. Kg3 R×d6 56. f×e6 R×e6. **52. Ne8+! Kf8 53. Nf6 b4 54. h5 Ke7 55. h6 Rd1 56. Rb7+ Kd6 57. h7 Rg1+ 58. Kh6 Rh1+ 59. Kg7 Rg1+ 60. Kf8 Rh1 61. R×b4 Bf5 62. K×f7?** Not the most precise. After 62. Rd4+! Kc6 63. Kg7 Rg1+ 64. K×f7 Rh1 65. Kg7 Rg1+ 66. Kh8 Rh1 67. Rd8, White's pawns are eventually unstoppable. **62. ... Kc5 63. Rb8 B×h7 64. N×h7** *(see diagram)*

64. ... R×h7+? Interestingly, Black's only chance for a draw was 64. ... Rf1! **65. Kg6 Rd7 66. f5 Kd6 67. f6 Kc7 68. Re8 Rd1 69. f7 Rg1+ 70. Kh5 1–0** [*Chess Player's Chronicle*, July 8, 1885; *Chess Monthly*, July 1885, pages 335–339]

After
64. Nf6×h7

49. Bird & Hewitt–MacDonnell & Pollock [A02]
BCA Meeting, London, Simpson's Divan, Consultation Game, 30 June/3 July 1885

1. f4 f5 2. e3 Nf6 3. b3 e6 4. Bb2 Be7 5. Nf3 0-0 6. Bd3 b6 7. 0-0 Bb7 8. Nc3 Na6 9. Bc4 c5 10. Ng5 h6 11. Nf3 Kh7 12. Ne5 Qe8 13. Be2 Nc7 14. Bf3 d5 15. a4 a6 16. Qe2 Bd6 17. Nd1 Rb8 18. Nf2 Rg8 19. h4 Ne4 20. B×e4 d×e4 21. Nh3 Nd5 22. g4 f×g4 *(see diagram)*

After
22. ... f6×g4

23. Ng5+?! Almost a bluff. 23. Q×g4 Nf6 24. Qg3 was safer. 23. ... h×g5 24. h×g5 B×e5! 25. B×e5 Rd8 26. Kg2 Rh8 27. Q×g4 Kg8 28. c4 After 28. Rh1 Qg6 29. R×h8+ K×h8 30. Rh1+ Kg8 31. Qh4 Kf7 32. Qg4 Nb4 Black takes the initiative anyway. 28. ... Nb4 29. Bc3 Bc8 30. Rh1 R×h1 31. R×h1 Qg6! 32. Rh5 Na2 32. ... Nd3 33. Qh4 Kf7 34. Rh8 Rg8! was a more natural approach. 33. Qh4 Kf7 *(see diagram)*

After
33. ... Kg8–f7

34. B×g7!? A vigorous blow. 34. ... R×d2+ If 34. ... K×g7 then 35. Rh6 Qf5 36. g6! R×d2+ 37. Kg3 Q×g6+ (forced) 38. R×g6+ K×g6 39. Qg5+ Kf7 40. a5! and White's chances are superior. 35. Kg3? An error. Better was 35. Kf1! 35. ... Nc1! 36. Rh7 Ne2+ 37. Kf2 N×f4+ 38. Kg1 Nh3+? 38. ... Kg8! 39. Rh8+ K×g7 40. R×c8 Rd1+ 41. Kh2 Qh5 was winning for Black. 39. Q×h3 Q×g5+ 40. Kf1 Qf5+ 41. Q×f5+ e×f5 42. Bc3+ Kg6 43. Rg7+ Kh6 44. Rc7 Rd3 45. Be5 Bd7 46. Bf4+ Kh5 47. Rb7 Kg4! 48. Ke2 Be8 49. R×b6 Bh5 50. R×a6 Kh3+ 51. Kf2 R×b3 52. Rh6 Kg4 52. ... Rb2+ would have secured a perpetual: 53. Ke1 Kh4 54. Rc6 Re2+ 55. Kf1 Rd2 56. R×c5 Rd1+ 57. Kf2 Rd2+. 53. a5 Bf7 54. a6 Ra3 55. Rh7 Ra2+ 56. Ke1 Ra1+ 57. Kd2 B×c4 58. a7 Bd5 59. Rd7 Ba8 60. Kc3 Kf3 61. Kc4 Ra5 61. ... Rc1+ 62. Kb5 c4 63. Rc7 c3 was a more promising defense. 62. Rf7 Bc6? 62. ... Ke2 63. Bd6 K×e3 64. R×f5 Ra4+ 65. Kb5 Rb4+ 66. K×c5 Rb7 67. Kc4 Ke2 68. Bc5 Rd7 and White maintains some winning chances, but not very substantial ones. 63. R×f5 Ke2 64. R×c5 Ra6 65. R×c6 Ra4+ 66. Kd5 R×a7 67. K×e4 Ra4+ 68. Kf5 Kf3 69. e4 Ra3 70. Be5 1–0 [*Chess-Monthly*, July 1885, pages 332–334; according to the *London Evening Standard* of July 4, 1885, the game was adjourned on June 30; when resumed on July 3, and under time pressure from the organizers to end all outstanding games, "Bird and MacDonnell played it out single-handed without their partners and Bird won."]

HAMBURG (JULY 1885)

50. Pollock–C. Doppler [C01]
Hamburg, Hauptturnier, Round 6, July 1885

1. e4 e6 2. d4 d5 3. e×d5 e×d5 4. Nf3 Nf6 5. Bd3 Bd6 6. 0-0 0-0 7. b3 Pollock: "An idea of Steinitz's but not to be recommended. The following moves occurred in a game between Messrs. Pollock and Skipworth (Hereford International Tournament 1885)." 7. ... Bg4 8. c4 c5 9. d×c5? Pollock: "Of course an oversight of the first magnitude." Better was 9. c×d5 c×d4 10. Bb2 Bc5 11. h3. 9. ... Be5 10. c×d5 B×a1 *(see diagram)*

11. d6 Pollock: "This game is a pretty good example of *sang froid*. Having lost a rook for two pawns in the opening, White, instead of resigning,

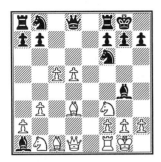

After
10. ... Be5×a1

After
16. Qd1–d4

coolly sets to work with might and main to win the game (or of course draw it should a chance offer) by making the best moves he can find on the board, and—succeeds!" **11. ... Nc6 12. Be2 Re8 13. Be3 Ne5 14. Na3 B×f3 15. g×f3** Pollock: "If 15. B×f3 N×f3+, 16. Q×f3 Be5 17. Q×b7 Ng4, and should win easily." **15. ... Bc3** Pollock: "If 15. ... Bb2 White could well reply with 16. Nb5." **16. Nb1 Ba5** Pollock: "Otherwise he loses the bishop or submits to a draw." **17. a3 Qd7** Pollock: "To make room for the bishop." **18. b4 Bd8 19. Nc3 a6** Pollock: "In order to prevent Bb5." **20. Kh1 Rc8 21. Rg1 g6 22. f4** Pollock remarked that White shouldn't fall for the trap 22. Bg5? Nfg4! **22. ... Qc6+?** Pollock: "Black instead is treated to a trap and falls right into it." 22. ... Nc6 23. Qc2 Qe6 24. f5 Qd7 25. Rg3 Kh8 26. f×g6 h×g6 27. f4 and although Black is temporarily restrained, the advantage should be on his side. **23. Rg2 Ned7 24. b5 a×b5 25. B×b5 Q×g2+?** 25. ... R×e3! 26. B×c6 R×c3 27. B×d7 N×d7 28. Qg4 f5 29. Qe2 N×c5 with chances for both sides. **26. K×g2 Re6 27. Bc4 Re8 28. Nd5 Ne4 29. Qg4 f5 30. Ne7+ Kh8 31. Bd4+ Nef6 32. Qg5 B×e7 33. d×e7** 33. Be6! was a nicer shot. **33. ... Kg7 34. Be6 h6 35. Qh4 g5** and White mates in 5 moves. **1–0** [*PM*, pages 83–84]

51. Pollock–A. Schottländer [C51]
Hamburg, Offhand Game, 18 July 1885

1. e4 e5 2. Nf3 Nc6 3. Bc4 Bc5 4. b4 Bb6 5. b5 Na5 6. Be2 Nf6 7. Nc3 d6 8. d4 e×d4 9. N×d4 0–0 10. Bg5 h6 11. Bh4 Re8 12. f3 Be6 13. g4 Nc4!? 14. N×e6 f×e6 15. B×c4 Ba5 16. Qd4 (*see diagram*)

16. ... d5! 17. e×d5 e×d5+ 18. Be2 Qe7 19. 0–0–0 Qa3+ 20. Kd2 B×c3+ 0–1 [*Bristol Mercury*, December 26, 1891; *Baltimore Sunday News*, May 13, 1893 (Pollock gave "March 18" in his column, very likely an error); *Brooklyn Standard-Union*, May 20, 1893; the first source noted,

rather bizarrely, that the game was "Played on Christmas Eve."]

HEREFORD (CCA, AUGUST 1885)

52. Pollock–A. Skipworth [C01]
Counties' Chess Association, Hereford, Round 1, 4 August 1885

1. e4 e6 2. d4 d5 3. e×d5 e×d5 4. Nf3 Nf6 5. Be2?! Too timid. **5. ... Bd6 6. 0–0 0–0 7. b3 Re8 8. Bb2 Bg4 9. c4 c6 10. Nc3 Nbd7 11. Qc2 Rc8 12. Rae1 Bb8 13. h3 Bh5 14. Nd1 Ne4 15. g4 Bg6 16. Bd3 Qf6 17. Kg2 h5 18. Ne3 Qf4 19. Bc1 Qd6 20. Rh1?** (*see diagram*)

After
20. Rf1–h1

White had to try to muddy the waters with 20. Nf5 B×f5 21. g×f5 Ndf6 22. Rg1 Qd7 23. Ne5 Q×f5 24. f3 R×e5 25. d×e5 Q×e5 26. Kf1 Ng3+ 27. Kg2 Qd6 28. c5 Qd7 29. Bg5. **20. ... N×f2! 21. Q×f2** 21. K×f2 Qg3+ 22. Ke2 Qg2+ 23. Kd1 Q×f3+ and Black has an easy task. **21. ... B×d3 22. g×h5 Be4 23. Ng4 f5 24. Ne3 Qf6 25. Bb2 Qg5+ 26. Kf1 Bd3+ 27. Re2 Q×e3 0–1** [*Hereford Times*, October 17, 1885]

53. Pollock–G.H. Mackenzie [C51]
Counties' Chess Association, Hereford, Round 3, 5 August 1885

1. e4 e5 2. Nf3 Nc6 3. Bc4 Bc5 4. b4 Bb6 5. b5

Na5 6. Bd3 d6 7. Nc3 Be6 8. Qe2 Nf6 9. Na4
Nh5 10. g3 g6 11. N×b6 a×b6 12. Nh4 Ng7
13. 0–0 Bh3 14. Ng2 Ne6 15. Bb2 Qe7 16. f4
0–0–0 17. Qf2 f6 18. Be2 Rhf8 19. Qe3 e×f4
20. g×f4 B×g2 21. K×g2 Nc5 22. d3 Kb8
23. Qd2 *(see diagram)*

After
23. Qe3–d2

23. ... d5! 24. e×d5 R×d5 25. Bf3 Rd7
26. Qb4 Qd6 27. Bc3 g5 28. d4 Ne6 29. Q×d6
c×d6 30. f×g5 Nf4+ 31. Kg3 f×g5 32. d5?! Best
was 32. B×a5 b×a5 33. c4 Rdf7 34. Rae1. **32. ...
Nc4 33. a4? h5?** Most probably signs of time trouble for both players. 33. ... Ne3! would have been
devastating. **34. Rfe1 Rdf7 35. Re4?** 35. h3!? gives
some hope of defending a bad position. **35. ... h4+
36. Kg4 N×d5 37. R×c4 Ne3+ 38. K×g5 N×c4?**
Missing a quicker finish: 38. ... Rg8+ 39. K×h4
Ng2+! **39. Bh5** 39. Be4! would have made things
more difficult for Black as White's bishops offer
some protection to the exposed king. **39. ... Rg8+
40. K×h4** 40. Kh6 Rf2 41. Bd4 R×h2 42. Bf7 Rg4
43. c3 Ne5 and Black should win nevertheless.
40. ... Rf4+ 41. Kh3 Ne5?! 41. ... Rf5! 42. Bg4
Rfg5. **42. Re1 Rf5 43. Bd1 Nf3 0–1** [*St. John
Globe*, January 21, 1898; *Baltimore Sunday News*,
May 10, 1891]

54. C.E. Ranken–Pollock [C84]
Counties' Chess Association, Hereford,
Round 4, 6 August 1885

1. e4 e5 2. Nf3 Nc6 3. Bb5 a6 4. Ba4 Nf6 5. d4
e×d4 6. 0–0 Be7 7. e5 Ne4 8. N×d4 0–0 9. c3 f6
10. Bb3+ Kh8 11. Bc2 N×d4 12. c×d4 d5 13. f3
Ng5 14. Nc3 f×e5 15. d×e5 d4! 16. Ne2 Bc5
16. ... c5!? 17. f4 Ne6 was interesting as well. **17. Kh1
Bf5 18. B×f5 R×f5 19. Qc2 R×e5** Far more incisive was 19. ... d3! 20. Q×c5 d×e2 21. Re1 Ne4!
22. Qc4 (22. Qa3? Nf2+ 23. Kg1 R×e5) 22. ... Qh4
with a powerful attack. **20. B×g5 R×g5** 20. ...
Q×g5!? 21. f4 Qf5 was good too. **21. Rad1 Bb6
22. Nf4 Qf6 23. g3 Re8 24. Rfe1 Rge5 25. R×e5
R×e5 26. Kg2** *(see diagram)*

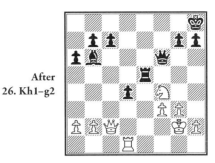

After
26. Kh1–g2

26. ... Re3 Vigorous play via 26. ... g5! 27. Nd3
Re3 28. Qf2 Qf5 29. Nc1 Qe6 was even more
promising. **27. Rd3 Qe5 28. R×e3 Q×e3 29. Qe2?**
The endgame is lost. White should have instead
gone for 29. Qf5! as his only chance for counterplay. **29. ... Q×e2+ 30. N×e2 g5 31. Nc1 Kg7
32. Kf1 c5 33. b3 Kf6 34. Ke2 Ke5 35. Nd3+
Kd5 36. Nb2 Bc7 37. a4 h5 38. Nc4 b5 39. a×b5
a×b5 40. Nd2 c4 41. b×c4+ b×c4 42. Ne4 d3+
43. Ke3 Bb6+ 44. Kd2 Kd4 45. N×g5 c3+
46. Kc1 Kd5 47. Ne4 Be3+ 0–1** [*BCM*, February
1886, pages 48–49]

55. E. Schallopp–Pollock [C22]
Counties' Chess Association, Hereford,
Round 7, 8 August 1885

1. e4 e5 2. d4 e×d4 3. Q×d4 Nc6 4. Qe3 Nf6
5. Be2 d6 6. Bd2 Be7 Steinitz: "This bishop is
now blocked. It was much better to open an outlet
for it at g7 by ...g6." **7. Nc3 0–0 8. 0–0–0 Be6
9. Qg3 Ne8 10. f4 f5** Steinitz: "Here it would have
gained time to attack the queen first by ...Bh4, for
in such case the White queen could not at once
occupy such a commanding position as subsequently when White had already brought the Nd5."
10. ... Bf6 11. Kb1 Nd4 was a good alternative to
the riskier text move. **11. e×f5 B×f5 12. Nd5**
12. Bc4+ Kh8 13. Nf3 Nf6 14. Rhe1 was a natural
path. **12. ... Bh4 13. Qb3** Steinitz: "Compare our
note to Black's 10th move." **13. ... Nd4 14. Q×b7
Be4** Steinitz: "A very good move. If perhaps 14. ...
Rb8, 15. Q×a7 Bf2 16. Be3 with an even game."
14. ... B×c2 could have been met by 15. Bc4! B×d1
16. N×c7+ Kh8 17. N×a8 Ba4 18. Q×a7, with unclear play. **15. Bc3 Rb8** *(see diagram)*

Steinitz: "His best play was here 15. ... B×g2,
which would have led to the following continuation: 16. Ne7+ B×e7 17. Q×g2 N×e2+ 18. N×e2
Bf6, with an even game." **16. Ne7+! Q×e7!** After
16. ... B×e7 17. Q×e4 N×e2+ 18. N×e2 White has

After
15. ... Ra8–b8

the clear edge. **17. Q×b8 N×e2+** Steinitz: "This turns out to be a miscalculation, but it was not easy to reckon how White would escape from the apparently vehement attack here initiated, as will be seen subsequently. His best plan was still ... B×g2." Possible too was 17. ... B×g2!? 18. B×d4 B×h1 19. Q×a7 R×f4 20. Bc4+ d5 21. Ne2 Rg4 22. R×h1 d×c4 23. Nc3 Qe6 with decent play. **18. N×e2 B×g2** It can be argued that 18. ... B×c2 19. K×c2 Q×e2+ 20. Rd2 Qe4+ 21. Kc1 R×f4 was more appealing. **19. Rhg1 Q×e2 20. Rd2 Qe3 21. Rg×g2 Be1 22. Qb3+** Steinitz: "By this fine move in conjunction with his after-play, White recovers ground and assumes a powerful attack." **22. ... Rf7** Steinitz: "Obviously, if the king moved, White would win the queen by B×g7+." **23. Rge2 B×d2+ 24. Kd1 Qg1+?** Steinitz recommended 24. ... Qf3! and he was correct. After 25. B×d2 Qh5 26. Qe6 Nf6 27. c4 h6 would have kept Black in the game. **25. K×d2 Kf8** Steinitz: "Fatal, but the game could only be prolonged at the expense of a most important pawn by 25. ... Nf6, whereupon followed 26. B×f6 g×f6 27. Qd5 c6 (Best, for otherwise the queen is lost or mate forced. If, for instance, 27. ... Qb6 28. Rg2+ Kf8 29. Qa8+ Ke7 30. Re2+ and mates ultimately by Qe8.) 28. Q×d6 with a winning game." **26. Qe6** Steinitz: "For the threatened mate can only be avoided by ...Kg8, whereupon White captures the knight, followed by Qe4, etc. We are indebted to Dr. Gold of Vienna for suggestions to most of the notes in this game" **1–0** [*tournament book*, pages 380–381; *BCM*, October 1885, pages 381–382; *ICM*, October 1885, page 304].

56. Pollock–J. Mason [A03]
Counties' Chess Association, Hereford, Round 8, 10 August 1885

1. f4 d5 2. e3 e6 3. Nf3 a6 Pollock: "This precaution is hardly necessary." **4. b3 c5 5. Bb2 Nc6 6. Nc3 Nf6 7. Bd3** Pollock: "A move sometimes

adopted by Chigorin and others, with the object of bringing the queen's knight round by e2. If Black replies Nb4 White allows the bishop to be captured, retaking with the pawn, which then keeps the other knight from entering e4." **7. ... Be7 8. 0–0 b5** Pollock: "In order to prevent Ne2 which would cost the bishop, through c5–c4." **9. Ne5 Bb7 10. a4 c4 11. a×b5 a×b5 12. Be2 R×a1** Pollock: "Black ought not to have neglected to castle; he is now subjected to a very harassing and enduring fire." **13. Q×a1 Qb6 14. b×c4 d×c4 15. Rb1 N×e5** Pollock: "The b–pawn is in danger, and a little examination will show that Black could not now castle." **16. f×e5** (*see diagram*)

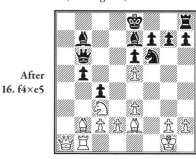

After
16. f4×e5

16. ... Nd7? Too passive. Better was 16. ... Ne4! 17. N×e4 B×e4 18. Bd4 Qc6 and if now 19. Qa7? then 19. ... B×g2 20. Qb8+ Bd8 21. Q×b5 Q×b5 22. R×b5 Be4 23. B×c4 B×c2 and Black's in no trouble at all. **17. Ba3! N×e5 18. R×b5** 18. N×b5! was even stronger: 18. ... Qc6 19. Bf1 f6 20. B×e7 K×e7 21. Qa3+ Kd7 22. Nd4! **18. ... Qc6 19. e4** 19. Bf1 Qa6! 20. R×e5 Q×a3 21. Q×a3 B×a3 and Black can put up some resistance. **19. ... f6?** Again, 19. ... Qa6! was the best defense: 20. Bb2 Nc6 21. Q×e7 K×e7 21. Qa7 Nd7 22. R×b7 Qd6 23. B×c4 Rd8** Pollock: "If 23. ... Q×d2 , 24. Nd5 Kf8 25. Rb8+ etc." **24. d4 Qf4 25. d5 Qc1+ 26. Bf1 e5 27. Qb6 Ke8 28. Qe6+ Kf8 29. d6 Qe3+ 30. Kh1 Qf2 31. Qe7+ 1–0** [*PM*, pages 32–33; *tournament book*, pages 18–19]

57. Pollock–E. Thorold [C30]
Counties' Chess Association, Hereford, Round 10, 11 August 1885

1. e4 e5 2. Nc3 Bc5 3. f4 d6 4. Nf3 Nc6 5. Bb5 Bg4 6. Na4 f6 7. N×c5 d×c5 8. 0–0 Nge7 9. f×e5 f×e5 10. h3 B×f3 11. Q×f3 Qd4+ 12. Kh2 0–0–0 13. d3 (*see diagram*)
13. ... Rdf8? Overlooking White's response. Better was 13. ... a6 14. Bc4 Ng6 15. Qg4+ Kb8 16. Rf7 Nf4! **14. Q×f8+ R×f8 15. R×f8+ Kd7**

After
13. d2–d3

After
21. Qc3–e1

16. c3 Qd6 17. Bg5 h6 18. Bh4 g5 19. Raf1 Qg6 20. R1f6 Qh5 21. Bc4 Nd8 21. ... Q×h4 leads to 22. Be6+ Kd6 23. Bg4 mate. **22. Bf2 g4 23. B×c5 a6 24. Be3 g×h3 25. R×h6 Qe2 26. R×h3 b5 27. Bb3 Q×b2 28. Bg5 Ndc6 29. Rh7 Q×c3 30. Bd5 Q×d3 31. Rf6 Kc8 32. B×c6 N×c6 33. R×c6 Kb7 34. Rh×c7+ Kb8 35. Rg7 Qe2 36. Rh6 1–0** [*tournament book*, pages 52–53]

58. I.A. Gunsberg–Pollock [C22]
Counties' Chess Association, Hereford, Round 11, 11/12 August 1885

1. e4 e5 2. d4 e×d4 3. Q×d4 Nc6 4. Qe3 Nf6 5. Be2 Be7 6. Nc3 Nb4 7. Qd2 d5 8. a3 (*see diagram*)

After
8. a2–a3

8. ... d4! 9. a×b4 B×b4 9. ... d×c3! 10. Q×c3 (10. Q×d8+?! K×d8! 11. e5 B×b4 12. b3 Ne4 favors Black.) 10. ... N×e4 11. Q×g7 Bf6 12. Qh6 Qd4 was an excellent alternative. **10. Bd3 Qe7 11. f3 d×c3 12. b×c3 Bc5 13. Ne2 0–0 14. Nd4 Bb6 15. Ba3 c5 16. Ne2 Rd8! 17. c4 Be6 18. Qc3 Qc7 19. Bb2 a5 20. 0–0 a4 21. Qe1** (*see diagram*) **21. ... Ba7?** Not the best idea here. 21. ... Nd7! was far more flexible: 22. f4 f6 23. Nc3 Ba5 24. Nb5 Qc6 25. Qh4 Nb6. **22. Qh4 b5 23. e5 Ne8** 23. ... b×c4 was losing too after 24. e×f6 c×d3 25. Qg5 Kf8 26. c×d3 c4+ 27. Kh1 g×f6 28. B×f6 c×d3 29. Nf4. **24. Q×h7+ Kf8 25. Qh8+ Ke7 26. Qh4+ Kd7 27. Be4 Rab8 28. c×b5 R×b5 29. Bc3 Rdb8**

30. **R×a4 Rb1 31. Nc1 c4+ 32. Kh1 Be3 33. Rd1+ Kc8 34. Ba5 Qd7 35. Qd8+ Q×d8 36. R×d8 mate 1–0** [*Leeds Mercury*, August 22, 1885; *Chess Player's Chronicle*, September 16, 1885]

Various Games (1884/1885)

59. F.J. Lee–Pollock
Match (Odds Game), London, Simpson's Divan, 27 August 1885
Remove f7 pawn

1. e4 d6 2. d4 Nc6 3. Nf3 Bg4 4. Bb5 a6 5. B×c6+ b×c6 6. 0–0 e6 7. c4 Be7 8. Nc3 Nh6 9. h3 Bh5 10. Qd3 Nf7 11. Ne2 0–0 12. Nf4 B×f3 13. N×e6 Qc8 14. N×f8 Bh5 (*see diagram*)

After
14. ... Bf3–h5

15. g4? This gives Black some counterplay. 15. N×h7! K×h7 16. f4 Kg8 17. f5 Ng5 18. e5 was winning for White. **15. ... B×g4! 16. h×g4 Q×g4+ 17. Kh2 R×f8 18. Rg1** 18. Qg3 Qh5+ 19. Kg2 was somewhat better. **18. ... Qh4+ 19. Kg2 Ne5!** **20. Qe2 Ng4** 20. ... Nf3! 21. Q×f3 R×f3 22. K×f3 d5 was even more forceful. **21. f4 Qh2+ 22. Kf1 Qh3+ 23. Ke1 Bh4+ 24. Kd1 Nf2+ 25. Kc2 Re8 26. e5 Qf5+ 27. Kb3 Rb8+ 28. Ka3 Nd3 29. Qg4 Qf8 30. e×d6?** 30. Q×h4 would have maintained the tension: 30. ... d×e5+ 31. c5 e×d4 32. Bd2 a5! 33. Qh5 Kh8 34. b3 N×c5 35. Kb2 a4. **30. ... Q×d6+ 31. c5 Q×d4 32. Q×g7+ Q×g7 33. R×g7+**

K×g7 **34. b4 R×b4 0–1** [*Illustrated Sporting and Dramatic News*, October 3, 1885; *Sheffield and Rotherham Independent*, March 20, 1886]

60. S. Tinsley–Pollock [A01]
London, Purssell's, 1884/1885

"Played some time ago at Purssell's Chess Rooms."
1. b3 Nf6 2. Bb2 d5 3. e3 e6 4. Nf3 c5 5. Nc3 Nc6 6. Bb5 Be7 7. Qe2 0–0 8. B×c6 b×c6 9. 0–0 Bd6 10. e4 d4 11. e5 Bc7? Safer was 11. … d×c3 12. d×c3 Bc7 13. e×f6 Q×f6. **12. e×f6 d×c3 13. B×c3?** Returning the favor. 13. f×g7! K×g7 14. B×c3+ f6 15. Ng5! would have left Black in a dire situation. **13. … g×f6 14. Qe4 Rb8 15. Qg4+ Kh8 16. Qh4 e5! 17. Rfe1 Rg8** (*see diagram*)

After
17. … Rf8–g8

18. Qh6 White missed 18. R×e5! f×e5 (18. … B×e5? 19. N×e5 Rg7 20. Nf3) 19. N×e5 R×g2+! (19. … Q×h4?? 20. N×f7 mate.) 20. K×g2 Q×h4 21. Ng6+ Kg8 22. N×h4 Be6 23. Nf3 with a clear pawn up. **18. … Bd6?** Allowing the same tactical opportunity as above. Best was 18. … Rg6! 19. Qe3 Be6. **19. Nh4** Again, White missed this tactical motif: 19. N×e5! B×e5 20. R×e5 Rg6 21. Qh4 h6 22. Rae1 with a winning advantage. **19. … Bf8 20. Qe3 Qd5 21. f4 h6?** 21. … c4! 22. b×c4 Q×c4. **22. Qf3** 22. f×e5! would have created serious problems for Black: 22. … Rb4!? (22. … f×e5? 23. B×e5+ Kh7 24. B×b8) 23. B×b4 c×b4 24. d4 f×e5 25. Q×e5+ Q×e5 26. R×e5 Bg7 27. Re4 c5 28. Rf1 B×d4+ 29. Kh1 Be6 30. Nf5 with a clear edge. **22. … Rg4 23. Q×d5 c×d5 24. Nf3 d4 25. Ba5 R×f4** (*see diagram*)
26. N×e5! Rb7 26. … f×e5 fails because of 27. Bc7. **27. Nd3 Rf5 28. Re8 Bd7 29. R×f8+ Kg7 30. Rd8 c4 31. Nb2 R×a5 32. N×c4 Rg5 33. Re1 Bc6 34. g3 Rd7 35. R×d7 B×d7 36. Re4 Rd5 37. Kf2 Bf5 38. Re7 B×c2 39. R×a7 Rf5+ 40. Ke2 d3+ 41. Ke3 Rf1 42. Kd4 Rf2 43. Kc3 R×h2 44. Nd6 Rh1 45. b4 1–0** [*The Field*, January 16, 1885]

After
25. … Rg4×f4

61. Pollock–A. Rumboll [C29]
London(?), 1885

1. e4 e5 2. f4 Nf6 3. Nc3 Nc6 4. f×e5 N×e5 5. d4 Nc6 6. e5 Ng8 7. Nf3 d5 8. Bb5 a6 9. Ba4 h6 10. 0–0 Be6 11. Qe1 Bb4 12. Qg3 Bf8 13. Be3 Nge7 14. Nh4 g5 15. Nf3 g4 16. Nd2 Nf5 17. Qf2 Rg8 (*see diagram*)

After
17. … Rh8–g8

18. N×d5!? g3 18. … Q×d5 19. Bb3 g3 20. h×g3 Qb5 (20. … Qa5 21. Nc4 Qb5 22. d5 B×d5 23. a4) 21. a4 Qb6 22. Nc4 B×c4 23. B×c4 Nce7 24. c3 with complicated play. **19. Q×f5! g×h2+ 20. Kh1 B×f5 21. Nf6+ Ke7?** 21. … Q×f6 22. e×f6 Bd7 23. c3 0–0–0 was the only defense. **22. d5 N×e5 23. Nde4?** 23. R×f5 or 23. N×g8+ was much simpler. **23. … Nd7?** Black missed a good defensive resource: 23. … B×e4 24. Bc5+ Qd6 25. N×g8+ Kd8 26. B×d6 c×d6 27. Rae1 Bg6! (27. … B×d5? 28. R×e5! d×e5 29. Rd1 and White wins.) 28. c3 Rc8. **24. Bc5+ N×c5 25. N×g8 mate 1–0** [*Hereford Times*, November 7, 1885].

62. J.N. Burt–Pollock [C80]
Bath, Athenaeum Club, 1885

1. e4 e5 2. Nf3 Nc6 3. Bb5 a6 4. Ba4 Nf6 5. 0–0 N×e4 6. Re1 Nc5 7. B×c6 d×c6 8. N×e5 Be7 9. d4 Ne6 10. c3 0–0 11. f4 f6 12. Nf3 Bd6?! More precise was 12. … Qd5 13. c4 Qh5 14. Nc3 Bd6; or 12. … Re8 13. f5 Nf8 14. Nh4 Bd6. **13. Qb3 a5?!** 13. … Kh8 directly was better. **14. a4** 14. R×e6!

a4 15. Qc4 B×e6 16. Q×e6+ Kh8 17. c4 with a clear edge for White. **14. ... Kh8 15. R×e6 B×e6 16. Q×e6 Re8 17. Qc4 Qd7 18. Kf2 Qf5 19. g3 Qc2+ 20. Nbd2** *(see diagram)*

After
20. Nb1–d2

20. ... b5? It is rather curious why Black didn't go for the obvious 20. ... Re7! 21. Qb3 Qd3 22. Kg1 Rae8 with equal play. **21. a×b5 c×b5 22. Q×b5 a4 23. Ne1 Qd1 24. Ndf3 a3 25. b4 Rab8** 25. ... a2 could have been tried, but White can keep it together with 26. Qd3 Qb3 27. Nc2 Bf8 28. Nd2. **26. Qd3 Q×d3 27. N×d3 1–0** [*Clifton Chronicle,* September 30, 1885].

1st Irish Chess Association Tournament (October 1885)

63. Pollock–W.W. Mackeson [C50]
1st Irish Chess Association Tournament, Dublin, Round 1, 6 October 1885

1. e4 e5 2. Nf3 Nc6 3. Bc4 d6 4. 0–0 Na5 5. Be2 c5 6. d3 Be7 7. Be3 Nf6 8. h3 h6 9. Nbd2 Be6 10. Nh2 Nc6 11. c3 a6 12. f4 e×f4 13. B×f4 b5 14. Qe1 Ra7 15. Qg3 g5 16. Be3 Nh7? An illfated manoeuvre. Both 16. ... Rc7 and 16. ... Qd7 were better choices. **17. d4! c×d4 18. c×d4 d5 19. Rac1 Qb6?** *(see diagram)* 19. ... Rc7 was forced.

After
19. ... Qd8–b6

20. R×c6! Qb7 20. ... Q×c6 allows the simple 21. Qb8+ Bd8 22. Q×a7 d×e4 23. Ng4 and White's

a full piece ahead. **21. e×d5 B×d5 22. R×h6 0–0 23. Bd3 f5 24. R×f5 Rc8 25. Rg6+ Kh8 26. Qe5+ Bf6 27. Rf×f6 Rc1+ 28. Rf1+ Qg7 29. R×c1 Q×e5 30. Rc8+ 1–0** [*BCM,* December 1885, pages 425–426]

64. Pollock–J. Murphy [C62]
1st Irish Chess Association Tournament, Dublin, Round 2, 7 October 1885

1. e4 e5 2. Nc3 Nc6 3. Nf3 Nf6 4. Bb5 d6 5. d4 e×d4 6. N×d4 Bd7 7. B×c6 b×c6 8. Qe2 c5 9. Nf3 Be7 10. 0–0 0–0 11. h3 h6 12. Be3 Bc6 13. Bf4 Qb8 14. b3 Qb4 15. Bd2 B×e4? 15. ... N×e4 fails too because of 16. Nd5!; But 15. ... Qb7! was best here. **16. Nd5! Qb7 17. N×e7+ Kh7 18. Ne1?** 18. Bc3! Rae8 19. B×f6 g×f6 20. Nh2 R×e7 21. f3. **18. ... c6?!** More precise was 18. ... Rfe8 19. Bc3 R×e7 20. B×f6 Re6! 21. Bc3 B×g2 22. Qg4 Rg6. **19. f3 Q×e7 20. f×e4 N×e4 21. Nf3 d5 22. Bf4 Rae8 23. Rae1 Qf6 24. Nd2 Nc3 25. Qd3+ Ne4 26. N×e4 d×e4 27. R×e4 Rd8 28. Rd4+ 1–0** [unidentified newspaper cutting]

65. J.A.P. Rynd–Pollock [C22]
1st Irish Chess Association Tournament, Dublin, Round 3, 10 October 1885

1. e4 e5 2. d4 e×d4 3. Q×d4 Nc6 4. Qe3 Nf6 5. e5 Nd5 6. Qe4 Nb6 7. f4 Be7 8. Nc3 d5! 9. e×d6 c×d6 9. ... Q×d6 10. Bd2 Bg4 11. Be2 f5 was more accurate. **10. Bd3 d5 11. Qf3 0–0 12. Nge2 Bc5 13. Bd2 Nb4 14. a3 N×d3+ 15. c×d3 Re8 16. Kf1 Bf5 17. Re1 d4 18. Nd1 Be6 19. Ng3 Bd5 20. Qg4 R×e1+ 21. B×e1 Qe8 22. Nh5 Qf8 23. Nf6+ Kh8 24. Bh4 g6 25. Bg5 Qg7 26. Qh4** *(see diagram)*

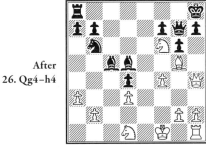

After
26. Qg4–h4

26. ... h5? Better was 26. ... Be7 27. Kf2 Be6 28. Re1 Rc8 with chances for both sides. **27. N×h5?** 27. g4! was a forceful way to break through Black's kingside. For example, 27. ... Bf3 28. g×h5 B×h5

29. N×h5 Qh7 30. Bf6+ Kg8 31. Rg1. **27. ... Qh7! 28. Nf6 Q×h4 29. B×h4 Bb3 30. Ke2 Be7! 31. Kd2?** 31. g3 promised some chances for a draw: 31. ... Kg7 32. Ne4 B×h4 33. g×h4 f5 34. Nd2 Re8+ 35. Kf2 Bc2 36. Nf3 B×d3 37. Re1 R×e1 38. K×e1 Nd5 39. Kd2 Ba6 40. N×d4. **31. ... Rc8** Good enough. Another alternative was 31. ... Nd5 32. N×d5 B×h4 and the knight on d5 has no safe square. **32. Nc3 d×c3+ 33. b×c3 Rc6 34. Rb1 Ba4 35. R×b6 R×b6 36. Nd5 Rb2+ 0–1** [*Dublin Evening Mail*, October 15, 1885; according to the *Dublin Daily Express* of October 12, the game lasted four hours.]

66. J. Murphy–Pollock [C50]
1st Irish Chess Association Tournament, Dublin, Round 4, 12 October 1885

1. e4 e5 2. Nf3 Nc6 3. Bc4 Bc5 4. 0–0 Nf6 5. Nc3 d6 6. d3 Bg4 7. Be3 Nd4 8. Kh1 h6 9. B×d4 B×d4 10. Ne2 Bb6 11. Ng3 h5 12. h3 h4! 13. Nf5 B×f5 14. e×f5 Qd7 15. Qd2 Rh5 16. Rae1 0–0–0 17. Ng5 d5! 18. Bb3 Re8 19. c3 Q×f5 20. Nf3 e4 21. Nh2 e×d3 21. ... c6! was even stronger. **22. R×e8+ N×e8 23. Bd1 Rg5 24. Bg4 R×g4 25. N×g4 Nd6** (*see diagram*)

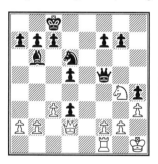

After
25. ... Ne8–d6

26. Ne3? Superior play was 26. Rd1 Ne4 27. Q×d3 c6 28. Qf3, but Black still has some compensation. **26. ... Ne4 27. N×f5 N×d2 28. Kg1 N×f1 29. K×f1 Kd7** A better version of the endgame was reached by 29. ... g6! 30. Ne7+ Kd7 31. N×d5 Kd6 32. Nf4 d2 33. Ke2 B×f2 34. K×d2 g5. **30. N×h4** The other alternative was 30. N×g7 c5 31. Ke1 Bd8 32. g3 Bg5 33. Kd1 c4 34. Nf5 h×g3 35. f×g3 Ke6 36. g4 Bf4 37. h4. **30. ... d2 31. Ke2 B×f2 32. Nf3 Be3 33. Ne5+** 33. N×d2 B×d2 34. K×d2 Ke6 35. Ke3 Ke5 seems a hopeless effort. **33. ... Ke6 34. Ng4 Bf4 35. Nf2 c5 36. Kf3 Bh6 37. Ke2 c4 38. Ng4 f5 39. N×h6 g×h6 40. K×d2 Ke5 41. Ke3 f4+ 42. Kf3 h5 43. g4 f×g3 44. K×g3 Kf5 45. Kf3 b5 46. Ke3 Kg5**

47. Kd4 Kh4 48. K×d5 K×h3 49. b3 Kg3 50. b×c4 b×c4 51. K×c4 h4 52. Kb5 h3 53. c4 h2 54. c5 h1Q 0–1 [*BCM*, December 1885, pages 423–424]

67. Pollock–A.S. Peake [C52]
1st Irish Chess Association Tournament, Dublin, Round 5, 12 October 1885

1. e4 e5 2. Nf3 Nc6 3. Bc4 Bc5 4. b4 B×b4 5. c3 Ba5 6. 0–0 Nge7 7. Ng5 d5 8. e×d5 N×d5 9. d4 e×d4? (*see diagram*)

After
9. ... e5×d4

9. ... 0–0 or 9. ... Be6 were better options. **10. N×f7! K×f7 11. Qh5+ Kf8 12. B×d5 Qf6 13. Re1 Bd7 14. Ba3+ Bb4 15. c×b4 b5 16. Nd2 Be8 17. Qf3 Rd8 18. Q×f6+ g×f6 19. R×e8+ 1–0** [*Weekly Times & Echo*, November 11, 1885; *Dublin Evening Mail*, October 15, 1885]

68. Pollock–J.A.P. Rynd [A03]
1st Irish Chess Association Tournament, Dublin, Round 6, 13 October 1885

1. f4 d5 2. e3 Bf5 3. Bd3 Nh6 4. Nf3 c5 5. 0–0 Nc6 6. Nc3 g6 7. b3 Bg7 8. Bb2 0–0 9. Qe2 Rc8 10. Rae1 Nb4 11. B×f5 N×f5 12. a3?! 12. d3 was better, even if it could have been met by 12. ... d4! 13. Nd1 Nd5 14. Bc1 d×e3 15. N×e3 N×f4. **12. ... N×c2 13. Rc1 d4! 14. R×c2** After 14. Na4 d3 15. Qd1 Qd5 16. B×g7 K×g7 17. R×c2 d×c2 18. Q×c2 f6 Black's position is much stronger. **14. ... d3 15. Qd1 d×c2 16. Q×c2 c4 17. b4 a6 18. Kh1 b5 19. Rg1 Qd3 20. Qc1 Rfd8 21. g4 B×c3 22. B×c3 Qe4 23. g×f5 Q×f3+ 24. Rg2 Rd3 25. f×g6 f×g6 26. Qa1 Kf8?!** 26. ... Rcd8! and if 27. Kg1 then there is 27. ... R×c3! 28. Q×c3 Qd1+ 29. Kf2 Q×d2+ and Black wins. **27. Kg1 e6 28. h4** Better was 28. Rg3 Qd5 29. Rg5 Qd7 30. Rg2 attempting a fortress. **28. ... Kf7 29. Kh2** Searching for some counterplay with 29. a4 Rc7 30. a×b5 a×b5 31. Qa5 was stronger. **29. ... Ke8** (*see diagram*)

After
29. ... Kf7–e8

30. Bf6? Best was 30. a4! Rcd8 31. a×b5 a×b5 32. Qa6. **30. ... c3! 31. B×c3 Rc×c3 32. d×c3 Q×e3 33. a4 Q×f4+ 34. Kg1 Q×h4 35. a×b5 Rh3 36. Kf1 Rh1+ 37. Rg1 Qh2 0–1** [*BCM*, December 1885, pages 424–425]

69. Pollock–W.W. Mackeson [C45]
1st Irish Chess Association Tournament (Handicap?), Dublin, 18 October 1885

1. e4 e5 2. Nf3 Nc6 3. d4 e×d4 4. N×d4 Bc5 5. Be3 Qf6 6. c3 Nge7 7. Qd2 B×d4 8. c×d4 d5 9. e5 Qg6 10. f4 0–0 11. Nc3 Bf5 12. a3? Further weakening of the light squares was not necessary. White could have tried 12. h3!? Nb4 13. g4 Nc2+ 14. Kf2 N×a1 15. g×f5 N×f5 16. Rg1 Qh6 17. Bd3, with some compensation and good attacking chances. **12. ... Na5! 13. Ra2 Bb1** (*see diagram*)

After
13. ... Bf5–b1

14. g4? 14. Kf2!? B×a2 15. N×a2 Nc4 16. B×c4 d×c4 17. Rc1 was to proper way to seek some compensation. **14. ... B×a2 15. N×a2 Qb1+ 16. Nc1 Nb3** Stronger was 16. ... Nc4! 17. B×c4 d×c4 18. Rg1 f6! **17. Qc3 N×c1 18. Q×c1 Q×c1+ 19. B×c1 Rfc8 20. Be3 a5 21. Bh3 b6 22. g5 Rd8 23. 0–0 c5 24. Rc1 c4 25. Bg4 g6 26. h4 b5 27. Kf2 Nf5 28. B×f5 g×f5 29. Bd2 Rdb8 30. Be1 b4 31. a4 Rc8 32. Ke2 Kg7 33. h5 h6 34. Kf3 34. Bh4 is met by 34. ... c3! 35. b3 Rc6 36. Kd3 Rh8. 34. ... Rh8 35. g6 f×g6 36. h×g6 K×g6 37. Bh4 Kh7 38. Rh1 Rhg8 39. e6 Rg6 40. Re1 Re8 41. e7 Rg4 42. Bf6 Kg6 43. Re6 Kf7 44. Rd6**

Rg6 45. Be5 R×d6 0–1 [unidentified newspaper cutting]

70. J.A.P. Rynd–Pollock [C45]
1st Irish Chess Association Tournament (Handicap), Dublin, October 1885

1. e4 e5 2. Nf3 Nc6 3. d4 e×d4 4. N×d4 Bc5 5. Be3 Qf6 6. c3 Nge7 7. Qd2 a6 8. f4 d5 9. e5 Qg6 10. Bd3 Qg4 11. 0–0 N×d4 12. B×d4 B×d4+ 13. c×d4 Bf5 14. Nc3 Qg6 15. Rf3 B×d3 16. R×d3 0–0 17. Rc1 f6 18. Na4 (*see diagram*)

After
18. Nc3–a4

18. ... f×e5 19. d×e5?! A dubious choice. More logical was 19. f×e5! to which Pollock could have responded with 19. ... Rf5!? (19. ... c6 20. Nc5 b6 21. Nd7 Rf7 22. Rdc3 and White has the initiative.) 20. Rg3 (20. R×c7? allows 20. ... Raf8 21. Rc1 Rf2 and Black wins.) 20. ... Qf7 21. h3 Ng6 with balanced play. **19. ... R×f4! 20. Q×f4 Q×d3 21. Nc5 Qb5 22. e6 Rf8 23. Qd4** 23. Qd2 was better as it prevented the intrusion of the White queen. **23. ... b6** An immediate 23. ... Qe2! 24. h3 c6 25. N×b7 Ng6 26. Kh1 Nf4 provided Black with a formidable attack. **24. Nd7 Rf5 25. h3 Qe2! 26. R×c7?** 26. Qc3 would have been met by 26. ... Rf2 27. Qg3 R×g2+ 28. Q×g2 Qe3+ 29. Qf2 Q×c1+ 30. Kh2 Kh8! 31. Qf8+ Ng8 and Black should win. **26. ... Qe1+ 27. Kh2 Rf1 28. g4 Rh1+ 29. Kg2 Qf1+ 30. Kg3 R×h3 mate 0–1** [*Sheffield Independent*, October 24, 1885]

71. A.S. Peake–Pollock
1st Irish Chess Association Handicap Tournament, Dublin, October 1885
Remove f7 pawn

1. e4 d6 2. d4 Nf6 3. Nc3 Nc6 4. Bb5 Bd7 5. d5 Ne5 6. B×d7+ Q×d7 7. Nge2 e6 8. d×e6 Q×e6 9. Nf4 Qf7 10. 0–0 c6 11. b3 Be7 12. Nd3 More solid play was offered by 12. f3! 0–0 13. Be3 Nh5 14. Nfe2. **12. ... 0–0 13. N×e5 d×e5 14. f3 Bc5+ 15. Kh1** (*see diagram*)

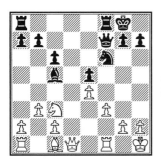

After
15. Kg1–h1

15. ... Ng4! 16. Bf4 16. Ba3!? B×a3 17. f×g4 Qe6 18. Rb1 was another clumsy way to seek a solution. **16. ... Bd4 17. f×g4 B×c3 18. Bg3 Qg6 19. R×f8+ R×f8 20. Rb1 Q×e4 21. h3 Bd4 22. c4 h6 23. a3 Bf2 24. Bh2 Bh4 25. Bg1 Rd8 26. Qf1 Rd3 27. Kh2** 27. Qf5 is met by 27. ... R×h3+ 28. Bh2 Re3 29. Q×e4 R×e4 30. Bg1 b6 and White's position is doomed. **27. ... Bg3+ 28. Kh1 Bf4 29. Re1 R×h3+ 30. Bh2 R×h2+ 31. Kg1 Qd4+ 32. Qf2 Rh1+ 0–1** [*BCM*, February 1886, pages 51–52]

Part Two, Section II
(January 1886–March 7, 1889)

VARIOUS

72. J.T. Heppell–Pollock
Odds Game, Purssell's, January 1886

1. e4 and d4 e6 2. Nf3 d5 3. Bd3 d×e4 4. B×e4 Nf6 5. Bd3 Nc6 6. c3 Bd6 7. Nbd2 0–0 8. Qc2 e5! 9. d×e5 N×e5 10. N×e5 B×e5 11. Nf3 Bd6 12. Be3 h6 13. h3 Nd5 14. 0–0–0 N×e3 15. f×e3 Qe8 16. e4 Be6 17. Kb1 f6 18. Nh4 Be5 19. Nf3 Bd6 20. Nd4 Bf7 21. g4 c5 22. Bb5 Qe5 23. Nf5 Bc7 24. Rd7 a6 *(see diagram)*

After
24. ... a7–a6

25. Be2 White could have gone for a sharper finish and a creditable result with 25. R×f7!? R×f7 (25. ... K×f7 26. Bc4+ Kg6 27. h4 Rad8 28. g5 Kh7 29. g6+ Kh8 30. Bd5 R×d5 31. e×d5 c4 was a sharper if unnecessary line.) 26. Bc4 Rd8 27. Bd5 R×d5 28. e×d5 Q×d5 29. Re1 Qd8 30. N×h6+ g×h6 31. Qg6+ Kf8 32. Q×h6+ with a clean draw. **25. ... Rfd8 26. Rhd1 b5 27. Ne7+ Kh8 28. Nc6 Qe6?** Best was 28. ... R×d7! 29. N×e5 R×d1+ 30. Q×d1 B×e5 and Black has a fighting chance. **29. R×d8+?** Missing 29. R×c7! Q×a2+ 30. Kc1 Bb3 31. Q×b3! Q×b3 32. N×d8 b4 33. Rb7 and White's position looks very strong. **29. ... R×d8** *(see diagram)*

After
29. ... Ra8×d8

30. N×d8? This gives it all away. Best was 30. R×d8+! B×d8 31. N×d8 Q×a2+ 32. Kc1 Bb3 33. Qb1 Qa5! and if 34. Nc6 Black has the powerful 34. ... Qc7! (If 34. Qd3, then 34. ... Bc4

J.T. Heppell (London Borough of Hackney Archives).

239

35. Qd2 Qa1+ 36. Kc2 Qa4+ with a perpetual.) **30. ... Q×a2+ 31. Kc1 Bf4+ 32. Rd2 Bb3 33. Qb1 B×d2+ 34. K×d2 Q×b1 0–1** [*Chess-Monthly*, February 1886, pages 180–181].

BRITISH CHESS CLUB MASTERS (FEBRUARY/MARCH 1886)

73. I.A. Gunsberg–Pollock [C77]
British Chess Club Masters, London, Round 2, 20 February 1886

1. e4 e5 2. Nf3 Nc6 3. Bb5 a6 4. Ba4 Nf6 5. d3 d6 6. h3 g6 7. Be3 Bg7 8. Qd2 h6 9. Nc3 b5 10. Bb3 Na5 11. g4 N×b3 12. a×b3 g5 13. Ne2 13. N×b5!? was not very convincing because of 13. ... B×g4 14. N×d6+ c×d6 15. h×g4 N×g4 16. Qb4 N×e3 17. f×e3 Qc7. **13. ... Qe7 14. Ng3 d5?** 14. ... c6! was more careful play. **15. Qc3! Bb7 16. Nf5 d4** (*see diagram*)

After
16. ... d5–d4

17. Qa5 17. N3×d4 e×d4 18. B×d4 was much stronger. **17. ... Qd8 18. N×g7+ Kf8 19. Nf5 d×e3 20. f×e3 Nd7 21. h4 g×h4 22. R×h4 Rc8 23. Ke2 Qf6 24. Rah1 c5 25. R×h6 1–0** [*Chess-Monthly*, May 1886, pages 274–275; *The Field*, March 6, 1886]

74. Pollock–G.A. MacDonnell [C54]
British Chess Club Masters, London, Round 4, 27 February 1886

1. e4 e5 2. Nf3 Nc6 3. Bc4 Bc5 4. b4 Bb6 5. a4 a6 6. c3 d6 7. d3 Nf6 8. Be3 B×e3 9. f×e3 0–0 10. 0–0 d5 11. e×d5 N×d5 12. Qe1 Be6 13. Na3 Qd6 14. Ng5 Nd8 15. Rd1 h6 16. Ne4 Qe7 17. Qg3 f6 Also possible was 17. ... f5!? **18. Nc5 f4 19. e×f4 N×c3 20. Rde1 B×c4 21. d×c4 b6 22. N×a6 R×a6 23. Q×c3 R×a4 24. c5 Ne6. 18. d4 Nb6?** 18. ... e×d4 19. e×d4 a5 was accurate. **19. Bd3** 19. d5! Bf7 20. N×f6+ Kh8 21. Ng4 and White's almost winning here. **19. ... f5! 20. Nc5 e4 21. Be2 Nd5**

22. Rc1 c6 23. Nc4 b5 24. Ne5 Qg5 25. Q×g5 h×g5 (*see diagram*)

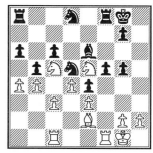

After
25. ... h6×g5

26. N×c6! N×e3 27. N×d8 Rf×d8 28. N×e6 Rd6 29. N×g5 N×f1 30. R×f1 Rc8 31. a×b5 a×b5 32. R×f5 R×c3 33. Rc5 R×c5 34. d×c5 Rd2 35. B×b5 e3 36. Kf1 Kf8 37. c6 Ke7 38. Ne4 Rc2 39. Ba4 Rc4 40. Bb5? R×b4 41. Nc3 Rb3 42. Nd5+ Kd6 43. c7 Rb1+ 44. Ke2 Rc1 45. Ba6 K×d5 46. c8Q R×c8 47. B×c8 Ke4 48. h4 Kf4 49. g4 Kg3 50. K×e3 K×h4 51. Kf4 g6 52. Bd7 1–0 [*Chess-Monthly*, May 1886, pages 275–276]

75. Pollock–H.E. Bird [B27]
British Chess Club Masters, London, Round 6, 6 March 1886

1. e4 c5 2. d4 c×d4 3. Nf3 g6 Pollock: "3. Nc6 is usually played here and is probably advisable." **4. Q×d4 Nf6 5. e5 Nc6 6. Qf4 Nd5 7. Qe4 e6** (*see diagram*)

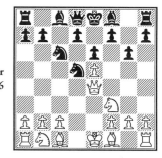

After
7. ... e7–e6

Pollock: "Black has not a good opening. As is well known, d6 and not e6 is the proper accompaniment to g6." **8. Nc3?!** Pollock: "Here 8. Bc4 is indicated, preserving the queen's knight for subsequent attack. Another line of play was 8. a3 Bg7 9. c4 Nde7 10. Nc3 a6 11. Bf4, with a very fine game. The course adopted may be compared with that in a game Pollock vs. Mortimer, the disadvantage of the doubled c–pawn being fully counterbalanced, especially in gain of time in development." **8. ... N×c3 9. b×c3 d5 10. e×d6 Bg7 11. Qd3 0–0**

12. Be2 e5 13. 0–0 Bf5 14. Qd1 14. Qd5 was better. **14. ... e4 15. Ne1 B×c3 16. Rb1** 16. Bf4 could have been met by 16. ... B×a1 17. Q×a1 Be6 18. f3 g5 19. Bg3 Qb6+ 20. Kh1 f5! **16. ... Be5 17. R×b7 B×d6 18. Kh1** Pollock: "This or 18. g3 is necessary here." **18. ... Rb8 19. Rb3?!** Pollock: "A good position for the rook, which would not suffer being exchanged." Better was 19. R×b8 Q×b8 20. c3 Qc7 21. Nc2 Be5 22. Nd4. **19. ... Qe7 20. Qd2 Rbd8 21. Qh6 Be5 22. Ba3 Bd6 23. g4** Pollock: "Although this gives some attack it was probably a case of miscalculation, White imagining it was unanswerable." **23. ... Be6 24. Rh3 f6 25. Bb2 Rf7 26. Ng2 Ne5** Pollock: "From this point Mr. Bird plays to the end with consummate skill." **27. Ne3 Qb7 28. Ba1 Rg7 29. c4 Nf7 30. Qh4 g5 31. Qh5 Be5 32. B×e5 N×e5 33. Nd5 B×d5 34. c×d5 Q×d5 35. Ra3 e3+ 36. f3** *(see diagram)*

After
36. f2–f3

36. ... Qd7? Pollock: "A really pretty situation; 'one of the olden time.'" Not quite so. 36. ... Qd2! 37. Bb5 e2 was immediately winning. **37. Rd1?** Pollock missed a fine resource: 37. R×e3! Qc6 38. Re4 Re7 39. Bc4+ Kg7 40. R×e5! R×e5 (40. ... f×e5? 41. Q×g5+ Kh8 42. Q×e7 and White wins.) 41. Qf7+ Kh8 42. Bd3 f5 43. B×f5 Qh6 44. Q×a7 Red5 45. Qe3 and White has at least equality here. **37. ... Q×d1+! 38. B×d1 R×d1+ 39. Kg2 Ng6 40. Ra4 e2 41. Re4 Nf4+ 42. R×f4 e1Q 43. Re4 Rd2+ 44. Kh3 Qf1+ 45. Kg3 Qg2 mate 0–1** [*Morning Post*, March 15, 1886; *PM*, pages 38–39]

76. J.H. Blackburne–Pollock
British Chess Club Masters, London, Round 7, 8 March 1886

1. e4 (...) 1–0 [Score not recovered][1]

Opposite: **Herbert Jacobs (London Borough of Hackney Archives).**

LONDON (JUNE 1886)

77. H. Jacobs–Pollock
London, London Chess Club, Spring Handicap, 23 June 1886
Remove f7 pawn

1. e4 Nc6 2. d4 d5 3. e×d5 Q×d5 4. Nf3 Bg4 5. Be2 0–0–0 6. c4 Qh5 7. Be3 e5 8. d5 Nf6 9. Qa4 Nd4! 10. B×d4 e×d4 11. Q×a7 Re8 12. Qa8+ Kd7 13. Qa4+ Kd8 14. Qa8+ Bc8 15. N×d4 Bb4+ A fascinating alternative was 15. ... Qe5!? 16. Ne6+ R×e6! 17. d×e6 Bb4+ 18. Nd2 B×d2+ 19. K×d2 Q×b2+ 20. Ke3 Qc3+. **16. Nc3 B×c3+ 17. b×c3** *(see diagram)*

After
17. b2×c3

17. ... R×e2+! 18. N×e2 Re8 19. 0–0 R×e2
20. Rad1? 20. Qa3! Qg6 21. d6 was the better way
to defend. 20. ... Ne4 Black missed the strong
20. ... Ng4! 21. h3 N×f2 22. R×f2 R×f2 23. Re1
Re2. 21. h3? 21. Qa3, 21. Rde1 or 21. Qa7 were all
good defensive choices. 21. ... N×f2! 22. R×f2
R×f2 23. K×f2 Q×d1 24. Qa3 Qd2+ 25. Kg1
Qf4 26. Qc5 Bd7 27. Qd4 Q×d4+ 28. c×d4 Bf5
29. Kf2 Bd3 30. c5 Bc4 31. a4 B×d5 32. a5 Kd7
33. g3 Kc6 34. Ke3 Kb5 35. Kf4 K×a5 36. Ke5
Bg2 37. h4 b5 38. c×b6 c×b6 39. d5 b5 40. d6
Bh3 41. Kf4 Bd7 42. Ke3 Kb4 43. Kd2 Kc5
44. Kc3 K×d6 45. Kd4 Be6 46. h5 h6 0–1 [*Leeds
Mercury*, July 24, 1886; *Chess Player's Chronicle*,
September 22, 1886; *BCM*, December 1886 pages
452–454]

BCA Congress (July 1886)

78. Pollock–J.H. Blackburne [C00]
BCA Congress, London, Round 1,
12 July 1886

1. e4 e6 2. e5 Pollock: "This was adopted several
times by Steinitz at the London Tournament of
1883. The idea is to exchange off the e–pawn for
the d–pawn, and by d2–d4 and f2–f4 to keep
Black's e6–pawn 'depressed' at e6, and his game
thereby cramped." Steinitz: "One of the Editor's
[Steinitz's] various experiments in this opening. It
was first adopted in the Vienna tournament of
1882." 2. ... f6 3. d4 c5 4. Bd3 Steinitz: "Up to
this the moves are identical with the first game
in the tie-contest between Steinitz (White) and
Winawer (Black) at the end of the above-mentioned tournament. But here the latter game proceeded 4. d×c5 B×c5 5. Nc3 Qc7 6. Bf4 Qb6
7. Qd2 B×f2+ 8. Q×f2 Q×b2 9. Kd2 Q×a1
10. Nb5 Na6 11. Nd6+ with a strong attack." 4. ...
g6 Steinitz: "If 4. ... c×d4, the game might have
gone on thus: 5. Qh5+ Ke7 6. e×f6+ N×f6 7. Qc5+
d6 8. Q×d4 Nc6 9. Qh4 etc." 5. h4 f5 Pollock: "If
5. ... c×d4, 6. h5 Qa5+ 7. Kf1 Q×e5 8. h×g6 h6
9. Nf3 Qd5 10. N×d4 Q×d4? [10. ... Nc6 11. Nb5!;
10. ... Qe5 11. Nb5 Na6 12. N1c3 f5 13. Qf3 and
White wins—authors] 11. g7 B×g7 12. Bg6+ and
wins." 6. Bg5 Pollock: "As will be seen it is excellent play to get rid of the adverse king's bishop."
6. ... Be7 Steinitz: "Obviously, much inferior to
6. ... Qb6. The exchange of the king's bishop which
the opponent with good judgment effects at once,

leaves a sore spot at d6, and is the source of all future trouble, as White, by clever manoeuvring,
fixes a knight on that square in a commanding position." 7. B×e7 Q×e7 (*see diagram*)

After
7. ... Qd8×e7

8. Na3! c×d4 9. Nb5 Kd8 9. ... Qb4+ 10. Qd2
Q×d2+ 11. K×d2 Kd8 12. Nd6 Nh6 13. f4 Rg8
was a better way to defend. 10. Qd2 Nc6 11. Nd6
b6 Pollock: "Of course, N×e5 would cost the
knight." Steinitz: "Of course he dare not capture
the pawn, on account of the reply 12. Qa5+."
12. Nf3 Steinitz: "Here, we believe, it was stronger
still to fortify the e5–pawn by 12. f4 first, in order
that he might afterward have more freedom of operation for his king's knight. He was then sure at
any rate to recover his pawn by Nf3, followed by
Bb5." 12. ... h6 Pollock: "Again, 12. ... N×e5
13. N×e5 Q×d6 14. Nf7+ winning the queen for
two knights." 13. c3 Qg7 Steinitz: "It was certainly
no improvement to his game to abandon the pawn
he had gained, and at all risks he ought to have
taken the pawn first." 14. c×d4 Nge7 Pollock: "If
14. ... N×d4, 15. N×d4 Q×e5+ 16. Be4 wins."
15. 0–0–0 Kc7 16. Nb5+ Kb8 17. Kb1 Bb7
18. Bc4 a6 19. Nd6 Nc8? Steinitz: "It was necessary to prevent the advance of the d–pawn and ...
Na5, or perhaps ...Rg8 first (in order to protect
the queen and to be enabled to capture the d–pawn,
in reply to d5, without fear from the answer Qc3)
was the better plan." A more exact defense was
19. ... Na5! 20. Be2 Be4+ 21. Ka1 Nb7. 20. N×b7!
K×b7 21. d5 e×d5 22. B×d5 N8a7 23. B×c6+
d×c6 24. e6 24. Qd7+ Q×d7 25. R×d7+ Kc8
26. Rg7 was even cleaner. 24. ... Rae8 25. Rhe1
Rh7 26. Qf4 Qc7 27. Qd4 Qg7 28. Qc4 Qf6
29. Rd6 Rc7 30. Ne5 b5 (*see diagram*)
31. Nd7! Pollock: "It is remarkable how persist-
ently White maintains his attack throughout this
game. A good move seems to be always forthcoming." Steinitz: "Simple as this rejoinder may appear,
it was most probably unforeseen by the adversary,
and it bears the mark of very high talent when its
consequences are analysed." 31. ... Qg7 31. ...

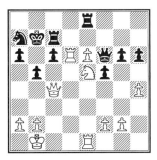

After
30. ... b6–b5

After
16. ... Qe7–f7

Q×b2+ 32. K×b2 b×c4 33. Rdd1 Re7 34. Kc3 leaves Black hopeless as well. Steinitz: "If 31. ... b×c4, 32. N×f6 Ree7 33. Ng8 Re8 34. e7 Kc8 35. R×g6, and wins." **32. Qc5 Nc8 33. Rc1!** Steinitz: "Mr. Pollock's attack in this game is quite worthy of any aspirant for the highest mastership." **33. ... R×e6** Steinitz: "The only resource, bad as it is. If 33. ... N×d6 34. Qb6+ and either mates by Qb8 or wins the rook and also the queen, as he afterward threatens Nb6 mate." **34. R×e6 Q×d7 35. R×g6 Qd3+ 36. Qc2 Qd5 37. R×h6 Nb6 38. Rf6 Nc4 39. R×f5** 39. Rd1 Q×g2 40. Q×f5 was more to the point. Steinitz: "If 39. g3, which otherwise looked promising, Black would answer 39. ... Nd2+ followed by ...Ne4." **39. ... Q×g2 40. Rh5 Qg7** Pollock: "Black certainly makes a heroic resistance." **41. Rg5 Qh8 42. h5 Rd7 43. Qc3 Qh6 44. f4 Nd2+ 45. Ka1 Ne4 46. Rg6** Steinitz: "Fine and unanswerable in its simplicity." **46. ... Q×g6 47. h×g6 N×c3 48. b×c3 Kc7 49. f5 Kd8 50. f6 Ke8 51. Rh1 Rd2 52. f7+ Ke7 53. Re1+ 1–0** [*BCM*, August & September 1886, pages 327–328; *Chess-Monthly*, June 1886, pages 295–296; *ICM*, August 1886, pages 244–245; *New York Clipper*, December 18, 1886; *PM*, pages 35–37]

79. I.A. Gunsberg–Pollock [A80]
BCA Congress, London, Round 2, 13 July 1886

1. d4 e6 2. Nf3 f5 3. e3 Nc6 4. Be2 Nf6 5. 0-0 Ne7 6. c4 Ng6 7. Nc3 b6 8. Ne5 Bd6 9. Bf3 c6 10. N×g6 h×g6 11. g3 Bb7 12. e4 Nh5 13. e5 Bc7 14. Re1 Qe7 15. a3 Bd8 16. b4 Qf7 (*see diagram*)
17. d5 Be7 18. d×c6 Another good possibility was 18. Nb5!? 0-0 (18. ... c×b5? 19. d×e6 d×e6 20. B×b7 Rd8 21. Bc6+ Kf8 22. Qc2 leaves White in full control.) 19. d×e6 d×e6 20. Nd6 B×d6 21. e×d6. **18. ... d×c6 19. b5! Rd8 20. Qc2 g5 21. b×c6 Ba8 22. Nb5 0-0 23. Nc7?** 23. Qa4! could have been met by very inventive play: 23. ... Rd3 24. Be2 f4!? 25. g4 (25. B×d3? f×g3 and

Black's attack is lethal.) 25. ... Rg3+!! 26. h×g3 f×g3 27. f3 Bc5+ 28. Kg2 B×c6 and Black's compensation is excellent. **23. ... g4! 24. Bg2 f4 25. N×a8 Bc5! 26. Ra2 R×a8 27. g×f4 N×f4 28. Be3 N×g2 29. K×g2 Qf3+ 30. Kg1 g3!? 31. h×g3 Rf5! 32. Qe2 Q×e2** 32. ... Q×c6!? **33. B×c5 Q×c5 34. Qd3 Raf8. 33. Ra×e2 B×a3?** 33. ... B×e3 34. R×e3 Rc8 35. Rd3 R×c6 36. Re4 Rf7, with approximate equality. **34. Ra1! Bc5 35. B×c5 b×c5 36. Ra5 Rf7 37. R×c5 Rc7 38. Ra2 Kf7 39. Rd2 Kg6 40. Rd7 Rac8 41. Rd6 Kf5 42. f3 a5 43. Kf2 a4 44. Ke3 a3 45. g4+ Kg5 46. Ra5 R×c6 47. R×c6 R×c6 48. Kd4 Kf4 49. R×a3 g5 50. c5 Rc8 51. Kc4 K×e5 52. Kb5?** 52. Rc3 Kf4 53. Kb5 e5 54. c6 e4 55. f×e4 K×g4 56. Kb6 Kf4 57. Rc4 was winning. **52. ... Kd5?** 52. ... Kd4! would have drawn: 53. c6 Rb8+ 54. Ka5 Ra8+ 55. Kb4 Rb8+ 56. Ka5 Ra8+ 57. Kb4 Rb8+. **53. c6??** Winning was 53. Rd3+ Ke5 54. c6 Kf4 55. Kb6. **53. ... Rb8+! 54. Ka5 Ra8+ 55. Kb4 Rb8+ 56. Ka4?** 56. Kc3 K×c6 would have been a draw. **56. ... Kc4! 57. Ka5 Ra8+ 58. Kb6 R×a3 59. c7 Rb3+?? 59. ... Ra8! gave Black the full point: 60. Kb7 Rf8 61. c8Q+ R×c8 62. K×c8 Kd4 63. Kd7 e5 64. Kd6 e4 65. f×e4 K×e4 66. Kc5 Kf4 67. Kd4 K×g4 68. Ke4 Kh3. 60. Ka7! ½–½** [*Supplement to the Nottinghamshire Guardian*, July 23, 1886; *Chess Player's Chronicle*, July 28, 1886]

80. J.H. Zukertort–Pollock [C62]
BCA Congress, London, Round 3, 14 July 1886

1. e4 e5 2. Nf3 Nc6 3. Bb5 d6 4. d4 Bd7 5. d×e5 d×e5 6. 0-0 Bd6 7. Nc3 Nge7 8. Bc4 0-0 9. Be3 Bg4 10. h3 Bh5 11. g4 Bg6 12. Nh4 Na5 13. Bd3 (*see diagram*)
13. ... Nd5! 14. Nf5 N×e3 15. N×e3 Qh4 16. Kg2 Nc6 17. Ne2 Rae8 18. Ng3 Nd4 19. Nef5 B×f5 20. g×f5 Kh8 21. c3 Nc6 22. Bb5 g6! 23. Qg4 Qf6 24. Kh2 Bc5 25. Rad1 Rd8 26. B×c6 Q×c6 27. f4?! 27. Qg5 R×d1 28. R×d1

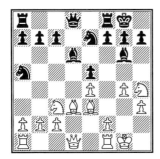

After
13. Bc3–d3

Re8 29. Rd2, with equal chances. **27. ... R×d1 28. R×d1 Bd6! 29. f×g6 f×g6 30. f5! Qb6 31. Qe2 Be7 32. Rd3 Bg5! 33. Kh1 Bf4 34. f×g6 Q×g6 35. Nf5 Rg8 36. Qf2 Qc6 37. Qe1 Qg6 38. Qf1 Qc6 39. Qe2 Qg6 40. Rd1 Qf6 41. Rd7 Qg6 42. Qg4 Qb6** Correctly avoiding 42. ... Q×g4? 43. h×g4 R×g4 44. R×c7 with excellent play for White, but 42. ... Qa6! would have been much stronger than the text. **43. Rg7! Qe6 44. b3 a5 45. c4 Bc1 46. a3** *(see diagram)*

After
46. a2–a3

46. ... c6? This gives White a clear edge now. Of course, 46. ... B×a3? is met by 47. R×h7+!; 46. ... h6!? 47. a4 Bd2 48. Qg3 Bf4 49. R×g8+ Q×g8 50. Qd3 Qe8 and Black may be able to draw this endgame without much difficulty. **47. c5 Bf4 48. b4 a4 49. R×g8+ Q×g8 50. Qd1 Bg5** 50. ... Qe8 would have been replied with 51. Qd6! **51. Qd7 Bf6 52. Q×b7 Bd8 53. Q×c6 Qf7 54. Qd5 Qf6 55. Qd7 h6 56. Qd6 Qg5 57. Q×h6+ Q×h6 58. N×h6 Kg7 59. Ng4 Bc7 60. c6 1–0** [*Chess-Monthly*, June 1886, pages 300–302; *The Field*, July 17, 1886; *New York Times*, July 30, 1886; *PM*, page 34; according to the *London Evening Standard*, July 15, 1886, the game lasted four hours and 45 minutes.]

81. S. Lipschütz–Pollock [A85]
BCA Congress, London, Round 4,
15 July 1886

1. d4 e6 2. c4 f5 3. Nc3 Nf6 4. Nf3 Bb4 5. Qb3

c5 6. Bf4 Ne4 7. e3 0–0 8. Bd3 Nc6 9. 0–0 B×c3 10. b×c3 Qe8 11. B×e4 f×e4 12. Nd2 c×d4 **13. c×d4 N×d4! 14. Qd1** 14. e×d4 R×f4 15. Qe3 Qf8 16. N×e4 b6 17. f3 Bb7 was playable too. **14. ... Qg6 15. Bg3 Nc6** 15. ... Nf5!? promised very little after 16. N×e4 N×e3 17. f×e3 R×f1+ 18. Q×f1 Q×e4 19. Qf3. **16. Bd6 Rf7 17. Qc2 e5 18. N×e4 b6 19. c5 Bb7 20. Qa4?!** *(see diagram)* 20. f3 Rc8 21. Rad1 was safer.

After
20. Qc2–a4

20. ... Nd4! 21. Ng3 21. e×d4 B×e4 22. f3 B×f3 23. R×f3 (23. Rf2 Bd5! 24. Qc2 Q×c2 25. R×c2 e4 and Black gets the better endgame.) 23. ... R×f3. **21. ... b5!? 22. Qa5 Ne2+ 23. Kh1 Nf4?** Interesting was 23. ... Qg4!? 24. Q×b5 B×g2+! 25. K×g2 Qf3+ 26. Kh3 Rf6 27. Qc4+ Kh8 forcing White to 28. Qh4 Rh6 29. Q×h6 g×h6 30. Rab1 Re8 and Black's advantage is close to winning. **24. e×f4 e×f4 25. Q×b5?!** 25. Qc7 Bc6 26. B×f4 h5 27. f3 h4 28. Ne2 h3 29. Rf2 h×g2+ 30. Kg1 Re8 (with chances for both) was perhaps clearer. **25. ... Bc6 26. Qc4 f3?** 26. ... f×g3! 27. B×g3 Re8 was the best way forward. **27. Rfe1 Kh8** 27. ... f×g2+ 28. Kg1 h6 29. f4 solves little. **28. Rac1 Qf6 29. Kg1 f×g2 30. Qe2 h6 31. Qe3 Qh4 32. Rcd1 Qh3 33. Rd4 Rf6 34. Rf4 Re6 35. Qd2 Kg8 36. Nf5** *(see diagram)*

After
36. Ng3–f5

36. ... Qd3! 37. Qc1 37. N×h6+! would have highlighted the flaws in Black's combination. 37. ... g×h6 38. Rg4+ Kh8 (38. ... Kf7 39. Qf4+ Rf6 40. Re7+ Kf8 41. Q×f6 mate.) 39. Qb2+. **37. ... Qc2 38. Ne7+ Kh8 39. N×c6 R×e1+ 40. Q×e1**

d×c6 41. Rg4 a5 42. K×g2 Q×a2 43. Qe7 Qd5+ 44. f3 Qg8 45. Be5 Re8 46. R×g7?? A stunning error. Easily winning was 46. B×g7+ Kh7 47. Qc7 Rc8 48. Qd7 Rd8 49. Qf5 mate. **46. ... R×e7 0–1** [*Morning Post*, July 16, 1886; *BCM*, August & September 1886, pages 319–320]

82. Pollock–J. Mortimer [C46]
BCA Congress, London, Round 6, 17 July 1886

1. e4 e5 2. Nf3 Nc6 3. Nc3 Bc5 4. N×e5 N×e5 5. d4 Bd6 6. d×e5 B×e5 7. Bd3 d6 8. 0–0 Nf6 9. Ne2 d5 10. f4 Bd6 11. e5 Bc5+ 12. Kh1 Ng4 13. Qe1 c6 14. h3 h5 15. Nc3 a6 16. f5 Qe7 17. Bf4 Bd7 (*see diagram*)

After
17. ... Bc8–d7

18. h×g4? Extremely risky. More energetic was 18. e6 Bc8 (18. ... f×e6? 19. f×e6 B×e6 20. Na4! Ba7 21. Bg6+ Kd7 22. Qa5 with a big plus.) 19. Na4! Ba7 20. c4! **18. ... h×g4+ 19. Bh2 0–0–0! 20. f6** 20. Qg3 was not a solution either: 20. ... Rh5 21. e6 Bd6! 22. e×d7+ K×d7 23. Rf4 Rdh8. **20. ... g×f6 21. g3 Rh3 22. Kg2 Rdh8 23. Bg1 f×e5 24. Nd1 B×g1 25. R×g1 Qf6 26. Nf2 Qf3+** Also possible was 26. ... R×g3+ 27. Kf1 R×g1+ 28. K×g1 g3. **27. Kf1 Rh1 28. Qe2 R×g1+ 29. K×g1 Q×g3+ 30. Kf1 Rh2 31. Rd1 Rg2 32. Ke1 f5** (*see diagram*)

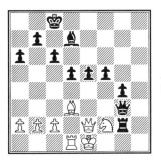

After
32. ... f7–f5

33. B×a6 Rg1+ 34. Kd2 Qf4+ 35. Kc3 Rg3+ 36. Nd3 b×a6 37. b3 e4 38. Rh1 e×d3 39. c×d3

Qe3 40. Rh8+ Kc7 41. Qh2 Q×d3+ 42. Kb4 Qc3+ 43. Ka3 f4 44. Qf2 Qc1+ 45. Kb4 a5+ 46. K×a5 0–1 [*Daily News*, July 19, 1886; *Chess Player's Chronicle*, July 28, 1886]

83. J. Taubenhaus–Pollock [C66]
BCA Congress, London, Round 7, 19 July 1886

Daily News: "The last game decided previously to the adjournment was a well-contested battle between Taubenhaus and Pollock, in which the former adopted the Ruy Lopez, Pollock playing a somewhat unusual defence which need not be further described, as we append this brilliant and instructive game below. After the sacrifice of a bishop for the king's rook's pawn, White found himself fully compensated in the game by the possession of four passed pawns in exchange for the pieces he had given up, and Pollock was at last forced to strike his colours at the 60th move. This game occupied three hours and 55 minutes." **1. e4 e5 2. Nf3 Nc6 3. Bb5 d6 4. c3 Nf6 5. d4 Bd7 6. 0–0 e×d4 7. c×d4 N×e4 8. Re1 d5 9. Ng5 Be7 10. N×e4 d×e4 11. R×e4 0–0 12. Nc3 f5 13. Re3 f4 14. Re4 Bd6 15. Bc4+ Kh8 16. Nb5 f3 17. g3 Bf5 18. N×d6 Q×d6 19. Rh4 Ne7?!** A very good alternative was 19. ... Rae8! 20. Bf4 Q×d4 21. Q×d4 N×d4 22. B×c7 Ne2+ 23. B×e2 R×e2. **20. Q×f3 h6 21. Bf4 Qb6** (*see diagram*)

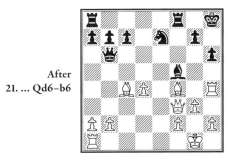

After
21. ... Qd6–b6

22. B×h6!? A violent attempt but not decisive by all means. **22. ... g×h6 23. Qe3 Ng8 24. B×g8 K×g8 25. R×h6 Rf6 26. Qg5+ Rg6 27. R×g6+ Q×g6 28. Qf4 Re8 29. Q×c7 Qg4 30. Qc3 Be4 31. Re1 Bc6 32. R×e8+ B×e8 33. f3 Qe6?!** Keeping the queens with 33. ... Qf5 was better. **34. Qb3 Q×b3 35. a×b3** (*see diagram*)

35. ... a5 36. Kf2 b5 36. ... Bf7 was best met by 37. b4! and White maintains clear winning chances. **37. Ke3 b4 38. d5 Kg7 39. Kd4 Bg6 40. f4 Kf6 41. g4 Bc2 42. Kc4 Bd1 43. h3 Be2+ 44. Kc5 Bd1 45. g5+ Ke7 46. f5 B×b3 47. d6+?!** Clearer

After
35. a2×b3

was 47. f6+! Kf7 48. h4 a4 49. K×b4 B×d5 50. K×a4. **47. ... Kd7 48. g6 Bc2 49. g7 Bb3 50. h4 Bg8??** 50. ... a4! 51. K×b4 K×d6 52. Kb5 Ke5 would have drawn. **51. h5 a4 52. K×b4 K×d6 53. K×a4 Ke5 54. b4 Kf6 55. h6 Bd5** 55. ... K×f5 still loses after 56. b5 Ke6 57. b6 Kd7 58. Kb5 Kc8 59. Kc6 Bh7 60. Kd6 Kb7 61. Ke7 K×b6 62. Kf7. **56. b5 Kf7 57. b6 Kg8 58. Kb5 Kh7 59. Kc5 Ba8 60. Kd6 1–0** [*Daily News*, July 24, 1886; *Chess-Monthly*, October 1886, pages 48–49]

84. Pollock–J.M. Hanham
BCA Congress, London, Round 8,
20 July 1886

Morning Post (July 21, 1886): "Pollock and Hanham played an irregular opening, the former developing his pieces rapidly, while his opponent played a close defence. There was much manoeuvring for position, and Pollock very ingeniously won a piece soon afterwards, forcing mate by a pretty combination." According to the *Standard* report (July 21, 1886), the game opened with **1. e4 d6** and "Pollock's game was rather dull, owing to the nature of the defence adopted to [by] the Major, viz. **...d6** (in answer to **1. e4**). Both masters maneuvered strategically, Pollock gradually gaining position. The ending somewhat compensated for the staleness of the preceding portion of the game. Pollock finished by a clever bishop's move, forcing a mate. The game was concluded soon after the adjournment."

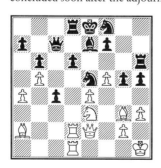

White to move

1. Nd5 Qc5 2. Bf2 Qc8 3. Bd4 Qb7 4. f6! B×f6 5. N×f6+ R×f6 6. B×e5 Re6 7. B×d6 R×e4 8. Q×h5 c3 9. Bc7! Ne6 and White mates in three moves. **1–0** [*Chess-Monthly*, August 1886, page 376]

85. H.E. Bird–Pollock [C45]
BCA Congress, London, Round 9,
21 July 1886

1. e4 e5 2. Nf3 Nc6 3. d4 e×d4 4. N×d4 Bc5 5. Be3 Qf6 6. c3 Nge7 7. Be2 B×d4 8. c×d4 d5 9. Nc3 Be6 10. e5 Qg6 11. 0–0 h5! Pollock: "This seems compulsory, as White threatened to win the queen for a minor piece by 12. Bh5 Qf5 13. g4." **11. ... Nf5 12. Bh5 N×e3 13. f×e3 Qg5 14. Qe2 0–0** was also possible. **12. Kh1 Rd8** Pollock: "A well opened game on both sides, considering its nature." **13. Na4 Nf5 14. Nc5 Bc8 15. Rc1 h4! 16. Bd3 h3?!** Pollock: "An advance of this kind ought to be made only with great caution. In the first place the pawn as it stood exercised considerable restraint on White's game, which would be enhanced by the advance of either of the three White pawns. In the second place, the advance pawn at h3 can now never be exchanged, and the kingside becomes partly blocked in favour of White. 16. ... h3 was not good." 16. ... b6 17. Nb3 a5 was a more sensible idea. **17. g3 b6 18. Nb3 Nb4** Pollock: "Initiating a long combination of moves that results only in the loss of a piece to Black." **19. Bb1 Ba6** *(see diagram)*

After
19. ... Bc8–a6

20. Qf3!? Pollock: "White plays very steadily and forcibly; if 20. Re1 Bd3 21. B×d3? N×d3 22. Q×d3? N×g3+ winning the queen." Interesting too was 20. R×c7 Rd7 21. Rc3 B×f1 22. Q×f1 Qh5 23. Bg5!! Q×g5 24. Rc8+ Rd8 25. Qb5+ Nc6 26. R×d8+ K×d8 27. Q×c6 with complicated play that seems to favor White. **20. ... Nd3?** Better was 20. ... Bd3! 21. B×d3 N×d3 22. Rc3 N×e3 23. Q×e3 N×b2 24. R×c7 0–0. **21. Rfd1** 21. R×c7! was decisive: 21. ... 0–0 (21. ... Rd7 22. R×d7 K×d7

23. Q×d5+) 22. Bd2! Nh6 23. B×h6 g×h6 24. Nd2.
21. ... N×e3 22. f×e3 Rd7 23. Nd2 Pollock: "Preventing Qe4." **23. ... f5?** A better defensive manoeuvre was 23. ... Qg5 24. B×d3 B×d3 25. Rc3 Bf5 26. Rf1 Be6. **24. Rc3 N×b2 25. B×f5 0–0** Pollock: "A very curious and interesting position." **26. B×g6 R×f3 27. Rb1** Pollock: "Quiet, but masterly." **27. ... Rf2 28. R×b2 Be2 29. e6 Re7 30. Bf7+ Kh7 31. Rc1 Bd3 32. Nc4!** Pollock: "Again, very ably played." **32. ... Rf3 33. Ne5 R×e3 34. N×d3 R×d3 35. Rf2 R×d4 36. Rf4 R×f4 37. g×f4 d4 38. Rg1 c5 39. f5 c4 40. Rg4 Kh6 41. R×d4 Rc7 42. Rd7 Rc5 43. e7 R×f5 44. Rd1 1–0** [*Standard*, July 22, 1886; *Chess Player's Chronicle*, September 1, 1886, pages 38–39; *PM*, pages 34–35; *BCM*, August & September 1886, pages 324–325; according to the *Daily News* of July 22, the game lasted three hours and ten minutes.]

86. Pollock–A. Burn [C00]
BCA Congress, London, Round 10, 22 July 1886

Western Daily Press (July 23): "...Burn's French Defence against Pollock realised the gain of a pawn for the second player, which, being skilfully nursed, proved victorious." *Daily News* (July 23): "The last game of the day in the Masters' Tournament, Pollock vs. Burn, was also decided previously to the adjournment. Pollock opened with **1. e4**, and Burn played the French defense of **1. ... e6**, Pollock continued with Steinitz's favorite move of **2. e5**, and on Black playing **2. ... d5**, captured the pawn *en-passant* [**3. e×d6 B×d6**] (*see diagram*).

After
3. ... Bf8×d6

Subsequently Black won an isolated centre pawn, and notwithstanding an ingenious combination commencing at Pollock's 33rd move, by which he nearly succeeded in averting defeat, the game was finally won by Burn in 47 moves. Time: 3h. 45m." The *Morning Post* (July 23) noted the game lasted

46 moves and the London *Times* of July 23 gave 45 moves. **0–1** [Full score not recovered]

87. E. Schallopp–Pollock [C29]
BCA Congress, London, Round 11, 23 July 1886

1. e4 e5 2. Nc3 Nf6 3. f4 d5 4. d3 d×e4 5. f×e5 Ng4 6. N×e4 N×e5 7. d4 Ng6 8. Bd3 Nc6 9. c3 Be7 10. Nf3 f5 11. Ng3 Bh4? A mistake. Better was 11. ... 0–0 12. Qb3+ Kh8 13. 0–0 f4 14. Ne4 Nce5!? **12. N×h4 Q×h4 13. 0–0 f4 14. Nh5** 14. Qb3!? Nce7 15. Ne4 Rf8 16. Bd2 would have placed Black in a very tough spot. **14. ... 0–0 15. Qb3+ Kh8 16. B×g6! h×g6 17. N×f4 Bf5 18. Q×b7 Be4** (*see diagram*)

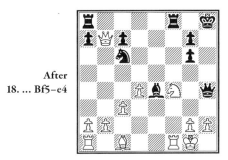

After
18. ... Bf5–e4

19. Q×c6! R×f4 20. R×f4? 20. Q×a8+! B×a8 21. B×f4 Qg4 22. Bg3 was a clearer path to winning. **20. ... Qe1+ 21. Rf1 Qe2 22. Rf2** Again, 22. Q×e4!? Q×e4 23. Bf4 was an efficient solution. **22. ... Qe1+ 23. Rf1 Qe2 24. Rf2 Qd1+ 25. Rf1 Qe2 26. Rf2 Qe1+ 27. Rf1 Qe2 28. Q×e4!** Finally, White realized the only way to play for a win was this sacrifice. **28. ... Q×e4 29. Bf4 Qb7 30. b3 Re8 31. Be5 Kg8 32. Rae1 Rf8 33. R×f8+ K×f8 34. Rf1+?** White shouldn't allow the possibility of the queen to infiltrate to e4. Instead, better was 34. c4! a5 35. Re3 g5 36. h3 Kf7 37. Kh2 a4 38. d5. **34. ... Ke7 35. B×g7 Qe4 36. Bh6 Qc2 37. c4 Q×a2 38. Rf3 Qa1+ 39. Kf2 Q×d4+ 40. Be3 Qb2+ 41. Kg3 a6 42. h4 Kd7 43. Bg5 Qe5+ 44. Kh3 a5 45. Rf6 Qc3+ 46. Rf3 Qc2 47. g4 Kc6 48. Bf6 Qd1 49. Kg2 Kc5 50. h5 g×h5 51. g×h5 c6 52. Bg7 Qd2+ 53. Kf1 Qd1+ 54. Kf2 Qd2+ 55. Kf1 Qd1+ 56. Kf2 Qd2+ 57. Kf1 Qc1+ 58. Kf2 Qd2+ 59. Kf1 Qc1+ 60. Kf2 Qd2+ 61. Kf1 Qd1+ 62. Kf2 Kd6 63. h6 Ke6 64. Kg2 Qd2+ 65. Kg3 Qg5+ 66. Kf2 Qd2+ 67. Kg3 Qg5+ 68. Kf2 Qh4+ 69. Kg2 Qg4+ 70. Kf2 Qh4+ 71. Kg2 Qe4 72. Kf2 Qh4+ 73. Kg2 c5 74. Rh3 Qe4+ 75. Kf2 Qc2+ 76. Kg1**

Qd1+ 77. Kg2 Qg4+ 78. Kh2 Qf4+ 79. Kg2
Qd2+ 80. Kg1 Qc1+ 81. Kh2 Qc2+ 82. Kg1
Qb1+ 83. Kh2 Qc2+ 84. Kg1 Qh7 85. Bc3 Kf5
86. Kg2 Qb7+ 87. Kf2 Qh7?! 87. ... Q×b3! 88. h7
Qc2+ 89. Ke1 Qc1+ with a perpetual was satis-
factory here. 88. B×a5 Kg4 89. Rg3+ Kf4
90. Bd2+ Ke4 91. Ke2 Ke5 92. Rd3 Kf5 93. Be3
Kg4 94. Kd2 Qa7 (see diagram)

After
94. ... Qh7–a7

95. h7! Now White gets concrete winning
chances. 95. ... Q×h7 96. B×c5 Qh2+ 97. Kc3
Qe5+ 98. Bd4 Qe1+ 99. Kc2 Qe2+ 100. Rd2
Qe4+ 101. Kb2 Kf5 102. b4 Ke6 103. b5 Kd6
104. c5+ Kc7 105. Kc3 Qb1 106. Kc4 Qf1+
107. Kb4 Qb1+ 108. Ka5 Qc1 109. Rd3 Qc4
110. Be5+ Kc8 111. Rd6 Qa2+ 112. Kb6 Qf7
113. Rc6+ Kd8 114. Bf6+ 1–0 [Chess-Monthly,
August 1886, pages 368–370]

88. Pollock–J. Mason [B40]
BCA Congress, London, Round 12,
26 July 1886

1. e4 e6 2. Nf3 c5 3. d4 c×d4 4. N×d4 Nf6
5. Nc3 Bb4 6. e5 Nd5 7. Ndb5 7. Bd2 N×c3
8. b×c3 Be7 9. Qg4 0–0 10. Bh6 g6 is a popular
line today. 7. ... a6 8. Nd6+ B×d6 9. e×d6 N×c3
10. b×c3 Nc6 11. Bd3 Qa5 12. 0–0 0–0 12. ...
Q×c3?! 13. Rb1 0–0 14. Rb3 Qc5 15. Ba3 Qd5
16. c4 Qe5 17. Bb2 Qf4 18. Re1 was too dangerous.
13. Re1 f5 (see diagram)

After
13. ... f7–f5

14. Qh5 b6 15. Re3 g6 16. Rg3 Ne5! 17. Bd2
Bb7 18. Re1 Rf7 19. Qg5 Raf8 20. c4 Qc5
21. Bc3 Ng4 Another way was the spectacular
21. ... N×d3!? 22. c×d3 f4 23. Q×c5 f×g3! 24. Qd4
g×f2+ 25. Kf1 f×e1Q+ 26. K×e1 e5! 27. Q×e5
Rf6 with chances for both, but seemingly easier
play for Black. 22. Re2 Nf6 23. h4! Q×d6? Best
defense was 23. ... Ne4! 24. B×e4 B×e4 25. h5 f4
26. Q×c5 b×c5 27. Rg4 Bf5 28. h×g6 B×g6 29. f3.
24. h5! Qe7 25. h×g6 h×g6 (see diagram)

After
25. ... h7×g6

26. Bb4?? Faulty calculation. White was winning easily with the less subtle 26. B×f5! Rg7
27. B×g6 Bc8 28. Qh4 d6 29. Bh7+! Kf7 30. R×g7+
K×g7 31. Re3. 26. ... Q×b4! 27. Q×g6+ Kh8
28. Rh3+ Rh7 29. Ree3 Qe7?! Not the most precise defense. Better was either 29. ... Qc5 or 29. ...
Bc6. 30. B×f5! Rff7 31. Bd3? White could have
stayed in the game with 31. Qg3! R×h3 32. Qb8+
Ne8 33. R×h3+ Kg8 34. Bg6. 31. ... Rfg7
32. R×h7+ N×h7 33. Qh6 Qg5 34. Q×g5 N×g5
35. f4 Nf7 36. g3 Nd6 37. Kf2 Kg8 38. Re1 Bc6
39. c5 b×c5 40. B×a6 Ne4+ 41. Ke2 R×g3 0–1
[Daily News, July 27, 1886; the source stated the
game lasted two hours and 50 minutes.]

89. G.H. Mackenzie–Pollock [C44]
BCA Congress, London, Round 13,
27 July 1886

1. e4 e5 2. Nf3 Nc6 3. Bb5 d6 4. d4 Bd7 5. c3
Nf6 6. Qe2 Be7 7. Nbd2 e×d4 8. c×d4 0–0 9. h3
Nb4 10. 0–0 c6 11. Ba4 Re8 12. a3 Na6 13. Bc2
Nc7 14. e5 Nfd5 15. Qd3 g6 16. Ne4 d×e5
17. N×e5 Bf5! 18. Qf3 Ne6 19. Rd1 Qb6 20. Be3
Q×b2! 21. g4 N×e3 22. f×e3 B×e4 23. Q×e4
Qb6 (see diagram)

24. N×f7? This doesn't work. White had to settle for something less ambitious, for instance
24. Rab1 Qc7 25. Rf1. 24. ... Bg5? The knight
could have been safely captured: 24. ... K×f7
25. Rf1+ Bf6 26. Qe5 Qd8 27. Rab1 Nc7 28. Qf4

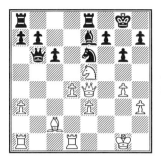

After
23. ... Qb2–b6

Kg7 29. R×b7 Rc8; But even stronger was 24. ...
Ng5! 25. N×g5 B×g5 26. Qg2 R×e3. **25. Ne5 Rad8
26. Rab1 Qc7 27. Bb3 Kg7 28. Rf1 Re7 29. B×e6
R×e6 30. Qf3 Rf6 31. Qe2 Rdf8 32. R×f6 B×f6
33. Nf3 Be7 34. Kg2 B×a3 35. Ra1 Qe7 36. e4
a5 37. e5 Bb4 38. Qe4 h6 39. Rd1 Qe6 40. d5
c×d5 41. R×d5 b6 42. Rd1 Qa2+ 43. Kg3 Bc5
44. Rf1 a4 45. h4 a3 46. h5 g×h5 47. g×h5 Kh8
48. e6 Rg8+ 49. Kf4 Qg2** 49. ... Bd6+ 50. Ke3
Qb3+ was equally strong. **50. Qe5+ Rg7 51. Qa1
Qg4+ 52. Ke5 a2 53. Kd5 Q×h5+ 54. Ne5 Rg5
55. Re1 Be7 56. Q×a2 Bf6** Most accurate was
56. ... Qf3+! 57. Kc4 b5+ 58. Kd4 Bf6. **57. Qa8+**
57. Kd6 would have prolonged the fight for a
while: 57. ... R×e5 58. Qa8+ Kh7 59. Qb7+ Bg7
60. R×e5 Q×e5+ 61. Kd7 Qd4+ 62. Ke8 Qc5
63. Qe4+ Kg8 64. Kd7 Qb5+ 65. Kc8 Qe8+
66. Kb7 b5 67. Ka6 b4 68. e7 Kf7. **57. ... Kh7?** 57. ...
Rg8 58. Qa4 Rd8+ was the way. **58. Qa7+ Bg7
59. Qa1?** After 59. Qc7! Qf3+ 60. Kd6 Qb3 61. e7
and Black has some real issues to solve requiring
maximum accuracy. **59. ... Qf3+ 60. Kd6 Qf8+**
60. ... Qf5! was best. **61. e7** 61. Kd7! would have
drawn: 61. ... Qc5 62. Qb1+ Kg8 63. e7 Qd5+
64. Kc8 R×e5 65. e8Q+ R×e8+ 66. R×e8+ Kf7
67. Re1 Qc6+ 68. Kb8 Be5+ 69. Ka7! **61. ... Qb8+
62. Kd5 Kg8 63. Ke6 B×e5 64. Qd1 Qc8+
65. Kd5 Qc5+ 66. Ke4 Qc4+ 0–1** [*Chess-Monthly*,
August 1886, pages 374–375; according to the
Daily News and *Morning Post* of July 28, 1886, the
game lasted seven hours.]

NOTTINGHAM (CCA, MASTERS, AUGUST 1886)

90. Pollock–A.B. Skipworth
**CCA Masters International, Nottingham,
Round 1, 3 August 1886**

1. e4 (...) 1–0 According to the *Nottingham*

Evening Post and *Morning Post* of August 4, the
game was adjourned and left unfinished. It was
scored as a victory for Pollock but the game was
cancelled when Skipworth withdrew from the
tournament.

91. J.H. Zukertort–Pollock [C33]
**CCA Masters International, Nottingham,
Round 2, 3 July 1886**

**1. e4 e5 2. f4 e×f4 3. Bc4 Nf6 4. Nc3 Nc6
5. Nf3 Be7 6. 0–0 N×e4 7. N×e4 d5 8. B×d5
Q×d5 9. d3 f5 10. Nc3 Qd6 11. d4 a6 12. d5 Nd8
13. Qe2 Nf7?** A clear mistake. 13. ... 0–0 was fine
even after 14. B×f4 because of 14. ... Qb6+ 15. Kh1
Bf6! **14. Re1 g5 15. N×g5 Qc5+ 16. Kh1 N×g5**
(see diagram)

After
16. ... Nf7×g5

17. B×f4?! More precise was 17. Na4 Qb4
18. Bd2 Qd6 19. B×f4 Qf6 20. Be5 Qf8 21. B×h8.
17. ... Ne4 17. ... Kf8 was another attempt to survive, but it's still over after 18. b4! Q×b4 19. Rab1
Qc5 20. Na4. **18. N×e4 f×e4 19. Q×e4?** Too com-
placent. 19. Qh5+! Kd8 20. R×e4 Re8 21. Bg5 and
White wins. **19. ... 0–0! 20. Bh6 Rf7?!** Black had
to try to get some activity by 20. ... Bd7 21. B×f8
R×f8 22. Rf1 (22. Q×e7? Rf1+) 22. ... Bf6 with
reasonable compensation. **21. Re3** *(see diagram)*

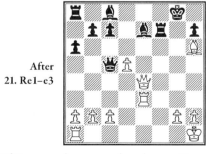

After
21. Re1–e3

21. Rf1! was much stronger than the text. **21. ...
Bf5?** This loses immediately. 21. ... Bd7! 22. Rg3+
Kh8 23. Be3 Qd6 24. c4 c5 and Black can be
optimistic here. **22. Rg3+ Kh8 23. Qe5+ Bf6**

24. Q×f5 Re8 25. Rf1 Qd4 26. c3 Qh4 27. Bg5 B×g5 28. Q×f7 Rd8 29. Qf5 h6 30. Qe5+ Kg8 31. Qe6+ Kh8 32. Rf7 1–0 [*Chess-Monthly*, July 1886, pages 326–327; *Morning Post*, August 9, 1886; *Chess Player's Chronicle*, October 27, 1887]

92. Pollock–I.A. Gunsberg [C24]
CCA Masters International, Nottingham, Round 3, 4 July 1886

1. e4 e5 2. Bc4 Nf6 3. Qe2 Bc5 4. f4?! e×f4 5. Nf3 0–0 6. d4 Bb6 7. 0–0 Nc6 8. c3 Re8 9. e5 Nh5 (*see diagram*)

After
9. ... Nf6–h5

9. ... d6! was even stronger. 10. Kh1 10. g4!? was worth trying: 10. ... Nf6 (10. ... f×g3? fails because of 11. B×f7+! K×f7 12. Ng5+ Kg8 13. Q×h5 h6 14. Qf7+ Kh8 15. Qg6 h×g5 16. Rf7 and White mates.) 11. Qg2 d5 12. e×f6 d×c4 13. f×g7 with better chances than in the game. 10. ... d6! 11. Nbd2 d×e5 12. Ne4 Be6 13. B×e6 R×e6 14. N×e5 Qh4! 15. g3? 15. Nf3 was likely to be met by 15. ... Ng3+ 16. N×g3 R×e2 17. N×e2 Qg4 18. B×f4, but it was White's only alternative. 15. ... N×g3+ 16. N×g3 f×g3 17. Rf4 Qh3 18. Qg2 Q×g2+ 19. K×g2 N×e5 20. d×e5 g×h2 21. K×h2 R×e5 0–1 [*Chess Player's Chronicle*, October 27, 1887]

93. J.M. Hanham–Pollock [C50]
CCA Masters International, Nottingham, Round 4, 5 August 1886

1. e4 e5 2. Nf3 Nc6 3. Bc4 Bc5 4. Nc3 Nf6 5. d3 d6 6. Ne2 Na5 7. Bb3 N×b3 8. a×b3 0–0 9. Ng3 Ne8? Adopting the wrong plan. 9. ... h6 was better. 10. 0–0 f5?! It was not too late for 10. ... h6 or 10. ... Be6. 11. Bg5! Nf6 12. e×f5 Qe8 13. d4! e×d4 14. Re1 Qb5 14. ... Qf7 15. N×d4 h6 16. Bh4 Qd5. 15. N×d4 B×d4 16. Q×d4 B×f5 17. Re7 B×c2 18. B×f6 R×f6 19. R×c7 B×b3 20. R×a7 R×a7 21. Q×a7 Bd5 21. ... Rf7 22. Qb8+ Rf8 23. Q×b7 Q×b7 24. R×b7 Be6 was not very appealing either. 22. Nh5 (*see diagram*)

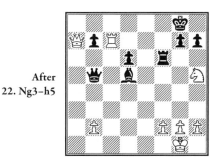

After
22. Ng3–h5

22. ... Rf8 22. ... Re6 23. R×g7+ Kf8 24. h3 Qc5 25. Qa4! loses too but in a less obvious way. 23. R×g7+ Kh8 24. Qd4 1–0 [*Irish Chess Chronicle*, 1 August 1887; C.N. 9796]

94. J.A.P. Rynd–Pollock [C45]
CCA Masters International, Nottingham, Round 5, 5 August 1886

1. e4 e5 2. Nf3 Nc6 3. d4 e×d4 4. N×d4 Bc5 5. Nb3 Bb6 6. Be2 Pollock: "Necessary, unless the risky advance 5. c4 be selected. For if 6. Nc3, Black may answer with 6. ... Qf6." 6. ... d6 7. 0–0 (*see diagram*)

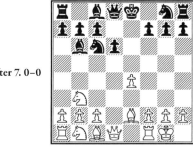

After 7. 0–0

7. ... Nge7 Pollock: "An exception to the rule against playing out the knights to self-protecting squares. Here it would not do to allow the knight to be pinned on f6, as Black has no very good means of keeping the knight from d5. Again, it is important, as will be seen, to be able to throw forward the f-pawn at an early stage." 8. Nc3 0–0 9. Na4 Pollock: "The bishop, indeed, is strong, but the exchange weakens White's a2-pawn, which causes loss of time on his 14th move." 9. ... f5! 10. N×b6 a×b6 Pollock: "Both Black's rooks are now brought passively into action." 11. e×f5 B×f5 12. c3 Be6 13. f4 Kh8 14. a3 Qe8 15. Nd2 Pollock: "A slip apparently." 15. ... Nd5 16. Ne4 Bf5 17. N×d6? Pollock: "This part of the game is incomprehensible." 17. ... c×d6 18. Bh5 g6 19. Q×d5

g×h5 **20. Bd2 Qg6 21. Rae1 Rae8 22. c4 Kg7?!**
22. ... Re6 was most accurate: 23. Bc3+ Kg8
24. Rf3 Be4 25. R×e4 Q×e4 26. Rg3+ Kf7 27. f5
Q×d5 28. c×d5 Re2 29. d×c6 b×c6 30. Kf1 Re4
with a clear edge. **23. Bc3+ Kh6 24. Rd1 Re2!**
25. Q×d6? A losing error. But it's hard to see anything for White even after 25. Rf2 R×f2 26. K×f2
Be6 27. Qd2 Qf5 28. g3 h4 29. b3 Kg6. **25. ...**
R×g2+ 26. Kh1 Be4 27. Q×f8+ Qg7!! *(see diagram)*

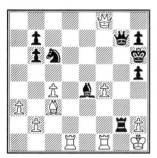

After
27. ... Qg6–g7

Pollock: "See diagram of this extraordinary position." **28. Rf3 B×f3 29. B×g7+ R×g7 mate 0–1**
[*Chess Player's Chronicle*, November 3, 1887; *PM*,
pages 39–40]

95. H.E. Bird–Pollock [C62]
CCA Masters International, Nottingham,
Round 6, 6 August 1886

1. e4 e5 2. Nf3 Nc6 3. Bb5 d6 4. 0–0 Bg4 5. h3
Bh5 6. d4 B×f3 7. Q×f3 e×d4 8. e5?! 8. c3!? d×c3
9. N×c3 a6 10. B×c6+ b×c6 11. Re1 was more accurate than the text. **8. ... Qd7! 9. e×d6 B×d6**
10. Nd2 *(see diagram)*

After
10. Nb1–d2

10. ... 0–0–0!? 10. ... Nge7!? 11. Ne4 0–0
12. N×d6 Q×d6 13. Bf4 Qc5 was better. **11. Nc4**
f6? Underestimating White's next move. Better
was 11. ... a6! 12. N×d6+ Q×d6 13. Bf4 Ne5!
14. Qg3 f6. **12. Na5! Nge7 13. Qb3 g5??** 13. ...
Qe8 was the only available defense: 14. B×c6 b×c6

15. Qb7+ Kd7 allows Black to continue fighting.
14. B×c6 Q×c6 15. N×c6 N×c6 16. Bd2 h5
17. Qe6+ Kb8 18. Q×f6 g4 19. h4 Be7 20. Qe6
B×h4 21. Rae1 Rdg8 22. b4 a6 23. a4 Rg7 24. b5
Nd8 25. Qe5 Rhh7 26. b6 Ka8 27. Bf4! 1–0 [*Nottinghamshire Guardian*. October 1, 1886; *Chess
Player's Chronicle*, November 3, 1887]

96. Pollock–A. Burn
CCA Masters International, Nottingham,
Round 7, 6 August 1886

1. e4 e5 2. Nc3 (...) 0–1 The *Derby Daily Telegraph* of August 9 noted that "Pollock, who
opened with a Vienna against Burn, resigned after
38 moves." The same was noted by the *Morning
Post* of the same day adding that it was an "interesting game." The *Nottingham Evening Post* (August 9) noted: "The Vienna Opening was played
by Mr. Pollock but Mr. Burn was too strong for
him and he resigned at the 38th move." [Full score
not recovered]

97. Pollock–E. Thorold [C38]
CCA Masters International, Nottingham,
Round 8, 6 August 1886

1. e4 e5 2. f4 e×f4 3. Nf3 g5 4. Bc4 Bg7 5. 0–0
d6 6. d4 h6 7. c3 Ne7 8. Na3 0–0 9. Bd2 c6
10. Qe2 Bg4 11. Rae1 Nd7 12. Bb3 Rc8 13. Kh1
b5 14. g3 Ng6 15. Qg2 f×g3 16. Q×g3 B×f3+
17. Q×f3 Qe7 18. Nc2 Nf6 *(see diagram)*

After
18. ... Nd7–f6

19. e5 d×e5 20. d×e5 20. Ne3 e4 21. Nf5 e×f3
22. R×e7 N×e7 23. N×e7+ Kh8 24. N×c8 R×c8
25. R×f3 Re8 could not have been appealing to
Pollock. **20. ... N×e5 21. Qg3 Nfd7** 21. ... Rce8!
was stronger. **22. Nd4 c5 23. Nf5 Qf6 24. Bd5**
Rce8 *(see diagram)*
25. h4! g4 26. N×h6+ Q×h6? 26. ... B×h6
27. R×f6 B×d2 28. R×e5 N×f6 29. Qd3! was insufficient but it would have been a better try than

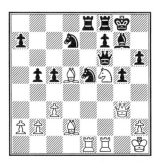

After
24. ... Rc8–e8

the text. **27. B×h6 B×h6 28. Rf5 Bg7 29. h5 Kh7 30. h6 Bh8 31. Be4 Ng6 32. Q×g4** 32. R×f7+ R×f7 33. B×g6+ K×g6 34. R×e8 was possible too. **32. ... Nf6 33. R×f6 B×f6 34. B×g6+ f×g6 35. Qd7+ 1–0** [*Illustrated Sporting and Dramatic News*, December 18, 1886]

98. J. Taubenhaus–Pollock [C39]
CCA Masters International, Nottingham, Round 9, 9 August 1886

1. e4 e5 2. f4 e×f4 3. Nf3 g5 4. h4 g4 5. Ng5 h6 6. N×f7 K×f7 7. d4 f3 8. Bc4+ d5 9. B×d5+ Ke8 10. g×f3 g3 11. f4 Nf6 12. Bc4 g2 13. Rg1 Bg4 14. Qd3 Nc6 (*see diagram*)

After
14. ... Nb8–c6

15. e5? 15. R×g2 N×d4 16. Nd2 Bc5 was safer than the text but Black's still much better. **15. ... Ne4! 16. Q×e4** After 16. R×g2 Black can force a quick win as follows: 16. ... Q×h4+ 17. Kf1 Qh1+ 18. Rg1 Bh3+ 19. Ke2 Qh2+ 20. Kf3 Q×g1 21. K×e4 Bg2+ 22. Kf5 Ne7+ 23. Kg4 h5+ 24. Kh4 Nf5+ 25. Q×f5 Qe1+ 26. Kg5 Qg3+ 27. Kf6 Rh6+ 28. Qg6+ Q×g6 mate. **16. ... Q×h4+ 17. Kd2 Qf2+ 18. Kc3 Q×g1 19. Be3 Qe1+ 20. Nd2 g1Q** 20. ... Q×a1 looks a bit risky because of 21. Qg6+, but Black is on safe ground even there: 21. ... Kd8 22. Qf6+ Ne7 23. Q×h8 Qe1 24. Q×f8+ Kd7 25. e6+ B×e6 26. B×e6+ Kd6! (26. ... K×e6? allows White a drawing opportunity: 27. Q×h6+ Kd7 28. Qh3+) 27. Q×a8 Q×e3+

28. Kb4 Q×d2+ 29. Kb3 Qe3+ 30. c3 Q×e6+. **21. B×g1 Q×a1** Most precise was 21. ... Bb4+! 22. Kb3 Q×d2 23. a3 Na5+ 24. Ka2 N×c4 25. a×b4 Q×b4 26. Qg6+ Kd8 27. Qf6+ Kd7 28. e6+ B×e6 29. d5 B×d5 30. Rd1 Nd2+. **22. Qg6+ Kd8 23. Qf6+ Kc8?** 23. ... Ne7 was best: 24. Q×h8 Ke8 25. Bf2 Qh1 26. Qh7 Qh3+ 27. Qd3 Q×d3+ 28. K×d3 h5 and White's pawns are not enough for the rook. **24. Q×h8 Kd7 25. Qh7+ Be7?** 25. ... Ne7! 26. Ne4 Rd8 27. Nc5+ Kc8 28. Bf2 Bf5 29. Qf7 Qd1 was once again the most exact play. **26. e6+! B×e6 27. B×e6+ K×e6 28. d5+!** (*see diagram*)

After 28. d4–d5

28. ... K×d5?? 28. ... Kd7! was the only move to keep Black in the game: 29. d×c6+ b×c6 30. Nf3 Rb8 31. Bc5 Q×b2+ 32. Kd2 Qf6 33. Ne5+ Ke6 34. Qe4 with an unclear position. **29. Qf5+** White missed a forced mate: 29. Qf7+ Kd6 30. Ne4+ Kd7 31. Nc5+ Kc8 32. Qf5+ Kb8 33. Nd7+ Kc8 34. Nb6+ Kb8 35. Qc8 mate. **29. ... Ne5 30. Q×e5+ Kc6 31. Q×e7 Q×g1?** Collapsing completely but there was little hope anyway; 31. ... b6 is met by 32. B×b6 a×b6 33. Qe4+ Kd7 34. Qd5+ Ke7 35. Q×a8. **32. Qe6+ Kb5 33. a4+ Ka5** and White mates in two. **1–0** [*Chess-Monthly*, July 1886, pages 336–337; *PM*, page 39]

99. Pollock–E. Schallopp [C52]
CCA Masters International, Nottingham, Round 10, 9 August 1886

Nottinghamshire Guardian (August 13, 1886): "...Mr. Pollock scored amidst great excitement after 29 moves." **1. e4 e5 2. Nf3 Nc6 3. Bc4 Bc5 4. b4 B×b4 5. c3 Ba5 6. 0–0 Nf6 7. d4 N×e4** Pollock: "6. ... Nf6 is inferior to 6. ... d6. It gives White the opportunity for the 'Richardson variation.' The only continuation after 7. d4 is 7. ... 0–0. The following would be a continuation: 7. ... 0–0 8. d×e5 N×e4 9. Bd5 N×c3 10. N×c3 B×c3 11. Ng5 N×e5 (If 11. ... B×a1, then 12. Qh5 wins.) 12. Qc2 Ng6

13. Q×c3 Qf6 14. Q×f6 wins. The variations springing from any alteration of Black's defence turn out in favour of White." Regarding the 11. ... B×a1 12. Qh5 line, it seems Pollock underestimated Black's chances after 12. ... Q×g5 13. B×g5 B×e5. **8. Re1** (*see diagram*)

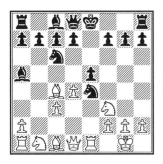

After
8. Rf1–e1

8. ... Nd6? Pollock: "The only chance now left is 8. ... d5. The text move brings him into hopeless trouble, and after some more moves he has to give up the queen for the rook and bishop, with the queenside entirely undeveloped. Any further comment would only be 'flogging a dead horse.' Black had a lost game in the opening, and it took its natural course." **9. Bg5! Ne7** 9. ... f6 fails to 10. d×e5 N×e5 11. N×e5 Kf8 12. Bb3 f×g5 13. Ng4! **10. N×e5 0–0 11. B×e7?** Best was 11. N×f7 N×f7 12. B×e7 Qe8 13. B×f8 Q×f8 14. Qh5 with an immediate win. The text move must have given Black hope. **11. ... Q×e7 12. N×f7 Q×e1+! 13. Q×e1 N×c4 14. Ne5 Re8 15. Qf1** 15. f4!? d6 16. Qf1 would have been slightly better. **15. ... N×e5 16. d×e5 R×e5 17. Nd2 b5!? 18. Nf3 Rc5 19. Qd3 Bb7 20. Q×d7 B×c3 21. Rd1 Bf6 22. Re1** (*see diagram*)

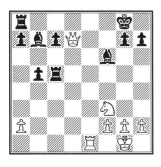

After
22. Rd1–e1

22. ... Kf8? With 22. ... h6! Black's position would have been perfectly sound. **23. Nd4! Bd5 24. Qf5 Re8 25. R×e8+ K×e8 26. Nb3 B×b3 27. Q×c5 B×a2 28. Q×b5+ Kd8 29. Qd3+ 1–0** [*Belfast News-Letter*, August 19, 1886; *Chess-Monthly*, July 1886, pages 339–340; *PM*, pages 71–72]

100. Taylor–Pollock
CCA Meeting (Handicap Tournament), Nottingham, August 1886
Remove f7 pawn

1. e4 and d4 d6 2. Bd3 Nc6 3. d5 Ne5 4. Be2 Nf6 5. f4 Nf7 6. Bd3 e6 7. c4 Be7 8. Nf3 e×d5 9. c×d5 0–0 10. 0–0 Kh8 11. Nc3 c6 12. d×c6 b×c6 13. Qe2 a5 14. Bd2 Nd7 15. Nd4 Bf6 16. Ne6 Qe7 17. N×f8 N×f8 18. Rac1 Ne6 19. Be3 Bb7 20. b3 Re8 21. Bb6 Bc8 22. Na4 c5 23. B×a5 Qa7 24. Bb6 Qb8 (*see diagram*)

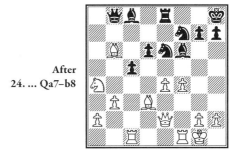

After
24. ... Qa7–b8

25. e5 d×e5 26. Qh5 Kg8 27. B×h7+ Kf8 28. B×c5+ N×c5 29. N×c5 e×f4 30. Kh1 Re5 31. Qd1 Ng5 32. Nd7+ B×d7 33. Q×d7 Re8 34. Bg6 Rd8 35. Qf5 f3 36. g×f3 Kg8 37. Qg4 Qd6 38. Be4 Kf8 39. Qf5 Kg8 40. Rc2 Qa6 41. Rfc1 Rf8 42. Qc5 N×e4 43. Qd5+ Kh8 44. Q×e4 Bg5 45. Rg1 Bh6 46. Rc6 Qa7 47. Rgg6 1–0 [*Chess Player's Chronicle*, September 29, 1886]

VARIOUS GAMES (LATE 1886)

101. Pollock–W. Cooke [C52]
Kingstown Chess Club, 24-board Simultaneous Exhibition, 27 August 1886

1. e4 e5 2. Nf3 Nc6 3. Bc4 Bc5 4. b4 B×b4 5. c3 Ba5 6. 0–0 Nf6 7. d4 N×e4 8. Re1 8. d×e5 was a continuation advocated by Jean Dufresne in the 1850s. **8. ... d5** (*see diagram*)

9. R×e4 An experiment against weaker opposition. **9. ... d×c4** 9. ... 0–0! would have been a good retort. 9. ... d×e4 was possible too: 10. Ng5 Rf8 (10. ... 0–0 allows 11. Qh5!) 11. d5 e3 12. B×e3 Bb6 and White's compensation is not very convincing. **10. Ba3** In the circumstances, 10. Qe2 was best: 10. ... 0–0 11. N×e5 Bf5 12. Rf4 N×e5 13. R×f5 Nd3 14. R×a5 N×c1 15. Qd2 Nd3 16. Na3, but

After
8. ... d7–d5

aggressive-looking moves by a master against an amateur worked very well. **10. ... Bf5** 10. ... Qd5! was much stronger: 11. R×e5+ (11. Re1 Bg4! 12. d×e5 0–0–0) 11. ... N×e5 12. N×e5 b5 13. Qe2 Be6 and White's in trouble. **11. Re1 Qd7** Again, 11. ... Qd5! was recommended. **12. d5?** It's odd that Pollock missed the simple 12. N×e5! N×e5 13. R×e5+ Be6 14. R×a5. **12. ... Nd8??** 12. ... 0–0–0! gave Black a won game: 13. d6 (13. N×e5 N×e5 14. R×e5 f6 15. Re1 Q×d5) 13. ... c×d6 14. Nbd2 Qe6. **13. N×e5 Qc8 14. Nd7+ K×d7 1–0** [*Illustrated Sporting and Dramatic News*, November 13, 1886]

102. Beaumont & Adamson & Zangwill–Pollock [C25]
Consultation Game, City of London Chess Club, 1 September 1886

Steinitz: "The following game is worthy of attention on account of its presenting a new feature in the defense of the Steinitz Gambit, hitherto not much noticed in analysis or practice. It was played on September 1st, 1886, in the City of London Chess Club, between Capt. Beaumont, Mr. Geo. Adamson and Mr. L. Zangwill (consulting) against Mr. W.H.K. Pollock." **1. e4 e5 2. Nc3 Nc6 3. f4 e×f4 4. d4 Qh4+ 5. Ke2 g5** Steinitz: "As far as we are aware this defense first occurred in some games played at Brooklyn between the Editor, who conducted the attack against Mr. Edwyn Anthony, about three years ago. It has also since been adopted by some Russian amateurs against Herr Chigorin who, we notice from the *Schachmatni Listock*, frequently plays the attack in this Gambit with success." **6. Nf3 Qh5 7. Nd5** Steinitz: "At this point we played against Mr. Anthony 7. g3 and the game proceeded: 7. ... g4 8. Nh4 f3+ 9. Kf2. The same idea of compelling the further advance of Black's pawns, and thus to obtain greater freedom for his pieces has since occurred to Herr Chigorin, but if

we recollect right he first played 7. Nd5 at this point, like the allies in the game before us, and on Black answering 7. ... Kd8, he advanced 8. g3." **7. ... g4** Steinitz: "With youthful dash Mr. Pollock seizes his opportunity for a counter-attack." 7. ... Kd8 was playable. **8. N×c7+** Steinitz: "But in White's place, we would probably have turned the tables by a counter-sacrifice, viz. 8. B×f4, which most likely would have led to the following continuation: 8. ... g×f3+ 9. g×f3 Bh6 10. Rg1 (threatening R×g8+) 10. ... Kf8 11. B×c7, with a fine attack." **8. ... Kd8 9. N×a8 g×f3+ 10. g×f3 Nf6** 10. ... f5!? 11. e5 Nge7 12. Rg1 Nd5 was interesting as well. **11. Qd3** *(see diagram)* Preferable was 11. B×f4 N×e4 12. Qd3 d5 13. Qe3 Bd6 14. B×d6 N×d6 15. Qf4.

After
11. Qd1–d3

11. ... d5! 12. B×f4 Steinitz: "Undoubtedly 12. e5 was much preferable." 12. e5 loses to 12. ... Bf5 13. Qd2 Ne4. **12. ... d×e4 13. Bc7+ Kd7 14. Qe3 Bh6** The simple 14. ... e×f3+ 15. Kd1 Nd5 16. Qe4 N×c7 17. N×c7 K×c7 leaves White's position in shambles. **15. Qf2 e3 16. Qg3 N×d4+** Even more energetic was 16. ... Qb5+! 17. Ke1 Qb4+ 18. c3 Q×b2 19. Rd1 Q×c3+ 20. Ke2 Nd5. **17. Kd1** *(see diagram)*

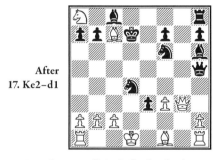

After
17. Ke2–d1

17. ... e2+? Steinitz: "Mr. Pollock who has so far shown fine form in his attack, relapses now with a won game in hand. 17. ... Ne4 was the proper move, and he could well afford the exchange of queens, which he apparently was afraid of, e.g., 18. Qh3+ (or 18. Qe5, 18. ... Q×f3+) 18. ... Q×h3

19. B×h3+ Kc6 20. f×e4 (if 20. B×c8 Black mates in two moves by 20. ... e2+ 21. Ke1 Bd2 mate.) 20. ... B×h3 21. Be5 Bg4+ 22. Kc1 (or 22. Ke1, 22. ... Nf3+ etc.) 22. ... Ne2+ 23. Kb1. **18. B×e2 Ne4! 19. Qg2?** Surprisingly, White can defend very well after 19. Qe5! Nf2+ 20. Ke1 N×c2+ 21. K×f2 Qh4+ 22. Kg2 Ne3+ 23. Kg1 Rg8+ 24. Qg3 R×g3+ 25. h×g3 Qd4 26. R×h6 Nc2+ 27. Kg2 N×a1 28. Bb5+. **19. ... N×e2** 19. ... Ke7! was stronger. **20. Q×e2 Qd5+ 21. Ke1 Nd2 22. Qd3 N×f3+ 23. Kf2 Nd4??** Pollock had now to accept the following endgame as his best chance: 23. ... Q×d3 24. c×d3 b5 25. K×f3 Bb7+ 26. Kg4 B×h1 27. R×h1 R×a8 28. Bg3. **24. Qh3+?** 24. Rad1 or 24. Rhd1 would have created insolvable problems for Black. **24. ... Kc6** 24. ... Qf5+! would have kept Black in the game. Steinitz: "Not much better was 24. ... f5 25. Rad1 Qe4 26. Qd3 and if 26. ... Qh4+, the bishop interposes. A piece is therefore lost anyhow." **25. Q×h6+ Be6 26. Qe3 R×a8 27. Qc3+ Kd7?** This loses but 27. ... Kb5 28. a4+ Ka6 29. Qd3+ Qc4 30. Q×c4+ B×c4 was pretty hopeless as well. **28. Rad1** Steinitz: "The White allies now score a victory, which is fully deserved by clever play after their opponent allowed them an escape on the 17th move." **28. ... Qf5+ 29. Kg1 h5** (Was 29. Kg1 actually played, and Pollock, as well as Steinitz, miss the conclusive 29. ... Qg4+, or was the given move a transcription error? 29. Ke3 is more likely.) **30. Q×d4+ 1–0** [*ICM*, December 1886, pages 379–380]

2ND ICA CONGRESS (BELFAST, SEPTEMBER 1886)

103. Pollock–E. Harvey [C14]
2nd ICA Congress, Belfast, Round 1, 21 September 1886

1. e4 e6 2. d4 d5 3. Nc3 Nf6 4. Bg5 Be7 5. B×f6 B×f6 6. e5 Be7 7. Qg4 g6 8. 0-0-0 c5 9. Bb5+ Another choice was 9. d×c5 B×c5 10. f4 0-0 11. h4 h5 12. Qg3 Nc6 13. f5!? 9. ... Bd7 10. B×d7+ N×d7 11. Nf3 Qb6 12. Rhe1 c4 12. ... Rc8 was a better idea. 13. Qf4 h6 14. h4 a5 15. a4 Qb4 16. Re3 Rc8 17. Kd2!? Nb6 18. Ra1 Rh7 19. Ke1 19. Kc1 Bd8 20. Ra3 was another defensive idea. 19. ... g5 Best was 19. ... Q×b2! 20. Ra2 Qc1+ 21. Ke2 Bb4 and Black has a clear advantage. 20. Qg3 Kd7 21. h5 Re8 22. Nd2 Na8 23. b3 c×b3 24. N×b3 Qb6 25. Rb1 Bb4 26. Nc5+

Kc6? 26. ... Ke7 was safer. **27. Kf1 Nc7 28. Na2 Na6** (see diagram)

After
28. ... Nc7–a6

29. Rc3! N×c5 30. R×c5+ 30. N×b4+! a×b4 31. R×c5+ Kd7 32. Rb5 was more precise. **30. ... Kd7** Black missed 30. ... B×c5 31. R×b6+ B×b6, but even then White takes over easily with 32. Qd3 Rhh8 33. c4! **31. c3 Qa6+?** But now 31. ... B×c5 was imperative: 32. R×b6 B×b6 33. Qd3 Rhh8 34. c4 d×c4 35. Q×c4 Rc8 and Black has at least equality here. **32. Rb5 Qc6 33. Qd3 Qc4 34. Q×c4 d×c4 35. c×b4 a×b4 36. R1×b4 Kc6 37. R×b7 Kd5 38. Rd7+ Kc6 39. Rbb7 Rd8 40. Nb4 mate 1–0** [*American Chess Review*, December 1886, pages 85–86].

104. Pollock–J.H. Blackburne [C51]
2nd ICA Congress, Belfast, Round 2, 22, 23 & 28 September 1886

Belfast News-Letter (September 23): "The great event of the day was the contest between Messrs. Blackburne and Pollock. Mr. Pollock opened offering the Evans Gambit, which was declined. The game was very closely contested for 32 moves, when, at eleven o'clock, it had to be adjourned, and will, we understand, be resumed during the morning sitting today. At the time of adjournment Mr. Pollock had won a pawn. A large number of spectators followed the game throughout its various stages." The same source recorded the following on September 24: "Blackburne and Pollock resumed their adjourned game shortly after two PM [on September 23]. After fifteen moves were played in an hour and three-quarters, when a second adjournment took place." The *Belfast News-Letter* of September 29 confirmed that the game was finished only on September 28: "In the morning Blackburne and Pollock resumed their game, adjourned for the second time at the forty-fifth move. This game was, perhaps, virtually over at the termination of the second sitting, during which queens had been exchanged, Mr. Blackburne's knight being imprisoned by his adversary's pawns at a4, and Mr. Pollock being a pawn ahead. It was finally decided at the fifty-sixth move. Pollock won by steady play in spite of his adversary's stubborn defence up to the last possible moment." **1. e4 e5 2. Nf3 Nc6 3. Bc4 Bc5 4. b4 Bb6 5. b5 Na5 6. Be2 Nf6** 6. ... d5!? Was an excellent retort at this point. **7. d3 d6 8. Bg5 h6 9. Bh4 Be6 10. Nc3 Qe7 11. Na4 Rd8 12. N×b6 a×b6 13. c4! g5 14. Bg3 Nd7 15. h4 g4 16. Nd2 h5 17. Qc2 Rg8 18. Nf1 Nf8 19. f3 g×f3 20. B×f3** (see diagram)

After
20. Be2×f3

20. ... Bg4?! 20. ... Kd7!? 21. Rd1 Kc8 was a better idea than the text even if Black still has problems with the knight on a5. **21. B×g4 R×g4 22. Ne3! Rg6** 22. ... R×g3 23. Nf5 Qf6 24. N×g3 Qg6 25. Nf5 Ne6 26. Ne3 Nd4 27. Qf2 seems to hold insufficient compensation. **23. Nd5 Qd7 24. Qf2 Nh7 25. 0–0 f6 26. Kh2! Kf7 27. Qf3 Kg7 28. Q×h5 Rh8 29. Ne3 Nf8 30. Nf5+ Kg8 31. Qf3 Ne6 32. Bf2 Qh7 33. g3** 33. g4 Ng5 34. Qe2 Kf8 35. h5 was more precise. **33. ... Kf7 34. Be3 Ke8 35. Kg2 Rhg8 36. Kf2 Ng7 37. h5 N×f5 38. Q×f5 Rg7 39. Q×h7 R×h7 40. Rh1 Kf7 41. Kf3 Ra8 42. Rag1 Kf8 43. Kg4 Rg7+ 44. Kf5 Kf7 45. h6 Rh7 46. g4 Rg8 47. g5! Rg6 48. g×f6 R×f6+ 49. Kg5 Ke7 50. Kh5 Rf3 51. Bg5+ Ke8 52. Rf1 Rff7 53. Kg4 Rd7 54. Rf6 d5 55. Re6+ Kf8 56. Rf1+ 1–0** [Chess-Monthly, November 1886, pages 78–79; BCM, November 1886, pages 428–430; PM, pages 87–88 (the latter source had 27. ... Rh8 and 28. ... Kg7 instead of the move order above)]

105. A. Burn–Pollock [A84]
2nd ICA Congress, Belfast, Round 3, 23 September 1886

1. Nf3 f5 Steinitz: "We do not like this, even for the first player, much less for the second." **2. e3 e6 3. d4 Nf6 4. c4 Bb4+** Pollock: "This is not a useless check, as Black thereby gains a little time." **5. Nbd2** Pollock: "If instead, 5. Bd2, Black could

exchange bishops without disadvantage. But if 5. Nc3, he would gain a theoretical 'pull' by 5. ... B×c3, subsequently fixing the double pawns by c7–c5." **5. ... 0–0 6. Be2 b6 7. 0–0 Bb7 8. Qc2 Nc6 9. Rd1 Qe8 10. Nf1 Ne4 11. Ne1** Steinitz: "White has formed his plan of development after the pattern of our defense of the Queen's Gambit Declined in the late championship match with the principal object of remaining passive on the kingside and preparing active operations in the centre and on the other wing. He had an excellent opportunity of improving his game consistent with his design by 11. a3, which move, we may remark in general, is no loss of time and often very advantageous when an adverse piece is thereby driven back, and when, as is here the case, it can be followed up by b4, forming a battle-order of pawns, which hampers the adverse pieces on the queenside." Too passive. White had to play active with 11. c5!? g5 12. a3 g4 13. N3d2. **11. ... Qg6 12. Nd3** (see diagram)

After
12. Ne1–d3

Pollock: "Leaving open an opportunity for a brilliant sacrifice, of which Black is not slow to avail himself. A few days later, in the Handicap Tournament of the same meeting, the eleven first moves between the same players were precisely the same, Mr. Burn again playing White. The game then switched off as follows: 12. f3 Ng5 13. Kh1 Bd6 14. a3 h5 15. b4 h4 16. c5 Be7 17. Bb2 h3 18. g3 Nd8 19. Nd2 Ndf7 20. Nd3 Nh6 21. Rf1 f4? Mr. Burn won the game." **12. ... N×f2!** Steinitz: "Somewhat speculative, not to say hazardous." **13. K×f2** Pollock: "If 13. N×f2 N×d4 equally; or if 13. Nf4 Nh3+ 14. N×h3 (14. Kh1 N×f4 etc.) 14. ... N×d4 15. Nf4 N×c2 16. N×g6 h×g6 17. Rb1 Bc5 and wins. Again, 13. d5 N×d3 (13. ... Nh3+ draws.) 14. d×c6 Ne1! (this beautiful move was overlooked by critics.) 15. R×e1 B×c6 and wins." **13. ... N×d4 14. N×b4** Pollock: "The sacrifice of the queen was by far the best resource, and indeed appears at first sight almost a sufficient one." **14. ... N×c2 15. N×c2 f4!** Steinitz: "This excellent move, which is by far superior to 15. Q×g2+, practically decides the game." **16. Ne1 f×e3+ 17. Kg1** *(see diagram)*

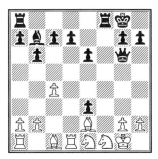

After
17. Kf2–g1

Pollock: "White overlooked his opponent's continuation, which is really as pretty as the previous play. However, if 17. K×e3 Qe4+ 18. Kd2 Rf2 19. Ng3 Qd4+ 20. Nd3 R×g2, and should win easily." **17. ... Rf2! 18. Ng3 R×e2!** Steinitz: "Another fine stroke. Mr. Pollock's play from the 15th move up to the end hardly requires any amendment." **19. N×e2 Qg4 20. Nc3 e2 21. Rd2 B×g2 22. N×e2 Bc6+** Pollock: "As the sequel shows, 22. ... Bb7+ would have been rather better." **23. Ng3 h5 24. Nd3 h4 25. Ne5 Qh3 26. N×c6 h×g3 27. Ne7+ Kf7 28. Rg2 g×h2+ 29. Kh1 K×e7 30. R×g7+ Kf6 31. Rg2 Qf3! 32. K×h2 Rh8+ 33. Kg1 Qd1+ 34. Kf2 Qd4+ 35. Be3 Q×b2+ 0–1** [*Belfast News-Letter*, October 1, 1886; *Chess-Monthly*, September 1886, pages 24–25; *The Field*, October 2, 1886; *Nottinghamshire Guardian*, October 15, 1886; *ICM*, November 1886, pages 339–340; *Chess Player's Chronicle*, October 20, 1886; *BCM*, November 1886, pages 425–427; *PM*, pages 86–87]

106. R.W. Barnett–Pollock [C29]
2nd ICA Congress, Belfast, Round 8,
29 & 30 September 1886

1. e4 e5 2. Nc3 Nf6 3. f4 d5 4. d3 Bb4 5. f×e5 d4 5. ... N×e4 6. d×e4 Qh4+ 7. Ke2 B×c3 8. b×c3 Bg4+ 9. Nf3 d×e4 10. Qd4 Bh5 leads to a chaotic position. **6. e×f6 d×c3 7. b3** 7. b×c3!? could have been met by 7. ... B×c3+ (7. ... Q×f6!?) 8. Bd2 Q×f6 (8. ... B×a1 9. Q×a1 Q×f6 10. Bc3 leaves White with clear compensation.) 9. Rb1 Nc6. **7. ... g×f6 8. Qh5 Nc6 9. Nf3 Be6 10. Be3 a5** 10. ... Qe7 11. d4 0–0–0! Was a better choice. **11. a4** White missed grabbing the initiative with 11. d4! **11. ... Qd7 12. h3 Rg8 13. Q×h7 0–0–0 14. Qh4 Bd6!** Setting up a trap for the White queen. **15. 0–0–0?** *(see diagram)*

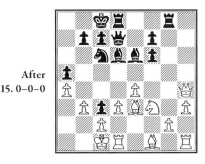

After
15. 0–0–0

15. g4 runs into the forceful 15. ... f5! 16. e×f5 Bd5. **15. ... Qe7** It's somewhat curious Pollock missed the following king assault: 15. ... Ba3+ 16. Kb1 Nb4! 17. Be2 Q×a4. **16. Re1 Bg3 17. Qh5 B×e1** 17. ... Qa3+ 18. Kd1 B×b3 19. Ke2 B×c2 was possible too. **18. N×e1 Qa3+ 19. Kd1 Rh8** 19. ... B×b3 was working again: 20. c×b3 Q×b3+ 21. Ke2 Qb2+ 22. Kf3 Ne5+ 23. Kf4 c2. **20. Qf3 Ne5 21. Q×f6 Qd6** Black slightly misplayed matters here. 21. ... Qa1+! 22. Bc1 (22. Ke2 Ng4) 22. ... Nc6 kept an edge. **22. Qf4 Rdf8 23. d4 Rd8?** 23. ... Ng4! was mandatory. **24. Ke2 Nc6? 25. Q×d6 R×d6 26. d5 Bg4+ 27. h×g4?** Unnecessary. 27. Kd3! was recommended: 27. ... Nb4+ 28. K×c3 Bf5 29. Bd3! (29. e×f5 N×d5+ 30. Kd2 N×e3+ 31. K×e3 Re8+ 32. Kf3 R×e1 33. h4 was unclear.) **27. ... R×h1 28. d×c6 Rd2+! 29. B×d2 c×d2 30. c×b7+ K×b7 31. K×d2 R×f1 32. Nd3 Rg1 33. Nf4 Rf1** Here, according to C.E. Ranken's notes in the December 1886 *BCM*, Barnett offered a draw which Pollock turned down. **34. Ke3 Rc1 35. Kd4 R×c2 36. Ke5 Rc3 37. Kf6 R×b3 38. e5 Rg3 39. g5 c5?!** This is risky. 39. ... Rg4! 40. Nd3 Rg3 41. e6 f×e6 42. Ne5 R×g2 43. g6 Kb6 44. g7 R×g7 45. K×g7 Kc5 would have secured the draw. **40. K×f7?** White kept serious winning chances with 40. g6 f×g6 41. e6 Re3 42. e7 Kc6 43. Kf7 Kd7 44. Nd5 Re2 45. Nf6+ Kc6 46. e8Q+ R×e8 47. K×e8 c4 48. Ne4 Kd5 49. Nc3+ Kd4 50. Na2 g5 51. Kf7 g4 52. Kf6 Kd3 53. g3 Kc2 54. Ke5 Kd3 55. Kf4. **40. ... R×g5 41. Kf6 Rg4 42. Kf5 Rg8 43. e6 Kc7 44. e7 Kd7 45. Kf6 Rg4 46. g3 R×g3 47. Kf7 Re3 48. Nd5 R×e7+ 49. N×e7 c4 50. Nd5 Kd6 51. Nc3 Kc5 52. Ke6 Kb4 53. Nb1 K×a4 54. Kd5 Kb4 55. Kd4 a4 56. Ke3??** This blunder loses a hard-fought game. 56. Nc3 a3 57. Na2+ Kb3 58. Nc3 would have drawn. **56. ... a3 57. N×a3 K×a3 58. Kd2 Kb2 0–1** [*BCM*, December 1886, pages 454–455; *Chess Player's Chronicle*, December 15, 1886]

107. W.C. Palmer–Pollock
2nd ICA Congress
(Handicap Tournament), Belfast, September 1886
Remove f7 pawn

1. e4 and d4 d6 2. Bd3 Nc6 3. c3 e5 4. f4?! e×d4 5. Nf3 d×c3 6. Ng5?! Qf6 7. N×c3 Nce7 8. 0–0 8. Nb5! would have been very unpleasant. **8. ... Nh6 9. Qc2 Bd7 10. a4 g6 11. Bd2 Bg7 12. Nf3 0–0 13. e5?!** 13. Qb3+ Nf7 14. Q×b7 Rfc8 15. Bc4 was better. **13. ... d×e5 14. N×e5 Qb6+ 15. Kh1 Be6 16. Rae1 Nhf5 17. Nb5 c6 18. Nc4 Qd8 19. Nbd6 Nd4 20. Qb1 Qd7 21. Bc3 b5! 22. a×b5 c×b5 23. B×d4 B×d4 24. N×b5 Bg7** 24. ... Q×b5 25. R×e6 Nf5 26. Qd1 Qc5 was fine too. **25. Ne5 Qb7 26. Nd6 Qb4** *(see diagram)*

After
26. ... Qb7–b4

27. f5!? Q×d6 28. f×e6? 28. N×g6! N×g6 (28. ... h×g6 29. R×e6 Qc7 30. f6 B×f6 31. Re×f6 R×f6 32. R×f6 Rf8 33. Re6 is clearly better for White.) 29. R×e6 Qd4 30. f×g6 Q×b2 31. R×f8+ R×f8 32. g×h7+ Kh8 33. Q×b2 B×b2 34. g4 and White has winning chances. **28. ... B×e5 29. Bc4 Kg7** 29. ... R×f1+ 30. R×f1 Qd4 31. Qd3 Q×d3 32. B×d3 Rf8 was a good alternative. **30. Rf7+ R×f7 31. e×f7 Bf6 32. Re6 Qd4 33. Qf1 Rd8 34. Re1 Q×b2 35. h4 Nf5 36. Re8 Ng3+ 37. Kh2 N×f1+ 38. Kh3 Qc3+ 0–1** [*Chess Player's Chronicle*, April 6, 1887]

108. R.W. Barnett–Pollock
2nd ICA Congress
(Handicap Tournament), Belfast, September 1886
Remove f7 pawn

1. e4 and d4 d6 2. f4 e6 3. c4 c5 4. Be3 c×d4 5. B×d4 e5 6. Be3 Nc6 7. Nf3 Nf6 8. Nc3 Ng4 9. Qd2 Be7 10. f5 N×e3 11. Q×e3 0–0 12. g4 Qa5 13. h4 Bd7 14. g5 14. 0–0–0! was even

stronger as the White king is evacuated from the center. **14. ... Rac8 15. Rh2** *(see diagram)*

After
15. Rh1–h2

15. ... a6?! 15. ... d5!? would have been immensely entertaining:16. c×d5 (16. e×d5? Bc5 17. Qd2 Nd4 18. Be2 Nb3) 16. ... Bc5 17. Qd3 Nd4 18. Rd2 Rfe8 (18. ... Nb3? 19. N×e5 N×d2 20. K×d2 Be8 21. Nc4 is good for White.) 19. Rc1 Qb6 with complicated play. **16. Rg2** Once again, 16. 0–0–0 was needed. **16. ... Kh8** The last opportunity for 16. ... d5! **17. h5 Nb4 18. Nh4 d5?** Now the timing is just poor. 18. ... Kg8 19. Qg3 Qd8 20. 0–0–0 gives White a winning edge. **19. Ng6+! Kg8 20. N×e7+ Kf7 21. N×c8 d4 22. g6+ h×g6 23. h×g6+ Ke8 24. Nd6+ Ke7 25. N×b7 Qc7 26. Qg5+ Rf6 27. Nd5+ N×d5 28. c×d5 Q×b7 29. 0–0–0 Ba4 30. Rdd2 Kd7 31. Q×f6** An elegant solution. **31. ... g×f6 32. g7 Qc8+ 33. Kb1 Qg8 34. B×a6 Ke7 35. Rd3 Qh7 36. g8Q Qh1+ 37. Rg1 Q×e4 38. Rg7+ Kd6 39. Qe6+ Kc5 40. Rc7+ Kb4 41. Qb6+ Bb5 42. Q×b5 mate 1–0** [*BCM*, December 1886, pages 458–459].

109. J.D. Chambers–Pollock
2nd ICA Congress
(Handicap Tournament), Belfast, September 1886
Remove f7 pawn

1. e4 and d4 d6 2. Bd3 Nc6 3. c3 e5 4. d5 Nce7 5. Nf3 Nf6 6. Ng5 Ng6 7. Bb5+ Ke7 8. Qe2 h6 9. Nf3 Kf7 10. 0–0 Be7 11. h3 Rf8 12. Nh2 Kg8 13. f4?! Better was 13. Be3 a6 14. Bd3 Nh7 15. Nd2 Bg5 16. Nc4 with balanced play. **13. ... e×f4 14. B×f4 Bd7** 14. ... c6! was very strong here. **15. B×d7 Q×d7 16. Bd2 Rae8 17. Na3 Bd8!? 18. Qd3** *(see diagram)*

18. ... R×e4? A miscalculation. 18. ... Ne5 19. Qc2 c6 20. Rae1 Bb6+ was the obvious way forward. **19. R×f6! Rfe8 20. R×g6 Qf5 21. Qg3 Bh4 22. R×g7+ Kh8 23. Rf1** Simplest is 23. Qf3! Q×f3 24. g×f3 Bf2+ 25. Kh1. **23. ... B×g3**

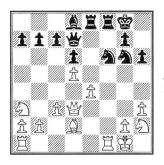

After
18. Qe2–d3

24. R×g3?? 24. R×f5 K×g7 25. Nf1 Be1 26. Nb5 maintained a clear edge for White. **24. ... Q×d5 25. B×h6 Kh7 26. Bf8** 26. Bg5!? Re1 27. Nc2 R×f1+ 28. N×f1 was playable. **26. ... Re1 27. Rgf3 R8e2! 28. Ng4?** and Black mates in four. 28. R×e1! R×e1+ 29. Nf1 Re2 30. Ne3 Q×a2 would have led to an unclear position. **0–1** [*Chess Player's Chronicle*, May 4, 1887; *New York Clipper*, July 2, 1887]

110. S.J. Magowan–Pollock
2nd ICA Congress
(Handicap Tournament), Belfast,
September 1886
Remove Nb8

1. d4 e6 2. e4 b6 3. Nf3 Bb7 4. Bd3 h6 5. Nc3 Ne7 6. Be3 a6 7. 0–0 g5 8. Ne5 d6 9. N×f7! K×f7 10. Qh5+ Kg7 11. f4! Qe8 12. Qg4 Bc8 13. f5 13. f×g5! was much stronger: 13. ... h5 14. Qf3 Kg8 15. e5 d5 16. g6 **13. ... e×f5 14. e×f5 N×f5 15. B×f5 Q×e3+ 16. Kh1 h5! 17. Qd1 Bb7** The objectively better 17. ... B×f5 18. R×f5 Be7 19. Nd5 Qe4 20. Qf3 was apparently not to Pollock's taste. **18. d5 Re8 19. Be6** *(see diagram)*

After
19. Bf5–e6

19. ... R×e6!? 20. d×e6 Q×e6 21. Qd4+ Qe5 22. Qc4? 22. Qd3! Qe6 23. Rae1 Qg6 24. Qd4+ was correct. The text move allowed Black serious counterplay. **22. ... d5! 23. Qd3 Bd6 24. Qg3** 24. Qh3 would have been answered with 24. ... Bc8! **24. ... Q×g3 25. h×g3 h4! 26. g4 h3?** Black misses 26. ... d4! Which would have won nicely.

27. Rae1? 27. Rf5! was White's only chance to complicate matters: 27. ... d4 28. R×g5+ Kf6 29. Rf5+ Kg6 30. Nd5 h×g2+ 31. K×g2 Rh2+ 32. Kf3 R×c2 33. b3 and things are not clear at all. **27. ... d4 28. Ne4 Re8 29. N×d6 h×g2+ 30. Kg1 g×f1Q+ 0–1** [*Morning Post*, January 3, 1887]

111. W.M. Nicholls–Pollock
2nd ICA Congress
(Handicap Tournament), Belfast,
September 1886
Remove Nb8

1. e4 e5 2. Nf3 d6 3. d4 f6 4. d×e5 f×e5 5. Bg5 Nf6 6. B×f6 Q×f6 7. Nc3 c6 8. Qd2 Be6 9. 0–0–0 Be7 10. h4 h6 11. Be2 b5 12. a3 a5 13. Nh2 b4 14. Nb1 b×a3 15. N×a3 0–0 16. f3 d5 17. Nb1 d4 18. g3 a4 19. Ng4 Qf7 20. N×e5 *(see diagram)*

After
20. Ng4×e5

20. ... a3 21. N×a3? 21. N×f7 a2 22. N×h6+ g×h6 23. Q×h6 Rf6 24. Qg5+ Kf7 25. Bd3 a1Q must have scared White, but it was the right choice: 26. e5! Ra2 27. Qh5+ Kf8 28. e×f6 Q×b2+ 29. Kd2 B×f6 30. Qh6+ Kf7 31. Rhe1 and Black is just lost. **21. ... R×a3! 22. Q×d4 Qf6 23. b3** 23. b×a3 B×a3+ 24. Kd2 Rd8 25. Q×d8+ Q×d8+ 26. Nd3 Bc4 leaves Black with sufficient play as well. **23. ... Ra2 24. Nc4?** 24. Bc4! is not an easy move to play: 24. ... Rd8 25. Qc3 Ba3+ 26. Kb1 Rb2+ 27. Ka1 Ra8 28. B×e6+ Q×e6 and, despite White's weak king position, he remains better with 29. f4 Bb4+ 30. K×b2 B×c3+ 31. K×c3 c5 32. Ra1 Re8 33. Rhd1. **24. ... Ra1+ 25. Kb2 Q×d4+ 26. R×d4 R×h1 0–1** [*Montreal Gazette*, November 10, 1886]

112. A. Burn–Pollock [A84]
2nd ICA Congress
(Handicap Tournament), Belfast,
September 1886

1. Nf3 f5 2. e3 Nf6 3. d4 e6 4. c4 Bb4+

5. Nbd2 0–0 6. Be2 b6 7. 0–0 Bb7 8. Qc2 Nc6 9. Rd1 Qe8 10. Nf1 Ne4 11. Ne1 Qg6 12. f3 Ng5 13. Kh1 Bd6 14. a3 h5 15. b4 h4 16. c5 Be7 17. Bb2 (see diagram)

After
17. Bc1–b2

17. ... h3! 18. g3 Nd8 An interesting alternative was 18. ... Bf6 19. b5 Ne7 20. Nd2 Qh5. **19. Nd2 Ndf7 20. Nd3 Nh6?!** 20. ... Qh6!? 21. Nf4 Nh7 22. e4 g5 23. Nd3 Nf6 was a more prescient way to keep up the pressure. **21. Rf1** (see diagram)

After
21. Rd1–f1

21. ... f4!? 22. e×f4 Nh7? Losing the thread. 22. ... Ngf7 23. Kg1 Bh4 24. g4 b5 maintained the tension. **23. Ne4 d5 24. Nef2** 24. Ne5 Qh5 25. Nf2 Nf7 26. c6 was even stronger than the text. **24. ... Nf5 25. Qd2** More precise was 25. c×b6 c×b6 26. Qc7 Rab8 27. Ne5 Qe8 28. Qd7. **25. ... Nf6 26. N×h3 Qh6 27. Kg2 Ne4!?** A last attempt to muddy the waters. **28. Qc1!** 28. f×e4?! d×e4 29. Kg1 e×d3 30. Bg4 Rad8 31. Rfe1 Bf6 32. Q×d3 N×d4 is unclear. **28. ... g5 29. f×e4 d×e4 30. Ne5 Bd5 31. f×g5 e3+ 32. Bf3 B×g5 33. B×d5 e×d5 34. N×g5 Q×g5 35. Rf4 Kh7 36. Qc2 Kh6 37. Raf1 e2 38. Q×e2 Rae8 39. R×f5 R×f5 40. Bc1 1–0** [*BCM*, November 1886, pages 427–428; *Chess-Monthly*, November 1886, pages 80–81]

Various Games (1886)

113. F.N. Braund–Pollock [C24]
London, Simpson's Divan,
25 October 1886

1. e4 e5 2. Nf3 Nc6 3. Bc4 Nf6 4. d3 d5!? Pollock's approach is very modern. **5. e×d5 N×d5 6. 0–0 Be7 7. Re1 f6** 7. ... 0–0!? Is considered an interesting alternative today. **8. h3 Bf5 9. Nc3 Nb6 10. Bb3 Nd4?** 10. ... Qd7 11. a4 Na5 12. Ba2 0–0–0 was much better than the text error. **11. N×d4 Q×d4 12. Be3** 12. Qf3! Qd7 13. a4 c6 14. a5 Nc8 15. a6 Nd6 16. a×b7 Q×b7 17. Nd5! would have weakened Black significantly. **12. ... Qd7 13. Qf3 0–0–0 14. a4 g5** (see diagram)

After
14. ... g7–g5

15. B×b6? 15. a5 g4 (15. ... Na8 16. a6! c5 17. Ba4 Qc7 18. a×b7+ Q×b7 19. Bc6) 16. a×b6! was an easy win. **15. ... a×b6** Black had to play 15. ... g4! 16. h×g4 B×g4 17. Qe3 c×b6! To stay in the game. **16. Nd5** 16. a5! b5 17. Nd5 Kb8 18. a6 would have given White a devastating attack. **16. ... Rde8 17. a5 b5 18. a6 b×a6 19. R×a6** A pretty finish: 19. N×e7+ Q×e7 20. Q×f5+ Kb7 21. Qe4+ c6 22. R×a6! K×a6 23. Q×c6+ Ka5 24. Ra1+ Kb4 25. Qc3 mate. **19. ... e4 20. d×e4 Bd8 21. Rea1 B×e4 22. Ra8+ Kb7 23. R1a7+ Kc6 24. Qc3+** 24. Ra6+ Kb7 25. Qe3 c5 26. Q×c5 would have mated more quickly. **24. ... Kd6 25. Ra6+ c6 26. R×d8 R×d8 27. Q×f6+ Kc5 28. Qc3+ Kd6 29. Nf6 Qf5 30. Qd4+ Kc7 31. Ra7+ Kc8 32. Ra8+ Kc7 33. Qa7+ Kd6 34. Qd4+ Bd5 35. N×d5 c×d5 36. Qb6+ Ke7 37. Qc5+?** 37. Qc7+ Rd7 38. Qc5+ Kf6 39. Qd4+ Ke6 40. R×h8 was a clean way to wrap it up. **37. ... Kf7 38. Ra7+ Rd7 39. B×d5+ Kf6 40. Ra6+ Ke5 41. Bc6+ 1–0** [*Chess-Monthly*, January 1887, pages 146–147]

114. Pollock–F.N. Braund [C59]
London, Simpson's Divan,
25 November 1886

1. e4 e5 2. Nf3 Nc6 3. Bc4 Nf6 4. Ng5 d5 5. e×d5 Na5 6. Bb5+ c6 7. d×c6 b×c6 8. Be2 h6 9. Nf3 e4 10. Ne5 Qd4 11. Ng4?! 11. f4 is a superior choice. **11. ... B×g4 12. B×g4** (see diagram)

12. ... e3! 13. Bf3 e×f2+ 14. Kf1 0–0–0 15. c3 Qd3+ 16. Qe2 Q×e2+ 17. K×e2 c5 18. K×f2

After
12. Be2×g4

Bd6 19. Re1 Nc4 20. d4! Rhe8 21. R×e8 R×e8 22. b3 Nb6 23. Be3 Preferable was 23. Ba3! B×h2 24. B×c5 (24. g3!? c×d4 25. c×d4 Ne4+ 26. B×e4 R×e4 27. Nd2 R×d4 28. Nf3 B×g3+ 29. K×g3) 24. ... Bb8 25. c4. 23. ... Nbd5 24. Bd2 Nf4 Black should have equalized quickly with 24. ... c×d4 25. c×d4 Ne4+ 26. B×e4 R×e4 27. Nc3 R×d4 28. Be3 N×e3 29. K×e3 Bc5 30. Ke2 f5. 25. Na3 Nd3+ 26. Kf1 c×d4 27. Nb5 Bc5? White keeps better options after 27. ... B×h2 as well, but it had to be tried: 28. N×a7+ Kc7 29. Nb5+ Kb6 30. N×d4 Ne4 31. B×e4 R×e4 32. Rd1 Bf4 33. B×f4 N×f4 34. c4. 28. c×d4 a6 29. d×c5 a×b5 30. Bc6 Re5 31. B×b5 N×c5 32. Rc1 Kd8 33. Ba5+ Ke7 34. Bb4 Nfe4 35. Bd3 Kf6 36. B×e4 N×e4 37. Bc3 N×c3 38. R×c3 Ra5 39. Rc2 Ke6 40. a4 f5 41. Ke2 Kd7 42. Ra2 Ra6 43. b4 g5 44. b5 1–0 [*Chess-Monthly*, January 1887, pages 148–149]

115. Pollock–F.N. Braund [C45]
London, Simpson's Divan,
25 November 1886

1. e4 e5 2. Nf3 Nc6 3. d4 e×d4 4. N×d4 Bc5 5. Be3 Qf6 6. c3 Nge7 7. Nc2 Bb6 8. Nba3 Nd8 9. Nb5 Ne6 10. Bc4 0–0 11. B×b6 a×b6 12. Ne3 Qg6 13. Qc2 13. B×e6 accomplishes little: 13. ... d×e6 14. N×c7 Ra5 15. Qd3 Rc5 16. Nb5 Nd5! 13. ... d6 14. 0–0 Kh8 (*see diagram*) 14. ... Bd7 15. a4 Bc6 was much better.

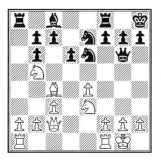

After
14. ... Kg8–h8

15. B×e6 f×e6 This leaves Black without much hope. 15. ... B×e6 16. N×c7 Ra5 had to be tried. 16. N×c7 Ra5 17. b4 Re5 18. f3 d5 19. Ng4 Rg5 20. Qd2 Bd7 21. Rae1 Rc8 22. Qf4 e5 23. N×e5 R×e5 24. Q×e5 Nc6 25. Qf4 d4 26. c×d4 N×b4 27. Rd1 h5 28. a3 Na6 29. N×a6 b×a6 30. d5 Ba4 31. Rc1 Rd8 32. e5 1–0 [*Chess-Monthly*, January 1887, pages 146–147]

116. Pollock–A. Burn [C47]
Offhand Game, London,
Simpson's Divan, November 1886

1. e4 e5 2. Nc3 Nf6 3. Nf3 Nc6 4. d4 e×d4 5. N×d4 Bb4 6. Nf5?! An optimistic choice, instead of the more conservative 6. N×c6. 6. ... 0–0 7. Bg5 B×c3+? 7. ... d5! would have highlighted White's problems. 8. b×c3 h6 (*see diagram*)

After
8. ... h7–h6

9. h4 Pollock: "The attack must be kept up at any cost. The game now becomes extremely animated." 9. ... d5! 10. Ng3 h×g5 11. h×g5 Ng4 12. Bd3 d×e4 13. N×e4 Re8 14. Qe2 Nce5 15. 0–0–0 N×d3+ 16. R×d3 Qe7 17. Rdh3 Nh6 18. Re3! Pollock: "The skilful combination of White's 17th and 18th moves wins back the knight, but against the best play it ought not to do more." 18. Nf6+ doesn't quite work: 18. ... g×f6 19. Q×e7 R×e7 20. R×h6 f×g5 21. g4 Re2 22. Rh8+ Kg7 23. R1h7+ Kf6 24. Rf8 B×g4 25. R×a8 Bf5; The same can be said of 18. R×h6 g×h6 19. Nf6+ Kf8 20. Q×e7+ R×e7 21. g×h6 Bf5. 18. ... Qa3+ 19. Kb1? 19. Kd2 Rd8+ 20. Rd3 Bg4 21. f3 R×d3+ 22. Q×d3 Qe7 23. Qe2 Rd8+ 24. Ke1 was unclear. 19. ... Bg4? Pollock was correct in pointing out that Black's best defense was 19. ... Be6 20. c4 Qb4+ 21. Kc1 Q×c4 22. Q×c4 B×c4 23. g×h6 f5 24. Ng3 R×e3 25. f×e3 g6. 20. Nf6+! g×f6 21. R×e8+ Kh7 and White mates in four. 1–0 [*Horncastle News*, April 2, 1887]

117. Pollock & Rynd–A. Burn [C33]
Consultation Game London,
December 1886

  **1. e4 e5 2. f4 e×f4 3. Bc4 d5 4. B×d5 Nf6
5. Nc3 Bb4 6. Nf3 B×c3 7. d×c3 c6 8. Bb3
Q×d1+ 9. K×d1 0-0 10. e5** 10. B×f4 N×e4
11. Ke2 Re8 12. Ne5 Be6 did not give White any
advantage either. **10. ... Nh5 11. Ke2 h6 12. Kf2
g5 13. g3! g4 14. Nh4 f×g3+ 15. h×g3 Re8
16. Ng6!?** A seemingly fine artifice, but 16. B×h6
R×e5 17. Rae1 R×e1 18. R×e1 was even stronger.
16. ... Bf5 17. R×h5 17. Nh8!? is the engines'
amusing recommendation: 17. ... K×h8 18. B×f7
Re7 19. B×h5 Kg7 20. Bf4 Nd7 21. Rae1. **17. ...
B×g6 18. R×h6 Be4** (see diagram)

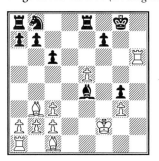

After
18. ... Bg6–e4

  19. Rh4 19. e6! f×e6 20. B×e6+ Kg7 21. B×g4
Rf8+ 22. Ke2 B×c2 23. Be3 would have favored
White; 19. Be3!? was equally strong. **19. ... Bf3
20. Bf4 Nd7 21. Re1 Nc5 22. Bg5 Kg7 23. Bf6+
Kg6 24. Bc4 b5 25. Bf1 Kf5 26. Bd3+ Ke6
27. Rh6 Kd5 28. Be7?** An hallucination. 28. Ke3
or 28. b3 would have continued to pose serious
problems for the Black king. **28. ... N×d3+
29. c×d3 R×e7 30. d4 Rd8 31. Ke3 a5 32. b3 Re6
33. Rh7 Re7 34. Rh4 Re6 35. Rh7 f5?** 35. ... f6!
was correct. **36. Rc1 Rg6 37. Re7! c5 38. c4+
b×c4 39. b×c4+ Kc6 40. d5+** (see diagram)

After
40. d4–d5+

  40. ... Kb6 A very risky choice. Black had to return the material to secure his king: 40. ... B×d5
41. c×d5+ (41. Rd1?! f4+ 42. g×f4 g3 43. c×d5+

R×d5 44. R×d5 K×d5 45. Rd7+ Kc6 46. Rd1 g2
47. Rg1 Kd5 48. Kf2 c4 49. Rd1+ Ke4 50. Kg1
K×f4 51. Rd4+ K×e5 52. R×c4) 41. ... R×d5
42. Kf4 Rh6 43. K×f5 Rh5+ 44. Kf6 Rd3.
41. Rb1+! Ka6 42. Rbb7?! Still playing for mate.
Instead, the advance of the central pawns should
have decided quickly: 42. e6! Be4 43. Rb2 a4
44. Kf4 Rgg8 45. Ke5 Rc8 46. d6 Bd3 47. Rc7.
42. ... Ra8 42. ... B×d5 was necessary to restore
the balance. **43. Rbc7! Kb6 44. Rb7+** 44. e6
would have forced an immediate resignation. **44. ...
Ka6 45. Rb5?** With 45. Red7 White's winning
chances are still significant. **45. ... B×d5! 0-1**
[*Horncastle News*, March 12, 1887]

118. Mr. R.–Pollock [C45]
Bath, 1886

  **1. e4 e5 2. Nf3 Nc6 3. d4 e×d4 4. N×d4 Bc5
5. Be3 Qf6 6. c3 Nge7 7. Nb5** Pollock: "Losing a
piece! Clearly a slip, but this is not a match game
and still retains its interest." **7. ... B×e3! 8. N×c7+?
Kd8 9. f×e3 K×c7 10. g3 h5 11. Na3 h4 12. Nb5+
Kd8 13. Qd6** Pollock: "A gallant effort to retrieve
his fortunes." **13. ... Qf3?** Pollock: "This is not a
good move." Unnecessary, indeed. Instead, 13. ...
Qe5! was best. **14. Qc7+ Ke8 15. Qf4! Q×f4** 15. ...
Q×h1 would have allowed White a draw with
16. Nd6+ Kd8 17. N×f7+ Ke8 18. Nd6+ Kd8
19. Nf7+ (19. 0-0-0?! is too risky because of 19. ...
Rh6 20. Nf7+ Ke8 21. N×h6 g×h6 22. g×h4 Qg1)
19. ... Ke8 20. Nd6+ etc. **16. e×f4 Kd8 17. Nd6
Rf8 18. Bc4** 18. 0-0-0! would have given White
clearer compensation. **18. ... Kc7** (see diagram)

After
18. ... Kd8–c7

  19. N×f7? Again, 19. 0-0-0 would have been
excellent. **19. ... b5** More exact was 19. ... Na5
20. Ne5 d6 21. b4 d×e5 22. b×a5 e×f4. **20. Bb3
Na5 21. Ng5 N×b3 22. a×b3 Bb7 23. Kf2 h×g3+
24. h×g3 Rh8 25. Rhb1** Pollock: "White has
fought pluckily after losing his knight. Still this is
a curious place for the rook." **25. ... d5! 26. e5
Rh2+ 27. Kg1 Rah8 28. Ne6+ Kb6 29. Nd4 g5**

Pollock: "It is now Black's turn for some elegant bit of chess." 29. ... R8h3! 30. Rf1 Nc6 was more forceful. **30. f5** The only fighting chance was 30. f×g5! R2h5 31. Rf1 R×g5 32. Rf6+ Nc6 33. Re1 R×g3+ 34. Kf2 Rg7 35. e6 N×d4 36. e7+ Kc7 37. e8Q R×e8 38. R×e8 N×b3. **30. ... N×f5!** Pollock: "This temporary sacrifice decides the game." **31. N×f5 d4 32. Nh4 Rc2 33. Rf1 g×h4 34. Rf6+ Bc6 35. c×d4 Kb7 36. Rd1 h3 37. R×c6 h2+ 38. Kh1 K×c6 0–1** [*Shoreditch Citizen*, August 11, 1888]

GAMES AGAINST BURN (EARLY 1887)[2]

119. Pollock–A. Burn [C45] London, Offhand Game London, January 1887

1. e4 e5 2. Nf3 Nc6 3. d4 e×d4 4. N×d4 g6 5. N×c6 Pollock: "The best duty for the knight, as the doubled pawns are troublesome to Black's game." **5. ... b×c6 6. Bc4 Bg7 7. Nc3 Ne7 8. Be3 0–0 9. Qd2 Re8 10. 0–0–0!** Pollock: "Quite sound. White now has a very fine game." **10. ... a5 11. h4 a4 12. h5 a3 13. h×g6** Always a touch-and-go tactician, Pollock had no patience for the more solid 13. Bd4! a×b2+ 14. K×b2 B×d4 15. Q×d4 Rb8+ 16. Ka1. **13. ... a×b2+ 14. Kb1 N×g6** Pollock: "On viewing the position after this race of rook pawns the Black king will be found to be the chief sufferer in position." **15. Bd4** Pollock: "Threatening, by the exchange of bishops, to make Black's position defenceless." **15. ... Ne5 16. Bb3 d6 17. f4 Ng4 18. B×g7 K×g7 19. f5!** 19. e5!? was the other critical choice. **19. ... Qf6 20. Qf4 Ne5 21. Qg3+ Kf8** Pollock: "If 21. ... Kh8, mate in eight moves." **22. R×h7 Ba6** (see diagram)

23. Rd5!? Highly imaginative, but 23. Rdh1! Ke7 24. R1h6 Rg8 25. Nd5+ c×d5 26. Qc3 would have won on the spot. Pollock: "White plays brilliantly, but incorrectly here. He ought to have played 23. Rdh1, threatening 24. R1h6, and he could not fail to win the game. 23. Rd5 has two points, it threatens 24. R×e5, and it defies the c-pawn, but it forgets that Black has at least two defences." **23. ...**

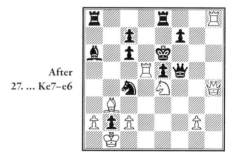

After
22. ... Bc8–a6

Nc4 Pollock: "Mr. Burn conducts this difficult game with unvarying 'sang froid' and defensive skill." **23. ...** Ke7 would have probably been met by 24. R×e5+ Q×e5 25. R×f7+ Kd8 26. Q×e5 d×e5 27. g4! **24. e5!** Pollock: "The rook at d5 was in imminent danger, for the White knight could not move, on pain of mate." **24. ... d×e5 25. Ne4 Q×f5 26. Rh8+ Ke7 27. Qh4+ Ke6** (see diagram)

After
27. ... Ke7–e6

28. Rh6+? Impatient play, neglecting the back rank. The simple retreat 28. Rd1 would have left Black hopeless: 28. ... Qf4 29. Rh6+. **28. ... K×d5 29. Nc3+ Kc5 30. Na4+ Kb4!** 30. ... Kb5 leads to a simple mate: 31. Q×c4+ Ka5 32. Qc3+ Kb5 33. Qc5 mate. **31. B×c4?** Now White's losing. After 31. Qe1+ Ka3 32. B×c4 K×a4 33. a3 Reb8 34. B×a6 Q×c2+ 35. K×c2 b1Q+ 36. Q×b1 R×b1 37. K×b1 R×a6 White had to fight hard for a draw. Pollock argued that he was winning with 31. a3+ K×a3 32. B×c4 B×c4 (32. ... K×a4? leads to a mate in eight.) 33. Q×c4, but he missed 32. ... Reb8! or 32. ... Qf4!, two fine defensive resources. **31. ... B×c4 32. a3+ Kb5 33. Nc3+ Kc5 34. Rf6 Qd7 35. Rd6** Pollock: "A despairing effort." **35. ... Q×d6!** Burn's finish is elegant. Pollock: "Had he taken the rook with pawn, he would have been

2. Most of this set of Pollock vs. Burn game scores was recovered by Richard Forster and given on pages 276–286 of his excellent *Amos Burn: A Chess Biography* (Jefferson, N.C.: McFarland, 2004). The 17 games presented here suggest two radically different styles of play, with Burn's skillful defensive chess contrasting sharply with Pollock's appetite for aggressive attacks. The overall score of the extant games for this period was 9–8 in Burn's favor, which is suggestive in terms of the comparative strength of these two masters at that particular moment in their careers.

mated on the move; with the king only drawn at best; but with the queen he secures the victory." **36. Ne4+ Kb5 37. N×d6+ c×d6 0–1** [*Horncastle News*, January 29, 1887]

120. Pollock–A. Burn [C29]
Offhand Game, London,
4 January 1887

1. e4 e5 2. Nc3 Nf6 3. f4 d5 4. e×d5 N×d5 5. N×d5 Q×d5 6. f×e5 Q×e5+ 7. Be2 Bg4 8. d4 Qe4 9. Nf3 B×f3 10. g×f3 Qh4+ 11. Kf1 Bd6 12. Qd3 0–0 13. Be3 (*see diagram*)

After
13. Bc1–e3

13. ... B×h2?! 13. ... Nc6 was far better than this greedy choice. **14. Bf2** 14. Qf5! was needed first. **14. ... Qh3+ 15. Ke1 Qg2 16. Kd2?** 16. Rf1 was forced. **16. ... Q×f2 17. Raf1 Qg3 18. Rfg1 Q×g1!** 18. ... Qd6 was fine as well. **19. R×g1 B×g1 20. Qb5 b6 21. Bd3 c6?!** After this, Black had real problems with developing his pieces. Best was 21. ... Bh2 22. Be4 c6 23. Qg5 Bd6 so as not to allow Qe7. **22. Qg5 Bf2 23. Qe7! g6 24. c3!** Better than 24. Qb7 Nd7 25. Q×d7 Rad8 26. Q×a7 B×d4. **24. ... Bg3 25. Qb7 Bf4+ 26. Kc2 h5 27. Q×a8 h4 28. Q×a7?!** 28. Bf1! was compulsory in order to stop the dangerous h–pawn. **28. ... h3 29. Qe7 h2 30. Qh4 Kg7 31. Kb3?** It is equally unlikely 31. Qe1 Nd7 32. Qh1 Rh8 would have saved White. **31. ... Rh8 32. Q×f4 h1Q 33. Qe5+ Kh7 34. Qc7 Q×f3 35. Qh2+ Kg7 36. Qe5+ Qf6 0–1** [*BCM*, July 1888, page 330]

121. Pollock–A. Burn [C51]
Offhand Game, London, February 1887

1. e4 e5 2. Nf3 Nc6 3. Bc4 Bc5 4. b4 B×b4 5. c3 Bd6 6. 0–0 Qe7 7. d4 Nf6 8. Ng5 0–0 9. f4!? h6 9. ... e×f4 10. Re1!? (A famous game known by both players continued: 10. e5?! B×e5 11. d×e5 Qc5+ 12. Kh1 N×e5 13. Bb3 Neg4 14. Nh3 d6 15. B×f4 Ne4 16. Qd4 Re8 17. Nd2 Q×d4 18. c×d4

N×d2 19. B×d2 Be6 20. Ng5 B×b3 21. a×b3 Re2 22. Nf3 a6 23. Rae1 Rae8 24. R×e2 R×e2 25. Re1 R×e1+ 26. B×e1 f6 27. Kg1 Ne3 28. Kf2 Nd5 29. Bd2 Kf7 30. Ke2 Ke6 31. Kd3 c5 32. g3 g5 33. Ke4 f5+ 34. Kd3 h6 35. Ne1 b5 36. Be3 Nb4+ 37. Kc3 Kd5 38. Nf3 g4 39. Ne1 h5 40. Nd3 N×d3 41. K×d3 c4+ 42. b×c4+ b×c4+ 43. Kc3 Ke4 44. Bd2 d5 0–1, A. Anderssen–L. Kieseritzky, London, 1851) 10. ... h6 11. e5 (11. Nf3 Ng4! 12. e5 Nc×e5 13. N×e5 B×e5 14. B×f4 d5!) 11. ... N×e5 12. d×e5 B×e5 should favor Black. **10. f×e5! h×g5?** Too optimistic. 10. ... N×e5 11. d×e5 B×e5 12. Nf3 Qc5+ 13. Kh1 Q×c4 14. N×e5 Q×e5 would have led to extremely complicated play: for example, 15. R×f6!? Q×e5 (15. ... g×f6 16. Ng4 Qe6 17. N×h6+ Kg7 18. Na3) 16. Rf1 d6 17. Bf4 Qc5 with sufficient compensation for Black. **11. e×f6** Objectively, 11. e×d6 Q×e4 (11. ... c×d6 12. B×g5 Q×e4 13. Nd2 Qh7 14. B×f6 g×f6 15. Rf3) 12. B×g5 leaves Black with no chances. **11. ... g×f6 12. Qh5 Q×e4?** (*see diagram*) 12. ... Kg7! was the correct defense.

After
12. ... Qe7×e4

13. B×g5! 13. R×f6 Qe1+ 14. Rf1 Qh4 15. B×f7+ Kg7 16. Qg6+ Kh8 17. B×g5 was straightforward too. **13. ... f×g5 14. R×f7 B×h2+ 15. Kh1 d5 16. B×d5 1–0** Richard Forster: "A drastic but just punishment for Burn's hazardous opening experiment." [*Illustrated London News*, May 28, 1887]

122. A. Burn–Pollock [C30]
Offhand Game, London, February 1887

1. e4 e5 2. Nc3 Bc5 3. f4 d6 4. Nf3 Bg4 5. Bb5+ c6 6. Bc4 Nd7 7. d3 f5!? Highly enterprising play. **8. Qe2 B×f3 9. Q×f3 Qb6 10. e×f5 0–0–0 11. Be6 Ngf6 12. f×e5 d×e5 13. Qg3 Kb8 14. Q×g7 Rhg8! 15. B×g8 R×g8 16. Qf7 Bg1!** An unusual attacking move. 16. ... R×g2! seems stronger: 17. Qb3 (17. Kd1 Bg1 18. Ne4 N×e4 19. Q×d7 Nf2+ 20. Ke1 a6!) 17. ... Bb4! 18. Rf1 Ng4 and Black has a very strong attack. **17. Nd1! R×g2 18. c3 B×h2 19. Be3 c5 20. Bf2 Qc6?!**

20. ... Bg3!? 21. B×g3 R×g3 22. Qe6 Qb5 was a critical alternative to the much slower choice in the text. **21. Ne3 Bg3! 22. N×g2 Q×g2** *(see diagram)*

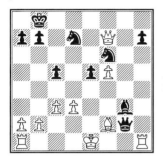

After
22. ... Qc6×g2

23. 0–0–0! Richard Forster: "The high art of defence. Burn gives up all his material advantage but maintains clear positional superiority. In this kind of endgame (with an open pawn structure) the rook is stronger than the minor pieces." **23. ... B×f2 24. R×h7!** Part of the fine exchange of attacking and defensive moves in this game. **24. ... N×h7?** This recapture is natural but not necessary. Among other moves, 24. ... Qg4! (threatening ... Be3+) was excellent: 25. Rhh1 Q×f5 26. Kb1 Kc7 and the position remains rather unclear. **25. Q×d7 Qg8 26. Rh1 Ng5 27. Qd6+ Ka8?** 27. ... Kc8 28. Q×e5 Nf7 had to be tried. **28. Q×e5 Nf7 29. Qe6 a6 30. Qg6 Qe8** 30. ... Qd8!? was worth trying since White had to find moves like 31. f6!! (31. Q×f7? allows 31. ... Q×d3 and Black is out of trouble.) 31. ... Qd5 32. Qe4 Qg5+ 33. Kb1. **31. Kb1 c4 32. Qe6 Qg8 33. Q×c4 Ka7 34. d4 Qg2 35. Rd1 Qe4+ 36. Qd3 Q×d3+ 37. R×d3 Kb6 38. Rh3 Kc6 39. Kc2 Kd5 40. Kd3 Ng5 41. Rh6 Bg3 42. c4 mate 1–0** [*Illustrated Sporting and Dramatic News*, March 5, 1887]

123. Pollock–A. Burn [C51]
Offhand Game, London,
5 February 1887

1. e4 e5 2. Nf3 Nc6 3. Bc4 Bc5 4. b4 B×b4 5. c3 Bc5 6. 0–0 d6 7. d4 e×d4 8. c×d4 Bb6 9. Nc3 Na5 10. Ng5 10. Bg5 seems stronger than this knight attack. **10. ... N×c4 11. Qa4+ Qd7 12. Q×c4 h6 13. Nf3 Nf6 14. e5 d5 15. Qb3 Nh7** *(see diagram)*

16. e6! A powerful idea. 16. N×d5 0–0 17. Ba3 Re8 18. Rac1 c6 posed his opponent lesser problems.**16. ... f×e6 17. Ba3 c6 18. Ne5 Qc7?** After 18. ... Qd8 Pollock must have intended to transfer his queen to the kingside via 19. Qd1 Qf6 20. Re1.

After
15. ... Nf6–h7

19. Rae1!? B×d4 20. N×d5! Richard Forster: "The attack is excellently played by Pollock. If 20. ... c×d5 21. Qa4+, followed by 22. Q×d4. Burn tries to escape with a queen sacrifice, but he fails to hold up the storm." **20. ... Q×e5!** This leads to an immediate collapse. 20. ... c×d5 is not much better either: 21. Qa4+ Bd7 22. Q×d4 Nf6 23. Re3! **21. R×e5 B×e5 22. Qb4** 22. Ne7! Nf8 23. Re1 Bf6 24. N×c8 R×c8 25. Q×b7! was most precise. **22. ... Kf7 23. f4 Bd4+ 24. Q×d4 e×d5 25. Re1 Nf6 26. Re7+ Kg6 27. R×g7+** 27. Bb2 was simpler. But the text can hardly be criticized. **27. ... K×g7 28. Be7 Kh7** 28. ... Rf8 29. B×f8+ K×f8 30. Q×f6+ Kg8 31. Q×h6 is just hopeless. **29. Q×f6 Rg8 30. Bf8 R×f8 31. Q×f8 1–0** [*Illustrated Sporting and Dramatic News*, March 12, 1887]

124. A. Burn–Pollock [C62]
Offhand Game, London, May 1887

1. e4 e5 2. Nf3 Nc6 3. Bb5 d6 4. 0–0 Bd7 5. c3 Nge7 6. Na3 Ng6 7. d3 Be7 8. Nc4 0–0 9. Ne3 f5! 10. Bc4+ Kh8 11. e×f5 B×f5 12. N×f5 R×f5 13. Be6 Rf8 14. g3 d5 15. Ne1 Bc5 *(see diagram)*

After
15. ... Be7–c5

16. Qb3? Neglecting the threat on f2. 16. Bh3 was advisable. 16. Qh5!? Qd6 17. Bh3 was also possible. **16. ... R×f2! 17. R×f2 B×f2+ 18. K×f2 Qf6+ 19. Ke2 Q×e6 20. Q×b7?** This second poor queen move really throws White into a ditch. But after 20. Kd1 e4! 21. Qc2 e×d3 22. Q×d3 Nge5 23. Qe2 d4! Black gets a strong attack anyway.

20. Qc2 is met by 20. ... e4 21. d4 Qg4+ 22. Kf2 Rf8+ 23. Kg1 Nh4! **20. ... Rf8 21. Be3 Rb8 22. Q×c7 R×b2+ 23. Kd1 d4 24. Bg1 d×c3 25. Nf3 h6 26. Be3 e4 27. Bd4 N×d4 28. N×d4 Qg4+ 29. Ke1 e×d3 30. Q×c3 Re2+ 31. Kd1 Rc2+ 0–1** [*Illustrated London News*, May 21, 1887]

125. A. Burn–Pollock [C01]
Offhand Game, London, May 1887

1. e4 e6 2. d4 b6 3. g3 Bb7 4. Bg2 f5 5. f3 f×e4 6. f×e4 Nf6 7. Nd2 Be7 8. c3 0–0 9. Nh3 d5?! 9. ... c5 is a better plan. **10. Ng5** 10. Nf4 seems more logical. **10. ... N×e4?** 10. ... Bc8 was necessary. **11. Nd×e4** (*see diagram*) 11. N×e6 Nf2 12. Qc2 Qe8 13. 0–0 gives White a clear edge.

After
11. Nd2×e4

11. ... Bc8! Richard Forster: "It is incredible that instead of recapturing the piece on e4 Black simply undoes the development of his bishop—and even gets away with it. Without a little help from his opponent this would not be possible, but his defensive resources are nevertheless extraordinary." **12. Qh5 h6 13. Nh3 d×e4 14. B×e4 c6 15. Qg6?!** If roles were reversed, it's very likely Pollock would not have missed 15. B×h6 Rf5 16. Qg6 Qf8 17. g4 with a crushing assault. **15. ... Rf6 16. Qh7+ Kf7 17. Nf4** Pollock: "Threatening to win the exchange." **17. ... Qg8 18. Nh5** Pollock: "This is not sound, as it allows Black to imprison and capture a bishop." **18. ... Q×h7 19. B×h7 g6 20. N×f6 B×f6 21. B×h6 Ba6 22. Kd2?!** 22. h4!? Nd7 23. h5 g5 24. Be4 Rh8 25. B×c6 Ke7 26. B×g5 B×g5 27. Kf2 was the alternative, leading to an unclear position. **22. ... Nd7** Now Black has enough compensation. **23. Rae1 Rh8 24. B×g6+ K×g6 25. Bf4 c5 26. Re4** The score given on page 2511 of the *Illustrated London News* appears corrupt, since it is difficult to accept that White did not play 26. R×e6 and Black did not play 26. ... Bb7 in response to the text move. Forster: "Either 25. ... Re8 26. Re4 c5 27. Rhe1 Kf5 or 25. ... Re8 26. Re4 Kf5 27. Rhe1 c5 would appear to have been the actual move order." **26. ...**

126. Pollock–A. Burn [C51]
Offhand Game, London, 1887

1. e4 e5 2. Nf3 Nc6 3. Bc4 Bc5 4. b4 B×b4 5. c3 Bc5 6. d4 e×d4 7. 0–0 d6 8. c×d4 Bb6 9. Nc3 Na5 10. Bd3 Ne7 11. e5!? d×e5 12. d×e5 0–0 12. ... Bf5 is best against White's current plan. **13. Bg5! Qe8** (*see diagram*) 13. ... h6 could have avoided White's vicious attack.

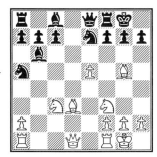

After
13. ... Qd8–e8

14. Bf6! g×f6 14. ... Ng6 was the safer alternative: 15. Re1 Be6 16. Ne4 Nc6. **15. e×f6 Ng6?** 15. ... Nf5! seems to be Black's only reliable defense: 16. Nh4 (16. Ng5!? Qe5! 17. Qh5 h6 18. Nce4!, with unclear play. 16. ... Qe5 17. Qg4+ Kh8 18. N×f5 Q×f6 19. Nd5 B×f5 20. B×f5 Qg7. **16. Ng5?!** 16. Qd2! was the correct way forward: 16. ... Qe6 17. Nd5!! Be3 18. N×e3 Q×f6 19. Q×a5. **16. ... h6?** This results in immediate collapse. 16. ... Qc6 loses too after 17. Nce4 Nf4 18. Qf3; 16. ... Nf4! was probably Black's best choice: 17. B×h7+ Kh8 18. Be4 Rg8 19. h4 c6 20. g3 and now the splendid 20. ... Qe6!! 21. g×f4 (21. N×e6? R×g3+ 22. Kh1 Rh3+ 23. Kg1 B×e6) 21. ... Q×f6; engines suggest another staggering defense: 16. ... Be3!! 17. N×h7! K×h7 18. Re1 Kg8 19. R×e3 Qd7 20. Qh5 Q×f6 21. Rg3 Kg7 22. Q×a5 b6 23. Qd5 c6 24. Qe4 Bb7. **17. Qh5 1–0** [*Illustrated Sporting and Dramatic News*, March 3, 1888]

127. Pollock–A. Burn [C51]
Offhand Game, London, 1887

1. e4 e5 2. Nf3 Nc6 3. Bc4 Bc5 4. b4 B×b4 5. c3 Bc5 6. d4 e×d4 7. 0–0 d6 8. c×d4 Bb6 9. Bg5! f6 9. ... Nf6 or 9. ... Nge7 were better choices. **10. B×g8 R×g8** 10. ... f×g5! was considerably stronger. **11. Qb3 Kf8 12. Be3 Qe7 13. Nc3**

Be6 14. Qa4 Bd7 15. Qc2 g5 16. Rae1 Re8
17. Nd5 Qd8 *(see diagram)*

After
17. ... Qe7–d8

18. e5! d×e5 19. Q×h7 Bg4 20. N×b6?
20. d×e5!? looks strong, but perhaps Black could
defend with 20. ... Rg7! (20. ... B×f3 21. N×f6!)
21. Qh6 f×e5 22. Nf6 B×f3 23. N×e8 Q×e8
24. g×f3 Nd4. Very provocative is 20. N×g5!?
Q×d5 (20. ... f×g5? 21. f4!!) 21. Ne6+ but Black
has enough resources after 21. ... R×e6 22. Bh6+
Ke8 23. Q×g8+ Kd7 24. Q×g4 e×d4 25. h4 Q×a2.
20. ... a×b6 21. Nh4? 21. N×e5!? was perhaps
worth trying: 21. ... N×e5! (21. ... f×e5 22. f4!)
22. d×e5 Qd7 23. Qh6+ Qg7 24. Q×g7+ K×g7
25. f4 with roughly equal chances. **21. ... Rg7!
22. Qe4 g×h4 23. Bh6 f5 24. Qb1 N×d4 25. f3
Bh5 26. f4 e4 27. Kh1 Qf6 28. B×g7+ K×g7
29. Rg1 Kh7 30. Re3 Bg4 31. Qb2 Qd6 32. h3
Bh5 33. Qf2 Qf6 34. Kh2 c5 35. a4 Ra8 36. Qa2
Bf7 37. Qb1 R×a4 38. Kh1 Ra2 39. g4 f×g4
40. R×e4 Nf3 41. Re2+ Kh6 42. R×a2 B×a2 0–1**
[*Illustrated London News*, February 11, 1888]

128. Pollock–A. Burn [C44]
Offhand Game, London, 1887

**1. e4 e5 2. Nf3 Nc6 3. c3 d5 4. Qa4 d×e4
5. N×e5 Qd5 6. Bb5 Nge7 7. f4 Bd7 8. N×d7
K×d7 9. 0–0 Nf5 10. d4 e×d3 11. Rd1 Bc5+
12. Kf1** 12. Kh1 runs into a simple mate after 12. ...
Ng3+. **12. ... Kc8** 12. ... Nd6 13. R×d3 Qh5
14. Rh3 Qg4 15. Be2 Qe6 16. b4 Rae8 was a more
aggressive approach. **13. R×d3 Qe6 14. B×c6?**
14. Qb3! accomplished more than the text. **14. ...
b×c6 15. Qd1 Re8 16. b4 Be3 17. Nd2 Kb7?!**
17. ... B×f4 18. Nb3 B×h2 would have made it very
difficult for White. **18. Nb3 Qh6?** 18. ... Bb6 or
18. ... Qe4 were fine for Black. **19. Na5+ Ka6** *(see
diagram)*
20. Qf3! Nh4 20. ... Re6 fails because of 21. R×e3!

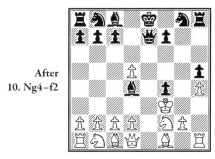

After
19. ... Kb7–a6

N×e3+ 22. B×e3. **21. Q×c6+ Q×c6 22. N×c6
B×c1 23. R×c1 Re4 24. g3 Nf5 25. Rd7 f6 26. a4
Rae8 27. Nd4 Ne3+ 28. Kg1 R8e7 29. b5+ Kb6
30. a5+ Kc5 31. R×e7 R×e7 32. Nc6 Re4
33. N×a7 Ra4 34. a6 Kb6 35. Re1 Nd5 36. c4
R×c4 37. Nc8+ K×b5 38. Ra1 c5 39. a7 1–0** [*Illustrated London News*, July 23, 1887]

129. Pollock–A. Burn [C39][3]
Offhand Game, London, 1887(?)

**1. e4 e5 2. f4 e×f4 3. Nf3 g5 4. h4 g4 5. Ne5
Bg7 6. N×g4 d5 7. e×d5?** 7. Qf3 h5 8. Nf2 d×e4
9. Q×f4 was better. **7. ... Qe7+ 8. Kf2 Bd4+
9. Kf3 h5 10. Nf2** *(see diagram)*

After
10. Ng4–f2

10. ... Nd7 There's a forced mate in ten moves
here: 10. ... Bg4+ 11. N×g4 h×g4+ 12. K×g4
(12. K×f4 Qe5+ 13. K×g4 Nf6+ 14. Kh3 R×h4+
15. K×h4 Bf2+ 16. Kh3 Qg3 mate.) 12. ... Nf6+
13. Kh3 R×h4+ 14. K×h4 Ne4+ 15. Kg4 Nf2+
16. Kh5 Qe5+ 17. Kh4 Qf6+ 18. Kh5 Qg6+ 19. Kh4
Bf6 mate. **11. g3 f×g3 12. Ne4 Ne5+ 13. Kg2 Bg4
14. Be2 0–0–0 15. c3 Bb6 16. d6** 16. d4 was
White's last chance to pose some resistance. **16. ...
R×d6! 17. N×d6+ Q×d6 18. B×g4+ N×g4
19. Qf3 N8f6 20. d4 Nf2 21. Bf4** After 21. Re1
Rg8 22. Bg5 Qd7 23. Q×f6! Qh3+ 24. Kf3 it's not
clear how Black can claim an edge. **21. ... Qd7**

---

3. On page 285 of *Amos Burn*, Richard Forster considered the possibility that this game was actually played on the
passage from Dublin to New York in March 1889.

22. Be5? 22. Nd2 N×h1 23. R×h1 Rg8 24. Rf1 with some hopes for White. **22. ... N×h1 23. B×f6 Re8 24. Nd2 Nf2 0–1** [*Warder and Dublin Evening Mail*, July 13, 1889]

130. Pollock–A. Burn [C37]
Offhand Game, London, 1887

1. e4 e5 2. f4 e×f4 3. Nf3 g5 4. Bc4 g4 5. Ng1!? Richard Forster: "An exceptionally rare move." **5. ... d5** Richard Forster: "5. ... Qh4+ is certainly not a bad reply to the knight move. Burn's mode of development fails to reveal the disadvantages of this experiment." **6. e×d5 Nf6 7. Nc3 Bd6 8. Qe2+ Kf8 9. d4 Kg7 10. Qf2 Re8+ 11. Nge2** 11. Kf1? should lose after 11. ... g3 12. h×g3 Ng4 13. Qf3 f×g3 14. Nge2 Nh2+ 15. R×h2 g×h2. **11. ... g3 12. h×g3 f×g3 13. Qf3 Bg4 14. Qd3 Nbd7 15. Bh6+ Kh8 16. 0–0–0! Rg8 17. Rdf1 Bh5** (see diagram)

After
17. ... Bg4–h5

18. R×h5! N×h5 19. R×f7 Ndf6 19. ... Rg6! 20. Bd2 Nb6 would have made things rather unclear. **20. Qf5 Rg6 21. Bd2** 21. Bg5 looks fine but Black has 21. ... R×g5! 22. Q×g5 Qg8 23. Q×g8+ K×g8 24. R×c7 B×c7 25. d6+ Kf8 26. d×c7 Ke7. **21. ... Qg8 22. R×f6! N×f6 23. Nf4 B×f4 24. B×f4 Qc8 25. Qd3 Qg4 26. Be5** 26. B×c7 was perhaps even stronger. **26. ... Qg5+ 27. Kb1 Qh4 28. Qf1 Re8 29. Bd3 Rh6 30. Ne4 R×e5?!** Interesting too was 30. ... Qh1 31. N×f6 R×e5 32. d×e5 Q×f1 33. B×f1 Rh1 34. c4 R×f1+ 35. Kc2 Rf2+ 36. Kd3 Kg7, with a wild endgame. **31. d×e5 Ng8 32. a3 Qh5?** Once again, Black's best chance was 32. ... Qh1 33. N×g3 Q×f1+ 34. N×f1 Rh5. **33. Qf4 Qh1+ 34. Ka2 Q×g2 35. Ng5?** A missed opportunity for a quick knockout. 35. e6 should have won: 35. ... Rg6 36. Qe5+ Rg7 37. d6. **35. ... Qf2! 36. Q×f2?** 36. Nf7+ Kg7 37. Qg4+ K×f7 38. d6 c×d6 39. Bc4+ Ke8 40. Qc8+ Ke7 41. Qc7+ secures at least a draw. **36. ... g×f2 37. Nf7+ Kg7 38. N×h6 N×h6 0–1** [*Dublin Evening Mail*, September 8, 1887]

131. Pollock–A. Burn [B00]
Offhand Game, London, 1887

1. e4 b6 2. d4 Bb7 3. Bd3 e6 4. Be3 Nf6 5. Nd2 Be7 6. f3 0–0 7. Ne2 c5 8. c3 d5 Giving a player like Pollock the whole kingside was not a good idea. **9. e5 Nfd7 10. g4 Nc6 11. f4 c4 12. Bc2 b5 13. Nf3 b4 14. h4 a5 15. f5! Nb6 16. Ng5!?** 16. f6 must have been tempting for Pollock too. However, after 16. ... g×f6 17. e×f6 B×f6 18. g5 Bg7 19. h5 Ne7 20. Bf4 Nf5 21. Ng3 Re8 things are far from clear. **16. ... h6** (see diagram)

After
16. ... h7–h6

17. f6! g×f6 Black cannot defend with 17. ... h×g5 18. h×g5 g6 because of 19. B×g6 f×g6 20. Qc2. **18. Nh7** 18. e×f6 B×f6 19. Nf3 was a less imaginative choice, but perhaps even more effective. **18. ... f×e5 19. N×f8** Uncharacteristically materialistic. Further complications were available via 19. B×h6 Re8 20. 0–0 e4 21. Ng5 Bf8 (21. ... B×g5 22. B×g5 Qc7 23. Qd2) 22. B×f8 R×f8 23. Nf4. **19. ... B×f8 20. g5 h×g5?** An immediate 20. ... e4 was necessary. **21. h×g5 e4?** An understandable decision but it opens other avenues for White's pieces. Instead, 21. ... Bg7 22. Bh7+ Kf8 23. g6 Nd7 secures an effective defense. **22. Nf4! a4 23. Qh5 Bg7 24. g6 Qf6 25. g×f7+ Q×f7 26. Ng6 Bf6 27. Bg5 Ne7 28. B×f6 Q×g6 29. Qh8+ Kf7 30. Rh7+ 1–0** [*Illustrated London News*, August 27, 1887]

132. A. Burn–Pollock [C60]
Offhand Game, London, 1887

1. e4 e5 2. Nf3 Nc6 3. Bb5 Na5?! An oddity tried by Pollock in a few games throughout his career. **4. 0–0 c6 5. Be2 f6?** At least Black should have tried 5. ... d5! **6. d4! e×d4 7. Q×d4 b6 8. Bf4 Ne7 9. c4** 9. Nh4 posed immediate problems: 9. ... d5 10. Nc3. **9. ... Nb7 10. b4 Ng6 11. Bd2 Bd6 12. Qb2 0–0 13. Nc3 Qe7 14. a3 Nd8 15. Nd4** (see diagram) White should have exercised a bit of caution here with 15. g3.

After
15. Nf3–d4

15. ... B×h2+!? 16. Kh1 16. K×h2 Qe5+ 17. f4 Q×d4 18. Rad1 Qd6 19. Qb3 Nf7 20. Be3 Qc7 21. c5 was good for White as well. **16. ... Bc7 17. Nf5 Qf7 18. f4 Ne6 19. g3 Bb7 20. Bh5 Rad8 21. Nh4 Qe7 22. N×g6!?** Signaling White's intention to play for mate. 22. B×g6 h×g6 23. N×g6 Qf7 24. N×f8 N×f8 was also fine. **22. ... h×g6 23. B×g6 d5 24. Be3 Rf7 25. Qh2 Nf8 26. f5?** 26. B×f7+ Q×f7 27. e×d5 c×d5 28. N×d5 was the most pragmatic decision here. 26. Kg2 is a pretty resource, but there is no mate: 26. ... N×g6 27. Rh1 Rff8 28. f5 Ne5 29. Qh7+ Kf7 30. Qh5+ g6 31. f×g6+ N×g6 32. Qh7+ Ke8 33. Q×g6+ Qf7 34. Q×f7+ R×f7. **26. ... d4! 27. Kg2 d×c3 28. Rh1 Q×e4+ 29. Kf1 Qf3+ 30. Bf2 Rd1+ 31. R×d1 Q×d1+ 32. Be1 Qf3+ 33. Kg1 Qe3+ 34. Kf1 Qd3+ 35. Kg1 Qd4+ 36. Kf1 Q×c4+ 37. Kg1 Qd4+ 38. Kf1 Qd3+** 38. ... Ba6+ was an easy win: 39. Kg2 Qe4+ 40. Kg1 Q×e1+ 41. Kg2 Qd2+ 42. Kh3 N×g6 43. f×g6 Re7. **39. Kg1 Qd4+ 40. Kf1 Qc4+ 41. Kg1 N×g6 42. f×g6 Kf8?** 42. ... Qd4+ 43. Qf2 Rd7 would have secured the full point. **43. Qh8+ Ke7 44. g×f7 Q×f7 44.** ... Qd4+ 45. Bf2 Qd1+ 46. Kh2 B×g3+ 47. B×g3 Qc2+ 48. Kg1 leads to a perpetual. **45. Rh7 c2 46. Bd2 Kd6 47. R×g7 Qe6 48. Qf8+?** 48. Bf4+ was accurate: 48. ... Kd5 49. Qh1+ Kd4 50. R×c7 Qe2 51. Qg2. **48. ... Kd5 49. Qf7 Q×f7 50. R×f7 B×g3 51. R×b7 Be1 52. Bc1** *(see diagram)*

After
52. Bd2–c1

52. ... c5? It is likely Pollock assumed this endgame was lost anyway. Interestingly, it was not completely hopeless. 52. ... Bh4!! (threatening ... Bg5) 53. Rd7+ Kc4 54. a4 (54. Rd2 Kc3 55. Rh2 Bg5 56. Rh3+ Kc4 57. Bb2 c1Q+ 58. B×c1 B×c1 59. Kf2 Kb5 60. Rc3 Bb2 61. Rb3 Be5 62. Kf3 Ka4 63. Re3 Bb2 64. Ke4 B×a3 with superior chances for Black.) 54. ... Bg5 55. Ba3 c1Q+ 56. B×c1 B×c1 57. b5 c×b5 58. a×b5 (58. Rc7+ can be risky for White: 58. ... Kb4 59. R×c1 b×a4 60. Kf2 a3 61. Ke3 a2 62. Kd2 Kb3 63. Rc3+ Kb2 64. Rc2+ Ka3 and White has to take the draw.) 58. ... Be3+ 59. Kg2 K×b5. **53. b×c5 b×c5 1–0** [*Belfast News-Letter*, June 14, 1888]

133. A. Burn–Pollock [C40]
Offhand Game, London(?), 1887

1. e4 e5 2. Nf3 f5 3. N×e5 Nc6 4. N×c6 Perhaps Burn considered 4. Qh5+ g6 5. N×g6 Nf6 6. Qh4 h×g6 7. Q×h8 Qe7 8. d3 f×e4 9. d×e4 N×e4 10. Be2 d5 11. Bh6 Nd4 not very clear. **4. ... d×c6 5. e5 Qh4 6. Nc3 Bc5 7. Qe2 Be6 8. d3 0–0–0 9. g3 Qe7 10. Bg2 g5?!** 10. ... h5 was more to the point. **11. 0–0 h5 12. Na4 g4?** Pollock's kingside attack is doomed from the start. **13. N×c5 Q×c5 14. c4 h4 15. Bg5 h×g3 16. h×g3!** 16. B×d8 g×h2+ 17. Kh1 K×d8 would have given Black some chances. **16. ... Rd7 17. b3 Rdh7** *(see diagram)*

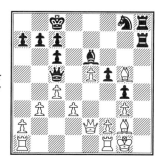

After
17. ... Rd7–h7

18. Qe3 18. d4! was a pretty tactical shortcut. **18. ... Qa3 19. d4 Ne7 20. Rfd1 Ng6** Even 20. ... Rd8 could have not stopped d4–d5: 21. Rd2 Kb8 22. Rad1 Rg8 23. d5. **21. d5 f4 22. g×f4 Bf5 23. e6 Qa6 24. e7 Bd7 25. d×c6 b×c6 26. R×d7 K×d7 27. Rd1+ Kc8 28. e8Q+ R×e8 29. Q×e8+ Kb7 30. Rd8 Qb6 31. Rb8+ 1–0** [*Albany Evening Journal*, September 5, 1896]

134. A. Burn–Pollock [C29]
Offhand Game, London, 1887

1. e4 e5 2. Nc3 Nf6 3. f4 d5 4. d3 Bb4 5. f×e5 N×e4 6. d×e4 Qh4+ 7. Ke2 B×c3 8. b×c3 Bg4+

9. Nf3 d×e4 10. Qd4 Bh5 11. Ke3 B×f3 12. Qa4+? Objectively, White had to go for 12. g×f3 Qe1+ 13. Kf4 Qh4+ 14. Ke3 and agree to a draw. **12. ... Nc6 13. Bb5** 13. g×f3 runs into 13. ... Qe1+ 14. Kf4 Q×c3 15. Q×e4 Rd8! 16. Be3 Q×a1 17. Rg1 g6 18. Bc4 Qc3 and Black should win. **13. ... Qg5+ 14. Kf2 Q×g2+ 15. Ke3 Qg5+ 16. Kf2 Qg2+ 17. Ke3** (see diagram)

After
17. Kf2–e3

17. ... 0–0–0! 18. B×c6 Qg5+ 18. ... Qe2+ also leads to mate: 19. Kf4 g5+ 20. Kf5 Bg4+ 21. Kf6 Qf2+ 22. Ke7 Qc5+ 23. Kf6 Rd6+! **19. Kf2 Rd2+!** **20. B×d2 Q×d2+ 21. Kg3 Qg2+ 22. Kf4 g5+ 23. Kf5** 23. Ke3 loses too after 23. ... Rd8! 24. B×b7+ Kb8 (24. ... K×b7?? loses to 25. Rhb1+ Kc8 26. Qa6+ Kd7 27. Rd1+ B×d1 28. R×d1+) 25. Bd5 Qe2+ 26. Kd4 Qd2+ 27. Kc5 Q×d5+ 28. Kb4 B×h1. **23. ... Qh3+ 24. Kf6 Qh6+ 25. K×f7 Bh5+ 26. Ke7 Qf8+ 27. Ke6 Qf7 mate 0–1** [*Illustrated Sporting and Dramatic News*, August 6, 1887]

135. A. Burn–Pollock [A00]
Offhand Game, London, 1887

1. g3 e5 2. Bg2 d5 3. d3 Pollock: "This stealthy opening is known as the original 'Indian Fianchetto.'" **3. ... Bd6 4. c3** Pollock: "White would have gained nothing by capturing the d-pawn." **4. ... Be6 5. Nf3 Nc6 6. Nbd2 f6 7. Nf1 Nge7 8. Qb3 Qd7!? 9. Q×b7** Pollock: "A hazardous move, but Mr. Burn is a mark on the b-pawn." **9. ... 0–0 10. Qb3 Kh8** 10. ... e4! was forceful too. **11. Qc2 Rae8 12. Bd2 e4 13. d×e4 d×e4 14. Nd4** Pollock: "14. Q×e4 might have been played, but the attack would have been very hot." **14. ... Bd5 15. Ne3 f5 16. Bh3 Ne5** Pollock: "This part of the game is conducted with much skill on both sides." **17. 0–0 Ba8! 18. f4 e×f3 19. e×f3 Bc5 20. f4 B×d4 21. c×d4 Nf3+ 22. Kf2?** 22. R×f3 B×f3 23. Rf1 Ba8 24. Qc5 was necessary. **22. ... Q×d4 23. Bc3** Pollock: "The

interest is vigorously sustained by these thrusts and parries." **23. ... Qb6 24. Qb3 Qh6! 25. Bg2** (see diagram)

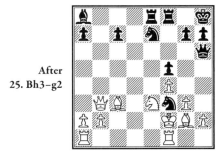

After
25. Bh3–g2

25. ... N×h2? 25. ... Nd5! was the way to create further threats: 26. N×d5 B×d5 27. Q×d5 Qb6+ 28. Bd4 N×d4 29. Kg1 Nc2+ 30. Kh1 N×a1 31. R×a1 Q×b2. **26. Rh1 B×g2?!** 26. ... Ng6! 27. R×h2 (27. B×a8 N×f4! 28. B×g7+ K×g7 29. Qc3+ Kg8 30. g×f4 Q×f4+) 27. ... Q×h2 28. Rh1 Q×h1 29. B×h1 B×h1 30. Qc4 Be4 was playable. **27. K×g2 Nd5 28. Q×d5** Pollock: "Compulsory." **28. ... R×e3 29. Rae1 R×e1 30. B×e1 Ng4! 31. R×h6 Ne3+ 32. Kf3 N×d5 33. Ra6 Ra8 34. a4 Kg8 35. Bf2 Rb8 36. Bd4** Pollock: "The endgame is consummately played by White." **36. ... Rb3+ 37. Kf2 Rb4 38. Be5 Nb6 39. R×a7 N×a4 40. R×c7 N×b2 41. R×g7+ Kf8 42. R×h7 Nd3+ 43. Kf3 N×e5+ 44. f×e5 Re4 45. Rh5 R×e5 46. Kf4 Ra5??** Pollock did not explain this blunder. 46. ... Rf1 (or other similar rook retreats) should have drawn easily. On page 284 of his Burn biography, Forster commented: "Despite the incomprehensible finish a magnificent battle and a fine specimen of Burn's extraordinary defensive skills. It seems that in skittle play he derived much more pleasure from defending difficult positions than from looking out for brilliancies." **47. R×f5+ 1–0** [*Illustrated London News*, February 18, 1888]

VARIOUS GAMES (EARLY 1887)

136. Pollock–Bailey
Odds Game, City of London Chess Club, London, January 1887
Remove Nb1

1. f4 d5 2. e3 a6 3. Nf3 Bg4 4. Be2 Nc6 5. b3 B×f3 6. B×f3 e5 7. f×e5 N×e5 8. Be2 Bd6 9. 0–0

Ne7 10. c4 c6 11. d4 N5g6 12. Bd3 Qc7 13. Qh5 Qd7 14. Bd2 0–0–0? 14. ... 0–0 would have been much safer. **15. c5! Bc7 16. b4 f6 17. a4 Nf8 18. b5 g6 19. Qe2 c×b5 20. a×b5 a×b5 21. Ra8+ Bb8 22. Be1! Ne6 23. Bg3 Nc7 24. R×f6 N×a8 25. B×b5** *(see diagram)*

After
25. Bd3×b5

25. ... Nc6? 25. ... B×g3! 26. B×d7+ R×d7 27. h×g3 Re8 gave decent survival chances. **26. R×c6+! b×c6 27. Ba6+ Qb7 28. Qg4+ Rd7 29. B×b7+ K×b7 30. Q×d7+ 1–0** [*Dublin Evening Mail*, February 10, 1887; *Morning Post*, September 22, 1887]

137. J.T. Heppell–Pollock [C33]
Dublin(?)/London(?), January 1887

1. e4 e5 2. f4 e×f4 3. Bc4 f5 4. Nc3 Nf6 5. e×f5 c6 6. d4 d5 7. Bd3 Bd6 8. Qf3 0–0 9. B×f4 B×f4 10. Q×f4 Qb6? Pollock tempted the White king to castle on the queenside and then launched an unsound attack. However, White's attack proved much faster. **11. 0–0–0! a5 12. Nf3 a4 13. a3 Qa5 14. g4 b5 15. g5 Ne8 16. f6 g6 17. Rde1 Ra7 18. Q×b8 Nc7** *(see diagram)*

After
18. ... Ne8–c7

19. Re7! Rb7 20. Rg7+ 20. B×g6 h×g6 21. Rg7+ Kh8 22. Ne5 would have been a pretty finish as well. **20. ... Kh8 21. Nh4 R×b8 22. B×g6 Ne6 23. R×h7+ Kg8 24. Nf5 1–0** [*Dublin Evening Mail*, February 3, 1887]

138. Pollock–F.N. Braund [C56]
London, Simpson's Divan,
7 April, 1887

1. e4 e5 2. Nf3 Nc6 3. Bc4 Nf6 4. d4 e×d4 5. N×d4 Bc5 6. Nf5? Too ambitious and unsound. 6. N×c6 b×c6 7. 0–0 was superior. **6. ... 0–0 7. Bg5 B×f2+!?** 7. ... d5! was just as good and principled. **8. Ke2** 8. K×f2 N×e4+ 9. Ke1 Q×g5 10. Rf1 d5 is hopeless for White. **8. ... Qe8 9. Nc3** 9. N×g7 was not working either: 9. ... Qe5! (9. ... K×g7? 10. B×f6+ K×f6 11. K×f2 Q×e4 12. Bd5 Qf5+ 13. Qf3 leaves White with some hope.) 10. K×f2 Q×g5 11. Rf1 K×g7. **9. ... N×e4 10. Ne7+ N×e7 11. N×e4 Ng6 12. Kf3 Ne5+** 12. ... Bb6! was even more accurate: 13. Re1 Ne5+ 14. Kg3 N×c4 15. Nf6+ g×f6 16. R×e8 R×e8 17. B×f6 Re3+ 18. Kf4 d6 19. Bd4 Re8. **13. K×f2 N×c4 14. Re1! Ne5** *(see diagram)*

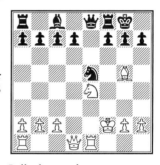

After
14. ... Nc4–e5

15. Qh5?! Here Pollock missed an opportunity for further complications: 15. Nf6+ g×f6 16. B×f6 Qe6! (16. ... d6? allows 17. R×e5!) 17. B×e5 f6 18. Bc3 and White has some chances for a good result. **15. ... f6! 16. Q×e8 R×e8 17. B×f6 d5?!** 17. ... Ng4+! leaves White with almost zero compensation: 18. Kg1 g×f6 19. h3 f5 20. Nc3 R×e1+ 21. R×e1 Nf6 22. Nb5 c6 23. Nd6 b5 24. N×f5 Ba6. **18. B×e5 R×e5 19. Nc3 Rf5+ 20. Kg1 Bd7 21. Re7 Bc6 22. R×c7 Re8 23. Rf1 Rg5 24. h4 Rg4 25. g3?** 25. Rf5! d4 26. Nd5 Re2 27. Rc8+ was necessary. **25. ... d4! 26. Nd1 R×g3+ 27. Kh2 Rg2+ 28. Kh3 R×c2 29. Rff7 Bg2+ 30. Kg3 R×c7 31. R×c7 Bc6 32. Nf2 Re3+ 33. Kg4 Re2 34. Nd1 d3 35. Kf4 Re1 36. Nc3 d2 37. Rc8+ Kf7 38. Rd8 Rh1 39. Kg4 h5+ 40. Kg3 Rg1+ 41. Kh3 Rh1+ 42. Kg3 g5 43. h×g5 h4+ 44. Kg4 Rh2 45. Kh5 Kg7 46. Rd3 Rh1?** 46. ... b5! was clearly better. **47. g6?** White should have grabbed this opportunity for a more stubborn defense: 47. Kg4! h3 48. R×d2 h2 49. Kh3 Rg1 50. K×h2 R×g5. **47. ... d1Q+ 48. N×d1 R×d1 0–1** [*Illustrated London News*, May 14, 1887]

139. Pollock–Mr. E.
London, Simpson's Divan,
Handicap Tournament(?), April 1887
Remove Nb1

1. f4 d5 2. e3 Nf6 3. Nf3 e6 4. Be2 Bd6 5. 0–0 0–0 6. b3 c5 7. Bb2 Nc6 8. h3 d4 9. Qe1 Bd7 10. a3 Re8 11. Qh4 e5 12. f×e5 N×e5 13. e×d4 N×f3+ 14. B×f3 Bc6 15. d×c5 B×c5+ 16. Kh1 B×f3 17. R×f3 Ne4 18. Qg4 Bf8 19. Raf1 Qg5 20. Qd7 Re7 21. Qd3 Q×d2 22. Qc4 Nd6 23. Qh4 Rc8 24. B×g7 Re4! 25. Qf6 Re6 26. Rg3 R×f6 27. B×f6+ Bg7 28. B×g7! The best practical chance. 28. ... Ne4 29. Rg4 *(see diagram)*

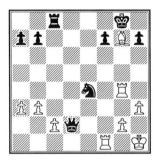

After
29. Rg3–g4

29. ... Ng5? Amusingly, Black had a variety of ways to win here, but he chose an unfortunate path. For example, 29. ... h5! 30. Bc3+ h×g4 31. B×d2 N×d2 32. Rf4 g×h3 33. g×h3 R×c2; Or 29. ... Qe2 30. Bh6+ Q×g4 31. h×g4 Ng3+ 32. Kg1 N×f1 33. K×f1 R×c2; or 29. ... f5 30. Bc3+ f×g4 31. B×d2 N×d2 32. Rd1 R×c2. 30. Bh6! f6?! 30. ... Rc5! 31. h4 Qe2 would have maintained winning chances: 32. Rff4 Q×c2 33. Kh2 Q×b3 34. B×g5 h5 35. Be7+ h×g4 36. R×g4+ Kh7 37. B×c5 Qe6. 31. R×f6 Rc6?? Overlooking a direct mate. After 31. ... Qe1+ 32. Kh2 Qe5+ 33. Rff4 Kh8 34. B×g5 Rf8 35. Bh6 Rg8! 36. Kg3 Qd6 37. R×g8+ K×g8 38. Bg5 Qg6 39. Kh4 h6 Black has at least good drawing chances, if not more. 32. Rf8 mate 1–0 [*Baltimore Sunday News*, July 15, 1893; *PM*, page 81]

140. Amateur–Pollock
London, Simpson's Divan,
Handicap Tournament, April 1887
Remove Nb8

1. e4 e5?! Perhaps this was not the best choice considering the missing knight on b8. 2. Nf3 d6 3. d4 e×d4 4. Q×d4! Nf6 5. e5! d×e5 6. Q×d8+ K×d8 7. N×e5 Bb4+ 8. c3 Re8 9. f4 Bd6 10. Bd3

Ng4 11. 0–0! Bc5+ 12. Kh1 Nf2+ 13. R×f2 B×f2 14. N×f7+ Ke7 15. Ne5 g6 16. Na3 Rd8 17. Be2 Bf5 18. Nac4 h5 19. Be3! Bh4 20. Bc5+ Ke8 21. Bf3 Rab8 22. g3 Be7 23. B×e7 K×e7 24. Re1 Kf6 *(see diagram)*

After
24. ... Ke7–f6

25. g4 h×g4 26. N×g4+ Kf7 27. Nh6+ Kf6 28. N×f5 K×f5 29. Kg2 K×f4 30. Re4+ Kf5 31. Ne3+ Kf6 32. Ng4+ Kf7 33. Ne5+ Kf6 34. Ng4+ Kf7 35. Rb4 1–0 [*Bristol Mercury and Daily Post*, April 7, 1887]

141. W. Wayte–Pollock [C48]
St. George's vs. City Match, London,
12 April 1887

1. e4 e5 2. Nc3 Nf6 3. Nf3 Nc6 4. Bb5 Bc5 5. 0–0 Qe7 6. d3 d6 7. Bg5 Bd7 8. Nd5 Qd8 9. c3 h6 10. B×f6 g×f6 11. Nh4 a6 12. Ba4 b5 13. Bb3 f5 14. Qh5 Qg5 15. N×f5 B×f5 *(see diagram)*

After
15. ... Bd7×f5

16. e×f5 Q×h5 17. Nf6+ Ke7 18. N×h5 Rag8 19. Kh1 Rg5 20. Ng3 Rhg8 21. Bd5 Nd8 22. f4 e×f4 23. R×f4 c6 24. Bf3 d5 25. a4 f6 26. a×b5 a×b5 27. d4 Bb6 28. Rh4 Nf7 29. Ra6 Rb8 30. Bh5 Nd6 31. Bg6 Nc4 32. R×h6 b4 33. c×b4 Kd6 34. Ne2 Ne3 35. g3 N×f5 36. B×f5 R×f5 37. Kg2 Re8 38. Nc3 B×d4 39. Nb5+ Ke5 40. R×c6 Rf2+ 41. Kh3 B×b2 42. Rh5+ f5 43. g4 Rg8 44. R×f5+ R×f5 45. g×f5 K×f5 46. Rc5 Ke4 47. Nd6+ Kf3 48. Kh4 Kf4 49. Kh5 d4 50. Rf5+ Ke3 51. Re5+ Kf3 52. Rf5+ Ke2

53. Re5+ ½–½ "In some quarters rumours were afloat that Mr. Pollock only accepted the draw believing the match was already decided in favor of the City. Whether that statement is correct or not we do not know, but, as matter of fact, we must declare that White had for a long time a decided advantage. He lost it finally, without, however, offering to his opponent any winning chances." [*Chess-Monthly*, July 1887, pages 343–344; *BCM*, July 1887, pages 279–281]

142. Pollock–J. Mortimer [C52]
London, Simpson's Divan, May 1887

1. e4 e5 2. Nf3 Nc6 3. Bc4 Bc5 4. b4 B×b4 5. c3 Ba5 6. 0–0 Nf6 7. d4 0–0 8. d×e5 N×e4 9. Re1 Nc5 It is somewhat dubious if White has sufficient compensation after 9. ... N×c3 10. N×c3 B×c3 11. Bg5 Qe8 12. Bd2 B×a1 13. Q×a1. **10. Bg5 Qe8** *(see diagram)*

After
10. ... Qd8–e8

11. Bf6!? Pollock was clearly fond of this motif. **11. ... Ne6** 11. ... g×f6 12. e×f6 Qd8 13. Qd5 could have been followed up with 13. ... Q×f6! 14. Q×c5 d6. **12. Nh4 Ne7 13. Qh5! Ng6 14. Qh6!?** Much more tempting than 14. Nf5. **14. ... g×h6 15. Nf5 Ng7 16. N×g7 d6! 17. N×e8 R×e8 18. Na3 Be6 19. Re3 c6 20. Rae1** 20. e×d6! Bd8 21. B×d8 Ra×d8 22. Rd1 was clearly better. **20. ... Bc7 21. h4 Rac8** and Black eventually won. **0–1** [*Illustrated London News*, June 11, 1887]

143. J.H. Blake–Pollock [C45]
London, Simpson's Divan, 30 May 1887

1. e4 e5 2. Nf3 Nc6 3. d4 e×d4 4. N×d4 N×d4 5. Q×d4 Ne7 6. Be3 Nc6 7. Qd2 Bb4 8. c3 Ba5 9. Na3 0–0 10. Nc4 Bb6 11. N×b6 a×b6 12. Bc4 d6 13. 0–0 Kh8 14. Rae1 f5? 14. ... Be6!? seemed a more reasonable choice. **15. Bg5 Qd7 16. e×f5 Q×f5 17. Be7 N×e7?** 17. ... Re8 fails to 18. B×d6! **18. R×e7 Qc5?** *(see diagram)* 18. ... b5 19. Bb3 Qc5 20. Qf4 Bf5 was recommended.

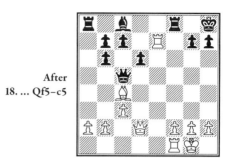

After
18. ... Qf5–c5

19. Qf4! Be6 19. ... Bf5 is met strongly by 20. b4 Qc6 21. Qd4 Rf6 22. Rfe1 h5 23. Bd5 Qa4 24. R×c7. **20. Qg3 Rf7 21. R×f7 B×f7 22. B×f7 1–0** [*Shoreditch Citizen*, March 31, 1888]

144. Pollock–R.J. Loman [C55]
London, Simpson's Divan, June 1887

1. e4 e5 2. Nf3 Nc6 3. Bc4 Nf6 4. Qe2 Be7 5. Nc3 d6 6. d3 Bg4 7. Be3 Qd7 8. h3 Bh5 9. g4 Bg6 10. 0–0–0 Na5 11. Bb3 N×b3+ 12. a×b3 a5 13. d4 13. g5 Nh5 14. d4 was more accurate. **13. ... e×d4** Possible too was 13. ... N×e4!? 14. d×e5 N×c3 15. b×c3 d5. **14. B×d4 Qc6?** *(see diagram)* 14. ... 0–0 was mandatory.

After
14. ... Qd7–c6

15. e5! Ne4 16. e×d6 c×d6 17. Rhe1 d5 18. B×g7 Rg8 19. Bd4 0–0–0 20. Ne5 Bg5+ 21. Kb1 N×c3+ 22. b×c3 Qd6 23. N×g6 h×g6 24. Qe5 Q×e5 25. B×e5 Rde8 26. Bd4 Re6 27. R×e6 f×e6 28. Re1 Kd7 29. Kb2 Rf8 30. Bb6 Bd8 31. B×d8 R×d8 1–0 It's unclear if the game lasted more than 31 moves. White's advantage in this rook endgame is not yet decisive. [*Dublin Evening Mail*, June 30, 1887]

145. Pollock–J. Burt [C44]
Simpson's Divan, June 1887

1. e4 e5 2. Nf3 Nc6 3. d4 N×d4 4. N×e5 Ne6 5. f4 f6? 6. Qh5+ g6 7. N×g6 h×g6 8. Q×h8 Nh6

9. f5 Nf7 10. Qg8 g×f5 11. e×f5 Nd4 12. Bd3 Qe7+ 13. Kd1 d5 14. Nc3 c6 15. Re1 Ne5 16. Bf4 Bd7 *(see diagram)*

After
16. ... Bc8–d7

17. R×e5!? 17. B×e5 f×e5 18. Qh8 0–0–0 19. Q×e5 was less artistic but more pragmatic. **17. ... f×e5 18. f6 Qe6** 18. ... Q×f6 19. Qg6+ Q×g6 20. B×g6+ Ke7 21. B×e5 leaves White with an extra pawn. **19. f7+ Ke7 20. Bg5+ Kd6 21. Kd2 e4?** 21. ... Bh6!? was a promising resource: 22. Q×a8 B×g5+ 23. Ke1 Q×f7. **22. Re1 Qg4 23. Be2 Qf5 24. Rf1 e3+ 25. K×e3 Q×c2 26. K×d4 c5+ 27. Ke3 d4+ 28. Kf2 d×c3 29. Rc1?** 29. Bf4+ Kc6 30. b×c3 should have settled the matter more quickly. **29. ... Q×b2?** 29. ... Qf5+!, followed by 30. ... c×b2, would have made things very difficult for White. **30. Qg6+ Kc7 31. Bf4+ Kc8 32. Qg8 Bg4 1–0** [*Dublin Evening Mail*, June 30, 1887]

146. Pollock–J. Burt [C51]
Clifton, June 1887

"A lively and amusing game played recently between Mr. 'Master' Pollock and Mr. Burt, one of our most ingenious amateurs." **1. e4 e5 2. Nf3 Nc6 3. Bc4 Bc5 4. b4 Bb6 5. b5 Na5** *(see diagram)*

After
5. ... Nc6–a5

6. B×f7+!? K×f7 7. N×e5+ Kf8 8. Ba3+ d6 9. d4 Be6 10. 0–0 Ne7 11. Qf3+ Ke8 12. Qh5+ g6 13. Qg5 d×e5 13. ... B×d4 14. Nd2 B×e5 was best. **14. Q×e5 B×d4 15. Q×e6 B×a1**

16. Nd2 Bc3 17. Rd1 Rf8 Simpler was 17. ... Qd7 18. Q×d7+ K×d7 19. Nb1+ Ke6 20. N×c3 Rad8. **18. Nf1 Rf7 19. R×d8+ R×d8 20. Ne3** 20. B×e7 R×e7 21. Qg8+ Kd7 22. Qd5+ Kc8 23. Qc5 would have kept the game going. **20. ... Rd2 21. h3 Rd×f2** 21. ... Bd4 was much safer. **22. Nd5** 22. B×e7! should have won: 22. ... R×e7 23. Qc8+ Kf7 24. K×f2. **22. ... Bd4 23. N×c7+ Kf8 24. Qc8+ Kg7 25. Ne6+ Kh6 26. Qb8 Rf1+ 27. Kh2 Bg1+ 28. Kg3 Bf2+ 29. Kg4 Nc6 30. Bc5 B×c5 31. N×c5 Ne3+ 32. Kg3 R7f2 33. Qe5 R×g2+ 34. Kh4 g5+ 35. Q×g5+ R×g5 0–1** [*Illustrated Sporting and Dramatic News*, July 9, 1887]

147. R.J. Loman–Pollock [C45]
London, Simpson's Divan, June 1887

1. e4 e5 2. Nf3 Nc6 3. d4 e×d4 4. N×d4 Qh4 5. Nb5 Bc5 6. Qf3 Nd4 7. N×d4 Pollock: "Or the following 7. N×c7+ Kd8 8. Qf4 Q×f4 9. B×f4 N×c2+ 10. Kd1 N×a1 11. N×a8, and in all probability 'Jack is as good as his master.'" **7. ... B×d4 8. Bc4 Nf6 9. 0–0 Be5 10. g3 Qh3** *(see diagram)*

After
10. ... Qh4–h3

11. Bg5!? Pollock: "An enterprising move which gives a lively character to the game. On the 12th move it is noteworthy that no fewer than four of White's pieces are *en prise*." **11. ... B×b2 12. e5** After 12. B×f6!? g×f6 13. Nc3 B×a1 14. R×a1 0–0 15. Nd5 White has sufficient (and appealing) compensation. **12. ... Qg4 13. B×f7+ K×f7 14. Qb3+ Nd5** Pollock: "This curious looking move ensures at least the gain of the exchange; the calculation is of course quite simple." **15. Q×d5+ Qe6 16. Q×e6+** 16. Nc3 Q×d5 17. N×d5 B×a1 18. R×a1 c6 19. Nc7 Rb8 20. Bf4 offered better resistance. **16. ... K×e6 17. Nd2 B×a1 18. R×a1 h6 19. Be3 K×e5 20. Re1 Kd5 21. c4+ Kc6 22. Bd4 Rg8 23. Re7 Kd6** Pollock: "It certainly seems as though Black would live to rue his venturesome play." **24. R×g7 R×g7 25. B×g7 h5**

26. Ne4+ Ke6 27. Nf6 Kf7 28. N×h5 Kg6 29. g4 d5 Pollock: "White ought to have included this move in his forecast. It decides the game." **30. h3 d×c4 31. f4 b5 32. Be5 c5 33. f5+ B×f5** Pollock: "Black is quite justified in the sacrifice, although it can hardly be called a sacrifice. The rook comes in at the death very neatly." **34. Nf4+ Kg5 35. g×f5 K×f5 36. Bc7 b4 37. Kf2 Rc8 38. Bd6 Rc6 39. Bb8 Ra6 40. Ng2 R×a2+ 0–1** [*PM*, page 42]

148. Pollock–F.J. Lee [C42]
London, Simpson's Divan, July 1887

1. e4 e5 2. Bc4 Nf6 3. Nf3 d5 4. B×d5 N×d5 5. e×d5 Q×d5 6. Nc3 Qd6 7. 0–0 Be7 8. Re1 Nc6 9. Nb5 Qd7 10. N×e5 N×e5 11. R×e5 f6 *(see diagram)*

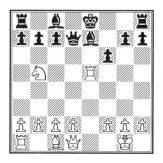

After
11. ... f7–f6

12. Rd5! Qc6 13. Qh5+ g6 14. Qe2 0–0 15. Q×e7! Re8? 15. ... Q×d5 16. N×c7 Qc6 17. d4 Bh3 18. d5 Q×c2 19. Bf4 Rf7 20. Qb4 R×c7 21. B×c7 Q×c7 22. g×h3 was Black's most precise option. **16. Rd8! Bd7 17. R×a8 R×a8 18. Nd4 Qd5 19. Q×f6 Re8 20. Nf3?** Panic or simple oversight? 20. f3 c5 21. Nb3 Re1+ 22. Kf2 would have assured the full point. **20. ... Q×f3! 21. g×f3 Bh3 22. Qd8 R×d8 ½–½** [*Illustrated London News*, July 9, 1887]

149. Pollock–J. Mortimer [C25]
London, July 1887

1. e4 e5 2. Nc3 Nc6 3. f4 e×f4 4. Nf3 Be7 5. Bc4 g5 6. d4 d6 7. h4 g4 8. Ng5 B×g5 9. h×g5 Q×g5 10. g3 Qg7 11. Nb5 Kd8 12. B×f4 a6 13. Nc3 N×d4 14. Qd3 Nf3+ 15. Kf2 Bd7 16. Rad1 h5 17. Nd5 17. B×d6 c×d6 18. Q×d6 looks tempting since White gets massive pressure after 18. ... Ne5 19. Rd5 f6 20. Qb6+ Kc8 21. Rhd1. **17. ... Ne5 18. Qc3 Ne7** *(see diagram)*

After
18. ... Ng8–e7

19. N×c7!! K×c7 20. R×d6! N7c6? 20. ... K×d6 loses after 21. Rd1+ Nd5 22. R×d5+ Ke7 23. Qb4+. **21. R×c6+! K×c6 22. B×e5** 22. Bb5+ was a pretty choice too: 22. ... Kd6 (22. ... K×b5 23. a4+ K×a4 24. Qb3+ Ka5 25. Bd2 mate) 23. B×e5+ Q×e5 24. Rd1+ Ke6 25. B×d7+ Kf6 26. Rd6+. **22. ... Qf8 23. Bd5+ Kb6 24. Qc7+ Kb5 25. Bc4+ Kb4 26. Bc3+ Ka4 27. Qa5 mate 1–0** [*Illustrated London News*, July 23, 1887]

A line-drawing of W.H.K. Pollock (*Baltimore Sunday News*, **April 19, 1891**)

CCA Meeting (Stamford, August 1887)

150. Pollock–C.D. Locock [C58]
CCA Meeting, Stamford, Round 1,
1 August 1887

1. e4 e5 2. Nf3 Nc6 3. Bc4 Nf6 4. Ng5 d5
5. e×d5 Na5 6. d3 h6 7. Nf3 e4 8. Qe2 N×c4
9. d×c4 Be7 10. Ne5 0–0 11. h3 Re8 12. Ng4 b5
13. Ne3 Bb7 14. Nc3 Bb4 15. Bd2 B×c3 16. B×c3
b×c4 17. B×f6 Q×f6 18. c3 Rab8 19. 0–0–0
Red8 20. Rd2 Qa6 21. a3 Qb5 22. Rhd1 Ba6 (see diagram)

After
22. ... Bb7–a6

23. Nf5! Qc5 24. Qg4 g6 25. N×h6+ Kg7
26. Nf5+!? Seemingly, Pollock was not interested
in 26. N×f7 K×f7 27. Qe6+ Kg7 28. Q×a6. 26. ...
Kf8 27. Nd4 R×d5? 27. ... Bb7 28. Qf4 Kg8
29. Nc2 B×d5 offered greater resistance. 28. Q×e4
Rd6 29. Qe3 Qa5 30. Qh6+ Kg8 31. Nc6! 1–0
[*Illustrated Sporting and Dramatic News*, August
27, 1887]

151. Pollock–E. Thorold [C42]
CCA Meeting, Stamford, Round 2,
2 August 1887

1. e4 e5 2. Nf3 Nf6 3. Bc4 d5 4. e×d5 Bd6
5. d4 e4 6. Ne5 Nbd7 7. N×d7 B×d7 8. Bg5 h6
9. Bh4 Qe7 10. Nc3 g5 11. Bg3 0–0–0 12. Qd2
a6 13. 0–0–0 b5 14. Bb3 Ne8 15. Qe3 f5 (see diagram)

16. Be5! Rf8 16. ... B×e5 17. d×e5 Q×e5 is not
playable because of 18. Qa7. 17. Rhe1 Kb7 18. f3
B×e5 19. d×e5 Q×e5 20. f×e4 Nd6 21. e×f5
Q×e3+ 22. R×e3 R×f5 23. Rde1 a5 24. a4
b×a4 25. Ba2 Rf2 26. R3e2 Rdf8 27. Nd1
R×e2 28. R×e2 Bb5 29. Re6 29. Rf2 Re8 30. Nc3
Re1+ 31. Kd2 Rh1 32. Ke3 R×h2 33. N×b5 N×b5
34. c4 was much stronger than the text. 29. ... h5

After
15. ... f7–f5

30. Kd2 Rf4 31. c3 Rf5 32. Ke3 Rf1 33. Kd2
Rg1 34. g3 Pollock's defense is not the best. Better was 34. Ne3 Rh1 35. Re7 R×h2 36. c4. 34. ...
Rg2+ 35. Ke3 a3! 36. Rg6 Re2+ 37. Kd4
Rd2+ 38. Kc5 R×d1 39. b×a3 Ka6 40. Re6 Ra1
41. a4 B×a4 42. Bc4+ Kb7 43. Bd3 Bb3 44. Rh6
a4 45. R×h5 Rd1 46. Be2 a3 47. R×g5 a2
48. B×d1 B×d1 0–1 [*Leeds Mercury*, August 13,
1887]

152. G.A. MacDonnell–Pollock [C62]
CCA Meeting, Stamford, Round 3,
3 August 1887

1. e4 e5 2. Nf3 Nc6 3. Bb5 d6 4. d4 Bd7 5. B×c6
B×c6 6. Nc3 f6 Pollock: "The maintenance of the
centre in this way has always been allowed by experts
to be in harmony with the spirit of this form of defence to the Ruy Lopez. At the same time they have
generally fought shy of adopting it in serious chess.
Steinitz has always laid it down as a principle that
the support of the e-pawn by f7–f6 is advisable when
there is no danger from the adverse king's bishop.
And at all events Black's game is not more cramped
than by ...e×d4, Be7, etc." 7. 0–0 Qe7 8. b4 Pollock:
"A much better preparation to meet Black's intention of castling on the queenside would be 8. Be3."
8. ... a6 9. Be3 Qf7 Pollock: "Naturally, a very good
place for the queen." 10. a4 g5?! 11. Qe2 Ne7
12. Rfd1 Ng6 13. b5 Bd7 14. b×a6 Pollock: "It
would be more advantageous to let Black capture
first, and here Nd5, supported by c4, looks more
consistent with the advance of the pawns." 14. ...
b×a6 14. ... R×a6 was superior. 15. Nd5! Be6
16. Qc4 B×d5 17. e×d5 Qd7 18. Rdb1 Pollock: "A
pretty sharp attack is now looming up." 18. ... Be7
19. Rb7 e4 Pollock: "If 19. ... Bd8 20. d×e5 d×e5
21. d6! We shall therefore have to confess that Black's
game is too backward and that his judgement was
at fault on the 10th move, the time for which he
could not afford." 20. Ne1?! Why not 20. Nd2 Rc8

21. N×e4?; Pollock: "It is not quite certain that White cannot play as follows: 20. R×c7 Qg4 21. h3 Qh5 22. Qc6+ Kf7 23. Q×d6 e×f3 24. Qe6+ Kg7 25. R×e7+ N×e7 26. Q×e7+ Qf7 27. Q×f7+ K×f7 28. c4 and should win." **20. ... Bd8 21. f3 e×f3 22. N×f3 0–0 23. Rf1 Qg4** Pollock: "Releasing the queen from the masked battery, and presumably intending an attack by ...Qe4 and ...Ne7 if allowed." **24. Qd3 f5 25. Bd2 Qh5 26. Qe2 Bf6 27. Qe6+ Kh8** *(see diagram)*

After
27. ... Kg8–h8

28. Q×f5!? Pollock: "Splendidly conceived and well meriting success." 28. R×c7 g4 29. Ne5! was more forceful: 29. ... N×e5 (29. ... d×e5? 30. R×f5) 30. d×e5 B×e5 31. Bf4. **28. ... B×d4+ 29. N×d4 R×f5 30. N×f5 Rc8** Pollock: "An abject looking defence!" **31. Bc3+ Kg8 32. h3 h6 33. Re1! Rf8?** 33. ... g4 34. h×g4 Qg5! would have maintained equal chances. **34. R×c7 Ne5 35. N×d6 Qh4 36. Ne4** Pollock: "If 36. R×e5 Black could draw by perpetual check." **36. ... Rf3!** Ingenious desperation. Pollock: "A happy resource indeed!" **37. Rb1?** White falters right at the key juncture. Instead, he could have won with 37. g×f3 N×f3+ 38. Kf1 Q×h3+ 39. Kf2 Qh2+ 40. K×f3 g4+ 41. K×g4 Q×c7 42. d6 Qd7+ 43. Kh4. **37. ... Q×e4 38. Rc8+** 38. Re1 Re3 39. Rb1 Rf3 40. Re1 Re3 (40. ... Q×c2 41. R×e5 Qf2+ 42. Kh1 Re3 43. Rc8+ Kf7 44. R×e3 Q×e3 45. Rc6, with equality.) 41. Rb1 would have forced a draw. **38. ... Rf8 39. R×f8+ K×f8 40. Re1 Nf3+! 41. g×f3 Q×d5 42. Bb4+ Kf7** and Black won. **0–1** [*PM*, pages 48–49]

153. Pollock–J.H. Blake [C58]
CCA Meeting, Stamford, Round 6, 4 August 1887

1. e4 e5 2. Nf3 Nc6 3. Bc4 Nf6 4. Ng5 d5 5. e×d5 Na5 6. d3 h6 7. Nf3 e4 8. Qe2 N×c4 9. d×c4 Bc5 10. h3 0–0 11. Ne5 b5 Pollock: "A very ineffective move in this position. The following variations are suggestive: 11. ... e3 12. f×e3! Re8

13. Ng4 Ne4 14. Qf3 Qh4+ 15. Nf2 N×f2 16. Q×f2 Q×c4; 11. ... c6 12. d×c6 Qa5+ 13. Bd2 B×f2+ 14. Q×f2 Q×e5." **12. Ng4 b×c4 13. Q×c4 B×g4 14. Q×c5 Bf5 15. Nc3** Pollock: "Thus White returns the pawn with a tolerably good game." **15. ... Nd7 16. Qd4 Re8 17. Be3 Qb8 18. 0–0–0 Qb6 19. Qa4 Qd6 20. Nb5 Qe5 21. g3 Nb6 22. Qb3 Rec8 23. Bf4 Qe7** *(see diagram)*

After
23. ... Qe5–e7

24. d6! Pollock: "White has fully assumed the attack, which he maintained with vigour. The heroic manner in which Black saves the game is astonishing and beyond all praise." **24. ... c×d6 25. N×d6 Rc5 26. Qa3! Nd7 27. N×f5 Qe6 28. g4** Pollock: "Surely 28. R×d7 would have cut short all further resistance?" **28. ... Rac8 29. c3 Rc4 30. Rd6** 30. Ne7+ Kh7 31. N×c8 R×c8 32. Qd6 was simple enough. **30. ... Qe8 31. Rhd1 Nc5 32. Q×a7 Nd3+ 33. R1×d3** Even 33. Kb1 N×f4 34. Ne7+ Kh8 35. N×c8 R×c8 36. Qd7 should have won. **33. ... e×d3 34. Qe7 Qa4 35. R×d3 R×f4 36. Qe5** Pollock completely missed 36. Rd8+! R×d8 37. Q×d8+ Kh7 38. Ne7 with a mate in six. **36. ... R×f5! 37. Q×f5 Re8 38. Kd2 Q×a2 39. Qb5 Qe6 40. Re3 Rd8+ 41. Kc2 Qg6+ 42. Kb3 Kf8 43. Qc5+ Kg8 44. Qc7 Ra8 45. Qb7 Rd8 46. f4 Qd6** Pollock: "A very strong move, threatening ...Rb8, ...Q×f4 and ...Qd1+." **47. Qf3 Qb6+ 48. Kc2 Qb5 49. b3?!** Pollock: "Extremely weak. 49. Re4 would still win with a little care." **49. ... Qa5 50. Kb1 Qa3 51. Rd3 Q×b3+ 52. Kc1 Re8 53. Re3?** 53. Rd4, 53. f5, and 53. Rd5 were all safer options. **53. ... Rd8** No mention was made of the fact that Black could have won with 53. ... Rb8! 54. Qe4 Qa2 55. f5 Rb2. **54. Rd3 Re8 55. Re3 Rd8 ½–½** [*PM*, pages 51–52]

154. Pollock–J.H. Blake [C47]
CCA Meeting (Handicap Tournament), Stamford, August 1887

1. e4 e5 2. Nc3 Nc6 3. Nf3 Nf6 4. d4 e×d4 5. N×d4 Bb4 6. Bg5 B×c3+ Pollock: "There is no necessity for this capture. Black should castle or play ...h7–h6." **7. b×c3 Qe7 8. Bd3 Qc5** *(see diagram)*

After
8. ... Qe7–c5

9. Nf5! Pollock: "Black must have overlooked this. It precludes castling, on account of the fatal reply B×f6." **9. ... Q×c3+ 10. Bd2 Qe5 11. N×g7+ Kf8 12. Nf5 N×e4?!** A risky approach. 12. ... d5 was necessary. **13. Bh6+ Ke8 14. Ng7+ Kd8 15. 0–0 Nc3** Pollock: "There was hardly another move in face of B×e4 and Re1." **16. Qd2 d6 17. Rae1 Qd4 18. Qg5+?!** Very strong was 18. Nf5!? B×f5 19. Qg5+ f6 20. Qg7. **18. ... f6 19. Qh5 Ne5 20. h3 c6 21. Bf5!** Pollock: "Keeping up the attack actively. If 21. ... B×f5, 22. Q×f5, threatening a fatal check with Ne6." **21. ... Qd5 22. f4 Nf7 23. Qh4 B×f5 24. Q×f6+ Kc7 25. Re7+ Kb6 26. R×f7** Missing the rather simple 26. Q×c3! N×h6 (26. ... Ka6 27. N×f5 Q×f5 28. Qa3+ Qa5 29. Q×a5+ K×a5 30. R×f7; 26. ... Bc8 27. Rb1+ Ka6 28. Qa3+ Qa5 29. Q×a5+ K×a5 30. R×f7) 27. Rb1+ Ka6 28. Re×b7. **26. ... Be4** Pollock: "The defence is valiant but clearly ineffectual." In fact, 26. ... Bg6 27. Rd7 Qc5+ 28. Kh2 Rhf8 was Black's last chance even if White's advantage is not in doubt. **27. Q×c3 Q×f7 28. Qb4+ Kc7 29. Q×e4 Rhg8 30. Ne6+ Kd7 31. f5** Pollock: "A subtle move." **31. ... Qh5 32. Nc5+! d×c5 33. Qe6+ Kc7 34. Bf4+ Kb6 35. Qb3+ 1–0** [*Chess-Monthly*, September 1887, pages 26–27; *PM*, pages 49–50]

155. H. Jacobs–Pollock [C29]
CCA Meeting (Handicap Tournament), Stamford, August 1887

1. e4 e5 2. Nc3 Nf6 3. f4 d5 4. d3 Nc6 5. f×e5 N×e5 6. d4 Ng6 7. e×d5 N×d5 8. Nf3 Bb4 9. Bd2 0–0 10. Be2 Ndf4! 11. 0–0 Bg4 12. Bc4 *(see diagram)* 12. g3 N×e2+ 13. Q×e2 Re8 14. Qc4 was the correct path.

12. ... N×g2!! 12. ... B×f3! 13. Q×f3 Q×d4+ 14. Be3 Q×c4 15. B×f4 Rfe8 gives Black a full pawn. **13. K×g2 Nh4+ 14. Kg3** 14. Kh1 is safer: 14. ...

After
12. Be2–c4

N×f3 15. R×f3 Q×d4 16. Rf4 Q×f4 17. B×f4 B×d1 18. R×d1 Rad8 19. Bd3 and White can be satisfied. **14. ... B×f3 15. R×f3 Q×d4 16. Bd3 Bd6+ 17. Bf4 f5!? 18. Nb5?!** 18. K×h4 looks dangerous, but it's not all that clear: 18. ... B×f4 (18. ... g5+?! 19. Kg3 [19. K×g5?? leads to a quick mate: 19. ... Qf6+ 20. Kh5 Qg6+ 21. Kh4 Qg4 mate] 19. ... B×f4+ 20. Kg2 g4 21. Rf2 and White has the edge) 19. Kh3 Rf6 20. B×f5! Rh6+ 21. Kg2 R×h2+ 22. Kf1 Rh1+ 23. Kg2 R×d1 24. R×d1 Qe5 25. Rd5 Qf6 26. R×f4 g6 27. Ne4 with a very unclear position. 18. Be2 was another good defensive idea. **18. ... Qf6** 18. ... B×f4+ was cold-blooded and good: 19. R×f4 Qe3+ 20. K×h4 Q×f4+ 21. Kh3 Rf6 22. Kg2 Rh6 23. h3 Qg5+ 24. Kh2 Qe3 25. Qf1 f4. **19. Rf1** The losing move but the situation is desperate. 19. Kh3 was to be met by 19. ... g5! 20. Bc4+ Kh8 21. B×d6 g4+ 22. Kg3 N×f3 23. N×c7 f4+ with a winning attack. **19. ... Qg5+ 20. Kh3 0–1** [*Glasgow Weekly Herald*, August 13, 1887]

VARIOUS GAMES (MID–1887)

156. T.J. Beardsell–Pollock [C21]
London(?), August 1887

1. e4 e5 2. d4 e×d4 3. c3 d×c3 4. Bc4 c×b2 Pollock: "The Danish gambit." **5. B×b2 Nf6 6. Nf3 Bb4+ 7. Kf1 N×e4** Pollock: "The opening is not played with particular care, both parties risking a good deal. Mr. Beardsell used to delight in these airy skirmishes, while displaying at other times talent for a steady and careful style of play." **8. B×g7 Rg8 9. Qd5 Qe7 10. Be5 Nf6 11. Qd4 Rg4 12. Qd3** Pollock: "White might have exchanged queens here for, though he would have been subjected to the embarrassment of central passed pawns against him, he would have some attack against his opponent's undeveloped queen's wing." **12. ... Nc6 13. Bb2 d5 14. Bb3 Ne4 15. Nbd2** *(see diagram)*

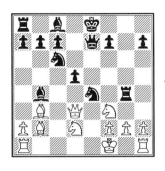

After
15. Nb1–d2

15. ... R×g2!! Pollock: "This sacrifice produces some highly animated chess; it was a good idea, and just about sound." **16. K×g2 Bh3+ 17. Kg1 0-0-0 18. Nf1 Rg8+ 19. Ng3 Bc5 20. Nd4 Ne5** 20. ... Qf6 21. Rf1 Ne5 was strong as well. **21. Qe3 Qg5** Pollock: "He might have played 22. Re1. Of course, White could not play 22. Q×g5 on pain of mate in two." **22. Bc2** After 22. Re1 c6! 23. Bd1 Qh4 Black maintains a winning offensive. **22. ... Q×e3 23. B×e4** Pollock: "If 23. f×e3, mate in two." **23. ... Q×e4 0-1** [*Belfast News-Letter*, September 21, 1887]

157. Pollock–E. Thorold [C30]
Bath, September 1887

1. e4 e5 2. Nc3 Bc5 3. f4 d6 4. Nf3 Bg4 5. h3 B×f3 6. Q×f3 Nc6 7. Bc4 Qh4+ 8. g3 Nd4 9. Qg2 Qh5 10. d3 Nf3+ 11. Kf1 Nd4 12. g4 Qh4 13. Be3 e×f4 14. B×f4 Ne7 15. e5 Ng6 16. Bg3 *(see diagram)*

After
16. Bf4–g3

16. ... N×c2?! 16. ... Qh6 or 16. ... Qd8 were better alternatives. **17. B×f7+** 17. Nd5! was more accurate than the text (if less spectacular). **17. ... Kf8** 17. ... K×f7!? 18. Qf3+ Ke8 19. B×h4 Rf8 20. Bf6 N×e5 was not exactly in White's favor. **18. B×g6 Ne3+ 19. Ke2 N×g2 20. Rhf1+ Qf6?** A miscalculation. 20. ... Ke7! 21. B×h4+ N×h4 22. Be4 c6 and White has no clear advantage. **21. Be4! Q×f1+ 22. R×f1+ Ke8 23. B×g2 Rf8 24. B×b7 R×f1 25. K×f1 Rb8 26. Bc6+ Kf8**

27. e6 g5 28. Ne4 Be3 29. N×d6 R×b2 30. Nf5 Bc5 31. Be5 1-0 [*Illustrated Sporting and Dramatic News*, September 24, 1887]

BCA MASTERS (NOVEMBER/ DECEMBER 1887)

158. J.H. Blackburne–Pollock [C40]
BCA Masters, London,
British Chess Club, Round 1,
29 November 1887

1. e4 e5 2. Nf3 f5 Steinitz: "A hazardous way of meeting the King's Knight opening. But ambitious tournament players, especially the young ones, will sometimes resort to inferior openings that are little known, even against great masters, and occasionally they succeed with such tactics." **3. d4** Steinitz: "Which takes the probably well-prepared opponent out of his books. But the innovation cannot be recommended, and 3. N×e5 or 3. Bc4, the recognized strongest moves at this juncture, are preferable." **3. ... f×e4 4. N×e5 Nf6 5. Bg5 Be7 6. Nc3** Steinitz: "An excellent preparatory move for a powerful and beautifully-conceived attack." **6. ... d6** 6. ... d5 is more solid. **7. B×f6 B×f6 8. Qh5+ g6** *(see diagram)*

After
8. ... g7–g6

9. N×g6!? h×g6 **10. Q×g6+ Kd7** Steinitz: "If 10. ... Kf8, 11. Bc4 Qe7 12. Nd5 and wins." **11. Nd5 Rf8?** 11. ... Be7 was offering reasonable defensive chances: 12. Q×e4 Qe8! 13. Be2 Kd8 14. h4 c6 15. Ne3 Nd7. **12. Be2! c5** 12. ... B×d4 is met by 13. 0-0-0! Qe8 14. Q×e8+ K×e8 15. R×d4 Kd8 16. R×e4 R×f2 17. Bf3; Steinitz: "His only chance was 12. ... Nc6; But he could only expect to prolong the fight even in that case, for White would have proceeded with 13. Q×e4 and if 13. ... Re8, then 14. Qf3 with an irresistible attack." **13. d×c5 B×b2?** Steinitz: "This makes matters worse, but there was no good move." 13. ... Kc6 is met by 14. Q×e4 Re8

15. Qa4+! K×d5 16. 0–0–0+ Ke6 17. R×d6+.
**14. Q×d6+ Ke8 15. Bh5+ Rf7 16. B×f7+ K×f7
17. Q×d8 Nc6 18. Qc7+ Ke8 19. Rb1 Be5
20. Qh7 Kd8 21. Qg8+ Kd7 22. 0–0 1–0** [*Leeds
Mercury*, December 3, 1887; *Nottinghamshire
Guardian*, December 10, 1887; *ICM*, January 1888,
page 25; *New York Clipper*, March 17, 1888]

159. Pollock–A.G. Guest [C51]
BCA Masters, London,
British Chess Club, Round 2,
30 November 1887

Morning Post (December 1): "The longest game
was an Evans Gambit, played by Pollock against
Guest, and won by the latter after 51 moves." *Daily
News* (December 1): "The only game unfinished at
the adjournment was that between Pollock and
Guest, the former selecting the Evans Gambit,
which the latter accepted and defended with conspicuous ability. Resuming play at 8 o'clock the contest was prolonged for another hour, when Pollock
finally resigned a struggle which had long been
hopeless." **1. e4 e5 2. Nf3 Nc6 3. Bc4 Bc5 4. b4
B×b4 5. c3 Bc5 6. d4 e×d4 7. 0–0 d6 8. c×d4 Bb6
9. Bg5 Nge7 10. Nc3 f6 11. Bh4 Bg4 12. Ne2 Ng6
13. Bg3 Na5 14. Qd3 B×f3 15. g×f3 N×c4
16. Q×c4 Qd7 17. a4 c6 18. a5 Bc7 19. Rfb1 Rb8
20. f4 Qf7 21. Qc2 Ne7 22. f5 g5 23. f4 g4 24. a6**
24. d5 0–0 25. Bf2 c5 26. Nd4!? was worthy of careful study. **24. ... Bb6 25. a×b7 R×b7 26. Kg2 h5
27. Bh4 0–0 28. Rf1 Rfb8 29. Rad1 Bd8 30. Rb1
Kg7 31. R×b7 R×b7 32. Ng3 Kh6 33. h3 g×h3+
34. Kh2 a5 35. Qe2 Ng8** (*see diagram*)

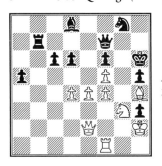

After
35. ... Ne7–g8

36. Rg1 36. e5!? must have been calculated:
36. ... d5 (36. ... d×e5 37. f×e5 Rb3 38. Rg1 is too
dangerous.) 37. K×h3 Rb3 38. Rc1 Qe8 39. Qc2
a4 40. Q×c6 Q×c6 41. R×c6 Kg7 42. Ra6 with
advantage for White. **36. ... a4 37. N×h5?** 37. e5!
was good enough. Pollock's sacrifice is too speculative. **37. ... a3!** It's likely that Pollock was betting

A.G. Guest (London Borough of Hackney Archives).

on 37. ... Q×h5? 38. Rg6+ Q×g6 39. f×g6 a3
40. K×h3 Rb2 41. Qc4 d5 42. Qc3. **38. K×h3**
38. Qg4 Rb2+ 39. K×h3 a2 40. e5 Rb3+ 41. Kh2
d×e5 42. f×e5 a1Q! 43. R×a1 Q×h5 doesn't look
too promising either. **38. ... Rb2 39. Qg4 a2
40. Q×g8 Rb3+ 41. Kh2 Q×g8 42. R×g8 K×h5
43. R×d8 a1Q 44. Bf2 Qa2 45. Kg2 Kh6
46. R×d6 Rb2 47. R×f6+ Kg7 48. Rg6+ Kf7
49. Kg1 R×f2 50. e5 R×f4 51. e6+ Kf8 0–1**
[*Daily News*, December 1, 1887]

160. Pollock–F.J. Lee [C14]
BCA Masters, London,
British Chess Club, Round 3,
1 December 1887

The *Daily News* noted this game was "a skirmish
of brief duration, finished in less than fifty minutes." **1. e4 e6 2. d4 d5 3. Nc3 Nf6 4. Bg5 Be7
5. e5 Nfd7 6. B×e7 Q×e7 7. f4 a6 8. Bd3 c5
9. Nf3 c×d4 10. N×d4 Qb4 11. Nde2 d4?!** 11. ...
Q×b2!? 12. 0–0 Nc6 13. Rb1 Qa3 14. Qe1 h6
15. Qg3 g5!? was the other critical choice here. So
was 11. ... Nc6. **12. a3 Qb6 13. Ne4** (*see diagram*)
13. ... Nc6? 13. ... 0–0 was compulsory: 14. Nd6

After
13. Nc3–e4

g6 15. Qd2 Nc6. **14. Nd6+ Ke7 15. 0–0 f5 16. Qe1 Q×b2 17. Qh4+ Kf8 18. Rfb1 1–0** [*Daily News*, December 2, 1887; *Ladies' Treasury: A Household Magazine*, January 1, 1888]

161. I.A. Gunsberg–Pollock [C41]
BCA Masters, London,
British Chess Club, Round 4,
2 December 1887

1. e4 e5 2. Nf3 f5 3. e×f5 d6 3. ... e4 4. Ne5 Nf6 is the main line. **4. d4 e4 5. Qe2 Nf6 6. Nc3 d5 7. Ne5 c6?!** *(see diagram)* 7. ... c5!? could have been tried as well: 8. Bg5 c×d4 9. B×f6 Q×f6 10. Qh5+ g6 11. f×g6 h×g6 12. Bb5+ Nc6 13. N×d5 g×h5 14. N×f6+ Ke7 15. N×c6+ b×c6 16. B×c6 Rb8 17. N×e4 R×b2.

After
7. ... c7–c6

8. g4! Now Black could be simply lost. **8. ... Bb4 9. g5 0–0 10. g×f6 Q×f6 11. Bh3 c5** 11. ... B×f5 12. B×f5 Q×f5 13. Rg1 Nd7 had to be given a go at any cost. **12. Be3 Nc6 13. N×c6 b×c6 14. Rd1 g6 15. f×g6! B×h3 16. Qh5 Q×g6 17. Q×h3 Rf3 18. Qf1 Qf6 19. Rg1+ Kf7 20. Qg2 Rb8 21. Qg4 Rf5 22. Qg3 Re8 23. Bg5 Qg6 24. a3 Ba5 25. Bf4 e3 26. f×e3 c×d4 27. R×d4 c5 28. Ra4 Bb6 29. Nb5 Q×g3+ 30. h×g3 Rf6 31. Nd6+ R×d6 32. B×d6 R×e3+ 33. Kd2 c4 34. Rf1+ Ke6 35. Bf4 Re4 36. Re1 Kf5 37. R×e4 K×e4 38. b3 h5 39. b×c4 d4 40. Bd6 a5 41. c5 Bd8 42. c3 1–0**
[*Daily News*, December 3, 1887; it also noted the game lasted two hours and a half.]

162. Pollock–J.H. Zukertort [C44]
BCA Masters, London,
British Chess Club, Round 5,
3 December 1887

1. e4 e5 2. Nf3 Nc6 3. c3 d5 4. Qa4 f6 5. Bb5 Nge7 6. 0–0 Bd7 Pollock: "Steinitz advocates playing the bishop to e6 where possible in this and similar positions." **7. e×d5 N×d5 8. d4 a6 9. Qb3 a×b5 10. Q×d5 e×d4 11. Re1+ Be7 12. Qh5+** Pollock: "12. c×d4 simply, followed, unless ...Bg4, by Nc3, would give White an excellent game." **12. ... g6 13. Qh6 Kf7! 14. Qh4 Ne5** *(see diagram)* 14. ... d3 15. Be3 Be6 16. Nbd2 Qd7 is even more forceful.

After
14. ... Nc6–e5

15. R×e5!? Pollock: "A very energetic stroke, but unsound." **15. ... f×e5 16. N×e5+ Ke8 17. Q×d4 Bf6 18. Bg5!?** A beautiful and provocative move but risky. **18. ... Rf8?!** As Pollock rightly noted in his annotations, Black had 18. ... B×g5 19. N×d7 Rg8! and White seems in trouble. **19. Bh6 Rh8 20. Nd2 Bf5 21. Qe3 Qe7 22. Re1 Q×e5 23. Q×e5+ B×e5 24. R×e5+ Kd7 25. g4 Be6 26. Ne4 R×a2 27. Nc5+ Kd6 28. Bf4 Bd5 29. Nb3?** Pollock: "The draw is extremely neatly brought about." In fact, the text move is poorer than 29. Nd3 Ra4 30. Re1+ Kc6 31. Nb4+ Kc5 32. B×c7. **29. ... Rha8** 29. ... Ra4 30. Nd4 c6 was keeping winning chances for Black. **30. Rh5+ Kc6 31. Nd4+ Kc5 32. Nb3+ Kc6 33. Nd4+ Kc5 34. Nb3+ Kc4 35. Nd2+ Kc5 36. Nb3+** Pollock: "Black can only escape the perpetual check by moving away from the protection of his bishop." ½–½ [*Chess-Monthly*, January 1888, pages 146–147; *PM*, pages 46–47]

163. H.E. Bird–Pollock [C53]
BCA Masters, London,
British Chess Club, Round 6,
5 December 1887

1. e4 e5 2. Nf3 Nc6 3. Bc4 Bc5 4. c3 Qe7 5. b4

Bb6 6. a4 a5 Pollock: "In the customary fashion of the Evans Gambit Declined (where the fourth moves of the present game are not made) this is not so good as ...a6, although adopted by some masters. For after b5 the knight must go to d4, whereupon White exchanges, with gain of time to form a strong centre." **7. b5 Nd8 8. 0–0 d6 9. d4 f6** Pollock: "The position is in favour of Black, who here plays correctly." **10. Ba3 Bg4 11. Be2 Ne6 12. Nh4 B×e2 13. Q×e2 e×d4** Pollock: "Rather short-sighted and losing his advantage. 13. ... Nh6 or 13. ... g6 are better moves." **14. Nf5 Qd7 15. Rd1 g6 16. N×d4** 16. c×d4!? was an interesting choice. **16. ... Nf4 17. Qf3 Ne6** (*see diagram*)

After
17. ... Nf4–e6

18. e5!? f×e5 19. N×e6 Q×e6 20. Q×b7 Rd8 21. Qc6+ Rd7 22. Nd2 Ne7 23. Qc4 Qd5 23. ... d5 24. Qh4 0–0 25. Nf3 Nf5 was excellent too. **24. Qe4 Qf7** Pollock: "The play on both sides is rather pretty. White's object is to play Nc4 and take the bishop, so long as he can oblige Black to recapture the pawn, leaving the d-pawn assailable." **25. Rf1 g5 26. Nc4 Qd5 27. Qe2 Ng6 28. Rfd1** Pollock: "Now 28. N×b6 would give Black a rather threatening attack on the kingside." **28. ... Qb7?** 28. ... Nf4!? is an interesting resource. **29. N×b6** 29. B×d6! c×d6 30. R×d6 Bc7 31. R×d7 K×d7 32. Rd1+ Ke7 33. Qg4 would have given White a very strong attack. **29. ... Q×b6 30. Bc1 Nf4 31. B×f4 g×f4 32. Rd5** Pollock: "Threatening R×e5+." **32. ... 0–0 33. Rad1** Pollock: "Again menacing the pawn." **33. ... Rg7 34. Qf3** Pollock: "Necessary to prevent ...f4–f3." **34. ... Qb8!** Pollock: "Black is aware that his queen is sitting shut out from the fun." **35. Kh1 Qe8 36. Qe4 Qh5 37. f3 Rf6 38. Qe1?!** 38. R5d2 was safer. **38. ... Rh6** Pollock missed 38. ... R×g2!! 39. K×g2 Rg6+ 40. Kf1 Q×f3+ 41. Qf2 Qh3+ 42. Ke1 Rg2 43. Qa7 Q×c3+ 44. R1d2 f3 45. R5d3 Qc1+ 46. Rd1 Qc2 with a clear win. **39. Qg1 Qh4** Pollock: "Apparently intending to push ...e5–e4."

40. b6! Pollock: "Very well played, although truly he has little else to do." **40. ... c×b6 41. R×d6 R×d6 42. R×d6 Rg6 43. R×g6+ h×g6 44. Qd1 Qf2 45. h3 Kh7 46. Qb1 Kh6 47. Qe4 Qc5 48. Qe1 Kg5 49. h4+ Kf6 50. Qd2 Ke7 51. Qd3 Kf6 52. Kh2 Qc6 53. Qe4? Qc5?** Pollock: "53. ... Q×e4 followed by 54. ... b5 wins at once." **54. Qd3 Qc6 55. Qc2 Ke7 56. Kh3 Qe6+ 57. g4 Qc4 58. Kg2 b5! 59. a×b5 Q×b5 60. c4 Qc5 61. g5 Qe3 62. Qb2 a4 63. Qb7+ Kd8 64. Qb8+ Kd7 65. Qb5+ Kd6 ½–½** [*PM*, pages 45–46; *Daily News* (December 6): "...this proved to be the longest battle of the day, terminating in a drawn game at 10:30 PM, after six and a half hours' struggle." *Standard* (December 6): "Bird vs. Pollock was given up as drawn at 10:45 in an ending of queen and equal number of pawns on both sides. After a protracted struggle Pollock forced the draw by perpetual check."]

164. Pollock–J. Mortimer [C46]
BCA Masters, London,
British Chess Club, Round 7,
6 December 1887

1. e4 e5 2. Nf3 Nc6 3. Nc3 Bc5 4. N×e5 N×e5 5. d4 Bd6 6. d×e5 B×e5 7. Bc4 B×c3+?! 7. ... Nf6 was more to the point. **8. b×c3 d6 9. 0–0 Ne7 10. Qh5 Ng6 11. Bg5 Qd7 12. h3 0–0 13. f4! Kh8?** Black could have played 13. ... Qc6 14. Bb3 Be6 15. f5 B×b3 16. a×b3 f6! with a decent game. **14. f5 Ne5** (*see diagram*)

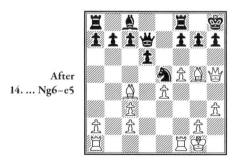

After
14. ... Ng6–e5

15. f6 Tempting and strong. But 15. Rf4! was even stronger: 15. ... Kg8 (15. ... h6 16. B×h6!) 16. Rh4 h6 17. B×h6 leads to mate. **15. ... g6** 15. ... Kg8 runs into the same idea as before: 16. Rf4 Re8 17. Rh4 h6 18. f×g7 Re6 19. B×h6. **16. Qh6 Rg8 17. Rf4! Nf3+ 18. R×f3 Qe8 19. Rf4 Qf8 20. Q×h7+ 1–0** [*Irish Chess Chronicle*, December 15, 1887; *Daily News*, December 7, 1887; it noted the game lasted one hour.]

165. J. Mason–Pollock [C40]
BCA Masters, London,
British Chess Club, Round 8,
December 1887

1. e4 e5 2. Nf3 f5 3. d4 f×e4 4. N×e5 Nf6
5. Bc4 d5 6. Bb3 Bd6 7. Bg5 c6 8. 0–0 0–0
9. Nc3 Qc7 10. Bf4 Kh8 11. Bg3 b6 12. Qd2 a5
13. a3 Ba6 14. Ne2 c5 15. c3 a4 16. Ba2 Nbd7
17. N×d7 Q×d7 18. Rae1 B×g3 19. f×g3 B×e2
20. R×e2 Rae8 21. Rf4 Qb5 22. Qe3 Rc8 *(see diagram)*

After
22. ... Re8–c8

23. g4? Due to back rank problems, 23. h3!?
c×d4 24. c×d4 Rc7 25. g4 Rfc8 26. Rf5 was more
accurate. 23. ... c×d4 24. c×d4 N×g4! 25. R×f8+
R×f8 26. Qd2 e3 27. Qc2 Qa6 27. ... Re8 was the
best way to maintain the pressure. 28. h3?! Rf2
28. ... Rc8! 29. Qd1 Nf2 30. Qf1 Qd3 31. B×d5
Q×d4 was very forceful. 29. Bb1 g6 30. Qd3 Qc4!
31. h×g4? 31. Q×c4 was how to fight for a draw:
31. ... d×c4 32. R×f2 N×f2 33. Kf1 Nd1 34. Ke2
N×b2 35. K×e3. 31. ... R×e2 0–1 [*Morning Post*,
December 8, 1887; *New York Clipper*, March 10,
1888; the *Daily News* of December 8 reported the
game lasted three hours and a half.]

166. Pollock–A. Burn
BCA Masters, London,
British Chess Club, Round 9,
8 December 1887

1. e4 e6 2. c4 *Daily News* (December 9): "Pollock having first move against Burn played 1. e4,
the second player adopting the French Defence,
which has been so popular in the present tournament. Through an oversight of White, Burn early
won the important advantage of a pawn, and soon
afterwards another, though in order to do so he
was obliged to submit for some time to a cramped
position, and to remain strictly on the defensive.
Possessing an unbroken array of four centre pawns,

he could well afford to wait his opportunity, whilst
gradually bringing his forces into the field and
preparing to assume the offensive. Meanwhile, in
the eagerness of his attack, White, at the 28th
move, was compelled to submit to the loss of a
rook in exchange for a minor piece, and shortly afterwards Black obtained a clear piece by giving up
a rook for a knight and bishop. Of course, barring
accidents, only one result could follow, and finding
the struggle completely futile, Pollock resigned at
the 38th move. Time, 3 hours 45 minutes." *Morning Post* (December 9): "Pollock played a somewhat eccentric opening—viz. 1. e4, 2. c4—against
Burn. The last-named player soon won two of his
opponent's pawns, and Pollock, conducting his
game indifferently, was defeated after some two
hours' play." A brief report in the *London Times*
(December 9) noted that Pollock resigned in 47
moves and the game took two hours and a half.
0–1 [Full score not recovered]

VARIOUS GAMES (1887)

167. Pollock–F.J. Lee [C00]
London, Simpson's Divan,
November 1887

1. e4 e6 2. c4 d5 3. c×d5 e×d5 4. e×d5 Q×d5
4. ... Nf6!? seems better. 5. Nc3 Qe6+ 6. Be2 a6
7. Nf3 h6?! 8. 0–0 Be7 9. d4 Nf6 10. Bf4! c6
11. Re1 Qg4 12. Qd2 12. B×b8! R×b8 13. Bc4
Qf5 14. Qb3 was even stronger. 12. ... Be6 13. Ng5
Qf5 14. Bd3 Qa5 15. N×e6 f×e6 16. R×e6 Kf8
17. Rae1 Bb4 *(see diagram)*

After
17. ... Be7–b4

18. R×f6+! g×f6 19. B×h6+ Kf7 20. Ne4!?
Nd7 20. ... B×d2 leads to a quick mate: 21. Nd6+
Kg8 22. Re8 mate. 21. Nd6+ Kg8 22. Bc4+ Kh7
and White mates in four moves. **1–0** [*Chess
Player's Chronicle*, March 1888, pages 274–275]

168. F.N. Braund–Pollock [C52]
London, British Chess Club,
1 December 1887

   1. e4 e5 2. Nf3 Nc6 3. Bc4 Bc5 4. b4 B×b4 5. c3 Ba5 6. d4 e×d4 7. 0–0 d×c3 8. Qb3 Qf6 9. e5 Qg6 10. N×c3 Nge7 11. Ne2 b5! 12. Bd3 12. B×b5 Rb8 13. Qa4 a6 14. B×c6 N×c6 offers Black plenty of activity. The same goes for 12. Q×b5 Rb8 13. Qc5 Bb6 14. Qa3 Bb7. **12. ... Qe6 13. Qb2 Nd5 14. Nf4 N×f4 15. B×f4 h6 16. Rad1 0–0 17. Bb1 Qc4 18. Bg3 Qc3 19. Qe2 f5?!** 19. ... Qc5 20. Qd3 g6 21. Rc1 Qe7 22. Bh4 Qe6 was safer. **20. e×f6 Q×f6 21. Qe4** (see diagram)

After
21. Qe2–e4

   21. ... Rb8? Losing immediately. After 21. ... g6 22. Q×g6+ Q×g6 23. B×g6 d6 24. Be4 Bb7 25. B×d6! c×d6 26. R×d6 Rac8 27. Bd5+ Kh8 28. Nh4 Bc7 29. B×c6 B×c6 30. Ng6+ Kg7 31. R×c6 Rf6 the game remains wide open. **22. Bh4 Qe6 23. Qh7+ Kf7 24. Nd4 Qg4 25. Nf5 Qg6 26. Nd6+ Q×d6 27. R×d6 c×d6 28. Bg6+ Ke6 29. Q×g7 Ba6 30. Q×h6** 30. Rd1!? would have created an artistic finish: 30. ... d5 (30. ... Bb6 31. Bf7+ R×f7 32. Qg6+ Ke5 33. Qh5+ Ke4 34. Qd5+ Kf4 35. Bg3+ Kg4 36. h3 mate) 31. Be8! **30. ... Ne5 31. Be4+ Kf7** and White mates in two. **1–0** [*Chess-Monthly*, March 1888, pages 216–217]

169. J. Morphy–Pollock [C57]
Dublin, Dublin Chess Club,
Simultaneous Exhibition,
14 December 1887

   1. e4 e5 2. Nf3 Nc6 3. Bc4 Nf6 4. Ng5 (see diagram)

   4. ... N×e4!? A Pollock favorite. **5. N×f7** 5. B×f7+ Ke7 6. d4 (6. d3!? Nf6 7. Nc3 d5 8. Qf3 Nd4 9. Qg3 Qd6 10. f4) 6. ... h6 7. N×e4 K×f7 8. d5 poses far more problems for Black than the text. **5. ... Qh4 6. 0–0 Bc5 7. N×h8 N×f2**

After
4. Nf3–g5

8. R×f2?! 8. Bf7+ Ke7 9. R×f2 B×f2+ 10. Kh1 d6 11. Qf1 was somewhat more stubborn. **8. ... Q×f2+ 9. Kh1 d5! 10. B×d5!** 10. Nc3 d×c4 11. Ne4 Bg4! 12. N×f2 B×d1 13. N×d1 0–0–0 was hardly satisfactory either but better than an immediate collapse. **10. ... Bg4 11. Bf3 B×f3 12. g×f3 Nd4 13. Qg1 Q×f3+ 14. Qg2 Qd1+ 15. Qg1 Q×g1+ 16. K×g1 N×c2+ 17. Kf1 N×a1 0–1** [*Dublin Evening Mail*, 20 December 1888; *PM*, pages 88–89]

170. Pollock–J. Hirschfeld [C46]
London, Simpson's Divan, 1887

   1. e4 e5 2. Nc3 Nc6 3. Nf3 Bc5 Pollock: "Not a good move." **4. N×e5 N×e5 5. d4 Bd6 6. d×e5 B×e5 7. Bd3 B×c3+ 8. b×c3 d6 9. 0–0 Qf6 10. Be3 Bd7 11. Rb1 Bc6 12. Bd4 Qh6 13. f4 Ne7 14. f5** Pollock: "Here 14. Qg4 is the *coup juste*." **14. ... f6 15. Qf3 g5?!** Black should have castled on either side in this position. **16. f×g6 h×g6 17. h3 Rf8 18. Qg4 f5 19. e×f5 g×f5** (see diagram)

After
19. ... g6×f5

   20. Bg7? Best was 20. Qe2 Rg8 21. Rf2 Kd7 22. Bc4 Be4 23. B×g8 R×g8 24. Qe3; 20. R×f5!? was playable too: 20. ... Rg8! (20. ... N×f5 21. B×f5 Kd8 22. Bf2!) 21. Q×g8+ N×g8 22. Re1+ Ne7 23. Bf6 0–0–0 24. R×e7 Rg8 25. Bg7 Qh4 26. Rff7. **20. ... Qe3+ 21. Kh2 f×g4 22. R×f8+ Kd7 23. R×a8** Pollock: "A rather ludicrous termination. There is, however, little to be done." Black mates in four. **0–1** [*PM*, pages 47–48]

171. Pollock–Block [C42]
London, Simpson's Divan, 1887

1. e4 e5 2. Nf3 Nf6 3. Bc4 N×e4 4. Nc3 Nf6
5. Qe2 Nc6 6. d4 Bb4? 6. ... d5 7. d×e5 d×c4
8. e×f6+ Be6 was evidently better. **7. d×e5 0–0**
After 7. ... Ng8 8. Ng5 Nh6 9. 0–0 Be7 10. Nd5
0–0 11. N×e7+ N×e7 12. Rd1 White has a winning advantage. **8. Bg5?!** 8. e×f6! was working as
well: 8. ... d5 9. Bd3 d4 10. 0–0 (10. a3 B×c3+
11. b×c3 Re8 12. Be4 Bf5) 10. ... d×c3 11. B×h7+
Kh8 12. Ng5 Qd7 13. h3! **8. ... Re8 9. 0–0–0**
B×c3 10. b×c3 Qe7 11. Rhe1 Qa3+ 12. Kb1 *(see
diagram)*

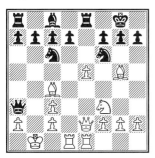

After
12. Kc1–b1

12. ... d5! 13. Bb3? White could have countered with 13. B×f6 d×c4 14. Ng5 Bf5 (14. ... g×f6
15. Qh5 f×g5 16. Q×g5+ Kf8 17. Qh6+ Ke7
18. Qf6+ Kf8 with a perpetual.) 15. Q×c4. **13. ...
Ne4 14. Qe3 Be6 15. Bf4 a5! 16. c4 a4 17. c×d5
a×b3 18. Q×e4 b×a2+ 19. Ka1 Qc3 mate 0–1**
[*Illustrated London News*, March 19, 1887]

172. Pollock–A.B. Skipworth [C70]
Horncastle, 1887

1. e4 e5 2. Nf3 Nc6 3. Bb5 a6 4. Ba4 Nge7
5. d4 e×d4 6. N×d4 N×d4 7. Q×d4 b5 8. Bb3
d6 9. c3 Be6 10. Bc2 Nc6 11. Qe3 Be7 12. 0–0
0–0 13. f4 Bc4 14. Rd1 Qb8 15. e5 Further patience with 15. Nd2 Be6 16. Nf3 was necessary.
15. ... Qa7 16. Be4 d5 17. Q×a7 N×a7 18. Bf3!
Taking the pawn with 18. B×d5 would have been
rather unpleasant: 18. ... Rad8 19. Bf3 R×d1+
20. B×d1 Bc5+ 21. Kh1 Rd8 22. Bf3 Bd5 23. Nd2
B×f3 24. g×f3 Be3. **18. ... b4 19. b3 b×c3
20. N×c3 Bc5+ 21. Kh1 Bb5 22. N×d5 Rad8**
(see diagram)

23. N×c7? 23. Bb2 was safer. **23. ... R×d1+
24. B×d1 Bd4 25. N×b5? N×b5 26. Rb1 Nc3
27. Bc2 N×b1 28. B×b1 B×e5!? 28. ... Rd8! was
a good alternative as well. **29. Bf5** White's position
is hopeless after 29. f×e5 Rd8 30. Bc2 Rc8

31. B×h7+ K×h7 32. Ba3 Rc2. **29. ... Rd8 30. Bg4
f5 31. Bf3 Bd4 0–1** [*Hereford Times*, February 19,
1887]

173. Sohlberg–Pollock [C55]
Netherlands, 1887

1. e4 e5 2. Nf3 Nc6 3. Bc4 Nf6 4. 0–0 N×e4
5. Bd5 Nf6 6. B×c6 d×c6 7. N×e5 Bd6 8. d4 Bf5
9. Nc3 0–0 10. Bg5 h6 11. B×f6 Q×f6 12. f4
Rad8 13. Qh5 B×c2 14. Qh3 Bf5 15. g4 Bh7
16. Rf2 Be7 17. g5 h×g5 18. Nd7 *(see diagram)*

After
18. Ne5–d7

**18. ... Q×d4! 19. N×f8 B×f8 20. Rd1 Q×d1+!
21. N×d1 R×d1+ 22. Kg2 Be4+ 23. Kg3 Bc5?**
It is unclear why Pollock would miss a straightforward mate: 23. ... Rd3+ 24. Kg4 f5+ 25. K×g5
Be7+ 26. Kg6 Rd6+ 27. Kh5 Rh6 mate. **24. Rd2?**
0–1 After 24. Qc8+ Kh7 25. f×g5 Kg6 26. Re2
the position remains highly complicated. [*Hereford Times*, July 23, 1887]

174. Pollock & [William] Cooke–
F.J. Lee & O.C. Müller [C14]
Simpson's Divan, London, January 1888

"The following game, remarkable for a rare and
beautiful mate, was played this year at the Grand
Divan, London, Messrs. Wm. Cook and W.H.K.
Pollock playing alternate moves (without consultation) against Messrs. F. Lee and O. Müller." **1. e4**

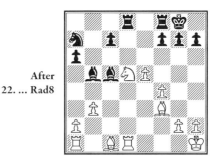

After
22. ... Rad8

e6 2. d4 d5 3. Nc3 Nf6 4. Bg5 Be7 5. B×f6 B×f6 6. e5 Be7 7. Bd3 0–0 8. Nf3 f5 9. 0–0 c5 10. d×c5 B×c5 11. Ne2 Nc6 12. Qd2 Bd7 13. Rae1 Qb6 14. c3 Rac8 15. Bb1 Nd8 16. Nf4 Bc6 17. Ng5 Bd7 18. b4 Be7 19. Nf3 a6 19. ... a5!? 20. a3 g5 was a more active option. **20. Re3!? g5?** Now, with the White rook on the third rank, this is a risky move. 20. ... Rc4!? was launching wild complications: 21. Nd4 B×b4 22. Nd×e6 B×e6 23. N×d5 B×c3 24. R×c3 Rd4 25. N×b6 R×d2 26. Rd3 Rb2 27. Rd6 B×a2 28. B×a2+ R×a2. **21. Nd3** 21. N×g5! was excellent: 21. ... B×g5 22. Rg3 Nf7 23. h4 N×e5 24. R×g5+ Kh8 25. Re1 Nc4 26. Qe2 with promising play on the kingside. **21. ... h6 22. Nd4 Be8 23. Rh3! Kg7 24. Kh1 Bg6 25. f4 g4 26. Re3 Kf7 27. h3 h5 28. Kg1 Rh8 29. Nf2 Nc6 30. a3! a5 31. h×g4** It seems Cook did not understand Pollock's 30. a3. He could have gone directly for 31. N×e6!! a×b4 (31. ... K×e6 32. Q×d5+ K×d5 33. Ba2 mate.) 32. a×b4 Ra8 33. Rd1. **31. ... h×g4?** *(see diagram)*

After
31. ... h5×g4

Oblivious to White's ploy. 31. ... N×d4 32. c×d4 first was necessary. **32. N×e6!! K×e6** 32. ... d4 33. N×d4 N×d4 34. Q×d4 Qe6 could have been met by the artistic 35. Ne4! Rhd8 (35. ... f×e4 36. f5) 36. Nd6+ B×d6 37. e×d6 Q×d6 38. Ba2+. **33. Q×d5+ K×d5 34. Ba2 mate 1–0** A report in the *American Chess Bulletin* of January 1911 (page 14) noted that in a lecture at the Brooklyn Chess Club, Hermann Helms referred to the finish of this game as the "the acme of chess artistry." [*Newark Sunday Call*, August 12, 1888; the position at White's 30th move was published in *Pollock Memories*, page 157; see also C.N. 9827]

175. C. Pearson–Pollock [C21]
Dublin, Dublin Chess Club,
Simultaneous Exhibition,
January 1888

1. e4 e5 2. d4 e×d4 3. c3 d×c3 4. Bc4 Nf6

5. N×c3 Nc6 6. Nge2 Bc5 7. Bg5 Pollock: "Here White should have castled." **7. ... B×f2+ 8. Kf1 Bb6 9. Nd5** *(see diagram)*

After
9. Nc3–d5

9. ... Ng4 Pollock: "Black's first intention was to play 9. ... N×d5, and after touching the piece he saw that it would be fatal." **10. B×d8 K×d8 11. Qd2 d6 12. N×b6 a×b6 13. Qg5+ Ne7 14. Q×g7 Rg8 15. Qd4 Nc6 16. Qd2 Nce5 17. Bd5 c6 18. B×c6** Pollock: "It is but just to remark that the two players were both unknown to each other; certainly each appears to have mistaken his opponent for a 'rank duffer'!" **18. ... Nc4 19. Qb4 Nge3+ 20. Kf2 R×g2+ 21. Kf3 Bg4+ 22. Kf4 B×e2** Pollock: "Threatening mate on the move." **23. Rhg1 Rf2+ 24. Kg5 Ke7** Pollock: "Again threatening mate." **25. Kh6 R×h2+ 26. Kg7 b×c6 27. Qc3 Rf2 28. b3 f6** Pollock: "Insidious. Nothing can save White now." **29. e5 Nf5+ 30. K×h7 N×e5** 30. Rh2+! 31. Kg6 Ke6 with a mate in three. **31. Qh3 Bd3 32. Rae1 Nh6+** Pollock: "There is no reply if 33. Q×d3, to 33. ... Rh2." **0–1** [*Leeds Mercury*, October 23, 1888; *PM*, page 54]

176. A.B. Skipworth–Pollock [C29]
London, Match Game, February 1888

1. e4 e5 2. Nc3 Nf6 3. f4 d5 4. f×e5 N×e4 5. Nf3 Bb4 6. Qe2 B×c3 7. b×c3 0–0 8. Bb2 c5 9. Qe3 Bg4 9. ... f5!? 10. e×f6 R×f6 11. d3 Re6 was worth a close study: 12. d×e4 R×e4 13. Q×e4 d×e4 14. Bc4+ Kh8 15. Ne5 Qh4+ 16. g3 Qe7 17. Nf7+ Kg8 18. Ng5+ Kh8 19. 0–0 h6. **10. Be2 Qb6 11. Rb1 c4 12. Q×b6 a×b6 13. d3 Nc5 14. d×c4 d×c4 15. B×c4 Nbd7 16. Bd5 B×f3 17. g×f3 N×e5 18. c4 Rfe8 19. Kf2 R×a2 20. Rhd1 Na4 21. B×e5** *(see diagram)*

21. ... R×c2+? Missing a tactical back rank motif. 21. ... R×e5 22. Rd2 Kf8 23. B×b7 Rc5 was the accurate continuation. **22. Kg3 R×e5 23. Be4! Re8 24. B×c2 Nc3 25. R×b6 N×d1 26. B×d1 Re7 27. Kf4 Re8 28. Bc2 Re7 29. Be4 Rc7**

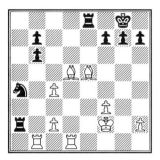

After
21. Bb2×e5

30. R×b7 g5+ 31. K×g5 R×c4 32. Kf6 1–0 [*Bristol Mercury and Daily Post*, March 24, 1888]

177. Pollock & Allies–A. Bird & Allies
Consultation Game, Stamford,
1 March 1888

The *Lincoln, Rutland and Stamford Mercury*, March 9, 1888: "On March 1st an interesting contest took place at the Stamford Institution between Mr. W.H.K. Pollock (assisted by two local players) and numerous members of the Stamford Institution. The match was hurriedly arranged, and, the games not being commenced until half-past eight, was as hurriedly played. The conditions were, Mr. Pollock, with Mr. H. Leonard (Ketton) and Mr. J.A. Tiffany, to play two simultaneous consultation games (giving the odds of the Queen's Rook, but reserving the right of first move) against all comers. Two teams were accordingly organized, the first being captained by Mr. A. Bird, whose assistants were Messrs. Dalton, Armstrong, and Gilbert, while at the second board there presided the local *pater-familias* in chess (Mr. M.W. Packer), supported by Messrs. George Siddons and Fred. Pollard, with the assistance during portions of the game of Messrs. Beale and Wilford. There were four boards in actual use, two being the property of White and two of Black. Pollock's team and the 'town' team had separate tables, and tellers called over the moves as they were made. For the first half-hour play was painfully slow on the part of the 'town' and extremely uninteresting, Pollock's team, with its professional captain, naturally playing a quick game. But afterwards matters went more smoothly, the only little contretemps being the insistence of Mr. Bird's team of the popular delusion among amateur players that White having given the queen's rook could not castle on the Queen's side. 'Well,' said Pollock, 'we have castled; you make the move in the meantime, and argue the point tomorrow.' At ten o'clock there was not

much in either of the games; but through the courtesy of the secretary, play was prolonged for half-an-hour, in which time there were developments of considerable importance. Pollock (perhaps influenced by the ill-advice of his lay assistants) gave Mr. Packer the King's gambit, which the local veteran readily accepted; and followed up the advantage with such ability as to make Pollock at one time observe to his assistants, with much naiveté, 'You devote your attention to Mr. Packer, and I'll manage Mr. Bird.' The King's gambit certainly proved a very bad opening for White, and by means of quick play in the last half hour, following upon his careful procedure and development of the first hour and a half, Mr. Packer had practically a won game. There was very little in the position after Black's 21st move, and it was in the next six moves that Mr. Packer showed some brilliant play and, White playing proportionately weak, on account of pressure of time, gained his advantage[...]." **1. e4 e5 2. Nf3 Nc6 3. Bc4 Nf6 4. Ng5 Nd5 5. e×d5 Q×g5 6. d×c6 Q×g2 7. c×d7+ B×d7 8. Rf1 Qe4+ 9. Be2 Bh3 10. Rg1 Qf5 11. d3 Bc5 12. Bf3 Qf6 13. Nd2 Bf5 14. Qe2 c6 15. Nb3 Bb6 16. Bg5 Qe6 17. 0-0-0 f6 18. Bd2 g5 19. a4 a5 20. Bh5+ Bg6 21. Bg4 f5 22. Bh3 g4 23. Bg2 f4 24. B×f4 0-0 25. Bg3 Rae8 26. Be4** [*see diagram*; abandoned for want of time].

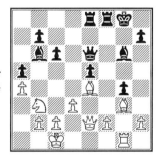

Abandoned after
26. Bg2–e4

178. Pollock–T.C. Gibbons
Odds Game, London, Simpson's Divan,
March 1888
Remove Nb1

1. e4 e5 2. Nf3 Nc6 3. Bc4 Bc5 4. b4 B×b4 5. c3 Ba5 6. 0-0 Nf6 7. Qc2 0-0 8. Ba3 d6 9. d4 e×d4 10. c×d4 Bb6 11. Rad1 Bg4 12. e5 B×f3 13. g×f3 Nh5 14. Qe4 Qg5+ 15. Kh1 Kh8 16. Bc1 f5 17. Qe2 f4 18. Rg1 Qh6 19. Bb2 Ne7 20. e×d6 Nf5 21. d7 Rf6 22. d5 Rf7 23. Rde1 (*see diagram*)

After
23. Rd1–e1

23. ... Be3?! Black could have won via this pretty sequence: 23. ... Nfg3+! 24. f×g3 N×g3+ 25. R×g3 f×g3 26. d6 Bf2! 27. B×g7+ Q×g7 28. h×g3 B×e1 29. B×f7 c×d6! (29. ... B×g3?? 30. Qe8+ Qf8 31. Q×f8+ R×f8 32. Be8) 30. Qe8+ Qf8. **24. Bd3 Nfg3+! 25. f×g3 N×g3+ 26. R×g3 f×g3 27. Bc1 R×f3 28. d6 Rf2 29. Q×f2 g×f2 30. R×e3 Qg6! 31. B×g6 f1Q mate 0–1** [*Montreal Herald*, April 20, 1895; *BCM*, November 1899, pages 474–475]

179. Pollock–Keogh
Simpson's Divan, Odds Game,
March 1888
Remove Nb1

1. e4 e5 2. Nf3 Nc6 3. Bc4 Bc5 4. b4 B×b4 5. c3 Ba5 6. Qb3 Qf6 7. d4 d6? 7. ... N×d4 8. N×d4 e×d4 9. 0–0 B×c3 was maintaining the substantial odds advantage. **8. d5 Nb8 9. Qb5+ Nd7 10. Q×a5 b6 11. Qa4 h6 12. Bb5 Qg6 13. 0–0 Ngf6 14. Bc6 Rb8 15. Q×a7 0–0 16. Q×c7 Q×e4 17. Q×d6 Ne8 18. Qe7 Nef6 19. Re1** (*see diagram*)

After
19. Rf1–e1

19. ... Re8? Losing on the spot. After 19. ... Qg6 20. N×e5 N×e5 21. Q×e5 Bd7 22. Ba3 Rfe8 23. Qd6 White keeps a winning edge. **20. Q×e8+ 1–0** [*Dublin Evening Mail*, March 22, 1888]

HANDICAP TOURNAMENTS (MID–1888)

180. J.H. Zukertort–Pollock [C59]
Handicap Tournament, London,
Simpson's Divan,
March/April 1888

1. e4 e5 2. Nf3 Nc6 3. Bc4 Nf6 4. Ng5 d5 5. e×d5 Na5 6. Bb5+ c6 7. d×c6 b×c6 8. Be2 h6 9. Nf3 e4 10. Ne5 Qc7 11. d4 Bd6 12. f4 0–0 Pollock: "If 12. ... e×f3, 13. N×f3 Bg4 14. 0–0 B×f3 15. B×f3 B×h2+ 16. Kh1, with a better game, and a likelihood of recovering the extra pawn again." **13. 0–0 c5 14. c3 Rb8!?** Pollock: "14. ... Bb7, with a view of occupying the centre files by ...Rad8, etc., would be more to the point." **15. Kh1 c×d4 16. c×d4 Nd5 17. Nc3** Pollock: "It will be seen how important was White's 15th move." **17. ... N×c3 18. b×c3 B×e5** Pollock: "An unpleasant necessity, if 18. ... Q×c3 19. Bd2 Qa3 20. B×a5 Q×a5, 21. Nc6 winning the exchange." **19. f×e5 Q×c3 20. Bd2 Qa3 21. Rc1** Pollock: "It is not difficult to see that White will be able to at once prosecute an overwhelming attack on the weak kingside. The text move threatens 'en-passant' to win the exchange by 22. Qe1 Nb7 23. Bb4." **21. ... Nb7?** (*see diagram*) Overlooking the transfer of the rook to g3. 21. ... Be6! 22. Be1 (22. Rc3 Q×a2 23. Rg3 Rb3!) 22. ... Rfc8 was better.

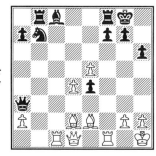

After
21. ... Na5–b7

22. Rc3! Qe7 23. Rg3 Kh7 24. Bc4 Nd8 25. Qh5 Rb6 26. d5 f5 Better was 26. ... Rg6, but White keeps a winning advantage still: 27. Bf4! R×g3 28. B×g3 g6 29. Qh4! **27. d6 Q×e5** Pollock: "If 27. ... Qe8, 28. R×g7+ and mates next move; If 27. ... Qd7 28. Qg6+ (or 28. B×h6) wins." **28. Qg6+ Kh8 29. B×h6! Rb7 30. Bf4** Pollock: "A beautifully played game on the part of Dr. Zukertort." 30. Qh5 or 30. Rh3 would have mated in four moves. **1–0** [*Chess-Monthly*, August 1888, pages 362–362; *PM*, page 61]

181. Pollock–Amateur
Handicap Tournament, London,
Simpson's Divan, March/April 1888
Remove Nb1

1. e4 e5 2. Bc4 Nf6 3. Qe2 Be7 4. d4 e×d4
5. e5 Ng8 6. Qh5 Bb4+ 7. c3 Qe7 8. Bg5 Q×e5+
9. Kf1 g6 10. Qf3 Q×g5 11. Q×f7+ Kd8 12. Re1
Be7 13. Qg7 Qf6 14. R×e7 Q×g7 15. R×g7 Ne7
16. Nf3 d5 17. Ng5 Ke8 18. Bb5+ c6 19. Bd3 h6
20. Nh7 Nd7 21. f4 Rg8 22. B×g6+ Kd8
23. R×g8+ N×g8 24. Kf2 Ndf6 25. Re1 N×h7
26. Re8+ Kc7 27. B×h7 Nf6 28. Rh8 *(see diagram)*

After
28. Re8–h8

28. ... Ne4+? A dramatic error that gave White
the needed respite. 28. ... d×c3 29. b×c3 Rb8!
would have ended White's quest. **29. B×e4 d×e4
30. c×d4 Kd6** 30. ... Rb8!? 31. R×h6 Bf5 32. h3
e3+ 33. K×e3 Re8+ 34. Kd2 would have been better. **31. Ke3 a5?** This is far too slow and gives
White serious winning chances. 31. ... Ke7 and
31. ... h5 were better moves. **32. g4! b5 33. h4 Ke7
34. h5 Bb7** 34. ... Kf7 was better but White has
the better game after 35. Rh7+ Kg8 36. R×h6 Bd7
37. Rd6 Be8 38. h6 Bf7 39. R×c6 B×a2 40. f5 b4
41. g5 a4 42. Rb6 a3 43. R×b4 Be6 44. b×a3 B×f5
45. a4. **35. Rh7+ 1–0** [*Bristol Mercury and Daily
Post*, May 26, 1888]

182. Pollock–Amateur
Handicap Tournament, London,
Simpson's Divan, March/April 1888
Remove Nb1

1. e4 e5 2. Nf3 Nc6 3. d4 e×d4 4. Bc4 Bc5
5. Ng5 Nh6 6. Qh5 Qe7 7. 0–0 d6 8. h3 Bd7 9. f4
0–0–0 10. f5 f6 11. Ne6 B×e6 12. B×e6+ Kb8
13. Kh1 Ng8 14. a3 Ne5 15. b4 Bb6 16. a4 c5
17. a5 Bc7 18. b5 Qe8 19. Qe2 Ne7 20. Bd2 b6?!
20. ... d3! 21. c×d3 Q×b5 was stronger. **21. a×b6
B×b6 22. Ba5 Kb7 23. c4 Ra8 24. Qa2 Qd8
25. Bd2 Qb8 26. Bf4 Kc7 27. Rfd1 Qb7 28. Qe2**

a5 29. Ra4 Ra7 30. Rda1 Rha8 31. Bd2 h6
32. Qe1 *(see diagram)*

After
32. Qe2–e1

32. ... Nd3?! 32. ... Re8 33. R1a3 Nc8 34. Bd5
Qb8 35. Qg3 Kd8 was more careful play. **33. Qg3!
Q×e4 34. Q×g7 Kb8?** 34. ... Re8! would have
maintained Black's advantage. **35. Qf8+ 1–0**
[*Bristol Mercury and Daily Post*, April 28, 1888]

183. Pollock–H.E. Bird [C48]
Handicap Tournament, London,
Simpson's Divan, March/April 1888

1. e4 e5 2. Nf3 Nc6 3. Nc3 Nf6 4. Bb5 Bc5
Pollock: "Inferior to 4. ... Bb4." **5. N×e5 N×e5
6. d4 Bb4 7. d×e5 N×e4 8. 0–0** Pollock: "8. Qd4
is the usual move, but the text move may be made
without danger." **8. ... B×c3** Pollock: "If 8. ...
N×c3, 9. b×c3 B×c3, White may obtain the advantage by 10. Qg4, while 10. Rb1 would also be
good play." **9. b×c3 N×c3** *(see diagram)*

After
9. ... Ne4×c3

10. Qg4! Qe7 Pollock: "Taking the bishop is
clearly out of the question." **11. Bg5** Pollock: "He
could also take the knight's pawn with 11. Q×g7
and 11. ... Qf8, exchange queens with a capital
game." Even stronger was 11. Q×g7 Qf8 12. Qf6
Ne4 13. Qf3 Qc5 14. a4 Q×e5 15. Re1! **11. ... Qe6
12. Qb4 N×b5 13. Q×b5 b6 14. f4 Bb7 15. Rad1
Qc6 16. Qe2 h6 17. Bh4 Qe4 18. Qg4 g5! 19. Rfe1
Qc6 20. f×g5 0–0–0** Pollock: "Both sides are evidently bent on attack. Owing, however, to the

bishops being on opposite colours little real progress can be made, and, as it turns out, but not before some very animated discussions, Black eventually loses by trying to force a win out of a drawn position." **21. g6 Rdg8 22. g7 Rh7 23. Bf6 h5 24. Qh3 Rh6** It is somewhat doubtful if Black has enough compensation after 24. ... Rg×g7 25. B×g7 R×g7 26. Re2 Rg5, but it is an interesting alternative. **25. Re3 Rg6 26. Rd2 Qb5 27. g3** Pollock: "White defends with commendable caution." **27. ... Qc6 28. Red3 Qc5+ 29. Kf1 Ba6?** 29. ... Bc6 was the correct move. **30. Q×d7+ Kb7 31. Q×f7 R×f6+ 32. Q×f6 Qe3 33. Kg2 B×d3 34. R×d3 Qe2+ 35. Qf2 Q×e5 36. Qf3+ Kb8 37. Qf8+ Kb7 38. Qf3+ Kb8 39. Rd5?** 39. Rd7 Re8 40. Rf7 wins. **39. ... Q×g7 40. R×h5 Qc3??** Pollock: "Although reputed as more or less reckless in play, it scarcely ever has occurred to Mr. Bird to make a blunder of this magnitude. The game, however, should, with a little care, be won in the end by White." **1–0** [*PM*, pages 59–60]

184. Pollock–F.J. Lee [C00]
Handicap Tournament, London,
Simpson's Divan, March/April 1888

1. e4 e6 2. Nc3 d5 3. Nf3 Nf6 4. e5 Nfd7 5. b3 Pollock: "Quite an unusual method of treating the French Defence." **5. ... a6 6. Bb2 c5 7. Bd3 Be7 8. 0–0 0–0 9. Qe2 Nc6 10. Rae1 Nb4 11. a3** Pollock: "White's position on the queenside would be safer with this pawn unmoved. It is, however, necessary to dislodge the knight in order to mass the forces for the attack on the other wing." **11. ... N×d3 12. Q×d3 b5 13. Ne2 Nb6 14. Ng3 Bd7 15. Kh1 a5 16. Ng1 a4 17. Nh3 a×b3 18. c×b3** Pollock: "Here White has to capture from the centre, while the a3-pawn is left weak." **18. ... c4 19. Qe3 c×b3 20. f4 g6** Pollock: "20. ... f5 is essential to a correct defence." In fact, after 20. ... Nc4! 21. Qd4 Qb6 White's position is very precarious. **21. f5 e×f5 22. Qh6** Pollock: "This is a most important point. White should have played 22. Bd4 (attacking the knight) whereby Black's d5-pawn would be fixed, thus frustrating ...d5–d4, which at the last moment in the actual game might have turned the tables. The time used in this move of the bishop was actually used in White's 25th move, which led to a startling finish only owing to Black missing his way." Indeed, after 22. Bd4! Black has to be very careful not to allow White too much play. Best seems to be 22. ... f4!! 23. N×f4 Nc4 24. Qc3 Be6. **22. ... Be6** (*see diagram*)

After
22. ... Bd7–e6

Pollock: "Of course, 23. e6 was threatened." **23. R×f5** Pollock: "Threatening to continue with 24. Rh5." **23. ... B×f5** Pollock: "Not 23. ... g×f5 on account of 24. Nh5." **24. N×f5 g×f5 25. Re3 Ra4?** Pollock: "The correct defence is 25. ... Kh8! after which the game should, with a little care, result decisively in Black's favour. After the text move White wins by force." The *New York Clipper* of June 16, 1888, noted that, during the *post-mortem*, Zukertort discovered 25. ... Kh8!! was Black's only move. 26. Bd4 (26. Rg3 Rg8 27. e6+ d4 28. R×g8+ K×g8 29. e×f7+ K×f7 30. Nf4 Qd6) 26. ... Rg8 27. e6+ f6 28. Ng5 R×g5 29. Q×g5 Ra4! **26. e6!** Pollock: "Not 26. Rg3+ Rg4 27. e6 d4!" **26. ... Rg4** Pollock: "Obviously 26. ... d4 now would shut out the rook, and White would win at once by Rg3+. Black will now have no time for ...d5–d4." **27. Ng5!** Pollock: "Utterly unexpected and a problem-like conclusion." **27. ... R×g5 28. Rh3** Pollock: "Mate is forced in three moves. The winner of this game was presented by the late Mr. F.H. Lewis, a most generous patron of chess, with a special 'brilliancy prize' of £1, which was awarded to him at a dinner held at Simpson's to celebrate the tournament." **1–0** [*New York Clipper*, June 16, 1888, and January 21, 1893; *Montreal Gazette*, February 4, 1893; *Newcastle Weekly Courant*, November 12, 1895; *PM*, pages 62–63]

185. O.C. Müller–Pollock [C41]
Handicap Tournament, London,
Simpson's Divan, March/April 1888

1. e4 e5 2. Nf3 d6 3. d4 e×d4 4. N×d4 Nf6 5. Nc3 Be7 Pollock: "According to some highly interesting statistics compiled from 1,500 match and tournament games by a correspondent in the *New York Sun*, Philidor's Defence was played but little over once in every hundred games, less frequently than any other of the 17 openings considered, and yet was only second to the Two Knights' Defence as the hardest defence to beat. By far the most frequently played openings were the Ruy Lopez, Queen's Pawn openings, and French Defence. The present form of the 'Philidor' is a safe one, and rather better than playing ...Nc6 early." **6. Bc4 0–0 7. 0–0 a6** Pollock: "This might mean a general advance on the queenside by ...b5, ...c5, etc., but White forestalls it." **8. a4 N×e4!** Pollock: "As usual, Black improves his game by this capture, which is a consequence of the opponent's sixth move, which was hardly his best." **9. N×e4 d5 10. Bd3 d×e4 11. B×e4 Nd7 12. c3 Bf6 13. Be3 Nc5 14. Bc2 Ne6 15. Qd3** Pollock: "White could exchange, leaving four bishops on the field, but he certainly would have no advantage." **15. ... g6 16. Rad1 Ng7 17. Qc4 Bd7 18. Rfe1 Qc8 19. Bf4 c5 20. Nb3 b6 21. Be4 Ra7** (*see diagram*)

After
21. ... Ra8–a7

22. a5 Pollock: "The position has worked itself out in a curious manner and is most difficult. But here White, thinking no doubt to gain a decisive advantage, falls right into a trap that loses the game forthwith." **22. ... Bb5 23. Qd5 Rd8?!** 23. ... Rd7! was correct. **24. Bd6?!** Not as promising as 24. a×b6! R×d5 25. b×a7 R×d1 26. R×d1 Bc6 27. N×c5 Ne6 28. B×c6 Q×c6 29. N×e6 f×e6 30. Rd6 Qb7 31. Rd7! **24. ... Ne8?** This error was left unquestioned by Pollock. 24. ... Rad7! was still very useful. **25. a×b6! R×d6 26. Q×d6?** 26. b×a7! R×d5 27. R×d5, rather, would give White a winning position, based on some fine tactics: 27. ... Qb7 28. Rd7!! **26. ... N×d6 27. b×a7 N×e4 28. R×e4 Qa8 0–1** [*PM*, pages 63–64]

186. J. Mortimer–Pollock [C57]
Handicap Tournament, London,
Simpson's Divan, March/April 1888

1. e4 e5 2. Nf3 Nc6 3. Bc4 Nf6 4. Ng5 N×e4!? 5. B×f7+ Ke7 6. N×e4 K×f7 7. d4 d5 8. Ng5+ Kg8 9. d×e5 N×e5 10. 0–0 h6 11. Ne4 Sharp play was offered too by 11. Re1!? h×g5 12. R×e5 c6 13. B×g5 Qc7 14. Qd4 Bc5 15. Qc3 Bg4. **11. ... Be6**

12. Ng3 Bc5 13. Qe2 Bd6 14. f4 Bg4! 15. Qb5 c6 16. Q×b7 Bc5+ 17. Kh1 Rb8 18. Qa6 Rb6 19. Qa5 Nd7 20. Qe1 Kh7 21. Qc3 Re8 22. Qd3+ Kh8 23. Nc3 Rb4 24. Qg6 Nf6 25. a3 Rb7 26. Na4 Bd6 27. Bd2 Rbe7 28. Bc3! Rg8 29. h3 29. B×f6 g×f6 30. Q×f6+ Reg7 31. Qc3 was much stronger. **29. ... Be6 30. B×f6 g×f6 31. Q×f6+ Kh7** (*see diagram*)

After
31. ... Kh8–h7

32. f5? This loses a piece. 32. Qc3 kept an edge for White. **32. ... Bf7! 33. Ne2 R×e2 34. Q×f7+ Rg7 35. Q×g7+** 35. Qh5 runs into 35. ... Rg×g2. **35. ... K×g7 36. f6+ Kf7 37. Nc3 R×c2 38. Ne2 d4 39. g4 c5 40. Nf4 Qa8+ 0–1** [*Leeds Mercury*, September 22, 1888]

187. Pollock–Amateur [C20]
Handicap Tournament, London,
Simpson's Divan, 28 April 1888

1. e4 e5 2. d3 Nc6 3. Nc3 Bb4 4. Bd2 B×c3 5. B×c3 d6 6. Nf3 f5 7. Be2 Nf6 8. e×f5 B×f5 9. Qd2 0–0 10. 0–0–0 Nd5 11. h3 h6 12. g4 Be6 13. g5 Nf4 14. g×h6 N×e2+ 15. Q×e2 Bd5 (*see diagram*)

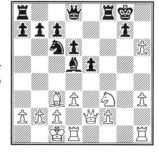

After
15. ... Be6–d5

16. Nh2 B×h1 17. h×g7! Re8 18. Qh5! Bd5?! If 18. ... Re7 White can follow up with 19. R×h1 (19. Qh8+ Kf7 20. Qh7 Qg8 21. Qh5+ Ke6 22. Qg4+ Kf6 23. Qf4+ Ke6 24. Qg4+) 19. ... R×g7 20. f4 Qe8 21. Qf3 with complicated play. **19. Rg1 Be6** 19. ... Re7 does not save Black but postpones the end: 20. Qh8+ Kf7 21. Qh7 Ke6 22. Ng4! R×g7 23. Q×g7 Qf8 24. Qg6+ Ke7 25. d4! **20. Nf3 Ne7 21. Qh8+ Kf7 22. Ng5+ Kf6 23. g8Q+** and mate in three. Some early 1890s columnists saw 23. g8N+ (mate in two). **1–0** [*Albany Evening Journal*, October 24 and September 12, 1896; *St. John Globe*, November 13, 1896]

188. Amateur–Pollock
Odds Game, London, Simpson's Divan, May 1888
Remove Ra8 and f7 pawn

1. e4 d6 2. Nf3 Nc6 3. Bb5 e5 4. B×c6+ b×c6 5. 0–0 g5 6. h3 h5 7. d3 g4 8. Ng5 g×h3 9. Qf3 Nf6 10. N×h3 Bg4 11. Qg3 h4 12. Qe3 Bh6 13. Ng5 Rg8 14. Ne6 B×e3 15. N×d8 *(see diagram)*

After
15. Ne6×d8

15. ... Bb6?! 15. ... Bf3! was best, objectively: 16. Kh2 R×g2+ 17. Kh3 Ng4 18. K×h4 B×f2+ 19. R×f2 N×f2 20. Bg5 Rg4+ 21. Kh5 Nh3 22. Ne6 R×g5+ 23. Kh4 Rh5+ 24. Kg3 Ke7. **16. N×c6 Bf3 17. Be3?** and Black mates in three moves. **0–1** Instead of the text error, 17. Kh2 was evidently best: 17. ... R×g2+ 18. Kh3 Ng4 19. K×h4 B×f2+ 20. R×f2 N×f2 21. Bg5 Rg4+ 22. Kh5 Nh3 23. Bh6 R×e4+ 24. Kg6 Rg4+ 25. Kf5 Rh4 26. N×e5 Rh5+ 27. Kf6 R×e5 28. Nc3 with a playable position. [*Dublin Evening Mail*, May 31, 1888; *New York Clipper*, January 4, 1890; *PM*, page 107; *Belfast News-Letter*, July 12, 1888]

189. H. Erskine–Pollock [C37]
London, Simpson's Divan, June 1888

Pollock in the *Baltimore Sunday News* (May 4, 1895): "We find the following game classed among 'Curiosities of Chess' in our MSS of nearly 3,000 games. It was played at Simpson's Divan, London, June 1888, and is here selected as a 'change of diet' and as having a suggestive ending, as well as some

lively play otherwise." **1. e4 e5 2. f4 e×f4 3. Nf3 g5 4. Bc4 g4 5. 0–0 g×f3 6. Q×f3 Qf6 7. e5 Q×e5 8. B×f7+** Pollock: "The 'Double Muzio Gambit.'" **8. ... K×f7** Pollock: "8. ... Kd8 is a safer move." **9. d4 Q×d4+** Pollock: "Here again 9. ... Qf5 is safer." **10. Be3 Qf6 11. Qd5+ Ke8 12. R×f4** *(see diagram)*

After
12. Rf1×f4

12. ... Bh6!? Pollock: "A venture, of course, but producing a very lively exchange of compliments." Highly imaginative but 12. ... Ne7! was best. **13. R×f6 B×e3+ 14. Kh1 N×f6 15. Qe5+ Kf7 16. Q×e3 Re8 17. Qb3+ d5 18. Nc3 Nc6?!** 18. ... c6 was most solid. **19. N×d5 Be6 20. c4 Na5?** Pollock: "This is, perhaps, after all, Black's best chance." However, engines suggest 20. ... Nd4 offered a safer path: 21. Q×b7 B×d5 22. c×d5 Rad8 23. Q×c7+ Rd7 24. Qc5 Nf5 25. Rf1 Re5. **21. Qf3 B×d5 22. c×d5 Rf8** Pollock: "Practically forced." **23. Rf1 Kg7 24. Qg3+ Kh8** Pollock: "This king, however, is to be heard from again." **25. Q×c7** The decisive 25. Qc3 was not difficult to spot. **25. ... b6 26. Qe7 Rae8 27. Q×a7 N×d5** Pollock: "Now some more fun begins." **28. R×f8+ R×f8 29. h3 Nc4 30. a4 Nce3** Pollock: "If 30. ... N×b2, 31. a5 b×a5 32. Qb7 winning one of the knights." **31. b4 Nf1 32. Qb7 Nc3 33. Q×b6?** Pollock: "Giving Black the option of draw by perpetual check." 33. Qe7! should have won. **33. ... Ng3+ 34. Kg1??** 34. Kh2 would have forced a draw. **34. ... Rf1+ 35. Kh2 Nce2** Engines reveal that 35. ... Nce4! wins for Black in a study-like manner: 36. Qd8+ Kg7 37. Qe7+ Kg6 38. Qe6+ Kg5 39. Qg8+ Kf4 40. Qg4+ Ke3 41. Qf3+ R×f3 42. g×f3 K×f3 43. b5 Kf2 44. h4 Nf1+ 45. Kh3 h5 46. a5 Kg1 47. a6 Nf2 mate. **36. Qd8+ Kg7 37. Qe7+ Kg6 38. Qe8+ Kf5 39. Qf7+ Ke4 40. Qc4+ Ke3 41. Qe6+ Kf2 42. Qf6+ Ke1 43. Qa1+ Kd2 44. Qb2+ Kd3 45. Qb3+ Kd4 46. Qb2+ Kc4** Pollock: "And after the king has taken a walk and captured the a and b-pawns, (which White must lose in order to retain the ever-lasting check) he crossed the board at leisure, attended closely by the White queen, until the following situation was arrived at (Black to move):

Black to move

The game continued: **1. … Rf7 2. Qe5+ Rf6 3. Qe7+ Kg6 4. Qe8+ Kh6 6. Qe3+ Kh5** and the game was abandoned as drawn." [*Baltimore Sunday News*, May 4, 1895; *PM*, pages 55–56]

190. Pollock–H.E. Bird [B34]
London, British Chess Club
(Handicap Tournament), July 1888

1. e4 c5 2. d4 c×d4 3. Nf3 Nc6 4. N×d4 g6 5. N×c6 b×c6 6. Qd4 f6 7. Nc3 Bg7 8. Bc4 Qb6 9. Qd3 Nh6 10. 0–0 Ng4 11. Qg3 d6 12. h3 Ne5 13. Bb3 Ba6 14. Be3 Qb7 (*see diagram*)

After
14. … Qb6–b7

15. f4!! B×f1?! It was best to refrain from this capture, and, instead, play 15. … Nc4 16. Bf2 0–0–0. **16. f×e5 Ba6 17. e×d6 Rd8 18. Bc5 e×d6 19. B×d6 Bf8 20. e5! B×d6 21. e×d6 Kf8 22. Ne4 Qb6+ 23. Kh1 Qd4 24. Re1 Kg7 25. c3 Qe5 26. Q×e5** Avoiding this trade with 26. Qf2 Rhe8 27. Q×a7+ Kh6 28. Bf7 Rf8 29. Qe7 was much stronger. **26. … f×e5 27. Nc5 Bc8 28. Rd1 Bd7 29. Be6 B×e6 30. N×e6+ Kf6 31. N×d8 R×d8 32. c4 c5 33. Rd5 1–0** [*Illustrated London News*, August 11, 1888; *PM*, page 59]

191. G.E. Wainwright–Pollock [C37]
Handicap Tournament, British Chess Club, London, June 1888

1. e4 and Nc3 e5 2. f4 e×f4 3. Nf3 g5 4. Bc4 g4 5. 0–0 Qe7? 5. … g×f3!? was perhaps best in the circumstances. **6. d4** Stronger was 6. Nd5! Qd8 7. Ne5 d6 8. N×f7 K×f7 9. N×c7+. **6. … g×f3 7. Q×f3 c6 8. B×f4 b5 9. Bd6! Q×d6 10. Q×f7+ Kd8 11. Q×f8+ Kc7 12. B×g8 Q×d4+ 13. Kh1 Na6 14. Rad1 Qb4 15. Qg7 R×g8 16. Q×g8 Q×b2 17. Qg3+** 17. R×d7+ B×d7 18. Q×a8 Q×c3 19. Q×a7+ Kd8 20. Q×a6 was an easy win as well. **17. … Kb6** (*see diagram*)

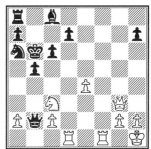

After
17. … Kc7–b6

18. Na4+ b×a4 19. Rb1 Qb5 20. c4 Qb4 21. a3 Qb3 22. R×b3+ a×b3 23. Q×b3+ Kc7 24. Rf7 Nc5 25. Qg3+ Kb6 26. R×h7 Ba6 27. Qc3 Rb8 28. h3 N×e4 29. Qb4+ Kc7 30. Qa5+ Kb7 31. R×d7+ Ka8 32. Q×a6 1–0 [*Morning Post*, July 23, 1888]

192. Pollock–J.H. Blackburne
Handicap Tournament, British Chess Club, June 1888[4]

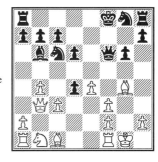

Black to move

---

4. On pages 234–235 of *Joseph Henry Blackburne: A Chess Biography* (Jefferson, N.C.: McFarland, 2015), Tim Harding noted this position was given in P. Anderson Graham's *Mr. Blackburne's Games at Chess* (1899, Game 229, page 196) and identified as being "from a game in the B.C.A. Handicap tournament of 1886." On page 259, while discussing the handicap tournament held at the British Chess Club in June 1888, Harding wrote: "None of Blackburne's games from the Handicap have survived." Harding was unaware that the same position and moves appeared on page 376 of the August 1888 *Chess-Monthly* as "played in the recent Handicap Tournament of the British Chess Club...."

12. ... Ne5 13. Bh3 13. c4 was more stubborn: 13. ... d3 14. Nd2 Bd4 15. Rb1 Nh6 16. Bb2 B×b2 17. R×b2 Nh×g4 18. f×g4 Qf4 19. f3 Kg7 20. c5 h5! but Black still gets a strong attack. **13. ... N×f3+ 14. Kg2 Nh4+! 15. Kg3 Qf3+ 16. K×h4 c6!** 16. ... h6! would have been more efficient but less pretty. **17. Bg5 h6 18. Be7+ N×e7 19. Bg4 Nf5+! 20. e×f5 Bd8+** "and mate next move." **0–1** [*Chess-Monthly*, August 1888, page 376]

193. Pollock–I.A. Gunsberg [C52]
Handicap Tournament,
British Chess Club, June 1888

1. e4 e5 2. Nf3 Nc6 3. Bc4 Bc5 4. b4 B×b4 5. c3 Ba5 6. d4 e×d4 7. Qb3 Qf6 8. 0–0 d×c3 9. Re1 9. e5 Qf5 10. N×c3 is better. **9. ... b5! 10. e5 Qg6 11. Bd5 Nge7 12. Be4 Qe6 13. Qc2 h6** 13. ... b4 would have made things difficult for White. **14. N×c3 Rb8 15. Re3 Bb6 16. Re1 b4 17. Ne2 Ba6 18. Nf4 Qc4 19. Qd1 Nd4 20. Bb2 N×f3+** An uninspired exchange. Best was 20. ... Ne6 21. N×e6 d×e6. **21. Q×f3 Bc8?** 21. ... 0–0!? 22. Bd3 Q×f4 23. Q×f4 B×d3 was playable as well. **22. Nd5! Ng6** (see diagram)

After
22. ... Ne7–g6

23. e6!! 0–0 24. B×g6 Bb7 25. e×f7+ with a quick mate after 25. ... Kh8 26. B×g7+. **1–0** [*The Field*, July 28, 1888]

194. I.A. Gunsberg–Pollock [C47]
Handicap Tournament,
British Chess Club, June 1888

1. e4 e5 2. Nc3 Nf6 3. Nf3 Nc6 4. a3 Pollock: "Mr. Gunsberg has adopted this move successfully against Blackburne and Zukertort." **4. ... d5** Pollock: "4. ... a6 would perhaps been safer." **5. Bb5 d4 6. Ne2 Bd6** Pollock: "Zukertort, who here played 6. ... Bd7, thinks 6. ... N×e4 best." **7. d3 h6** Steinitz: "Loss of time, as usual." Pollock: "This shuts off the queen's bishop. Zukertort played here

7. ... Bd7." **8. 0–0** Pollock: "Apparently very strong." Steinitz: "White could also get a good game by 8. Ne×d4, followed by e5." **8. ... 0–0 9. Ng3 Ne7 10. Nh4** Steinitz: "This move is all the more faulty as he could greatly improve his position by 10. N×e5 B×e5 11. f4 Bd6 12. e5 Ng6 13. e×f6 Q×f6 14. Ne4, followed by N×d6 and f5, with much the superior game." **10. ... g5!?** Steinitz: "The proper rejoinder, which ought to give Black the advantage." **11. Nhf5** Steinitz: "By allowing his pawns to be doubled he subjects himself to a strong attack, but Nf3 was also inconvenient, as Black could reply ...Ng6 followed by ...Nf4 either at once, or perhaps better still, after some preparatory move like ...Kh7." **11. ... B×f5 12. e×f5** Pollock: "12. N×f5 would leave him nothing with which to attack the weakened kingside, the king's bishop being out of play." **12. ... Qc8 13. Qf3 g4** Steinitz: "Black could not well afford to protect the h6-pawn first. If 13. ... Kg7 White would protect himself by 14. h3, and Black's h-pawn could not advance without leaving the g5-pawn en prise. 13. ... Kh7 was still more unfavourable, as White would reply 14. Ne4." **14. Qe2 N×f5 15. N×f5** Pollock: "Mr. Gunsberg thought 15. Ne4 would have been stronger; but after 15. ... Qd8 the game is still in Black's favour." **15. ... Q×f5 16. B×h6 Rfd8 17. f3** Pollock: "Overlooking the force of Black's reply." Steinitz: "This bad continuation compromises his game seriously. Either 17. g3 or 17. Bd2 were correct. If, however, 17. Qd2 Kh7 18. Qg5 Qg6 19. Q×g6+ K×g6 and Black has freed his h-file for an immediate attack of the rooks, or he may remove his knight followed by ...f5." **17. ... Qh5 18. Qd2** Pollock: "Forced." **18. ... Kh7** Pollock: "If 18. ... e4, 19. Qg5+ etc." **19. Bg5** (see diagram) Pollock: "Again he has no option."

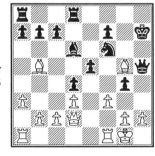

After
19. Bh6–g5

19. ... e4! Steinitz: "Very fine play." **20. f4** Pollock: "He had the alternative of 20. h4, but it is doubtful whether this would have improved matters." Steinitz: "No doubt his best. If 20. d×e4, 20. ... Q×h2+ 21. Kf2 g×f3 22. Bd3 (if 22. K×f3, then obviously 22. ... Qh5+ wins; or if 22. B×f6, 22. ... f×g2 23. Rg1 Bf4 24. R×g2 Be3+ and wins.) 22. ... Qg3+ 23. Kg1 Ng4 24. e5+ Kg8 25. R×f3 Qh2+ 26. Kf1 Qh1+ 27. Ke2 Q×g2+ 28. Ke1 Q×f3 29. e×d6 Re8+ 30. Be2 c×d6 and wins." **20. ... e3** Pollock: "20. ... e3 would not have been so good." **21. Qe2** Pollock: "He cannot avoid the exchange of queens." **21. ... g3!?** 21. ... Nd5!? 22. h3 f6 23. h×g4 Qf7 24. Bh4 N×f4 25. Qf3 Qd5 was the other key alternative here. Steinitz: "But this is hardly as sound as 21. ... Kg6, making room for a treble attack on the open h-file, which White could scarcely defend." **22. Q×h5+ N×h5 23. B×d8** Steinitz: "White could have maintained a simple advantage by 23. h×g3, for if 23. ... N×g3 24. Rf3 f6 25. B×f6 Rf8 26. R×g3 R×f6 27. Rh3+ with a pawn ahead, and although the bishops are of opposite colors, and Black has a passed pawn far advanced, the latter will have great difficulty to draw the game." **23. ... g×h2+ 24. K×h2 R×d8 25. Kg1?!** Pollock: "If 25. g3, 25. ... Rg8 and if the [White] rook defends, 26. ... N×g3; 25. Rf3 is better but useless." 25. Rf3! would have made things very complicated: 25. ... N×f4 26. g3 Nh5 27. R×f7+ Kh6 28. Kg2 Rg8 29. Rh1 R×g3+ 30. Kf1. **25. ... B×f4** 25. ... N×f4 was accurate. **26. Rae1** Pollock: "If 26. g3, 26. ... N×g3!" **26. ... Rd6** Steinitz: "A very fine move, which wins at least another pawn." **27. Bc4?** Pollock: "27. g3 or 27. g4 would have prolonged the fight, but the attack is too strong." Steinitz: "His only chance of prolonging the fight was 27. g4, when of course Black would have pinned the pawn by ...Rg6 and would have won it, but still there would have been some play left. But 27. Rf3 was of no use, as Black could still reply 27. ... Ng3." **27. ... Ng3 0–1** Steinitz: "A beautiful coup which forces the game. The only defense is now 28. Rf3 and then follows 28. ... Rh6 29. R×g3 B×g3 30. Re2 (If the rook moves elsewhere, Black of course advances ...e2) 30. ... Bf2+ 31. R×f2 Rh1+ 32. K×h1 e×f2 and wins." [*Belfast News-Letter*, June 21, 1888, and August 9, 1888; *Chess-Monthly*, August 1888, pages 370–371; *ICM*, August 1888, pages 246–247]

195. W.M. Gattie–Pollock [C30]
Handicap Tournament,
British Chess Club, 28 June 1888

1. e4 e5 2. Nc3 Nc6 3. Bc4 Nf6 4. f4 Bc5 5. Nf3 d6 6. d3 Bg4 7. Na4 Nd4 8. N×c5 B×f3 9. g×f3 d×c5 10. c3 Nc6 11. Qb3 0–0 12. Q×b7 Qd6 13. f5 a5 14. Qb3 a4 15. Qd1 Rfb8 16. h4 Na5 17. h5 h6 18. Qe2 N×c4 19. d×c4 Nh7 20. Be3 Qb6 21. Rh2 Qa5 22. Rc1 a3 23. b3 *(see diagram)*

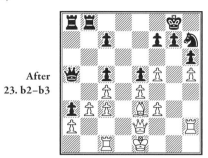

After 23. b2–b3

23. ... R×b3? This is not sound. 23. ... Rd8 was a better move. **24. a×b3 a2 25. Q×a2 Q×a2 26. R×a2 R×a2 27. Rd1! Nf6 28. B×c5** Somewhat more forceful was 28. Rd8+ Kh7 29. Rf8 Rb2 30. R×f7 R×b3 31. Kd2 Rb2+ 32. Kd3 Rh2 33. R×c7 R×h5 34. R×c5 Rh3 35. Ke2 and White's c-pawn decides the game. **28. ... N×h5 29. Rd8+ Kh7 30. Rd7 Nf4 31. R×c7 h5! 32. Rd7 h4 33. Rd2 Ra1+?!** Black had a draw in hand with 33. ... Ng2+ 34. Ke2 Nf4+ 35. Ke3 Ng2+. **34. Kf2 Rh1?** Black had to start fighting for a draw with 34. ... Rc1. **35. Be3! h3 36. Kg3 g5 37. f×g6+ f×g6 38. B×f4 e×f4+ 39. K×f4 Rg1 40. Rh2 g5+ 41. Ke5 Rg3 42. Rf2 Rg2 43. Rf1 h2 44. Rh1**

Isidor A. Gunsberg (John G. White Chess and Checkers Collections, Cleveland Public Library).

Kh6 **45.** c5 g4 **46.** f×g4 **1–0** [*The Field*, July 14, 1888]

196. O.C. Müller–Pollock [C67]
London, Purssell's Restaurant, July 1888

1. e4 e5 **2.** Nf3 Nc6 **3.** Bb5 Nf6 **4.** 0–0 N×e4 **5.** d4 Be7 **6.** d5 Nd6! **7.** B×c6 d×c6 **8.** N×e5 c×d5 **9.** Q×d5 0–0 **10.** Nc3 Be6 **11.** Qf3 f6 **12.** Nd3 c6 **13.** Nc5 Bc4 **14.** Rd1 Qe8 **15.** b3 Bf7 **16.** Re1 Bh5 **17.** Qe3 Qg6! **18.** N3e4 18. Q×e7 doesn't work: 18. ... Rfe8 19. Nd3 R×e7 20. R×e7 Bf3 21. g3 Re8 22. R×e8+ Q×e8 23. Bb2. **18. ... Nf5 19.** Qc3 (*see diagram*)

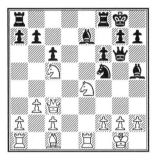

After
19. Qe3–c3

19. ... Rfe8!? Sacrificing two pawns for the attack. **20.** N×b7 Rab8 **21.** Q×c6 Bf3! **22.** g3 Qg4 **23.** Qc4+? 23. Bf4! would have maintained the tension: 23. ... Nd4 24. Qc4+ Kh8 25. Ned6! B×d6 26. N×d6 Rf8 27. Re3 Qh3 28. Qf1 Qh5 29. Qd3 Ne2+ 30. R×e2 B×e2 31. Qe3 with unclear play. **23. ...** Kh8 **24.** Nbc5 B×c5 **25.** Bf4 Nh4! **26.** B×b8 B×e4 **27.** R×e4 B×f2+! **28.** K×f2 Qf3+ **0–1** [*Leeds Mercury*, September 8, 1888]

Bradford (August 1888)

197. M. Weiss–Pollock
International Masters, Bradford,
Round 1, 6 August 1888

1. e4 e5 **2.** Nf3 Nc6 **3.** Bb5 (...) **1–0** *Belfast News-Letter* (August 7): "A very hotly-contested game was that between Weiss and Pollock. In the endgame, however, Weiss forced a win after 50 moves." *Leeds Mercury* (August 7): "This was the last game finished, and concluded at 9:00 PM; Weiss, who had succeeded in winning a pawn, sacrificing in the endgame a rook for bishop." The *Standard* (August 7): "The game between Weiss and Pollock after the adjournment looked like a

draw, each side having rook and bishops of different colour. Weiss, however, was a pawn ahead, and finally sacrificing a rook for bishop and pawn, he remained with a bishop and two pawns against his opponent's rook, and after a hard struggle won the game." [Full score not recovered]

198. Pollock–I.A. Gunsberg [C54]
International Masters, Bradford,
Round 2, 7 August 1888

1. e4 e5 **2.** Nf3 Nc6 **3.** Bc4 Bc5 **4.** c3 Nf6 **5.** d3 d6 **6.** Bg5 Qe7 **7.** Nbd2 Bd7 **8.** Nf1 h6 **9.** Be3 Bb6 **10.** Ng3 Ng4 (*see diagram*)

After
10. ... Nf6–g4

11. Qd2?! 11. B×b6 a×b6 12. h3 Nf6 13. 0–0 was better than the text. **11. ...** N×e3 **12.** f×e3 Na5 **13.** Bb3 N×b3 **14.** a×b3 g6 **15.** Qe2 c6 **16.** Nd2 h5 **17.** Qf2 a6 **18.** Rf1 Rf8 **19.** 0–0–0 h4! **20.** Ne2 f5! **21.** d4 0–0–0 **22.** Nc4 Ba7 **23.** d×e5 d×e5 **24.** Qe1 b5 **25.** Nd6+ Kc7 **26.** c4 Be6 **27.** e×f5 g×f5 **28.** Qc3 R×d6 **29.** Q×e5 Rf7 **30.** Nc3 Bc8 **31.** Rd5 B×e3+ **32.** Kb1 Q×e5 **33.** R×e5 Bd4 **0–1** [*Bradford Observer*, August 8, 1888; *Leeds Mercury*, August 11, 1888]

199. J.H. Blackburne–Pollock [C77]
International Masters, Bradford,
Round 3, 7 August 1888

1. e4 e5 **2.** Nf3 Nc6 **3.** Bb5 a6 **4.** Ba4 Nf6 **5.** Qe2 Pollock: "A sound move, somewhat favoured by Blackburne." **5. ...** b5 **6.** Bb3 Bc5 **7.** c3 0–0 **8.** 0–0 d5 **9.** d3 Bg4 Pollock: "9. ... d×e4, followed by 10. ... Qe7 is safer." **10.** Bg5 Ne7 **11.** Nbd2 d4 Pollock: "The necessity of such a move, where his game should be developing, ought not to arise. Black must be conceded to have the worst of the opening." **12.** h3 B×f3 **13.** N×f3 Ng6 **14.** Rac1 d×c3 **15.** b×c3 h6 (*see diagram*)

16. Nh4!? N×h4 As Pollock suggested, tempting White into some tactical complications with

After
15. ... h7–h6

16. ... h×g5 17. N×g6 Re8 was another possibility.
17. B×h4 Ba3? Pollock: "Some sort of attempt at
a diversion, but quite purposeless. His best course
was now 17. ... Be7." **18. Rcd1 c5 19. f4!** This advance underscores Black's kingside weaknesses.
19. ... Qb6 20. f×e5 Nd7 21. Bd5 Rae8 22. R×f7!
Pollock: "A fine stroke of play." Steinitz: "A charming sacrifice in Blackburne's happiest style." **22. ...
R×f7 23. B×f7+ K×f7 24. Qh5+ g6** 24. ... Qg6
25. Rf1+ Nf6 26. Q×g6+ K×g6 27. e×f6 is pretty
hopeless too. **25. Q×h6 Re6 26. Rf1+ Kg8
27. Bf6 c4+** Pollock: "There is no escape from the
vice-like grip." **28. d4 N×f6 29. Q×g6+ Kf8
30. e×f6 Qa7 31. Qh6+ Ke8 32. f7+ Kd7 33. f8N+
B×f8 34. Q×f8 Re7 35. Rf7 Ke6 36. R×e7+
Q×e7 37. Q×e7+ 1–0** [*Chess-Monthly*, September
1888, pages 18–20; *ICM*, October 1888, page 315;
PM, pages 66–67]

200. Pollock–A. Rumboll [C44]
International Masters, Bradford,
Round 4, 8 August 1888

1. e4 e5 2. Nf3 Nc6 3. c3 Pollock: "This attack
has been seldom adopted in games of importance
since the Rosenthal–Zukertort match. It was played
in tournaments within the last year by Gunsberg
vs. Mortimer, and by Pollock vs. Zukertort, both
games resulting in a draw. It is by no means so
sound for White as the more regularly played attacks in the Royal Opening." **3. ... d5** Pollock:
"The strongest defence." **4. Qa4 f6 5. Bb5 Nge7
6. e×d5** Pollock: "6. d3 should be sounder, but it
is obviously too defensive a continuation." **6. ...
Q×d5 7. d4 Bd7** Pollock: "If 7. ... e4, 8. Nfd2 e3(?)
9. Nf3 e×f2+ 10. K×f2, with the better game."
8. 0–0 e4 9. Ne1 Pollock: "The knight is played
on this square for a defensive purpose. The plan of
campaign is as follows: Black will not easily be able
to castle on the kingside, therefore he will affect
that operation on the queenside, and vigorously
attack on the other. As will be seen, White's game

will prove the stronger, (1) because his queen will,
unlike Black's, aid both in attack and defence;
(2) because of the position of the king's knight;
(3) because of the greater activity of the bishops."
**9. ... Nf5 10. Bc4 Qa5 11. Qc2 Nd6 12. b4! Qf5
13. Bb3 0–0–0 14. Be3 h5 15. d5 Ne5 16. Nd2**
Pollock: "If 16. B×a7, 16. ... h4 (16. ... b6 17. a4
Kb7 18. a5 Ra8 19. a×b6 c×b6 20. Qa2 Bb5 21. c4
Ne×c4 22. Nc3, with a strong attack.) 17. Nd2 h3
18. g3 g5, and Black has a good chance." **16. ...
Qg6 17. c4 Nd3** *(see diagram)* 17. ... Nf5! was
stronger: 18. c5 N×e3 19. f×e3 Ng4 20. Qc3 Kb8
21. a4 h4.

After
17. ... Ne5–d3

18. N×e4! Bf5 19. Q×d3 B×e4 Pollock: "19. ...
N×e4 would have been greatly preferable, as the
queen must move at once, and Black regains the
pawn (by ...B×b4)." **20. Qe2** 20. Qd4! b6 21. c5
was even more potent. **20. ... h4 21. f3! Bf5 22. c5**
Pollock: "White has now a telling advantage in
force and position." **22. ... Nf7 23. c6! Bd6** Pollock: "This square must imperatively be reserved
for the knight in order to defend b7." **24. c×b7+
Kd7** 24. ... K×b7 is not sufficient: 25. Qb5+ Kc8
26. B×a7 h3 27. g3 Rde8 28. Rc1. **25. B×a7
B×h2+ 26. K×h2 Qg3+ 27. Kg1 h3 28. Ba4+ c6
29. B×c6+ Kd6 30. Bc5+ Kc7 31. Qb5** Pollock:
"Best. 31. Qe7+ is inferior, as the king need not go
to b8." 31. Qa6! would have mated in seven moves,
but the text is almost as good. **31. ... R×d5 1–0**
[*Leeds Mercury*, August 10, 1888; *BCM*, August
1888, pages 376–378]

201. J. Owen–Pollock [A80]
International Masters, Bradford,
Round 5, 9 August 1888

**1. Nf3 f5 2. d4 Nf6 3. e3 e6 4. Bd3 b6 5. 0–0
Bb7 6. c4 Be7 7. Nc3 0–0 8. d5 Na6 9. a3 Nc5
10. Bc2 Qe8 11. Nd4 Qg6 12. f3** *(see diagram)*
12. ... Qh5? 12. ... a5 first was useful. **13. b4!
Na6 14. d×e6 Bd6 15. g3 d×e6 16. N×e6 Rf7?!**
16. ... Rfe8 17. Nd4 Be5 would have given Black

After
12. f2–f3

something back for the pawn. **17. Nd5! N×d5 18. c×d5 Re8 19. Bb3 Nb8 20. Bb2 Nd7 21. f4 Qg6 22. Qd3 Nf6 23. B×f6 R×f6 24. N×c7 Re7 25. Ne6 Qg4 26. Rac1 Rh6 27. Rf2 Rh3 28. Ng5 Rh5 29. Bd1 1–0** [*tournament book*, page 21; *BCM*, August–September 1888, page 378; *PM*, page 65]

202. Pollock–A. Burn
International Masters, Bradford, Round 6, 9 August 1888

1. e4 e6 (…) 0–1 *Glasgow Herald* (August 10): "Burn obtained an overwhelming position in his game with Pollock, and won in thirty-nine moves." *Morning Post* (August 10): "Burn defeated Pollock who lost a piece at the end and resigned." *Leeds Mercury* (August 10): "Burn adopted the French Defence, and Pollock, with a novelty (**4. f3**[5]) on the fourth move, brought the game into complication; but at the loss of a pawn both sides were somewhat pressed for time, and Burn, wisely keeping strictly to his defensive, utilised this advantage, and in spite of his opponent's strenuous exertions to maintain the attack here initiated, finally, with all his pieces in play, achieved a win after 34 moves, the game having been very interesting from start to finish." [Full score not recovered]

203. J. Taubenhaus–Pollock [C49]
International Masters, Bradford, Round 7, 10 August 1888

1. e4 e5 2. Nc3 Nc6 3. Nf3 Nf6 4. Bb5 Bb4 5. d3 d6 6. 0-0 Bg4 Pollock: "Not very orthodox, but admissible." **7. Nd5 Bc5 8. Bg5 a6** Pollock: "This, or 8. … h6, is apparently the only available move, for if 8. … Be6 White could obtain a dangerous attack after 9. d4." **9. B×c6+** Pollock: "If the bishop retreats, Black will get a good game by

9. … b5 and 10. … Nd4." **9. … b×c6 10. B×f6** Pollock: "Not necessary here nor advisable, as the doubling of the pawns only strengthens Black's centre, thus rendering castling unnecessary, as the king will be secure from any attack for a long time to come." **10. … g×f6 11. Ne3 Qd7?!** 11. … h5!? was worth considering. **12. c3** 12. N×e5! f×e5 (12. … B×d1? 13. N×d7 K×d7 14. Ra×d1 B×e3 15. f×e3 Ke7 16. Rf5) 13. N×g4 Qe6 14. Qf3 would have favored White. **12. … Rg8 13. N×g4 Q×g4 14. Ne1** Pollock: "White bases his hopes on having a knight against a bishop for the ending, the former piece being generally very deadly to doubled pawns. Black on the other hand trusts to his powerful pawn centre." **14. … h5 15. Q×g4 h×g4 16. g3** Pollock: "To guard against …g3, but as that advance could not be made at once on account of 17. h×g3 R×g3 18. d4, he would have done perhaps better with 16. Nc2." **16. … f5!?** **17. Kg2** Pollock: "If 17. e×f5, 17. … Rg5 recovers the pawn." **17. … f×e4 18. d×e4 Ke7 19. Nd3 Bb6 20. f4 f6 21. Nb4** Pollock: "Very questionable, as he cannot take the c-pawn, and therefore loses valuable time." **21. … a5 22. Nd3 Raf8 23. Rac1 Kd7 24. f×e5 f×e5 25. R×f8 R×f8 26. Rf1 R×f1 27. K×f1 Ke6 28. Nf2 B×f2 29. K×f2 c5 30. Ke3?!** (*see diagram*) 30. b3! c6 31. Ke3 d5 32. Ke2 would have kept the edge.

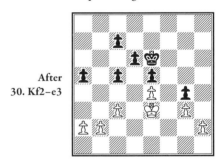

After
30. Kf2–e3

30. … d5! Pollock: "The endgame is most interesting. Black is practically a pawn ahead and although it is, per se, a badly doubled one it wins the game by gaining a move." **31. e×d5+** Pollock: "Probably 31. b3 would have drawn the game." **31. … K×d5 32. Kd3** 32. b3 was met by 32. … c4! 33. b4 a×b4 34. c×b4 Kc6 35. a4 Kd5 36. Kd2 e4 37. Kc2 e3 38. Kc3 Ke4. **32. … c4+ 33. Ke3 a4 34. a3 c6 35. Ke2 Ke4 36. Kf2 Kd3 37. Kg2 e4 38. h4 g×h3+ 39. K×h3 e3 0–1** [*tournament book*, page 32; *Bradford Observer*, August 11, 1888;

---

5. Richard Forster: "…presumably after **1.e4 e6 2.d4 d5 3. Nc3 Nf6**" (*Amos Burn*, page 334).

the endgame from move 29th onwards was featured in *ICM*, September 1888, page 283; *PM*, pages 69–70]

204. Pollock–C.D. Locock [C45]
International Masters, Bradford,
Round 8, 11 & 13 August 1888

1. e4 e5 2. Nf3 Nc6 3. d4 e×d4 4. N×d4 Bc5 5. Nb3 (...) 0–1 The game was adjourned once and resumed on August 13. *Yorkshire Post* (August 13): "The gambit pawn was immediately recovered by 4. N×d4, as is now almost invariably the case in the important games. Upon Black moving 4. ... Bc5 Pollock retreated 5. Nb3, instead of supporting it by Be3 and c3, as is generally done. Getting out his queenside pieces, White castled on this side and Black immediately invited exchange of queens, which was declined. On the 14th move Black castled on the kingside, leaving his b2-pawn *en prise* to the adverse queen. It was promptly taken, and Locock seizing the open file with his queen's rook opened a brilliant attack." *Leeds Mercury* (August 14): "Pollock adopting the 'modern' Scotch Gambit against Locock playing 5. Nb3, instead of the usual 5. Be3, soon obtained an advantage, each side castling with the opposite rook. In castling Locock sacrificed a pawn, and obtained a fine attack by a subsequent sacrifice of a piece, and this, barring an after miscalculation, was fine enough to have won. However, Locock's error was capped by a later one on the part of his opponent, who fell into an ingenious trap, and resigned on the 52nd move." [Full score not recovered]

205. G.A. Mackenzie–Pollock [A41]
International Masters, Bradford,
Round 9, 11 August 1888

1. Nf3 d6 2. d4 Bg4 3. e3 Nd7 4. c4 e5 5. Nc3 f6?! Pollock: "A novel method of opening certainly. The text move seems at least unnecessary, and 5. ... Ne7 preferable." Too eccentric. 5. ... Ngf6 was normal and good. **6. Be2 Ne7 7. Qb3 b6?!** This unjustified weakening of the light squares is soon to be regretted. Pollock: "7. ... Rb8 is the proper reply. Black however is bent on upsetting all the canons of opening, and devises a (suicidal) scheme to lure the White queen to destruction." **8. 0–0 Nc6 9. Qb5! Na5 10. b4 Nb7 11. Qc6 Qc8 12. d×e5** 12. N×e5 and 12. Nd5 were both possible as well. **12. ... f×e5 13. Nd5 Kd8 14. e4! h6**

15. Nd4!? Searching for a brilliant finish. But developing the bishop on c1 was much stronger. **15. ... B×e2 16. N×e2 g5** Pollock: "To prevent f4." **17. Nec3 Rh7 18. Be3 a5 19. h3 a4?** Pollock: "The idea of still ensnaring the queen, while himself under attack, is unsound. 19. ... Ra6 at once is a better move, or possibly 19. ... Nb8." Black had to grab the given opportunity by 19. ... a×b4! 20. N×b4 Na5 21. Qd5 Nf6 22. Qd3 g4. **20. N×a4 Nb8 21. Qb5 Ra6** *(see diagram)* Pollock: "White threatened N×b6."

After
21. ... Ra8–a6

22. Na×b6! c6 23. N×c8 K×c8 23. ... c×b5 24. c×b5 Ra3 25. Rfc1 is a simple win. **24. Rfc1 Rf7 25. a4 Kd8 26. Qb6+ R×b6 27. B×b6+ Ke8 28. Ne3 Nd7 29. a5 d5 30. e×d5 1–0** [*Leeds Mercury*, August 13, 1888 (the first ten moves); *PM*, page 66]

206. Pollock–J. Mason [C54]
International Masters, Bradford,
Round 10, 13 August 1888

1. e4 e5 2. Nf3 Nc6 3. Bc4 Bc5 4. b4 Bb6 5. c3 Nf6 6. d3 d6 7. Bg5 h6 8. Bh4 g5 Pollock: "A very bold continuation, to be explained, doubtless, by the fact that Mr. Mason had, in previous match games, found the attacking style to succeed best against his present opponent." **9. Bg3 Ne7 10. Qb3** Pollock: "Best. White has indisputably the stronger position." **10. ... 0–0 11. Nbd2 Ng6 12. h4!** Pollock: "Compelling Black to weaken his pawns, which are unsoundly posted on the fifth rank." **12. ... g4 13. h5 Nf4 14. B×f4 e×f4 15. Nh4 c6** Pollock: "Obviously Ng6 is the bone of contention hereabouts." **16. Qc2** *(see diagram)*

16. ... d5! 17. Bb3 a5 17. ... Re8!? was a strong continuation. **18. b×a5 B×a5 19. 0–0–0 Be6 20. d4 Rc8 21. e5 Nh7** 21. ... c5!? could have been tried: 22. e×f6 c×d4 23. Kb1 R×c3 24. Qb2 Q×f6 gives a powerful initiative. **22. Nf5** Pollock: "By this an entire 'time' is lost at a most important moment. The position is very intricate and full of

After
16. Qb3–c2

variations. As it is part of Black's plan to sacrifice the exchange, the proper course is to attack the king's rook in one, rather than the queen's in two moves. Thus, if 22. Ng6! Qg5 (best) 23. N×f8 N×f8. Now White may proceed with 24. Nf3, for if 24. ... g×f3, 25. g×f3 Kh8 26. Rdg1 Qe7 27. Qd2 c5 28. Q×f4; or 27. ... f5 28. Q×f4 Qh7 29. Rg6 N×g6 30. h×g6 Qg7 31. Qg5 and wins. And if 24. ... Qe7, 25. Nh4 Qg5 26. Nf3. White must be content to draw, his position, after castling, being otherwise defenceless." A further point to Pollock's comment: 22. Ng6!? would have led to some complicated play with chances for both sides: 22. ... c5! (22. ... f×g6 23. Q×g6+ Kh8 24. Q×e6) 23. N×f8 Q×f8 24. Nb1 Ng5. **22. ... Qg5 23. Nd6 c5!** Pollock: "Finely played, and full of force up to the resigning point." **24. N×c8 R×c8 25. c4 c×d4 26. Ba4 B×d2+ 27. K×d2 R×c4 0–1** [*Bradford Observer*, August 1888; *Leeds Mercury*, August 14, 1888; *Morning Post*, September 17, 1888; *BCM*, August 1889, pages 330–331]

207. J. Mortimer–Pollock [C59]
International Masters, Bradford,
Round 11, 14 August 1888

1. e4 e5 2. Nf3 Nc6 3. Bc4 Nf6 4. Ng5 d5 5. e×d5 Na5 6. Bb5+ c6 7. d×c6 b×c6 8. Be2 h6 9. Nf3 e4 10. Ne5 Qc7 11. f4 Bd6 12. d4 0–0 13. 0–0 c5 14. c3 Bb7 15. Be3 Nd5 16. Qd2 c×d4 17. B×d4 Rad8 17. ... f6 18. Ng6 e3 19. Qe1 Rfe8 is an exciting possibility for Black. **18. Qe1?** 18. g3 was necessary. **18. ... N×f4 19. R×f4 B×e5 20. B×e5 Q×e5 21. Rf1 e3 22. Qg3 Qe7** 22. ... Nc6 was even better: 23. Q×e5 N×e5 24. c4 f5 25. Nc3 Rd2 26. b3 f4. **23. b4 Nc6 24. Rf3 Rfe8 25. Qe1 N×b4!? 26. c×b4 B×f3 27. g×f3 Qg5+ 28. Kh1 Qf6 29. Nc3 Rd2 30. Rc1 Qd4** (*see diagram*)

31. Nb1? 31. Ne4 was better but Black had available a powerful shot here as well: 31. ... R×e4! 32. f×e4 Q×e4+ 33. Kg1 Rd6 34. Bh5 Rd5 35. Rc5

R×h5 36. R×h5 Qg4+. 31. Qf1 was a more stubborn choice, but Black's edge remains clear after 31. ... Q×b4 32. Ne4 R×a2 33. Bc4 Rd2! **31. ... Qb2 32. Nc3 Rc8 0–1** [*tournament book*, page 50; *PM*, page 71].

208. C. von Bardeleben–Pollock [A80]
International Masters, Bradford,
Round 13, 15 August 1888

1. d4 f5 A definite preference of Pollock's. **2. Nc3 d5 3. Bf4 e6 4. e3 Nf6 5. Nf3 Bb4 6. a3 B×c3+ 7. b×c3 Ne4 8. Nd2!?** 8. Ne5 0–0 9. f3 Nd6 10. Bd3 was another good plan. **8. ... N×c3 9. Qh5+ g6 10. Qh6 Qe7 11. h4 Rg8 12. Nf3 Ne4 13. Bd3 Nc6 14. B×e4 f×e4 15. Ne5** 15. Ng5 Rg7 16. h5 could be met by 16. ... e5! **15. ... N×e5 16. B×e5 Bd7 17. Qg5 Qf7!? 18. Rb1 Rf8 19. Qg3 Bc6 20. B×c7 Qd7 21. h5 g5 22. Be5?!** 22. 0–0! was useful right away. **22. ... Bb5!** This retains the White king in the center and provides Black with plenty of compensation for the material deficit. **23. Q×g5 Ba6 24. Bf4 Rc8 25. Rb2 Qc6** (*see diagram*)

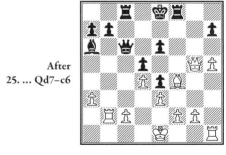

After
25. ... Qd7–c6

26. Kd1? 26. Qe5! was forced: 26. ... Qc3+ 27. Kd1 R×f4 28. e×f4 Q×b2 29. Q×e6+ Kd8 30. Qd6+ Ke8 31. Qe6+ Kd8. **26. ... Bd3! 27. Bd6 Q×d6 28. Qe5** 28. c×d3 was still impossible because of 28. ... Q×a3! and White can't escape mate. **28. ... Q×e5 29. d×e5 R×f2 30. R×b7 Rc×c2 31. Rb8+ Kd7 1–0** [*Yorkshire Post*, August 16,

After
18. ... Nf6–d7

19. Ne3!? Pollock: "Bold indeed, but almost justifiable in the close state of the game, and in face of ...c5, by which Black would have obtained a good position." **19. ... N×e5 20. f×e5 Qd8 21. g4 f5** 21. ... c5! was another way of keeping active. **22. e×f6+ R×f6 23. g5 Rf7 24. Q×e6 Qd6 25. Q×d6 c×d6 26. Bc2 Raf8 27. Bb3 Rf4 28. h3 h6 29. g×h6+ K×h6 30. N×d5 N×d5 31. B×d5 g5 32. f3 Rb8?** Too passive. 32. ... Re8 was more accurate. Pollock: "Black ought to have been a little more conservative with his pawns, for his opponent has now a full equivalent for the loss of the exchange." **33. Re1! Kg6 34. Re7 b5 35. Ra7 Rb6 36. Ra8 Rf6 37. Rg8+ Kf5 38. Kf2 a5 39. Kg3 Rh6 40. Rf8+ Kg6 41. Be4+ Kg7 42. Rf5 Rh5 43. Bd3 b4 44. c4!** It's clear White has reasons to play for a win. **44. ... a4 45. Ra5 a3 46. b3 Kf6 47. Be4 Rb8 48. Ra6** 48. Rd5! was most precise. Now 48. ... Rbh8 can be met by 49. Bf5. **48. ... Rbh8 49. R×d6+ Ke7 50. c5 R×h3+ 51. Kg4 Rh2 52. Ra6 Rd8 53. d5 R×a2?** 53. ... Rf8! would have kept Black in the game. **54. Kf5** Pollock: "Mr. Thorold plays the latter part of the game exceedingly well." **54. ... Rh2 55. d6+ Kf8 56. c6 Rh7 57. c7 Rf7+ 58. Kg4 Rc8 59. Ra8 1–0** [*PM*, pages 67–69]

209. Pollock–F.J. Lee [C14]
International Masters, Bradford,
Round 14, 16 August 1888

The *Sheffield Daily Telegraph* (August 17): "The game between Pollock and Lee was exceedingly slow." **1. e4 e6 2. d4 d5 3. Nc3 Nf6 4. Bg5 Be7 5. e5 Nfd7 6. B×e7 Q×e7 7. Nf3 a6 8. Qd2 c5 9. d×c5 Nc6 10. 0–0–0 N×c5 11. Bd3 Bd7 12. Rhe1 b5 13. Kb1 Rc8 14. Ne2 h6 15. Ned4 N×d4 16. N×d4 Rc7 17. f4 g6 18. g4 Kd8?!** A dubious idea. 18. ... Qh4 19. h3 0–0 (19. ... Q×h3? 20. Rh1 Q×g4 21. Rdg1) 20. Qe3 b4 could have been tried. **19. Qa5! Na4** *(see diagram)* 19. ... h5 20. g5 Re8 was better, but Black's position remains poor.

After
19. ... Nc6–a4

20. f5! g×f5 21. g×f5 Qc5 22. Nb3 Qb6 23. Qd2 e×f5 24. Qf4 Rc4? This was not necessary. 24. ... Kc8 25. B×f5 Be6!? should have been played instead. **25. B×c4 b×c4 26. R×d5 Qb7 27. Red1! Nb6 28. R×d7+ 1–0** [*Yorkshire Post,* August 17, 1888]

210. E. Thorold–Pollock [D02]
International Masters, Bradford,
Round 15, 17 August 1888

1. Nf3 d5 2. d4 Bg4 3. Bf4 B×f3 4. e×f3 Pollock: "Taking with the g-pawn is generally preferred in similar positions. It is better to double pawns 'towards' the centre than 'from' it." **4. ... e6 5. Bd3 Bd6 6. Qd2 Nc6 7. c3 Nf6 8. 0–0 Nh5** Pollock: "Black has now the better game." **9. B×d6 Q×d6 10. Na3 a6 11. g3 0–0 12. Qg5 g6 13. f4 Kg7 14. Rae1 Qd8 15. Qg4** Pollock: "The exchange of queens would give Black the best of the ending, on account of White's doubled pawns." **15. ... Nf6 16. Qh3 Qd6 17. Nc2 Ne7 18. Re5 Nd7** *(see diagram)*

211. Pollock–J.E. Hall
International Masters, Bradford,
Round 16, 17 August 1888

White to move

Leeds Mercury (August 18): "The Bradfordian played an irregular defence, the opening moves being 1. e4 d6 2. d4 f5 3. e×f5 B×f5 4. Bd3 B×d3 5. Q×d3 Nf6, and the game went on very equally until about the 28th move, when Hall obtained an advantage on the queenside, but five moves later he gave his opponent a chance, of which he immediately availed himself, the position and the concluding moves being as follows": **1. Qa8+ Ke7 2. Qa7 Ke6 3. Ng5+ Kd5 4. Qa8+ Kc4 5. Qg8+ Kd4 6. Qb3 Ne5 7. Qd1+ Nd3 8. Qg4+ Kd5 9. Qe4 mate 1–0** [*Leeds Mercury*, August 18, 1888]

212. Pollock–H.E. Bird [C41]
International Masters, Bradford, Round 17, 18 August 1888

1. e4 e5 2. Nf3 d6 3. d4 f5 An attempt for a clever last-round surprise by Bird. **4. d×e5! f×e4 5. Ng5 d5 6. e6!? Nf6 7. Nf7 Qe7 8. N×h8 B×e6 9. Be2 Nc6 10. Bh5+ Kd7 11. Nc3 Rd8 12. 0–0 Kc8 13. Bg5 Ne5?!** Better was 13. ... Qd7 14. Re1 Bd6. **14. Qe2 g6 15. f4 Nc6 16. f5!? g×f5 17. Rad1** 17. Nf7!? B×f7 18. B×f7 Q×f7 19. R×f5 Bc5+ 20. Kh1 Qg6 21. B×f6 Q×f5 22. Rf1 Qe6 23. B×d8 N×d8 was the other key line, with unclear play. **17. ... Qg7 18. Nf7** (*see diagram*)

After
18. Ng5–f7

18. ... B×f7? A critical error. Much stronger was 18. ... Bc5+! 19. Kh1 N×h5! 20. Q×h5 (20. B×d8 Q×f7; 20. N×d8 Q×g5!) 20. ... Rg8. **19. B×f6 Q×f6 20. R×f5 B×h5 21. Q×h5 Qe6 22. Qh3** 22. Rf×d5 was much simpler. **22. ... Bc5+ 23. Kh1 Bd6 24. Rf×d5 Q×h3 25. g×h3 e3 26. Re1 Re8 27. Rd3 Bf4 28. Nd5 Bh6 29. N×e3 Nb4 30. Rb3 c5 31. a3 Nc6 32. Kg2 b5 33. Rd3 Bf4 34. Kf2 B×h2 35. Nf5 Rf8 36. Rf3 Kd7 37. Rd1+ Kc7 38. Ng7 R×f3+ 39. K×f3 Nd4+ 40. Ke4 Ne2 41. Ne6+ Kc6 42. Rd2 Ng3+ 43. Kf3 Nf1**

44. Rf2 Be5 45. c3 Nh2+ 46. Kg2 h5 47. Ng5 Kd5 48. Rf5 b4 49. a×b4 c×b4 50. c×b4 Kd4 51. R×e5 K×e5 52. K×h2 Kd4 53. Ne6+ Kc4 54. Nd8 a6 55. Nc6 1–0 [*tournament book*, pages 73–74].

In London and Ireland (Late 1888–Early 1889)

213. Pollock–O.C. Müller [C42]
London, Simpson's Divan, 9 September 1888

1. e4 e5 2. Nf3 Nf6 3. N×e5 d6 (*see diagram*)

After
3. ... d7–d6

4. N×f7!? A dangerous gambit attributed to John Cochrane. Interestingly, there's no other game of Pollock's on record with this sacrifice. **4. ... K×f7 5. Bc4+ Be6 6. B×e6+ K×e6 7. d4 Kf7 8. f4 Nc6 9. Be3 Be7 10. Qf3 Rf8 11. Nc3 Kg8 12. g4 a6 13. 0–0–0 Qe8 14. h4 b5?! 15. h5** 15. e5! would create serious problems for Black: 15. ... d×e5 16. d×e5 b4 17. Ne2 and White recovers his piece, with advantage. **15. ... Rc8 16. g5** 16. e5 was still appealing. **16. ... Nd7 17. Rdg1 Na5 18. Nd5 Bd8 19. f5! c5 20. Qg3?** A lethal loss of time. Best was 20. f6! Nc4 21. Bf2 c×d4 22. h6 g6 23. B×d4; another appealing possibility was 20. h6!? g6 21. b3!?. **20. ... c×d4 21. B×d4 Ne5?** 21. ... Q×e4! would have ended the fight instantly. **22. Nf6+!?** 22. f6! Qe6 23. Kb1 Nac4 24. Rg2 a5 25. Nf4 Qf7 26. f×g7 was possibly more powerful than the text. **22. ... R×f6 23. g×f6 B×f6 24. h6 Qc6 25. Rg2?** 25. Qc3 b4 26. Q×c6 Na×c6 27. B×e5 N×e5 was a consideration, but even here Black retains the upper hand. **25. ... Q×e4 26. Bc3 b4 27. B×b4 Nd3+ 28. Kb1 N×b4 29. h×g7 N×c2 0–1** [*Chess Player's Chronicle*, January 16, 1889; *Hampshire Telegraph*, November 29, 1890]

214. Pollock & Lee–Bird & Rushworth [C39]

Consultation Game, London, Simpson's Divan, November 1888

1. e4 e5 2. f4 e×f4 3. Nf3 g5 4. h4 g4 5. Ne5 h5 6. Bc4 Nh6 7. d4 d6 8. Nd3 c6 9. g3? 9. B×f4 was normal. **9. ... f5 10. Nc3 f×e4 11. N×e4 Nf5 12. Kf2 Bg7 13. Re1 B×d4+ 14. Kf1 d5!** (*see diagram*)

After 14. ... d6–d5

15. B×d5? 15. Nd6+ would secure excellent play for White: 15. ... Kf8 16. N×f5 B×f5 (16. ... d×c4 17. N×d4 Q×d4 18. Qe2!) 17. N×f4 d×c4 18. Re5! **15. ... Q×d5?** 15. ... c×d5! 16. Nd6+ Kf8 17. Re8+ Q×e8 18. N×e8 K×e8 favors Black. **16. Nf6+ Kd8 0–1** The newspaper's columnist recorded that White resigned in this position. It is unclear why since 17. N×d5 wins for White. It could be a clerical error in reporting the result. The columnist also added that "both parties seem in this game to play more for the 'fun of the thing' than for glory of victory." [*Illustrated Sporting and Dramatic News*, February 2, 1889]

215. Pollock–Mr. M.

Odds Game, London, Simpson's Divan, November 1888

Remove Nb1

1. e4 e5 2. Nf3 Nc6 3. d4 e×d4 4. Bc4 Bc5 5. Ng5 Nh6 6. Qh5 Qf6 7. 0-0 d6 8. h3 Ne5 9. Bb3 Qg6 10. Qe2 f6 11. Ne6 B×e6 12. B×e6 f5 13. Qb5+ Ke7 14. B×h6 K×e6 15. e×f5+ Q×f5 (*see diagram*)

16. f4 g×h6 16. ... Nc6! was better. **17. B×g7 d3+ 18. Kh1 Rhg8. 17. f×e5 Qe4?** 17. ... Qg5 18. e×d6 Rhg8 19. Rae1+ K×d6 20. Q×b7 d3+ 21. Kh1 c6 would have allowed Black to play for a win. **18. Rae1 Qc6 19. e×d6+ Kd7 20. Rf7+ Kd8 21. d×c7+ Kc8 22. Qd3 Re8?? 1–0** 22. ... Qg6!

After 15. ... Qf6×f5

was the correct defense: 23. Rf5 Bd6 24. Q×d4 Rg8 25. Qd5 B×c7 26. Rf7. [*Dublin Evening Mail*, December 6, 1888]

216. Pollock–Mr. N.

Odds Game, London, Simpson's Divan, November 1888

Remove Nb1

1. e4 e5 2. c3 Nf6 3. Bc4 N×e4 4. Qb3 Qf6 5. Nh3 c6 6. d4 e×d4 7. 0-0 Nc5 8. Qc2 d5 9. Bg5 Qg6 10. Rae1+ Ne6 10. ... Be6! was the correct move. **11. Bd3 Qh5 12. f4 Be7?** Far superior was 12. ... h6 13. f5 h×g5 14. f×e6 g4! **13. Be2 d3 14. Q×d3 Qg6 15. f5 Nc5?** 15. ... Q×g5! 16. N×g5 Bc5+ 17. Kh1 N×g5 18. Bh5+ Kd8 kept the game alive. **16. f×g6 N×d3 17. g×f7+ Kd7 18. Bg4+ Kc7 19. R×e7+ Kb6 20. B×c8 Na6 21. R×b7+ Ka5 22. b4+ Ka4 23. Bg4 Ne5 24. Bd1+ Ka3 25. Bb3 Nd3 26. Nf4 h6 27. N×d3 h×g5** (*see diagram*)

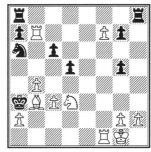

After 27. ... h6×g5

28. f8Q Rh×f8 29. R×f8 R×f8 30. R×a7 1–0 [*Dublin Evening Mail*, December 6, 1888]

217. Jones & Newcomb–Pollock

Simultaneous/Consultation Game (6 Boards), Dublin, Dublin Chess Club, 14 December 1888

White to move

1. **Qb3** and Black mates in five moves. **0–1**
[*Belfast News-Letter*, February 21, 1889]

218. Drury & Fitzpatrick–Pollock [C23] Simultaneous/Consultation Game (6 Boards), Dublin, Dublin Chess Club, 14 December 1888

1. **e4 e5 2. Bc4 Bc5 3. c3 Nf6 4. d4 e×d4
5. c×d4 Bb4+ 6. Bd2 B×d2+ 7. N×d2 N×e4!?
8. B×f7+** Pollock: "This line of play costs the allies
a piece, though in a manner which is not at first
obvious." **8. ... K×f7 9. Qb3+?** 9. N×e4 Re8
10. Qh5+ Kg8 11. Qd5+ Kh8 12. 0–0–0 was better. **9. ... d5 10. N×e4 Re8 11. f3 Kf8** Pollock: "If
11. ... Be6, 12. Ng3 saving the piece. Black had a
still stronger move here in 11. ... Re6. The latter
move, although apparently uncouth, is a very powerful one." **12. Ne2 d×e4 13. f×e4 Be6?!** More
precise was 13. ... Qh4+ 14. g3 Q×e4 15. 0–0+ Ke7
16. Rf2 (16. Rf7+? Kd8) 16. ... Be6 17. Qb4+ Kd8
18. Nc3 Na6! **14. 0–0+ Kg8 15. d5 Bf7** (*see diagram*) 15. ... Bc8 or 15. ... Bg4 were recommended.

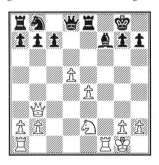

**After
15. ... Be6–f7**

16. **Ng3?** As Pollock remarked in his notes, the
White players missed a fine tactic here: 16. R×f7!!
K×f7 17. d6+ Kg6 18. Nf4+ Kf6 19. Qc3+ Kf7
20. Qc4+ Kf6 21. Qd4+ Kf7 22. Qd5+ Kf8 (22. ...
Kf6 23. Qf5 mate) 23. Rf1 and White wins. **16. ...
Nd7 17. Rf4 Nf6 18. Raf1 Qd6 19. Qc3 Re5**

20. **Nf5** Pollock: "In spite of the oversight on their
sixteenth move, they conduct their attack with
spirit and determination." **20. ... Qb6+ 21. Kh1
Rae8 22. Qg3** At least 22. Nh6+ Kf8 23. Ng4 had
to be tried even if eventually proven insufficient:
23. ... N×g4 24. R×f7+ Kg8 25. h3 Nf6 26. Q×c7
Q×c7 27. R×c7 R×e4 28. d6 Rd4 29. R×b7 a6
30. Rb6. **22. ... Bg6 23. Nh6+ Kf8** Pollock: "23. ...
Kh8 seems safer." **24. Ng4 R×e4 25. N×f6 R×f4**
Pollock: "A fine stroke of play, evidently premed-
itated. The position is one of a highly instructive
nature." **26. Nd7+** Pollock: "White must now still
remain a piece to the bad, play as they may." **26. ...
Ke7 27. R×f4 K×d7 0–1** [*Belfast News-Letter*,
February 7, 1889; *Dublin Evening Mail*, December
20, 1888; *PM*, page 90]

219. C. Newsome–Pollock [A01] Simultaneous Exhibition, Dublin, Dublin Chess Club, 15 December 1888

1. **b3 f5 2. e3 Nf6 3. Bb2 e6 4. f4 b6 5. Be2
Bb7 6. Bf3 Nc6 7. c4 Bc5 8. d4 Bb4+ 9. Bc3
B×c3+ 10. N×c3 0–0 11. d5!? e×d5 12. N×d5
Re8 13. Kf2 Ne4+ 14. B×e4 R×e4 15. Nf3 Re8
16. Re1 Ne7 17. N×e7+ Q×e7 18. Qd3 Be4
19. Qd2 Qf6 20. Rad1 Re7 21. Qd4 Qh6 22. Rh1
Rae8 23. Rde1** (*see diagram*)

**After
23. Rd1–e1**

23. **... d6** 23. ... c5 24. Qd2 d5 25. c×d5 Rd7
was one possibility to break through. **24. h3 Re6
25. Ng5 Rg6 26. N×e4 f×e4 27. Reg1 ½–½**
[*Belfast-News Letter*, January 24, 1889]

220. Pollock–R.H. Fawcett [C38] Simultaneous Exhibition (19 Boards), Kingston Chess Club, December 1888

1. **e4 e5 2. f4 e×f4 3. Nf3 g5 4. Bc4 Bg7 5. c3
Qe7 6. d4 d6 7. 0–0 Be6 8. d5?!** This offers Black
a good game. 8. B×e6 f×e6 9. Qb3 was better. **8. ...**

Bg4 9. b4 Nd7 10. a4 B×f3 11. Q×f3 Ngf6 12. Nd2 0–0 13. Bb3 a5 14. b5 Nc5 15. Bc2 Qd7 16. Bb2 Ng4 17. Nc4 Ne5 18. N×e5 d×e5 **18. …** B×e5 was naturally superior. **19. Ba3 b6 20. Rad1 Rad8 21. Rd2 Rfe8 22. Rfd1 Bf8 23. c4 Bd6 24. Bb2 g4! 25. Qf2 f6 26. Qh4 Qg7 27. Kh1 Qg5 28. Qe1 Kf7 29. Rf2 h5 30. Qd2 Nb7 31. Rdf1 Bc5 32. Re2 Nd6** (*see diagram*)

After
32. … Nb7–d6

33. Bc1!? Setting up a small trap. **33. … N×c4?!** Black should have ignored this capture and carried on his kingside push with 33. … h4! 34. Qc3 Rg8 35. Bb3 Qh5. **34. Qd3 Nd6 35. g3! Qg6 36. g×f4 e×f4 37. B×f4 ½–½** [*Dublin Evening Mail*, December 27, 1888]

221. Pollock–A. Stephens [C25]
Simultaneous Exhibition,
Clontarf Chess Club,
December 1888

1. e4 e5 2. Nc3 Nc6 3. f4 e×f4 4. Nf3 g5 5. h4 g4 6. Ng5 (*see diagram*)

After
6. Nf3–g5

6. … Nh6 Pollock: "The correct move is 6. … h6, compelling the sacrifice of the knight. The mistake, however, is not in departing from the 'books' here, but in departing from the 'principles' on the next move." **7. d4 Qf6?** Pollock: "The career of the Black queen in this game is a striking illustration of the importance of the rule not to develop that piece prematurely." **8. e5 N×e5 9. d×e5 Qc6**

10. Nd5 Bg7 11. Bb5 Qc5 Pollock: "Taking the bishop would obviously cost Black his queen." **12. B×f4 c6 13. Nc7+ Kd8 14. e6** 14. Nge6+ f×e6 15. N×e6+ Ke8 16. N×c5 c×b5 17. B×h6 B×h6 18. Rf1 was a somewhat less artistic path. **14. … Re8** Pollock: "This is much better chess, and more like Mr. Stephens." **15. Qd2 B×b2 16. Ne4** Pollock: "A very strong move, containing four or five distinct points." **16. … Qe7 17. Rd1** Pollock: "Curiously, 17. Bd6 would here have won the adverse queen the same as on the next move." **17. … d5 18. Bd6 Q×e6 19. N×e6+ R×e6 20. 0–0 (…) 1–0** Pollock: "Black, even thus handicapped, fought the game out, and was one of the last to succumb to the single player." [*Dublin Evening Mail*, December 20, 1888; *PM*, pages 89–90]

222. W.H.S. Monck–Pollock [C49]
Simultaneous Exhibition (11 Boards),
Dublin, Dublin Chess Club,
December 1888

1. e4 e5 2. Nc3 Nf6 3. Nf3 Nc6 4. Bb5 Bb4 5. 0–0 B×c3 6. d×c3 Qe7 7. Bg5 d6 8. h3 h6 9. B×f6 Q×f6 10. B×c6+ b×c6 11. Qe2 0–0 12. c4 Be6 13. Rad1 Kh7 14. b3 Rg8 15. Nh2 g5 16. Qh5 Rg6 17. Rd3 Rag8 18. Rf3 Qe7 (…) 1–0 [*Dublin Evening Mail*, December 27, 1888; the full score proved impossible to decipher].

223. S. Van Gelder–Pollock [C27]
Location/Occasion Unknown, 1888

1. e4 e5 2. Bc4 Bc5 3. Nc3 Nf6 4. d3 (*see diagram*)

After
4. d2–d3

4. … b5!? A provocative gambit idea. **5. B×b5 c6 6. Bc4 0–0** 6. … d5!? 7. e×d5 c×d5 8. Bb5+ Bd7 9. B×d7+ Nb×d7 10. Nf3 0–0 11. 0–0 Qc7 and Black would have some compensation for the pawn. **7. Be3 B×e3 8. f×e3 Qb6 9. Qc1 d5?!** 9. … Ng4! was a better idea: 10. Nd1 Bb7 11. Nf3 d5

12. h3 Nf6 13. e×d5 c×d5 14. Bb3 e4. **10. e×d5 c×d5 11. B×d5 N×d5 12. N×d5 Qa5+ 13. Nc3 Bb7 14. Qd2 Rc8 15. Nf3 Qb4 16. Nd1 Qc5 17. Rc1 Na6 18. 0–0 Rab8 19. Qf2 Nb4** Pollock's opening experiment backfired as he was two pawns down. His search for complications remains instructive, however. **20. Nc3 Rc6 21. Ne4 Qe7 22. N×e5 R×c2 23. R×c2 N×c2 24. Ng5** 24. Qg3! would have been a lethal blow: 24. … Rf8 25. Nf6+ Kh8 26. Nfd7. **24. … f6 25. Q×c2?** 25. Qh4! f×g5 26. Qc4+ Kh8 27. Nf7+ Kg8 28. N×g5+ Kh8 29. Nf7+ Kg8 30. Nd6+ Kh8 31. Nf5 Qe5 32. Q×c2 would have maintained an edge for White. **25. … Q×e5 26. Nh3 Q×e3+ 27. Nf2 Qg5 28. Ne4 Qe5 29. Nc3 h6 30. Qf2 Ba6! 31. Re1 Qa5! 32. Q×a7 R×b2 33. Re7 Qg5! 34. Re2?** Pollock's powerful series of active moves bear fruit. 34. Qa8+ Kh7 35. Qf3 was the way forward. **34. … Qc1+ 35. Kf2 B×d3 36. Qc5 B×e2** 36. … R×e2+ was simpler. **37. Qd5+ Kf8 38. Qd8+ Kf7 39. Qd7+ Kg6 40. Qe8+ Kg5 41. h4+ K×h4 42. g3+ Kh3 43. N×e2 Qc5+ 44. Kf3 Qd5+ 45. Kf2 Qg2+ 46. Ke1 Rb1+ 0–1** [*Dublin Evening Mail*, 26 January 1888]

224. Pollock–I.A. Gunsberg [C51]
London, Simpson's Divan
(Handicap Event?), 1888

1. e4 e5 2. Nf3 Nc6 3. Bc4 Bc5 4. b4 Bb6 5. b5 Na5 6. Na3 Qf6 7. d4 e×d4 8. 0–0 d6 9. e5 d×e5 10. N×e5 N×c4 11. Na×c4 Ne7 12. Qh5?! 12. N×b6 a×b6 13. Q×d4 0–0 14. Bb2 is a more practical choice. **12. … Qf5 13. Qh4 Bc5 14. Re1 Be6 15. Bb2?** A direct 15. Ba3 was advisable. **15. … 0–0–0! 16. Ba3 B×a3 17. N×a3 Ng6 18. Qg3 Nf4 19. Nd3** (see diagram)

After
19. Ne5–d3

19. … g5! 20. Nb4 h5 21. c3 d3 22. Qe3 Rhg8 23. Rad1 23. Q×a7 wasn't of much help either: 23. … Qg4 24. Qa8+ Kd7 25. Q×b7 Bd5. **23. … Qg4 24. g3 Qh3! 25. Qe4 Bf5 26. Qh1 Ne2+**

27. R×e2 d×e2 28. Re1 Rd1 0–1 [*Morning Post*, December 10, 1888]

225. H. Jacobs–Pollock
London, City of London Chess Club
(Handicap?), 1888
Remove the f7 pawn

1. e4 Nc6 2. d4 d5 3. e×d5 Q×d5 4. Nf3 Bg4 5. Nc3 (see diagram)

After
5. Nb1–c3

5. … B×f3? This renders the game hopeless. 5. … Qf5 had to be played. **6. N×d5 B×d1 7. N×c7+ Kd7 8. N×a8 B×c2 9. d5 Nb4 10. Bb5+ Kd6 11. Bf4+ K×d5 12. Nc7+ Ke4 13. Bg3 e5 14. 0–0 Bd6 15. Ne8 Bb8 16. Rac1 Ne7 17. a3 Bd3 18. Rfe1+ Kd4 19. Red1 a6 20. Rc4+ Kd5 21. R×b4 a×b5 22. R×d3+ Ke6 23. Rd8 1–0** [*Shoreditch Citizen*, March 10, 1888]

226. J. Burt–Pollock [C45]
Offhand Game, Location Unknown,
1888

1. e4 e5 2. Nf3 Nc6 3. d4 e×d4 4. N×d4 Bc5 5. Be3 Qf6 6. c3 Nge7 7. f4 d5! 8. e5 Qh4+ 9. g3 Qh6 10. Bg2 10. N×c6 B×e3 11. N×e7 K×e7 12. Bg2 g5! gives Black excellent play. 10. Qd2 was probably better. **10. … Bh3** Very good too was 10. … N×e5!? 11. Qe2 Nc4 12. Bf2 0–0 13. 0–0 Re8 14. B×d5 Nd6 15. Bg2 B×d4 16. B×d4 Nc6. **11. 0–0 B×g2 12. K×g2** (see diagram)

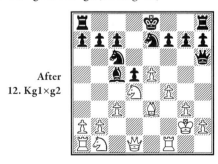

After
12. Kg1×g2

12. ... 0–0–0! 13. b4 B×d4 14. B×d4 N×d4 15. c×d4 Nf5 16. Qd2 Qb6 17. Rd1 h5 18. Na3 h4 19. Nc2? 19. g4 h3+ 20. Kh1 Nh4 21. Rac1 Kb8 22. Rc3 f5! was uncomfortable but necessary. **19. ... Qg6! 20. Qd3 h×g3 21. h×g3 Qh7 0–1** [*Belfast News-Letter*, January 19, 1888]

227. A. Burn–Pollock [C50]
Offhand(?) Game, London, 1888

1. e4 e5 2. Nc3 Bc5 3. Bc4 Nc6 4. Nf3 d6 5. d3 Bg4 6. Ne2?! B×f3 7. g×f3 Qh4 8. Ng3 0–0–0 9. B×f7 Nf6 10. 0–0 Rdf8 11. Be6+ Kb8 12. c3 g6 13. b4 (*see diagram*)

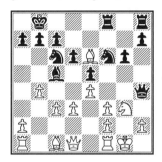

After
13. b2–b4

F. Anger (London Borough of Hackney Archives).

13. ... Bb6 13. ... h5! was an imaginative try: 14. Kg2 (14. b×c5? Ng4!; 14. Bg5 Q×g5 15. b×c5 h4) 14. ... Ng4! 15. Rh1 (15. f×g4 h×g4 16. Rh1 Qh3+ 17. Kg1 B×f2 mate) 15. ... N×f2 16. Qe2 N×h1 17. b×c5 Qf6 18. Bd5 N×g3 19. h×g3 h4 and Black wins. **14. a4 a5** 14. ... h5! was still an option. **15. b×a5 Ba7 16. Rb1 Nd8 17. Qb3 Nh5! 18. N×h5 g×h5?!** 18. ... R×f3! first would have been the correct path. **19. Be3** 19. a6! Qf6 20. Bf5 Rhg8+ 21. Kh1 Qg7 22. Bh3 B×f2 23. Bf4! R×f4 24. R×f2 gives White the edge. **19. ... B×e3 20. f×e3 Qg5+ 21. Kf2 Qf6 22. Bf5 Rhg8 23. Ke2 Rg2+ 24. Rf2 R×f2+ 25. K×f2 Qh4+ 26. Kf1 Q×h2 27. a6 Rf7 28. a×b7??** 28. Qb2! keeps the game going: 28. ... Qh1+ 29. Ke2 Qg2+ 30. Ke1 Q×f3 31. Qe2. **28. ... Rg7 29. Bg4 h×g4 0–1** [*Shoreditch Citizen*, April 14, 1888]

228. F. Anger–Pollock [C54]
London, 1888

1. e4 e5 2. Nf3 Nc6 3. Bc4 Bc5 4. c3 Nf6 5. d3 d6 6. h3 Be6 7. Bb5 0–0 8. 0–0 Ne7 9. d4 e×d4 10. c×d4 Bb6 11. e5 d×e5 12. d×e5 Nfd5 13. Bg5 c6 14. Bc4 Qd7 15. Qb3 Rad8 16. Nc3 h6 17. N×d5 c×d5 18. Bb5 Qc7 19. Rac1 Bc5? 19. ... Nc6 was best. **20. Qc2?** 20. R×c5 Q×c5 21. Rc1 Qb6 22. B×e7 should have won easily. **20. ... h×g5 21. Q×c5 Q×c5 22. R×c5 a6 23. Bd3 f6 24. Nd4 Bc8 25. e×f6 g×f6 26. Re1 Rfe8 27. Rc7 Rd7 28. Rc2 Kf7 29. Rce2 Rc7 30. Ne6 B×e6 31. R×e6 Rd7 32. b4 Rc8 33. g3 Nc6 34. Bf5 Nd4 35. R×f6+ K×f6 36. B×d7 Nf3+ 37. Kf1 Rc2** 37. ... Rc7 would have led to a draw just as well: 38. Re6+ Kf7 39. Re3 Nh2+ 40. Kg2 R×d7 41. K×h2 d4 42. Rd3 Ke6 43. Kg2 Kd5 44. Kf3 Kc4 45. Ke2 Re7+ 46. Kd2 Rf7. **38. Re6+ Kf7 39. Rb6 d4 40. R×b7** Strong was 40. Bf5! Rc3 41. Ke2. **40. ... Kf6 41. Rb6+ Ke7 42. Be6 d3 43. Bb3 Rc1+ 44. Kg2 Ne1+ 45. Kh2** (*see diagram*)

After
45. Kg2–h2

45. ... d2! 46. R×a6 Nc2 47. Ra7+ Kd6 48. Ra6+ Ke5 49. Re6+ Kd4 50. Rd6+ Kc3

51. b5 d1Q 52. R×d1 R×d1 53. B×c2 53. h4 g×h4 54. g×h4 Rd2 55. Kg3 Nd4 56. h5 N×b3 57. a×b3 Rd6 58. Kf4 draws as well. **53. ... K×c2 54. Kg2 Ra1 55. Kf3 R×a2 56. Kg4 Kd3 57. K×g5 R×f2 58. g4 Rb2 59. h4 R×b5+ 60. Kf6 Ke4 ½–½** [*Belfast News-Letter*, August 2, 1888]

229. J.E. Imbrey–Pollock [C60]
London, November/December 1888/
Early 1889(?)

"Played during Mr. W.H.K. Pollock's sojourn in London." **1. e4 e5 2. Nf3 Nc6 3. Bb5 g6 4. 0–0 Bg7 5. c3 Nge7 6. d4 e×d4 7. c×d4 0–0 8. Nc3 d6 9. Be2 f5 10. Qb3+ Kh8 11. e5 d×e5 12. d×e5 N×e5 13. Bg5 c6 14. Rfe1 Qc7 15. N×e5 B×e5 16. h3 Bg7?!** 16. ... Kg7 was more consistent: 17. Rad1 h6 18. Be3 f4 19. Bd4 B×d4 20. R×d4 Nf5. **17. Bc4! Ng8?** 17. ... b5 could have been tried: 18. R×e7 b×c4 19. Q×c4 Qb6, but White has 20. R×g7! K×g7 21. Re1, with a winning attack. **18. B×g8 R×g8 19. Re7 Qb6 20. Qf7 Q×b2** (*see diagram*)

After
20. ... Qb6×b2

White mates in three moves. **1–0** [*Oldham Standard*, June 27, 1891; *Hampshire Telegraph*, August 8, 1891; *Chess Player's Chronicle*, July 4, 1891]

230. Pollock–H.E. Bird [B34]
London, Simpson's Divan, Handicap
Tournament (?), November/
December 1888/Early 1889

1. e4 c5 2. Nc3 Nc6 3. Nf3 g6 4. d4 c×d4 5. N×d4 Bg7 6. Be3 h5 7. Be2 d6 8. 0–0 Nf6 9. h3 h4 10. f4 Nh5 11. N×c6 b×c6 12. B×h5 R×h5 13. f5!? Rh8 14. Bd4 14. Qf3!? maintained the tension. **14. ... B×d4+ 15. Q×d4 Qb6 16. Q×b6 a×b6 17. f×g6 f×g6 18. Rae1 Ra5 19. a3 Re5 20. Na2 c5 21. Nc3 Be6 22. Na4 b5 23. Nc3 b4 24. a×b4 c×b4** (*see diagram*)

J.E. Imbrey (London Borough of Hackney Archives).

After
24. ... c5×b4

25. Ra1 Kd7! 25. ... b×c3 26. Ra8+ Kd7 27. R×h8 c×b2 28. Rb8 R×e4 29. R×b2 was a possibility as well. **26. Ra7+ Kc6 27. Na4 Bc4 28. Re1 Rf8 29. b3 Bb5 30. c4 B×a4 31. R×a4 Kc5 32. Rd1 R×e4 33. Ra6 Rf5 34. Ra5+ Kc6 35. Ra6+ Kd7 36. Rb6 Re2! 37. Rf1 Rg5 38. Rf2 Re3 39. R×b4 R×h3** and Black eventually won. **0–1** [*Hereford Times*, February 2, 1889]

231. Pollock & Downing–
Cumming & Gamble & Harvey [C39]
Consultation Game, Belfast,
Belfast Chess Club, January 1889

1. e4 e5 2. f4 e×f4 3. Nf3 g5 4. h4 g4 5. Ng5

h6 6. N×f7 K×f7 7. d4 d5 8. B×f4 d×e4 9. Nc3
Nf6 10. Bc4+ Kg7 11. 0–0 Bd6 12. B×d6 Q×d6
13. Nb5 Qg3 14. Qe2 Nc6 *(see diagram)* In view
of White's next move, 14. ... Rf8 or 14. ... Nbd7
were better options.

After
14. ... Nb8–c6

15. R×f6! K×f6 16. Rf1+ Ke7 17. Q×e4+ Kd8
18. Rf7! Bd7 19. R×d7+ Spectacular, but not the
most accurate. Better was 19. Be6! Kc8 20. B×d7+
Kb8 21. B×c6 b×c6 22. N×c7. **19. ... K×d7**
20. Qe6+ Kd8 21. Qf6+ Ne7 22. Q×h8+ Kd7
23. Q×h6 23. Q×a8 allows a perpetual: 23. ...
Qe3+ 24. Kh2 (Not 24. Kf1?? because of 24. ...
Nf5!) 24. ... Qf4+. **23. ... Qe1+ 24. Kh2 g3+**
25. Kh3 Qh1+ 26. Kg4 Qd1+ 27. Kh3 Re8? An
attempt to play for a win instead of accepting the
draw, but it backfires. **28. Be6+** Even stronger was
28. Qf4 Qh1+ 29. K×g3 Qe1+ 30. Kh2. **28. ...**
Kd8 29. Qf4 Q×c2?? Missing the only way out:
29. ... Qh1+ 30. K×g3 Nf5+! 31. B×f5 (31. Q×f5!?
Qe1+ 32. Kh3 R×e6 33. Qg5+ Kc8 34. Kh2) 31. ...
Rg8+ 32. Bg4 Qe1+ 33. Kh3 Qh1+ and Black secures the draw. **30. Nd6!! Nf5 31. Qg5+ Re7**
32. Nf7+ Ke8 33. Qg8 mate 1–0 [*Belfast News-
Letter,* January 24, 1889]

232. Pollock–Knox & Thompson [C51]
Consultation Game, Belfast,
Belfast Chess Club, January 1889

1. e4 e5 2. Nf3 Nc6 3. Bc4 Bc5 4. b4 B×b4
5. c3 Bc5 6. 0–0 d6 7. d4 e×d4 8. c×d4 Bb6
9. Nc3 f6 10. e5 d×e5 11. Ba3 N×d4?! 11. ... B×d4
12. Qb3 Nge7 13. Rad1 Bg4 was safer. **12. N×d4**
12. N×e5! f×e5 13. Qh5+ g6 14. Q×e5+ Be6
15. Ne4 would have given White the attack he
wanted. **12. ... Q×d4?** 12. ... B×d4 13. Nb5 c5 was
the correct defense. **13. Qb3 Nh6 14. Rad1! Qg4**
15. Nb5 Bd7 16. h3 Qf5 *(see diagram)*

17. R×d7! Q×d7 17. ... K×d7 is met by 18. Rd1+
Kc8 19. Nd6+ c×d6 20. Be6+. **18. Nd6+?!** Elegant
but imprecise. 18. Rd1 Qf5 19. N×c7+ was best.
18. ... Q×d6! 19. B×d6 c×d6 20. Bd5 0–0–0?!

20. ... Ke7! 21. B×b7 Rab8 22. Qd5 Rhd8 23. Rc1
Kf8 gave Black at least equality. **21. a4 Rhe8 22. a5**
B×f2+ 23. K×f2 Re7 24. Rb1 Rdd7 25. Be6
R×e6 26. Q×e6 Kd8 27. a6 b6 28. R×b6 a×b6
29. Q×d7+ K×d7 30. a7 1–0 [*Belfast News-Let-
ter,* February 21, 1889]

233. Pollock–Godwin [C22]
Simultaneous Exhibition (?), Belfast,
Belfast Chess Club, January 1889

1. e4 e5 2. d4 e×d4 3. Q×d4 Nc6 4. Qe3 d6
5. Nc3 Be7 6. Bd2 Nf6 7. h3 h6 8. 0–0–0 a6 9. f4
Na7?! 10. Nf3 c5 11. g4 Bd7 12. Bg2 Bc6
13. Rhe1 Nd7 *(see diagram)*

After
16. ... Qg4–f5

After
13. ... Nf6–d7

14. e5! d5 14. ... 0–0 was imperative, even if
White's position remained superior, after 15. e×d6
B×d6 16. Qd3 Nf6. **15. e6! Nf8 16. e×f7+ K×f7**
17. Ne5+ Ke8 18. N×d5 Qd6 18. ... B×d5 runs
into 19. Ba5! Q×a5 20. B×d5. **19. N×c6 N×c6**
20. Bc3 Kf7 21. N×e7 Q×e7 22. Bd5+ 1–0
[*Belfast News-Letter,* February 28, 1889]

234. Pollock–Thompson [A03]
Belfast, Belfast Chess Club, January 1889

1. f4 d6 2. e4 Nc6 3. d4 e6 4. Nf3 Nge7 5. c3
d5 6. e5 Ng6 7. Bd3 Be7 8. 0–0 a6 9. Qe2 Na7
10. Be3 Bd7 11. Nbd2 Qc8 12. Rae1 c5 13. Kh1
c4 14. Bb1 b5 15. g4 *(see diagram)*

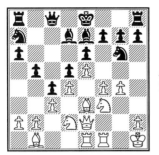

After
15. g2–g4

15. ... f5 Too weakening. 15. ... b4!? was better since Black did not have to fear 16. f5! because of 16. ... e×f5 17. g×f5 B×f5 18. B×f5 Q×f5 19. Ng5 Qc8 20. N×f7 0–0! **16. e×f6 B×f6 17. f5 e×f5 18. Bg5+ Kf7** 18. ... Kd8 19. g×f5 Re8 20. Qg2 Ne7 21. Ne5 would also have left Black in a difficult position. **19. B×f6 g×f6 20. g×f5 Nf8 21. Qe7+ Kg8 22. Rg1+ Ng6 23. f×g6 1–0** [*Belfast News-Letter*, February 28, 1889]

235. R. Boyd–Pollock
19-board Simultaneous Exhibition, Belfast, Belfast Chess Club, 9 January 1889

Black to move

18. ... Nf3 19. Qh6 Rg6 20. Qf4 Kg8 21. g×f3 Nh5 22. Q×g4 R×g4 23. f×g4 Ng7 24. Bh6 Qf6 25. g5 Qf3+ 26. Kg1 Nf5 27. Nd1 Nd4 27. ... Nh4 or 27. ... Re8 mates in six. **28. Nc3 Ne6 29. g6 Rf8 30. Rae1** 30. Ne4! was a fine defensive resource. **30. ... Rf4** "and Black mates in a few moves." **0–1** White's defense was left unmentioned: 31. Ne2 Rh4 32. Ng3 Qg4 33. g×h7+ K×h7 34. R×e6 Q×e6 35. Bg5 [*Belfast News-Letter*, February 7, 1889; *PM*, page 156].

236. Pollock–W.A. Chapman [C41]
18-board Simultaneous Exhibition, Dublin, Dublin Chess Club, January 1889

1. e4 e5 2. Nf3 Nc6 3. d4 d6 4. d×e5 Bg4!? 5. e×d6 B×d6 6. Be3 Qe7 7. Nc3 Bb4 7. ... 0–0–0!? was more consistent with Black's fourth move. **8. Bd3 Rd8 9. 0–0 Ne5** (*see diagram*)

After
9. ... Nc6–e5

10. Qe2 10. Nd5! would give White the initiative, i.e., 10. ... B×f3 11. g×f3 Qd6 12. Bf4 Bc5 13. B×e5 Q×e5 14. f4 Qd6 15. b4 B×b4 16. N×b4 Q×b4 17. Rb1. **10. ... B×c3 11. b×c3 B×f3 12. g×f3 Qd7 13. f4 N×d3 14. c×d3 Q×d3 15. Qg4?!** 15. Q×d3 R×d3 16. B×a7 b6 17. a4 Ne7 kept things balanced. **15. ... Nf6! 16. Qg3 Q×e4** 16. ... 0–0 17. e5 Ne4 18. Qf3 Nd2 was slightly more ambitious. **17. Rfe1 Qf5 18. B×a7+ Kf8 19. Bd4 b6 20. B×f6 Q×f6 21. Re5 Rd6 22. Rae1 Re6 23. Qg5 R×e5 24. R×e5 Q×g5+ 25. f×g5 f6 26. g×f6 g×f6 27. Re6 Kf7 28. Rc6 Rc8 29. Kg2 Kg6 30. Kf3 Ra8 31. R×c7 R×a2 ½–½** [*Belfast News-Letter*, March 7, 1889]

237. Morgan & Fischer & Crum–Pollock [C56]
Consultation Game, Argham, January 1889

1. e4 e5 2. Nf3 Nc6 3. Bc4 Nf6 4. d4 e×d4 5. e5 d5 6. Bb5 Ne4 7. N×d4 Bd7 8. N×c6 b×c6 9. Bd3 Nc5 10. 0–0 Be7 11. Be3 0–0 12. Nd2 N×d3 13. c×d3 c5 14. f4 d4 15. Bf2 Rb8 16. b3 Bc6 17. Qe2 f5 18. e×f6 Qd5 19. Bg3 B×f6 20. Rae1 Rbe8 21. Ne4 Bd8 22. Qf3 a5 23. Rc1 Be7 24. Rc4 Kh8 25. a4 Rb8 25. ... Qf5!? 26. Rcc1 Rb8 was perhaps a more constructive plan. **26. Qd1 Rb6 27. Qc2 Rfb8** 27. ... Qf5!?, and if 28. N×c5, then 28. ... Bd5! **28. N×c5 Rb4?** Envisioning a grand combination which actually does not work. **29. Na6 R×b3 30. N×b8 Ba3 31. Rf3!** 31. N×c6 Rb2 32. R×d4 also refutes Black's play. **31. ... Rb2 32. Qd1** 32. Q×b2 B×b2 33. N×c6 was more confident play. **32. ... Bb7** 32. ... R×b8 33. f5 Rb2 was Black's last chance. **33. Qe1?** 33. R×c7 was correct. **33. ... R×g2+! 34. Kh1** (*see diagram*)

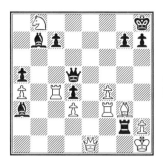

After
34. Kg1–h1

34. ... Rb2? It is somewhat surprising that Pollock missed grabbing the following opportunity: 34. ... Qh5! 35. Nc6 (35. K×g2?? Q×f3+ 36. Kh3 Bc8+) 35. ... B×c6 36. R×c6 R×h2+ 37. B×h2 Q×f3+ 38. Kg1 Q×c6 39. Q×a5 Bc1 and Black can play for a win. By contrast, 34. ... R×g3 35. Q×g3 Q×f3+ 36. Q×f3 B×f3+ 37. Kg1 c5 38. Nd7 is not appealing enough. **35. Qe8+ Qg8 36. Q×g8+ K×g8 37. Nc6 Rb6 38. N×d4 c5 39. Kg1 c×d4 40. Rf1 Rc6 41. R×c6 B×c6** and eventually White won in about 50 moves. **1–0** [*Belfast News-Letter*, February 14, 1889]

238. M. Crum & R.M. Cracke–Pollock [C56]
Consultation Game, Portadown, 10 January 1889

Pollock gave two exhibitions in Portadown on January 10, 1889: in the first he had the White pieces and in the second he took the Black pieces, scoring 26 wins, 5 losses and 2 draws.

1. e4 e5 2. Nf3 Nc6 3. Bc4 Nf6 4. d4 e×d4 5. e5 Pollock: "An old combination which cannot lead to more than an even game with best play." **5. ... d5 6. Bb5** Pollock: "Much better than 6. e×f6." **6. ... Ne4 7. N×d4 Bd7 8. N×c6 b×c6 9. Bd3 Bc5 10. B×e4 Qh4 11. Qe2 Q×e4 12. Q×e4 d×e4** Pollock: "As appears from the ensuing positions the game is now about equal." **13. Nc3 Bf5 14. Ne2 0–0 15. Bf4 Rab8 16. b3 Rfe8 17. 0–0 Rbd8 18. c3 Rd3 19. Rfd1 Red8 20. Re1 Bg6 21. Ng3 e3** Pollock: "The best means of disposing of the weak e-pawn." **22. B×e3 B×e3 23. R×e3 R×e3 24. f×e3 Rd3 25. e4 R×c3 26. Rd1 Kf8 27. Nf5** Pollock: "As Black must take, and leave White with pawns too far advanced to be strong here, 27. Rd7 was the *coup juste*." **27 ... B×f5 28. e×f5 Ke8** Pollock: "If 28 ... Ke7, 29. f6+ g×f6 30. e×f6+ K×f6 31. Rd7." **29. f6 g6 30. Re1 Rc2** Pollock: "30. ... Kd7 is sounder." **31. e6 R×a2 32. e7** Pollock: "White has now a strong position." **32 ... Rd2 33. Re3 Rd6**

34. Rf3 c5 35. g4 Pollock: "Very well played." **35 ... h5 36. g5** (*see diagram*)

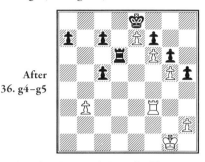

After
36. g4–g5

36. ... c4 37. b×c4 a5 38. h4 1–0 [*Belfast News-Letter*, January 17, 1889]

239. Pollock–F.J. Lee [C11]
London, Simpson's Divan, February 1889

1. e4 e6 2. d4 d5 3. Nc3 Nf6 4. e5 Nfd7 5. f4 c5 6. d×c5 B×c5 7. Qg4 g6 8. Nf3 Nc6 9. a3 Nb6 10. Bd3 Bd7 11. Bd2 a6 12. b4 Be7 13. 0–0 Na7 Pollock: "These manoeuvres with single pieces waste valuable time, while the adversary is preparing an attack." **14. Rae1 Rc8 15. Nd4 Nc4 16. Bc1** (*see diagram*) Pollock: "A snare, in which Black sets his foot."

After
16. Bd2–c1

16. ... N×a3?! This was tempting but Pollock had something prepared against it. **17. N×d5!** e×d5 18. e6! f×e6? 18. ... B×e6 19. N×e6 f×e6 20. B×a3 Rc6 was mandatory. **19. B×g6+! h×g6 20. Q×g6+ Kf8 21. f5 e×f5 22. Re6!** Pollock: "A crushing 'finale.'" **1–0** [*PM*, pages 72–73]

3RD ICA CONGRESS (MARCH 1889)

240. Pollock–J. Mason [C10]
3rd ICA Congress, Dublin, Round 2, 5 March 1889

1. e4 e6 2. d4 d5 3. Nc3 Nc6 4. Nf3 Bb4 5. e5
Qe7 6. Bd3 h6 7. 0–0 Ba5 8. Be3 Bd7 9. a3 B×c3
10. b×c3 Na5 11. Qe2 b6 12. c4 N×c4 13. B×c4
d×c4 14. Q×c4 Qd8 15. Rad1 15. d5 promised
little: 15. ... e×d5 16. Q×d5 Ne7 17. Qb3 0–0.
**15. ... Ne7 16. Bc1 Bc6 17. Ne1 Qd7 18. Qe2 Nf5
19. Bb2 Bb7 20. c4 Rd8 21. Nc2 Qc6 22. d5!
e×d5 23. c×d5 R×d5 24. Nb4 Qb5 25. Qc2
R×d1 26. R×d1 c5 27. Q×f5 c×b4 28. Qg4!?
0–0! 29. a×b4 Bc8** *(see diagram)*

After
29. ... Bb7–c8

Interestingly, at this point Mason proposed a
draw and Pollock agreed to it. However, with
30. e6!, the latter could have obtained a winning
position: 30. e6! f6 31. B×f6!! R×f6 32. Rd8+ Rf8
33. e7 Re8 34. R×c8 Kf7 35. Qf4+ Ke6 (35. ...
K×e7? 36. Rc7+ Ke6 37. R×g7!) 36. Qe4+ Kf7
37. Rc7 with a winning edge for White. ½–½
[*Chess Player's Chronicle*, May 1, 1889; *Belfast News-
Letter*, March 19, 1889]

241. M.S. Wollett–Pollock [C45]
3rd ICA Congress, Dublin, March 1889

1. e4 e5 2. Nf3 Nc6 3. d4 e×d4 4. N×d4 Nf6
5. N×c6 b×c6 6. Bd3 d5 7. Nc3 Bc5 8. Bg5 0–0
9. 0–0 Bd4 *(see diagram)*

After
9. ... Bc5–d4

10. Ne2? Poor play. White should have tried
10. e×d5 h6 11. B×f6 Q×f6 12. d×c6 B×c3 13. b×c3
Q×c6. **10. ... B×b2 11. Rb1 d×e4 12. B×f6 Q×f6
13. B×e4 Ba6! 14. B×c6 Rad8 15. Qe1 Q×c6
16. R×b2 Rfe8! 17. c3 Qc4 18. Rd2 R×d2**

19. Q×d2 Q×e2 20. Q×e2 R×e2 21. Rd1 Kf8 0–1
[various databases; historical source unavailable]

242. Pollock–S. Fitzpatrick [B29]
3rd ICA Congress, Dublin, March 1889

1. e4 c5 2. d4 c×d4 3. Nf3 Nf6 4. e5 Nd5 5. c4
Nb6 6. c5 Nd5 7. Q×d4 e6 8. Bd3 Qa5+ 9. Bd2
Q×c5 10. Qe4 Nb4 11. 0–0 N×d3 12. Q×d3
Be7?? 12. ... Nc6 13. Qe2 d5 was correct. **13. Rc1
Qd5 14. R×c8+ Bd8 15. Bg5 f6 16. Q×d5 e×d5
17. e×f6 1–0** [various databases]

243. Pollock–A. Burn [C67]
3rd ICA Congress, Dublin, Round 7,
7 March 1889

1. e4 e5 2. Nf3 Nc6 3. Bb5 Nf6 Richard
Forster: "Burn's first recorded Berlin Defence in
tournament play. After the French it was to become
his main weapon against 1. e4." **4. 0–0 N×e4 5. d4
a6 6. B×c6 d×c6 7. Qe2 Bf5** *(see diagram)*

After
7. ... Bc8–f5

8. g4? True to Pollock's provocative and dashing
style, but this weakening of the kingside can't be
advisable, and this especially so not in a decisive
game, against a solid player like Burn. 8. Re1 or
8. Rd1 were more reasonable continuations. **8. ...
Bg9 9. N×e5 Q×d4 10. Nf3?!** Since it opens the
h-file, 10. N×g6 seems risky but it's better than the
text: 10. ... h×g6 11. Nc3 f5 12. N×e4 f×e4 13. Bf4.
**10. ... Qd7! 11. Ng5 Qe7 12. N×e4 Q×e4
13. Q×e4+ B×e4 14. Bg5?** 14. Re1 is best replied
to with 14. ... 0–0–0! 15. Bg5 f6 16. B×f6 g×f6
17. R×e4 Rd1+ 18. Kg2 Bd6 with a clear advantage
for Black. **14. ... f6 15. Nc3 B×c2 16. Rfe1+ Kf7
17. Bf4 Bd6 18. B×d6 c×d6 19. Rac1 Bg6 20. f4
f5** With no compensation for the deficit of two
pawns, White is simply lost. **21. g5 Rhe8 22. Ne2
Re4 23. h4 Rae8 24. Kf2 Bh5 25. Rc2 B×e2
26. Rc×e2 R×f4+ 27. Kg3 Rg4+ 28. Kh3 Rge4
29. R×e4 R×e4 0–1** [*Warder and Dublin Evening
Mail*, March 30, 1889]

Part Two, Section III
(March 25–May 1889)

6TH AMERICAN CHESS CONGRESS (MARCH–MAY 1889)

244. S. Lipschütz–Pollock [C29]
6th American Chess Congress,
New York, Round 1, 25 March 1889

1. e4 e5 2. Nc3 Nf6 3. f4 d5 4. f×e5 N×e4 5. Qf3 N×c3 6. b×c3 Be6 7. d4 c5 8. Rb1 Qc7 9. Bb5+ Nc6 10. Ne2 0-0-0 Steinitz: "Black treats this variation in an original way that seems to lead to an early equalization." 11. 0-0 Be7 12. Be3 h5 13. Nf4 Bg5 Steinitz: "Best. If 13. ... Bg4, 14. N×d5, etc." 14. N×e6 B×e3+ 15. Q×e3 f×e6 16. B×c6 Q×c6 17. Rf7 Rd7 18. Rbf1 Rhd8 19. Qg5 c×d4 20. c×d4 R×f7 21. R×f7 *(see diagram)*

After
21. Rf1×f7

21. ... Q×c2? Steinitz: "The game was still even and a draw was almost declared by 21. ... Qc3 22. Qf4 Qe1+ 23. Qf1 Qe3+ 24. Qf2 Qc1+, and draws. The text move loses." 22. Rf1! Steinitz: "This is a *coup de repos* of the kind, that, in our opinion, denotes greater mastery than the conception of brilliant terminations. Such a winning re-

treat with all its consequences in actual play alone could not be easily conceived nor anticipated by the opponent. Black's game is now absolutely lost." 22. ... Qh7? Best was 22. ... Kd7! 23. Q×g7+ Kc8 24. Qe7 Qc6. 23. Qe7 Qh6 24. h3 24. Rb1 Qe3+ 25. Kh1 Rd7 26. Qf8+ Kc7 27. Qa8 was very strong as well. 24. ... h4 25. Kh2 Qe3 Steinitz: "Black can only wait for his doom. If 25. ... Rd7 26. Qf8+ Rd8 27. Qc5+ Kb8 28. Rf7 Rc8 29. Qd6+ Ka8 30. Rf8 and wins." 26. Q×e6+ Rd7 Steinitz: "If 26. ... Kb8, White wins easily by 27. Qf7 followed by the advance of the e-pawn." 27. Rf3 Qe1 28. Qf5 Kc7 29. Qc2+ Steinitz: "The finish may be called artistic and scientific as well." 29. ... Kd8 Steinitz: "If 29. ... Kb6 30. Qc5+, followed by Ra3+, and mate next move." 30. Qc5 Steinitz: "Unless he gives up the queen by 30. ... Qg3+, 30. ... Re7 is the only move to delay mate, and then White proceeds with 31. Rf8+, followed by 32. Qc8+." 1-0 [*tournament book*, page 283]

245. Pollock–J.H. Blackburne [C54]
6th American Chess Congress,
New York, Round 2, 26 March 1889

1. e4 e5 2. Nf3 Nc6 3. Bc4 Bc5 4. c3 Nf6 5. d3 d6 6. Nbd2 Qe7 7. Nf1 Be6 8. Bb3 0-0-0 Steinitz: "The game has opened on both sides on most approved methods, but it is more usual for either party to take refuge with the king on the kingside." 9. B×e6+ Pollock: "A change of tactics. White is obliged to attack as he does, to prevent his opponent from obtaining dangerous further development by the immediate advance of ...d5." 9. ... f×e6 10. b4 Bb6 11. a4 a5 Pollock: "In similar positions it is generally advisable to lock up

the queenside against attack, as Mr. Blackburne does here." **12. b5 Nb8 13. Ne3 Nbd7 14. 0–0 Rhg8** Pollock: "A dark move." **15. Nc4 Qe8 16. N×b6+ N×b6 17. Be3 Nbd7** (*see diagram*)

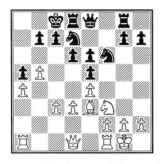

After
17. ... Nb7–d7

18. b6!? Steinitz: "The attack obtained by this sacrifice lasts long, but by proper management the pawn ahead on the other side should outlive the assault." Pollock: "As Black would block by ...b6, this sacrifice is the only way to obtain an attack." **18. ... N×b6 19. Qb3 Na8** Steinitz: "Best, if he wants to keep the pawn, and good enough, we think. If, however, 19. ... Nbd7, 20. Qb5 b6 21. Qa6+ Kb8 22. Rab1, with a fine attack." **20. Rab1 b6 21. d4** Pollock: "White prosecutes his attack with spirit, but it is a question whether he could improve on his 24th move." 21. Ng5!? was an interesting attempt: 21. ... d5 (21. ... Kd7 22. f4! Ng4 23. Bc1 h6 24. Nf3 e×f4 25. B×f4 Rf8 26. Bg3) 22. Nf3 d×e4 23. N×e5 e×d3 24. Rfd1. **21. ... N×e4 22. d×e5 d5** Steinitz: "The adversary is thus allowed to open another file for his rooks by his next pawn advance. 22. ... Nc5 23. B×c5 d×c5 24. Ng5 Rd5 and if 25. Rfd1, 25. ... R×e5 was safe enough." **23. c4 g5 24. c×d5 g4 25. Nd4** Steinitz: "25. Ne1, followed by Nd3 was much better. If, however, 25. Qc4 g×f3 26. Q×e4 R×g2+ 27. Kh1 R×h2+ 28. K×h2 Qh5+, and wins." **25. ... Nc5 26. Qc2 R×d5 27. Nb5 Qg6 28. Qc1 Rgd8 29. B×c5 b×c5?!** Steinitz: "Black allows his strongly fortified position of pawns to be broken up, probably in order to get his knight into play. With a little more patience he need not have minded his knight being shut up nor any attack on his king after 29. ... R×c5 30. Na7+ Kd7 (Of course, not 30. ... Kb7 on account of the reply 31. Q×c5) 31. Rd1+ Ke8 etc., whereas now the opponent obtains the better game, with a sure draw at least." Pollock gave the same variation and assessment here. **30. Na7+** 30. Qc3 was a strong option: 30. ... Kd7 31. Q×a5 Ke8 32. Rbe1, with a clear edge. **30. ... Kd7 31. Qc4 Ke8 32. Qb5+** Steinitz: "If 32. Nc6, 32. ... Q×b1 33. R×b1 (or

33. N×d8 Qb6, and wins.) 33. ... Rd1+, with a superior game." **32. ... Kf7 33. Nc6 R8d7 34. Nb8 Rd8 35. Nc6 R8d7 36. Nb8** Pollock: "With such a strong weakness in pawns, White would have welcomed a 'repetitive draw,' but Blackburne did not 'see it.'" **36. ... Rd8 37. Nc6 Re8** Steinitz: "Black is not justified in the present position to refuse the draw." **38. Qb7?!** 38. Q×a5! would have secured White's advantage based on the a-pawn. **38. ... Kg8 39. Rb3 Qc2 40. Ne7+** Steinitz: "This loses, while 40. Rg3 with the probable continuation 40. ... h5 41. f3 Rd7 42. f×g4 h4 43. Ne7+ gave White a winning advantage." **40. ... R×e7 41. Qc8+** Steinitz: "Loss of time. If he meant to hold out, 41. Q×a8+ saved a move at any rate." Pollock: "An *ignis fatuus*! Black now winds affairs up like a Blackburne." **41. ... Kg7** (*see diagram*)

After
41. ... Kg8–g7

42. Rg3? Pollock: "42. Rb8, the original intent, will be found to result in smoke." Not quite. Pollock's intuition was correct: 42. Rb8! was White's only chance and a very interesting one: 42. ... Qf5 (42. ... Nb6?? 43. Qf8+ Kg6 44. Q×e7; 42. ... Rd1 43. Qg8+ Kh6 44. Q×g4 R×f1+ 45. K×f1 Qc1+ 46. Ke2 Qc2+ with a likely perpetual.) 43. Qh8+ Kh6 44. Rf8 Rf7 45. R×f7 Q×f7 46. Q×a8. **42. ... h5 43. Q×a8 Rd1** Steinitz: "All hope of escape is now cut off for White." **44. Qf3 Red7 45. R×g4+ h×g4 46. Qf6+ Kh7 47. Qh4+ Kg8 48. Q×g4+ Kf8 49. Qf3+ Qf5 0–1** [*tournament book*, pages 204–205]

246. I.A. Gunsberg–Pollock [C77] 6th American Chess Congress, New York, Round 3, 27 March 1889

1. e4 e5 2. Nf3 Nc6 3. Bb5 a6 4. Ba4 Nf6 5. d3 b5 6. Bb3 d5 Steinitz: "The defence is similar to the one adopted by Morphy against Anderssen, but the former did not play ...d5 until he had developed ...Bf8–c5 in reply to White's c2–c3. The difference of position is, we believe, greatly in favor of White, who, we hold, ought to obtain at least a slight advantage anyhow if Black attempt an early advance of the d-pawn." **7. e×d5 N×d5 8. a4** Steinitz: "Quite in accordance with modern principles of play. By compelling the adversary to advance a pawn further into his own camp he is likely to obtain an advantage in the end." **8. ... b4 9. 0–0** Steinitz: "White could have won a pawn here by 9. Qe2 Qd6 10. d4 f6 11. d×e5 f×e5 12. N×e5 N×e5 (Or 12. ... Q×e5 13. B×d5) 13. f4, etc." **9. ... Be7 10. Re1 Qd6 11. Nbd2 Bg4 12. h3 B×f3 13. Q×f3 Rd8 14. Ne4 Qd7 15. Bc4 0–0 16. Be3** Steinitz: "Superfluous. 16. B×a6 Nd4 17. Qd1, were good enough to leave White with an advantage." **16. ... N×e3 17. f×e3 Na5** Steinitz: "Remarkably clever." **18. B×a6 Qe6 19. Bc4 N×c4 20. d×c4 Q×c4 21. Qf5 f6 22. b3 Qc6** Steinitz: "Obviously, if 22. ... Q×c2, he would lose the queen by 23. N×f6+." **23. Rac1 g6 24. Qf3 f5 25. Nd2 Qc3 26. Nc4 e4 27. Qe2 Bc5 28. Kh1 Rd5 29. Rf1 c6 30. Rf2 Ba7 31. Rcf1 Bb8 32. g4** *(see diagram)*

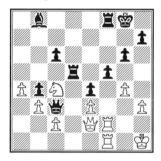

After
32. g2–g4

32. ... f4! Steinitz: "A very interesting attack is here formed by Black, which called for the greatest caution of the opponent to meet its difficulties." **33. e×f4 R×f4 34. Ne3** Steinitz: "If 34. R×f4 Q×h3+ 35. Kg1 (or 35. Qh2 Q×h2+ 36. K×h2 g5 etc.) 35. ... B×f4 and if 36. R×f4, 36. ... Qg3+, and wins." **34. ... g5 35. Kg2 Qe5 36. Kh1 Qc3 37. Kg2 Qe5 38. Kh1 Rf3! 39. R×f3 e×f3 40. Qf2 Rd4 41. Nf5 Re4! 42. Qd2** Steinitz: "Both parties have exercised their ingenuity in attempts to win, but each player was carefully on the watch, and a forced draw is now the result." **42. ... Re2??** 42. ... Bc7! was a very subtle try to play for a win: 43. Q×g5+ Kh8 and White has nothing better than 44. Qg7+ Q×g7 45. N×g7 K×g7 46. R×f3 Re2. **43. Q×g5+ Kf8 44. Qh6+ Kg8 45. Qg5+ Kf8 46. Qh6+ Kg8 47. Qg5+ Kf8 48. Qd8+ Kf7 49. Qd7+ Kf8 50. Qc8+ Kf7 ½–½** [*tournament book*, pages 157–158]

247. Pollock–M. Chigorin [C47]
6th American Chess Congress, New York, Round 4, 28 March 1889

1. e4 e5 2. Nc3 Nf6 3. Nf3 Nc6 4. d4 e×d4 5. N×d4 Bb4 6. N×c6 b×c6 7. Bd3 Steinitz: "7. Qd4 Qe7 8. f3 d5 9. Bg5 brings about a position of the Scotch Gambit which is demonstrated in the International Chess Instructor, in favour of White." **7. ... d5 8. e5?** Steinitz: "Wrong on principle, as it allows Black a strong majority of pawns on the queenside. 8. e×d5 c×d5 9. Bb5+, as played by Señor Golmayo against Captain Mackenzie, is the right play." **8. ... Ng4 9. 0–0 0–0 10. h3** Steinitz: "The attack against the adverse king which he aims at by giving up the e5-pawn in exchange for Black's h-pawn is worthless and only damages additionally his position, on account of the counter-attack which the opponent obtains on the e-file with his rooks. Black also gains the combination of the two bishops against bishop and knight, the latter being besides badly posted for any purpose. Much better was 10. Bf4 Re8 11. Re1 Bc5 (or 11. ... d4 12. a3 Ba5 13. b4) 12. Re2." **10. ... N×e5 11. B×h7+ K×h7 12. Qh5+ Kg8 13. Q×e5 Re8 14. Qg3 Bf5 15. Bg5 Qd7 16. Rac1 Re6 17. Qf4 B×c3** Steinitz: "Though the parties remain with bishops of opposite colours, Black obtains a very strong attack, which places great difficulties in the way of the defence." **18. b×c3 Re2 19. Qa4 Rae8 20. Be3?** *(see diagram)* Steinitz: "Overlooking a beautifully-conceived and finely worked-out combination. 20. Q×a7 B×h3 21. Bf4 would have given good prospects of parrying the attack."

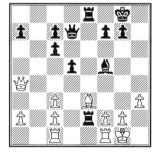

After
20. Bg5–e3

20. ... B×h3! 21. g×h3 R8×e3 Steinitz: "This and the foregoing move of Black are played in most admirable style, and leave no hope for the opponent." **22. Rce1** Steinitz: "Of course, if 22. f×e3, 22. ... Q×h3 23. Rf2 Qg3+, and wins." **22. ... Q×h3 23. R×e2 R×e2 24. Rb1 Re5 0–1** [*tournament book*, pages 44–45; *ICM*, November 1889, page 336]

248. H.E. Bird–Pollock [B01]
6th American Chess Congress,
New York, Round 5,
29 March 1889

1. e4 d5 2. e×d5 Nf6 3. Bb5+ c6 Steinitz: "Not as good as 3. ... Bd7 4. B×d7+ Q×d7, and if 5. c4 c6." **4. d×c6 b×c6 5. Be2 e5 6. d3 Bc5 7. Nf3 e4 8. d×e4 Qb6 9. 0–0 N×e4 10. Qe1 0–0 11. Nbd2 Re8 12. N×e4 R×e4 13. Qd1 Nd7 14. Bd3 Re7 15. c3 a5 16. Qc2 h6 17. Bf4 Nf6 18. Rae1 Be6 19. Be5** Steinitz: "It could in no way improve his position to give up the a2-pawn, and, moreover, it would have greatly strengthened his queenside to advance 19. b3." **19. ... B×a2 20. B×f6 R×e1 21. R×e1 g×f6 22. c4** Steinitz: "The attempt to shut out the adverse queen's bishop is futile, and he only exposes himself to greater attack on that wing." **22. ... Rd8 23. Bf1 Bb3 24. Qe2** (see diagram)

After
24. Qc2–e2

24. ... B×c4! Steinitz: "Finely played, for if 23. Q×c4, 23. ... B×f2+ 24. Kh1 B×e1 25. N×e1 Qf2, followed by ...Rd1 and wins." **25. Qc2 B×f1 26. R×f1 Qb5 27. Nh4 Rd5 28. g3 Qd3** Steinitz: "Much better was 28. ... Bd4." **29. Qa4 Qb5 30. Qg4+ Rg5 31. Qc8+ Kh7 32. Qd7 Qc4 33. Rd1 Qe6 34. Qd3+ Kg7 35. Qc2 Re5 36. Kg2 Bb6 37. Rd2 Rc5 38. Qd1 Rd5 39. f3 Re5 40. f4 Re1?** 40. ... Rb5 or 40. ... Rc5 were the correct moves here. **41. Nf5+** Steinitz: "Black's last move was a grave error, and White takes hold of the attack with great ingenuity. He must win the exchange, for if Black moves the king, White answers Qg4, winning still more easily. The rest of the game is a struggle against hope on Black's part." **41. ... Q×f5 42. Q×e1 a4 43. Qe2 h5 44. Qd3 Qc5 45. Qf3 Kh6 46. Re2 Qd4 47. Q×c6 Qg1+ 48. Kh3 Qf1+ 49. Qg2 Qd1 50. f5 Bd4 51. Qf3 Kg7 52. Q×h5 Qf1+ 53. Kh4 Qc1 54. Qg4+ Kf8 55. Qf4 Qc5 56. Qh6+ 1–0** [*tournament book*, page 405]

249. Pollock–N. MacLeod [C68]
6th American Chess Congress,
New York, Round 6,
30 March 1889

1. e4 e5 2. Nf3 Nc6 3. Bb5 a6 4. B×c6 d×c6 5. N×e5 Qd4 6. Ng4 Steinitz: "Original as well as strong." **6. ... Q×e4+ 7. Ne3 Bd6 8. d4 Nf6 9. 0–0 0–0–0 10. Nc3 Qg6** Steinitz: "10. ... Qe7 was better." **11. f4 Ng4 12. Nc4** 12. f5 runs into 12. ... B×f5! 13. N×f5 B×h2+ 14. Kh1 Qh5 15. Q×g4 Q×g4 16. K×h2 Rae8, with better chances for Black. **12. ... f6 13. Rf3 Qh5 14. Rh3 Qf7 15. Qd3 Nh6 16. Rf3** 16. R×h6!? was certainly playable but not without risks: 16. ... g×h6 17. Bd2 Qg6 18. Ne4 Bf5 19. Nc×d6 c×d6 20. Qb3+ d5 21. Ng3 B×c2 22. Q×b7 Qd3. **16. ... Bf5 17. Qf1 c5 18. d5 b5 19. Ne3 b4 20. Ne2 Be4 21. Rh3 Nf5 22. Ng3!? N×e3 23. B×e3 Q×d5?** Steinitz: "Faulty and causing the loss of a piece, whereas 23. ... B×d5 gave him a safe superiority of material." **24. Rd1 Qe6** (see diagram)

After
24. ... Qd5–e6

25. f5! Qe8 25. ... B×g2 was not sufficient either: 26. f×e6 B×f1 27. K×f1 Rae8 28. Rd5 c4 29. Nf5 R×e6 30. Rd4. **26. Qc4+ Kh8 27. N×e4 Rd8 28. N×d6 c×d6 29. Qh4 Kg8 30. Q×h7+ Kf7 31. Bh6 1–0** [*tournament book*, page 412]

250. Pollock–J.W. Baird [C52]
6th American Chess Congress,
New York, Round 7, 1 April 1889

1. e4 e5 2. Nf3 Nc6 3. Bc4 Bc5 4. b4 B×b4 5. c3 Ba5 6. d4 e×d4 7. N×d4 Steinitz: "There is always refreshing originality in Mr. Pollock's play. The innovation will hardly strengthen the attack theoretically, but in practice it was well worthy adopting exceptionally." **7. ... Ne5** Steinitz: "Much inferior to 7. ... Nge7 or 7. ... Nf6." **8. Bb3 d6 9. 0–0 Ne7 10. f4 N5c6 11. Qh5 0–0 12. f5 N×d4** Steinitz: "12. ... Bb6, and if 13. Bb2 (or if 13. Be3,

13. ... d5) 13. ... Ne5 was his correct defence."
13. c×d4 Bb6 14. Bb2 d5 *(see diagram)*

After
14. ... d6–d5

After
13. ... c6×d5

15. f6 Ng6 16. e5 Re8 17. Kh1 g×f6 18. Nd2!
c6 Steinitz: "If 18. ... f×e5 or 18. ... f5, then equally
19. Nf3, threatening Ng5, with a fine attack."
19. e×f6 Very strong was 19. Ne4!! Re6 [19. ...
d×e4 20. B×f7+ Kg7 (20. ... K×f7 21. Q×h7+ Ke6
22. R×f6+) 21. e×f6+ K×f7 22. Q×h7+ Ke6
23. Q×g6 Kd5 24. Qh5+ Kd6 25. f7 and White
wins.] 20. Nf6+ R×f6 21. e×f6 Qf8 22. Rae1.
19. ... Re6 20. Nf3 Re4 21. Bc2 Rg4 21. ... Bg4
would have not stopped White's attack: 22. Qg5
(22. Qh6 Qf8 23. Qg5 h6 24. Qd2 Rae8) 22. ...
B×f3 (22. ... Re2? 23. B×g6! h×g6 24. Q×g4 R×b2
25. Qh4!) 23. R×f3 Re6 24. B×g6 h×g6 25. Raf1.
22. h3 R×g2! 23. Ng5 Steinitz: "Of course, White
dare not take the rook on account of the reply ...
Nf4+." Even stronger was 23. B×g6 R×g6 (23. ...
h×g6 24. Qh4!) 24. Ng5 h6 25. N×f7! K×f7
26. Rae1. **23. ... R×c2?** Steinitz: "A blunder, but
his game was anyhow gone." Steinitz was correct.
For example, 23. ... R×g5 24. Q×g5 Ba5 (24. ...
Qf8 25. h4! Qd6 26. h5 Bc7 27. Rf2) 25. Ba3! Kh8
26. Qh6 Qg8 27. Rg1 Be6 28. h4. **24. Q×h7+ Kf8**
25. Q×f7 mate 1–0 [*tournament book*, page 403]

251. E. Delmar–Pollock [C48]
6th American Chess Congress,
New York, Round 8, 2 April 1889

1. e4 e5 2. Nf3 Nc6 3. Nc3 Nf6 4. Bb5 a6
Steinitz: "There is no better play at this juncture
than to form the Double Ruy Lopez by 4. ... Bb4."
5. B×c6 d×c6 6. N×e5 N×e4 7. N×e4 Qd4
8. 0–0 Q×e5 9. Re1 Be6 10. d4 Qf5 Steinitz:
"Not as good as 10. ... Qd5." **11. g4 Qg6 12. Bg5**
Steinitz: "Initiating a pretty combination, but
hardly as efficient, and even safe, as 12. Ng5." **12. ...**
h5 Steinitz: "For Black would have obtained a better game by 12. ... h6 13. f4 (if 13. Bh4, 13. ... h5
etc.) 13. ... h×g5 14. f5 Qh6 15. Qe2 0–0–0
16. f×e6 f×e6 etc." **13. d5 c×d5** *(see diagram)*

14. Q×d5 Bd6 Steinitz: "Best. If 14. ... B×d5
15. Nf6+ double check, and mates next move."
15. N×d6+ c×d6 16. Qf5 Kd7 17. Q×g6 f×g6
Steinitz: "Nothing more than a draw should ensue
from this position." **18. Rad1 Rac8 19. Rd2 h×g4**
20. b3 b5 21. Bf4 Rc6 22. Be5 b4 Steinitz: "22. ...
Rh5, with the view of offering the exchange of
rooks by ...Rd5 if White took the g7-pawn, was
much superior." **23. B×g7 Rg8 24. Be5 Rgc8**
Steinitz: "Loss of time. 24. ... Re8 was the proper
play." **25. Kg2 Bf5 26. Kg3 Re8 27. Re3 g5**
Steinitz: "His kingside becomes very weak through
this, and his bishop loses support at an important
post. 27. ... Kc7 was the best plan." **28. Bf6 R×e3+**
29. f×e3 R×c2 30. Rd4 Ke6 31. B×g5 a5 32. Bd8
R×a2 33. e4 Bh7 34. Bc7 Ra3 35. R×d6+ Ke7
36. Ra6 Kd7 37. B×a5 B×e4 38. K×g4 Bb7?
Steinitz: "Overlooking the adverse ingenious reply.
38. ... Bd5 would have drawn with ease." 38. ...
R×b3 was sufficient too. **39. Rd6+ K×d6** Steinitz:
"His game was gone. If 39. ... Ke7, 40. B×b4 followed accordingly by a discovered check with the
rook and wins; or if 39. ... Ke8 (of course, he is
mated if he plays 39. ... Kc8) 40. Rd8+ Ke7
41. B×b4+ and wins in a manner similar to that
which occurred in actual play." **40. B×b4+ Kc6**
41. B×a3 Kb6 42. Be7 Bd5 43. b4 Be4 44. h4
Kc6 45. Kf4 Bd3 46. h5 Kd7 47. Bc5 Ke6 48. h6
Kf6 49. Ke3 Bh7 50. b5 Ke6 51. b6 Kd7 52. Kf4
Kc8 53. Ke5 Kd7 54. Kf6 Kc6 55. Kg7 Be4
56. h7 B×h7 57. K×h7 and White won. 1–0
[*tournament book*, pages 371–372]

252. Pollock–A. Burn [C54]
6th American Chess Congress,
New York, Round 9, 3 April 1889

1. e4 e5 2. Nf3 Nc6 3. Bc4 Bc5 4. c3 Nf6 5. d4
e×d4 6. Bg5!? Steinitz: "A new venture that involves the sacrifice of a pawn for an attack which
seemingly presents great difficulties to the opponent for a long time." This aggressive move was

used a few times in the early 1850s. **6. ... h6 7. B×f6 Q×f6 8. e5 Qe7** Steinitz: "If 8. ... N×e5, 9. Qe2 d6 10. c×d4, and wins a piece." **8. ... Qf4!** is a more ambitious choice. **9. 0–0 d×c3 10. N×c3 0–0 11. Nd5 Qd8 12. Qb1** Steinitz: "Threatening Nf6+, followed by Qg6+, which would win in a few moves." **12. ... Be7** Steinitz: "We prefer 12. ... Kh8, with the view of retreating ...Ne7." **13. Qe4 d6 14. Rad1 Be6** 14. ... N×e5!? 15. N×e5 d×e5 16. Nb6 a×b6 17. R×d8 R×d8 18. Q×e5 Bd6 was an acceptable variation too. **15. Bd3 g6** (*see diagram*)

After
15. ... g7–g6

16. Ne3 16. Nf4 Bf5 17. Qc4 Qd7 18. Rfe1 was much better. **16. ... Kg7 17. Bb1 Qe8 18. Nd4 N×d4 19. Q×d4 Kh7 20. f4 d×e5 21. Q×e5 Bd6 22. Qd4 Rd8 23. Rde1** Steinitz: "If 23. Q×a7, 23. ... Qc6 threatening ...Bc5." **23. ... Qc6 24. Rc1 Qb6 25. Qc3 Bb4 26. Qe5 Rd5 27. Qe4 Bd2 28. Rce1** Steinitz: "28. Kh1 would not save the exchange, as Black could answer 28. ... Rd4." **28. ... f5 29. Qf3 B×e1 30. R×e1 Rd2** Steinitz: "It is now an easy matter for Black to win." **31. Kh1 Rfd8 32. g4 R×b2 33. Bc2 R×c2 34. g×f5 g×f5 35. Ng4 Bd5 36. Re7+ Kh8 0–1** [*tournament book*, page 245]

253. J.M. Hanham–Pollock [C24]
6th American Chess Congress, New York, Round 10, 4 April 1889

1. e4 e5 2. Nf3 Nc6 3. Bc4 Nf6 4. d3 d5 Steinitz: "His e-pawn becomes weak and subject to inconvenient attack after this." **5. e×d5 N×d5 6. 0–0 Be7 7. Re1 Bg4 8. Bb5 Qd6 9. Nbd2 f6 10. Ne4 Qd7 11. c4?!** 11. d4 was the accurate move here. **11. ... Ndb4 12. c5 0–0–0 13. a3** (*see diagram*)

13. ... N×d3 Steinitz: "The two pawns that he obtains for the exchange are separated on the two wings and, especially so early in the game, they are no equivalent." **14. B×d3 Q×d3 15. Nd6+ R×d6**

After
13. a2–a3

16. c×d6 Q×d1 17. R×d1 B×d6 18. h3 Bh5 19. g4 Bg6 20. Be3 h5 21. g5 h4 22. b4 Steinitz: "An error which allows the opponent to recover the exchange, with a pawn ahead. It was high time to withdraw 22. Nd2." **22. ... Bh5 23. Kg2 e4 24. Nd2 B×d1 25. R×d1 Re8 26. Nc4 Rd8 27. g×f6 g×f6 28. Rd5 Be5 29. Rc5** Steinitz: "29. R×d8+, followed by b5, gave better prospects in fighting for a draw." **29. ... Bd4 30. Rh5 B×e3 31. N×e3 Rg8+ 32. Kf1** Steinitz: "Feeble. 32. Kh1 was his only salvation." **32. ... Ne5** Steinitz: "Beautiful play. He wins the exchange by force." **33. R×h4?** This was the actual losing move. Best was 33. Nd5! Rf8 (33. ... Nf3? 34. Ne7+) 34. N×f6! R×f6 35. R×e5 Rf4 with excellent chances for a draw. **33. ... Nf3 34. Rg4** Steinitz: "Mate by ...Rg1 and ...Re1 being threatened, he had no other resource. If 34. R×e4, he loses a clear rook by the answer 34. ... Nd2+." **34. ... Nh2+ 35. Ke2 N×g4 0–1** [*tournament book*, page 410]

254. Pollock–J. Taubenhaus [C58]
6th American Chess Congress, New York, Round 11, 5 April 1889

1. e4 e5 2. Nf3 Nc6 3. Bc4 Nf6 4. Ng5 d5 5. e×d5 Na5 6. d3 h6 7. Nf3 e4 8. Qe2 N×c4 9. d×c4 Bc5 10. h3 0–0 11. Ne5 Steinitz: "New, but a questionable experiment." **11. ... Qe7** Steinitz: "For by 11. ... Re8 12. Ng4 N×g4 13. h×g4 e3 14. B×e3 B×e3 15. f×e3 Qg5, Black would have obtained a strong attack." **12. Ng4 Nh7 13. Nc3 f5 14. Nh2 Bd7 15. Bf4 Be8 16. 0–0–0 a6 17. Kb1 g5?!** 17. ... b5! was an excellent attempt to seek counterplay: 18. c×b5 a×b5 19. N×b5 B×b5 20. Q×b5 Rfb8 21. Qc4 Bd6 with sufficient compensation for Black. **18. Be3 Nf6 19. B×c5 Q×c5 20. g4! f4 21. N×e4 N×e4 22. Q×e4 b5** (*see diagram*)

23. d6 Steinitz: "White had a won game in hand either simply by 23. Qd4 or by pressure of a

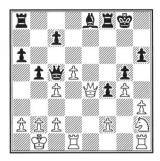

After
22. ... b7–b5

After
17. Nc3–d5

kingside attack, commencing with 23. h4. The sally adopted was not accurately enough reckoned out." **23. ... c×d6 24. Rd5** Steinitz: "He probably saw that if 24. Q×a8 Bc6 25. Q×a6 Ra8, winning the queen." 24. Qe6+ Bf7 25. Q×h6 was stronger option. **24. ... Q×c4 25. Q×c4 b×c4 26. R×d6 Kg7 27. Re1 Bf7 28. Kc1 Rfe8 29. R×e8 R×e8 30. Kd2** Steinitz: "Better than 30. R×a6 Re2, with a strong attack." **30. ... Rb8 31. Kc3 Re8 32. Nf3 Re2 33. Rd2 Re4 34. Nd4 Kf6 35. Re2 R×e2 36. N×e2 Bd5 37. Kd4 Bg2 38. Ng1 Bf1 39. b3 c×b3 40. a×b3 Ke6 41. Kc5! Ke5 42. Nf3+ Kf6 43. Ng1 Ke5 44. f3?** Steinitz: "Weak play, for this pawn, where it stood, was less liable to be attacked and also kept the adverse king aloof in case White's king had to move off." 44. c4 gave White an easy win. **44. ... Bg2 45. c4 Bf1 46. b4 Bd3 47. b5 a×b5 48. c×b5 B×b5!!** Steinitz: "Black's play for a draw is very ingeniously conceived." **49. K×b5 Kd4 50. h4 g×h4 51. Nh3 Ke3 52. g5 h×g5 53. N×g5 Kf2 54. Kc4 Kg2 55. Kd4 h3 56. N×h3 K×f3 57. N×f4 ½–½** [*tournament book*, pages 416–417]

255. Pollock–D.M. Martinez [C52]
6th American Chess Congress,
New York, Round 12, 6 April 1889

1. e4 e5 2. Nf3 Nc6 3. Bc4 Bc5 4. b4 B×b4 5. c3 Ba5 6. 0–0 d6 7. d4 e×d4 8. Qb3 Qf6 9. c×d4 Steinitz: "An obsolete form of this opening. Waller's attack by 9. e5 d×e5 10. Re1 is the only way to keep up the pressure." **9. ... Bb6 10. e5 d×e5 11. d×e5 Qg6 12. Ng5 Nd8 13. Nc3 h6 14. Nge4 Ne7 15. Ba3 Nec6 16. Rae1 Be6 17. Nd5** (*see diagram*)

17. ... N×e5? 17. ... B×d5 18. B×d5 Ne6 was mandatory. **18. N×b6** 18. Nc5! gave White a winning edge. **18. ... a×b6 19. f4?!** 19. B×e6! N×e6 20. f4 was very forceful. **19. ... B×c4 20. Q×c4 R×a3** Steinitz: "If 20. ... N×c4, 21. Nf6

mate." (Steinitz's note read "21. Nf6 and mates next move," not noting Nf6 came with a mate.) **21. Qb4?** White had to try 21. Q×c7 0–0 22. f5 Qg4 23. Q×e5. **21. ... R×a2 22. Ng3 Ndc6 23. Qb3 Ra5 24. f×e5 Qe6 25. Qf3 0–0** Steinitz: "Practically this ends the fight, as White's sacrifice of pawns could only be compensated by an attack direct against Black's knight which, however, has now taken safe refuge." **26. Nf5 Ne7 27. Nd4 Qd5 28. Qg4 Ra4 29. Re4 Ng6 30. e6 f5 31. N×f5 Q×e4 32. Q×g6 R×f5 33. Q×f5 Q×f5 34. R×f5 Re4 35. Rf7 c5 36. Re7 g6 37. Kf2 Kf8 38. Rf7+ Ke8 39. Rf6 Ke7 40. R×g6 R×e6** Steinitz: "The stronghold of White's last hope is gone." **41. Rg7+ Kd6 42. R×b7 Kc6 43. Rf7 c4 44. g4 b5 45. h4 c3 46. Kg3 c2 47. Rf1 b4 48. g5 h×g5 49. h×g5 b3 50. Rc1 Kd7 0–1** [*tournament book*, pages 413–414]

256. M. Judd–Pollock [C83]
6th American Chess Congress,
New York, Round 13, 8 April 1889

1. e4 e5 2. Nf3 Nc6 3. Bb5 a6 4. Ba4 Nf6 5. 0–0 N×e4 6. d4 b5 7. Bb3 d5 8. d×e5 Be6 9. c3 Be7 10. Bc2 0–0 11. Re1 f6 12. Nd4 N×d4 13. c×d4 f×e5 14. f3 Nf6 15. R×e5 Bf7 16. Nc3 Bd6 17. Bg5!? Steinitz: "The position would have been fairly balanced but for this venture which turns out unfavourable, owing to the opponent's very ingenious play. 17. Re2 was the correct move." **17. ... B×e5 18. d×e5 d4! 19. Ne4 d3 20. N×f6+?** Steinitz: "He was bound to lose the exchange, but the sacrifice of a rook, though he gets three pawns for it and some attack, was not justified. 20. e×f6 was his only good move." **20. ... g×f6 21. B×f6 d×c2 22. Q×c2 Qd4+ 23. Kh1 Bg6 24. Q×c7 Rf7 25. Qc6 Raf8 26. Q×a6 Q×b2 27. Rd1 Qc2 28. Qd6 Q×a2 29. h4 Qc4** Steinitz: "Threatening ...R×f6, followed by ...Q×h4+." **30. Rd4 Qc1+ 31. Kh2 Qc7 32. Qd5 Qb7 33. Qb3 h5 34. Rb4**

Rb8 35. f4 Bf5 Steinitz: "Black sees in advance the adverse ingenious trap. If 35. ... Kh7 at once, 36. f5 B×f5 37. R×b5 and wins. We believe that 35. ... Qc6, followed by 36. ... Qc2 would have better answered all purposes." **36. Qg3+ Kh7 37. Qg5 Bg4 38. e6** (see diagram)

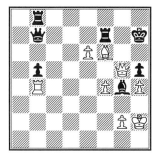

After
38. e5–e6

38. ... Rg7 Steinitz: "Excellent and correct play which breaks all attack and produces a winning ending for Black." In fact, even more accurate was 38. ... R×f6! 39. Q×f6 Qg7 40. Qg5 Q×g5 41. h×g5 B×e6. **39. B×g7** Judd missed the brilliant 39. Qe5!! Rgg8 40. Rd4 which would have erased Black's advantage: 40. ... Rbe8 41. Rd7+ Q×d7 42. Qe4+ Kh3 43. Bg5+ Kg7 44. Qe5+ Kh7 45. Qe4+ Kh8 46. Bf6+ Qg7 47. Qg6 Q×f6 48. Q×f6+ Kh7 49. Qf7+ Kh8 with chances for both. **39. ... Q×g7 40. R×b5 R×b5 41. Q×b5 Qf6 42. Qb7+** Steinitz: "If 42. Qb6, Black would still win more quickly by 42. ... Q×h4+, followed by ...Qe1+ and ...Q×e6." **42. ... Kh6 43. g3 Q×e6 44. Qb2 Qe2+ 45. Q×e2 B×e2 46. Kg2 Kg6 47. Kf2 Ba6 48. Ke3 Kf5 49. Kd4 Kg4 50. Kd5 Bd3 51. Ke5 K×g3 52. f5 K×h4 53. f6 Bc4 0–1** [*tournament book*, pages 344–345]

257. Pollock–J. Mason [C54]
6th American Chess Congress,
New York, Round 14, 9 April 1889

1. e4 e5 2. Nf3 Nc6 3. Bc4 Bc5 4. c3 Nf6 5. d3 d6 6. Be3 Bb6 7. Nbd2 Ne7 8. Qb3 0–0 9. 0–0–0 Steinitz: "Rather bold, for we believe Black has the first chance of instituting an attack after this." **9. ... c6 10. d4 e×d4** Steinitz: "10. ... Ng4 11. Nf1 d5 were superior." **11. N×d4 d5 12. e×d5 c×d5 13. Bd3 Bg4 14. f3 Bh5 15. g4 Bg6 16. B×g6 N×g6 17. Kb1** Steinitz: "Hardly necessary for pursuing his attack. 17. Nf1 at once was necessary." **17. ... Re8 18. Nf1 Qd7 19. Nf5 B×e3 20. N1×e3** Steinitz: "White conducts the attack remarkably well." **20. ... Re5 21. g5** 21. h4 Rae8 22. h5 Ne7 23. N×e7+ R8×e7 24. Nf5 Re8 25. h6 g6 26. Nd4

was aggressive but not decisive at all. **21. ... R×f5 22. g×f6 R×f3** 22. ... R×f6! 23. R×d5 Qc7 was safer. **23. N×d5! Qf5+ 24. Ka1 g×f6 25. Q×b7 Re8** (see diagram)

After
25. ... Ra8–e8

26. Rhg1 Steinitz: "This and the next move are superfluous. A systematic advance of the c-pawn was more likely to succeed, as Black could form no attack in the meanwhile." 26. h4! h5 27. Rhg1 was the right sequence. **26. ... Kg7 27. a3 Rf2 28. c4 Ree2 29. Rb1 Qd3 30. Qb4 Re4 31. Rbc1 R×h2 32. Rge1** Steinitz: "Black makes the better bargain, for after 32. Qc3 we still prefer White's game." **½–½** [*tournament book*, page 318]

258. C.F. Burille–Pollock [C29]
6th American Chess Congress,
New York, Round 15, 10 April 1889

1. e4 e5 2. Nc3 Nf6 3. f4 d5 4. f×e5 N×e4 5. Qf3 N×c3 6. b×c3 Be7 7. d4 0–0 8. Bd3 f5 9. Ne2 (see diagram)

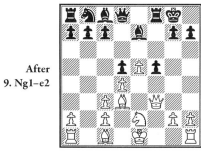

After
9. Ng1–e2

9. ... c5 Steinitz: "If played on the last move, it would have been very good, as it threatened ...c5–c4, but now it is quite a mistake, whereby the key of his centre is delivered." **10. Nf4 c×d4 11. c×d4 Bb4+ 12. Bd2 B×d2+ 13. K×d2 Bd7?** Premature capitulation. After 13. ... Nc6! 14. c3 Ne7 15. h4 Qb6 16. N×d5 N×d5 17. Q×d5+ Be6 Black still had a decent game. **14. Q×d5+ Kh8 15. e6 Qg5** Steinitz: "Virtually losing a piece, though he may delay its capture for one move." **16. Qd6 Rf6 17. Rae1 Nc6 18. e×d7** Steinitz: "For all practical purposes the game which has been well-played by White is finished with this threat of a mate in two moves by Re8." **18. ... h5 19. Re8+ Kh7 20. Qc7 Rd8 21. h4 Qh6 22. g3 Rf8 23. d5 Qf6 24. d×c6 1–0** [*tournament book*, page 407]

259. Pollock–M. Weiss [D00]
6th American Chess Congress, New York, Round 16, 11 April 1889

1. d4 d5 2. Qd3 Steinitz: "Eccentric and not commendable." **2. ... Nf6 3. Bf4 e6 4. Nc3 a6** Steinitz: "As usual, we object to the early advance of a wing pawn on either side. 4. ... c5 was quite safe, and if 5. Qb5+ (or if 5. Nb5, 5. ... Na6) 5. ... Nbd7, etc." **5. a3 c5 6. d×c5 B×c5 7. e3 Nc6 8. Nf3 b5 9. Be2 Bb7 10. 0–0 0–0 11. Nd4 Qb6** Steinitz: "We should have preferred 11. ... Ne7, with the following probable continuation: 12. Bg3 Nd7 13. f4 Nc8 14. Bf3 Nd6 15. b3 Rc8, with the superior game." **12. N×c6 B×c6 13. b4 Be7 14. Be5 Nd7 15. Bd4 Qc7 16. f4** Steinitz: "White has cleverly retrieved the inferiority of his position in the opening and takes the initiative for a counter attack." **16. ... Rac8 17. e4 d×e4 18. N×e4 B×e4 19. Q×e4 Nf6 20. B×f6** Steinitz: "We think that the position of two bishops and their bearing against the adverse king was quite worth a pawn, and he ought to have avoided the exchange. After 20. Qf3, 20. ... Q×c2 21. Bd3 Qc6 22. Qh3 Rfd8 23. Be5 g6 24. Rf3 Nh5 (24. ... Ne8 subjects him to mate in three moves: 25. Q×h7+ K×h7 26. Rh3+ Kg8 27. Rh8 mate.) 25. f5 e×f5 26. B×f5, etc." This interesting line given by Steinitz can be successfully refuted by Black: 26. ... Qb6+! 27. Kh1 Rc4 28. g4 Bf6! **20. ... B×f6 21. Bd3 g6 22. Rad1 Rfd8 23. Qf3 Qb6+ 24. Kh1 Rc3 25. g4 R×a3 26. f5! e×f5 27. g×f5 Kg7 28. f×g6 f×g6 29. Rde1 Rf8 30. Qg4 Rc3 31. Rg1** Preoccupied with his sacrificial idea, Pollock missed 31. Qd7+ Rf7 32. Re6!, with at least an equal position. **31. ... Kh8** (*see diagram*)

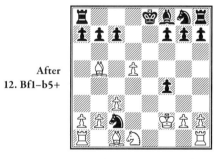

After 31. ... Kg7–h8

32. B×g6? Steinitz: "This sacrifice is unsound against such a formidable opponent." 32. h4 Qd4 33. h5 Q×g4 34. R×g4 g×h5 35. Rf4 Kg7 36. Re6 was objectively best. **32. ... h×g6 33. Q×g6 Qb7+ 34. Rg2 Bg7 35. Reg1 Rc7 36. Qh5+ Kg8 37. Qg6 Re7 38. Qg3 Rf3 39. Qd6 Rfe3 40. Qd8+ Kh7 41. Qd2 Qe4 42. Qd6 Re1** Steinitz: "Black has concentrated his forces both for defence and attack in an admirable manner, and he now fin-ishes off with a few vigorous attacks." **43. Qc5 R×g1+ 44. Q×g1 Bd4 45. Qf1 Rg7 46. Qd3 Q×d3 0–1** [*tournament book*, pages 107–108]

260. G.H.D. Gossip–Pollock [C25]
6th American Chess Congress, New York, Round 17, 12 April 1889

1. e4 e5 2. Nc3 Nc6 3. f4 e×f4 4. d4 Qh4+ 5. Ke2 d5 6. e×d5 Bg4+ 7. Nf3 B×f3+ 8. K×f3 Steinitz: "It was not alone safe, but in fact better to retake with the pawn, which would practically compel Black to sacrifice his knight and to play ... 0–0–0, with one strong piece less for the usual attack. Any attempt at harassing the king further by 8. g×f3 Qe7+ 9. Kf2 Qh4+ 10. Kg1 Qg5+ 11. Bg2 would only help to consolidate White's forces." **8. ... Qh5+ 9. Kf2 Q×d1 10. N×d1 N×d4 11. c3 Nc2 12. Bb5+** (*see diagram*)

After 12. Bf1–b5+

12. ... c6 Steinitz: "After queens are off the board, such a sacrifice of a pawn becomes, of course, still more hazardous." 12. ... Kd8 13. Rb1 Bc5+ 14. Kf3 Ne3 15. N×e3 B×e3 16. B×e3 f×e3 17. K×e3 Nf6 18. Kd4 was a possible alternative. **13. d×c6 Bc5+ 14. Kf3 0–0–0 15. c×b7+ K×b7 16. Rb1 g5 17. Ba4** Steinitz: "Still stronger was 17. h4." **17. ... g4+ 18. K×f4 Nd4 19. Re1** 19. c×d4? invites 19. ... R×d4+ 20. Kg3 R×a4 21. b4 Bd6+ 22. K×g4 Nf6+ 23. Kf3 Rc8. **19. ... Ne6+ 20. K×g4 Nf6+ 21. Kh3 Rd5 22. g3 Rg8**

23. Bb3 Rh5+ 24. Kg2 Nd5 Steinitz: "24. ... Ng4 25. h3 Ne5, might have made it more difficult for White to make his game quite safe." **25. B×d5+ R×d5 26. b4 Bd6 27. Nf2 h5 28. Ne4 Be7 29. Be3 Rg6 30. Rbd1 Kc6 31. c4** Steinitz: "Very well played." **31. ... R×d1 32. b5+ Kc7 33. R×d1 f5 34. Nc3 Bd6 35. Nd5+** Steinitz: "35. b6+ Kc6! (obviously, if 35. ... a×b6, 36. Nb5+ and wins.) 36. b×a7 Rg8 37. Nb5, was more forcible, but, of course, he is also bound to win in the way he plays." **35. ... Kb7 36. Rf1 h4 37. Nf4 B×f4 38. B×f4 h×g3 39. h×g3 Rg4 40. Kf3 Nd4+ 41. Ke3 Ne6 42. Rd1 Rg6 43. Rd5 Ng7 44. c5 Nh5 45. Kf3 Rf6 46. Rd7+ Kc8 47. R×a7 Re6 48. c6 N×f4 49. K×f4 1–0** [*tournament book*, pages 408–409]

261. Pollock–J.W. Showalter [C55]
6th American Chess Congress, New York, Round 18, 13 April 1889

1. e4 e5 2. Bc4 Nf6 3. Nf3 Nc6 Steinitz: "3. ... N×e4 is the proper play, as the answer 4. Nc3 has been proved unsound beyond doubt." **4. d4** Steinitz: "An ordinary position of the Two Knights' Defence is here formed, in which 4. Ng5 is recognized as the strongest continuation." **4. ... N×e4 5. 0–0 d5 6. Bb5 e×d4 7. N×d4 Bd7 8. B×c6 b×c6 9. f3 Nf6** Steinitz: "9. ... Nc5, in order to play ...Ne6 sooner or later, was superior." **10. Re1+ Be7 11. Qe2 c5 12. Nb3** 12. Bf4!? is interesting but promised little after 12. ... 0–0 (12. ... c×d4? 13. B×c7! Bb5 14. Q×b5+ Qd7 15. R×e7+ K×e7 16. Qc5+ Ke6 17. Nd2 and the Black king is in real danger.) 13. Q×e7 c×d4 14. Q×d8 Rf×d8 15. B×c7 Rdc8 16. Be5 R×c2 17. B×d4 Re8. **12. ... Be6 13. f4 c4 14. f5?** 14. Nd4 was better. **14. ... B×f5 15. Nd4 Be4 16. b3 c×b3 17. a×b3 0–0 18. Bb2 Bc5 19. Kh1 Qd7 20. Nd2 Rfe8 21. Rf1 Qg4** Steinitz: "He has tenaciously kept the two pawns which the adversary had sacrificed for the attack, and it was to his advantage to exchange, but still better was clearly to capture the c2-pawn." **22. N×e4 R×e4 23. Q×g4 N×g4 24. Ra4 Rae8 25. h3 Nf6 26. Nf5 R×a4 27. b×a4 Re6 28. g4 Ne8 29. g5 Re4** Steinitz: "Losing sight of the adverse ingenious reply 29. ... Nd6, and if 30. N×g7 Rg6, kept his superiority of position and material." **30. B×g7 Nd6** Steinitz: "If 30. ... N×g7, White has perpetual check with his knight." **31. N×d6 B×d6 32. Bf6 R×a4 33. Rb1 Rb4 34. Ra1 h6 35. c3 Rb2 36. R×a7 Rh2+ 37. Kg1 R×h3 38. Ra5 h×g5 39. R×d5 Rg3+ 40. Kf2 Bf4** *(see diagram)*

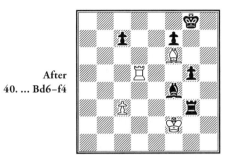

After 40. ... Bd6–f4

41. Rf5! Steinitz: "A very curious and most cleverly conceived position has been brought about by White, who threatens B×g5, and then to recover at least the piece, no matter how Black might retake." **41. ... Rg4 42. Kf3 Rg1 43. Kf2 Rg4 44. Kf3 Rg3+ 45. Kf2 Kf8 46. Rd5 Kg8 47. Rf5 Rd3 48. B×g5 B×g5 49. R×g5+ Kf8 50. Rc5 Rd7 51. Ke3 Ke7 52. Rc6 Kd8 53. Rf6 Kc8 54. Ke4 Kb7 55. c4 c6 56. Rf5 Kb6 57. Re5 c5 58. Rf5 Rd4+ 59. Ke3 R×c4 60. R×f7 Rd4 61. Rf1 Rd8 62. Rb1+ Ka5 63. Ra1+ Kb4 64. Rb1+ Ka3 65. Rc1 Kb4 66. Rb1+ Ka4 67. Rc1 Kb5 68. Rb1+ Kc6 69. Rb2 c4 70. Rd2 Rh8 71. Kd4 Rh4+ 72. Kc3** Steinitz: "White's defence was a masterpiece of end play. He has now reached with his king his goal in front of the adverse passed pawn, and the draw is theoretically forced and easy." **72. ... Kc5 73. Rd8 Rh3+ 74. Kc2 Rg3 ½–½** [*tournament book*, pages 396–397]

262. D.G. Baird–Pollock [C29]
6th American Chess Congress, New York, Round 19, 15 April 1889

1. e4 e5 2. Nc3 Nf6 3. f4 d5 4. f×e5 N×e4 5. Qf3 Nc6 6. Bb5 Bc5 7. N×e4 Steinitz: "It was probably better to play 7. Nge2 and not to accept at once the ingenious sacrifice of the pawn, which gives the opponent a strong attack for a long time." **7. ... d×e4 8. B×c6+ b×c6 9. Q×e4 0–0 10. Nf3 Be6 11. c3 Bd5 12. Qe2 Qe7 13. d4 Bb6 14. 0–0 f6 15. Bf4 Rae8 16. Kh1 c5 17. a3?** Steinitz: "Loss of time. Either 17. Qd3 or 17. Rae1 were better." **17. ... c×d4 18. c×d4 f×e5 19. B×e5** *(see diagram)* **19. ... R×f3!?** Steinitz: "Black wins two minor pieces and a pawn for the adverse rook by this very pretty sacrifice, but the weakness of his position on the queenside soon acts as a set-off against the advantage which he now gains." **20. R×f3 B×d4 21. Re1** 21. Rf5 Qe6 22. B×d4 Q×e2 23. R×d5 Qd2 24. Rd7 Re1+ 25. R×e1 Q×e1+ 26. Bg1 was

After
19. B×e5

an interesting choice as well, but the queen seems stronger. **21. ... Q×e5 22. Q×e5 R×e5 23. R×e5 B×f3** Steinitz: "Obviously, if he take the other rook, White would have won by 25. Rf5." **24. Re8+ Kf7 25. Rd8 Bf6 26. Rd7+ Ke6 27. R×c7 Be4 28. R×a7 B×b2** Steinitz: "A long and rather uninteresting struggle ensues now, in which neither side can make a winning impression." **29. a4 Bd4 30. Rc7 Kd6 31. Rc1 Bb6 32. Rc4 Bd5 33. Rg4 g6 34. Rh4 h5 35. Rb4 Kc5 36. Rb5+ Kc6 37. Rb1 Bc4 38. Rb4 Kc5 39. Rb2 Ba5 40. Rb8 Bc7 41. Rb1 Bb6 42. Rb2 Ba5 43. Rb8 Bb6 44. Rc8+ Kd5 45. Ra8 Kc6 46. Rc8+ Bc7 47. Rf8 Kb7 48. Rf3 Bd5 49. Rd3 Be4 50. Rd4 Bf5 51. Rb4+ Ka6 52. Rb5 Bd7 53. Rb4 Bb6 54. Rf4 Ka5 55. Rf6 Bf5 56. Rd6 Be3 57. Rc6 K×a4** and the game was drawn at move 75. **½–½** [*tournament book*, pages 400–401]

263. Pollock–S. Lipschütz [C62]
6th American Chess Congress,
New York, Round 20, 18 April 1889

1. e4 e5 2. Nf3 Nc6 3. Bb5 d6 4. d4 Bd7 5. 0–0 Be7 6. Nc3 Nf6 7. Be3 0–0 8. Qe2 Bg4 Steinitz: "Black's defense has kept the game quite even up to this, which is disadvantageous to his queenside. 8. ... Re8 and if 9. Rad1, 9. ... Qc8 would have left the position still well balanced." **9. B×c6 b×c6 10. d×e5 d×e5 11. h3 B×f3 12. Q×f3 Qd6 13. a3 Qe6 14. Rad1 a5 15. Rd3 Rab8 16. Bc1 Ne8** Steinitz: "This retreat loses time, for he cannot afford to open the game by ...f5, which, no doubt, was intended to be prepared by this move, as this plan would leave his e-pawn isolated." **17. b3 Bd6 18. a4 Nf6 19. Nd1 Rb4** Steinitz: "Again a lost move, for he has immediately to retreat in order to guard against the loss of a valuable pawn by Bd2." **20. Re1 Rbb8** Steinitz: "A little better was perhaps 20. ... Ra8 21. Bd2 Rbb8, but not 21. ... Rd4, on account of 22. R×d4 e×d4 23. e5 B×e5 24. Bf4 Nd7 25. B×e5 N×e5 26. Qe4 and wins."

21. Ne3 Nd7 22. Nf5 Nc5 23. Qg4 23. Rc3 appears to offer more. **23. ... Qg6 24. Rg3** Steinitz: "White has obtained the superior position on both wings, but he overlooks here a plan which we believe was quite decisive. 24. Rc3 threatening accordingly Ba3 or Rc4, followed by Be3, must have gained a valuable pawn that would have been sufficient to give White a winning game." **24. ... Q×g4 25. h×g4 Ne6 26. Bd2 Ra8 27. Rd3 Rfd8 28. Bc3 f6 29. N×d6** Steinitz: "No necessity for this, and it could do no good either to undouble the adverse pawns and to strengthen the hostile centre. The right play was 29. f3, with the view of manoeuvring his knight via e3–c4." **29. ... c×d6 30. g3 Kf7 31. Red1 Ke7 32. f3 Nc5 33. R3d2 Ke6 34. Bb2 Nb7 35. f4 Nc5 36. Re2 Ke7 37. Ba3 Ne6 38. Red2 c5 39. Rf2 Nd4 40. Rdf1 Nc6 41. Bc1 h6 42. g5!? h×g5 43. f×g5 Rf8 44. g4 Ke6 45. Bd2 Rf7 46. g6** Steinitz: "White has kept up a spirited attack very skilfully, but he goes too far with the same in virtually sacrificing the pawn by advancing it thus." **46. ... Rff8 47. g5 Ne7 48. g×f6 R×f6 49. R×f6+ g×f6 50. g7 Kf7** (*see diagram*)

After
50. ... Ke6–f7

51. Kf2 The start of a remarkable walk. **51. ... K×g7 52. Ke3 Kf7 53. Kd3 Ke6 54. Kc4 Nc6 55. Kb5 Nd4+ 56. Kb6 N×c2 57. Kb7 Rg8 58. B×a5 Rg3** Steinitz: "Black in turn had now a won game, but 58. ... Nd4 59. Rb1 (if 59. b4, 59. ... Nb3 etc.) 59. ... Rg3 60. b4 Nb3 61. Ka6 c4 was his best plan; for if now, for instance, 62. Bb6 c3 63. R×b3 c2, and wins. The play in the text gives the opponent an opportunity for a highly ingenious counter-attack that still keeps Black's king in jeopardy, though forces are already much reduced." **59. Kc8?** 59. Bd8 Kd7 (59. ... R×b3+ 60. Kc7) 60. Bb6 R×b3 61. a5 Na3 62. Rh1 maintained the tension. **59. ... Nd4 60. Bd8 f5 61. e×f5+ N×f5 62. Rb1 Nd4 63. a5 Rg8** Steinitz: "With this his winning prospects are altogether abandoned, while 63. ... Rg7, followed accordingly by ...Nc6 or ...Nb5, made it still difficult, if not impossible, for

White to escape with a draw." **64. Kc7 R×d8** Steinitz: "This involves also the sacrifice of the knight within a few moves, leaving Black with three pawns for the rook. But the pawns are not advanced well enough to secure victory, and a draw ought to have been the legitimate result." **64. ... Nb5+!** 65. Kc6 Na3 66. Ra1 Nc2 67. Rc1 Nd4+ 68. Kc7 N×b3 was an amusing way to secure the full point. **65. K×d8 Nc6+ 66. Kc7 N×a5 67. Kb6 N×b3 68. R×b3 e4 69. Kb5 Kd5 70. Rb1 e3 71. Rd1+ Ke4 72. Kc4 e2 73. Rh1 Ke3 74. Kc3 d5 75. Rh3+ Kf2 76. Rh2+ Kf1??** Steinitz: "Black, most injudiciously, is not satisfied with a draw which he could easily secure by 76. ... Ke3, and he has to bear the usual penalty for attempting to win a game drawn by its nature, for after the opponent's reply his own game can no more be saved." **77. Rh1+ Kf2 78. Kd2 Kf3 79. Re1 Ke4 80. R×e2+ Kd4 81. Rh2 Kc4 82. Rh4+ d4 83. Rh5 Kb4 84. Kd3 Kb5 85. Rh8 Kc6 86. Kc4 1–0** [*tournament book*, pages 284–285]

264. J.H. Blackburne–Pollock [C28]
6th American Chess Congress, New York, Round 21, 19 April 1889

1. e4 e5 2. Nc3 Nc6 3. Bc4 Nf6 4. d3 Bb4 5. Nge2 Steinitz: "In consequence of Black's last irregular move a sort of Lopez defence with a move ahead might have been formed by White here, by 5. Nf3." **5. ... d6 6. 0–0 Bg4** Steinitz: "The two players have taken each other quite out of the books. Though not much harm is done by the last move, it can be no advantage to induce the opponent to fortify his K centre." **7. f3 Be6 8. Bb5** Steinitz: "White being some moves ahead and, being well guarded in the centre, might have tried here 8. Nd5, a move which used to be much in favour with the late Mr. Zukertort in similar positions that sometimes arose from the Three Knights' Game or the Double Ruy Lopez." **8. ... 0–0 9. Bg5 h6 10. Bh4 Bc5+ 11. Bf2 Bb6 12. Qd2 d5 13. e×d5 N×d5 14. N×d5 Q×d5 15. Nc3 Qd6 16. Ne4 Qe7 17. B×c6** Steinitz: "White now obtains by this a fairly promising attack against the adverse weakened queenside." **17. ... b×c6 18. Qc3 Bd5 19. Rae1 f6 20. Nc5 a5** Steinitz: "The advance of this pawn only exposes the same still more for the end. 20. ... Qf7 at once, followed by ...Rfe8, were better." **21. a4 Qf7 22. Kh1 Rfe8 23. Qd2 Qh5 24. Nd7 Ra6** Steinitz: "A curious and ingenious resource but for which Black's game would be broken up, for the latter would be compelled to exchange his Bb6 in order not to lose a

pawn, and White would retain knight against bishop for the ending in a most favourable position for his side, on account of Black's isolated and doubled pawns on the queen's wing." **25. Qe2 Qf7 26. Nc5 Raa8 27. c4 B×c5 28. B×c5 Be6 29. Qe4 Qd7 30. Rd1 Rab8** Steinitz: "Loss of time, as will soon be seen." **31. Rf2 Bf5 32. Qe1 Ra8** Steinitz: "Of course he is bound to retreat again, as he cannot afford to lose the a-pawn." **33. Rfd2 Bg6 34. Qg3 Qf7 35. f4!? Rab8 36. f×e5 R×e5 37. Bd4 Rg5 38. Qf2 Rf5 39. Qg1 Qd7 40. Bc3 Re8 41. Re1 R×e1 42. Q×e1 Rh5 43. d4 Qd6 44. h3 Kh7 45. Re2** (*see diagram*)

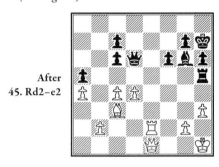

After 45. Rd2–e2

45. ... c5?! Steinitz: "The long manoeuvring of both parties did not effect any impression, and by the nature of the game a draw ought to have ensued, chiefly on account of the bishops being of opposite colors. The move in the text, however, greatly compromises Black's position, for it shuts out the rook from protecting the important a-pawn and provoke the further advance of a hostile pawn that in the ending would have had difficulty to assert itself if Black's c-pawn would have kept unmoved at c6. 45. ... Bf7 46. b3 Qa3 47. Qb1+ Bg6 48. Qb2 Qd6 were his proper defence for a draw." **46. d5 Qf4?** 46. ... Bf5 47. Kg1 Bd7 48. b3 c6 was more accurate than the text. **47. b3 Bf5 48. Re3 Bc2 49. B×a5 Re5** Steinitz: "His game was now bad already, but he deprives himself of all chance of a good resistance by this blunder." **50. R×e5 Q×e5** Steinitz: "No better was 50. ... f×e5 51. B×c7, and if 51. ... B×b3 52. Qb1+ Kh8 53. Q×b3 Qc1+ 54. Kh2 Qf4+ 55. Qg3, and wins." **51. Q×e5 f×e5 52. B×c7 B×b3 53. a5 B×c4 54. d6 Bb5 55. a6 1–0** [*tournament book*, pages 206–207]

265. Pollock–I.A. Gunsberg [B00]
6th American Chess Congress, New York, Round 22, 20 April 1889

1. e4 b6 2. d4 Bb7 3. Bd3 Nc6 Steinitz: "A novel idea in this opening. Most practitioners of this debut develop this knight at d7 after advancing ...d7–d6, or else play ...e6 and ...c5 first, before bringing out ...Nc6." **4. c3** Steinitz: "Best, undoubtedly. If 4. Ne2, Black may answer 4. ... Nb4 and exchange the important king's bishop on d3." **4. ... e5 5. d5 Nce7 6. Ne2** Steinitz: "A weak move. He ought to have foreseen the opponent's clever reply, which either breaks White's centre or much relieves the cluster of Black's pieces on the kingside. 6. c4 was the right play." **6. ... f5 7. 0–0** Steinitz: "He gives up a pawn designedly, but the attack on which he speculates as a compensation proves unsatisfactory. His best plan was now either 7. f3, in which case Black could not advance ...f4 on account of the rejoinder 8. g3, or he might have played also 7. e×f5, whereupon, after 7. ... B×d5 8. Ng3, Black dare not play 8. ... B×g2 on account of 9. Qh5+ g6 10. f×g6 Nf6 11. g7+ N×h5 12. g×h8Q and wins." **7. ... f×e4 8. B×e4 Nf6 9. Ng3 N×e4 10. N×e4 B×d5 11. Qh5+ Ng6 12. Bg5 Be7 13. B×e7 Q×e7 14. Nbd2 0–0 15. Ng5** Steinitz: "The upshot of all this is that White has lost a fine centre pawn and remains with the inferior position." **15. ... Rf5** Steinitz: "Black might have been satisfied with this plain winning advantage, which he could have retained simply by ...h6, but he plays for higher game, and on the merits of position judgment his aim was as correctly measured as it was ingeniously conceived." **16. Q×h7+ Kf8 17. h4 R×g5! 18. h×g5 Q×g5 19. g3 Kf7 20. Qh3 Rh8 21. f4 N×f4** Steinitz: "The moves on both sides from the 15th, the point of our last comment, were probably foreseen by both players, as they were pretty nearly forced for each party. At this critical juncture, however, Black impetuously goes astray in the pursuance of his attack. He could have made much more sure of his victory by 21. ... Qe7, threatening ...Qc5+, 22. f×e5+ (Steinitz failed to mention 22. Qf5+! Kg8 23. Ne4!) 22. ... Kg8 23. Qg4 N×e5 24. Qd4 (there seems nothing better) 24. ... Rh1+ 25. Kf2 Rh2+. Black wins with ease accordingly by ...Rg2+ or ...Nd3+." **22. R×f4+ e×f4** *(see diagram)*

After
22. ... e5×f4

23. Q×d7+? Steinitz: "White allows himself to be unduly intimidated. 23. Q×h8 was his only chance, and, moreover, a good one for drawing purposes. The game must then have proceeded: 23. ... Q×g3+ 24. Kf1 Bg2+ (if 24. ... f3, 25. Qh5+ Kf6 26. Qh1 etc.) 25. Ke2 Qe3+ 26. Kd1 Qg1+ 27. Kc2 Q×a1 (thus far we follow in the main variation the analysis of the *Deutsche Schachzeitung*), and now White has a chance of drawing by 28. Qh2." **23. ... Kg6 24. Ne4 f×g3!** Steinitz: "A very neat surprise. Of course, White dare not take the queen, for he is mated by ...Rh1." 24. ... Qh5 was the less artistic finish. **25. Re1 Qh4 26. Nf2** Steinitz: "Leaving open a little brilliant which his clever opponent immediately seizes upon, but there was no salvation for his game under any circumstances." **26. ... Qh1+ 27. N×h1 R×h1 mate 0–1** [*tournament book*, pages 158–159; *ICM*, October 1889, pages 305–306]

266. M. Chigorin–Pollock [C51]
6th American Chess Congress,
New York, Round 23, 22 April 1889

1. e4 e5 2. Nf3 Nc6 3. Bc4 Bc5 4. b4 B×b4 5. c3 Bc5 6. 0–0 d6 7. d4 e×d4 8. c×d4 Bb6 9. Nc3 Na5 10. Bg5 f6 11. Bf4 Steinitz: "11. Be3 is, we believe, preferable." **11. ... N×c4 12. Qa4+ Kf7** Steinitz: "This novelty is the invention of Mr. Pollock and has a great deal in its favour, on general principles. It seems better anyhow than the usual continuation, 12. ... Qd7 13. Q×c4 Qf7 14. Nd5 threatening N×b6, or else Qa4." **13. Q×c4+ Be6 14. Qe2** Steinitz: "In a subsequent game between the same players Mr. Chigorin played here 14. d5." **14. ... Ne7 15. e5 Ng6 16. Be3 d5 17. e×f6 g×f6 18. Nd2 Qd7** Steinitz: "We much prefer ...Re8, followed soon by ...Kg8." **19. f4 Bf5 20. Qf3 c6 21. Nb3 Rae8 22. Rae1 Re7 23. h3 Rhe8 24. Bd2 R×e1 25. B×e1 Bc2 26. Qh5 Kg7 27. f5** *(see diagram)*

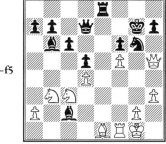

After 27. f4–f5

27. ... Re5! Steinitz: "An excellent move which,

by attacking the f-pawn once more, compels White to shut his queen out of play by the advance of the g-pawn." **28. g4 B×b3 29. a×b3 B×d4+ 30. Kh1 B×c3** Steinitz: "Black has played up to this remarkably well, but fails at this critical moment. There were two clear and simple ways of winning here, namely, in the first place, 30. ... R×e1 31. R×e1 B×c3 32. f×g6 h×g6, and wins with ease. Secondly, 30. ... Nf4 31. Qh4 B×c3 32. B×c3 d4 33. R×f4 d×c3, and wins." **31. B×c3 d4 32. Bd2 Qd5+ 33. Kg1 Re2 34. Rf2 R×f2?** Pollock missed 34. ... R×d2! 35. R×d2 Qe4 36. Rf2 Nf4 37. R×f4 Q×f4 38. Qh4 Qc1+ 39. Kg2 Qc2+ 40. Kh1 Q×b3 with a winning position. **35. K×f2 Nf8 36. Bh6+ Kg8 37. Qe8 Qd6 38. Qc8 Qh2+** Steinitz: "The series of checks that follow could do no good by proper play of the opponent whereas we believe that simply 38. ... d3 would have won, for if 39. B×f8, 39. ... Q×f8 40. Q×b7 Qe8 and wins." **39. Ke1 Qg3+ 40. Ke2** Steinitz: "40. Kd2 would have compelled Black to retreat again by 40. ... Qd6. By the play in the text, however, he still leaves winning chances for Black (for if 40. ... Qc3+ 41. Ke2 d3+ 42. Kf1 Qc5 43. Q×b7 and wins). **40. ... d3+ 41. Kd1 Qg1+ 42. Kd2 Qg2+ 43. Kc3 Qc2+ 44. Kd4 Qb2+ 45. Ke4 Qe2+ ½–½** Steinitz: "A strange consummation such as sometimes, but rarely, occurs between masters. Mr. Pollock could hardly have bestowed much attention to this position, or else he would not have consented to a draw. After 46. Kd4 (if 46. Kf4, 46. ... Qd2+ wins the bishop) 46. ... Qe7, threatens ...Qd7+, 47. B×f8 (47. Kc3! was left unmentioned by Steinitz: 47. ... d2 48. B×d2 c5 49. Qb8 b6 50. Bh6 and Black can't make real progress.) 47. ... Q×f8 48. Qe6+ (if 48. Q×b7, 48. ... Qd8+, followed by ...d2, and wins) 48. ... Qf7 49. Qc8+ Kg7, and should win" [*tournament book*, pages 45–46].

267. Pollock–H.E. Bird [B72]
6th American Chess Congress, New York, Round 24, 23 April 1889

1. e4 c5 2. d4 c×d4 3. Nf3 Nc6 Steinitz noted that after 3. ... e5 4. c3 White will obtain a "good attack." **4. N×d4 d6 5. Be3 g6 6. Nc3 Bg7 7. Be2 Nf6 8. Qd2 h5 9. h3 0–0 10. 0–0–0 Bd7 11. f4 N×d4 12. B×d4 Bc6 13. Bd3 Qa5 14. Kb1 e5 15. Be3 Rfd8 16. f5!?** Steinitz: "Premature and misjudging the position which required Qf2 to be played first." **16. ... d5 17. Bh6?!** 17. f×g6!? was a rather interesting try: 17. ... d4 18. Nd5 Q×d2 19. N×f6+ B×f6 20. g×f7+ K×f7 21. B×d2 Rg8

22. Rhg1 Rg3 23. Rdf1 Kg6 24. Rf3. **17. ... d×e4 18. B×g7?** 18. N×e4 Q×d2 19. N×f6+ B×f6 20. B×d2 was advisable although Black remains in the lead. **18. ... K×g7 19. N×e4 Q×d2 20. N×d2 e4! 21. Bc4 g×f5 22. Kc1 b5** Steinitz: "Black, after having won a pawn by hard play, commences an artificial line of attack that in the end involves him in difficulties, whereas the simple ...e3 at this junction, with the view of entering soon with the knight to e4, would have won in an easy manner." **23. Be2 Nd5 24. Rdf1 Ne3 25. Rf4 Kg6 26. Re1 Kg5 27. Rf2 Nd5 28. g4!** Steinitz: "Excellent, and practically decisive, as it recovers the pawn, with much the superior game." **28. ... h×g4 29. h×g4** *(see diagram)*

After
29. h3×g4

29. ... e3? 29. ... Nf4! was stronger: 30. Bd1 R×d2! 31. K×d2 (31. R×d2 f×g4 32. Rf2 f5) 31. ... f×g4 32. Ref1 e3+ 33. K×e3 Re8+ 34. Kd2 Rd8+ 35. Kc1 Rd4 with superior chances for Black. **30. R×f5+ Kg6 31. Nf3 f6 32. Nh4+ Kg7 33. g5! Rh8 34. g×f6+ N×f6?** This loses material. 34. ... Kf7 35. Nf3 N×f6 36. B×b5 B×b5 37. R×b5 Rae8 was a possible defense but White keeps the material edge. **35. Rg1+ Kf7 36. Rg6** Steinitz: "The telling blow. It wins a piece." **36. ... R×h4 37. Rg×f6+ Ke7 38. R×c6 Rh2 39. B×b5 Rh1 40. Rf1 R×f1+ 41. B×f1 Rf8 42. Be2 Rf2 43. Kd1 Rg2 44. Ke1 1–0** [*tournament book*, page 406]

268. N. MacLeod–Pollock [C20]
6th American Chess Congress, New York, Round 25, 24 April 1889

1. e4 e5 2. c3 d5 3. Nf3 Nc6 4. Bb5 f6 5. Qa4 Nge7 6. 0–0?! 6. e×d5 was the main move. **6. ... d×e4! 7. Q×e4 Bf5 8. B×c6+ b×c6 9. Qa4 Bd3 10. Re1 Qd7 11. c4** Steinitz: "A badly played opening further degenerates with this move which costs a piece." **11. ... e4 12. Re3 e×f3 13. R×f3 Qe6 14. Re3 Q×c4 15. Qd1 Bc2 16. Qf3 Qd5 17. Qe2 B×b1 18. R×b1 Q×a2 19. Qd3 Qd5**

20. Qa6 Kf7 21. Qb7 Qa2 22. Q×a8 Q×b1 23. Re1 Qa2 24. Qb8 Qa5 25. Qb3+ Qd5 26. Qb8 Qd7 27. Q×a7 Nd5 28. Qb8 Rg8 29. Qb3 Bb4 30. Qc2 Re8 31. Rf1 Re2 32. Q×h7 Nf4 33. Qc2 Qd5 34. f3 R×g2+ 35. Kh1 *(see diagram)*

After
35. Kg1–h1

35. ... R×h2+ Steinitz: "Black announced here mate in nine moves. The finish is worthy of a much better game." 35. ... Rg1+ would have mated in eight moves: 36. K×g1 Qg5+ 37. Kf2 Qg2+ 38. Ke3 Qe2+ 39. K×f4 Bd6+ 40. Kg4 Qg2+ 41. Kh4 g5+ 42. Kh5 Qh3 mate. **36. K×h2 Qh5+ 37. Kg3 Qg5+ 38. Kf2 Qg2+ 39. Ke3 Qe2+ 40. K×f4 Bd6+ 41. Kg4 Qg2+ 0–1** [*tournament book*, pages 412–413]

269. M. Chigorin–Pollock [C51]
6th American Chess Congress, New York, Replayed Game, 25 April 1889

1. e4 e5 2. Nf3 Nc6 3. Bc4 Bc5 4. b4 B×b4 5. c3 Bc5 6. 0–0 d6 7. d4 e×d4 8. c×d4 Bb6 9. Nc3 Na5 10. Bg5 f6 11. Bf4 N×c4 12. Qa4+ Kf7 13. Q×c4+ Be6 14. d5 Bd7 15. Ne2 Qe8 Steinitz: "It was better to develop the kingside by 15. ... Ne7 and ...Re8 or ...Rf8. The queen should have been reserved for a better post." **16. a4 Ne7 17. Be3 Ng6** Steinitz: "17. ... Qd8, in order to be enabled to retake with the a-pawn in reply to B×b6, seems better. Now his d-pawn becomes isolated and weak and is the mark of the hostile attack for a long time." **18. B×b6 c×b6 19. Qb4 Qe7 20. Ng3 Rhc8 21. Nd4 Rc5 22. f4 Rac8 23. Qd2** Steinitz: "We do not see the object of this preparation, and 23. Ne6 at once appears stronger." **23. ... Rc4** Steinitz: "Black ought to have now retreated 23. ... Nf8 in order to prevent White's strong entrance of Ne6." **24. Ne6 Nh4** Steinitz: "If 24. ... B×e6, 25. d×e6+, and should the queen retake, he loses a piece by f5." 24. ... Rc2!? was interesting but White could have replied with

25. Q×c2 R×c2 26. Nf5 B×e6 (26. ... R×g2+!? 27. K×g2 Nh4+ 28. N×h4 B×e6 29. d×e6+ Q×e6 30. Kg3 h5 was another interesting possibility for Black) **27. N×e7 N×e7 28. d×e6+ K×e6 29. Rac1 Rc5 30. Kf2** with unclear play. **25. Qd1 B×e6 26. d×e6+ Kg8** Steinitz: "Again he could not take with the queen on account of f5, followed by Qh5+." **27. Qg4** Steinitz: "The kingside attack is congenial to Mr. Chigorin's style, and he pursues it here with consummate mastery." **27. ... Ng6 28. Nf5 Qc7** Steinitz: "Of course, if 28. ... Q×e6, he loses the queen by 29. Nh6+." **29. e7 Kf7?** Steinitz: "29. ... Re8 with the intention eventually of sacrificing the exchange for the advanced pawn, would have given him a better chance of making a longer fight. But if 29. ... R×e4, White could have answered 30. N×d6." **30. Rad1 Qc5+ 31. Kh1 Rc6** *(see diagram)*

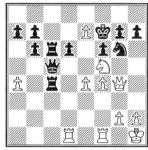

After
31. ... Rc8–c6

32. e5! Steinitz: "The initiation of a splendidly conceived attack." **32. ... f×e5** Steinitz: "If 32. ... d×e5 33. Rd8 N×e7 (or 33. ... Re6 34. e8Q+ R×e8 35. Nd6+, and wins.) 34. Q×g7+ Ke6 35. N×e7 and wins." **33. N×d6+** Steinitz: "The crushing stroke." **33. ... R×d6 34. f×e5+ Rf6 35. e8Q+** Steinitz: "Finishing with accuracy and elegance." **35. ... K×e8 36. Qd7+ Kf8 37. e×f6 1–0** [*tournament book*, pages 47–48; *ICM*, May 1889, pages 147–148]

270. J.W. Baird–Pollock [C83]
6th American Chess Congress, New York, Round 26, 26 April 1889

1. e4 e5 2. Nf3 Nc6 3. Bb5 a6 4. Ba4 Nf6 5. 0–0 N×e4 6. d4 Steinitz: "6. Re1 might strengthen the attack in a continuation similar to the one that occurred in the match between Messrs. Steinitz and Zukertort, viz. 6. ... Nc5 7. B×c6 b×c6 8. N×e5 Be7 9. Qe2 Ne6 10. Nc3, with the better game." **6. ... b5 7. Bb3 d5 8. d×e5 Be6 9. c3 Be7 10. Re1 0–0 11. Nbd2 N×d2 12. Q×d2** Steinitz: "In order to place sooner the king's bishop and queen on the same diagonal with threats of mate. Compare White's fourteenth move." **12. ... Qd7 13. Qd3 Rfd8 14. Bc2 g6 15. Nd4 N×d4 16. c×d4 c5 17. Qe3** Steinitz: "He ought to have exchanged pawns at once, followed by Bg5." **17. ... Rac8 18. Bd3 c×d4 19. Q×d4 Bc5 20. Qf4 d4 21. Bd2 Bc4 22. Be4 Bd5 23. Bd3 Qe6 24. b3 Qe7 25. Qh6 Bb4 26. Bg5 Qf8 27. Qh4** *(see diagram)*

After 27. Qh6–h4

27. ... B×e1 Steinitz: "Overlooking the force of the adverse reply. 27. ... Rd7, in order to make room for ...Qd8 and afterward accordingly ...Be7 or ... Bf8 was imperative." **28. Bh6 Q×h6** Steinitz: "This desperate resource was his only one, as White threatened Qf6." **29. Q×h6 Bc3 30. Rf1** Steinitz: "Much better was 30. Rd1." **30. ... Re8 31. f4 Bd2 32. h4?** Steinitz: "He could hardly do much worse, as he not alone loses a most valuable centre pawn, but he is also compelled by the opponent's reply, which threatens to win the queen by ...Rh5, to compromise altogether his kingside with the advance of the g-pawn." 32. Qh3! was keeping White's position together: 32. ... Be3+ 33. Kh1 Rc3 34. Qd7 Bc6 35. Qd6. **32. ... R×e5 33. g4 Re3 34. Qg5 Bb7 35. Kh2** Steinitz: "If 35. Bb1, 35. ... Rg3+ 36. Kh2 Rg2+ 37. Kh3 Rc3+, and wins." **35. ... R×d3 36. h5 Be3 0–1** [*tournament book*, page 404]

271. Pollock–E. Delmar [C50]
6th American Chess Congress,
New York, Round 27, 27 April 1889

1. e4 e5 2. Nf3 Nc6 3. Bc4 Be7 4. d4 d6 5. Nc3 Nf6 6. Be3 Bg4 7. Bb5 Steinitz: "A sort of Philidor's Defence, in which White is a move behind, has resulted from the opening. White would have done better on the fourth move to play c2–c3." **7. ... e×d4 8. Q×d4 0–0 9. Qd2 Ne5 10. N×e5 d×e5 11. Bd3 c6 12. f3 Be6 13. 0–0 Qc7 14. Kh1 Rad8 15. Qf2 b6 16. a4 Nd7 17. Qg3 Nc5** Steinitz: "17. ... Kh8 instead would have saved him

much trouble." **18. Bh6 Bf6 19. f4 N×d3 20. c×d3 Kh8 21. f×e5 Q×e5 22. Bf4 Qh5 23. e5 Bh4 24. Qe3 g5** Steinitz: "His king's bishop is a sore point of his game after this advance, and his king becomes much exposed." **25. Bg3 B×g3 26. Q×g3 Rd4 27. Ne4 Rfd8 28. Qf2** Steinitz: "More solid and, therefore, presumably more effective on its merits was 28. Nd6." **28. ... Qg6 29. Nd6 R×d3 30. a5 c5 31. a×b6 a×b6 32. Ra7 Rf8 33. Qe2 Rd4 34. g3 g4 35. Kg1 Bd5** Steinitz: "The simple 35. ... Qd3 would have given him a telling superiority of position, and he is already a pawn ahead for the ending." **36. e6?!** Almost a bluff. Better was 36. Rf6 Qd3 37. N×f7+ R×f7 38. Q×d3 R×d3 39. Ra×f7 B×f7 40. R×f7 Re3 41. Rb7, with equal play. **36. ... Q×e6** Steinitz: "Dropping into an ingeniously laid trap. There was no reason against 36. ... B×e6." **37. Rf×f7** Steinitz: "Charming play. He threatens R×h7+, followed by mate with the other rook." **37. ... R×f7 38. N×f7+ Kg8 39. Q×e6 B×e6 40. Ng5 Bf5 41. Kf2 h6** Steinitz: "Uselessly throwing away a pawn, whereas we believe that after 41. ... Rd2+ 42. Ke3 R×b2 followed by the advance of ...c5–c4, he could win without difficulty." **42. Nf7 Rd7?** 42. ... Kg7! 43. Nd6+ Kg6 44. N×f5 K×f5 still keeps some winning chances. **43. N×h6+ Kh7 44. R×d7+ B×d7 45. Nf7 Kg7 46. Ne5 Be6 47. Ke3 Kf6?** 47. ... b5 was probably more accurate: 48. Nd3 c4 49. Nb4 Kf6 50. Kd4 Bd7. **48. Kf4! b5 49. N×g4+ Ke7 50. Ne3 Kd6 51. Ke4 Bf7 52. Kf5 c4 53. g4 b4 54. Kf6 Bd5 55. g5 c3 56. b×c3 b×c3 57. g6 Be4 58. g7 Bh7 59. h4 Kc5 60. h5** Steinitz: "This goes very near to letting the victory slip, while 60. Kd4 would have given him time to advance the rook's pawn further, and then his winning was assured." Steinitz's assessment is incorrect. White still has a completely winning position. **60. ... Kd4 61. Nc2+ Ke4 62. h6?** 62. Kg5! was most precise: 62. ... Kd3 63. Kh6 Bg8 64. Na3 Bd5 65. Kg6 Kd2 66. h6+ Be4 67. Kf6 Bh7 68. Kf7. **62. ... Kf4 63. Nb4 Kg4 64. Nd5 Kh5 65. N×c3 K×h6 66. Nd5 Bg8 67. Ne7 Kh7 68. Ng6 Ba2 69. Ne5 Kg8** Steinitz: "At last he walks into the trap which his astute opponent had still held in reserve. The point of this very curious position is just that he should not move ...Kg8, but rather keep him at h6 or h7, and also, as long as possible, to guard g8 with the bishop at a distance." **70. Kg6** *(see diagram)*

70. ... Be6? Steinitz: "His game is lost now as White also threatens Nd7 or Ng4 with the same effect." Black had an interesting resource here, left unmentioned: 70. ... Bf7+! 71. Kh6 Bb3 72. Ng4

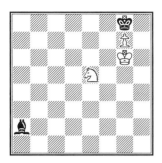

After
70. Kf6–g6

Kf7 73. Kh7 Ke7. **71. Nc6 Bf5+ 72. Kh6** Steinitz: "For if 72. ... Kf7, White still answers 73. Ne7." **1–0** [*tournament book*, pages 372–373]

272. A. Burn–Pollock [C77]
6th American Chess Congress, New York, Round 28, 29 April 1889

1. e4 e5 2. Nf3 Nc6 3. Bb5 a6 4. Ba4 Nf6 5. d3 Bc5 6. c3 b5 7. Bc2 d5 8. Qe2 0–0 9. e×d5 N×d5 Steinitz: "We prefer 9. ... Q×d5, followed as soon as possible by ...Bg4." **10. 0–0 Re8 11. Re1 Bb7** Steinitz: "This bishop is not well placed on this diagonal. 11. ... Bf5 would have had more bearing against the adverse queenside and also afforded more protection to his own kingside." **12. Nbd2 Nf4 13. Qf1 Bb6 14. Ne4** (*see diagram*)

After
14. Nd2–e4

14. ... f5?! Steinitz: "This loses a pawn without necessity. 14. ... Ng6 was certainly better." 14. ... Ne6!? 15. Be3 h6 16. b4 f5 was a good alternative too. **15. B×f4 f×e4** Steinitz: "15. ... e×f4 16. Bb3+ Kh8 17. Neg5 would have lost the exchange." **16. Bg5 Qd6 17. d×e4 h6 18. Rad1 Qg6 19. Bh4 Rf8 20. Bg3 Rae8 21. Nh4 Qh5 22. Qe2 Qg5 23. Qd2 Qh5 24. Nf5 g6?** Steinitz: "Black plays more desperately than was called for by the situation. Though he was a pawn behind, he held still a fair position. 24. ... Nd8, followed by ...Ne6, was his best play." **25. Bb3+** Steinitz: "Winning another pawn by force." **25. ... Kh8 26. Q×h6+**

Q×h6 27. N×h6 Bc8 28. Nf7+ Kg7 29. Ng5 Kh6 30. h4 Na5 31. Bd5 Bg4 32. Rd2 Rd8 33. Rc2 c6 **34. Be6** Steinitz: "He sees through the adverse clever scheme. Better than 34. Nf7+ Kh5 35. N×d8 c×d5 36. b4 Nc4 37. Nc6 d×e4, threatening ...e3, and Black, though the exchange behind, has still some fight left." 37. ... d4! was more problematic. **34. ... Rd3 35. Kh2 Bd1 36. Rc1 Bh5 37. f3 Rd2 38. Rcd1 Be3 39. Nf7+ Kh7 40. R×d2 B×d2 41. Rd1 Nc4 42. Kh3 g5** Steinitz: "It was all hopeless, and he could only speculate on some blunder on the part of the opponent, which, however, does not occur." **43. N×e5 N×e5 44. B×e5 Re8 45. Bf5+ Kg8 46. R×d2 R×e5 47. h×g5 1–0** [*tournament book*, page 246]

273. Pollock–J.M. Hanham [C41]
6th American Chess Congress, New York, Round 29, 3 May 1889

1. e4 e5 2. Nf3 d6 3. d4 Nd7 4. c3 Be7 5. Bc4 Ngf6 6. Qe2 0–0 7. h3 c6 8. Bb3 d5 9. e×d5 e4 10. Ne5 c×d5 11. Ng4 Steinitz: "11. Nd2, with the view of playing Nf1, was, we believe, preferable." **11. ... Nb6 12. Bf4 Be6 13. Nd2 a5 14. a4 Nfd7** Steinitz: "Anderssen's favorite retreat for the knight, viz. e8, would have served Black's purpose better, as it would have given no opportunity to the adversary on the seventeenth move to effect an exchange." **15. 0–0 f5 16. Ne5 Bg5 17. N×d7 N×d7 18. B×g5 Q×g5 19. f3 Rfe8** Steinitz: "If 19. ... e3, 20. f4 isolates the advanced pawn which must soon fall." **20. f×e4 f×e4 21. Rae1 Nf6 22. Qe3 Qg6 23. Rf2 Rac8 24. Bc2 Bd7** (*see diagram*)

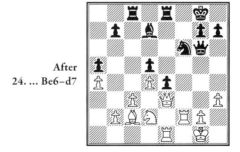

After
24. ... Be6–d7

25. c4! d×c4 26. N×e4 Bf5? Steinitz: "An error of which the opponent avails himself most beautifully. 26. ... Kh8 was his best defence. If, however, 26. ... N×e4, the game might have proceeded 27. B×e4 Qh5 28. g4 Qh4 29. Bd5+ Kh8 30. Q×e8+ R×e8 31. R×e8+, and mates next move." **27. N×f6+ g×f6 28. B×f5 R×e3 29. R×e3 Qg5 30. Rff3 Qh4 31. Re4 Qh6 32. B×c8 Qc1+**

33. Kh2 Q×b2 34. R×f6 Kg7 35. Rf3 h5 36. Re7+
Steinitz: "The mating net could have been drawn
tighter here by 36. Ref4." **36. ... Kg6 37. B×b7
Q×d4 38. Be4+ Kh6 39. Rh7+ Kg5 40. Rg7+
Kh6 41. Rg6+ Kh7 42. Rf7+** Steinitz: "A much
shorter and finer finish is here missed by 42. Rf4
Kh8 (42. ... Qa1 43. Rff6, etc.) 43. Rf5 Qd1 44. Bf3,
and wins." Steinitz did not mention 44. Rf8+ Kh7
45. Rg3+ Kh6 46. Rf6 (or h8) mate. **42. ... Kh8
43. Re6 Kg8 44. Rb7 Kf8 45. Ra6 Qd8 46. Rh6
Qd4 47. Rh8+ Q×h8 48. Rb8+ Kg7 49. R×h8**
and White won. **1–0** [*tournament book*, page 411]

274. J. Taubenhaus–Pollock [C83]
6th American Chess Congress,
New York, Round 30, 4 May 1889

**1. e4 e5 2. Nf3 Nc6 3. Bb5 a6 4. Ba4 Nf6
5. 0-0 N×e4 6. d4 b5 7. Bb3 d5 8. d×e5 Be6 9. c3
Be7 10. Re1 0-0 11. Nd4 N×d4 12. c×d4 Bf5!?
13. f3 Ng5 14. Nc3 c6 15. h4 Ne6** (*see diagram*)

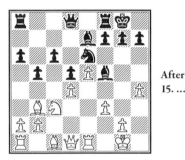

After
15. ... Ng5–e6

16. g4 Steinitz: "White had, we believe, the better game at this point, where he unwisely rushes at
a bait which his deep-sighted adversary has very
ingeniously thrown, and which draws him on to a
perilous line of play." **16. ... B×h4 17. g×f5 B×e1
18. f×e6 Qh4! 19. Be3?** Steinitz: "19. e7 forced
the adversary to draw, and this was probably his
best plan." **19. ... Bf2+ 20. Kf1 Rfe8 21. Ne2 R×e7**
offered a complicated position for both. **19. ...
Qg3+ 20. Kf1** Steinitz: "If 20. Kh1, 20. ... f×e6
21. Q×e1 Qh3+ 22. Kg1 R×f3 with a fine attack."
**20. ... f×e6 21. Q×e1 R×f3+ 22. Bf2 R×f2+
23. Q×f2 Rf8 24. Q×f8+ K×f8 25. Ne2?** Steinitz:
"A fatal error. 25. Rd1 left still much scope for a
good fight, in which Black, however, had the advantage with his two passed pawns on the kingside,
and many prospective opportunities of drawing by
perpetual check in case of emergency." **25. ... Qf3+
26. Kg1 Q×e2 0–1** [*tournament book*, pages 417–
418]

275. D.M. Martinez–Pollock [C77]
6th American Chess Congress,
New York, Round 31, 6 May 1889

**1. e4 e5 2. Nf3 Nc6 3. Bb5 a6 4. Ba4 Nf6 5. d3
Bc5 6. Nc3 0-0 7. 0-0 d6 8. Bg5 Ne7 9. Qd2 Be6
10. Nh4 Ng6 11. Nf5 B×f5 12. e×f5 Ne7
13. B×f6 g×f6** Steinitz: "Black has the better position after the exchanges with the strong centre
which he can form, and the open g-file that, as will
be seen, can be utilised for the attack with heavy
pieces." **14. g4 d5 15. Qh6 Qd6 16. Rad1 Kh8
17. Kh1 Rg8 18. f3 Rg5 19. Bb3 c6 20. Rde1
Rag8 21. Nd1 R8g7 22. c3 Bb6 23. Bc2 Ng8
24. Qh4 h5 25. Nf2 Rh7 26. Qg3 B×f2** Steinitz:
"26. ... Bc7, threatening ...Qd8 or Qe7, followed
by e5–e4, was much stronger." **27. R×f2 h×g4
28. f×g4 Nh6 29. Bd1 Rhg7 30. Rg1 N×f5
31. Qh3+ Rh7 32. Qf3 Nh4 33. Q×f6+ Q×f6
34. R×f6 Ng6 35. Rgf1 Nf4** Steinitz: "The more
simple 35. ... Kg8 was more safe too." **36. d4 Ne6
37. R1f5** Steinitz: "37. d×e5, followed by Bc2, was
better." **37. ... R×f5 38. g×f5 Ng5 39. Rd6 e×d4
40. f6 Ne6 41. Bg4 Rh6** (*see diagram*)

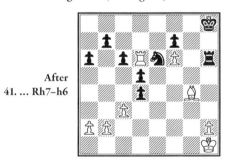

After
41. ... Rh7–h6

42. B×e6 R×f6 Steinitz: "A very clever resource
whereby he obtains pawns sufficient for the piece
given up, besides a strong attack." **43. Rd8+ Kg7
44. Bg4 d3 45. c4** Steinitz: "White defends with
remarkable ingenuity in an apparently hopeless
position." **45. ... d×c4** Steinitz: "No more than a
draw could have resulted after 45. ... d2 46. c×d5
Rf1+ 47. Kg2 d1Q 48. B×d1 R×d1 49. Rd7, etc."
**46. Kg2 c5 47. Bd1 Rg6+ 48. Kf2 Rf6+ 49. Kg2
Rg6+ 50. Kf2 Rf6+ ½–½** [*tournament book*,
pages 414–415]

276. Pollock–M. Judd [C51]
6th American Chess Congress,
New York, Round 32, 7 May 1889

1. e4 e5 2. Nf3 Nc6 3. Bc4 Bc5 4. b4 Bb6 5. b5

Na5 6. N×e5 Nh6 7. d4 d6 8. B×h6 d×e5 9. B×g7 Q×d4 Steinitz: "A new idea, and, as far as can be judged from the present game, a very good one, for it clearly and quickly equalizes forces and position, which, we believe, is not the case in most forms of this opening." 10. Q×d4 B×d4 11. B×h8 B×a1 12. Bd3 Steinitz: "Black likewise regains the pawn after 12. Bb3 Ke7 13. Bg7 Bd7 14. Bh6 B×b5, etc." 12. ... Ke7 13. Bg7 Be6 14. Bh6 B×a2 15. 0–0 Bd4 16. Bd2 Nc4 17. Bb4+ Nd6 18. c3 Bb6 19. c4 B×b1 Steinitz: "19. ... Bd4 at once was decidedly better." 20. R×b1 Bd4 21. c5 Ne8 22. Ba3 Kf6 23. Bc4 Ng7 24. Rb3 Ne6 25. Rf3+ Kg6 26. Rg3+ Kf6 27. Rf3+ Kg6 28. h4 Steinitz: "White is not satisfied with a draw, and the result does not justify his conclusion." 28. ... h5 29. Rf5 Re8 30. Be2 Rh8 31. g3 c6 32. b×c6 b×c6 33. Bc4 Rb8 34. Kg2 Rb1 Steinitz: "An excellent move which transfers the attack to Black." 35. Be2 Ng7 36. Rf3 Steinitz: "If 36. Rg5+?, 36. ... Kh6, followed by ...f6, and wins." 36. ... a5 37. Bd3 Rb3 Steinitz: "We would have preferred 37. ... Ra1 38. Bc4 Ne6 39. Kh3 (or 39. B×e6 f×e6, followed by ...a4, then ...Rb1 and ...Rb3, winning.) 39. ... Nd8, followed by ...f6 and ...Nb7." 38. Bc4 R×f3 39. K×f3 Kf6 40. Ke2 Ne6 41. f3 N×c5 42. B×c5 B×c5 43. g4 h×g4 44. f×g4 Be7 45. Bb3 Kg7 46. h5 Steinitz: "46. Ba4 at once, followed immediately by Kd3, would have drawn without difficulty." 46. ... f6 47. Ba4 c5 48. Kd3 Kh6 49. Kc4 Kg5 50. Bd7 Steinitz: "The true cause of his disaster, whereas 50. Kd5 K×g4 51. Ke6 Bf8 52. K×f6, would have drawn with ease." 50. ... Bf8 Steinitz: "The manner in which Black now wins, though bishops are of opposite colours and his own bishop is blocked, makes this ending one of the finest of that description." 51. Kb5 Kf4 52. Bf5 Ke3 53. h6 Kd4 54. h7 Bg7 55. Be6 K×e4 56. K×c5 Kf3 (see diagram)

After
56. ... Ke4–f3

57. Bf5? This was Pollock's fatal error. 57. Kd6 would have still provided substantial drawing chances: 57. ... Kf4 (57. ... e4 58. Ke7 e3 59. Bc4 e2

60. B×e2+ K×e2 61. Kf7 Bh8 62. Kg8 a4 63. K×h8 a3 64. Kg8 a2 65. h8Q a1Q) 58. Ke7 Kg5 59. Bc4 Kh6 60. Ke6 K×h7 61. Kf5 a4 62. g5 f×g5 63. K×g5. 57. ... e4 58. Kd5 e3 59. Ke6 e2 60. Kf7 Bh8 61. Kg8 e1Q 62. K×h8 a4 63. Bg6 Qe7 64. Kg8 a3 65. Bf7 K×g4 66. Kg7 f5 67. Kg8 Qe5 0–1 [tournament book, pages 345–346]

277. J. Mason–Pollock [C77]
6th American Chess Congress,
New York, Round 33, 8 May 1889

1. e4 e5 2. Nf3 Nc6 3. Bb5 a6 4. Ba4 Nf6 5. d3 Bc5 6. c3 b5 7. Bb3 d5 8. Qe2 0–0 9. Bg5 Steinitz: "The pinning is useless and even disadvantageous under the circumstances that Black's king's bishop is still in communication with the kingside and White is liable to be driven back and cut off from his queenside, as happens. 9. Nbd2 was better." 9. ... d×e4 10. d×e4 Qe7 11. Nbd2 Rb8 Steinitz: "11. ... h6 was preferable now that White could have been compelled either to exchange or to fall back on the kingside at h4." 12. Nf1 h6 13. Bh4 Steinitz: "He would have done better to retreat 13. Bd2." 13. ... Na5 14. Bc2 Steinitz: "Here is an instance to show that Bc2 is generally preferable in this form of opening on the 7th move." 14. ... b4 15. a3 Steinitz: "Ingenious, as Black obviously dare not capture either pawn without subjecting himself to the loss of a piece by the reply 16. b4." 15. ... b3 16. Bd3 Rb6! 17. h3 Steinitz: "White fails to see through the adverse highly-ingenious scheme. 17. Ne3 with the view of castling, was his only good play." 17. ... Rd8 18. g4 Rbd6 19. Rd1 19. 0–0–0 was White's only practical chance but Black's attack remains strong: 19. ... Nc4 20. Ng3. 19. ... Nc4! Steinitz: "Ingenious and powerful. He threatens ...N×b2." 20. Nd4 Steinitz: "There was hardly anything better, bad as this is." 20. ... e×d4 21. B×c4 d×c3 22. R×d6 Q×d6 23. b×c3 b2 24. Ba2 N×e4 25. Bg3 (see diagram)

After
25. Bh4–g3

25. ... Qe6 Steinitz: "A regular gem of a game on Mr. Pollock's part. The termination is charming." **26. Bb1** Steinitz: "If 26. Q×b2, 26. ... N×c3+, followed by ...Rd1 mate; and, of course, if 26. B×e6 b1Q+, and mates next move." **26. ... N×c3 27. Q×e6 Rd1 mate 0–1** [*tournament book*, pages 318–319; *PM*, page 154 (endgame)]

278. D.M. Martinez–Pollock [C40]
6th American Chess Congress, New York, Replayed Game, 9 May 1889

1. e4 e5 2. Nf3 f5 Steinitz: "Mr. Pollock is very partial to this dangerous opening which he sometimes adopts against the strongest players in important tournament games." **3. d4** Steinitz: "3. e×f5 brings about, by a transposition of moves, a variation of the Philidor, for the reply 3. ... d6 is considered best by all authorities, after which *The Modern Chess Instructor* proceeds with 4. d4 e4 5. Qe2 Qe7 6. Nfd2!, etc." **3. ... f×e4 4. N×e5 Nf6 5. Ng4** Steinitz: "The line of play initiated here and pursued in the next two moves is new, we believe, but hardly advisable, as Black's pawns form a strong centre that becomes all the more formidable after the exchange of queens." **5. ... d5 6. N×f6+ Q×f6 7. Qh5+ Qf7 8. Q×f7+ K×f7 9. Bf4 c6 10. Nd2 Bf5 11. 0-0-0 Nd7 12. Be2** (*see diagram*)

After
12. Bf1–e2

12. ... c5?! Steinitz: "With this advance Black gratuitously loosens his centre, and the weakness of his d-pawn gives him the inferior position. He ought to have played ...Be7, followed by ...Rf8 and ...Kg8, and his game was still slightly preferable." **13. Be3 Rc8 14. Nf1** Steinitz: "An excellent move for the defence as well as for the preparation of a counter-attack in the centre." **14. ... c×d4** Steinitz: "This capture is unwise. He ought to have abandoned his plan of operations against the adverse king, and secured his own game by ...c4." **15. B×d4 Bc5 16. Ne3** Steinitz: "Well played. He gains a pawn by force, with an excellent position." **16. ...**

Be6 17. B×c5 N×c5 Steinitz: "If 17. ... R×c5, White equally wins a pawn by 18. b4." **18. N×d5 Na4 19. Nf4** Steinitz: "White conducts the attack with vigour and accuracy." **19. ... B×a2** Steinitz: "The opponent threatened N×e6 followed by Bg4+, and he could scarcely do better than what he did. If 19. ... Bf5, 20. g4 g5 21. Nh3 etc.; or if 19. ... Rhe8, 20. Bb5, and wins; or if 19. ... Nc5, 20. b4 Nd3+ 21. B×d3 e×d3 22. R×d3 remaining with two pawns ahead." **20. Rd7+ Kf6** Steinitz: "The retreat of the king to the last row also left little hope of saving the game, for White might simply sweep off the pawns on the queenside and win easily." **21. Nh5+ Kg6 22. Rhd1** Steinitz: "It is rarely seen that such a fine position arises in the ending after the exchange of queens. White has very cleverly driven the opponent into a mating net. He threatens now an elegant mate by 23. R×g7+ Kf5 (or 23. ... Kh6 24. Rd6+, and mates next move) 24. Bg4+ Ke5 25. Rg5 mate." **22. ... Rc6 23. R×g7+ Kh6 24. g4 Rg6 25. h4** Steinitz: "A masterly finish." **25. ... R×g7 26. Rd6+ Rg6 27. g5 mate 1–0** [*tournament book*, pages 415–416; *ICM*, July 1889, pages 205–206]

279. Pollock–C.F. Burille [C42]
6th American Chess Congress, New York, Round 34, 10 May 1889

1. e4 e5 2. Nf3 Nf6 3. Bc4 N×e4 This idea could not have surprised Pollock since he was one of its earliest advocates. **4. Nc3 Nf6 5. N×e5 d5 6. Qe2 Be6 7. Bb3 c6 8. d4 Bd6 9. 0-0 0-0 10. Bg5 Re8 11. f4 Qb6 12. Qf2 Ne4** Steinitz: "His previous move would have greatly helped him out of his difficulties into which he got, chiefly owing to his omission on the third move to exchange knights, if he has now pursued what at any rate should have been its object: viz., 12. ... Bf5, and if 13. B×f6 g×f6 14. Qg3+ Kf8, etc. But he has now aggravated his bad situation by the text move." **13. N×e4 d×e4** (*see diagram*)

After
13. ... d5×e4

14. c4! Steinitz: "This fine move prepares a victorious onslaught on either of the wings, and Black cannot cover both." **14. ... Bc7** Steinitz: "If 14. ... Qc7, 15. f5 Bc8 16. N×f7, with an excellent attack." 14. ... Na6 was possible: 15. Kh1 B×e5 (15. ... f6 16. B×f6 g×f6 17. c5) 16. f×e5 Nb4 17. Qg3 Q×d4 18. Bf6 g6 19. Qf4 Qc5 20. Q×e4 a5, although White's position is superior. **15. f5! B×e5 16. c5 Qc7 17. f×e6 B×h2+ 18. Kh1 f6 19. B×f6 Qf4 20. Be5 1–0** Steinitz: "Wit and science are combined in White's play. He wins a piece now, for he threatens e7+, followed by Rf8+, and mates next move" [*tournament book*, pages 407–408].

280. M. Weiss–Pollock [C77]
6th American Chess Congress, New York, Round 35, 11 May 1889

Steinitz: "For winning this game Mr. Pollock was awarded the special prize of $50 donated by Professor Isaac L. Rice for the most brilliant game in the second round." **1. e4 e5 2. Nf3 Nc6 3. Bb5 a6 4. Ba4 Nf6 5. d3 b5 6. Bb3 Bc5 7. c3 d5 8. e×d5 N×d5 9. Qe2** Steinitz: "The opening is the same as occurred in two match games between Anderssen and Morphy, excepting that Anderssen retreated his Bc2 on the 6th move. White has obtained the superior position chiefly owing to Black's 7th move, ...d5, which loosens the e-pawn. Instead of the text move we would prefer, however, 9. 0–0 Bg4 10. h3 Bh5 (or 10. ... B×f3 11. Q×f3 Nce7 12. Re1, with a fine attack.) 11. g4 Bg6 12. Qe2, winning at least a pawn with a very good game." **9. ... 0–0** Pollock: "We base this form of development on the principle that 'counter-attack is the soul of defence,' v. Anderssen vs. Morphy, games II and IV of match." **10. Qe4 Be6** Pollock: "Black was fully alive to the claims of soundness of either knight to e7 here, for if now 11. Ng5 g6! (if 11. ... f5 12. N×e6 f×e4 13. N×d8, leaving the knight pinned)." **11. N×e5** Steinitz: "He could have obtained much the best of the game by 11. Ng5 g6 12. N×e6, etc." **11. ... N×e5 12. Q×e5** (see diagram)

12. ... Nb4!! Steinitz: "The soundness of this sacrifice is questionable." Pollock: "This rather dazzling idea occurred to me, as it were, by inspiration; curiously enough, some of the ensuing positions were at first analyzed as an effect of ...Nf4. A good many critics insist on the absolute soundness of such an adoption, forgetting the attractions of 'to venture,' the brilliancy prize, and the time-

After 12. Qe4×e5

limit." In fact, Pollock's sacrifice was indeed quite correct. **13. 0–0** Steinitz: "For after 13. c×b4 B×b4+ 14. Kd1 Q×d3+ 15. Bd2 we think that the attack against White's king could not be sustained, and Black had only two pawns for the piece, and, therefore, the worst as regards material." Analysis shows Black's attack had actual strength to it. For instance, 15. ... Rad8! 16. Qe3 Qd6 17. Kc1 B×b3 18. a×b3 Rfe8 19. B×b4 Q×b4 20. Qf3 Qc5+ 21. Nc3 (21. Qc3? Q×f2) 21. ... b4 22. Kc2 b×c3 23. b×c3 h6 and the White king remains rather exposed. Pollock: "We shall be happy to say all we know of the consequences of 13. c×b4, on receipt of stamped envelope." **13. ... N×d3 14. Qh5** Steinitz: "Not good. 14. Qg3 Bd6 15. Qf3 would have been superior." **14. ... B×b3 15. a×b3 Re8 16. Nd2** Pollock: "Black's intention was to play ... Re5 to defend the bishop, and next ...N×f2." White probably had to go for the uncomfortable 16. Be3 B×e3 17. f×e3 Qe7 18. Kh1 Qe6 with a poor position. **16. ... Qe7 17. b4** Steinitz: "He had no means of saving the pawn, for if 17. Nf3, 17. ... N×f2, and White dare not take with the rook on account of ...Qe1+ and mate next move." **17. ... B×f2+!** Steinitz: "Beautiful play. It will be easily seen that White cannot recapture the two pieces on account of the mate in two moves impending afterward by ...Qe3+ and ...Qe1 mate." **18. Kh1** (see diagram)

After 18. Kg1–h1

18. ... Qe1!! Steinitz: "The prelude to a most ingenious and splendidly conceived line of attack."

19. h3 N×c1! Steinitz: "This sacrifice of the queen for no more than two pieces is based on a most profound and brilliant idea, such as has very rarely occurred in actual play." **20. R×e1 R×e1+ 21. Kh2 Bg1+ 22. Kg3** 22. Kh1 loses to 22. ... Bc5+! 23. Kh2 Bd6+ 24. g3 Rae8 25. Qf3 R8e2+ 26. Qg2 R×g2+ 27. K×g2 Re2+. **22. ... Re3+** Pollock: "Here we finally determined to go in for a checkmate, and the most problematic one we could conceive of." **23. Kg4** Pollock: "The three other alternatives expose White to another check and immediate ruin." Steinitz: "Best. If 23. Nf3, 23. ... Ne2+ 24. Kg4 Re4+ 25. Kg5 Be3+ 26. Kf5 Ng3 mate." **23. ... Ne2! 24. Nf1** 24. Qd5 would have lost to 24. ... h5+! 25. Kg5 (25. K×h5 Nf4+; 25. Q×h5 Rg3+ 26. Kh4 g5+ 27. Q×g5+ R×g5 28. K×g5 Be3+) 25. ... Rg3+ 26. Kf5 Re8! 27. Nf3 Be3!; 24. Qf5 loses quickly too to a similar idea: 24. ... h5+ 25. Kg5 f6+ 26. Kg6 Re5. **24. ... g6 25. Qd5** Steinitz: "Very tempting but no doubt overlooking the beautiful surprise which Black has in store. His best play was 25. Qh6, with the following probable continuation: 25. ... f5+ 26. Kg5 Rf8 27. Q×f8+ (but if 27. R×a6, 27. ... Rg3+ 28. N×g3 (28. Kh4 R×g2) 28. ... Be3+ 29. Kh4 g5+ and wins.) 27. ... K×f8 28. N×e3, followed by Kf6, with legitimate hopes of drawing." In fact, Pollock has a stylish win even after 25. Qh6: 25. ... Rd3!! 26. h4 (26. Kg5 Re8 27. R×a6 Ng3 28. N×g3 Be3+ 29. Kh4 B×h6) 26. ... Re8 27. g3 Re4+ 28. Kh3 Nf4+ 29. Q×f4 R×f4 30. Kg2 Rf2+ 31. K×g1 R×b2. **25. ... h5+! 26. Kg5** *(see diagram)*

After
26. Kg4–g5

26. ... Kg7! Steinitz: "Truly magnificent." This forces a mate in nine. **27. N×e3** Steinitz: "There was actually no defence. If 27. Q×a8 (or 27. Qd7 Re5+ 28. Kh4 Kh6, and wins.) 27. ... f6+ 28. Kh4 Bf2+ 29. g3 R×g3, and White has only one useless check by sacrificing the queen, after which mate follows by ...Rg4+ or by ...B×g3+ if N×g3." **27. ... f6+** and "mates in two moves." **0–1** Steinitz: "Mr. Pollock's play from the 17th move renders this

game one of the finest monuments of Chess ingenuity, and altogether it belongs to the most brilliant gems in the annals of practical play. The mate is effected after 28. Kh4 by 28. ... Bf2+ 29. g3 B×g3 mate." [*tournament book*, pages 2–3; *Albany Sunday Express*, June 30, 1889; *Baltimore Sunday News*, July 7, 1889; *BCM*, July 1889, pages 284–285; *ICM*, May 1889, pages 142–143; *New York Clipper* of June 8, 1889, published this game and called it "magnificent beyond praise" and called 12. ... Nb4 an "electric coup."]

281. Pollock–G.H.D. Gossip [C54] 6th American Chess Congress, New York, Round 36, 13 May 1889

1. e4 e5 2. Nf3 Nc6 3. Bc4 Bc5 4. c3 Nf6 5. d3 d6 6. h3 Be6 7. Bb3 Qe7 8. Be3 B×e3 9. f×e3 0–0 10. c4 Nh5 Steinitz: "Useless, as he cannot enter at g3 after White's reply." **11. g4 Nf6 12. Nc3 Rae8 13. Qe2 Nd7 14. 0–0–0 Nc5 15. Bc2 Nb4 16. Bb1** Steinitz: "He ought to have carefully guarded his bishop against being exchanged for the knight, as the majority of his pawns stand on white squares, and his opponent retained a bishop commanding that colour." **16. ... Bd7 17. d4 Na4 18. Qd2 N×c3 19. Q×c3 Nc6 20. Bc2 a5 21. Kb1** 21. a3 a4 22. Kb1 was more accurate. **21. ... Nb4 22. d×e5? N×c2 23. Q×c2 d×e5** *(see diagram)*

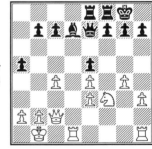

After
23. ... d6×e5

24. Rd5 Steinitz: "The pawn does him no good, as the opponent is sure to recover it, with the stronger position." **24. ... Bc6! 25. R×a5 Qf6 26. Nd2** Steinitz: "If 26. Rf1, 26. ... Qh6, etc." **26. ... Qf2 27. Rd1 Q×e3 28. Ra3 Qe2 29. Rg3 Rd8 30. Rgg1 Rd4 31. Rge1 Qg2 32. Kc1 Rfd8 33. h4 Q×g4 34. Rg1 Qf4 35. Rge1 Q×h4 36. b4** Steinitz: "The fate of the game was decided even without this blunder." 36. Re2 Qf4 37. b3 Bd7 and the game is over. **36. ... R×d2 0–1** [*tournament book*, pages 409–410]

282. J.W. Showalter–Pollock [C80]
6th American Chess Congress, New York, Round 37, 14 May 1889

1. e4 e5 2. Nf3 Nc6 3. Bb5 a6 4. Ba4 Nf6 5. 0-0 N×e4 6. d4 b5 7. Bb3 d5 8. d×e5 Ne7 9. Re1 Steinitz: "Threatening 10. R×e4 and 11. B×f7+." **9. ... Bb7** Steinitz: "9. ... Nc5 was better." **10. Be3 Nf5 11. c3 N×e3 12. R×e3 Bc5** Steinitz: "12. ... c5 was the right play." **13. Nd4 Qg5 14. Qe2 Bb6 15. Nd2 N×d2 16. Q×d2 0-0 17. Qe2 Rae8 18. Re1** *(see diagram)*

After
18. Ra1–e1

18. ... f5 Steinitz: "It is difficult to see how he could expect any good from this, while it was very obvious that White's strong centre pawn must become dangerous. 18. ... c5, with the view of soon following it up by ...Bc7, was clearly superior." **19. Rg3 Qf4 20. Rf3 Qg4 21. h3 Qh5 22. e6 Re7 23. Qe5 B×d4 24. c×d4 c6 25. g4 Qg6 26. Bc2 Bc8 27. R×f5 R×f5 28. B×f5 Qh6 29. Qd6 Qf6 30. Qd8+ 1-0** Steinitz: "The termination has been vigorously conducted by White who now wins the interposing queen by the reply 31. B×h7+" [*tournament book*, page 397].

283. Pollock–D.G. Baird [C45]
6th American Chess Congress, New York, Round 38, 15 May 1889

1. e4 e5 2. Nf3 Nc6 3. d4 e×d4 4. N×d4 Qf6 5. Nf3 Steinitz: "A remarkable novelty." **5. ... Bc5 6. Nc3 Bb4** Steinitz: "As he cannot well afterward exchange, this bishop is still worse placed now. 6. ... Nd4 was his best play." **7. Bd2 Nge7 8. a3 Ba5 9. Bd3 d6 10. h3 Ne5 11. N×e5 Q×e5 12. 0-0 a6** Steinitz: "Much inferior to 12. ... c6, with the view of playing ...Bc7." **13. Kh1 B×c3 14. f4 Qf6 15. B×c3 Qh6 16. f5! Nc6 17. Qe1 Bd7 18. Qg3 Rg8 19. Bc4! Kf8 20. Rad1 Re8 21. Rf4 Ne5 22. Rh4 Q×h4** Steinitz: "The result justifies his speculating on making a better fight with two pieces

for the queen than with a pawn behind and a very bad game after 22. ... Qf6 23. R×h7." **23. Q×h4 N×c4** *(see diagram)*

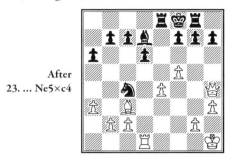

After
23. ... Ne5×c4

24. e5 Steinitz: "Of course, an error. 23. Re1 was the right play." After 24. b3! Ne3 (24. ... N×a3 25. f6 Nb5 26. f×g7+ R×g7 27. B×g7+ K×g7) 25. Rd3 White has an easy win. 24. f6!? was better than the text as well. **24. ... Ne3 25. Re1 N×f5 26. Qb4 Bc6 27. Kh2 h5! 28. e×d6 c×d6 29. Re5** 29. R×e8+ K×e8 30. Qf4 g6 31. g4 was, once again, a facile win. **29. ... R×e5 30. B×e5 Ke7 31. g4 h×g4 32. h×g4 Kd7 33. Bf4** 33. Qf4! was better. **33. ... g5 34. g×f5 g×f4 35. Q×f4 Rg2+ 36. Kh3 R×c2 37. Qd4 Rc5 38. Qf6 Bd5 39. Qd4 Bb3 40. Qb4 Rb5** Steinitz: "Black has guarded all his points, and the adverse king cannot gain any effective entrance into his game. His defence with two pieces against the queen is a very fine specimen of play in a position of that character." **41. Qe4 ½-½** [*tournament book*, pages 401–402]

284. Pollock–D.G. Baird [C50]
6th American Chess Congress, New York, Replayed Game, 17 May 1889

1. e4 e5 2. Nf3 Nc6 3. Bc4 Be7 4. d4 d6 5. c3 Nf6 6. Qd3 0-0 7. d5 Nb8 8. Bb3 a5 Steinitz: "We disapprove on general principles of White's early advance on the seventh move. Black's retort at this juncture is all the more feeble, as he could have obtained the superiority of position at once by 8. ... Nfd7 9. Bc2 (or 9. Be3 Na6) 9. ... Nc5 10. Qe2 f5, etc." **9. h3 h6 10. Be3 Nh7 11. g4 c5 12. c4 a4 13. Bc2 Bd7 14. Nc3 Na6 15. a3 Nc7** *(see diagram)*

16. B×c5!? d×c5 17. N×e5 Steinitz: "He might have been well satisfied with recovering the piece and getting the superior game by 17. d6, but the plan adopted is of doubtful value." **17. ... Bh4** Steinitz: "He should have not allowed his adversary to free at once his e-pawn for action. 17. ...

After
15. ... Nc7

Be8 18. Nf3 Bh4 19. e5 g6 made it more difficult for the opponent to proceed with his attack." **18. N×d7 Q×d7 19. e5 g6 20. 0–0–0** Steinitz: "It was hardly advisable to give up a pawn, and he could well adopt 20. Ke2 with the view of playing 21. f4 soon." Steinitz's 20. Ke2 is just as provocative as Pollock's 20. 0–0–0: 20. ... b5! 21. f4 Rab8 22. Rab1 Rfd8 23. Rhd1 Nf8 24. Qe3. **20. ... B×f2 21. d6** 21. e6 N×e6 22. Qe2 Bd4 23. d×e6 Q×e6 24. Q×e6 f×e6 25. B×g6 Ng5 creates no problems for Black. **21. ... Ne6 22. Nd5 Nd4** Steinitz: "22. ... Qd8 was the simplest defence, but if he in-

tended to give up the exchange, it was only justifiable in this position if he had played ...Bd4, instead of the text move." **23. Nb6 Qd8 24. N×a8 Qg5+ 25. Kb1 R×a8 26. Rhf1 Bh4 27. Qe4 N×c2?** Steinitz: "He abandons his stronghold in the adverse centre without cause, ...Qd8, which made room for ...Ng5, was by far better." **28. K×c2 Rf8 29. Rd5 Qd8 30. R×c5 Ng5 31. Q×b7 Ne6 32. Rd5 Qc8 33. Qb5** Steinitz: "33. Q×c8, followed by Kc3, would have worked quicker toward the winning end." **33. ... Qa8 34. Qa5 Qc6 35. Kc3 Rb8 36. Rb5 Rc8 37. Q×a4 Qe4 38. Rd1 Be1+ 39. Kb3 Nd4+** 39. ... Ra8! was much stronger: 40. Q×a8+ Q×a8 41. R×e1 Nd4+ 42. Ka2 N×b5 43. c×b5 Qd5+ 44. Kb1 Q×b5 45. Rd1 Qd7 and Black has excellent winning chances. **40. Ka2 N×b5 41. Q×b5 Bh4 42. d7 Rd8 43. Qd5 Qf4 44. c5 Qf2 45. c6 Rb8 46. d8Q+** Pollock: "One of Mr. Pollock's bright surprises. Black cannot afterward stop the adverse c-pawn from queening." **46. ... B×d8 47. Q×d8+ R×d8 48. R×d8+ Kh7 49. c7 1–0** [*tournament book*, pages 402–403]

Part Two, Section IV
(May 31, 1889–March 1890)

In Brooklyn, Baltimore and Washington (May 1889–February 1890)

285. P. Richardson & G.F. Murray-Pollock & C.A. Gilberg [C25]
Consultation Game, Brooklyn, Brooklyn Chess Club, 31 May 1889

1. e4 e5 2. Nc3 Nc6 3. f4 e×f4 4. Nf3 g5 5. h4 g4 6. Ng5 h6 7. N×f7 K×f7 8. d4 f3 9. g×f3 Be7 10. Bc4+ Ke8 11. Be3 B×h4+ 12. Kd2 Na5 13. Bd3 d6 14. f×g4 Bg5 15. Qe2 c5! 16. d×c5 d×c5 17. Nd5 c4!? 18. Qh2? Weaker than 18. B×c4 B×e3+ 19. K×e3 Qg5+ 20. Kd3 Nf6 21. Raf1 N×g4 22. Kc3 Qe5+ 23. Kd2 Qd4+ 24. Bd3 Nc4+ 25. Ke1 N×b2 26. Bb5+. **18. ... B×e3+ 19. N×e3** 19. K×e3 does not solve White's problems: 19. ... Qg5+ 20. Kf2 c×d3 21. Nc7+ Kf7 22. N×a8 Nf6 23. Raf1 d2 24. Qc7+ Kg6 25. Kg2 B×g4 and Black wins. **19. ... Qg5 20. Qc7 Nf6** *(see diagram)*

After
20. ... Ng8–f6

21. e5 21. B×c4 loses to 21. ... N×e4+ 22. Ke2 Rh7! **21. ... Q×e3+! 22. K×e3 Nd5+ 23. Kf3 N×c7 24. Bf5 Nc6 25. Ke4 Be6 26. Rad1 Ke7 27. Rd6 Rad8 28. Rhd1 h5 29. g5 Rhf8 30. B×e6**

N×e6 **31. Kd5 Rf5 32. R×d8 R×e5+ 33. K×c4 b5+ 34. Kc3 Nc×d8 0–1** [*Brooklyn Daily Eagle*, June 6, 1889; *Boston Weekly Post*, June 21, 1889]

286. Pollock–J.H. Park [C29]
Simultaneous Exhibition (12 Boards), Brooklyn, Brooklyn Chess Club, 31 May 1889

1. e4 e5 2. Nc3 Nf6 3. f4 e×f4 4. e5 Qe7 5. Qe2 Ng8 6. d4 Nc6 7. Nf3 d6? 8. B×f4 8. Nd5! was stronger yet more difficult to calculate in a simultaneous exhibition: 8. ... N×d4 (8. ... Qd7 9. e×d6+) 9. N×e7 N×e2 10. Nd5 c6 11. Nc7+ Kd8 12. N×a8 N×c1 13. R×c1 Be6 14. Ng5. **8. ... Bg4 9. Nd5! B×f3 10. g×f3 N×d4 11. Qe4?** 11. Qf2 was correct: 11. ... Qd7 12. Q×d4 c6 13. Bh3! **11. ... Qh4+ 12. Kd1 Ne6** *(see diagram)* 12. ... 0–0–0 was mandatory.

After
12. ... Nd4–e6

13. e×d6? Pollock missed the pretty 13. N×c7+! Kd8 (13. ... N×c7 14. e×d6+ Kd7 15. d×c7; 13. ... Kd7 14. N×e6 f×e6 15. Q×b7+ Kd8 16. Bb5, with a quick mate.) 14. e×d6 B×d6 15. N×e6+ f×e6 16. B×d6 Q×e4 17. f×e4. **13. ... 0–0–0! 14. Qa4** 14. Bd2 Q×e4 15. f×e4 B×d6 16. Bh3 was White's

337

only way to fight for a draw. **14. ... R×d6 15. c4 Q×f4 16. Q×a7** Still insufficient, but better than the text, was 16. Qe8+ Rd8 17. Q×d8+ K×d8 18. N×f4 N×f4. **16. ... Qd4+ 17. Q×d4 N×d4 18. Bh3+ f5 19. Re1 Nf6 20. Re5 N×d5 21. c×d5 g6 22. Rc1 N×f3 23. Re8+ Rd8 24. Re6 R×d5+ 25. Ke2 Nd4+ 26. Kf1 Bh6 0–1** [*Cincinnati Commercial Tribune*, June 22, 1889]

287. Pollock–J. Uhthoff
Baltimore, Baltimore Chess Association, July 1889

White to move

1. R1h6 B×c3 1. ... Qe7? loses to 2. Qh2!! (Even stronger than 2. Rh8+ B×h8 3. R×h8+ Kg7 4. R×e8 Q×e2 5. R×e2 Nd3+ 6. Kd1 a5) 2. ... Qd8 and now either 3. Qh5 or 3. Rg6. **2. R×f6 R×e2 3. B×c3?** This loses immediately, but Pollock had a drawing solution: 3. Rf×f7+! Kg8 (3. ... Ke8? fails to 4. R×c7! Kd8 5. Ra7 B×d2+ 6. Kd1) 4. B×c3 b×c3 5. Rhg7+ Kh8 6. Rh7+ Kg8. **3. ... b×c3 4. Rf×f7+ Ke8! 0–1** [*Baltimore Sunday News*, July 28, 1889]

288. Pollock & J. Hinrichs–
H.E. Bird & J. Uhthoff [C51]
Consultation Game,
Baltimore Chess Association, July 1889

1. e4 e5 2. Nf3 Nc6 3. Bc4 Bc5 4. b4 B×b4 5. c3 Bc5 6. d4 e×d4 7. c×d4 Bb6 8. 0–0 Pollock: "One of Bird's favorite lines of attack (revived by him lately, but practised years ago by Boden and MacDonnell) is to proceed with 8. Bb2 and postpone castling, in some cases even castling on the queenside later on." **8. ... d6 9. Nc3 Bg4 10. Qa4** Pollock: "The old Fraser attack, long discarded in favor of 10. Bb5 but adopted by the White allies for the sake of variety." **10. ... Kf8** Pollock: "The retreat 10. ... Bd7 leads into the

mazes of the historical Fraser–Mortimer attack analyzed in nearly every modern work on chess." **11. d5 Na5 12. Be2 B×f3 13. g×f3 Ne7 14. Kh1 h5 15. Be3 Ng6 16. Rac1 Ne5 17. Rg1** Pollock: "The development of White's game is thorough and in accordance with the principles of the gambit." **17. ... Qh4** Pollock: "A somewhat premature rally, resulting in a slight loss of time." **18. Rg3** Pollock: "Threatening Bg5. 18. Rg2 would also be good play." **18. ... Qe7 19. Nb5 h4?** 19. ... a6 20. Nd4 g6 was better. **20. Rgg1 a6 21. Nd4 Qd7** 21. ... g6? runs into 22. f4! Nec4 23. R×c4! N×c4 24. Q×c4 Q×e4+ 25. Bf3. **22. Qa3** 22. Qb4! Qd8 23. f4 Nd7 24. e5 Nc5 25. f5 was more forceful. **22. ... Rh7** 22. ... c5 had to be tried even if White keeps a clear edge after 23. Nf5 g6 24. f4 Nec4 25. B×c4 g×f5 26. Qb2. **23. f4 Ng6** (*see diagram*)

After 23. ... Ne5–g6

24. f5 The White players missed a powerful continuation here: 24. R×g6! B×d4 (24. ... f×g6 25. Ne6+ Kg8 26. B×b6 c×b6 27. Rc7 Qe8 28. Q×d6 was actually mentioned by Pollock in his game notes adding the following: "The White allies adopt a brilliant but less decisive course.") 25. B×d4 f×g6 26. Q×a5 Rc8 27. e5. **24. ... Ne7** Pollock: "If 24. ... Ne5, 25. f4 and the horse is lost." **25. Bg4 Qe8 26. f6! g×f6 27. Ne6+?!** Pollock: "A daring sacrifice to occur in consultation chess." 27. Nf5! was best. **27. ... f×e6 28. B×e6 Qh5 29. B×b6 c×b6 30. Rc7 Re8 31. Qc3** 31. R×e7!? K×e7 32. Qc3 runs into 32. ... Nc4! **31. ... Qe5 32. Q×e5** Pollock: "Best. Such is the strength of White's position that they can afford to exchange queens, although a piece and a pawn minus." Pollock also noted that 32. Rg8+ N×g8 33. R×h7 runs into 33. ... R×e6. **32. ... f×e5 33. f4** 33. Rg8+ N×g8 34. R×h7 Re7 35. B×g8 R×h7 36. B×h7 b5 is pretty hopeless too. **33. ... e×f4 34. e5** Pollock awarded an exclamation point for White's 33rd move and two for White's 34th move. In truth, Black's position is winning regardless of White's energetic attempts. **34. ... d×e5 35. d6 Nac6** Pollock: "The *coup juste*; the defense has been conducted with great skill." **36. R×b7 Rg7?** It was the Black players' turn to miss a clear win: 36. ... Ng6! 37. R×h7 R×e6 38. d7 Rd6 39. Rc1 Nge7. **37. R×g7 K×g7 38. Bd7 Rd8 39. B×c6 R×d6 40. R×e7+ Kf6 41. Rh7** Pollock: "The Black party has not included this near move in their calculations. The game is now a draw, by correct play." **41. ... Kg5 42. Bf3 Rd2 43. Rh5+ Kf6 44. R×h4 R×a2 45. Rh6+ Kf5 46. Rh5+ Kf6** Pollock: "Here the game was drawn by mutual consent." ½–½ [*Baltimore Sunday News*, July 14, 1889; *St. John Globe*, August 2, 1889]

289. A.W. Schofield & E.L. Torsch–Pollock [C44]
Consultation Match, Game 2, September 1889

1. e4 e5 2. Nf3 Nc6 3. d4 N×d4 4. N×e5 Ne6 5. Bc4 Nf6 6. Nc3 Bb4 7. 0-0 B×c3 8. b×c3 0-0 Pollock: "The opening is uncommon. Black cannot take the e-pawn on account of 9. B×e6 followed by 10. Qh5+." **9. Qe2 d6 10. Nd3 Re8 11. f3 Bd7 12. Bb3 Bb5 13. Bb2 d5** Pollock called this "weak." **14. Qf2 B×d3 15. c×d3 Nf4 16. Rad1 Re5?!** A dubious idea. 16. ... c6 was safer. **17. Qh4 Ne2+ 18. Kh1** Pollock: "If 18. Kf2, the queen is lost." **18. ... Rh5** 18. ... Nh5!? 19. Q×d8+ R×d8 20. g3 Nh×g3+ 21. h×g3 N×g3+ 22. Kg2 N×f1 23. R×f1 d×e4 24. f×e4 was unclear. **19. Qf2 Qd6?** (*see diagram*) 19. ... Nf4 had to be played but White kept the upper hand with 20. c4 d×c4 21. d×c4 Qe7 22. e5!

After
19. ... Qd8–d6

20. g4! Ng3+ 21. Kg1 Rh3 22. Rfe1 Pollock: "The allies very skilfully win a piece. Black's attack was too precipitate and his knight is securely caged." 22. h×g3? R×g3+ 23. Kh1 Rh3+ leads to a perpetual. **22. ... Nd7 23. f4 Qh6 24. Re3 N×e4 25. d×e4 1-0** [*Baltimore Sunday News*, October 20, 1889]

290. Pollock–A.W. Schofield & E.L. Torsch [C52]
Consultation Match, Game 4, Baltimore, September 1889

1. e4 e5 2. Nf3 Nc6 3. Bc4 Bc5 4. b4 B×b4 5. c3 Ba5 6. d4 e×d4 7. 0-0 d6 8. c×d4 Pollock: "White can get a strong attack by 8. Ng5 Ne5 9. N×f7 (or 9. c×d4 N×c4 10. Qa4+) 9. ... N×f7 10. B×f7+ K×f7 11. Qh5+, etc." **8. ... Bg4 9. Bb5** Pollock: "Or 9. Qa4 Bd7 10. Qb3, followed by Nc3 with a favourable position." **9. ... Bd7 10. e5 Nce7** Pollock: "10. ... N×e5 would cost Black a piece in the following curious manner: 11. Qe2 B×b5 12. Q×b5+ Nc6 (12. ... c6 13. Qe2) 13. d5 a6 14. Qa4 b5 15. Qa3 Nb4 16. Q×a5 Nc2 17. Qc3." **11. B×d7+ Q×d7 12. Ng5 Nh6 13. Ne4 Nhf5 14. g4 N×d4** Pollock: "Highly ingenious, as if White took the knight the allies would have drawn by perpetual check, making their score 2½–1½, thus ½ nearer the goal of 5, with a pawn and move partie to follow." **15. e×d6 c×d6 16. Bb2 Nec6 17. h3?** Too risky. If Pollock wanted to keep the game going (instead of settling for a draw with 17. B×d4), he should have tried 17. Na3 Bb6 18. Nc2. **17. ... Bb6 18. Nbc3 h5?** Pollock: "The allies are now two pawns to the good. Here, ...d5 was not only essential, but left them with a distant superiority every way." 18. ... f5! was very powerful. **19. Nd5** Pollock: "As a matter of course." **19. ... 0-0-0 20. N×b6+ a×b6 21. B×d4 h×g4 22. B×b6 f5** (*see diagram*)

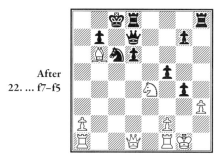

After
22. ... f7–f5

23. Qa4! Kb8 24. Ng3 Pollock: "After this solid defensive move (the knight has an eye on the weak h1 square!) White gets time to use his rooks and bring the contest to a rather pretty finale." **24. ... Rde8 25. Rfc1 R×h3** 25. ... f4 loses to the excellent 26. Rc3! f×g3 27. Ra3 g×f2+ 28. Kg2 g×h3+ 29. Kh2. **26. Rc3 Re4 27. N×e4 f×e4 28. Ba7+ Kc8 29. Be3 g3 1-0** Pollock: "Dies biting like a game and hardshell market crab. White now mates by force in eight moves, all checks. The mate is instructive and very pretty." [*Baltimore Sunday News*, January 12, 1890]

291. Pollock–A.W. Schofield & E.L. Torsch [C30]
Consultation Match, Game 8, Baltimore, October 1889

Pollock: "The consultation match at the Rooms resulted as follows: Pollock, 5; Schofield and Torsch, 3. The Allies won the first two games played, but the tide then turned, and subsequently they only added two draws to their score. Most of the eight games were interesting, original and keenly contested. The final one was very eccentric." **1. e4 e5 2. f4 Bc5 3. f×e5?** Pollock's "eccentric" comment cited above explains this move. **3. ... Qh4+ 4. g3 Q×e4+ 5. Qe2 Q×h1 6. Nf3 Nc6 7. c3 Nge7 8. d4 Bb6 9. Kd2 Nf5 10. Bg2 N×g3 11. h×g3 Qh5 12. a4 0-0 13. b4 a5 14. b5 Ne7 15. Ba3 Re8 16. B×e7 R×e7 17. c4 d6 18. Nc3 Qh6+ 19. Kc2 Bf5+ 20. Kb3 c6 21. Rh1** (*see diagram*)

After 21. Rh1

21. ... Qg6? 21. ... Qe6 22. d5 Qc8 was still winning for Black. **22. Nh4 Qe6 23. N×f5 Q×f5 24. Be4 Qe6** 24. ... Qg5 25. B×h7+ Kf8 26. Be4 g6 27. Rh8+ Kg7 28. R×a8 Q×g3 was hopeless as well. **25. B×h7+ Kf8 26. Bf5 1-0** [*Baltimore Sunday News*, December 29, 1889]

292. Pollock–Prangley [C25]
Simultaneous Exhibition (14 Boards), Baltimore, 26 September 1889

1. e4 e5 2. Nc3 Nc6 3. f4 e×f4 4. Nf3 g5 5. d4 Bg7 6. Bc4 d6 7. h4 h6 8. h×g5 h×g5 9. R×h8 B×h8 10. Ne5?! d×e5 11. Qh5 Qf6 12. Nd5 Qg7 13. N×c7+ Kd8 Even stronger was 13. ... Kf8 14. N×a8 Nf6 15. Qh2 N×e4. **14. N×a8 e×d4?** 14. ... N×d4 15. Bd3 Nf6 16. Qh2 Qf8! was Black's

best way forward for an advantage. **15. Bd2 Ne5 16. Ba5+ b6 17. N×b6! a×b6 18. B×b6+ Ke8 19. B×d4 Nf6** 19. ... Bg4 20. Q×g4 N×g4 21. B×g7 B×g7 22. c3 Ne3 remained double-edged. **20. Bb5+ Bd7** (*see diagram*) 20. ... Kf8 21. Qh1 N×e4 22. 0-0-0 Nd6 was clearly superior.

After 20. ... Bc8–d7

21. Qh3! B×b5? After 21. ... Kf8 22. B×d7 Nf×d7 23. 0-0-0, White keeps a winning advantage. **22. Qc8+ Ke7 23. Bc5 mate 1-0** [*Baltimore Sunday News*, October 6, 1889]

293. Pollock–Newcomb [C42]
Baltimore, September 1889

1. e4 e5 2. Nf3 Nf6 3. Bc4 N×e4 4. Nc3 Nf6 5. N×e5 Pollock: "Black must recover his lost time by ...d5 presently. Here if 5. d4, 5. ... e4." **5. ... d5 6. Qe2 Be6** Pollock: "White, of course, threatened to play Nc6+." **7. Bb3 c6** Pollock: "7. ... a6, followed by ...c5, is more promising." **8. d4 Bd6 9. 0-0 Nbd7 10. Bf4** Pollock: "Threatening play with knight from e5." **10. ... Qc7 11. Rfe1 0-0-0** (*see diagram*)

After 11. ... 0-0-0

12. N×c6 Pollock: "A very pretty little sacrifice, if sound." **12. ... Q×c6** Pollock revealed the following brief variations: 12. ... B×f4 13. Nb5 Qb6 14. Nb×a7+ Kc7 15. N×d8; 12. ... b×c6 13. Qa6+ Kb8 14. Nb5. **13. Nb5 Bb8 14. Rac1 Nb6?** Pollock: "A fatal, though not very obvious slip. 14. ... Rde8 was best, and White must then play 15. Qf1 before advancing c4." **15. B×b8! Qd7 16. Qe5! Qe7** Pollock: "If 16. ... Rdf8, 17. B×a7 Q×b5 18. Qb8+ Kd7 19. Q×b7+ Ke8 20. B×b6." **17. c4! Kd7 18. c×d5 Nb×d5 19. B×d5 N×d5 20. Q×d5+! B×d5 21. Rc7+! Ke8 22. Rc×e7+ Kf8 23. Bd6 1–0** [*Baltimore Sunday News*, September 22, 1889; *St. John Globe*, November 8, 1889]

294. Pollock–J. Hall [C55]
Offhand Game, Baltimore, 5 October 1889

Pollock: "A Saturday night skittle." **1. e4 e5 2. Nc3 Nc6 3. Nf3 Bb4 4. Bc4 Nf6 5. 0–0 d6 6. Nd5 Bg4 7. c3 Ba5 8. d3 Ne7** *(see diagram)*

After
8. ... Nc6–e7

9. N×e5 B×d1 10. N×f6+ g×f6 11. B×f7+ Kf8 12. Bh6 mate 1–0 [*Baltimore Sunday News*, October 13, 1889]

295. A.W. Schofield–Pollock
Handicap Tournament, Baltimore Chess Association, December 1889
Remove f7 pawn

1. e4 d6 2. Nf3 Nf6 3. Nc3 e5 4. d4 e×d4 5. N×d4 Nc6 6. Bb5 Bd7 7. 0–0 Be7 8. N×c6 b×c6 9. Bc4 Qb8 10. Qe2 Ng4 11. h3 Ne5 12. Bb3 c5 13. f4 Nc6 14. Nd5 Nd4 15. Qf2 N×b3 16. a×b3 Bd8 17. f5 0–0 18. Qg3 Kh8 19. Bg5 Bf6 20. B×f6 g×f6 21. Qh4 Rf7 22. Rf3 c6 23. Nf4 c4 24. Rg3 Qb6+ 25. Kh1 Rd8 26. Qh6 Qf2 27. Rg4 Rg8 *(see diagram)*

After
27. ... Rd8–g8

28. Ng6+! R×g6 29. f×g6 Rg7 30. Rf4 Qe3 31. Rh4 Qf2 32. b×c4 and after a few more moves Black resigned. **1–0** [*Baltimore Sunday News*, February 9, 1890; *PM*, page 112]

296. A.W. Schofield–Pollock
Handicap Tournament, Baltimore Chess Association, December 1889
Remove f7 pawn

1. e4 Nc6 2. d4 e5 3. Nf3 d5 4. d×e5 d×e4 5. Q×d8+ K×d8 6. Ng5 Nd4 7. Kd2 Bf5 8. Kc3 Bc5 9. Be3 h6 10. Nf7+ Ke8 11. N×h8 Rd8 12. Na3 Ne7 13. Bc4 Nec6 14. B×d4 B×d4+ 15. Kb3 Na5+ 16. Ka4 N×c4 17. N×c4 b5+ 18. K×b5 Bd7+ 19. Ka6 Rb8 *(see diagram)*

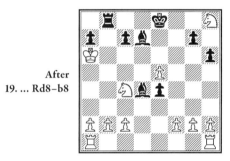

After
19. ... Rd8–b8

20. a4? This leads to a mate in five. White had a large number of winning moves available, among them: 20. Rhd1, 20. Rad1, 20. c3 B×f2 21. b3. **20. ... Be6 20. ... Bc8+ 21. Ka5 Bc5 22. c3 Rb3** would have made a pretty mate. **21. b3 Bc8+ 0–1** [*Baltimore Sunday News*, December 29, 1889]

297. Knight–Pollock [C24]
Simultaneous Exhibition (22 Boards), Washington, 14 December 1889

1. e4 e5 2. Nf3 Nc6 3. Bc4 Nf6 4. d3 d5 5. e×d5 N×d5 6. 0–0 Be7 7. Re1 Bg4 8. Bb5 0–0! 9. B×c6 b×c6 10. R×e5 Bd6 11. Re1 Qf6 12. Nbd2 Rae8 13. c4 13. h3 R×e1+ 14. Q×e1 Bd7 15. Ne4 was much safer. **13. ... Nf4 14. Ne4 Qf5 15. Be3 Qh5** *(see diagram)*

16. c5? 16. Ng3 was better. **16. ... R×e4! 17. d×e4 Nh3+** 17. ... N×g2! 18. K×g2 Qh3+ 19. Kg1 B×f3 20. Q×f3 B×h2+ 21. Kh1 Q×f3+ 22. K×h2 f5 was the most exact finish. **18. Kh1 N×f2+ 19. B×f2 B×f3** and White resigned here. But after 20. c×d6 B×d1 21. Ra×d1 things are not that simple. **0–1** [*Baltimore Sunday News*, Decem-

After
15. ... Qf5–h5

ber 22, 1889; *Atlanta Sunny South*, January 11, 1890]

298. Pollock–S. Newcomb [C52]
Simultaneous Exhibition (12 Boards), Washington, 21 February 1890

1. e4 e5 2. Nf3 Nc6 3. Bc4 Bc5 4. b4 B×b4 5. c3 Ba5 6. 0–0 Nf6 7. d4 e×d4 8. Ba3 d6 9. e5 Ng4 10. e×d6 c×d6 11. Re1+ Ne7 12. h3 Nf6 13. Qa4+ Bd7 14. Qb3 *(see diagram)*

After
14. Qa4–b3

14. ... Qc7? 14. ... 0–0 15. B×d6 Nf5 16. B×f8 Q×f8 was leaving Black with sufficient compensation. 15. B×f7+ Kd8 16. N×d4 Bb6 17. Bc4 Re8 18. Nd2 Rc8 19. Rac1 B×d4 20. c×d4 Nc6 21. R×e8+ N×e8 22. Qe3 b5 23. Qg5+ Nf6 24. Q×g7 b×c4 25. Q×f6+ Ke8 26. Re1+ Ne5 27. R×e5+ 1–0 [*Baltimore Sunday News*, March 2, 1890]

3RD USCA CONGRESS (ST. LOUIS, FEBRUARY 1890)

299. W.A. Haller–Pollock [C27]
3rd USCA Congress, St. Louis, Round 2, 4 February 1890

1. e4 e5 2. Nc3 Nf6 3. Bc4 Steinitz: "A weak move in this opening. 2. f4 is the strongest con-

tinuation." 3. ... N×e4! Steinitz: "The correct reply that gives Black at least a little the better game." 4. N×e4?! Not the most effective response to Black's surprising choice: 4. Qh5 Nd6 5. Q×e5+ Qe7 6. Q×e7+ B×e7 7. Bb3 was a much safer path. Steinitz: "Under the circumstances that his game was somewhat spoiled already, his best play was 4. Bd3; If, however, 4. B×f7+, 4. ... K×f7 5. N×e4 d5 6. Qf3+ Kg8 7. Ng5 Qd7, followed soon by h6, with the superior game." 4. ... d5 5. Qh5 d×c4 6. Q×e5+ Be6 7. Nf3 Nc6 8. Qf4 Nb4! 9. Kd1 Qd7 10. Re1 Steinitz: "Losing valuable time that might have been better used for b3 at once." 10. ... 0–0–0 11. b3? Steinitz: "Too late now and merely giving the brilliant opponent the desired opportunity for a display of his rare powers in positions where sacrifices are in order." 11. a3 Nd5 12. Qg3 Bg4 13. h3 was superior, even if Black keeps a clear edge. 11. ... c×b3 12. a×b3 N×c2! Steinitz: "Highly ingenious. Of course the knight cannot be taken on pain of mate by 13. ... Qd3+, followed accordingly by ...B×b3 mate." 13. R×a7 Kb8 14. Ne5 Qb5 15. Nc3 *(see diagram)*

After
15. Ne4–c3

15. ... B×b3!! Steinitz: "At first sight this would seem to be played merely 'for the gallery,' as taking with the queen would equally threaten mate at once by ...Nd4, but there was an actual necessity for the brilliant coup, for if 15. ... Q×b3, the fine key move pointed out by Mr. Pollock, 16. Nc6+, would win thus: 16. ... Kc8 17. Ra8+ Kd7 18. R×d8+ K×c6 19. Qe4+, followed by 20. Q×c2." 16. Bb2 16. N×b5 allows a mate in one. 16. ... Nb4+ 17. Kc1 Q×e5 Steinitz: "A charming termination to a beautifully played game." F.J. Lee: "The finish is played in Mr. Pollock's usual brilliant style." 18. Q×e5 Nd3+ 19. Kb1 N×e5 20. Ra5 Nc4 21. Rb5 N×d2+ 22. Kc1 Bc4 23. Rbe5 Bd6 24. Rh5 Bf4 25. Rh4 g5 26. R×f4 g×f4 27. Ne4 Rhe8 28. Bf6 Rd6 29. f3 N×e4 30. f×e4 Bd5 0–1 [*St. Louis Republic*, February 6, 1890; *Baltimore Sunday News*, February 16, 1890; *New York Clipper*, March 8, 1890;

tournament book, pages 17–18; *ICM*, February 1890, page 57]

300. Pollock–L. Uedemann [C44]
3rd USCA Congress, St. Louis, Round 3, 5 February 1890

1. e4 e5 2. Nf3 Nc6 3. c3 d5 4. Qa4 Bd7 5. e×d5 Nd4 6. Qd1 N×f3+ 7. Q×f3 Nf6 8. d4 e×d4 9. c×d4 Bb4+ 10. Nc3 Qe7+ 11. Be3 0–0 12. h3 c6 13. d×c6? 13. Bd3 N×d5 14. 0–0 N×c3 15. b×c3 B×c3 16. Rab1 was better than the risky capture on c6. **13. ... B×c6 14. Qf5 Nd5 15. Qd3 Nf4** 15. ... Rfe8 was another strong possibility. **16. Qd2 N×g2+! 17. B×g2 B×g2 18. Rg1 B×h3** 18. ... Bd5 19. 0–0–0 Rfc8 was more logical. **19. Kd1** *(see diagram)* Perhaps Pollock was afraid of 19. 0–0–0 Bf5! but his choice is equally poor.

After
19. Ke1–d1

19. ... Rfc8?! 19. ... Rfd8! was more to the point. The text move allows White to simplify and consolidate. **20. Nd5 Qe6 21. N×b4 Bg4+ 22. Ke1 Bf5 23. Nd3 b6 24. Ke2 Re8 25. b3 Rad8 26. Nf4 Qe4 27. Kf1 Qf3 28. Qe2 Qe4 29. Rd1 h6 30. Qd3 Q×d3+ 31. N×d3 Bh3+ 32. Ke2 R×d4 33. Kf3 Rd6 34. Nf4 R×d1 35. R×d1 Bf5 36. Rd4 g5 37. Nd5 Kg7 38. Nc7 Re7 39. Nb5 Bb1 40. Ra4 Bd3 41. R×a7 R×a7 42. N×a7 b5 43. Bd4+ Kg6 44. Nc6 Kf5 45. Ne5 Bb1 46. a4 b×a4 47. b×a4 Be4+ 48. Kg3 Bd5 49. a5 h5 50. a6 Ke6 51. a7 f5 52. Nc4** 52. f4 g4 (52. ... g×f4+ 53. K×f4 Be4 54. Nc4 h4 55. Nb6 h3 56. Bg1) 53. Nc4 was easily winning as well. **52. ... f4+ 53. Kh3 g4+ 54. Kh4 g3 55. f×g3 f×g3 56. K×g3 h4+ 57. K×h4 Ke7 58. Nb6 Bb7 59. a8Q B×a8 60. N×a8 Ke6 61. Kg4 Kd5 62. Bf2 Ke4 63. Nb6 Ke5 64. Bc5 Ke4 65. Bd6 Ke3 66. Kf5 Kd4 67. Kf4 Kd3 68. Bc5 Ke2 69. Ke4 Kf1 70. Kf3 Ke1 71. Bd4 Kf1 72. Nc4 Ke1 73. Bc5 Kf1 74. Nd2+ Ke1 75. Ke3 Kd1 76. Kd3 Ke1 77. Bg1 Kd1 78. Bf2 Kc1 79. Nc4 Kd1 80. Nb2+ Kc1 81. Kc3 Kb1 82. Kb3 Kc1 83. Be3+ Kb1 84. Nc4 Ka1 85. Bf4 1–0** [*tournament book*, pages 20–23]

301. Pollock–A.H. Robbins [C46]
3rd USCA Congress, St. Louis, Round 4, 5 February 1890

1. e4 e5 2. Nf3 Nc6 3. Nc3 f5 4. Bc4 Nf6 5. Ng5 d5 6. e×d5 Na5 7. Bb5+ c6 8. d×c6 b×c6 9. Ba4 Qd4? This impetuous queen move makes little sense. Best was 9. ... Bc5 or 9. ... h6. **10. 0–0 Bd6 11. d3 0–0 12. a3! f4 13. Nf3 Qb6 14. b4 Nb7 15. Bb3+ Kh8 16. Ng5 Bg4 17. Qe1 Nd8 18. Bb2 Qc7 19. f3 Bh5 20. Rd1 Bg6 21. Kh1 Re8 22. Rd2 Nf7 23. Nge4 Qe7 24. Re2 N×e4 25. N×e4 Qc7 26. N×d6 Q×d6** *(see diagram)*

After
26. ... Qc7×d6

27. d4!? The simpler 27. B×f7 B×f7 28. B×e5 must not have been to Pollock's taste. **27. ... e4 28. f×e4 Qf6 29. e5 Qg5 30. Bc1 Bh5 31. B×f4 Qg4 32. Re3 Rad8 33. c3 Nh6 34. B×h6 g×h6 35. Rg3 Qd7 36. e6 Qd6 37. Re3 Re7 38. Qh4 Bg6 39. Qf6+ Kg8 40. Rg3 a5 41. R×g6+! 1–0** [*tournament book*, pages 25–26]

302. Pollock–J.W. Showalter [C47]
3rd USCA Congress, St. Louis, Round 5, 6 February 1890

1. e4 e5 2. Nf3 Nc6 3. Nc3 Nf6 4. d4 e×d4 5. N×d4 Bb4 6. f3 0–0 7. Bg5 Re8 8. Be2 d5 9. N×c6 b×c6 10. 0–0 Bb7 11. Bd3 Qd6 12. Bd2 Rad8 13. a3 Bc5+ 14. Kh1 Nh5 *(see diagram)*

After
14. ... Nf6–h5

15. f4?? Black mates in three moves. **0–1** [*St. Louis Republic*, February 7, 1890; *New York Clipper*, March 1, 1890, and September 5, 1891; *Turf, Field & Farm*, March 14, 1890; *tournament book*, page 26]

303. S. Lipschütz–Pollock [C25]
3rd USCA Congress, St. Louis,
Round 6, 6 February 1890

1. e4 e5 2. Nc3 Nc6 3. g3 Bc5 4. Bg2 d6 5. d3 Be6 6. Na4 Bb6 7. N×b6 a×b6 8. Ne2 Nf6 9. 0-0 Qd7 10. f4 Bh3 11. f5 B×g2 12. K×g2 d5! 13. Nc3 d×e4 14. d×e4 Q×d1 15. R×d1 Nd4 16. Bg5 c6 17. B×f6 g×f6 18. Rd2 Ke7 19. Rad1 Rhd8 20. a3 Rd7 21. Kf2 Rad8 22. Rc1 Rd6 23. Rd3 Kf8 24. Na4 c5 25. Nc3 Kg7 (*see diagram*)

After
25. ... Kf8–g7

26. g4!? 26. Nd5 was met by 26. ... N×f5! 27. N×b6 Ne7 28. Ke2 Nc6 29. Nd5 Nd4+ 30. Kf2 f5. **26. ... b5 27. Nd5 Nc6 28. Rg3 Kf8 29. Rh3 Ne7 30. N×e7 Rd2+ 31. Kf3 K×e7 32. R×h7 c4 33. Rh4 R8d4 34. Rh8 Rd7 35. Rh6 b6 36. h4 Rh2 37. g5 Rdd2 38. R×f6 Rdf2+ 39. Ke3 Re2+** ½–½ [*tournament book*, pages 28–29]

304. H.C. Brown–Pollock [C56]
3rd USCA Congress, St. Louis,
Round 7, 7 February 1890

1. e4 e5 2. Nf3 Nc6 3. Bc4 Nf6 4. d4 e×d4 5. e5 d5 6. Bb5 Ne4 7. N×d4 Bd7 8. N×c6 b×c6 9. Be2? 9. Bd3 was correct. **9. ... Bc5 10. 0-0 0-0 11. c3 f6!? 12. Nd2?** 12. e6 B×e6 13. Nd2 f5 14. N×e4 f×e4 15. Be3 was not ideal, but best in the circumstances. **12. ... N×f2! 13. R×f2 f×e5 14. Nf3 B×f2+ 15. K×f2 e4 16. Kg1 e×f3 17. B×f3 Qe7 18. Bd2 Qc5+ 19. Kh1 Qf2 20. Qe2** (*see diagram*)
20. ... R×f3! 21. Q×f3 Q×d2 0–1 [*tournament book*, page 30]

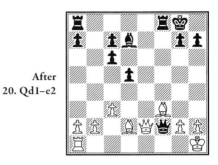

After
20. Qd1–e2

305. L. Uedemann–Pollock [C22]
St. Louis, 3rd USCA Congress,
Round 9, 8 February 1890

1. e4 e5 2. d4 e×d4 3. Q×d4 Nc6 4. Qe3 Nf6 5. f4?! A dubious experiment duly punished by Pollock. **5. ... Be7 6. e5 Ng4 7. Qf3 d5! 8. c3 Bc5 9. Nh3 0-0 10. Bd3 f6!** 11. e×f6 N×f6 11. ... R×f6 was even more forceful. **12. Nf2 Qe7+ 13. Kd1 B×f2 14. Q×f2 Ne4 15. B×e4 d×e4 16. Be3 Bg4+** The immediate 16. ... Ne5!? was the other attractive possibility. **17. Ke1 Ne5! 18. Qg3 Qd7 19. Nd2 Qd3 20. Kf2 Qe2+ 21. Kg1** (*see diagram*)

After
21. Kf2–g1

21. ... Nf3+!! 22. g×f3 Q×e3+ 23. Qf2 Q×f4 24. N×e4 B×f3 25. Ng3 Rf6 26. Rf1 Raf8 27. Q×a7 b6! 28. Qa6 Qe3+ and Black mates in five moves. **0–1** [*St. Louis Republic*, February 9, 1890; *tournament book*, page 35]

306. Pollock–W.A. Haller [C51]
3rd USCA Congress, St. Louis,
Round 10, 9 February 1890

1. e4 e5 2. Nf3 Nc6 3. Bc4 Bc5 4. b4 B×b4 5. c3 Ba5 6. d4 e×d4 7. 0-0 Bb6 8. c×d4 d6 9. Nc3 Na5 10. Bg5 f6 11. Bh4 N×c4 12. Qa4+ Qd7 13. Q×c4 Qf7 14. Nd5 Be6 15. Qa4+ Bd7 16. Qa3 Rc8 17. Rfe1 Ne7? Black's first mistake after the "book has closed." 17. ... Nh6 18. e5

0–0 led to some scary complications: 19. Ne7+ Q×e7 20. e×f6 Qf7 21. Re7. **18. N×e7 Q×e7 19. Bg3** The immediate 19. e5! was very strong: 19. ... d×e5 20. R×e5! Be6 21. R×e6 Q×e6 22. Re1. **19. ... c5?!** *(see diagram)* In view of White's transparent intentions, Black had to castle as soon as possible and return the pawn if needed: 19. ... 0–0! 20. e5 f×e5 21. d×e5 Qf7 22. e×d6 c×d6 23. B×d6 Rfe8.

After
19. ... c7–c5

20. e5! d×e5 21. N×e5! f×e5 22. R×e5 Be6 23. Rae1 0–0 24. d5 Qf6 25. R×e6 Qf7 26. Qc3 c4 27. R1e2 Rfe8 28. R×e8+ R×e8 29. Q×c4 Rd8 30. Rd2 h6 31. h3 Rd7 32. Kh2 Bc7 33. B×c7 R×c7 34. Qd4 Now White converts his extra pawn with ease. **34. ... Qf6 35. Q×f6 g×f6 36. Kg3 Kf7 37. Kf4 Kg6 38. d6 Rc4+ 39. Kg3 Rc8 40. Kf4 Rc4+ 41. Ke3 Rc8 42. Kd4 Kf7 43. Re2 Re8 44. R×e8 K×e8 45. Kd5 Kd7 46. g4 b5 47. Kc5 b4 48. h4 a5 49. f4 a4 50. K×b4 K×d6 51. K×a4 Kd5 52. g5 h×g5 53. h×g5 1–0** [*tournament book*, page 38]

307. A.H. Robbins–Pollock [A85]
3rd USCA Congress, St. Louis, Round 11, 9 February 1890

1. d4 f5 2. c4 e6 3. e3 Nf6 4. Nc3 b6 5. Nf3 Bb7 6. Bd3 Be7 7. d5 e×d5!? Pollock's intention was to gambit away the f-pawn. **8. c×d5 0–0 9. Qb3 Kh8 10. B×f5 c6 11. d×c6 N×c6 12. 0–0 Qe8 13. Nb5 Qh5 14. Nbd4 Bd6! 15. h3 g6 16. Qd1?** *(see diagram)* Utter panic. White must have been worried about 16. Bd3 N×d4 17. N×d4 B×g2! 18. K×g2 Qg5+ 19. Kh1 Qh5, but there was no reason to fear it.

16. ... N×d4! 16. ... g×f5 was also sufficient: 17. N×c6 Rg8!! 18. Q×d6 R×g2+ 19. K×g2 Rg8+. **17. Q×d4 g×f5 18. Q×d6 B×f3 19. Kh2 B×g2! 20. K×g2 Rg8+ 21. Kh2 Ng4+ 22. Kg3 Ne5+ 23. Kf4 Qf3+ 24. K×e5 Qe4+ 25. Kf6 0–1** [*tournament book*, page 41]

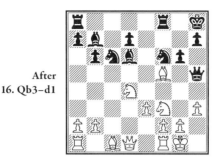

After
16. Qb3–d1

308. J.W. Showalter–Pollock [C82]
3rd USCA Congress, St. Louis, Round 12, 10 February 1890

Pollock: "The subjoined (hitherto unpublished) game (played in the second round, Feb. 10) is the only one which Champion Showalter failed to win." **1. e4 e5 2. Nf3 Nc6 3. Bb5 a6 4. Ba4 Nf6 5. 0–0 N×e4 6. d4 b5 7. Bb3 d5 8. d×e5 Be6 9. c3 Bc5** Pollock: "In the New York Tournament 9. ... Be7 proved disastrous, on account of 10. Bc2 followed by Nd4 and f3." **10. a4 0–0 11. a×b5 a×b5 12. R×a8 Q×a8 13. Bf4** Pollock: "If 13. B×d5, 13. ... Rd8 14. B×c6 R×d1 15. B×a8 and Black mates in three moves." **13. ... Ne7 14. Qe2 Ng6 15. Be3 B×e3 16. Q×e3 c5!?** 16. ... Qa1 17. Qc1 Ra8 was an equally ambitious choice. **17. Nbd2 N×d2 18. N×d2 Qc6** Pollock: "Black might obtain a better game by ...d4, and after exchanging bishops, ...Qd5." **19. f4 Ne7 20. Bd1 Nf5 21. Qf3 c4 22. Kh1 Qb6 23. Re1 d4! 24. Qf2 Rb8 25. Nf3** *(see diagram)*

After
25. Nd2–f3

25. ... d×c3 25. ... d3! was preferable: 26. Q×b6 R×b6 27. Nd2 Bd5 28. Kg1 Ra6, with a clear edge for Black. **26. Q×b6 R×b6 27. b×c3 b4** Pollock: "He ought to have seized this opportunity to play the king across to the queenside. The passed pawn is too weak." **28. c×b4 R×b4 29. Bc2 c3 30. Rd1 g6 31. Rd3 Rc4 32. Kg1 Kf8 33. g3 Ke8 34. Kf2 Ne7 35. Rd4 R×d4 36. N×d4 Bc4 37. Ke1 Kd7 38. Ba4+ Kc7 39. Nb5+ B×b5 40. B×b5 Nd5 41. Kd1 Kb6 42. Be8 f6 43. Bf7 Ne3+ 44. Ke2**

c2 45. Kd2 f×e5 46. f×e5 Kc5 47. Kc1 Nf1
48. K×c2 N×h2 49. Kd3 Nf1 50. Ke4 N×g3+
51. Kf4 Nh5+ 52. Kg5 Kd4 53. e6 Ke5 Pollock:
"Either side can draw, neither can win." ½–½ [*Baltimore Sunday News*, March 23, 1890; *St. Louis Republic*, March 30, 1890; *tournament book*, page 43]

309. Pollock–S. Lipschütz [C51]
3rd USCA Congress, St. Louis, Round 13, 11 February 1890

1. e4 e5 2. Nf3 Nc6 3. Bc4 Bc5 4. b4 Bb6 5. b5
Na5 6. N×e5 Qf6 7. B×f7+ Kf8 (*see diagram*)

After
7. ... Ke8–f8

8. d4 d6 9. B×g8 d×e5 10. Bd5 c6 11. Qh5 g6
Obviously, 11. ... c×d5? loses to 12. Ba3+. **12. Qh6+
Ke8 13. Bg5 Qf8 14. b×c6?!** Pollock's best way to
continue the attack was 14. Qh4 c×d5 15. 0–0 B×d4
16. c3 Bb6 17. Bf6. **14. ... b×c6 15. Bb3 B×d4
16. Q×f8+ R×f8 17. c3 B×f2+ 18. Kd2 Bc5 19. Be3
B×e3+** 19. ... Bb6 20. Na3 Ba6 was somewhat
stronger. **20. K×e3 Ba6 21. Na3 Rd8 22. Rad1 Ke7
23. c4 Rb8 24. Rd3 Rfd8 25. Rhd1 R×d3+
26. R×d3 Rb4 27. Rc3 c5 28. Kd3 Rb8 29. Nc2
Rf8 30. Ke2?** 30. Ne3 Nc6 31. Nd5+ Kd6 32. Rc1
Rf2 33. Rc2 offered clear drawing chances. **30. ... Rf4
31. g3 R×e4+ 32. Ne3 Rd4 33. Ke1 Kd6 34. h4 e4
35. h5 Ke5 36. h6 Kf6 37. Rc2 Kg5 38. Rf2 K×h6
39. Rf7 B×c4 40. B×c4 N×c4 41. Ng4+ Kg5
42. Nf6 h5 0–1** [*tournament book*, page 45]

ODDS GAME

310. Pollock & Euphrat–N.N.
Odds Game, Cincinnati Chess Club, March 1890
Remove Ra1

1. e4 e5 2. Nf3 Nc6 3. Bc4 Bc5 4. b4 B×b4
5. c3 Bc5 6. 0–0 d6 7. d4 e×d4 8. c×d4 Bb6
9. Nc3 Na5 10. Bg5 f6 11. Bh4 N×c4 12. Qa4+
Qd7 13. Q×c4 Qf7 14. Nd5 c6 15. Qa4 Bd8
16. Re1 b5 17. Qc2 Bb7 18. Nc3 Ne7 19. e5 d×e5
20. Ne4 Qd5 21. d×e5 0–0 22. e×f6 Ng6
23. f×g7 R×f3 24. B×d8 (*see diagram*)

After
24. Bh4×d8

24. ... R×f2? The simple 24. ... R×d8 25. g×f3
K×g7 was sufficient. **25. Q×f2 Q×d8 26. Qb2!
Qb6+ 27. Kh1 Ne7?** 27. ... c5 28. Nf6+ Kf7
29. Rf1 Qc6 30. Rf2 was better, but White is still
superior. **28. Nf6+ Kf7 29. Qe5** 29. Nd7! was the
other key alternative, this one forcing a mate in
twelve. **29. ... Qd8** 29. ... Kg6 loses too after
30. Qh5+ K×f6 31. Qe5+ Kg6 32. Qd6+ Kg5
33. Q×e7+ Kg6 34. Qd6+ K×g7 35. Re7+ Kf8
36. Qf6+ Kg8 37. Qg7 mate. **30. Qe6+ K×g7
31. Nh5+ Kf8 32. Rf1+ Ke8 1–0** [*Baltimore Sunday News*, March 23, 1890]

Part Two, Section V
(May 1890–April 1891)

---

311. Spencer–Pollock [C29]
Baltimore Chess Association
Championship, Baltimore, May 1890

1. e4 e5 2. Nc3 Nf6 3. f4 d5 4. e×d5 e×f4 5. Bc4 Bb4 6. Nf3 0–0 7. 0–0 c6 8. d×c6 N×c6 9. d4 a6 10. Ne2 Nh5 11. d5 Ne7 12. Kh1 Nf5 13. Nfd4 Qh4! 14. N×f5 B×f5 15. Qd4? 15. B×f4 Rae8 16. Ng3 N×f4 17. N×f5 Qg5 18. Qf3 was White's best choice. **15. ... Rfe8! 16. Qf2** (see diagram)

After
16. Qd4–f2

16. ... Ng3+! 16. ... Q×f2 17. R×f2 Rac8 18. b3 R×c4 19. b×c4 Bc5 was possible as well. **17. Kg1 Rac8 18. B×f4 N×e2+ 19. Kh1 Q×f2 0–1** [*Baltimore Sunday News*, June 1, 1890; *PM*, page 93]

312. Pollock–A.H. Robbins [C52]
Offhand Game, St. Louis, May 1890

"A lively little bit of Evans played between Dr. W.H.K. Pollock, the Irish champion, and the talented St. Louis problemist, Mr. A.H. Rob-bins, during the former's late visit in this city." **1. e4 e5 2. Nf3 Nc6 3. Bc4 Bc5 4. b4 B×b4 5. c3 Ba5 6. d4 e×d4 7. 0–0 d6 8. Qb3 Qf6 9. c×d4 Bb6 10. e5 d×e5 11. N×e5 N×e5 12. d×e5 Qg6 13. e6 f×e6 14. Re1 Bd7 15. B×e6 0–0–0 16. Bb2 B×e6 17. R×e6 Rd1+?** 17. ... Nf6 18. Nc3 Qf5 19. Rf1 Rhe8 was obviously better. **18. Q×d1 Q×e6 19. B×g7 B×f2+! 20. Kh1 Nf6! 21. B×h8 Nh5?** 21. ... Ne4! (threatening ...Ng3) was the correct move here: 22. g4 Qc6! 23. Kg2 Be3 24. Qf3 Qc2+ 25. Kf1 Qd3+ with clear compensation for Black. **22. h3** 22. Qd2 Be3 23. Qb4 c5 24. Qh4 was more precise. **22. ... Ng3+ 23. Kh2 Ne2** (see diagram)

After
23. ... Ng3–e2

24. Na3? 24. Nc3! N×c3 25. B×c3 was easily winning. **24. ... Qe4** 24. ... Bg1+ 25. Kh1 Qe3 would have forced 26. Q×e2 Q×e2 27. R×g1 Q×a2, with superior chances for Black. **25. Qd2?** Drawing with 25. Kh1 Ng3+ 26. Kh2 Ne2 was White's best option. **25. ... Be3! 26. Qe1 Bc5?!** 26. ... Qf4+! 27. g3 Qf3 28. Nb5 Bf2 should have won here. **27. Nb5 Be3?** 27. ... Bg1+! 28. Kh1 Qf4 would have still kept things unclear. **28. Rd1! Qf4+ 29. g3 Qf3 30. Bd4 1–0** [*St. Louis Republic*, June 22, 1890]

313. J.W. Showalter & A.H. Robbins– Pollock & Hulse [C45]
Consultation Game, St. Louis Chess Club, St. Louis, June 1890

1. e4 e5 2. Nf3 Nc6 3. d4 e×d4 4. N×d4 Nf6 5. N×c6 b×c6 6. Bd3 Bc5 7. 0–0 d5 8. e5 Ng4 9. h3 N×e5! 9. ... N×f2?! 10. R×f2 B×f2+ 11. K×f2 Qh4+ 12. Kg1 B×h3 was met by 13. Qe2 (13. g×h3 Qg3+ 14. Kh1 Q×h3+ 15. Kg1 Qg3+ 16. Kf1 Qh3+ leads to a draw.). 13. ... Bg4 14. Qf2. **10. Re1 Qf6 11. Be3 d4 12. Bc1 0–0 13. B×h7+ K×h7 14. Qh5+ Kg8 15. R×e5 Bd6 16. Re4 g6 17. Qh6 c5** 17. ... Bf5 18. Rh4 Rfe8 19. Nd2 Qg7 was better. **18. Rh4 Re8 19. Qh7+ Kf8 20. Bh6+ Ke7 21. Nd2 Kd7 22. Bg7** (see diagram)

After
22. Bh6–g7

22. ... Qe7? A costly imprecision. 22. ... Qf5! would have given Black powerful threats. For instance, 23. Nc4 Re2 24. Rf1 Ba6 25. N×d6 c×d6 26. Bh6 Bc4 27. b3 Bd5 28. Rf4 Q×c2. **23. Re4 Qg5 24. R×e8 K×e8 25. Qg8+ Kd7 26. Q×f7+ Kc6** 26. ... Qe7 was better but, ultimately, unsatisfactory as well: 27. Q×g6 Bb7 28. Qf5+ Qe6 29. Q×e6+ K×e6 30. Re1+ Kf7 31. Be5. **27. Qe8+ Kb6** and White mates in two moves. **1–0** [*Baltimore Sunday News*, June 8, 1890]

314. J.W. Beebe & L.K. Thatcher & G.A. L'hommêdé–Pollock [A00]
Consultation Game, Kansas City, June 1890

1. c3 e5 2. d4 e×d4 3. Q×d4 Nc6 4. Qa4 Nf6 5. Nf3 d5 6. Bg5 Bd6 7. e3 0–0 8. Nbd2 h6 9. Bh4 g5 10. Bg3 Bf5 11. Be2 Ne4 12. B×d6 Q×d6 13. Nd4! N×d4 14. c×d4 N×d2 15. K×d2 Rac8 16. Rac1 Bg6 17. h4 f5?! 17. ... Rfe8 18. h×g5 h×g5 was more careful play. **18. h×g5 h×g5 19. Rh6 f4?** Once again, too optimistic. 19. ... Rf6 20. Bd3 Kg7 21. Rch1 a6 was needed. **20. Rch1 f×e3+ 21. f×e3 Kg7** (see diagram)

After
21. ... Kg8–g7

22. Bd3! Rf2+ 23. Kd1! Rf6 24. R×g6+ R×g6 25. B×g6 b5 Desperation. 25. ... K×g6 loses after 26. Qc2+! Kg7 27. Qh7+ Kf8 28. Qf5+, with a mate in six. 25. ... Q×g6 loses material after 26. Qd7+. **26. Q×b5 c6 27. Qb7+ 1–0** [*Kansas City Journal*, October 18, 1890]

315. Pollock–L. Uedemann [C49]
Chicago Tournament, Chicago Chess and Checker Club, June 1890

1. e4 e5 2. Nf3 Nc6 3. Nc3 Nf6 4. Bb5 Bb4 5. Nd5 N×d5 6. e×d5 e4 7. d×c6 d×c6 8. B×c6+?! 8. Bc4 e×f3 9. Q×f3 Qe7+ 10. Qe3 was cleaner play. **8. ... b×c6 9. Qe2 0–0! 10. Ne5 Qd5 11. Nc4 f5 12. b3 a5** 12. ... f4!? 13. Bb2 Bf5 14. 0–0–0 a5 was more forceful. **13. a4 Ba6 14. Bb2 Rfd8 15. 0–0–0 B×c4** 15. ... Qf7 would invite 16. f3! e×f3 17. g×f3 Re8 18. Qf1 Rab8 19. Rg1 and White gets some counterplay. **16. Q×c4 Q×c4 17. b×c4 Bd6 18. g3 Bc5 19. Rhf1 Rab8 20. d4 Be7 21. c3 Rb3 22. Kc2 Rdb8 23. Rb1 Kf7 24. Rfe1 Kg6 25. c5 Kh5 26. h3 g5 27. g4+! Kg6 28. g×f5+ K×f5 29. f3 e3 30. R×e3 Bf6 31. Ree1 h5 32. Re4 h4 33. Re2 R3b7 34. Ree1 Rb3 35. Rf1 R3b7 36. c4 Rb4 37. Bc3 R×b1 38. R×b1 R×b1 39. K×b1 Kf4 40. B×a5 B×d4 41. B×c7+ K×f3 42. a5 g4 43. h×g4 K×g4 44. Kc2 h3 45. Kd3 B×c5 46. Ke4 Bf2 47. Bh2 Ba7 48. a6 Bc5 49. Ke5 Kf3 50. Ke6** (see diagram)

After
50. Ke5–e6

50. ... Ke4! 50. ... Kg2?! would have caused significant problems for Black that require precision: 51. Bb8! Ba7! (51. ... h2 52. B×h2 K×h2 53. Kd7 Kg3 54. K×c6 Ba7 55. Kd5 Kf4 56. c5 Bb8 57. c6) 52. Bd6 Bc5! 53. Bc7 Bb6 54. Kd7! B×c7! 55. a7 h2 56. a8Q Bg3 57. Q×c6+ Kg1 58. Qf3, even if White cannot win. **51. Kd7 Kd3 52. K×c6 K×c4** Drawn by mutual consent. ½–½ [*Chicago Times*, October 5, 1890]

316. Blanchard–Pollock [C55]
Chicago Tournament, Chicago Chess and Checker Club, June 1890

1. e4 e5 2. Nf3 Nc6 3. Bc4 Nf6 4. Nc3 N×e4 5. B×f7+? 5. 0–0 was better. So was 5. N×e4 d5 6. Bd3 f5 7. Nc3 e4 8. Be2. **5. ... K×f7 6. N×e4 d5 7. Neg5+ Kg8 8. d4 h6 9. Nh3 Bg4 10. d×e5 N×e5 11. Nhg1 Bc5 12. Bf4 Ng6 13. Bg3 Kh7 14. Qd3 Re8+ 15. Kf1 Re4 16. Re1 Qe7** (*see diagram*)

After
16. ... Qd8–e7

17. **Q×d5?** This leads to an immediate collapse. 17. Ne2 Re8 18. h3 Bh5 19. c3 was more stubborn play. **17. ... R×e1+ 18. N×e1 Rd8 19. Qc4 Q×e1+ 20. K×e1 Rd1 mate 0–1** [*Albany Sunday Express*, June 21, 1890; *ICM*, June 1890, page 184; *New York Sun*, July 10, 1892, *New York Clipper*, September 24, 1892; *PM*, pages 93–94]

317. Pollock–Hermann [C44]
Chicago Tournament, Chicago Chess and Checker Club, June 1890

1. e4 e5 2. Nf3 Nc6 3. c3 Nf6 Steinitz: "We have often expressed our preference for 3. ... d5 at this juncture." 4. d4 d6 Steinitz: "4. ... N×e4 is the correct move." 5. Bb5 Steinitz: "White could now obtain the superior game by 5. Bd3." **5. ... Bd7 6. Qe2 Nb8** Steinitz: "Giving up a pawn without cause." 7. Bc4 Steinitz: "And it is still more strange that White does not accept the offer by 7. d×e5

d×e5 8. N×e5 etc." **7. ... Qe7 8. Ng5 Be6 9. N×e6 f×e6 10. 0–0 Nbd7 11. f4 0–0–0 12. Bd3 e×f4 13. B×f4 e5 14. Bg3 h6 15. Nd2 g5 16. d5 Qh7 17. b4 h5 18. a4 h4 19. Bf2 Nh5 20. Qe3 Nf4** (*see diagram*)

After
20. ... Nh5–f4

21. **Bb5** 21. Q×a7! was an excellent choice: 21. ... N×d3 22. Qa8+ Nb8 23. Ba7 Kd7 24. Q×b7 Nf4 25. B×b8 Rc8 26. a5 and White wins. **21. ... Qh5 22. Nf3 Qg4 23. Ne1 h3 24. g3 Ng2?** Steinitz: "Black has obtained the superior game and could have secured keeping it by ...a6 at this point, followed eventually by ...Kb8." **25. Q×a7 N×e1 26. Bc6** Steinitz: "A splendid coup that is now decisive." 26. Qa8+ Nb8 27. Ba7 would have forced a mate too. But Pollock's solution is more artistic. **26. ... b×c6** and White gave mate in five moves. **1–0** [*Albany Sunday Express*, June 21, 1890; *Baltimore Sunday News*, June 22, 1890; *ICM*, June 1890, pages 184–185, *Bristol Mercury*, January 3, 1891; *The Week* (Toronto), November 6, 1891]

MATCH AGAINST MOEHLE (JUNE 1890)

318. C. Moehle–Pollock [C24]
Match, Game 1, Cincinnati, 24 June 1890

1. e4 e5 2. Nf3 Nc6 3. Bc4 Nf6 4. d3 d5 5. e×d5 N×d5 6. 0–0 Be7 7. Qe2 Bg4 8. c3 0–0 9. h3 Bh5 Pollock: "The sacrifice of the pawn in this position is unusual, and not a bad idea." **10. g4 Bg6 11. N×e5 N×e5 12. Q×e5 Nb6 13. Qg3** Pollock: "Best, for if 13. b3 B×d3 14. Rd1 N×c4 15. b×c4 Bd6." **13. ... N×c4 14. d×c4 Bd6 15. f4** Pollock: "After this Black ingeniously regains the pawn with the better game. However, if 15. Bf4 B×f4 16. Q×f4 Qd3 17. Re1 and we prefer Black's position." **15. ... Bd3 16. Re1 B×c4 17. Be3 Re8 18. Nd2 Bd5 19. Nf3 g5!?** Pollock: "Who would say 'unsound' of this? Yet White almost proves it

so." **20. Nd4 Re4 21. Rf1 Qe8 22. Nf5?!** *(see diagram)* 22. Rf3 was safer, so as to prevent Black's next move.

After
22. Nd4–f5

22. ... R×e3!! Pollock: "And this. Curiously, if here 22. ... g×f4 then 23. Qh4." **23. N×e3 Bc5 24. Rae1 Qe4 25. Kh2** A direct 25. b4 was more exact. **25. ... Bc6?** Pollock must have missed 25. ... B×e3 26. R×e3 g×f4! 27. R×e4 f×g3+ 28. K×g3 B×e4. **26. b4 Rd8?** Pollock: "Hoping to draw. Black's attack is broken, if the bishop retreats, then b5 [and] if ...B×b5, Qf3." 26. ... B×e3 27. R×e3 g×f4! was still possible. **27. b×c5 Rd2+ 28. Rf2 g×f4 29. Qh4 f×e3 30. Qg5+ Kf8 31. R×d2 Qg6 32. Rd8+ 1–0** [*Baltimore Sunday News*, July 13, 1890; *St. Louis Republic*, July 20, 1890; *The Lincoln, Rutland and Stamford Mercury*, September 5, 1890; *ICM*, July 1890, pages 213–214; *PM*, pages 114–115]

319. Pollock–C. Moehle [B32]
Match, Game 4, Cincinnati, 25 June 1890

1. e4 c5 2. d4 c×d4 3. Nf3 e6 4. N×d4 Nc6 5. Nb5 d6 6. Bf4 e5 7. Be3 f5 8. N1c3 a6 9. Nd5 a×b5 10. Bb6 *(see diagram)*

After
10. Be3–b6

10. ... Ra4? A fatal miscalculation. Black could try to exempt himself from immediate resignation: 10. ... Qh4 11. Nc7+ Kf7 12. N×a8 Q×e4+ 13. Qe2 Qa4 14. Nc7 Nd4 15. B×d4 Qa5+ 16. Bc3 Q×c7. **11. B×d8 R×e4+ 12. Ne3 K×d8** and White won

in 44 moves. **1–0** [*Baltimore Sunday News*, August 3, 1890]

320. Pollock–C. Moehle [C59]
Match, Game 10, Cincinnati, June 1890

For this game, Moehle was awarded half of the brilliancy prize. **1. e4 e5 2. Nf3 Nc6 3. Bc4 Nf6 4. Ng5 d5 5. e×d5 Na5 6. Bb5+ c6 7. d×c6 b×c6 8. Be2 h6 9. Nh3** Pollock: "Steinitz's novelty. *Instructor*, page 94." **9. ... B×h3 10. g×h3 Qd5 11. Bf3 e4 12. Bg2 Qe5 13. Qe2 Bd6** Pollock: "We prefer 13. ... 0–0–0, if 14. Nc3 Bc5 15. N×e4 N×e4 16. B×e4 Rhe8 17. d3 f5 18. Bf3 Qf6." **14. Nc3 0–0 15. b3** Pollock: "Steinitz gives 15. d3. The text move is sound." **15. ... Nd5 16. Bb2 Nf4 17. Qf1 f5 18. 0–0–0** Pollock: "The position is not without its dangers. For instance, if 18. Nd1, Black might reply 18. ... Nd3+." **18. ... Qe7 19. Rg1** Pollock: "A most critical question. Is not this the time to play 19. Qa6, instead of a move later?" **19. ... Ba3 20. Qa6** Pollock: "Mr. Moehle condemns this move and considers White's best to be 20. B×a3." **20. ... Qc5 21. Bf1 Rfb8 22. Na4** *(see diagram)*

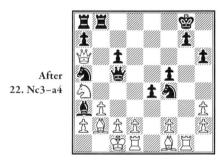

After
22. Nc3–a4

22. ... Qe5 23. c3 B×b2+ 24. K×b2 Qd5 Pollock: "To prevent White posting his bishop to c4." **25. c4?** 25. b4 was best: 25. ... Nd3+ 26. B×d3 e×d3 27. Ka1 Nc4 28. f4. **25. ... Qe5+ 26. Ka3** Pollock: "If 26. Kb1 N×b3 27. a×b3 R×b3+ 28. Kc2 (Or 28. Ka2, 28. ... Rab8) 28. ... Ra3." **26. ... Ne6 27. c5 Nd4 28. Rc1 Nb5+ 29. B×b5 R×b5 30. b4** Pollock: "A fatal error, though it is very hard to escape the effects of ...Qd4, which Black threatens in any case, now that his knight is defended. 30. Nb6 looks like a resource, as Black cannot sacrifice with advantage. He might, however, reply 30. ... Rd8." **30. ... Qd4! 31. Q×a5 R×a5 32. b×a5 Rb8 33. Rb1 Rb5 34. a6 Ra5 35. Rb4 Q×d2 36. Rb8+ Kh7 0–1** [*Baltimore Sunday News*, July 20, 1890; *St. Louis Republic*, July 27, 1890; *St. John Globe*, August 8, 1890; *Al-*

bany Sunday Express, August 2, 1890; *ICM*, July 1890, pages 214–215; *PM*, pages 115–116]

321. C. Moehle–Pollock [C47]
Match, Game 11, Cincinnati, 29 June 1890

Pollock: "In this partie, 'Ajeeb' was autotomized through getting mixed up in a rather complicated opening." **1. e4 e5 2. Nf3 Nc6 3. d4 e×d4 4. N×d4 Nf6 5. Nc3 Bb4 6. N×c6 b×c6 7. Qd4 Qe7 8. f3 d5 9. Bg5 c5 10. B×f6** Pollock: "Bad for White's endgame. The 'given' is 10. Bb5+ Kf8 (not a simple position; Gunsberg once lost a tourney game to Blackburne through playing 10. ... Bd7 here, which costs a pawn.) 11. Qd3 d×e4 (Black must do better than 11. ... d×e4; Would 11. ... c4 or 11. ... Rb8 meet the case?) 12. f×e4 Q×e4+ 13. Q×e4 N×e4 14. Bc6, and wins." **10. ... c×d4 11. B×e7 K×e7 12. a3 Ba5 13. b4 d×c3 14. b×a5 d4 15. Rb1 Be6 16. Rb4 c5 17. Rb7+ Kd6 18. a6 Rhb8 19. f4 R×b7 20. a×b7 Rb8 21. Ba6 Bd7 22. Ke2** Pollock: "Castling might be a little better, but play as he may, Black's superior pawn position must eventually carry the day." **22. ... Bc6 23. Kd3** *(see diagram)*

After 23. Ke2–d3

23. ... B×b7 Pollock: "If 23. ... R×b7, 24. e5+! Kd5 25. B×b7 B×b7 26. Ke2, and should win." **24. B×b7 R×b7 25. Kc4 Rb2 26. Rc1 a5** Pollock: "In order to play ...a4 and ...Ra2, for if ...Ra2 at once, 27. Kb3." **27. a4?** White had to try 27. e5+ Kc6 28. f5 g6 29. f6 g5 30. g3 h6 31. g4 a4 32. h3 with excellent drawing chances. **27. ... Rb4+ 28. Kd3 R×a4 29. Rb1 Rb4 30. Ra1 a4 31. g4 g5!** Pollock: "White was unable to prevent Black from breaking up his rank of infantry and so occupying d5 or e5 with the king, for the final pawn advance." **32. f×g5 Ke5 33. Rf1 c4+ 34. Ke2 K×e4 35. R×f7 d3+ 36. c×d3+ c×d3+ 0–1** [*Baltimore Sunday News*, July 27, 1890; *Albany Sunday Express*, August 2, 1890; *PM*, pages 116–117]

322. Pollock–C. Moehle [C29]
Match, Game 12, Cincinnati, 29 June 1890

Pollock's "strong candidate" for his best game in this match. **1. e4 e5 2. Nc3 Nf6 3. f4 d5 4. f×e5 N×e4 5. Nf3** Pollock: "The New York experts are very fond of 5. Qf3. Boston's Burille defeated both Burn and Pollock with it in the late tournament." **5. ... Bc5 6. Qe2** Pollock: "To form a centre. But what becomes of the king's bishop? We prefer 6. d4." **6. ... N×c3 7. b×c3 0–0 8. d4 Be7 9. g3** Pollock: "Intending, if Black played 9. ... f6, 10. e6, followed by Bh3." **9. ... c5 10. Bg2 c×d4 11. c×d4 Bb4+ 12. Bd2 B×d2+ 13. Q×d2 Be6 14. 0–0 Nc6 15. Rf2** Pollock: "An excellent preparation for bringing all the forces to bear on the Black king." **15. ... Rc8 16. Bf1 Na5 17. Bd3 Nc4 18. Qf4 h6 19. Raf1 f6 20. Nh4!** The *Baltimore Sunday News* offered a diagram here, "of this intellectual treat." **20. ... Bh3** *(see diagram)* Pollock: "20. ... f×e5 clearly loses the exchange; and if 20. ... g5, 21. Qc1 g×h4 22. Q×h6, with a winning attack."

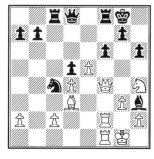

After
20. ... Be6–h3

21. Nf5!! B×f1 Pollock: "Again best. If 21. ... g5 22. N×h6+, followed by Qf3 and Qh5." **22. Qg4 Kf7?** Pollock: "'Ajeeb's' deliberations over this more occupied about 45 minutes, yet he strays. Still we have found no real defense in 22. ... Qc7 and 22. ... Rf7. Thus: 22. ... Qc7 23. R×f1 Nb2 24. e6 (24. e×f6) 24. ... Rce8 25. N×h6+ Kh8 26. Nf7+ and wins; secondly, 22. ... Rf7 23. R×f1 Kh8 24. e6 Qe8 25. Re1, followed by Nh4 and if possible Qf5." **23. Q×g7+ Ke6 24. R×f1 Rc7 25. Ne7!!** Pollock: "Quite a decisive idea, which forces a simple endgame. White could also win by 25. Qg4, [and if] 25. ... Kd7 26. e6+." **25. ... f5 26. R×f5 R×e7 27. Q×f8 Q×f8 28. R×f8 1–0** [*St. Louis Republic*, July 27, 1890; *St. John Globe*, August 12, 1890; *Baltimore Sunday News*, July 20, 1890; *Stamford Mercury*, December 19, 1890]

Various Baltimore Games (July 1890–February 1891)

323. A.W. Schofield–Pollock & R. Hall
Odds Game, Chesapeake Outing,
July 1890
Remove f7 pawn

1. e4 e6 2. Nf3 d5 3. e×d5 e×d5 4. d4 Nf6
5. Bg5 Bd6 6. Bd3 0–0 7. 0–0 Nc6 8. c3 Bg4
9. Nbd2 Qd7 10. Qc2 h6 11. Be3 Nh5 12. Nh4
Ne7 13. Rae1 Rf6 14. Bh7+ Kh8 *(see diagram)*

After
14. ... Kg8–h8

15. h3? A provocation that must have been quickly regretted. 15. f3 Be6 16. Bd3 was much safer. **15. ... B×h3! 16. B×h6** 16. g×h3 loses immediately to 16. ... Q×h3 17. f4 Q×h4 18. Re2 Qg3+ 19. Kh1 B×f4! or 19. ... g6. **16. ... Qg4** 16. ... R×h6 17. Ndf3 B×g2! 18. N×g2 Qh3 was fine too. **17. R×e7 B×e7 18. Bf5 R×f5 19. Q×f5 Q×f5 20. N×f5 B×f5 21. Be3 Bd6 22. Nf3 Nf4 23. Ng5 Rf8 24. g3 Nh3+ 25. Kg2 N×g5 26. B×g5 Bd3 27. Rh1+ Kg8 28. Rh4 Be4+ 29. Kg1 Rf3 30. Rg4 Rd3 0–1** [*Baltimore Sunday News*, November 15, 1891]

324. Pollock & R. Hall–Three Allied Players
Consultation Game, Baltimore Chess
Association, July 1890
Remove Nb1

1. e4 e5 2. Nf3 Nc6 3. Bc4 Bc5 4. b4 B×b4
5. c3 Ba5 6. 0–0 Nf6 7. Ng5 0–0 8. f4 d6 9. d3
B×c3 10. Rb1 Bd4+ 11. Kh1 Rb8 12. f5 Ne7
13. Qf3 c6 14. Qh3 h6 15. Qh4 h×g5 16. B×g5
d5 17. Bb3 Qd6 18. Rf3 *(see diagram)*
18. ... d×e4? 18. ... Rd8 or 18. ... Re8 would have maintained Black's advantage. **19. Rh3 Ng6 20. f×g6 B×h3** and White mates in four moves. **1–0** [*Baltimore Sunday News*, August 3, 1890]

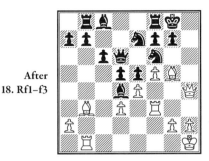

After
18. Rf1–f3

325. Pollock–B.H. Lutton [C45]
Simultaneous Exhibition (10 Boards),
Pittsburg, Allegheny Chess Club,
2 December 1890

1. e4 e5 2. Nf3 Nc6 3. d4 e×d4 4. N×d4 Qh4
5. Nf5?! 5. Nc3 and 5. Nb5 are better choices here.
**5. ... Q×e4+ 6. Ne3 Bc5 7. Bd3 Qe7 8. 0–0 B×e3
9. B×e3 d6 10. Nc3 Be6 11. Re1 h6** *(see diagram)*

After
11. ... h7–h6

12. Nd5? Premature. 12. f4!? was recommended.
**12. ... B×d5 13. Bg5 h×g5 14. R×e7+ Ng×e7
15. Qg4 f6 16. Re1 Ne5 17. Qa4+ c6 18. Bf1
N7g6 19. c4 Be6 20. Qa3 c5 21. g3 Kf7 22. Bg2
B×c4 23. B×b7 Rae8 24. Re3 Re7 25. Bc4 f5
26. B×f5 Nf3+ 27. R×f3 Re1+ 28. Kg2 Bf1+
29. Kg1 Bh3 mate 0–1** [*Pittsburg Dispatch*, December 6, 1890; *Dallas Morning News*, December 28, 1890]

326. Pollock–Watt [C39]
Simultaneous Exhibition (10 Boards),
Pittsburg, Allegheny Chess Club, 2
December 1890

1. e4 e5 2. f4 e×f4 3. Nf3 g5 4. h4 g4 5. Ne5
Nf6 6. Bc4 d5 7. e×d5 N×d5 8. d4 Be6 9. Qe2
Be7 10. 0–0 Nc6 11. Bb5 Qd6 12. c4 0–0–0
13. B×c6 *(see diagram)*
13. ... b×c6? A complicated position for an amateur in a small simultaneous exhibition. 13. ... Nb4!

After
13. Bb5×c6

would have launched some tactical complications keeping Black in the game: 14. B×b7+ (14. d5 f3! 15. Qe4 b×c6 16. d×e6 Q×e6 17. Q×g4 Q×g4 18. N×g4 Nc2) 14. ... K×b7 15. R×f4 Nc6 16. N×c6 Q×c6. **14. c5 f6 15. Qa6+ 1–0** [*Quebec Morning Chronicle*, December 18, 1890 (cites as source *Pittsburgh Chronicle*)]

327. Pollock–J.L. McCutcheon [C12]
Simultaneous Exhibition (4 Boards),
Pittsburg Library Chess Club,
3 (13?) December 1890

1. e4 e6 2. d4 d5 3. Nc3 Nf6 4. Bg5 Bb4 McCutcheon was credited with patenting this line in the French Defense, and in his December 21 *Baltimore Sunday News* column, Pollock noted that this line "is being further tested by a series of three postal games with Mr. Pollock." **5. e5 h6 6. Be3 B×c3+** Today, 6. ... Ne4 7. Qg4 is one of the key mainlines. **7. b×c3 Ne4 8. Qg4! g6 9. Bd3 N×c3 10. Nf3 h5 11. Qh3 Ne4?** 11. ... c5!? 12. d×c5 Nc6 was better. **12. 0–0 Nc6 13. B×e4 d×e4 14. Ng5 b6 15. N×e4 Bb7 16. Rad1 Nb4** *(see diagram)*

After
16. ... Nc6–b4

17. Bg5! 17. d5!? was ingenious and strong: 17. ... N×d5 (17. ... B×d5 18. Nf6+ Kf8 19. c4) 18. Bg5 Qb8 19. c4. **17. ... Qc8 18. Nf6+ Kf8 19. Qa3 c5 20. d×c5 b×c5 21. Rd6 N×c2 22. Qc1 Nd4 23. Bh6+ Ke7 24. Q×c5! Ne2+ 25. Kh1 B×g2+**

26. K×g2 Qb7+ 27. Rd5 mate 1–0 [*Baltimore Sunday News*, December 21, 1890; *Pittsburg Dispatch*, December 27, 1890; some reports said this game was played December 13, not December 3]

328. Pollock–J. Uhthoff
Handicap Tournament,
Baltimore Chess Association,
December 1890/January 1891
Remove Nb1

1. f4 f5 2. Nf3 Nf6 3. e3 e6 4. b3 Nc6 5. Bb2 Be7 6. Rc1 Nb4?! 7. a3 Nbd5 8. c4 Nb6 9. Be2 h5?! 9. ... a5 or 9. ... d6 in order to offer some shelter to the knight on b6 were necessary. **10. 0–0 Rh6 11. Ng5 g6 12. Qe1 Bf8 13. d3 h4 14. Bf3 Bg7 15. e4 Qe7 16. c5 Nh7 17. B×g7 Q×g7 18. c×b6 c×b6 19. Qe3 Qe7 20. Rc7 N×g5 21. f×g5 Rh7 22. Rfc1 Qd8 23. e×f5 g×f5 24. g6 Rh8 25. g7 Rg8** *(see diagram)*

After
25. ... Rh8–g8

26. Q×e6+! Pollock: "Mate in the middle or on either side." **1–0** [*Baltimore Sunday News*, March 1, 1891; *PM*, pages 108–109]

329. Pollock–J. Uhthoff
Handicap Tournament,
Baltimore Chess Association,
December 1890/January 1891
Remove Ng1

1. e4 e5 2. d4 d6 3. Bc4 Nf6 4. 0–0 Be7 5. f4 e×d4 6. e5 d×e5 7. f×e5 Nd5 8. Qf3 Be6 9. Nd2 c6 10. Ne4 Nd7 11. Qg3 Qb6 12. Bg5 0–0–0 13. B×e7 N×e7 14. R×f7 d3+ 14. ... B×f7 was also in Black's favor: 15. Nd6+ Kb8 16. N×f7 d3+ 17. Kh1 Q×b2 18. e6+ Ka8 19. Qe1 d2. **15. Kh1 B×c4?** 15. ... B×f7 16. Nd6+ Kb8 17. N×f7 Q×b2 was, once again, the best. **16. Nd6+! Kb8 17. N×c4 Qc5 18. c×d3 Ng6** Black had to navigate some complications starting with 18. ... Nf8! in order to keep some edge: 19. e6+ Ka8 20. a4 N×e6

21. Qe1 R×d3 22. Q×e6 Rhd8 23. Raf1 Rd1 24. Ne3 R×f1+ 25. N×f1 Nd5. **19. e6+ Nde5 20. e7 R×d3 21. N×e5 N×e5** *(see diagram)*

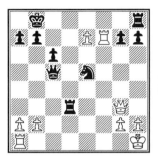

After
21. ... Ng6×e5

22. Rf8+!? 22. Q×g7 was stronger: 22. ... N×f7 23. Q×h8+ N×h8 24. e8Q+ Kc7 25. Q×h8. **22. ... R×f8 23. Q×e5+ Q×e5 24. e×f8Q+ Kc7 25. Rf1 Qd4 26. b4 Kb6 27. h3 Qc3 28. Qf5 g6??** 28. ... a6 or 28. ... Rd5 would have kept the game wide open. **29. Qa5 mate 1–0** [*Baltimore Sunday News*, March 22, 1891; *Stamford Mercury*, April 10, 1891; *PM*, page 109]

330. Pollock–J.W. Dallam
Handicap Tournament,
Baltimore Chess Association,
12 December 1890
Remove Nb1

1. f4 e6 2. Nf3 d5 3. e3 c5 4. Be2 Bd6 5. 0–0 h6 6. b3 Nc6 7. Bb2 Nf6 8. Kh1 Qe7 9. c4 Bd7 10. Rc1 0–0–0 11. Ne5 d4 12. b4 B×e5 13. f×e5 N×e5 14. e×d4 c×d4 15. B×d4 Qd6 Pollock: "If 15. ... Ba4, 16. Q×a4 R×d4 17. Q×a7, with a good attack." **16. Bc5 Qc7 17. d4** Pollock: "White suffers for this violation of the principle that 'Bishops fight best at a distance.'" **17. ... Bc6 18. b5 b6 19. b×c6 b×c5 20. d5 N×c6 21. Qa4 Nd4 22. Rb1 Rd6 23. Bd3 Ng4 24. Be4** *(see diagram)*

After
24. Bd3–e4

24. ... Kd8? Pollock: "Though this move which

threatens now ...Ra6, was studied by Dallam [with] care and sealed (the game being adjourned), it is an oversight!" It is somewhat bizarre that Pollock said nothing of 24. ... R×d5! 25. g3 Rh5 26. Qa6+ Kd8 27. Rb2 Q×g3. **25. R×f7! Q×f7 26. Rb8+ Ke7 27. Rb7+ Kf6 28. R×f7+ K×f7 29. Q×a7+ Kf6 30. Q×c5 Nf2+ 31. Kg1 N×e4 32. Q×d4+ Kf5 33. Q×g7 Rb6?** Pollock: "A more serious oversight." 33. ... Rhd8! would have kept things very complicated. **34. g4+ Kf4 35. Q×h8 e×d5 36. c×d5 K×g4 37. a4 Kf3 38. Qf8+ Nf6 39. Qa3+ Ke4 40. a5 1–0** [*Baltimore Sunday News*, January 11, 1891]

331. Pollock–J.W. Dallam
Handicap Tournament,
Baltimore Chess Association,
27 December 1890
Remove Ra1

1. e4 e6 2. d4 Pollock: "The old masters when ceding odds of queen's rook or knight used to play 2. f4, or if 2. ... d5, then 3. e5—safer line of attack." **2. ... d5 3. Nc3 c5 4. Bf4** Pollock: "4. e×d5 gains a pawn, but leaves the game too open and easy at such odds." **4. ... Qb6 5. Nb5 Na6 6. e×d5 e×d5 7. Nf3 Bd7 8. a4 B×b5 9. B×b5+ Kd8 10. Ng5 Nh6 11. 0–0 Bd6** Pollock: "Black should play 11. ... Nc7 here." **12. d×c5** Pollock: "A very strong move, whichever way Black retakes the pawn." **12. ... Q×c5** *(see diagram)*

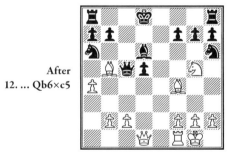

After
12. ... Qb6×c5

13. Ne4!! d×e4 14. B×d6 Qf5 Pollock: "The only move." **15. Qd2 Nc7** Pollock: "Losing the queen, on pain of some elegant checkmates. But if 15. ... Kc8 or 15. ... Qe6, White would win by 16. Rd1." **16. Be5+ Kc8 17. Qc3 Q×e5 18. Q×e5 N×b5 19. a×b5 f6 20. Qc5+ Kd8 21. Rd1+ Ke8 22. Qc7 Kf8 23. Rd8+ R×d8 24. Q×d8+ 1–0** [*Baltimore Sunday News*, January 4, 1891; *PM*, pages 107–108]

332. H.S. Habershom–Pollock
Handicap Tournament,
Baltimore Chess Association,
December 1890/January 1891
Remove Ng8

"A very curious game played in the ... winter handicap tournament...." **1. e4 e6 2. Nf3 b6 3. Bc4 Bb7 4. Nc3 Bb4 5. d3 d5 6. e×d5 e×d5 7. Qe2+ Kf8 8. Bb3 d4 9. a3 Ba5 10. Qe5 d×c3 11. 0–0 Nc6 12. Qf5 Qf6 13. Qd7 Re8 14. Bg5 Qg6 15. Rae1 f6 16. Nh4 Qh5** (*see diagram*)

After
16. ... Qg6–h5

17. g4 White missed a mate in seven, starting with 17. Nf5! **17. ... Ne5 18. R×e5 R×e5 19. B×f6?** "The move sealed at adjournment; but Mr. Habershom did not return to finish. It ought to lose the game." **0–1** 19. Bh6!! would have won prettily: 19. ... g×h6 20. Qd8+ (20. g×h5?? loses to 20. ... Rg5+ 21. Ng2 R×g2+ 22. Kh1 Rg7+) 20. ... Kg7 21. Nf5+ Kg6 22. g×h5+ K×f5 23. Q×h8 [*Baltimore Sunday News*, July 5, 1891; *New York Clipper*, August 1, 1891; *PM*, pages 111–112].

333. Pollock–D. Kemper
Handicap Tournament,
Baltimore Chess Association,
14 January 1891
Remove Ra1

1. e4 e5 2. f4 e×f4 3. Bc4 g5 4. Nf3 h6 5. Ne5 Rh7 6. 0–0 Nf6 7. B×f7+ R×f7 8. N×f7 K×f7 9. e5 Ng8 10. Qh5+ Kg7 11. b4 Be7 12. Bb2 Nc6 13. h4 N×b4?! 14. h×g5 B×g5 15. R×f4 (*see diagram*)

15. ... B×f4? and White mates in eight moves starting with 16. e6+. Instead of 15. ... B×f4?, 15. ... Qe7! would have maintained Black's advantage even if some precision was still required: 16. Rf7+ Q×f7 17. e6+ Qf6 18. B×f6+ B×f6 19. Qg4+ Kh8 20. e×d7 B×d7 21. Q×d7 Na6 22. c3 Rd8. **1–0** [*New York Clipper*, April 11, 1891; *PM*, page 108]

334. A. Maas–Pollock
Handicap Tournament,
Baltimore Chess Association,
January 1891
Remove Ra8

After
15. Rf1×f4

1. d4 f5 2. Nf3 Nf6 3. e3 e6 4. Bd3 b6 5. Ne5 Bb7 6. f3 Be7 7. Nc3 a6 8. 0–0 g5 9. e4 f4 10. Ng4 Nh5 11. e5 Nc6 12. Be4 d5 13. e×d6 c×d6 14. B×c6+ B×c6 15. d5 Bb7 16. d×e6 d5 Pollock: "Plain sailing so far for White. Black's idea is to shield his king behind the White pawn while creating complications." **17. Re1 0–0 18. Nh6+ Kg7 19. Nf7 Bc5+ 20. Kh1 Qf6 21. N×d5 B×d5 22. Q×d5 R×f7** (*see diagram*)

After
22. ... Rf8×f7

23. e×f7? Black mates in two. **0–1** Pollock: "White falls in his opponent's one and only trap (prepared fully half an hour before). He had ... many ways of breaking it up...." 23. g4! or 23. g3 wins for White. [*Baltimore Sunday News*, June 14, 1891; *Chess Player's Chronicle*, June 20, 1891]

335. Pollock–F.W. Koch
Handicap Tournament,
Baltimore Chess Association,
16 January 1891
Remove Nb1

1. e4 e5 2. Nf3 Nc6 3. Bc4 Nf6 4. Ng5 d5 5. e×d5 Na5 6. d3 a6 7. 0–0 b5 8. Bd2 N×c4

9. d×c4 b×c4 10. Qe2 Q×d5 11. Rad1 Bd6 12. Bc3 Qc6 13. f4 Bg4 14. Nf3 Bc5+ 15. Kh1 e4 16. h3 B×f3 17. R×f3 0–0 18. Rg3 *(see diagram)*

After
18. Rf3–g3

18. ... Rad8 and Black eventually won. Pollock noted that in case of 18. ... a5?? he had planned 19. R×g7+ K×g7 20. Qg4+ Kh8 21. Qg5 Be7 22. Rd7 Q×d7 23. B×f6+ but the text move ruined the plot. **1–0** [*Baltimore Sunday News*, January 25, 1891]

336. E.L. Torsch–Pollock
Handicap Tournament,
Baltimore Chess Association,
February 1891

Black to move

1. ... N×e4! 2. f×e4 B×e4 3. Ka1 R×b2 0–1 [*Baltimore Sunday News*, February 8, 1891]

337. D. Melamet–Pollock
Handicap Tournament,
Baltimore Chess Association,
February 1891
Remove f7 pawn

Pollock: "A game that will repay examination." **1. e4 and d4 c5 2. Qh5+ g6 3. Q×c5 Nc6 4. d5 e5 5. Qe3 Nd4** Pollock: "If 5. ... Bh6 6. Qc3 B×c1 7. d×c6, etc." **6. Qd3 a6** Pollock: "To save the knight which is threatened by c3." **7. a4** 7. f4! Bh6 8. Na3 was best. **7. ... Nf6 8. Bd2 Bc5 9. b4** Pol-

lock: "All part of his scheme to win that knight." **9. ... Ba7 10. h3 0–0 11. Ra3 Qb6 12. a5 N×c2+ 13. Kd1** Pollock: "Otherwise he would lose a bishop for a knight." **13. ... Q×f2 14. K×c2 d6 15. Nf3 N×e4 16. Kc1?** Pollock: "Obviously 16. Q×e4 would cost the queen." 16. Q×e4 was perhaps White's best try anyway: 16. ... Bf5 17. Nc3 Rac8 18. Kb2 R×c3! 19. Qe2 Rc2+ 20. Kb3 Rfc8 21. Q×f2 B×f2 22. b5. **16. ... Bf5 17. Qe2 Rac8+ 18. Nc3 N×c3** 18. ... Ng3 was simpler. **19. R×c3 R×c3+ 20. B×c3 Rc8?** 20. ... Qg3 was imperative. **21. Kb2** Pollock: "White must be rattled; why not here 21. Q×f2?" **21. ... Qg3!** Pollock: "Threatening to gain a piece by ...e4." **22. Qd2 e4 23. Nd4 e3 24. Qd1 Qf2+ 25. Ne2** Pollock: "Forced! If else, ...B×d4 wins a piece." **25. ... Be4 26. Rg1 Rc4 27. Kb3 Rc7 28. g4 Bf3** Pollock: "Menacing ... Q×g1." **29. Qe1 B×d5+ 30. Ka3 Q×e1 31. B×e1 Rc2 32. Nc3 e2** Pollock: "Attack and counterattack demand attention." **33. Bg2 Bc4 34. Rh1 Bd4 35. Bd5+ B×d5 36. N×d5 Rc1 37. Nf4 Bc3 38. Nd3** 38. N×e2 R×e1 39. R×e1 B×e1 40. Nd4 was a better try. **38. ... Rd1** *(see diagram)*

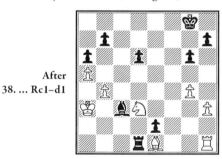

After
38. ... Rc1–d1

39. B×c3? Pollock: "This is fatal yet fate impels him." 39. Kb3 was an interesting defensive attempt: 39. ... B×e1 40. N×e1 d5 41. Kc2 Kf7 42. Rh2 with some reasonable hopes for a draw. **39. ... R×h1 40. Kb3 R×h3 41. Kc4 Rg3 42. Ne1 h5 43. g×h5 g×h5 44. Bf6 Rh3 0–1** [*Baltimore Sunday News*, February 22, 1891]

338. Pollock–Salomon
Handicap Tournament,
Baltimore Chess Association,
March 1891
Remove Ra1

1. e4 e5 2. Nf3 Nc6 3. Bc4 Nf6 4. Ng5 d5 5. e×d5 N×d5 6. N×f7 K×f7 7. Qf3+ Ke6 8. Nc3 Ncb4 9. 0–0 c6 10. d4 Qf6 11. Qe2 Bd6 12. f4 Rf8 13. Ne4 *(see diagram)*

After
13. Nc3–e4

13. ... Qf5? 13. ... Qg6! 14. d×e5 Bc7 15. a3 b5 16. Bb3 Na6 maintained the edge. **14. g4! Qg6 15. f5+ R×f5 16. R×f5 Kd7?!** 16. ... h6 17. d×e5 Bc7 was needed. **17. Rg5 Qh6 18. d×e5** 18. N×d6 Q×d6 19. R×g7+ Ke8 20. c3 was more exact. **18. ... B×e5** 18. ... Be7 was superior, of course. **19. Nc5+! Kd6 20. Q×e5+ K×c5 21. Be3+ K×c4 22. Qc3+ Kb5 23. R×d5+! N×d5 24. Qc5+ Ka6 25. Qa3+ Kb5 26. c4+ 1–0** [*Baltimore Sunday News*, April 19, 1891]

339. A. Maas–Pollock
Handicap Tournament,
Baltimore Chess Association,
March 1891
Remove Ra8

1. d4 f5 2. Nf3 Nf6 3. c4 e6 4. a3 b6 5. e3 Bb7 6. Nc3 a6 7. Bd3 Bd6 8. h3 Nc6 9. b4 0–0 10. e4 f×e4 11. N×e4 N×d4 12. N×d6 N×f3+ 13. g×f3 c×d6 14. Rg1 Qa8 15. Bb2 e5 16. Be2 Qb8 17. Qd2 Rf7 18. 0–0–0 d5 19. Qg5 d4 20. Rde1 d6 21. h4 a5 22. h5 a×b4 23. h6 b×a3 24. B×a3 Qa8 25. Kb2 Qa5 26. Rc1 Bc6 27. B×d6 Ra7 28. Q×g7+ R×g7 29. R×g7+ Kh8 30. Rf7 Ng8 *(see diagram)*

After
30. ... Nf6–g8

31. Bf8? This only draws. 31. f4 or 31. Rf5 were winning. **31. ... N×h6 32. B×h6 Qb4+ 33. Ka2 Qa4+ ½–½** [*Baltimore Sunday News*, February 14, 1892; *PM*, pages 110–111]

340. Pollock–J. Hinrichs
Handicap Tournament,
Baltimore Chess Association,
March 1891
Remove Nb1

1. e4 e5 2. Nf3 Nc6 3. Bc4 d6 4. c3 Bg4 5. Qb3 Qd7! 6. B×f7+ Q×f7 7. Q×b7 *(see diagram)*

After
7. Qb3×b7

7. ... Kd7! Pollock: "Very well played, this and all the game." **8. Q×a8 B×f3 9. g×f3 Q×f3 10. Rg1 Q×e4+ 11. Kf1** Pollock: "White cannot escape the draw by 'perpetual' if 11. Kd1 Qf3+ 12. Kc2 Nd4+. Still 11. Kd1 is safer than the text move." **11. ... Nge7 12. Qb7** Pollock: "Here we prefer 12. b4." **12. ... g6 13. Qb5 Bg7 14. d3 Qf3 15. Be3 Nd5 16. Re1 Rf8 17. B×a7 Nf4** Pollock: "This powerful stroke wins by force." **18. Rg3 Qh1+ 19. Rg1 Q×h2 20. f3 Nh3 21. Re2 R×f3+ 22. Ke1 Qf4 23. Re4 Qc1+ 24. Ke2 N×g1+ 25. B×g1 Qf1+ 0–1** [*Chess Player's Chronicle*, July 4, 1891; *PM*, page 110]

341. Pollock–I.A. Gunsberg [C29]
Exhibition Game, Baltimore,
4 February 1891

1. e4 e5 2. Nc3 Nf6 3. f4 d5 4. f×e5 N×e4 5. Nf3 Nc6 6. Bb5 Bb4 7. Qe2 B×c3 8. b×c3 0–0 9. 0–0 Qe7 10. a4! Re8 11. Ba3 Qe6 12. c4 Nd6? *(see diagram)*

After
12. ... Ne4–d6

13. B×d6 13. e×d6!! Q×e2 14. c×d5 was a remarkable resource: 14. ... Q×f1+ 15. R×f1 a6

16. Bd3 Ne5 17. d×c7 N×d3 18. c×d3 b5 19. a5 f6
20. d6. **13. … Q×d6?** 13. … c×d6 14. Ng5 Qg6
15. N×f7 Bd7 had to be played, but with a poor
position. **14. e×d6 R×e2 15. c×d5 1–0** [*Baltimore
Sunday News*, February 8, 1891; *Albany Evening
Journal*, February 21, 1891; *Philadelphia Times*,
March 15, 1891]

342. Pollock–I.A. Gunsberg [C44]
Exhibition Game, Baltimore,
5 February 1891

1. e4 e5 2. Nf3 Nc6 3. c3 Nf6 4. d4 e×d4 5. e5
Nd5 6. a3 d6 7. Bb5 Bd7 8. c×d4 a6 9. Ba4 Nb6
10. Nc3 d×e5 11. d×e5 N×a4 12. Q×a4 Be7
13. Qc2 Bg4 14. Bf4 B×f3 15. g×f3 Qd4 16. Ne2
Qd5 (*see diagram*)

After
16. … Qd4–d5

17. Qc3? Pollock should have tried the more
courageous 17. Rd1 Q×f3 18. Rg1, with clear compensation. **17. … 0–0–0! 18. Rg1 g5?!** 18. … Rhg8
19. Rc1 g5 20. Be3 Q×e5 was more patient play.
19. Be3? 19. B×g5 B×g5 20. R×g5 Rhe8 21. Kf1
R×e5 22. R×e5 N×e5 23. Rc1 c6 24. Nf4 Q×f3
25. Q×f3 N×f3 26. Kg2 offered some slight drawing chances. **19. … Qb5 20. Rc1 Rd3 21. Qc2
Rhd8** and Black won shortly. **0–1** [*Baltimore Sunday News*, February 15, 1891]

343. Pollock & Gunsberg & Schofield–
"Nine Strong Fighters"
Odds Game in Consultation
(After Banquet), Baltimore,
5 February 1891
Remove Nb1

1. f4 Nf6 2. b3 e6 3. Bb2 d5 4. e3 c5 5. Nf3
Nc6 6. Bd3 Ne4 7. 0–0 Qc7 8. c3 Bd7 9. Rc1
0–0–0 10. Ba3 Qa5 11. Bb2 f6 12. c4 Kb8 13. a3
Rg8 14. Rb1 g5 15. f5 g4 16. b4 c×b4 17. Nd4
Qc7 18. f×e6 N×d4 19. B×d4 B×e6 20. Rc1 Qa5
21. a×b4 Q×b4 22. Rb1 Qe7? 22. … Q×d2
23. Qb3 Bc8 was sound. **23. B×e4 d×e4 24. B×f6**

Qd6 25. B×d8 Q×d8 26. Qa4 Bc5 27. Qc6 Qc8
28. Q×e4 (*see diagram*)

After
28. Qc6×e4

28. … Bb6? 28. … Re8 was needed. **29. Rf6**
29. R×b6! a×b6 30. Qe5+ Qc7 31. Q×e6 Rd8
32. d4 was more accurate. **29. … B×c4?** Again,
29. … Re8 was the correct defense. **30. Rc1! Rg7
31. Q×c4 1–0** [*Baltimore Sunday News*, February
15, 1891]

344. Torsch & von Haften–Pollock &
de Conin
Odds Game in Consultation,
Baltimore, 14 February 1891
Remove f7 pawn

1. e4 and d4 c5 2. d×c5 Nc6 3. Bd3 e5 4. Be3
Nf6 5. Nc3 b6 6. Nd5 B×c5 7. N×f6+ Q×f6
8. Bc4? 8. Qf3 was better. **8. … B×e3 9. f×e3
Qh4+ 10. Kd2 Q×e4 11. Qe2 d5 12. Bd3 Qb4+
13. Kc1 0–0 14. c3 Qc5 15. Kd2 e4 16. Bc2 Ne5
17. h3** (*see diagram*)

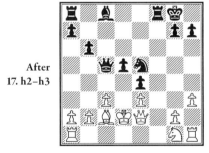

After
17. h2–h3

**17. … Ba6! 18. Q×a6 Nc4+ 19. Ke1 Q×e3+
0–1** [*Baltimore Sunday News*, February 22, 1891]

345. Pollock & de Conin–Hinrichs &
Waitjen
Odds Game in Consultation,
Baltimore, 21 February 1891
Remove Ra1

"The wet weather of the 21st ult. affected the Saturday Consultation game, and Messrs. de Conin and Pollock were rather over-weighted in rendering a Rook to Messrs. Hinrichs and Waitjen." **1. e4 e5 2. Nc3 Nc6 3. f4 e×f4 4. Nf3 Bc5 5. d4 Bb4 6. Bc4 g5 7. 0–0 B×c3 8. b×c3 d6 9. Ba3 Bg4 10. h3 B×f3 11. Q×f3 Qf6 12. e5 d×e5 13. Rb1 Rb8 14. Bb5 Nge7 15. d5 0–0 16. d×c6 b×c6 17. B×c6 Q×c6** "Drawn owing to lateness of the hour." ½–½ [*Baltimore Sunday News*, March 1, 1891]

In Brooklyn and Manhattan

346. Pollock–C. Thompson [C58]
Simultaneous Exhibition (12 Boards), Brooklyn Chess Club, 3 April 1891

"Game at Board 7: Mr. Thompson won his game in Mr. Gunsberg's simultaneous performance at the Manhattan in 1889, being then only 15 years of age. He is now a strong player." **1. e4 e5 2. Nf3 Nc6 3. Bc4 Nf6 4. Ng5 d5 5. e×d5 Na5 6. d3 h6 7. Nf3 e4 8. Qe2 N×c4 9. d×c4 Bd6 10. h3 0–0 11. Nd4 Nh7 12. Nc3 f5 13. g4 Bc5 14. Nb3** (*see diagram*) It's likely that Pollock considered 14. N×f5 B×f5 15. g×f5 R×f5 16. N×e4 risky, but after 16. ... Re5 17. Bf4 B×f2+ 18. Kd2 Re8 19. Raf1 White has the advantage.

After
14. Nd4–b3

14. ... B×f2+!? 15. Q×f2 15. K×f2 f×g4+ 16. Kg1 g×h3 17. N×e4 Qh4 gives Black a seemingly strong attack. **15. ... f×g4 16. Bf4! g5 17. h×g4 R×f4 18. Qh2 Qf6 19. 0–0–0! B×g4 20. Rde1 Bf3 21. Rhg1 Nf8 22. Nc5 Kh7?** 22. ... Re8 holds Black's play together nicely. **23. N3×e4 B×e4 24. N×e4 R×e4 25. Q×c7+ Kg6 26. R×e4 1–0** [*Baltimore Sunday News*, April 12, 1891]

347. Pollock–J.D. Elwell
Simultaneous Exhibition (12 Boards), Brooklyn Chess Club, 3 April 1891

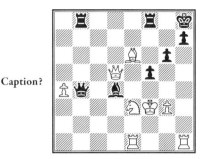

Caption?

In the *Baltimore Sunday News* of April 12, 1891, Pollock gave this position with the remark that "White mated in five moves." While there is no forced mate, White wins with **1. R×h7+ K×h7 2. Rh1+ Kg7 3. Qd7+ Kf6 4. Nd5+ 1–0**

348. Pollock–R. Bonn [C39]
Simultaneous Exhibition?, Brooklyn Chess Club, 3 April 1891

Pollock: "A peculiar finish." **1. e4 e5 2. f4 e×f4 3. Nf3 g5 4. h4 g4 5. Ng5 d5 6. e×d5 Q×d5 7. Nc3 Qd8 8. d4 Bd6?!** 8. ... h6 was more principled. **9. Bc4 Nh6 10. 0–0 0–0 11. B×f4 Nc6 12. Nd5 B×f4 13. R×f4 Bf5 14. Qd2** 14. R×f5 N×f5 15. Q×g4 Nh6 16. Qe4 f5 17. Qf4 was a pretty solution. **14. ... b6 15. Raf1 Na5** (*see diagram*)

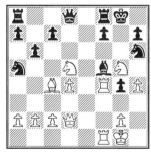

After
15. ... Nc6–a5

16. Bd3 B×d3 17. Nf6+ Kg7 18. Q×d3 Rh8 19. Nf×h7 19. Nh5+ Kg8 20. N×f7, with a mate in six. **19. ... f5 20. R×f5 Qd6** and White mates in three. **1–0** [*Baltimore Sunday News*, April 12, 1891; *PM*, page 95]

349. E.N. Olly–Pollock [C32]
Brooklyn Chess Club, April 1891

1. e4 e5 2. f4 d5 3. e×d5 e4 4. Nc3 Nf6 5. Bc4

Bc5 6. Nge2 0–0 7. d4 e×d3 8. Q×d3 Re8 9. h3
Nbd7 10. Bd2 Nb6 11. 0–0–0 a5 12. Ng3 Bf2
13. Nge4? Bf5 Most precise was 13. ... N×e4
14. N×e4 Bf5 15. Rhe1 N×c4 16. Q×c4 b5 17. Qd3
B×e1 18. R×e1 Qe7. 14. N×f6+ Q×f6 15. Qf1
Qd4 16. Bb5 c6?! A dubious sacrifice. 16. ... Bd7
was better. 17. d×c6 b×c6 18. B×c6 Rab8 After
18. ... Nc4!? 19. B×a8 R×a8 Black had a modicum
of compensation. 19. B×e8 Nc4 20. b3 20. Bb5!
was best. 20. ... N×d2 (see diagram)

After
20. ... Nc4×d2

21. Qc4? Failing to make sense of the unraveling
tactics. 21. Nb5 kept White's edge: 21. ... Qb6
22. R×d2 Be3 23. Qe2 B×d2+ 24. Q×d2 R×e8
25. Nd6 Rd8 26. Rd1. 21. ... N×c4 22. R×d4
B×d4 23. Nd5 23. b×c4 B×c3 24. Bb5 Be4 25. Rd1
B×g2 is hopeless for White. 23. ... R×e8 24. b×c4
Re2 25. c3 Bc5 26. g4 Bc2 0–1 [The World, April
21, 1891; Charleston Sunday News, May 3, 1891]

350. Pollock–J.S. Ryan [C21]
Manhattan Chess Club, 5 April 1891

Pollock: "Two 'Irish Champions' meet." 1. e4
e5 2. d4 Nf6 3. Nf3 N×e4 4. d×e5 Be7 5. Bc4
Nc6 6. Nc3 0–0 7. 0–0 d6 8. Nd5 Bg4 9. b4 Ne6
10. Bb2 Ng5? 10. ... d×e5 11. h3 B×f3 12. Q×f3
Nd7 was correct. 11. Qd4 B×f3 (see diagram)

After
11. ... Bg4×f3

12. e×d6 Bf6 13. Ne7+! Kh8 14. Q×f6 Rg8
15. Q×g5 Nd7 16. B×f7 1–0 [Baltimore Sunday

News, April 12, 1891; Bristol Mercury, July 14,
1891; New York Clipper, November 28, 1891]

351. F. Mintz & E.A. Ford & others–
Pollock & Holladay & Euphrat [C56]
Consultation Game,
Manhattan Chess Club,
5 April 1891

1. e4 e5 2. Nf3 Nc6 3. Bc4 Nf6 4. d4 e×d4
5. 0–0 Bc5 Pollock: "Bringing the opening into
the famous Max Lange Attack. 5. ... N×e4 is rather
better for Black." 6. e5 d5 7. e×f6 d×c4 8. Re1+
Be6 9. f×g7 Pollock: "9. Ng5 at once is much
stronger." 9. ... Rg8 10. Ng5 Pollock: "Threatening to win a piece by N×e6." 10. ... Qd5 11. Qg4
0–0–0 Pollock: "If 11. ... R×g7, 12. N×e6 R×g4
13. N×c7+." 12. N×e6 f×e6 13. R×e6 13. Bh6
was better. 13. ... R×g7! Pollock: "This fine move
gains time for Black." 14. Rg6+ Rgd7 15. Rg5
Ne5 16. Qf5 Re8 17. Nd2 (see diagram) Pollock:
"To obviate the effects of ...Nf7."

After
17. Nb1–d2

17. ... Ng6 Pollock: "A very pretty stroke.
White, however, rightly considered 17. ... Kb8 as
more conclusive." 17. ... h6 18. Rh5 d3 19. c3 Kb8
20. h3 Rf7 would have given Black a winning edge.
18. Q×d5 R×d5 19. R×d5 Nf4 20. Ne4 Pollock:
"The coup juste, for if 20. ... R×e4, 21. B×f4 wins."
20. ... N×d5 21. f3 Bb6 22. Kf1 Nb4 23. c3 Nc2
24. Rb1 d3 25. b3 Be3 26. B×e3 c×b3 Pollock:
"Retaking the bishop at once costs a pawn."
27. a×b3 N×e3+ 28. Kf2 Ng4+! 29. f×g4 R×e4
30. Kf3 Re2 31. Rd1 Rb2 32. b4 c5 33. b×c5 a5
34. R×d3 a4 35. c4 Kc7 36. h4 Kc6 37. g5 K×c5
38. h5 Rb6 39. Ra3 Kb4 40. Ra1 a3 and the game
was drawn "owing to the lateness of the hour." It
was reported that Mintz had thought White was
winning here, but that's not the case. ½–½ [Balti-
more Sunday News, April 26, 1891]

Part Two, Section VI
(July 1891)

352. Pollock–E. Delmar [C25]
**NYSCA Meeting Match, Game 1,
Skaneateles, 20 July 1891**

**1. e4 e5 2. Nc3 Bc5 3. f4 d6 4. Nf3 Bg4 5. Bc4
Nc6 6. Bb5** Steinitz: "Serious loss of time. The
right play is 6. f×e5 d×e5 (or 6. ... N×e5, 7. Be2
etc.) 7. d3, and if 7. ... Nd4 8. B×f7+ Kf8 (or 8. ...
K×f7, 9. N×e5+ and should win) 9. N×d4 B×d1
10. Ne6+, and ought to win. The last variation was
played by the editor in Havana in 1889." **6. ... a6**
Steinitz: "6. ... Nge7 was preferable." **7. B×c6+
b×c6 8. d3 Ne7** *(see diagram)*

After
8. ... Ng8–e7

9. Ne2?! Pollock: "This appears to give Black
the upper hand." **9. ... Ng6 10. f×e5 d×e5**
Steinitz: "We believe that Black might have given
up the pawn and instituted a strong attack by 10. ...
Nh4, with the probable continuation 11. N×h4
Q×h4+ 12. g3 Qh3 13. d4 Qg2 14. Rg1 Q×g1+,
and wins." **11. Ng3 Nh4 12. Qe2 0–0** Pollock: "If
12. ... Qf6 13. Bg5 equalizes matters." **13. h3**
Steinitz: "13. Bd2, with the view of castling, was
more likely to relieve him." **13. ... B×f3 14. g×f3
f5** Steinitz: "Not as strong as 14. ... Qf6 followed,
if the rook defended the pawn, by ...Qg6 or ...
Qe6." **15. e×f5 N×f5 16. N×f5 R×f5 17. Qe4 Qf8**

18. Ke2 Rd8 19. c3 Re8 20. Rf1 Pollock:
"20. Q×c6 would be met by 20. ... e4." **20. ... Kh8
21. Bd2** Steinitz: "We see no clear reason why
White on this and the next move does not capture
the c6-pawn." **21. ... Qf7 22. Rae1 Rf8 23. b3** Pollock: "The same holds good here." Steinitz: "Now
23. Q×c6 would have been dangerous on account
of the rejoinder 23. ... e4." **23. ... Bb6 24. Kd1
R×f3** Pollock: "This made White feel happy, but
Mr. Steinitz thinks the advantage of the pawn is
not balanced by the shutting off of the Black
bishop." **25. R×f3 Q×f3+ 26. Q×f3 R×f3
27. R×e5 h6 28. d4 R×h3 29. Ke2** *(see diagram)*

After
29. Kd1–e2

29. ... g5 Steinitz: "Premature. He ought to
have played 29. ... Rh1, with the view of attacking
at b1, which would have the important effect of
driving back the adverse king, as White had hardly
anything better than Kd3, and then to defend at
c2." Pollock: "For here the very fine move of 29. ...
Rh1 should come in. The text move is weak anyway." **30. a4 a5 31. Be3 g4 32. c4** Steinitz: "A powerful stroke that comes in at the right time after
ingenious preparations." **32. ... Rh2+ 33. Kd3 g3
34. c5 Ba7?** 34. ... g2 35. c×b6 c×b6 36. Bg1 Rh1
37. Re1 h5 was Black's best chance. **35. Ke4 Kg7
36. Kf3?** Pollock: "Enclosed at the adjournment.

White should have played 36. Re7+." Steinitz: "The sealed move, the game having been adjourned after Black's previous move. White could have won easily now by 36. Re7+ Kg6 37. R×c7 Bb8 38. R×c6+ Kg7 39. Rb6 etc." **36. ... Kf7 37. K×g3 Rb2 38. B×h6 R×b3+ 39. Kf4 Rb4 40. Ke4 R×a4 41. Bg5 Rb4 42. Bd8 a4 43. B×c7 a3 44. Bd6** Steinitz: "White's game is gone and the rest is a struggle against fate." **44. ... Kf6 45. Rf5+ Ke6 46. Re5+ Kf6 47. Rf5+** Pollock: "To gain little 'clock time.'" **47. ... Ke6 48. Rh5 Ra4 49. Rh6+ Kd7 50. Ke5?** Pollock: "This loses. 50. Rh1 draws easily." **50. ... a2 51. Rh7+ Kc8 52. Rc7+ Kd8 53. Ke6 a1Q 54. Rd7+ Kc8 55. Rc7+ Kb8 56. R×c6+ Kb7 57. Rc7+ Ka6 58. d5 Re4+ 59. Kd7 Qa4+ 60. c6 Re2 61. Be7 Qg4+ 62. Kd8 Qg8+ 63. Kd7 Q×d5+ 64. Bd6** and Black mates in two. **0–1** [*ICM*, June 1891, pages 173–174; *New York Tribune*, July 21, 1891; *Baltimore Sunday News*, July 26, 1891; *New York Clipper*, August 22, 1891]

353. E. Delmar–Pollock [C77]
NYSCA Meeting Match, Game 2,
Skaneateles, 20 July 1891

1. e4 e5 2. Nf3 Nc6 3. Bb5 a6 4. Ba4 Nf6 5. d3 Bc5 6. Nc3 Pollock: "Not considered so good as 6. c3." Steinitz: "If 6. B×c6, 6. ... d×c6 7. N×e5 B×f2+ 8. K×f2 Qd4+, recovering the pawn with the superior game, but 6. c3 is preferable." **6. ... 0–0 7. 0–0 b5 8. Bb3 Bb7** Steinitz: "A mode of development for this bishop which was first introduced by Paulsen in a similar position, but is rarely adopted by masters." **9. Bg5** Steinitz: "9. Be3 or 9. Ne2 was better adapted to assist his developments." **9. ... Be7 10. Ne2 Nh5 11. Be3 Kh8 12. Bd5 Bd6 13. Ng5 Qf6 14. a4** Pollock: "14. c3 at once seems preferable." **14. ... Nf4 15. Nf3** (*see diagram*)

After
15. Ng5–f3

15. ... g5!? 16. c3 g4 17. Ne1 N×d5 18. e×d5 Ne7 19. c4 Steinitz: "White has cleverly counterbalanced the adverse attack on the kingside, as well

as the superiority of the two bishops, by his pressure on the other wing, and he obtains much the better game by this advance." **19. ... c5** Steinitz: "Black is forced to block his queen's bishop thus, for he cannot afford to allow the opponent the advance of c5, followed by d6, which would have formed a strong chain of pawns for White that must have ultimately given the latter a telling advantage." **20. Ng3 Qg6 21. f4 f5 22. Qe2** Pollock: "22. f×e5 was surely better—White now permits his opponent not only to establish a passed pawn but to form a strong defensive blockade." Steinitz: "Better than 22. f×e5 B×e5 23. B×c5 d6, followed by ...f4, with a strong attack." **22. ... b×c4 23. d×c4 e4 24. b3 a5 25. Bc1** Pollock: "The sealed move at the adjournment." **25. ... Kg8 26. Bb2 Qh6 27. Qd2** 27. Be5?! looks interesting but doesn't offer much: 27. ... B×e5! 28. f×e5 Qg7 29. Qb2 d6 30. Rb1 Q×e5 31. Q×e5 d×e5 32. Rd1 Rad8. **27. ... Ng6 28. Ne2 Ra6 29. g3** Steinitz: "Ill-advised and overlooking the adverse fine sally. 29. Qc3 would have given him free hand for further operations on the queen's wing as clearly Black could not answer 29. ... N×f4, on account of 30. N×f4 B×f4 31. R×f4 and Black could not retake since mate is impending by Qg7. White would thus have gained time for manoeuvring Nb5, via c2 and a3." Pollock: "Perhaps overlooking the reply. It would have been stronger to move 29. Qc3." **29. ... Ne5 30. Nc3 Nf3+ 31. N×f3 g×f3 32. Nb5 Be7 33. Rae1 Qh3?!** Steinitz: "Impetuously throwing away his advantage, which he could have easily maintained by the preliminary precaution of 33. ... Rf7." Pollock: "The correct play was 33. ... Bd8 followed by ...d6." **34. R×f3** Steinitz: "Highly ingenious and strong enough for a draw at least." Pollock: "A very fine move and unanswerable." **34. ... e×f3 35. R×e7 Rg6 36. Qf2 Qg4 37. Qe3** Steinitz: "We believe that White could have won here by 37. R×d7 Bc8 38. Re7 h5 39. Re3, etc." **37. ... h5 38. Qe5 Rgf6 39. Re8 R×e8** Steinitz: "Best as White threatened Q×f6." Pollock: "Forced. White threatened Q×f6 or R×f8+." **40. Q×e8+ Rf8 41. Qe7** 41. Q×d7 Bc8 42. Qe7 h4 43. Kf2 wins for White as well. **41. ... h4 42. Kf2 h×g3+ 43. h×g3 Rf7 44. Qe8+ Rf8 45. Qe7 Rf7 46. Qe8+ Rf8 47. Qe7 Rf7 48. Qe3** Steinitz: "In rejecting a draw he exercises good judgment, for it appears that he had a won game in the ending though he was the exchange behind." **48. ... Qh5** Pollock: "There was no other defense, and White now properly exchanges queens." **49. Qe8+ Kh7 50. Qh8+ Kg6 51. Q×h5+ K×h5 52. Nd6 Re7** *(see diagram)* Steinitz: "Black makes the most of a bad case and he succeeds with his desperate ingenuity."

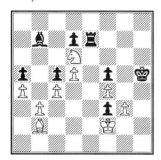

After
52. ... Rf7–e7

53. Be5? Steinitz: "If he has realized his danger he would not have grudged the adverse rook the open file. 53. Bf6, which was pointed out by Mr. Gilberg, would have won the game without much difficulty." Pollock: "A fatal mistake, either 53. K×f3 or 53. Bf6, as pointed out by Mr. Gilberg, wins easily." **53. ... Kg4** Steinitz: "Exceedingly fine and decisive." **54. N×b7 Rh7 55. N×c5 Rh2+ 56. Ke3?** 56. Ke1 or 56. Kf1 should have drawn. **56. ... Re2+ 57. Kd3 Re1 58. Bd4 Rd1+ 59. Ke3 R×d4!** Steinitz: "Black's conduct of the ending belongs to the masterpieces of play in positions of similar description." **60. K×d4 f2 61. N×d7 f1Q 62. Ne5+ K×g3 63. d6 Q×f4+ 64. Kd5 Qe4+ 65. Ke6 Kf4 0–1** [*Baltimore Sunday News*, August 3, 1891; *ICM*, June 1891, pages 176–177; *New York Tribune*, July 22, 1891; *PM*, pages 120–122]

354. Pollock–E. Delmar [C30]
NYSCA Meeting Match, Game 3, Skaneateles, 21 July 1891

1. f4 e5 2. e4 Steinitz: "It is quite safe to accept From's Gambit by 2. f×e5, though Black obtains some temporary attack after 2. ... d6 3. e×d6 B×d6 4. Nf3 Nf6, which, however, ought not to last long by proper play on the other side. The text move transforms the position into one of a regular King's Gambit." **2. ... Bc5 3. Nf3 d6 4. c3** Pollock: "Hardly the best continuation." **4. ... Nc6** Steinitz: "4. ... Bg4 is the authorized defence." **5. d4 e×d4 6. c×d4 Bb6 7. Bb5 Bd7 8. 0–0 Nge7 9. Nc3 0–0 10. Kh1 Bg4 11. Be3** Pollock: "Very objectionable. 11. Ne2 is necessary." **11. ... d5** Steinitz: "Injudicious, as the doubled pawn which the opponent promptly forms in reply ought to have hampered his game all along up to the ending and White had, therefore, a manifest advantage after the reduction of forces." **12. B×c6 b×c6 13. e5 Nf5 14. Bf2 Qd7**

15. Ne2 Steinitz: "More to the point, for operations against the adverse queenside was 15. Na4, followed soon by Rc1." **15. ... Rae8** Pollock: "Most players would take off the knight while there is time, but Delmar plays for mate." **16. Neg1 Re6 17. a4 Rh6 18. Qe1** Pollock: "Perceiving the snare. If 18. a5 B×d4 19. B×d4 Ng3 mate." Steinitz: "Parrying a neat thrust which the shrewd opponent had designed. If 18. a5 B×d4 and White dare not recapture with the bishop on account of the terrible rejoinder ...Ng3 mate, while White's knight is obviously pinned." **18. ... a5 19. h3 Ne7 20. Ra3 Bf5 21. Nd2** Pollock: "His move was sealed and the game adjourned." **21. ... Ng6 22. Rf3 Qe7 23. Qe3 Rd8 24. Rg3** Steinitz: "His game deteriorates after this ill-judged move. It was high time to stop the dangerous advance of the c-pawn which the adversary was evidently preparing. 24. Rc1 was sufficient for the purpose, for if then 24. ... c5, 25. f×c5 d4 26. Qa3 etc." **24. ... c5! 25. d×c5 d4 26. Qb3 B×c5 27. Rg5 Be6 28. Qg3 Bd5** *(see diagram)*

After
28. ... Be6–d5

29. Qg4 29. f5! would have been an interesting try that would have balanced the game: 29. ... Bb4 30. Be1 N×e5 31. f6!? R×f6 32. R×e5 Re6 33. R×e6 B×e6 34. Ne4 B×e1 35. R×e1. **29. ... f6 30. e×f6 g×f6 31. Re1** Pollock: "If 31. R×d5, 31. ... R×d5 32. f5 Qd7 33. Bg3 was perhaps as good." **31. ... Qg7** Steinitz: "Black has played exceedingly well after his release on the 24th move, but here he might have more efficiently simplified matters by 31. ... Qd7 32. Q×d7 (or if 32. Rf5, 32. ... Be6 33. R×e6 Q×e6 and White dare not take the bishop, as he would lose the queen, his h3-pawn being pinned.") 32. ... R×d7 33. Rf5 Kg7, and wins." **32. R×d5** Pollock: "The exchange was lost anyway." **32. ... R×d5 33. Re8+ Nf8 34. Qc8 Qd7 35. Qb8 Kf7 36. Rc8 Ne6 37. Ne4 Be7 38. Nf3 d3** Steinitz: "Here and for some moves later Black ignores the following combination, which Delmar afterward pointed out, namely: 38. ... N×f4 39. R×c7 R×h3+ 40. Kg1 (or 40. Nh2 Qg4, and should win.) **39. Be1 Bd8 40. Bd2 Rhh5 41. Ng3 Rhf5** 41. ... Nd4! 42. N×h5 (42. Ng1 Rh4) 42. ... N×f3 43. R×d8 Q×d8 44. Q×d8 R×d8 45. g×f3 Rb8 was better. **42. N×f5** Pollock: "Black thus had to return the exchange." **42. ... R×f5 43. Qa8 Rd5 44. Rb8 Be7 45. b4?!** 45. B×a5 d2 46. N×d2 R×d2 47. B×d2 Q×d2 48. Qc6 N×f4 49. Qe8+ would have secured at least a draw. **45. ... B×b4?** Steinitz: "45. ... a×b4 was undoubtedly by far superior." **46. B×b4 a×b4 47. Rh8 Rh5** Pollock: "Absolutely fatal. 47. ... Kg7 should have been played." Steinitz: "The climax of indecision and, in fact, little short of a blunder, considering the standing of the two players. 47. ... Kg7 48. Qg8+ Kh6, a line of play pointed out by Mr. Rose, would have made the king safe and he could then win easily." **48. f5** Steinitz: "The surprise is certainly ingenious but a player of Delmar's strength ought to have foreseen it." **48. ... Kg7** (see diagram) Steinitz: "The knight has no sensible move without leaving a mate open by Qg8+, and if 48. ... R×f5 49. Qg8+ Ke7 50. R×h7+, and after capturing the queen he also wins the rook by Qh7+."

After
48. ... Kf7–g7

49. f×e6 Qe7 Steinitz: "Nothing was good, if 49. ... Q×e6 50. Qf8+ Kg6 51. Rg8+ Kf5 52. Nd4+, winning the queen." **50. Qg8+ Kh6 51. Qf7 1–0** [*Baltimore Sunday News*, August 2, 1891; *Pittsburg Dispatch*, August 8, 1891; *ICM*, June 1891, pages 179–180; *PM*, pages 122–124]

355. E. Delmar–Pollock [C44]
NYSCA Meeting Match, Game 4, Skaneateles, 21 July 1891

Baltimore Sunday News (August 2): "The fourth game was a short affair, finished off prettily by the Manhattan player in 2½ hours. Pollock adopted a brilliant variation, but, running short of time near the end of his first hour, played his queen wrong and speedily collapsed. The variation in question was unknown to, or, more probably forgotten, by Delmar, who, nevertheless, almost proved it un-

sound before his opponent became suddenly demoralized. The game made the score 'two all.'" **1. e4 e5 2. Nf3 Nc6 3. c3 Nf6** Steinitz: "We consider this opening favourable for the second player if Black here adopts 3. ... d5. The text move only leads to an even game." **4. d4 N×e4 5. d5** (see diagram)

After
5. d4–d5

5. ... Bc5!? Pollock: "Very bold—in a match game of such importance." Steinitz: "Too hazardous for a match game. 5. ... Nb8, as played by Weiss against Chigorin in the Sixth American Chess Congress, is the proper move." **6. d×c6 B×f2+** Pollock awarded this move with a "!" **7. Ke2 b×c6 8. Qa4 f5 9. Nbd2 Bb6** Pollock: "The old masters castled here, and after 10. N×e4 f×e4 11. K×f2 e×f3 White escapes further inconvenience by 12. g3." Steinitz: "Both parties played according to book up to this, which is new. Usually the game proceeds 9. ... 0–0 10. N×e4 f×e4 11. K×f2 e×f3 12. g3, etc." **10. N×e4 f×e4 11. Q×e4 0–0 12. Ng5 g6 13. Kd1 d5 14. Qh4** Steinitz: "14. Q×e5 Bg4+ [14. ... Rf5! 15. Qg3 Bf2 16. Qg4 Re5 17. Qf3 Re1+ 18. Kc2 Bf5+ 19. Bd3 R×h1 20. B×f5 g×f5 21. Q×f2 R×c1+ 22. R×c1 Q×g5 was stronger and fine for Black—authors] 15. Be2 Re8 16. Q×e8+ Q×e8 17. B×g4, with three minor pieces against the queen, was also safe." **14. ... Qe7 15. Be2 Bf5 16. Rf1 Rad8?!** 16. ... e4!? 17. Bf4 e3 18. g4 Be4 seems much stronger than this normal but momentarily useless rook move. **17. Nf3 Qe6?** Pollock: "The error above alluded to. 17. ... Qd6 was much better. If then 18. Bh6 Rfe8 19. Ng5 does not attack the queen, and consequently Black has not lost a 'tempo,' though in the end perhaps his attack should fail." **18. Bh6 Rfe8 19. Ng5 Qd7 20. g4 d4** Steinitz: "Desperate and fatal, but the only other alternative, 20. ... Be6 21. Rf6, left also little hope of retrieving fortunes." **21. Bc4+** Steinitz: "White grasps the winning opportunity vigorously." **21. ... Kh8** Steinitz: "If 21. ... Be6, 22. Rf8+ R×f8 23. B×e6+ and wins." **22. Nf7+ Kg8 23. N×d8 1–0** [*ICM*, June 1891, page 183; *Baltimore Sunday News*, August 2, 1891;

New York Clipper, 15 August 1891; *St. John Globe*, August 21, 1891; *PM*, pages 124–125]

356. Pollock–E. Delmar [C47]
NYSCA Meeting Match, Game 5, Skaneateles, 22 July 1891

1. e4 e5 2. Nf3 Nc6 3. Nc3 Nf6 4. d4 e×d4 5. N×d4 Bb4 6. N×c6 b×c6 7. Bd3 Steinitz: "The usual continuation is here 7. Qd4." **7. ... d5 8. e×d5 c×d5 9. 0–0 0–0 10. Bg5 B×c3** Steinitz: "This exchange is disadvantageous, for the strength of White's two bishops outweighs the slight drawback of the doubled pawn on the latter's queenside. Moreover, White can hardly be stopped from advancing c4, at a later stage with at least an equal game." **11. b×c3 Qd6** Steinitz: "11. ... c6 was now imperative." **12. Qf3** Steinitz: "Strange to say White overlooks the gain of an important pawn by 12. B×f6 Q×f6 13. Qh5 which threatened mate, and attacked the d-pawn." Pollock: "As pointed out by Steinitz, White could have won a pawn by 12. B×f6, followed by 13. Qh5." **12. ... Bg4 13. Qg3 Q×g3 14. f×g3** Steinitz: "14. h×g3 was more superior." **14. ... Nd7 15. Bf4 c6 16. Rab1 Rfe8 17. Rfe1 Be6 18. Bd6 Nb6 19. Ba6** Pollock: "The defense requires great care here." **19. ... Bd7 20. Kf2 R×e1 21. K×e1 Bc8 22. Bd3 f6 23. Rb4 Kf7** Steinitz: "If he attempted the capture of the h-pawn, he would have been blocked in by ...g6." **24. a4 g6 25. a5 Nd7 26. Rh4 Kg7** Pollock: "If 26. ... h5, 27. g4 would follow." **27. c4 Ne5 28. Kd2** Steinitz: "We believe that White could now have obtained a superior game by 28. B×e5 f×e5 29. c×d5 c×d5 30. Rb4 threatening c4, with a view of entering with the bishop at e4." **28. ... Be6 29. c×d5 B×d5 30. Rb4 N×d3 31. Rb7+** (see diagram)

After
31. Rb4–b7+

31. ... Kh6 Pollock: "Black gets into a dangerous corner." **32. c×d3 a6 33. Ke3 B×g2 34. Kf4 Bf1 35. Rf7 g5+ 36. Kf5 B×d3+ 37. K×f6 Kh5** Steinitz: "Necessary, as White threatened g4, followed by h4, and it would have been fatal for his

game if he had given time for those two moves, which confine him in a mating net." Pollock: "The only move. If 37. ... Bg6, 38. g4 B×f7 39. h4 and mates next move." **38. h3 Re8 39. Rg7** Pollock: "39. Kg7 gives the rook more freedom and maintains the attack." **39. ... Bg6 40. Rb7 Rd8 41. Be5 Rf8+ 42. Kg7 Re8 43. Bf6 Re3 44. Rb6** Steinitz: "White has pursued a dangerous plan, for Black's combined two passed pawns, which can now be formed, are certainly stronger than White's isolated a-pawn." **44. ... R×g3 45. R×a6 R×h3 46. R×c6 Rd3** Steinitz: "Quite contrary to general ending maxims. The rook ought to have attacked the hostile pawn in the rear by ...Ra3, and the hostile pawn could then hardly become dangerous, while his own pawns could march on freely after a few precautions." **47. a6 Rd7+ 48. Kf8 Be4 49. Rc5 h6 50. Ra5 Kg6 51. Be7 Ra7 52. Bc5 Ra8+ 53. Ke7 g4 54. Be3 Bc6 55. a7 Re8+ 56. Kd6 Bf3** Steinitz: "56. ... Bh1 was the easiest way of avoiding all danger and of gaining time for the advance of his own pawns." **57. Bf4 Rf8 58. Be5 h5 59. Ke6** 59. Bg3 was best, with equal play. **59. ... h4 60. Rb5 Re8+ 61. Kd7** (see diagram)

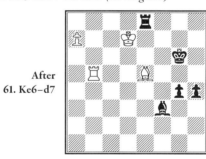

After
61. Ke6–d7

61. ... Rf8 Pollock: "61. ... R×e5 62. R×e5 h3 63. Rc5 h2 seems to be the winning process." Steinitz: "As pointed out by Mr. Gilberg, Black could have drawn at least here and two moves later, retaining good winning prospects by 61. ... R×e5 62. R×e5 h3. On examination we find that this line of play leads to a sure win for Black; who can now retreat ...Ba8 and the advance of his pawns cannot be stopped." Gilberg, Steinitz and Pollock were incorrect here. White can still draw as follows: 63. Re6+ Kg5 64. Re2!! Bg2 (64. ... g3? 65. Re3 g2 66. R×f3 g1Q 67. a8Q) 65. Ke6 g3 66. Rc2 Kf4 67. Rc4+ Ke3 68. Rc3+ Kf4 69. Rc4+ Ke3 70. Rc3+ Kf2 71. Rc1 h2 72. Rc2+ Kf1 73. Rc1+; 61. ... Ra8!? was the way to fight for an advantage but White could still defend: 62. Bf4 g3 (62. ... R×a7+ 63. Ke6 Ra6+ 64. Ke7 h3 65. Rg5+ Kh7 66. Kf7) 63. Ke6 g2 64. Rg5+ Kh7

65. Bb8 h3 66. Bh2 R×a7 67. Rg3 Bb7 68. R×h3+ Kg6 69. Rg3+ Kh5 70. Kf5 Ra5+ 71. Kf4 Ra4+ 72. Ke3 Bc6 73. Rg8 etc. **62. Ke6 Re8+ 63. Kd7 Rg8 64. Ke7 Bc6 65. Rb6 Kf5 66. Bb8 Bg2??** Pollock: "After Black's blunder mate must follow curiously and quickly." Steinitz: "An extraordinary error, 66. ... Ba8 was now the only move and good enough for a sure draw, with winning chances. Most likely it would have led to an ending with rook and bishop against rook, as White would have had to sacrifice his bishop for the two advancing pawns." **67. Rf6+** Steinitz: "The position is a very curious one. If 67. ... Kg5 68. Bf4+ and mates next move by 69. Rh6. Black therefore has no other move than 67. ... Ke4, whereupon White queens with check." **1–0** [*ICM*, June 1891, pages 185–187; *Baltimore Sunday News*, August 9, 1891]

357. E. Delmar–Pollock [C84]
NYSCA Meeting Match, Game 6, Skaneateles, 23 July 1891

Baltimore Sunday News (August 9): "A novel and ingenious Ruy Lopez adopted by Delmar. A novel and ingenious combination by Pollock on the 12th move to obtain a counterattack gave the latter almost a winning position and a pawn to the good. Delmar, however, emerged most skilfully and won a good game of 53 moves' duration. This made the score 3 all." **1. e4 e5 2. Nf3 Nc6 3. Bb5 a6 4. Ba4 Nf6 5. 0–0 Be7 6. d4** Steinitz: "6. d3 gives a more retentive attack." **6. ... e×d4 7. e5 Ne4 8. N×d4 0–0 9. Re1 Nc5 10. B×c6 d×c6 11. Nc3 Ne6 12. Nf5 Bg5 13. Qg4** *(see diagram)*

After
13. Qd1–g4

13. ... Nd4! Pollock: "An original combination, bright and sound." Steinitz: "A fine novelty. In conjunction with his 15th move, it obtains the superiority for his side." **14. B×g5 B×f5 15. Qh4 f6** Pollock: "A perfectly safe continuation for Black." **16. e×f6 g×f6 17. Bh6 Rf7 18. Rad1 c5 19. Re3** 19. Ne4! was much stronger. **19. ... Kh8 20. Rde1 Bg6** Pollock: "By this Black obtains a decisive ad-

vantage, whereas 20. ... N×c2 would be met by the ingenious reply 21. Re7!" Indeed, but Black also had available 21. ... Qg8!, with excellent play. **21. Qf4 N×c2 22. Rd1 Nd4 23. Kf1** Steinitz: "A necessary preparation for his next move, and, as will be seen, he calculates very deeply in taking that precaution (...)." **23. ... Qd7** Steinitz: "23. ... Qc8 was by far superior." **24. b4 b6 25. b×c5 b×c5 26. h4** Pollock: "Merely desperation. White is simply waiting for a blunder." **26. ... Qc6** Steinitz: "A useless speculation for an attack on the kingside. 26. ... Qf5 was the right play." **27. f3 Nc2** Pollock: "Black ought to have played to exchange off the rooks." **28. Re2 c4** Steinitz: "This pawn is only more weakened than before its further advance." **29. Ne4** Pollock: "Mr. Delmar gets in some effective work now and completely turns the tables on his opponent." **29. ... Nb4 30. Qd2 Nd3 31. Qc3** Steinitz: "Threatening R×d3." **31. ... B×e4** Steinitz: "If 31. ... Ne5, 32. N×f6 etc." **32. R×e4 Ne5** 32. ... Qb5!? 33. Bg5 Raf8 34. Kg1 a5 was better. **33. Bf4 Qa4 34. Rd2 Nd7 35. R×c4 Qb5 36. Kf2 Re8 37. B×c7 Qb1?** 37. ... Rfe7 was a more stubborn defense. **38. Qc1** 38. R×d7! R×d7 39. Q×f6+ Rg7 40. Be5 Qg6 41. Rg4 wins immediately. **38. ... Qf5 39. Bg3 Rg8 40. Bf4 Ne5! 41. B×e5 f×e5** Steinitz: "He could have made a better fight for a draw by retaking with the queen, and he could then stand exchanging pieces, as his king would afford protection for his pawns in the ending. His weak e-pawn now becomes the mark of attack and must soon fall, which practically ends the game." **42. Qc3 Rfg7 43. Kg1 Qb1+ 44. Qc1 Qb6+ 45. Kh1 Qe3 46. Re4 Qh6 47. Qb2 Qc6 48. R×e5 Qc4 49. Re4 Qf1+ 50. Kh2 h6?** 50. ... Qb5 51. Qf6! Qa5 52. Rde2 Qc7+ 53. Kh1 Qb8 54. Re7 Qb1+ 55. Kh2 Qg6 56. Qe5 Rf8 was more ambitious but without improving his survival chances. **51. Rg4** Steinitz: "There is no escape from the effect of this powerful blow." 51. Re6 would have forced a mate: 51. ... Kh7 52. Qc2+ Rg6 53. Re7+ Kh8 54. Qc3+ R6g7 55. R×g7 R×g7 56. Rd8+ Kh7 57. Qc2+ Rg6 58. Rd7+ etc. **51. ... Qe1 52. Rd7 h5 53. Rd×g7 1–0** [*Pittsburgh Dispatch*, August 8, 1891; *Baltimore Sunday News*, August 9, 1891; *ICM*, June 1891, pages 187–188; *PM*, pages 127–128]

358. Pollock–E. Delmar [C05]
NYSCA Meeting Match, Game 7, Skaneateles, 24 July 1891

Baltimore Sunday News (August 9): "The seventh game looked like being the shortest of the series in two senses, as Pollock was all but mated after three hours' play on Thursday evening, July 23 [*sic*], of which time Delmar had consumed but 35 minutes. The Baltimore player escaped, however, a pawn minus, and prolonged the game on the following day up to the 64th move. The game was a very brilliant achievement on the part of Delmar, whose play was characterized by a good deal more continuity than he usually exhibits." **1. e4 e6 2. d4 d5 3. Nd2** Steinitz: "Dr. Tarrasch introduced this remarkable novelty at the Manchester tournament of last year. It is, however, curious to note that the editor tried the same experiment in a game played against Major Hanham in a simultaneous performance at the Manhattan Chess Club only a few weeks later and without knowing of its previous adoption by Tarrasch." Pollock: "Introduced by Tarrasch in the Manchester Tournament, 1890, and independently by Steinitz in simultaneous play against Hanham." **3. ... c5** Pollock: "This appears to be Black's best reply." **4. Ngf3** Pollock: "But, if so, it then follows that Dr. Tarrasch's innovation must be very good indeed for, as Mr. Steinitz points out, 4. d×c5 B×c5 5. Nb3, isolating Black's d-pawn, gives the first player a sufficient pull." Steinitz: "4. d×c5 B×c5 5. Nb3 would have at least effected the isolation of the d-pawn with the superior game for White." **4. ... Nf6 5. e5 Nfd7 6. c3 Nc6 7. Bd3 Be7 8. 0–0 0–0 9. Re1 Re8 10. Nf1 f5 11. e×f6 B×f6** *(see diagram)*

After
11. ... Be7×f6

12. Qc2 Steinitz: "This excellent move much augments White's superiority of position." **12. ... Nf8** Pollock: "Forming a rather pretty gambit—his best defense though. 12. ... h6 being very weakening, and if 12. ... g6 then probably 12. B×g6 h×g6 13. Q×g6+ Bg7 (13. ... Kf8 14. Bh6+ Ke7 16. R×e6+ K×e6 17. Ng5+) 15. Bh6 Re7 16. B×g7 R×g7 17. Qe6+ and should win." Steinitz: "This loses a pawn, but Black obtains a strong attack. It was anyhow his best resource, for 12. ... h6 would have allowed White to get a strong hold of the adverse position by the reply 13. Bg6, and if 12. ... g6, 13. B×g6 with a fine attack." **13. d×c5 e5 14. Bf5** Pollock: "Mr. Gilberg, a close

observer of the games, rightly condemns the bad judgment shown in this move. 14. Bb5 is much superior, it restraining an aggressive knight, while the text move aids the development of the Black's queenside rook; again, the Black queen's bishop was not dangerous, and the White king's bishop might help the attack on Black's d-pawn." **14. ... e4 15. B×c8 R×c8 16. N3d2 Ne5 17. Nb3** Pollock: "If 17. b4 Nd3 18. Rd1 N×b4." **17. ... Nd3 18. Rd1 Ng6 19. Be3 Be5 20. g3** Steinitz: "This is weak. Here and later on, White ought to have sacrificed the rook for the knight, gaining another extra pawn with an excellent attack on a third pawn on the queenside, which he could still more strengthen by Bd4 and Ne3." Pollock: "Steinitz considers the entire plan of White's defense to be faulty and recommends 20. R×d3, with an attack on the d-pawn which might be augmented afterwards by Bd4 and Ne3." **20. ... Bb8 21. f4 Qd7 22. Rd2 Qh3 23. Rad1 Rc6 24. Nc1** *(see diagram)* Pollock: "Still imagining Black's attack to be unsound. 24. R×d3 is again available."

After
24. Nb3–c1

24. ... Ng×f4 Steinitz: "A very fine sacrifice and quite sound." Pollock: "A very fine sacrifice, even if obligatory." **25. g×f4 Rg6+ 26. Rg2 B×f4 27. B×f4** Steinitz: "If 27. N×d3, 27. ... B×e3+ 28. N×e3 Q×e3+ 29. Nf2 R×g2+ 30. K×g2 Qf3+, followed by ...e3 with a winning game; (Pollock agreed and his suggestion continued with 31. Kg1 e3 32. Nh1 h5 adding that "it seems to win for Black, but the variation is not very obvious." In fact, Black's best hope is 32. ... e2 33. Re1 h5 34. Ng3 h4 35. R×e2 Re3 36. R×e3 Q×e3+ 37. Qf2 Qg5 38. Qe1 h×g3 39. h×g3 Qg6 and he could only hope for a draw.) Or, if 27. R×g6, 27. ... B×e3+ 28. N×e3 Q×e3+ 29. Kh1 Nf2+, and wins." **27. ... N×f4 28. R×g6 h×g6 29. Rd4?** Steinitz: "It is difficult to find anything good, but this is evidently bad." Pollock: "This should prove quickly fatal; the only possibility, bad as it is, appears to be 29. Rd2, then 29. ... e3 30. Re2, and then 30. ... Qf3, equally breaks off." Both Pollock and Steinitz underestimated White's defensive potential at this juncture. 29. Ng3! maintained the balance: 29. … e3 30. Nd3 e2 31. N×f4 e1Q+ 32. R×e1 R×e1+ 33. Kf2 Q×h2+ 34. Ng2 Rg1 35. Kf3 g5, with a complicated position with chances for both. **29. … Qf3** Pollock: "29. … Qg4+ 30. Ng3 Qf3 wins right off." Steinitz: "Delmar afterward pointed out that he could have won here straight off by 29. … Qg4+ 30. Ng3 Qf3, etc." **30. h3 Re5 31. h4 Nh3+** Steinitz: "31. … Qg4+, followed by …Rh5, would have won soon with heavy forces on the board, which most likely would have led to a more elegant termination. The line of play chosen gives White an opportunity of exchanging queens, and the ending which follows hardly requires further explanation, for some pretty situations which arise during its progress will be easily appreciated." **32. Kh2 Q×f1 33. Qg2** (see diagram)

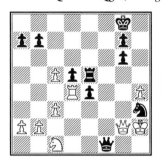

After
33. Qc2–g2

33. … Q×g2+? Not as precise as the spectacular 33. … Qe1!! 34. K×h3 (34. Q×h3 Rf5!) 34. … Rh5 35. Qg3 Qh1+ 36. Kg4 R×h4+ 37. Q×h4 Qf3+ 38. Kg5 Qf5 mate. **34. K×g2 Nf4+ 35. Kg3 Ne6 36. Ra4 N×c5 37. R×a7 Rf5 38. Ne2 Rf3+ 39. Kg4 Kh7** Pollock: "A beautiful move, subtly menacing various mates by either …Nd3 or …Ne6." 39. … Rf2 40. Nd4 R×b2 was more effective. **40. Nd4 Rf2 41. b4 Nd3 42. Ne6?** Pollock: "The only move as Black threatened another little perfectum by …Rg2+ and …Nf4." 42. Kg3! would have held the game. **42. … Kh6** Pollock: "The game is virtually over as the king must now enter." **43. Ra8 Ne5+ 44. Kg3 Rf3+ 45. Kg2 Kh5 46. Rd8 Nc4 47. Nd4 Ne3+ 48. Kh2 Rf4?** 48. … Ng4+ 49. Kg1 R×c3 50. R×d5+ K×h4 was best. **49. Kg3! Rg4+ 50. Kf2 Nd1+ 51. Ke2?** The final error left unmentioned by the key contemporary annotators. 51. Ke1! Rg1+ (51. … N×c3?? runs into 52. Rh8 mate.) 52. Kd2 K×h4 53. R×d5 keeps things very unclear. **51. … N×c3+ 52. Kd2 Rg3 53. Ne6 K×h4 54. Rd7 b5 55. R×g7 N×a2 56. Nf4 g5 57. Ne6 d4 58. Rh7+ Kg4 59. Rg7 Kh5 60. Ke2 d3+ 61. Kf2 Rf3+ 62. Kg2 d2 63. R×g5+ Kh4 0–1** [*New York Tribune*, July 25,

1891; *ICM*, June 1891, pages 189–190; *Baltimore Sunday News*, August 9, 1891; *PM*, pages 128–129]

359. E. Delmar–Pollock [B23]
NYSCA Meeting Match, Game 8, Skaneateles, 24 July 1891

1. e4 c5 2. Nc3 e6 3. Nf3 b6 4. d4 a6 5. d5 Bb7?! 5. … d6 was better. **6. Bf4! Ne7 7. Be2 Ng6 8. Bg3 Qc8 9. h4! Ne7 10. Na4 Qd8 11. c4** 11. d×e6! f×e6 12. Ng5 h6 13. N×e6 d×e6 14. Q×d8+ K×d8 15. 0-0-0+ Ke8 16. N×b6 was another forceful possibility. **11. … Ng8 12. d×e6** Steinitz: "The initiation of a masterly planned attack." **12. … f×e6** Steinitz: "If 12. … d×e6 13. Q×d8+ followed by N×b6." **13. Ng5 Be7** 13. … Nc6! was a good try since 14. Bh5+ g6 15. N×h7 R×h7 16. B×g6+ Rf7 17. B×f7+ K×f7 18. Qf3+ Kg7 was not that clear. **14. Bh5+ g6** (see diagram)

After
14. … g7–g6

15. N×h7 Steinitz: "Alike elegant and correct." **15. … B×e4** Steinitz: "If 15. … R×h7 16. B×g6+ Rf7 17. Qh5 and wins; Of course, if 15. … g×h5 16. Q×h5 mate." **16. Qg4** Steinitz: "White's game is now won." **16. … R×h7 17. Q×e4 R×h5 18. Q×g6+ Kf8 19. Q×h5 Nc6 20. 0-0-0 b5** Steinitz: "The attempt of a counterattack against such superior force and in such a position could not possess much vitality." **21. N×c5 Qa5 22. N×d7+ Kg7 23. Be5+** Steinitz: "For quicker winning purposes 23. Ne5 N×e5 24. B×e5+, followed by Rd7, was much superior." **23. … N×e5 24. Q×e5+ Kh6 25. Qe4+ Kg7 26. Ne5 Rf8** Steinitz: "White threatened mate in two moves by Qg6+, followed by Nf7 or Qf7." **27. Qg6+ Kh8 28. Nf7+ R×f7 29. Q×f7 Q×a2** Steinitz: "Black gains only a short reprieve by this counter demonstration." **30. Qh5+ Kg7 31. Rh3 Q×c4+** Steinitz: "If 31. … Qa1+ 32. Kd2 and the king soon escapes pursuit from checks." **32. Kb1 Qe4+ 33. Rdd3 Nf6 34. Qg5+ Kf7 35. Rhe3 Qc4 36. h5 b4 37. Qg6+ Kf8 38. Rf3 Qh4 39. g3 Qh1+ 40. Ka2 1–0** [*ICM*, July 1891, pages 211–212; *PM*, pages 130–131]

Part Two, Section VII (August–December 1891)

A Correspondence Match (December 1890–August 1891)

360. Pollock–J.L. McCutcheon [C12]
Correspondence Match, Game 1,
December 1890–August 1891

1. e4 e6 2. d4 d5 3. Nc3 Nf6 4. Bg5 Bb4 5. e5 h6 6. Bd2 B×c3 7. B×c3 Pollock: "Aiming at novelty; 7. b×c3 is as good." **7. ... Ne4 8. Bb4 c5!** **9. d×c5 Qc7** 9. ... N×f2! 10. K×f2 Qh4+ 11. g3 Q×b4 clearly favors Black. **10. Nf3 Bd7 11. c3 Nc6** Pollock: "Both sides play the opening very carefully." **12. Bd3 Ng5 13. 0–0 N×f3+ 14. Q×f3 N×e5** Pollock: "Or 14. ... Q×e5 15. Rae1 Qg5! 16. Qe2 and White has a strong position." **15. Qg3 0–0–0 16. Be2 g5 17. c4** Pollock: "Black's last move renders this sacrifice especially strong, as the bishops have now great power." **17. ... N×c4 18. Q×c7+ K×c7 19. Bc3 Rhg8 20. b3 Na3 21. Rfc1 Kb8** Pollock: "It is absolutely necessary to vacate this square for the knight." **22. Bb2 Nb5 23. a4 Nc7 24. b4** (see diagram)

After
24. b3–b4

24. ... Ne8?! Too passive. Black had to free his game with 24. ... d4!! 25. B×d4 Bb5. **25. b5 Rc8?** 25. ... Bc8 26. Be5+ Ka8 27. c6 f6 was necessary. **26. a5 a6 27. b×a6 Bc6 28. Be5+ Ka8 29. a×b7+ B×b7 30. c6** Pollock: "A combination which Black did not foresee in time." **30. ... R×c6 31. a6 f6 32. a×b7+ K×b7 33. Rcb1+ Rb6 34. Ba6+ Kc6 35. Rc1+ Kd7 36. Bc8+ Ke7 37. Ra7+ Kf8 38. Bd4 Rb5 39. Bd7 1–0** [*Baltimore Sunday News*, September 27, 1891]

361. Pollock–J.L. McCutcheon [C12]
Correspondence Match, Game 4,
December 1890–August 1891

Pollock: "A match of four games by correspondence for a stake of $20 a side, between Messrs. J.L. McCutcheon of Pittsburg and W.H.K. Pollock, commenced last December, is now drawing to a close. The match was played to test the McCutcheon Defence in the French Defence—originated by the Pittsburg player in the game won by him against Mr. Steinitz in simultaneous play. We never thought much of the merits of Mr. McC.'s variation, but it is singularly productive of fresh and unheard of positions—the match in question swarms with them. Subjoined is the fourth game." **1. e4 e6 2. d4 d5 3. Nc3 Nf6 4. Bg5 Bb4** Pollock: "Mr. McCutcheon's variation and the point of his challenge." **5. e5** Pollock: "Adopted by White in three of the four games." **5. ... h6 6. Bh4** Pollock: "We hold as best 6. Bd2 B×c3 7. b×c3 Ne4 8. Bd3, quietly developing everything." **6. ... g5 7. Bg3 Ne4 8. Nge2 c5 9. a3** Pollock: "Asking the bishop a question about the game." **9. ... Ba5** Pollock: "Here, as in all the games, the Pittsburgher played for beauty, chess and complications, but really his safety lay in exchanges." **10. Qd3 c×d4 11. N×d4**

369

N×c3 **12. b×c3 Qc7 13. Nb5 Qc6 14. Be2** Mc-Cutcheon: "Instead of the text move, 14. Nd6+ would really have promised much for White, but would really have accomplished almost a winning position for Black." **14. ... Nd7** Pollock: "Still hoping for 15. Nd6+ Kf8, then 16. Kd2 Nc5, etc." Pollock expected "14. ... 0–0 15. 0–0 a6 16. Nd6 Q×c3 17. Rad1 Q×d3 18. R×d3 Nc6 19. f4 with a view of mating the Black king." **15. 0–0 Bc7?!** Mc-Cutcheon: "With this move Black abandoned his attack, deeming himself fortunate to find so good a move to cover his retreat." 15. ... 0–0 or 15. ... Nc5 were better options. Pollock: "If 15. ... Nc5 16. Qf3 Ne4 17. c4, if now 17. ... d×c4 (17. ... Nd2 18. Qf6; 17. ... d4 18. Q×e4) 18. Q×e4. **16. f4 g×f4?** 16. ... Nc5!? 17. N×c7+ Q×c7 18. Qe3 Ne4 19. c4 Bd7 was better. **17. B×f4** Pollock: "17. R×f4 is possibly lofty but without foundation." **17. ... b6** McCutcheon: "Esteemed a lucky discovery, as any other move seemed to lead to Black's inevitable defeat." **18. Bh5!** Pollock: "The four moves made by this bishop during the partie are singularly telling." **18. ... B×e5** *(see diagram)*

After
18. ... Bc7×e5

19. B×f7+! Ke7 20. Rae1 Ba6 21. c4! Mc-Cutcheon: "I consider this White's finest move of the game. The expediency of it was quite beyond anticipation. With any other move White's apparently resistless attack would possibly have failed." **21. ... B×b5** Pollock: "If 21. ... d×c4, 22. Qg6 Nf8 23. Bg5+ h×g5 24. Q×g5+ Kd7 25. Rd1+ and wins." **22. c×b5 Qd6 23. R×e5** 23. Bg3! was slightly stronger. **23. ... N×e5 24. Qd4 Q×a3** Mc-Cutcheon: "A gambler's move taken in a sort of desperation, and under the circumstances considered preferable to forcing the exchange of queens." **25. B×e5** Pollock: "25. Q×e5, as pointed out by Mr. McCutcheon, is much more crushing." **25. ... Rhf8 26. Qf4** Pollock: "Threatening to mate in six moves." **26. ... Kd7 27. Q×h6 Qc5+ 28. Kh1 Qe7 29. Qg7 a6** *(see diagram)*

Pollock: "Here White announced a mate in 18 moves." **1–0** Engines indicate it is actually a mate

After
29. ... a7–a6

in 15. Pollock gave the following variation: 30. B×e6+ K×e6 31. Qg6+ Rf6 32. R×f6+ (32. B×f6 mates more quickly: 32. ... Qe8 33. Re1+ Kd7 34. Qg7+ Kd6 35. Be7+ Kc7 36. Bh4+ Kd6 37. Qf6+ Kc7 38. Qc3+ Qc6 39. Q×c6+ Kb8 40. Bg3+ Ka7 41. Re7 mate.) 32. ... K×e5 33. Qg5+ Kd4 34. Qd2+ Kc4 35. Qd3+ Kc5 36. Qc3+ K×b5 37. Qc6+ Kb4 38. Q×b6+ Kc3 39. Qb3+ Kd4 40. Qa4+ Kc3 41. Rf3+. [*Baltimore Sunday News*, July 12, 1891; *St. John Globe*, July 17, 1891; *New York Clipper*, August 1, 1891; *PM*, pages 140–141]

Training Match against Showalter (July/August 1891)

362. J.W. Showalter–Pollock [C33]
Training Match, Game 1, Georgetown, Kentucky, 31 July 1891

1. e4 e5 2. f4 e×f4 3. Bc4 f5 4. e5 Qh4+ 5. Kf1 f3! 6. d4 f×g2+ 7. K×g2 Nc6 7. ... b5!? 8. B×b5 Bb7+ 9. Nf3 g5 was a more suitable continuation for Pollock. **8. Nf3 Qg4+ 9. Kf2 Be7 10. h4?** 10. Rg1 Qh3 11. R×g7 was best. **10. ... d6** Pollock: "After 10. ... f4, 11. Qg1 and the exchange of queens, Black might lose the advanced pawn." 10. ... N×e5! was a powerful blow: 11. N×e5 (11. d×e5 Q×c4; 11. B×g8 N×f3 12. Q×f3 R×g8 13. Q×g4 f×g4) 11. ... B×h4+ 12. R×h4 Q×d1 13. Bf7+ Kf8 14. Nc3 Q×c2+ and Black is better. **11. Bg5 B×g5 12. h×g5 f4 13. Rg1 Qh5 14. e6!?** Pollock: "White has extricated himself very well from the results of his aberration on the fourth move." **14. ... Nge7 15. Nc3 b6** Pollock: "Castling would be highly perilous." **16. Ne2 Rf8 17. Qd2 d5 18. Bb5 B×e6 19. N×f4 Qf7 20. N×e6 Q×f3+** Pollock: "If 20. ... Q×e6, 21. Rae1 Qd6 22. B×c6+ Q×c6 23. Qe3, followed by Kg2 or g6 with a strong attack." **21. Ke1 Qe4+**

22. Qe2 Qh4+ 23. Kd1 Rf2! 24. Qe5 Pollock: "The winning line of play." **24. ... Kf7! 25. B×c6 N×c6** (see diagram)

After
25. ... Ne7×c6

26. Q×c7+? 26. g6+! h×g6 27. Ng5+ would have secured a draw. **26. ... K×e6?** Best was 26. ... Ne7! 27. Qe5 Qh5+ 28. Ke1 Qh2 29. Rg3 Nf5 and White is almost lost. **27. Re1+ Kf5 28. Qf7+ Kg4 29. Rg1+ Kh3 30. Rh1+ Kg3 31. Q×f2+ K×f2 32. R×h4 Re8 33. Rh2+ Kg3 34. R×h7 N×d4 35. c3 Nf3 36. Kc2 Re2+ 37. Kb3 Nd2+** Pollock: "A valiant fight, but now soon over." **38. Kb4 Ne4 39. b3 a5+ 40. Kb5 N×c3+ 41. K×b6 d4 42. R×g7 d3 43. Rd7 Re3 44. g6** and White won. **1–0** [*Baltimore Sunday News*, November 15, 1891; *PM*, page 131]

363. Pollock–J.W. Showalter [C44] Training Match, Game 2, Georgetown, Kentucky, 31 July/1 August 1891

1. e4 e5 2. Nf3 Nc6 3. c3 d5 4. Qa4 f6 5. Bb5 Nge7 6. e×d5 Q×d5 7. 0–0 Bd7 8. d4 e×d4 9. c×d4 Ne5 10. Nc3 N×f3+ 11. g×f3 Qf5 12. B×d7+ Q×d7 13. Qb3 0–0–0 14. Be3 Nf5 (see diagram)

After
14. ... Ne7–f5

15. Nb5?! A risky experiment. 15. Rac1 or 15. Rfc1 were much better options. **15. ... a6! 16. a4 Nh4! 17. Rfc1 N×f3+ 18. Kh1 Bd6 19. N×c7 B×c7 20. Bf4** Pollock must have intended 20. R×c7+ K×c7 21. Bf4+ but Black has

21. ... Ne5 22. d×e5 Qd4 23. Rc1+ Kb8. **20. ... N×d4! 0–1** [*PM*, page 132]

364. Pollock–J.W. Showalter [C56] Training Match, Game 4, Georgetown, Kentucky, August 1891

1. e4 e5 2. Nf3 Nc6 3. Bc4 Nf6 4. d4 e×d4 5. 0–0 N×e4 6. Re1 d5 7. B×d5 Q×d5 8. Nc3 Qh5 9. N×e4 Be6 10. Bg5 Bb4 11. c3 d×c3 12. b×c3 Be7 13. B×e7 13. Ng3!? Qg6 14. B×e7 N×e7 15. Qa4+ c6 16. Qa3 seems a more precise try. **13. ... N×e7 14. Qa4+ Nc6 15. Rab1 Qa5 16. Q×a5 N×a5 17. Nc5** (see diagram)

After
17. Ne4–c5

17. ... 0–0 18. N×e6 f×e6 19. R×e6 Rae8 20. Rbe1 R×e6 21. R×e6 Rd8 22. Kf1 Nc6 23. Ke2 h6 24. Ne5 N×e5 25. R×e5 Kf7 26. Ke3 ½–½ [*PM*, page 132]

365. J.W. Showalter–Pollock [C31] Training Match, Game 5, Georgetown, Kentucky, August 1891

1. e4 e5 2. f4 d5 3. Nf3 d×e4 4. N×e5 Bc5 5. Bc4 Nh6 6. Nc3 Qd4 7. Rf1 0–0 8. Qe2 Nc6 (see diagram)

After
8. ... Nb8–c6

9. N×c6?! 9. N×e4 N×e5 10. f×e5 Bg4 11. Qd3 Q×e5 12. Qd5 was more stable. **9. ... b×c6 10. Q×e4 Qd7 11. Be2 Re8 12. Qc4 Qe7 13. d4 Bb4 14. Bd2 B×c3 15. b×c3 c5 15.** ... Bg4! 16. Rf2

Qh4 17. g3 B×e2 18. R×e2 Q×h2 was more force-ful. **16. Qd3?** Mandatory was 16. Kf2 Bb7 17. Bf3. **16. ... Bf5 17. Qc4 B×c2** 17. ... Bg4 was best, once again. **18. Kf2 Nf5 19. Ke1** 19. Bf3! Ne3 20. B×e3 Q×e3+ 21. Kg3 Re4 22. Q×c5 Q×f4+ 23. Kf2 Qe3+ 24. Kg3 offered some survival chances. **19. ... Nd6 0–1** [*PM*, page 132–133]

366. Pollock–J.W. Showalter [C67] Training Match, Game 6, Georgetown, Kentucky, August 1891

1. e4 e5 2. Nf3 Nc6 3. Bb5 Nf6 4. 0–0 N×e4 5. d4 Be7 6. Qe2 Nd6 7. B×c6 b×c6 8. d×e5 Nb7 9. Nd4 0–0 10. Nc3 Nc5 11. Rd1 Qe8 12. Nf5 Bd8 Pollock: "Hardly time for this. White might play 13. Qg4 at once, instead of the weak text move." **13. b4 Ne6 14. Rd3** 14. b5!? was stronger. **14. ... f6 15. Rg3 f×e5** (*see diagram*)

After
15. ... f6×e5

16. N×g7? Pollock: "Unsound, though very tempting." **16. ... N×g7 17. Bh6 Rf7 18. Qh5 Bf6 19. Ne4 Qe7 20. B×g7 R×g7** Pollock: "20. ... B×g7, 21. Ng5." **21. Rf3 Rg6?** Pollock: "Allows White a curious draw; the proper move was 21. ... Bg5." **22. N×f6+ R×f6 23. Qg5+ Kf7 24. Qh5+ Ke6 25. Qg4+ Kf7 ½–½** [*Baltimore Sunday News*, November 29, 1891; *PM*, page 133]

367. J.W. Showalter–Pollock [C30] Training Match, Game 7, Georgetown, Kentucky, 7 August 1891

1. e4 e5 2. f4 Nf6 3. f×e5 N×e4 4. Nf3 d5 5. d3 Nc5 6. d4 Ne6 7. Bd3 c5 8. c3 Nc6 9. 0–0 c×d4 10. c×d4 Nc×d4 11. N×d4 Pollock: "Instead of this exchange, 11. Nc3 would have yielded White a strong developing game." **11. ... N×d4 12. Qa4+ Nc6 13. Qf4 Bc5+ 14. Kh1 Be6 15. Nd2 Qc7 16. Nf3 0–0–0 17. Qa4 h6** Pollock: "'A country move,' observed Black, 'but it may come in useful later on.'" **18. Bd2 Kb8 19. b4 Bb6 20. Rfc1 Qd7**

21. b5 Ne7 22. Bb4 Rc8 23. Bd6+ Ka8 24. Qa3 R×c1+ 25. R×c1 Rc8 26. R×c8+ N×c8 27. Bf8 Pollock: "'I suppose,' observed White, 'that this is where your country move comes in useful.'" **27. ... Bf5 28. B×g7 Be4 29. Be2 d4 30. B×h6 d3 31. Bd1 Q×b5 32. Qf8 Qc4** (*see diagram*)

After
32. ... Qb5–c4

33. Bb3? Pollock: "Completely overlooking the pretty surprise (...) 'Had I played 33. Bd2,' said White, 'the game would have been perfectly even.' 'True,' replied Black, 'but that bishop, I thought was too busy *in the country*.'" **33. ... d2** The *Baltimore Sunday News* recorded that White resigned here and so did Steinitz in the *International Chess Magazine*. But Rowland's *Pollock Memories* gave further moves: **34. h4 B×f3 35. g×f3 Qf1+ 36. Kh2 Qf2+ 37. Kh3 Q×f3+ 38. Kh2 Kb8 39. B×d2 Qf2+ 40. Kh3 Q×d2 41. Q×f7 Qe3+ 42. Kg4 Q×e5 43. h5 Bc7 44. h6 a6 45. Qg8 Qg3+ 46. Kf5 Qf4+ 47. Kg6 Qe4+ 48. Kf7 Qf5+ 49. Ke8 Qf6 50. Qg7 Nd6+ 51. Kd7 Qd8+ 52. Ke6 Qe8+ 53. Qe7 Q×e7+ 54. K×e7 Nf5+ 55. Kf6 N×h6 56. Be6 Bf4 57. a4 Kc7 0–1** [*Baltimore Sunday News*, November 22, 1891; *ICM*, September 1891, pages 274–275; *PM*, pages 133–135]

368. Pollock–J.W. Showalter [C44] Training Match, Game 8, Georgetown, Kentucky, August 1891

Steinitz: "...a very interesting game..." **1. e4 e5 2. Nf3 Nc6 3. c3 d5 4. Qa4 f6 5. Bb5 Nge7 6. e×d5 Q×d5 7. 0–0 Bd7** Steinitz: "7. ... e4 is now stronger and if 8. Nd4 then 8. ... Bd7 is more in time." **8. d4 e×d4 9. c×d4 Ne5! 10. B×d7+** Pollock: "In a subsequent game occurred 10. Nc3 N×f3+ 11. g×f3 Qf5 12. B×d7+ Q×d7 13. Qb3 0–0–0 14. Be3 Nf5 15. Nb5 a6 16. a4 Nh4, and Black, Showalter, won." **10. ... Q×d7 11. Q×d7+ N×d7 12. Nc3 0–0–0 13. Bf4 Nb6 14. Rac1 Nbd5 15. Bg3 Nf5** Steinitz: "Quite safe and very good play." **16. Rfe1** Steinitz: "If 16. N×d5, 16. ... N×g3 17. N×c7 (17. R×c7+ Kb8 and wins.) 17. ... Ne2+ and wins." **16. ... N×g3 17. h×g3 Bb4 18. N×d5 B×e1** Pollock: "Black overlooked something in his forecast or he overrated the position which he actually arrives at in a few moves. He could have easily maintained the better game by simply retaking the knight." **19. Ne7+ Kd7 20. R×e1 Rhe8 21. Nf5 R×e1+ 22. N×e1** *(see diagram)*

After
22. Nf3×e1

22. ... g5?! Steinitz: "22. ... g6 was much superior." **23. g4 Kc6 24. Kf1 Kd5 25. Ke2 Re8+ 26. Kd2 Rh8 27. Nc2 h5 28. Nce3+ Kc6** Pollock: "If 28. ... Ke4, White mates in three; or if 28. ... Ke6, Black at least loses the h-pawn." **29. Ne7+ Kb5** Steinitz: "The only move. If 29. ... Kd7, 30. N7d5, etc.; or if 29. ... Kd6, 30. N3f5+ Ke6 (or 30. ... Kd7 31. Nd5, etc.) 31. g×h5 and Black evidently dare not retake on account of Ng7+, winning the rook." **30. g×h5** Steinitz: "White's next move was better applied here at once. Black had no better answer than ...c5, as later on in a similar situation, and it then made the difference that White could sooner clear the kingside from adverse pawns and need not have allowed the Black rook attacking entrance against White's pawns on the queenside." **30. ... R×h5 31. N7d5 c5 32. d×c5 K×c5 33. N×f6 Rh4 34. g4** Steinitz: "34. f3, threatening Ne4, with or without check, was more confining to Black's forces and must have soon gained the g-pawn." **34. ... Rh2 35. Ke2 Kd4 36. Kf3 Rh1 37. Ne4 Rb1 38. b4 Ke5 39. a3 Rb3 40. N×g5 R×a3 41. Nf7+ Kf6 42. Nd8 Rb3** Steinitz: "Not as good as 42. ... b6, which would have enabled him to make a counter demonstration with the a-pawn quicker. Probably he overlooked that on the next move he would have to lose time with his king in order to provide against the double edged Nd5+, which prevented his taking the pawn." **43. N×b7 Kg6** Pollock: "It certainly looks grossly careless like or incompetent on White's part to fail

any way to win from so palpably a favourable position as this. Perhaps the result would have been different in an important match. Again many of these games were played out to save time at very peculiar hours, some being commenced even at 3:00 a.m., for ten games were played within six days." **44. Na5 R×b4 45. Nc6 Ra4 46. Nc4** Steinitz: "A pretty move, and it is obvious that Black dare not take, but more strategical was 46. Kg3 (threatening f4) 46. ... Ra3 47. Kh4 a5 48. Nc4 Ra2 49. f4." **46. ... Kg5 47. N6a5?** 47. N6e5 was best: 47. ... Ra1 48. Ke4 Rf1 49. f3 a5 50. Ne3 Rf2 51. Nd3 Rh2 52. f4+. **47. ... Ra2! 48. Kg3** *(see diagram)*

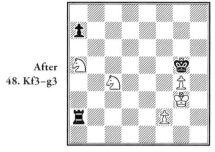

After
48. Kf3–g3

48. ... R×f2 Steinitz: "An ingenious resource which makes it at least difficult for White to win." **49. K×f2 K×g4 50. Ne3+ Kg5 51. Kg3 Kf6 52. Kf4 Kg6 53. Ng4 a6** *(see diagram)*

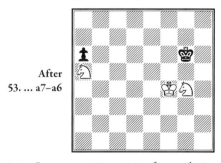

After
53. ... a7–a6

Steinitz: "...a rare position arising from a choice ending. Though the two knights could not mate if Black had only the king alone on the board this extra pawn should have been disastrous for him, for he could not hope to be stalemated." Pollock: "The game was abandoned as a draw. White, of course, was outwitted in allowing his opponent to sacrifice the rook. But anyway the win is surely easy from this point. White has to hold the king in a corner till he can release the other knight; only the Black pawn must not be allowed to go beyond the 5th square." Indeed, according to the Nalimov Endgame Tablebases, White mates in 43 moves

from the diagrammed position with 54. Ke5. ½–½
[*ICM*, September 1891, pages 273–274; *New York Tribune*, January 3, 1892; *PM*, pages 135–136]

LEXINGTON EVENTS (AUGUST 1891)

369. J.W. Showalter–Pollock [C82]
4th USCA Championship, Lexington, Round 1, 4 August 1891

1. e4 e5 2. Nf3 Nc6 3. Bb5 a6 4. Ba4 Nf6
5. 0–0 N×e4 6. d4 b5 7. Bb3 d5 8. d×e5 Be6 9. c3
Bc5 10. Nbd2 0–0 11. Bc2 Bf5 12. Nb3 Bb6
13. Nbd4 N×d4 14. N×d4 Bg6 15. Qg4?! 15. f3
Nc5 16. Be3 seems better. **15. ... f5 16. Qe2 Qe8**
17. f3 Nc5 18. b4 Ne6 19. Bb2 Rc8 20. Kh1 c6
21. f4 Qe7 22. Qd2 N×d4 22. ... c5!? 23. N×e6
Q×e6 24. b×c5 B×c5 25. a4 b4 was a more attractive option. **23. c×d4 Qe6 24. a4 Ra8 25. Rf3 Ra7**
26. Bb3 Rfa8 27. Rc1 Be8 28. a5 Bd8 29. Rh3
Rc7 30. Bc3 Bg6 31. Qe3 Be7 32. Be1 Raa7
33. Qc3 Rc8 34. Bd1 Qf7 35. Bh4 B×h4 35. ...
Bf8!? was a more careful choice so not to weaken
the dark squares even more. **36. R×h4 Qe7 37. Rh3**
Qf7 38. Qc5 Qe7 39. Q×e7 R×e7 40. Rhc3 Rec7
(see diagram)

After
40. ... Re7–c7

41. e6?! Premature. White should have built up
more with 41. Bf3 Bf7 42. g4! g6 43. g×f5 g×f5
44. Rg1+ Kf8 45. Rg5 Be6 46. Kg2. **41. ... Be8**
41. ... Kf8, followed by ...Ke7, was more precise.
42. Bf3 42. g4 was strong: 42. ... g6 43. g×f5 g×f5
44. Rg3+ Rg7 45. Bc2 Bg6 46. Rcg1 Rcc7 47. h4
Rce7 48. R1g2. **42. ... Rd8 43. Re3 Re7 44. g4**
g6 45. Re5 Kg7 46. g×f5 g×f5 47. R×f5 47. Rg1+
Kf6 48. Rg8 accomplishes nothing after 48. ...
Rd6! **47. ... R×e6 48. Rg1+ Bg6 49. Rfg5 Kf6**
(see diagram)
50. f5? Risky. 50. Re5 or 50. Rc1 were normal

After
49. ... Kg7–f6

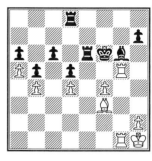

moves and sufficient to maintain the balance.
50. ... B×f5 51. R×f5+ K×f5 52. Bg4+ Kf6
53. B×e6 K×e6 54. Rg7 Rd7 55. Rg8 Kf5!
56. Ra8 Ke4 57. R×a6 Rc7 58. Rb6 K×d4 59. a6
Kc4 60. Rb7 Rc8 61. a7 Ra8 62. R×h7 K×b4
63. h3 Ka3 64. Kg2 b4 65. Rc7 b3 66. R×c6
R×a7 0–1 [*tournament book*, pages 14–15; *New York Sun*, August 30, 1891]

370. S.F.J. Trabue–Pollock [C45]
4th USCA Championship, Lexington, Round 2, 4 August 1891

1. e4 e5 2. Nf3 Nc6 3. d4 e×d4 4. N×d4 Bc5
5. Be3 Qe7 5. ... Qf6 is the more established move.
6. Nc3 Nf6 7. f3 *(see diagram)*

After 7. f2–f3

7. ... d5! 8. Bb5 Bd7 9. B×c6 b×c6 10. Nf5?
10. Qd3 0–0 11. 0–0 was necessary. **10. ... B×f5**
11. B×c5 Q×c5 12. e×f5 0–0 13. Qd3 13. Ne2
loses a pawn after 13. ... Rfe8 14. Kf1 Re5 15. Qd4
Qd6! 16. Kf2 R×f5 17. Rhe1 c5. **13. ... Rfe8+**
14. Kd2 Nd7 15. f4 d4 16. Ne2 16. Ne4 was superior, but Black maintains a decisive edge after
16. ... Q×f5 17. Rae1 Q×f4+ 18. Kd1 Ne5 19. Qg3
Qh6. **16. ... Re3 17. Qa6 Nf6 18. h3 Qb4+** 18. ...
Ne4+ 19. Kc1 d3 was more direct. **19. Kc1 Rae8**
20. c3 d×c3 21. N×c3 R×c3+! 22. b×c3 Q×c3+
0–1 [*tournament book*, page 20; *New York Sun*,
August 6, 1891; *New York Post*, August 7, 1891;
Times-Picayune, August 8, 1891]

371. Pollock–J.M. Hanham [C23]
4th USCA Championship, Lexington, Round 3, 5 August 1891

1. e4 e5 2. Bc4 d6 3. c3 c6 4. Qb3 Qc7 5. a4 Bg4 6. Na3 Bh5 7. d3 Nd7 8. Ne2 Ngf6 9. Ng3 Bg6 10. 0–0 h5! 11. Be3 Ng4 12. h3 N×e3 13. f×e3 f6 14. Nf5 Nc5 15. Qc2 Bf7 16. b4 Ne6 17. b5 h4 18. b×c6 b×c6 19. Qf2 *(see diagram)*

After
19. Qc2–f2

19. ... g5? 19. ... Nc5 was better. **20. Rab1** Pollock would have been pleased to discover that taking on d6 earlier was best: 20. N×d6+! Q×d6 (20. ... B×d6 loses to 21. Q×f6 Rh7 22. B×e6 B×e6 23. Q×e6+ Re7 24. Qg8+ Kd7 25. Q×a8) 21. Q×f6 Rh7 22. Nb5! Qe7 (22. ... c×b5? 23. B×b5+ Qd7 24. Q×e5) 23. Qf5 Rg7 24. Q×e5 a6 25. Rf6! **20. ... a6 21. N×d6+** At this point, 21. Nd4! was even stronger: 21. ... N×d4 (21. ... e×d4 22. B×e6 B×e6 23. Q×f6) 22. B×f7+ Q×f7 23. c×d4, with a clear edge. **21. ... Q×d6 22. Q×f6 Rh7 23. Rb7 Be7 24. Qf5 Rg7 25. d4 Nd8 26. Rb3 Bg6 27. Qf3 e×d4 28. c×d4 Qg3 29. Q×g3 h×g3 30. Bd3 Bf7 31. Nc4 g4! 32. Rb6 g×h3 33. g×h3 Be6 34. Kg2 Kd7 35. Ne5+ Kc7 36. a5 Bd6 37. Nf3** 37. R×a6 R×a6 38. B×a6 B×e5 39. d×e5 Rg5 40. Bd3 R×e5 41. Ra1 would have made it very difficult for Black to win. **37. ... Nb7 38. e5 Be7 39. Ng1?** 39. R×a6 R×a6 40. B×a6 N×a5 41. e4 was still White's best chance. **39. ... N×a5 40. R×a6 R×a6 41. B×a6 Bd5+ 42. Nf3 Nc4 43. Re1 Nd2 44. Be2 Bg5 45. Bd1 Rf7 46. K×g3 N×f3 47. B×f3 R×f3+ 48. Kg4 B×e3 49. h4 B×d4 50. h5 Re3 51. R×e3 B×e3 0–1** [*tournament book*, pages 24–25; *New York Post*, August 6, 1891]

372. Pollock–W.H. Ripley [C51]
4th USCA Championship, Lexington, Round 4, 5 August 1891

1. e4 e5 2. Nf3 Nc6 3. Bc4 Bc5 4. b4 B×b4 5. c3 Bc5 6. 0–0 d6 7. d4 e×d4 8. c×d4 Bb6

9. Nc3 Na5 10. Bg5 f6 11. Bf4 N×c4 12. Qa4+ Qd7 13. Q×c4 Qg4 14. Nd5 c6? 14. ... Ne7 15. h3 Qd7 was better. **15. N×b6 a×b6 16. B×d6 Be6 17. Qb4 b5** *(see diagram)*

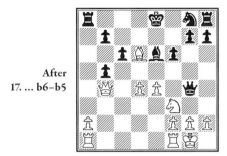

After
17. ... b6–b5

18. a4!? 18. d5! was strong as well: 18. ... Ra4 19. Qd2 Bf7 20. Rae1. **18. ... Q×e4 19. Rfe1 Qd5 20. R×e6+ Q×e6 21. Re1 Kf7 22. R×e6! K×e6 23. d5+ c×d5 24. Q×b5 K×d6 25. Qb6+ 1–0** [*tournament book*, page 30; *Baltimore Sunday News*, August 16, 1891; *New York Sun*, August 30, 1891]

373. L. Uedemann–Pollock [C44]
4th USCA Championship, Lexington, Round 5, 6 August 1891

1. e4 e5 2. Nf3 Nc6 3. c3 Nf6 4. d4 N×e4 5. d5 Bc5 *(see diagram)*

After
5. ... Bf8–c5

6. d×c6 B×f2+ 7. Ke2 b×c6 8. Qa4 f5 9. Nbd2 Bb6 10. N×e4 f×e4 11. Q×e4 0–0 12. Kd1 d5 13. Q×e5 Bg4 14. Qg3 Qd7 15. Bd3 d4 16. c4 Bc5 17. Kc2 Bf5 18. Ne5 Qe6 19. B×f5 R×f5 20. Ng4?! Pollock: "Fearing the loss of a piece by ...Bd6." 20. Re1 Bd6 21. Bf4 Raf8 22. c5 d3+ 23. Kc3 d2 24. Re3 B×c5 25. Nd3 was White's best choice. **20. ... Q×c4+ 21. Kb1 d3 22. a3 Qc2+ 23. Ka2 Bd6** Pollock: "23. ... Bf2 has its points also." **24. Ne3 Qc5 25. Qg4 Rf4 26. Qe6+ Kh8 27. Ng4 Ra4 28. Ne3** Pollock: "Neither party had any idea of drawing tactics throughout the game.

White could force a draw by 28. Nh6." **28. ... d2** Pollock: "This could not well be delayed on account of 29. Rd1. White calculates the ensuing variation more accurately." **29. B×d2 R×a3+ 30. b×a3 Q×a3+ 31. Kb1 Rb8+ 32. Kc2 Rb2+ 33. Kd1 Q×a1+ 34. Ke2 Qa6+ 35. Nc4** Pollock: "Not as good as interposing the queen." **35. ... Rb8 36. Rf1 c5** Pollock: "A fine move preventing the escape of the White king by any black squares." **37. Rf4 Qb5 38. Re4 B×h2?** 38. ... Rf8 was superior. **39. Bc3!** Pollock: "Menacing to mate in three by B×g7+." **39. ... Rg8 40. Rg4** Pollock: "Again threatening a speedy issue." **40. ... Qb8 41. g3 Bg1 42. Ne5 Qb5+ 43. Rc4?** With some precise play, White should have won here: 43. Kd2 Rd8+ 44. Kc2 Qe2+ 45. Kb3 c4+ 46. R×c4 Qd1+ 47. Ka3. **43. ... Re8!** Pollock: "A most peculiar position. If now, 44. Nf7+, Kg8 45. Nh6 Kf8 and wins." **44. Qf7 Bd4! 45. Kf3 Qb7+ 46. Kg4?** 46. Kf4! was the only move: 46. ... g5+ 47. Kg4! (47. K×g5 R×e5+) 47. ... Qe4+ 48. Kh3 Qh1+ 49. Kg4 Qe4+ 50. Kh3 (50. Kh5 Q×e5 51. R×d4 c×d4 52. B×d4 Q×d4 53. Q×e8+ Kg7 54. Qe7+ Kg8 55. Qe8+) 50. ... Qh1+ 51. Kg4 with a perpetual check **46. ... Qe4+ 47. Kh3 Qh1+ 48. Kg4 Qe4+ 49. Kh3 Q×e5** *(see diagram)*

After
49. ... Qe4×e5

50. R×c5 Pollock: "Most ingenious—there is but one reply." **50. ... Qe4! 51. Rf5 Qh1+ 52. Kg4 Re4+ 53. Rf4 h5+ 54. Kg5 Re5+ 55. Rf5 Be3+ 56. Kg6 Qc6+ 0–1** Pollock: "White actually resigned on the 56th move, though, probably not seeing the long-winded 'mating net' that was on the tapis. On the 60th move, Black's check with the bishop is most instructive—careless play would even here produce a draw. The mate is now effected by...." **57. K×h5 Qh6+ 58. Kg4 Re4+ 59. Kf3 Qh1+ 60. Ke2 Bd4+ 61. Kd3 Qb1+ 62. Kc4 Be5+** [Engines suggest a quicker mate with 62. Be3+ 63. Bd4 (63. Kd5 Qb7 mate) 63. ... R×d4+ 64. Kc3 Rd3+ 65. Kc4 Qb3 mate.] **63. Kd5 Qb7+ 64. Ke6 Qc6+ 65. Ke7 Bf6+ 66. Kf8 Qa8+ 67. Qe8 Q×e8 mate.** Miron Hazeltine (*New York Clipper*): "The

most amusing specimen I ever came across of a king trying to cuddle up to a rook and bishop in hopes of getting one of them; and the performance of the queen in ordering him 'out of that!' reminds me of the story of the Irish soldier, who, single-handed and alone, brought in three prisoners. Asked how he managed it, Pat replied: 'Faith and I surrounded them'" [*tournament book*, pages 32–33; *Baltimore Sunday News*, August 23, 1891; *Pittsburg Dispatch*, August 15, 1891; *St. John Globe*, September 7, 1891; *New York Clipper*, October 24, 1891; *PM*, pages 96–97].

374. Pollock–O. Fick [C50]
4th USCA Championship, Lexington, Round 6, 7 August 1891

1. e4 e5 2. Nf3 Nc6 3. Bc4 Be7 4. d4 d6 5. c3 Nf6 6. Qe2 0–0 7. 0–0 Bg4 8. d5 Nb8 9. Bd3 Nbd7 10. Be3 h6 11. Nbd2 Nh7 12. h3 Bh5 13. Kh2 g5 14. g4 Bg6 15. Rg1 h5 16. g×h5 Pollock: "To prevent a blocked game, which Black might bring about by ...h4. White's construction is superior generally, Black's 3rd, 7th, 8th and 11th moves being opposed to the harmonious or symmetrical development of pieces." 16. N×g5!? B×g5 (16. ... N×g5? 17. g×h5 Bh7 18. h4 f6 19. h×g5 f×g5 20. Nf3) 17. g×h5 B×e3 18. Q×e3 Qf6 19. h×g6 f×g6 20. Rg2 was appealing as well. **16. ... B×h5 17. Rg2 Kh8 18. Nf1 Rg8 19. Ng3 Bg6 20. Rh1 Bf6 21. Kg1 Qe7 22. Kf1 c6 23. d×c6** Pollock: "Centrifugal pawn exchanges are generally unadvisable, but here 23. c4 would lose a time [*sic*]–and perhaps the whole kingside attack." **23. ... b×c6 24. Rgh2 d5! 25. e×d5 c×d5** *(see diagram)*

After
25. ... c6×d5

26. h4! g×h4? 26. ... g4 27. Ng5 Rab8 was much more logical. **27. N×h4 B×h4 28. R×h4 Ndf6?** 28. ... Ndf8 29. B×g6 f×g6 30. c4 Rg7 was Black's last hope. **29. Bg5 Rg7** Pollock: "If 29. ... e4 White might make the very curious rejoinder 30. Qf3. Black could not then either take or leave either piece without loss." **30. f4** 30. Qf3 Ne4 31. N×e4 d×e4 32. B×e7 e×f3 33. B×g6 f×g6 34. Bf6 was another possibility. **30. ... B×d3 31. Q×d3 Kg8** 31. ... e4 runs into 32. Qd4. **32. Nf5 Qd7 33. B×f6** Pollock: "For if 33. ... e4 34. R×h7 R×h7 35. R×h7 K×h7 36. Qh3+ Kg6 37. Qh6+ K×f5 38. Qg5+ and mates next move." **1–0** [*tournament book*, pages 34–35; *Baltimore Sunday News*, August 23, 1891]

375. J.W. Showalter–Pollock [C55]
4th USCA Championship, Lexington, Tiebreak Game, 7 August 1891

Baltimore Sunday News (August 16): "Although 9 o'clock at night they started to play off the tie, and after three hours' hard work Mr. Showalter won." **1. e4 e5 2. Nf3 Nc6 3. Bc4 Nf6 4. d4 e×d4 5. Ng5** Pollock: "This certainly has the merits of novelty." Steinitz: "Quite a refreshing novelty." **5. ... Ne5!** Steinitz: "5. ... d5 6. e×d5 N×d5 7. 0–0 [runs] into a variation which is given in favor of White in *The Modern Chess Instructor* with the following main continuation: 7. ... Be6 8. Re1 Qd7 9. N×f7 K×f7 10. Qf3+ and wins either [by] R×e6 or B×d5 accordingly." **6. Q×d4 N×c4 7. Q×c4 d5! 8. e×d5 Q×d5 9. Qe2+ Be7 10. 0–0 h6 11. Re1 0–0!?** Pollock: "Risky but not to the extent of audacity." Steinitz: "The only other alternative was 11. ... Qd8, after which he could not castle for a long time and the opponent could develop his attack still more effectively." **12. Q×e7** Steinitz: "He could have also proceeded very advantageously with 12. Nc3, for if 12. ... Qa5, 13. Q×e7 h×g5 14. Re5." **12. ... h×g5 13. Q×c7 Bd7 14. Nc3 Rfe8 15. R×e8+ R×e8 16. Be3 Qe6 17. Q×b7 Bc6 18. Qc7** (*see diagram*)

After
18. Qb7–c7

18. ... Nh5? Instead, 18. ... Ne4! was excellent: 19. Bd4 N×c3 20. B×c3 Qe4 21. f3 Qe3+ 22. Kh1 and now 22. ... B×f3! would have kept the balance. **19. Rd1!** Pollock: "White now breaks the slight counter-attack completely." Steinitz: "This excel-

lent move breaks the attack and White's superiority of material asserts itself after the exchange of queens which is practically forced, in consequence of this development." **19. ... Nf4 20. Rd6 Rc8 21. R×e6 R×c7 22. B×f4 g×f4 23. Rd6 Kf8** Steinitz: "He would have probably made a better fight by advancing 23. ... f3, while White was compelled to take, and then the broken kingside would have afforded some attacking opportunities for Black that might have enabled him to give some trouble, in spite of White's superiority on the other wing." **24. f3** Steinitz: "White properly closes the door against the entrance of the adverse pawn." **24. ... Ke7 25. Rd4 g5 26. Kf2 Ke6 27. Ke2 Ke5 28. Rd8 g4 29. f×g4 B×g2 30. h4 Bc6 31. h5 f6 32. Kf2 Rg7 33. Rc8** Pollock: "There is still some play in this ending, but White has no real chances open." **33. ... Bb7** (*see diagram*)

After
33. ... Bc6–b7

34. h6! Steinitz: "...pretty position. Evidently Black dare not take either the pawn or the rook without losing immediately." **34. ... Rh7 35. Rc5+ Kd4 36. Rh5 f3** Steinitz: "A fatal error. He could have still made some hard struggle by 36. ... Bc6 followed soon by ...Bd7 attacking the adverse g-pawn." **37. Nb5+ Ke4 38. Nd6+ Kf4 39. N×b7 K×g4 40. Rh1 f5 41. Nd6 Re7 42. h7 Re2+ 43. Kf1 R×c2 44. h8Q 1–0** [*tournament book*, pages 37–38; *Baltimore Sunday News*, August 16, 1891; *New York Tribune*, August 23, 1891]

376. J.W. Showalter–Pollock [C56]
[Event Unclear], Lexington, August 1891

In his *New York Tribune* column of August 30, 1891, Steinitz introduced this game as "played at Lexington in the general context of the championship tournament of the United States Chess Association." In his *Baltimore Sunday News* column of August 16, Pollock gave the bare score of this game without other relevant information. The discrepancy in status between this game and **Game**

375 remains unclear. **1. e4 e5 2. Nf3 Nc6 3. Bc4 Nf6 4. d4 e×d4 5. 0–0 N×e4 6. Re1 d5 7. B×d5 Q×d5 8. Nc3 Qh5** Steinitz: "8. ... Qd8 is rightly preferred by the authorities." **9. N×e4 Be7 10. Ng3 Qd5 11. Re4** Steinitz: "Under the circumstances, well played. Though he does not recover the pawn he creates a weakness in the adverse centre by inducing the opponent to advance the f-pawn." **11. ... f5 12. Re1 0–0** Steinitz: "12. ... Be6 was now the correct play." **13. Bf4** Steinitz: "If 13. N×d4, he would have a hard game after 13. ... Rd8 14. c3 Bf6 etc." **13. ... Qd8 14. Qd3 g5?!** 14. ... g6 15. Rad1 Bf6 was a more balanced approach. **15. Qc4+ Kg7** (*see diagram*)

After
15. ... Kg8–g7

16. R×e7+!? Steinitz: "A high-spirited sacrifice that gives White a lively attack for a long time." 16. Be5+ N×e5 17. N×e5 h6 18. Rad1 c5 19. c3 was stronger. **16. ... Q×e7 17. N×g5 h6 18. Nh3** Steinitz: "The knight is here out of play and should have retreated to f3." **18. ... Be6 19. Qd3 Qf7 20. Qd2 Qg6 21. B×c7 Kh7 22. Bf4 Rae8 23. Ne2 Bd5 24. Ng3** Steinitz: "Time lost. 24. Bg3 was much better." **24. ... Re6 25. f3 Rfe8 26. b3 R6e7 27. c4 Bf7 28. a3 Rd7 29. Qd3 Ne5!** Steinitz: "Black challenges battle at the cost of another pawn, and, as will be seen, he has deeply forecalculated its recovery." **30. Q×f5 Q×f5 31. N×f5 Nd3 32. Bd2** Steinitz: "If 32. B×h6, Black wins a piece by the rejoinder 32. ... Be6." **32. ... Re2 33. B×h6 Kg6 34. g4** Steinitz: "34. Ng3 at once was better. He only weakens the f-pawn by this advance." **34. ... Be6 35. Ng3 Rb2 36. Nf4+ N×f4 37. B×f4 R×b3 38. Re1 B×c4 39. Re5 R×f3 40. Rg5+ Kf7 41. Rf5+ Ke8?!** Steinitz: "Inferior to 41. ... Kg8, whereupon if 42. Ne4 Rf1+ 43. Kg2 Rf7 44. R×f7 (or 44. Nf6+ Kg7 etc.) 44. ... K×f7 45. Nd6+ Ke6, and should win." **42. Ne4 R×a3 43. Bd6?** Steinitz: "There was evidently more hope, if any, after 43. Nf6+, and taking the exchange. He confines Black's king for a while by the text move, but the adverse pawns are anyhow too strong for him." **43. ... Ra1+ 44. Kg2 Rf7 45. Nf6+ Kd8**

46. g5 d3 47. Bb4 Ra2+ 48. Rf2 Steinitz: "Wherever the king went Black's d-pawn would advance and cost a piece. Of course, it is also all over after the move in the text and the exchange of rooks, which is its natural result." **48. ... R×f2+ 49. K×f2 b6 50. h4 a5 51. Bc3 Re7 52. h5 Re2+ 53. Kf3 d2 54. B×d2 R×d2 55. g6 Ke7 0–1** [*Baltimore Sunday News*, August 16, 1891; *New York Tribune*, August 30, 1891]

377. J.M. Hanham–Pollock [C24]
Triangular Tournament, Lexington, August 1891

Pollock: "White's temporary sacrifice of a pawn by his 13th move was well calculated to equalize the positions. On resumption of play the next morning Mr. Pollock, who was accidentally 59 minutes late in arriving, endeavoured to make his remaining 20 moves in the single minute left, in other words instantaneously, lost a rook on the 21st move and resigned. The excessively 'sharp' work accomplished by the judges in 'clocking' belated players on each occasion led to the ill success and disruption of the triangular tournament." **1. e4 e5 2. Nf3 Nc6 3. Bc4 Nf6 4. d3 d5 5. e×d5 N×d5 6. 0–0 Be7 7. Re1 Bg4 8. Nbd2 0–0 9. c3 Kh8 10. Nf1 Nb6 11. Bb3 Qd7 12. h3 Bh5** (*see diagram*)

After
12. ... Bg4–h5

13. Be3 B×f3 14. Q×f3 Q×d3 15. Rad1 Qg6 16. B×b6 a×b6 17. Rd7 Rac8 18. Bd5 Bd6 19. R×f7 R×f7 20. Q×f7 Qg5 1–0 [*Baltimore Sunday News*, September 13, 1891]

Various Games

378. Pollock–Amateur
Handicap Event, Manhattan Chess Club, 17 September 1891
Remove Nb1

1. e4 e5 2. Nf3 Nc6 3. Bc4 Bc5 4. b4 Bb6 5. b5

Na5 6. N×e5 N×c4 7. N×c4 B×f2+ 8. K×f2 Qf6+ 9. Qf3 Q×a1 Pollock recommended 9. ... Qd4+ 10. Ne3 Q×a1. **10. Bb2** *(see diagram)*

After
10. Bc1–b2

10. ... Q×a2? Pollock: "Taking the other rook is perfectly safe." 10. ... Q×h1 was the move and White has no real breakthrough: 11. B×g7 Q×h2 12. Ne3 Qd6 13. d4 Ne7 14. B×h8 a6 15. Be5 Qg6. **11. Qc3** 11. Qd3! was more precise: 11. ... f6 12. Ra1 Q×a1 13. B×a1 d6 14. Ne3. **11. ... Nf6** 11. ... Qa4 12. Ra1 Q×b5 13. Ra5 Nf6! would have given Black the edge. **12. d3?** 12. Qd4! was correct. Pollock: "Palpably if 12. Ra1 N×e4+ wins. The next move is a 'waiter.'" **12. ... d5!? 13. e×d5 Qa4! 14. Re1+ Kd8?** Pollock: "White gave forced mate in five moves." **1–0** 14. ... Kf8! was the correct defense and White does not have a decisive blow: 15. d6 Q×b5 16. d×c7 Qc5+ 17. Kf1 Kg8 18. Qe5 Q×e5 19. R×e5 h5 20. Nd6 a5. [*Baltimore Sunday News*, January 24, 1892]

379. Pollock & J.W. Dallam & Kenney–Uhthoff & S. Adler & G.C. Witmer [C22]
Christmas Alternation Game,
Baltimore Chess Association,
16 December 1891

Baltimore Sunday News (December 20): "An amusing game was played last Wednesday at the club rooms specially for THE NEWS. In turned out to be (as far as it went) of the right sort. Messrs. Pollock, J.W. Dallam and Kenney manipulated White's moves in turn (without consulting) and Messrs. Uhthoff, S. Adler and Witmer the Black men similarly." **1. e4 e5 2. d4 e×d4 3. Q×d4 Nc6 4. Qe3 d6 5. Nf3 Nf6 6. Bd3 Be7 7. Nc3 0–0 8. 0–0 h6 9. h3 Bd7 10. b3 Nh7 11. Nd5 f5 12. Bb2** *(see diagram)*

12. ... Bg5 13. Bc4 Kh8 14. N×g5 N×g5 15. e×f5 B×f5 16. Rae1 N×h3+ 17. g×h3 a6 1–0 [*Baltimore Sunday News*, December 20, 1891]

After
12. Bc1–b2

380. Allies–Pollock
Odds Game, Baltimore Chess
Association, 1891
Remove f7 pawn

1. e4 d6 2. d4 Nf6 3. Bd3 Nc6 4. c3 e5 5. d5 Ne7 6. Be3 Ng6 7. Ne2 Bd7 Pollock: "A highly useful waiting move." **8. Na3** Pollock: "The knight is needed on the kingside, Black has just got what he wanted, as we shall see." **8. ... Nh4 9. 0–0 Ng4 10. Bd2** *(see diagram)*

After
10. Be3–d2

10. ... N×g2 11. h3 Pollock: "Somewhat weak calculations, as Black can play now ...Qh4, forcing h×g4. The next move only gives Black a choice, and he chooses." **11. ... Nh4 12. Ng3 Nf6 13. Nf5 N×f5 14. e×f5 g6** Pollock: "A little venturesome, 14. ... Qe7 equally attacks a pawn and is safe." **15. Qf3 g5 16. Kh2 h5!** Pollock: "To check at g4 if White plays B×g5." **17. Qg2 Rg8 18. Rae1** Pollock: "If 18. B×g5, 18. ... R×g5." **18. ... g4! 19. h4 N×d5 20. Bc4?** 20. Bg5 was White's best chance even if Black maintains a strong offensive: 20. ... R×g5! 21. h×g5 Nf4 22. Qe4 Q×g5 23. Q×b7 Rc8 24. Re3 h4. **20. ... Q×h4+ 21. Kg1 g3 22. f3** Pollock: "Had they played 22. f4, Black would have won by the terrible move 22. ... Bc6." **22. ... c6 23. Re4 Qf6 24. f4 0–0–0** Pollock: "This practically decides the event, but White makes a clever fight yet, and produces pretty positions." **25. b4 B×f5 26. f×e5 B×e4 27. Qh3+ Bf5 28. R×f5 Qe6**

Pollock: "Coming out of what looked like a trap, with the gain of the exchange." **29. Q×h5 d×e5 30. R×e5 Qg4 31. Qf5+ Q×f5 32. R×f5 g2 33. B×d5 c×d5 34. Nb5 a6 35. Nd4 Bd6 36. Bg5 Rde8 37. Nf3 Re2 38. R×d5 Bc7 39. c4 Rh8 40. Nh4 R×a2 41. N×g2 Rf8 42. Rd1 Rg8** Pol-

lock: "A singular and effective manoeuvre is that of this rook." **43. Rd5 R×g2+ 44. K×g2 Bf4 45. Rd8+ R×d8 46. B×f4 Rd4 0–1** [*New York Daily Tribune*, February 21, 1892; *ICM*, November 1891, pages 344–345]

Part Two, Section VIII
(January–December 1892)

In Baltimore

381. Pollock–G.C. Witmer [C50]
Simultaneous Exhibition, Baltimore,
21 January 1892

Pollock noted that he gave "special attention" to this game, Witmer "being a strong and promising player." **1. e4 e5 2. Nf3 Nc6 3. Bc4 Be7 4. d4 d6 5. d×e5 d×e5 6. Q×d8+ B×d8 7. 0-0 Nf6 8. Nc3 0-0 9. Be3 a6 10. a4 Be7 11. h3 Bd6 12. Rad1 Nd8 13. Nh4 Ne6?** 13. ... Be6 was superior. **14. Nf5 Bb4** *(see diagram)*

After
14. ... Bd6–b4

15. Nd5! N×d5 16. R×d5 f6? 16. ... Nd4 17. N×d4 e×d4 18. R×d4 Bc5 19. Rd3 was better than the outright error in the text, but Black remains a pawn down for nothing. **17. c3 c6 18. Rd2 b5 19. Ba2 Ba5 20. Ne7+ Kh8 21. N×c8 1–0** [*Baltimore Sunday News*, February 7, 1892]

382. S. Adler–Pollock [C80]
Simultaneous Exhibition, Baltimore,
21 January 1892

Pollock: "A curiosity at board IV. Black's king's knight makes seven moves in succession." **1. e4 e5 2. Nf3 Nc6 3. Bb5 a6 4. Ba4 Nf6 5. 0-0 N×e4 6. Re1 Nc5 7. c3 Nd3 8. Re3 N×c1 9. d4 N×a2 10. B×c6 N×c3 11. B×d7+ B×d7** *(see diagram)*

After
11. ... Bc8×d7

12. R×e5+ 12. N×c3 Be7 13. d×e5 Be6 14. Rd3 was much stronger. **12. ... Be7 13. b×c3 0-0 14. Qe2 Bd6 15. Rh5 Re8** 15. ... Bg4 was a greedier choice. **16. Qd3 g6 17. Rh4 Bb5 18. c4 Q×h4 19. c×b5 Re1+ 20. N×e1 Q×h2+ 21. Kf1 Qh1+ 22. Ke2 Re8+ 23. Kf3** and Black mates in two moves. **0–1** [*Baltimore Sunday News*, February 7, 1892]

In Brooklyn and Manhattan

383. Pollock–A.B. Hodges
Brooklyn Chess Club Championship,
Round 1, 5 March 1892

1. f5 1. Bf3 Q×d2 2. Q×d2 R×d2 3. Bc1 was most precise. **1. ... R×f5 2. Ra8+ Nd8 3. Qg3 Rg5 4. Bg4 h5 5. Be6+ Kh7?** 5. ... Kh8! was best: 6. B×d5 R×g3 7. B×c4 b×c4 8. Bc3, gives White a slight edge. **6. B×d5 R×g3 7. Be4+ Kh6** 7. ... Kg8

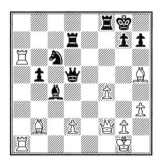

White to move

loses a piece after 8. Be5 Rb3 9. Bf5 R×d2 10. Bc7 Rbb2 11. Be4. **8. R1a6+** Hodges sealed his move and then resigned. Pollock: "If 8. … Kg5 (best), White would probably continue with 9. Be5." **1–0** [*Baltimore Sunday News*, March 20, 1892]

384. Pollock–A.J. Souweine [C51] Brooklyn Chess Club Championship, 20 March 1892

1. e4 e5 2. Nf3 Nc6 3. Bc4 Bc5 4. b4 B×b4 5. c3 Bc5 6. 0–0 d6 7. d4 e×d4 8. c×d4 Bb6 9. Nc3 Nf6 Pollock: "A radical error in the Evans when the centre pawns have been exchanged. The knight should not be deployed until measures have been taken, either by …Na5 or …Bg4, to prevent the cooperation of White's king's knight and bishop against the f7-pawn." **10. e5 d×e5** Pollock: "If 10. … d5, 11. e×f6 d×c4 12. Re1+ Kf8 13. Ba3+ Kg8 14. d5, with a powerful attack." **11. Ba3 Na5?** 11. … B×d4 was best here. **12. Re1 N×c4 13. Qa4+ c6 14. Q×c4 Be6 15. R×e5 Qd7** (see diagram)

After
15. … Qd8–d7

16. R×e6+!! Pollock: "The sacrifice of the exchange is necessary to prevent Black from castling on the queenside. Had the latter played …Qc8, it would have been useless." **16. … f×e6** Pollock: "If 16. … Q×e6 17. Re1 follows." **17. Ne5 Qc8 18. Re1 Nd5?** Pollock: "Fatal. Black overlooked the ensuing mate. The game could hardly be saved, however; if 18. … Bc7 (to prevent 19. Nb5), might continue

19. N×c6; and if 18. … a6, either 19. N×c6 or 19. Na4." In fact, 18. … Bc7 19. Qb4! Bd8 20. Nb5! c×b5 21. Q×b5+ Nd7 22. N×d7 was even more spectacular. **19. N×d5 c×d5 20. Qb5+ Kd8** and White mates in two moves. **1–0** [*Baltimore Sunday News*, March 20, 1892; *PM*, pages 97–98]

385. E. Delmar–Pollock [A84] Brooklyn Chess Club Championship, March 1892

1. d4 f5 2. e3 Nf6 3. c4 e6 4. Bd3 Bb4+ 5. Bd2 B×d2+ 6. N×d2 0–0 7. Ne2 b6 8. 0–0 Bb7 9. f3 c5 10. a3 Nc6 11. Rb1 Nh5 12. b4 c×d4 13. e×d4 Qg5 14. f4 Qh6 15. Rf2 Ne7 16. Nf1 Ng6 17. Qd2 Nf6 18. h3 Nh4 19. Qe3 Rae8 20. Neg3 Kh8! 21. a4 Rg8 22. a5 (see diagram)

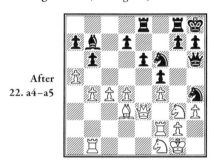

After
22. a4–a5

22. … g5 23. f×g5 R×g5 24. Rbb2 Reg8 25. a×b6?! 25. d5 was mandatory: 25. … e×d5 26. N×f5 N×f5 27. B×f5 d×c4 28. Qd4 and White had a fighting chance. **25. … a×b6** 25. … N×g2 26. R×g2 R×g3 27. R×g3 Q×e3+ 28. N×e3 R×g3+ 29. Kf2 Rf3+ 30. Ke2 a×b6 must not have seemed sufficient for Pollock. **26. Qe5?** Once again, 26. d5 was necessary. **26. … B×g2 27. Kh2 B×h3! 28. Kh1 B×f1 29. B×f1 R×g3 0–1** [*Brooklyn Standard-Union*, April 23, 1892; *PM*, pages 98–99]

386. Pollock–J.M. Hanham [A03] Brooklyn Chess Club Championship, March 1892

1. f4 d5 2. c4 Pollock: "Benoni's move, adopted by St. Amant in the Queen's Pawn opening (1. d4 c5) against Staunton." **2. … e6 3. e3 Nf6 4. Nc3** Pollock: "With a view to the ensuing sacrifice of the f-pawn, which leads to a lively game." **4. … d4 5. e×d4 Q×d4** (see diagram) **6. Nf3! Q×f4 7. d4 Qg4 8. Bd3 Be7** Pollock: "A very inadequate defense. 8. … Q×g2 would,

After
5. ... Qd8×d4

indeed, have been dangerous, if not fatal, but we prefer 8. ... Qh5 or 8. ... Bd6, or almost anything to the move adopted." **9. Kf2! Nh5?** Pollock: "After this it is probable that Black's game cannot be saved." 9. ... Bd6 was best. **10. Ne2 f5** Pollock: "If 10. ... Nf6 11. h3 Qh5 12. Bd2 and must win." **11. h3 Qg6 12. g4 Qf6** Pollock: "If 12. ... Nf6, 13. Ne5 wins the queen." **13. g×h5 0–0 14. Bg5 Qf7 15. B×e7 Q×e7 16. Qd2 Nc6 17. Rag1 Bd7 18. h6 g6 19. h4 e5 20. d×e5 N×e5 21. N×e5 Q×e5 22. Qc3 Qe7 23. c5 Be6 24. Nf4 Rf6 25. N×e6 R×e6 26. Bc4 Q×c5+ 27. Kf1 1–0** [*Baltimore Sunday News*, April 10, 1892]

387. E. Kemény–Pollock [A85]
Brooklyn Chess Club Championship, March 1892

1. d4 f5 2. c4 e6 3. Nf3 Nf6 4. e3 Bb4+ 5. Nc3 c5 6. Be2 0–0 7. 0–0 B×c3 8. b×c3 b6 9. Ba3 d6 10. Qc2 Qc7 11. Rad1 Bb7 12. d5 e5 13. Q×f5 e4 14. Ng5 Bc8 15. Ne6 Qe7 16. f3 Na6 17. f×e4 Nc7 (*see diagram*)

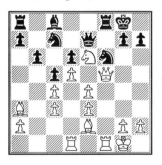

After
17. ... Na6–c7

18. e5 N×e6? 18. ... d×e5 was forced here: 19. Bf3 (19. Q×e5 N×e6 20. d×e6 Q×e6 21. Q×e6+ B×e6) 19. ... N×e6 20. Q×e5 Bd7 21. d×e6 Rae8! **19. e×f6 R×f6 20. Qe4 Qb7** 20. ... R×f1+ 21. R×f1 Qb7 was useless as well, thanks to 22. Qf3 or 22. Qf5. **21. R×f6** This is sufficient. The surprising 21. B×c5! involved some pretty tactics: 21. ... d×c5

(21. ... b×c5 22. R×f6 g×f6 23. Rb1) 22. d×e6! R×f1+ 23. B×f1 Kf8 24. Rd8+ Ke7 25. Rd7+. **21. ... g×f6 22. Rf1 Qg7 23. d×e6 1–0** [*Brooklyn Standard-Union*, March 19, 1892; *New York World*, March 20, 1892]

388. S. Lipschütz–Pollock [C33]
Offhand Game, Manhattan Chess Club, 6 March 1892

1. e4 e5 2. f4 e×f4 3. Bc4 f5 4. Qe2 f×e4?! A dubious idea. 4. ... Qh4+ 5. Kd1 f×e4 6. Nc3 Kd8 7. N×e4 c6 leads to some really wild play. **5. Qh5+ g6 6. Qe5+ Qe7 7. Q×h8 f3?** 7. ... Nf6 8. Nc3 c6 9. Nge2 d5 was a more reliable way to get some compensation. **8. g×f3 e×f3+ 9. Kd1 f2 10. Nf3 d5 11. B×d5** 11. Q×g8 d×c4 12. Q×c4 Bh3 13. Rf1 B×f1 14. Q×f1 was possible too. **11. ... Bg4 12. Rf1** 12. Q×g8?! is not quite sufficient: 12. ... Nc6! 13. h3 Nd4! **12. ... Nf6** (*see diagram*)

After
12. ... Ng8–f6

13. Nc3? An understandable desire for further development, but 13. B×b7! was the best move. The tactics, admittedly, are difficult to spot: 13. ... Ne4 14. Ke2! c6 15. Qd4 Nd6+ 16. K×f2 B×f3 17. Qe3. **13. ... Ne4** Even stronger was 13. ... N×d5 14. R×f2 Nf6 15. d4 Nbd7 16. Bg5 0–0–0. **14. B×e4 Q×e4! 15. R×f2 B×f3+ 16. Ne2 Nc6 17. d3 0–0–0** 17. ... Qg4 was stronger. **18. Bd2?** White had to try something much faster. For instance, 18. Qf6 B×e2+ 19. R×e2 Qh1+ 20. Re1 Q×h2 21. Bf4 with complicated play. **18. ... Qg4** 18. ... B×e2+ 19. R×e2 Qf3 20. c3 Qf1+ 21. Re1 Q×d3 was more to the point. **19. Qf6 B×e2+** 19. ... Nd4! 20. Bg5 Re8 was most exact. **20. R×e2 Re8 21. Be3 R×e3 22. Q×f8+ Kd7 23. Qf2 Rf3 24. Qe1 Nd4 25. Re7+ Kd8 26. Re8+ Kd7 27. Qe7+?!** This was unjustified. 27. Re7+ Kd8 (27. ... Kc6?? walks into a mate: 28. Qc3+ Kb6 29. Q×c7+ Ka6 30. Q×b7+ Ka5 31. Q×a7+ Kb4 32. Rb7+ Nb5 33. Qa3 mate) 28. Re8+ Kd7 29. Re7+ would have drawn. **27. ... Kc6 28. Qe4+ Q×e4 29. R×e4 Rf1+ 30. Re1?** Naturally, best was 30. Kd2 Nf3+ 31. Ke3 R×a1

32. K×f3 R×a2 33. Rc4+ Kd7 34. b4, with solid hopes for a draw. **30. ... R×e1+ 31. K×e1 N×c2+ 0–1** [*Brooklyn Standard-Union*, March 12, 1892]

BACK TO BALTIMORE

389. J.W. Showalter–Pollock [C51]
Offhand Game, Baltimore, April 1892

1. e4 e5 2. Nf3 Nc6 3. Bc4 Bc5 4. b4 B×b4 5. c3 Bc5 6. 0–0 d6 7. d4 e×d4 8. c×d4 Bb6 9. Nc3 Na5 10. Bg5 Ne7 11. Nd5 f6 12. B×f6 g×f6 13. N×f6+ Kf8 14. Ng5 N×c4 15. Qh5 Kg7 16. Qf7+ Kh6 17. Ng4+ B×g4 18. Qf6+ Kh5 19. Nf7 Ng6 20. N×d8 Ra×d8 (*see diagram*)

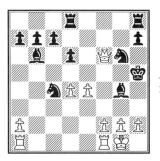

After
20. ... Ra8×d8

Pollock: "We offer a 'Torsch Chess Button' as a badge of honor for the best suggestion as to White's line of play from the point diagrammed." **21. f3?** 21. h4 was best: 21. ... N×h4 (21. ... Kh6 22. Qg5+ Kg7 23. Q×g4 h5 24. Qe2 Na5 25. Rad1) 22. g3 Bf3! (22. ... Nf3+? 23. Kg2 and Rh1+ decides.) 23. Rac1 (23. g×h4 Rhg8+ 24. Kh2 Rdf8 25. Qe7 h6 26. Rg1 Bg4 27. R×g4 R×f2+ 28. Kg3 R×g4+ 29. K×f2 B×d4+ 30. Ke2 B×a1 favors Black; 23. Q×h4+ Kg6 24. Rac1 d5 25. e×d5 Nd6 26. Rfe1 is a calmer possibility.) 23. ... d5 would have been very edgy play. **21. ... Bd7 22. h4 Kh6 23. Rad1 Rhg8 24. f4 Ne3 25. h5 N×d1 26. R×d1** 26. h×g6 was correct: 26. ... Rdf8 27. Qg5+ Kg7 28. Qe7+ K×g6 29. f5+ Kh6 30. R×d1. **26. ... Rdf8 27. Qg5+ Kg7 28. f5 Rf6 0–1** [*Baltimore Sunday News*, July 17, 1892]

390. J.W. Showalter–Pollock [C56]
Offhand Game, Baltimore, April 1892

"A skirmish played during Mr. Showalter's recent visit to Baltimore." **1. e4 e5 2. Nf3 Nc6 3. Bc4 Nf6 4. d4 e×d5 5. Ng5 Ne5 6. Q×d4** Pollock: "The attack introduced by Showalter at Lexington, 1891, and pronounced excellent by Steinitz." **6. ... N×c4 7. Q×c4 d5 8. e×d5 N×d5** Pollock: "Much better

than the more obvious 8. ... Q×d5 to which White replies 9. Qe2+." **9. 0–0 Be7 10. Rd1 c6 11. Qe2 0–0 12. N×h7** Pollock: "Sacrificing development for material." **12. ... K×h7 13. c4 Bd6 14. c×d5 Re8 15. Qh5+** Pollock: "If 15. Qd3+, 15. ... Kg8 16. d×c6 Re1+ 17. R×e1 B×h2+, winning the queen for rook and bishop." **15. ... Kg8 16. d×c6 Re4?!** Pollock: "With this move Black at least equalizes matters. White's 18th move being forced, on account of the attack on two spots." 16. ... g6 17. Qf3 Qc7 was more sensible. **17. h3** 17. Nc3 was much stronger since 17. ... Rh4 is not possible due to 18. R×d6! **17. ... Qe7 18. Be3** (*see diagram*)

After
18. Bc1–e3

18. ... R×e3!! 19. f×e3 Q×e3+ 20. Kh1 Qg3 21. R×d6 Q×d6 22. c×b7 B×b7 23. Nc3 Pollock: "Slow stick! Though come'st too late!" **23. ... Qg3 24. Rg1?** Pollock: "Fatal! The queen should have been played." 24. Qe2 Q×h3+ 25. Kg1 Qg3 26. Rd1 was necessary. **24. ... Re8!** Pollock: "White resigns, as if he stops the mate by Nd5 he loses a piece. The position is quite a little study." **0–1** [*Baltimore Sunday News*, June 21, 1892]

391. G.C. Witmer–Pollock
Handicap Event, Baltimore Chess
Association, May 1892
Remove f7 pawn

1. e4 and d4 d6 2. e5 d×e5 3. Qh5+ g6 4. Q×e5 Nf6 5. Nf3 Bg7 6. Bf4 0–0 7. Q×c7 Qe8 8. Bc4+ Kh8 (*see diagram*)

After
8. ... Kg8–h8

9. Ng5?! Very tempting but not the best. 9. 0–0 and 9. Nc3 were much stronger. **9. ... Na6 10. B×a6 Nd5! 11. Qc4 N×f4 12. Bb5 N×g2+ 13. Ke2 Nf4+ 14. Ke1 Qd8 15. Nf7+ R×f7 16. Q×f7 Bf5 17. c3 e6** 17. ... e5 was even stronger. **18. h4?** 18. Q×b7 Rb8 19. Qf3 R×b5 20. Q×f4 seems better, but then White runs into 20. ... e5!, with an excellent attack for Black. **18. ... Qd5 0–1** [*Baltimore Sunday News*, June 26, 1892]

392. Pollock–M. Baumgarten
Handicap Event, Baltimore Chess
Association, May 1892
Remove Nb1

1. e4 e5 2. Nf3 Nf6 3. d4 e×d4 4. Bd3 Bc5 5. e5 Nd5 6. 0–0 d6 7. Bg5 f6 8. e×f6 N×f6 9. Re1+ Kf7 10. c3 d×c3 11. b4 Bb6 12. Qb3+ Kf8 13. Rad1 Bg4 *(see diagram)*

After
13. ... Bc8–g4

14. Ne5 d×e5 14. ... Bh5 was correct. **15. Bg6! 1–0** [*Baltimore Sunday News*, July 10, 1892]

393. Em. Lasker–Pollock [C68]
Baltimore, Double Blindfold Game,
29 November 1892

Baltimore Sunday News (December 4): "The subjoined game as played on the 29th of November as a substitute for the proposed simultaneous blindfold exhibition, which Lasker requested to be excused from." **1. e4 e5 2. Nf3 Nc6 3. Bb5 a6 4. B×c6** Steinitz: "An old continuation which leads to equality." **4. ... d×c6** Steinitz: "We would recommend here the trial of the novelty 4. ... b×c6 with the sequence 5. d4 f6 6. d×e5 f×e5 7. N×e5 Qe7 8. f4 (if 8. Qh5+, 8. ... g6 9. N×g6 Q×e4+, and wins.) 8. ... d6 9. N×c6 Q×e4+ 10. Qe2 Q×e2+ 11. K×e2 Bb7 etc." **5. d4** *(see diagram)*

5. ... Bg4 Steinitz: "The unsoundness of the sacrifice of a pawn at this stage would have been illustrated by a [more] minor star than Lasker. 5. ...

After
5. d2–d4

e×d4 was the only move." **6. d×e5 Q×d1+ 7. K×d1 Bc5 8. Ke2 0–0–0 9. Be3 Be7 10. h3 Bh5 11. Nbd2 f6 12. Rhd1 f×e5 13. g4 Be8 14. N×e5 Nf6 15. f3 h5 16. Nf1** Steinitz: "Every point skilfully guarded and all that is left of Black's attack is the pawn ahead for White." **16. ... h×g4 17. h×g4 Nd7 18. N×d7 B×d7 19. Kf2 Rdf8 20. Kg2 Bd6 21. Ng3 Rf7 22. Nf5?!** Steinitz: "Either an oversight or deep beyond ordinary measure. 22. Rd3 seems good enough." **22. c4 c5 23. Rh1 Re8 24. Rad1** was superior. **22. ... B×f5! 23. e×f5 Rh2+ 24. Kg1 R×c2 25. Rd2 R×d2 26. B×d2 Rd7** Steinitz: "Ill-considered. 26. ... Be5 must have gained most important time, for if White opposed Bc3 Black would capture, followed by ...Rd7, threatening ...Rd3." **27. Bc3 Bc5+ 28. Kg2 Bd4 29. B×d4 R×d4 30. Rh1 b5 31. Rh7 c5** Steinitz: "The beauty of White's play is hidden by Black's correct perception. If 31. ... Rd7, 32. g5 Kd8 33. f6 g×f6 34. g6 and wins." **32. R×g7 c4 33. Kg3** Steinitz: "Unnecessary. The march of the f-pawn might have been started at once with quieter effect we believe." **33. ... b4 34. f6 c3 35. b×c3 b×c3 36. f7 Rd8 37. Rg8 c2** Steinitz: "A surprise with still deeper views." **38. R×d8+ Kb7 39. f8Q** Steinitz: "Many would have been tempted to check by 39. Rb8+ when Black of course would have retreated Ka7 with hopes of a longer fight." **39. ... c1Q 40. Qb4+ Kc6** *(see diagram)*

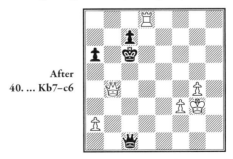

After
40. ... Kb7–c6

41. Qd6+ Steinitz: "Straight to the core. If Black takes, White recovers the queen by Rc8+."

41. ... Kb7 42. Qd5+ Steinitz: "For if 42. ... c6, 43. Qb3+ and mates next move; Or if 42. ... Kb6, 43. Rb8+ and mate follows." **1–0** [*Baltimore Sunday News*, December 4, 1892; *New York Tribune*, December 11, 1892; *Pittsburg Dispatch*, December 23, 1892; *New York Clipper*, December 24, 1892]

394. Em. Lasker–Pollock [C60]
Baltimore, Simultaneous Game in
Consultation, 30 November 1892

1. e4 e5 2. Nf3 Nc6 3. Bb5 Na5?! 4. 0-0 c6 5. Be2 Qc7?! 5. ... d5 was more logical. **6. d4 f6 7. a3 b6 8. Be3 d6 9. Nc3 Ne7 10. Qd2 Ng6 11. Ne1 Be7 12. b4 Nb7 13. f4** 13. b5 was somewhat stronger. **13. ... e×f4 14. B×f4 N×f4 15. Q×f4 0-0 16. Bg4 B×g4 17. Q×g4 Rfc8?!** 17. ... Nd8 18. Nf3 Nf7 19. Nh4 Rae8 20. Nf5 g6 was much better. **18. Nd3 a5 19. b5 Nd8 20. b×c6 N×c6 21. Nd5 Qd8 22. c3 Kh8 23. N3f4 Bf8** (*see diagram*)

After
23. ... Be7–f8

24. Rf3 White missed a pretty mate in seven: 24. Ng6+ h×g6 25. Qh3+ Kg8 26. Qe6+ Kh7 27. Rf3 g5 28. Qf7 g4 29. Rf5 and mate follows. **24. ... Ra7 25. Qe6** 25. Ng6+ was possible again: 25. ... h×g6 26. Qe6. **25. ... g5 26. N×f6! Rg7 27. Rh3 Q×f6 28. Q×f6 g×f4 29. R×h7+ K×h7 30. Qf5+ Kg8 31. Q×c8 1–0** [*London Chess Fortnightly*, January 30, 1893, pages 94–95]

CORRESPONDENCE GAMES

395. Pollock–J.L. McCutcheon [C37]
Game by Correspondence, 1892

1. e4 e5 2. f4 e×f4 3. Nf3 g5 4. Bc4 g4 5. 0-0 g×f3 6. Q×f3 Qf6 7. e5 Q×e5 8. B×f7+ K×f7 9. d4 Qf5 Pollock: "Considered better than 9. ... Q×d4+." **10. B×f4 Nf6 11. Nc3 d6 12. Rae1 Rg8** (*see diagram*)
13. Qe2! Qg6 14. Nd5 Nbd7 Pollock: "If 14. ... N×d5 15. Bh6+ Qf5!. 16. R×f5+ B×f5 17. Qh5+

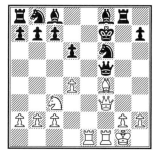

After
12. ... Rh8–g8

and must win." **15. N×c7 Rb8 16. Ne8 Q×g2+** Pollock: "Again 16. ... N×e8 loses to 17. Bh6+." **17. Q×g2 R×g2+ 18. K×g2 N×e8 19. B×d6+ Nef6 20. B×b8 N×b8 21. R×f6+ K×f6 22. Re8 Bd6 23. R×c8 Nc6 24. c3 h5 25. h3 h4 26. Kf3 Ke6 27. Ke4 Kd7 28. Rh8 Bg3 29. Rh7+ Ne7 30. c4 1–0** [*Baltimore Sunday News*, August 5, 1893]

396. J.L. McCutcheon–Pollock [C25]
Game by Correspondence, 1892

1. e4 e5 2. Nc3 Nc6 3. f4 e×f4 4. Nf3 g5 5. Bc4 g4 6. 0-0 g×f3 7. Q×f3 Pollock: "The moves thus far, inclusive, were stipulated by White." **7. ... Qf6**

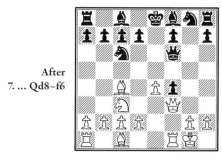

After
7. ... Qd8–f6

8. Nd5 Pollock: "Reckless of his minor pieces." **8. ... Qd4+ 9. Kh1 Q×c4 10. d3 Qd4 11. N×c7+ Kd8 12. B×f4 d6 13. c3 Qg7 14. N×a8 Bg4 15. Qf2 Kc8 16. b4 Kb8** Pollock: "If 16. ... Q×c3 17. Rfc1 Q×b4 18. Q×a7 etc." **17. b5 Nd8** Pollock: "If 17. ... Na5, White wins the knight by the text continuation." **18. Nb6 a×b6 19. Q×b6 Ne6** Pollock: "19. ... Qf6 is probably better, as the reply 20. Be5 is not greatly to be feared." **20. Be3 Nc5 21. d4** Pollock: "A very fine continuation." **21. ... N×e4 22. d5 Nc5 23. B×c5 d×c5 24. d6 f6 25. Qd8+ Bc8 26. Rae1 B×d6** Pollock: "Black has nothing better. Mr. McCutcheon finishes in great style." **27. Q×d6+ Qc7 28. Qf8 h5 29. Re8 h4 30. Rd1 h3 31. R×c8+ Q×c8 32. Rd8 h×g2+ 33. K×g2 Q×d8 34. Q×d8+ Ka7 35. Qa5+ Kb8 36. b6 1–0** [*Baltimore Sunday News*, August 5, 1893]

397. Albany Chess Club–
Baltimore Chess Association [C70]
Match by Correspondence, Game 1, 1892

1. e4 e5 2. Nf3 Nc6 3. Bb5 a6 4. Ba4 b5 5. Bb3 Bb7 6. c3 d6 7. d3 Qe7 8. Nbd2 Nd8 9. Nf1 g6 10. Ng3 Bg7 11. Be3 Nf6 12. 0–0 0–0 13. Qe2 Ne6 14. Rac1 Kh8 15. Ng5 h6 16. N×e6 f×e6 *(see diagram)*

After
16. ... f7×e6

17. f4 e×f4 18. R×f4 Nd7 19. Rcf1 R×f4 20. B×f4 Rf8 21. Qg4 ½–½ [*Albany Evening Journal*, January 14, 1893; *Baltimore Sunday News*, January 22, 1893][1]

398. Baltimore Chess Association–
Albany Chess Club [C52]
Match by Correspondence, Game 2, 1892

1. e4 e5 2. Nf3 Nc6 3. Bc4 Bc5 4. b4 B×b4 5. c3 Ba5 6. 0–0 d6 7. d4 Bg4 *(see diagram)*

After
7. ... Bc8–g4

8. Qb3 Pollock: "Neither this nor 8. Bb5 is quite satisfactory. 8. Bb2 might be tried." 8. ... B×f3 9. g×f3 e×d4 Pollock: "Black wisely decline to protect the f7-pawn; if 9. ... Qd7 10. B×f7+ Q×f7 11. Q×b7." 10. B×f7+ Kf8 11. Bh5 Pollock: "11. B×g8 only transfers the attack to the opponent." 11. ... Qd7 12. Bg4 Qe8 13. c×d4 N×d4 14. Qd3 Bb6 15. Bb2 Nc6 16. Kh1 Pollock: "Instead of this useless move, White might at least have enlivened the game by 16. f4 (a necessary precaution) 16. ... Qg6 17. Kh1 Q×g4 18. Rg1 Qd7 19. B×g7+ Q×g7 20. R×g7 K×g7 21. Nc3 Nf6 22. Rg1+, with a fair attack." 16. ... Ne5 17. Qc3 Pollock: "Of course, 17. Qe2 is far better." 17. ... Nf6 18. Bf5 Qb5 19. Nd2 Qd3 20. f4 Q×c3 21. B×c3 Ng6 22. Nf3 Pollock: "Exchanging both knights was a little better, but would not achieve salvation." 22. ... N×f4 1–0 [*Albany Evening Journal*, January 14, 1893; *Baltimore Sunday News*, January 29, 1893][1]

1. Pollock played for the Baltimore Chess Association in **games 397** and **398**.

Part Two, Section IX
(January–August 1893)

In Buffalo

399. Pollock–J.L. McCutcheon
Pittsburg, Allegheny Chess Club,
10 March 1893

Black to move

An endgame sequence rich in errors on both sides. **1. ... Nb8?** 1. ... Ne7 2. K×a5 Kc5 3. g3 Nd5 4. Bd2 Kc6 would have kept the balance. **2. K×a5 Nd7 3. Kb4?** 3. Kb5! Nc5 4. a5 should have won. **3. ... Nc5! 4. a5 Nb3 5. Bd2?** 5. Kb5 N×c1 6. a6 d2 7. a7 d1Q 8. a8Q+ Ke6 9. Qe8+ Kf6 10. Qf8+ would have secured a perpetual check. **5. ... N×d2 6. a6 Ke4? 7. a7 Ke3** and the game was drawn several moves later. **½–½** Objectively, White should win this as follows: 8. a8Q Ne4 9. Qa7+ Ke2 10. Qg7 d2 11. Q×g6 Nf2 (11. ... d1Q 12. Q×h5+ Ke1 13. Q×d1+ K×d1 14. h5 Nf6 15. h6 Kc2 16. K×c4 K×b2 17. Kd4 and White wins) 12. Q×f5 d1Q 13. Q×h5+ Ke3 14. Q×d1 N×d1 15. f5 N×b2 16. Kc5 Na4+ 17. K×c4 and Black cannot stop the pawns. [*Baltimore Sunday News*, March 13, 1893]

400. Pollock–T.N. Wilcox [B32]
Buffalo Chess Club, 13 March 1893

1. e4 c5 2. d4 c×d4 3. Nf3 Nc6 4. N×d4 N×d4 5. Q×d4 e6 6. Nc3 Ne7 7. Nb5 (*see diagram*)

After
7. Nc3–b5

7. ... d5? 7. ... Nc6 8. Nd6+ B×d6 9. Q×d6 Qe7 was necessary. **8. Bf4** 8. Qc3! Nc6 9. Qg3 e5 10. e×d5 Nb4 11. Q×e5+ Qe7 12. Q×e7+ B×e7 13. Nc7+ was possible too. **8. ... f6** Mandatory was 8. ... Nc6. **9. Nd6+ Kd7 10. Bb5+ Nc6 11. e×d5 Qa5+** 11. ... B×d6 loses too after 12. d×c6+ Ke7 13. 0-0-0 e5 14. B×e5 f×e5 15. Rhe1. **12. c3 Q×b5 13. d×c6+ Q×c6 14. Nf7+ Ke8 15. N×h8 Bc5 16. Qd3 f5 17. 0-0-0 Bb6 18. Rhe1 Bd7 19. Q×f5 1–0** [*Baltimore Sunday News*, March 18, 1893, and April 1, 1893; *Buffalo Courier*, March 14, 1893; *PM*, page 100]

401. H.E. Perrine–Pollock [A84]
Buffalo Chess Club, 14 March 1893

"At 4:00 pm Mr. H.E. Perrine sat down at the board and played one of the most brilliant games ever contested in Buffalo. In the middle of the game Dr. Pollock sacrificed his queen, but came off the victor after 40 minutes of hard play." **1. d4**

f5 2. c4 e6 3. e3 Bb4+ 4. Bd2 B×d2+ 5. Q×d2
Nf6 6. Nc3 0–0 7. Nf3 b6 8. Be2 Bb7 9. 0–0 Qe8
10. d5 Na6 11. a3 Nc5 12. Rad1 Rd8 13. b4 Nce4
14. N×e4 f×e4 15. Ne1 15. Nd4 e×d5 16. c5!? was
a better idea. **15. ... e×d5 16. c×d5 B×d5 17. Qc3
c6 18. Nc2 Be6 19. h3 Qg6 20. Kh2 Kh8 21. Nd4
Bd5 22. Qc2 b5 23. f4 e×f3 24. Q×g6 f×e2!?
25. Qb1** *(see diagram)*

After
25. Qg6–b1

25. ... Bc4? Creative but imprecise. 25. ... e×f1Q
26. R×f1 Rde8 was fine. So was 25. ... Be4 26. Qa1
e×f1Q 27. R×f1 Rde8 28. Rf4 Bg6. **26. Rg1**
26. R×f6! offered White a clean win: 26. ... R×f6
27. Re1 Rf2 28. Kg3 Rdf8 29. Qc2 Rf1 30. R×e2.
**26. ... e×d1Q 27. Q×d1 Ne4 28. Qc2 Bd5
29. Nf3 Rf6 30. Qb2 Rdf8 31. Qd4 a6 32. Rb1
h6 33. Rb2 Kh7 34. Qd1** 34. Nd2 Re8 35. N×e4
R×e4 36. Qa7 was a more active try. **34. ... g6
35. Qd4 h5 36. Qe5 d6 37. Qd4 g5! 38. Qd3 Kh6
39. Qd4?** 39. Nd2 could have given White some
hopes in the endgame: 39. ... Rf2 40. Qd4 R×g2+
41. K×g2 N×d2+ 42. Q×d5 c×d5 43. R×d2. **39. ...
g4 40. Nh4 g3+ 0–1** [*Buffalo Morning Express*,
March 15, 1893]

402. Pollock–S. Langleben [C51]
Buffalo Chess Club, 15 March 1893

**1. e4 e5 2. Nf3 Nc6 3. Bc4 Bc5 4. b4 B×b4
5. c3 Bc5 6. 0–0 d6 7. d4 e×d4 8. c×d4 Bb6
9. Nc3 Bg4 10. Bb5 B×f3 11. g×f3 Qf6 12. d5**
12. Nd5 Qg6+ 13. Kh1 0–0–0 14. Rg1 was a worthy option. **12. ... Q×c3 13. d×c6 b×c6** *(see diagram)*

**14. Bb2! Qc5 15. B×c6+ Q×c6 16. B×g7 d5
17. B×h8** 17. Q×d5 was less appealing: 17. ... Q×d5
18. e×d5 f6 19. B×h8 Kf7 20. Rfd1 Bc5 21. Rac1
Bd6 22. Rc4 Ne7 23. B×f6 K×f6. **17. ... 0–0–0
18. e5 h5** 18. ... d4!? 19. Qd3 Qg6+ 20. Q×g6
h×g6 21. a4 c5 gave Black sufficient compensation.
19. Qd3 Qe6?! 19. ... Qh6! 20. Bf6 N×f6 21. e×f6
Q×f6 was much stronger. **20. f4 a5 21. Rab1!
Qg4+ 22. Kh1 Q×f4 23. Rfc1 Kb7 24. Qc3**

After
13. ... b7×c6

Q×f2? 24. ... Ne7 was recommended: 25. Bf6
(25. Q×c7+ Ka8!) 25. ... Rd7 26. B×e7 R×e7
27. Qc6+ Ka7 28. Q×d5 Q×e5. **25. Q×c7+ Ka8
26. Q×b6 Qf3+ 27. Kg1 Qg4+ 28. Kf1 Qf3+
29. Qf2 Qh1+ 30. Ke2 Qe4+ 31. Kd2 Nh6
32. Rc7** 32. Rc6 was very powerful as well. **32. ...
d4 33. Qf1 Qe3+** 33. ... d3 fails too because of
34. Rc5 Rd5 35. Rc8+ Ka7 36. Qf2+. **34. Kd1
1–0** [*Buffalo Morning Express*, March 16, 1893;
Buffalo Courier, March 16, 1893]

403. Pollock–H.E. Perrine [C52]
Buffalo Chess Club, 16 March 1893

**1. e4 e5 2. Nf3 Nc6 3. Bc4 Bc5 4. b4 B×b4
5. c3 Ba5 6. 0–0 h6 7. d4 e×d4 8. c×d4 Bb6
9. Bb2 Qf6?!** 9. ... Nge7! 10. d5 Na5 11. Bd3 0–0
was more accurate. **10. e5 Qg6?** This gets Black in
trouble quickly. The alternative was not great either: 10. ... Qf4 11. Nc3 Nge7 12. Ne2 Qe4 13. Ng3
Qg6 14. d5 Na5 15. Bd3 Qg4 16. d6! **11. d5 Na5
12. Bd3 Qh5 13. Re1 Ne7 14. d6** 14. Re4! g5
(14. ... c6? 15. Rh4) 15. e6 was even stronger. **14. ...
Nec6** 14. ... Ng6 was not that much better: 15. Qa4
Nf8 16. Nc3 Ne6 17. Ne4 0–0 18. d×c7 B×c7
19. Ng3. **15. Re4 Qf5 16. Nc3 Qh7 17. Nd5 Kd8
18. Rg4 Qg8 19. Qd2 Qf8 20. Re1 c×d6 21. e×d6
f6** *(see diagram)* 21. ... Q×d6 was losing after
22. Bf1 Re8 23. R×g7 R×e1 24. N×e1 Ne7 25. Bf6.

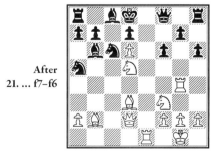

After
21. ... f7–f6

**22. R×g7 Q×d6 23. B×f6+ Q×f6 24. N×f6
Nd4 25. N×d4 B×d4 26. Q×a5+ b6 27. Qd5**

B×f6 28. R×d7+ B×d7 29. Bf5 1–0 [*Buffalo Morning Express*, March 17, 1893; *Buffalo Courier*, March 17, 1893]

404. S. Langleben–Pollock [B10]
Buffalo Chess Club, 17 March 1893

Pollock: "...the shortest game of the series...."
1. e4 d5 2. e×d5 Nf6 3. c4 c6 4. Nc3 c×d5
5. c×d5 N×d5 6. Bb5+ Nc6 7. Qa4 N×c3
8. B×c6+ b×c6 9. Q×c6+?! 9. d×c3 is a safer option. 9. ... Bd7 10. Q×c3 Rc8 11. Qb3 Qa5
12. Nf3 (*see diagram*)

After
12. Ng1–f3

12. ... Bb5! 13. Ne5 13. Qa3 Q×a3 (13. ... Qb6!?
14. Qe3 Qa6 15. b3 Q×a2 16. Qe5 a6 17. Qb2
Q×b2 18. B×b2 e6) 14. b×a3 f6 15. Nd4 Bd3 16. f4
was the lesser evil. 13. ... e6 14. Qf3 Qc7 14. ... f6
15. Qb7 Qa6 16. Q×a6 B×a6 17. Nf3 Kf7 was possible as well. 15. Qe4?? 15. Qc3 was needed, but
Black keeps a clear advantage after 15. ... f6
16. Q×c7 R×c7 17. Nf3 Bd3! 15. ... Q×c1+ 0–1
[*Buffalo Courier*, March 19, 1893; *Baltimore Sunday News*, March 25, 1893]

405. Pollock–N.N.
Odds Game, Buffalo Chess Club, March 1893
Remove Ng1

"Played at Buffalo Chess Club against a strong opponent." 1. e4 e5 2. Bc4 Nf6 3. d4 e×d4 4. 0–0
d6 5. a4 Be7 6. Ra3 d5 7. Rd3 d×c4 8. R×d4 Bd7
9. e5 Ng4? Evidently, 9. ... Ng8 was safe. 10. R×g4
B×g4 11. Q×g4 0–0 12. Bh6 g6 13. Nc3! c6
14. Rd1 Qc7 14. ... Qc8 15. Q×c4 Rd8 was best.
15. e6! f5 16. Q×c4 Rd8 (*see diagram*) 16. ... Qe5!
still gave Black a clear edge: 17. B×f8 K×f8 18. Qb3
b6.
17. Rd7! Qa5 17. ... N×d7 leads to a quick mate:
18. e×d7+ Kh8 19. Qd4+. 18. Qd4 and White
mates in six moves. 1–0 [*Baltimore Sunday News*, April 1, 1893]

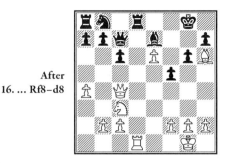

After
16. ... Rf8–d8

406. Pollock–Allies [C56]
Simultaneous Exhibition
(6 Boards; Consultation),
Buffalo, March 1893

1. e4 e5 2. Nf3 Nc6 3. Bc4 Nf6 4. d4 e×d4
5. 0–0 N×e4 6. Re1 d5 7. B×d5 Q×d5 8. Nc3
Qf5 9. N×e4 Be6 10. N×d4 N×d4 11. Q×d4 h6?!
This loss of time will prevent Black from fully developing. 11. ... Be7! was much better: 12. Bg5
(12. Q×g7 0–0–0!) 12. ... B×g5 13. Q×g7 0–0–0
14. Q×g5 Q×g5 15. N×g5 Bd5. 12. b3 a6 13. Bb2
a5? (*see diagram*) 13. ... Rd8 14. Qe3 Qg6 15. Qc3
Rd7 16. Rad1 was better, but White keeps a clear
advantage.

After
13. ... a6–a5

14. Rad1! f6 and White mates in five moves.
1–0 [*Baltimore Sunday News*, March 25, 1893;
New York Clipper, April 22, 1893; *PM*, page 140]

IN MONTREAL

407. D.C. Robertson–Pollock [C80]
Montreal Chess Club, 25 March 1893

1. e4 e5 2. Nf3 Nc6 3. Bb5 a6 4. Ba4 Nf6
5. 0–0 N×e4 6. Re1 Nc5 7. N×e5 N×e5 8. R×e5+
Ne6 9. d4 (*see diagram*)
9. ... Bd6? 9. ... b5! was first necessary: 10. Bb3
Bd6 11. Bg5 f6 12. Qh5+ g6 13. Qf3 B×e5 14. d×e5
Bb7! 15. Q×b7 f×g5 16. Nc3 Qb8 17. Qe4 with

After
9. d2–d4

rich and complicated play. **10. Bg5! Q×g5** 10. ... f6 fails to 11. R×e6+ Kf8 12. R×d6 c×d6 13. Bf4 Qe7 14. Nc3 and White has a crushing position. **11. R×g5 N×g5 12. Qe2+ Kd8 13. Nc3 Re8 14. Qd2** 14. Qg4 f6 15. h4 Ne6 16. d5 was perhaps more forceful. **14. ... Ne6 15. Nd5 b5 16. Bb3 Bb7 17. Re1 a5 18. a3 Ra6 19. c4 Bf8 20. c×b5 Rd6 21. Q×a5 R×d5 22. B×d5 B×d5 23. b6 c5 24. b7+ Ke7 25. Q×c5+ Kf6 26. Q×d5 d6 27. Qc6 1–0** [*Montreal Gazette*, April 1, 1893]

408. J.N. Babson & D.C. Robertson–Pollock [C34]
Blindfold Simultaneous (6 Boards), Montreal, 29 March 1893

1. e4 e5 2. f4 e×f4 3. Nf3 Nf6 4. e5 Nh5 5. d4 d5 6. Bd3 g5 7. 0–0 c5 8. c3 Nc6 9. b3 Be6 10. Bb2 g4 11. Nbd2? A dubious decision, but 11. Ne1 Qb6 12. Kh1 0–0–0 gave Black a strong attack. **11. ... g×f3 12. Q×f3 Qg5 13. Be2 Rg8 14. Rf2** (see diagram)

After
14. Rf1–f2

14. ... Bg4?! In a normal contest, Pollock would not have missed 14. ... Ng3!! 15. Bd3 (15. h×g3 f×g3 16. Rff1 Qh6 17. Qh5 Q×d2) 15. ... Bh6 16. Rd1 0–0–0 with an irresistible assault. **15. Q×d5 Rd8 16. Qe4** 16. Qc4 B×e2 17. R×e2 c×d4 18. c×d4 was more accurate. **16. ... c×d4 17. c×d4 Qg6 18. B×g4 Q×e4 19. N×e4 R×g4 20. h3 Rg6 21. Rd2 f6 22. e×f6 N×f6 23. Re1 N×e4 24. R×e4+ Be7 25. R×f4 Rgd6 26. Re4**

R×d4 Ingenious (especially for a blindfold contest) but ultimately ineffective. 26. ... Rd5 27. Rde2 R8d7 28. Rh4 h5 maintained winning chances. **27. B×d4 R×d4 28. Rd×d4 N×d4 29. Kf2 Nc6** Here White offered a draw, but Black refused. **30. Kf3 Kf7 31. Kg4 Kg6 32. Re6+ Bf6 33. Kf4 Nd4 34. Rd6 Nc6?** 34. ... Ne2+ 35. Ke3 Nc1 36. g4 h6 37. h4 b6 was keeping the balance. **35. g4 h6 36. h4 Kf7 37. Rd7+! Ke6 38. Rh7 Kd5 39. R×h6 Be5+ 40. Ke3 b5 41. g5 a5 42. Rh7 b4 43. g6 Nd4 44. Rd7+ Kc5 45. Ke4 Bf6 46. Rd5+ 1–0** [*Montreal Herald*, April 15, 1893; *New York Clipper*, May 20, 1893]

409. E.B. Cook–Pollock [C29]
Offhand Game, Montreal Chess Club, March 1893

1. e4 e5 2. Nc3 Nf6 3. f4 d5 4. f×e5 N×e4 5. Qf3 Nc6 6. N×e4 d×e4 7. Q×e4 Bc5 8. Nf3 0–0 8. ... Nd4 would have equalized easily. **9. c3! Be6 10. d4 Bb6 11. Be2** 11. Ng5! g6 12. N×e6 f×e6 13. Bh6 Rf5 14. 0–0–0! was the best possible continuation. **11. ... Bd5 12. Qe3 f6! 13. e×f6 Q×f6 14. 0–0 Rae8 15. Qf2?!** (see diagram) 15. Qd2 was most precise. The text move allows a tactical shot which Pollock missed.

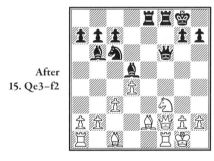

After
15. Qe3–f2

15. ... Qe6 15. ... N×d4!! gave Black a clear advantage: 16. c×d4 (16. N×d4? allows 16. ... Qg6 17. Qg3 R×e2 18. R×f8+ K×f8 19. Q×g6 h×g6 20. g4 Rg2+ 21. Kf1 R×h2) 16. ... B×f3 17. Bc4+ (17. Q×f3 Q×d4+ 18. Be3 R×f3 19. B×d4 B×d4+ 20. Kh1 R×f1+ 21. B×f1 B×b2 22. Rb1 Bd4) 17. ... Kh8 18. Q×f3 Q×d4+ 19. Be3 R×f3 20. B×d4 B×d4+ 21. Kh1 R×f1+ 22. R×f1 B×b2 23. g3 Bf6 and Black has two extra pawns. **16. Bd1 Bc4 17. Re1 N×d4** 17. ... Q×e1+!! was even stronger: 18. N×e1 (18. Q×e1 R×e1+ 19. N×e1 Rf1 mate.) 18. ... N×d4! 19. Be3 R×e3! 20. c×d4 B×d4 21. Be2 B×e2 22. Nc2 Ref3 (or 22. ... R×f2 23. K×f2 B×b2 24. K×e3 B×a1 25. K×e2 Bf6) 23. g×f3 B×f2+ 24. K×f2 B×f3 and Black wins the endgame.

18. R×e6 N×f3+ 19. g×f3 R×e6 20. Q×b6 Re1+? Pollock: "He should have taken the queen at once." 20. ... a×b6 21. Kf2 Bd5 would have conserved Black's winning position. **21. Kf2 Rf1+ 22. Kg2 a×b6 23. Bb3 B×b3** "This resource left bishops on opposite colors and Black shortly afterwards proposed a draw, which was of course accepted." **½–½** [*Baltimore Sunday News*, April 8, 1893]

410. Pollock–D.C. Robertson [C55]
Simultaneous Exhibition,
Montreal Chess Club, March 1893

1. e4 e5 2. Nf3 Nc6 3. Bc4 Nf6 4. Qe2 Be7 5. d4 d6 6. d5 Na5 7. Bd3 b6 8. 0–0 0–0 9. h3 Nb7 10. Be3 Ne8 11. g4 h5 12. Nh2 Bg5 13. Nc3 B×e3 *(see diagram)*

After
13. ... Bg5×e3

14. f×e3!? Qh4 15. Qg2 h×g4 16. h×g4 a6 17. Rf3 Nf6 18. Raf1 Nh7 19. Rh3 Qe7 20. Nf3 Ng5 21. Rh5 N×f3+ 22. R×f3 g6? The critical error. 22. ... f6 was the correct move, although White maintains the pressure with 23. g5 g6 24. Rh2 Nc5 25. Qf1. **23. Rh1 Qg5** 23. ... f6 24. Rfh3 Qg7 25. Qh2 B×g4 26. Rh7 is hopeless too. **24. Qh2 1–0** [*PM*, page 143]

411. J.N. Babson–Pollock
Simultaneous Exhibition,
Montreal Chess Club, March 1893

White to move

29. R×e7 K×e7 30. Kg2 30. Kf3 was stronger: 30. ... a5 31. B×e6 R×e6 32. R×e6+ K×e6 33. Ke4. **30. ... Kd6 31. R×e6+ R×e6 32. B×e6 K×e6 33. Kh3** and Black resigned at move 49. It is unclear if Pollock continued with 33. ... Bd8!, which seems to hold the game. **1–0** [*PM*, page 143]

IN ALBANY

412. Pollock–A. Rathbone [C56]
Simultaneous Exhibition (15 Boards),
Albany Chess Club, 7 April 1893

1. e4 e5 2. Bc4 Nf6 3. Nf3 Nc6 4. d4 d6 5. 0–0 e×d4 6. Ng5 Ne5 7. Q×d4 h6 8. f4? Too optimistic. 8. Nf3 was safest. **8. ... N×c4 9. Q×c4 h×g5 10. f×g5 d5! 11. e×d5 N×d5 12. Nc3 Be6 13. g6! Qd7?** A costly hesitation. 13. ... c6 was best: 14. g×f7+ B×f7 15. Re1+ Be7 16. N×d5 B×d5 17. Qf4 Rf8. **14. g×f7+ B×f7 15. Bg5! Nf6 16. Rae1+ Kd8** 16. ... Be7!? 17. Qb4 Be6 18. Q×b7 0–0 was a serious alternative. **17. Qe2 Bc5+ 18. Kh1 Re8 19. Ne4 Kc8 20. B×f6 g×f6 21. R×f6 Bd5** *(see diagram)*

After
21. ... Bf7–d5

22. N×c5 22. Nd6+!? was an interesting choice, but after 22. ... c×d6 23. Q×e8+ Kc7 24. Q×a8 Qg7 25. Rf3 B×f3 26. g×f3 Qf7 27. Kg2 Qg6+ Black has a clear draw in hand. **22. ... B×g2+ 23. Kg1 Qd4+ 24. Qf2 R×e1+ 25. K×g2 Q×f2+ 26. K×f2 Re8 27. Rf7** An immediate 27. h4 b6 28. Nd3 Rh8 29. Kg3 was promising too. **27. ... Rb8 28. h4** The endgame arising after 28. Ne6 R×e6 29. Rf8+ Kd7 30. R×b8 could have offered a winning try. **28. ... Kd8 29. h5 b6 30. Na6** 30. Nd7 offered a double-edged alternative: 30. ... Ra8 31. Nf6 Rh8 32. Kg3 Kc8 33. Kg4 Kb7 34. Kg5 Rad5 35. h6 Rd2. **30. ... Rc8 31. Nb4 Rh8 32. Nd5 c6 33. Nf4 Re8?** Leaving the h-pawn could have proved dangerous. 33. ... a5 was recommended instead. **34. R×a7** 34. h6! was winning: 34. ... Re7

35. h7 Kd7 36. R×e7+ K×e7 37. Ng6+ Kf6 38. h8Q+ R×h8 39. N×h8 Kg7 40. Kg3 c5 41. Kf4. **34. ... Re7 35. Ra6 Rb8 36. Kg3 Kc7 37. Kg4 Rg7+ 38. Ng6 Kb7 39. Ra4 Rd8 40. Rf4 Rd6 41. Kg5 Rh7 42. Re4 Ka6 43. h6 Rd2 44. Ne5 R×c2 45. Kg6 R×h6+ 46. K×h6 R×b2 47. N×c6 Kb5 48. Na7+ Kc5** ½–½ [*Albany Evening Journal*, April 15, 1893]

413. Pollock–H.J. Rogers [C52]
Simultaneous Exhibition (15 Boards), Albany Chess Club, 7 April 1893

1. e4 e5 2. Nf3 Nc6 3. Bc4 Bc5 4. b4 B×b4 5. c3 Ba5 6. 0–0 d6 7. d4 e×d4 8. c×d4 Bd7 9. Bb2 Nh6 10. d5 Ne5 11. N×e5 d×e5 12. f4? Qh4 12. ... Ng4! 13. g3 (13. B×e5 Qh4 14. h3 N×e5 15. f×e5 Q×e4) 13. ... Bb6+ 14. Kh1 Ne3 15. Qe2 Bh3 was even more forceful. **13. Be2 Bb6+ 14. Kh1 e×f4 15. B×g7 Rg8 16. B×h6?!** 16. Bd4 was necessary. **16. ... Q×h6 17. Nc3?** 17. Nd2 Qg5 18. Bf3 Rg6! 19. Rb1 Rh6 would have forced White to play 20. R×b6, and after 20. ... a×b6 enter a hopeless position. **17. ... Qg7 18. Bf3 Q×c3 19. Rc1 Qe5 20. Qb3 Rg6 21. a4 a5 22. Rc2 Rh6 23. Rd1 Qf6 24. h3** *(see diagram)*

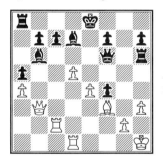

After
24. h2–h3

24. ... B×h3! 25. g×h3 R×h3+ 0–1 [*Albany Evening Journal*, April 15, 1893]

414. Pollock–N.N. [C56]
Blindfold Simultaneous Exhibition (5 Boards), Albany, 8 April 1893

1. e4 e5 2. Nf3 Nc6 3. Bc4 Bc5 4. 0–0 d6 5. c3 Nf6 6. d4 e×d4 7. c×d4 Bb6 8. Nc3 0–0 9. h3 h6 10. Be3 a6 Pollock: "10. ... N×e4 seems to be the proper continuation here." **11. Qd2 Qe7 12. Rae1 Bd7** 12. ... N×e4 13. N×e4 Q×e4 14. B×h6 Qg6 was an interesting alternative. **13. Bd3 Rae8 14. B×h6 N×d4** Pollock: "14. ... g×h6 would be very dangerous on account of 15. Q×h6 threaten-

ing Ng5 with Nd5 and e5." **15. N×d4 B×d4 16. Bg5 c6 17. Ne2 Qe5?** 17. ... Bc5 or 17. ... Bb6 were better choices. **18. Bf4** The immediate 18. N×d4 Q×d4 19. e5 was powerful as well. **18. ... Qc5 19. N×d4 Q×d4** *(see diagram)*

After
19. ... Qc5×d4

20. e5! d×e5 21. B×e5 Qh4 Pollock: "Of course, if 21. ... R×e5 22. Bh7+ wins the queen." **22. Bc3 Bc8 23. Bb1 Ne4?** 23. ... Rd8 or 23. ... Be6 had to be played. **24. B×e4** Pollock: "There seems to be more in 24. Qd4." **24. ... R×e4 25. R×e4 Q×e4 26. Re1 Qd5 27. Qe3 Qd6 28. Qg5 Qg6 29. Qh4 Qd6** Pollock: "A little aimless on both sides perhaps but while White was handicapped by having to conduct four other games sans voir, Black had, according to the rules, to make his move instantly when it came his turn to play." **30. Re3 Bf5 31. Rg3 Bg6 32. f4 Qd5?** Best was 32. ... Re8 33. f5 Qc5+ 34. Qd4 Q×d4+ 35. B×d4 B×f5 36. R×g7+ Kf8. **33. Rg5! Qe4 34. Qg3! Kh7 35. f5** 35. Rh5+ Kg8 36. f5 was another possibility. **35. ... B×f5 36. R×g7+** 1–0 [*Baltimore Sunday News*, April 15, 1893; *PM*, pages 101–102]

VARIOUS

415. Pollock–M. Schapiro & E.L. Torsch [C52]
Consultation Game, Baltimore, Columbia Social Club, 23 May 1893

1. e4 e5 2. Nf3 Nc6 3. Bc4 Bc5 4. b4 B×b4 5. c3 Ba5 6. d4 e×d4 7. 0–0 d6 8. c×d4 Bd7 Pollock: "A novel and interesting defense." **9. Ng5** Pollock: "Tempting, but premature. 9. Bb2, 9. a4 or 9. e5 suggest themselves here." **9. ... Nh6 10. f4 Bb6 11. Bb2 Qf6 12. e5 d×e5 13. N×f7** *(see diagram)* Pollock: "13. Re1 was perhaps better."

13. ... N×d4 Pollock: "This, with the next move, is exceedingly well played by Black." **14. f×e5?**

After
13. Ng5×f7

Pollock: "If 14. Kh1, 14. ... e×f4 15. N×h8 0–0–0, with great superiority." Pollock's suggestion was still far better than the text. **14. ... Ndf5+** The direct 14. ... Qh4! 15. Kh1 Ng4 would win on the spot. **15. Kh1 Qh4 16. Qd3 Ng4 17. Q×d7+** Pollock: "He has already nothing better." **17. ... K×d7 18. e6+ Kc8 19. Be5 N×e5 20. R×f5 N×c4** 20. ... Ng4 21. h3 Qg3 would force a quick mate. **21. Nc3 Re8 22. Rd1 Ne3 23. g3 Qh3 24. Rf2 N×d1 25. Rf4 R×e6** Pollock: "[White] Resigns—and well he might!" **0–1** [*Baltimore Sunday News*, June 3, 1893; *New York Clipper*, July 8, 1893]

416. Pollock–W.H. Gwyer Jr. [C38]
Simultaneous Exhibition (24 Boards), Washington, 31 May 1893

Pollock: "...an uncommonly beautiful, though not quite original game...." **1. e4 e5 2. f4 e×f4 3. Nf3 g5 4. Bc4 Bg7 5. d4 d6 6. h4 h6 7. h×g5 h×g5 8. R×h8 B×h8 9. Nc3 c6** (*see diagram*) Pollock: "9. ... Nc6 is better play."

After
9. ... c7–c6

10. Ne5 d×e5 11. Qh5 Qf6 12. d×e5 Qg7 13. e6 Nh6 13. ... B×e6! 14. B×e6 Nf6 was more accurate; Pollock: "Or 13. ... Nf6 14. e×f7+ and Black must be careful not to play 14. ... Kf8 on account of 15. B×f4 mating if either queen or bishop be taken." **14. e×f7+ Kf8?** 14. ... N×f7 15. B×f7+ Ke7 was correct. **15. B×f4! N×f7** The original score had 15. ... Nd7 16. 0–0–0 but it's very un-

likely a mate in one had been missed by both sides. **16. 0–0–0 Nd7 17. Rd6 g×f4 17. ... Nf6 18. Q×f7+ Q×f7 19. B×f7 Ke7!** would have given Black a winning position. **18. Rg6 Q×g6 19. Q×g6 Nde5 20. Qh5 Bg4** 20. ... N×c4 21. Qc5+ Ncd6 was an easy win. **21. Qh4 Bg7 22. Be2 f3 23. g×f3 B×f3 24. B×f3 N×f3** Pollock: "Hereabouts White preferred a draw, as it seemed impossible to find anything to win with. The draw was refused, to Black's subsequent regret, after a long fight." **1–0** [*Baltimore Sunday News*, June 24, 1893]

417. E. Hymes–Pollock [A85]
Albany Chess Club, July 1893

"Edward Hymes, the young player who distinguished himself by winning all his games in the Intercollegiate Chess Tournament, has just returned from Albany, where he met the Irish chess champion, W.H.K. Pollock. The game was a Dutch opening, in the course of which Pollock sacrificed two minor pieces for rook and pawn in a troublesome attack. [...]" **1. d4 f5 2. c4 e6 3. Nc3 Nf6 4. e3 b6 5. Be2 Bb7 6. Bf3 c6 7. a3 Na6 8. d5 c×d5 9. c×d5 e5 10. e4 f4 11. Be2 Bc5 12. Nf3 Qe7 13. 0–0 Rc8?!** 13. ... 0–0 or 13. ... Nc7 were more accurate alternatives. **14. Bd2** 14. Qa4! was difficult to deal with. **14. ... 0–0 15. Rc1 Nc7 16. Bd3 Ng4 17. Nb5 N×b5 18. B×b5** (*see diagram*)

After
18. Be2×b5

18. ... N×f2!? 18. ... Ne3!? was even more imaginative, especially for a player like Pollock. **19. R×f2 B×f2+ 20. K×f2 R×c1 21. Q×c1 Rc8 22. Bb4 d6 23. Qd2 g5 24. Bc6 Ba6 25. h3 h5 26. Nh2 g4! 27. h×g4 h×g4 28. g3** Of course, 28. N×g4 is not possible: 28. ... Qh4+ 29. Kf3 Qg3 mate. **28. ... Rf8 29. Qd1 Bc8! 30. Bb5?** 30. N×g4? runs into 30. ... Qg5; 30. Qd3 was White's best chance: 30. ... Qh7 31. Kg1 f3 32. Be1 f2+ 33. B×f2 R×f2 34. K×f2 Q×h2+ 35. Kf1 Q×b2 36. Bb5. **30. ... Qg5** 30. ... Qh7! was strong:

31. N×g4 (31. Kg1 f×g3 32. N×g4 Qh4) 31. ... Qh3 and Black wins. **31. Qe1 Qh5 32. Kg1 Qh3 33. Bf1 Q×g3+ 34. Q×g3 f×g3 35. N×g4 B×g4 36. B×d6 Rd8** 36. ... Rf2 37. B×e5 Bf3 38. d6 B×e4 39. B×g3 R×b2 offered some winning chances. **37. B×e5 Re8 38. B×g3 R×e4 39. Bb8 ½–½** [*New York Evening Post*, August 2, 1893]

NYSCA CONGRESS (STATEN ISLAND, AUGUST 1893)

418. Pollock–J. Halpern [C00]
NYSCA Congress, Staten Island, August 1893

1. e4 e6 (*see diagram*)

After
1. ... e7–e6

2. Qe2!? A seemingly new idea by Pollock which was later used extensively by Chigorin in important matches and tournaments. In annotating the second game of the Chigorin vs. Tarrasch 1893 match, in his November 19, 1893, *Baltimore Sunday News* column, Pollock wrote about 2. Qe2: "Introduced by the Editor. See News August 19. The object is to stop ...d5. Mason calls it 'but a harmless violation of principle, yielding a strange game, a confusion of the Sicilian, Fianchetto and French.'" While annotating the same game for the October 25, 1893, *New York Sun*, Chigorin said nothing about 2. Qe2. However, the newspaper columnist remarked: "Chigorin introduced a novel move in the French game, namely 2. Qe2, and as a matter of course the game becomes doubly interesting, inasmuch as it might completely alter the theory of this defence. Chigorin in his notes, taken especially for the *Sun*, does not make any remarks regarding the move." The October 27, 1893, edition of the *Sun* published the following from Pollock: "To the editor of the *Sun*: Sir: The move of 2. Qe2 in the French defence, which in your admirable report of today is described as novel and

introduced by Chigorin, was played by myself against J. Halpern in the recent Staten Island cup tournament. Yours respectfully, W.H.K. Pollock." **2. ... d5 3. e×d5 Q×d5 4. Nc3 Qd8 5. Nf3 Nf6 6. d4 Nc6 7. Qc4 Bb4 8. Bd2 B×c3 9. b×c3 Bd7 10. Bd3 Qe7 11. 0–0 Nd5 12. Qb3 Nb6 13. a4 Na5 14. Qa2 0–0 15. c4 Nc6 16. a5 Nc8 17. Rab1 b6 18. Rfe1 b×a5 19. Rb5 Nb4 20. R×b4 a×b4 21. Qa5** "The game was scored by White by default, Mr. Halpern being unable to attend the following morning." **1–0** [*Baltimore Sunday News*, August 19, 1893; *PM*, pages 102–103]

419. Pollock–E.N. Olly [B01]
NYSCA Congress, Staten Island, August 1893

1. e4 d5 2. e×d5 Q×d5 3. Nc3 Qd8 4. Nf3 Nc6 5. Bb5 Bd7 6. 0–0 e6 7. d4 Bd6 8. Re1 Nge7 9. d5!? e×d5 10. N×d5 0–0 11. Bg5 f6 (*see diagram*)

After
11. ... f7–f6

12. Bc4! Kh8 12. ... f×g5 was not as lethal as it seems: 13. N×c7+ (13. N×e7+ Kh8 14. N×c6 [14. N×g5?! N×e7 15. Qh5 Bf5] 14. ... B×c6 15. Ne5 Qf6!) 13. ... Kh8 14. Q×d6 Nf5 15. Q×f8+ Q×f8 16. N×a8 Q×a8 17. Rad1 Qc8 18. N×g5 g6 with a complicated position. **13. Bd2 Ng6 14. Bc3 Bg4 15. Qd2?** An unnecessary concession that leads to a complete loss of initiative. 15. Ne3 kept White's chances intact. **15. ... B×f3 16. g×f3 Nce5 17. Be2 c6 18. Ne3 Nh4 19. Qd1 Qc7 20. Ng2 Neg6 21. Bd2 B×h2+ 22. Kh1 N×g2 23. K×g2 Rad8 24. Rh1 Nf4+ 25. B×f4 R×d1?** 25. ... B×f4 was more accurate. **26. B×c7 R×h1 27. R×h1 B×c7 28. Bd3 h6 29. Re1 Be5 30. Kh3 b6 31. Kg4 B×b2 32. Kf5 Ba3 33. Re6 Bc5 34. R×c6 Kh7 35. Rc7** 35. Kg4+ Kg8 36. Rc7 a5 37. Kf5 maintained the balance. **35. ... h5! 36. R×a7 Re8 37. a4?** 37. Kf4+ Kh6 38. Kg3 was necessary. **37. ... B×f2** 37. ... Kh6! would have created a mating net around the White king: 38. a5 (38. f4 Bd4!) 38. ...

Re5+ 39. Kf4 B×f2. **38. Kf4+?** Walking right into the subtle mating net. 38. f4! was mandatory. **38. … Kh6! 39. a5 Re5 40. Bg6 b×a5 41. Ra8 K×g6 42. c4 Kf7 0–1** [*Brooklyn Standard-Union*, August 11, 1893]

420. E.N. Olly–Pollock [A80]
NYSCA Congress, Staten Island,
August 1893

1. d4 f5 2. Nc3 Nf6 3. Nf3 e6 4. Bg5 Bb4 5. Qd3 0–0 6. Nd2 c5 7. a3 B×c3 8. Q×c3 c×d4 9. Q×d4 Nc6 10. Qd6 b5!? 11. e4! f×e4 12. B×f6?! 12. B×b5 Bb7 13. 0–0 was more logical. **12. … Q×f6 13. 0–0–0 Q×f2 14. N×e4 Qe3+ 15. Nd2 Bb7 16. B×b5 Nd4 17. B×d7 Rab8** 17. … Bd5 was an interesting alternative: 18. Rhe1 Ne2+ 19. Kb1 Rab8 20. Nb3 Rb6 21. Qg3 Qe4. **18. Rhe1** 18. Rde1 was more accurate since 18. … Ne2+ could have been met by 19. Kd1. **18. … Ne2+ 19. Kb1 Bd5 20. Nf1 Qe4!?** 20. … R×b2+ 21. K×b2 Qc3+ 22. Kb1 Ba2+ 23. K×a2 Q×c2+ offered only a perpetual. **21. Qc5 Qe5 22. B×e6+ Q×e6** (see diagram) 22. … Kh8 is not good because of 23. Q×f8+! R×f8 24. B×d5 Rd8 25. Bc4 R×d1+ 26. R×d1 g6 27. Rd8+ Kg7 28. Rd7+ Kh8 29. Rd2 and White has no problems.

After
22. … Qe5×e6

23. Ne3? White has lost his way in the complications. Best was 23. R×d5 Nc3+ 24. Q×c3 Q×d5 25. Ne3. **23. … Rfc8! 24. Q×c8+ R×c8 25. R×e2 B×g2 26. Rde1 Bf3 27. Rf2 Rf8 28. Ng2 Qg6 29. Nh4 Qh5 30. N×f3 R×f3 31. Rfe2 Rf1 0–1** [*Brooklyn Standard-Union*, August 19, 1893]

421. Pollock–J.M. Hanham [A03]
NYSCA Congress, Staten Island,
August 1893

1. f4 d5 2. e3 e6 3. Nf3 Nf6 4. c4 Bd6 5. Nc3 a6 6. b3 Nbd7 7. Bb2 b6 8. Be2 c6 9. 0–0 0–0 10. Rc1 Re8 11. Nd4 c5 12. Nf3 Bb7 13. c×d5

e×d5 **14. Qc2 Nf8 15. Bd3 b5 16. Ne2 Ne4 17. Ng3 N×g3 18. h×g3 c4 19. Bf5 f6** (see diagram)

After
19. … f7–f6

20. g4 g6 21. g5 g×f5 22. g×f6 Bc8 23. Ng5 Ra7 24. f7+? Impatient play. Instead, 24. Qd1 Be6 25. Qh5 Bf7 26. Qh6 Bg6 27. g4 was very promising. **24. … R×f7! 25. Qc3?** Pollock had to settle for the lesser of two evils: 25. N×f7 K×f7 26. Rf3 Ng6 27. Rh3 Kg8 28. Qc3 Bf8 29. Rg3. **25. … Be5!** This leaves White in a hopeless position. 25. … Ng6 was possible too, but the text move is much stronger: 26. N×f7 K×f7 27. Qg7+ Ke6 28. Q×h7 Rg8. **26. f×e5 Q×g5 27. b×c4 Rg7 28. Rf2 d×c4 29. d4 c×d3 30. Q×d3 Be6 31. Rc6 Rd8 32. Bd4 Bd5 33. Rcc2 Ne6 34. R×f5 Qg6 35. e4 Bc4 36. Qc3 R×d4 37. Qf3 Qg4 0–1** [*Albany Evening Journal*, August 12, 1893; *New York Clipper*, September 2, 1893]

422. Pollock–A.B. Hodges [C44]
NYSCA Congress, Staten Island,
11 August 1893

1. e4 e5 2. Nf3 Nc6 3. c3 d5 4. Qa4 f6 5. Bb5 Nge7 6. e×d5 Q×d5 7. 0–0 Be6 8. d4 e4 9. Nfd2 f5 10. Nb3 Bd7?! 11. c4 11. Nc5 b6 12. N×d7 Q×d7 13. Bg5 was a powerful continuation. **11. … Qd6 12. Nc5 Q×d4** (see diagram)

After
12. … Qd6×d4

13. Be3!? Q×b2 14. Nb3? White had to go for the complications arising from 14. Nc3 Q×c3

15. Rad1 f4 16. B×f4 Bg4 17. N×b7. **14. ... Rd8!**
15. B×a7? This makes things even worse. 15. Na3
was uncomfortable as well because of 15. ... a6
16. Nc5 a×b5 17. N×b5 Kf7! **15. ... b6 16. c5 Ra8**
17. c×b6 17. Qc4! R×a7 18. Nc3 g6 19. Rab1 Qa3
20. Rfd1 offered White real compensation. **17. ...**
c×b6 18. Qc4 R×a7 19. Nc3 Qa3 20. Rac1 Qb4
21. Qe2 g6 22. Rfd1 Bg7 23. Nd5 N×d5 24. R×d5
Rc7 25. Qd1 Qe7 26. Rd6 Be5 27. Rd×c6 B×c6
28. B×c6+ Kf7 29. Nd4 Qd6 30. Qb3+ Kf6
31. Nb5 R×c6! 32. Rd1 Qe6 33. Qh3 Kg7 34. Qa3
Re8 0–1 [*Albany Evening Journal*, August 26, 1893;
Brooklyn Standard-Union, September 2, 1893]

423. A.B. Hodges–Pollock [C70]
NYSCA Congress, Staten Island,
11 August 1893

1. e4 e5 2. Nf3 Nc6 3. Bb5 a6 4. Ba4 b5 5. Bb3
Bb7 6. c3 Nf6 7. Qe2 Bc5 8. d3 0–0 9. Be3 B×e3
10. f×e3 a5 11. 0–0 a4 12. Bc2 d5! 13. e×d5
N×d5 14. d4 (*see diagram*)

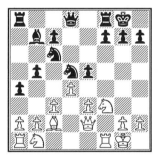

After
14. d3–d4

14. ... a3?! A puzzling pawn sacrifice, but not
without some logic. 14. ... Re8 was appropriate as
was 14. ... e×d4!? 15. e×d4 b4 16. c4 Re8 17. Qd3
Nf6 18. d5 Ne5. **15. N×a3 e×d4 16. e×d4** 16. Qx×b5
was possible as well: 16. ... Ba6 17. Q×c6 B×f1
18. R×f1 N×e3 19. c×d4 N×f1 20. K×f1. **16. ...**
b4 16. ... N×c3!? 17. b×c3 R×a3 was not a bad alternative. **17. c×b4 Nc×b4 18. Qd2 Ra6!?** It's possible that Pollock had concluded that 18. ... R×a3
was insufficient for an advantage: 19. b×a3 N×c2
20. Q×c2 Ne3 21. Qb2 N×f1 22. Q×b7. **19. Ne5**
Qh4 20. Nd7 Rd8 21. Nc5 N×c2 22. N×c2 Rh6?
Naturally, this was tempting and seemingly compelling but, in truth, it's a waste of time now. 22. ...
Rb6 23. N×b7 R×b7 24. b3 Rb6 25. Rae1 Rg6 was
correct. **23. g3 Nf4** A flawed combination that un-
derlines Pollock's poor form. **24. R×f4** Of course,
24. g×h4 runs into 24. ... Nh3 mate. **24. ... Q×g3+**
25. h×g3 Rh1+ 26. Kf2 Rh2+ 27. Ke3 Re8+
28. Kd3 1–0 [*New York Recorder*, August 18, 1893;

Baltimore Sunday News, August 26, 1893; *Brooklyn
Standard-Union*, September 2, 1893]

424. Pollock–J.M. Hanham [B23]
NYSCA Congress, Staten Island,
Handicap Tournament, 8 August 1893

1. e4 e6 2. Nc3 c5 3. Nf3 Nc6 4. Bd3 a6 5. 0–0
Qc7 6. b3 Be7 7. Bb2 d6 8. Qe2 b5 9. Rae1 Nf6
10. Kh1 Bb7 11. a4 b×a4 12. N×a4 e5 13. Nh4 g6
14. Bc4 0–0 15. f3 Na5 16. Bd3 Nh5 17. Qf2 Nf4
18. Be2 c4 19. b4 Nc6 20. Bc3 Nd8 (*see diagram*)

After
20. ... Nc6–d8

Pollock: "This complicated position is a good
example of the play of knights to B5, the strong
post, against a castled king. It appears here as if
White could neither dislodge the Black knight nor
extricate his own from a rather awkward position.
Appearances, however, prove deceptive." **21. Nf5!**
Bf6 Pollock: "If 21. ... g×f5 22. Qg3+ Kh8 (or 22. ...
Ng6 23. e×f5, with a good game.) 23. Q×f4 safely."
22. Nh6+ Kg7 23. Ng4 Be7 Pollock: "23. ... N×e2
should have been played here." **24. Nb6 Rb8**
25. N×c4 N×e2 26. Q×e2 f6 After 26. ... h5
27. Nge3 Ne6, 28. f4! was still very potent. **27. f4**
Rc8 28. f×e5 Q×c4 29. e×f6+ B×f6 30. Qf2 Qe6
31. N×f6 Rf7 32. Qh4 h6 33. Ng4+ R×c3
34. d×c3 g5 35. R×f7+ N×f7 36. Qg3 B×e4
37. Kg1 d5 38. Ne3 Qb6 39. Qf2 Qc6 40. Rf1
Bg6 41. Qf3 Q×c3 42. Nf5+ 1–0 [*Brooklyn Standard-Union*, August 12, 1893; *Montreal Gazette*,
August 26, 1893; *New York Clipper*, September 2,
1893; *Baltimore Sunday News*, September 23, 1893]

425. J.M. Hanham–Pollock [A00]
NYSCA Congress, Staten Island,
Handicap Tournament, August 1893

1. a3 e5 2. e3 d5 3. d4 Nc6 4. Nf3 e4 5. Nfd2
f5 6. c4 d×c4 7. N×c4 Nf6 8. Nc3 Be6 9. Be2 Be7
10. Qc2 0–0 11. 0–0 Qe8 12. b4 Qg6 13. b5 Nd8
14. Ne5 Qh6 15. f4 Nf7 16. N×f7 B×f7 17. Nd1
Bd6 18. a4 Kh8 19. Nf2 Rac8 19. ... g5!? 20. Nh3

Rg8 21. f×g5 R×g5 22. Nf4 Rag8 23. Rf2 Qh4 was a commanding continuation. **20. Nh3?!** *(see diagram)* 20. Ba3 was a better try.

After
20. Nf2–h3

20. ... c5! 21. Ng5 Bg8 22. d×c5? B×c5 23. Qd2 Nd5 24. Ra3 Rfd8! 25. Qb2 N×f4 26. R×f4 B×a3 26. ... Q×g5 27. Rc3 Q×f4 28. R×c5 Qg5 was another possibility. **27. Q×a3 Q×g5 28. Bb2 Rc2 29. Rf2 R×e2 30. R×e2 Rd1+ 0–1** [*Brooklyn Standard-Union*, August 9, 1893]

426. H. Helms–Pollock
NYSCA Congress, Staten Island,
Handicap Tournament, August 1893

White to move

"Mr. Pollock, who displayed poor form in the silver business, came within half a game of tying for first prize in the handicap. He had, however, one remarkable slice of luck in his second game with Mr. Helms, who received pawn and two moves. White, who had achieved this position by a very fine sacrifice of the exchange had only to play Q×h6 to win. He played, however, **1. a5** whereupon the Black obtained a drawing position by **1. ... Qe4.** The game proceeded now with **2. Qd8+ Kh7 3. Qd7+ Kh8 4. Qg4 R×g2+!** This draws, after 5. Q×g2 Q×f4+, but Black [*sic*: White] perpetrated the astonishing crime of capturing the rook with the king and had to pay the sorrowful penalty of moving that piece into the corner [where] he was instantly slain." **0–1** [*Baltimore Sunday News*, August 19, 1893]

427. W. Frère–Pollock [C60]
NYSCA Congress, Staten Island,
Handicap Tournament,
12 August 1893

1. e4 e5 2. Nf3 Nc6 3. Bb5 Na5?! Another eccentricity occasionally tried by Pollock (**see Game 394**). **4. d4 a6 5. Bd3 e×d4 6. N×d4 g6 7. Bd2 c5 8. Nf3 Bg7 9. Bc3 Nf6 10. 0–0 b5** 10. ... d6 or 10. ... Nc6 were better ideas. **11. e5 Nh5 12. B×a5 Q×a5 13. Qd2 Q×d2 14. Nb×d2 0–0 15. c4 Rb8 16. c×b5 a×b5 17. Ne4 c4 18. Bc2 f6 19. e×f6 N×f6 20. Nd6 Ba6 21. Rab1 Ne8 22. Rfd1 Nc7 23. b3 c3 24. b4 Ne6** *(see diagram)*

After
24. ... Nc7–e6

25. Rb3 R×f3!! 26. g×f3 Nd4 27. R×d4 B×d4 28. Kf1 Rb6 29. Ne4 Rc6 30. Ke2 d5 31. Kd3 Rc4 32. N×c3 Bc8 33. Kd2 B×f2 34. N×d5 Bh3 35. Bd3 Rd4 36. Nc7 Bd7 37. Kc3 Rh4 38. B×b5 Bf5 39. Kd2 R×h2 40. Be2 h5 41. b5 h4 42. b6 B×b6?! 42. ... Bg3! 43. Nd5 Be6 44. Rb5 h3 45. b7 Bb8 46. Ne3 Kf7 was a more sensible continuation. **43. R×b6 h3 44. Rb8+** 44. Nd5! maintained serious winning chances for White after 44. ... Rg2 45. Ne7+ Kh7 (45. ... Kf7? 46. N×f5 h2 47. Rb7+ Kf6 48. Ng3 R×g3 49. Rh7 Rg2 50. a4 and Black's h-pawn is worthless.) 46. N×f5 h2 47. Rb7+ Kh8 48. Rb4 h1Q 49. Rh4+ Q×h4 50. N×h4. **44. ... Kh7 45. Ne6 B×e6 46. Rb1 Bc4 0–1** [*Brooklyn Standard-Union*, August 14, 1893; *PM*, pages 103–104]

Café Bondy Handicap (August 1893)

428. S.G. Ruth–Pollock
Handicap Tournament, Café Bondy,
August 1893
Remove f7 pawn

Pollock: "After the terribly dull chess weather which seems to have prevailed everywhere of late, the chess editor found the activity of the game in New York both a delight and a surprise. More chess seemed to be going on in the various cafes and resorts than ever before. The Café Bondy, formerly Longeling's, 49 Bowery, is crowded from morning to midnight. There are about thirty entrants for the handicap tourney, Captain Pinkham and J. Halpern playing in class A. The proprietors and chess managers are doing their utmost to make the Café Bondy the Divan of the New World." **1. e4 and d4 d6 2. Bc4 e6 3. Nc3 c6 4. Qh5+ g6 5. Qf3 Bg7 6. Nge2 d5 7. e×d5 e×d5 8. Bb3 Nf6 9. Bg5 0–0 10. Qd3** Pollock: "Although there is no real harm done yet, White has played the opening with great illiteracy." **10. ... Bf5 11. Qd2 Nbd7 12. h3 Qe8 13. 0–0–0 b5 14. f3 a5 15. a3 b4 16. Nb1 a4 17. Ba2 b×a3** Pollock: "He had much better have sacrificed the bishop here than immolated it in so senseless a manner a few moves later: 17. ... B×c2 18. Q×c2 b3 19. B×b3 a×b3 20. Qd2 Nb6." **18. N×a3 Rf7 19. Rde1 Qb8 20. g4 Be4** Pollock: "Of course, if 20. ... Be6, 21. Nf4 wins a piece." **21. B×f6?!** 21. Ng1! or 21. Bf4 were more reliable choices. **21. ... N×f6 22. f×e4 N×e4 23. Qe3** (*see diagram*)

After
23. Qd2–e3

23. ... Qf8 Pollock: "A very potent resource." **24. h4** Pollock: "To prevent ...Bh6." White missed the exceptional 24. Q×e4!! d×e4 25. Ref1 Raa7 26. R×f7 R×f7 27. Rf1 Kh8 28. R×f7 Qd8 29. c3, with a clear advantage. **24. ... Kh8** Pollock: "Not ...Rf3 at once, as the queen could take the knight in reply." **25. Ng1 Rb8 26. Rh3** Pollock: "26. c3 was absolutely necessary." **26. ... Qb4 27. Bb3 B×d4 28. Qe2 Rf2** Pollock: "Mr. Devide pointed out an immediate and very beautiful win by 28. ... a×b3 whereupon if 29. R×b3 (or if 29. c3, 29. ... N×c3) 29. ... B×b2+." **29. Qd1 Rd2 30. Qf3 a×b3 31. R×e4 d×e4 32. Q×b3 B×b2+ 33. K×b2 Qd4+ 34. Ka2 R×b3 35. R×b3 Q×g1 36. h5 g×h5 37. g×h5 e3 38. h6 e2 39. Rb8+ Qg8+ 0–1** [*Baltimore Sunday News*, September 16, 1893; *Brooklyn Standard-Union*, September 2, 1893]

429. Pollock–M. Lissner [C55]
Handicap Tournament, Café Bondy, August 1893

1. e4 e5 2. Nf3 Nc6 3. Bc4 Nf6 (*see diagram*)

After
3. ... Ng8–f6

4. Qe2 Pollock: "Puzzling the problemist." **4. ... Bc5 5. Ng5 0–0** Pollock: "5. ... Nd4 might be played, for if 6. B×f7+ Kf8 7. Qc4 Qe7 and White may lose a piece by ...h6." **6. N×f7 Qe7** Pollock: "Fearful of losing the exchange." **7. N×e5+ d5 8. e×d5 B×f2+** Pollock: "This beautiful resource saves a hopeless looking game." **9. Kd1 N×e5 10. d6+ N×c4 11. d×e7 Bg4 12. e×f8Q+ R×f8 13. Q×g4 N×g4 14. h3 Nf6 15. Rf1** Pollock: "A flaw. By replying ...Nh5 Black would recover the exchange and actually have the better game. He played, however, 15. ... Bb6 and White eventually won." 15. d3! was keeping a solid advantage. **15. ... Bb6 16. b3 Nd6 17. Bb2 Nh5 18. R×f8+ K×f8 19. Be5 Nf7 20. Bh2 Bd4 21. c3 Be5 22. B×e5 N×e5 23. d4 Nc6 24. Ke2 Nf4+ 1–0** [*Baltimore Sunday News*, August 26, 1893; *New York Clipper*, October 7, 1893; *PM*, pages 106–107]

430. Pollock–Bondy [C30]
Handicap Tournament, Café Bondy, August 1893

1. e4 e5 2. f4 Bc5 3. Nc3 d6 4. Nf3 Nc6 5. Bc4 Nge7 (*see diagram*)

After
5. ... Ng8–e7

6. Ng5! Be6? 6. ... Rf8 7. N×h7 e×f4 8. N×f8 K×f8 9. Rf1 Ng6 was a valid option. **7. B×e6 f×e6 8. N×e6 Qd7 9. N×g7+ Kd8 10. f5 Kc8 11. d3 Nd8 12. g4 Ng8 13. Nh5 Qe7 14. h4 h6 15. g5 h×g5 16. h×g5 c6 17. Qg4 Kc7 18. Ne2 Nf7** Pollock: "Black defends himself well and is looking out for a chance to exchange a minor piece for some of the advanced pawns." **19. Neg3 Qd7 20. g6 Nfh6 21. Qh4 Qd8 22. Bg5 Qe8 23. Ng7 Qd7 24. Ne6+ Kb6 25. Nh5 d5 26. Bf6 Be7 27. Qf2+ d4 28. B×e5 Ng4 29. Q×d4+ Q×d4 30. B×d4+ c5 31. B×h8 1–0** [*Baltimore Sunday News*, August 26, 1893]

431. Pollock–S.H. Pretzfelder
Handicap Tournament, Café Bondy, August 1893
Remove Ra1

1. e4 e5 2. f4 d5 3. e×d5 Q×d5 4. Nc3 Qe6 5. Nf3 e×f4+ 6. Kf2 Bc5+ 7. d4 Bd6 8. Bb5+ Pollock: "Very familiar old trap." **8. ... c6 9. Re1 Q×e1+ 10. Q×e1+ Ne7 11. Ne4 Bc7 12. d5 N×d5** Pollock: "Attack and defense as spiritedly maintained. Black does not seem to know how to fear either double check." **13. Nd6+ Kd7 14. N×f7 Re8 15. N3e5+ B×e5 16. N×e5+ Kc7 17. c4 Ne3 18. B×e3 f×e3+ 19. Q×e3** (*see diagram*)

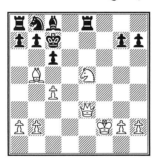

After
19. Qe1×e3

19. ... c×b5? 19. ... Nd7 was keeping a big advantage. **20. c×b5 Nd7 21. Qc3+ Kd6 22. Nf7+**

Pollock: "Overlooking that if 23. Q×g7, 23. ... Rf8 would pin the knight. After 23. Ng5 Nf6, White drew by perpetual check, with 24. Qc5+ Kd7 25. Qd4+ Kc7 26. Qc5+ etc." **22. ... Ke7 ½–½** [*Baltimore Sunday News*, September 30, 1893]

432. Loeb–Pollock
Handicap Tournament, Café Bondy, August 1893
Remove f7 pawn

1. e4 Nc6 2. d4 e5 3. d×e5 N×e5 4. Qh5+ Ng6 5. Bc4 Nf6 6. Qe2 Ne5 7. Bb3 Bc5 8. f4 Pollock: "White misjudges the position in undertaking an immediate attack." **8. ... Nc6** Pollock: "Best." **9. e5** Pollock: "9. Qc4, threatening mate, the bishop, and e5, all of which things Black's forced reply obviates." **9. ... Nd4 10. Qc4 Qe7 11. Ne2** (*see diagram*)

After
11. Ng1–e2

11. ... d5 12. Qd3 N×e2 Pollock: "If 12. ... Bf5, 13. Qd1 N×e2 14. e×f6 and Black loses a piece." **13. Q×e2** Pollock: "Here if 13. e×f6 N×c1 14. f×e7 N×d3+ 15. c×d3 c6 with an excellent game." **13. ... Bg4 14. Qd3 Ne4 15. B×d5** Pollock: "Losing offhand. White calculates seemingly on either ...Nf2 or ...0–0–0 as replies, neither of which would avail much." **15. ... Qh4+ 16. g3** and Black mates in two moves. **0–1** [*Baltimore Sunday News*, September 2, 1893; *PM*, pages 113–114]

Part Two, Section X
(October 1893)

433. Pollock–J.W. Showalter [C26]
New York, Impromptu Tournament,
Round 1, 4 October 1893

Pollock (*Baltimore Sunday News*, October 7, 1893): "Although it was not generally expected that the 'Impromptu International Tournament' would be set in motion before October 2 at the Manhattan Chess Club, the committee, in order to save time, adhered to their originally proposed date, and the first round was commenced last Saturday at 2:00 pm. Pollock and Showalter, who had not arrived, were permitted by the committee to begin on Monday, their game of the first round to be played on the 4th inst., that being an off-day set apart for finishing adjourned games." **1. e4 e5 2. d3** Pollock: "A strong waiting move, rarely adopted." **2. ... Nf6 3. f4** Pollock: "White has the Greco Gambit, with the important move of d3 superseded." **3. ... d6** Pollock: "If 3. ... Bc5, 4. f×e5 N×e4 5. d×e4 Qh4+ 6. Kd2 at least drawing." **4. Nf3 Nc6 5. Be2 Be7 6. c3 0–0 7. f5** Pollock: "Apparently a feasible continuation." **7. ... d5 8. Qc2 a5** Pollock: "Intending to play ...Bc5." **9. Bg5 d×e4 10. d×e4 Ng4 11. h3 B×g5 12. h×g4 Bf4 13. Rh3** Pollock: "Stronger is 13. Kf2 Qe7 14. g3 Qc5+ 15. Kg2." **13. ... Qe7 14. Na3 Rd8 15. Bd3 Qc5 16. Qe2 b6** Pollock: "Threatening ...R×d3 followed by Ba6 with a lively attack." **17. Rd1 f6** Pollock: "White threatened to win a piece by g3." **18. Bc4+ Kh8 19. R×d8+ N×d8** (*see diagram*)

20. g5! B×g5? 20. ... f×g5 was forced: 21. g3 g4 22. R×h7+! K×h7 23. g×f4 g6 24. Qh2+ Kg7 25. f6+ K×f6 26. Qh8+ with a strong attack for

White. **21. R×h7+?** Pollock: "Overlooking that the knight cannot check on f7. 21. N×g5 wins..." 21. N×g5 h6 (21. ... f×g5 22. R×h7+) 22. Rd3 was indeed an easy win. **21. ... K×h7 22. N×g5+ Kh6 23. Nf3** 23. Qf3 Qg1+ 24. Kd2 Qh2 25. Nh3 Bd7 26. Nc2 was more accurate. **23. ... g5! 24. f×g6 Bg4 25. Qd2+ Kg7** Pollock: "Much inferior to 25. ... K×g6." **26. Nh4 Nb7 27. Qf2** Pollock: "The only move." **27. ... Rd8 28. Bd5 c6 29. Q×c5 N×c5 30. B×c6 Rd1+ 31. Kf2 Nd3+ 32. Kg3 Be6 33. Nb5 N×b2 34. Nc7 Rd3+** Pollock: "A useless check." **35. Kh2 B×a2** (*see diagram*)

36. Bd5! Pollock: "After this White ought, with proper play, to win, we believe." Objectively, this edgy position is roughly equal. **36. ... B×d5**

37. e×d5 Kh6 38. Ne8 R×d5 39. g7 Kh7
40. N×f6+ K×g7 41. N×d5 Nd1 42. N×b6
42. Nf5+ Kf7 43. Nfe3 was a much better try.
**42. ... N×c3 43. Nf5+ Kf6 44. Ne3 e4 45. g4
Kg5 46. Kh3 a4 47. Nbc4 Ne2 48. Nc2 Nf4+**
½–½ [*New York Sun*, October 5, 1893; *New York
Times*, October 5, 1893; *Baltimore Sunday News*,
October 14, 1893]

434. A. Albin–Pollock [C77]
New York, Impromptu Tournament,
Round 2, 2 October 1893

1. e4 e5 2. Nf3 Nc6 3. Bb5 a6 4. Ba4 Nf6
5. Qe2 b5 6. Bb3 Bc5 7. c3 0–0 8. d3 d5 9. Bg5
d×e4 10. d×e4 Qd6 11. Nbd2 h6 12. Bh4 Ne7
13. Rd1 Ng6 14. Nf1 14. Nc4 could have tempted
Pollock to play 14. ... b×c4 (14. ... N×h4!? was interesting as well: 15. N×d6 N×g2+ 16. Kf1 Nf4
17. N×f7!? Bh3+ 18. Ke1 N×e2 19. N7g5+ Kh8
20. N×h3 Nf4 21. N×f4 e×f4 22. e5 Rae8)
15. R×d6 c×d6 16. B×c4 Nf4. **14. ... Qe7 15. Bg3
Nh5! 16. Ne3 c6 17. 0–0 Nhf4 18. Qc2 Qf6
19. Nf5 B×f5?** 19. ... a5 or 19. ... Re8 20. a4 Ra7
were superior options. **20. e×f5 Ne7** (*see diagram*)

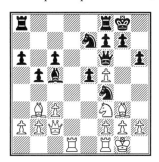

After
20. ... Ng6–e7

21. Bh4 21. Rfe1! N×f5 22. N×e5 would have
given White a winning advantage. **21. ... Q×f5!
22. B×e7 Qg4 23. g3 Nh3+ 24. Kg2 Nf4+
25. Kg1 Nh3+ 26. Kg2 Nf4+ 27. Kg1 Q×f3!?
28. g×f4 Qg4+ 29. Kh1 Qf3+ 30. Kg1 Qg4+
31. Kh1 Qf3+ 32. Kg1 B×e7 33. Rd3?** A critical
mistake caused by missing Black's tactics on f2.
Best was 33. f×e5! Rad8 34. Rfe1 Qg4+ 35. Kf1
R×d1 36. Q×d1 Qh3+ 37. Kg1 (37. Ke2? c5! is
too risky.) 37. ... Bc5 38. Qe2, with equal chances.
**33. ... Q×f4 34. Rg3 e4 35. Re1 Bc5! 36. R×e4
B×f2+ 37. Kg2 B×g3 38. R×f4 B×f4 39. Qf5
Bg5 40. Qg4 Rad8 41. h4 Rd2+ 42. Kf1 Be3** 0–1
[3:00–3:08] [*New York Sun*, October 3, 1893; *New
York Recorder*, October 6, 1893; *Albany Evening
Journal*, October 14, 1893]

435. Pollock–G.H.D. Gossip [C51]
New York, Impromptu Tournament,
Round 3, 3 October 1893

Edward N. Olly: "Among the impromptu curiosities of the impromptu congress, the following
game should be entitled to take the cake. Mr. P. says
he was afraid of Mr. G. What kind of feeling was
predominant on the other side is unknown. However, the honors were finally divided by a most unexpected manoeuvre of Mr. P." **1. e4 e5 2. Nf3 Nc6
3. Bc4 Bc5 4. b4 Bb6 5. b5 Na5 6. Be2** 6. N×e5
Nh6 7. d4 d6 8. B×h6 d×e5 9. B×g7 Rg8 10. B×f7+
K×f7 11. B×e5 is a more modern alternative. **6. ...
d6 7. 0–0 Nf6 8. Nc3 Be6 9. d3 c6 10. a4 Qc7
11. Ba3 0–0 12. Qd2 Rfd8 13. Qg5 d5 14. Bb2 d4
15. Nd1 Nd7 16. Qg3 f6 17. c3 Nb3 18. Rb1 c×b5
19. c×d4 Qc2** (*see diagram*)

After
19. ... Qc7–c2

20. Nc3?! 20. d×e5!? offered some interesting
possibilities: 20. ... Bc7 21. Ne3 Q×e2 22. d4 b×a4
(22. ... f×e5 23. d5 Bf7 24. d6 B×d6 25. Nf5) 23. d5
Bf7 24. d6. **20. ... b4** 20. ... e×d4! was much
stronger: 21. Ne1 Q×b2 22. R×b2 d×c3 23. Rc2
Nd4 and Black has the edge. **21. Bd1 Q×d3 22. Be2
Qc2 23. Bd1 Qd3 24. Be2 Qc2 25. Bd1 Qd3
26. Be2 Qc2** and the game was drawn. ½–½
[1:37–1:00] [*New York Sun*, October 4, 1893; *New
York Recorder*, October 7, 1893; *British Chess Magazine*, November 1893, pages 478–479]

436. J.M. Hanham–Pollock [C24]
New York, Impromptu Tournament,
Round 4, 5 October 1893

1. e4 e5 2. Bc4 Nf6 3. d3 d5 4. e×d5 N×d5
5. Nf3 Nc6 6. 0–0 Bg4 7. c3 Be7 8. Re1 0–0
9. Nbd2 Qd7 10. Nf1 Rad8 10. ... Nb6 11. Bb5 f6
12. h3 Be6 13. d4 Rad8 was more accurate. **11. h3
Bf5 12. Ng3** 12. N×e5 N×e5 13. R×e5 Nb6 14. Qf3
N×c4 15. d×c4 Be6 16. b3 Qd3 would have offered
Black some compensation. **12. ... Bg6 13. Bb5 f6
14. d4 a6 15. Ba4 Kh8?!** 15. ... e×d4 was better:

16. N×d4 b5 17. N×c6 Q×c6 18. Bb3 Bc5. **16. d×e5 b5 17. Bb3** 17. e×f6 would have won a pawn, but Black seems to have enough resources in terms of piece activity: 17. ... B×f6 18. Bb3 Na5 19. B×d5 Q×d5 20. Q×d5 R×d5 21. Ne4 B×e4 22. R×e4 Rd1+ 23. Re1 R×e1+ 24. N×e1 Rd8 25. Bf4 Nc4. **17. ... f×e5 18. N×e5 N×e5 19. R×e5 c6 20. B×d5 c×d5 21. Bg5** (*see diagram*)

After
21. Bc1–g5

21. ... B×g5 21. ... Bc5!? 22. B×d8 (22. Be3!? B×e3 23. R×e3 Qa7 24. Qd4) 22. ... B×f2+ 23. Kh2 R×d8 was an interesting try. **22. R×g5 Qf7** 22. ... d4 should have offered solid drawing chances: 23. c×d4 Q×d4 24. Q×d4 R×d4 25. Re5 Rd2 26. Re2 Rfd8 27. Rae1 Kg8. **23. Qd4 Be4 24. f3 Bg6 25. Rd1 Rfe8 26. R×d5 R×d5 27. Q×d5 Qc7 28. Kf2 Bf7 29. Qd4 B×a2 30. Ra1** 30. Qd6 or 30. Ne4 were stronger. **30. ... Bc4?** 30. ... Rd8 31. Qe3 Qf7 32. Kg1 h6 33. Ne4 Qb3 was a more stubborn choice. **31. R×a6 Rd8 32. Qe3 Qd7 33. Ne4 Qd1 34. Ra7 h6 35. b4 Bf1 36. Kg3 Qc2 37. Qf2 Be2 38. Kh2 Qd3 39. Ra2 1–0** [1:50–1:58] [*New York Sun*, October 6, 1893]

437. Pollock–J.S. Ryan [C44]
New York, Impromptu Tournament, Round 5, 6 October 1893

1. e4 e5 2. Nf3 Nc6 3. c3 Nf6 4. d4 e×d4 5. e5 Nd5 6. a3 h6 7. c×d4 Nce7 8. Bc4 b6 9. Nc3 Bb7 10. 0–0 N×c3 11. b×c3 Nd5 12. Qb3 c6 13. Ne1 Be7 14. Nc2 0–0 15. B×d5 c×d5 16. Ne3 Rc8 17. f4 d6 18. Nf5 d×e5 19. f×e5 Rc6 (*see diagram*)

After
19. ... Rc8–c6

20. Q×d5 Qc7 21. Qb3 Rg6! 22. Rf2 Bg5? 22. ... Qd7 23. Raa2 Be4 24. N×e7+ Q×e7 25. Rae2 Bb7 was better. **23. B×g5 R×g5** (*see diagram*)

After
23. ... Rg6×g5

24. Raf1 Natural and good. 24. Nd6!?—going after the f7-pawn—was perhaps more precise but a long series of exact manoeuvres are difficult to see in full in over-the-board play: 24. ... Rg6 25. Raf1 Qc6 26. N×b7 Q×b7 27. Rf3 Qe4 28. Qa2 Kh7 29. a4 Rc8 30. Qb1 Qd5 31. R1f2 Rc7 32. Rg3 Rcc6 33. h3 a5 34. Qd3 Kg8 35. Qf3. **24. ... Ba6 25. Re1 Bc4 26. Qb4 Be6 27. Ne7+ Kh8 28. d5!?** The simple 28. Ng6+ R×g6 29. Q×f8+ Kh7 30. Re3 was perhaps more straightforward. **28. ... Re8 29. d6?** 29. d×e6! should have made things far easier: 29. ... R×e7 30. e×f7 R×f7 31. R×f7 Q×f7 32. e6 Qe8 33. e7 Rc5 34. Qe4. **29. ... Qd7 30. Qh4 Rg4 31. Qh5 R×e7!** 31. ... Qb5, or similar feeble attempts, lose to 32. R×f7! Qc5+ 33. Kh1 B×f7 34. Q×g4 Q×c3 35. Qg3. **32. d×e7 Q×e7 33. h3 Rg3 34. Rf3??** Overlooking Black's simple tactical idea. 34. Ref1 should have easily secured a draw. **34. ... Rg5 35. R×f7** 35. Qh4 loses after 35. ... R×g2+. **35. ... Qc5+ 0–1** [1:03–1:10] [*New York Times*, October 7, 1893; *New York Sun*, October 7, 1893]

438. E. Delmar–Pollock [C48]
New York, Impromptu Tournament, Round 6, 7 October 1893

1. e4 e5 2. Nf3 Nc6 3. Nc3 Nf6 4. Bb5 Bc5 5. 0–0 0–0 6. d3 d6 7. Bg5 Ne7 8. Qd2 c6 9. Bc4 Be6 10. Bb3 Ng6 11. Na4 Bb6 12. N×b6 a×b6 13. Nh4 N×h4 14. B×h4 B×b3 14. ... N×e4 did not promise Black anything: 15. d×e4 Q×h4 16. B×e6 f×e6 17. Q×d6 Q×e4 18. Q×e6+. **15. B×f6 Q×f6 16. a×b3 Rfc8 17. Qe3 Qd8 18. Rab1 b5 19. f4 f6 20. f5 d5 21. e×d5?!** An unjustified attempt to destabilize the position. 21. Ra1 was recommended. **21. ... Q×d5 22. Rf3 Rd8 23. Qe2 Ra2! 24. h3** 24. Qf2 was more careful play. **24. ... R×b2 25. Rbf1?** 25. R×b2 Qd4+ 26. Kh2 Q×b2 27. Rg3 Kh8 28. Qg4 Rg8 29. Qb4

was correct. **25. ... Q×b3 26. R1f2 Qc3 27. Kh2 b4 28. Rg3 Rd7 29. Qh5 Rf7 30. Rg4 R×c2 31. Rf3 Qc5 32. Rfg3** *(see diagram)*

After
32. Rf3–g3

32. ... Rc1?! 32. ... Qd6 33. Qh6 Qd7 34. R×b4 Q×f5 was most accurate. **33. d4 e×d4** Olly: "From sheer greediness Black kills another pawn, and in so doing commits an error as big as Brooklyn Bridge. 33. ... Qe7 was the right move." 33. ... Qe7 34. Rh4 Kf8 35. Q×h7 Ke8 36. d×e5 f×e5 37. Rd3 kept the game wide open. **34. Qh6! Kf8?** Black panicked and ruined it all with this move. 34. ... Qe7! required some calculation but Black seems to be able to hold it: 35. Q×c1 c5 36. Qc2 Kf8 37. Rh4 h6 38. Re4 Qc7 and Black's four queenside pawns are difficult to deal with. **35. R×g7 R×g7 36. Q×f6+ Ke8 37. R×g7 Rh1+ 38. K×h1 Qc1+ 39. Kh2 Qf4+ 40. Rg3 h5 41. Qg6+ Kd7 42. Q×h5 d3 43. f6 b3 44. Qh7+** and White won at move 62. **1–0** [2:00–2:05] [*New York Sun*, October 8, 1893; *New York Recorder*, October 9, 1893]

439. Pollock–L. Schmidt Jr. [C25]
New York, Impromptu Tournament, Round 7, 8 October 1893

1. e4 e5 2. Nc3 Bc5 3. Nf3 d6 4. d4 e×d4 5. N×d4 Nc6 6. Bb5 Bd7 7. Be3 Nf6 8. Qd2 Bb4 9. f3 0–0 10. N×c6 b×c6 11. Bc4 Re8 The direct 11. ... d5!? was an interesting resource: 12. e×d5 (12. e5 Re8! 13. e×f6 Q×f6) 12. ... c×d5 13. B×d5 N×d5 14. Q×d5 Re8 15. Kf2 B×c3 16. b×c3 Qh4+ 17. g3 Qh3. **12. 0–0–0 c5 13. a3 Ba5 14. g4 Be6 15. Bb5 Bd7 16. Bc4 Be6 17. Bb5 Bd7 18. Bd3 Rb8 19. h4 c6 20. h5 Qb6** *(see diagram)*

21. b4 21. b3 Be6 22. g5 invites 22. ... N×e4! 23. B×e4 B×b3! **21. ... B×b4 22. a×b4 Q×b4 23. Nb5?!** White could have simplified en masse beginning with 23. Qe1 d5! 24. Nb5! (24. g5 invites unfavorable complications after 24. ... Ng4!? 25. f×g4 Qb2+ 26. Kd2 d4) 24. ... Q×e1 25. Rh×e1 c×b5 26. e×d5 N×d5 27. B×h7+ K×h7 28. R×d5 Bc6 29. R×c5 B×f3 30. Rf5 B×g4 31. R×f7 B×h5

After
20. ... Qd8–b6

32. R×a7. **23. ... Q×d2+** After 23. ... Qa4!? White seems to have sufficient resources: 24. Qc3 c×b5 25. g5 b4 26. Qb2 Nd5 (26. ... Rec8 27. Bc4 Ne8 28. g6!) 27. e×d5 R×e3 28. h6 Qa3 29. B×h7+ K×h7 30. h×g7+ Kg6 31. Rh6+ K×g5 32. Q×a3 b×a3 33. Rh8 Ree8 34. R×e8 R×e8 35. Rg1+ Kf5 36. g8Q R×g8 37. R×g8 Bb5 38. Ra8 a6 39. Ra3 f6 40. Re7. **24. K×d2 c×b5 25. g5 c4! 26. g×f6 c×d3 27. Rdg1 d×c2?** 27. ... Be6! had to be played: 28. R×g7+ Kh8 29. c×d3 a5 30. Bf4 Rb6 31. Rc1 b4 32. d4 d5 33. Bc7 Rb5 34. Kc2 a4 35. Bd6 Rc8+ 36. Kb1 R×c1+ 37. K×c1 a3 38. Rg1 h6. **28. R×g7+ Kh8 29. R×f7 Be6 30. R×a7 Rg8 31. Bd4** 31. Re7! Rg2+ 32. Kc1 Bb3 33. f7 was the correct play for a win. **31. ... Rg2+ 32. Kc1 Kg8 33. Rg1 R×g1+ 34. B×g1 Bf7 35. K×c2 b4 36. Bd4 b3+ 37. Kb2 Rc8 38. Bc3 h6 39. Rd7 Ra8 40. R×d6 Ra2+ 41. Kb1 B×h5 42. e5??** Another collapse from Pollock that took him from a superior position into a completely lost one. 42. Rd8+ Kf7 43. Rd7+ Ke8 44. Re7+ Kf8 45. Rb7 Ke8 46. R×b3 Rf2 47. e5 would have maintained some winning chances. **42. ... Bg6+ 43. Kc1 Rc2+ 44. Kd1 R×c3** and Black won at move 63. **0–1** [2:21–2:00] [*New York Sun*, October 10, 1893]

440. E.N. Olly–Pollock
New York, Impromptu Tournament, Round 8, 10 October 1893

The game was scored against Pollock without play based on a disagreement between the two players regarding the actual starting time of the game. Pollock's appeal against this decision was rejected by the tournament committee. **1–0**

441. Pollock–J.F. Lee [B01]
New York, Impromptu Tournament, Round 9, 12 October 1893

1. e4 d5 2. e×d5 Q×d5 3. Nc3 Qd8 4. d4 c6 5. Nf3 Bg4 6. Be3 e6 7. Bd3 Nf6 8. Ne2 Nd5

9. Qd2 Nd7 10. 0–0–0 Nb4 11. Kb1 N×d3 12. c×d3?! It's difficult to find a reason for this eccentricity. **12. ... Be7** 12. ... B×f3 13. g×f3 Nb6 seems more logical. **13. Ne5 N×e5 14. d×e5 Qd5 15. f3 Bf5 16. Qc3 f6 17. g4 Bg6** (*see diagram*)

After
17. ... Bf5–g6

18. h4?! 18. Nf4!? Q×f3 19. N×e6 Q×e3 20. Rhe1 was something more to Pollock's taste. **18. ... Q×f3 19. Qd2 Rd8** 19. ... 0–0–0! 20. Nd4 Qd5 21. h5 f×e5 was even stronger. **20. Nf4 c5 21. e×f6 g×f6 22. h5?** 22. g5 was more accurate: 22. ... f×g5 23. N×g6 h×g6 24. Rhf1 Qd5 25. B×g5. **22. ... Bf7 23. Rdf1 Qc6 24. Qc3 e5 25. Nh3 Qa4 26. Nf2 Q×a2+ 27. Kc1 Qb3 28. g5 Q×c3+ 29. b×c3 f×g5 30. Ng4 Bd5 31. Rhg1 e4 32. d4 Rf8 33. R×f8+ K×f8 34. d×c5 Rc8 35. Rf1+ Ke8 36. h6 Bc4 37. Rf2 Be6 38. Nf6+ B×f6 39. R×f6 Kd7 40. Bd4 Ke7 41. Rf2 Rf8 42. c6 b6 43. R×f8 K×f8** and Black won "after 60 moves." **0–1** [2:56–2:08] [*New York Sun*, October 13, 1893]

442. Em. Lasker–Pollock [C67]
New York, Brooklyn Chess Club, Impromptu Tournament, Round 10, 13 October 1893

1. e4 e5 2. Nf3 Nc6 3. Bb5 Nf6 4. 0–0 N×e4 5. d4 Nd6 6. B×c6 b×c6 7. d×e5 Nb7 8. Bg5 Be7 9. B×e7 Q×e7 10. Nc3 0–0 11. Re1 Nc5 12. Qd2 Rb8 13. b3 f6 14. Rad1 Ne6 15. e×f6 Q×f6 16. Ne4 Qf5 17. Ng3 Qf6 18. Ne4 Qf5 19. Qc3 (*see diagram*)

After
19. Qd2–c3

19. ... Nf4!? 19. ... d6!? was worth exploring in great depth: 20. Nd4 (20. Q×c6 promised little: 20. ... Bb7 21. Qc4 d5 22. Ng3 Q×f3 23. g×f3 d×c4 24. R×e6 B×f3) 20. ... N×d4 21. Q×d4 c5 22. Qc4+ Be6 23. Qd3 Rbe8. **20. Ng3 Nh3+ 21. g×h3 Q×f3 22. Q×f3 R×f3 23. Kg2 Rf8 24. Re7 c5 25. Ne4** (*see diagram*)

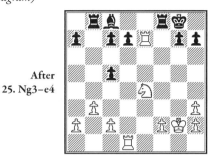

After
25. Ng3–e4

25. ... Rb6!? L.D. Broughton: "Lasker remarked later that had Pollock played 25. ... c4, Black would have at least drawn. White's best continuation being 26. Rd5." **26. N×c5 Rg6+ 27. Kf1 d6 28. Nd3 B×h3+ 29. Ke1 Bg4** L.D. Broughton: "Lasker suggested later that 29. ... Bf5 at once was better; or 29. ... Re6+, forcing the exchange of rooks, would have drawn." **30. Rc1 c5** A highly ambitious approach. 30. ... Re6+ was the safer alternative: 31. R×e6 B×e6 32. Kd2 Rf3 33. Re1 Kf7. **31. R×a7 Re6+ 32. Kd2 Re2+ 33. Kc3 Bf5 34. a4 B×d3 35. K×d3 Re×f2 36. Kc4 R×h2 37. Kd5** (*see diagram*)

After
37. Kc4–d5

37. ... Rh5+?! Wasting valuable time. 37. ... h5! was more effective: 38. a5 h4 39. a6 (39. K×d6!? Rd2+ 40. K×c5 h3 41. Re7 h2 42. c4 Ra8 43. b4 g5) 39. ... Rd2+ 40. Kc6 h3 41. Rb7 h2 42. a7 R×c2 43. Rh1 Ra2 with, despite appearances, a likely draw. **38. Kc6 Rhf5?! 39. a5 h5 40. a6 h4 41. Rb7 Ra8 42. a7 Rf7** 42. ... Rff8 is met by 43. Rg1! **43. Rb8+ Rf8 44. R×f8+ R×f8 45. Rh1** L.D. Broughton: "Lasker took no chances in this position; if 45. Kb7, and Black exchanges the rook for pawn, the White king is so far away that the king's pawns become dangerous." **45. ... g5 46. Rg1 Kh7 47. R×g5 Kh6 48. Rd5 h3 49. Rd3 1–0** [1:45–2:05] [*Brooklyn Standard-Union*, October 14, 1893; *New York Sun*, October 14, 1893; *Brooklyn Daily Eagle*, October 14, 1893]

443. Pollock–H.N. Pillsbury [C26]
New York, Brooklyn Chess Club,
Impromptu Tournament, Round 11,
13 and 16 October 1893

1. e4 e5 2. d3 Bc5 3. Nf3 d6 4. Nc3 Ne7 5. d4 e×d4 6. N×d4 Nbc6 7. Be3 B×d4 8. B×d4 0-0 9. Be3 f5!? 10. Qd2 f×e4 (*see diagram*)

After
10. ... f5×e4

11. 0-0-0!? 11. N×e4 d5 12. Ng5 d4 13. 0-0-0 Qd5 leads to very sharp play. **11. ... Bf5 12. Be2 Qd7 13. h3 Rae8 14. g4 Bg6 15. h4 Nc8 16. h5 Bf7 17. g5 g6?!** 17. ... Nb6 was more prudent. **18. h×g6 B×g6** 18. ... h×g6 loses to 19. Bd4! Ne5 20. Rh6. **19. Bc4+** 19. Nd5! Nb6 20. Nf6+ R×f6 21. g×f6 Qf5? would have allowed a fine tactic: 22. B×b6 a×b6 23. R×h7!! B×h7 24. Rg1+ Kf7 (24. ... Kh8 25. Qh6 Qd7 26. Qg7+ Q×g7 27. f×g7+ Kg8 28. Bc4+) 25. Qh6 Rf8 26. Bh5+. **19. ... Kh8 20. Nd5 Nb6 21. B×b6 a×b6 22. Nf6 R×f6 23. g×f6 Qf5 24. Qc3 Ne5 25. Bb3 Rc8 26. f7! Kg7 27. Rdg1 Kf8 28. Qe3** The attractive 28. R×h7 was insufficient: 28. ... B×h7 29. Rg8+ Ke7 30. f8Q+ R×f8 31. Q×c7+ Nd7 32. Rg7+ Kf6 33. Q×d7 Q×d7 34. R×d7 Bg8. **28. ... N×f7 29. Rh4 d5 30. Rf4 Qe6 31. Qd4 Rd8 32. Rf6 Qe7** (*see diagram*) 32. ... Qd7 was more accurate.

33. B×d5! R×d5 34. Rf×g6 h×g6 35. Q×d5 e3 36. Qf3 e×f2 37. Q×f2 Kg7 38. Re1 Qd7 39. Qf3 Nd6 40. Qc3+ Kf7 41. Rh1 Ke7 42. Qg7+ Kd8 43. Rh8+ Ne8 44. Q×g6 Qe7 45. Qd3+ Kc8 46. c3 Qe1+ 47. Kc2 Qe5 48. Qh3+ Kd8 49. Qh4+ Kc8 50. Qg4+ Kd8 51. Qd4+ Q×d4 52. c×d4 and Pillsbury resigned at move 81. **1–0** [3:09–3:15] [*New York Tribune*,

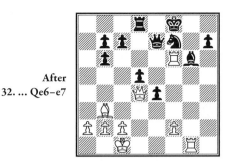

After
32. ... Qe6-e7

October 17, 1893; *New York Sun*, October 17, 1893]

444. J. Taubenhaus–Pollock [C67]
New York, Impromptu Tournament,
Round 12, 16 October 1893

1. e4 e5 2. Nf3 Nc6 3. Bb5 Nf6 4. 0-0 N×e4 5. d4 Be7 6. Qe2 Nd6 7. B×c6 d×c6? 7. ... b×c6 8. d×e5 Nb7 is correct. **8. d×e5 Nf5 9. Rd1 Bd7** (*see diagram*)

After
9. ... Bc8-d7

10. e6! f×e6 11. Ne5 Bd6 12. Qh5+ g6 13. N×g6 Ng7 14. Qh6 Nf5 15. Qh3 Rg8 16. Q×h7 Rg7 17. Qh5 17. Qh8+? Kf7 18. Q×d8 R×d8 19. Nf4 Nh4 20. g3 e5 offers Black plenty of compensation as well. **17. ... Qf6 18. Ne5+ Ke7 19. Ng4 Qh4 20. Q×h4+ N×h4 21. h3 e5 22. f3 Bc5+ 23. Kf1 Bf5** 23. ... Be6 24. Nc3 Bc4+ 25. Ne2 Ke6 26. Bd2 Nf5 27. Ke1 Be7 28. g3 Rf8 was a good alternative. **24. Be3 Bd6** 24. ... B×e3 25. N×e3 Rg3 26. Kf2 Rag8 27. Rg1 B×h3 was much stronger. **25. Rd2 e4! 26. Bf2 Ng6 27. Ne3 Be6 28. f×e4 Rf8 29. Nc3 Nf4 30. Bh4+ Ke8 31. Rf2 Bc5 32. Ncd1 N×g2 33. R×f8+ K×f8 34. N×g2?** 34. Bf2 was forced: 34. ... B×h3 35. N×g2 B×g2+ 36. Ke2 Be7 37. Bd4. **34. ... Bc4+ 35. Ke1 R×g2 36. b3 Bb4+ 37. c3 Re2+ 38. Kf1 R×a2+ 39. b×c4 R×a1 40. Ke2 Bc5 41. Bf6 a5 42. Kd2 a4 43. Kc2 a3 44. Bd4 B×d4 45. c×d4 R×d1 0–1** [1:54–1:58] [*New York Tribune*, October 17, 1893; *New York Sun*, October 18, 1893]

445. Pollock–N. Jasnogrodsky [C51]
New York, Impromptu Tournament,
Round 13, 17 and 18 October 1893

1. e4 e5 2. Nf3 Nc6 3. Bc4 Bc5 4. b4 Bb6 5. b5
Na5 6. Bd3 d6 7. Nc3 Ne7 8. 0–0 0–0 9. Na4 f5
10. N×b6 a×b6 11. c3?! 11. e×f5 B×f5 12. B×f5
N×f5 13. d3 was correct. **11. ... f×e4 12. B×e4 Bf5**
12. ... d5! 13. Bc2 Bg4 would have made things very
uncomfortable for White. **13. Qe2 B×e4 14. Q×e4
Ng6 15. d3 Qd7 16. c4** 16. Rb1 d5 17. Qe2 was
recommended. **16. ... Nb3** *(see diagram)*

After
16. ... Na5–b3

17. a×b3 R×a1 18. Q×b7 h6 19. Be3 R×f1+
20. K×f1 Qf5 21. Ke2 Rf7 22. Qa8+ Kh7
23. Qd5 Re7 24. Kd2 Rf7 25. Ne1 Nf4! 26. Qf3

Ne6 27. Qd5 Nf4 28. Qf3 g6 29. Kc3 Qe6
30. Qc6 Qg4 31. f3 Qf5 31. ... Qh4 was more to
the point. **32. Kd2 Ne6 33. Qd5 Nf4 34. Qc6
Qh5 35. Bg1 N×g2!?** An interesting but risky attempt in a balanced position. **36. N×g2 Qg5+
37. f4!** e×f4 38. Qf3 Qe5 39. d4 Qf5 40. Bf2 Qb1
41. Ne1 Qa2+ 42. Nc2 Qb1 43. d5 Qf1 44. Qe2
Qg2 45. Kc3 Qg5 46. Qf3 Re7 47. Nd4 Qe5
48. Kd3 Re8 49. h4 Ra8 50. Qe4 Ra2 51. Be1
Q×e4+ 52. K×e4 g5 53. h×g5 h×g5 54. Kf5 Kh6
55. Kg4 Rg2+ 56. Kf3 Rg1 57. Bf2 Rf1 58. Ne6
g4+ Best was 58. ... Kh5 59. b4 Rb1 60. N×c7
R×b4 61. Ne8 R×c4 62. N×d6 Rb4 63. Nf5 g4+
64. Kg2 R×b5 65. Ng7+ Kg6 66. Ne6 Rb2.
**59. Kg2 Rb1 60. N×f4 R×b3 61. Ne6 Rc3
62. N×c7 R×c4 63. B×b6 Rb4 64. Bf2** and
White won at move 114. **1–0** [4:46–4:06] Pollock
(*Baltimore Sunday News*, October 28, 1893):
"With the 114-game between Pollock and
Jasnogrodsky, in which the latter claimed the 50-
move rule (in a case of king vs. king, knight and
bishop), but resigned after 23 moves, the 'Impromptu International Tournament' at the Manhattan Chess Club became a matter of history."
[*New York Sun*, October 19, 1893]

Part Two, Section XI
(May 1894–July 1895)

In New York

446. Pollock–J.M. Hanham [C00]
New York, NYSCA Midwinter Meeting, Round 1, 22 February 1894

1. e4 e6 2. Qe2 c6 3. Nc3 d5 4. d4 Pollock: "The variations introduced by White's pawn sacrifices are quite original." **4. ... d×e4 5. Bf4 Nf6 6. 0-0-0 Qa5 7. Kb1 Qf5** Pollock: "Black gets into difficulties through trying to hold the pawn but it should be remembered that the time-limit was 30 moves an hour, from which cause White suffered later." **8. g3 Bb4 9. Bh3 Qg6** *(see diagram)*

After
9. ... Qf5–g6

10. Nb5!? Pollock: "Unexpected. If 10. ... c×b5, 11. B×b8 etc." **10. ... Na6** After 10. ... c×b5 11. B×b8 Black had 11. ... Bd7 12. Be5 Bc6 13. Bg2 Ng4, with excellent play. **11. Nd6+ B×d6 12. B×d6 Bd7 13. Bf1** Pollock: "Obtaining time to release the knight. If now 13. ... 0-0-0, of course White wins by 14. Q×a6." **13. ... Rd8 14. Nh3 Bc8 15. Ba3 Nc7 16. Nf4 Qg4 17. Qe1** Pollock: "Threatening Qa5." **17. ... b6 18. c4 Rd7 19. Bh3 Qg5 20. Qc3 Bb7 21. Rhe1 h6 22. f3 e×f3 23. Re5?** 23. Q×f3 was correct. **23. ... Q×e5! 24. d×e5 R×d1+ 25. Kc2**

Ne4 **26. Q×f3 Rd2+** 26. ... Rd4 27. Bf1 Nd2 28. Qf2 c5 was most accurate. **27. Kc1 c5** Pollock: "The major has now an advantage, which he pursues steadily to the finish." **28. Nh5 R×h2 29. Bg2 Rg8 30. g4 Ke7?** 30. ... Ba8 was needed. **31. b4?** 31. Ng3! R×g2 (31. ... N×g3? 32. Q×b7 Rd8 33. Q×c7+ Rd7 34. B×c5+ b×c5 35. Q×c5+ Kd8 36. Qf2 Rd3 37. Q×a7 with extremely complicated play.) 32. Q×g2 Rd8 33. N×e4 Rd4 34. Qg1 R×c4+ 35. Nc3 was White's way back into the game. **31. ... Na6 32. b5 Nb4 33. B×b4 c×b4 34. Qf1 Nd2! 35. K×d2 R×g2+ 36. Ke3 R×g4 37. Nf4 Rd8 38. Qe1 Rg5 39. Q×b4+ Ke8 40. Qb2 Rg3+ 41. Ke2 g5 42. Qc1 g×f4 43. Q×f4 Rgd3 0-1** [1:40–1:15] [*Baltimore Sunday News*, March 10, 1894]

447. Pollock–J. Halpern [C00]
New York, NYSCA Midwinter Meeting, City Chess Club, Round 4, 23 February 1894

1. e4 e6 2. Ne2 d5 3. f3 Bd6 4. Nbc3 c6 5. d4 Bd7 6. e5 Bc7 7. Ng3 c5 8. Nb5 c×d4 9. N×c7+ Q×c7 10. f4 f5 11. Bd3 Nc6 12. a3 Qd8 13. Bd2 a6 14. 0-0 Qh4 15. Qe2 Nh6 16. Rf3 0-0 17. Raf1 g5?! 17. ... Rac8 was more accurate. **18. Nh1** 18. N×f5! was an excellent tactical shot: 18. ... R×f5 (18. ... e×f5 19. Rh3 Qg4 20. Rff3 Kg7 21. Rhg3) 19. B×f5 N×f5 20. Rh3 d3 21. c×d3 Ncd4 22. Qd1 Ba4 23. Q×a4 Qg4 24. Qd7 with an indisputable edge. **18. ... g4 19. Rg3 Kh8 20. Be1 Qe7 21. Bf2 Rg8 22. Rc1 Rac8 23. Qd2 Nf7 24. Re1 h5 25. Bf1 h4 26. Rb3 b5 27. g3 h3 28. Rc1 Nfd8 29. a4?!** 29. B×d4 N×d4 30. Q×d4 Nc6 31. Qb6 was best. **29. ... b4** 29. ... b×a4!? was

408

more ambitious: 30. Rb6 a3 31. b×a3 Q×a3 32. R×a6 Qb2 33. Rca1 Rb8. **30. B×a6 Rc7 31. Bb5 Qc5 32. Qd3 Na5 33. B×d4 B×b5 34. a×b5 Qe7 35. Ra1 N×b3** 35. ... Ndb7 36. Bb6 Nc5! was even stronger. **36. Q×b3 Rc4 37. c3?!** Perhaps White's best chance resided in an attempt to sacrifice a knight on g4: 37. Qd3 Qc7 38. c3 Nb7 39. Nf2 Nc5 40. Qd1 b×c3 41. b×c3 Rb8 42. N×g4 f×g4 43. Q×g4 Qh7 44. B×c5 R×c5 45. Q×e6 Rc×b5. **37. ... Qe8 38. b6 Nc6 39. Be3 Qd7 40. Nf2 Qb7 41. Nd3 Ra8 42. Re1** *(see diagram)*

After
42. Ra1–e1

42. ... Na5 42. ... d4! would have made a fine finish: 43. Nc5 (43. Q×c4 N×e5; 43. c×d4 N×d4 44. B×d4 Qg2 mate.) 43. ... R×c5 44. Q×e6 d×e3 45. Qh6+ Kg8 46. Qg6+ Qg7 47. Qd6 N×e5 48. f×e5 R×e5. **43. Qc2 b×c3 44. b×c3 Qc6 45. Rc1 Rc8 46. Nb4 Qb5 47. Na2 d4 48. Rb1 Qd5 49. Rd1 R×c3 50. N×c3 R×c3 51. b7 R×c2 52. b8Q+ Kh7 0–1** [*New York Times*, February 24, 1894]

In Montreal

448. Pollock–F.J. Marshall [C20]
**Montreal, Montreal Chess Club,
Simultaneous Exhibition (19 Boards),
22 September 1894**

1. e4 e5 2. Nf3 Nc6 3. c3 d5 4. Qa4 Bd7 5. e×d5 Nce7?! 5. ... Nd4! 6. Qd1 N×f3+ 7. Q×f3 Nf6 8. Bc4 Bc5 was far better than the text. **6. Qb3 Ng6 7. Bc4 Bd6 8. d3 h6 9. Be3 Nf6 10. Nbd2 0–0 11. 0–0–0?** Overly optimistic. 11. a4 was stronger. **11. ... Qe8** 11. ... b5! would have given Black a clear advantage: 12. B×b5 Rb8 13. a4 a6 14. c4 a×b5 15. a×b5 N×d5! **12. Qc2 b5! 13. Bb3 a5 14. a3 b4 15. a4 b×c3 16. b×c3 Ba3+ 17. Kb1 Bd6** 17. ... Qe7 18. Ka1 Rfb8 was more logical. **18. Ka2 Ne7 19. c4 Rb8 20. Rb1 c6 21. Ne4** 21. c5!? would have launched some tactical fireworks: 21. ... Ne×d5 22. B×d5 c×d5 23. c×d6 Rc8 24. Qb2 d4! with rich play for both. **21. ... N×e4 22. d×e4 c×d5 23. c×d5 Rb4 24. Bd2 Rb8 25. Rhc1 f5!** *(see diagram)*

After
25. ... f7–f5

26. N×e5! B×e5 27. d6+ 27. f4! was more forceful: 27. ... Bd4 28. Qc4 Ba7 29. e5. **27. ... Kh8** 27. ... R×b3! was a fine resource that would have allowed Marshall to play for a win: 28. Q×b3+ Rf7 29. d×e7 Be6! 30. Rc4 (30. Q×e6? Q×a4 mate.) 30. ... f×e4 31. Re1 R×e7 32. R×e4 Qf7 33. B×a5 Rb7 34. Bb6 R×b6 35. Q×b6 B×c4+ 36. R×c4 Q×c4+. **28. d×e7 Q×e7 29. f4 Bd4 30. Qc4 Q×e4 31. Re1 Rbc8 32. R×e4 R×c4 33. Re7 Rc7 34. B×a5 Ra7 35. Bb4 Rfa8?** 35. ... Rb8 allowed Black some hopes: 36. Ka3 B×a4 37. R×a7 B×b3 38. Bd6 B×a7 39. B×b8 B×b8 40. K×b3 B×f4. **36. a5?** 36. Rd1! B×a4 37. R×d4 R×e7 38. B×e7 was an immediate win. **36. ... Bf6** and White won at move 56. **1–0** [*Montreal Herald*, September 29, 1894]

449. Pollock–R.P. Fleming [C56]
**Montreal, Bobson's Residence,
Blindfold Game, October 1894**

"We are indebted to Mr. Pollock for the score and notes of the following pretty game, played recently in the house of Mr. Babson, both players playing without the sight of the boards and men." **1. e4 e5 2. Nf3 Nc6 3. Bc4 Nf6 4. d4 e×d4 5. 0–0 N×e4 6. Re1 d5 7. B×d5 Q×d5 8. Nc3 Qd8** 8. ... Qa5 is the more established alternative. **9. R×e4+ Be7 10. N×d4 0–0** 10. ... f5!? is a challenging response: 11. R×e7+ Q×e7 12. Nd5 Qd7 13. Ne6 Kf7 14. Ng5+ Kg8 15. c3 with complicated play. **11. N×c6 b×c6 12. Qe2 Re8 13. Bg5 Be6 14. Rd1 Qc8 15. B×e7 R×e7** *(see diagram)*

16. f4?! 16. Na4 Qf8 17. Nc5 was a more suitable plan here. **16. ... Bg4! 17. R×e7 B×e2 18. N×e2 Qg4** 18. ... Qf5! was a better try: 19. Rdd7 g6

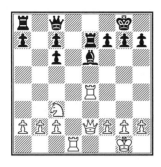

After
15. ... Re8×e7

20. Kf2 Q×c2 21. R×f7 Q×b2 22. R×h7 Re8 23. Rde7 R×e7 24. R×e7. **19. Rdd7 f6 20. h3 Qg6 21. f5 Q×f5 22. R×g7+ Kh8 23. Nd4 Qe4 24. Rge7 Qg6 25. Ne6 Q×c2 26. Nd4 Qc1+ 27. Kh2 Qf4+ 28. Kh1 Qf1+ ½–½** [*Montreal Gazette*, October 27, 1894]

450. F.J. Marshall–Pollock [C55]
Montreal, Montreal Chess Club,
Simultaneous Exhibition (22 Boards),
10 November 1894

1. e4 e5 2. Nf3 Nc6 3. Bc4 Nf6 4. Nc3 N×e4 5. B×f7+ 5. N×e4 d5 6. B×d5 Q×d5 7. Nc3 is the other key alternative. **5. ... K×f7 6. N×e4 d5 7. Neg5+ Kg8 8. d3 h6 9. Nh3 B×h3 10. g×h3 Qd7 11. Qe2 Q×h3 12. Bd2 Bd6 13. Rg1 Kh7 14. Rg3 Qf5 15. 0-0-0 Rhf8** (*see diagram*)

After
15. ... Rh8–f8

16. B×h6? 16. Rdg1! Qf6 (16. ... Rf7? 17. Nh4 Q×f2 18. Qh5!) 17. R×g7+ Q×g7 18. R×g7+ K×g7 was seemingly better. **16. ... g×h6 17. Ng5+ Kh8 18. Rdg1 e4 19. Qh5 B×g3?** 19. ... Bf4+ 20. Kb1 Rf6 was the correct defense (20. ... B×g5 was less convincing: 21. R×g5 Qh7 22. Rg6 Rg8 23. d×e4 d×e4 24. b4!): 21. d×e4 d×e4 22. R3g2 Nd4 with a winning advantage. **20. Q×h6+ Kg8 21. R×g3 Rf6 22. N×e4+ Kf7 23. Rg7+ Ke6 24. N×f6 Rh8** 24. ... Q×f6 25. Rg6 Rf8 26. Qh3+ Kd6 27. R×f6+ R×f6 28. Qg3+ Kc5 29. Q×c7 offered no real resistance either. **25. Nh7+ Ke5 26. Rg5**

Nd4 **27. Qf6+** There was another four-move mate here: 27. f4+ K×f4 28. Rg3+ Ke5 29. Re3+ Qe4 30. Qf6 mate. **27. ... Kf4 28. Q×d4+ Qe4** and White mates in two moves. **1–0** [*St. John Globe*, December 7, 1894]

451. Pollock–G.H.D. Gossip [C25]
Montreal, Private Chess Séance,
22 November 1894

1. e4 e5 2. Nc3 Nc6 3. f4 e×f4 4. Nf3 g5 5. h4 g4 6. Ng5 Pollock: "The Hamppe-Allgaier gambit. White has the option of retreating Ng1." **6. ... h6 7. N×f7 K×f7 8. d4** Pollock: "Sometimes known as the 'Thorold' attack. This is considered stronger than 8. Bc4+." **8. ... f3** Pollock: "Probably best, as keeping the f-file closed against the operation of the White rook." **9. Bc4+ d5 10. B×d5+ Ke8 11. g×f3 Be7 12. Be3 B×h4+ 13. Kd2 Bg5 14. f4 Bf6 15. e5 Bg7** Pollock: "The line of defence selected is rather tardy and yields White a well-supported pawn centre. As an offset to this White's king is awkwardly situated." **16. Qe2 Nge7 17. B×c6+ N×c6** Pollock: "We consider 17. ... b×c6 much better and certainly more economical from a time saving point of view." **18. Qd3 Ne7** (*see diagram*)

After
18. ... Nc6–e7

Pollock: "White threatened to advance d5 or f5. Either 18. ... Rf8 or 18. ... Be6 would, of course, have lost a piece by 19. Qg6+." **19. Rae1** Pollock: "The pawn should have been pushed at once." **19. ... c6** Pollock: "For Black might have practically raised the siege here by 19. ... Bf5, when if 20. Qb5+ Bd7 White dare not capture on b7 on account of 21. Q×b7 Bc6." **20. e6?** Pollock: "To open the e-file." 20. Rh5!? Rf8 21. Qh7 Rf7 22. Ne4 Bf5 23. R×f5 N×f5 24. e6 was worth trying out here. **20. ... B×e6 21. Bf2 Qd6** Pollock: "If 21. ... Qd7 the reply is 22. Ne4." **22. Qe3** (*see diagram*)

22. ... Q×d4+?! Pollock: "Although this is a

After
22. Qd3–e3

After
9. Qg4–g3

heavy sacrifice and probably leads only to equality, it is almost imperative to break the attack. 22. ... Rd8 would probably result in the same position as in the text, while if 22. ... Bf7 23. Bh4 with a violent attack." 22. ... Bf5 23. Bh4 Bf6 was more effective. **23. Q×d4 B×d4 24. B×d4 Rd8 25. R×e6** Pollock: "Best." **25. ... R×d4+ 26. Ke3 Rd7 27. f5** Pollock: "Overlooking a strong continuation in 27. Rh5." **27. ... Kf7 28. Kf4 h5 29. Ke5?** 29. Ne4 Rd4 30. Re1 Nd5+ 31. Ke5 was correct. **29. ... Rd2! 30. Rf6+ Kg7 31. Ke6?** Pollock: "Another oversight and this time a fatal one of which Black takes prompt advantage. The rook should return to e6, when the game would probably be drawn, as Black's best plan would be to play 31. Re6 Kf7 (For if 31. ... Nd5 32. N×d5 R×d5+ 33. Kf4 with an excellent game.)" **31. ... Rd6+ 32. K×d6 K×f6 33. Ne4+ K×f5 34. Ng3+ Kf4 35. N×h5+ Kg5 36. K×e7 R×h5 37. Re1 g3 38. Ke6 g2 39. Rg1 Rh2 40. Ke5 Kg4 41. Ke4 Kg3 0–1** [*Montreal Herald*, December 1, 1894]

452. Pollock–W.T. Lindsay [C50]
Montreal, Montreal Chess Club,
Simultaneous Exhibition (21 Boards),
29 November 1894

1. e4 e5 2. Nf3 d6 3. d4 Bg4 4. Bc4 Nc6 5. Nc3 Pollock: "Playing for a well-known trap." **5. ... N×d4 6. N×e5 d×e5** Pollock: "Avoiding the trap. If Black now takes the queen, White mates in two moves." **7. Q×g4 N×c2+ 8. Ke2 Nf6** Pollock: "8. ... N×a1 is simpler and should leave Black with an ample superiority, although White might gain a smart attack by 9. Bg5 when, if 9. ... f6 10. Qe6+ probably better than (10. Rd1) 10. ... Qe7 11. Bb5+ etc." **9. Qg3** (*see diagram*)
9. ... Nd4+ After 9. ... N×a1!? 10. Rd1 Nd7 11. Qg4 Black has to be careful not to lose immediately. For instance, after 11. ... Nc2 (11. ... Bd6!?

12. Q×g7 Qf6 13. Q×f6 N×f6 14. Bg5 Be7 15. B×f6 B×f6 16. Nd5 Bd8 17. R×a1) White has 12. B×f7+ K×f7 13. R×d7+ Q×d7 14. Q×d7+. **10. Kf1 Nc6** Pollock: "He might have braved ... Bd6." **11. Bg5 Bd6 12. Rd1 0–0 13. h4** Pollock: "An excellent continuation." **13. ... Nd4** Pollock: "13. ... Kh8 is a safer move." **14. Nd5** Pollock: "To induce Black to dig a pit and then fall into the middle of it himself." **14. ... N×e4** Pollock: "He tumbles." **15. Qd3 N×g5?** Pollock: "Fatal, as we shall find: 15. ... Nf6 is his only help, but he would lose the exchange through 16. N×f6+ g×f6 17. Bh6." **16. h×g5 Q×g5** Pollock: "Of course a blunder. Black, in this pretty position, is quite lost. If f-pawn moves mate follows in two; if ...g6, he loses by Nf6+, and if ...h6, 17. Nf6+ g×f6 18. Qg6+ and mates next move." **17. Q×h7 mate. 1–0** [*Montreal Herald*, December 8, 1894]

453. Pollock–R.L. Beecher [C29]
Montreal, Montreal Chess Club,
Simultaneous Exhibition (21 Boards),
29 November 1894

1. e4 e5 2. Nc3 Nf6 3. f4 Bb4? 4. f×e5 B×c3 5. d×c3 Ng8 6. Nf3 Ne7 7. Bc4 h6 8. 0–0 Nbc6 (*see diagram*)

After
8. ... Nb8–c6

9. Be3 9. B×h6!! is a very surprising and effective riposte: 9. ... g×h6 (9. ... R×h6 10. Ng5 d5 11. N×f7 Qd7 12. N×h6 d×c4 13. Qh5+ g6 14. Qf3 Nf5

15. e×f5) 10. B×f7+ Kf8 (10. ... K×f7 11. Nh4+ Nf5 [11. ... Ke6 12. Qg4+ K×e5 13. Qf4+ Ke6 14. Qf6 mate; 11. ... Kg7 12. Qg4+ Kh7 13. Rf7 mate] 12. R×f5+ Kg7 13. Qg4+) 11. Nh4 N×e5 12. Qh5. **9. ... Na5 10. B×f7+! K×f7 11. Ng5+ Kg8 12. Ne6 Qe8 13. N×c7 Qd8 14. Ne6 Qe8 15. Rf8+ Q×f8 16. N×f8 K×f8 17. e6 Ke8 18. Qh5+ g6 19. Q×a5** and White won after a few more moves. **1–0** [*Montreal Gazette*, December 8, 1894; *Montreal Herald*, November 24, 1894]

454. Pollock–C.C. Wheeldon [A03]
Montreal Chess Club,
Simultaneous Exhibition (21 Boards),
29 November 1894

1. f4 d5 2. e3 Bf5 3. Nf3 e6 4. Nc3 Nf6 5. b3 c6 6. Bb2 Bd6 7. Bd3 B×d3 8. c×d3 0–0 9. g4 N×g4 10. Rg1 f5 11. Ng5 h6 12. h3 After 12. N×e6 Qh4+ 13. Rg3 Rf6 the knight is trapped. **12. ... h×g5 13. h×g4 Nd7** 13. ... g×f4 14. Qe2 Qh4+ 15. Kd1 f×e3 16. d×e3 e5 was much better. **14. g×f5 R×f5 15. Qg4 Nc5 16. Ke2 d4 17. Ne4 d×e3 18. d×e3** *(see diagram)*

After
18. d2×e3

18. ... N×e4? The exquisite 18. ... Be5!? would have assured equality: 19. N×c5 (19. f×e5? Q×d3+ 20. Ke1 Q×e3+; 19. Rad1 B×b2 20. N×c5 Qe7 21. d4 Ba3) 19. ... B×b2 20. Rab1 Qd5. **19. d×e4 Rc5** 19. ... Rf7 20. Q×e6 Qd7 21. Q×d7 R×d7 22. R×g5 would have prolonged the game for a while. **20. Rab1?** White could have mated with 20. Q×e6+ Kf8 21. Rh1 Rc2+ 22. Kf1! **20. ... Qe7 21. f×g5?!** 21. Rbd1 Bc7 22. Bd4 Ra5 23. a4 Rd8 24. f×g5 was correct. **21. ... Rc2+ 22. Kd3 Rh2 23. Rg2 Rd8 24. Ke2 Bb4 25. Bd4?** 25. R×h2 Rd2+ 26. Kf3 R×h2 27. g6 had to be played. **25. ... R×g2+ 26. Q×g2 e5 27. g6 Qe6** 27. ... e×d4 was correct. **28. Rh1?** 28. Qg5! would have allowed White back in the game. **28. ... e×d4 29. Qg5 Qf6 30. Qh5 d3+ 31. Kd1 Qa1 mate 0–1** [*Montreal Gazette*, December 8, 1894]

455. Pollock–G.H.D. Gossip [C44]
Montreal, J.W. Shaw's House,
November 1894

"Played at a chess gathering at the house of Mr. J.W. Shaw, Montreal, for a small prize offered by the host." **1. e4 e5 2. Nf3 Nc6 3. c3 Nf6** Pollock: "The move now generally adopted is 3. ... d5 with the usual continuation 4. Qa4 Nge7 5. Bb5 f6. Considerable attention has been paid to the latter form of debut, from time to time by Messrs. Steinitz, Chigorin, Alapin, Showalter, Pollock and others, the legitimate outcome being still very much in doubt." **4. d4 N×e4** Pollock: "4. ... e×d4 may also be played. White then continues 5. e5 and Black can reply with either ...Nd5 or ...Ne4. In the former event White may then play 6. c×d4 or possibly 6. Bb5 or 6. a3 without disadvantage. In the latter, 5. ... Ne4 6. Qe2 Nc5 7. c×d4 Na6 8. Nc3 seems to give White the advantage." **5. d5** Pollock: "Or 5. d×e5 and if then 5. ... Bc5 6. Qd5." **5. ... Nb8** Pollock: "Black may obtain a lively but scarcely sound attack by 5. ... Bc5, giving up the knight for two pawns. 5. ... Ne7 is generally preferred to the text move." **6. Bd3** Pollock: "If 6. N×e5 at once, Black wins by 6. ... Qe7." **6. ... Nc5 7. N×e5 N×d3+ 8. N×d3** Pollock: "If 8. Q×d3 Black replies 8. ... Qe7." **8. ... Be7 9. 0–0 0–0 10. Be3 c6 11. Qb3** Pollock: "White, no doubt with good reason, directs his immediate attention to the queenside." **11. ... d6 12. Na3 Qc7 13. c4 Bf5 14. Rac1 B×d3 15. Q×d3 Nd7 16. Rfd1 Ne5 17. Qe2 f5 18. Bd4 Rae8** *(see diagram)*

After
18. ... Ra8–e8

Pollock: "If 18. ... Bf6 19. c5 d×c5? 20. d6 Q×d6 21. B×c5." **19. c5** Pollock: "If 19. B×a7 b6 of course follows." **19. ... Bg5** Pollock: "Black, pretty clearly, dare not take either of the advanced pawns. White's attack is by no means easy to parry satisfactorily." **20. c×d6 Q×d6 21. Bc5 Qh6 22. B×f8 B×c1 23. Bc5 Kf7** Pollock: "An awkward looking defense for Black, as White could now win a pawn by Qc2." **24. d×c6** Pollock: "This pins the knight, on pain of Rd7+. Probably however Qc2 is superior." **24. … Bf4!** Pollock: "24. … Qe6 would, truly enough, threaten to win by Nf3. White would win however by 25. f4." **25. g3 Q×c6** Pollock: "The only resource, apparently, but a very good one." **26. Qh5+?** 26. Qb5 Qe4 27. Qb3+ Kg6 28. g×f4 Nf3+ 29. Kh1 b6 30. Qc2 was necessary. **26. … Kg8 27. g×f4** Pollock: "The only move by which White can hope to play for a win is 27. Rd6 followed immediately by Qd1." **27. … Nf3+ 28. Kf1 Qe4?** Pollock: "A singular oversight, which costs the game. Black can draw by 28. … Nd2+ for if 29. R×d2 Qh1 mate, and if 29. Kg1 Nf3+ 30. Kg2? Nh4+ 31. Kh3 Qg2+ 32. K×h4 Q×h2+ 33. Kg5 h6+ 34. Kg6 Re6+ 35. K×f5 Rf6+ and wins." **29. Be3 g6 30. Qh3 Qc6 31. Ke2 1–0** [*Montreal Gazette*, November 10, 1894]

456. F.J. Marshall–Pollock
Handicap Game, Montreal Chess Club, December 1894
Remove f7 pawn

1. e4 and d4 d6 2. Bd3 Pollock: "I find in my MS collection of some 3,000 games the following continuations: 2. f4 Nh6 (2. … e6 3. Bd3 Nc6 4. e5 Nge7 [4. … Qh4+ 5. g3 Qe7 6. Nf3 d×e5 7. f×e5 h6] 5. c3 Nf5 6. Nf3 d5 7. Qe2 Be7 8. Be3 0–0 9. Ng5 h6 10. Nf3 Bd7 11. g4 N×e3 12. Q×e3 Qe8 13. g5 Qh5 14. Nbd2 Rf7) 3. f5 Nf7 4. Qh5 e6 5. Nf3 Be7 6. Bd3 e×f5 7. e×f5 Bf6 (Divan Tournament, 1888; Sellon vs. Zukertort, Gunsberg vs. Pollock, respectively.)" **2. … Nc6 3. e5?!** This is premature. 3. Nf3 Nf6 4. c3 e5 5. 0–0 was best. **3. … g6** Pollock: "Something rash would be 3. … d×e5 4. Qh5+ g6 5. B×g6+ h×g6 6. Q×h8 N×d4 7. Na3 Qd5." **4. f4 N×d4 5. c3 Nf5 6. g4 Ng7 7. f5 d×e5!** Pollock: "Decidedly the best." **8. f×g6** *(see diagram)*

After 8. f×g6

8. … h5!? Pollock: "Following Steinitz's principle: 'When you have found a good move, don't

make it but look for a better one.' The text move is much stronger than 8. … h6, which is purely defensive." 8. … B×g4!? would generate massive exchanges: 9. Bb5+ c6 10. Q×g4 Nf6 11. Qg2 c×b5 12. Q×b7 Rb8 13. Qc6+ Qd7 14. Q×d7+ N×d7 15. g×h7 R×h7. **9. Qf3 Nf6 10. Bc4** Pollock: "A very curious position already. White calculated on 10. g5 and sees, just in time, that the reply 10. … e4 followed by …Bg4 if 11. B×e4, would more than upset his plans. The next move was sealed and the game adjourned." **10. … Qd6 11. Bf7+ Kd8 12. Nd2?** Pollock: "White is in great difficulty as …Bg4 is threatened. His attack was quite premature." 12. g5 e4 13. Qg3 Ng4 14. Nd2 Nf5 15. Q×d6+ N×d6 was better. **12. … h×g4 13. Qg2 Bd7 14. Nc4 Qc6** Pollock: "The game was again adjourned here." **15. Q×c6 B×c6 16. Bg5 B×h1 17. N×e5 c6** Pollock: "A few cautious defensive measures and the day is won." **18. Ne2 Kc7 19. Nd4 Bd5 20. c4 B×f7 21. N×f7 Rh5 22. Bf4+ e5** Pollock: "A neat stroke, for which White was quite unprepared. Now another piece goes." **23. B×e5+ R×e5+ 24. N×e5 Re8 25. Kd2 R×e5 26. Rf1 Be7 27. b4 B×b4+ 28. Kd3 Be7 29. a4 a6** Pollock: "Preparing to dislodge the knight with …c5." **30. Ne2 Kd6 31. Nc3 Ke6 32. Rb1 b5 33. a×b5 a×b5 34. c×b5 c×b5 35. N×b5 Kf5 36. Nd4+ K×g6 37. h4 g×h3 38. Nf3 Rd5+ 39. Ke2 Bc5 40. Rh1 Ngh5 41. Nh2 Ng3+ 42. Ke1 Nfe4 43. Nf3** Pollock: "As a mate was also threatened by …Bb4, it cannot be staved off." **43. … Bf2 mate 0–1** [*St. John Globe*, March 29, 1895; *Montreal Herald*, March 23, 1895]

Match with Gossip

457. G.H.D. Gossip–Pollock [C30]
Montreal Chess Club, Match, Game 1, 15 December 1894

1. e4 e5 2. Nc3 Bc5 3. f4 d6 4. Nf3 Nf6 5. Bc4 Nc6 6. d3 a6 7. Qe2 Bg4 8. Be3 e×f4 9. B×c5 d×c5 10. Qf2 0–0 11. Ne2 Qe7 11. … b5! was an interesting choice: 12. Q×c5 (12. Bb3 c4) 12. … b×c4 13. Q×c6 c×d3 14. N×f4 B×f3 15. g×f3 N×e4! 16. N×d3 Qh4+ 17. Ke2 Qh5. **12. 0–0 B×f3 13. g×f3 Nh5 14. a3** *(see diagram)* **14. … Rad8! 15. Nc3 Rd6 16. Nd5?** 16. Kh1 Rh6 17. Ne2 Nd4 was a difficult choice but White had nothing better. **16. … Qg5+ 17. Qg2** 17. Kh1 was met by the powerful 17. … Ng3+! 18. h×g3 (18. Kg1 N×f1+ 19. K×f1 Rh6 20. Re1 Qh5) 18. …

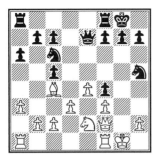

After
14. a2–a3

f×g3 19. Qg2 Rh6+ 20. Kg1 Rh2. **17. ... Qh4
18. Kh1 Rg6 19. Q×g6** 19. Qd2 loses quickly too:
19. ... Ng3+ 20. Kg2 N×e4+. **19. ... h×g6 20. Kg2
Ne5 21. Bb3 Rd8 22. Rae1 c6 23. Nc3 g5 24. Ne2
g4 25. f×g4 N×g4 0–1** [*St. John Globe*, December
21, 1894; *Albany Evening Journal*, July 7, 1894]

458. Pollock–G.H.D. Gossip [C23]
**Montreal Chess Club, Match, Game 2,
18 December 1894**

**1. e4 e5 2. Bc4 Nc6 3. Ne2 Nf6 4. 0–0 Bc5
5. Ng3 d6 6. c3 0–0 7. d3 Ng4?! 8. h3 Nf6** 8. ...
B×f2+ 9. R×f2 N×f2 10. K×f2 Na5 11. Bb3 N×b3
12. Q×b3 Qf6+ 13. Kg1 does not offer Black anything. **9. Bb3 d5 10. Bg5 d×e4 11. d×e4 Q×d1
12. R×d1 Be6 13. Bc2 Be7 14. Nd2 h6 15. Be3
g5 16. Kh2 Rad8 17. b3 a5 18. f3 b5** (*see diagram*)

After
18. ... b7–b5

19. Nf5? Impatience. 19. Ndf1 was more thoughtful play. **19. ... B×f5 20. e×f5 Nd5 21. Nf1 N×c3
22. R×d8 R×d8 23. Ng3 Nb4 24. f6 Bf8** 24. ...
B×f6 25. Be4 N×e4 26. N×e4 Bg7 was fine too.
25. Bf5 Nbd5 25. ... Nb×a2 should have been
played. **26. Bd2 b4 27. a3 N×f6 28. a×b4 a×b4
29. Bc1 Bc5 30. Bc2 Bd4?!** 30. ... Nfd5 was
Black's last chance to preserve his advantage:
31. Nf5 Bf8 32. h4 f6. **31. Ra6 e4 32. Nf5 Be5+
33. g3 Ne2 34. N×h6+ Kg7 35. Nf5+ Kf8
36. B×g5 B×g3+??** A crass oversight. 36. ... e×f3
would have maintained the balance. **37. N×g3**

Nd4 **38. B×f6 N×f3+ 39. Kh1 1–0** [*St. John Globe*,
January 11, 1895]

459. G.H.D. Gossip–Pollock [C28]
**Montreal Chess Club, Match, Game 3,
20 December 1894**

**1. e4 e5 2. Nc3 Nc6 3. Bc4 Nf6 4. d3 Bb4
5. Bg5 h6 6. B×f6 Q×f6 7. Nge2 d6 8. 0–0 B×c3
9. N×c3 Be6 10. Bb3 0–0–0 11. Ne2 g5!? 12. c3**
(*see diagram*)

After
12. c2–c3

**12. ... d5! 13. f3 Qg6 14. Qc2 f5! 15. e×d5
B×d5 16. Rfd1 f4 17. d4 Q×c2 18. B×c2 Bc4
19. Bf5+ Kb8 20. Bd3 B×d3 21. R×d3 e×d4
22. c×d4 Rd5 23. Rad1 Rhd8 24. b3** 24. g3 was
probably a better idea. **24. ... Nb4 25. R3d2 c5!
26. Kf2 Nc6 27. g3 f×g3+ 28. h×g3 N×d4
29. N×d4 R×d4 30. R×d4 R×d4 31. R×d4?**
31. Rc1 Rd2+ 32. Ke3 R×a2 33. R×c5 Rg2 34. g4
would likely secure a draw. **31. ... c×d4 32. Ke2
h5 33. g4 h4 34. f4 h3 0–1** [*St. John Globe*, January 11, 1895]

460. Pollock–G.H.D. Gossip [C51]
**Montreal Chess Club, Match, Game 4,
22 December 1894**

**1. e4 e5 2. Nf3 Nc6 3. Bc4 Bc5 4. b4 Bb6 5. b5
Na5 6. N×e5 Nh6 7. d4 d6 8. B×h6 g×h6** 8. ...
d×e5 9. B×g7 Rg8 10. B×f7+ K×f7 11. B×e5 Nc4
was the other key alternative. **9. B×f7+ Ke7** (*see
diagram*)

After
9. ... Ke8–e7

10. Bd5?! 10. Nc3!? was worth considering too: 10. ... d×e5 11. Qf3 Bg4! 12. Q×g4 K×f7 13. d×e5 Qg5 14. Qd7+ Kf8 15. f4 Rd8 16. Qh3. **10. ... d×e5 11. Qh5 B×d4 12. c3 c6 13. Qf7+ Kd6 14. c×d4 c×d5 15. Nc3** 15. d×e5+ was stronger: 15. ... Kc5 (15. ... K×e5 16. 0–0! Re8 17. Nc3 Be6 18. Qg7+ Kd6 19. Rac1) 16. 0–0! Re8 17. Rc1+ Kb6 18. e×d5 R×e5 19. Nc3 Bf5 20. f4. **15. ... e×d4 16. e5+?!** 16. Qf4+ Kc5 17. N×d5 Nc4 18. Rc1 Be6 19. Nc7 was better. **16. ... Kc5 17. Na4+ K×b5** *(see diagram)*

**After
17. ... Kc5×b5**

18. Rb1+! Kc6 18. ... K×a4? would be met by 19. Qf3 Bf5 20. Qd1+ Ka3 21. Rb3+ Ka4 22. R×b7+ Ka3 23. Rb3+ Ka4 24. Rb8+ Ka3 25. R×d8; 18. ... Kc4 loses on the spot too after 19. Qf3! Qf8 20. Qe2+ d3 21. Qb2. **19. 0–0 b5! 20. Nb2?** 20. Qf4 was correct even if Black can hold: 20. ... b×a4 21. Q×h6+ Kc7 22. Qg7+ Bd7 23. e6 Rg8 24. Qe5+ Kc6 25. e×d7 Q×d7 26. Q×d4 Nc4 27. Rfc1. **20. ... Qf8! 21. Rfc1+ Nc4 22. N×c4 d×c4 23. R×c4+ b×c4 24. Q×c4+ Qc5 25. Qf1 Bf5?** 25. ... Q×e5 wins with ease. **26. Qa6+ Kc7 27. Qb7+ Kd8 28. Q×a8+ Bc8 29. Qe4 Re8 30. Rd1 R×e5 31. Q×h7 Qe7 32. R×d4+ Bd7 33. Qh8+ Kc7 34. h3 Re1+ 35. Kh2 Qe5+ 36. Q×e5+ R×e5 37. Rh4 h5 38. Rc4+ Bc6 39. Rc2 Kd6 40. f4 Ra5 41. g4 h×g4 42. h×g4 Bd5 43. Kg3 R×a2 44. R×a2 B×a2 45. Kf3 Kc5 46. Ke3 Kb4 47. Kd2 Bb1 48. Kc1 Be4 49. Kb2 a5 50. f5 a4 51. Ka2 a3 52. Ka1 Kb3 53. g5 B×f5 54. g6 Be6 55. g7** "After a few more moves the game ended in a draw by stalemate." ½–½ [*St. John Globe*, January 18, 1895; *Montreal Gazette*, December 24, 1894]

461. G.H.D. Gossip–Pollock [C29]
**Montreal Chess Club, Match, Game 5,
22 December 1894**

1. e4 e5 2. Nc3 Nf6 3. f4 d5 4. d3 Bb4 5. Bd2 d×e4 6. f×e5 Ng4 7. N×e4 B×d2+ 8. Q×d2 Nc6 9. Nf3 Ng×e5 10. N×e5 N×e5 11. d4 Qh4+ 12. Ng3 Ng4 13. Qf4 0–0 14. 0–0–0 g5? A seri-

ous weakening of the kingside. 14. ... Qe7 was safer. **15. Qd2 N×h2 16. R×h2! Q×g3 17. Rh5 f6 18. Bc4+ Kg7** *(see diagram)*

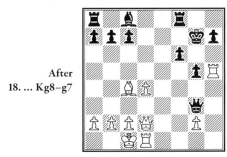

**After
18. ... Kg8–g7**

19. Qb4? 19. Qe2! would have left Black defenseless: 19. ... Qd6 20. R×h7+ K×h7 21. Qh5+ Kg7 22. Rh1 Qf4+ 23. Kb1. **19. ... Qe3+ 20. Kb1 Bg4 21. Re1 Q×e1+! 22. Q×e1 B×h5 23. Qe7+ Bf7 24. B×f7?!** An ill-conceived exchange. 24. b3 Rac8 25. Kb2 a6 26. a4 h5 27. c3 h4 28. Qd7 was a superior choice. **24. ... R×f7 25. Qe4 c6 26. g4 Rd8 27. c3 Rdd7 28. Kc2 Rde7 29. Qf3 h5! 30. g×h5 f5 31. c4 Re4 32. Kd3 Kf6 33. d5 c×d5 34. c×d5 Rd7 35. Kc2 R×d5 36. Qc3+ Ree5 37. b4 Rd6 38. b5 Rdd5 39. Qb4 Rc5+ 40. Kd3 f4 41. a4 f3 42. Qb1 f2 43. b6 a6 44. Qf1 Rf5 45. h6 Rc1 0–1** [*St. John Globe*, February 8, 1895]

462. Pollock–G.H.D. Gossip [C51]
**Montreal Chess Club, Match, Game 6,
27 December 1894**

1. e4 e5 2. Nf3 Nc6 3. Bc4 Bc5 4. b4 Bb6 5. b5 Na5 6. N×e5 Nh6 7. Qf3?! Qf6 8. Q×f6 g×f6 9. Nf3 Ng4 9. ... N×c4 10. d3 Ng4 11. d×c4 N×f2 12. Rf1 N×e4 was in Black's favor. **10. Bd3 B×f2+ 11. Ke2 Bc5 12. Bb2 d6 13. Nc3! Be6 14. h3 Ne5 15. Nd5 B×d5 16. N×e5 f×e5 17. e×d5 Ke7 18. Raf1 Rag8 19. g4 h5! 20. Kf3 Rg5 21. Bc3 Bb6 22. Bf5 Nc4 23. Re1 Ba5** 23. ... Bc5 was marginally better: 24. d4 h×g4+ 25. B×g4 f5 26. d×c5 d×c5! **24. B×a5 N×a5 25. d3 b6 26. h4 h×g4+ 27. B×g4 Rg7** *(see diagram)*

**After
27. ... Rg5–g7**

28. h5? Rh6 28. ... Rg5! 29. h6 f5 would have given Black a big advantage. **29. Reg1 Nb7 30. Bc8 R×g1 31. R×g1 Nc5 32. Rg8?** Playing for a win was too ambitious here. 32. Rh1 or 32. Rg5 would have kept the balance. **32. ... R×h5 33. Bg4 Rh2 34. Ra8 R×c2 35. R×a7 N×d3 36. a4 Kf6 37. Bd7 e4+ 38. Ke3 Ke5 39. Ra8 Nc5 40. Re8+ K×d5 41. Bc6+ Kc4 42. Re7 Rc3+ 43. Ke2 f5 44. R×c7 Kb4 45. Rf7 Rf3 46. Rf6 N×a4 47. R×d6 Nc3+ 48. Ke1 N×b5 0–1** [*St. John Globe*, February 15, 1895]

463. G.H.D. Gossip–Pollock [B73]
Montreal Chess Club, Match, Game 7,
December 1894

1. e4 c5 2. Nc3 Nc6 3. Nf3 g6 4. d4 c×d4 5. N×d4 Bg7 6. Be3 d6 7. Be2 Nf6 8. 0–0 0–0 9. Qd2 Bd7 10. Rad1 a6 11. a4 Rc8 12. h3 Ne5 13. f4 Nc4 14. B×c4 R×c4 15. b3 *(see diagram)*

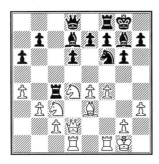

After
15. b2–b3

15. ... Rc8 Sacrificing the exchange with 15. ... R×c3!? 16. Q×c3 N×e4 17. Qd3 f5 was certainly more in the spirit of this Sicilian. **16. e5!?** Ne8 **17. e×d6** 17. Nd5!? is forceful and obliges Black to a careful defense: 17. ... d×e5 18. f×e5 B×h3! (18. ... B×e5?! 19. Nf3 Bd6 (19. ... Bg7? 20. Bb6!) 20. Bb6 Bc5+ 21. Kh1 B×b6 22. Qh6!, with a strong attack.) 19. c4 Bg4 20. Qb4 B×d1 21. N×e7+ Kh8 22. N×c8 Bg4. **17. ... N×d6 18. Nd5 e6** 18. ... B×a4! 19. Qb4 (19. b×a4 Ne4 20. Qb4 Q×d5 21. Nf3 Qe6) 19. ... Bd7 20. c4 b5 was most precise. **19. Nb6!** Ne4 **20. Qb4 a5 21. Q×a5 Nc3?** 21. ... Qc7 was first needed: 22. Qb4 Nc3 23. Rd3 Nd5 24. N×d5 e×d5 25. f5 Rfe8. **22. Rd3** White must have missed 22. N×e6! B×e6 23. R×d8 Rc×d8 24. Qb4 with a clear edge. **22. ... Nd5 23. Nb5 R×c2 24. Rfd1 Rc6** 24. ... N×e3 25. R×e3 R×g2+ 26. K×g2 Bc6+ 27. Kh2 Q×d1 was even more potent. **25. Na7 Rc2 26. R×d5?!** e×d5 **27. Q×d5 Qe7 28. Qf3 Bf5 29. Nd5 Qe4** 29. ... Qe6!—threatening ...Be4—30. Qg3 Rd8 was lethal.

30. Q×e4 B×e4 31. Ne7+ Kh8 32. Nb5 R×g2+ 33. Kf1 Rg3 34. Bc5 R×h3 35. Rd7 Rf3+ 36. Ke2 R×f4 37. Nd6 Bf6? Black could hang on pretty easily with 37. ... Bf3+ 38. Ke3 Rf6 39. Ne4 B×e4 40. K×e4 b6 41. Bd4 Re6+ 42. Kd3 B×d4 43. K×d4 h5. **38. N×e4** 38. Ke3 was even clearer. **38. ... R×e4+ 39. Kf3 Re6 40. N×g6+ h×g6 41. B×f8 Kg8 42. Bc5 b6 43. Be3 Be7 44. Rb7 Bc5 45. B×c5 b×c5 46. Rb5 Rc6 47. Ke4 f5+ 48. Kd5 Rf6 49. Ke5 Rc6 50. Kd5 Rc8 51. R×c5 Rf8 52. Rc1 g5 53. Rg1 g4 54. a5 Kg7 55. b4** *(see diagram)*

After
55. b3–b4

55. ... Kf6? 55. ... Rb8! would have maintained the balance. **56. b5 Ra8 57. a6 Kg5 58. Kc6 f4 59. Kb7** White could have won this endgame with 59. Ra1! f3 60. b6 f2 61. a7 Rc8+ 62. Kd6 Rd8+ 63. Kc5 g3 64. b7 g2 65. a8Q R×a8 66. b×a8Q f1Q 67. Qg8+. **59. ... Rg8 60. a7 f3 61. a8Q?** This gives away half a point. 61. Rf1! was still winning: 61. ... Kf4 62. a8Q R×a8 63. K×a8 g3 64. b6 g2 65. Rb1 f2 66. b7 f1Q 67. b8Q+. **61. ... R×a8 62. K×a8 f2 63. Rb1 g3 64. b6 g2 65. b7 f1Q 66. R×f1 g×f1Q 67. b8Q Qa1+ 68. Qa7 ½–½** [*Montreal Gazette*, January 12, 1895; *St. John Globe*, January 25, 1895]

464. Pollock–G.H.D. Gossip [C38]
Montreal Chess Club, Match, Game 8,
27 December 1894

1. e4 e5 2. f4 e×f4 3. Nf3 g5 4. Bc4 Bg7 5. 0–0 d6 6. d4 Nc6 7. N×g5? Too adventurous. 7. ... B×d4+ 8. Kh1 Q×g5 9. R×f4 Qg6? 9. ... Nf6 was strongest: 10. Qf1 Rg8 11. c3 Be5 12. Rf3 Qh4. **10. B×f7+ Q×f7 11. R×f7 K×f7 12. Qh5+ Ke6 13. Bg5+ Bf6 14. Nc3 Be6 15. Rf1 Rf8 16. Bh4 B×h4 17. R×f8 K×f8 18. Q×h4 Bf7 19. Nd5 B×d5?!** This practically gives away the queenside pawns. 19. ... h5 20. N×c7 Rh6 would have given Black hopes for counterplay. **20. e×d5 Nce7 21. Qd4 Ng6 22. Q×a7 Nf6 23. Q×b7 Ne8 24. a4**

Kg7 25. a5 Rf8 26. Kg1 Rf5 27. a6 Nf4 28. g3 N×d5 29. a7 Ne3 30. h4 Rf1+ 31. Kh2 *(see diagram)*

After
31. Kg1–h2

31. ... Rf2+ After 31. ... Nf6, White has to still be careful: 32. Q×c7+! (32. a8Q? Nfg4+ 33. Kh3 Nf2+ 34. Kh2 Nfg4+) 32. ... Kg6 33. Q×d6 Neg4+ 34. Kh3 Rf2 35. h5+! K×h5 36. Qc5+ Kg6 37. Q×f2 N×f2+ 38. Kg2. **32. Kh3 h5 33. a8Q 1–0** [*St. John Globe*, February 22, 1895; *Nottinghamshire Guardian*, September 21, 1895; this game's result was cancelled by the committee.]

465. Pollock–G.H.D. Gossip [C68]
Montreal Chess Club, Match, Game 9, 16 January 1895

1. e4 e5 2. Nf3 Nc6 3. Bb5 a6 4. B×c6 d×c6 5. N×e5? Qd4 6. Ng4 Q×e4+ 7. Ne3 Bd6 8. 0–0 Nf6 9. d4 0–0 10. Nc3 Qh4 11. g3 Qh3 12. f3 Re8 13. Ne2 Be6 14. Rf2 Rad8 15. Kh1? 15. c4 h5 16. Qc2 h4 17. g4 had to be tried. **15. ... c5! 16. Ng1 Qh5 17. g4 Qh4 18. Rg2 c×d4 19. Nf1 Bc4 20. Ng3 B×g3 21. R×g3 c5 22. b3 Bd5 23. Qd2 N×g4 24. Qg2** *(see diagram)*

After
24. Qd2–g2

24. ... f5 "The game was adjourned, Pollock having enclosed a sealed move. At the next period for play Pollock declined to proceed any further with the match and made default. The umpire produced the sealed move." **25. Nh3 Re1+** "And at

the end of the hour the game was scored in favor of Gossip." **0–1** [*Montreal Gazette*, January 26, 1895]

466. G.H.D. Gossip–Pollock
Montreal Chess Club, Match, Game 10, January 1895

"The tenth game was also scored in favor of Gossip, Pollock having failed to appear at the time fixed for play or for one hour thereafter." **1–0** [*Montreal Gazette*, January 26, 1895]

467. Pollock–G.H.D. Gossip [C45]
Montreal Chess Club, Match, Game 11, January 1895

1. e4 e5 2. Nf3 Nc6 3. d4 e×d4 4. N×d4 Bc5 5. Nb3 Bb6 6. Nc3 Qf6 7. Be3 B×e3 8. f×e3 Nh6 9. Qd2 d6 10. 0–0–0 Ng4 11. Nd5 Qd8 12. h3 Nge5 13. Be2 Be6 14. Nd4 0–0 15. g4 N×d4 16. e×d4 B×d5 17. e×d5 Nd7 18. Bd3 Qh4 19. Rde1 a6 20. Be4 Nf6 21. Bg2 Rfe8 22. Kd1 R×e1+ 23. R×e1 Re8 24. R×e8+ N×e8 25. Qe3 Kf8 26. c4 Qe7 27. Qd3 g6 28. b4 Qh4 29. Qe3 Nf6 30. a4?! 30. Qe1 was safer. **30. ... h5! 31. g×h5 N×h5 32. a5 Nf4 33. Bf3?** 33. Bf1 Qf6 34. Qf2 g5 35. Kd2 was a better defense. **33. ... N×h3 34. c5** *(see diagram)*

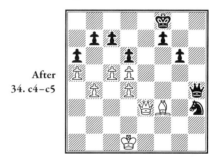

After
34. c4–c5

34. ... g5 34. ... Ng5 could have been met by 35. c6! b×c6 36. Be2! c×d5 37. B×a6 Ne6 38. b5 N×d4 39. b6 and Black has serious problems to solve. **35. c6?!** 35. b5! had to be tried as a last resort: 35. ... g4 (35. ... a×b5? 36. c6 b×c6 37. a6; 35. ... d×c5 36. b6 c×b6 37. d6 Q×d4+ 38. Q×d4 c×d4 39. a×b6 Ke8 40. B×b7 Kd7 41. Bg2 K×d6 42. B×h3) 36. Bg2 (36. c6!? g×f3 37. c×b7 f2 38. b8Q+ Kg7 39. Qf3 Q×d4+ 40. Kc2 Ng5 41. Qe2 Q×d5 42. b×a6 Qf5+ 43. Kb2 Qf6+ 44. Kc2 f1Q 45. Q×f1 Q×f1 46. a7) 36. ... Qh7

37. Kc1 d×c5 38. b6! and White has excellent
chances to save the game (if not more). **35. ...
b×c6 36. d×c6 g4 37. Bg2 g3 38. b5 Nf4! 39. Bf3
g2 40. Kd2 Qh2 41. B×g2 Q×g2+ 42. Kc1 Qf1+
43. Kd2 a×b5 44. a6 Qg2+ 45. Kd1 Qh1+
46. Kd2 Qg2+ 47. Kd1 Qh1+ 48. Kd2 Q×c6**
48. ... Ne6 was best: 49. a7 Q×c6 50. Qa3 Qa8
51. Qa5 Ke7. **49. Q×f4 Q×a6 50. Qh6+ Ke8
51. Qh8+ Kd7 52. Qh3+ Kc6 53. Qf3+ Kb6
54. Q×f7 Qa5+ 55. Ke2 b4 56. Qg8 Kb7
57. Qg2+ d5 58. Qf2 Qa2+ 59. Kd3 b3 0–1**
[*Montreal Gazette*, February 2, 1895]

468. G.H.D. Gossip–Pollock [C48]
**Montreal Chess Club, Match, Game 12,
February 1895**

**1. e4 e5 2. Nf3 Nc6 3. Nc3 Nf6 4. Bb5 a6
5. B×c6 d×c6 6. N×e5 N×e4 7. N×e4 Qd4
8. 0–0 Q×e5 9. d4 Qf5 10. Re1 Be6 11. Bg5 Qg6**
11. ... h6 12. Qd3!? Kd7! 13. Bh4 Re8 14. c4 Kc8
was a good alternative. **12. Qe2 Kd7 13. Rad1
Re8 14. c4 Bb4 15. Nc5+ Kc8 16. Bd2 B×c5
17. d×c5 Bg4** 17. ... Qc2!? was worthy of serious
consideration. **18. Q×e8+ R×e8 19. R×e8+ Kd7
20. Rde1 Be6 21. Rb8 Qd3 22. Ba5 Q×c4
23. R×b7 Q×c5 24. R×c7+ Ke8 25. Rc8+ Kd7
26. Rc7+ Kd6 27. Rd1+ Bd5 28. b4 Qc2 29. Re1
Qd2** *(see diagram)*

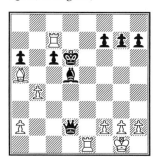

After
29. ... Qc2–d2

30. Ra1? 30. Rf1 Q×a2 31. Ra7 Bc4 32. Rd1+
Ke6 33. h3 was correct. **30. ... Qg5! 31. g3 Qe5?**
31. ... Qg4! should have won: 32. Re1 Qh3 33. f3
B×f3 34. Kf2 Bd5. **32. Rf1 Qe4 33. f3 Qe3+
34. Rf2 g5 35. Rb7 Bc4 36. Bb6 Qe1+ 37. Kg2
Ke6 38. Bc5 Kf6 39. Re7 Be6 40. g4 Kg6 41. h3
Qc3 42. Re8 h6 43. Rg8+ Kh7 44. Re8 a5
45. Rb8 a4 46. Rd8 Bd5 47. Bf8 a3 48. Rd6 Qe1
49. R×h6+ Kg8 50. Bc5 Kg7 51. Rd6 Kh7
52. Rd7 Qa1 53. Ra7 Qc3 54. Re7 Be6 55. Ra7
Kh6 56. Re7 Kg6 57. Re8 ½–½** [*St. John Globe*,
May 24, 1895]

469. Pollock–G.H.D. Gossip [C44]
**Montreal Chess Club, Match, Game 13,
February 1895**

**1. e4 e5 2. Nf3 Nc6 3. c3 Nf6 4. d4 N×e4 5. d5
Nb8 6. Bd3 Nc5 7. N×e5 N×d3+ 8. N×d3 Be7
9. 0–0 d6 10. c4 0–0 11. Nc3 Bf5 12. Be3 Nd7
13. f4 Nf6 14. Nf2 Qd7 15. h3 h5 16. Qf3 a6
17. Kh2?!** Pushing the g-pawn is not the best plan.
Safer was 17. Rfe1 Rae8 18. Rad1 Bd8 19. Nd3 Re7
20. Bf2. **17. ... h4 18. Rg1 g6 19. g4 h×g3+
20. R×g3 c5 21. Rag1 Rae8 22. Ng4 Kg7 23. Bd2
Rh8!** 24. Nf2 Rh4 Even stronger was 24. ... b5!
25. b3 Nh5 26. R3g2 Bf6. **25. Nce4 N×e4
26. N×e4 Reh8 27. Bc3+ f6 28. Nf2 Kf7** 28. ...
b5!? was an interesting try although the position
remains balanced: 29. b3 (29. R×g6+?! B×g6
30. f5 R4h5 31. R×g6+ Kf7 32. Rg4 R×f5) 29. ...
b×c4 30. b×c4 Kf7. **29. Qg2 R8h6 30. Qf3 b5
31. b3 Bd8 32. Kg2 b4 33. Bb2 a5 34. Rh1 a4
35. Ng4 B×g4 36. R×g4 R×g4+ 37. h×g4 R×h1
38. K×h1 a×b3 39. a×b3 Qe8 40. Kg2 Qe1
41. Qd3 Be7 42. Qc2 Bf8 43. Bc1 Bh6 44. g5
Bg7** *(see diagram)*

After
44. ... Bh6–g7

45. f5! g×f5 46. Q×f5 Qe5?! 46. ... Qe2+
should have assured a draw quite easily. **47. g6+
Ke7 48. Q×e5+ d×e5 49. Kh3 f5 50. Bg5+ Kd6
51. Kg3 Kd7 52. Kh4 e4?** This loses immediately.
52. ... f4 was a better attempt even if White main-
tains a very solid advantage: 53. Kh5 Bf8 54. Bh6
B×h6 55. K×h6 f3 56. g7 f2 57. g8Q f1Q 58. Qe6+
Kd8 59. Qd6+ Ke8 60. Q×e5+ Kd7 61. Qe6+
Kd8 62. Kg7. **53. Be3 Kd6 54. Bf4+ Ke7 55. Kg5
Bd4 56. K×f5 e3 57. d6+ 1–0** [*St. John Globe*,
May 31, 1895]

470. G.H.D. Gossip–Pollock [C48]
**Montreal Chess Club, Match, Game 14,
February 1895**

**1. e4 e5 2. Nc3 Nf6 3. Nf3 Nc6 4. Bb5 Bc5
5. 0–0 0–0 6. d3 d6 7. Bg5 Ne7 8. d4 e×d4**

9. N×d4 Ng6 **10.** Nb3 Bb6 **11.** Nd5 Kh8
12. N×b6 a×b6 **13.** Qd4 Be6 **14.** f4 c5 14. ... c6
15. Bd3 c5 was better. **15.** B×f6 c×d4? Best was
15. ... Q×f6 16. Q×f6 g×f6 17. f5 B×b3 18. a×b3
Ne5 19. Rfd1 Kg7. **16.** B×d8 B×b3 **17.** c×b3
Rf×d8 **18.** a4 *(see diagram)*

After
18. a2–a4

18. ... **Ne7?** 18. ... d5! 19. e5 Rac8 20. g3 Rc2
would have given Black sufficient counterplay.
19. Rad1 Rac8 **20.** R×d4 Rc2 **21.** Rfd1 g5 **22.** f5
d5 **23.** f6 Ng6 **24.** R×d5 R×d5 **25.** R×d5 h5 **26.** g3
R×b2 **27.** R×g5 h4 **28.** Bc4 h3 **29.** B×f7 Rb1+
30. Kf2 Rb2+ **31.** Ke3 Nf8 **32.** Rh5+ Nh7
33. R×h3 1–0 [*Montreal Gazette*, February 9, 1895]

471. Pollock–G.H.D. Gossip [C54]
Montreal Chess Club, Match, Game 15,
February 1895

1. e4 e5 **2.** Nf3 Nc6 **3.** Bc4 Bc5 **4.** c3 Nf6 **5.** d4
e×d4 **6.** c×d4 Bb4+ **7.** Bd2 B×d2+ **8.** Nb×d2 d5
9. e×d5 N×d5 **10.** Qb3 Nce7 **11.** 0–0 0–0
12. Rfe1 c6 **13.** Ne4 Qc7 **14.** Rac1 Qb6 **15.** Qc2
Bf5 **16.** Qd2 B×e4 **17.** R×e4 Ng6 **18.** Rce1 Qc7
19. Ne5 Rae8 **20.** f4 *(see diagram)*

After
20. f2–f4

20. ... **f6?** Sliding into a difficult position right
away. 20. ... Rd8! was best. 20. ... Re7?! gives White
a strong attack: 21. f5 N×e5 22. d×e5 Qb6+ 23. Kh1
Rfe8 24. Qg5. **21.** N×c6! R×e4 **22.** B×d5+ Kh8
23. B×e4 b×c6 **24.** f5 24. g3! was more accurate.
24. ... Ne7 **25.** Qc3 g6 **26.** f×g6 h×g6 **27.** d5 Qb6+
28. Kh1 c×d5 **29.** Bc2 Qf2 **30.** Qh3+ Kg8

31. Qe6+ Rf7 **32.** Ba4 Qf5? 32. ... Kf8 33. Be8 Rh7
was Black's best defense. **33.** Bd7 Qf2 **34.** Be8
Q×e1+ **35.** Q×e1 Rg7 **36.** Qe6+ Kf8 **37.** Q×f6+
K×e8 **38.** Q×g7 Kd7 **39.** h4 1–0 [*Montreal
Gazette*, February 16, 1895; *Albany Evening Journal*,
February 16, 1895; *St. John Globe*, May 3, 1895]

472. G.H.D. Gossip–Pollock [B73]
Montreal Chess Club, Match, Game 16,
February 1895

1. e4 c5 **2.** Nc3 Nc6 **3.** Nf3 g6 **4.** d4 c×d4
5. N×d4 Bg7 **6.** Be3 d6 **7.** Be2 Nf6 **8.** 0–0 0–0
9. h3 Bd7 **10.** Qd2 a6 **11.** a4 Rc8 **12.** f4 Ne8
13. Rad1 Nc7 *(see diagram)*

After
13. ... Ne8–c7

14. f5 g×f5? 14. ... Ne8 or 14. ... Ne5 were better
ideas here. **15.** N×f5 B×f5 **16.** R×f5 Ne5 **17.** Bh6
Ng6 **18.** B×g7 K×g7 **19.** Rh5 Rh8 **20.** Qh6+ Kg8
21. Bd3 Qf8 **22.** Qe3 Qg7 **23.** Rf1 Ne6 **24.** Rhf5
f6 24. ... Nh4! **25.** R5f2 Qg5 was a much stronger
resource. **25.** Nd5 h5 **26.** Qb6 White missed the
rather obvious 26. R×f6! Nef4 (26. ... e×f6
27. N×f6+ Kf8 28. N×h5+) 27. R6×f4 N×f4
28. R×f4 Rf8 29. e5! **26.** ... **Nh4** **27.** R5f2 Re8
28. Bc4 28. e5!! was a beautiful solution: 28. ... Rh6
(28. ... f×e5 29. Bc4) 29. e×f6 e×f6 30. Qb4! Qg3
31. Qd2 Ng5 32. N×f6+ R×f6 33. R×f6. **28.** ... **Rh6**
29. Nf4 Kh7 **30.** B×e6 Kh8 **31.** Q×b7 a5 **32.** Qd7
Rf8 **33.** c4 Rh7 **34.** Bf5 N×f5 **35.** Q×f5 Rh6
36. Ne6 1–0 One of Pollock's worst games of his
entire career. [*Montreal Gazette*, February 16, 1895]

VARIOUS GAMES
(MONTREAL AND ST. JOHN)

473. Pollock–Amateur
Handicap Game, Montreal Chess Club,
March 1895
Remove Nb1

1. e4 e5 **2.** Nf3 Nc6 **3.** Bc4 Nf6 **4.** Ng5 d5

5. e×d5 N×d5 6. N×f7 K×f7 7. Qf3+ Ke8 7. ...
Ke6 had to be played. **8. B×d5 Qf6 9. B×c6+**
Q×c6 10. Qh5+ g6 11. Q×e5+ Qe6 12. Q×e6+
B×e6 13. 0–0 Bg7 14. d3 Kf7 15. Bf4 c6 16. Rfe1
Rhe8 17. c3 Bf5 18. d4 Re4 19. R×e4 B×e4
20. Re1 Bd5 21. b3 b5 22. Rc1 Re8 23. Be3 Be4
24. Re1 a5 25. f3 Bb1 26. a3 Bc2 27. b4 a×b4
28. a×b4 Bh6 29. Kf2 B×e3+ 30. R×e3 R×e3
31. K×e3 Ke6 32. Kd2 Bb3 33. Ke3 h5 34. h4
Kf5 35. g3 Bc4 36. Kf2 Bb3 37. Ke3 Bc4? The
repetition is unjustified. Black can win with 37. ...
Ke6 38. g4 (38. Kf4 Kd5 39. Kg5 Bd1 40. f4 Bc2)
38. ... Kd5 39. Ke2 Bc2 40. Kd2 Bb1 41. Kc1 Bd3
42. Kd2 Kc4. **38. Kf2 ½–½** [*Montreal Herald*,
March 30, 1895]

474. C. Gerstner–Pollock
Handicap Game, Montreal Central Club,
December 1894 / March 1895
Remove f7 pawn

"Played in the Central Club tournament between Pollock and Mr. C. Gerstner. It is well to
note that the game began in the middle of December and was not finished till Saturday last." **1. e4**
and d4 d6 2. Bd3 Nc6 3. Be3 e5 Pollock: "The
object of either ...d6 or ...Nc6—or both—in this
opening, is the early advance of ...e5, blocking
White's centre." **4. c3** Pollock: "Black has now almost reduced the odds to pawn and move." **4. ...**
Nf6 5. Ne2 Be7 6. Nd2 0–0 7. Qc2 Pollock:
"White's development may, however, be said to be
so far faultless." **7. ... e×d4 8. B×d4** Pollock: "The
best way to retake." **8. ... N×d4 9. c×d4 Ng4?!**
Pollock: "9. ... Kh8 as a waiting move appears very
strong at this juncture." **10. Nf3 Bg5 11. h3 Nh6**
12. h4 Bf4 13. N×f4 R×f4 14. 0–0–0 Pollock:
"White has opened with manifestly good judgement." **14. ... Bg4** Pollock: "Threatening to win
the h-pawn." **15. Rdg1 d5** Pollock: "If White had
no better move than this ...B×f3 threatening to
win a pawn would have been better. Black's object,
which is admirably frustrated, is to allow the plant-
ing of a bishop at f5." **16. Ng5! d×e4 17. B×e4**
Q×d4 18. f3 Bd7 19. Rd1 Qe3+ 20. Kb1 Bf5
21. B×f5 R×f5 22. Rd3 Pollock: "In reserving his
obvious move of 22. g4 White makes the utmost
out of this position." **22. ... Qe7 23. Rc3 Rd8**
24. g4 Re5 25. Q×h7+ Kf8 26. Qh8+ Ng8
27. Rhc1 c6 28. f4 Re2 *(see diagram)* Pollock: "Adjourned at this point for two months."
29. f5 Rdd2 Pollock: "Black perceiving that the
hostile queen on whose imprisonment he has

After
28. ... Re5–e2

counted is about to set fire to her prison resorts to
a bluff." **30. Rb3 Qe5** Pollock: "Again threatening
mate." **31. Ne6+ Ke7 32. R×b7+ Kd6 33. Q×g7**
Qe4+ 33. ... R×b2+ is insufficient as well: 34. R×b2
R×b2+ 35. Ka1 Rh2+ 36. Q×e5+ K×e5 37. Re1+
Kf6 38. Nd4 R×h4 39. g5+ Kg7 40. f6+ Kg6
41. N×c6. **34. Ka1** Pollock: "The bluff has failed,
and White who has throughout played an admirable game wins the well-deserved laurels." **1–0**
[*Montreal Gazette*, March 2, 1895]

475. R. Short–Pollock
Handicap Game, Montreal Chess Club,
March 1895
Remove f7 pawn

1. e4 and d4 Nf6 2. e5 Nd5 3. c4 Nb6 4. Bd3
d5 5. Qh5+ Kd7 6. c5 6. e6+! Kc6 (6. ... K×e6
7. Qf5+ Kd6 8. c5+ Kc6 9. Nc3) 7. Qe2 was another fine possibility. **6. ... Nc4** *(see diagram)*

After
6. ... Nb6–c4

7. e6+! Kc6 8. Qe2 b6 9. b3 Na5 10. b4 Nc4
11. B×c4 d×c4 12. Qe4+ Kb5 13. a4+ K×b4
14. Bd2+ c3 15. B×c3+ Kc4 16. d5+ Kb3 17. Ra3
mate 1–0 [*St. John Globe*, April 1, 1895]

476. Pollock–G. Breeze
Odds Match, Montreal, 26 March 1895
Remove Ra1

"Played March 26th, 1895, between Messrs.

W.H.K. Pollock and G. Breeze in a little match of three games, arranged by Mr. J.W. Shaw, in which Mr. Pollock conceded Mr. Breeze the odds of pawn and two moves, won by Pollock; knight in the second game, drawn; and queen's rook in the third game, won by Pollock." **1. e4 e5 2. Nf3 Nc6 3. Bc4 Nf6 4. d4** Pollock: "A move well calculated to puzzle the receiver of odds." **4. ... d6** Pollock: "Somewhat objectionable, at all events it would be so in an even game." **5. Ng5** Pollock: "Promptly seizing the opportunity for an early attack." **5. ... d5** Pollock: "Black had other courses: for instance, even 5. ... N×e4 when if 6. B×f7+, 6. ... Ke7 7. Bb3 d5 (or 7. ... N×f2 8. Qh5); Not a bad course was 5. ... Be6 6. d5 Na5 7. d×e6 N×c4 8. N×f7 Qc8 9. N×h8 Q×e6 10. Nc3 Be7, castling on the queenside and a knight ahead." **6. e×d5 N×d5** Pollock: "Considerably safer was 6. ... Na5." **7. N×f7 K×f7 8. Qf3+ Ke8** Pollock: "8. ... Ke6 is very dangerous here." **9. B×d5 Qf6 10. Qd1** Pollock: "Partly to avoid the routine of the other game, no. 3 in the same match." **10. ... N×d4 11. 0–0 Bc5 12. Nc3** Pollock: "Clearly the best course." **12. ... Ne6** Pollock: "Loses time, preferable much is 12. ... c6." **13. Ne4 Qe7 14. Qh5+ g6** Pollock: "Not nearly as good as moving the king at once it seems." **15. Q×e5 Ng7 16. Qg3 Nf5 17. Qb3** *(see diagram)* Pollock: "I think these moves are the best. If 17. Qc3, 17. ... Bd4. White wishes to keep the Black king's bishop on the present diagonal."

After
17. Qg3–b3

17. ... Kf8? Pollock: "His game is very difficult. The b7-pawn was threatened, etc. The text move loses the game." 17. ... Nd4! was best: 18. Qc4 c6 19. Re1 c×d5 20. Q×d5 Ne6 21. N×c5 Kf7 and White doesn't have a winning attack. **18. Bg5 Qe8** Pollock: "If 18. ... Qe5, 19. Bf6 best." **19. N×c5 Nd4** Pollock: "Fatal." **20. Bh6+ Ke7 21. Re1+ Kd6 22. Bf4+ Qe5 23. B×e5+ K×c5 24. Qc4+ Kb6 1–0** [*Montreal Gazette*, April 6, 1895]

477. J. de Soyres–Pollock [C44]
Montreal, Montreal Chess Club,
14 May 1895

"The following highly interesting game was played at the Montreal Chess Club May 14, 1895, between the Rev. John de Soyres, of this city, and Dr. W.H.K. Pollock. The game is of interest inasmuch as Dr. Pollock, on being challenged to the conflict, observed that they had not enjoyed a game together for ten years. Mr. de Soyres, then in London, played two beautiful games with his present opponent in the first congress of the British Chess Association, 1885. Our older readers will remember from the chess records that the Rev. de Soyres's name in London chess annals of the first class dates a good deal further back than even his talented opponent's." **1. e4 e5 2. Nf3 Nc6 3. d4 e×d4 4. Bc4 Bc5 5. 0–0 d6 6. Ng5** Pollock & de Soyres: "White, not having regained the gambit pawn, is almost 'condemned' to a premature attack. If 6. c3 Bg4 7. Qb3 B×f3 with advantage in every variation. However, 7. Bf4 has been tried without disadvantage for White, and, perhaps, it is a good move." **6. ... Nh6 7. h3** Pollock & de Soyres: "In faint hopes that Black would castle, when 8. Qh5 would yield a formidable attack, the advance of the f-pawn following quickly." **7. ... Qe7 8. c3 Bd7** Pollock & de Soyres: "Black defends after the most approved fashion." **9. Bf4?!** 9. Nf3 d×c3 10. N×c3 0–0–0 11. Re1 was safer. **9. ... 0–0–0** Pollock & de Soyres: "If 9. ... f6 at once, White might reply with 10. Qh5+." **10. Nd2 f6 11. Ngf3 g5 12. Bh2** Pollock & de Soyres: "White has the option of 12. c×d4, and if Black recapture, of posting this bishop on e3 instead." **12. ... d×c3** Pollock & de Soyres: "Here ...d3 has great merits, as it may give the second player later on more leisure for his kingside attack." **13. b×c3 g4 14. Nd4** Pollock & de Soyres: "Take all my pawns but let me have at your King!" **14. ... N×d4 15. c×d4 B×d4 16. Rb1 g×h3 17. Qb3 Bb6 18. Bd5 h×g2** Pollock & de Soyres: "Probably underestimating the force of his opponent's designs." **19. Rfc1 Ng4 20. Bg3** Pollock & de Soyres: "20. Nc4 deserves consideration." **20. ... Ne5 21. Nc4 Kb8** Pollock & de Soyres: "21. ... N×c4 would give Black an easier defense." **22. a4** *(see diagram)*

Pollock & de Soyres: "A very strong, if obvious, advance." **22. ... Nc6?!** 22. ... N×c4! seems better but Black has to be careful still: 23. R×c4 c6! (not 23. ... Bc8? 24. a5! B×a5 25. Q×b7+ B×b7

After
22. a2–a4

26. R×b7+ Kc8 27. R×a7 Bb6 28. Ra8+ Kd7 29. Bc6+ Ke6 30. Bd5+ with a perpetual.) 24. a5 c×d5 25. a×b6 a6 26. Rc7 Q×e4. **23. a5 Nd4?** Pollock & de Soyres: "Black's intention, if 24. Qb2, was to play ...Bh3, threatening mate on the move, and if 25. Kh2 Qd7, or if 25. Nd2 Ne2+, breaking the attack." **23. ... N×a5 24. N×a5 Bc8 25. Nc4 h5** was Black's only chance. **24. a×b6** Pollock & de Soyres: "This brilliant stroke almost deserved victory." **24. ... N×b3 25. b×c7+** Pollock & de Soyres: "If 25. b×a7+ Ka8 26. R×b3 Bc6! and we cannot see a win for White." **25. ... K×c7 26. R×b3** Pollock & de Soyres: "If 26. N×d6+ N×c1 27. R×c1+ [the players missed 27. R×b7 mate in their analysis—authors] 27. ... Bc6 28. Nf5+ Qd6 and Black wins." **26. ... Bc6 27. Na5! Rb8** (see diagram)

After
27. ... Rd8–b8

28. N×c6? 28. R×b7+! R×b7 29. R×c6+ Kb8 (29. ... Kd8 30. R×d6+ Ke8 31. N×b7) 30. B×d6+ Q×d6 31. R×d6 Rg7 32. R×f6 should have won. **28. ... b×c6 29. R×c6+ Kd7 30. Ra3 Rb7** 30. ... a5! 31. R×a5 Ra8 32. B×d6 R×a5 33. B×e7 K×e7 was much better. 30. ... Ke8!? was another possibility. **31. Rc1?** Pollock & de Soyres: "White seems to miss his way to victory here. After 31. B×d6! Rb1+ [the players missed the beautiful 31. ... Rg8!! 32. Ra1 Qg7 with equal chances—authors] 32. K×g2 Q×d6 33. R×a7+ Black is lost." 31. Raa6! was giving White a clear edge. **31. ... Rhb8** 31. ... Rc8 32. Rca1 Rbc7 33. K×g2 Ke8 was more precise. **32. Bc6+?** Pollock & de Soyres: "32. B×b7

was surely better." 32. Rc6! would have kept the game going. **32. ... Kd8 33. Rd3 Rb1 34. R×b1 R×b1+ 35. K×g2 Kc7 36. Bd5 Rb4** Pollock & de Soyres: "Threatening to simplify matters by ... R×e4." **37. Rc3+ Kb8 38. Rc6 Rb6 0–1** [*St. John Globe*, May 17, 1895; *PM*, pages 144–146]

478. de Bury & Palmer & Ring– Pollock [C57]
Consultation Game, Saint John, July 1895

1. e4 e5 2. Nf3 Nc6 3. Bc4 Nf6 4. Ng5 N×e4 5. N×e4 d5 6. B×d5 Q×d5 7. Nbc3 Qd8 8. d3 b6 9. 0–0 Bb7 10. f4 f5 11. Ng5 Bc5+ 12. Kh1 Qd7 13. f×e5 0–0 14. Bf4 Rae8 15. Qh5 g6 15. ... h6!? would have allowed White a pretty but insufficient continuation: 16. e6 Qc8 17. Qf7+ R×f7 18. e×f7+ Kh8 19. f×e8Q+ Q×e8 20. Rae1 Qa8 21. Nh3 Nd4. **16. Qe2 Nd4 17. Qd2 Qc6 18. Rae1 h6** (see diagram)

After
18. ... h7–h6

19. Nf3 19. Nh3 was mandatory: (19. ... g5?! allows 20. B×g5! h×g5 21. Q×g5+ Kh8 22. Ne4 f×e4 23. Rf6 e×d3 24. Qh4+ [24. R×c6 B×c6 25. Qh4+ Kg8 26. Qg5+] 24. ... Kg8 25. Qg4+, with at least an easy draw for White) **19. ... N×f3 20. g×f3 Q×f3+ 21. R×f3 B×f3+ 22. Qg2 B×g2+ 23. K×g2 g5 24. Bd2 c6 25. a3 Bd4 26. e6 Rf6 27. Nd1 Rf×e6 28. R×e6 R×e6 29. Kf1 Kg7 30. c3 Be5 31. Kg2 B×h2 32. Ne3 Bf4 33. N×f5+ Kf6 34. B×f4 K×f5 35. Bb8 Kg4 36. B×a7 Re2+ 37. Kf1 R×b2 38. Bb8 Kf3 39. Kg1 g4 0–1** [*St. John Globe*, August 9, 1895]

479. Pollock–R. de Bury
Handicap Game, Saint John, July 1895
Remove Nb1

1. e4 e5 2. Nf3 Nc6 3. Bc4 Nf6 4. Ng5 d5 5. e×d5 N×d5 6. N×f7 K×f7 7. Qf3+ Ke8?! 7. ... Ke6 was safe. **8. B×d5 Qf6 9. Qd1 Bc5 10. 0–0

Rf8 **11. d4 B×d4 12. Qh5+ Qg6 13. Qh4 Q×c2**
13. ... Qg4! was strongest: 14. Q×g4 (14. Q×h7
R×f2) 14. ... B×g4 15. Be3 Rd8. **14. Bg5 h6**
15. Qh5+ g6 16. Q×h6 *(see diagram)*

After
16. Qh5×h6

16. ... B×b2?? Black had to start defending with
16. ... Qf5 17. Rae1 Ne7 18. Qh4 Qd7. **17. Qg7! e4?**
17. ... Ba3 was met by 18. Rae1! **18. B×c6+ b×c6**
19. Qe7 mate 1–0 [*Montreal Daily Herald*, July 20,
1895]

480. Pollock–C.F. Stubbs [C51]
Simultaneous Exhibition, Saint John, July 1895

1. e4 e5 2. Nf3 Nc6 3. Bc4 Bc5 4. b4 Bb6 5. b5
Na5 6. N×e5 N×c4 7. N×c4 B×f2+? Naive and
materialistic. 7. ... d5 or 7. ... Ne7 were more reasonable choices. **8. K×f2 Qf6+ 9. Qf3 Q×a1**
10. Nc3 Nf6 11. Re1 0–0 12. e5 Ng4+ 13. Q×g4
d5 14. Qg3 d×c4 15. Ba3 Q×e1+ 16. K×e1 Re8
17. Nd5 Re6 *(see diagram)*

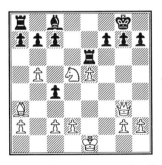

After
17. ... Re8–e6

18. Nf6+! Kh8 19. Bf8 g6 20. Qg5 1–0 [*St.*
John Globe, undated (*circa* 1895) cutting]

481. Pollock–A.L. Palmer [C44]
Simultaneous Exhibition (13 Boards), Saint John, July 1895

1. e4 e5 2. Nf3 Nc6 3. c3 d5 4. Bb5 Qd6
5. e×d5 Q×d5 6. Qa4 Bd7 7. 0–0 Bc5 8. d4 e×d4?

C.F. Stubbs (*Le Monde Illustré*, October 13, 1894,
page 286).

8. ... e4 9. Re1 Be7 10. c4 Qf5 was correct. **9. c×d4**
Bb6 10. Nc3 Qf5 11. Re1+ Nge7 12. d5 Nb8
13. d6! c×d6 14. B×d7+ 14. Bf4 was even
stronger. **14. ... Q×d7** *(see diagram)*

After
14. ... Qf5×d7

15. Nb5 15. R×e7+! K×e7 16. Nd5+ Kd8
17. N×b6 Q×a4 18. N×a4 gives White a winning
edge. **15. ... 0–0 16. Bf4 Nf5 17. Rad1 a6 18. Nc3**
Nc6 19. Nd5 Ba7 20. g4 Nfd4 21. N×d4 Q×g4+
22. Kh1 N×d4? 22. ... B×d4 was the correct move.
23. Nf6+! g×f6 24. Rg1 f5 25. R×g4+ f×g4
26. R×d4 1–0 [*Montreal Herald*, July 20, 1895]

482. Pollock–C.E. Harding [C39]
Simultaneous Exhibition, Saint John, July 1895

1. e4 e5 2. f4 e×f4 3. Nf3 g5 4. h4 g4 5. Ng5

d5 6. d4 h6 7. N×f7 K×f7 8. B×f4 Be7 9. Nc3 Nf6 10. e5 Nh5 11. Bd3 Rf8?! 11. ... B×h4+! 12. g3 N×g3 13. B×g3 B×g3+ 14. Ke2 Nc6 was very strong. **12. 0–0 Kg7 13. Qd2 N×f4 14. R×f4 R×f4 15. Q×f4 B×h4?!** 15. ... Nc6 16. Rf1 Qg8 17. Nb5 Be6 was more precise. **16. Rf1 Be6** (*see diagram*)

After 16. ... Bc8–e6

17. **N×d5!! B×d5 18. Qf5 Qg8** and White mates in three moves. **1–0** [*St. John Globe*, July 26, 1895]

483. C.E. Harding–Pollock [A80]
Offhand (?) Game, Saint John, July 1895

"Played during Pollock's recent trip to Saint John. An interesting example of this master's adventurous style of play." **1. Nf3 f5 2. d4 e6 3. Nc3 Nf6 4. Bf4 Bd6 5. Bg5 0–0 6. e3 b6 7. Bc4 Bb7 8. d5 e×d5?** 8. ... e5 was more natural and logical. **9. Bb3?** 9. B×f6! should have won for White since the White queen cannot be trapped: 9. ... Q×f6 10. B×d5+ B×d5 11. Q×d5+ Qf7 12. Q×a8 Nc6 13. Qb7 Qc4 14. 0–0–0! Rb8 15. Nd2. **9. ... c6** (*see diagram*) 9. ... Kh8 10. N×d5 Be7 11. N×e7 Q×e7 was more accurate.

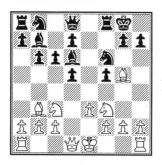

After 9. ... c7–c6

10. **N×d5!? c×d5 11. B×f6 Q×f6 12. B×d5+ B×d5 13. Q×d5+ Kh8 14. Q×a8 Nc6 15. Qb7 Rb8 16. Q×d7** 16. Qa6 was possible too: 16. ... b5 17. 0–0–0 Qf8 18. R×d6 Q×d6 19. Rd1 Qc5 20. c3. **16. ... Rd8 17. Q×d8+?** Unnecessary. 17. Qb7 Bb4+ (17. ... Rb8 18. Qa6 Q×b2 19. 0–0) 18. Ke2

was sufficient for White to keep a clear edge. **17. ... N×d8 18. 0–0** 18. 0–0–0 was preferable. **18. ... g5 19. Rad1 g4 20. Nh4 B×h2+ 21. K×h2 Q×h4+ 22. Kg1 Ne6 23. Rd6 Ng5 24. Rd8+ Kg7 25. Rd7+ Kh6 26. Rd4 Ne4 27. Rd5 g3 28. f×g3 N×g3 29. Rfd1 Qh1+ 30. Kf2 Ne4+ 31. Kf3 Qh5+ 32. Kf4 Qg5+ 33. Ke5 Nf6 34. Rd6 f4+ 35. Ke6 f×e3 36. Rf1 e2 37. R×f6+ Q×f6+ 38. K×f6 e1Q 0–1** [*Montreal Daily Herald*, July 21, 1895]

484. Pollock–J. de Soyres [C56]
Simultaneous Exhibition (7 Boards), Saint John, 15 July 1895

1. **e4 e5 2. Nf3 Nc6 3. Bc4 Nf6 4. d4 e×d4 5. 0–0 d6 6. Ng5 Ne5 7. Q×d4 h6 8. f4?** A tricky but flawed idea. 8. Nf3 was mandatory. **8. ... N×c4 9. Q×c4** (*see diagram*)

After 9. Qd4×c4

9. **... Qe7** After 9. ... h×g5! 10. f×g5 d5! 11. e×d5 Q×d5 12. Qe2+ Ne4 13. Nc3 Qd4+ 14. Kh1 Bf5!! 15. R×f5 0–0–0 16. N×e4 Q×e4 17. Qf1 Bd6 Black has a solid advantage. **10. Nc3?!** 10. Nf3 was again best. **10. ... d5! 11. Qd3 Bd7** 11. ... h×g5 was safe and sound: 12. e×d5 Ng4 13. h3 Qc5+ 14. Kh1 Nf2+ 15. R×f2 Q×f2 16. Bd2 g×f4 17. Re1+ Be7 18. d6 c×d6 19. Nd5 f3! 20. R×e7+ Kd8. **12. e5 h×g5 13. e×f6 Q×f6 14. f×g5 Bc5+ 15. Kh1 Qc6 16. Q×d5 0–0–0 17. Q×c6?!** 17. R×f7 was more accurate. **17. ... B×c6 18. Bf4 Rh4 19. Bg3 Rh3** Pretty, but nowhere near as effective as 19. ... Rd2! **20. Ne2** 20. Rad1 was a must. **20. ... Re8** 20. ... R×g3!? was powerful: 21. N×g3 (21. h×g3 Rh8 mate.) 21. ... Rd2 22. Rf3 B×f3 23. g×f3 R×c2. **21. Rae1! Bd6! 22. B×d6 c×d6** 22. ... Rhe3!? 23. R×f7 c×d6 24. Rf2 Bb5 25. c4 B×c4 26. Rc1 d5 27. Ng1 Kd7 was another possibility. **23. Kg1 Rhe3 24. Kf2 B×g2 25. K×g2 R×e2+ 26. R×e2 R×e2+ 27. Rf2 R×f2+ 28. K×f2 Kd7 29. h4 Ke6 30. h5?** With 30. Kf3 Kf5 31. c4, the game would have been drawn. **30. ... Kf5 0–1** [*St. John Globe*, August 16, 1895]

485. Pollock–W.G. Hanbury [C51]
Simultaneous Exhibition, Saint John, 16 July 1895

1. e4 e5 2. Nf3 Nc6 3. Bc4 Bc5 4. b4 Bb6 5. b5 Na5 6. N×e5 Qf6 7. B×f7+ *(see diagram)*

After
7. Bc4×f7+

7. ... Kd8? 7. ... Kf8 was forced. **8. d4 d6 9. B×g8 R×g8 10. Bg5 Q×g5 11. Nf7+ Ke7 12. N×g5** "Prof. Hanbury, who is well known to Saint John players, missed the train, and rather than miss the opportunity of meeting a chess master, walked up from Musquash, about 18 miles. We seldom hear of an equal display of chess enthusiasm." **1–0** [*St. John Globe*, October 4, 1895]

486. J. de Soyres–Pollock [C27]
Offhand Game, Saint John, 17 July 1895

1. e4 e5 2. Bc4 Nf6 3. Nc3 c6 4. d4 b5 5. Bb3 b4 6. Nce2 6. d×e5!? b×c3 7. e×f6 Bb4 8. b×c3 B×c3+ 9. Bd2 B×a1 10. Q×a1 Q×f6 11. Bc3 was

an interesting possibility. **6. ... N×e4 7. d×e5 Bc5 8. Nh3 d5! 9. 0–0** 9. Ng3 Qh4 10. Qf3 Bg4 11. Qf4 was much better. **9. ... B×h3 10. g×h3 Qh4 11. Be3 B×e3 12. f×e3 Qg5+ 13. Kh1 Q×e3** *(see diagram)*

After
13. ... Qg5×e3

14. B×d5 Nf2+! 14. ... c×d5 15. Q×d5 0–0 16. Q×a8 Q×e2 17. Rae1 Nf2+ 18. Kg2 is not very convincing. **15. R×f2 Q×f2 16. Bg2 0–0 17. Ng3 Na6 18. Ne4 Qf4 19. Qe2 Q×e5** 19. ... Nc7 was correct: 20. Nd6 f6! 21. B×c6 Rad8. **20. Q×a6 Qb5?** 20. ... Q×b2 was Black's only way to play for an advantage, although White's kingside push appears to be very threatening: 21. Rg1 Rfd8 (21. ... Q×c2 22. Nf6+ Kh8 23. Be4 Qc3 24. N×h7 Rfe8 25. Qe2 Re7 26. Ng5 g6 27. Qg4 Qc4 28. Qh4+ Kg7 29. Qh7+ Kf6 30. Qh4) 22. Ng5 Qf6 23. Be4 h6 24. Nf3 Rd6. **21. Q×b5 c×b5 22. Rg1 Rad8 23. Bf1 f5 24. Ng5 Rd5 25. Bd3 g6 26. h4 Re8 27. Nf3 Kg7 28. Kg2 h6 29. Re1 R×e1 30. N×e1 a6 31. Nf3 Kf6 32. Kg3 g5 33. h×g5+ h×g5 34. Kf2 g4 35. Nd2 ½–½** [*St. John Globe*, July 19, 1895]

Part Two, Section XII
(August 1895–September 2, 1895)

At Hastings

487. C. Schlechter–Pollock [C77]
Hastings Tournament, Round 1,
5 August 1895

**1. e4 e5 2. Nf3 Nc6 3. Bb5 a6 4. Ba4 Nf6
5. Nc3 Bb4** Schiffers: "The *Handbuch* considers that Black's best move here is 5. ... Be7, when White continues 6. 0–0 b5 7. Bb3 d6 8. a3 or 8. a4." **6. Nd5** Pollock: "6. B×c6 d×c6 7. N×e5 N×e4 8. N×e4 Qd4 9. 0–0 yields White a better attack." **6. ... Bc5** Schiffers: "After 6. ... Be7 would follow 7. d3 h6 with an even game. It would not be good to play 6. ... N×d5 7. e×d5 Ne7 8. c3 Ba5? 9. N×e5." Pollock: "Here Black ought to play 6. ... N×d5, followed by ...e4, or else simply 6. ... Be7 at once." **7. d3** Schiffers: "The *Handbuch* gives the continuation 7. c3 N×e4 8. d4 e×d4 9. c×d4 Bb4+ 10. Kf1 in White's favour." **7. ... h6 8. Be3 B×e3 9. f×e3** Schiffers: "Also good would have been 9. N×e3." **9. ... d6 10. 0–0 Be6?!** Pollock: "Rather risky, but Black had calculated the consequences." Schiffers: "10. ... Bg4 is better." **11. N×f6+ Q×f6** 11. ... g×f6?! 12. B×c6+ b×c6 13. Nh4 Rb8 14. b3 Rg8 15. Qh5 clearly favors White. **12. Nd4!** Pollock: "12. d4 was also strong." **12. ... Qg5** The only move. **13. N×c6** Schiffers: "After 13. N×e6 f×e6 (13. ... Q×e3+ 14. Kh1 f×e6 15. Qh5+) 14. B×c6+ b×c6 15. Qf3, White's game is preferable." **13. ... Q×e3+ 14. Kh1 Bd7** (*see diagram*) 14. ... b×c6 15. B×c6+ Ke7 16. B×a8 R×a8 17. Qe1 is not really a valid option.

15. N×e5? Pollock: "Probably best; 15. Nb4 B×a4 15. Nd5, however, was tempting." Schiffers: "And other moves still do not give White the superiority, e.g., 15. Nb4 B×a4 16. Nd5 Qc5, etc."

After
14. ... Be6–d7

Actually, 15. Nb4! was an excellent idea: 15. ... B×a4 16. Nd5 Qc5 17. b4 Qc6 18. Qg4! (18. R×f7!? is tempting but not quite decisive: 18. ... K×f7 19. Qh5+ g6 20. Qf3+ Kg8 21. Ne7+ [21. Rf1 Rh7 22. Nf6+ Kg7 23. N×h7 Qd7 24. Nf6 Qe6 25. Rf2 Bc6] 21. ... Kg7 22. N×c6 Rhf8 23. Qe3 B×c6) 18. ... g6 19. Rf2, with a winning advantage. **15. ... B×a4 16. N×f7 0–0!
17. Qh5 Be8 18. Rf3 B×f7** Pollock: "The 18th moves are forced on both sides, and the game now becomes even." The more materialistic 18. ... Qd2 was possible too although it looks very risky: 19. Raf1 B×f7 20. R×f7 Q×c2 21. Qd5 R×f7 22. R×f7 Kh7 23. h4 Q×b2 24. Qf5+ Kg8 25. R×c7 Rf8. **19. Q×f7+ R×f7 20. R×e3 Rf2
21. Rae1** Pollock: "If 21. Rc1 Raf8 22. Kg1 Rd2 23. Rf3 R×f3 24. g×f3 Kh7, with the better game." Schiffers: "21. Rc1 Raf8 followed by ...Rd2 and ...Rff2 would have been worse, as White would then get into difficulties, whereas now the draw is secure." **21. ... Raf8 22. Kg1 R×c2 23. R3e2 R×e2
24. R×e2 Rf4 25. Rc2 c6 26. Rc3 Kh7** Pollock: "Not 26. ... Kf7, on account of 27. Rb3 b5 28. Ra3, etc." **27. g3 Rf7 28. Kg2 Kg6 29. d4 Kf6 30. Kf2
Ke6+ 31. Ke3 Rf1 32. Rc2 Re1+ 33. Kd3 Rd1+
34. Ke3 Re1+** Pollock: "Both sides persisting in

426

their moves, the game was drawn by perpetual check." ½–½ [*tournament book*, pages 16–17; *Baltimore Sunday News*, August 31, 1895]

488. G. Marco–Pollock [C62]
Hastings Tournament, Round 2, 6 August 1895

1. e4 e5 2. Nf3 Nc6 3. Bb5 d6 4. d4 Bd7 5. Nc3 Teichmann: "At this juncture, 5. c3 is preferable; it has been played very successfully in this tournament against the Steinitz defence to the Ruy Lopez." **5. ... Nge7 6. d5** Teichmann: "We do not like this early advance of the d-pawn, but White seems to have had a preconceived plan of a very early attack." **6. ... Nb8 7. Ng5** Teichmann: "This in connection with the somewhat adventurous-looking sally of the queen next move forms a novel kind of attack in this opening, which even if not quite correct certainly makes the defence very difficult." **7. ... Ng6 8. Qh5 B×b5 9. N×b5 a6** *(see diagram)*

After
9. ... a7–a6

10. Nc3 10. f4 was a brutal attempt but with little effect: 10. ... a×b5 11. f5 Qf6 12. Ne6?! (12. f×g6 Q×g6 13. Q×g6 h×g6 14. 0–0 Be7 15. N×f7 Rf8) 12. ... f×e6 13. Bg5 Qf7 14. f×e6 Qg8 15. 0–0 Be7 16. B×e7 K×e7 17. Qg5+ Ke8 18. Rf7 Na6 19. Raf1 Nc5 20. R×c7 N×e6! 21. d×e6 Q×e6. **10. ... h6** Teichmann: "But this is a strange mistake, which loses the game very soon. The natural move 10. ... Nd7 and to f6 would have enabled Black to drive the White pieces back with a good development of his own. White could not, of course, capture the h7-pawn; e.g., 11. N×h7 Be7 and 12. ... Nf8, winning a piece." In fact, Pollock's last move was not a classic error as many initially thought. It is just as good as 12. ... Nd7 or 12. ... Be7. **11. Ne6! Qe7?** This was Pollock's first critical mistake. Instead, 11. ... Qc8! 12. 0–0 Nd7 offered Black decent chances. **12. 0–0 Kd7?** Teichmann: "A futile attempt to save the game. But 12. ... f×e6 13. Q×g6+ Qf7 14. Q×e6+ would also have left

him with a bad game and a pawn minus." In the circumstances, 12. ... Nf4 should have been tried: 13. N×f4 e×f4 14. B×f4 Nd7 even if White can force matters with 15. e5! d×e5 16. Rae1 g6 17. B×e5 N×e5 18. Q×e5 Q×e5 19. R×e5+ Kd7 20. Rfe1, with a clean extra pawn for White. **13. f4 e×f4 14. B×f4** 14. N×f4 N×f4 15. R×f4 g6 16. Qh3+ Kd8 17. Be3 Bg7 18. Raf1 was more natural. **14. ... N×f4?** 14. ... Kc8! was mandatory. **15. R×f4 f×e6** Teichmann: "If 15. ... f6, then 16. Ne2 and d4, to f5, or almost anything, all the Black pieces being blocked in." **15. ... g6 16. Qf3 Ke8 17. Rf1! f×e6 18. d×e6! Nc6 19. Nd5 Nd4 20. Qf2 leaves Black in a completely hopeless position as well. **16. Rf7 e5 17. Raf1 Kd8 18. R×e7 B×e7 19. Rf7 Bf6 20. Qf5 Re8 21. Ne2 Be7 22. Ng3 Nd7 23. Nh5 g6 24. Q×g6 Rf8 25. Ng7 R×f7 26. Q×f7** and Black resigned. Teichmann: "For he is quite helpless against the threatened Nf5 or Ne6+, if the Black knight should move." **1–0** [*tournament book*, pages 38–39]

489. Pollock–B. Vergani [B21]
Hastings Tournament, Round 3, 7 August 1895

1. e4 c5 2. d4 c×d4 3. Nf3 e5 von Bardeleben: "This move is not to be recommended, since it does not further Black's development. The book-move is 3. ... e6." **4. Bc4 h6** von Bardeleben: "Obviously with the intention of preparing ...Nf6 or ...Ne7, but the move 4. ... h6 loses too much time, and therefore gives the opponent the advantage of by far quicker development. Better would be 4. ... Be7 5. 0–0 d6, etc." **5. 0–0** 5. B×f7+ is attractive but not very efficient: 5. ... K×f7 6. N×e5+ Kf6 7. Q×d4 Qa5+ 8. Nc3 Q×e5 9. Nd5+ Ke6 10. Nf4+ (10. Qc4? Nc6! 11. Nc7+ Ke7 12. N×a8 Nf6 13. 0–0 b5) 10. ... Kf6 11. Nh5+ Ke6 12. Nf4+. **5. ... Nc6 6. c3 Bc5?!** 6. ... Qc7 7. Qb3 d6 was a good option. **7. b4 Bd6** von Bardeleben: "A weak move. Preferable would be 7. ... Bb6." **8. c×d4 e×d4 9. N×d4 Nge7** 9. ... Qf6!? could have launched some complications for White: 10. Nf5!? (10. Be3 Be5 11. Nb5 Nge7 12. f4 B×a1 13. Nc7+ Kd8 14. N×a8 Bd4; 10. Nf3! Q×a1 11. Q×d6 Qf6 12. Qd2 d6 13. Bb2 Qg6 14. Nh4 Qg4 15. Q×d6 Nge7, with unclear play.) 10. ... Be5 11. f4! Bc7 12. Qd2! d5 13. Bb2 Bb6+ 14. Kh1 d4. **10. N×c6 d×c6 11. Bb2** *(see diagram)*

11. ... 0–0? von Bardeleben: "Black would defend himself for a longer time by 11. ... Rg8, although Black's game at length could not be sufficiently

After
11. Bc1–b2

After
20. Ra1×c1

defended." **11. ... Ng6!** was an excellent defensive resource since 12. B×g7?! may be very risky. For instance, 12. ... Rg8 13. e5! (13. Bb2? B×h2+ 14. K×h2 Qh4+ 15. Kg1 Nf4 and Black wins) 13. ... B×e5 14. B×e5 N×e5 15. Na3 Bg4 16. Q×d8+ K×d8! (16. ... R×d8? 17. Rfe1) 17. Rfe1 Nf3+! 18. g×f3 Bh3+. **12. Qd4! B×h2+ 13. K×h2 Q×d4 14. B×d4 Rd8 15. Rd1 c5 16. b×c5 Nc6 17. Bd5 Nb4 18. Nc3 N×d5 19. e×d5 Bd7 20. Rab1 Bc8 21. Re1 Kf8 22. d6 Rd7 23. Nd5 1–0** [*tournament book*, page 46]

490. H.N. Pillsbury–Pollock [C83]
Hastings Tournament, Round 4,
9 August 1895

1. e4 e5 2. Nf3 Nc6 3. Bb5 a6 4. Ba4 Nf6 5. 0–0 N×e4 6. d4 b5 7. Bb3 d5 8. d×e5 Be6 9. c3 Be7 10. Re1 0–0 11. Nd4 N×d4 Tinsley: "With slight transpositions we arrive here at precisely the same position and by the same moves as those made in the memorable games by Tarrasch v. Zukertort, 1887, and Gunsberg, 1890, in Frankfurt and Manchester respectively. If now 11. ... Qd7 12. N×e6 and wins a piece and the game, for whether 12. ... Q×e6 or 12. ... f×e6, 13. R×e4, wins. 12. ... N×e5 is also out of question, as White replies 13. f3." **12. c×d4 c6** Tinsley: "A bolder course is 12. ... c5, but the text move strengthens Black's pawn position." **13. f3 Ng5 14. Nc3** Tinsley: "Attempts to win the knight by 14. h4 would with an undeveloped queenside probably prove dangerous, but it is noticeable that h4 is possible at this stage." **14. ... Bf5 15. g4 Bc8 16. f4 b4 17. Na4 Ne4 18. f5 Bg5 19. Qf3 B×c1** 19. ... h5 was probably met by 20. R×e4 d×e4 21. Q×e4 Ra7 22. e6 Kh8 23. Nc5. **20. Ra×c1** (*see diagram*)

20. ... Qh4 Tinsley: "The game suddenly reaches a critical point. Except for the presence of the Black queen White might safely dispose of the strongly posted knight. But 21. R×e4 d×e4 22. Q×e4 h5, would break up White's game on the

kingside completely." **21. Re2** 21. R×e4!? d×e4 22. Q×e4 h5 23. e6 was very appealing: 23. ... f×e6 (23. ... Q×g4+? 24. Q×g4 h×g4 25. R×c6 f×e6 26. f×e6 leaves Black tied down completely.) 24. Nb6 Rb8 25. N×c8 Rf×c8 26. B×e6+ Kh8 27. B×c8 R×c8 28. b3 Q×g4+ 29. Q×g4 h×g4 30. Kg2 Rd8 31. R×c6 R×d4 32. R×a6. **21. ... Ng5 22. Qg3** Tinsley: "The consequences are evidently foreseen. They give Black a momentary advantage." **22. ... Q×g3+ 23. h×g3 Nf3+ 24. Kf2 N×d4 25. Rd2 N×b3 26. a×b3** Tinsley: "And Black is a pawn to the good in the end game. It will be seen however that White's turn is yet to come, and that he must speedily regain lost material." **26. ... Bb7** Tinsley: "Not 26. ... Bd7, because of 27. Nb6, regaining at least a pawn." **27. Nc5 Bc8 28. Ke3 h5 29. Kf4 g6 30. Kg5** Tinsley: "We assume that White, having established his position, and being able pro tem. to keep Black confined closely, is playing for a mating position with his rooks. Supposing, for instance, Black plays here 31. ... h×g4, then 32. f6, followed soon by Rh2." **30. ... Kg7?!** 30. ... Re8 was probably best: 31. Re2 Ra7 32. Nd3 a5 33. R×c6 Ba6 34. Rd2 h×g4 35. f×g6 B×d3 36. R×d3 R×e5+. **31. f6+ Kh7 32. Nd3?!** 32. e6! f×e6 33. Re2 was winning. **32. ... B×g4 33. R×c6 Rfe8 34. Rc7 Kg8 35. Kh6 Bf3 36. Re7 Kf8 37. R×e8+ R×e8 38. Kg5 Be4 39. Kf4** (*see diagram*)

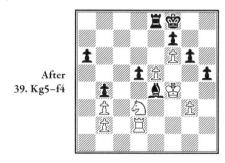

After
39. Kg5–f4

39. ... Rc8 Tinsley: "Another critical point of a very interesting game is here reached. Black scarcely rises to the occasion. He might as well have gone on with 39. ... a5 or perhaps better; 39. ... g5+ 40. K×g5 (best) 40. ... B×d3 41. R×d3 R×e5+ 42. Kf4 Re6 43. Kg5 Re5+, and would apparently either draw or win." **40. N×b4 Rc5 41. N×a6 Rb5 42. Ke3** Tinsley: "The charming audacity of this bold bid for a win is very noticeable. It is probably safe to say that there is no other way to win and that this is the only chance left." 42. Rd4! was correct: 42. ... Bg2 43. Ra4 Kg8 44. Rb4 R×b4+ 45. N×b4. **42. ... R×b3+ 43. Kd4 R×g3 44. Nc5** Tinsley: "Necessary to prevent Black winning by giving up a piece by ...Rd3+ etc., later; also to capture the bishop presently, and furthermore to guard the outlet of the Black king at his d7. See his 46th move. ...Rb3 is also now guarded against." **44. ... h4** 44. ... Bg2!? was better but White has some resources of his own: 45. e6! f×e6 46. Nd7+ Kf7 47. Rf2 Bf3 48. b4 g5 49. b5 g4 50. b6 Rg1 51. Rb2. **45. b4 h3??** 45. ... Bg2 would have maintained the balance. **46. Ra2 Kg8 47. Ra8+ Kh7 48. e6! f×e6 49. N×e4 d×e4 50. f7 Rf3 51. f8Q R×f8 52. R×f8 g5 53. K×e4 g4 54. Rf1 e5 55. b5 g3 56. Rh1 1–0** Tinsley: "I have found this game, and especially the ending, exceptionally difficult. One gains the impression gradually as it proceeds that Black should have won, but where is not easy to detect in a brief space of time. Of its absorbing interest after about move 26 there can be no question. Those addicted to analyses will here find a rare opportunity" [*tournament book*, pages 62–64].

491. Pollock–R. Teichmann [C44]
Hastings Tournament, Round 5,
10 August 1895

1. e4 e5 2. Nf3 Nc6 3. c3 d5 4. Bb5 d×e4 Schiffers: "Here the move recommended by Steinitz, 4. ... f6, is more frequently played or 4. ... Nge7, followed by ...f6 if 5. Qa4." **5. N×e5 Qd5 6. Qa4 Nge7 7. f4** Schiffers: "To 7. N×c6 the correct answer would be 7. ... N×c6 (and not 7. ... b×c6 8. Be2)." **7. ... e×f3 8. N×f3 Be6** Schiffers: "8. ... Bd7 can be played here; after 8. ... a6 might follow 9. Be2, but not 9. Bc4 Qh5, and Black threatening ...b5 gains time. If 9. ... Qe4+?, then 10. Kf2 Be6 11. d3, with a good game." **9. 0-0 a6 10. c4** 10. Na3! 0-0-0 11. Bc4 was superior. **10. ... Qd8?!** 10. ... Qd3! 11. Re1 0-0-0 was stronger. **11. B×c6+ N×c6 12. d4 Bd7 13. Qb3 Be7 14. d5!** Schiffers: "Here and in the succeeding move White can apparently take the b-pawn with impunity." In truth,

14. Q×b7?! Rb8 15. Q×a6 Rb6 16. Qa4 N×d4 was not necessary. **14. ... Na7 15. Be3 b6 16. Nc3 0-0 17. Rae1 Nc8 18. Bd4 Nd6 19. Ne5 Be8 20. Nc6 B×c6 21. d×c6 Nf5 22. Nd5** Schiffers: "Here White could play 22. B×b6 although the c6-pawn cannot be maintained, still White obtains the attack afterwards by Nd5"; 22. B×b6!? could have been met by 22. ... Rb8! 23. Nd5! R×b6 24. N×b6 Bc5+ 25. Kh1 Nd4 26. Qc3 c×b6 27. b4 B×b4 28. Q×b4 Nc2 29. Qe7 N×e1 30. R×e1 g6. **22. ... N×d4 23. N×e7+ Kh8** 23. ... Q×e7?! seems uncomfortable for Black after 24. R×e7 N×b3 25. a×b3 Rac8 26. Rd7 f6 27. Re1 Rf7 28. Ree7 R×e7 29. R×e7 Kf8 30. Rd7. **24. Qc3 Qd6 25. Qd3** Schiffers: "Defending the c6-pawn." **25. ... Rae8** *(see diagram)*

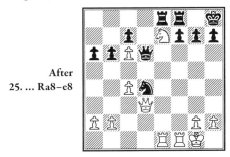

After
25. ... Ra8–e8

26. R×f7!? Schiffers: "Prettily conceived." **26. ... Ne2+** If 26. ... R×f7 27. Ng6+ h×g6 28. R×e8+ Rf8! (28. ... Kh7 29. Qh3 mate.) 29. R×f8+ Q×f8 30. Q×d4, with a pawn ahead. 26. ... Qc5!? was an interesting (and simpler) defense: 27. R×f8+ R×f8 28. Kh1 N×c6. **27. Q×e2 R×f7 28. Ng6+ h×g6 29. Q×e8+ Rf8 30. Qd7 Qc5+ 31. Kh1 Q×c4 32. h3** Schiffers: "Now 32. ... Rf1+ 33. R×f1 Q×f1+ 34. Kh2 Qf4+ is drawn." ½–½ [*tournament book*, pages 82–83]

492. W. Steinitz–Pollock [C53]
Hastings Tournament, Round 6,
12 August 1895

Pollock (*Baltimore Sunday News*, September 3, 1895): "Steinitz's defeat at the hands of Pollock was received with tremendous applause. The game, which I append, was a very fine one, and of course the checking of a victorious career lends fresh interest to the race. It was the first game ever between the two masters. By the bye, rightly or wrongly, a game won against any of the favourites in this tournament inevitably evokes loud applause, which is spontaneous and quite irrepressible." **1. e4 e5 2. Nf3 Nc6 3. Bc4 Bc5 4. c3** Pollock: "A favourite opening with Mr. Steinitz in this tournament, in which he has beautifully demonstrated the efficiency of some new ideas contained in the last section of *The Modern Chess Instructor*." **4. ... Qe7** *(see diagram)* Pollock: "Strangely enough, this valid old defence of the days of the Berlin 'Pleiades' has escaped all notice in the work referred to. A little story comes in here: previous to the championship match between Steinitz and Lasker, at the request of the latter I played the defence to the Giuoco in a few offhand games with him at the Manhattan Chess Club. I adopted this old defence without success, although Lasker admitted it was new to him. But I told him that Steinitz would play it against him and beat him if he did not play the attack differently. (It is no easy matter to reply correctly to Lasker's bad moves.) Lasker good humoredly suggested that we submit the theoretical question to Showalter. However he did *not* adopt this attack against Steinitz. The points of the defence are well shown in the present game." Pillsbury: "Perhaps not as good as ...Nf6, but favoured by Dr. Pollock."

After
4. ... Qd8–e7

5. d4 Bb6 6. a4 Pillsbury: "Advances of this character so early seem premature, and only weaken the position later on. Although this includes a trap—viz. if in answer 6. ... d6 7. a5, winning two pieces for rook and pawn, yet it is no exception to the foregoing rule. Any developing move, as 6. 0–0, would be better." **6. ... a5 7. 0–0 d6 8. d5** Pollock: "This is, as usual, a questionable advance." Pillsbury: "Rather than this advance, which allows Black later on to open the game at his leisure on the king's side, the lesser evil of the two, 8. h3, would be preferable. Black could form no immediate assault upon this point, and his somewhat weakened queen's wing would scarcely permit him to castle on that side, with intent of a pawn attack on the White king." **8. ... Nd8 9. Bd3 Nf6** Pollock: "White's ninth move was in order to prevent ...f5. Without doubt Black should now have played for the advance by ...g6." Pillsbury: "The position would

permit of a direct assault upon the castled king, should Black desire, by 9. ... f5, followed soon by ...g5 and ...h5. In answer, 10. Nh4 would be disastrous by 10. ... g5 11. Qh5+ Nf7 12. Nf3 Bd7(!), followed by ...0–0–0, now permissible owing to the displacement of the White queen." **10. Na3 c6 11. Nc4 Bc7 12. Ne3 Nh5** Pollock: "If 12. ... c×d5, 13. Bb5+ followed by N×d5. Nor can Black well castle, on account of Nh4 threatening to establish a knight at f5." **13. g3** 13. N×e5! Nf4 14. N5c4 was in White's favor. **13. ... g6 14. b4** Pollock: "Intending no doubt 15. d×c6 b×c6 16. b5, when it would be difficult to prevent the posting of the White knight at d5." **14. ... f5** Pollock: "It is necessary for Black to attack, but the situation is a critical one." **15. Ng2** Pollock: "15. d×c6 might have been tried as an alternative to prevent ...f4, for if then 15. ... f4, 16. c×b7, followed by Bb5+ and Nd5." **15. ... c×d5 16. e×d5** Pollock: "Preferable certainly seems 16. Bb5+ and if 16. ... Bd7 17. e×f5 with the threat N×e5 or Bg5 presently." **16. ... Nf7 17. Re1 0–0** Pollock: "Black has now an excellent position." Pillsbury: "With a fine position for attack; a direct evidence of the weakness of White's 8th move." **18. Nd4 Qf6 19. Nb5 Bb6 20. b×a5** Pillsbury: "Only still further weakening his pawns." **20. ... B×a5 21. Be2 Ng7 22. Bd2 Bd7 23. Rf1 Rac8 24. c4 Bb6 25. Be3** Pillsbury: "25. Qb3 with intent to force matters on the queenside, seems better." **25. ... B×e3 26. f×e3 Ng5** Pollock: "Of course an attack by ...g5 might be in the cards, but Black prefers the safer plan of ...Ne4 and ...Nc5, thus first securing the queenside." **27. Nc3** *(see diagram)* Pollock: "Bad, as yielding the opponent a splendid opportunity for a kingside assault." Pillsbury: "A violation of an old-time principle 'that the pieces should not be left loose and unguarded.' Black takes advantage of this misplay with great precision, and from this point obtains a winning advantage. White should have played 27. Qc2 and if 27. ... Ne4, 28. Nc3 Nc5 39. a5 with a fair prospect of attack on the weak b-pawn."

After
27. Nb5–c3

27. ... **f4! 28. Qc2** Pollock: "If 28. e×f4, 28. ... e×f4 attacking the knight." **28. ... f3 29. Nh4** Pollock: "If the bishop moves, 29. ... Nh3+ followed by 30. ... f×g2+." **29. ... Nf5** Pillsbury: "Perhaps 29. ... Bh3 was quicker, for 30. Rf2 Bg2 wins without much trouble." **30. R×f3** Pollock: "If 30. N×f5 B×f5 31. Bd3 f2+ etc." **30. ... N×f3+ 31. N×f3 N×e3** 31. ... e4 32. Nd2 N×e3 33. Nd×e4 N×c2 34. N×f6+ R×f6 35. Ra2 Nd4 was just as effective. **32. Qb1 N×c4 33. Ne4 Qd8 34. Q×b7 Na5?!** 34. ... Bg4 was more accurate. **35. Qb4 Bg4 36. Rf1 Bh3 37. Re1 Rb8?!** 37. ... Rc2 38. Q×d6 Q×d6 39. N×d6 R×e2 40. R×e2 R×f3 was the best way forward. **38. Q×d6 Q×d6 39. N×d6 Rb2 40. Bd1** 40. Bf1 B×f1 41. R×f1 Rb6 42. Ne4 offered stronger resistance. **40. ... Rg2+ 41. Kh1** 41. Kf1 is met by 41. ... Nb3 42. Ne4 Nd4 43. Nf2 N×f3 44. N×h3 R×h2. **41. ... Rf2 42. Ne4 R2×f3 43. B×f3 R×f3 44. d6 Rf1+ 45. R×f1 B×f1 46. Kg1 Bd3** Pollock: "Not 46. ... Bh3, on account of 47. g4." **47. Nf6+ Kf7 48. N×h7 Ke6 49. Kf2 K×d6 50. Ke3 Bc2 51. h4 Nc4+ 52. Ke2 Kd5 53. g4 Kd4** Pollock: "The ending is a good one for the 'gallery,' either the king or the pawn must advance with immediate effect." **54. Nf8 Bd3+ 55. Ke1 Ke3 56. h5 g×h5** Pollock: "Unnecessary, Black has a mate in four moves here." 56. ... Be2 57. Ne6 Na3 58. h×g6 Nc2 mate. **57. g×h5 Be2 58. Nd7 Na3 0–1** Pillsbury: "Rather an amusing finish to a very interesting game" [*tournament book*, pages 93–94; *Baltimore Sunday News*, September 8, 1895; *BCM*, September 1895, pages 396–397].

493. Pollock–Em. Lasker [C51]
Hastings Tournament, Round 7,
13 August 1895

1. **e4 e5 2. Nf3 Nc6 3. Bc4 Bc5 4. b4 Bb6** Tarrasch: "It is noteworthy that Lasker usually declines the Evans Gambit, although he has declared that he knows a winning defence." **5. c3 d6 6. a4 a6 7. a5 Ba7 8. b5?!** 8. d3 was a calmer approach. **8. ... a×b5 9. B×b5 Nf6** Tarrasch: "9. ... Nge7 seems preferable." **10. a6** Tarrasch: "Instead of developing, White makes premature attempts at attack, which finally only facilitate and hasten the development of his opponent." **10. ... 0–0** Tarrasch: "10. ... N×e4 would be bad, on account of 11. Qa4 Nc5 12. a×b7." **11. d3 Ne7 12. a×b7 B×b7 13. Na3** *(see diagram)* Tarrasch: "...B×f2+ was threatened."

13. ... d5! Tarrasch: "Black is so far advanced in development that he can at once begin the attack." **14. 0–0 Ng6 15. e×d5 N×d5 16. Qe1** Tarrasch:

"All of White's pieces are in bad positions, with the exception of the king's knight at f3. White's game is thus no longer capable even of defence." **16. ... Qf6 17. Bg5** Tarrasch: "With this and the mistake immediately following the bishop gets also exposed. It would have been better to interrupt the file of the adverse queen's bishop with Ng5 and Ne4." **17. ... Qf5 18. Nc2 N×c3** 18. ... Ndf4! was even stronger. For example, 19. B×f4 N×f4 20. Ne3 B×e3 21. f×e3 N×g2 22. K×g2 R×a1 23. Q×a1 Qg4+. **19. R×a7** Tarrasch: "He may well despair." 19. Q×c3 B×f3 20. Qd2 Qg4 21. Ne1 was White's last attempt. **19. ... B×f3 20. Ne3** Tarrasch: "After 20. Be3, 20. ... Qg4 wins." **20. ... Q×g5 21. R×a8 R×a8** In this position, even a direct 21. ... Nf4 wins. **22. Q×c3 Nf4 23. Ra1 Ne2+ 0–1** [*tournament book*, page 115]

494. A. Albin–Pollock [C50]
Hastings Tournament, Round 8,
14 August 1895

1. **e4 e5 2. Nf3 Nc6 3. Bc4 Nf6 4. d3 Bc5 5. Nc3 d6 6. Bg5** Teichmann: "To pin the knights with the bishops is, in Giuoco Piano as a rule, bad, and this is proved again in this game." **6. ... h6 7. Be3 Bb6 8. a3** Teichmann: "Another weak move, and loss of time." **8. ... Be6 9. B×e6** Teichmann: "These ill-judged exchanges seem to be the consequence of his last bad move, as he could not now retire his bishop to b3." **9. ... f×e6 10. B×b6 a×b6 11. 0–0 0–0 12. h3** *(see diagram)*

12. ... Qe8! Teichmann: "A very good move, bringing the queen into action, and enabling him to play ...Nf6–Nh5 and ...Nh5–Nf4." **13. Nh2 Nh5 14. Kh1?!** 14. Nb5 Rc8 15. g3 Nd4 16. N×d4 e×d4 17. Qe2 was much better. **14. ... Nd4! 15. Ne2 N×e2 16. Q×e2 Nf4 17. Qe3 Qg6 18. Qg3** Teichmann: "A decisive mistake, which ought to lose the game. But there was no more a defence against Black's powerful attack." **18. ... Q×g3 19. f×g3 Ne2 20. R×f8+ R×f8 21. Nf1** Teichmann: "If 21. g4, then 21. ... Rf2 threatening ...Nf4, and winning at least a pawn." White had to try 21. Nf3 N×g3+ 22. Kh2 Ne2 23. a4. **21. ... R×f1+** Teichmann: "Black is too eager to simplify the game and reduce it to what he most likely thought an easily won pawn ending. His two doubled pawns on the queenside, however, ought to have given him some apprehensions about the possibility of winning. 21. ... Nd4, followed by ...Rf2 would have given Black a won game in a few moves." Indeed, 21. ... Nd4 or 21. ... Rf2 were stronger options. **22. R×f1 N×g3+ 23. Kg1 N×f1 24. K×f1 Kf7 25. Kf2 Ke7 26. Ke3 Kd7 27. Kf3 Kc6 28. Ke2 Kc5 29. Kd2 d5 30. Ke3 b5** (see diagram)

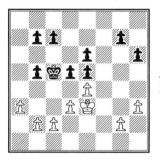

After
30. ... b6–b5

31. e×d5 Teichmann: "Suicidal; he could have forced the draw at once with 31. b4+ after which we fail to find a winning continuation for Black; e.g., 31. ... Kd6 32. Ke2 b6 33. Ke3 c5 34. Ke2 c4 35. Ke3. White only moves his king, and never exchanges any pawns; we cannot see how Black can do anything. Clearly he gains nothing by playing the king over to the other side, as the White king is also free, and will always be able to keep the opposition or to block the pawns. An interesting question arises whether Black, without the mistake on the 30th move, could have won this ending. After a very careful analysis of the position I have come to the conclusion that, in spite of being a pawn to the good and having the king well in play, Black cannot force a win against the best defence, as the two doubled pawns can never be dissolved. The following variation shows the resources of the attack and the defence: 30. ... Kb5 31. b3 Kc5 32. c3 (best) b5 33. b4+ (best; Black threatened 34. ... d4+ 35. Kd2 d×c3+ 36. K×c3 b4+ 37. a×b4 Kb5, winning.) 33. ... Kd6 34. Kf3 b6 35. Ke3 c5 36. Ke2 c4 37. Kd2 d4 38. Kc2, and Black cannot win, because, as soon as he plays his king over to the kingside, White would force a passed pawn on the other, and win." **31. ... e×d5 32. d4+** 32. c3 was only a temporary solution: 32. ... Kd6 33. Kf3 Ke6 34. g3 c5 35. g4 g5 36. Ke3 d4+ 37. Ke4 Kd6 38. c×d4 e×d4 39. b3 b6 40. Kf3 c4 and wins. **32. ... e×d4+ 33. Kd3 Kd6 34. K×d4 c5+ 35. Kd3 Ke5 36. Ke3 d4+ 37. Kf3 c4 38. g3 g5 39. g4 b6 40. c3 Kd5 41. c×d4 K×d4 42. Ke2 c3 43. b×c3+ K×c3 44. Ke3 Kb3 45. Ke4 K×a3 46. Kf5 b4 47. Kg6 b3 48. K×h6 b2 49. K×g5 b1Q 0–1** [*tournament book*, pages 135–137]

495. C. von Bardeleben–Pollock [A43] Hastings Tournament, Round 9, 16 August 1895

1. d4 c5 Blackburne: "This bizarre defence is not to be commended." **2. d5 g6 3. e4 Bg7 4. Bd3 Na6** Blackburne: "One of Pollock's favourite manoeuvres; if now 5. B×a6, then 5. ... Qa5+ and 6. ... Q×a6." **5. a3 Nc7 6. Ne2 d6 7. 0–0 Nh6** The direct 7. ... b5 was fine for Black. **8. f3 e6** Blackburne: "Black's scheme is evidently to advance the pawns on the queenside; therefore it would, perhaps, have been advisable to play ...b5 before attempting to break up the centre." **9. c4** (see diagram)

After
9. c2–c4

9. ... b5!? A highly provocative game by Pollock here, reminiscent of the more modern Blumenfeld/Volga/Benko themes. 9. ... f5!? was quite an appealing choice as well. **10. c×b5 e×d5 11. e×d5 Bb7 12. Bc4 Nf5 13. Nbc3 0–0 14. Qd3 Qe7** Blackburne: "Lost time; 14. ... Re8 is better." **15. Bd2 Rfe8 16. Rae1 Qh4!?** Poorly conceived after excellent if unorthodox opening play. 16. ... Ne3?! 17. Nf4 Bd4 18. Kh1 is uncomfortable for Black; Instead, 16. ... Qd7!? 17. Ne4 Nd4 18. N×d4 c×d4 19. Bf4 N×d5 offered some interesting complications. **17. Ne4! h6 18. Bc3 Nd4?** 18. ... B×c3 was forced, but it leaves White in a dominating position: 19. b×c3 Rad8 20. g3 Qe7 21. Nf4. **19. N×d4 c×d4 20. g3** Blackburne: "He could play 20. B×d4 at once with perfect safety; for instance, 20. ... f5 21. B×g7 f×e4 22. Qc3, and White has two pawns ahead." **20. ... Qh5 21. B×d4 N×d5** Blackburne: "Leading to still further loss, but his game is hopelessly gone." **22. B×g7 K×g7 23. N×d6 R×e1 24. R×e1 Nb6 25. Qd4+ Kh7 26. Ne8 1–0** [*tournament book*, pages 148–149]

496. Pollock–D.M. Janowski [C44]
Hastings Tournament, Round 10, 17 August 1895

1. e4 e5 2. Nf3 Nc6 3. c3 Nf6 von Bardeleben: "I prefer the usual defence, 3. ... d5." **4. d4 N×e4 5. d5 Nb8 6. Bd3 Nc5 7. N×e5 N×d3+ 8. N×d3 Be7 9. 0–0 d6 10. c4** von Bardeleben: "White would have a very good game if he played 10. Qf3 in order to prevent Black developing the queen's bishop." **10. ... 0–0** von Bardeleben: "10. ... Bf5 would be better." **11. Nc3** von Bardeleben: "Now again White should have played 11. Qf3." **11. ... Bf5** von Bardeleben: "After this move has been made, the game is equalised." **12. Qf3** von Bardeleben: "Too late (!)." **12. ... Bg6 13. Bf4 Nd7 14. Rfe1 Bf6 15. Rac1 B×c3 16. R×c3 Qf6 17. Qe3 h6 18. Bg3 Rae8** von Bardeleben: "White threatened to play 19. Qe7, and therefore Black rightly gives two rooks for the queen." **19. Q×e8 R×e8 20. R×e8+ Kh7 21. Re3 Qd4 22. h3 h5 23. Ne1 Be4 24. Nf3 B×f3 25. R×f3 Nf6 26. Rfd3 Qe4 27. f3 Qe2 28. Rb3 g5 29. Rd4 h4 30. Bf2** (*see diagram*)

After
30. Bg3–f2

30. ... Nh5 30. ... b6! first was stronger. **31. Re4 Qd2 32. R×b7** von Bardeleben: "This looks very dangerous, but Black's attack is not so strong as it seems to be." **32. ... Qc1+ 33. Kh2 Qf1 34. Bg1 Ng3 35. Rg4 Kg6** 35. ... Q×c4 could have secured

Black an immediate draw. **36. R×c7?** 36. f4! was mandatory to prevent Black's next play. **36. ... f5! 37. Rd4 Ne2 38. Be3 f4?** von Bardeleben: "If Black takes the rook with the knight, the White pawns become very strong, and Black would have no better chance than after the line adopted." **38. ... Qe1! 39. Rd3 Qg3+ 40. Kh1 g4** gave Black serious winning chances. **39. Re4** von Bardeleben: "Very cleverly played. Of course now Black cannot capture the bishop because of 40. Re6+, and mate on the next move." **39. ... Qb1** von Bardeleben: "The only way to defend the king against the threatening 40. Re6+ Kh7 41. Rh7 mate." **40. Re6+ Kh5 41. Bf2** 41. Rc8 Q×b2 42. Bd4!! would have assured Pollock a splendid win: 42. ... Q×d4 43. R×e2 Kg6 44. Re6+ Kf7 45. Rc7+ Kf8 46. R×d6 Ke8 47. Rdd7 Qf2 48. Re7+ Kd8 49. Rcd7+ Kc8 50. R×a7. **41. ... Ng3 42. Be1?** White could have still pressed on with 42. Re1 Q×b2 43. Rh7+ Kg6 44. Rd7. **42. ... Nf1+ 43. Kg1 Ne3 44. Kh2 Nf1+ 45. Kg1 Ne3 46. Kh2 ½–½** [*tournament book*, pages 159–160]

497. A. Burn–Pollock [A43]
Hastings Tournament, Round 11, 19 August 1895

1. d4 c5 Blackburne: "A favourite defence of Pollock's, and one which he occasionally plays in tournaments, but it is of doubtful merit." **2. d5** Blackburne: "2. e4 turning it into an old form of the 'Sicilian,' may also be played." **2. ... g6 3. e4 Bg7 4. f4 Na6 5. Nf3** Blackburne: "If 5. B×a6, then 5. ... Qa5+ and 6. ... Q×a6." **5. ... Nc7 6. c4 d6 7. Bd3 e6 8. 0–0 e×d5 9. c×d5 Nf6 10. Nc3 0–0 11. Qc2 Re8 12. Bd2 Bd7** An immediate 12. ... b5!? was interesting as well: 13. N×b5 (13. Rfe1 c4 14. Bf1 a6) 13. ... N×b5 14. B×b5 R×e4 15. Ng5 Re7 16. Bc3 h6 17. Nf3 Bf5. **13. Rae1 b5!** Blackburne: "A good move if properly followed up." **14. Qb1** Blackburne: "This, or 14. b3, appears the only move to avoid the loss of a pawn." **14. ... b4** Blackburne: "Instead of this, he certainly ought to have played 14. ... c4, followed by ...b4 and ...a5. His only hope was in breaking through with the pawns on the queenside." **15. Nd1 a5 16. Nf2 Nb5** Blackburne: "16. ... Bb5, threatening ...c4, was more forcing." **17. Bc1 Rc8** Blackburne: "Losing too much time with this rook; rather have gone on with 17. ... a4." **18. Nd2 Nd4 19. Nc4 Bb5 20. Bd2 Ra8** 20. ... a4 21. f5 Rc7 was somewhat more precise. **21. Qd1 Ra7 22. b3 a4! 23. Be3** 23. ... Nh5! was an excellent try. **24. B×d4**

c×d4 25. a×b3 B×c4 26. B×c4 Ra2 27. Qf3 Blackburne: "27. Q×d4 would be answered by 27. ... Ng4, followed by ...N×f2, then ...Qb6 and ...Bd4, winning." **27. ... Nd7 28. Nd3 Qb6 29. e5 Nf8** (*see diagram*) 29. ... f5 throws Black into a completely passive position as well: 30. e×f6 R×e1 31. R×e1 N×f6 32. Qh3 h6 33. Qe6+ Kh7 34. f5 g5 35. Qf7 Ra7 36. Qg6+ Kg8 37. h3 Rf7 38. Re6 Qd8 (38. ... Qb8 39. Ne5! d×e5 40. d6 Kf8 41. Re7).

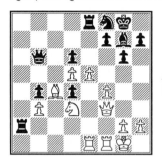

After
29. ... Nd7–f8

30. f5! Blackburne: "A very fine move, to which there is no satisfactory reply." **30. ... d×e5 31. d6 Kh8 32. f6** Blackburne: "32. f×g6 was equally good." Indeed, especially if 32. ... f6 was to be met by 33. N×e5! R×e5 (33. ... f×e5 34. Qf7) 34. R×e5. **32. ... Bh6 33. R×e5 Be3+ 34. Kh1 Rea8 35. Re7 R8a5 36. R×f7 Q×d6 37. Rg7 h5 38. Qb7 1–0** [*tournament book*, pages 175–176]

498. J. Mason–Pollock [C62]
Hastings Tournament, Round 12,
20 August 1895

1. e4 e5 2. Nf3 Nc6 3. Bb5 d6 4. Nc3 Bd7 Schiffers: "This move seems futile, as doubling of pawns on the c-file is not dangerous for Black. The correct move is 4. ... Nf6, and after 5. d4 Nd7 (Chigorin's Defence)." **5. d3** Schiffers: "The natural continuation here would be 5. 0–0 in conjunction with 6. d4." **5. ... Nf6 6. Bg5 Be7 7. Qd2 h6 8. Be3 a6** Schiffers: "Here Black might advantageously play 8. ... Ng4, in order to exchange the knight for the bishop on e3." **9. Ba4 b5 10. Bb3 Na5 11. 0–0 N×b3 12. a×b3 c6 13. Ne2 Nh7 14. Ng3 Ng5 15. Ne1 f6 16. f4 Nf7 17. f5 d5 18. Qe2 d4 19. Bd2 0–0** Schiffers: "A very dangerous castling position; Black ought to have made earlier preparation to move ...c5, in order to ease his game, which is extremely hampered at present." **20. Nf3 Kh7?!** 20. ... a5 21. Nh4 Nh8 22. Qg4 g5 23. Nf3 Be8 was more accurate. **21. Nh4 Nh8 22. Nh5 Rg8 23. Kh1 Qe8 24. Ng3 Qf7 25. Qg4 Bf8** (*see diagram*)

After
25. ... Be7–f8

26. Ng6 Bc8 Schiffers: "Clearly, if 26. ... N×g6, then 27. f×g6+ Q×g6 and Black loses the bishop on d7." **27. N×f8+ Q×f8 28. Nh5 g6?** A losing move. 28. ... Nf7 29. b4 Kh8 30. c3 Ra7 was better. **29. f×g6+ N×g6 30. Qe2** Schiffers: "If 30. N×f6+, then 30. ... Q×f6." **30. ... f5 31. e×f5 Nf4 32. B×f4 e×f4 33. Qe5! Rg5 34. Nf6+ Kh8 35. R×f4 Bb7** Schiffers: "The Bishop is in sad straits." 35. ... Ra7 is insufficient as well: 36. Ne4+ Kh7 37. N×g5+ h×g5 38. Rf3 g4 39. Q×d4. **36. Ne4+ Rg7** Schiffers: "After 36. ... Qg7, would follow 37. N×g5 Q×e5 38. Nf7+ and 39. N×e5." **37. Rh4 1–0** [*tournament book*, page 189]

499. Pollock–S. Tarrasch [C00]
Hastings Tournament, Round 13,
21 August 1895

1. e4 Pollock: "My first idea was to play an attacking game of an original nature and to be only careful not to be premature nor to overshoot the mark. I had no notion as to what defence my opponent would be likely to adopt." **1. ... e6 2. e5** von Bardeleben: "This continuation was first adopted by Steinitz against Winawer in the Vienna Tournament, 1882. I do not think it quite sound." Pollock: "I played this move not only to take my opponent but *myself* 'out of the books.' I had not the remotest idea that Dr. Tarrasch would work into a variation played by me before (against Blackburne in 1886). It was the stranger that he was acquainted with that game. He either unconsciously followed the English master's false track in acting prematurely against the White's centre pawns and recollected it later on, or else, as I fancy, his memory was misled by Steinitz's notes on the game in question in the *International Chess Magazine* and other notes of smaller calibre which erroneously declared White's attack unsound. It is a good plan to take *yourself* clear out of the beaten track, so long as you keep the principles in view, in order to cultivate originality." **2. ... f6** von

Bardeleben: "The simple move 2. ... d5 seems to be the best answer to the irregular second move of White." **3. d4 c5** Pollock: "These moves are, I believe, a premature attempt to break up White's centre. Especially in a close game like the 'French' the pawn centre is the business which first occupies the minds of both players." **4. Bd3 f5** *(see diagram)*

After
4. ... f7–f5

von Bardeleben: "I prefer 4. ... g6." Pollock: "Black's second and third moves seem to constitute a premature operation against White's forming a pawn centre. The logical continuation would be 4. ... c×d4 5. Qh5+ Ke7 6. Nf3 Qe8 7. Qh4 Nc6 8. 0–0 but Black will hardly maintain the pawn gained, while White has a capital position; A well-known game (Pollock vs. Blackburne, London, 1886) proceeded 4. ... g6 5. h4 f5 (In this variation, if 5. ... c×d4 6. h5 Qa5+ 7. Kf1 Q×e5 8. h×g6 h6 9. Nf3 Qd5 10. N×d4, would have given White a winning attack (in spite of the critics of that day), for if 10. ... Q×d4 11. g7 B×g7 12. Bg6+) 6. Bg5 Be7 7. B×e7 Q×e7 8. Na3 c×d4 9. Nb5 Kd8 10. Qd2 Nc6 11. Nd6 b6 12. Nf3 h6 13. c3 Qg7 14. c×d4 Nge7 15. 0–0–0, White winning after a very pretty game. Dr. Tarrasch admitted that he was acquainted with the London game." **5. g4!** Pollock: "Having gained a move in the opening, White can safely act thus at once against the adverse pawn centre. [...] The real difficulty that confronted, and I might say confused, Black was to determine whether this was a sound or an unsound advance, and, if the latter, how to prove it so. As I won this game, the move was 'of-coursed' by the London press. Had I lost it, be sure the adverse result would both have been laid to the account of this very move, and the move itself set down as another of Mr. Pollock's ingenious but ridiculous vagaries. There is a risk in it, but I was convinced that the risk lay in my being unable to follow it up properly." von Bardeleben: "An excellent move." **5. ... c×d4 6. g×f5 Qa5+ 7. c3** Pollock: "With this move White had to take into consideration the plan of castling, and afterwards playing Re1.

The c-pawn, which Black never has time to capture, becomes a most important factor in the attack, and the whole line of play is far superior to 7. Kf1, which would avoid the second check from the queen." **7. ... Q×e5+ 8. Ne2! Nc6** Pollock: "Dr. Tarrasch consumed a whole hour over the first nine moves (the time limit being 30 moves in the first two hours), and was at this stage plunged in a very brown study indeed.... So much impressed was I with his reflecting that I had to make several excursions around the hall to watch the ceiling and the other games, in order to avoid being infected with it and so changing my more rapid tactics into too much unprofitable analysing." von Bardeleben: "I prefer 8. ... e×f5 9. c×d4 Qf6 10. Nbc3 Ne7, though in any case Black's position would be precarious." **9. 0–0 Bc5 10. Re1 Qf6** Pollock: "He could not, even if he desired, obtain a perpetual check by 10. ... d×c3 and 11. ... B×f2+." **11. Nd2** von Bardeleben: "White plays with great energy and sound judgement." Pollock: "This is now the only difficult piece to bring into play." **11. ... e×f5** Pollock: "11. ... d5, the alternative, to keep the knight from e4, would have been very hazardous indeed, as the reply 12. Nf4 would attack both the e and d-pawns." **12. c×d4 Be7** Pollock: "Clearly he dare not recapture, nor does 12. ... Bb4 hold out pleasant prospects." Actually, 12. ... Bb4 13. a3 B×d2 14. B×d2 Nge7 was likely to be Black's best option. **13. Nf3 Kd8?** von Bardeleben: "If 13. ... Qg6+ then 14. Kh1 Nf6 [14. ... d5 15. Nf4 Qd6 16. Nh5 Kf8 17. Bf4 Qd8 was equally depressing—authors] 15. Nf4 Qf7 16. Ng5 Qf8 17. B×f5 and White will win." Pollock: "Possibly 13. ... Kf8 might have turned out better." **14. Bg5** Pollock: "Hereabouts the little circle of spectators around the roped off table began to increase, although it never really approached the size of that which watched some other of the games in which I was engaged." **14. ... Qf7 15. B×e7+ Ng×e7 16. Qd2** Pollock: "This seizes important diagonals and unites the rooks, besides defending b2 preparatory for playing Rc1 and Bc4 in certain contingencies." **16. ... h6 17. Ne5! N×e5** Pollock: "This exchange, which indeed can hardly be avoided, plays the opponent's game, as it opens up a more important file for him than the e-file." **18. d×e5 b6?** von Bardeleben: "18. ... g5 would be better in order to prevent White's next move." Black had 18. ... Nc6! available: 19. Rad1 Re8 20. f4 g5 21. Ng3 g×f4 22. Q×f4 Qg7 23. B×f5, with some realistic hopes for survival. 23. ... R×e5. **19. Nf4** Pollock: "The winning move, cutting off Black's possible chances of attack by ...Qg6+ etc." **19. ... Bb7 20. Bb5 Nc6 21. e6 Qe7** von Bardeleben: "Suicide, but the game is beyond all remedy. If 21. ... Qe8 22. Qc3 Rg8 23. e×d7 or 23. Rd1 and White wins easily." Pollock: "If 21. ... Qe8, 22. Rad1 also winning immediately." **22. Ng6 Qg5+ 23. Q×g5+ h×g5 24. N×h8 Nd4 25. e7+** and Tarrasch resigned. Pollock: "If 25. ... Ke8, 26. B×d7+ K×d7 27. Rad1 R×h8 28. R×d4+ etc." Pollock: "My opponent asked a question as to the game referred to already and, after a little analysis of the opening moves, observed with a slight sigh: 'Sehr strong attack.' He took his defeat, a serious one for him at that stage, as a perfect gentleman should, but as some of the best of us in that sorrowful 'second Battle of Hastings' did not always, although we were generally pretty quiet about it—inside the Congress Hall. I consider this by far my best game at Hastings, in spite of the help which I undeniably received from my antagonist and of my better acquaintance with the exact nature of the opening that even his, that of a so distinguished a master of theory. In conclusion, I can only ask my readers to forgive any appearance of conceit in these notes, which from their nature must savour all too strongly of the pronoun 'ego.'" **1–0** [*tournament book*, pages 213–214; *BCM*, September 1895, pages 491–492; *St. John Globe*, April 10, 1896]

500. I.A. Gunsberg–Pollock [C26] Hastings Tournament, Round 14, 23 August 1895

1. e4 e5 2. Nc3 Pollock: "In his notes to the game between Chigorin and Janowski, in the *Daily News*, Mr. Gunsberg remarks at this point: 'We have over and over again expressed ourselves unfavorably regarding this opening, while, as in the present game, we have seen numerous instances in which the defence does well, we seldom came across a game played at this opening in which the first player is successful.' The gambits and games springing from the opening are inexhaustible. It was adopted at Hastings more often than any of the 20 openings (*BCM*, page 407) except the QP, Ruy Lopez, and French, with a percentage of 41. 66. We merely quote the note as a curiosity worth preserving. The 'Vienna,' in some of its countless forms, will always be a favourite with chess-players, as is the case with every opening that has held its ground steadily for half a century." **2. ... Nf6 3. g3** Pollock: "'The only feasible continuation leading to a sound game.'—*Daily News*. This is as much as

saying that it is a fatal disadvantage to have the option of playing two moves in succession as second player. The text move is a favourite with many masters, but it is a question whether it is as strong as 3. f4 or 3. Nf3. White has also the choice of a pretty gambit, 3. Bc4 N×e4 4. Nf3, or of adopting some such waiting move 3. Be2 or 3. a3." **3. ... Bc5 4. Bg2 0–0 5. Nge2** (*see diagram*)

After
5. Ng1–e2

Albin: "5. Na4 is the usual and best move in this position." **5. ... d5!?** Pollock: "White here humorously remarked, 'Did you mean to go two squares or one?' But Black, having experience, replied 'Ich sage nichts.' The gambit here instituted gives the second player a splendid development, and is exempt from the flaw of a possibility of being refused." **6. e×d5** Albin: "6. N×d5 is better." **6. ... c6 7. d×c6 N×c6 8. d3 Bg4 9. f3** Albin: "9. h3 is more correct, in order not to open the diagonal for the Black bishop." Pollock: "9. h3 Be6 10. 0–0 Qd7 11. Kh2 would have White helpless on the kingside, at all events for attack, while the second player, absolutely secure on that wing, might even proceed to operate on the other by ...Rac8 and ...Rfd8 in some cases." **9. ... Be6 10. a3** Pollock: "An insidious and cunning move, which makes it difficult for Black to discover the very best continuation." Albin: "Why not 10. Ne4?" **10. ... Bb6** Pollock: "This is a half waiting move too, both anticipating 11. Na4 and clearing the c-file for the rook. Another idea was to be prepared to answer 11. Bg5 with 11. ... h6, when, if 12. B×f6 Q×f6 13. Ne4 Qe7, followed by ...f5. But we think 10. ... Nd5 (and if 11. Na4, 11. ... Ne3) much more attacking." **11. Bd2 a5 12. Qc1 Rc8 13. Nd1 Nd5 14. Nf2 f5 15. 0–0 f4! 16. Kh1** Pollock: "The effects of capturing the pawn are interesting. For instance, 16. g×f4 Qh4 (or 16. ... e×f4 17. B×f4 [17. N×f4 R×f4 18. B×f4 N×f4 19. Q×f4 Nd4, etc.] 17. ... R×f4 18. N×f4 N×f4 19. Q×f4 Nd4 20. Kh1 Bc7 and should win.) 17. f×e5 N×e5 18. Bg5 Qa4." **16. ... f×g3 17. h×g3** Albin: "17. N×g3, followed by Ne4 and Rg1, was the only way to obtain any chances." **17. ... Rf5 18. c4** Albin:

"18. g4 seems to be stronger, for if 18. ... Qh4+, 19. Kg1 followed eventually by Bg5." Pollock: "Bad. The position is exceedingly complicated. White has two main lines of defence here, 18. Bh3 and 18. g4. First: 18. Bh3 Rh5 19. Kg2 Qd7 20. Rh1 B×h3+ 21. R×h3 R×h3 22. N×h3 Rf8 with a lasting attack; Second: 18. g4 Qh4+ 19. Nh3 Rf4 20. Ne×f4 e×f4 21. B×f4 Nd4 22. Bg5 Qg3 23. Bf4 N×f4 24. Q×f4 Ne2 and Black will at least equalise the game." **18. ... Rh5+ 19. Kg1** *(see diagram)*

After
19. Kh1–g1

19. ... Nf4! Pollock: "This somewhat unexpected coup results in the temporary loss of a second pawn, but so strong is Black's position that it is doubtful if the game can be saved from this point." **20. B×f4** Pollock: "If 20. g×f4, 20. ... Qh4 and wins; And 20. N×f4 e×f4 21. B×f4 Q×d3 is also bad for White." **20. ... e×f4 21. N×f4 Nd4! 22. Qe3?!** Pollock: "No doubt 22. Re1 is better than this." Albin: "22. Re1, to make room for the king, and to disengage finally the knight, was preferable." **22. ... Rh6 23. Rac1?** Albin: "Why not 23. Rfe1?" **23. ... Qg5** Pollock: "The right move, deciding the issue. White was now much pressed which would account for the rather ludicrous termination of the game." **24. Rfe1** Albin: "Too late; White is helpless." **24. ... Q×g3 25. Ne2 N×e2+ 26. Q×e2 Bh3** Pollock: "Black could win the queen here by 26. ... B×f2+ 27. Q×f2 (best) 27. ... Rh1+, but the text move is more decisive." **27. Qf1** Albin: "Black has played the whole game in a masterly manner." **27. ... Rg6** 27. ... Bg4 would have led to a mate in seven. **28. c5 B×g2 29. Q×g2** 29. Ne4 fails too to the obvious 29. ... Qh3. **29. ... Q×g2 mate 0–1** [*tournament book*, pages 232–233; *BCM*, September 1895, pages 527–528]

501. Pollock–H.E. Bird [C29]
Hastings Tournament, Round 15,
24 August 1895

1. e4 e5 2. Nc3 Nf6 3. f4 d5 4. f×e5 N×e4 5. Nf3 Be7 von Bardeleben: "The usual move is better, 5. ... Bb4." **6. d4 0–0 7. Bd3 f5 8. e×f6 Bb4?** von Bardeleben: "This sacrifice is not sound. The right move was 8. ... N×f6." **9. 0–0** 9. f×g7 K×g7 10. 0–0 N×c3 11. Qe1 was the precise refutation. **9. ... B×c3 10. b×c3 R×f6** von Bardeleben: "Better would be 10. ... N×f6." **11. c4 Bg4 12. c×d5 B×f3** von Bardeleben: "If 12. ... Q×d5, then 13. Qe2 Nd6 14. c4 and White has the better game." **13. g×f3** 13. R×f3! was best. For example, 13. ... Nc3 14. B×h7+ K×h7 15. Qd3+ Kg8 16. Q×c3 Q×d5 17. R×f6 g×f6 18. Bh6. **13. ... Nc3 14. Qe1 N×d5 15. Kh1 Nf4** von Bardeleben: "A mistake, which costs the game. In order to prevent Bg5, Black should have played 15. ... Rf8, but White would in any case have the superior game with his two bishops and the open g-file." **16. Bc4+ Kh8 17. Qe4** *(see diagram)*

After
17. Qe1–e4

17. ... Qd6? von Bardeleben: "Now Black's game is hopeless. If 17. ... Ng6, then 18. Bg5, winning the exchange." 17. ... Qf8 could have been met by 18. Ba3! Q×a3 19. Q×b7 Rf8 20. Q×a8 with a clear edge for White. **18. Q×b7 Nc6 19. Q×a8+ Rf8 20. B×f4 Qf6 21. Be5 1–0** [*tournament book*, page 239]

502. C.A. Walbrodt–Pollock [C28]
Hastings Tournament, Round 16,
26 August 1895

1. e4 e5 2. Nc3 Nc6 3. Bc4 Nf6 4. d3 Bb4 Teichmann: "Avoiding the complications arising from 4. ... Bc5, after which White may turn into the King's Gambit declined with 5. f4." **5. Nge2** Teichmann: "This development of the knight appears a little unnatural; I prefer 5. Nf3." **5. ... d6 6. 0–0 Bg4 7. f3 Be6 8. Bb5** Teichmann: "This I cannot approve of. 8. Bb3 is much better, as Black then cannot exchange the bishops without allowing one of the White knights to enter at f5." **8. ... 0–0 9. B×c6 b×c6 10. Kh1 d5 11. a3 Bc5 12. Qe1 Ne8 13. f4 f6 14. f5 Bf7 15. Qh4 Nd6 16. Rf3**

d×e4 **17. d×e4 g5 18. f×g6** Teichmann: "Necessary, because if 18. Qh6, then 18. ... N×e4." Teichmann must have underestimated White's 19. Be3! in this line. **18. ... B×g6 19. Bh6 Rf7 20. Raf1 f5** Teichmann: "Too aggressive. 20. ... Ne8 would have given him a safe position, with good prospects of taking advantage of the weakness in White's game (e4-pawn)." **21. Bg5 Qd7 22. e×f5 N×f5 23. Qc4 Bb6 24. Ne4** (see diagram)

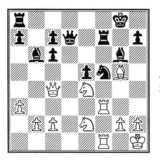

After
24. Nc3–e4

24. ... Qd5! Teichmann: "Very ingenious. By the sacrifice of the exchange he frees himself from all difficulties, and gets even winning chances." **25. Nf6+ R×f6 26. Q×d5+ c×d5 27. B×f6 Ne3 28. Rc1 Re8 29. c3?!** 29. Bg5! would have kept the game edgy: 29. ... N×c2 30. Bh6 d4 31. b4 Be4 32. Rf6 Ne3 33. B×e3 d×e3 34. Nc3 Bb7. **29. ... e4** 29. ... Bh5! was even stronger: 30. Rf2 Ng4 31. Rf5 Bg6 32. Rf3 Nf2+ 33. R×f2 B×f2. **30. Rf4 c5 31. b4 Bc7 32. Rf2 Ng4 33. Rff1 N×h2 34. Rfe1 Ng4 35. Bh4 e3 36. b×c5 Nf2+ 37. Kg1** Teichmann: "It is curious to agree to a draw in this position, which certainly would admit of much play. We think Black has slightly the best of it, but after a careful analysis of the position I have come to the conclusion that he has not enough to win." ½–½ [*tournament book*, page 258]

503. Pollock–J. Mieses [C68]
Hastings Tournament, Round 17, 27 August 1895

1. e4 e5 2. Nf3 Nc6 3. Bb5 a6 4. B×c6 d×c6 5. 0–0 von Bardeleben: "Better is 5. d3 or 5. d4." **5. ... Bg4 6. h3 h5 7. d3 Bc5** (see diagram)

von Bardeleben: "I prefer 7. ... Qf6; if White then plays 8. h×g4, Black answers with 8. ... h×g4 9. Ng5 (or 9. Bg5 Qg6 10. N×e5 [if 10. Nh2?, then 10. ... Qh5!] 10. ... Q×g5 11. f4 g×f3 12. N×f3 Qh6, having the better position.) 9. ... Qh6 10. Nh3 Qh4 11. Kh2 g×h3 12. g3 Qh7 being a pawn ahead." **8. h×g4 h×g4 9. Ng5 g3 10. Qf3 g×f2+ 11. R×f2 Nf6 12. Nc3 Qe7 13. Nh3 B×f2+ 14. K×f2** von

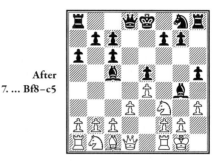

After
7. ... Bf8–c5

Bardeleben: "This brings the king into a bad position. Better would be 14. N×f2 Nh5 15. Be3 Qh4 16. Ne2." **14. ... Nh5 15. Bg5 f6 16. Be3 g5 17. Rf1 0–0–0 18. Ke1 Nf4 19. Nf2 Kb8 20. g3** von Bardeleben: "A weak move, which drives the hostile knight to a very good square. White should have played 20. Kd2, in order to bring his king to c1." **20. ... Ne6 21. Ng4 Qb4 22. Q×f6 Nd4 23. N×e5** von Bardeleben: "If 23. Kd2, 23. ... Rhf8." **23. ... N×c2+ 24. Kd2 N×e3 25. K×e3 Qd4+ 26. Kd2 Rhe8 27. N×c6+** von Bardeleben: "Better would be 27. Rf5." **27. ... b×c6 28. Q×d4 R×d4 29. Ke3 c5 30. Ne2 Rd7 31. Rf5** 31. b3! was an excellent prophylactic move. **31. ... Red8 32. Nc1** (see diagram)

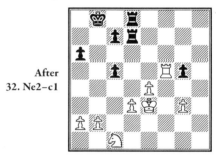

After
32. Ne2–c1

32. ... c4! von Bardeleben: "Very well calculated." **33. d×c4 Rd1 34. Nb3 Re1+ 35. Kf3 Rd3+ 36. Kf2 Rb1! 37. R×g5 R×b2+ 38. Ke1 R×a2 39. Nc1 Re3+ 40. Kd1 Rg2 41. Ra5 Re×g3 42. R×a6 Rh3 43. Ne2 Rh1+ 44. Kd2 Rhh2 45. Kd3 R×e2 46. Kd4 Kb7 47. Re6 Rd2+ 48. Kc5 Rd6 49. R×d6 c×d6+ 50. K×d6 Rd2+ 51. Kc5 Kc7 52. e5 Rd1 53. e6 Rd2 54. Kb5 Re2 0–1** [*tournament book*, pages 270–271]

504. Pollock–J.H. Blackburne [C41]
Hastings Tournament, Round 18, 28 August 1895

1. e4 e5 2. Nf3 d6 3. d4 Bg4 4. d×e5 Nd7 Pillsbury: "The sacrifice of a pawn so early in the game, merely to secure a slightly quicker development, should not be sound." **5. Be2** Pillsbury: "5. e×d6 B×d6 6. Be2 was perfectly safe, with a pawn plus." **5. ... B×f3 6. B×f3 d×e5 7. Nc3 c6 8. 0–0 Ngf6 9. Qe2 Qc7 10. Qc4?!** Pillsbury: "This attack is premature and results in loss of valuable time. 10. Be3 was the correct developing move." **10. ... Nb6 11. Qb3 Be7 12. a4 0–0 13. Be3 Nbd7 14. Rad1** Pillsbury: "14. Rfd1 was the proper move, more especially after having commenced a pawn advance upon the queen's wing." **14. ... Nc5 15. Qc4 Ne6 16. Ne2 Rfd8 17. Ng3 g6 18. Be2 h5 19. f3 Nf4 20. B×f4?** Pillsbury: "This capture involves White in grave difficulties; he should have moved 20. Rfe1"; Perhaps White had to settle for 20. Qc3 h4 21. B×f4 e×f4 22. Nh1 Nd7 23. Nf2 Bc5 24. Kh1 B×f2 25. R×f2 Ne5 26. Rff1 even if Black's knight on e5 is stronger than White's bishop on e2. **20. ... e×f4 21. Nh1 Qb6+ 22. Nf2 R×d1 23. B×d1** 23. R×d1 Bc5 24. Rf1 Nd7 was unpleasant. **23. ... Bc5** Pillsbury: "After 23. ... Q×b2 24. Nd3 Qb6+ 25. Kh1 Qc7 26. c3, White obtains a good counter-attack for the lost pawn." **24. b4** Pillsbury: "There appears to have been no necessity for this, and Black could have safely replied 24. ... Q×b4 25. Q×b4 B×b4 26. Nd3 Bd2, with a fine game. White could still have obtained a fair game by 24. c3 Rd8 25. Bb3 Rd7 26. g3 etc." **24. ... B×f2+ 25. R×f2 Rd8 26. Qf1** *(see diagram)*

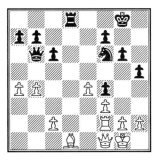

After
26. Qc4–f1

26. ... Rd2! Pillsbury: "Black plays for a deep game; he could simply win the queen's wing pawns, and his opponent could obtain no counter-attack to compensate for their loss." **27. g3 f×g3 28. h×g3 Qd4 29. c3 Qe3 30. c4 Qd4** 30. ... h4! was a clever resource: 31. g×h4 (31. g4 h3 32. Be2 Rc2 33. b5 Rc1 34. Bd1 Qd4) 31. ... Qd4 32. Bb3 Rb2. **31. Be2 Ra2** 31. ... h4! was still powerful: 32. g4 (32. g×h4 Nh5 33. Kh2 Nf4 34. b5 N×e2 35. R×e2 Q×c4) 32. ... Ra2 33. g5 Nh5 34. Kh2 Ng3 35. Qg2 N×e2 36. R×e2 Qe5+ 37. Kh1 Ra1+. **32. Kh2 R×a4 33. b5 Ra1 34. Qg2 Ra2 35. Qf1 Nd7** Pillsbury: "With the entrance of the knight Black soon wins

a second pawn, after which the result is merely a question of time." **36. Rg2 Nc5 37. Qf2 Q×f2 38. R×f2 Nd3 39. Rg2 Ne1 40. b×c6 b×c6** Naturally, not 40. ... N×g2? 41. c7! R×e2 42. c8Q+ Kg7 43. Kg1 and Black's winning chances are gone. **41. Rf2 N×f3+ 42. Kg2 Nd4 43. Bd1 Ra1** Pillsbury: "43. ... R×f2+ would have saved time; the two pawns plus would have settled matters in a shorter time." **44. Rd2 c5 45. Kf2 a5** Pillsbury: "45. ... f6 at once, followed by ...Kf7 and ...Ke6 would have shortened matters also." **46. Ke3 Kf8 47. Kf4 f6 48. e5 Ke7 49. Ke4 f×e5 50. K×e5 Ra3 51. Rb2 Nc6+ 52. Kf4 Nb4 53. Rd2 Rd3 54. R×d3 N×d3+ 55. Kg5 Ne5 56. Bb3 Kf7 57. Bd1 Kg7 58. Bb3 Nf7+ 59. Kf4 Kf6 60. Ke4 Ke6 61. Bd1 Nd6+ 62. Kf4 Kf6 63. Bb3 g5+ 64. Kf3 Ke5 65. Ke3 Ne4 66. g4 h4 67. Bc2 Nf6 68. Bd1 h3 69. Kf3 Kd4 0–1** [*tournament book*, pages 281–283]

505. Pollock–M. Chigorin [C51]
Hastings Tournament, Round 19, 30 August 1895

1. e4 e5 2. Nf3 Nc6 3. Bc4 Bc5 4. b4 B×b4 5. c3 Ba5 6. d4 e×d4 7. 0–0 d6 8. c×d4 Bb6 9. Nc3 Na5 10. Bg5 f6 11. Bh4 von Bardeleben: "I prefer 11. Bf4." **11. ... Ne7 12. Re1** von Bardeleben: "A weak move. White should have played 12. Qe2 and if Black answers 12. ... Bg4 13. Rad1; by this line of play White would prepare the advance of the e-pawn better than by 12. Re1." **12. ... Bg4 13. e5** von Bardeleben: "This proves to be disadvantageous." **13. ... d×e5 14. d×e5 Q×d1 15. Ra×d1 N×c4 16. e×f6 g×f6 17. B×f6** von Bardeleben: "If 17. Nd5, then 17. ... 0–0–0 18. N×e7+ Kb8 and Black has the better game." **17. ... Kf7 18. B×e7 B×f3 19. g×f3 Ba5** *(see diagram)*

After
19. ... Bb6–a5

20. Rd7 20. Re4! was stronger: 20. ... Rhg8+ 21. Kf1 Rge8 22. Bg5 R×e4 23. N×e4 Re8 24. Rd7+ Kg6 25. h4 h5 26. Kg2 with equal chances. **20. ...**

Nb6! von Bardeleben: "An excellent move, which practically decides the game in Black's favour." **21. R×c7 Rhc8 22. R×b7 B×c3 23. Ba3+ Kf6 24. Ree7 Rg8+ 25. Kf1 Rad8 26. Rf7+ Kg6 27. Kg2 Nc4 28. Bc5 Rd5 29. Bf8 Nd2 30. Ba3 Rf5 31. Rfc7 Rg5+ 32. Kh3 Bf6 33. f4 Rh5+ 34. Kg2 Kf5+ 35. Kh1 Nf3 36. Rb5+ Ke6 37. f5+ R×f5 38. Rc6+ Kd7 39. Rd6+ Kc7 40. Rb1 Rh5 0–1** [*tournament book*, pages 291–292]

506. S. Tinsley–Pollock [A90]
Hastings Tournament, Round 20, 31 August 1895

1. d4 f5 2. c4 e6 3. g3 Nf6 4. Bg2 Bb4+ Teichmann: "In this variation the Black king's bishop cannot be well used otherwise; it seems therefore best to exchange it for the White knight, a course which in other variations cannot be recommended." **5. Nc3 0–0 6. Qb3 c5 7. e3 Nc6 8. a3 c×d4** Teichmann: "8. ... B×c3+, followed by ...Qe7, seems to be preferable." **9. a×b4 d×c3 10. b×c3 Ne5 11. Nf3 Nd3+ 12. Ke2 N×c1+ 13. Rh×c1** Teichmann: "White has now a very good development." **13. ... b6 14. Nd4 Ne4 15. Rd1 Qg5 16. h4 Qg6** Teichmann: "16. ... Qf6 would have been much better." **17. Bf3 Bb7 18. Nb5 d5 19. c×d5 e×d5 20. R×a7 R×a7 21. N×a7 Kh8 22. b5 Qf6 23. Rc1 Ra8 24. Nc6 B×c6 25. b×c6 Q×c6 26. Rc2 h6 27. Kf1 Ra1+ 28. Kg2 b5 29. Qb4 Kh7 30. Be2 Nd6 31. Bf3 Ra4 32. Qb1 Rc4 33. Rd2 Ne4 34. Rd3 Rc5 35. h5 Kg8** Teichmann: "With a view to taking the c-pawn, which he could not do before, on account of 35. ... N×c3 36. R×c3! R×c3 37. Q×f5+, drawing at least. But he ought to have played ...Kh8 instead, after which I find no satisfactory defence for White." **36. Qa2 Kh8 37. Qa5 Kh7 38. Qd8 N×c3 39. Qf8 Qc8 40. Qf7 b4 41. g4** (*see diagram*)

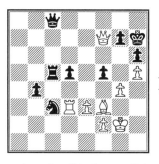

After
41. g3–g4

41. ... f×g4 Teichmann: "There was no necessity for taking this pawn, but even taking it ought not

to result in any disadvantage." **41. ... b3!** seems stronger than the text: 42. g×f5 b2 (42. ... Kh8 43. Qe7! Q×f5 44. Q×c5 b2! [44. ... Q×d3 45. Qc8+ Kh7 46. Bg4 b2 47. Bf5+ Q×f5 48. Q×f5+ Kh8 49. Qc8+ Kh7 50. Q×c3 b1Q with equality] 45. Q×c3 Qg5+ 46. Kh3 b1Q 47. Qc8+ Kh7 48. Rd1 Qbf5+ 49. Q×f5+ Q×f5+ 50. Kg2, with roughly equal chances.) 43. f6 Qg8 44. Qg6+ Kh8 45. f7 Qf8 46. R×c3 R×c3 47. Qb6 Q×f7 48. Q×b2. **42. Qg6+ Kh8 43. B×g4 Qd8 44. f4 Qf6??** Teichmann: "A blunder, which loses the game at once. Black could have drawn the game easily if he simply kept the queen on the last row; whenever White threatened mate with Bf5, then ...Kg8 or ...Qg8." **44. ... Ra5 45. Bf5 Qg8 46. Rd4 Ra2+ 47. Kf3 b3 48. Be6 Qd8 49. Bf5 Qg8 50. Be6** would have forced a draw. **45. Qe8+ Kh7 46. Be6 Q×e6 47. Q×e6 b3 48. Qb6 Ne4 49. Qg6+ Kg8 50. R×d5 Rc2+ 51. Kf3 Rd2 52. Q×e4 1–0** [*tournament book*, pages 314–315]

507. Pollock–E.S. Schiffers [C55]
Hastings Tournament, Round 21, 2 September 1895

1. e4 e5 2. Nf3 Nc6 3. Bc4 Nf6 4. d4 e×d4 5. Ng5 d5 6. e×d5 Na5 Tarrasch: "The usual move here is 6. ... Ne5." **7. Q×d4** Tarrasch: "The game is about equal for the two players." **7. ... N×c4 8. Q×c4 Q×d5 9. Qe2+** Tarrasch: "The exchange of queens was preferable." **9. ... Be6 10. 0–0 0–0–0 11. N×e6 Q×e6 12. Q×e6+ f×e6** Tarrasch: "After a dozen moves the players have reached the endgame. Black being in possession of the open d-file, has a slight advantage and makes the best use of it." **13. Nc3 Bb4** (*see diagram*)

After
13. ... Bf8–b4

14. Bg5? 14. Ne2 was structurally more sensible. **14. ... B×c3 15. b×c3 Rd5 16. Be3 Rhd8** Tarrasch: "Now the superiority of Black's game is evident." **17. c4 Ra5 18. a4 Rd6 19. Rfb1 Ng4 20. Rb5?** Tarrasch: "Even without this blunder White cannot prevent some loss." Indeed, even after 20. h3 N×e3 21. f×e3 Rda6 22. Rb4 b6 23. c5 b5 24. c3 b×a4 25. Ra3 R×c5 26. Kf2 Rca5 Black's advantage is indisputable. **20. ... R×a4 21. Rab1 N×e3 22. f×e3 Rb6 23. Rf1 R×c4 24. Rg5 g6 25. Rf8+ Kd7 26. Rf7+ Kd6 27. R×h7 Rb1+ 28. Kf2 R×c2+ 29. Kg3 b5** Tarrasch: "Now follows the race of the pawns and White arrives too late. The final moves need no comment; besides which the whole game is easily understood." **30. R×g6 Rb3 31. Kf4 Rc4+ 32. Kg5 R×e3 33. Rgg7 Re5+ 34. Kh6 Rh4+ 35. Kg6 R×h7 36. R×h7 b4 37. g4 b3 38. Rh3 Rb5 39. Rd3+ Ke7 40. Rd1 b2 41. Rb1 a5 42. h4 a4 43. h5 a3 44. h6 a2 0–1** [*tournament book*, pages 330–331]

Part Two, Section XIII
(September 18, 1895–May 1896)

In England and Ireland

508. Pollock–Amateur [C52]
Bristol, Simultaneous Exhibition
(12 Boards), 18 September 1895

**1. e4 e5 2. Nf3 Nc6 3. Bc4 Bc5 4. b4 B×b4
5. c3 Ba5 6. 0-0 Nf6 7. d4 N×e4 8. Re1 N×c3**
8. ... d5 was correct. **9. N×c3 B×c3** (*see diagram*)

After
9. ... B×c3

10. Qb3 B×a1? Taking the wrong rook. After
10. ... B×e1 11. B×f7+ Kf8 12. Bg5 (12. Ba3+?
Bb4!) 12. ... N×d4! Black has a fine position.
11. B×f7+ Kf8 12. Bg5 Ne7 12. ... N×d4 was
hopeless too: 13. Qa3+ K×f7 14. N×e5+ Kg8
15. B×d8 d6 16. Nf3 Be6 17. B×c7. **13. R×e5**
13. N×e5 was more precise: 13. ... d6 14. Bh5 d5
15. Qf3+ Bf5 16. B×e7+. **13. ... d6 14. Bh5?**
14. B×e7+ Q×e7 15. R×e7 K×e7 16. Bg8 was correct. **14. ... d5!** After 14. ... g6! 15. B×e7+ Q×e7
16. R×e7 K×e7 17. Qe3+ Kf6 18. Qg5+ Kf7
19. Bg4 c5 it's not clear what exactly is White's advantage. **15. B×e7+ Q×e7 16. R×e7 K×e7
17. Q×d5 Be6 18. Qe5 1-0** [*Western Daily Press*,
September 23, 1895]

509. Pollock–H.L. Leonard [C25]
Bristol, Simultaneous Exhibition
(14 Boards), 20 September 1895

"Game played in a simultaneous contest by Mr.
W.H.K. Pollock against fourteen picked players
of the district, at the rooms of the Bristol Literary
and Philosophical Institute." **1. e4 e5 2. Nc3 Nc6
3. f4 e×f4 4. Nf3 Bc5 5. d4 N×d4 6. N×d4 Qh4+
7. g3?** 7. Ke2 was mandatory. **7. ... f×g3 8. Bg2
g×h2+ 9. Kf1 Nf6 10. Qd2 d5** 10. ... d6 was better. **11. Nf3 Qg3 12. Qe1 Q×e1+ 13. N×e1 d×e4
14. N×e4 N×e4 15. B×e4 Bd6 16. Nd3 Bh3+
17. Kf2 0-0-0 18. Nf4?!** 18. Bf4 was correct: 18. ...
B×f4 19. N×f4 Rhe8 20. Kf3 f5 21. N×h3 R×e4
22. R×h2. **18. ... B×f4 19. B×f4 Rd4 20. Rae1
f5! 21. Kg3 f×e4 22. K×h3 Re8 23. R×h2 h6
24. Rd2 R×d2 25. B×d2 Re6 26. Kg4 Kd7** (*see
diagram*)

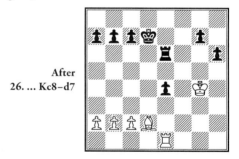

After
26. ... Kc8–d7

27. Kf4 g6 28. R×e4 R×e4+? 28. ... g5+ 29. Kf5
R×e4 30. K×e4 Ke6 was a better version of this
rook exchange. **29. K×e4 h5 30. Bf4 c6 31. Ke5
Ke7 32. Bg5+ Kf7 33. Kd6 c5! 34. K×c5?** Falling
into a clever trap. Better was 34. a4 a5 35. c4 b6
36. Kd5 without a hope for Black. **34. ... Ke6
35. c4 Kf5 36. Be3?** 36. Bd8 maintained the

balance. **36. ... h4! 37. Kd5 h3 38. Bg1 Kf4 39. Bh2+ Kf3 40. b4 g5 41. c5 g4 42. b5 g3 43. B×g3 K×g3 44. c6 b×c6+ 45. b×c6 h2 46. c7 h1Q+ 47. Kd6 Qd1+ 48. Kc6 Qc2+ 49. Kb7 Qe4+ 0–1** [*Western Daily Press*, September 23, 1895; *Newcastle Weekly Chronicle*, October 5, 1895; *Dublin Daily Express*, October 11, 1895; *Bristol Mercury and Daily Post*, October 19, 1895; *Chess Player's Chronicle*, February 5, 1896, pages 11–12; *St. John Globe*, March 10, 1899]

510. Pollock–"Leeds Allies" [C25]
Newcastle, Consultation Game, October 1895

1. e4 e5 2. Nc3 Nc6 3. f4 e×f4 4. Nf3 g5 5. h4 g4 6. Ng5 h6 7. N×f7 K×f7 8. Bc4+ d5 9. B×d5+ Kg7 10. d4 Nf6 11. B×f4 Be7 12. 0–0! Nb4 13. Be5 Rf8 14. Qd2 c6 15. Bb3 Na6 16. Rf4 Kg6 17. Raf1 Nc5 18. Bc4 18. B×f6! R×f6 19. e5 R×f4 20. Q×f4 h5 21. Bf7+ Kg7 22. Ne2 was another decisive possibility. **18. ... Ncd7?** 18. ... Be6 was a better defense. **19. B×f6 N×f6** (*see diagram*) 19. ... B×f6 20. Qe3 B×h4 21. e5 was losing too.

After
19. ... Nd7×f6

20. e5! Nd5 21. R×f8 B×f8 22. N×d5 c×d5 23. Bd3+ Kh5 23. ... Kg7 was no better: 24. Rf6 Kg8 25. Rg6+ Bg7 26. Q×h6 Qe7 27. c4! **24. Rf6! Qe8 25. Qf4 1–0** [*Montreal Herald*, November 16, 1895]

511. Pollock–H.G. Lee [C44]
Bath, Simultaneous Exhibition (13 Boards), 2 October 1895

1. e4 e5 2. Nf3 Nc6 3. c3 d5 4. Bb5 Bg4 5. Qa4 Qd6 6. N×e5 Q×e5 7. B×c6+ b×c6 8. Q×c6+ Ke7 9. f3! Rd8 10. f×g4 Q×e4+ 11. Kf2 Qf4+ 12. Kg1 Q×g4 13. Q×c7+ Rd7 14. Qe5+ Kd8 15. Qb8+ Ke7 16. h3 Qe6 17. d4 f6 18. Bf4 Kf7 19. Nd2 19. Na3 was safer. **19. ... g5! 20. Be5?** 20. Bg3 loses the knight too, but White gets some activity and material in return: 20. ... Qe3+

21. Kh2 Q×d2 22. Qb5 Re7 23. Rhf1 Kg7 24. Rf2 Qe3 25. Q×d5. **20. ... Bg7?!** There was no reason to fear 20. ... f×e5 21. Nf3 Kg7! 22. N×e5 (22. N×g5 Qd6) 22. ... Bd6! 23. Qb5 Re7 24. Re1 Nf6. **21. Nf3** (*see diagram*)

After
21. Nd2–f3

21. Rf1 was good too. **21. ... Kg6?** Exposing the king on the b1–h7 diagonal was not a good idea. 21. ... Qa6! was better: 22. Bg3 Rb7 23. Qd6 Q×d6 24. B×d6 R×b2. **22. Bg3 Ne7 23. Qb3 Nf5 24. Re1** The direct 24. Qc2 allows 24. ... Qe4! **24. ... Qc6 25. Qc2 h5 26. h4** 26. Bh4!!, with the idea of playing g2–g4 next—was a pretty conclusion: 26. ... g4 27. Nh2 g×h3 28. Nf3 h×g2 29. Rh2. **26. ... Qc8?** 26. ... g4 was better but it still left Black in a dire situation after 27. Nh2 Qc8 28. N×g4! **27. Re6! Rf8 28. Ne5+ 1–0** [*Albany Evening Journal*, October 26, 1895]

512. Pollock–S. Highfield [C39]
Bath, Simultaneous Exhibition (13 Boards), October 1895

1. e4 e5 2. f4 e×f4 3. Nf3 g5 4. h4 g4 5. Ng5 d5 6. d4 h6 7. N×f7 K×f7 8. Nc3 Bb4 9. B×f4 Nf6 10. e5 Ne4 11. Bd3! N×c3 (*see diagram*)

After
11. ... Ne4×c3

12. Qd2 N×a2?! 12. ... Ne4 13. Q×b4 Nc6 was better. **13. c3 N×c3 14. b×c3 Be7 15. 0–0 Kg7?** 15. ... Be6! 16. B×h6+ Ke8 17. Bg7 Kd7! was an excellent defensive resource. **16. B×h6+! R×h6 17. Rf7+ K×f7 18. Q×h6 Ke8** 18. ... Qg8 is also hopeless: 19. Qh5+ Kf8 20. Rf1+. **19. Qg6+ 1–0** [*Bristol Mercury and Daily Post*, October 19, 1895; *Albany Evening Journal*, December 21, 1895; *Dublin Daily Express*, October 11, 1895]

513. Leeds Chess Club–Pollock [C80] Leeds, Consultation Game, 19 October 1895

1. e4 e5 2. Nf3 Nc6 3. Bb5 a6 4. Ba4 Nf6 5. 0–0 N×e4 6. Re1 Nc5 7. N×e5 Be7 8. B×c6 d×c6 9. d4 Ne6 10. c3 0–0 11. f4 f6 12. Nd3 Kh8 13. Qb3 Qd7 14. Be3 b6 15. Qc2 Bb7 16. Nd2 Rae8 17. Nb3 Bd6 18. Rad1 Qf7 19. Qf2 Qh5 20. Qf3 Q×f3 21. g×f3 *(see diagram)*

After
21. g2×f3

21. ... c5?! 21. ... g6 22. Nd2 Ng7 23. Bf2 Nf5 was perhaps a more logical plan. **22. d×c5 b×c5 23. Nb×c5 B×f3 24. N×e6 R×e6 25. Rd2 Rfe8 26. Bf2 R×e1+ 27. B×e1 Bc6 28. Bf2 Bb5 29. Bg3 Rd8 30. Nf2 f5! 31. b3 Rd7 32. c4 Bc6 33. Re2 h6 34. Kf1 Kh7 35. Nd3 Bf3 36. Re3 Be4 37. Ke2 ½–½** [*St. John's Globe*, July 7, 1900]

514. Pollock–H.E. Beater [C50] Dublin Chess Club, Simultaneous Exhibition (15 Boards), 2 January 1896

1. e4 e5 2. Nf3 Nc6 3. Bc4 Bc5 4. 0–0 d6 5. c3 h6 6. d4 e×d4 7. c×d4 Bb6 8. Nc3 Na5 9. Bd3 Nc6 10. Be3 Nf6 11. Rc1 0–0 12. Qd2 Ne7 *(see diagram)*

After
12. ... Nc6–e7

13. B×h6!? 13. e5 was a less risky alternative: 13. ... d×e5 14. d×e5 Nfd5 15. N×d5 Q×d5 16. Rfd1 Bg4 17. B×b6 a×b6 18. Qe2. **13. ... N×e4?** There was no reason not to accept the sacrifice: 13. ... g×h6 14. Q×h6 Ng4 15. Qh5 Kg7 16. h3 Nf6 17. Qg5+ Ng6, with good chances for Black. **14. N×e4 Bf5 15. Qg5 Bg6 16. Nf6+** Spectacular, but 16. Ng3! was even stronger: 16. ... g×h6 17. Q×h6 B×d3 18. Nh5 Nf5 19. Nf6+ Q×f6 20. Q×f6 B×f1 21. Q×f5 Be2 22. Ng5 Kg7 23. Rc3. **16. ... g×f6** 16. ... Kh8 would lose swiftly to 17. Qh4 Ng8 18. Bf4+ Nh6 19. B×h6 g×f6 20. B×f8+ Kg8 21. B×g6. **17. Q×f6 Nf5! 18. Q×d8 Rf×d8 19. Rfe1?** 19. Bg5 was correct and after 19. ... N×d4 20. N×d4 B×d3 21. Rfd1 Be4 22. B×d8 R×d8 White could have tried to convert the advantage. **19. ... N×h6 20. B×g6 f×g6 21. Re6 Kh7 22. Rce1 Nf5 23. Ng5+ Kh6?!** 23. ... Kg7 24. d5 Rf8 was even more accurate. **24. Nf7+ Kg7 25. N×d8 R×d8 26. d5 Rf8 27. R1e4 Nd4 28. Re7+ Rf7 29. Kf1 R×e7 30. R×e7+ Kf6 31. Re8 Ba5 32. Rc8 b5 33. g3 Nf3 34. Kg2 Ne5 35. f4 Nf7 36. Kf3 g5 37. Kg4 g×f4 38. g×f4 Nh6+ 39. Kh5 Kg7 ½–½** [*Bristol Mercury and Daily Post*, January 18, 1896]

515. Pollock–Miss Lynam [C38] Dublin Chess Club, Simultaneous Exhibition (15 Boards), 2 January 1896

1. e4 e5 2. f4 e×f4 3. Nf3 g5 4. Bc4 Bg7 5. 0–0 d6 6. d4 h6 7. g3 g4 8. Nh4 f3 9. c3 Be6 10. B×e6 f×e6 11. Qb3 Qc8 12. Ng6 Rh7 13. Nf4 Nc6 14. N×e6 b6? Overlooking a simple tactic. 14. ... Bf8 or 14. ... Nge7 had to be played. **15. N×c7+ Q×c7 16. Q×g8+ Bf8 17. Bf4** 17. Q×g4 was simplest. **17. ... h5?** 17. ... Qd7 18. Qg6+ Rf7 was better than this immediate collapse. **18. B×d6 Q×d6 19. Q×h7 N×d4 20. Q×h5+ Kd8 21. c×d4 Q×d4+ 22. Kh1 Q×b2 23. Nd2 1–0** [unidentified newspaper cutting]

516. Pollock–F.S.B. [C33] Dublin Chess Club, Simultaneous Exhibition (15 Boards), 2 January 1896

1. e4 e5 2. f4 e×f4 3. Kf2? An eccentricity without precedent among extant Pollock games. **3. ... Bc5+** A tempting move but not the best. Instead, 3. ... Nf6! 4. Nf3 N×e4+ 5. Kg1 d6 6. d3 Bc5+ 7. d4 Bd6 secures a clear advantage. **4. d4 Bb6 5. B×f4 Qf6 6. Ke3 c5! 7. Be5 c×d4+ 8. B×d4 B×d4+**

9. Q×d4 Q×f1 10. Nc3 Q×g2 10. ... Q×a1 was possible too: 11. Q×g7 Qc1+ 12. Ke2 Q×c2+ 13. Kf3 d5! **11. Nf3 Nc6 12. Qd6 Qg6 13. Nb5 Q×d6 14. N×d6+ Ke7 15. Rad1 Nh6 16. Rhf1 f6 17. Rg1 Rg8 18. Rg2 b6 19. Nb5 Kd8 20. Rgd2 Ng4+ 21. Ke2 Nge5 22. Nbd4 N×d4+ 23. N×d4 Re8 24. Kf1 Nc4 25. Re2 N×b2 26. Rb1 Nc4 27. Kf2 Bb7 0–1** [*Bristol Mercury and Daily Post*, January 18, 1896]

In Montreal

517. Pollock–J. Pelletier [C55]
Montreal, St. Dennis Chess Club,
Simultaneous Exhibition, May 1896

1. e4 e5 2. Nf3 Nc6 3. Bc4 Nf6 4. d4 e×d4 5. 0–0 Bc5 6. e5 d5 7. e×f6 d×c4 8. Re1+ Be6 9. Ng5 Qd6? 9. ... g6 or 9. ... Qd5 were the respectable choices. **10. Ne4** 10. R×e6+! f×e6 11. f×g7 Rg8 12. Qh5+ Kd7 13. Ne4 wins. **10. ... Qe5 11. f4 Qf5 12. g4 d3+ 13. Kf1?!** 13. Kh1 d×c2 14. g×f5 c×d1Q 15. R×d1 B×f5 16. N×c5 g×f6 17. Nc3 was superior. **13. ... Qd5?** The very pretty 13. ... Qh5!! was best. **14. f×g7 0–0–0 15. g×h8Q R×h8** (*see diagram*)

After
15. ... Rd8×h8

16. Nbc3 16. f5 was winning: 16. ... Rg8 17. f×e6 Qf5+ 18. Kg2 R×g4+ 19. Ng3 Qf2+ 20. Kh3 (20. Kh1? Rh4) 20. ... f5 21. Re2! **16. ... Qh5!! 17. Be3** Pollock failed to find the only defensive move here: 17. Nf2! Q×h2 18. Be3 B×e3 19. R×e3 Q×f4 20. Qf3. **17. ... Qh3+ 18. Kg1? B×e3+**

J. Pelletier (*Le Monde Illustré*, July 9, 1898, page 159).

19. Kh1 B×f4 0–1 [*Albany Evening Journal*, May 30, 1896]

518. Pollock–G.W. Falconer [C51]
Montreal Chess Club, Simultaneous
Exhibition, May 1896

1. e4 e5 2. Nf3 Nc6 3. Bc4 Bc5 4. b4 Bb6 5. b5 Na5 6. N×e5 Qf6 7. B×f7+ Kf8 8. d4 d6 9. B×g8 d×e5 10. Bd5 B×d4 11. Qd2 B×a1 12. Q×a5 Bd4 13. 0–0 Bb6 14. Ba3+ Ke8 15. Qb4 a6 16. b×a6 R×a6 and Black eventually won. **0–1** [*Albany Evening Journal*, May 30, 1896]

PART THREE

Appendices, Bibliography, Indices

Appendix A: Pollock and the 1890s American Chess Clubs

The following extensive Pollock article appeared in the British Chess Magazine, *Christmas Number, 1893, pages 23–30. The spelling of some chess players' names appearing in the text has been standardized according to Gaige's* Chess Personalia. *The old-style chess notation within the original text has been standardized using algebraic notation. The italics are kept as in the original.*

"American Chess Clubs That I Belong To"
By W.H.K. Pollock

I cannot apologise for this head-line, for be it understood that I write to orders! The fact is that I was requested by the editors to make a few interesting remarks about "American Chess Clubs that I have visited." Now, out of rather over a score of such societies, I may boast of "belonging to," the majority either as an active member, an honorary member, or perambulating peripatetic circus member, a press member (tolerated as calling in occasionally to see the hon. sec., and write up the club in the papers), or a non-member; there are in the first category the Albany and Baltimore Clubs; in the second the Brooklyn, St. Louis, Buffalo, Montreal, and Hagerstown; the third the Kansas City, Indianapolis, and Springfield; the fourth the Manhattan, City, and Chicago; the fifth the Café Bondy, Schneider's, and other resorts.

The first chess club I visited in the United States was the MANHATTAN, in its old quarters close by the historic Union Square. This was on March 25th, 1889. The club looked something like business on that Friday night, as nearly all the contestants in the Sixth American Chess Congress were assembled. There I first met Steinitz, Delmar, the brothers Baird, and many other lights. Recently (during the past twelve months) the club has been located in magnificent rooms, at the top of the United Charities' Building. It has its own cuisine,

its own waiters, club monogram, library, pictures, and other splendid furnishings. One of its sofas is the most luxurious thing of the kind I have ever seen. You plunge into it as into a warm bath. Its effect in assuaging the dolorous pangs of losing a dead-won game is magical. But this is partly accountable to its being in the snug writing room, retired from the din of the battle. Losing a game is not, however, so mortifying in such a club as the Manhattan, its members are too good players to even unintentionally vex the susceptible soul of the vanquished. The chessmen of the premier club have thick india-rubber bases, rendering their movements peculiarly stealthy and undisturbing. To this circumstance I attribute losing three important games in the "Impromptu" Tournament!

The Manhattan Chess Club is the Mecca of European experts, and since 1889 its roll of match players and visitors has included the names of Steinitz, Chigorin, Mackenzie, Gunsberg, Weiss, Bird, Blackburne, Burn, Albin, Lee, Jasnogrodsky, Schottländer, Mortimer, Taubenhaus. Lasker, Walbrodt, Judd, Showalter, Mason, Gossip, the writer, and many other fine players, quite apart from its own list of members, such as Lipschütz, Delmar, Hodges, Hanham, etc., etc.

The BROOKLYN CHESS CLUB, centrally situated in the enormous "City of Churches," is the Scholars' Club. Its membership is well over one hundred, and their peculiarity is that very nearly all are *players*. This is readily seen by a glance at one of the immense cardboard score sheets; one of which was "built" to contain the names of over eighty players. This refers to the "Continuous" or "Perpetual" Tournaments, introduced by Mr. E. Olly. The Brooklyn Chess Club ranks in importance and strength second only to the Manhattan. It is a nursery for young players, and turns them out very fast—that is to say, they don't remain "young" very long. English is spoken in this club. Its principal members figure so often in the pages of the *B.C.M.* that they need not be mentioned here. My friend, Charles A. Gilberg, president of the club, will I am sure agree with me that it must necessarily be invidious to mention names in an article of this nature. And let no reader who fails to read his name here, fail to see that the cause is never forgetfulness, neglect, or ingratitude. I simply mention names just as they are incidental to the narrative. Still, I must risk mentioning, to instance the "literary work" done by members of the club, that the chess editors of the *New York Sun, Recorder, Staatszeitung, Brooklyn Standard-Union, Brooklyn Eagle, Albany Journal, Baltimore News,* are all members of the Brooklyn Chess Club.

The CITY CHESS CLUB consists principally of members of the old Columbia and New York Clubs. It is situated in the region of the better class of German cafés. The "Citizens" are a very sociable lot, and, headed by the immortal Samuel Loyd, perhaps the strongest problemists to be found in any club in the United States. Although I am probably more indebted for hospitality to this club than any other—for I cannot boast of having rendered it any service of myself—I am obliged to give it but a brief notice. It has only just moved again to cosy quarters at the leading chess café, the Café Manhattan, and I do not know at the time of writing what its programme or membership is. Dr. O. Jentz and Mr. C. Nugent, both fine players, and as fine problemists, are its mainstay, Mr. F.G. Janusch having deserted to the camp of the Manhattan C.C., where he is extremely active in the general management of affairs.

I do not "belong to" the STATEN ISLAND CHESS CLUB, where the sceptre of great Hodges holds sway, except in so far as having received an invitation to a dinner given by it to the ex–Tennessee, to celebrate the winning of the *Staatszeitung* Silver Rook for his Islanders, 1893–1894. G.A. Barth is another leading spirit of that club, and a missionary of chess on the breezy sea-girt isle. He is chess editor of the *Staten Islander*, a good solver, musician, and deservedly a popular young man; not too German, but just German enough. The subjoined

three-move problem will best convey some idea of Mr. Barth's skill as a problem composer.

White to mate in three

It was on Staten Island that I invented and discovered the move of **2. Qe2** in the French, since "spoiled" by the hibernations of the bear in the St. Petersburg match. My old Richmond (Va) friend of the *Daily News*, and other London players, decry the move as inducing, instead of seducing the "Frenchman" to reply **...d5.** Witness **3. e×d5 Q×d5 4. Nc3 Qd8 5. Nf3 Nc6 6. d4** (a curious and sound gambit), (if) **6. ... N×d4 7. N×d4 Q×d4 8. Nb5**, and *must* win *(see diagram).*

I might just as well quit the Metropolitan Chess Clubs right here and take a trip up the Hudson River and through the Empire State. The guide book will be of service to us as regards the scenery, although I don't propose to be as rude as that Yankee, M. Twain, who gave all his "weather" in the introduction of one of his novels.

Having been bowled over the most perfect urban tracks of America, northward, we escape from New York's confines at Yonkers, where there used to be a chess club, presided over by Dr. R.J. Southworth, son of Mrs. Hannah Southworth, one of America's greatest serial and novel writers. I have visited that club in the company of James Mason, but it is heard of no more.

We are using the tracks of the New York Central R.R., now champion of the world for fast schedule time, and we hug closely the East shore of the Rhine of America (passing Tarrytown, the home of the hermit G.E. Carpenter, a famous local engineer and a big bit of a problemist still), gliding athwart the embattled cliffs of the Palisades to the serene glory of the Highlands, where autumn hues indescribably mingle gold, and orange, and crimson, and saffron, now sobering into drab and maroon, now flaring up into solferino and scarlet. Reaching Albany (143 miles in 2¾ hours) we readily find the classic little club of some twenty members. In proportion to its size, no chess club in the New World has done more to encourage the game. Profs. Deyo and Rogers have long been leading spirits, but the latter in resigning the editorial chair in favor of the writer, described Albany as a "sleepy old Dutch town." Bird, Gunsberg, Lasker, Lipschütz, Mackenzie, and many other well-known performers have given blindfold and other exhibitions here. The Albany players have supported the State Chess Association nobly, and the *Evening Journal*, with which I have the honor to be connected at this moment as chess editor, general reporter, etc., is the official organ of the association.

The enterprising and prosperous city of Syracuse is a sort of quarter-way-house from New York to Chicago. It was once famous for salt, the presence of which was known to the Indians, and was by them imparted to the Jesuits, in 1654. This may be taken *cum grano salis*! I only spent about twenty minutes in the Syracuse Chess Club. It happened thus: Returning from the Skaneateles Congress of the N.Y.C.A. in 1891, I happened to be engaged ceding the odds of a Queen's Knight to Mr. Searle, of Rome. [New York State, it may be incidentally observed, is notorious for three styles of topical nomenclature: Dutch, Graeco-Roman, and Indian. We have Amsterdam, Dutchess, Rensselaerville (Dutch); Troy, Rome, Athens, Syracuse (Graeco-Roman); Niagara, Otsego, Owego, Oswego, Hotsago, Owendontwantogo (Indian). But this is a deplorable digression.] When the train drew up at Syracuse I accepted a draw, having won three Pawns for the piece. On our way to the club (we had about an hour in Syracuse before taking the East-bound train) a very curious "pute" (I cannot class it either as a dispute or a computation) arose or rather sprung up. Neither player could, in re-perusing the game *sans voir*, find *where Black* had lost a piece, the pieces being found even. We went clear through the game, but not till we set up the position at the club did we find that *White's*

Queen's Knight had been used throughout. Yet we both thought all through the game that White was giving the odds of that piece. This mistake is not of infrequent occurrence. It reminds one of Bird's having once to refund a shilling. The veteran had been giving Pawn and two to an amateur in Purssell's. He had had occasion to move his Rh1, to protect his g2-pawn; soon afterwards the Rook went back to h1, in order to occupy the open Rook file; some minutes later he Castled with that Rook, and won the game. Well—two years later I tried to recover the 10-cent stake from Mr. Searle, on Staten Island, but found that I had in the meantime forgotten that he was a lawyer.

And now for the "Bisons," the Buffalo Chess Club. Its rooms have a rental of over $500 per annum. They are very comfortable and beautifully furnished. This thriving club was founded last February, through the exertions of Gen. J.A. Congdon, one of the America's oldest "traveling champions." On the evening of its formation I was playing a game of chess at Baltimore, with Mr. A.S. Richmond, a friend and former school-mate of president Cleveland. After the game, which resulted in a draw (Mr. R. being a player of considerable skill), a conversation ensued about chess in Buffalo, and I commented on the pity of an old chess center so near the Niagara Falls having no organized chess club. Endorsed. "But," said Mr. R., "if you ever come to Buffalo, be sure to visit the Acacia Club, you will be welcomed and will be sure of getting a game, though you may not get it from me." On that very evening he was elected president, not of the United States, but of the Buffalo Chess Club, which had been formed on that very evening. On my visit there in March, I had the honor of being elected the first honorary member of the club, which then numbered nearly seventy members. One of the most dangerous of these is S. Langleben, a pupil of Winawer's, at Warsaw. He "does things" such as the following: **1. e4 e5 2. Nf3 Nc6 3. Bc4 Bc5 4. b4 Bb6 5. a4 a6 6. b5 a×b5 7. B×b5**. With this curious "Evans-Ruy-Lopez" he won two very pretty games against Schottländer recently. G.C. Farnsworth and G.H. Thornton, the problemists, are not inferior to Langleben in strength.

Montreal has six chess clubs, three of which are good. The leading one is the Montreal Chess Club, which contains a number of fine players, probably about as good as the "Bisons" just spoken of. J.N. Babson is the leading spirit in chess at the Canadian metropolis. Montreal has three regular weekly chess columns, in the *Gazette* (J. Henderson), the *Herald* (J.N. Babson), and *La Presse*, a French-Canadian paper. All three are very well edited. The French-Canadian Chess and Checker Club has two good rooms of its own. I gave a simultaneous blindfold performance there (a complimentary one), and essayed six games, all of which I lost except one Evans Gambit. Since then I have drawn the line at five games. The six games were hard fought, and I never saw an audience better pleased. It was a novelty, and the jolly Frenchmen (who mostly did not know my nationality) were delighted at seeing a supposed son of Uncle Sam badly whipped at his own game. I have the honor of being a hon. member of the Montreal C.C. Montreal has been visited by Bird, Gunsberg, Mackenzie, Lasker and other masters, and at the time of writing Steinitz is there.

We may now take a run as far West as Ashtabula, which must be halfway between New York and Chicago. There is no chess club there, and we shall have to leave Lake Erie and go down South to Pittsburgh to find the next one. The PITTSBURGH C.C. meets in the library, while the ALLEGHENY C.C., just across the river, occupies a rather comfortable hall, used also as a lecture room, etc. Messrs.

John Henderson, the chess editor of the *Montreal Gazette* (*Le Monde Illustré*, February 10, 1894, page 491).

Lutton and McCutcheon are the rival giants of "Smoky City" over the board, and Messrs. Collins and Grier do the "literature" for Western Pennsylvania. While much cannot be said of the club-rooms and general arrangements, Pittsburgh is a good home for chess as well as for checkers. I have been treated with great hospitality by my Scotch-Irish friends there (Pittsburgh is a strong Scotch-Irish settlement), everybody, chess-player or not, giving the impression of being interested in the welfare of the game.

Pittsburgh is one of *the* cities in which I do not recollect having ever been asked the (to an Englishman) disagreeable question, "Have you taken out your papers (of naturalization) yet?" No Briton should visit America and omit Pittsburgh; he will find the Pittsburghers thorough Americans, but he will find himself at home there, and if he is the right sort he will find the Pittsburghers at home with and—to him.

The CHICAGO CHESS AND CHECKER CLUB is a strong one in numbers and force, in respect to both games. Louis Uedemann, chess editor *Chicago Times*, is, next to Amos Burn, late of Liverpool, England, probably the strongest player of the "Windy City." Chicago chess is, however, considerably disjointed at present, and it will take considerable time before the city is sufficiently disengaged from the whirlpool of business to admit of the introduction of the German Café and its concomitants, peace, order, coffee, cigars, and chess. To the greater Germany, and the introduction of her systems of orderly recreation, New York is chiefly indebted for her position as a really great chess centre. It will be long before the game will thrive in the United States to anything like the extent to which it does in New York. Chess players of the New World, for the most part, require something between the repulsive coarseness of the American bar-room or saloon, and the uncomfortable primness of the Sunday School, and of any institution at all public, the Continental Café, and the Continental Café alone, will fill the bill—outside New York at all events.

KANSAS CITY has had a good and bright Chess and Checker Club for some years past. A peculiarity of the Kansas City players is the varied hours at which they commence and finish play. It may be a sign of the approach to the Western liberty, for Kansas City must be nearly 1,500 miles from New York by most routes. Some of the Kansas City players often start operations long before 12:00 noon, while others prefer a corresponding hour at midnight. Messrs. Beebe, Merriam, and Shaw were the leading lights at the time of my visit; and G.A. L'hommêdé, now in Chicago, is becoming widely known as a correspondence expert. In one of his Canadian games (a Bishop's Gambit), not long ago, he independently discovered and announced a very long-winded mate from a position in the game which is dismissed by the *Handbuch* as a win for the other party!

Springfield, Mo., a town of some 30,000 souls, away down near Indian territory, has a small chess club in connection with the Y.M.C.A.E.W. Grabill is the leading player, and X. Hawkins the problem maker. American Y.M.C.A.'s do not in the large cities seem greatly to differ from similar institutions in England; but in the small towns of the interior they are curious and useful. Most of the country chess clubs owe their first existence to the local Y.M.C.A.'s; the latter are very often not intimately connected with religion, and are equally open to all creeds, positive or negative. Were they to depend solely on the devout for support, they would soon rust out. They generally have fair libraries and reading rooms, and often gymnasia, etc. Before leaving this part of the country, I cannot refrain from offering this little "sui," as a Xmas box from Grand Rapids, Mich., the home of the immortal Shinkman, and his talented nephew Würzburg.

by Otto Würzburg
White compels Black to mate in five

The St. Louis Chess Club has already been partly described in the *British Chess Magazine*, in connection with the battles of Judd and Showalter. It is very strong in strength of play, and few chess-playing travellers are there who have not enjoyed its genial society on some occasion. It was founded by Max Judd, and among its greatest supporters recently have been Messrs. J.W. Hulse and E.S. Rowse. Under the auspices of the club, one of the best meetings ever held in the interior was that of the United States Chess Association, in 1890, in which the prizes aggregated over 500 dollars. It was surprising that this liberal amount of prize-money should have induced no Eastern players to compete, excepting the ubiquitous A. Ettlinger, S. Lipschütz, and the writer.

The Indianapolis Chess Club meets at the Hotel English. Its quarters are not private, but are in the public parlour of the cosy old-fashioned hotel. It has seen some good chess a few years back, but is less celebrated as a regular club than as the nucleus of the Indiana State Chess Association, which promoted the Lasker–Showalter match; and, containing such active players and workers as Ballard, Brown, Jackson, and Ripley, has done and continues to do great things for that section of the country in chess. A tribute should be paid, in this connection, to the Ohio Association, led by Cincinnati. Chess in the last named city is poorly organized at present, though containing many fine players. Major Lowe, once a hustling patron saint of the game there, has removed to the oil regions of Pennsylvania, and is now one of the strong men of the Pittsburgh clubs. The Mount Auburn Chess Club, of Cincinnati, entertained me on my 32nd birthday. I found it, as a club, austere and classical. Its members met once a week in a school-room upon the beautiful Walnut Hills and they met for chess. The winner of its tournament was, after the custom of our Universities, elected president for the year. Sometimes, as in the case of W. Strunk, Jun., the president would be in his teens. I found the Auburn a thorough lot to beat, and I do not remember my score in the "simultaneous." Outside the club I have never met a more sociable crowd. Among Cincinnati's other great players and patrons have been Messrs. Cochran, Smith, Moehle, Nordhoff, Euphrat, Cameron, Kinzbach, Bachrach, H. and E. Bettmann, and Burgoyne.

The Washington Chess Club was not long ago re-organized, and now has a new room in a central situation. Mr. F.M. Wright, who once captained the Cambridge University Chess Club, is secretary. The club numbers about forty, all players. The membership is largely composed of government clerks and men of letters, the commercial element being of a minor importance in Washington. A peculiar "institution" of this club is that every member plays on even terms with the rest. The names are posted on a black-board, the strongest at the top, the weakest at the bottom. The grading is determined by a sort of continuous (but not skittle) tournament, the object of which is to select the best players for "the next team match." Their only important rivals in Washington are the players of the Cosmos Club—a social club comprising a large number of the first literary and scientific men of the city.

The BALTIMORE CHESS ASSOCIATION is another club of which *B.C.M.* readers have from time to time heard a good deal. Its president, E.L. Torsch, has in a quiet way done untold good labor in Caissa's vineyard, at home and abroad, for many years, from a pure love of the game and its surroundings. He has less time to devote to its practice than to its organization. He is the hero of original chess articles (many of which have appeared anonymously in the *Baltimore News* and other papers), humorous, instructive, and pathetic; of the "Torsch chess recognition buttons," of countless chess excursions, chess matches, chess dinners, and he seldom misses an opportunity of joining in the local tournament, in which he received Pawn and two moves from the writer. Although the old shipmates, Fuechsl, Hinrichs, R.C. Hall, Hughes, Schofield, Uhthoff, etc., stick to the old club like stout-hearted mariners to the pumps of a leaking vessel, they receive no encouragement from outside. There has been practically no new blood in the association for nearly ten years. No association has worked harder, under the captaincy of Mr. Torsch, in the interest of local chess. A large chess club was formed in the Young Men's Hebrew Association—it never took root. At the Y.M.C.A.'s it had the same fate. Weekly exhibitions were given free to the public, at the club-rooms—no lasting result. Bird, Blackburne, Gunsberg, Lasker (twice), Mackenzie, Pollock, Sellman, Showalter, Steinitz, Zukertort, have all by invitation given special exhibitions of play, attended frequently by over one hundred spectators, but the membership does not increase. In all respects except that of *making new blood*, the Baltimore Association thrives. It has constant revivals, fetes, and tournaments—it has almost everything that a plain chess club could desire. Matches are played over the board with Washington, correspondence matches with Albany and Boston, and for ordinary play the members meet nightly. Were the Baltimore Chess Club to be transplanted, members and all exactly as it is, to New York City it would within a year have five hundred members instead of fifty.

South of Baltimore there is hardly a chess club, properly so-called, in the United States. Atlanta, New Orleans, and Washington are the exceptions. It all tends to prove that some entirely new system of chess club should be adopted. That the good

work done in Baltimore has borne fruit elsewhere the writer knows well. It has created the Maryland Chess Association (now practically defunct), stimulated chess in Washington, gladdened the hearts of Albany, Boston, and Wilmington, left lasting impressions of good-will among the champions named above, started chess in Hagerstown and the Eastern Shore, produced innumerable contributions to the literature of the game, perhaps more especially in the problem line, with which the names of Arnold, Dennis, and Wieman [original had "Wiemann"] are connected; and beyond all, shewn forth that true spirit of chess masonry which is one of the noblest attributes of the practice of the game.

The latest effort of the Baltimore Association was the organizing of a Jewish Chess Resort, in connection with C. Schneider's German Restaurant. Something of a novelty, surely, in a club starting and supporting by its kindly interest a Jewish Chess Club and a Restaurant Chess Club, almost in the same block, and all three clubs within a stone's throw of each other!

The POLLOCK CHESS CLUB, of Hagerstown, Md., is the only chess club, properly so-called, in Maryland, excepting the Baltimore Chess Association. It was founded last winter, shortly after I had paid a visit to Hagerstown (a little town of some 15,000 inhabitants, but, excepting of course Baltimore, of equal importance with any town in the State). It derived its name from my having in a measure helped in its formation, in the circumstance of my having represented Maryland for some years as champion of that State, and from the fact of my editing the chess column in the *Baltimore News*, the official organ of the Maryland Chess Association. The club consists of a charming class of gentlemen, not very strong as yet, but improving through study, correspondence play, and occasional practice with the Baltimore players.

The FRANKLIN CHESS CLUB, Philadelphia, is a very powerful organization. I may here state that several of these clubs have moved into new quarters since I visited them, and there seems little advantage in describing their old nests. In this category are the Franklin, Montreal, New York City, Kansas City, and Hagerstown. The Franklin C.C. has fine new rooms, centrally situated, and among the best known members to English readers are Messrs. G. Reichhelm (*Philadelphia Times*), W.P. Shipley, Prof. Morley (late of the Bath College), Emil Kemény, Persifor Frazer, Martinez (father and son), Barbour, etc.

And now without further apology or prologue I will, after the good old English manner, wish to all the readers and staff of the *British Chess Magazine* "A Merry Christmas and a Happy New Year." May the bonds of masonry and mutual friendship between all chess players both in England and America grow stronger and stronger throughout 1894, and may the doings of a prosperous chess year more than ever prove to the outside world that the game is not only without a rival in its literary possessions, but beyond rivalry from any other mundane pursuit in its power to bind hearts and hands together with the strong cords of good fellowship and brotherly love.

KEYS TO PROBLEMS:

1. **Barth's Chess Problem:** the existence of different three solutions (1. Rf6; 1. Rb8; 1. Rc8) questions the accuracy of the diagram given in the original.

2. **Würzburg's self-mate problem: 1. B×a2 h4 2. Qh8 h3 3. Bg8+ Ba7+ 4. Nb6+ Kb8 5. Rg7 B×b6 mate.**

Appendix B: Pollock Obituaries

In addition to several obituary notices appearing in Chapter 14, below are the transcripts of others that saw print in the English, American and Canadian press.

Western Daily Press, October 7, 1896

DEATH OF A FAMOUS BRISTOL CHESS PLAYER. We regret to record the death of Mr. William Henry Krause Pollock, one of the most famous of modern English chess players, which occurred in this city yesterday morning. Mr. Pollock was the son of the Rev. William Pollock, who was formerly rector of St. Saviour's, Bath, and is now chaplain to the Bristol Blind Asylum. He was educated at Clifton College, under Dr. Percival, and was intended for the medical profession, but though he was a licentiate of the Royal College of Surgeons, Ireland, he practiced but little. It was in 1878 that he first began to show signs of exceptional talent as a chess player. He joined the Bath Chess Club, which in those days was remarkably strong, and a year or two later he began to rise into prominence in chess circles. Eventually, in 1883, he went to London, and from that time he took rank as one of the leading players of the country. Curiously enough, he was not very successful as a prize-winner, for in the great tournaments in which he entered he gained distinction rather by the brilliancy of individual games than by the scoring of a successive number of victories over his opponents. He took part in matches all over England, and he was especially popular in Ireland, where he played a large number of exhibition games. In 1889 he went to the United States to play in the great New York tournament, and it was there that he accomplished his most famous achievement. The game in which he beat Weiss of Vienna, in this tournament, is generally considered to be one of the finest ever played. He resided in America for some years afterwards, living first in Baltimore, where he edited the chess column of the *Baltimore News*, a work he continued up to the present year. After residing at Albany for some time, he crossed the border, and went to live at Montreal. Last summer he came back to England to play in the Hastings tournament as the representative of Canada, but his health had already began to fall, and he was not in his best form. He stayed in England until the commencement of the present year, and returned to Canada in February. During the summer his condition grew worse, and he decided to re-visit England again. Unfortunately, the vessel on which he was leaving Canada collided with another steamship in the St. Lawrence. The damage sustained by the steamer was serious, and it is believed that the shock so affected Mr. Pollock, in his weak state of health, as to hasten his end. The steamer put back into dock, and a week elapsed before he was able to leave for England on another steamer.

He reached this country six weeks ago, and was taken straight to his father's house, 5, Berkeley Square, Clifton, where he has remained ever since. It was soon realised that he was in a rapid consumption, and he died yesterday morning, beginning his 38th year. Mr. Pollock was an extremely good cricketer about fifteen years ago, and one of the most valuable members of the Bath Association team at that date. He was unmarried. His brother is the Rev. J. Pollock, vicar of St. Gabriel's, Swansea.

Pall Mall Gazette, October 9, 1896

Mr. W.H.K. Pollock, who has just died at Bristol from rapid consumption, was one of the most famous of modern English chess-players. It was in 1878 that he began to exhibit exceptional talent in the game, and from this time he rapidly rose into prominence, taking part in matches all over England and Ireland, in which country he was especially popular. Up to a few weeks ago the deceased held a distinguished position in literary and chess circles in America, and it was at the great New York Tournament of 1889 that he accomplished his most famous achievement—the defeat of Weiss, of Vienna. He was only thirty-seven.[1]

Bristol Mercury and Daily Post, October 10, 1896

It is with deepest regret—a regret which all chess players, not only in this country but in America will share—that we have to announce the death of Mr. W.H.K. Pollock, the brilliant chess player, who has delighted members of the Clifton Chess Club and others further afield, especially by his feats of simultaneous play. Mr. Pollock, who was the son of the Rev. William James Pollock, M.A., chaplain of the Blind Asylum, died on Tuesday at his father's residence, No. 5, Berkeley Square. Three or four weeks ago we mentioned his return from America, where ill-health compelled him to resign a prominent position he held in literary and chess circles. It was known when he reached his father's

residence that his recovery was hopeless, so seriously were his lungs affected, and despite every medical care and good nursing he succumbed on Tuesday. Mr. Pollock, who was 37 years of age, spent his early life in Bath, whence his father came to Bristol some few years ago.

Leeds Mercury (Weekly Supplement) October 10, 1896

W.H.K. POLLOCK:—The genial thorough Englishman, W.H.K. Pollock, left Canada lately for his parents' home to die. He perhaps thought it might end thus when he penned his "Farewell" letter in the Baltimore News chess column a month or two ago, but it was the heartfelt wish of all the readers of it that his sojourn for a time in the South of England would prove a lasting benefit. It is with deep regret we learn of his death on Monday evening last, at his father's residence in Berkeley-square, Bath [sic]. Though his malady seemed to increase, and it was believed would eventually end fatally, the suddenness came as a great shock to his friends, it was so unexpected. A brilliant man was poor Pollock, an enemy to no one but himself, and decidedly a chess genius, in whose company none could be for a moment dull. He has left many marks of his brilliant chess genius, and it may be possibly the work of some enthusiast to gather his gems together, and present them to the chess world as a most appropriate monument to his memory. Mr. Pollock was born at Cheltenham, February 21, 1859, being in his 38th year at the time of his death.

Morning Post, October 12, 1896

We regret to announce the death of Mr. W.H.K. Pollock, which occurred at Clifton on Tuesday. Mr. Pollock was born in 1858 [sic], and, after completing his education at Clifton College, took up the study of medicine and obtained a degree. Chess, however, had an extraordinary fascination for him, and he eventually abandoned the medical profession in order that he might devote himself to the game, of which he proved a highly original and ingenious exponent. He distinguished himself in the New York Tournament of 1889 by winning

---

1. One can already note, in the Pall Mall Gazette, the tendency toward uplifting the deceased. His chess columns and other writing in America, which barely kept him from a pauper's fate, were by now being referred to as "a distinguished position in literary and chess circles in America." Pollock himself would likely have smiled at such an appellation.

the Brilliancy Prize, and took up his residence in America, becoming the chess editor of the *Baltimore News*. Afterwards he settled in Montreal, whence he travelled to England to take part in the Hastings Tournament last year. A brief sojourn in this country was followed by his return to Canada; but the breakdown of his health induced him to come to England once more, and after staying with his father, the Rev. W. Pollock, at Clifton, he passed away, the cause of his death being consumption. Mr. Pollock was highly esteemed by chess players on both sides of the Atlantic, and his loss will be mourned by many friends.

The Times, October 13, 1896

English chess, properly so called, has sustained severe losses recently, in the deaths of Mr. Edward Freeborough, of Hull, and Mr. W.H.K. Pollock, of Bristol, both of whom had made excellent contributions to the literature of the game. (...) Mr. Pollock has been for some time in failing health. He had resided for the last 10 or 12 years [*sic*] in the United States and Canada. His analyses and notes, published mostly in the *Baltimore News*, were widely read and appreciated. It will be remembered that Mr. Pollock was one of the 22 Hastings competitors. After that event he returned to Montreal, but soon had to come home, and, as it turned out, to die last week at his father's house at the early age of 37. Mr. Pollock lived too exclusively for chess; but he has left a multitude of friends. He was at times a most brilliant player.

Bath Chronicle, October 15, 1896

The funeral took place on Friday at Arno's Vale Cemetery, Bristol, of Mr. W.H.K. Pollock, well known throughout the country as one of the most famous English chess players. The deceased gentleman arrived in this country about five weeks ago from America, where he has been staying several years. He went straight to the residence of his father, the Rev. William Pollock, chaplain to the Bristol Blind Asylum (formerly rector of St. Saviour's, Bath), being in a very weak state of health. It was soon realised that he was in a rapid consumption, and that the end was not far distant. Deceased was 38 years of age. He was educated at Clifton [College].

Dublin Daily Express, October 16, 1896

POLLOCK MEMORIES. [A Pollock chess problem was given here.] Irish chess players, particularly those of Dublin and Belfast, justly grieve for the sudden and unexpected death of their brilliant friend, Dr. William Henry Krause Pollock, who, in the prime of his life, passed away at his father's residence, Berkeley square, Clifton, Bristol, on the 5th inst.

He was born at Cheltenham, 21st Feb. 1859, was educated at Somersetshire College, Bath and Clifton College, and took his medical qualification in Dublin in 1882. We became acquainted with him in the year 1880, at which time he was a resident pupil of Steevens Hospital and a member of the City and County of Dublin Chess Club—now the Dublin Chess Club—where he was wont to meet such players as Messrs. R.F. Hunt, W.H.S. Monck, Parker Dunscombe, J.B. Pim, Capt. M.S. Woollett, and the late Major Shaw.

His friendly and genial manner, ever pleasant and agreeable, endeared him to the hearts of all and made him for ever afterwards a welcome guest and a popular favourite. About this time the only newspaper in Dublin containing chess was one issued by Messrs. W. and H.M. Goulding, entitled *The Practical Farmer*. In this his first published game and his first problem appeared. How many of his brilliant games have enriched the columns of other papers since?

After a sojourn in Bath, where he and his brother, the Rev. John Pollock, who is also a fine player, were well known, he returned to Dublin and competed in the tournaments of the Irish Chess Association Congress in October 1885, with the result that he won first prize in the even tournament, and second prize in the handicap.

In 1886 he played for Ireland in a correspondence match against Sussex, his opponent being L. Leuliette. During the same year he competed at the London Chess Congress, the Counties' Chess Association meeting at Nottingham, and the Belfast Congress which was held during September. In the even tournament of the latter he won the first prize, and title of Irish champion, J.H. Blackburne was second and Amos Burn third. In the handicap of the same, Dr. Pollock won second prize.

His next visit to Ireland was in 1888, when, in the month of December, he was accorded the warmest welcome in Dublin. Then, in addition to giving exhibitions of his gifted simultaneous play at the City, the Clontarf, the Dublin, the Kingstown, and the Rathmines Chess Clubs, he gave a performance to a large audience at the Leinster Hall, Molesworth Street. He also received a most cordial and enthusiastic reception from the chess-players of Belfast, Portadown, Londonderry, and Armagh, each of which town he visited during the month. From all accounts he met opponents equally as strong as those in Dublin, and it is worthy to record that most of the games played were remarkable for their style, dash, brilliancy and finish.

Dr. Pollock was then elected by the Dublin and the Northern players to represent Ireland at the Sixth American Chess Congress. At that great Congress he nobly represented us by winning the brilliancy prize of the tournament. On the eve of his departure for America he contested in a tournament of the I.C.A. in Dublin with the result that he won second prize; A. Burn won first by one game, and J. Mason was third. There were nine competitors. He resided in America for some years afterwards, living first at Baltimore, where he edited the chess column of the *Baltimore News*, a work he continued up to the present year. After residing at Albany for some time, he crossed the border, and went to live at Montreal. Last summer he came back to England to play in the Hastings tournament as the representative of Canada, but his health had already began to fail, and he was not in his best form. He stayed in England up to the middle of December last, when he came over to visit (alas! the farewell one) his many friends in Dublin, Blackrock (where his uncle, Dr. J.T. Pollock resides) and Kingstown. His failing health was then noticeable and caused much anxiety amongst his friends and relations. He then, against advice, returned to Canada. During the summer his condition grew worse, and he decided to re-visit England again. Unfortunately, the vessel on which he was leaving Canada collided with another steamship in the St. Lawrence. The damage sustained by the steamer was serious, and it was believed that the shock so affected Mr. Pollock in his weak state of health, as to hasten his end. The steamer put back into dock, and a week elapsed before he was able to leave for England on another steamer. He reached England

just seven weeks ago, and was taken straight to his father's house, 5 Berkeley square, where he remained up to the time of his death. It was soon realised that he was in a rapid consumption, and he died on the 5th inst., being in his 38th year. Mr. Pollock was an extremely good cricketer about 15 years ago, and was one of the most valuable members of the Bath Association team at that date. He was unmarried, eldest son of the Rev. W.J. Pollock, M.A. His brother is the Rev. J. Pollock, Vicar of St. Gabriel's Swansea.

Why Dr. W.H.K. Pollock did not follow the medical profession we do not know. It may have been that it was distasteful to him, or it may have been that his great love for chess caused him to give up all other pursuits. As it was, the course he adopted did not serve him, and we do not know of a single instance of any man being successful as a chess professional.

The remains were interred at Arno's Vale Cemetery on Friday morning. The funeral left Berkeley square at noon, and reached the cemetery shortly before one. The mourning coaches were occupied as follows: first coach, the Rev. W.J. Pollock, the Rev. J. Pollock and Miss Pollock; second coach, the Rev. Marcus Bickerstaff and Mrs. Bickerstaff; third carriage, the Revs. Leonard Bickerstaff and S. Day. The service was conducted by the Revs. Marcus and Leonard Bickerstaff. Amongst those at the graveside were the following gentlemen: Messrs. N. Berry and T. Furber, representing the Clifton and Literary and Philosophic Clubs; and Mr. H.H. Davies, representing the City Chess Club, and a number of local chess players. Amongst the many floral offerings and wreaths was one "In loving memory" from T.B. and F.F. Rowland, Kingstown, Ireland.

[This obituary ended with the score of Pollock's 1889 brilliancy against Max Weiss.]

Westminster Budget, October 16, 1896[2]

DEATH OF A NOTED CHESS-PLAYER. The death is announced to have taken place last week at

---

2. Pollock's passion for cricket was mentioned by Rowland in her *Pollock Memories* (page 7) by citing private correspondence: "[...] In a letter received from Mr. F.J. Lee he says: 'A very interesting fact concerning the young days of W.H.K.P. was his undoubted ability as a "Cricketer." Long before he went to America, and at the time of his first appearance in London, Pollock often went with me to witness great cricket matches at Lord's ground in London. On one notable occasion, previous to the commencement of a match—"M.C.C. and ground v Australians," Mr. A.G. Steel (at that time about amateur champion bat of England) was practising at the nets. Mr. Steel made a gigantic lofty drive, and Pollock caught the ball, to the astonishment and applause of a large assembly'."

Clifton, at the early age of thirty-seven, of Dr. William Henry Krause Pollock, a noted chess-player and cricketer years ago in the West of England. Mr. Pollock was the son of the Rev. William Pollock, the present chaplain at Bristol Blind Asylum. Mr. Pollock was a licentiate of the Royal College of Surgeons, but seldom [*sic*] practiced, having of recent years devoted the principal part of his time to chess. In 1876, when only seventeen, he began to show exceptional skill at the game, but it was not until 1883 that he became a leading player. In 1889 he took part in the great New York tournament, and his victory over Weiss, the Austrian champion, is still regarded as one of the best if not the best game played during the present century. Mr. Pollock subsequently went to reside at Baltimore, and took over the editorship of the chess column of the *Baltimore News*, a work in which he was still engaged at the time of his death. Two years ago he went to reside at Montreal, and all chess-players will remember the position he took in last year's tournament at Hastings, where he played as the representative of Canada. For some time Dr. Pollock had suffered from consumption, and a few weeks ago he decided to return to England, as the Canadian climate seemed to be increasing the disease. Just after the vessel started for Montreal it collided with another steamer, and the shock was keenly felt by the doctor. He had to go back, and a week passed before he was well enough to start again. He took up his residence in this country at Clifton, but was confined to his rooms the whole time since his arrival six weeks ago until his death. Some years ago the dead gentleman tried to take a serious interest in cricket, but his health failed him. Dr. Pollock was never married, but his nephew has already shown signs of following the deceased's love for chess.

Illustrated London News,
October 17, 1896

The news of the death of Mr. W.H.K. Pollock will be received with sincere regret by everyone who knows what a peculiar place he filled in the Chess world. While not a successful player as

counting by results, he was one of the finest the game has yet known, and some of his performances will not readily be forgotten. His classic contest with Weiss in the New York Congress is familiar to everybody, and raised him to the fellowship of the "Immortals," while even as recently as the Hastings Tournament last year he scored off both Steinitz and Tarrasch in a scarcely less striking fashion.

Nottinghamshire Guardian,
October 17, 1896

We regret to hear of the death of Mr. W.H.K. Pollock from consumption. He was one of the most brilliant of chess players, and the most charming of men. It has been suggested that a suitable memorial, in the shape of a collection of games, should be issued. We are sure that his devotion to chess was such that he would esteem this the highest testimonial to his career. He was the chess editor of the *Baltimore News*, and under his care the chess column of that paper was one of the best; full of good chess matter, always arranged in his inimitable style. The English chess world is a great loser by his death.

Newcastle Weekly Courant,
October 17, 1896[3]

We regret to announce the death of W.H.K. Pollock, which took place at his father's residence, Bristol. The distinguished master had returned recently from Canada in a delicate state of health. As a player Mr. Pollock's style was brilliant, and he has enriched the pages of chess literature with many delightful games. His notable encounters with Steinitz, Dr. Tarrasch, and Gunsberg in the Hastings tournament will be well remembered by our readers. Only a year ago this week Mr. Pollock was with us in Newcastle, when he gave striking examples of his skill as a simultaneous player—his score reading 34 wins, 2 losses and 2 draws. He was only in his thirty-eighth year, and his early

---

3. On October 17, the *Bristol Mercury and Daily Post* published three chess problems composed by Pollock and his victory over Steinitz at Hastings, with Pillsbury's notes. On the same day, the *Hampshire Telegraph and Sussex Chronicle* (a newspaper column that on September 27 published Pollock's win over Tarrasch from Hastings) announced Pollock's death "of consumption."

death robs the chess world of a kind, gentle and noble-hearted man.

Weekly Irish Times, October 17, 1896

(in addition to giving the score of Pollock's victory over Steinitz at Hastings)

At his father's residence, Berkeley square, Clifton, on Monday evening 5th inst., passed away W.H.K. Pollock, eldest son of the Rev. W.J. Pollock, M.A., well known to all our Dublin chess-players as one of the most popular and beloved of the masters. Educated at Somersetshire College, Bath, and Clifton College, he took his medical qualification in Ireland, 1882, where he acquired much of his chess, being a favorite of the Dublin Chess Club, especially on account of his great ability in the direction of simultaneous play. Later, he and his brother (the Rev. J. Pollock) were well-known in Bath. In 1885 he took the first prize at the meeting of the Irish Chess Association. He left England for America in 1889 and resided in Baltimore. He subsequently settled in Montreal, Canada, and became the chief representative of that country at the International Tournament held at Hastings, England, in August 1895. After the Hastings Tournament he returned to his father's home in Bristol, and gave several simultaneous exhibitions at the Bristol and Bath Chess Clubs. Subsequently he went on tour to the Northern Counties, and played successfully at Leeds, Newcastle, &c. He visited Dublin last Christmas, and played at Blackrock and Booterstown Chess Club simultaneously on December 21st and gave an exhibition at the Coffee Palace, Townsend street, on the evening of January 2, where he encountered many strong players. He returned to Montreal on February 29, where he was warmly received and gave several exhibitions of play there, and also object lessons and lectures at the famous clubs there.

His last public exhibition of simultaneous play was at the Montreal Chess Club on May 14 last, when he encountered a very strong team and played with great success. Immediately after this, the symptoms of the insidious disease to which he eventually fell a victim were developed, and though the summer months were favourable to him, he finally decided on returning home for rest and medical treatment. He arrived at Bristol on August 27, after a very perilous and prolonged voyage, which un-

doubtedly hastened the course of the disease. Still his friends hoped that with care and the very best treatment his life might be prolonged. But he passed away rather suddenly on Monday evening.

The remains were interred at Arno's Vale Cemetery on Friday morning. The funeral left Berkeley square at noon and reached the cemetery shortly before one. The mourning coaches were occupied as follows:—First Coach, the Rev. W.J. Pollock, the Rev. J. Pollock, and Miss Pollock; second coach: the Rev. Marcus Bickerstaff and Mrs. Bickerstaff and S. Day. The service was conducted by Revs. Marcus and Leonard Bickerstaff. Amongst those at the graveside were the following gentlemen: Messrs. N. Berry and T. Furber, representing Clifton and Literary and Philosophic Clubs; and Mr. H.H. Davis, representing City Chess Club and a number of local chess players. Amongst the many floral offerings and wreaths was one "In Loving Memory" from T.B. and F.F. Rowland, Kingstown, Ireland.

In the remarks on Mr. Pollock's play, the Book of the Hastings Tournament says—"He could probably take a better position by treating the game more seriously. Pleasant in manners, brilliant in style, and an agreeable companion, he still lacks staying power. Many of his games are of the highest order, and the one against Weiss, at the 1889 Congress has become historic. He has won many "brilliancy prizes" and was one of the deepest and cleverest in analysis, his annotations to some of the games in the *British Chess Magazine* being very valuable. As a chess editor and an original writer he had few equals."

This obituary ended with the following inscription, which very well may have been carved on Pollock's gravestone:

WILLIAM HENRY KRAUSE POLLOCK,
Born February 21st, 1859.
Died October 5th, 1896.

The brilliant chess master.
The keen analyst.
The original writer.
The beloved friend.

"He is not dead, but sleepeth."

Montreal Witness, October 16, 1896

The news of his death, though more sudden than expected, will hardly be unexpected; though it will bring grief to the heart of many a friend in and out of Montreal Chess circles, not to mention that far wider circle whom his genial and kindly ways drew around him at every point of his Bohemian wanderings. [...]

As a chess editor and analyst Pollock was also in the front rank, and his columns in the *Baltimore News* and *Albany Journal* were eagerly sought after by Chess editors the world over, and his opinions were quoted and referred to with a deference most flattering. For some time in the early nineties he was intimately associated with Steinitz in the preparation of his "Modern Chess Instructor," which owes much both in analysis and literary polish to Pollock's indefatigable enthusiasm wherever Chess was concerned. [...]

Albany Evening Journal, October 18, 1896

W.H.K. Pollock, the famous chess player, died in Bristol, England, his old home, October 5, aged 37 years. Up to a year ago he had been resident of Albany for a few years. He was the chess editor of "The Journal," and did admirable work on the local staff, having a style of writing which was peculiarly his own. In addition to his work on "The Journal" he conducted chess departments for Baltimore and Montreal newspapers, leaving America to take part in the international tournament in which Pillsbury first astonished the chess world. Mr. Pollock made a fine showing at that time in competition with the great masters of the game. He was of a quiet, lovable disposition and during his stay in Albany won many friends.

Brooklyn Daily Eagle/New York World/New York Times, October 18, 1896

Death of W.H.K. Pollock: A Noted Chess Player and Writer Passes Away. W.H.K. Pollock, the eminent chess player, died at Bristol, England, on October 5. For a number of years and till his last illness he made the United States his home. He was born on February 20, 1859, at Chitenham [*sic*: Cheltenham], educated at Clifton college and took his medical qualification in Ireland, where he acquired much of his chess at the Dublin Chess Club. It was early in the spring of

1889 that Pollock came to America as one of the British representatives at the sixth American chess congress, where he gained the brilliancy prize in a game with Weiss that has become historic. Of this game William Steinitz in the book of the congress says: "Mr. Pollock's play from the seventeenth move renders this game one of the finest monuments of chess ingenuity, and altogether it belongs to the most brilliant gems in the annals of practical play." [The game was reproduced at this point.] Since that congress Mr. Pollock occupied himself with his profession of journalism, playing much brilliant chess and competing at the Hastings international tournament of 1895. In 1891 he won the championship of the Brooklyn Chess Club in a field of exceptionally strong players.

Brooklyn Standard-Union, October 19, 1896

Death of W.H.K. Pollock. Dr. W.H.K. Pollock, the eminent chess player, died in Bristol, England, on Oct. 5. For a number of years, and till his illness, he made the United States his home. He was born on February 21, at Chitenham [*sic*: Cheltenham]. He was educated at Clifton College and took his medical qualification in Ireland, where he acquired much of his chess at the Dublin Chess Club.

It was early in the spring of 1889 that Pollock came to America as one of the British representatives at the Sixth American chess congress, where he gained the brilliancy prize in a game with Weiss that has become historic. Of this game, William Steinitz, in the book of the congress, says: "Mr. Pollock's play from the seventeenth move renders this game one of the finest monuments of chess ingenuity, and altogether it belongs to the most brilliant gems in the annals of practical play." Since the congress Mr. Pollock occupied himself with the profession of journalism, playing much brilliant chess and competing at the Hastings international tournament of 1895.

Belfast News-Letter, October 22, 1896

Chess players in our own province, especially those who remember the brilliant performance of Mr. William Henry Krause Pollock at the Belfast Congress in 1886, heard with regret of his decease.

Born in Cheltenham in 1859, he studied at Bath and Clifton College, coming to Dublin to study medicine. We find him in 1880 a member of the Dublin Chess Club, where his genial manner rendered him a universal favourite. His first problem and his first published game appeared in *The Practical Farmer*, a paper issued by Messrs. W. & H.M. Goulding, the only paper in Dublin containing then a chess column. His first visit to Ulster was in 1886 to attend the Chess Congress, held in the Examination Hall, Queen's College, when he carried off the first prize of the handicap. He paid a second visit to our province in 1888, and received a most enthusiastic welcome from the chess players of Belfast, Portadown, Londonderry, and Armagh. He went to America to take part in the sixth American Congress, and for his remainder of a too brief a life that country became his home. He edited with marked success and ability the chess column of the *Baltimore News*, and his pathetic farewell appeared in this column a few weeks ago. He played last year at Hastings, but though the brilliancy of his genius was still apparent, failing health prevented him taking a high place. After returning to America his health became worse, and he came home to his father's house to die. Mr. Pollock was a kind friend, a genial companion, and his loss is greatly deplored by all who had the pleasure of his acquaintance.

Knowledge, December 1, 1896 (page 288)

By the death of Mr. W.H.K. Pollock, at the age of thirty-seven, Anglo-Canadian chess loses its leading representative, and the *British Chess Magazine* an able contributor. Mr. Pollock made his first public appearance as a player in the second class of the Counties' Chess Association about fourteen years ago. On that occasion Mr. Pollock took the first prize, without losing a single game, Mr. Locock (who also made his *début* on this occasion) being second. After this Mr. Pollock rapidly rose to the position of an acknowledged expert, and was a regular attendant at the meetings of the Counties' Chess Association (to which he usually went on foot) and other first-class tournaments, both national and international. Though he never took a very high place in these latter, he was always reckoned a dangerous competitor; witness his brilliant victories over Steinitz and Tarrasch in the Hastings Tournament last year. Outside the chess world Mr. Pollock was a man of educated tastes, a licentiate of the College of Surgeons, and, like Mr. Blackburne, as fond of cricket as of chess. This latter taste he acquired no doubt at Clifton College, where he was educated for a short time, and afterwards at Somersetshire College, Bath.

Appendix C: *Pollock Memories*: Inception and Reception

Following Pollock's death, F.F. Rowland proved instrumental in putting together material for a small biography of her friend. In her October 31, 1896, column in the Weekly Irish Times, *she commenced a section titled "Pollock Memories," a series which continued to 1899. In November 1896, Rowland began a concentrated effort to collect relevant material on Pollock's life and games from the United States, Canada and England.[4] She wrote personal letters to the men with whom Pollock interacted, asked for personal recollections and appealed for help in their columns.*

---

4. From the *Irish Times* of November 21, 1896: "A few friends are co-operating in collecting the brilliant games and other various interesting articles, by the above lamented Chess master, with the view of publishing them in book form, as a tribute to his memory. Any games, reminiscences, &c, sent to the Chess Editor of this paper will be carefully copied and, if requested, returned to the senders. American and Canadian exchanges kindly notice." Both American and Canadian columnists eagerly helped the project. The same announcement appeared in the December 10, 1896, issue of the *St. John Globe,* and no doubt elsewhere by way of the chess exchanges.

Her appeal sparked some fine recollections of Pollock. The below appeared in the St. John (New Brunswick) Globe *of February 19, 1897*:

A POLLOCK ANECDOTE—He was once paired with an opponent in a tournament in Ireland, to whom he had to concede the odds of pawn and two moves. His vis-à-vis moved at once P–K4, and then paused. Time went on—a half-hour, three quarters had passed, but no other move was made. The hour was nearly completed, and Pollock ventured—"My friend, it is about time you made your second move." "What other move?" asked his companion. "Why, I gave you pawn and two moves, and as yet you have made only one." "That is my business," said the other, "the rules do not compel me to make the second move now, and I reserve the right to make two consecutive moves at any time during the game, according to my choice, and when I think such play will be of greater advantage to me." An argument ensued, during which the obstinate player insisted that there was no rule which stated that the two moves should be made immediately at the commencement of the game. As this was his first experience in tournament play, Pollock eventually convinced him of his error, and the game proceeded on orthodox lines.

Presumably in the weeks after Pollock's death, she also obtained Pollock's manuscripts, including his original notebooks containing nearly 3,000 games played by various masters and amateurs, with Pollock's own annotations. Unfortunately, this wealth of material appears not to have survived.[5] The news of Rowland's work on a tribute to Pollock in book form was received with enthusiasm in Canada as well. The following appeared in the St. John (New Brunswick) Globe *of January 21, 1898*:

Mrs. F.F. Rowland, 6 Rus-in-Urbe, Kingstown, Ireland, announces the early publication of "Pollock Memories," a memorial to the lamented W.H.K. Pollock. We are indebted to Miron, of the *New York Clipper,* for the announcement. Mr. Pollock was a brilliant man in many ways. Some of his games are gems of the first water. His pathetic farewell to his American friends, followed so soon by his death in the home where he vainly sought

health, was one of the saddest events in American chess. Mrs. Rowland's work is a labor of love, which should meet with wide favor.

The January 1898 issue of the American Chess Magazine *(vol. I, no. 8, page 455) contained details of Rowland's book, calling it "nearly completed." The editor added: "Pollock was well liked in this country. He was a genial, kindly man, and always willing to give from the large share of chess knowledge he possessed. His games had a sparkle that was most enchanting, and the collection of them in one volume will be hailed with pleasure by many Americans." But there were financial problems with preparing the book, as Rowland revealed to the chess editor of the* Manchester Times *(September 16, 1898)*:

Dear Sir—This work [*Pollock Memories*] is in the press, but the publication is deferred until sufficient funds are guaranteed to pay the expenses. I am quite sure, if the chess-playing public are made aware of the cause of the delay, that the money will be at once provided. The work is compiled as a tribute to the memory of the late "Brilliancy Master," and contains 200 of his selected games in England, Ireland, Holland, Germany, America, and Canada, with portrait, biography, problems, endgames &o. Subscription forms can be had on application to me, on receipt if money is sent (2s. 9d. post free).—Yours faithfully, (Mrs.) Frideswide F. Rowland, 6, Rus-in-Urbe, Kingstown, Ireland.

After some delay apparently caused by an inability to raise sufficient subscriptions, F.F. Rowland's Pollock Memories: A Collection of Chess Games, Problems, &c., &c. *was finally published in Dublin at the end of 1899 or in the first two months of 1900.[6] Just prior to being sent to printers, it was priced at two shillings and nine pence before publication (on subscription basis). After publication, the price was increased to five shillings. The project was endorsed by the* British Chess Magazine *which noted in its September 1899 issue (page 373)*:

POLLOCK MEMORIES
Mrs. T.B. Rowland, 6, Rus-in-Urbe, Kingstown,

---

5. An appeal on "the Pollock notebooks" to fellow researchers and archivists in Edward Winter's widely-read *Chess Notes* column at *www.chesshistory.com* (C.N. 6134) led to no results. ● **6.** In 1998, in an article for ChessCafe.com ("A Chess Idealist," reprinted on pages 227–233 in his *A Chess Omnibus*), Edward Winter brilliantly recollected Pollock's chess based on Rowland's work. Winter noted Pollock enjoyed the posthumous distinction of "being one of the very few players to be the subject of a biographical games collection in the nineteenth century." Around 2001, Moravian Chess Publishing House (Czech Republic) reprinted Rowland's work.

Ireland, who is editing the selection of games played by the late W.H.K. Pollock, with a brief sketch of his career, informs us that the printer has promised that the work will be ready for the subscribers sometime during the present month.

We have seen some forward sheets, and have pleasure in advising those of our readers who have not subscribed for the book to do so at once, as the price after publication will be raised from 2/9 to 5/–.

The March 1900 issue of the British Chess Magazine *(page 97) published the following:*

"Pollock Memories"

The long-promised book has appeared at last, but with no explanation for its lateness. The delay in publication will, of course, not affect the merits of the work; it will rather enhance them, as giving greater opportunity for editorial revision; but we

fear it may somewhat prejudice the sale to non-subscribers, for it is now more than three years since Mr. Pollock's death. The book is edited by Mrs. Rowland, the well-known chess player and problem composer of Kingstown, Ireland, and is divided into two parts. The first part contains a portrait and biography of the late Mr. Pollock, and 70 of his games, played in England, Ireland, and Holland, which were selected, noted, and diagrammed by himself. The second part consists of a selection of games played by Mr. Pollock in the United States and Canada, including his match games with Messrs. Delmar, Showalter, and Gossip, also various consultation and correspondence games, together with several end-games of the deceased master, and a few specimens of his problems. The book is clearly printed on good paper, and bound in cloth. As it has only just come into our hands, we have not had time to play through the 145 games, with a view to ascertaining their accuracy of record, but great care seems to have been taken as to this matter throughout the whole work, and as there is no list of errata, we presume there is nothing to correct. To all Mr. Pollock's old friends this volume will be a welcome reminiscence, and to those who never knew him, but have only heard his fame, we commend the book as a valuable collection of instructive games, well worth possessing at its moderate price.

After a minor mention in the London Standard's *column,[7] the book was reviewed in W.H.S. Monck's chess column in the* Common Sense *of March 1900 (page 56):*

Pollock Memories has appeared at last, and I think it was worth waiting for. Pollock had all the brilliancy of Morphy, but without his steadiness. Morphy hardly ever played a brilliant combination that was not sound, but Pollock often did, and still more frequently he got a bad position in trying to bring about a combination that did not come off. In this last respect, as in others, Morphy stands supreme. Had his adversary seen through the projected sacrifice, and prepared for it, he would have still found Morphy with an even game, and few of his contemporaries could play an end game better. This fact, however, does not render Pollock's games less worth study. In some of those which he lost we may fail to see what he was aiming at, but we

Frideswide F. Rowland (F.R. Gittins, *The Chess Bouquet; or, The Book of the British Composers of Chess Problems*, **London, 1897, page 77).**

---

7. "Mrs. F.F. Rowland has published a selection of games played by the late W.H.K. Pollock, 'as a small tribute to the memory of a dear friend.' The games have been corrected by the late Mr. Pollock and annotated, probably with a view to eventual publication" (February 20, 1900).

Pollock Memories:

A collection of

CHESS GAMES, PROBLEMS,

&c., &c.

Part I—Portrait, Biography, and 70 Games, played in England, Ireland, and Holland, selected, annotated, and illustrated by the late W. H. K. POLLOCK.

Part II—A selection of Games played in the United States, and Canada, including his matches with EUGENE DELMAR, JACKSON SHOWALTER, and G. H. D. GOSSIP; End Games, Problems, and items of interest connected with the Chess career of the late Master.

EDITED BY MRS. F. F. ROWLAND.

DUBLIN:
MRS. F. F. ROWLAND, 6 RUS-IN-URBE, KINGSTOWN.

1899.

Solvers Prize
Presented to Charles Barry
by Chess Editor
"Weekly Irish Times"
Jan 7th 1903
H. Rowland

The title page of F.F. Rowland's *Pollock Memories* **and a personal inscription by the author (courtesy Edward Winter).**

may feel assured that he was trying for something that did not come off. If I were to add another to the number of chess maxims I would be disposed to say: Always play with an object and not merely because it is your turn to play.

> 'Tis better to have tried and lost
> Than never to have tried at all

[*Monck then gave the score of a game Burn–Pollock from* Pollock Memories, *with Pollock's notes.*]

The Illustrated London News *chess column of February 17, 1900, commented*[8]:

"Pollock Memories" (Dublin: Mrs. F.F. Rowland)—This is a short sketch of the life of the late W.H.K. Pollock and a selection of his games. Together they form a not unworthy memorial of one of the most brilliant players of our time, who, if occasionally uncertain, was never dull, and from whom the very foremost champion was seldom

safe. His game with Weiss at New York ranks as the classical masterpiece of this generation, and his defeat of Tarrasch at Hastings was little inferior in its surprising effects. To those who wish to possess a permanent record of a fascinating personality this book can be well commended. The price is five shillings, and the work can be obtained from the editor-publisher, Mrs. F.F. Rowland, 6, Rus in Urbe, Kingston, Dublin.

A very positive review appeared in the Pall Mall's *March 13, 1900, column:*

"Pollock Memories," edited by Mrs. F.F. Rowland, is a book which charms us almost on every page to which we turn. There is an idealism pervading the splendid collection of games, which strongly reminds one of the finest traits of character of the deceased chess player when at his best. The notes are mostly by Pollock himself and taken

---

8. The same was reproduced in the *Literary Digest* of March 17, 1900.

from a large collection of games which he left behind. They will be found very valuable to the student. The book also contains a collection of end games played by the deceased master, as well as a few problems, and a biographical sketch of his career. Owing to the fact that the late Mr. Pollock was engaged in various tournaments in which he met most of the best players of the world, the book really forms a most representative collection of games. The book is also published by the able editress, Mrs. F.F. Rowland, King's Town, Dublin.

The book was also warmly received in the May 14, 1900, column of the Morning Post. *The latter published an extensive presentation, which*

included the following, perhaps best summing up Pollock's finest traits as a chess player:

Pollock's reputation, however, rests not so much on the winning of games as on his extraordinary inventive power and the abundance of charming and surprising combinations that characterised his play. If these did not always lead to victory they usually illustrated the subtle beauties of the game, and this was invariably Pollock's aim rather than the mere defeat of his opponent. He played more as an artist than as a combatant, and his games, on this account, are the more capable of affording entertainment, and not the less worthy of preservation.[9]

Appendix D: A Pollock Essay on Time Limits

The following brief article by W.H.K. Pollock appeared in the Irish Times *of August 21, 1897. It was originally published much earlier. (See, for instance, Hazeltine's* New York Clipper, *where the text below appeared in the July 9, 1892, issue.) It is worth noting the rate of play in two of the strongest tournaments Pollock took part in: the Sixth American Chess Congress (1889)—15 moves an hour; Hastings Tournament (1895)—30 moves in 2 hours.*

A QUESTION OF THE CHESS AGE

Can anyone devise a time limit that shall dispense with the debilitating effect of stop-clocks? Stop-clocks are the ruin of the first class chess, because the clock is a more pressing agent in match and tournament play than the game itself, than glory, gains, or ambition. Every modern combination is subservient to time. Steinitz has shown the highest art in accommodating his genius to this agent, but will it glorify his record when, long hence, comparison of his games is instituted to those of Morphy's? Morphy used no time limit, and there would be plenty of games, not merely a

few here and there, played equal to Morphy's finest efforts were modern masters equally untrammeled. We want a modification of the absurd 15 or 20 moves an hour system. Let the time limit be a limit to inconveniently slow play, not a spur to the practice of ingenious arts and tricks in order "to get into the second hour." A time limit might be imposed after a game, say of 30 moves' duration had already occupied about five hours. Games, would, therefore, be increased in speed, on the average, and there would be no more clap-trap about the weakness of the modern dog, and superlativeness of the dead lions.

---

9. On page 304 of *The Steinitz Papers: Letters and Documents of the First World Chess Champion* (McFarland, 2002) Kurt Landsberger inexplicably wrote the following bizarre note on F.F. Rowland: "A resident of Ireland and a problem composer, she completed a biography and games collection of Pollock in 1898, which may not have been published (probably because of a lack of funding)."

Appendix E: A Question of Originality

*W.H.K. Pollock was an original player who often dared innovative ideas in the openings. For instance, his **2. Qe2** (after 1. e4 e6) concept in his 1890 game against J. Halpern [**see Game 418**] was quickly adopted by Chigorin that very year, and it is still seen today in high level tournament play as a surprise line. Pollock has written on the issue of opening originality in an article which subsequently appeared serialized in several chess columns. It also appeared in full in Rowland's* Pollock Memories, *pages 152–153, citing the* Baltimore Sunday News. *It is reproduced below in full; it first appeared in the April 18, 1896, edition of the* Baltimore Sunday News[10]:

QUEER MOVES IN CHESS

It is astonishing what bizarre and unexpected moves can be found right in the opening of a game—nay, as early as the first, second, or third moves. I refer to such as can be made without danger, and even with advantage. Anderssen made a great hit with **1. a3** in his match with Morphy, and Boden took the great New Orleans player "out of the books" with good results by **1. f3**. Some moves that have occurred in my own experience will be less well known, and, therefore, amusing.

On entering Simpson's Divan one morning some years ago I gave out that I had discovered an entirely new move for White in giving the odds of a piece, viz., on the first move. Veteran Bird, who fears not to start a game with any move whatever, got up on his hind legs at this, but when I took off the QKt and moved the R to the vacant square he sat quite still. A gentleman shortly after came in, and a well-known professional player remarked "sotto voce" that he would like to tackle him for the customary shilling stake, but he always exacted the odds of Knight, and was just strong enough to make it very poor market. "Go in and try my new move," said I, and he did so and won four games straight!

I once told Showalter that in the great New York Tournament of 1889 I played **1. d4** against Weiss, who replied also **1. ... d5**."Now," said I (as soon as my old friend had acknowledged that he did not recollect the game), "I will give you 18 guesses as to what my second move was." He failed to guess it. The move was **2. Qd3**. (A good game, too. See Tournament book.) There must be some sort of mind reading in this kind of bluff, for I tried the same on Arthur Peter, who won the "free-for-

all" at Lexington, Kentucky, and his first guess was **2. Qd3** *(see diagram)*.

After
2. Qd1–d3

Another time I allowed a young New York player (who was smart enough, anyway, to have gained one of Loyd's gold chess pins for solving), no fewer than 27 guesses as to what a certain new defence which I had discovered to the Ruy Lopez was. He did not find it, and finally besought me to tell him. It was **3. ... Na5!** *(see diagram)* Quite a feasible move, too. I have played it against Lasker and Burn.

After
3. ... Nc6–a5

Now, Alapin, the Russian master, comes out

---

10. The present authors have added several diagrams for ease of visualization.

with four or five pages of analysis in *La Stratégie* to prove that the correct defence to the Ruy Lopez is **3. ... Bb4!** It is even worse than my move, if only because less ridiculous.

Two or three years ago I showed Babson, the renowned problemist, a new opening which I had invented on the street. I called it the "King's Own Gambit." It was **1. e4 e5 2. f4 e×f4 3. Kf2!** *(see diagram)* "I'll try it on Short" (a strong player with whom he had had little success), said he, and he won 11 games straight at the opening.

After
3. Ke1–f2

I have been reduced to such desperation when rendering the odds of a Kt to a player who had "got on to" all my opening tricks that I have had to make double fianchettos with the Rooks instead of the Bishops, getting the latter on the Rooks squares.

To get Staunton out of his grooves in the QP opening St. Amant repeatedly answered **1. d4** with **1. ... c5.** I played thus twice in the Hastings Congress and would do so again. I usually play the Kt to a6 and subsequently to c7.

There is hardly any hopelessly bad move in answer to **1. e4,** except if be **1. ... f5.** Delmar is fond of opening with **1. g4** in skittles, and **1. b4** has produced fine games.

Steinitz has been defending the Ruy Lopez with

3. ... Bc5 and **4. ... Qf6** with excellent results in his matches.

I have seen the King moved—as Black's first move, i.e., **... Kf7**—as a defence in a Pawn and move game.

I have seen Bird win a dead-lost game in a handicap tournament by taking a Pawn "en passant" with a Rook; in other words, "jumping it." Neither player noticed it, and the bystanders thought they had no right to interfere.

And many other curious moves too numerous to be related here. But I should like to see a position which Mr. Loyd told me he had constructed some years ago—or, at least, was constructing. It was a sort of problem in which both Kings were in perpetual check, and neither could escape, nor could either side either win or lose the game. He called it "The Whirlpool."

One of Alapin's leading variations is curious:

After
11. Rf1–e1

1. e4 e5 2. Nf3 Nc6 3. Bb5 Bb4 4. 0–0 Nge7 5. c3 Ba5 6. B×c6 N×c6 7. b4 Bb6 8. b5 Na5 9. N×e5 0–0 10. d4 Qe8 11. Qd3 and White is made to get into trouble by f5 and d6. It is strange that so good a player should have failed to notice the great superiority of **11. Re1**. Many other of his variations are very ingenious, and more carefully worked out.

Appendix F: Pollock's Chess Problems

W.H.K. Pollock was also attracted to chess artistry of a different kind: the composition of chess problems. He excelled at problem solving or created problems of his own. The problem solving section of many British columns of the 1880s often published his name as one of the solvers. Toward encouraging such practice among his readers, the chess columnist of the Belfast News-letter *of March 14, 1889, wrote: "It is worthy to note that Mr. W.H.K. Pollock owes much of his proficiency as a player to solving problems. He competed in one of the solution tourneys of the* Sheffield Independent *and* Bristol Mercury, *and retained a place in the front rank throughout." In addition to the Pollock problems published in chapters 5 and 8 of the present work, page 158 of* Pollock Memories *offered four of Pollock's original chess problems:*

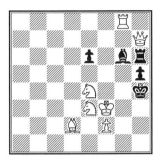

1. White mates in two
by W.H.K. Pollock

2. White mates in two
by W.H.K. Pollock

3. White mates in two
by W.H.K. Pollock & Samuel Gold

4. White mates in three
by W.H.K. Pollock & T.B. Rowland

The problem below appeared in the Dublin Daily Express, *October 16, 1896, and in the* Bristol Mercury and Daily Post, *October 17, 1896:*

5. White mates in five
by W.H.K. Pollock

KEYS & FURTHER NOTES:

Problem 1: 1. Ng5. This problem appeared in the *Bristol Mercury and Daily Post*, October 17, 1896.

Problem 2: 1. Nd6 About this problem *Pollock Memories* also states at page 158: "This very peculiar and highly original problem was composed by Mr. Pollock on the occasion of giving a lesson on the art of composing at the Baltimore Chess Association." We can now add that it first appeared in the *Baltimore Sunday News*, June 29, 1890.

Problem 3: 1. Kd3

Problem 4: 1. N3f4

Problem 5: 1. Ng6+

Appendix G:
Pollock's Review of Steinitz

In his August 25, 1889, Baltimore Sunday News *column, W.H.K. Pollock reviewed the first volume of W. Steinitz's* The Modern Chess Instructor *(1889) (punctuation follows the original)*

The Modern Chess Instructor
BY WILLIAM STEINITZ
(Part I, Published by G.P. Putnam's Sons, New York, 27 and 29 West Twenty-third St.; and London, 27 King William St., Strand)

Steinitz's long expected work is at last before the public, and we may honestly say that, taking the First Part as an average of the whole, it surpasses anticipation. To avow that the analytical result of the author's thirty odd years of laborious industry smashes up every preconceived idea of Chess Openings and the theory of the game in general, would involve an amount of research utterly beyond our present scope or field, for there are about fifty solid pages devoted to *Ruy Lopez* and its modern developments alone, but it is fair to state right away that this is, in our opinion, the first part of an altogether original and unique campaign upon the accepted theory of the intricacies of chess, and perhaps the first attempted complete treatise on the game in any language, since that of Howard Staunton.

The volume contains 234 large pages (including index of games), and is divided into four chapters of general description and laws of the game, an article on the Ethics of Chess, one chapter defining the ideas of the "Modern School," a splendid epitome of "the principles," and the 192 pages of analysis and games proper divided among the Ruy Lopez and its kind, the Scotch, Two Knights, Petroff, Philidor and lastly twenty games, very fully annotated, including the recent Steinitz–Chigorin match and other Havana match and consultation games.

The author in the preface makes no bones of distinguishing his plans of "reasoning out the opening moves by comparison of different maxims," from *empirical* methods long pursued by "the authorities," but to avoid misapprehension we may here state that he has also grasped a distinction between his meth-

ods of conducting a polemic department of a chess magazine and elaborating a Standard Work on the game, the tone of which is faultless, as we ourselves expected it would be, for Mr. Steinitz's devotion to and enthusiasm for his work has drowned even references to feuds or factions, personal or general.

The explanations of the movements of the pieces, notation, technical terms, etc., are clear and stamped with thoroughness, and quite sufficient for the guidance of beginners, and the Laws of the Game given are mainly those of the British Chess Association, as adopted in congresses, with some few hints and amplifications.

In Chapter V, an able treatise on "Chess as a Training of the Mind and How to Improve," the author devotes a few remarks as to the advantages of the study of Problems, which he considers, although not absolutely necessary, to be especially useful (in solving if *thoroughly* worked out) for strengthening the mind in the exercise of precision and conception of fresh ideas in actual play.

Chapter VI may be called a definition of the "Modern School" of practice, but the succeeding chapter of the "Relative Value of Pieces and Principles of Play" is most important. The author follows Staunton in his approximate estimate of the value of the pieces (Pawn 1, Queen, 9.94); about the Bishop and Knight, however, respectively 3.50 and 3.05, we are at variance, and imagine that recent developments in Openings, Endings and Problems have tended to ring the possibilities of power in those pieces much closer together.

"The King is considered *invaluable*." Now this is thoroughly "Steinitzian!" but no less so are the Author's elucidations of the power possessed by this piece, in accordance with the principles of the modern school. We have often heard Mr. Blackburne when in a humorous vein comment on the worn aspect of his opponent's King compared with that of other figures of his private set of chessmen, but the renowned English master is as ready to recognize its serious scientific phase. But this is a chapter that should be made a careful study by every player who wishes to be able to acquire an intellectual and interesting style of chess.

Further on, we hope to say a little about the six main openings treated in this book, and to conclude our present observations, it will be [prescient] to remark that the volume is dedicated to the Hon. R. Steel, of Calcutta, well-known as a member of the executive council of the Viceroy of India, and a generous patron of chess and chess masters as well as a first-class chess player himself, and that the book has a noble appearance, and paper and type being eminently suitable and the 170 diagrams well placed and clearly printed. The notation is that most approved in recent works, Cook's Synopsis, American edition, and German Handbuch.

In his September 8, 1889, column, Pollock wrote: "Mr. Steinitz desires us to state that copies of The Modern Chess Instructor *can be obtained from him direct. Address: P.O. Box 2937, New York City."*

Opposite: The title page of the first volume of W. Steinitz's *The Modern Chess Instructor* (1889) (courtesy Edward Winter).

THE

MODERN CHESS INSTRUCTOR

BY

W. STEINITZ

PART I.

CONTAINING ELEMENTARY EXPLANATIONS FOR BEGINNERS—THE DESCRIPTION OF NOTATIONS—A TELEGRAPHIC CHESS CODE—AN ESSAY ON THE PRINCIPLES OF THE GAME AND ANALYSES OF SIX POPULAR OPENINGS, WITH ILLUSTRATIVE GAMES TO EACH OPENING, ETC., ETC., ETC. THE APPENDIX CONTAINS THE GAMES OF THE CONTEST BETWEEN MESSRS. STEINITZ AND TSCHIGORIN PLAYED AT HAVANA IN JANUARY AND FEBRUARY, 1889 WITH ANNOTATIONS BY THE AUTHOR

G. P. PUTNAM'S SONS
NEW YORK   LONDON
27 & 29 WEST 23D STREET   27 KING WILLIAM ST., STRAND
1889

Printed in U.S.A.

Appendix H: Reviewing Mason

The following brief review appeared in W.H.K. Pollock's April 7 and 21, 1894, Baltimore Sunday News *columns:*

Mason's Great Chess Work

(*The Principles of Chess in Theory and Practice* by James Mason,[11] London: Horace Cox, Windsor House, Breams Buildings, E.C., 1894, Price 2s. 6d. net)

Without even opening this book, probably the greatest work on chess ever written by an American citizen, two things strike the observant eye with considerable force—the fascination of the title and the extraordinarily low price of the volume, which contains nearly 300 pages. Dismissing

11. W.H.K. Pollock wrote the following in his *Baltimore Sunday News* column of June 30, 1894: "Mr. Mason was the other day pleasantly surprised, says the *Hereford Times*, to receive a four-page autograph letter from Lord Randolph Churchill complimenting him on his book, *The Principles of Chess*."

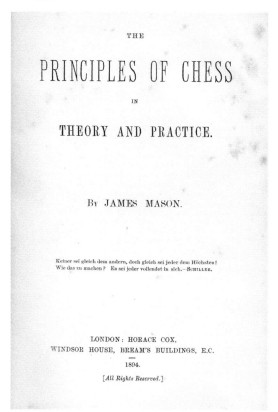

THE

PRINCIPLES OF CHESS

IN

THEORY AND PRACTICE.

By JAMES MASON.

Keiner sei gleich dem andern, doch gleich sei jeder dem Höchsten!
Wie das zu machen? Es sei jeder vollendet in sich.—Schiller.

LONDON: HORACE COX,
WINDSOR HOUSE, BREAM'S BUILDINGS, E.C.
—
1894.
[*All Rights Reserved.*]

The title page of James Mason's *The Principles of Chess in Theory and Practice* (1894) (courtesy Edward Winter).

the latter item, to which we hope to return as soon as the author has completed his arrangements for the publication and sale for the work in this country, it may be said, the title, as indicating the contents, is a very model of truth and honesty, Mr. Mason's industrious application of his enormous experience and magnificent creative ability has at length practically resulted in relegating the great majority of works on the game in the rank of elementary text-books, annotated compilations of games and collections of openings.

The author, in a preface which alone is sufficient to show his superb style and mastership of the English language, explains his intentions thus: "Chess is a science as well as an art. In its exercise the tendency is to premature mechanical facility rather than in a clear perception of principles; though upon this, of course, all true and lasting faculty

necessarily depends. In the present treatise this tendency is taken into account. The intention is to afford a concise yet comprehensive view of the 'principles' underlying the 'art' of chess, as exemplified by the foremost practice in these closing years of the century. As a consequence, the method pursued conforms as much as possible to the logical requirements of the subject, and therein differs from any hitherto employed."

The four main divisions of the book are: I. Elements of Chess, II. General Principles, III. Combination, IV. Master Play: Games. The first division contains a highly original sub-chapter on Terms, Resistance, Obstruction, Restraint, the Opposition, Exchanging, Winning and Endplay. The section on Combination is profusely illustrated by no less than 50 large diagrams. Master-play consists of a masterly article on "Opening" rather than "Openings," with 31 games annotated as only Mason can annotate, occupying about 100 pages of the work. As regards the printing and general make-up of the volume, we need only say it is distinctly first-class and believe that the only misprints that can be found are some three, which the author has pointed out to us in a private letter.

We hope next week to mention Mr. Mason's arrangements for the sale of his new work on chess. The elementary chapters evince the greatest care in compilation. There is a most interesting artifice on the knight's tour, but some knowledge of mathematics is required to appreciate its tour. The "opposition" of Kings is ably defined. The author's expressions are charmingly fresh. Under "General Principles" we quote examples of style: "Carefully consider the recoil. The gain of force is seldom secured in the mere act of capture. Inattention to this fact fully accounts for the difficulty found in "winning a won game." "A wandering rook"; "The pawns block and resist the rook more than they do any other piece. But if the Rook once gets in among or behind the hostile Pawns he soon changes all that. The Rooks doubled are more than doubly strong"; "The pawn is the knight's worst enemy."

The work contains a good portrait of the author with autograph and the only flaw we can discover, except a misprint of Witlek for Wittek,[12] is the unreasonable omission, which may be mistaken for suppression, of any of Lasker's games in the "Examples of Masterplay."

---

12. On page 193 of the first edition the heading to a Berlin 1881 game was "A. Witlek," but the spelling was corrected to Wittek in all subsequent editions.

Appendix I: A Call for Original Research

The following brief review appeared in W.H.K. Pollock's September 23, 1893, Baltimore Sunday News *column:*

We have received an advance edition of Part II of J[ohn] W. De Arman's *Guide to the Chess Openings.* The *Guide* is published at 40 cents a part and that just issued treats solely of the Evans Gambit. Buy of the author, Franklin, Pa. Mr. De Arman's work appears in pamphlet form, being printed by a new process from type-written copy. When complete and bound the work will be valuable as a reference chart. The "Evans" part contains a large amount of careful analysis of the ever green gambit and nearly 200 variations from the accepted best authorities. Beginners, however, must expect to find little or no instruction here—there is nothing to show the reason for moves new or old—while advanced students will of course find no "replies" to the badger-holes made in their tracks by the cunning expert. Badger-holes are to be avoided by the application of "principles." A perusal of this painstaking work would repay any lover of the game, but something written in original style, even if not original in premises, will always go further than compilations from books. A chess-smith, too, must go into the forge and strike the iron on its white-hot places; he has no time to forage around for pieces of old metal to burnish up and weld into marketable shape—they are too thin and twisted and torn for use.

Appendix J: War Whoops

The following Pollock write-up appeared in his December 21, 1890, Baltimore Sunday News *column. The last paragraph appeared twice in the* Chess Player's Chronicle *for 1891 (January 31, 1891, page 346, and December 16, 1891, page 203, under the heading "ADVICE TO YOUNG PLAYERS"). The italics in the original have been kept. Pollock signed this piece as "SITTING BULL."*

WAR WHOOPS

According to the "Laws" of chess, recent London edition, problems are the cream of the royal game, a kind of triple-extract of beauty and excellence in mating. But while they are the most artistic development of chess, they belong to the theoretical rather than the real. They are too rich for the blood of the average player. To mate his opponent is his object, whether the mate come slowly or quickly, awkwardly or prettily. He is too anxious to attain it, to risk danger and difficulty in making it problem-like. How few games in actual play end with the intricacies, beauties and difficulties of problems? Only in the games of masters do we find an approach thereto. And even in their finest mates, the effect is sometimes weakened because the preceding moves unavoidably indicate the point of culmination. The beauty of his endings is some measure of a player's strength. That of the expert is like the completion of a pyramid: while the weak players blunders through, wasting time and effort, as if torturing a victim or mutilating a corpse.

It is said that composers are seldom great players. It may be because, like the minstrels' *end* men, they handle the *bones*, not the quivering flesh of the openings. But solving undoubtedly improves the *analytical* powers of any player.

As between problems or theoretical endings and actual endings, so between tournament play and off-hand games or skittles, one may trace a distinct line. The one is earnest and beneficial. The other is careless and superficial. *Where there is no incentive to carefulness the lessons of the blunders are forgotten.* But where a prize or record is at stake every game will instruct and improve. The player concentrates his faculties, and brings into play memory, vigilance, caution, courage, reason. He thinks carefully and thoroughly and acts decisively. In ordinary English, he makes up his mind and sticks to it. He realizes that every move counts, and mistakes once made can never be "taken back." He plays with a purpose and aims right at the bull's eye. At the close of a tourney game he is often able to say he has no blunders to regret. That is the difference between "wood-shifting" and chess play.

A man has only to step once on a banana peel to remember it a long time. He always afterwards regards one with respectful attention, and, after treading on a slippery and dangerous spot in the game, the beginner will always look with caution on a similar one. For example, after the spider-legged knight has once made what the brokers call "straddle," and forked his king and queen, he always despises that piece for his duplicity. When a little pawn happens to extend its right hand to a

rook and its left to a bishop, and he sees that one of them must vanish, he calls it the "dirty snake." When it becomes a passed pawn and reaches the eighth square, he no longer considers it little and insignificant.

When a bishop gets upon the same diagonal with his rook and queen the loss of quality makes a lasting impression. A doubled pawn is often a useless one. But if it enables your rook to command an open file, it is good; and doubled rooks are still better. Young man, beware of the discovered check. Do not advance your queen too early in the game. It is too liable to attack by an inferior piece. Do not try to win the game in the first dozen moves. You cannot overwhelm your adversary at one jump. Develop your pieces instead. Do not move all along the line at once, but concentrate your energy in one direction. Beware of the perpetual check, the stalemate, the brilliant combination, the ambush, the pin, the capturing eye— and the mate. Clear vision through a long vista of moves is acquired only with time and experience. Do not block the retreat of your pieces with your own pawns. Do not depend on your opponent making an error. It is putting a premium on blunders. When he leaves a piece *en prise* beware lest you fall into a trap. Some of Mr. Blackburne's prettiest mates were when his adversaries thought he was overlooking the loss of his queen. And, finally, do not play out a lost game. Some men will not resign until they have forced the sacrifice of their last pawn. They have evidently forgotten Dr. Zukertort's advice on the subject.

Appendix K: Undated Games (519–530)

The following Pollock games proved impossible to accurately identify as to venue and date. They are presented here in the chronological order of their source.

519. Pollock–E. Thorold [C42]
Venue and Date Unknown

"A skirmish played some years ago between Pollock and E. Thorold." **1. e4 e5 2. Nf3 Nf6 3. N×e5 d6 4. Nf3 N×e4 5. d4 d5 6. Bd3 Be7 7. 0–0 Nc6**

8. c4 Be6 9. c×d5 B×d5 10. Re1 f5 11. Nc3 N×c3 12. b×c3 0–0 13. Ne5 Bd6 14. Bf4 g5?! 14. ... N×e5 15. B×e5 (15. d×e5 Bc5) 15. ... Qg5 16. g3 Rae8 was more sensible. **15. Bg3 B×e5** 15. ... f4? loses to 16. Qh5. **16. B×e5 g4 17. Qd2 Qh4 18. Bg3 Qf6 19. c4** 19. B×c7 was fine too. **19. ...**

f4 19. ... B×g2 was not a valid solution either: 20. K×g2 f4 21. Re4 f×g3 22. R×g4+ Kh8 23. f×g3 N×d4 24. Rf1 Qc6+ 25. Be4. **20. c×d5 f×g3 21. Re4** Too rushed. Best was 21. h×g3 N×d4 22. Rac1 Rac8 23. Re4. **21. ... N×d4?** 21. ... g×f2+! 22. Kf1 g3! would have posed some problems: 23. h×g3 Ne7 24. Re5 Ng6. **22. R×g4+ Kh8 23. h×g3** *(see diagram)*

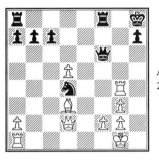

After
23. h2×g3

23. ... Nf3+ 23. ... Ne2+! assured equality: 24. Q×e2 Q×a1+ 25. Kh2 Rae8 26. Be4 Qd4 27. f3 Rg8 28. Rh4 Rg7. **24. g×f3 Q×a1+ 25. Kg2 Qf6 26. Rf4 Qg7?** 26. ... Qe5 offered more resistance: 27. Rh4 Rf7 28. Qc2 Qf6 29. Rf4 Qg7 30. R×f7 Q×f7 31. Qb2+ Kg8 32. Q×b7 Rd8 33. Be4. **27. Rh4 Rf6 28. R×h7+ Q×h7 29. B×h7 K×h7 30. Qc2+ Kg7 31. Q×c7+ Rf7 32. Qe5+ Kh7 33. d6 Raf8 34. f4 Rd7 35. f5 Rfd8 36. f6 Kg6 37. Qe7 R×d6 38. f7 1–0** [*Illustrated London News*, July 2, 1887]

520. R.J. Loman–Pollock [C45]
London, Date Unknown

1. e4 e5 2. Nf3 Nc6 3. d4 e×d4 4. N×d4 Bc5 5. Be3 Qf6 6. c3 Nge7 7. Qd2 a6 8. Be2 B×d4 9. c×d4 d5 10. e5 Qg6 11. 0–0 0–0 12. Bd3 Bf5 13. B×f5 N×f5 14. Nc3 Rad8 15. Ne2 Nh4 *(see diagram)*

After
15. ... Nf5–h4

16. Bg5?! 16. Ng3 was a more stable alternative. **16. ... N×g2! 17. K×g2 h6 18. h4 h×g5 19. h×g5 f6! 20. Rh1** White's overextension on the kingside

demands a price: 20. f4 f×g5 21. f×g5 Qe4+ 22. Kh2 Qh4+ 23. Kg2 Qg4+ 24. Kh2 g6! 25. Rf6 Kg7 26. Ng3 Rh8+ 27. Kg2 Qh3+, with a strong attack. **20. ... f×e5 21. Rag1 Qe4+ 22. Kf1 R×f2+! 23. K×f2 Rf8+ 24. Ke1 N×d4 25. Kd1** 25. Rh3!? was a more stubborn defense, but Black remains in the lead: 25. ... Nf3+ 26. R×f3 R×f3 27. Qc1 Qh4+ 28. Kd2 Qb4+ 29. Kd1 Rd3+ 30. Kc2 Qe4 31. Nc3 Qf5 32. Re1 b5. **25. ... Rf2 26. Rf1 R×e2 27. Rf8+ K×f8 28. Qb4+ Kg8 29. Rh8+ K×h8 30. Qf8+ Kh7 31. g6+ Q×g6 0–1** [*Illustrated London News*, March 29, 1890]

521. Pollock–[O.C.?] Muller [C55]
Simpson's, Handicap, Date Unknown

1. e4 e5 2. Nf3 Nf6 3. Bc4 N×e4 4. Nc3 Nc6 5. 0–0 Be7 6. N×e4 d5 7. Bb5 d×e4 8. N×e5 Qd5 9. N×c6 b×c6 10. Ba4 0–0 11. Qe2 Bd6 12. Bb3 Qe5 13. g3 Bh3 14. Re1 Kh8? The simple 14. ... Rae8 15. d3 e×d3 16. Q×e5 R×e5 17. R×e5 B×e5 18. c×d3 Bf5 gives Black good play. **15. d3** *(see diagram)*

After
15. d2–d3

15. ... Rae8?! 15. ... f5! made perfect sense. For instance, after 16. d×e4 f×e4 17. Q×e4 Rae8 18. Q×e5 B×e5 the obvious 19. c3 fails because of 19. ... B×g3! **16. Q×e4 Q×e4 17. R×e4 R×e4 18. d×e4 Re8 19. Be3!** 19. f3 is insufficient due to 19. ... Bc5+ 20. Kh1 Rd8 21. Bf4 f6! 22. Bc4 g5 23. B×c7 Rd2. **19. ... f6 20. f3 f5 21. Ba4 Rb8 22. e×f5 R×b2 23. Bb3 Be5 24. Rd1 h5?** 24. ... Bf6 25. g4 h6 26. Kf2 Bh4+ 27. Ke2 Bf6 28. Rd7 was winning for White just as well. **25. Rd8+ 1–0** [*The Lincoln, Rutland and Stamford Mercury*, May 2, 1890]

522. Pollock–F.J. Lee [C14]
Simpson's Divan, Date Unknown

1. e4 e6 2. d4 d5 3. Nc3 Nf6 4. Bg5 Be7 5. e5 Nfd7 6. B×e7 Q×e7 7. f4 a6 8. Qg4 g6 9. 0–0–0 c5 10. d×c5 N×c5? 10. ... Nc6 was correct. **11. Nf3**

Did Pollock really miss 11. N×d5 f5 (11. ... e×d5 12. Q×c8+ Qd8 13. Q×c5; 11. ... h5 12. Qh3) 12. N×e7 f×g4 13. N×c8? **11. ... Nc6 12. Bd3 Bd7 13. h4 0-0-0 14. Kb1 Kb8 15. Qg5 Q×g5 16. h×g5 Ne7 17. Nd4 N×d3 18. R×d3 Rdg8 19. Rdh3 Rg7 20. Nd1 Ng8 21. Ne3 h5?** 21. ... Ne7 22. Ng4 Nc6 would have prolonged the game. **22. g×h6 Rgh7 23. Ng4 f5 24. e×f6** *(see diagram)*

After
24. e5×f6

24. ... e5 25. f7 R×f7 26. N×e5 R×f4 27. N×d7+ Kc8 28. Nb6+ Kb8 29. Ne6 Re4 30. Ng5 1-0 [*Chess Player's Chronicle*, August 30, 1890]

523. N.N.–Pollock
Odds Game, Venue and Date Unknown
Remove f7 pawn

1. e4 c5 2. Qh5+ g6 3. Q×c5 Nc6 4. c3 e5 5. Qe3 Bh6 6. Qf3 Nf6 7. Na3 d5 8. Bb5 Bg4 9. Qg3 Bf4 10. B×c6+ b×c6 11. Qd3 N×e4 12. g3 Qb6! 13. Qf1 *(see diagram)*

After
13. Qd3–f1

13. ... Q×b2!! 14. Qa6 14. g×f4 Q×a1 15. Ne2 0-0 16. Nc2 Qb1 17. Na3 Qd3 was equally hopeless. **14. ... B×d2+ 15. Kf1 0-0! 16. f3 B×f3!?** There was a fine mate in eight here: 16. ... R×f3+!! 17. N×f3 Bh3+ 18. Ke2 B×c1+ 19. Ke1 Bd2+ 20. Ke2 Bf4+ 21. Kd1 Nf2+ 22. Ke1 Q×c3+ 23. K×f2 Qe3 mate. **17. B×b2** 17. Qd3 would have met with the same fate: 17. ... Bg4+ 18. Nf3 R×f3+ 19. Q×f3 Bh3+ 20. Qg2 Rf8+ 21. Ke2 N×c3+

22. Kd3 Bf5+ 23. Qe4 B×e4 mate. **17. ... Bg4+ 18. Nf3 R×f3+ 19. Kg1 Bh3** Pollock must have wished for a certain mate pattern here since there are many quicker options. **20. Q×c6 Rf1+ 21. R×f1 Be3+ 0-1** [*The Lincoln, Rutland and Stamford Mercury*, December 12, 1890]

524. J.D. van Foreest–Pollock [C21]
Venue and Date Unknown

"Played some time since between van Foreest and Pollock." **1. e4 e5 2. d4 e×d4 3. c3 d×c3 4. Bc4 c×b2 5. B×b2 Bb4+ 6. Nd2 B×d2+ 7. Q×d2 Nf6 8. 0-0-0 0-0 9. f4 N×e4 10. Qc2 Nf6 11. g4 d5 12. g5 Qd6 13. g×f6** 13. Ne2 Qc5 14. g×f6 d×c4 15. f×g7 Re8 favors Black too. **13. ... Q×f4+ 14. Kb1 Q×c4 15. Bc3 Qe4 16. Q×e4 d×e4 17. Ne2 Na6 18. h4 h5 19. Nf4 Bg4 20. Rdg1 g6 21. R×g4 h×g4 22. h5 g5 23. Ng6** f×g6 23. ... Rfd8 24. Ne5 Rd5 25. N×g4 Rad8 was much easier to handle. **24. h×g6 Rf7! 25. g7!** R×g7 25. ... R×f6! 26. B×f6 Kf7 27. Bc3 e3 28. Kc2 e2 29. Rh8 Rg8 30. Kd2 c5 31. K×e2 Nb4 was more accurate. **26. f×g7 Kf7?** 26. ... Rb8 would have maintained some advantage: 27. Rh8+ Kf7 28. Rh5 Rd8 29. R×g5 b6 30. R×g4 Nc5 although White's g7-pawn remains a big asset. **27. Rf1+ Ke7 28. Bf6+ Ke6?** *(see diagram)* 28. ... Kf7 was forced.

After
28. ... Ke7–e6

29. Bd8!! R×d8 30. Rf8 R×f8 31. g×f8Q 1-0 [*Montreal Herald*, June 1, 1895]

525. Pollock–J. Mortimer [C52]
Venue and Date Unknown

The two sources for this score gave conflicting clues about the occasion of this game: *Albany Evening Journal*—"How Mortimer, now on a visit to this country, was quickly beaten in his own variation by Pollock"; *Montreal Gazette*—"Played some years ago at Simpson's Divan." **1. e4 e5 2. Nf3 Nc6 3. Bc4 Bc5 4. b4 B×b4 5. c3 Ba5 6. 0-0 Nf6 7. d4**

0–0 8. d×e5 N×e4 9. Re1 Nc5 10. Ng5 Ne6 11. Qh5 N×g5? 11. ... h6 was forced: 12. N×e6 f×e6 13. B×h6 Qe7 14. Be3 (14. Bg5? Rf5; 14. Bd2 Bb6) 14. ... Qf7 and White has no attack. **12. B×g5 Qe8** *(see diagram)* 12. ... Ne7 loses as well after 13. Re3 b5 14. Bd3 h6 15. Rg3!

After
12. ... Qd8–e8

13. Bf6!! g×f6 13. ... Ne7 loses too because of 14. Re3 Ng6 (14. ... d5 15. e×d6 c×d6) 15. Rh3 h6 16. Q×g6. **14. Bd3 1–0** [*Albany Evening Journal*, May 27, 1893; *Montreal Gazette*, January 19, 1895]

526. Pollock–Mr. B. [C54]
Venue and Date Unknown

1. e4 e5 2. Nf3 Nc6 3. Bc4 Bc5 4. c3 Nf6 5. d4 e×d4 6. c×d4 Bb4+ 7. Bd2 Qe7 8. 0–0 0–0? 8. ... B×d2 9. Nb×d2 d6 had to be played. **9. e5 Ne4 10. Be3** It is likely that Pollock saw 10. B×b4 N×b4 11. Qe1 c6 and now if 12. Q×e4 Black has 12. ... d5. However, after 12. Bb3! Black loses a piece. **10. ... d6 11. Bd5 Bf5 12. a3 Ba5 13. g3 Bg6 14. Nh4 Ng5 15. f4 B×b1?** 15. ... d×e5 16. f×g5 e×d4 17. Bf4 d3 was Black's last resort, albeit a desperate one. **16. R×b1 Ne6 17. f5** 17. Nf5! was correct. **17. ... Ne×d4** *(see diagram)*

After
17. ... Ne6×d4

18. Ng6 18. B×d4 N×d4 19. f6 (19. Q×d4? Bb6) 19. ... Q×e5 was not to Pollock's taste. **18. ... h×g6 19. f×g6 Ne6?** 19. ... Q×e5 was forced and sufficient to resist White's mounting pressure: 20. B×f7+ R×f7 21. g×f7+ Kf8 22. Qd3 Qh5

23. B×d4 N×d4 24. Rbd1 Bb6. **20. Qh5! f×g6 21. Q×g6 N×e5 22. B×e6+ Nf7 23. Bd4 1–0** [*Bristol Mercury*, March 21, 1896]

527. Pollock–W. Stewart
Odds Game, Venue and Date Unknown
Remove Ra1

"We present the readers an unpublished game by the late W.H.K. Pollock and W. Stewart of Lancaster." **1. e4 e5 2. Nf3 Nc6 3. Bc4 Bc5 4. b4 B×b4 5. 0–0 d6 6. c3 Bc5 7. d4 e×d4 8. c×d4 Bb6 9. Nc3 Nf6 10. e5 d×e5 11. Ba3 B×d4 12. Qb3 Qd7 13. Re1 B×c3?!** 13. ... Na5 or 13. ... Ng4 were stronger alternatives. **14. Q×c3** *(see diagram)*

After
14. Qb3×c3

14. ... h6? A fatal misapprehension. With 14. ... e4! 15. Ne5 N×e5 16. Q×e5+ Kd8 17. Bb3 Qe8 18. Qg5 Rg8 19. Rd1+ Bd7 Black would have kept the material advantage with ease. **15. N×e5 N×e5 16. Q×e5+ Kd8 17. Be7+ Ke8 18. B×f6+ Kf8 19. B×g7+ Kg8 20. B×h8 Qg4 21. Qe8+ Kh7 22. Q×f7+ K×h8 23. Re8+ Qg8 24. Q×g8 mate 1–0** [*Orillia Packet and Times*, March 30, 1899]

528. Pollock–E.L. Torsch
Baltimore, Odds Game, Date Unknown
Remove Nb1

1. f4 e6 2. e3 d5 3. Nf3 Nc6 4. b3 Bd6 5. Bb2 Nf6 6. Bb5 a6 7. B×c6+ b×c6 8. 0–0 Bb7 9. Qe1 Qe7 10. a3 0–0–0 11. b4 h5 12. Qe2 Ng4?! 12. ... h4 was better. **13. B×g7 Rhg8 14. Bd4 f6 15. Rfb1 e5 16. Ba7 Kd7 17. h3 Ra8 18. Bc5 Nh6 19. Nh4 Qf7** 19. ... Qe6 was more consistent: 20. Kh1 Nf5 21. N×f5 Q×f5 22. Rf1 Rae8. **20. a4 Rae8 21. f5 e4 22. B×d6 K×d6 23. b5 c×b5 24. a×b5 a×b5 25. Q×b5 Bc6?** 25. ... Rb8 was required. **26. Qb4+?** It appears both sides missed 26. Ra6! Qd7 27. Qb4+ Ke5 28. d4+ e×d3 29. Qf4 mate. **26. ... Kd7 27. Ra7 Qg7 28. Qb6** *(see diagram)*

After
28. Qb4–b6

28. ... Rc8 28. ... Qg3! was impossible to parry: 29. Rb3 (29. Rba1 Rb8 30. Qa5 Rb5 31. Qc3 Rgb8 32. Rf1 Rb1 33. Ra1 R×f1+ 34. R×f1 Q×h4) 29. ... Rb8 30. Qa5 R×b3 31. c×b3 Rg5. **29. c4?** 29. Ng6 N×f5 30. Nf4 Ng3 31. Re1 h4 32. Ne6 was still insufficient, but better than the text. **29. ... N×f5 30. c×d5 B×d5?** 30. ... N×h4 31. Q×c6+ Kd8 was an easy win. **31. Qb5+** 31. Rb5! was the correct defense: 31. ... Ne7 32. R×d5+ N×d5 33. Qb5+ Ke6 34. Qc6+ Ke5 35. d4+ e×d3 36. Ra6 Rge8 37. Nf3+ Kf5 38. Q×d5+ Kg6 39. Q×d3+ Kf7. **31. ... Ke6 32. Rba1 N×h4 33. R1a6+ Ke5 34. g4 Nf3+** 34. ... h×g4 makes things infinitely easier. **35. Kf2 h×g4 36. h×g4 Q×g4??** Overlooking a simple mate. Instead, 36. ... c6! was still winning: 37. R×g7 c×b5 38. Re7+ Be6 39. Re×e6+ Kd5 40. Rad6+ Kc5 41. d4+ e×d3 42. K×f3 Rgd8. **37. Qb2+ Nd4 38. Q×d4+ 1–0** [*PM*, pages 112–113]

529. Pollock–Amateur [C55]
Dublin, Date Unknown

Pollock: "In some positions the king should not always be 'checked to death,' or he may 'escape alive.' The following is a very fine example, known in Dublin years ago as the 'Monck Gambit.'" **1. e4 e5 2. Nf3 Nc6 3. Bc4 Nf6 4. Nc3 N×e4 5. B×f7+ K×f7 6. N×e4 d5 7. Nfg5+ Kg6 8. Qf3 d×e4 9. Qf7+ K×g5** (*see diagram*) Pollock: "White now mates in ten moves." After 9. ... Kh6 White still

gets a big advantage with 10. d4 Q×g5 (10. ... e×d3 11. Ne6+) 11. B×g5+ K×g5 12. d5 Nd4 13. h4+ Kh6 14. Q×c7.

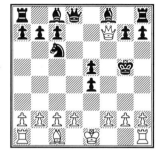

After
9. ... Kg6×g5

10. d4+ Kh4 11. h3 Bb4+ If 11. ... g6, then 12. g3+ Kh5 13. g4+ Kh4 14. Qb3 with a mate in six. **12. Kf1 g6 13. g3+ Kh5 14. g4+ Kh4 15. Qb3 Bc3 16. Q×c3 e3 17. Q×e3 B×g4 18. h×g4+ K×g4 19. Qh3 mate 1–0** [*PM*, page 157]

530. J.H. Blackburne–Pollock
Venue and Date Unknown

White to move

1. R×f7 R×f7 2. B×f7+ K×f7 3. Qh5+ g6 4. Q×h6 Re6 5. Rf1+ Kg8 6. Bf6 c4+ 7. d4 N×f6 8. Q×g6+ Kf8 9. e×f6 Qa7 10. Qh6+ Kg8 11. Qg5+ Kf8 12. f7 1–0 [The position was given in P. Anderson Graham's *Mr. Blackburne's Games at Chess* (1899, Game 249, page 204) and identified as being "Played in the B.C.A. Handicap."]

Appendix L: Six Pollock Endgames

A number of endgames and combinations won by Pollock appeared on pages 154–157 of Pollock Memories *without providing precise sources. Presumably, they come from Pollock's own notebooks or various
chess columns. Below are six game finishes that do not appear in the game section of this book.*

531. White to play

532. White to mate in seven

533. White to mate in nine

534. White to play and win

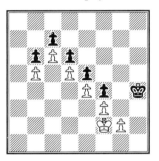

535. Pollock vs. John L. McCutcheon
1. ... Nb8 and White (Pollock) drew

536. Pollock vs. John D. Elwell
White mates in three

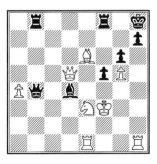

Solutions:

531: 1. Qh7+ K×h7 2. h×g7+ Kg8 3. Rh8 Kf7 4. g8Q mate.

532: 1. Bb8 Kg1 2. Ba7+ Kh1 3. Nb6 Kg1 4. Nd5+ Kh1 5. Ne3 Kg1 6. Nf5+ Kh1 7. Ng3 mate.

533: 1. Nf4 Kg8 2. Ne6 Kh8 3. Nb3 Kg8 4. Nbc5 Kh8 5. Nd7 Kg8 6. Nef8 Kh8 7. Kf7 g5 8. Nf6 g4 9. Ng6 mate (An alternative path: 3. Nc2 Kg8 4. Ne3 Kh8 5. Kf7 Kh7 6. Ng4 Kh8 7. Nf8 g5 8. Ne5 g4 9. Neg6 mate).

534: 1. g3+ f×g3+ 2. Kg2 Kh5 3. K×g3 Kg5 4. f4+ e×f4+ 5. Kf3 Kg6 6. K×f4 Kf6 7. e5+ d×e5+ 8. Ke4 Kf7 9. K×e5 Ke7 10. d6+ c×d6+ 11. Kd5 Ke8 12. K×d6 Kd8 13. c7+ Kc8 14. Ke6 K×c7 15. Ke7 Kc8 16. Kd6 Kb7 17. Kd7 Kb8 18. Kc6 Ka7 19. Kc7 Ka8 20. K×b6 and wins easily.

535: F.F. Rowland: "The following fine ending arose in a game played in Pittsburg, between Mr. Pollock, of Albany, New York, and Mr. John L. McCutcheon. Black drew elegantly, as follows: **1. ... Nb8 2. K×a5 Nd7 3. Kb5 Nc5 4. a5 Nb3 5. Bd2 N×d2 6. a6 Ke4 7. a7 K×f4 8. a8Q Ke3** and the game is drawn." A few notes by the authors: 1) Black can win with 1. ... e4! 2. Be3 Ne7 3. Bd2 Nc8 4. K×a5 Kc5 5. Be3+ Kc6 6. Kb4 Nb6 7. Bd2 e3 etc. 2) **3. ... Nc5** is an error that gave White winning chances; best was 3. ... e4 with a draw in hand; 3) Instead of **4. a4**, even stronger was 4. f×e5! Nd7 5. e6 K×e6 6. a5; 4) Instead of **5. Bd2**, 5. a6! was more precise for a clear win.

536: 1. R×h7+ K×h7 2. Rh1+ Kg7 3. Qd7+ Qe7 4. Q×e7+ Rf7 5. Q×f7 mate; This fragment also appeared in the *Baltimore Sunday News* of April 12, 1891, where it was said to have been played in a simultaneous exhibition at the Brooklyn Chess Club in April 1891.

Appendix M:
Pollock's Tournament and Match Record

Tournaments[13]	Date	+	–	=	Place	%
CCA Meeting, Birmingham (Div. II, Class II)	July/August 1883	11	3?	0	1	78.57
CCA Meeting, Bath (Class I, Div. II)	July/August 1884	7	3	0	1	70.00
1st British Chess Association (Masters)	June 1885	10	4	1	4	70.00
1st BCA—Lord Tennyson Tournament	June 1885	6	0	1	1	92.85
Hamburg (Hauptturnier, Group A)	July 1885	4	2	1	3	64.28
CCA Meeting, Hereford (Masters)	August 1885	3	7	0	9/11	30.00
1st ICA Congress, Dublin	October 1885	8	1	0	1	88.88
British Chess Club Masters, London	Feb./March 1886	3	4	0	4/5	42.86
BCA Congress, London	July 1886	4	7	1	10	34.61
CCA Masters, Nottingham	August 1886	3	6	0	7	33.33
2nd ICA Congress, Belfast	September 1886	8	0	0	1	100
CCA Meeting, Stamford	August 1887	2	2	2	3–5	50.00
BCA Masters, London	Nov./Dec. 1887	3	4	2	5	44.44
International Masters, Bradford	August 1888	7	9	0	9–10	43.75
3rd ICA Congress, Dublin	March 1889	6	1	1	2	81.25
6th American Congress, New York	March–May 1889	15	18	5	11	46.05
3rd USCA Congress, St. Louis	February 1890	8	2	2	2	64.29

13. Playoff games not counted; handicap tournaments are not included.

(Tournaments)	(Date)	(+	–	=	Place	%)
Chicago Tournament	June 1890	7	2	2	3	57.14
4th USCA Congress, Lexington	August 1891	8	2	2	2	75.00
Brooklyn Chess Club Championship	March 1892	15	3	0	1	83.33
Impromptu Tournament, New York	October 1893	4	7	2	9–11	38.46
Hastings Tournament	August 1895	6	11	4	19	38.09
		148	**98**	**26**		
		54.41%	**36.02%**	**9.55%**		

Matches	Date	+	–	=	Score	%
Charles Moehle (Cincinnati)	June 1890	7	6	1	7½–6½	53.57
Eugene Delmar (Skaneateles)	July 1891	3	5	0	3–5	37.5
G.H.D. Gossip, Montreal	Dec. 1894–Jan./Feb. 1895	6	6	3	7½–7½	50.00

Bibliography

Books

Cheshire, Horace F. *The Hastings Chess Tournament, 1895*. London: Chatto & Windus, 1896.

Emanuel Lasker: Denker, Weltenbürger, Schachweltmeister. Edited by Richard Forster, Stefan Hansen, Michael Negele. Berlin: Exzelsior Verlag, 2009.

Forster, Richard. *Amos Burn: A Chess Biography*, Jefferson, N.C.: McFarland, 2004 and 2014.

Fourth Annual Report by the United States Chess Association with Twenty-Six Games Played at the Lexington, Ky., Meeting. Cincinnati: Keating, 1893.

Gaige, Jeremy. *Chess Personalia: A Biobibliography*. Jefferson, N.C.: McFarland, 1987.

Gilberg, Charles A. *The Fifth American Chess Congress*. New York, 1881.

Hilbert, John. *Emil Kemeny: A Life in Chess*. Jefferson, N.C.: McFarland, 2013.

_____. *Essays in American Chess History*. Yorklyn, Del.: Caissa Editions, 2002.

_____. *The New York State Chess Association Congresses Buffalo 1894 and 1901*. Yorklyn, Del.: Caissa Editions, 1996.

_____. *Walter Penn Shipley: Philadelphia's Friend of Chess*. Jefferson, N.C.: McFarland, 2003.

_____. *Young Marshall: The Early Chess Career of Frank James Marshall with Collected Games, 1893–1900*. Olomouc: Moravian Chess, 2002.

Landsberger, Kurt. *William Steinitz, Chess Champion: A Biography of the Bohemian Caesar*. Jefferson, N.C.: McFarland, 1993.

Rogers, Howard J. *New York State Chess Association 1878–1891: History and Report*. Albany, N.Y., 1891.

Rowland, Frideswide F., *Pollock Memories: A Collection of Chess Games, Problems, &c, &c*. Rowland, Dublin, 1899.

Steinitz, William. *The Book of the Sixth American Chess Congress: Containing the Games of the International Chess Tournament held at New York in 1889*. Zurich: Edition Olms reprint, 1982.

_____. *The Steinitz Papers: Letters and Documents of the First World Chess Champion*. Edited by Kurt Landsberger. Jefferson, N.C.: McFarland, 2002.

The United States Chess Association: Its History and Objects. 1892.

The United States Chess Association: Second Annual Report. 1890.

Third Annual Report by the United States Chess Association with Forty-Two Games Played at St. Louis and Seven Games Played at Indianapolis. Indianapolis. Carlon & Hollenbeck, Printers and Binders, 1891.

Urcan, Olimpiu G. *Adolf Albin in America: A European Chess Master's Sojourn, 1893–1895*. Jefferson, N.C.: McFarland, 2008.

White, Alain C. *Sam Loyd and His Chess Problems*. Leeds: Whitehead and Miller, 1913.

Whyld, Kenneth. *The Collected Games of Emanuel Lasker*. Nottingham: The Chess Player, 1998.

Winter, Edward. *A Chess Omnibus*. Milford, Conn.: Russell Enterprises, 2003.

_____. *Chess Explorations*. London: Cadogan Books, 1996.

_____. *Chess Facts and Fables*. Jefferson, N.C.: McFarland, 2006.

_____. *Kings, Commoners and Knaves*. Milford, Conn.: Russell Enterprises, 1999.

Journals and Magazines (1880s–1910s)

American Chess Bulletin
American Chess Magazine
The British Chess Magazine
Checkmate
The Chess Player's Chronicle
The Chess World
The Chess-Monthly
Columbia Chess Chronicle
Four Leaved Shamrock
International Chess Magazine
Irish Chess Chronicle
London Chess Fortnightly

Newspapers (1850s–1910s)

Albany Evening Journal
Atlanta Sunny South
Baltimore Sunday News
Bath Chronicle
Bath Chronicle and Weekly Gazette
Belfast News-Letter
Birmingham Daily Post
Blackburn Standard
Brighton Guardian
Bristol Mercury and Daily Post
Brooklyn Daily Eagle
Brooklyn Standard-Union
Buffalo Morning Express
Chicago Daily News
Chicago Tribune
Cincinnati Commercial Tribune
Daily Mail
Dublin Daily Express
Dublin Evening Mail
Dundee Advertiser
Dundee Courier
Evening Mail (Dublin)
The Falkirk Herald
The Field (London)
The Fortnightly Review
Freeman's Journal and Daily Commercial Advertiser (Dublin)
The Hastings and St Leonards Observer
Illustrated London News
Illustrated Sporting and Dramatic News
Irish Times
Jackson's Oxford Journal
Knowledge
Leeds Mercury
Lincolnshire Chronicle
London Daily News
London Standard
Manchester Courier and Lancashire General Advertiser
Manchester Guardian
Montreal Daily Herald
Montreal Daily Star
Montreal Witness
Morning Herald (Montreal)
Morning Post
Morning Transcript
New York Clipper
New York Evening Post
New York Herald
New York Recorder
New York Sun
New York Times
New York Tribune
New York World
New Yorker Staats-Zeitung
Newcastle Weekly Courant
Northern Echo
Nottinghamshire Guardian
The Observer
Oxford Journal
Pall Mall Gazette
Philadelphia Inquirer
Pittsburg Dispatch
Sheffield and Rotherham Independent
Sheffield Independent
St. John's Globe
St. Louis Globe-Democrat
St. Louis Republic
Stamford Mercury
The Times (London)
Washington Post
The Weekly Irish Times
Western Daily Gazette
Western Daily Press
Westminster Budget
Worcester Journal
Yorkshire Evening Post

Digital Repositories

Ancestry (www.ancestry.com)
British Newspaper Archive (www.britishnewspaper archive.co.uk)
Brooklyn Daily Eagle On-Line, 1841–1955 (www.bk lyn.newspapers.com)
Chronicling America: Historic American Newspapers (www.chroniclingamerica.loc.gov)
Edward Winter's *Chess Notes* (www.chesshistory.com)
Gale Databases (www.cengage.com)
Genealogy Bank (www.genealogybank.com)
ProQuest Historical Newspapers (www.proquest.com)

Archives & Libraries

John G. White Chess and Checkers Collections, Cleveland Public Library
Library and Archives Canada
Library of Congress (U.S.)
National Archives of the UK
National Archives, Washington, D.C.
National Library of Ireland
New York Public Library
Royal Library in the Hague
Widener Library, Harvard College Library

Index of Pollock Opponents
(by Game Number)

References are to game numbers involving Pollock given in Part II and Appendix K.
Numbers in **bold** indicate Pollock had White. Numbers in *italics* and ***bold italics*** indicate consultation games
(with ***bold italics*** indicating Pollock's team had White). Numbers underlined indicate Pollock wins.

Index of Historical Annotators
(by Game Number)

All references are to game numbers in Part II and Appendix K.

Index of Openings—Traditional Names (to Game Number)

References are to game numbers in Part II and Appendix K. Numbers in **bold** and ***bold italics*** indicate Pollock had White. Numbers in *italics* indicate consultation games (with ***bold italics*** indicating Pollock's team had White). Numbers *underlined* indicate Pollock wins.

Index of Openings—ECO Codes (to Game Number)

References are to game numbers in Part II and Appendix K.
Numbers in **bold** and ***bold italics*** indicate Pollock had White. Numbers in *italics* indicate consultation games (with ***bold italics*** indicating Pollock's team had White). Numbers underlined indicate Pollock wins.

491

General Index
(to Page Numbers)

Specific references to Pollock's games appear in the Index of Pollock Opponents.
Numbers in **bold italics** indicate illustrations.

493